A

Philip E. Lilienthal

BOOK

The Philip E. Lilienthal imprint
honors special books
in commemoration of a man whose work
at the University of California Press
from 1954 to 1979
was marked by dedication to young authors
and to high standards in the field of Asian Studies.
Friends, family, authors, and foundations have together
endowed the Lilienthal Fund, which enables the Press
to publish under this imprint selected books
in a way that reflects the taste and judgment
of a great and beloved editor.

The publisher gratefully acknowledges the generous contributions to this book provided by the Philip E. Lilienthal Asian Studies Endowment Fund of the University of California Press Foundation, which is supported by a major gift from Sally Lilienthal, and by The University of Chicago.

The Language of the Gods in the World of Men

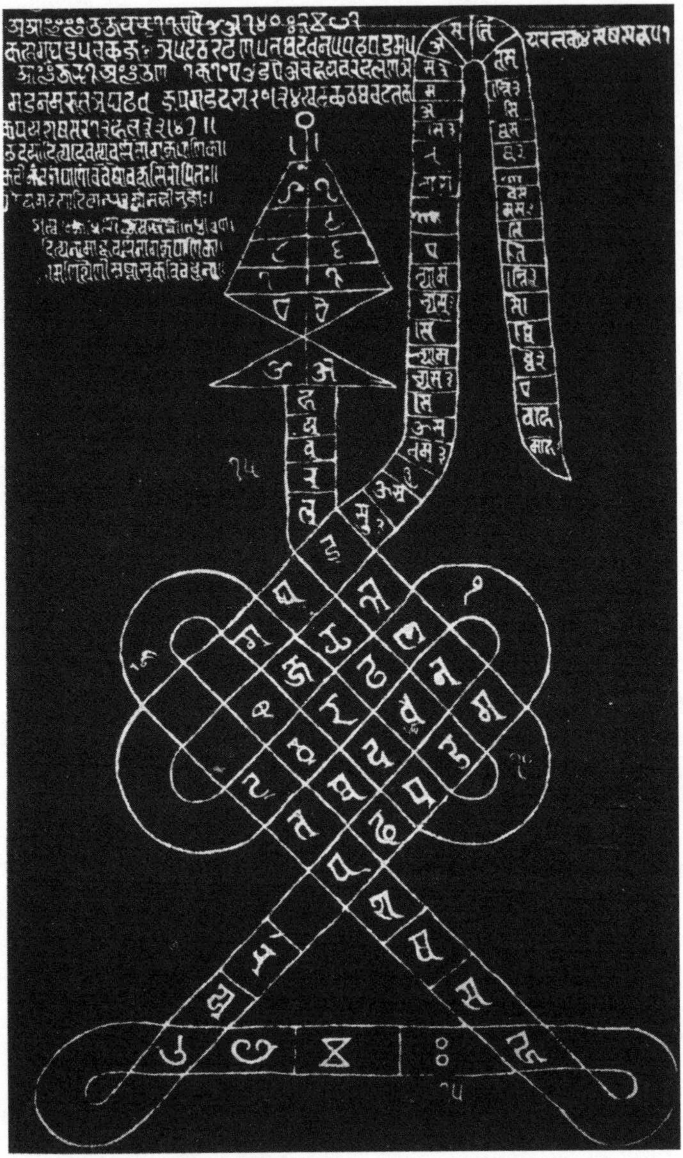

Serpentine Scimitar of King Udayāditya (Mahākāleśvara Temple, Ujjain, early twelfth century; photo courtesy Archaeological Survey of India); see p. 177.

The Language of the Gods in the World of Men

Sanskrit, Culture, and Power in Premodern India

Sheldon Pollock

UNIVERSITY OF CALIFORNIA PRESS
Berkeley Los Angeles London

University of California Press, one of the most distinguished university presses in the United States, enriches lives around the world by advancing scholarship in the humanities, social sciences, and natural sciences. Its activities are supported by the UC Press Foundation and by philanthropic contributions from individuals and institutions. For more information, visit www.ucpress.edu.

University of California Press
Berkeley and Los Angeles, California

University of California Press, Ltd.
London, England

First paperback printing 2009

Library of Congress Cataloging-in-Publication Data

Pollock, Sheldon I.
The language of the gods in the world of men : Sanskrit, culture, and power in premodern India / Sheldon Pollock.
p. cm.
"Philip E. Lilienthal Asian studies imprint."
Includes bibliographical references and index.
ISBN 978-0-520-26003-0 (pbk. : alk. paper)
1. Sanskrit literature—To 1500—Political aspects. 2. Sanskrit literature—To 1500—History and criticism. 3. Indic literature—To 1500—History. 4. Indic literature—To 1500—Political aspects. 5. Politics and literature—India—History. 6. Literature and society—India—History. I. Title.
PK2907.P65P65 2006
891A'.209—dc22 2005013461

Manufactured in the United States of America
15 14 13 12 11 10
10 9 8 7 6 5 4 3

The paper used in this publication meets the minimum requirements of ANSI/NISO Z39.48-1992 (R 1997) *(Permanence of Paper)*.

For my mother,
Elsie Russ Pollock

CONTENTS

PREFACE AND ACKNOWLEDGMENTS *xi*

Introduction *1*

Culture, Power, (Pre)modernity 2

The Cosmopolitan in Theory and Practice 10

The Vernacular in Theory and Practice 19

Theory, Metatheory, Practice, Metapractice 30

PART 1. The Sanskrit Cosmopolis

Chapter 1. The Language of the Gods Enters the World *39*

1.1 Precosmopolitan Sanskrit: Monopolization and Ritualization 39

1.2 From Resistance to Appropriation 51

1.3. Expanding the Prestige Economy of Sanskrit 59

Chapter 2. Literature and the Cosmopolitan Language of Literature *75*

2.1. From Liturgy to Literature 75

2.2. Literary Language as a Closed Set 89

2.3. The Final Theory of Literary Language: Bhoja's Poetics 105

Chapter 3. The World Conquest and Regime of the Cosmopolitan Style *115*

3.1. Inscribing Political Will in Sanskrit 115

3.2. The Semantics of Inscriptional Discourse: The Poetics of Power, Mālava, 1141 134

3.3. The Pragmatics of Inscriptional Discourse: Making History, Kalyāṇa, 1008 148

Chapter 4. Sanskrit Culture as Courtly Practice 162

4.1. Grammatical and Political Correctness: The Politics of Grammar 162

4.2. Grammatical and Political Correctness: Grammar Envy 177

4.3. Literature and Kingly Virtuosity 184

Chapter 5. The Map of Sanskrit Knowledge and the Discourse on the Ways of Literature 189

5.1. The Geocultural Matrix of Sanskrit Knowledge 189

5.2. Poetry Man, Poetics Woman, and the Birth-Space of Literature 200

5.3. The Ways of Literature: Tradition, Method, and Stylistic Regions 204

Chapter 6. Political Formations and Cultural Ethos 223

6.1. Production and Reproduction of Epic Space 223

6.2. Power and Culture in a Cosmos 237

Chapter 7. A European Countercosmopolis 259

7.1. Latinitas 259

7.2. Imperium Romanum 274

PART 2. The Vernacular Millennium

Chapter 8. Beginnings, Textualization, Superposition 283

8.1. Literary Newness Enters the World 283

8.2. From Language to Text 298

8.3. There Is No Parthenogenesis in Culture 318

Chapter 9. Creating a Regional World: The Case of Kannada 330

9.1. Vernacularization and Political Inscription 330

9.2. The Way of the King of Poets and the Places of Poetry 338

9.3. Localizing the Universal Political: Pampa Bhāratam 356

9.4. A New Philology: From Norm-Bound Practice to Practice-Bound Norm 363

Chapter 10. Vernacular Poetries and Polities in Southern Asia 380
10.1. The Cosmopolitan Vernacularization of South and Southeast Asia 380
10.2. Region and Reason 397
10.3. Vernacular Polities 410
10.4. Religion and Vernacularization 423

Chapter 11. Europe Vernacularized 437
11.1. Literacy and Literature 437
11.2. Vernacular Anxiety 452
11.3. A New Cultural Politics / 460

Chapter 12. Comparative and Connective Vernacularization 468
12.1. European Particularism and Indian Difference 468
12.2. A Hard History of the Vernacular Millennium 482

PART 3. Theory and Practice of Culture and Power

Chapter 13. Actually Existing Theory and Its Discontents 497
13.1. Natural Histories of Culture-Power 497
13.2. Primordialism, Linguism, Ethnicity, and Other Unwarranted Generalizations 505
13.3. Legitimation, Ideology, and Related Functionalisms 511

Chapter 14. Indigenism and Other Culture-Power Concepts of Modernity 525
14.1. Civilizationalism, or Indigenism with Too Little History 525
14.2. Nationalism, or Indigenism with Too Much History 539

Epilogue. From Cosmopolitan-or-Vernacular to Cosmopolitan-and-Vernacular 567

APPENDIX A
A.1 Bhoja's Theory of Literary Language (from the Śṛṅgāraprakāśa*) 581*
A.2 Bhoja's Theory of Ornamentation (from the Sarasvatīkaṇṭhābharaṇa*) 583*
A.3 Śrīpāla's Bilpaṅk Praśasti *of King Jayasiṃha Siddharāja 584*

A.4 The Origins of Hemacandra's Grammar
(from Prabhācandra's Prabhāvakacarita*)* *588*

A.5 The Invention of Kāvya
(from Rājaśekhara's Kāvyamīmāṃsā*)* *591*

APPENDIX B

B.1 Approximate Dates of Principal Dynasties *597*

B.2 Names of Important Peoples and Places with Their Approximate Modern Equivalents or Locations *597*

PUBLICATION HISTORY *601*

BIBLIOGRAPHY *603*

INDEX *649*

MAPS FOLLOW PAGE *xiv.*

PREFACE AND ACKNOWLEDGMENTS

A number of the ideas in this book began to germinate as long ago as 1990, when I delivered my inaugural lecture as Bobrinskoy Professor of Sanskrit and Indic Studies at the University of Chicago. Three years later I reformulated that presentation as a series of lectures at the Collège de France. A year's fellowship under the auspices of the National Endowment for the Humanities and the American Institute of Indian Studies, 1995–1996, enabled me to work closely with the greatest living scholar in the field of Old Kannada, T. V. Venkatachala Sastry, professor emeritus of the Institute of Kannada Studies, University of Mysore. It was only then that I began to conceive of this book the way it is today, having come to understand more fully than ever before that just as the history of Sanskrit makes less sense the less we understand of its relationship to local forms of culture and power, so the vernacular revolution in second-millennium South Asia makes less sense the less we understand of the shaping role played by Sanskrit.

Also in the mid-1990s, I began a collaborative research project involving seventeen scholars on three continents, the end result of which was the volume *Literary Cultures in History: Reconstructions from South Asia*. A number of the central ideas for this project emerged out of my earlier work on Sanskrit and my new interests in Kannada. The Literary Cultures project claimed large amounts of my time and effectively stalled my personal research, but the questions it raised were obviously of fundamental concern to this study. I learned much from my colleagues, and traces of their learning may be found throughout this book.

The issues raised here are of such scope that I could have studied forever and still not have discovered, let alone mastered, all of the relevant material in all the relevant languages. The book was long enough in coming, but it would never have been finished unless I stopped reading for it, which I did when completing the first full draft of the book in 2001–2. It has therefore not always been possible to take complete account of specialist monographs and articles that have been published since.

With respect to the spelling of names, the standard transcription schemes for Kannada and other vernacular forms are used when Kannada and other vernacular authors and works are under discussion: thus I write "Kēsirāja" rather than "Keśirāja," "Nāgarvarma" rather than "Nāgavarman," but "Someśvara" and not "Sōmeśvara," since he wrote his *Mānasollāsa* in Sanskrit. Names of languages and scripts are given without diacritics. Place names cited from texts are typically permitted to retain the variation they show in the texts themselves; no attempt to impose uniformity has been made. Providing modern names as equivalents of premodern ones is often problematic not only cognitively (where, after all, are the borders of Jambūdvīpa?) but also politically (where, after all, are the borders of Kannaḍanāḍu?). In fact, the contrast between the reductive cartographic exactitude of modernity and the accommodation of nominal pluralism in premodernity (where the slogan seems almost to have been: Let there be many Gaṅgās!) speaks to one of the core problems of this book. I have nonetheless decided to include modern names (and without diacritics) when there is not too much uncertainty about the identification, in order to give at least some local habitation to what for many readers might otherwise be a blank abstraction. These are relegated to an appendix for fear of clogging the text even further. I use "India" and "South Asia" more or less interchangeably, but "southern Asia," when Southeast Asia is specifically meant to be included.

Texts are cited in the original as a rule only when the language itself is the point of the discussion, the translation problematic, or the text rare enough not to be generally available to scholars. To have done otherwise would have swollen this book well beyond its already distended present state.

In a work like this, in which the problematics, while coherent and unified—at least as I see them—are incredibly complex, the author cannot possibly be an authority in every area of literary culture examined, and he must to some degree rely on the learning of his colleagues. In addition to Venkatachala Sastry, with whom I carried on daily conversations for a year that is a precious memory for me, I must thank a number of scholars of very different orientations. Allison Busch graciously shared her deep knowledge of Brajbhasha literature with me. She also read the final draft of the manuscript in its entirety and made countless suggestions for improvement. The late Norman Cutler discussed many issues of early Tamil literary history with me over the decade and a half in which we were colleagues, until his premature death deprived the world of Tamil scholarship of this learned and gentle man. Anne Feldhaus drew on her remarkable knowledge of early Marathi to help me with a number of thorny questions in the inscriptional record. Gérard Fussman, preeminent scholar of early Indian epigraphy, was my host at the Collège de France, and in the years since my visit I have continued to profit greatly from our discussions on the complicated historical issues addressed in chapter 1. The Latinist Robert Kaster, a scholar whose generosity is as deep as his learning, helped me think more sharply about the "countercosmopolis" (a formulation for which he should not be held responsible) described in chapter 7. Roger Wright, the pathbreaking sociophilologist of early Romance, was always ready with scholarship, criticism, and great goodwill when I raised questions concerning the materials in chapter 11—a chapter also read, with a critical eye for which I am very grateful, by the historian Robert Moore.

Arjun Appadurai and Dipesh Chakrabarty have been the closest of colleagues, friends, and conversation partners for going on two decades. While we have sometimes agreed amicably to disagree on certain questions, their perspectives have proved invaluable to me, especially with regard to the thinking that went into part 3.

I am also grateful to two outside readers for University of California Press for their suggestions for improving the work.

My former student Steven Heim helped me enormously in preparing the materials that Bill Nelson transformed into the splendid maps that grace this book.

Research assistants who aided me over the years include Prithvidatta Chandrashobhi, Xi He, Guy Leavitt, Lawrence McCrea, and Samuel Wright.

To Reed Malcolm, my editor at the University of California Press, I owe an immense debt of gratitude. It was Reed who insisted years ago that I begin this book, and who showed great patience and support in the period of research and writing. When in the end he got far more than he had ever bargained for, his gentle prodding and understanding help me turn this *megalon biblion* into what I hope is not so *megalon* a *kakon*.

At the University of California Press, Cindy Fulton was the perfect project editor, moving this complicated work along with great proficiency, and Carolyn Bond, the perfect copyeditor, showing unflagging care as well as infinite patience.

Each of the following friends and colleagues contributed in various ways, and I regret I do not have the space to explain how valuably: U. R. Ananthamurthy, Benedict Anderson, Johann Arnason, Rick Asher, Homi Bhabha, Bronwen Bledsoe, Carol Breckenridge, Johannes Bronkhorst, Steven Collins, Tony Day, the late Edward Dimock, Jr., Shmuel N. Eisenstadt, Matthew Kapstein, Sudipta Kaviraj, Stuart McGregor, Christopher Minkowski, Kathleen Morrison, Janel Mueller, Christian Novetzke, V. Narayana Rao, Susanne and Lloyd Rudolph, Joseph Schwartzberg, Bulbul Tiwari, Ananya Vajpeyi, Blake Wentworth, Björn Wittrock, Dominik Wujastyk, Yogendra Yadav.

Warm thanks go to Howard Bass and Elizabeth Voyatzis, whose affection and companionship during a sabbatical in 2002 enabled me to complete the first full draft of this book. I am grateful, too, to my daughters: Mica, for her helpful conceptual and stylistic criticism on some earlier essays that formed the background of this book, and Nira, for her patient explanation of some issues of evolution that troubled me in chapter 13.1, and both for their loving support over the long period of this work's gestation.

In closing, I remember two men of Karnataka whose deaths took away not only friends but teachers: A. K. Ramanujan, with whom I had the wonderful if all too brief pleasure of exchanging Sanskrit for Kannada instruction in the early 1990s, and D. R. Nagaraj, from whom I learned how great are the stakes of the knowledge of culture-power, yet how joyful, too, such knowledge can be.

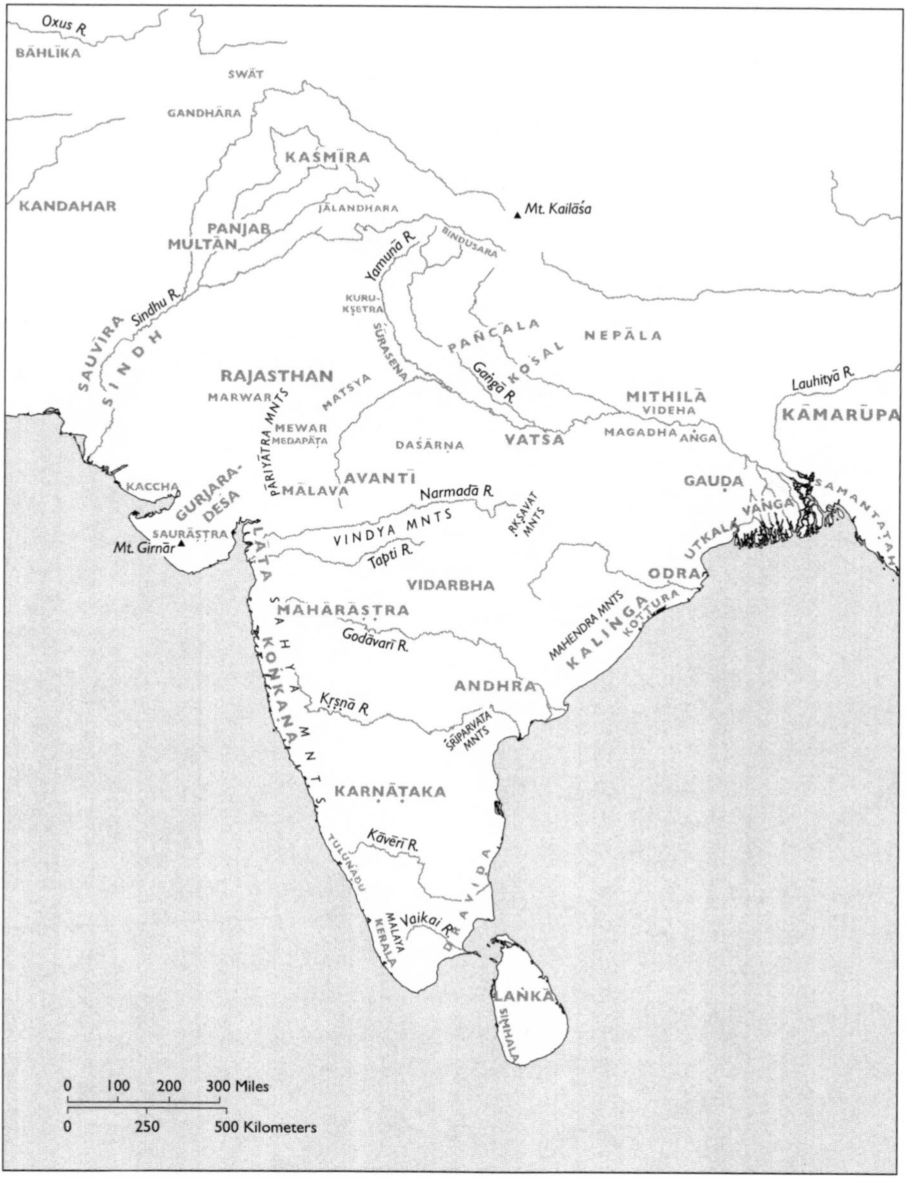

MAP 1. Premodern South Asia: Regions and Physical Features

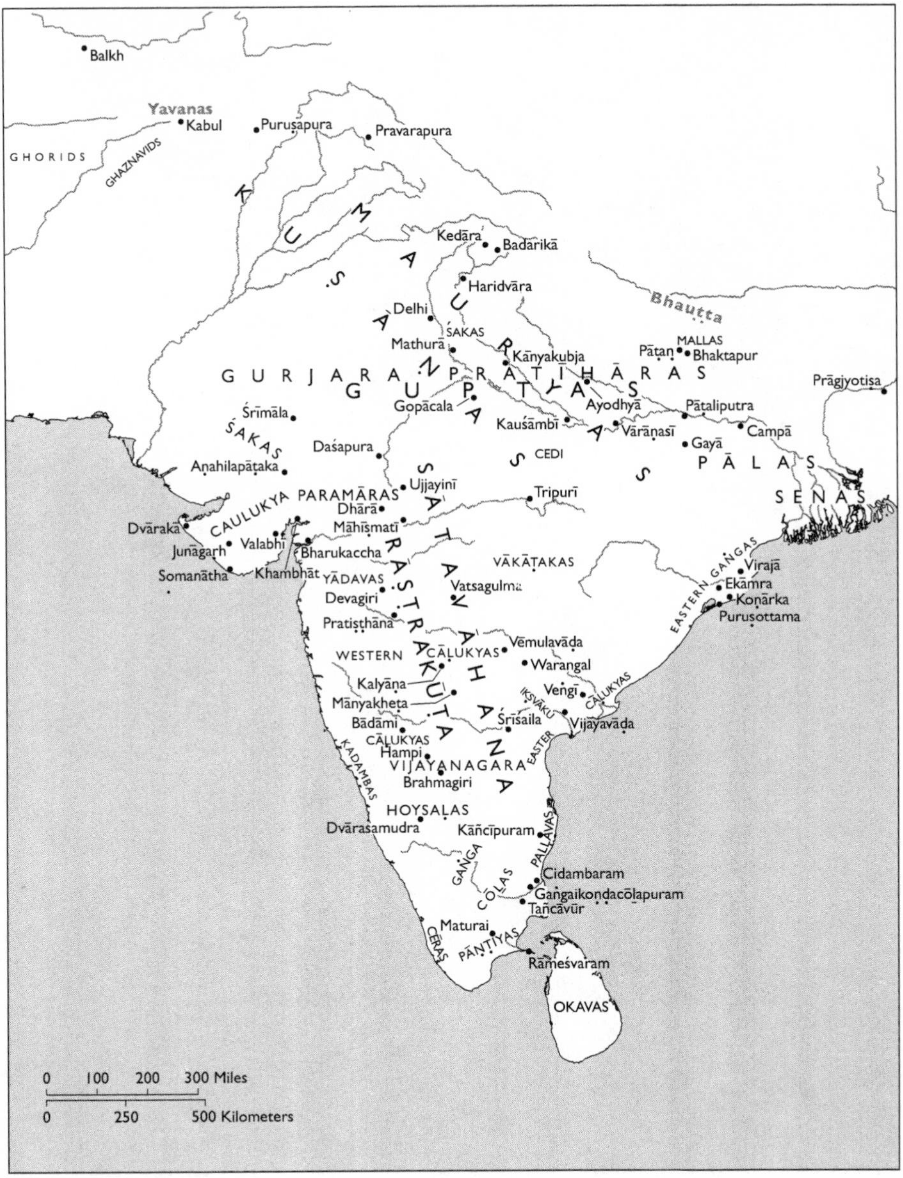

MAP 2. Premodern South Asia: Dynasties and Cities

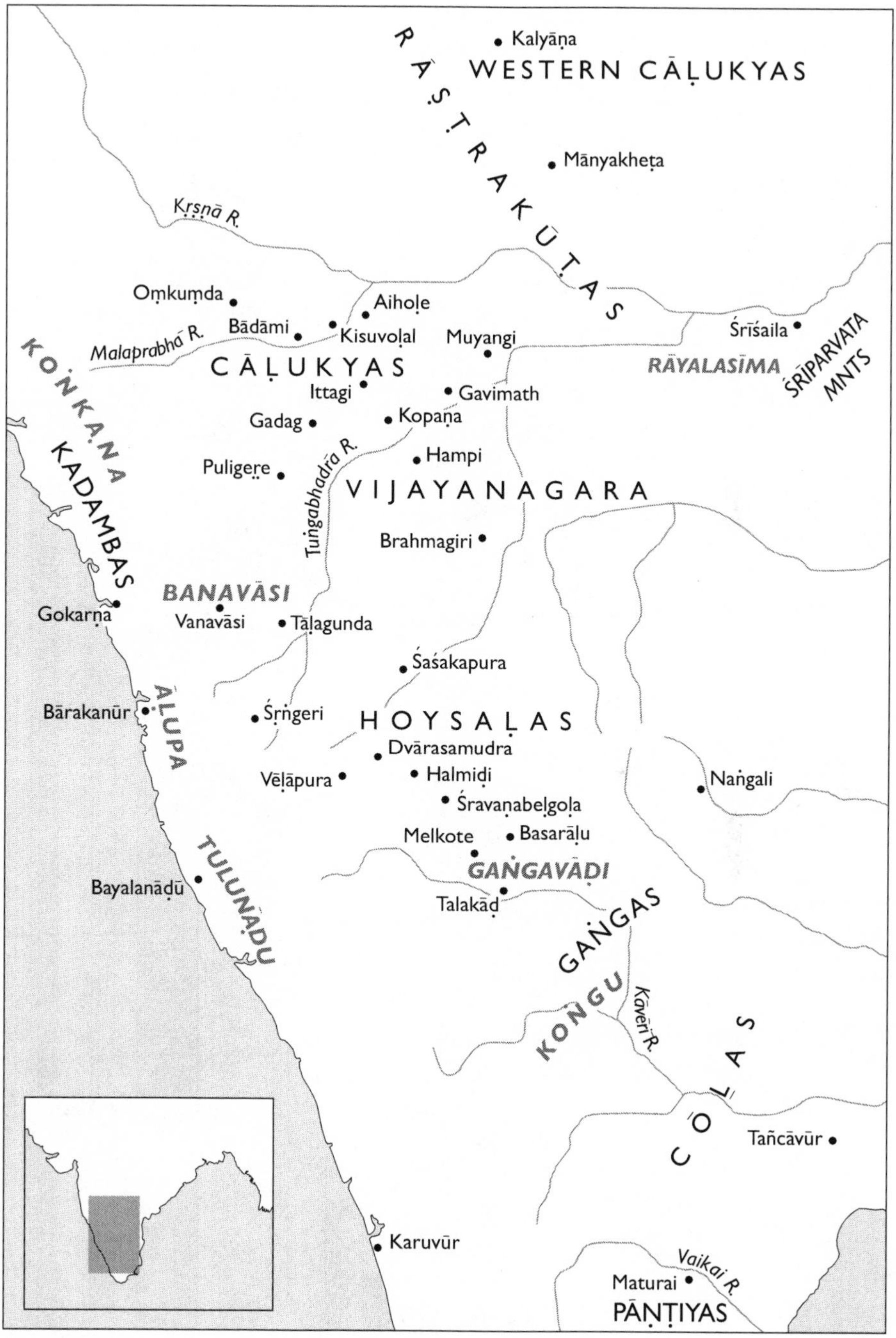

Map 3. Premodern Karnataka

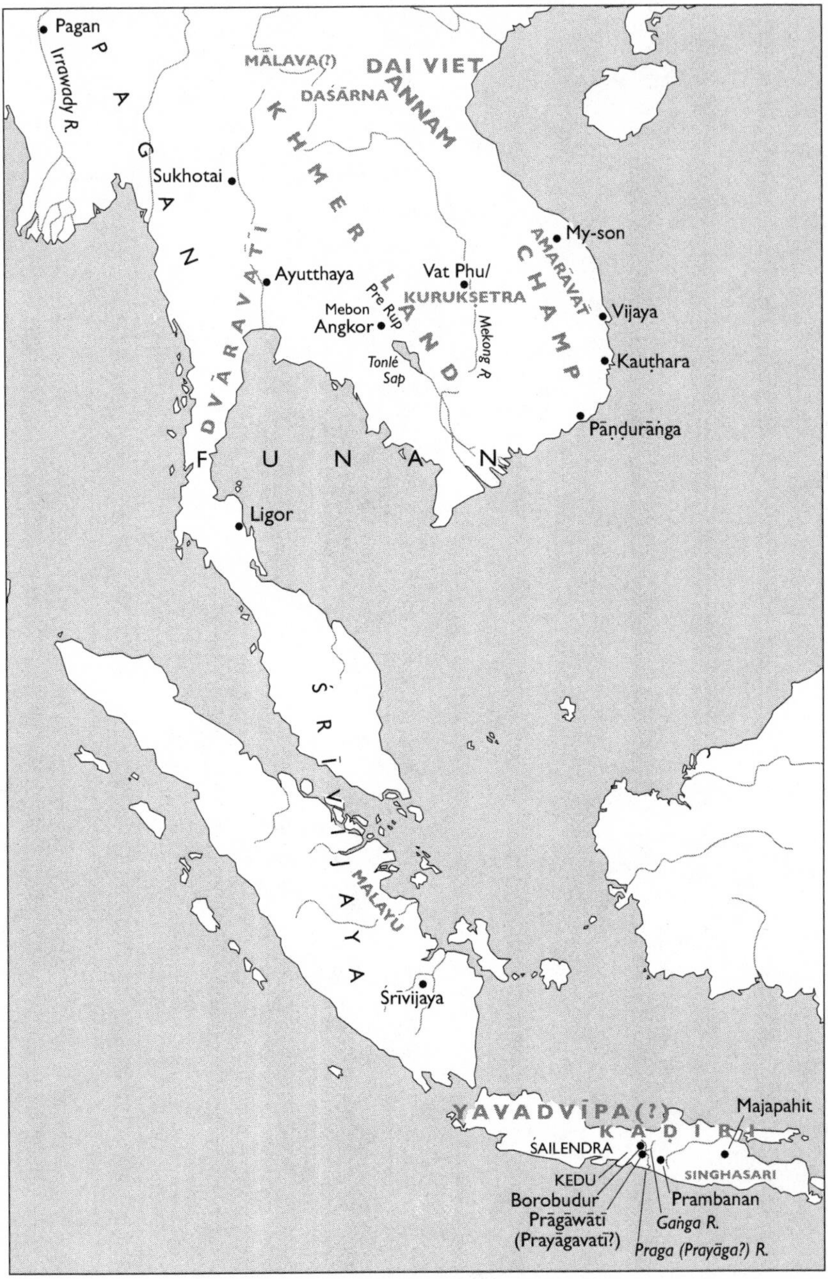

MAP 4. Premodern Southeast Asia

Introduction

> I feel that if language is understood as an element of culture, and thus of general history, a key manifestation of the "nationality" and "popularity" of the intellectuals, this study is not pointless and merely erudite.
>
> GRAMSCI, *selections from Cultural Writings*

> Das Sein verstimmt das Bewusstsein.
>
> GRAFFITO, *East Berlin, November 1989*

This book is an attempt to understand two great moments of transformation in culture and power in premodern India. The first occurred around the beginning of the Common Era, when Sanskrit, long a sacred language restricted to religious practice, was reinvented as a code for literary and political expression. This development marked the start of an amazing career that saw Sanskrit literary culture spread across most of southern Asia from Afghanistan to Java. The form of power for which this quasi-universal Sanskrit spoke was also meant to extend quasi-universally, "to the ends of the horizons," although such imperial polity existed more often as ideal than as actuality. The second moment occurred around the beginning of the second millennium, when local speech forms were newly dignified as literary languages and began to challenge Sanskrit for the work of both poetry and polity, and in the end replaced it. Concomitantly new, limited power formations came into existence. Astonishingly close parallels to these processes, both chronologically and structurally, can be perceived in western Europe, with the rise of a new Latin literature and a universalist Roman Empire, and with the eventual displacement of both by regionalized forms. But the parallels are complemented by differences, too, in the specific relationships between culture and power in the two worlds. Today, the vernacular epoch that began in India and Europe a millennium ago seems to be mutating, if not ending, as the local cultures then created are challenged by a new and more coercive globalism. It may be only now, therefore, that we are able to identify the shape of these past events and to ask whether from their old differences we might learn any new ways of acting in the world.

This is a very large set of issues—the book might have carried as a second subtitle (if it hadn't already been taken by Charles Tilly) "A Study of Big Structures, Large Processes, and Huge Comparisons." A map of the inquiry into these structures, processes, and comparisons with respect to both their logic and their substance is certainly in order. So is some discussion of the basic terms employed. Three key words, "culture," "power," and "(pre)modernity," can be reviewed briskly, since rough-and-ready understandings of these categories have proved adequate for organizing this historical study. In fact, going with rather than against the dominant conceptual grain has seemed a methodological prerequisite, since the dominant conceptualizations in both Europe and South Asia have been the historically consequential ones; whether they are true in some transcendental sense is a secondary issue. More clarification is needed for two other core terms of this study, "cosmopolitan" and "vernacular," as well as for the culture-power critique that constitutes the grander objective of this historical reconstruction.

CULTURE, POWER, (PRE)MODERNITY

There should be nothing problematic about using the term "culture" to refer specifically to one of its subsets, language, and especially language in relation to literature. Sometimes the collocation "literary culture" is used here to describe a set of dynamic practices by which languages are produced as distinct entities and literatures created within a context of social and political life that helps to shape these practices even while being shaped by them. In premodern India it was in the activities of literary culture and the representations of literature, as much as anywhere else, that power and culture came to be constituted as intelligible facts of life.

What should be problematic, however, at least from the vantage point of contemporary theory, is claiming to know and define "literary." There are good reasons for arguing—and many have argued this for the past two decades or more—that anything can be literature; that the term needs to be understood pragmatically rather than ontologically, as pointing to ways certain texts are used rather than defining what those texts inherently and essentially are. Yet from the vantage point of premodern South Asia, most certainly not everything could be *kāvya,* the text genre for which the closest English translation is poetry and literary prose; and with respect to the history of *kāvya,* contemporary arguments about the nonessentialized nature of literature show themselves to be unhistorical essentializations.[1] This raises a point of method basic to this study, which might best be explained by the distinction Indian philosophers draw between *pāramārthika sat* and *vyāvahārika* (or, *saṃvṛti*) *sat,* or what the eighteenth-century Italian thinker Vico called *verum* and

1. Derrida 1992: especially 40–49, illustrates this well.

certum. The prior term points toward the absolute truth of philosophical reason, the second, toward the certitudes people have at different stages of their history that provide the grounds for their beliefs and actions.[2] It is these workaday truths, these certitudes, that are granted primacy in this book, in the conviction that we cannot understand the past until we grasp how those who made it understood what they were making, and why. By the standards of *vyāvahārika sat,* literature in the world of premodern South Asia was radically differentiated from nonliterature for all participants in literary culture, writers, critics, and audiences alike. What substantively constitutes *kāvya* and how literariness comes into being were naturally matters of ongoing debate, and various elements were proposed as the essence of *kāvya.* But the fact that *kāvya* has an essence—a "self" or "soul," as it was phrased—something marking it as different from every other language use, was never doubted by anyone.

At the heart of the premodern Indian conception is a distinction not unknown to modern literary theory, though variously formulated: between expression and content, performance and constatation, imagination and information. In Heidegger's philosophical aesthetics, a text's "workly" dimension—the aesthetic object's ability to reveal "a particular being, disclosing what and how it is"—may thus be differentiated from its documentary dimension. The same distinction underlies the different strategies phenomenologists identify for generating possible meanings in different kinds of texts: workly and documentary texts may be distinguished by the "degree to which one expands on [their] schematic structure to derive an expanded interpretation," or by the "kind and level of self-consciousness with which one checks one's reading against textual form and standards of interpretation."[3] Precisely these demarcations were made both theoretically and practically in premodern South Asia. At the high-water mark of Sanskrit literary theory in the eleventh century, the principal dichotomy in discourse was between *kāvya* and *śāstra,* or literature and science; a comparable distinction was operationalized in inscriptions by the use of one language for the expressive and imaginative, and another for the contentual and informational. In general, then, there is broad enough agreement on the *differentia specifica* of literature and nonliterature to make modern Western distinctions largely unobjectionable for describing the history of South Asian literary cultures.

Literature was distinguished not only by its content but also by its form. One thing that could not be *kāvya* was the purely oral. Although the fact is

2. On the distinction in India see Kapstein 2001: 215ff.; on Vico, Auerbach 1967: 238, 245, 265.

3. See respectively Lotman and Uspensky 1978, especially 217ff.; Austin 1962, especially 3, 6, 133ff., and Kloss 1967: 33. For Heidegger's *das Werkhaftes des Werkes* see 1960: 30. LaCapra introduces the useful complement of the "documentary" (1983: 30). For Ingarden's phenomenology I reproduce Hanks's typology (1996: 122–28).

rarely appreciated, not only is *kāvya* defined practically if not explicitly by writing for us modern readers who cannot know an unwritten literary past, but it was so for the premodern actors themselves. The invention of literacy and the growth of manuscript culture occurred in India a little before the beginning of the Common Era; from that point on, writing, the symbolic elevation of what is written, and the internal transformations the literary text undergoes by the very fact of being written down would become increasingly prominent features of literary culture. No convenient term exists in English for the breakthrough to writing; I will call it "literization" (by analogy with the German *Verschriftlichung*). The written differs from the oral in a variety of ways. For one thing, even in cultures like those of premodern South Asia that hypervalue orality—an attitude possible only given the presence of literacy, by the way—writing claims an authority the oral cannot. The authorization to write, above all to write literature, is no natural entitlement, like the ability to speak, but is typically related to social and political and even epistemological privileges (chapters 8.2, 11.1). For another, writing enables textual features far in excess of the oral; for literature it renders the discourse itself a subject for discourse for the first time, language itself an object of aestheticized awareness, the text itself an artifact to be decoded and a pretext for deciphering.[4] In addition, writing makes possible the production of a history of a sort the oral is incapable of producing. These and other features mark the written as a distinct mode of cultural production and communication. It is a core component in the process of vernacularization explained in part 2; without appreciating the role of writing, vernacularization cannot even be perceived as a historical phenomenon. Nietzsche was certainly right to locate in the origin of such *objektive Schriftsprache* (objective written language) a "prejudice of reason" in favor of "unity, identity, permanence, substance"; indeed, this is something fully borne out by the history of vernacular languages in South Asia. But he was wrong to judge as an error literary history's concern with written texts in preference to spoken linguistic art.[5] The first development made the second inevitable. Written literature in premodern South Asia, as in western Europe, undoubtedly preserved features realized only in oral performance, and listening to rather than reading literature long remained the principal mode of experiencing it. Yet with the introduction of writing, a new boundary was drawn between the purely oral and *kāvya*. Writing was never essential to literature—until literature *became literature*.

It is not I, then, who denies what several generations of scholars have argued—that something reasonable people would call literature can be pro-

4. See the discussion of "entextualization" in Bauman and Briggs 1990: 72 ff., and Silverstein and Urban 1996: 1–17. An interesting theoretical view of the passage from oral to literate is Bourdieu 1990: 94–105; the fullest field study, at least of Indian materials, is Honko 1998.

5. On Nietzsche see Nyíri 1996: 73–75.

duced in ignorance of writing, or at least without its use; that nonliterature can become literature if we choose to take it as such; or indeed, since the latently imaginative can always be detected in the overtly informational and vice versa, that the very binaries just mentioned are inadequate and literature as such must remain indefinable.[6] It is the theorists and practitioners of the dominant forms of verbal art in premodern South Asia who denied these claims. The theorists explicitly rejected the idea that language has any aesthetic dimension outside the realm of *kāvya*—even the hymns of the Veda were never thought of as *kāvya* before modernity—and they derived from actual practices a relatively stable paradigm of literary properties that in addition to lexical, metrical, and thematic features included writing as a fundamental component. The reality and effectiveness of this literary paradigm was demonstrated repeatedly in the history of Indian literary cultures. Indeed, it was by achieving conformity with it—a process that is often referred to here as "literarization" (to be distinguished from it close cousin, literization)—that new literatures first arose in the vernacular epoch.[7]

It will become clear that this definition of the literary in South Asia was not a fact of nature but an act in a field of power, no less so than any other cultural definition. As such, it would be repudiated often, sometimes so broadly as to constitute a *second* vernacular revolution (see chapter 10.4). Only previous acquiescence in the dominant definition of what may count as literature made contestation such as this possible, and perhaps necessary, in the first place. We understand less of the history of culture in South Asia the less we understand of these dominant conceptions, including the essentialization of literature and the primacy granted to writing in the constitution of literature. And it is hardly stating the obvious to say that both conceptions could only come to be displaced in modern scholarship because they had first been put in place by traditions like those of premodern India. Thus a sharp distinction between literature and nonliterature was both discursively and practically constructed by those who made, heard, and read texts in premodern South Asia, and it is with that construction—out of a methodological commitment to *vyāvahārika sat,* to taking seriously what they took seriously—that a history of their culture and power must begin.[8]

Few questions in premodern South Asian history are more unyielding to coherent and convincing answers than the nature of political power and the character of polity. At the most general level, what makes for some of the graver difficulties here (besides the uncommonly bad data noted below) is

6. Compare Hanks 1996: 184–91.

7. I felt forced to coin (I thought) the rebarbative term "literarization" (Pollock 1998), but others also seem to have found it unavoidable (e.g., Casanova 1999: 188–93).

8. A number of the issues of literariness raised here are discussed in detail in the introduction and various chapters of Pollock ed. 2003.

a kind of epistemological determinism embedded in the very categories that have to be used to make sense of the premodern forms—a situation curiously different from the realm of culture just described. Already a generation ago historians of Asia were attacking what they called "intellectual imperialism" in the imposition of Euro-American models and presuppositions for studying non-Western polities. Yet the old critique was itself contradictory. At the same time as it challenged the epistemic domination of the West it sought to give precedence to an analysis that "discerns a general order . . . and organization for India and elsewhere." It accordingly rejected as futile the idiographic (since it leads to "an endless series of noncomparable and culture-specific 'patterns'") and as pernicious any categorization that renders the non-West radically different. While the phrase "intellectual imperialism" may have a dated ring today, the problem it flags has not vanished, and the contradictions of the critique are those we are still living with.[9]

Was the political order segmentary in the African sense or feudal in the European? Did the polity consist of hierarchically parcellated authority with ritual hegemony at the center, or did it wither away under vast transfers of wealth to a feudal nobility? Was the state the Great Beast, the Great Fraud, or the Great Drama?[10] Or was India, as Max Weber thought, "prepolitical" before the coming of British colonialism? Can we even use for India a terminology—"empire," "state," "politics"—so saturated with the particularities of European history? These large problems have occupied scholars for generations, and no one book is going to solve them. Nor does this one even attempt to; it has far more modest objectives. The word "power" here often translates the Sanskrit *rājya* (the state of being, or function of, a king), and it is largely insofar as *rājya* stood in some relationship to *kāvya* that the phenomenon is pertinent to my concerns. How *rājya* and *kāvya* interacted, how the one underwrote or did not underwrite the other, how the one did or did not presuppose, condition, foster the other—these are the problems of "power" central to this book.

Central, too, is the character of political *imagination:* the ideas of rule, for instance, and the changing aspirations of rule over the course of time, from universality or near-universality toward something far more bounded. Again, the cognitive production of such political orders—the certitudes of the primary actors—is taken here as no less important than any absolute truths about these orders ascertainable by the historian. The creation of vernacular literature, for example, was intimately related to new conceptions of communities and places, which in turn correlated with a new kind of vernacular political order. And we can see that these were new because the world of

9. Fox 1977: ix–ix. For the vitality of the question see Reynolds 1995, especially p. 429.
10. Aung-Thwin 1995: 86.

cosmopolitan language and literature had known very differently defined spaces, communities, and aspirations of rulership, little concerned with self-differentiation or self-limitation.

Data on material practices that might give more concrete shape to the cosmopolitan and vernacular domains of premodern India are uncommonly poor. Aside from inscriptions and formal texts, not a single document from any royal archive has been preserved for the period covered in this book. Representations accordingly have much work to do here, and so we need to be clear about the value representations hold for this historical analysis of the constitution of forms of power. It is often assumed that textualized representations (conceptual spaces, for example) are somehow less real than material practices (circulatory spaces, for example), less consequential in actuality, and so less worthy of historiographical scrutiny and analysis. Much of the discussion of texts and representational practices, especially among critics of Orientalism during the era of excess in the 1990s, has been marked by a curious naiveté on this subject. It is a simple category error to reject such representations on the grounds that they are not "true," or to argue that, whereas a person's civilizational identification is a matter of great importance, an analysis of the historical etiology, activity, and meaning of that identification proves it unacceptable "as a true representation of people in history." On the contrary, among the "true representations" of the thought world of premodern South Asia are those believed to be true by the actors in that world. To contrast such representations with "history" is to ignore something crucial about the actual historicity of representation itself. To suggest that historical significance is established on the basis of numbers—as when we are told that "agricultural workers might not have even noticed" when the cultural-political elite in their texts represented the cosmopolitan age as coming to an end in the late medieval period—is to mix apples and oranges of different kinds and scales of historical significance.[11] Within the horizon of geological history, what agricultural workers might or might not have noticed does not count either; and in any case, if concentrating on elite representations means we miss the role of "the people" in history, we do capture something of the ideas that ultimately transformed the people's world. Moreover, to believe truth to be a kind of solid is to misconstrue the power and real consequentiality of representations, which can create what they appear merely to designate. As we acknowledge the normativity of the actual (which often manifests itself in the textualization of reality), so we need to acknowledge the actuality of the normative (which manifests itself in the realization of texts).[12] Finally, it is not clear that what people do is always more

11. Ludden 1994: 21, 11.

12. An instance of the latter would be the text-based traditionalization of reality under colonialism (see for example Dirks 1992 and 2001).

important than what people think—or indeed, that thinking itself is not a form of doing.

Granting all that has just been said, and even while concentrating on *rājya* and *kāvya,* it is both difficult and unwise to avoid other issues that have been considered pertinent to the analysis of power—domination, exploitation, violence—from at least the time of Weber. "Like the political institutions historically preceding it," he says in a famous passage, "the state is a relation of men dominating men, a relation supported by means of legitimate (i.e., considered to be legitimate) violence." The state, as well as every other political association, is for Weber defined by the means peculiar to it, namely, the use of political force. But such issues enter into consideration here only in their relationship to culture, that is, only to the degree it is possible to establish some role for culture in legitimating force, in answering Weber's basic question of when and why people obey. Determining the actual mechanisms of force or the material conditions for power do not concern me here; rather, I am interested in establishing, in a spirit as open as possible to historical difference, the specific contours of culture's place in power, and measuring the distance, if there is a distance, it has traveled to reach the place it occupies today.

Equally hard questions confront the Indologist in thinking about periodization, especially the caesura of modernity. When is this caesura to be drawn? What in fact is modernity? The concept is notoriously unclear even in social theory, the science of modernity; so, too, then, must its periodization be. For some, modernity began with capitalism, for others, with industrialization or colonialism or nationalism (whenever each of these may have begun). It has yet to begin for still others, who believe no vast rupture with the past has occurred, but rather only "small extensions of practices, slight accelerations in the circulation of knowledge, a tiny extension of societies, miniscule increases in the number of actors, small modifications of old beliefs."[13]

Modernity is a contrastive historical concept and therefore implies some understanding of what is counted as premodern. But much of the work on modernity (from Karl Marx to present-day scholars, such as Anthony Giddens, Jürgen Habermas, Niklas Luhmann, and so down the alphabet) offers little in the way of a convincing account of the nature of the "premodern," at least in the case of South Asia. The actual modernity of a number of phenomena included on lists of things considered modern remains uncertain. Some are probably modern beyond dispute: commodities that incorporate abstract labor as a unit of value, the sovereign state, the abstract individual. But consider the following criteria: the preponderance of formal over sub-

13. Latour 1993: 47–48.

stantive rationality (in, say, the organization of work or systems of accounting), the division of manual and mental labor, the abstraction of the social as a totality that can be acted upon, the economy conceivable as an independent domain, "embedded affinity to place," a reflexive appropriation of knowledge, the rise of expert systems that remove social relations from particular contexts, the questioning of moral frameworks that had once been accepted unhesitatingly, a new worry about the meaninglessness of life, loneliness. These have all been posited as elements of modernity but none has been shown to be unequivocally so, or to be entirely unknown to premodernity. By the same token, many of the properties ascribed to premodernity (e.g., "a just sense of security in an independently given world") seem to have been identified not through empirical historical work but rather by simply imputing counterpositive features required by the very narrative of modernity (with its "calculation of risk in circumstances where expert knowledge creates the world of action through the continual reflexive implementation of knowledge").[14] Just as we often conceive of the premodern by uncritically accepting the discourse of modernity, so we sometimes transfer to the past ideas or practices originating in modernity itself, and so produce a premodernity that is not premodern. Moreover, European modernity and South Asian premodernity are obviously uneven and not absolute categories; the former displays premodern features, the latter modern ones, and this is borne out no matter what definitions we invoke.

There are, as a consequence, entirely legitimate issues in cultural and political history to be raised through notions of "early modernities," "multiple modernities," "alternative modernities"—I have raised some myself. If one of the defining or enabling features of European modernity was the vernacularization of the cultural and political spheres, the same occurred in South Asia altogether independently of European influence.[15] Not only did Indian "premodernity" contain elements of European modernity, but in some key areas of culture, such as the analysis of language, it might even be said to have provided a stimulus to the development of that modernity (see chapter 4.1).

In this book, however, no attempt is made to set such received ideas on their head and find an Indian modernity (or nationalism or capitalism or whatever) *avant la lettre*. My concerns lie elsewhere. First, I want to understand the differences, if any, between the culture-power practices and their associated theories—legitimation, ideology, nationalism, civilizationalism, and the like—that came into being in modern Europe and the world of South Asia before the arrival of these practices and theories on the heels of Euro-

14. For most of these properties see Giddens 1990; the quoted passage is found on p. 84.
15. See Pollock 1998b.

pean expansion. These are what I have in mind when identifying what I contrastively and commonsensically call "premodern" South Asian materials, without fretting too much over how "premodern" or "modern" is to be defined or who has the right to define them. Second, I want to determine whether it is possible to conceptually work around such theories of culture-power and to understand what alternative practices may once have been available.

THE COSMOPOLITAN IN THEORY AND PRACTICE

The intensifying interactions today between local and translocal forms of culture and ways of political being, which have become truly global for the first time, have generated renewed scholarly interest in the idea of the "cosmopolitan."[16] As many have recognized, the processes at work in contemporary globalization are not altogether unprecedented. But our understanding of what exactly is new and different about them, beyond the sheer fact of their temporal speed and spatial reach, depends on our capacity to grasp the character of the earlier processes of globalization—of a smaller globe, to be sure—and the cosmopolitan identities that have characterized other historical epochs.[17]

The labels by which we typically refer to these earlier processes—Hellenization, Indianization, Romanization, Sinicization, Christianization, Islamization, Russification, and the like—are often used crudely and imprecisely. Yet they do serve to signal the historically significant ways in the past of being translocal, of participating—and knowing one was participating—in cultural and political networks that transcended the immediate community. These ways varied widely. In Hellenization, the dominant commitment was to a language, a culture, and even an aesthetic; in Christianization, by contrast, to a certain set of beliefs, in Islamization, to a certain set of practices, and in Romanization, to a particular political order—or so one might speculate, and speculation is all one can do for the moment. The comparative study of premodern processes of cosmopolitan transculturation—of how and why people may have been induced to adopt languages or life ways or modes of political belonging that affiliated them with the distant rather than the near, the unfamiliar rather than the customary—is very much in its infancy, even for a phenomenon as significant in the creation, or construction, of the West as Romanization. And when these earlier processes do come under scholarly scrutiny, they are typically not seen as processes at all, ones

16. See for example Pollock 2002.

17. Arjun Appadurai has rightly cautioned against a "rush to history" meant to neutralize the "special anxiety about its own not-newness" that contemporary globalization seems to provoke (Appadurai 1999). An example is Hopkins 2002.

through whose dialectical interaction the global and the local are brought into being simultaneously and continuously. Rather, they tend to be thought of as pregiven, stable, and sharply defined—the global or cosmopolitan as the exogenous, great tradition over against the local or vernacular as the indigenous, little tradition. They have taken on the character of stable entities that interact in thinglike ways, rather than being seen as constantly changing repertories of practices.

The local culture-power formations that displaced these quasi-global processes are examined in part 2 of this book, whereas part 3 considers the new cultural theory we are prompted to formulate on the basis of the historical materials supplied by premodern globalism and localism. Prerequisite to these discussions is the analysis in part 1 of the quasi-global formation that characterized early southern Asia—one that came into being around the start of the Common Era and at its height a thousand years later extended across all of South and much of Southeast Asia—and the problems that must be addressed to make some sense of it. The story of how this formation arose—how Sanskrit traveled the vast distance it did and came to be used for literary and political texts, and what such texts meant to the worlds of power in which they were produced—has never been told in the historical detail it merits. Indeed, it is unclear whether the fact that there is a story to tell has been fully recognized.

A number of factors account for this neglect. The temporal and spatial magnitude of the Sanskrit cultural and political order; the conceptual otherness of the subject matter; the apparent anomalousness vis-à-vis peer formations such as Confucian China or Latinate Europe, which has served to make the South Asia case almost invisible; the difficulty of the languages involved; the risk of provoking specialists of the particular regions where such study has always been parceled out; the almost immediate discovery of countercases to any tendency one believes to have discerned—all these obstacles have combined to induce a powerful resistance to generalization and large-scale interpretation.[18] In addition, Sanskrit studies, heir to a brilliant and imperious intellectual tradition that had set its own agenda in the important issues of the human sciences, has had grounds to rest content with addressing the questions predefined by this tradition—and the historical expansion of the realm of Sanskrit culture was not one of them.

Symptomatic of the many problems of understanding this realm and its history is the question of how even to refer to it. The phrase adopted here, "Sanskrit cosmopolis," is not without its drawbacks. Besides being hybrid and ahistorical, it is actually uncosmopolitan in the cultural specificity of the form

18. Heine had a sense of this resistance 150 years ago: "Es ist zu wünschen, dass sich das Genie des Sanskritstudiums bemächtige; tut es der Notizengelehrte, so bekommen wir bloss—ein gutes Kompendium" (Heine 1964: 113).

of citizenship implicit in it: membership in the *polis,* or the community of free males. But the very need for such a coinage reveals a social fact of some theoretical importance. Other great globalizing processes of the past found emic formulation and conceptualization, whether in terms of a cultural particularity (Hellenismos or Arabīya or Fārsīyat) or a political form (*imperium romanum* or *guo,* the Sinitic "fatherland"). But for neither the political nor the cultural sphere that Sanskrit created and inhabited was there an adequate self-generated descriptor. Even the word *saṃskṛti,* the classicizing term adopted for translating "culture" in many modern South Asian languages, is itself unattested in premodern Sanskrit in this sense. We will find Indian theory distinguishing the great Way, *mārga,* from Place, *deśī* (see chapters 5.3, 10.2), but both terms refer, significantly, only to cultural practices and never to communities of sentiment. If we are therefore obliged to invent our own expression for the transregional culture-power sphere of Sanskrit, the fact that Sanskrit never sought to theorize its own universality should not be seen as lack or failure. On the contrary, it points to something central about the character and existence of the Sanskrit cosmopolis itself: a universalism that never objectified, let alone enforced, its universalism.

The phrase "Sanskrit cosmopolis" carries three additional implications that make it especially useful here. The first is its supraregional dimension ("cosmo-"), which directs attention toward the expansive nature of the formation. The second is the prominence given to the political dimension ("-polis"), which was of particular importance in this form of global identification. Last, the qualification provided by "Sanskrit" affirms the role of this particular language in producing the forms of cultural and political expression that underwrote this cosmopolitan order. These different features are examined in the first six chapters of the book.

The history of the Sanskrit language and its social sphere has long been an object of interest to Sanskritists, for this is a curious history that holds considerable theoretical interest. The Sanskrit cosmopolis did not come into being simultaneously with the appearance of the Sanskrit language. Its development was slow and tentative, and for it to come about at all the very self-understanding of the nature and function of the "language of the gods," as Sanskrit was known, had to be transformed. Chapter 1 delineates the circumscribed domain of usage and access that characterized the language from its earliest appearance in history to the moment when this field was dramatically expanded around the beginning of the Common Era. Ritualization (the restriction of Sanskrit to liturgical and related scholastic practices) and monopolization (the restriction of the language community, by and large, to the ritual community) gave way to a new sociology and politicization of the language just around the time that western Asian and central Asian peoples were entering into the ambit of Sanskrit culture. Whether these newcomers, the Śakas (Indo-Scythians) in particular, initiated these processes or simply reinforced those already under way cannot be determined from the available evidence. What is not in doubt is that it was then that a new era—a cosmopolitan era—began.

Two key inventions, the second a subspecies of the first, marked the commencement of the cosmopolitan era in the literary-cultural domain and would continue to mark its expansion: *kāvya,* or written literature, and *praśasti,* or inscriptional royal panegyric. Chapter 2 sets out the grounds for thinking of Sanskrit *kāvya*—a category, as noted earlier, that was clear and distinct in premodern South Asia—as a new phenomenon in Indian cultural history when it first appeared a little before the beginning of the Common Era. From the first, *kāvya* was almost certainly composed and circulated (though not typically experienced) in writing; it was this-worldly *(laukika)* in its themes, even when these concerned the divine (no *kāvya* was incorporated into temple liturgy until the waning centuries of the cosmopolitan order); it was directed above all toward investigating the elementary forms of human emotional experience; at the same time (and for the same reason) it was centrally concerned with the nature of language itself, with its primary phonic and semantic capacities. In all these features *kāvya* was demonstrably something new in the historical record—something startlingly new to the participants in Sanskrit culture. Its novelty was thematized in the Sanskrit tradition itself with the story of the invention of *kāvya* told in the prelude to what came to be called the "first poem," the *Vālmīki Rāmāyaṇa.* In reflexively framing its own orality in a way that would be impossible in a preliterate world, and in doing so around the narrative of human response to problems of a human scale, the *Rāmāyaṇa* account captures some central features of the new expressive form that was *kāvya.*

Central to the theorization of *kāvya* in the cosmopolitan epoch was the restriction on the languages capable of producing it (chapter 2.2). The literary conquest of cosmopolitan space by Sanskrit produced a conception of literature as something able to be embodied only in language that was itself cosmopolitan. This was, of course, preeminently Sanskrit, though two other closely related idioms—Prakrit, the "natural" or informal language, and Apabhramsha, the dialectal (literally, decayed)—were counted as legitimate vehicles for *kāvya* from the first appearance of literary-theoretical reflection in the seventh century. Both Prakrit and Apabhramsha were in fact constituted as transregional koinés through the production of literary texts and grammatical descriptions, and they were used for literary production (almost exclusively so) across the subcontinent, the former from about the second or third century, the latter from about the fifth or sixth. (Since neither was spatially circumscribed, or reflexively understood to be so circumscribed, in the production of literary and political texts, neither qualifies as an instance of vernacularization.) But both languages occupy a much more subordinate position in literary history than Sanskrit, having never achieved anything like

Sanskrit's density of textual production or its spatial spread—neither was ever used for the production of literary texts outside the subcontinent. Sanskrit was the transregional code that filled the domain of the literary. The closed set of literary languages meant in principle that *kāvya* could not be made in other, localized languages; in this thought world, the very idea of *deśī kāvya,* "vernacular literature," would have constituted a contradiction in terms. And in practice it was never produced—until the vernacular moment came, when it was. These propositions, along with others that define the literary as distinct from all other language use, are explored on the basis of the comprehensive analysis of literature offered by King Bhoja of Mālava in the first quarter of the eleventh century (chapter 2.3).

Once Sanskrit emerged from the sacerdotal environment to which it was originally confined, it spread with breathtaking rapidity across southern Asia (chapter 3). Within three centuries Sanskrit became the sole medium by which ruling elites expressed their power from as far west as Puruṣapura in Gandhāra (Peshawar, in today's northwest Pakistan) to Pāṇḍurāṅga in Champa (central Vietnam) and Prambanan on the plains of Java. Sanskrit probably never functioned as an everyday medium of communication anywhere in the cosmopolis—not in South Asia itself, let alone Southeast Asia—nor was it ever used (except among the literati) as a bridge- or link- or trade-language like other cosmopolitan codes such as Greek, Latin, Arabic, and Chinese. And aside from the inscriptions, which have larger purposes, there is little evidence that it was ever used as the language of practical rule; tasks such as chancery communication or revenue accounting seem to have been accomplished by informal uses of local language. The work Sanskrit did do was beyond the quotidian and the instrumental; it was directed above all toward articulating a form of political consciousness and culture, politics not as transaction of material power—the power of recording deeds, contracts, tax records, and the like—but as celebration of aesthetic power. This it did in large part through the new cultural-political practices that came to expression in the *praśasti,* which not only arose coevally with Sanskrit *kāvya* but from the first exploited the full range of resources of the language-centered aesthetic of literature. Inscribed on rock faces or copperplates or, at a later date, temple walls, and thus to varying degrees publicly available, the *praśasti* was the literary expression of political selfhood. To a large extent, the Sanskrit cosmopolis consisted of precisely this common aesthetics of political culture, a kind of poetry of polity in the service of what was in some measure an aesthetic state. An examination of the semantics of inscriptional discourse aims to illuminate these concerns and illustrate its procedures (chapter 3.2). To foreground aesthetics, however, is not to argue with Weber (or Clifford Geertz) that culture is all that constituted polity in the nonmodern non-West and that other core issues of power were never addressed. A case study of the pragmatics of inscriptional discourse among the Kalyāṇa Cāḷukya dynasty is meant to show how seriously matters of real power were taken and how carefully memory was manufactured in its interests.

Even in such cases, however, we must be cautious about reducing the relationship between culture and power in the Sanskrit world to one of simple instrumentality. Things are much more complicated, and more interesting, than that. Chapter 4 shows that a vision of grammatical and political correctness—where care of language and care of political community were mutually constitutive—was basic to the cosmopolitan ethos from the very beginning. Something of the character of this linkage will have become apparent already in the history of the inscriptional habit, and further dimensions are brought to light by an examination of royal practices in the domain of grammar and literature. Sanskrit philology was a social form as well as a conceptual form, and it was inextricably tied to the practices of power. Overlords were keen to ensure the cultivation of the language through patronage awarded to grammarians, lexicographers, metricians, and other custodians of purity, and through endowments to schools for the purpose of grammatical studies. They were also responsible for commissioning many of the most important grammars. For a polity to possess a grammar of its own was to ensure its proper functioning and even completeness, so much so that a competitive grammaticality, even grammar envy, can be perceived among kings in the Sanskrit cosmopolis, as the narrative of Jayasiṃha Siddharāja of Gujarat illustrates (chapter 4.2). Kings also evinced consuming interest in demonstrating their Sanskrit virtuosity in literary matters. An encyclopedia of royal conduct from early-twelfth-century Karnataka, the *Mānasollāsa,* demonstrates how literary-theoretical competence *(śāstravinoda)* was as central to kingliness as military competence *(śastravinoda).* Episodes of grammatical and literary correctness such as these are not idiosyncratic tendencies of the persons or places in question. They point toward an ideal of proper rule and proper culture being complementary—an ideal in evidence throughout the cosmopolitan age, from the earliest recorded evidence in the second century, and beyond into the vernacular epoch, when so many cosmopolitan values of culture and power came to find local habitations and names.

Even if the transregional formation for which Sanskrit was the communicative medium was never named in the language, the transregionality of both culture and power decisively manifested itself in shaping Sanskrit discourse. The analytical matrices employed in much Sanskrit systematic thought—from the typology of females in the *scientia sexualis* to instrumental and vocal music and dance—are effectively geocultural maps of this vast space (chapter 5). The basic geographical template by which culture was conceptualized was, for its part, established only in the early centuries of the cosmopolitan era, reaching its final form in a mid-sixth-century work on astral science, and was transmitted more or less invariantly for the next ten centuries. Of particular interest is the spatialization of Sanskrit literature itself, through the discourse on the "Ways" of literature, modes of literariness conceived of as regional styles within a cosmopolitan space. The regionality of the cosmopolitan language was qualified, however. It was the same Sanskrit everywhere—an elementary aspect of the language ideology of Sanskrit is its invariability across time and space—though differently realized in terms of phonological, semantic, or syntactic registers. But these regional differences were in fact part of the repertoire of a global Sanskrit, with writers everywhere using them to achieve different aesthetic ends (the southern style for erotic verse, for example, or the northern for martial), and thus they constituted a sign precisely of Sanskrit's ubiquity. This idea is beautifully captured in a tenth-century tale of the origins of literary culture: Poetry Man is pursued by his wife-to-be, Poetics Woman, and in the process creates literature across South Asia—and only there. Literature is decidedly transregional if not quite universal.

But where was this "South Asia"? As represented in such treatises, the Sanskrit cosmopolitan order appears smaller than the cosmopolis was in actuality, for aside from the very occasional mention in Sanskrit texts of Suvarṇabhūmi (Malaysia), Yavadvīpa (probably Java), Śrīvijaya (Palembang), and the like, Southeast Asia never formed part of the representation (the same holds true of Tibet and parts of central Asia, which participated in a more limited fashion in the Sanskrit cosmopolitan order). The conceptual space of Sanskrit texts was slow to adjust, or so one might think, to the new and larger circulatory spaces through which people had increasingly begun to move. Indeed, these actual spaces were vast, and so was the spread of Sanskrit culture, enabled by the diffusion of *kāvya* and *praśasti* on the part of peripatetic literati and the cultivation everywhere of a literarily uniform Sanskrit. Accordingly, in the first millennium it makes hardly more sense to distinguish between South and Southeast Asia than between north India and south India, despite what present-day area studies may tell us. Everywhere similar processes of cosmopolitan transculturation were under way, with the source and target of change always shifting, since there was no single point of production for cosmopolitan culture. Yet just as Southeast Asia was included in the circulatory space of the cosmopolitan order, so it came to be included in its conceptual space thanks to the transportability, so to speak, of that space. In their own geographical imagination the imperial polities of Southeast Asia—Angkor around 1000 is exemplary here—made themselves part of the cosmopolitan order by a wholesale appropriation of its toponymy. With Mount Meru and the Gaṅgā River locatable everywhere, there was no spatial center from which one could be excluded; the Sanskrit cosmopolis was wherever home was. There is nothing in the least mystical about this replicability; it is a function of a different, plural, premodern logic of space.

While modern-day equivalents to places mentioned in these spatializations are often provided here so that some geographical image will form in the mind's eye of the reader, establishing positive concordances is not the objective. The goal instead is learning to understand how people conceptualized macrospaces in the past, and what work in the spheres of culture and power such conceptualization was meant, or not meant, to do. To explore this topic is not to presuppose a seamless continuity from the sixth century to today's representations of Akhaṇḍ Bhārat, "Undivided India," that have produced the "cartographic anxiety" behind so much of contemporary Indian political action.[19] The very appropriation and concretization of a sometimes imaginary and often vague geographical past in a precise and factual present constitute one of the deadly weapons of nationalism and a source of the misery of modernity. Premodern space, whether cosmopolitan or vernacular, is not the nation-space—and yet it was no less filled with political content than it was with cultural content. The attempt to recover knowledge of this space is not fatally distorted by the discourse of nationalism. Far from disabling a history of the premodern politics of space, the distortion of national narratives is precisely the condition that makes it necessary. Such a history need not be crippled by teleology; it can instead be seen as a history of the teleological. The national narrative is a second-generation representation only made possible by the existence of a first-generation representation—one informed, however, by a very different logic that nationalism often seeks to elide.

That the space promulgated by Sanskrit analytical matrices was conceived of not just as a culture-space but also as a power-space is demonstrated by the Sanskrit *Mahābhārata*. In this *itihāsa* (narrative of "the way it once was"), or "epic" in Western parlance (genre identity is no trivial matter, given the modern discourse on "nation," "epic," and "novel" discussed in part 3), the transregional frame of reference structures the entire work. Moreover, the dissemination of its manuscripts and the distribution of royal endowments for its continual recitation actualized literary spatiality, turning representations into components of popular consciousness: people recited and listened to the *Mahābhārata*'s story of a macrospace of power even while they inhabited that very space. The evidence assembled to demonstrate this claim (chapter 6.1) aims to correct errors old and new: for instance, that it was only on mountaintops that the language of the gods touched the earth, or that it was nationalist modernity that invented the cultural-political salience of Indian epic discourse.[20]

Whatever else the *Mahābhārata* may be, it is also and preeminently a work of political theory—the single most important literary reflection on the prob-

19. The phrase is that of Krishna 1994.

20. The first is Sylvain Lévi's assessment (cited in Bloch 1965: 14–15); the second is standard-issue postcolonial theory (see chapter 14.2).

lem of the political in southern Asian history and in some ways the deepest meditation in all antiquity on the desperate realities of political life—and to mention it with reference to the ecumenical culture of the Sanskrit cosmopolis naturally raises the question of how the cultural order articulated with political practice. As noted earlier, understanding the character of polity in premodern South Asia is far more difficult than describing its cosmopolitan culture, and scholars have generated wildly discrepant accounts of what polity meant. While some of these are examined briefly, more attention is given to the modes and character of political imagination (chapter 6.2). This is not, however, a *pis aller*. Almost as important as what polities did—and just as real—is what they aspired to do. In its aspirations the imperial polity of the Sanskrit cosmopolis was marked by several consistent if elusive features. It was territorially expansive, though territoriality in premodern South Asia remains an underdefined concept. It was politically universalistic, though what political governance actually meant is hard to pin down. It was ethnically nonparticularized, if the term "ethnic" may be used when it is not even certain that ethnies in the political-science sense actually existed. The fact that these aspirations were embedded in a set of cultural practices like *kāvya* and *praśasti* suggests that the practice of polity was to some degree also an aesthetic practice. *Kāvya* and *rājya* were mutually constitutive; every man who came to rule sought the distinction of self-presentation in Sanskrit literature, typically in the permanent public form of the *praśasti*. This constitutive relationship, however, presents interpretive challenges. The single available explanation of the social function of Sanskrit cosmopolitan culture is legitimation theory and its logic of instrumental reason: elites in command of new forms of social power are understood to have deployed the mystifying symbols and codes of Sanskrit to secure popular consent. Absolute dogma though this explanatory framework may be, it is not only anachronistic but intellectually mechanical, culturally homogenizing, theoretically naive, empirically false, and tediously predictable—or at least such are the claims argued out later in this book on the basis of the data assembled here.

The peculiar character of the Sanskrit cosmopolis as a cultural and political order becomes clear only through comparative analysis. "Beware of arriving at conclusions without comparisons," said George Eliot. I agree, though perhaps not for her reasons. Comparison always implicitly informs historical analysis, given that the individual subjectivity of the historian inevitably shapes his research questions. And these questions can be more sharply formulated and better answered if the comparison behind them is explicit.[21]

21. Curiously, little good theoretical work seems to be available on cultural and political comparison. See for now Bowen and Peterson 1999: 1–19 and especially Urban's essay in that volume, pp. 90–109.

Moreover, there is a natural proclivity to generalize familiar forms of life as universal tendencies and common sense, and comparison serves to point up the actual particularity, even peculiarity, of such supposed universalisms.

The account of the Roman Empire and the place of Latin within it (chapter 7) is the first of two comparative studies undertaken here; the second (chapter 11) concerns the vernacularization of Europe. Both are more central to the larger argument of the book than the space they have been allotted might suggest. If some similarities link the Roman and the Sanskrit cultural-political orders, the differences are such that the one presents itself as a kind of countercosmopolis to the other. In both worlds, literature, after making a more or less sudden irruption into history, became a fundamental instrument for the creation of a cosmopolitan culture, with literati across immense space being trained according to comparable standards and producing literature that circulated across this space. But Latin interacted with local idioms in a way radically different from that of Sanskrit. Radically different, too, were the origin and character of the empire form, as well as the modalities of affiliation to Roman culture, or Romanization.

The Sanskrit cosmopolis was characterized by a largely homogeneous language of political poetry along with a range of comparable cultural-political practices. Constituted by no imperial state or church and consisting to a large degree in the communicative system itself and its political aesthetic, this order was characterized by a transregional consensus about the presuppositions, nature, and practices of a common culture, as well as a shared set of assumptions about the elements of power—or at least about the ways in which power is reproduced at the level of representation in language. For a millennium or more, it constituted the most compelling model of culture-power for a quarter or more of the inhabitants of the globe. And it only ended, at various times and places in the course of the first five centuries of the second millennium, under pressure from a new model. If the Sanskrit cosmopolis raises hard questions for political and cultural theory, so do the forms of life that superseded it. The fact that this later transformation occurred at all, however, has been of scarcely more interest to historical research than the Sanskrit cosmopolis itself.

THE VERNACULAR IN THEORY AND PRACTICE

The problem of the vernacular claims some attention in the first part of this book, for without this contrastive category, and the contrastive reality of both cultural and political self-understanding toward which it points, the cosmopolitan has no conceptual purchase. Like "cosmopolitan," "vernacular" is not something that goes without saying, and not only because of its own scalar ambiguities (how small qualifies as vernacular?). A range of conceptual and historical problems have combined to effectively conceal the very process of people knowledgeably becoming vernacular—what is here termed "vernacularization"—leaving it largely unhistoricized and even unconceptualized in scholarship. And until these problems are clarified and some reasonable working hypotheses framed, vernacularization itself cannot even be perceived, to say nothing of its cultural and political ramifications. The problems here are in fact not all that different from those presented by cosmopolitanism, though they are perhaps denser. Besides considering the pertinent relational boundaries, we need to be clear about what the process of vernacularization entails, in particular what role to assign to writing and to the creation of expressive texts. Only when we gain some clarity about the intelligibility and reality of the object of analysis, and how this object exists in time, can we begin to ask why it has the particular history it does. These issues are addressed in chapter 8.

Simply to define the vernacular over against the cosmopolitan and leave it at that—even to make unqualified use of any of the kindred terms or phrases adopted here, like "regional" and "transregional"—elides some important aspects of their relativity. An obvious one is the potential of a local language to become translocal, and the consequences this can have for codes that are yet more local, so to say. The extreme case is offered by the cosmopolitan languages themselves. All of them began their careers as vernaculars: Latin in the third century B.C.E. was firmly rooted in Latium (central Italy) before setting out on its world conquest in lockstep with the advance of Roman arms. Sanskrit is the great anomaly here, since long before the onset of the cosmopolitan era it had become transregional—though not yet cosmopolitan—through the spread of Vedic culture.[22]

An expansion of the vernaculars in the post-cosmopolitan era occurred, too, but of an altogether different order of magnitude. Take the language now called Old Kannada. This developed from the prestige dialect of an area in northwest Karnataka into a unified medium for literary and political communication over a limited zone of southern India late in the first millennium. The intellectuals who cultivated the language clearly understood these spatial limitations and harbored no illusions about or aspirations toward its universalization. They defined a literary culture, and along with it a political order, in conscious opposition to some larger world, in relationship to which they chose to speak more locally. And they were fully aware they were doing so. And yet Kannada in fact became transregional—sometimes domineeringly transregional—for writers in still smaller zones marked by other idioms, such as Tulunadu and the southern Konkan on the west coast; as a result neither Tulu nor Konkani was committed to writing, let alone elaborated for

22. On the early history of the transregionality of this culture, which is not addressed in this book, the work of Michael Witzel is central; see for example Witzel 1987.

literature, until the colonial era. A precisely similar dynamic reveals itself in the history of vernacularization in western Europe. The vernacular that came to be called French first acknowledged spatial limits as compared with the limitless Latin, and later evinced an expansiveness into narrower spaces—or what were thereby transformed into narrower spaces—such as Brittany or Provence.[23]

If a certain transregionality thus characterized the vernaculars that attained cultural-political salience, this was on an entirely different scale from the cosmopolitan codes they displaced. This difference can be plotted along both the axis of material practice and that of subjective understanding. Sanskrit literary texts came to circulate from Sri Lanka to Sorcuq in central Asia, and from Afghanistan to Annam in Southeast Asia (just as Latin literary texts circulated from Iberia to Romania and Britain to Tunisia). They filled all the available cultural space, their expansion as literary-political media limited only by other cosmopolitan cultural formations; in northern Vietnam, for example, from the fifth century on, Sanskrit's advance was arrested by Chinese, as that of Latin was arrested by Greek in the eastern Mediterranean a few centuries earlier. The vernaculars inhabited much smaller zones; the limits they confronted, or rather helped to produce, were certain cultural-political isoglosses, so to speak, whose history and character are probed in the course of the second part of this work.

The objective dimensions of vernacular place over against those of cosmopolitan space were also registered within the subjective universes of the vernacular intellectuals. To participate in Sanskrit literary culture was to participate in a vast world; to produce a regional alternative to it was to effect a profound break—one the agents themselves understood to be a break—in cultural communication and self-understanding. It was in conscious opposition to this larger sphere that these intellectuals defined their regional worlds. They chose to write in a language that did not travel—and that they knew did not travel—as easily and as far as the well-traveled language of the older cosmopolitan order. The new culture-power places they projected, which were the conceptual correlates of the isoglosses just mentioned, fully testify to this sense of limit and contrast sharply with the spatial matrices at work in Sanskrit culture.

The localization in question is reflected in the South Asian term for the vernacular. If "Sanskrit cosmopolis" is a phrase hobbled by its hybridity, its

23. An impatience not unlike that sometimes felt by Kannadigas (and Kannada scholars) toward Tamilians (and Tamilists) who pretend to represent "south India" (see Gopal 1986 and 1992, and cf. e.g., Kulke ed. 1995: 165) is found among Tulavas (and specialists in Tulu) toward the Kannadigas who pretend to represent "Karnataka." See Honko 1998: 245 ff. Comparable responses in Provence and Brittany are well known; a memorable account is Hélias 1978.

adoption is an adversity that cannot be avoided and that anyway has uses in foregrounding the quasi-global, the political, and the cultural. "Vernacular" has similar liabilities and benefits. To be sure, a pejorative connotation haunts the Latin etymon—it refers to the language of the *verna,* or house-born slave, of Republican Rome—which has little political-cultural relevance to premodern South Asia. However, in a more common, indeed classical, sense the Latin *vernacularis* is "local," "native," "inborn," even "Roman" (in contrast to *peregrinus,* "foreign"). Apart from the fact that the cosmopolitan culture of Rome could be conceived of as native (another of its radical differences from the Sanskrit order, deriving from Latin's very different history), the sense of local does map well against the South Asian idiom. In many South Asian languages the conceptual counterpart to the cosmopolitan is *deśī,* the "placed," or "[a practice] of Place." Yet it is critical to register at once the paradox that what was *deśī* was not often thought of as native, inborn, or sometimes even local (as the discussion of region and reason in chapter 10.2 makes clear). Not only was the creation of local places a cultural process consequent upon literary vernacularization, but the very ubiquity of the self-same term *deśī* across South Asia is a sign of the *cosmopolitan* origins of the literary vernacular itself.

Finding vernacularization in history presupposes not just a sense of relevant orders of magnitude but also a clear conceptualization of the vernacularizing process and of the very idea that this process can begin. The question of beginnings raises a range of cognitive, conceptual, and ideological problems explored in chapter 8.1. A postmodern anxiety now attaches to the question of beginnings, the ominous phrase "quest for origins" conjuring up intellectual failings ranging from theoretical innocence to fundamentalism. There are older anxieties, too. The possibility of vernacular beginnings is often denied since, in a positivist historical sense, a beginning is always hostage to the fortune of historical preservation. Beginnings are held as suspect, produced by the machinations of modern (or premodern) inventors of tradition. They are historically unintelligible, since producers of culture often think they are beginning the new when they are continuing the old, or (more often in India) the reverse. They are undefinable, since boundaries between new and old, especially language boundaries, can be very blurry. And they are illogical because they cannot escape circularity: an absolute historiographical beginning has already organized the evidence required for its own justification.

Such problems might seem fatal, but far from weakening a historical account of the vernacularization process, they can strengthen it if they form part of the substance of that account. Beginnings are not only a *pāramārthika sat* according to some absolute historiography but a *vyāvahārika sat* according to the actors' understanding of their own life experiences. Thus, many vernacular literary cultures acknowledge and commemorate a beginning (as the cosmopolitan Sanskrit tradition does), and the memories developed around that beginning are themselves significant. Traditional accounts have certain vested interests, of course, and will often misrepresent what seems to us the truth of the matter. Yet misrepresentation is real, and falsification is true, in the sense that both have a historical reality. And for many literary cultures in South Asia evidence is available, far richer than that for Europe, in fact, that allows us to see vernacularization actually taking place—one of the few great historical changes in premodern India that we can actually document with some precision.

Vernacularization is here understood—not a priori or stipulatively but from tendencies visible in the empirical record—as the historical process of choosing to create a written literature, along with its complement, a political discourse, in local languages according to models supplied by a superordinate, usually cosmopolitan, literary culture. The process can thus be broken down into three connected components. Two have already been introduced: literization, and literarization. The third, closely related to the latter, is "superposition," or the presence of a dominant language and literary formation. While literarization and superposition can be briskly reviewed, literization needs additional attention.

Gaining access to writing, the resulting symbolic elevation of what is written, and the transformations to which the written text becomes subject by the very fact of its being written—such literization is the component without which vernacularization cannot be perceived as historical fact. Local languages of course existed in oral prehistory but only in a phenomenological rather than a conceptual sense, as "Language" or language continua rather than as defined languages. One such continuum, Kannada—or what in later literized discourse was named Kannada—merged imperceptibly into what in later discourse was named Marathi and Telugu, just as preliterate French merged into preliterate Spanish and Italian. In such a lifeworld, Kannada and the other languages should not even be regarded as pregiven points on a spectrum: the division of that continuum is an effect of, among other things, the cognitive revolution of writing that was part of the vernacularization process itself.

Although the materials assembled in this book will often be seen to contradict the views of Mikhail Bakhtin, they confirm his argument that "unified" or "unitary" language is "not something given" but something "posited" in opposition to "the realities of heteroglossia"; it "constitutes the theoretical expression of the historical processes of linguistic unification and centralization." What enables this positing, unification, and centralization to begin is literization and the processes of literary elaboration (Nietzsche's *objektive Schriftsprache*). Writing "creates" a language discursively as well as factually, promoting its regularization and, above all, its conceptual differentiation.[24] These are processes of which, again, premodern South Asian vernacular writers were fully aware, as the great monuments of vernacular unification demonstrate (chapters 9.2, 10.1). In this sense, vernacularity is not a natural state of being but a willed act of becoming. When cultural actors "choose a vernacular language" for literature and so inaugurate the vernacularization process, it is important to understand that they are choosing something that doesn't exist yet as a fully formed, stable totality; instead, Language is constituted as *a language*, as a conceptual object, in part by the very production of texts. Choosing at the inaugural moment means to begin to create such a totality out of the continuum of patois that constitutes language in a preliterate world.

To write at all in premodernity, let alone to write literarily, always meant writing in a language that was both learned and learnéd, endowing it with new norms and constraints and, inevitably, the new social status associated with constraint and normativity. Thus one definition of vernacular found in sociolinguistics, the "unstandardized native language of a speech community," is not relevant here, for in many cases the creation of a literary vernacular carried with it a powerful imperative toward standardization, often accompanied by formal grammaticization. It is the technology of writing that first began to unify the vernaculars, a process only intensified and not inaugurated by print. Historically speaking, what counted in the history of vernacular literary culture—what made history not only for us, by providing historical objects, but for the primary agents themselves, by marking a rupture in the continuum of history—was the committing of local language to written form.[25] Yet central to understanding the history of vernacularization is the fact that more than inscription was required for its achievement. Also essential was the creation of a vision of power and culture made possible only by the elaboration of a literary corpus. This rarely occurred at the inaugural moment of literization; as the South Asian materials show unequivocally, that moment was always *documentary*, nonliterary. Contrary to what we commonly assume, the history of a language and its literature are not coextensive.

The claim that literary vernacularization can begin and thereby become

24. This is sometimes referred to in sociolinguistics as Ausbau (elaboration) after Kloss 1967, which Kloss himself conceived of as the process whereby language differentiation is created, as between Swedish and Danish, which are therefore Ausbausprachen, or "languages by design," as opposed to Abstandsprachen, or "languages by distance," such as English and French. Bakhtin's observation is found in 1981: 270.

25. Two scholars who have rethought technologies and beginnings in European literature are Zumthor (1987), who locates the critical moment in script culture, and Gumbrecht (1988), who finds it in print culture, each technology possessing its particular textual and performative consequences. On writing and language naming see Janson 1991: 23–28. The sociolinguistic definition is that of Fasold 1984: 62 (following Charles Ferguson).

historically meaningful as a category of cultural analysis would indeed be unintelligible if either of two assumptions dealt with earlier were true—that the oral can be literature or that literature can be anything that is written. Neither proposition was historically the case for the societies under consideration in this book. Writing was constitutive of the process that made the vernacular literary, because the "literary" in these societies was the written production of expressive forms of language use, for the most part the sort prescribed in the dominant cultural formation against which the regional was defining itself. Accordingly, literization, the development of a written form of the vernacular, may have been a necessary condition for vernacularization but it was not a sufficient one; also required was literarization, the development of imaginative, workly discourse.

The fundamental differentiation between documentary and workly literization, as well as the gulf that eventually arose between orality and written literature, are made manifest in a range of South Asian narratives of vernacular self-assertion and risk (8.2). When the cultural notables of his town punished a seventeenth-century Marathi poet by throwing his texts in a river, it was because what he had written in the language of Place was no mere document but *kāvya.* And his anguish that his work may have been lost was not misplaced: literature *could now be lost* since it was something written and impermanent rather than something oral and stored lastingly in the memory: When the text-artifact was gone, the text was gone.

A prevalent feature in the vernacularization process is the time lag between literization and literarization. Many languages, from Marathi to Khmer, reveal long histories prior to their literary transformation. In all cases, literization was mediated by Sanskrit. Sometimes this happened simultaneously with the introduction of cosmopolitan literary culture, sometimes centuries later; inscriptions in Khmer are found from as early as the seventh century, within a few generations of the appearance of Sanskrit in Cambodia, those in Marathi from only at the end of the tenth century, after a millennium of Sanskrit literary culture in the region. Yet it was only much later—for Marathi, around the fourteenth century, for Khmer, around the sixteenth or seventeenth—that those languages came to be used for literary forms of writing. The possibility that languages could be speciated through initial documentary elaboration and yet remain indefinitely restricted to nonliterary functions by a firm division of linguistic labor was the norm in the Sanskrit cosmopolitan world. Four hundred years of Marathi literature, and a thousand of Khmer, did not disappear without trace. Rather, until Khmer and Marathi vernacular newness entered their worlds, Sanskrit occupied the entire space of literate literature and literate political expression, a fact we see registered in the Sanskrit theory of literary language as a closed set. Some of the earliest textualizations of the languages of Place are found in the twelfth-century encyclopedia mentioned earlier: these are presented not in the section on literature, however, but in that on song; the author is clear that "literature" is a cosmopolitan practice; all the rest is just music (chapter 8.2). Only once we have established the fact that vernacular literature did begin, by reason of newfound literariness wedded to literacy, can we ask the all-important questions why it began when it did and why at this or that particular social site.

If nationalists and other indigenists are predisposed to discover an ever-deeper history for the literature of the Folk, reaching back to a golden moment of pure autochthony, historical analysis shows that literatures typically arise in response to other literature *superposed* to them in a relation of unequal cultural power. In premodern India this other literature was preeminently Sanskrit, but also to some degree Prakrit and Apabhramsha (which were particularly rich sources of metrical forms for the vernaculars to appropriate), Tamil in some areas of south India, and, much later, Persian in some areas of the north. Conformity with the superposed matrix and its norms was the goal of those vernacular textbooks meant to "ornament" the language. Indeed, they were part of a literary apparatus that was adopted wholesale during the crystallizing moments of many vernacular literary cultures and formed a core component in the creation of what is here named the "cosmopolitan vernacular," that register of the emergent vernacular that aims to localize the full spectrum of literary qualities of the superposed cosmopolitan code (chapter 8.3).[26]

Chapter 9 offers a case study of all the elements of vernacularization just described in abstract terms. Few literary cultures anywhere permit the degree of historicization we can achieve for Kannada, due to the density of inscriptions and of texts recopied with singular devotion for more than ten centuries. Whereas Kannada was first literized as early as the fifth century, it did not come to be used for the production of *praśasti* until the ninth, when the elaboration also began of what, by the end of the thirteenth, would be a complete array of the elements of a literary culture. When the process of literarization was inaugurated, it occurred in one place only: the royal court. The first literary text in Kannada, and one of the great documents in the history of South Asian vernacularization, the *Kavirājamārgar* (Way of the King of Poets), was produced at the court of the ruling dynasty in ninth-century Karnataka. It adopts and adapts a cosmopolitan poetics, the great Way of writing, from an earlier Sanskrit treatise and makes it serve as the framework for a theory of the literary practices of Place, creating in the process one of

26. Texts that "adorn" the South Asian vernaculars by framing grammatical and rhetorical norms (the *Siyabaslakara* of ninth-century Sri Lanka, the *Kannadabhāṣābhūṣaṇam* of eleventh-century Karnataka, the *[Braj]Bhāṣābhūṣaṇ* of seventeenth-century Jodhpur; see chapters 9 and 10 in this book) are precisely equivalent to those meant to "illustrate" the European vernaculars (chapter 11.2).

the earliest examples of the cosmopolitan vernacular that in many regions would become the preeminent register of regional literary expression until the coming of colonialism (chapter 9.2)

To speak of a cosmopolitan vernacular is not just to acknowledge that "different languages are penetrated by each other, thus revealing every language's intimate discord with itself, the bilingualism implicit in all human speech"; nor even to try to update the idea of "vernacular humanism," of "using the ancient languages as models and so making the vernacular languages into worthy vehicles for literature and culture."[27] It is to point to the historical creation of a medium of culture that was not only new in itself but appropriate to a new vision of power—a medium of Place for a political vision of Place, but fashioned according to the time-honored model of *kāvya* and *rājya* of the great Way, which had been tied to no one place but were inclusive of them all. The existence of such a vision, and the fact that political power was centrally interested in sustaining a vernacular literary culture to produce it, find repeated corroboration in Kannada. Just as the *Kavirājamārgam* particularizes a global aesthetic, so the Kannada *Mahābhārata* of Pampa (c. 950) localizes a translocal narrative in the service of a new (or newly self-conscious) regional power formation, shrinking the space of the Sanskrit epic and its political vision to a narrower place, Kannaḍanāḍu, the culture-land of Kannada, which had already been announced in the *Kavirājamārgam*. The philological impulse of the *Kavirājamārgam* was also elaborated in a whole new set of vernacular subdisciplines, above all, grammar, which found its supreme expression at the Hoysaḷa court in the thirteenth century with the composition of one of the greatest regional-language grammars of India, the *Śabdamaṇidarpaṇam* (Jeweled Mirror of Language). Especially important here is the new cultural consciousness, unknown to the Sanskrit world, exhibited in the claims of the vernacular grammarian to legislate literary norms (chapter 9.3, 4).

Virtually all of the traits explored in the Kannada world—the time lag between literization and literarization, the place of the court in the creation of literary culture, the epicization of regional political space, the character of vernacular philology—mark the histories of vernacularization across southern Asia and their conceptualization, the rationalizations of regionality (chapter 10.1, 2). The historical material itself presents few serious challenges of interpretation. More difficult to explain is the transformation that was concurrently under way in the political sphere and the nature of its relationship to developments in literary culture (10.3). Choosing a language for literary and political text production implies affiliating with an existing sociotextual community or summoning such a community into being. For

27. Agamben 1999: 59; Auerbach 1965: 319.

it is in part from acts of reading, hearing, performing, reproducing, and circulating literary and political texts that social groups come to produce themselves and understand themselves as groups. This is especially the case when a notable feature of the texts in question, what might be termed an indexical rather than referential feature, is the very use of vernacular language for producing literary and political discourse. Whatever else it may be, the vernacularization of literature and political discourse is a social act, and one that typically bears major geocultural and political entailments.

While it is no easier to understand the practices of power in the second millennium than in the first, it is clear that during the period 1000–1500 these practices took on far more distinctively regionalized traits than ever before. Whether crystallizing culture spheres were the cause or consequence of crystallizing power spheres, or whether the two arose through a kind of dialectical dynamic, a new symmetry between the domains was patently being created. Functional regions began to coincide with formal regions—those new and coherent representations of place in vernacular literature that superseded the vast geocultural spaces prevalent during the preceding millennium. Understanding the nature of the new political order that arose with vernacularization is as difficult as understanding the nature of "empire" in the cosmopolitan epoch, and it has seemed preferable, therefore, to name this new political form neutrally as the "vernacular polity" rather than try to shoehorn it into some given European conceptual category (such as "protonation"). But one thing is certain: however much the fact may conflict with dominant social-science theory, especially of nationalism, power and culture had indeed a very considerable, if sometimes obscure, inclination for each other in premodern South Asia.

That the context of power fundamentally shaped the process of vernacularization in South Asia sits awkwardly with the unchallenged scholarly consensus regarding its origins as essentially religious, a kind of Indian Reformation (chapter 10.4). This view is as erroneous as is the one that locates the origins of European vernacularization in the real Reformation (sometimes Protestant presuppositions do not even work for Europe). Virtually all the reasons adduced for explaining vernacularization in South Asia as originating in a socioreligious rebellion are dubious. The presumed concomitance between Sanskrit and Brahmanism on the one hand and vernacularity and non-Brahmanism on the other does not hold for much of the period under discussion. The vision of Sanskrit as a sacred language "jealously preserved by the Brahmans in their schools" may not be the pure illusion of the colonial officer who gave it expression, yet it is undoubtedly something that developed late in this history of the language, when, for reasons very likely having to do with vernacularization itself, language options shrank for many communities and Brahmanical society reasserted its archaic monopolization over the language (the Catholic Church's eventual monopolization of Latin is an instructive parallel both historically and structurally).[28] In most cases, vernacular beginnings occurred independently of religious stimuli strictly construed, and the greater portion of the literature thereby created was produced not at the monastery but at the court. Only after vernacularization had been consolidated, and in reaction to an already-existing courtly literary and political culture, did a more demotic and often more religiously insurgent *second* vernacular revolution take place (as in twelfth-century Karnataka, fifteenth-century Gujarat, sixteenth-century Assam, and elsewhere). Here the cosmopolitan vernacular was challenged and in some cases displaced by a regional vernacular, a register far more localized in everything from lexicon to metrics to themes. The present account, by foregrounding the role of power in creating both the Sanskrit cosmopolis and the various regional worlds that succeeded it, aims to redress an interpretive balance that for too long has been skewed toward the religious.

In the nexus of poetry and polity we also encounter what is most salient and most neglected for a cross-cultural historical analysis of vernacularization. This analysis is initiated in chapter 11, where parallels between India and Europe in cultural and political regionalization are examined. Temporal, spatial, and other synchronies and symmetries abound. The tempo and structure of Dravidian and Germanic vernacularization, for example, form a striking contrast with those of north Indian and Romance languages. Many of the textual components in European vernacularization are comparable to those found in South Asia, such as the localization of superposed literary forms, genres, and themes. The social milieus are similar, too. The European vernaculars achieved literary expressivity—and often did so with astonishing abruptness—through the agency of courtly elites: whereas vernacular culture was undoubtedly in some sense popular culture in its origins, the process of full vernacularization was decidedly not. Yet there are important differences, too, and some of these are explored in chapter 12.1. In Europe the vernacular's admission to literacy was more contested, both linguistically and ideologically; vernacular distinction was slower in coming and was attended with greater anxiety; the cosmopolitan formation was more stubborn in its claim to primacy. A far more significant divergence is found in the development of polity. In both areas the political order that emerged in conjunction with vernacularization offered a regional alternative to the transregional imperial formation. But the specific character of the European form, and its endpoint, the nation-state, was unlike anything found in South Asia. The cultural and political theory designed to make sense of the European nation-state is often, and too facilely, applied to the premodern world out-

28. See Grierson 1927: 1129 for the quote. The gradual decrease in language options in early-modern South Asia is touched on in Pollock 2003: 73 ff.

side of Europe, distorting thinking about language and identity, and identity and polity, and thereby occluding the specificity of the Indian case and its misfit with models designed to explain the European. The comparative turn is therefore imperative for a history and theory of vernacularity in southern Asia.

The transformations in culture and power that began concurrently in India and Europe around the start of the second millennium were consolidated by its midway point. The rules of the new vernacular game of polity and poetry had largely been drawn up; the cosmopolitan order in both worlds was almost completely supplanted by the seventeenth century. If it is becoming possible to recognize vernacularization as a key historical problem only now that it is ending, the recognition is the easy part. Far more difficult is understanding the hard history of its origins, why across much of Eurasia the world abandoned cosmopolitanism and empire in favor of vernacularity and regional polities, and why this happened when it did (chapter 12.2). Whereas we can identify some factors that clearly contributed—reinvigorated trading networks in the early second millennium concentrated wealth in local power centers, the expansion of Islam on its western and eastern frontiers offered new cultural stimuli—a unified explanation of the historical origins of vernacularism is as improbable as a unified explanation of the cosmopolitanism that preceded. Yet the lack does not preclude learning lessons from these events, both for the theory of culture and power and for their practice.

To study the history of vernacularization is to study not the history of the emergence of primeval and natural communities of peoples and cultures but the historical inauguration of the naturalization of peoples and cultures through new conceptual and discursive practices. This naturalization took place by a double procedure of reduction and differentiation: as unmarked dialect was turned into unifying standard, heterogeneous practice into culture, and undifferentiated space into place, new regional worlds were created. What was inside these worlds would eventually be seen as the indigenous and natural; what was outside, as the exogenous and artificial. This did not happen everywhere in a similar manner; not all ways of the cultural production of vernacular sameness and difference have been the same, any more than all cosmopolitanisms have been the same. Figuring out what may have been distinctive about these vernacular and cosmopolitan practices is a precious if elusive prize.

THEORY, METATHEORY, PRACTICE, METAPRACTICE

The rise of the Sanskrit cosmopolitan culture-power formation and its supplementation and eventual supersession by vernacular orders constitute an important chapter in the story of human thought and action. The value of this story, from the standpoint of this book, lies not in its sovereign particularities but in its capacity to enrich the historical record of large-scale cultural and political processes, and thereby to help prove, improve, or perhaps even disprove and replace, existent theories as only such enriched historical records enable us to do. Several related questions concerning these processes have therefore been implicit in the organization of this exposition from the start, and the very materials have reinforced them at every step of the way. These have long been items on the agenda of social and political analysis and theory, but not often have they been the explicit objects of the empirical histories of the premodern world. It will be useful to restate them as clearly as possible.

First, in accounting for cultural and political change in South Asia over the first millennium and a half of the Common Era, what role is to be attributed to human agency and choice? Why did people choose—and a choice it most decidedly was—to invent entirely new forms of culture? Why did they adopt from others what must often have seemed the less intimately related, cosmopolitan cultural forms—especially in the case of a form so unintimate and unforgiving as that of Sanskrit—while abandoning older language routines and associated life conceptions that had become habitual? And why did they later reverse course and reject those quasi-global, illustrious, and by then long-familiar practices for other, local ones that were, according to prevailing standards, as yet undistinguished and new, if often made to appear customary? This large problematic is embedded in my term "transculturation," which has suggested itself in preference to more common ones like "acculturation" precisely because of the sense of agency it seems to connote.

Second, how does culture relate to political orders—culture in the sense of language and the production of texts, and especially texts denominated as *kāvya, sāhitya, poesis, literae, literature,* and the like, which have expressive, imaginative, workly ends? And why were these orders themselves similarly remade over the course of this millennium and a half, with the old aspiration of attaining "power to the horizons" and "empire without end"—*diganta rājya, imperium sine fine*—being re-placed, literally, by a new concern for locality? This second problematic, culture's link with power—call it politicization for want of a better term—comprises two closely connected issues. One relates to the reproduction of power and thus to what is familiar in Western social theory as legitimation of authority, ideology, hegemony, and like notions. The other issue relates to the constitution of power and thus to the organization of communities in general and to the two great kinds of organization in particular: (1) empire (as political form) and civilization (as cultural form), as they are called in the West, usually termed in this work the cosmopolitan culture-power complex; and (2) the nation, or here, the vernacular polity and cultural order.

If the purpose of knowing the history reconstructed in the first two parts of this book is to elaborate higher-order theories of power and culture, especially concerning the large themes of politicization and transculturation, in order to achieve this elaboration it is still necessary to have a more general theory of theory itself and its relationship to empirical work. How in fact is cultural-political theory fashioned from particulars, and how do newly elaborated models stand in relationship to earlier ones? Here we enter into a rather complex logic—a kind of Moebian strip, it sometimes seems—where finding where to begin is no easy thing. One (usually unstated) purpose of social or humanistic theory, whether concerning the development of polity or the place of expressive textuality, is to discover lawlike patterns in human behavior; these are then supposed to be put to use to order and make sense of new data. Such nomothetic theory can be of a very general sort, like Weber's dictum on how societies cohere: "In no instance does domination voluntarily limit itself to the appeal to material or affectual or ideal motives as a basis for its continuance. In addition every such system [of domination] attempts to establish and to cultivate the belief in its legitimacy." Or it can be quite specific, as in Bakhtin's dictum on the nature of epic discourse: "The epic world is constructed in the zone of an absolute distanced image, beyond the sphere of possible contact with the developing, incomplete and therefore re-thinking and re-evaluating present."[29] Much of what may sound distant and obscure when characterized as nomological thought of this sort tends to mutate into common sense. Epic worlds are now typically seen as perfected and distant from the present; domination is now typically thought to require legitimation. Conceptions of this sort—generalizations extrapolated from what always and of necessity are highly limited sets of particulars—can often inhibit rather than enable thought.[30] Yet the tendency to approach every problem in the history of culture and power with such conceptions firmly shaping one's understanding is hard to shake.

At the most general level of analysis, all perception is admittedly theory-laden, as many sociologists and philosophers have explained. We cannot cognize the world around us without simultaneously fitting our cognitions—or prefitting or retrofitting them, whichever is the true sequence—into the linguistic and conceptual schemata that constitute our world; the formulation of empirical observations becomes possible only within some referential framework. Theory at so intimate a level is very hard indeed to resist. Coupled with this, however, is the belief that already-available higher-order conceptualizations *ought* to structure our empirical work. The dominance of theory has been such that, in the human sciences at least, we often set out not

29. Weber 1978, vol. 1: 213; Bakhtin 1981: 17.

30. I examine one such conception in chapter 13.2 ("the history of all hitherto existing societies is the history of class struggle") but must ignore others completely (e.g., "a situation which every child is destined to pass through and which follows inevitably . . . the Oedipus complex").

to test it systematically but to deploy it while blithely assuming its truth. We thus do Weberian or Bakhtinian "readings" of political or cultural processes when, as those theories sometimes quite explicitly suggest, we should be examining such processes precisely to evaluate and, if necessary, revise Weber or Bakhtin.

If the examination of empirical materials is the horse to theory's cart, the horse should not be allowed to follow behind, let alone to wander off without pulling any theoretical load at all (a common failing of philology in general and Indology in particular). For one thing, theory is there to be tested; for another, the whole reason to study new particulars, after all, is to learn something from them—to frame new theory, which will itself become subject to testing. Other objections to prioritizing theory can be found. Leave aside the disarray of contemporary theory itself,[31] more important is the fact that the conditions that have made possible theory as we know it are the very conditions that must limit it, at least for a book like this one. Theories of power and culture—on legitimation of political authority, epic distance in literature, and a host of other questions—have their origins in the West in capitalism and modernity and were devised to make sense of the behavior of power and culture under Western capitalist modernity, the first political-economic and cultural order to theorize its own emergence and specificity. These are the particulars from which larger universalizations have typically been produced, in association with the universalization of Western power under colonialism and globalization. Given the conditions that made them possible, however, extrapolating from these particulars needs serious justification. For understanding the noncapitalist, nonmodern non-West, the theory problem that confronts us is acute. Trapped in the dichotomy of economism and culturalism peculiar to thinking through our own world, scholars typically reduce culture to power or power to culture and miss what may have been different about their relation to each other in the past. It is no easy thing to theorize premodernity without deploying the theoretical instruments forged by modernity, since they are the only ones we have.

These problems can be illustrated by previewing the questions raised by the problem of ideology (chapter 13.3). What role if any should be assigned, in the case of precapitalist South Asia, to the notion of ideology in its strong formulation, as a discourse of false necessity that through systematic distortion naturalizes and reproduces relations of unequal power? Is the problem of how social and political orders cohere, and of the mechanisms at work in their coherence, uniform throughout history? Or does the particular tension between capital and labor under the conditions of unfree freedom in capitalism engender a specific instability along with new ideational forms to

31. One recent review is Dirks 1998.

manage it? Aren't there presuppositions and unwarranted extensions of the particularities of capitalist modernity that one accepts as soon as one begins the search for ideological effects, inhibiting in advance the production of new theory from the empirical matrix—precisely what is required to account for precapitalist cultural and political formations? Theoretical openness would be required even if a consensus about ideology reigned today. How much more so when its usefulness for understanding social cohesion in capitalism itself has been increasingly thrown into doubt.[32]

Here a vast realm of inquiry opens before us. It is at once too fundamental to pass over in silence, as if we knew all the answers to begin with, and too complex to pretend to examine comprehensively; for any single question it is impossible even to summarize current standpoints. What is offered in part 3 are reflections on a few theoretical positions relevant to understanding premodern South Asia and an assessment of how well these positions fit with our materials and where the theoretical seams need to be let out. Among these perspectives are "cultural naturalism," the view that culture evolves and can be understood through evolutionary biology; several core conceptions about culture in society, especially the place of and commitment to language ("linguism") and the sense of peoplehood ("ethnicity"); and perhaps most important because it is the most widespread, functionalist approaches to explaining culture in relation to power (chapter 13).

This review is followed by a discussion of the two complementary paradigms of Western thinking about culture-power formations: civilization and nation (chapter 14). The former is the usual conceptual framework for understanding cosmopolitan culture and imperial polity, the latter for understanding vernacular culture and national polity. Both frameworks share assumptions about autochthony, but in constituting it they employ opposite historiographical practices. The theory of civilization, or as it is called here, civilizationalism, needs historical scarcity; nationalism, by contrast, requires historical surplus. No civilization wants its origins searched, and every nation does. Civilizationalism promotes a vision of always already perfected formations, which, depending on the historical epoch of the interpreter, either confer their gifts on "retarded or primitive cultures" or confront other already-perfected formations that merely add a foreign bauble here and an exotic bangle there—transculturation as either development or accessorizing. The theory of nations narrows thinking even more dramatically. If for constructivists nations are new and Western and all the rest are deficient and derivative, for nationalists old non-Western nations exist with even deeper and more authentic roots. Both theories of civilizations and theories of nations typically ignore complexity, heterogeneity, and historical

32. An important statement is found in Abercrombie et al. 1990: xv–xvi, 230.

process—precisely what the materials from premodern South Asia compel us to acknowledge.

Following this assessment of some universalizing frameworks for understanding the relationship of culture and power, and their inadequacy in accounting for data provided in the first two parts of this book, an epilogue recapitulates the larger trends identified in the history of this relationship before modernity and weighs the implications of these trends for shaping future practices. An ancient theory of practice in South Asia teaches that thought (figured as spirit, *puruṣa*) is inert unless embodied in action (figured as matter, *prakṛti*), whereas action without thought is blind. In keeping with this formulation I hold that a historical reconstruction of past practices, if considered apart from their potential to effect future practices, is an empty enterprise, however obscure the linkage may be between knowledge, especially knowledge of the past, and practices, especially practices yet to come.

An analysis of how, and how variously, people in the past have practiced being cosmopolitan and being vernacular requires therefore a further step, one toward a consideration of what might be called metapractice: learning in some reflexive, self-monitoring, and self-correcting way possibilities of practice different from those of the present through the resources opened up by studies of the nonpresent. The world of capitalist modernity enforces the hard logic of *either/or* in the domain of both the global and the local—the indigenism of civilizationalism and nationalism can tolerate no less—whereas ways of being *both/and,* however antinomic this may appear as an abstract proposition of logic, are shown by actual histories of cosmopolitan and vernacular in South Asia to not have been impossible. Learning that other practices have been available in the past may enable us to practice differently in the future.

The possibility of such knowledge is what makes the study of the South Asian past matter to the present. For much of their careers Sanskrit and the high vernaculars were no doubt the voices through which power spoke in South Asia—the voices of the powerless were often silenced in both the literary and the documentary records. But power is always relative, and the powerful of South Asian premodernity became the powerless in the force field of colonialism and capitalist modernity. Understanding the voice of power in premodern South Asia thus requires positive as well as negative critique. The target of negative critique is the violence—it is not too strong a word—exercised by Sanskrit discourses of domination, and although these are not the object of inquiry here, the kind of analysis they require merits comment.[33] Domination does not disappear simply by forgetting or destroying the lan-

33. See for example Pollock 1990, 1993a.

guage of domination, as some today believe who burn Sanskrit libraries. The past will not go away by ignoring it or pretending it is past: either we master it through critical historical analysis or it will continue to master us. Complementary to this position is the "cautious detachment" of Walter Benjamin's historian, so often quoted and so often ignored, which we need to cultivate when we examine the texts of power, whether cosmopolitan or vernacular, whether in South Asia or elsewhere: "For without exception the cultural treasures he surveys have an origin which he cannot contemplate without horror. They owe their existence not only to the efforts of the great minds and talents who have created them, but also to the anonymous toil of their contemporaries. There is no document of civilization which is not at the same time a document of barbarism."[34]

The targets of positive critique are those alternative possibilities of culture and power in South Asia that disappeared with modernity and capitalism but whose traces are preserved in the languages of premodern India. A story is told about the great ascetic Śaṅkara, how by leaving his own body and entering into the corpse of the dead king Amaru, he was able to reanimate him long enough to learn the ways of love. In the same way, if we can enter into these languages in some deep way, by acts of critical philology, historical sensitivity, and reflexive interpretation, they may be able to tell us something about ways of life vital for our future.

34. Benjamin 1969: 256.

PART ONE

The Sanskrit Cosmopolis

CHAPTER ONE

The Language of the Gods Enters the World

1.1 PRECOSMOPOLITAN SANSKRIT: MONOPOLIZATION AND RITUALIZATION

The transformation of the social life of Sanskrit around the beginning of the Common Era constitutes one of the most momentous events in the history of culture and power in Asia. It is also one of the least discussed and as a result, unsurprisingly, the least understood.

From around the beginning of the first millennium B.C.E., when the earliest form of Sanskrit appeared in South Asia, until around the beginning of the first millennium C.E., Sanskrit functioned as a communicative medium that was restricted both in terms of who was permitted to make use of the language and which purposes the language could subserve. Access to Sanskrit was reserved for particular orders of society, and it was employed predominantly in connection with the liturgy of the Vedic ritual and associated knowledge systems such as grammar, phonetics, and metrics. Its transformation, around the beginning of the first millennium C.E., into a far more broadly available language, with new and unprecedented expressive purposes to execute—above all, *kāvya* and *praśasti,* courtly literature and royal praise-poetry—led to the creation of a culture-power formation that would exhibit an astonishing stability over the following ten or more centuries. The aim of this chapter is to try to grasp this moment of expansion and transformation not only by identifying its salient dimensions but by establishing the very fact that it can be seen as constituting a historical event, indeed, a rupture in time. The existence of this event can emerge only against the background of the long prehistory of Sanskrit in its sacerdotal isolation. In order to capture something of this prehistory and get a sense of the social and discursive boundaries—symmetrical in their structure and related in their logic—that would be crossed around the beginning of the Common Era, it is most efficient to organize the exposition around two notions: social monopolization, especially as enunciated in Pūrvamīmāṃsā, the "prior analytic" of the nature of Vedic textuality, and discursive ritualization, especially as this becomes manifest in the early grammatical tradition.

One key characteristic of Sanskrit in the precosmopolitan period, explicit in the texts themselves whenever the problem of language and culture is raised, is that it was a code of communication not everyone was entitled to use, and fewer still were able to use. It is not just that some people did and some did not employ Sanskrit, but rather that some were permitted to do so and some—the majority, who otherwise might have been able to do so—were prohibited. Given the nature of the primary sphere for the application of Sanskrit, it is not surprising that this constraint was formulated as a restriction on participation in the rituals and liturgical practices of the Sanskrit speech community, whose members called themselves Āryas. And, again not unexpectedly, it is the Pūrvamīmāṃsā that most explicitly argues out this language monopolization. The foundational text of the system, the *Mīmāṃsāsūtra* attributed to Jaimini, dates to the last centuries (most probably third or second) B.C.E. There is good reason to believe that the reflexivity, even anxiety, about Vedic authority evinced in the work, of which the restriction on access to the corpus and its language is only one (if a decisive) component, would have been unthinkable in the absence of the broad religious and social critique that Buddhism had enunciated in the preceding two centuries and the "disenchantment of the world" that critique had signaled (section 2 below).[1] But if the reflexivity of the *Mīmāṃsāsūtra* was new, relatively speaking, the restrictions it promulgates were not.

The Mīmāṃsā discussion most pertinent to an analysis of the monopolization of Sanskrit culture occurs in the chapter "On Rights" *(adhikāra)*. This addresses a person's entitlement to possess the results of an act of *dharma*—the right, in other words, to participate in the moral universe and engage in the principal modes of conduct aimed at actualizing the worldview of early Sanskritic India. Although explicitly treated in a section seemingly buried in the middle of a vast treatise, this chapter by no means has the minor status its location might imply. It is foundational to the entire system and implicitly underwrites many of its doctrines from the very first aphorism of the *Mīmāṃsāsūtra* onward.[2] Especially pertinent to the question of the sociality of Sanskrit is the section "On the Exclusion of the Shudra" *(apaśūdrādhikaraṇa)*. The term "Shudra" refers to the fourth and lowest *varṇa*, or rank, in the an-

1. On the early history of Mīmāṃsā and Buddhist critique, see Pollock 1990 and Bronkhorst 2001; and on the historical formation of the system, Parpola 1981, 1994.

2. See the *adhikārādhikaraṇa* in *PMS* 6.1.27–38. Verpoorten 1987 rightly points to the centrality of the subject for the Mīmāṃsā system as a whole. The discussion that follows is adapted from Pollock 1993a: 109ff.

cient hierarchical social ordering, an ideal taxonomy often far messier in practice than in theory, but real enough throughout Indian history as a conceptual grid for organizing social status and privilege. It is in the Mīmāṃsā discussion that one of the key differences of the *varṇa* ordering is first articulated: the right of access to the Sanskrit Vedic texts and thereby to the ethical realm of *dharma*. There are certain prerequisites to the right of participation in *vaidika* practices (though these are not necessarily enunciated explicitly in the rules coded in the Veda). An individual must be in possession of the ritual instruments for performing the rite, for example, and must have the financial resources at his disposal, as well as the requisite knowledge. The mere desire to gain the results of ritual action—the various benefits the rites can confer, such as fathering a son, reaching heaven, and so on—does not suffice to qualify one for participation. Mīmāṃsā argues this out with interesting complexity.

The prototypical commandment of ritual action, contained in the Veda itself, runs simply, "He who desires heaven should sacrifice." This would appear to sanction a universal applicability, even demand compliance universally. The act of sacrificing, however, presupposes possession of the means of sacrifice, preeminently the ritual fires. And in the scriptural injunction for setting up these fires only the first three social orders are mentioned, not the Shudra. It is true, Jaimini continues, that according to some authorities the fire injunction is intended only to specify the conditions that must be met when actually building the fire, not to ordain who could do it, for surely, as the scholar Bādari declared, "The Shudra desires heaven, too . . . and what is it in a sacrifice that any man [of the three higher orders] can do but the Shudra is incapable of doing?"[3] Yet the insistence that only those actually mentioned have the right is confirmed in the eyes of Mīmāṃsā by way of one more condition: possessing the requisite knowledge, including knowledge of the language used in the rite. For yet another scriptural injunction mentions specific seasons for the initiation into studentship *(upanayana)* of Brahman, Kshatriya, and Vaishya boys, whereas the Shudra and all the others below him are again omitted. The objection that these others might study the texts of the Veda—and the Sanskrit language in which the Veda was composed along with the Sanskrit knowledge systems that understanding the Veda required—on their own, without initiation, is dismissed. Even if the Veda did not explicitly prohibit this, the knowledge thereby acquired would be inefficacious anyway.[4]

3. According to Bādari the injunction is conditional *(nimittārtha)* not constitutive *(prāpika)* (*PMS* 6.1.27; for the *siddhāntin*'s endorsement of the latter see 6.1.37). The quotation in the text is from the *pūrvapakṣa* in Śabara, see 6.1.32 (Bādari's own works are lost).

4. The rule for establishing the sacred fires is given in *Taittirīya Brāhmaṇa* 1.1.2.6, for the *upanayana* in *Āpastambadharmasūtra* 1.1.1.19. Uttaramīmāṃsā, or Vedānta, seamlessly extends

The argument for establishing inequality of cultural rights in the Vedic world has the circuitousness and tortured complexity characteristic of arguments for inequality everywhere. But its overall thrust and its implications regarding the status of Sanskrit in early South Asia are reasonably clear. To learn Sanskrit, the *saṃskṛta* language, and so to participate in the cult and its benefits presupposed access to the *saṃskāra,* or ritual purification, of initiation (the semantic linkage here will be revisited below). But how is the restriction of initiation to the three higher orders itself validated? This answer, for most *mīmāṃsakas*, is that the restriction is ultimately self-validating since we cannot otherwise explain it.[5] It cannot, for example, be prompted by social interests, since for Mīmāṃsā the commandments of the Veda are transcendent and not concerned with everyday motivated action—what worldly interests could possibly be served, the argument runs, by the many duties and costs associated with participating in Vedic culture? It may not make common sense to exclude from the world of Sanskrit knowledge certain groups of people who may be as capable of learning as anyone among the three higher orders. But then, neither does it accord with common sense to destroy food in a ritual fire, let alone to slaughter animals at the cultic altar, and yet the Veda authorizes doing just this. Indeed, precisely like sacrificial violence, the rules on the exclusivity of Sanskrit knowledge and the ritual domain to which it relates are warranted precisely because they are incomprehensible: "The purpose of the Veda *(śāstra)* is to inform us of what we cannot possibly otherwise know." Vedic commandment is meaningful to the degree that it enunciates something that transcends the phenomenal and is thus inaccessible to observation, inference, or other forms of empirical reasoning—something, in fact, nonrational, if not irrational.[6]

In brief, then, according to the theory of the most sophisticated circle of Sanskrit intellectuals in late Vedic India, the discursive and social domain of the Sanskrit language was bounded and limited. The limits on discourse were ritual, and the boundaries of society were those established by what might be called a theodicy of privilege.[7] No doubt the actual sociolinguistic situation was far more complex than the Mīmāṃsā theory of exclusion would lead

the Pūrvamīmāṃsā argument from the prohibition against the Shudra's sacrificing to the prohibition against his acquiring sacred knowledge *(vidyā)* in general (*Brahmasūtra* 1.3.34 ff.). In the late medieval period some scholars sought to temper this judgment (Appayya Dīkṣita [fl. 1550], *Śāstrasiddhāntaleśasaṃgraha* pp. 313–19, though contrast his *Nyāyarakṣāmaṇi* pp. 291–320).

5. Śabara does claim to find an explicit Vedic injunction, however—"The Shudra shall not recite the Veda" (quoted on *PMS* 6.1.37)—but its source is untraceable.

6. "The purpose of the Veda. . . ," *aprāpte śāstram arthavat* (first in *PMS* 6.2.18). As the equally rationalistic Tertullian would have put it, *credibile quia ineptum est:* It is reason that dictates belief in a thing in direct proportion to the thing's improbability (Sider 1980).

7. On the logic of such rules see further in Pollock 1989. "Theodicy of privilege" is an idea borrowed from Weber by Bourdieu (1977b: 188).

us to believe, and the borders around the sacred sphere were probably far more porous. The most basic linguistic data show this unequivocally. Some have argued that the oldest stratum of the Veda shows phonological and lexical convergence between Sanskrit and non-Sanskrit languages, indicating that a significant degree of intercommunity contact, both social and discursive, occurred early on.[8] More generally, the very existence of the Mīmāṃsā discourse on the restriction of rights betrays not just a moment of disenchantment when the rules of everyday life cease to be transparent and require reflexive grounding but a possible concern that the monopolization of Sanskrit itself was not only contentious but contested.[9] For as noted by Śabara, the great commentator on the Mīmāṃsā of perhaps the fourth century, it makes no sense to prohibit something no one does.[10] Ambivalence about the status of Sanskrit over against other languages, and concomitantly, about who was permitted to use it and for what purposes, was deeply rooted and would continue to mark the social, cultural, and intellectual history of Sanskrit for centuries, even after the moment of historical rupture had long come and gone.

Consider only two instances of such ambivalence from a much later period, when the cosmopolitan order of Sanskrit was already far eroded and the changes that had come about were too obvious to deny, and therefore, paradoxically, all the more necessary to deny. Anxiety over participation in Sanskrit culture on the part of those outside the *vaidika* order is captured in a verse, found in a thirteenth-century literary anthology, that praises the Sanskrit poetry of a simple potter named Ghroṇa by proclaiming, "Caste is no constraint for those rendered pure by the Goddess of Speech." Here (by a kind of Freudian *Verneinung*) the author reaffirms old restrictions on access to Sanskrit in the very act of seeking to deny them.[11] The second example, from the very end of our period of study, comes from a sixteenth-century Sanskrit manual on the social and moral practices required of Shudras. No one outside of the three higher orders, the text declares, can have anything to do with the Vedas, Sanskrit grammar, *smṛti* texts, even *purāṇas*; more than this,

8. On the effects of early bilingualism on Sanskrit, see Emeneau 1974; more recently, Hock 1996. Mīmāṃsā itself problematizes the interpretation of non-Sanskrit words in the Veda (see *PMS* 1.3.10), though without ever asking how they got there in the first place.

9. "A Shudra is a cremation ground; one must never perform Vedic recitation in his presence," according to a *śruti* text cited by Śaṅkara on *Brahmasūtra* 1.3.38; teaching a Shudra Sanskrit grammar and related sciences is famously denounced, along with the selling of learning, in *Manusmṛti* 3.156 (but see also Puṇyarāja on *Vākyapadīya* 2.79).

10. *na hy aprāptasya pratiṣedho 'vakalpate* (on *PMS* 6.1.43).

11. See *Sūktimuktāvalī* p. 45 no. 69. The verse is ascribed to Rājaśekhara, as is the following: "Ah, what power of the Goddess of Speech, that the untouchable *(caṇḍāla)* Divākara should have been a member of the literary circle of King Śrīharṣa, and the equal of Bāṇa and Mayūra" (no. 70).

"a Shudra is never to utter a Sanskrit word."[12] Here we have a late restatement of a very ancient postulate under visibly new social conditions (when, for example, so-called *sat-śūdra* communities in Maharashtra were claiming the right to use Sanskrit liturgy in their life-cycle ceremonies), the very novelty of which may have prompted this stubborn reassertion of archaic monopolization.[13] But the key point to stress here is that the many responses to the restrictions that had long hedged in Sanskrit show both how actual these restrictions were and how significant was the act of challenging them.

The discursive boundaries of Sanskrit in the archaic period are symmetrical with, or indeed even narrower than, the social boundaries just mapped. It is no cause for wonder that the domain of what could be said in Sanskrit should have been shaped by who was permitted to speak and for what purposes. Discourse typically owes its most important characteristics to the relations of language production within which it is generated.[14] The redrawing of the discursive boundaries of Sanskrit at the beginning of the Common Era occurred concurrently with a marked shift in its social boundaries. The older limits of the sayable are most powerfully indicated by the name itself that comes to be given to the language, *saṃskṛta,* and the epithets applied to it, such as "language of the gods." The latter may not be attested until relatively late, perhaps not before Daṇḍin's seventh-century work on literary theory, *Kāvyādarśa* (Mirror of Literature): "The language called Sanskrit is the language of the gods, taught [to men] by the great sages of old." (How humans were first able to learn this language is rarely discussed; one of the few direct observations is that of Daṇḍin's tenth-century Buddhist commentator on this passage: "The great sages themselves spoke the languages of Place *[deśabhāṣā],* but they were able to teach Sanskrit thanks to their extraordinary attainments. As a result, while the Prakrits are multiform, Sanskrit is uniform.")[15] But Sanskrit's apotheosis, along with the unique status thereby conferred on it, can be found far earlier than Daṇḍin. It is significant that the richly associative term *saṃskṛta* as an adjective qualifying speech or language *(saṃskṛtā vāg)* occurs for the first time in the *Vālmīki Rāmāyaṇa,* a work of the last centuries before the Common Era. The demon king Rāvaṇa

12. *Śūdracintāmaṇi* of Śeṣa Kṛṣṇa (c. 1580), pp. 41–47, especially 44: *śūdrasyāpi viśeṣeṇa saṃskṛtaśabdoccāraṇapratiṣedhāt.*

13. Hints of this claim are found earlier, as when the eleventh-century *ŚP* (p. 500) denies the right of access to *vaidika* culture only to *kṣudraśūdras* (low Shudras, as opposed to *sat* Shudras).

14. See Bourdieu 1977a: 647.

15. See *KĀ* 1.33 and Ratnaśrījñāna there. The claim to be the "language of the gods" or "speech of the noble" *(ārya)*—and with it, the assertion to historical primevality—has a long afterlife. Hemacandra, the Jain scholar of late-twelfth-century Gujarat, represents Ardhamagadhi, the language of the Jain canon, as the source from which all other languages developed (an argument he makes, however, in Sanskrit, *Kāvyānuśāsana* 1–2). Pali is projected as the "root-language of all beings" in postcanonical literature (Collins 1998: 49).

had disguised himself as a Brahman and abducted the princess Sītā, and when at last Hanumān, the monkey scout of Prince Rāma, discovers her he pauses before speaking, wondering what language he should use:

> If like a Twice-born [Brahman] I address Sītā using *saṃskṛta* speech
> she may think I am Rāvaṇa, and will be frightened.
> Far better to speak a human language, one that will make sense to her.[16]

The artifice of the narrative may aim to direct attention away from the fact, but Hanumān proceeds to subvert his own announced intention. Whatever language he presumably was using with Sītā, what we find the learned monkey speaking—we and everyone else, Brahman or not, who has ever read or heard the work—is of course Sanskrit.

It is no coincidence that in this first recorded use of *saṃskṛta* as the name of the language, allusion should be made to both the language's monopolization by a particular social group and the peculiar restrictions on its use that distinguished it from "human language." The *Vālmīki Rāmāyaṇa,* which both literary tradition and the text itself regard as the first Sanskrit *kāvya,* represented an entirely new genre in Indian literary history (chapter 2.1), and its reflexive understanding of the social and discursive peculiarities of the language it employed became possible only at a moment that marked the beginning of a new cultural order. Moreover, both of Hanumān's allusions—to the social limits and the discursive limits on the use of Sanskrit—make perfect sense when we keep in mind its liturgical functions in the early period. It is entirely in keeping with the monopolization of the language along these two axes that the oldest connotations of *saṃskṛta*—in the word's earliest appearances in the Vedic corpus around the beginning of the first millennium B.C.E. and resonant for centuries thereafter—are invariably ritual. An analysis of the semantic field demonstrates that "*saṃskṛta* speech" not only bears the literal sense that would eventually come to predominate in scholarly circles of ancient India—that of speech items "put together" from nominal and verbal morphemes, a process subjected to penetrating analysis in the grammatical tradition culminating in Pāṇini's *Aṣṭādhyāyī* (The Eight Chapters) sometime in the third or fourth century B.C.E—but also, and even more strongly in the early period, *saṃskṛta* conveys a derived meaning: it is speech "made fit" for sacrificial functions. The language was named *saṃskṛtā [vāg* or *bhāṣā],* or, at some later date, *saṃskṛtam,* because like other instruments or objects of liturgical practice it was rendered and kept ritually pure.[17]

16. *Rām.* 5.28.18–19. There is some textual confusion here (which the Baroda edition does little to alleviate), but the traditional reading of the verse (see *Tilaka* and *Bhūṣaṇa*) is unambiguous.

17. See Thieme 1982, 14. According to Cardona, grammatical description is viewed as a *saṃskāra* in two ways: "as a derivational explanation of correct speech forms" and "as a purification of speech, since correct speech forms are thereby segregated from corrupt ones"

There is no tension, however, between the ritual and grammatical meanings of *saṃskṛta.* The sacerdotal associations of the name of the language are in complete harmony with grammar's understanding of its own purposes, which were initially to describe and conserve sacred usage. In the conceptual universe in which *vyākaraṇa* (grammar, or perhaps more strictly, language "analysis") arose and functioned as a foundational intellectual discipline, a strong distinction was drawn between two kinds of action: instrumental and this-worldly, and noninstrumental and other-worldly *(dṛṣṭārtha* or *laukika,* and *adṛṣṭārtha* or *alaukika).* During the epoch of its formation as a knowledge system, grammar, and with it its first and originally sole analytical object, Sanskrit, were affiliated exclusively with the latter. Like everything else in this world, the character of language analysis would gradually change, but from an early period it functioned as an auxiliary science in the service of the revealed texts, as one of the six "limbs of the Veda."[18] In the *Aṣṭādhyāyī,* this sacerdotal function characterizes both registers of the language: on the one hand, the idiom actually used for the Vedic texts themselves, what Pāṇini calls *chandaḥ,* verse, or better, "the Verse" (albeit not all texts classified as Veda are versified); on the other, the rigorously normative idiolect restricted to (Vedic) pedagogical environments, which he calls *bhāṣā,* speech.[19] That both had largely sacral associations as late as the beginning of the Common Era is shown in Patañjali's *Mahābhāṣya,* the *Great Commentary* on Pāṇini's grammar.

Patañjali (his date is considered in chapter 2.1) appears to have lived at a moment of transition in intellectual history when the tradition of systematic study of grammar had somehow been disrupted. In the old days, he explains in his famous preface, Brahmans learned Sanskrit grammar directly after their initiation into studentship and before learning the Veda; today they study the Veda first and consider grammar useless. It is because of this state of affairs, in addition to the fact that declaring one's purpose is an essential prelude to every *śāstra,* that Patañjali finds it necessary to review the reasons for studying the grammar of Sanskrit. The most important are the following five: pre-

---

(Cardona 1988: 653–55). If this were strictly and narrowly true, we might expect to find the term applied also to the explanations and purifications of Prakrit grammars or those of other languages, for these after all have "correct speech forms," insofar as that is precisely what grammar is intended to present (only *apabhraṣṭa* language, but not the Apabhramsha literary language, does not). But this is never the case.

18. The term is as old as the *Nirukta* (400 B.C.E.?), see 1.20 (where it is used without further specification). The commandment *ṣaḍaṅgo vedo 'dhyeyaḥ*—"The Veda along with its six limbs is to be studied"—is not found in the Veda itself; *Mahābhāṣya* vol. 1: 1 attributes it to *āgama;* see also *Āpastambadharmasūtra* 2.8.10.

19. The precise limits of this term are of course problematic and very much tied up with the question of an everyday Sanskrit. Renou 1942 (part 2): 53–54, for example, largely skirts the question.

serving *(rakṣā)* the Veda; mastering morphological analogy *(ūhā)* for the performance of ritual; obeying scriptural injunction *(āgama),* which requires familiarity with grammar and the other five liturgical knowledges (phonetics, etymology, metrics, ritual performance, and astral or calendrical science); attaining facility of understanding *(laghu)* of more complex forms from simpler forms; and resolution of doubts *(asaṃdeha)* about the interpretation of sacrificial prescriptions. Patañjali goes on to cite a number of Vedic passages that identify additional functions of grammatical knowledge. These include the ability to distinguish between those who employ correct language forms and the "antigods" *(asura)* with their deviant usage; avoiding the potentially fatal consequences of the improper use of a word; acquisition of true learning, which consists in understanding and not just reproducing; gaining "infinite victory in the other world"; observing propriety in social interaction especially between preceptor and student; attainment of parity with the "Great God of language that has entered mortals"; and last, fulfilling the obligation of performing the naming ceremony of one's son.[20]

Not all of these reasons may be entirely clear to us, but there can be little doubt that for Patañjali, principal heir and final arbiter of the *vaidika* grammatical tradition, the purposes of Sanskrit language analysis were more or less exclusively tied to sacred performance and to the pedagogical practices, both social and discursive, pertaining to knowledge of the sacred. The same conception is shared by Kātyāyana, the major exegete of grammar who lived between the time of Pāṇini and Patañjali, and whose additions to and criticisms of Pāṇini are minutely scrutinized in the *Mahābhāṣya.* For Kātyāyana, the Sanskrit language is not something invented by humans but rather is *lokasiddha,* always already preexistent in the world. Accordingly, the only possible purpose of knowing this language as systematized in grammar is to impose constraints on its usage in the service of sacred action *(dharmaniyama).*[21] Kātyāyana's view, for its part, is in complete accord with Mīmāṃsā doctrine on the authority of grammar, which is explicitly and powerfully argued out in a section of the system devoted entirely to this topic.[22] And it correlates with yet another core Mīmāṃsā conception, that of the *autpattika,* "originary" or natural, connection between words and meanings. It is because the Sanskrit language is uncreated and without origin that the Veda itself could be considered beginningless and uncreated, and so immune to the kinds of error, and unconstrained by the kinds of limits, to which all other human communication is subject.

20. Patañjali describes the need for restating the purposes of grammar in *Mahābhāṣya* 1: 5 lines 5 ff.; the five principal reasons are discussed on 1: 1 lines 14 ff., and the supplemental ones on 1: 2 lines 10 ff.

21. Kātyāyana's *siddhānta* is given in *Mahābhāṣya* 1: 8 lines 3 ff.

22. See *PMS* 1.3.24–29, and the remarkable exegesis in Kumārila's *Tantravārttika.*

Again, entirely in keeping with this ritual view is the account that Patañjali proceeds to give of the domain of language usage *(śabdasya prayogaviṣaya)*, that is, the domain of the language that is the object of grammatical analysis. It comprises only the following: the four Vedas and their auxiliary sciences and mystical knowledges, texts all geared toward ritual action; the dialogue *(vākovākya)* portions of the Veda, which exemplify (rather than command) such action; narratives of "the way it once was" and accounts of the past *(itihāsa, purāṇa)*; and life science *(āyurveda)*. In the same spirit, Patañjali adds a further restriction on what constitute "constraints on (linguistic) practice" *(ācāre niyama)*, namely, sacrificial action *(yājñe karmaṇi)*. Outside of this sphere—and this is the clear implication here and of all that has gone before—there is no ritual sanction on language usage. Thus the employment of dialectal or vernacular forms in everyday life—and it was these forms that, we infer, were used in everyday life—does not produce spiritual demerit *(adharma)*. In short, for Patañjali, the communicative world within which Sanskrit and its grammar function is not simply coextensive with the lifeworld in general, as experience with other languages and their practices would lead us naturally to assume. The sphere of Sanskrit is markedly narrower: it is in essence the sphere of sacred textual knowledge, with only the most tentative moves toward textual practices beyond the sacred.[23]

Patañjali's identification of the functions of Sanskrit grammar and their pertinent realm of language practices is broadly consistent with what we know to have been the discursive domain of Sanskrit in concrete historical terms. The basic question here, usually formulated as whether or to what degree Sanskrit was ever an everyday spoken language, has long been debated, and current sociolinguistic opinion seems rather muddled. The fact that our data force us to even ask this question may be taken as already implying some actual limitation on the sphere of usage. It is significant that, with the exception of the *Rāmāyaṇa*, no remains of a nonsacral, this-worldly Sanskrit are extant from the early epoch of literacy (from the third century B.C.E to, say, the first century C.E.), when, as some believe, Sanskrit was still supposed to have been an everyday idiom, whereas vast amounts of such Sanskrit are available from the later period when Sanskrit "had ceased to be truly a current language."[24] It is not easy to believe that virtually every scrap of early evidence of such a usage has been lost. The mate-

23. The domain of language usage is detailed in *Mahābhāṣya* 1: 9 lines 20ff., and 11: 11. See also Cardona 1988: 639: the language that constitutes the object of the grammar was held to be "used for purposes such as ritual performance," as opposed to a "more vernacular speech"; similarly Deshpande 1985: 137.

24. Cardona 1988: 646. The testimony typically adduced to show the contrary, such as the grammarian's argument with the *sūta* (*Mahābhāṣya* on 2.4.56, 1: 488 lines 18ff.), may not be so straightforward as it seems if the *sūta* were less a rikshawallah than a ritual figure (a *rājakartṛ* in *Atharvaveda* 3.5.7; or perhaps comparable to the *rathakāra* of *PMS* 6.1.44ff.), or a personage

rials from the early age of literacy are decidedly non- or un-Sanskrit, whereas everything in Sanskrit from this period indicates a radically delimited arena of use.

Moreover, all that we can infer about the sociality of the language from the moment we can glimpse it provides further counterevidence to the belief that Sanskrit ever functioned as an everyday medium of communication. Never in its history was Sanskrit the vehicle for memories of childhood and adolescence, or for a whole range of comparable life experiences associated with this-worldly language use. Sanskrit was never bound to the land, to the village, or to any specific regional community. Indeed, when Sanskrit was finally constituted as the vehicle for political expression in inscriptions, the business of land or village—the specifics of a grant or endowment or bequest—came increasingly to be done in non-Sanskrit languages, especially in south India and Southeast Asia. Given such traits, Sanskrit in precolonial India has sometimes been analogized to postcolonial English, as being in some fundamental sense "inauthentic" (a judgment with respect to consciousness) or "illegitimate" (a judgment with respect to class location). But we will see throughout the course of this study that such judgments constitute a conceptual anachronism, as does the application of most of the language dichotomies borrowed from the contemporary West, such as living *versus* dead, learnéd *versus* natural.[25] These are all too crude to enable us to make sense of the language world of premodern South Asia, where linguistic options were far more multiple than in modernity, notions such as mother-tongue were absent (chapters 8.3, 12.1), and the very capacity to escape the limitations of the local place and the temporal moment of the individual life memory—the inauthenticity and illegitimacy of Romantic language theory—was considered a defining virtue of Sanskrit.

Accordingly, the most plausible assessment of Sanskrit's social and discursive world for perhaps the first thousand years of its existence on the subcontinent seems to be the following: At least two species of the language family usually called Indo-Aryan were in use as far back as we can see. One of these, Sanskrit, was a formal speech, viewed as correct by the custodians of the language and employed in particular contexts broadly related to *vaidika* ritual activity; the other was a demotic speech with what are usually called Middle-Indic characteristics.[26] Sanskrit thus had a mutually self-limiting re-

---

like Lomaharṣaṇa of the *MBh.* The situation depicted by Patañjali thus may well have ceremonial aspects. The one exception to the absence of early *laukika* Sanskrit is the *Vālmīki Rāmāyaṇa* (see chapter 2.1).

25. See chapter 8.3. The metaphor of language death was first used in Italian humanism (Agamben 1999: 50). It has no currency in premodern India. See also Pollock 2001a: 393.

26. See again Cardona 1988: 638 (though contrast pp. 639 and 646). The case has yet to be made for an "everyday Sanskrit" at this period (with the epics preserving an "underlying col-

lationship with textualized discourse on liturgy and liturgical knowledges: this discourse was composed exclusively in Sanskrit, and Sanskrit culture consisted entirely of this discourse. The point is worth repeating that for most of the first millennium or more of Sanskrit's existence in South Asia, we have virtually no indubitable evidence for its employment in any domain we would call, along with the *mīmāṃsakas*, this-worldly, the realm outside the practices of the sacred and the forms of knowledge necessary for the sacred. Like its very name, the character of its discursive functions situates Sanskrit far beyond the arena of everyday social existence.

We might be inclined, accordingly, to think of Sanskrit during this period as the higher pole of a classic diglossic situation, where the lower pole is constituted by protoregional speech forms (probably not the Prakrits as we know them, which, given their relatively early grammaticization and restricted literary uses, were equally high diglossically).[27] But the split in standards between Sanskrit and local language was such that "diglossia" seems an entirely inadequate category to describe it. For what we encounter is not an internal split (di-) in registers and norms, typically between literary and colloquial usage, in what local actors conceived of as a single language, but a relationship of extreme superposition (hyper-) between two languages that local actors knew to be entirely different. This modality, which I will call "hyperglossia," was ubiquitous in southern Asia before the vernacular revolution and derived ultimately from the discursive restrictions and social monopolization, the extreme compartmentalization of usage as well as the difference in cultural opportunity, that characterized Sanskrit from the earliest epoch. If the former attribute was one that Sanskrit would never entirely renounce—indeed, its function specialization as the preeminent language of literature and systematic thought would continue to constitute a large portion of its enduring prestige and appeal—its social monopolization was soon to be challenged and eventually destroyed.

---

loquial dialect," an "epic-vernacular substratum which at this period may have still been a living force"), let alone for a "Sanskrit for the common man" (Salomon 1989a: 277–78, 283, 284). Deshpande's assessment of the *Aṣṭādhyāyī* ("a description by a Brāhmaṇa grammarian of the male Brāhmaṇa's second language, for the benefit of male Brāhmaṇa learners") is a probable account of Sanskrit in the first millennium B.C.E. But his further argument, that the narrowing of the "sociolinguistic parameters" of Sanskrit—the momentous restriction of Sanskrit to liturgical contexts—was a later development occurring in the few centuries between the time of Pāṇini and Patañjali and for no discernible historical reason, is dubious, to say the least (1992, especially 119–21).

27. For a recent argument about Sanskrit diglossia see Houben 1996; and for diglossia in India more generally, Shapiro and Schiffman 1983: 164ff. On the distinction between the grammaticized Prakrits and the protoregional languages compare Nitti-Dolci 1938: 8, and for a more recent statement, Masica 1991: 53ff. On literary restrictions see chapter 2.

1.2 FROM RESISTANCE TO APPROPRIATION

It is only within the context of the social monopolization and discursive ritualization of Sanskrit—the restrictions on who may use the language and the purposes for which it may be used—that we can make sense of the first explicit and systematized assaults on the *vaidika* cultural order. At the same time, these critiques serve to establish the reality of the foregoing description of that order. The most important of them for our purposes here are embodied in the language theory and practices of early Buddhism, though these were in fact only part of a larger process, a transvaluation of values, that occurred in the last centuries before the Common Era.

An adequately detailed and historically sensitive account of just what the critique enunciated by early Buddhism meant within the larger intellectual and cultural history of the subcontinent remains an important desideratum for Indological scholarship.[28] A simple inventory of the strategies, from basic terminology to core notions of culture and society, by which early Buddhists sought to appropriate, redefine, and transform the very elements of the late *vaidika* conceptual order shows both how profound this critique was and how much it can tell us about the nature of its target. The dynamic at work here is familiar from other oppositional movements in the domain of religion and culture more generally and is well captured by the phrase "normative inversion," whereby one group turns another's obligations into abominations, and often vice versa.[29]

A preeminent instance of a substantive sort is the Buddhist proscription of one of the great sacred mysteries in the Vedic world, animal sacrifice. At the more intimate level of doctrinal terminology other illustrations abound. Consider the name chosen for the Buddha's teaching, *dharma* (Pali *dhamma*), or even more combatively, *saddharma,* the real or true *dharma* (already in the oldest parts of the Pali canon). An ancient, even primary, meaning of *dharma,* the key word of Vedic ritualism, is sacrifice—it is to sacrifice that the *Mīmāṃsāsūtra* is referring when it opens with the words "Now, then, the inquiry into *dharma.*"[30] Early Buddhism thus sought to annex and redefine the term that expressed what Buddhism most fundamentally rejected. (Even *dharma*'s somewhat later sense of "duty" as an expression of one's essential

28. Much of the best current work in early Buddhism (Schopen 1997 or Collins 1998) has been concerned with making sense of Buddhist social and intellectual history itself, an obvious prerequisite to any larger analysis.

29. See Assmann 1997.

30. For *dharma* as "sacrifice" see, e.g., *Ṛgveda* 10.90.16. Mīmāṃsā sought for centuries to limit the enlargement of the term's semantic realm; exemplary is the *Pūrvottaramīmāṃsāvādanakṣatramālā* pp. 254–57, a treatise of the sixteenth-century thinker Appayya Dīkṣita. See Pollock 2004c.

nature is turned upside down in the antiessentialist Buddhist appropriation.) Similarly transgressive redefinitions pertain to *ārya,* recoded from its old meaning, "noble," a member of the "twice-born" social order, to "adherent" of the Buddhist spiritual order. More striking is *sutta* for referring to the discourses of the Buddha: this is probably a dialectal variant not of Sanskrit *sūtra* (that is, a précis of any form of systematic knowledge) but rather of Sanskrit *sūkta,* a Vedic hymn. The Buddhist idea of three knowledges *(vijjā)*—of one's former lives, of the lives of others, and of the Four Noble Truths—may very well have been intended "to parallel and trump" the Brahmans' *vidyātraya,* or the knowledge constituted by the three Vedas. More subtly, the notion of (ritual) action at the heart of the term *karma* in the *vaidika* world was replaced by (spiritual) intention in Pali *kamma.*[31] These positive transvaluations in early Buddhism of core *vaidika* values were complemented by a range of pure negations, beginning with *an-atta (an-ātma),* the denial of a personal essence, whereby the core conception of Upanishadic thought was cancelled. All this evidence suggests that at the semantic level, to start with, Buddhism sought to turn the old *vaidika* world upside down by the very levers that world provided.

The same impulse toward inverting the normative reveals itself at a more fundamental level of thinking. It is fully in harmony with Buddhism's central analysis of the human predicament—the discovery of the origins of suffering in desire and the concept of dependent origination *(pratītyasamutpāda)* to explain the functioning of desire—that Buddhism developed a wider-ranging understanding of contingency or conventionalism in human life. This stood in radical opposition to the naturalism of the *vaidika* thought world, one of pure Bourdieuean *doxa,* where both the order of society and one's place in it went without saying. The new conventionalism came to have application not only to individual psychology but to the social world at large and, more important in the present context, to language. Against the Mīmāṃsā tenet that the relationship between word and meaning is *autpattika,* originary or natural—a position sometimes absurdly reduced by its opponents to a mechanical, even magical theory of reference—Buddhists typically argued for a relationship based on pure convention *(saṅketa,* sometimes *avadhi).* What was at stake for Mīmāṃsā in asserting the uncreated, eternal nature of language was the possibility that *vāṅmaya,* or a thing-made-of-

31. On *ārya (ariya),* see Deshpande 1979: 40–41; for *sūkta (sutta),* Gombrich 1990: 23; *vijjā* and *karma/kamma,* Gombrich 1996: 29 and 51–52, respectively. Additional examples include *dakṣiṇā,* a "payment to a priest for sacrificial services" in the Vedic world, becoming "merit accrued from giving gifts" in the Buddhist; *ārṣa,* "relating to the sages *(ṛṣi)*" of the Veda, appropriated as an epithet of the Buddha (Lüders 1940: 712–714); *nhātaka/snātaka,* "one who engages in ritual bathing," becoming "one who washes off evil by means of the Eight-fold Path" (Norman 1993: 276). The textual articulations of early Buddhism recapitulate many of these trends (see Gombrich 1990: 23–24).

language—that is, a text, like the Veda—could be eternal too, something the Buddhists sought fundamentally to reject. About the notion that nothing in language generally or in Sanskrit particularly is transcendent, Buddhist doctrine is unambiguous. Here once more is heard the subversive inversion of *vaidika* terminology in a way that must have resonated scandalously in the minds of twice-born candidates for membership in the new order: As the oft-repeated Buddhist formula has it, "All mental formations" *(sarve saṃskārāḥ, sabbe saṃkhārā)*—in fact, all things formed, no doubt including all Vedic rites *(saṃskāra)* and perhaps even Sanskrit itself *(saṃskṛta)*—"are noneternal"; they arise and, having arisen, disappear. Indeed, like social formations in general, language itself came to be regarded by Buddhists as a human invention. As a later Pali grammar puts it, "The signifier is related to the signified as a matter of pure convention," a position that contrasts as profoundly as possible with Mīmāṃsā postulates of a primal, necessary, and nonarbitrary relationship between the two.[32]

Two observations on the Buddhist critique noted earlier merit restating here. First, a dialectical process seems to have been at work. It was almost certainly in response to the disenchantment of the *vaidika* world effected by Buddhism, perhaps in particular by the altogether new kind of reflexivity and sense of human agency it offered, that *vaidika* thought itself developed some of the distinctive characteristics that were to mark it long into the future. The explicit formulation of what are now rightly viewed as axioms that naturalized the social world and the world of discourse—restrictions on the right to sacrifice and on the originary relationship of word and meaning (the *adhikāra* and *autpattika* doctrines discussed earlier) as well as the notion of an authorless and eternal Veda existing entirely outside of history—were likely developed in response to the Buddhist critique: neither makes sense without the arguments to the contrary. Second, even though the basic oppositions at issue in categories such as *autpattika/kṛtaka* (natural/factitious) may remind us of similar disputes elsewhere in the ancient world—such as the fifth-century Greek argument (in Plato's *Cratylus*) over whether signifiers and signifieds were connected by nature *(physis)* or convention *(nomos)*—the stakes of the debate in early South Asia were far higher. The Greek contro-

32. The Pali grammar is *Saddanīti* 636.26, 786.5: *saṅketaniruḷho saddo atthesu ti.* The Mīmāṃsā doctrine is found in theoretical discourse first in *PMS* 1.1.5. No adequate historical scholarship on the Buddhist view is available (it is not homogenous; one later commentator strikingly calls Pali *opapātika* [Collins, forthcoming]). The notion of *saṅketa* as well as related terms was nowhere elaborated; the relatively late and thin references include *Abhidharmakośa* 2.47 (pp. 272, 275), and *Pramāṇavārttika* 1.92; early Pali texts do not comment on the matter. The Buddhist *saṅketa* approximates the *samaya* of early Nyāya (*Nyāyasūtra* 2.1.55; only later *naiyāyikas*, such as Vācaspati Miśra, ascribed the convention to God). For the relativization of societal relationships in early Buddhism see *Cakkavatti Sihanāda Sutta* or, even more pointedly, the *Aggañña Sutta* (Collins 1998: 480ff.), almost a social *pratītyasamutpāda* analysis.

versy may also have extended beyond the bounds of language analysis to include important questions of justice, but the philosophical positions in India were expressions of radically different visions of life, of separate and apparently irreconcilable understandings of human existence and destiny.

In light of these broad tendencies, there was every reason for Buddhism to reject Sanskrit in the course of its confrontation with the social-religious practices for which Sanskrit was the principal vehicle. The logic of this rejection and the alternative codes that were recommended instead are brought out in the following text on Buddhist monastic discipline (fourth to third century B.C.E.?), the most famous, and probably most vexed, passage of any work in early India pertaining to the "question of the language":

> Two monks, Brahmans by birth, were troubled that other monks of various clans, tribes, and families, were corrupting the Buddha's words by repeating them each in his own dialect *(sakāya niruttiyā).* They asked the Buddha, "Let us put the Buddha's words into [Vedic-Sanskrit] verse *(chandaso āropema).*" But the Blessed One, the Buddha, rebuked them, saying, "Deluded men! This will not lead to the conversion of the unconverted . . ." And he commanded (all) the monks: "You are not to put the Buddha's words into [Vedic-Sanskrit] verse. To do this would be to commit an infraction. I authorize you, monks, to learn the Buddha's words each in his own dialect."[33]

Scholarly disagreement persists about what exactly the Buddha is telling his disciples to do here, in large part because of uncertainty about the meaning of the phrase *sakāya niruttiyā.*[34] But there is not much doubt about what he is telling them not to do. However we wish to characterize the critique that early Buddhism enunciated, it clearly was not, and perhaps could not have been, enunciated in the Sanskrit language. The resistance to Sanskrit, which has a very rich later history (discussed throughout part 2 of this study),

33. *Vinayapiṭaka* 2: 139; I follow but slightly modify Edgerton's version, agreeing instead with the commentator he cites, "like the Veda, in the Sanskrit language" (contrast Edgerton 1953: 1 n. 4). Collins, forthcoming, may be right to translate "in a (fixed) recitational form, as the Vedas are in Sanskrit," leaving the referent indeterminate, but Sanskrit was the only fixed recitational game in town. Brough 1980 correctly notes that Vedic and Sanskrit would not have been considered two separate languages at this period (contrast Renou 1956, 84 n. 1); indeed, for Pāṇini *chandaḥ* and *bhāṣā* constituted the two poles of a single language (so Rau 1985: 104). The Chinese translation of the *Mahīśāsaka Vinaya* by Buddhajīva of Kashmir (423 B.C.E.) represents the Brahmans as reciters of the "Chandoveda," and has the Buddha tell them: "Let [the disciples] recite according to the speech of the country" [the Chinese represents Skt. *deśabhāṣā*] . . . It is forbidden to regard the words of the Buddha as the language of the outsiders *[bāhyaka],*" which the context strongly suggests means "to present in a Sanskrit form" (cited Mair and Mei 1991: 390–91; see also Mair 1994: 722–23, and more generally Lamotte 1976: 610ff.).

34. Norman 1980: 62 translates as "explanatory gloss."

is perceived for the first time in the Buddha's rejection here. Scholarship has often exaggerated the importance, and minimized the contingency, of language choice in effecting or signaling religious change and, more generally, in defining religious communities (chapter 10.4). But there is no question that sometimes new ways of thinking did require new ways of speaking, whether for reasons of ideology or efficacy, and early Buddhism is the first and most celebrated case in point.

What the Buddha refused to allow his disciples to do, most scholars agree, was to transmit his doctrine by redacting it in Sanskrit, the form that had hitherto defined authoritative discourse on the transcendent for an influential community in South Asia. In fact, for the following four centuries or more the Buddha's words would be redacted in a range of languages other than Sanskrit. Some of these were very local (such as Gandhari in the far north of the subcontinent, or Sogdian and Tocharian in western and central Asia), a fact that gives us one answer to the question of how *sakāya niruttiyā* was pragmatically understood. At the same time, other Buddhists further south invented a new and parallel sacred language: Pali. This language combined elements of such geographical disparity that it would never have constituted the "native" language of anyone, certainly not the Buddha.[35] It is worth noting in passing that a similar rejection of Sanskrit occurred among the Jains, who employed an actual form of the northeast-Indian spoken language (so-called Ardhamagadhi) for their scriptural texts, without, however, attributing to Mahāvīra, the founder, any clear injunction to do so.

The very character of these languages of early Buddhist scripture provoked trenchant criticism among *vaidika* authors, who argued that such dialectal features undermined its doctrinal authority. In order to make just this point, the most brilliant and fearsomely polemical theoretician among these authors in early medieval India, Bhaṭṭa Kumārila, the "Lion's Roar" of Brahmanical learning, cites a passage from what appears to be a Buddhist canonical text, which includes, not coincidentally, the scandalous phrase *ime saṃkhaḍā dhammā saṃbhavanti sakāraṇā akāraṇā vinassaṃti* ("These *saṃskṛta* entities come into being when their cause is present, and perish when it is absent"):

> The scriptures of the Buddhists and Jains are composed in overwhelmingly incorrect *(asādhu)* language, words of the Magadha or Dakshinatya languages or their even more dialectal forms *(tadapabhraṃśa)*. And because they are therefore false compositions *(asannibandhana)*, they cannot possibly be true knowledge [or, holy word, *śāstra*]. When texts are composed of words that are [gram-

35. Von Hinüber 1983: 4. For earlier arguments, see Renou 1957: 79 n. 276.

matically] false *(asatyaśabda)*, how can they possibly communicate meaning that is true *(arthasatyatā)*? And how could they possibly be eternal [as true scripture must be] if we find in them forms that are corrupted *(apabhraṣṭa)*? . . . By contrast, the very form itself of the Veda proves its authority to be independent and absolute.[36]

The conviction enunciated here, which links intelligibility and truth of content to intelligibility and "truth" of form—and links truth of form to Sanskrit—would prove immensely influential in Indian history. For it articulates the grounds of resistance to the development of vernacular literary cultures, and, after the vernacular revolution, the grounds for restricting that revolution to the sphere of expressive literature such that Sanskrit remained the primary language of science up to the very eve of colonial rule. But equally remarkable is Kumārila's apparent historical ignorance. For by the time he was writing in the mid-seventh century, a vast Buddhist canon in Sanskrit, a "quite definite translation into Sanskrit," as one scholar has called it, had been in existence for centuries.[37]

The Buddhist turn to Sanskrit for the transmission of the word of the Buddha is attested already from the second century C.E.; portions of a canon (for which the Sarvāstivāda school appears to have been principally responsible) might have existed from as early as the third century. Canonical texts from several centuries prior to this period are found redacted in various forms of Middle Indic mixed with Sanskrit (sometimes called Buddhist Hybrid Sanskrit), an idiom that seems less a failure to achieve Sanskrit than a continuing reluctance to use it fully.[38] From about the second century, however, Buddhist discourse in north India, and perhaps in much of South Asia excluding the peninsula, where Pali preserved a modest mainland presence, seems to have largely meant discourse in Sanskrit. What exactly

36. *Tantravārttika* on *PMS* 1.3.12, p. 164 lines 8–15, rearranging slightly the verse and the prose gloss (the passage Kumārila goes on to cite is not Pali); p. 166 lines 1–2 (see also *Nyāyasudhā* p. 236 lines 10ff. and the broader linking of correct language and truth in *Śāstradīpikā* pp. 46–47). For Kumārila, the transcendent character of the Veda is revealed in part by its lexical and semantic uniqueness (e.g., words like *īḷe* [*ṚV* 1.1.1], which no human being could ever have invented, cf. p. 164 lines 18ff., 165 line 6). Already by Kumārila's time Dakshinatya Prakrit (assuming this refers to Maharashtri) and perhaps even Magadhi had been grammaticized, as in the version of the *Prākṛtaprakāśa* commented on by Bhāmaha (cf. von Hinüber 1986: 54, Scharfe 1977: 192). Accordingly, there would be no paradox in Kumārila's speaking of their "corrupt forms."

37. Brough 1954: 362, 367–68.

38. Evidence for a canon in Sanskritized Middle Indic in the first century C.E. is discussed in Salomon and Schopen 1984: 116–117. In the northwest, Gandhari continued to be in use for centuries. A medieval Buddhist commentary refers to the intentional "use of occasional solecisms in verses in order to loosen the fixation on standard language on the part of those who believe in the absolute language standards [of Sanskrit]" (*teṣāṃ ca suśabdavādināṃ suśabd[ā]grahavināśāyārthaśaraṇatām āśritya kvacid vṛtte 'paśabdaḥ*, from the *Vimalaprabhā*, a commentary on the *Śrī Kālacakra*, cited in Newman 1988: 125).

prompted the Buddhists to abandon their hostility to the language after half a millennium—the first instance of giving up resistance to Sanskrit and giving into its power, a process that would be reenacted time and again in Indian history—and finally adopt it for scripture, philosophy, and a wide range of other textual forms, some of which they would help to invent, is a question for which no convincing arguments have yet been offered.[39]

Various interpretations are common and recurrent, but none is entirely persuasive. One simply identifies Sanskrit as "the language of learning" to which all others had to conform. Another points toward "a desire to emulate the practices of the Brahman communities"—a "'keeping up with the Joneses' syndrome of competition with Brahmanical communities for popular esteem"—coupled with anxiety at the "gossip about the perceived inferior linguistic habits of the Buddhist monks." Neither explanation takes us very far, only replacing one question with another: why, after nearly five centuries, was it suddenly necessary or desirable for Buddhists to participate in such learning, or to achieve such emulation and avoid opprobrium, when it had long been perfectly acceptable to adopt a separate cultural style and to transmit a rather considerable amount of learning in regional speech forms? A third explanation, a variant on the first, assumes that Sanskrit has a natural communicative superiority that made it irresistible: the "technical precision of Sanskrit," according to Etienne Lamotte, "knowledge of which continually grew among diverse strata of society, made it an ideal instrument for presenting doctrines and ideas." But Lamotte unwittingly refutes himself by what he proceeds to demonstrate: that such materials could be, and in fact were, equally well presented in Pali, Gandhari, and other languages. And in any case, the assumption behind this explanation is dubious: neither Sanskrit nor any other prestige dialect has an inherent capacity qualifying it for tasks of complex expression, let alone an "inherent beauty and force" that somehow naturally "fulfilled the intellectual requirements of the Indian Man."[40] The value of a language resides, in part at least, in the social value of those who speak it. When natural superiority is attributed to Sanskrit, it is usually for the same reason (or unreason) why Heidegger believed that when a Frenchman begins to think philosophically he inevitably does so in German.

Other accounts of the Sanskrit turn among the Buddhists are more firmly grounded in some kind of sociology or history yet still remain problematic.

39. See in general Mishra 1993, Gombrich 1990, and for earlier literature, Lin Li-kouang 1949, 176ff.

40. So S. K. Chatterji (cited in Shapiro and Schiffman 1983: 143). The ideology of "natural superiority" among languages is discussed in Joseph 1987: 30ff., 41. On Sanskrit as the language of learning, see Brough 1954: 362, 367 (and cf. 368), Lamotte 1976: 646ff.; for Brahman emulation, Salomon 2001: 250.

Thus one scholar takes as his point of departure the fact that many of Sanskrit Buddhism's major teachers were converted Brahmans. But the same may be said of many Pali Buddhist teachers, including the greatest among them, Buddhaghosa. The assumption that Buddhists realized they could not win over the Brahmans, the "bearers of culture," to the teachings of the Master unless they presented their holy texts in the language of the *śiṣṭa,* the learned, begs the question why this realization dawned only centuries after the Buddha, and leaves us to wonder how the many Brahmans mentioned in Pali texts had themselves been won over. More recently it has been argued that the relevant condition in the adoption of Sanskrit as a canonical language was Buddhism's penetration westward to Mathurā and the heart of Āryāvarta, the core region of *vaidika* culture. But Buddhists had been located in other areas where, we are told, the "dominant culture was Hindu, Brahmanical, and Sanskrit" without adopting Sanskrit; then, too, at least according to the social imaginary of the Vinaya text recounted earlier, the use of "Vedic-Sanskrit verse" for the word of the Buddha was a conceptual possibility far to the east. Indeed, some early Buddhist records composed in Sanskrit give no indication that they were written in Mathurā but show vocabulary with eastern characteristics and suggest a "seemingly independent Sanskritization." Moreover, the presence of Buddhists in Mathurā seems to be in evidence long before the period when they began to adopt Sanskrit.[41]

The history of the Jain relationship to Sanskrit, for its part, also throws into doubt many of the assumptions underlying explanations of the Buddhist turn. For one thing, the Jains never considered their eastern Prakrit inadequate for communicating their ideas, since their canonical texts were never redacted in Sanskrit. On the contrary, throughout history a tacit prohibition against any such undertaking remained in force. The story of the monk Siddhasena, from a twelfth-century collection of tales, shows this clearly. When, like the Brahmans of the Vinaya tale, Siddhasena suggests rendering the holy texts into Sanskrit, he is excommunicated from his religious order until he repents. This attitude maintained itself despite the notable presence of Brahman converts in the Jain community throughout its history, and even despite the existence of a community of Jain Brahmans in medieval Karnataka (chapter 10.4). While it is true that the Jains adopted Sanskrit relatively early for philosophical disputation (at least from the time of Umāsvāti, author of the *Tattvārthādhigamasūtra,* in perhaps the third or fourth century), for centuries to come they remained reluctant to commit fully to Sanskrit for other

41. For Mahāyāna teachers, see Deshpande 1979: 42; for winning over the Brahmans, Lüders 1940: 713. The role of Mathurā is considered in Fussman 1980b: 425; easternisms in Buddhist Sanskrit are noted in Norman 1979: 294. Fussman has commented further on Sanskrit as a link language among Indian Buddhists whose Middle-Indic dialects had ceased to be mutually intelligible (1982a: 38–39).

kinds of moral or aesthetic texts. No Sanskrit biography of Mahāvīra was produced before the *Vardhamānacarita* of Asaga in 853 (whereas Aśvaghoṣa's Sanskrit "Life of the Buddha" dates probably to the mid-second century C.E.), and the first universal history in Sanskrit is Raviṣena's *Padmapurāṇa* of 678 (a rendering of Vimalasūri's Prakrit work of four centuries earlier).[42]

The fact that many Buddhist communities in the north of the subcontinent abandoned their long-standing language pluralism in favor of Sanskrit, the language they had rejected for centuries, therefore awaits better explanations. What we can be certain of, in view of all the evidence we have seen so far, is that their choice represented an astonishing expansion of the realm of Sanskrit, far beyond the *vaidika* sanctum to which it had been restricted for a millennium and in the most unanticipated directions, including the textualization of ideas fundamentally opposed to the *vaidika* world. Yet this is fully in keeping with other, equally momentous developments that took place at the same time, in the one or two centuries just before and after the beginning of the Common Era.

1.3 EXPANDING THE PRESTIGE ECONOMY OF SANSKRIT

Our ability to trace the lineaments of the expansion of Sanskrit's social and discursive domain, and to understand something of the new cultural-political order this generated, takes on an altogether different degree of historical precision once we enter the age of writing. This commenced around the middle of the third century B.C.E. with the records issued by Aśoka, the third overlord of the Maurya dynasty (320–150 B.C.E.). This has long been known. An emerging scholarly consensus, however, now regards the Brahmi syllabary, the first South Asian writing system (and the parent script for almost every other writing system in southern Asia), as the deliberate creation of Aśoka's chancery for the promulgation of his edicts on moral governance (in both the epigraphical idea itself and some of its formulaic language Aśoka was imitating Achaemenid practices).[43] The convention thereby inaugurated among southern Asian courts—the public display of inscribed texts on rock faces, free-standing pillars, temple walls, or, after about the mid-fourth century, copperplates—was to continue from this point on uninterruptedly to the middle of the second millennium. As we will see, these texts are valuable indices of not only a new kind of political imagination but, equally impor-

42. The Siddhasena episode is recounted in *Prabhāvakacarita* p. 58; cf. also Granoff 1992. On Asaga, see Upadhye 1983: 284–94. A general account of Jain views of Sanskrit is provided in Dundas 1996; the Jain turn to Sanskrit for writing *kāvya* is an important understudied question.

43. On the invention see, above all, Falk 1993, especially p. 339; Salomon 1995; on the Achaemenids (550–330 B.C.E.) model, Benveniste 1964: 144–45, and Pollock 2004a: 417.

tant, a new kind of literariness, as well as the new-old language in which literary expression could be coded. We find repeatedly throughout South Asian history that inscriptions functioned as synecdoches of the larger literary and political cultures of which they were products, and that they came to be transformed in tandem with these larger cultures.

If students typically know that written texts in India appeared first with Aśoka, they are not always aware that these texts were composed not in Sanskrit but in various Middle-Indic dialects, sometimes referred to as Prakrits. While closely related to Sanskrit, these dialects were considered entirely distinct from it by premodern Indian thinkers, who developed a set of clear categories to frame the distinction (chapter 2). As noted in section 1, for the first three to four centuries of literacy, next to nothing was inscribed except in the Prakrits. Moreover, the records in question, in stark contrast with what was to come, are entirely documentary and not literary in character, a distinction again fully intelligible according to local conceptual schemes. Not a single literary inscription of the sort to be found later in such abundance was produced in Sanskrit during this period, while the very few inscriptions that do aim toward expressivity were composed instead in Prakrit. In fact, a mere handful of inscriptions in Sanskrit are available, in contrast to the many Middle-Indic texts, and these Sanskrit epigraphs are by and large exiguous: one- or two-line records commemorating a *vaidika* or quasi-*vaidika* rite. These early Sanskrit documents are worth a glance in order to establish a baseline for the dramatic changes that were soon to occur.

What appear to be the earliest documents, from probably the first century B.C.E., announce the founding of a temple enclosure *(pūjāśilāprākāra)* in one case, and the dedication of a water tank in the other; the next two oldest, from the early first century C.E., record the establishment of sacrificial post memorials *(yūpa)*.[44] These are typical of the rest of the small corpus in being private rather than public gestures. Although, strictly speaking, all inscriptions are public in the sense of being open proclamations available to all with eyes to see or ears to hear (save Buddhist reliquary inscriptions meant to be deposited inside *stūpas*), only a couple of these early Sanskrit records were issued from royal courts. One of the latter is the sole Sanskrit document of the Śuṅgas, the dynasty that succeeded the Mauryas to the north (their one other extant record, and the only one to mention the dynasty's name, is in Prakrit). It is a very brief stone inscription from Ayodhyā in the northeast of what is today Uttarpradesh (dated no earlier than the first century C.E.), mentioning King Dhana[deva], "who twice offered the royal horse sacrifice" *(dviraśvamedhayājin)*, and memorializing the construction of a tomb.[45] One does not want to minimize the importance of such documents as these and the first inti-

44. See *EI* 16: 27; *JA* 1993: 113; *ASI A/R* 1910–11: 40ff.; and *EI* 22: 198–205 respectively.
45. *EI* 20: 57. The Prakrit Śuṅga inscription is published in *BI* p. 11.

mation they offer, however reticent and tentative, of some new desire—for publicity, permanence, or whatever—in the old *śrauta* world that the technology of inscription in Sanskrit satisfied, or perhaps created, as technology can do. But the main point to register is that these inscriptions were very isolated occurrences. They did not mark any kind of historical break in Sanskrit cultural consciousness or inaugurate a new public or civic discourse; they remained fully internal to the *vaidika* world. The moment of discontinuity was still on the horizon, and when it did come, it would be vast and total.

Prior to that moment, however, the state of affairs just recounted is very curious, and very suggestive of larger cultural tendencies. To put a fine point on it: For the first time, beginning in the mid-third century B.C.E., the possibility was widely available not only of actually writing Sanskrit—the older *vaidika* world having been one of pure and carefully regulated orality—but of writing it publicly. Yet how to explain the fact that, for the following four centuries or more, nothing of a public Sanskrit has been found and almost certainly was never produced, whereas epigraphs in Middle Indic abound? For Louis Renou, the leading French Indologist of the previous generation, the question why Middle Indic should have appeared in epigraphy centuries earlier than Sanskrit constitutes "the great linguistic paradox of India." And he insisted on explaining it, as so many other scholars have explained so many other problems in Indian history, in religious terms: as a convert to Buddhism, Aśoka supposedly adopted the Buddhist hostility toward Sanskrit described earlier, and the "epigraphical habit, thus primed would continue for many centuries."[46]

Yet this explanation seems to be refuted by a simple fact, one that is no mere artifact of our data: in the early period of literacy in South Asia, no dynasty, regardless of how *vaidika* it was—and therefore, according to the logic of the religious argument, both willing and able to use Sanskrit—employed that language for its public records. Exemplary here are the cultural practices of the Sātavāhanas. This lineage exercised some form of rule over a wide area of southern India from about 225 B.C.E. to 250 C.E. From the large body of Sātavāhana inscriptional and numismatic evidence available to us now, a very striking kind of cultural politics emerges. This was a lineage of rulers who unequivocally saw themselves inhabiting a Vedic world, as evidenced by both their continual performance of the solemn ceremonies of the *śrauta* tradition and their explicit self-identification as Brahmanical.[47] Yet

46. Renou 1956: 84.

47. Their Brahmanism is indubitable, notwithstanding uncertainties about the nuances of *ekabahmaṇa* ("exclusively Brahmanic," "alone worthy of the name of Brahmanic," "the one support of the Brahmans," etc., Mirashi 1981: 13, 35; the suggested translations include those of Georg Bühler and R. G. Bhandarkar). Additional references to the Brahmanism of the Sātavāhanas were first collected in Lévi 1904: 172.

every scrap of text they produced—documentary, *praśasti,* literary—is in Prakrit. There is no evidence for their use of Sanskrit in any nonliturgical domain.

Besides the complete absence of Sanskrit inscriptions, not a single Sanskrit work in any of the new textual forms of *kāvya* that were coming into being around this time is associated with the court, or indeed, found anywhere within the space-time world of the Sātavāhanas, which comprised most of the Deccan (the area between the Narmadā and Kṛṣṇā rivers) and much of peninsular India over a period of some four centuries. Two Sanskrit texts that are associated with the court (or at least were written within its penumbra), and point toward the same conclusion, are examined more closely below. One, the *Yugapurāṇa* (Lore of the Cosmic Ages), actually announces the momentous historical changes in literary culture that were about to take place on the subcontinent, and to do so it had to employ a sacred-prophetic register for which Sanskrit was the only appropriate vehicle. The second is the grammar named the *Kātantra* (Brief System). Although the career of its author, Śarvavarman, was later to become the stuff of legend, the work can be located with reasonable certainty in the Sātavāhana world of perhaps the second century C.E. What makes this grammar remarkable is that it is clearly a work of popularization in both its mode of presentation and its substance. It almost totally eliminates the complex metalinguistic terminology of its Paninian model (which it clearly sought to displace, and successfully displaced for many reading communities for centuries) and excludes all rules pertaining to the Vedic register of the language—a striking modification in a knowledge form that for a millennium had regarded itself as a limb of the Veda and, as Patañjali showed, was above all intended to ensure the preservation of Veda. With these innovations the *Kātantra* seems to have been contributing to a wider movement of desacralization of the use of Sanskrit that was manifesting itself in other regions of South Asia at that moment. As for the Sātavāhanas themselves, everything we know about their dynasty and their world indicates that they maintained a very conservative attitude toward Sanskrit and rigorously confined it to the domain of *vaidika* ritual and related scholastic contexts; their commitment to Prakrit outside these contexts was therefore anything but an "ex post facto fabrication" of modern scholarship.[48]

Elsewhere, too, it is not only common but absolutely regular to find Prakrit used in the early period for inscriptional materials of the public domain on

48. On Śarvavarman and the *Kātantra*'s relationship to Kumāralāta's grammar, see chapters 2.2, 4.1. It was Renou who argued "Que les Śātavāhanas aient été prākritisants . . . a pu être fabriqué après coup d'après des déductions fondées sur l'existence du Kātantra et de l'anthologie de Hāla" (1956: 99 and n.). He was, moreover, in error in viewing Sātavāhana records as purely "bureaucratic"; some of their inscriptions show unmistakable *praśasti* style (see chapter 2 n. 11). Nāgārjuna's *Suhṛllekha,* an epistle of spiritual counsel addressed to a Sātavāhana king, was purportedly written in Sanskrit (only Tibetan and Chinese translations survive).

the part of ruling families clearly committed to a *vaidika* and Brahmanical culture. Instructive here are the earliest inscriptions of the Pallavas (300–900), the first epigraphically attested rulers over the northern regions of Tamilnadu. Their oldest records, from the late-third and early-fourth centuries, are in Prakrit, but an unusual form of Prakrit ("in no way absolutely pure," as one scholar described it; it shows phonological preservations of Sanskrit forms and certain other "gross irregularities"). In fact, it seems an unfamiliar, almost reluctant Prakrit, certainly used because Sanskrit was thought inappropriate for public records. The first document records a ritual payment *(dakṣiṇā)* to one [Jīvasi]vasami (Jīvaśivasvāmin) for his performance of various apotropaic rituals (the *santisathiyāyaṇa, śāntisvastyāyana*). The second record was issued a decade later by *yuvamahārājo bhāradāyasagotto palavānaṃ sivakhaṃdavammo* ("crown prince Śivaskandavarman of the Bharadvāja [i.e., a Vedic] lineage") in assigning a gift of land to a Brahman community (a *brahmadeya*). Notably, the legend on the seal of the Prakrit record is in a somewhat different alphabet from that of the grant itself and renders the name of the king in the Sanskrit form *śivaska[ndavarmmaṇaḥ]*, in contrast to the orthography on the plate itself. In 338 the third extant Pallava record, a copperplate land grant again in Prakrit, was issued by the same Sivakhaṃdavamo, whose Vedic ritual accomplishments the record celebrates with a title in Prakrit: he is an *aggiṭṭhoma-vājapeyasamedhayājī*, that is, a performer of the *agniṣṭoma, vājapeya,* and *aśvamedha* sacrifices, among the greatest of the Vedic rites. Again, the seal bears the king's name in Sanskrit: *śivaskanda[varmaṇaḥ];* also in Sanskrit is the benediction at the end: *svasti gobr[ā]h[m]aṇalekhakavācakaśrotṛbhya iti* (Welfare to cows, Brahmans, the engraver, the reciter, and the audience [of the grant]). A last example comes from the latter half of the fourth century. This copperplate is entirely in Prakrit except for two verses cited at the close and attributed to "Vyāsa"—verses that would be repeated in land-grant documents for the next thousand years—which are composed in entirely normative Sanskrit:

> *bahubhir vasudhā dattā bahubhiś cānupālitā* |
> *yasya yasya yadā bhūmis tasya tasya tadā phalam* ||
>
> *svadattāṃ paradattāṃ vā ye haranti vasūndharāṃ* |
> *gavāṃ śatasahasrasya hantuḥ pibati duṣkṛtam* ||

> Many have gifted land and many have protected it. Whoever possesses the land, and so long as he possesses it, possesses the fruit thereof. Whoever steals land, whether he gave it or another did, drinks the sin of a man who has slain a thousand cows.[49]

49. The four records are reedited in *IP:* 29–41. For the remarks on the Prakrit of the Pallavas, see Pischel 1965: 8; see also Lévi 1904: 170, who first noted the significance of Śivaskandavarman's seal. The Pallavas' list of *vaidika* rituals (which was used formulaically elsewhere and later) harkens back to third-century Ikṣvāku records (Cāṃtamūla I is *agihot-āgiṭhoma-vāja[peya-*

The concomitance between content such as this, which emerges from a purely *vaidika* milieu, and the use of Prakrit for its public dissemination is not encountered in Sātavāhana and Pallava records alone; it is standard in the inscriptions of ruling groups across South Asia over the first four or five centuries of literacy. One conclusion is unavoidable: The choice of Prakrit for public inscription cannot have been conditioned by the religiously grounded conviction, as conveyed by the Buddhist theologians in the Vinaya account and embodied by the language choices of the writers of early scriptural texts, that Sanskrit was tied to Brahmanism and for that reason was to be avoided for purposes of non-*vaidika* (let alone anti-*vaidika*) communication. Brahmanism itself avoided Sanskrit, too, for purposes of nonliturgical cultural discourse. A second conclusion is that the choice of Prakrit cannot have been the result (as it is often supposed to be) of the sheer inability to write proper Sanskrit, since it is obvious that proper Sanskrit could be written when proper Sanskrit was desired.

Now, of course, when we use terms like the "choice of Prakrit" and "proper Sanskrit," we are presupposing that Sanskrit and Prakrit are distinct, and that the distinction between them was registered on the cognitive map of the people who chose Prakrit and employed proper Sanskrit. But it is not unreasonable to ask whether such a distinction can confidently be ascribed to the period in question. If it cannot, then Renou's "paradox" turns out to be an artifact of modern notions of razor-thin boundaries between languages that are simply inappropriate for a premodern world, with its supposedly broad language zones and their hazy borders. In fact, some scholars, questioning the "unitary" character of post-Vedic Sanskrit and positing the existence of so-called vernacular Sanskrits, have sought to weaken or even erase the distinction between Sanskrit and Prakrit and instead represent them as mere "poles of a dialectic spectrum."[50] Such an understanding would mean that no language choice was being made in the epigraphical record.

Here lie complexities about modern and premodern kinds and categories that will be encountered throughout the course of this study, not just in matters of language identity but in everything from the conceptual status of literary genres (like "epic") and political formations (like "empire") to encompassing notions of time and space. Again, we need to distinguish methodologically between the absolute truth of linguistics and the certitudes of lan-

āsamedha-yājisa] hiraṇakoṭi-go-satasahasa-hala-[satasahasa-padāyisa], etc.) (*EI* 20: 17 ff.; cf. Sircar 1939c: 384). With the Sanskrit of the Pallava seals compare the contemporaneous charter of Jayavarman, Kistna district, Tamilnadu (*EI* 6: 315–19; possibly the oldest copperplate record in South Asia). The charter is in Prakrit, whereas the seal reads: *bṛhatphalāyanasagotrasya mahārājaśrījayavarmmaṇaḥ;* contrast this with lines 4–5 of the plate itself: *bṛhatphalāyanasagoto rājā sirijayavammo.* The Sanskrit is also written in different characters from the Prakrit.

50. See Salomon 1989a: 277; Deshpande 1993b: 33–52.

guage users that provide the grounds for their beliefs and actions. No one would deny that a modest spectrum of variation in Sanskrit (though hardly a "dialectology") can be identified from the variety of Sanskrit registers available in Indian literary history; such a spectrum is easily explained by the influence of living speech on a literary language in a diglossic or hyperglossic (or just polyglossic) environment. But this has little bearing on the conceptual or cognitive status of the Sanskrit language in premodernity, both for those who participated in Sanskrit literary culture itself and for those who regarded it from the outside. From both perspectives, the speciation of Sanskrit from its linguistic others was as clear as any could be before the rise of unified languages under the modern regime of print-generated standardization.[51]

At its borders, every language may appear to merge into something else; the fact that it can be defined, cognitively and discursively, as a *language* in the first place, rather than continuing to exist as unmarked jargon, is largely due to the presence of a body of grammatical, literary, and other texts that provide it with norms and hence stability (a fact repeatedly corroborated by the evidence in part 2 of this book). And it was precisely by means of the vast production of philological, scriptural, and eventually literary texts that the tradition itself insistently thematized Sanskrit as such and distinguished it from non-Sanskrit. Moreover, even if various kinds of Sanskrit are found in use—nonnormative or informal Sanskrit; Sanskrit influenced by Apabhramsha or later Persian; Sanskrit transitional between the cosmopolitan and vernacular, which late inscriptions show in abundance—they were employed not indiscriminately in the production of texts by writers floating unselfconsciously on a wide dialectal sea but quite intentionally and restrictedly; wholly normalized Sanskrit would be produced for the specific arenas for which it was appropriate. Furthermore, Sanskrit was everywhere conceptualized as an identifiable and unified entity. Buddhist and Jain language preferences for scriptural text production would be unintelligible in the absence of the acknowledged distinctiveness of Sanskrit. In short, when the absolute perspective of science *(pāramārthika sat)* is at odds with the representations produced from within the traditions of language thought *(vyāvahārika sat),* it is to the latter that we must defer if we are to understand the history made by knowledgeable agents.[52] And according to the *vyāvahārika sat* of premodern South Asia, Sanskrit was an indubitable unity. This is something attested

51. There is much uncertainty about the history of "standardization." Joseph 1987 constructs his entire paradigm around the modernity of the notion (cf. p. 7), and yet koiné Greek is taken as a "prototype" and Latin as the first standardized language (p. 50). See also chapter 14.2 and n. 49.

52. Though in fact the disagreement is trivial. Emeneau's view from outside, if somewhat overstated, remains largely correct: "We find in [Sanskrit] no dialects, no chronological development, except loss and at times invasion from the vernaculars of the users, and no geographical divergences" (1966: 123).

to by everything from the repeated injunctions in scriptural texts themselves "to use correct language [i.e., Sanskrit] and not incorrect language [i.e., dialectal forms]" to the view of the tenth-century commentator cited earlier, that "whereas the Prakrits are multiform, Sanskrit is uniform."[53] Indeed, by the period under discussion in this book—and precisely in this period and through the processes with which it confronts us—even the earlier categories for constituting different kinds of Sanskrit, such as Pāṇini's distinctions between *chandaḥ* and *bhāṣā* (the language of the Veda and that of learned discourse) or *udīcya* and *prācya* (morphological differences marked as northern and eastern) had been almost completely abandoned.[54]

There seems, accordingly, to be little to recommend any of the available explanations for "the great linguistic paradox of India." There is no reason to believe that the various sorts of Prakrit hybrids that we find in epigraphy are evidence of an "intermediate stage in the popularity of Sanskrit and the decline of Prakrit," as if a half-realized Sanskrit were somehow a half-popular Sanskrit; or that the Prakrit that some call epigraphical hybrid Sanskrit, which makes its appearance around the middle of the first century C.E. in Mathurā (where Buddhist migration is supposed to have been a condition for a Buddhist appropriation of Sanskrit), marks the failure of an attempt to achieve Sanskrit; or that the Sātavāhana court used Prakrit in sheer ignorance of Sanskrit.[55] As we have seen, epigraphs from other parts of India might be composed wholly in Prakrit while ending with a benediction or citation from a *dharma* text in normative Sanskrit. When standard Sanskrit was desired, standard Sanskrit was written; and for the public, political document, Sanskrit was evidently not desired. The Prakrit inscriptions, and perhaps even early Buddhist Hybrid Sanskrit texts, might be taken as evincing a reluctance or refusal to write Sanskrit far more readily than an inability to do so.

If to speak of "proper Sanskrit" and "the choice of Prakrit," therefore, does not invoke categories that were anachronistic or unintelligible to premodern Indian conceptions, and does not presuppose language practices that no one practiced, and if religious affiliation was not the decisive factor in choosing Prakrit over Sanskrit, then clearly some other set of cultural factors must have conditioned the choice of language for public inscription in the first four or five centuries of South Asian literacy. It seems most reason-

53. Injunctions such as *nāsādhu vadet* ("One should not speak ungrammatically") and *sādhubhir bhāṣeta* ("One should use grammatical speech") are discussed repeatedly in Mīmāṃsā, especially on *PMS* 1.3.5 ff. *(śiṣṭākopādhikaraṇa)* and 1.3.10 ff. *(pikanemādhikaraṇa)*.

54. For the second, see for example Agrawal 1963: 39. The question of regional variation in the *Aṣṭādhyāyī* has attracted surprisingly little notice; see also chapter 5.3 and n. 35.

55. On the "intermediate stage" theory see Sircar, 1965–83, vol. 1: 430 n. 2; for "epigraphical hybrid Sanskrit" (though there is nothing especially inscriptional about the dialect) see Damsteegt 1978. For the Sātavāhanas see Mirashi 1981: 177 ("Their knowledge of Sanskrit must have been very meager," etc.).

able to assume that these factors pertained above all to the social value of Sanskrit and the reluctance—taboo may not be too strong a word—to employ it for the new public documentary mode. Very likely, this reluctance would have been most powerfully stimulated, and thence generalized as a value of high culture, precisely in contexts where both the agent and the act were fully embedded in the *vaidika* world (like Sivakhaṃdavamo, an *aggiṭṭhoma-yājī*, awarding a *dakṣiṇā* or granting a *brahmadeya*). The reality and salience of such reluctance seem to be corroborated by everything we know or can infer about the nature of Sanskrit culture for the entire first millennium B.C.E.: the prevalence of its liturgical dimension, the forms of knowledge necessary for liturgy, and the restriction of its use to those alone who participated in this form of life.

Such was the steady state of literary-cultural convention that was exploded in the early centuries of the first millennium. It was then that ruling elites made the first experiments in the inscription of texts in standard Sanskrit that would become dominant convention in the public expression of royal power across a large part of southern Asia for centuries to come. The beginnings of the formation of this new Sanskrit order are to be located in the cultural-political events of this epoch in the same way that its eventual breakup is to be located in the cultural-political events that occurred during the first half of the second millennium. The radical reinvention of Sanskrit culture seems to have occurred—at least, it is here that we can actually watch it occurring—precisely where one might expect it, in a social world where the presuppositions and conventions of *vaidika* culture were weakest: among newly immigrant peoples from the far northwest of the subcontinent (and ultimately from Iran and Central Asia), most importantly the Śakas (the so-called Indo-Scythians), especially a branch of the Śakas known as the Western Kṣatrapas, and the Kuṣāṇas.[56]

Large-scale generalizations about these peoples are exceedingly difficult. The same ethnonym, "Śaka," was borne by various groups who may have differed considerably in their lifeways. The major transformation with which we are concerned here was inaugurated by the Śakas of what is now Gujarat; to what degree others shared their cultural aspirations remains unclear. It was signaled by a celebrated inscription composed by a Western Kṣatrapa overlord named Rudradāman around 150 C.E. (year 72 of the Śaka era). Prior to this point, Śaka inscriptions (as well as coins) had by and large conformed to the cultural model in place everywhere else. Rudradāman made a departure from this model, and a radical one. The size and place of his document befit its historical importance: It is engraved in massive dimensions (the whole measures eleven by five feet) on a huge rounded granite boulder at

56. For a brief summary of recent scholarship on these peoples see Wink 1997: 52–59.

Junāgaṛh on the Kāṭhiāwāḍ peninsula, a site long marked by cultural distinction (eventually it would become part of a major pilgrimage circuit of the Śvetāmbara Jains). Juxtaposed to Rudradāman's inscription are fourteen earlier Ashokan Prakrit edicts; Rudradāman actually mentions the events of four centuries earlier that occasioned these records: the building activities of "the Maurya king, Candragupta," and of "Aśoka Maurya" and his subordinate, "the Yavana king Tuṣāsphena" (line 8). A Sanskrit inscription by the Gupta king Skandagupta would be added three hundred years later (457 C.E.). The Junāgaṛh rock thus carries, inscribed on its surface, seven centuries of Indian cultural-political history, thereby both demonstrating the capacity of certain objects, natural or man-made, to embody and preserve political charisma, and instantiating one form of the historical imitation and emulation that would prove central to the imperial mode across time and space (see chapters 6, 7). But it is first and foremost the content of Rudradāman's inscription that arrests attention: It is a Sanskrit *praśasti,* approximating *gadyakāvya,* or art-prose, whereby the king, on the occasion of repairing a great public waterworks, the reservoir called Sudarśana (Lake Beautiful) that had been damaged in a storm, celebrates his own political and cultural achievements. And it is like nothing the Sanskrit world had seen before:

> The water, churned by a storm wind with an awesome force like the wind at the end of time, leveled the hills, uprooted trees, and tore down embankments, turrets, towers, shelters—scattered and broke to pieces < . . . > and the stones and trees and shrubs and vines lay strewn about everywhere . . . He who from the womb possessed the splendor of consummate royalty, whom all castes resorted to and chose as their lord; who has made a vow—a vow he kept—to take no life except in battle < . . . > but never hesitates to strike an equal foe who faces him in combat; who rules as lord of eastern and western Ākarāvantī, Anūpa country, Ānarta, Surāṣṭra, Śvabhara, Maru, Kaccha, Sindhusauvīra, Kukura, Aparānta, Niṣāda, and other areas gained by his valor, and everywhere—town, market, countryside—is untouched by trouble from robbers, snakes, wild beasts, or disease. . . ; who [composes] prose and verse, clear and pleasant, sweet and charming, adorned with figures of speech and stamped by proper use of language; whose body is beautiful and marked with most excellent marks and signs . . . He, Mahākṣatrapa Rudradāman . . . by a vast sum of money from his own treasury and in a timely manner, strengthened the dam and lengthened it, three times greater than before < . . . > and far more beautiful now has Lake Beautiful become.[57]

The text of this inscription has been known for more than a century and a half; James Prinsep, the British colonial administrator and decipherer of the Ashokan inscriptions, first published it in 1838. What is not always appre-

57. Sircar 1965–83, vol. 1: 176ff. lines 6–16. Angle brackets indicate lacunae in the inscription.

ciated adequately, however, is its historical distinctiveness. The hundred and fifty years since Prinsep's work have witnessed an intensive hunt for inscriptions throughout South Asia, resulting in forty-four volumes of *Epigraphia Indica,* ten books of *Corpus Inscriptionum Indicarum,* and countless reports of as yet unpublished inscriptional finds from archaeological investigations around the subcontinent—by some estimates amounting to as many as one hundred thousand records. Yet nothing whatever has been discovered to unsettle the certainty that Rudradāman's text marks a true break in cultural history. For the first time, self-consciously expressive Sanskrit, with all the enormous authority, power, and cultural value garnered by the very fact of its centuries-long monopolization and ritualization, was used in a public space, in bold letters for all to see, for the self-presentation of a living overlord.

To what degree Rudradāman's inscription was part of a larger cultural-political initiative of the Śakas is impossible to determine with any precision. Only the merest scraps of their writing have been preserved; all told, we have no more than several dozen records or portions of records, none anywhere close to Junāgaṛh in size, and only a handful that point to the Sanskrit turn so magnificently on display here. But if we have only remnants of that culture, they are nonetheless suggestive remnants. Consider the fact that the next oldest inscription (279 C.E.) after Rudradāman, composed according to the formal conventions of what, precisely during this period, was coming to be called *kāvya,* is found at the close of a record of one Śrīdharavarman, who describes himself as a Śaka appointed as principal governor *(mahādaṇḍanāyaka).* But the predilection of the Śakas for the use of Sanskrit seems to be evident from even earlier documents, which show "learned or pretentious borrowings" from Sanskrit, and a Middle Indic markedly "infiltrated" by the language. And the new ruling lineages to the east, the Kuṣāṇas, seem to some extent to have shared the Śaka view of cultural politics.[58]

There is no little significance in the fact that while the Śakas helped transform the world of Sanskrit culture, they stood at a considerable remove from the old *vaidika* order. Whereas Rudradāman celebrates his own proficiency in various forms of Sanskrit knowledge *(vidyā),* including grammar, the Western Kṣatrapas themselves were scarcely "Brahmanized," as one scholar puts it. They did not adopt a *vaidika* lineage title (a *gotra* affiliation) until a century after Rudradāman. There is no indication of their offering special pa-

58. The earliest securely datable evidence for the complex metrical structures that mark *kāvya* as a literary form apart from all others is a step-well inscription from the time of Śoḍāsa, son of Rājūvula, the Śaka lord ruling in Mathurā c. 50 B.C.E., part of which is in the *bhujaṅgavijṛmbhita* meter (*EI* 24: 195 ff.; this is the dedication of a *vaidika* structure and not composed by a Śaka, but it is within their cultural ambit and so conforms to their norms). Not all Kṣatrapa inscriptions following Rudradāman are in Sanskrit, as Lévi believed (1904: 169), see *EI* 37: 142 ff. For the Śakas' "learned borrowings" see Fussman 1980a: 9; for Śrīdharavarman's inscription, which ends with a *śārdūlavikrīḍita* verse, *EI* 16: 230 ff.

tronage to Brahmans; instead, their administration largely relied on non-Brahmans: Pahlavas (Parthians), Ābhīras, and others outside the *vaidika* world.[59] The Junāgaṛh inscription itself demonstrates this at its close in a passage that also hints at a developing cosmopolitan culture in which the old right *(adhikāra)* to participate in moral and political action *(dharma* and *artha)* was scandalously being expanded beyond its archaic restrictedness to the twice-born: the minister of the Mahākṣatrapa, "the Pahlava Suviśākha, son of Kulaipa," is praised as having "duly enhanced loyalty *(anurāga)* by his political and moral action and views *(arthadharmavyavahāradarśanaiḥ),* and increased the moral quality, fame, and glory of his master."

Though the data are scant in the extreme, making any grand generalization hazardous, such a milieu does seem a likely place where the desacralization of Sanskrit would first be attempted.[60] Although the Śakas' contemporaries to the east, the Kuṣāṇas, may not have incorporated the Sanskrit idiom in their political discourse, various large and small bits of circumstantial evidence indicate their predilection for the same cultural-political practices as the Śakas. For example, credible tradition places the Sanskrit poet Aśvaghoṣa, the earliest known author and perhaps even inventor of both the courtly epic *(mahākāvya)* and dramatic genres, at the court of the Kuṣāṇa king Kaniṣka. And in Kuṣāṇa inscriptions, even Middle-Indic inscriptions, a Sanskritized form of the king's name and title (e.g., *mahārājasya kāṇiṣkasya*) is typically used.[61]

Viewed through the lens of the traditionalism reigning in the cultural-political sphere of the Sātavāhanas, the Śakas' principal competitors to the south, the appropriation of Sanskrit language and culture must have seemed like a sign of the world turned upside down. Such at least is strongly suggested by the Sātavāhana text mentioned earlier, the *Yugapurāṇa.* The only South Asian work to refer in any detail to the coming of the Śakas (and also one of the earliest accounts of the *yuga* theory), the *Yugapurāṇa* is likely to have been composed in Ujjayinī—that is, within the cultural sphere of the Sātavāhanas—and possibly not long after the arrival of the Śakas in the middle of the first century B.C.E.[62] The part of the text especially relevant here is couched as a historical prediction (a convention of the genre *purāṇa,* or "ancient lore," whereby knowledge of the present and immediate past can only be presented as foreknowledge and not as remembrance). This pre-

59. Pingree 1978: 4.

60. Yet note that for Patañjali, Śakas and Yavanas were non-outsiders *(aniravasita),* even though they lived outside Āryāvarta (*Mahābhāṣya* on 2.4.10; a reference that may suggest a later date for Patañjali than typically assumed, see chapter 2.1).

61. Fussman 1988: 19 contrasts the Middle-Indic form of the name of a noncourtly monk, *bhikhasa sihaksa.*

62. Mitchiner 1986: 81–82.

diction, spoken by God, describes the Kali Age commencing after the *Mahābhārata* war (v. 37), and the coming of the Yavanas (Indo-Greeks) and the Śakas (vv. 42 ff.). The conflicts predicted upon their arrival, coupled with or perhaps triggering a vast catastrophe, would bring about *yugānta,* the end of the cosmic epoch, and an apocalypse eventually ushering in a golden age. The text foretells, however, that before then the entire structure of the *vaidika* social order will be disrupted:

> All four social orders will adopt the same dress and the same ways . . . Outcastes, quick to invert the proper disposition of things, will perform sacrifice to the triple fire with *mantras* embellished by the sacred Sanskrit syllable *oṃ* when the end of the age is near. Shudras will observe the vows of the fire sacrifice and recitation of *mantras,* when the end of the Kali Age is near. Shudras will call Brahmans "fellow," and Brahmans will call Shudras "Ārya" . . . The *mleccha* king Āmrāṭa, red-eyed and dressed in red . . . will destroy the four social orders, recognizing all those that had previously gone unrecognized . . . The Śaka will destroy the good conduct of his subjects and their devotion to their proper tasks.[63]

These political evils would be followed by cosmic destruction, but "those who still remain, and who hold the moral law dear and cleave to *dharma,* however diminished they are by thirst and hunger" will survive the apocalypse if they betake themselves to one of the twelve political regions *(maṇḍala)* that will have been created out of solicitude for them.[64] These regions comprise an area that corresponds reasonably closely to what we know as the Sātavāhana political order at its largest extent.[65] It is here that people will preserve *dharma: vaidika* liturgy and the rules of comportment, especially the right of participation *(adhikāra)* reserved for certain social orders and the access to and command of Sanskrit that this right entailed. Here Sanskrit will not be "turned upside down" *(-vikriya)* but will be used the way the *Yugapurāṇa* itself uses Sanskrit: in the service of Vedic-puranic *(ārṣa)* status and authority, the one function for which it was used by the Sātavāhanas, within whose cultural sphere the *Yugapurāṇa* was composed.

63. Vv. 50, 53–55, 69 (the correct reading here may be *kṛtvāpūrvavyavasthitān,* "disrupting in an unprecedented way all the old established orders"), 88. "Quick to invert . . . " *laghuvikriyāḥ* (uncertain). The term *mleccha* (generally translated as "uncultured" in this book) refers to those outside *vaidika* society. Some of the *Yugapurāṇa* here corresponds with what is probably the oldest of the "prophecies of the past" in the *purāṇa* tradition, *Harivaṃśa* book 3 (e.g., 116.13 ff., All will recite the Veda *(brahma),* all will be Vājasaneyins, Shudras will use the word *bhoh*). But there the threat is not the Śaka but the Śākya, the Buddha (v. 15: "Shudras will perform *dharma* in dependence on the Śākya Buddha"), and the geographical orientation is, predictably, northern and eastern (vv. 28–29, Kauśiki River in Bihar, Aṅga, etc., Kashmir).

64. Vv. 98–99.

65. The domain between the Vindhya Mountains and the Kṛṣṇā River (today's Maharashtra and Madhya Pradesh), the Eastern Ghats of Orissa, and the Kāverī River system. See Mitchiner 1986: 75–79.

The remarkable incongruity in general language practices—the Brahmanical Sātavāhanas generally using Prakrit, except where a Vedic aura was sought, as in the *Yugapurāṇa,* and the outsider Śakas, their competitors for power, using Sanskrit—seems from this perspective rather less enigmatic than scholars have typically taken it to be.[66] The former attempted to preserve Sanskrit in its ancient and pristine sacral isolation and to use Prakrit for political and other *laukika* communication (a habit continued by all their successors to as late as the fourth century, see chapter 3.1), and they produced an end-of-time narrative spelling out the consequences of doing otherwise. The latter sought to turn Sanskrit into an instrument of cultural-political power of a new sort that did in fact mark the end of an era. If not the only answer to the great language paradox of early India, these data certainly offer a cogent one.

The Śakas' appropriation of Sanskrit for public political purposes at the beginning of the Common Era is an event symptomatic or causative of a radical transformation in the historical sociology of Sanskrit. It is comparable in character and very possibly related to the Buddhist appropriation of Sanskrit after half a millennium of rejection. Exactly what role in this whole process is to be assigned to the newly settled immigrants from outside the subcontinent has long been a subject of debate. Earlier scholars may have been right to argue that the new overlords only consecrated the vogue of literary Sanskrit and did not create it, though the evidence to prove this conclusively does not exist. A caution has been raised against adopting any mechanistic model and in favor of viewing the factor of political change as mere concomitance (and, we are rightly warned, "concomitance is not causality"), yet the synchrony of the two events is striking, and it may ultimately prove correct to locate in the Śaka practices a truly "innovating force."[67] What is historically important is not so much that new power-seekers in the subcontinent began to participate in the prestige economy of Sanskrit—other groups had sought and found inclusion even in *vaidika* communities—but rather that Śakas, Kuṣāṇas, and the poets and intellectuals they patronized, often Buddhist poets and intellectuals, began to expand that economy by

66. Mirashi expressed astonishment at the "contrast in the attitudes of the indigenous Hindus and the foreign Śakas," given that "followers of the Vedic religion" produced their records in Prakrit and the Śakas theirs in Sanskrit (and "fairly correct Sanskrit" at that) (1981: 66).

67. See, respectively, Renou and Filliozat 1947 vol. 1: 244 (also Renou 1956: 98–99), Fussman 1980b: 425, and Damsteegt 1989: 306. Damsteegt's argument is not carried further. Here, as in his 1978 work, some confusion remains. In Mathurā, as elsewhere, "the inscriptions of the pre-Kṣatrapa age," which includes "Hindu," that is, "Brahmanic," inscriptions, are all rightly said to be composed in Middle Indic, and the use of Sanskrit appears only after the arrival of the Kṣatrapas. But then the Sanskrit turn is illogically ascribed "not to the fact that [some Sanskrit] records are connected with the court, but to the fact that they are under the influence of Brahmanic culture" (p. 302).

turning Sanskrit into an instrument of polity and the mastery of Sanskrit into a source of personal charisma. If this kind of Sanskrit has a prehistory, no one has found it.

There seems to be something new here, therefore, and we must try to understand what it is. When we are asked to consider the extraordinary prestige that "the Indian civilization of the Madhyadeśa could have held for the tribal chiefs of Swāt," we might be inclined to assume that these tribal chiefs just picked up Indian civilization as if it were set out in a display case, already fully formed.[68] But the epigraphic record suggests something quite different: that these chiefs helped to create a central component of this civilization by employing Sanskrit in hitherto unprecedented ways. It is true that there are associations of great antiquity between kingly power and Sanskrit. But the greater part of the texts, from among the Vedic *saṃhitas* and *brāhmaṇas*, that establish these associations had for centuries been embedded in an entirely ritual context and accordingly could not be dissociated from it, whereas the "epic" materials, to the degree that they were not in fact one element of this historical transformation (chapter 2.1), were imaginative accounts. What Rudradāman appears to have inaugurated is something entirely different: Here is political poetry in a language that had never been used for such a purpose before—for the publicly inscribed celebration of a living ruler. Moreover, from that point onward for a thousand years and more, political poetry would be made only in that language. Perhaps it was as much for the Śakas' cultural innovations as for their political dominion that a new era came to be named after them, the Śaka era, beginning in 78 C.E. (the date of the putative capture of Ujjayinī); this era was later to be adopted widely across southern Asia (chapter 3.1).

It may ultimately be impossible to decide whether long-standing discursive restrictions rather than religious preferences explain the absence of Sanskrit from early Indian epigraphy, or whether recently arrived ruler lineages were the first to break with *vaidika* convention and desacralize Sanskrit in the interests of a new cultural politics. But without question a true historical caesura confronts us here. The arresting fact bears repeating, however familiar it may be to scholars: It is only in the second century, and with real prominence only in the third and fourth centuries—some three to four hundred years after public writing is found in the subcontinent—that texts expressing royal power in literary Sanskrit made their appearance, along with a new politics of culture and culture of politics connected with this language choice and discursive move. Prior to this period, not a single example is to be found anywhere in South Asia from Peshawar to Tamilnadu, though we have so much Sanskrit otherwise and, relatively speaking, so many inscriptions. The moment

68. Fussman 1980a: 9.

of rupture, in other words, is no mere illusion, no simple artifact of the hazards of preservation. And it marks not the *terminus ante quem* for the existence of a worldly Sanskrit stretching back into the mists of time yet unaccountably vanished without trace, but the *terminus post quem*, a real inauguration.

The standard account of Sanskrit cultural-political history purports to explain these developments by postulating a "resurgence of Brahmanism" leading to a "reassertion" or "revival" of Sanskrit as the language of literature and administration after the Maurya period.[69] The more plausible interpretation is that a new cultural-political formation, a Sanskrit cosmopolitan formation, was on the point of being invented. The textbook narrative posits the resurgence of a community we have no reason to believe was in need of resurgence; it assumes a reassertion at the expense of Buddhism, which in fact hardly suffered a subsequent decline (quite the contrary, it expanded markedly); it asks us to believe in the revival of cultural forms that cannot be shown to have preexisted in the first place. Sanskrit of the kind under discussion had not died; rather, it had not yet been born, at least not for the uses to which it was about to be put—*laukika,* or this-worldly, uses, such as political discourse, beyond the domain of the liturgy and its sacral auxiliaries.[70]

Many uncertainties continue to obscure our insight into the origins of the Sanskrit cultural-political formation, the agents involved, and their social goals. But at least the fact that this formation *did* begin should now be beyond dispute. The development of the second of its components, the public expression of political will, which has claimed our attention so far, is the focus of chapter 3. There we will see how the Sanskrit idiom of power came to be consolidated, with Prakrit forever banished from the domain of the political, everywhere and almost simultaneously, in the rush toward worldly Sanskrit. What had now begun, however, was not only *praśasti* but also the genus of which that discourse is a species. In other words, what began when Sanskrit escaped the domain of the sacred was literature.

69. See respectively Norman 1988: 17–18 (the claim that "the Prakrits remained in use only as the languages of the early texts of non-brahmanical religions" is likewise in need of correction), Kulke and Rothermund 1986: 85, and Falk 1988: 117. A Sanskrit renaissance was first described by F. Max Müller: The political-historical break effected by the Śaka "interregnum" was accompanied by a "blank" in Brahmanical literary culture already weakened by Maurya hostility. The reborn literature was "artificial" in contrast to the "natural" literature of the Vedic age (Müller 1882: xviii ff., 84 ff.).

70. Or coinage. Whereas coins of the second and first centuries B.C.E. found across the north are all in Prakrit, there is a clear move to Sanskrit for the first time in the Śaka period. The Śakas themselves eschewed the use of Sanskrit on their coinage—legends in pure Sanskrit are few, and the kings who issued such coins also issued coins in Prakrit (on the dialect see Bloch 1911: 16). But this changed quickly: within two centuries, the commercialization of Sanskrit among the Guptas was complete. See Diskalkar 1957: 186; Jha and Rajgor 1992: 48.

CHAPTER TWO

Literature and the Cosmopolitan Language of Literature

2.1 FROM LITURGY TO LITERATURE

The astonishing expansion of the discursive realm of Sanskrit in the century or two around the beginning of the Common Era occurred not only at the level of royal inscriptional eulogy. The *praśasti* itself was intimately related to, even a subset of, a new form of language use that was coming into being in the same period and would eventually be given the name *kāvya*.[1] It was only when the language of the gods entered the world of men that literature in India began.

To speak of beginnings, especially literary beginnings, is to raise a host of conceptual problems. The beginnings of vernacular literatures are especially vexatious—in part because indigenist or nationalist thinking strives to find the deepest historical roots possible—and require separate theoretical discussion (chapter 8.1). But in the case of Sanskrit literature, too, most scholars resist acknowledging invention. Assuming the truth of the schoolmen's tag *ex nihilo nihil fit,* they have long sought to provide an infinitely receding history to Sanskrit *kāvya,* or at least a very long genealogy leading back into the Vedic period. From one perspective—though it was one never adopted or even registered by people in premodern South Asia—Veda and *kāvya* do share certain traits. The ancient seers of the Veda are often referred to as *kavi,* the term later adopted for poet; their creations were sometimes called *sūkta,* "well-spoken," a descriptor close to one of the later words for poetry *(sūkti);* a number of formal features, not least certain elementary meters, are held in common; some Vedic genres (such as the materials collected in the *Ṛgvedasaṃhitā*)

1. Further reflections on the beginnings and character of Sanskrit literature are found in Pollock 2003, from which portions of the following are adapted.

are unmistakably concerned with exploring the nature of language as such—a hallmark of *kāvya,* which derives a measure of its power from its echoes of this archaic concern. To this degree, at least, it is correct to refer to *kāvya* as the "direct descendant of the Vedic mantra" or even as its rival, insofar as it seeks a "Vedic effect" by means of a vocabulary and a density that can often be traced back to Veda.[2] This is one reason some scholars might conceive of Sanskrit's historical development less as a departure from the sacral discursive domain than as an extension of that domain to include such new concerns as the aestheticization of actually existing political power.

While some commonalities with what preceded it must clearly be acknowledged, the form of language usage called *kāvya* nonetheless represents something profoundly new in Indian cultural history. In the Sanskrit critical tradition itself *kāvya* came to be theorized as a species of discourse fundamentally different from the Veda, the consummate instance of this conceptualization being the account by the great synthesizer King Bhoja, discussed below (section 3). Both theoretically and pragmatically the tradition drew a clear and untranscendable line dividing Veda from *kāvya,* and in fact from every other kind of textuality. According to the influential tenets of Mīmāṃsā (the last centuries B.C.E.), the Veda was produced by no agent human or divine; as such, it cannot have any authorial intention (*vivakṣā,* literally, desire to speak), which is a constitutive element of *kāvya.* The same strong distinction between Veda and *kāvya* was made pragmatically, too. Before the modern era, the Veda was never read as *kāvya,* never cited in anthologies, never adduced as exemplary in literary textbooks; in fact, the Veda was expressly denied to be *kāvya:* "It is not the mere capacity for producing meaning as such that enables a text to be called *kāvya,*" argued the philosopher Abhinavagupta in the early eleventh century. "That is why we never apply the term to everyday discourse or the Veda."[3] This is so, as Sanskrit theory takes pains to point out, because the rhetorical, discursive, aesthetic, and affective purposes of *kāvya* are entirely different from those of the Veda. Although Indian thinkers, like their Western counterparts, argued incessantly over how to frame an absolute and essential definition of this new and different kind of language usage—they were unsure whether this essence was to be located in figuration *(alaṅkāra),* style *(rīti),* suggestion *(dhvani),* aestheticized emotion *(rasa),* propriety *(aucitya),* or something else altogether—they all agreed that it could be specified within a system of contrasts. It is something different from *śāstra* (the discourse of systematic thought), from *itihāsa* (accounts of the way things were), and from *śruti,* the extant Vedic texts (those still available to be "heard"). Accordingly, if we are to grasp what premodern Indians understood

2. Renou 1956: 169 n.; 1959: 16. See also Smith 1985: 96 ff.

3. *Dhvanyālokalocana* p. 44: *na tarhy arthamātreṇa kāvyavyapadeśaḥ laukikavaidikavākyeṣu tadabhāvāt.*

by *kāvya*—the *vyāvahārika sat* of the term—and reconstruct its particular history, we must be careful to not make *kāvya* a continuation of the Veda by this-worldly means and must avoid incautious generalization about its "Vedic effect," to which much *kāvya* anyway shows complete indifference.

To argue that the specific and differential language use called *kāvya* at some point in time *began* is to claim the first occurrence of a confluence of conceptual and material factors that were themselves altogether new. These include new specific norms, both formal and substantive, of expressive, workly discourse; a new reflexive awareness of textuality; a production of new genre categories; and the application of a new storage technology, namely, writing. The historical copresence of this same complex of factors, moreover, conditioned the beginning of every other literary culture considered in this book, not just Sanskrit literary culture. Indeed, however legitimate it may be to stress the changeableness of the idea of "literature" transhistorically and transculturally, the factors of normativity, reflexive textuality, genre, and inscription may be taken to constitute a large part of what we mean by "literary culture" everywhere.

The fact that *kāvya* began in Sanskrit is not, however, merely an extrinsic (or etic) historical judgment. The Sanskrit literary tradition itself fully grasped the newness of *kāvya* and understood that it was actually invented at some point in time. For Indian writers from at least the second century C.E. onward, Vālmīki was explicitly the first poet *(ādikavi)* and his *Rāmāyaṇa* the first poem *(ādikāvya):* "Vālmīki created the first verse-poem," says the second-century Buddhist poet Aśvaghoṣa.[4] The belief that his masterpiece marked the invention of *kāvya* was reproduced in all the literary genealogies with which writers from the time of Bāṇa in the mid-seventh century prefaced their works. These demonstrate unequivocally that, in the eyes of working poets, *kāvya* was in no way a continuation of something old but rather was a new phenomenon entirely different from all earlier language uses, and that it began with Vālmīki. [5] The prologue of the *Rāmāyaṇa* itself provides a luminous account of the origin of *kāvya* which demonstrates the clear understanding that something unparalleled was being invented. Here we are told how, after being given a brief and prosaic account of the hero Rāma (almost as if receiving it from the folk tradition), Vālmiki utters the primal metrical line when he witnesses an act of violence in the forest. He then has a vision of the god Brahmā, the ultimate repository of the Sanskrit tradition, and sinks into meditation. Gaining knowledge of Rāma's "full story, public and private" he renders it as *kāvya* by means of the meter and "elegant speech" just produced through Brahmā's will.[6]

4. *Buddhacarita* 1.43: *vālmīkir ādau ca sasarja padyam.*
5. Pollock 2003: 76–80, and 1995a.
6. *Rāmāyaṇa* 1.2. On Brahmā and Sanskrit see for example *Vikramāṅkadevacarita* 1.31.

It is no simple thing, however, to identify what is first about the first poem. By the logic of its own tale of invention, what is new and makes the work "literature" is the poet's recording a personal response to real—and not mythic—human experience; poetry arises from pity ("I was overcome with 'pity,'" says Vālmīki, "and this [metrical line] issued forth from me—it must be 'poetry' and nothing else").[7] But this may not be the only kind of newness toward which the prelude is pointing. The *Rāmāyaṇa*'s highly self-conscious assertion of primacy may very likely be alluding to the fact that it was the first *kāvya* to be composed in Sanskrit rather than some other form of language available in South Asia.

Two other considerations bear on the question of the *Rāmayaṇa*'s firstness. The verse-form that the text celebrates as Vālmīki's invention (the eight-syllable *anuṣṭubh*) in fact antedates the work by a millennium or more. Since later Sanskrit poets such as Rājaśekhara in the early tenth century continued to frame Vālmīki's primacy in terms of metrics (chapter 5.2), they likely meant this as a kind of synecdoche for the formal innovations of the work as a whole, and these are indeed substantial. Another dimension of newness may lie in its being one of the first major texts committed to writing after the invention of writing in the mid-third century B.C.E. (as already noted and argued further later), the earliest credible date of the text.[8] The carefully constructed image of a purely oral culture in the prelude—a text unquestionably dated later than the main body of the work—cannot mean what it literally says. When Vālmīki is shown to compose his poem after meditating and to transmit it orally to two young singers, who learn and perform it exactly as he taught it to them, we are being given not a realist depiction but a sentimental "fiction of written culture" (as the phenomenon has been described in the case of the *chansons de geste*). For it clearly cognizes orality as such from outside orality, so to speak, and in a way impossible to do in a world ignorant of any alternative—ignorant, that is, of writing. Nostalgia for the oral and a desire to continue to share in its authenticity and authority, with the same lingering effects of remembered oral poetry, mark other first moments of literary invention across Eurasia. The actual manuscript history of Vālmīki's poem, then, should be seen as a record of just how difficult and discrepant such inscription turned out to be in the moment of transition to a new, literate, literary culture.[9]

7. *Rāmāyaṇa* 1.2.17: *śokārtasya pravṛtto me śloko bhavatu nānyathā*. In the old Indian conceptual universe the phonetic echo indicates an ontological connection.

8. The monumental text by Vālmīki shares too much of the Ashokan spirit to push it back earlier, see Pollock 1986: 23 ff.

9. On the "staging" of an oral communicative situation in vernacularizing Europe, see chapter 11.1 and n. 5 (the quote here is from Gumbrecht 1983, especially 168). A brief account of the manuscript tradition of the *Rāmāyaṇa* is given in Pollock 1984. A very different state of af-

Whatever may be the primary element in Vālmīki's innovation according to either a positivist or an ethnohistorical explanation, his masterpiece and the *kāvya* tradition it inaugurated present themselves as unprecedented in Indian history by every criterion of literary analysis: formal complexity, genre organization, rhetorical character, affective objectives, sociohistorical referentiality, authorial voice, and mode of textual transmission.[10] For all these reasons, even if the question of literary invention and beginnings is rarely addressed directly in later tradition, there is not much dispute about the innovation that *kāvya* represents. At issue, rather, is when and under what social and political circumstances it began. The dispute here has been vigorous for a century, though in all this time little new evidence has been discovered that affects the outcome in any significant way. There is no need to summarize this controversy in detail; only a minimal framework for analysis is needed, based on considerations that are or should be beyond doubt.

We have seen that for the first three centuries of literacy in South Asia, Sanskrit was virtually absent from the epigraphical record, even among Brahman communities, and that this situation was dramatically altered around the beginning of the Common Era in the domains ruled by new lineages recently immigrated from western and central Asia. Within a few centuries Sanskrit would become the sole vehicle for ever more extraordinary *kāvya*-like inscriptional works in praise of royal persons and practices. Nothing suggests that any remotely comparable Sanskrit texts existed prior to this time and have since been lost. Rather, the world of courtly texts had been a world of Prakrit until the complete disappearance of this language from the royal record across South Asia by the fourth century (chapter 3.1). Indeed, inscribed literary verse in Prakrit is attested from the time of Aśoka, and a genre of what is unmistakably political prose-poetry in Prakrit is found among the early Sātavāhanas.[11]

To repeat, what epigraphical evidence therefore establishes is not the date

---

fairs confronts us with the Sanskrit *Mahābhārata,* where the majority of *parvan*s (*Virāṭa* and *Karṇa* excepted) clearly descend from a written archetype. The faux orality of textual performance is preserved in the narrative framework, however, with such devices as listener's questions and narrator's answers.

10. For further detail on the specificity of *kāvya* see Pollock 2003: 41 ff.

11. See the painstaking reconsideration of the Rāmgaṛh evidence by Falk 1991. For the quasi *praśasti* of the Sātavāhana Śātakarṇi by Gautamī Bālaśrī, already considered by Bühler in 1890, see Sircar 1965–83, vol. 1: 203 ff., and Mirashi 1981: 178 (who oddly claims that the inscription was first written in Sanskrit and then converted into Prakrit notwithstanding his view that the Sātavāhanas knew little Sanskrit). Lévi more reasonably observes that the authors of these inscriptions "seem rather to guard against [writing Sanskrit] than try to write it; but they resolutely avoid overstepping the precise limit which separates their Prākrit from classical Sanskrit" (1904: 170). Compare also the nearly contemporaneous inscription of King Khāravela (*EI* 8: 60 ff.; chapter 6.2), which differs from classical prose poetry only in dialect (Bloch 1965: 22).

before which we must assume that Sanskrit *kāvya* existed (and from that point backward into a limitless past), which is the standard Indological assumption, but only the date *after which* we can say it unquestionably existed.[12] And we must accept the possibility of the sudden invention of new literary forms that this revised view entails (and that the history of vernacular literary cultures attests to in abundance, chapters 9–11). To be sure, some earlier scholars, equally uncomfortable with the conventional view, directly linked the origins of *kāvya* with the great first-century cultural-political transformation inaugurated or at least encouraged by the Śakas and other newcomers. Sylvain Lévi, basing himself on a repertory of royal titles found in Śaka inscriptions that had passed into early literature and that (he believed) were originally "foreign to current custom," argued that *kāvya* and more specifically literary drama ("really literary Sanskrit literature") was actually invented at the court of the Śakas. D. C. Sircar used stylistic arguments drawn from epigraphy to reject as impossible the existence of *kāvya* before the beginning of the Common Era. Although evidence is too scant to allow Lévi's pinpointing of the location of *kāvya*'s invention, while Sircar's argument is essentially one from silence, their doubts about the antiquity of *kāvya* have yet to be fully resolved.[13] And other evidence shows that the doubts they raise are serious.

Large quantities of early Sanskrit texts survive, and nothing they report conclusively establishes the existence of *kāvya* before the last centuries B.C.E. Some of the oldest textual citations from Sanskrit *kāvya* are found in Patañjali's *Mahābhāṣya*. These materials, if astonishingly meager for a treatise on the Sanskrit language some 1500 printed pages long, do attest to a culture of *kāvya* reasonably developed in form and convention.[14] The problem here is not the data but the date of the *Mahābhāṣya* itself. The evidence usually adduced for placing Patañjali around 150 B.C.E. is subject to a number of uncertainties, not least the possibility that the grammarian might have been citing predecessors in the passages taken as grounds for early dating. Arguments placing him as late as the middle of the second century C.E. are entirely credible.[15]

12. The former view has prevailed since Bühler. A recent history gives the standard narrative, dating *kāvya* to the sixth century B.C.E. (Lienhard 1984: 53 ff.).

13. Lévi 1904 (with more cautious allusion to Greek influence, p. 174, but see chapter 7.1); Sircar 1939b.

14. The line "The cocks are crowing, my lovely" (in *mālatī* meter), for example, likely formed part of an aubade; "sword in hand, he ran in pursuit of the Pāṇḍava" (in *vaṃśasthavila* meter) probably comes from a *Mahābhārata*-derived poem (*Mahābhāṣya* vol. 1: 283 and 426). All the literary citations are collected in Kielhorn 1885.

15. Patañjali refers only once to a poet by name, *vāraructaṃ kāvyam* (on 4.3.101, which is also his sole use of the word *kāvya* in the sense of literature), and he refers to only three literary works (*ākhyāyikās*, on 4.2.60). Since the grammarian could be citing older grammatical materials (even as he elsewhere cites older philosophical materials) in two key historical passages

All the other reasons offered for dating *kāvya* much before the beginning of the Common Era are even less tenable. No convincing evidence has been offered for a pre-Ashokan date of the *Rāmāyaṇa* in its monumental form (the common denominator of all our manuscripts), let alone a date before the Buddha (c. 400 B.C.E.). The attributions of individual verses, or whole *kāvyas*, to "Pāṇini," whose own date is largely conjectural (convention puts him in the mid-fourth century B.C.E.), are late and without a shred of reliability. The recent assessment of the so-called Bhāsa plays, which were once fantastically dated as early as the fourth century B.C.E., convincingly places the oldest of them at the Pallava court after the mid-seventh century.[16] The fact that literary theory as a self-consciously organized body of knowledge does not begin before the sixth century C.E. (though dramaturgical theory is perhaps several centuries earlier) also suggests that the object of its analysis, too, is late. In Kashmir, for example, the earliest literary work we can date with any confidence is that of Bhartṛmeṇṭha in the mid-sixth century, and the fervid creativity in the production of literary theory that was to have such a powerful influence across all of India did not begin until the eighth century at the earliest.[17]

Inscriptions, *testimonia,* citations in literature, philology, the history of literary theory—every piece of evidence hard and soft thus requires locating the origins of *kāvya* in the very last centuries B.C.E., perhaps as much as a millennium after the Sanskrit language is believed to have first appeared in the subcontinent. Only an ideology of antiquity and the cultural distinction conferred by sheer age have induced scholars to move them back appreciably before this date—a move that requires conjecture every step of the way and the most fragile gossamer of relative dating.

One factor in determining the beginnings of Sanskrit *kāvya* that has been mentioned so far only in passing needs detailed consideration: the place of writing in the constitution of this particular cultural form and the date of the invention of writing itself in India.[18] We have seen that a new scholarly consensus places the latter at the Maurya chancery around 260 B.C.E. (chapter 1.2). Whether or not this consensus is true in all particulars, nothing suggests

---

(see chapter 4.1), Frauwallner argues for a mid-second-century C.E. date (1960, especially pp. 111 ff.); so Sircar 1939a. If the *Mahābhāṣya* is taken as a composite work (denied by Cardona 1978), any precise dating of course becomes impossible. At all events, Patañjali's is hardly "the only really firm initial date known in Sanskrit writing" (Zvelebil 1992: 102).

16. See Tieken 1993. For a pre-fifth-century B.C.E. date for the *Rāmāyaṇa* see Goldman 1984: 18–23; on "Pāṇini," Warder 1972: 103 ff.; equally credulous is his early-third-century B.C.E. dating for a Sanskrit drama by "Subandhu" (pp. 110–11).

17. The date of one poet thought to be earlier, Candra[ka], cannot be fixed with any certainty.

18. On the literacy of *kāvya,* see Pollock 2003: 88 ff. This issue, crucial to the history of vernacularization, is revisited in part 2.

a date for Indic writing before that period, and much evidence from after that date serves to sustain the consensus.[19] Where confusion begins, however, is in the relation of writing to *kāvya.* This stems in part from doubts, legitimate in themselves, about whether notions inherited from European cultural history should be generalized to early South Asia. Despite some recent muddying of the conceptual waters, the linkage that has long existed in the West among literacy, grammar, and "literature" in the widest sense is deep and formative and hardly open to dispute. The *litteratus* of the Latinate world was "literate" both because he was grammatically educated and because, being grammatically educated, he knew how to read and interpret Latin. *Litteratura* was what he produced as a result of both literacy and grammaticality, the "discipline of the written." The *illitteratus* was accordingly associated, from an early date, not just with rusticity but with ignorance.[20]

By contrast, in the world of Sanskrit culture, grammaticality was divorced from literacy to a far greater degree, and accordingly, literacy and learning were never directly correlated. Whether or not Pāṇini's grammar was composed in a nonliterate environment continues to be debated, but there is no doubt that the outright memorization of the grammar and associated texts such as dictionaries remained a feature of elementary Sanskrit education into the modern era. Long after writing became an everyday practice in the Sanskrit world, a bias toward the oral persisted; knowledge that is *kaṇṭhastha,* "in the throat," or memorized, was invariably privileged over knowledge that is *granthastha,* "in a book." Moreover, the representation of knowledge (or understanding or awareness) itself as impregnated by language-as-speech—and never language-as-text—radically differentiates the medieval Indian world from Latinate Europe of the same epoch. In perhaps the sixth century Bhartṛhari, the great philosopher of language, declared that "Understanding has the form of speech, and if everlasting speech were to disappear, light would go out. For it is speech that reflects. Speech-informed awareness is the foundation of all knowledges, arts, and artisanal practices." This sentiment was echoed a few generations later by the literary theorist Daṇḍin: "This entire triple world would become pitch darkness if ever to the end of days the light called speech should cease to shine." Contrast with these normative statements the view of Latin grammarians of the ninth century that "letters are the foundation of all learning," and "the foundation of wisdom is the letter."[21] It is possible to chart how these two very different perspectives derived

19. For example, Gombrich 1990 links the rise of Mahāyāna Buddhism (second to first century B.C.E.) to the new availability of writing, which preserved doctrinally innovative texts that in an oral age would simply have vanished.

20. See Irvine 1994 passim, especially pp. 2 ff.

21. *Vākyapadīya* 1.117–18, "understanding has the form of speech," *vāgrūpatā avabodhasya; KĀ* 1.4, "the light called speech," *śabdāhvayaṃ jyotiḥ.* Such terminology admittedly refers to lan-

from a far more archaic conceptual divergence: between a moral order revealed at a moment in history through inscription on tablets, and one whose existence (according to the dominant tradition enunciated by Mīmāṃsā) is oral-aural and beginningless. The learned man in old India was therefore the *vāgmin,* the master of speech, and not, as in Europe, the *litteratus,* the lettered man.

The contrast many draw between India and Europe on the place of writing in culture, then, clearly contains some truth, but it should not be exaggerated. Orality in India sometimes seems as much an ideology as a fact of practice, for the oral ideal persisted long after writing had become fundamental to the Sanskrit tradition itself. The Daṇḍin and Bhartṛhari who celebrated the spoken lived in a world where the written had permeated both *kāvya* and *śāstra* for centuries. Many of the foundational texts of the Sanskrit intellectual tradition were composed in a literate environment even as they bear the shadow of the oral. We have already seen how Vālmīki's *Rāmāyaṇa* purports to offer an account of its own oral creation, though a reflexive representation of orality of this sort is possible only in a world aware of literacy as an alternative. Something similar is found in the *Mahābhāṣya,* a core work of Sanskrit systematic thought that, although indubitably a written text from the first, stylistically memorializes, even mimics, an oral pedagogy.[22] There is thus no little irony in the fact that Sanskrit culture, in the form in which it became *Sanskrit*—and not just *vaidika*—culture, was centrally based on writing, given the *idée reçu* long dominant in Indology of the culture's allegiance to orality.[23] What made *kāvya* historically possible as a cultural practice at all was writing itself; indeed, one could say that *kāvya* was the name given to an expressive text that was written down—and the text was the kind it was precisely because it was written down.

guage as such, rather than spoken language, but the fact that no distinction is made between the two (and written language is ignored altogether) corroborates the contrast I want to draw. For the (anonymous) Latin grammarians see Irvine 1994: 461.

22. Which was in fact based on writing. When discussing *tantra* (where two agents use one object simultaneously), Bhoja cites an exemplum, "those studying grammar [can do so by using] a single lamp in the study hall" (*ŚP* 492), that goes back to Śabara (see Raghavan ed., ad loc.). For comparable arguments about Plato's dialogue genre in relation to a consolidating culture of literacy see Havelock 1963, especially 97.

23. The various components of this belief—whether the supposed prohibition on transmitting the Veda in written form, the valorization of the disembodied *śabdabrahma,* or the indifference to calligraphy—need not testify to primary orality. The Mīmāṃsā argument that the Veda's efficacy was destroyed if the text was learned *anyāyavijñātād vedāl lekhyādipūrvakāt,* "in ways contrary to reason, as for example through a written text," rather than by the rightful *gurumukhoccāraṇānūccāraṇa,* "repeating what has been pronounced by the mouth of the guru" (*Tantravārttika* on *PMS* 1.3.7, p. 123), implies that literate Vedic learning occurred (which it did, as early as the fifth century C.E., see Falk 1993: 284). Some scholars seem overcredulous in accepting the reality of the image of orality in Sanskrit texts (e.g., Rocher 1994).

This is not necessarily to claim that, in cognitive terms, the Sanskrit poet created in exactly the same way as a contemporary writer might do. While literate authors certainly wrote down their compositions or dictated them to a scribe—and thus birch bark and palm leaf, ink, the stylus, and the rest were regarded as "basic equipment of poetry" (if secondary to genius)[24]—we still have no good models for understanding the various ways literacy affected the character of the poetry that literate authors composed. Even less does the association between *kāvya* and writing imply that the product of the literate poet was experienced primarily, let alone exclusively, through private reading. Much evidence shows, to the contrary, that literature in South Asia retained a prominent oral dimension long after it had become irreducibly literate.

Consider first the old binary of Sanskrit literary theory—dating from the seventh century at the latest and never questioned in the tradition—that represents *kāvya* as one of only two types, something seen (*dṛśya,* i.e., drama) or something heard (*śravya,* i.e., recitative); there is no category for literature as something read. The great Jain writer Jinasena II in his vast, complex, and thoroughly literate poem on universal history, the *Ādipurāṇa* (837), is typical in describing the virtues of poets, listeners, and reciters—but never readers. When the eleventh-century king Bhoja, who lived in a world suffused with literacy, wrote about poetry that is heard, he no doubt meant what he said. Discussing *rasa,* or the representation of emotion in literature, in the *Śṛṅgāraprakāśa* (Light on Passion), his encyclopedia of literary theory, Bhoja says:

> When displayed *(pradarśyamāna)* by skilled actors in correctly performed dramatic presentations *(abhinaya), rasa* can be grasped by spectators; when properly declaimed *(ākhyāyamāna)* by great poets in their compositions it can become accessible to the minds of the learned. However, things are not so sweetly relished when they are actually observed as they are when cognized through the language of masters of language. As it has been said,
>
> > Profound meanings never penetrate the heart so intensely
> > as when they flash forth from the words of great poets
> > when we carefully listen.
>
> Therefore we prize poets far more than actors, and poetry more than dramatic representations.[25]

A century later, the Kashmiri poet and lexicographer Maṅkha (fl. 1140) in his courtly epic, the *Śrīkaṇṭhacarita,* shows that a poem was "published" only

24. *KM* p. 50 line 18. The ready availability of palm leaf and other writing materials (preferred even after the introduction of paper in the thirteenth century) contrasts sharply with the high cost of parchment in Europe, which constituted a serious obstacle to literacy (see chapter 11.1).

25. *ŚP* pp. 5–6.

when it was recited before an audience. Without an audience to hear it, a literary work is like a ship on the open sea without a helmsman: it will sink without a trace. Yet the poem was recited from a written text. Here is how Maṅkha describes his own performance:

> He spread out his manuscript-book . . . The letters—black pearls of the jewelry of the Goddess of Speech—irresistibly attracted his eyes. And having spread the book out he calmly recited *(paṭhan)* his poem in a voice *(vyāhāreṇa)* that rang like the anklets of the Goddess of Knowledge dancing inside his mind.[26]

Indeed, as every Sanskritist knows, a common word for "read," *vācayati*, literally means to make [a text] speak.

The importance of oral performance is also widely attested in Sanskrit literary theory. Rājaśekhara's tenth-century *Kāvyamīmāṃsā* (Inquiry into Literature) devotes a whole chapter to the foundations of recitation. It opens with a discussion of *kāku*, intonation, understood in all its complex functionality as communicating emotional, grammatical, informational, and other aspects of the message. The reciter is then described: he may be someone other than the author but he must possess as perfect a command of language as the author. He should modulate his voice depending on the emotional register of the text (even and steady when the action is slow and calm, shriller when the action is faster), pause when the sense demands it, distinctly articulate the sounds the way a tigress carries her cubs in her jaws, careful not to harm them and ever anxious lest they fall and hurt themselves. Even people who do not know the language, from cowherds to women, should be able to enjoy an accomplished recitation. Using a format that recapitulates the spatial domain of Sanskrit systematic knowledge and literary culture (chapter 5), Rājaśekhara closes with a geography of recitative styles.[27] Whereas authors like Maṅkha often performed their own works, the recitation of *kāvya* was also the business of professionals, much as the performance of the *Mahābhārata*, *Rāmāyaṇa*, and the *purāṇa*s was in the hands of professionals.[28] One last but by no means least significant feature of this oral-performative dimension, as Maṅkha's account so dramatically demonstrates, is that it rendered Sanskrit *kāvya* a preeminently social, almost congregational, phenomenon. There was a content to this form, too: whatever particular narrative concerns it might have, thematically a *kāvya* typically spoke to the concerns of the social collectivity as such—

26. See respectively *Ādipurāṇa* ch. 1, esp. 126ff.; *Śrīkaṇṭhacarita* 25.10 and 25.143.

27. The various topics are discussed in *KM* pp. 28–34; cf. chapter 5.2.

28. Professional reciters of Sanskrit poetry figure in the twelfth-century *Mānasollāsa* (see chapter 4.3); the *Harṣacarita* of Bāṇa (c. 650) describes a professional *purāṇa* reader (Pollock 2003: 89). From Bengal to Tamil country we find families who specialized in the recitation and exposition of the *Mahābhārata* (chapter 6.1), as in vernacular epics like Kampaṉ's *Rāmāyaṇa* (see chapter 14 n. 61).

a collectivity that, accordingly, became a matrix of Sanskrit cultural theory as such.[29]

The persistent oral aspect of *kāvya* should therefore not be minimized. At the same time, there is no doubt that the written form of *kāvya* was central to its existence and that it was also read, perhaps even read in private, from a very early date. Among the oldest Sanskrit manuscript remains are second-century palm-leaf fragments of Buddhist drama and poetry preserved from Chinese Turkestan, some of which carry interlinear glosses of a Tocharian reader. These texts were disseminated across central Asia in purely written form and, evidently, were privately studied. Nothing suggests that in the following centuries the great Sanskrit genres of *kāvya* ever circulated orally, in any sense of that term familiar to us from preliterate societies. If many individual verses *(muktaka)* were included in the citation repertory of cultural virtuosos, the transmission history evinced by manuscripts of the great genres—*mahākāvya*s (courtly epics), *campū*s (prose-verse narratives), *ākhyāyikā*s (dynastic prose-poems), even *nāṭaka*s (epic dramas)—is completely literate. The textual biography of one of Kālidāsa's *mahākāvya*s (fourth or fifth century), for example, differs utterly from that of the *Virāṭaparvan* of the *Mahābhārata*, a book transmitted orally for centuries. The stability, even inviolability, of the *kāvya* text removes it entirely from the world of primary orality. Moreover, the fact that, generally speaking, the participants in Sanskrit literary culture—at the latest, from the time of the Tocharian reader—were thoroughly familiar with writing is repeatedly confirmed by casual references in *kāvya* itself. While almost never mentioned in the earlier era (until we reach the more recent strata of the *Mahābhārata* and the later *dharma* texts), literacy is referred to in *kāvya* almost from the beginning. In the works of Kālidāsa, again, reading and writing are represented as entirely commonplace skills. Moreover, some basic features of Sanskrit literary art can be properly understood only when read, and not when heard. This phenomenology of the constitutive literacy of *kāvya* is entirely consistent with the historical argument in favor of placing the beginnings of *kāvya* after the technology of writing was disseminated in the subcontinent in the last centuries B.C.E.[30]

29. See chapter 5; on the social foundations of *kāvya* generally, Pollock 2001c.

30. For the Tocharian manuscripts of Aśvaghoṣa see Hartmann 1988. References in *kāvya* to literacy are collected in Malamoud 1997. No scholarship exists on the demographics of premodern Indian literacy, but the casualness with which it is mentioned (see also chapter 8.2 at n. 45) implies that it was far more widespread than the mass illiteracy of modern India might suggest (compare the suggestive revisionist account of "Dark Age" literacy in Europe in McKitterick 1989). The phenomenological literacy of *kāvya* is entirely unstudied. One kind of paronomasia, *sabhaṅgaśleṣa* (e.g., *a-sv-āpa-phala; a-svāpa-phala*) cannot, by the system's own rules on accentuation (however obsolete), be transmitted efficaciously in speech (likewise, some forms of *prāsa* in medieval Telugu texts are meaningful only visually, according to V. Narayana Rao, in conversation).

In short, the world of *kāvya* was a world of literacy, and was so from the very first. A poem no longer resided exclusively in the incorporeal word of the oral epoch: it was now a text-artifact. Accordingly, it could be presented in book form to patrons, the way Maṅkha offered his manuscript to the god Śiva at the conclusion of his public recitation; it could be swept off in a river's current or lost in a flood, ending the poem's existence (a motif favored in legends of vernacular beginnings, chapter 8.2); or it could be burned. At the same time, it was never completely divorced from the archaic mode of oral reproduction. A story told about the *Tilakamañjarī*, a complex *campū* of the celebrated Jain poet and lexicographer Dhanapāla, touches on all these themes:[31]

> Dhanapāla was completing his soon-to-be famous tale, the *Tilakamañjarī*, when one day he brought to court the manuscript of the first part. King Bhoja had him read it out and explain it, and then insisted the poet make him the hero of the story, promising to pay any price if he agreed. Dhanapāla flew into a rage and burned the sole exemplar of the original. But his daughter rewrote the first half, since she remembered it from having written out the first manuscript; the second half the poet had to write anew.[32]

Writing thoroughly conditioned the Sanskrit literary text in both its production and its preservation, so much so that a work ceased to exist when separated from its physical embodiment. At the same time, literature was something orally performed—Dhanapāla, like Maṅkha, recites his work (no doubt from the manuscript copy), simultaneously providing the running commentary expected of the poets themselves and often an essential complement to the literary text.[33] In addition, as the account of Dhanapāla's daughter and her feat of reconstructing the work from memory are meant to suggest (and note that in its modern edition the first half of *Tilakamañjarī* covers 125 densely printed pages), *kāvya* was conceived of as remaining, ideally, within the sphere of memorization that informs a tradition in which texts are objects for listening.

31. Dhanapāla's literary activity covered more than three decades, from the time of Vākpatirāja (r. c. 975–95), who awarded him the title "Sarasvati," to that of Bhoja (contrast Vogel 1979: 322).

32. *Purātanaprabandhasaṃgraha*, p. 41. no. 60 ("the first manuscript," *prathamādarśaprati-*; "exemplar of the original," *mūlaprati-*). Bhoja was partially successful, for although he was not made the hero—it was impossible for a great Śaiva devotee to be the protagonist in a tale of Jain moral perfection—Dhanapāla made him the principal recipient of the work (*Tilakamañjarī* v. 50). Another version of their disagreement (*Prabhāvakacarita* p. 145; see also Granoff 1995: 372–75) is hard to reconcile with Dhanapāla's statement in his own book.

33. Poets were traditionally expected to explain their own poems (*sadā svakāvyavyākhyānam*, Kṣemendra, *Kavikaṇṭhābharaṇam* 2.14 [in *Kṣemendralaghukāvyasaṃgraha*]). In the *Prabhāvakacarita*, when Hemacandra recited a poem before King Jayasiṃha Siddharāja, "he adorned it with a commentary, as good conduct is adorned with [good] accounts of it" (185.17).

How the written, the performed, and the memorized interacted to give Sanskrit literary culture its unique character is brought out even more dramatically in a tale from the end of the cosmopolitan Sanskrit epoch concerning the twelfth-century poet and philosopher Śrīharṣa, author of what is often considered the last of the great courtly epics in Sanskrit, the *Naiṣadhīyacarita* (The Life of Nala, King of Niṣāda):

> One day the poet, realizing that
>
> > Gold is tested in fire, and poetry in the assembly of literary critics.
> > What use is his poem to a poet if the experts do not esteem it?
>
> left Bengal for the famed literary circle of Vārāṇasī, taking his poem with him. There he recited it to a scholar named Koka. Every day when the scholar would set off for his mid-day ablutions, he would hear Śrīharṣa reciting his poem as he followed behind. But never receiving any response, Śrīharṣa one day spoke up: "Dear sir, I took great pains with this poem and traveled a great distance to come to you, despite my love for my native land, so that you could judge it. I follow behind you as you walk along the way, reciting it in hopes of finding out what is or is not commendable in it. But, good sir, you neither praise nor blame it. I have to think you are not even listening." Koka replied: "How can you say I have not been listening? On the contrary, I have heard the whole thing, and will tell you in detail what I have determined about correcting the entire work through a full analysis of its words and meanings. I'm not speaking from mere impressions—rather, I listened to the entire poem and have it all by heart. If you don't believe me just listen." He then recited all the verses he had heard over the entire preceding month. Śrīharṣa listened with joy and amazement, and fell at his feet.[34]

Like the account of oral performance at the beginning of the *Rāmāyaṇa,* whose very reflexivity undercuts the authenticity of its orality, the focus here on mnemonic feats shows they had become rare enough to make a good story. Like other values associated with Sanskrit culture, the arts of memory were gradually eroded by a new and different kind of cultural practice. The undoubted importance of writing in creating and transmitting the literary work, the continuing commitment to memory as a pedagogical value, and the undiminished centrality of performance in the publication and consumption—the copresence of such factors throughout the long history of Sanskrit literary culture suggests how complex was the status of literacy in premodern South Asia, and how unfamiliar to modern sensibilities.

The point of historicizing the invention of *kāvya* is not to gratuitously debunk claims to antiquity for Indian culture, as a certain old Orientalism sought

34. *Puruṣaparīkṣā* of Vidyāpati (c. 1400), 2.10, pp. 68–69.

to do in a way that pained Indian intellectuals from an early date.[35] It is to enable us to grasp the novelty of the cultural form, its place in the wider developments of culture and power in the Śaka-Kuṣāṇa era, and some of its meanings and effects, including a new secularization—not too strong a word, and no anachronism—of the gods' language, a new medium, and a new cultural politics. The worldly transformation of Sanskrit made the language's enormous expressive resources available for describing the world of human action; writing preserved its new products and made possible the dissemination of Sanskrit culture across vast reaches of Asia. The new order of culture and power, dimly visible in the fragmentary inscriptional record of the new dynasties of western and northern India, set the fashion for an unprecedented way of using Sanskrit for political and literary ends that would dominate in the centuries to follow. We need not go as far as Lévi and Sircar, though inscriptional evidence published since their day tends to confirm their arguments, and not one new find has contradicted them. In the end it matters little who invented Sanskrit *kāvya* or the imperial inscriptional style that forms one of its most important subgenres. What matters is the cultural-political transformation this invention brought about. From this moment onward for the next millennium, just as southern Asian rulers would invariably express their political vision in Sanskrit, they would underwrite the development of a cosmopolitan literary culture in Sanskrit that gave this vision cultural coherence.

2.2 LITERARY LANGUAGE AS A CLOSED SET

The components of the literary culture that came into being at the beginning of the Common Era, helping to establish the Sanskrit cosmopolis and define its character, themselves became the object of systematic analysis only some five or six centuries later. While the lateness of literary theory *(alaṅkāra-* or *sāhitya-śāstra)* may well indicate the lateness of *kāvya* itself, it is still unclear how to account for the time lag between them—something especially curious in the Sanskrit thought world, where successful enactment of any cultural practice presupposed mastery of local theorization, conceived of as an organized and usually textualized body of knowledge.[36] There is no evidence that important early works have been lost; the oldest extant text, Bhāmaha's *Kāvyālaṅkāra* (Ornament of Literature) of the seventh century,

35. The Maharashtrian scholar R. G. Bhandarkar noted in 1887 the "very strong disinclination" on the part of European scholars "to admit the high antiquity of any book, thought, or institution [in India], and a tendency to trace Greek influence everywhere in our literature" (Bhandarkar 1933: 349).

36. This postulate is argued out in Pollock 1985. For a clear statement in the realm of literature, see the *KM,* cited in chapter 5.2 and n. 27.

does mention several predecessors in tropology and dramaturgy, but we have no knowledge of their contributions, or of any work earlier than the *Nāṭyaśāstra* (Treatise on Drama) of perhaps the third or fourth century (not mentioned by Bhāmaha). So far as we know, it was Bhāmaha (or more likely an immediate predecessor from whom Daṇḍin also drew) who roughed out the major themes and categories of the discipline, beginning a conversation that maintained its coherence to the end of the seventeenth century. We must, accordingly, understand these themes if we are to understand what Sanskrit literary culture meant to those who practiced it. This does not require starting from scratch; the brilliance of Sanskrit literary theory has attracted scholarly attention for a century. Yet some key issues have yet to receive the kind of historical treatment they merit.

The major areas of literary analysis charted by Bhāmaha and his immediate successors, some revisited later in this book, include the categorization and characterization of *guṇa*s, or the text's "qualities," or language properties—what in semiotic theory are sometimes called the expression-forms—relating to phonology, syntax, and lexicon (see chapter 5.3); *doṣa*s, or language "faults"; *alaṅkāra*s themselves, the "ornaments," tropes or figures of sound and sense; and *rasa* (an increasingly important topic for later writers, though Bhāmaha just touches on it). Theorists were also concerned with the actual languages of literature, and their basic conception is crucial to the theory and practice of premodern cosmopolitanism in South Asia. It can be stated succinctly: The literary function, however it may be described—as figuration, suggestion, aestheticized emotion, propriety—is not an inherent capacity of language as such but is something restricted to a few languages alone. Theorists were fully aware of the complex language environment of the everyday world, but the codes they regarded as qualified for literature constituted a dramatically smaller set, indeed, a closed set. What did qualify some languages and not others for participation in the literary sphere needs to be extrapolated from the discourse of *alaṅkāraśāstra,* which only lists the languages and does not analyze their shared properties.

Kāvya, says Bhāmaha, framing a definition with which scholars centuries later would still be contending as they devised alternative formulations, is "a unity of word and meaning," a text where form and content require and receive equal attention. "It is twofold in being either prose or verse, and threefold in being composed in Sanskrit, Prakrit, or Apabhramsha."[37] A generation or two later, in his *Kāvyādarśa,* Daṇḍin, who disputes with Bhāmaha repeatedly on other topics (the place of expression-forms in framing a definition of literature, for example, or genre rules), endorses him fully on the restriction of literary languages to those three. He merely enlarges on Bhāmaha's remarks and makes a few slight modifications.

37. *Kāvyālaṅkāra* 1.16.

The more expansive definitions of both Prakrit and Apabhramsha that Daṇḍin offers merit attention. He does not provide any explication of the term "Prakrit" as he does for "Apabhramsha," though there was some uncertainty in the tradition about its meaning. (While all thinkers concurred that "Prakrit" connotes a linguistic process, it was variously etymologized. Some took it to mean the language "derived from the *prakṛti*," or the primal language substance, that is, Sanskrit; others, the language "existing in, or derived from, or being the primal language substance," that is, pregrammaticized speech, of which Sanskrit itself was only a later development.)[38] What instead interests Daṇḍin is Prakrit's regional dimension:

> The language of Mahārāṣṭra is the best Prakrit, a very ocean of beautiful verse. In it are composed the *Setubandha* and other works. Shauraseni, Gaudi, Lati, and other such languages come into play under the rubric "Prakrit" in conversations [represented in literary texts].[39]

According to this prescription, it is only in Maharashtri, which is what most subsequent writers took the term "Prakrit" to signify, that works of literature are composed. The other forms of Prakrit, the dialects of Śūrasena (the Midlands), Gauḍa (Bengal), Lāṭa (southern Gujarat), or elsewhere—what the commentator Ratnaśrījñāna here calls general or common language *(sāmānyabhāṣā)*—find a place in literature only in a secondary capacity. This key point, which has implications beyond the narrow spectrum of the stylized literary Prakrits, would be even more strongly restated by Bhoja, who describes this secondary capacity as a purely mimetic one: these are speech styles used only to suggest regional character types within a literary work; they are never used as a work's primary language. And literary history itself fully bears this out. No works are extant that are composed wholly in any Prakrit but Maharashtri, and probably none ever did exist.[40] This is why Daṇḍin modestly expands on Bhāmaha's definition to include literary texts composed in a mixture of the three literary languages *(miśra)*, like the polyglot Sanskrit drama and Prakrit *kathā*.[41]

Daṇḍin's definition of Apabhramsha explains the term's etymological

38. The former is more common generally; see for example Siṃhadevagaṇi on *Vāgbhaṭālaṅkāra* 2.3: *prakṛteḥ saṃskṛtād āgataṃ prākṛtam;* or Mārkaṇḍeya, *Prākṛtasarvasva* 1.1: *prakṛtiḥ saṃskṛtaṃ tatra bhavaṃ prākṛtam ucyate;* so Śeṣakṛṣṇa in the *Prākṛtacandrikā* 1.4. The latter is more common among Jain scholars (Namisādhu on *Kāvyālaṅkāra* of Rudraṭa 2.12; cf. Cardona 1999: 112 n.); so also, however, Abhinavagupta: *prakṛter asaṃskārarūpāyā āgatam,* "derived from the primal linguistic matter that is devoid of grammatical refinement" (on *NŚ* 17.3).

39. *KĀ* 1.34–35: "come into play . . . ," *yāti prākṛtam ity eva vyavahāreṣu sannidhim.* The *Setubandha* is a fifth-century courtly epic by Pravarasena of the Vākāṭaka dynasty.

40. Aside from the rare experiment, such as Rājaśekhara's *Karpūramañjarī,* which is usually held to be composed mainly in Shauraseni (but see von Hinüber 1986: 51 and references there).

41. Such as Uddyotanasūri's *Kuvalayamālā* discussed later in the section. See *KĀ* 1.32 and 1.37.

signification in order to neutralize its negative connotations: "What is called 'Apabhramsha' is the language of the Ābhīras and others when used in literary works; whereas in scholarly discourse anything that deviates from correct Sanskrit is so named."[42] The word *apabhraṃśa* refers, once again, to a linguistic trait: deviation or even degeneration from the Sanskrit standard by simplification of phonology and morphology. It is this sense alone that it has in the (fifth-century?) Sanskrit dictionary, the *Amarakośa* ("'Apabhramsha' means deviation [from Sanskrit]"), and the same derogatory connotation is found two centuries later in Kumārila's denunciation of the Buddhists' scriptural language noticed earlier.[43] Daṇḍin, writing around the same time as Kumārila, may well have been among the first to distinguish between the two meanings of the term. But next to nothing is known about the process by which the speech of the Ābhīras and other pastoral peoples of western India was able to develop into a literary language with subcontinental presence (Daṇḍin was a southerner), since virtually all the early texts have disappeared (the Apabhramsha songs in one of Kālidāsa's plays are among the oldest extant materials). When in the twelfth century Vāgbhaṭa defined Apabhramsha as "a pure form of language spoken in the different regions," the very obscurity of his formulation suggests how difficult it remained for the literary system to slot Apabhramsha into the language taxonomy.[44] Yet Vāgbhaṭa is also saying something essential about its place in this system. Whatever its early history, Apabhramsha's qualification for *kāvya* had something to do with its having escaped the local confines of its origins and become available across "the different regions" of South Asian cultural space.

In addition to these definitional elaborations on Bhāmaha, Daṇḍin includes a fourth language for literature, Bhutabhasha, elsewhere known as Paishachi (the speech of the Bhūtas/Piśācas). Linguists have identified this as everything from an eastern Middle-Indic dialect close to Pali to a Munda language of inhabitants of the Vindhya Mountains; traditional commentators invariably understand it to be the language of the semidivine attendants of Śiva, the *pramathas* or *gaṇas*. In fact there is little reason to bother to choose between science and tradition. Paishachi is the joker in the deck of South Asian discourses on language, having an exclusively legendary status, since it is associated with a single lost text, the *Bṛhatkathā* (The Great Tale), which seems to have existed less as an actual text than as a conceptual category signifying the *Volksgeist*, the Great Repository of Folk Narratives, which may indeed be the source of its entry into the literary language taxonomy. In any event, aside from this legendary work (which "survives" only in one Jain Ma-

42. *KĀ* 1.36.

43. *Amarakośa* 1.6.2: *apabhraṃśo 'paśabdaḥ syāt* (curiously Amara does not define Prakrit). For Kumārila on Buddhist Apabhramsha, see chapter 1.1.

44. *Vāgbhaṭālaṅkāra* 2.3 (see n. 95 for the Sanskrit).

harashtri and several Sanskrit embodiments), Paishachi is irrelevant to the actual literary history of South Asia.[45]

Although written probably some two to three centuries earlier than Bhāmaha and Daṇḍin, the account of the division of languages in Bharata's *Nāṭyaśāstra* makes somewhat better sense once we place it in the later writers' conceptual universe. Bharata, too, discusses only three types of language: Sanskrit, Prakrit, and, in place of Apabhramsha, what he calls "languages of Place" *(deśabhāṣā)*—one of the earliest uses of a term that was to have a great afterlife in South Asian intellectual history. This division construes even more patently than Bhāmaha's and Daṇḍin's with something else that Bharata is one of the earliest to mention and that would emerge as a cornerstone of Indian philological thought: the threefold division of word species into Sanskrit-identical *(samānaśabda),* Sanskrit-derived *(vibhraṣṭa),* and of a Place *(deśīgata).*[46] Bharata adds a fourth, dialectal form that he (and he alone) calls *vibhāṣā* (perhaps meaning sublanguage). The point of the *Nāṭyaśāstra*'s discussion of the languages of Place in particular, as in its discussion of language generally, concerns not permissible literary languages but the speech forms that are to be represented on the stage, and who can use them:

> [A poet] may show [anyone] from among any of the pure castes making use of the Shauraseni language in literary texts. Or playwrights can employ the languages of Place as they will, for poetry in the drama can happen to arise in any number of places. These languages [of Place] are seven: Magadhi, Avanti, Eastern, Shauraseni, Ardhamagadhi, Vahika, and Southern. There are moreover [seven] sublanguages *(vibhāṣā)* used in drama: those deriving from the Śakāra, Ābhīra, Caṇḍāla, Śabara, Dramila, Āndhra, and the low language of forest-dwellers.[47]

45. "Mixed" in *KĀ* 1.32 (see at n. 41, this chapter) does not include Paishachi, pace Ratnaśrījñāna, which is defined only in 1.38. Ratna does refer to other Paishachi texts but none is extant (at 1.38 he mentions a *Ratnaprabhā;* see also v. 32 [an "altogether pure form," read *śuddhyadhikā;* the reference is to a monoglot text; Rudraṭa gives a verse combining Paishachi with Sanskrit, *Kāvyālaṅkāra* 4.19]); Raghavan believed Bhoja cited the opening of the *Bṛhatkathā* (see *ŚP* 167 n. 2); and Nannaya, among others, was credited with mastery of Paishachi (in an inscription of 1053, *EI* 4: 302 ff.). Von Hinüber takes Guṇāḍhya's Paishachi to represent the failed attempt to turn an eastern dialect of "Buddhist Middle Indic" into a "worldly literary language" (1986: 69–70; cf. Lin 1949 cited in n. 56, this chapter); so already Master 1943, who believed this was Pali (which in fact had hardly any *kāvya* tradition until the early second millennium, see Collins 2003).

46. See *NŚ* 17.3. The later history of the three-part division of lexemes—*tatsama, tadbhava,* and *deśī* (with this terminology first it seems in *KĀ* 1.33)—is discussed in chapter 10.2.

47. *NŚ* 17. 46–49. Abhinava here calls the *bhāṣās* "dialects of Sanskrit" *(saṃskṛtāpabhraṃśa)* and the *vibhāṣās* "dialects of the *bhāṣās*"; a subsequent verse prohibits the use of "Barbara, Kirāta, Āndhra, Dramila" and related languages for poetry in drama (17.57; discussed in section 3), and Abhinava tries to reconcile this with v. 17.49, but it is clear there was some uncertainty

After listing the languages, Bharata proceeds to apportion them among various characters in a drama, just as he does with Sanskrit and Prakrit (Magadhi is used in the king's harem, Ardhamagadhi by royal servants, military men, merchants; Eastern by the Brahman fool, and so on). Again, the important point, for the present discussion, is that all these speech forms are to be used solely in a secondary, socially mimetic capacity and never as the primary language of literary composition.

The restriction of literary language to three languages (or four if Paishachi is included) continued to be asserted as a matter of course by later theorists. Rudraṭa, writing perhaps in the early ninth century, describes the languages of the literary utterance as sixfold, not in contradiction with Bhāmaha but because he identifies Prakrit with Maharashtri *tout court* (as others, like Bhoja, were to do later) and so must include the two other Prakrits, Magadhi and Shauraseni, that are required by this narrower identification.[48] Even "sixfold," in and of itself, leaves little doubt that for Rudraṭa, too, the set of literary languages was strictly delimited, that the literary function was not a capacity shared by all languages across the board (if one may even speak of different "languages" in the absence of the literary function that differentiates them). Rājaśekhara, too, a century later, in his highly suggestive tale of the origins of cosmopolitan literary culture (chapter 5.2), imagines as the psychophysical source of *kāvya* a Primal Being of Literature, or Poetry Man *(kāvyapuruṣa),* whose mouth consists of Sanskrit, arms of Prakrit (Maharashtri), groin of Apabhramsha, feet of Paishachi, and chest of mixed language (the various dramatic Prakrits). And Rājaśekhara reaffirms the limitation of literary language later in his treatise when discussing the nature of literary subjects: "A given topic will be best treated in Sanskrit, another in Prakrit, or Apabhramsha, or the language of the spirits (*bhūtabhāṣā,* Paishachi); others still in two, or three, or all four languages. The writer whose mind is sharp enough to distinguish [among these possibilities] will win such fame as spreads across the universe."[49]

This conception of a closed set of literary languages, proclaimed at the very beginning of the critical tradition and undoubtedly present from the

---

about whether south Indian languages should appear at all in northern drama. "Vāhīkā," i.e., from the Punjab, v. l. Bāhlīkā, "from Balkh" (the two names are often interchanged, the latter usually falsely driving out the former). Languages of the northwest, such as Gandhari (Swat Valley), to say nothing of those of more distant areas like Balkh, eventually dropped out of the cultural-linguistic consciousness of South Asia after contacts with the region diminished, presumably with the breakup of the Kuṣāṇa empire. They are never discussed by grammarians and are absent from most language lists. See von Hinüber 1986: 54. On the dramatic Prakrits as "nonreal dramaturgical components" *(alaukikī nāṭyadharmī),* see Bansat-Boudon 1992: 161 ff., and Bhoja's discussion in section 3.

48. Contrast Namisādhu's comment on Rudraṭa's *Kāvyālaṅkāra* 1.11–12.

49. *KM* 48.25–26.

very commencement of the era of *kāvya,* remained in force for Sanskrit intellectuals even when, with new forms of vernacular literary culture everywhere making their appearance from the beginning of the second millennium, it became indisputable that the notion was not the result of some natural incapacity on the part of excluded languages but an artifact of the literary system itself. The persistence of the old Sanskrit formulation in the face of overwhelming evidence to the contrary is especially apparent in Śāradātanaya, whose *Bhāvaprakāśana* (Treatise on Feelings in Literature) was written most likely in the environs of Maturai in the heart of the Tamil-speaking south, probably sometime in the late twelfth century.[50] In a survey of language and region at the end of the work, the author acknowledges the variety of languages spoken in the vast world where Sanskrit literary culture had come to reign supreme:

> There are eighteen languages by which the various people [of the sixty-four regions of Bhāratavarṣa (see chapter 5.1)] communicate with each other, the languages being named after a few from among these regions. The bearers *(āśraya)* of these languages are the people of Dramiḍa, Kannaḍa, Āndhra, Hūṇa, Himmīra, Siṃhala . . . These languages are everywhere known as the uncultured *(mleccha)* languages.

As Śāradātanaya goes on to declare, in full agreement with the consensus of Sanskrit cultural theory, these languages are not equally capable of bearing the full literary function:

> The languages used for drama *(nāṭya)* are the following five, six, or seven [depending on how one categorizes languages]. Sanskrit, Prakrit [i.e., Maharashtri], Paishachi, Magadhi, Shauraseni make five; they are six if one includes their dialectal forms *(apabhraṃśa)* [as a separate collective category]. And some people reckon Apabhramsha as an [independent] seventh language.[51]

It is only because he happens to be writing a work on drama that Śāradātanaya frames his remarks in terms of that genre; his conception of language (like that of *bhāva,* the affective components of *rasa*) extends to the literary system as a whole. And this conception is unequivocal: literature is a competence that belongs not to language qua language but only to a small and select group of languages—which did not include even Tamil.

The restrictions that found expression in literary theory for centuries from

50. Śāradātanaya's residence was "the village of Māṭhara, to the south of the great people-place *[janapada]* of Merūttara" (*Bhāvaprakāśana* 1.5–6; Merūttara is probably Uttarameru; that he goes on to locate this in Āryāvarta indicates how vastly that geographical category had expanded by this time (compare chapter 5.1)

51. *Bhāvaprakāśana* 10.172–77, pp. 452–53. Introducing a distinction between *apabhraṃśa* and Apabhramsha (as in Daṇḍin) seems necessary. The one cultural role for the remaining languages is song; see further chapter 8.1, 2.

the time of Bhāmaha are echoed in the works of poets themselves. In his *Kuvalayamālā,* a *saṃkīrṇakathā* (mixed prose-verse tale) completed in Jalor, Rajasthan, in 779 C.E., Uddyotanasūri explicitly acknowledges the existence of three literary languages only, Prakrit, Sanskrit, and Apabhramsha, and he refers to them as the only vehicles of literary production throughout his book. His most forceful expression is found at the beginning of the text:

> This work is composed in the Prakrit language, written down in the letters of the Marahattha [Maharashtra] Place, the whole tale *(sakalakathā)* being pure and communicating the teachings of the great ascetic Jina. As a curiosity *(koūhaleṇa),* the story is also told in Sanskrit when needed for [imitating] another's speech, and here and there made with Apabhramsha, as well as demonstrating the Paishachi speech.[52]

In other words, besides the primary language of the *Kuvalayamālā,* which is Maharashtri Prakrit, the two (or three) other languages enter the tale "only as a curiosity" for reporting dialogue. The fact that Uddyotana observes this literary-language constraint becomes all the more striking in light of his awareness of the large and varied universe of linguistic codes—even more realistically depicted than Śāradātanaya's, since Uddyotana actually reproduces examples of local speech forms—that were potentially available for literary employment, had literary employment been available to them. During his travels the hero wanders through the great bazaar of Vijayapura (Bījāpur?), where he hears people speaking sixteen different languages of Place *(desabhāsā).* For each of these Uddyotana provides a snippet of conversation, in many cases the earliest documentation of their existence.[53] But again, these are purely mimetic usages; literature itself, which is something above and beyond such supplements, is manifestly not a capability that all languages were thought to share equally.

Identical presuppositions about the languages of literature underlie the account of the origins of the Paishachi *Bṛhatkathā* as found in the Sanskrit

52. *Kuvalayamālā* p. 4. vv. 12–13: *pāiyabhāsāraiyā marahaṭṭhayadesivaṇṇayaṇibaddhā* | *suddhā sayalakaha cciya tāvasajiṇasatthavāhillā* || *koūhaleṇa katthai paravayaṇavaseṇa sakkayaṇibaddhā* | *kiṃci avabbhaṃsakayā dāviyapesāyabhāsillā* || (cf. Master 1949–51: 1003, who, however, understands v. 12c as "in some parts in Sanskrit under the influence of alien expressions"; though *sakalakathā* later becomes the name of a specific genre, it probably does not have that sense here). See also 16.22, where (as Upadhye 1965: 317 takes it) "bards reciting in these [three] languages are introduced in the *Āsthāna* of King Dṛdhavarman." For the interesting "reportage" of the *apabhraṣṭa* language of Vedic students see Master 1949–51: 1009 ff.

53. *Kuvalayamālā* 152.22 ff. (cf. Master 1949–51: 414). The languages are those of the Golle (Ābhīra pastoralists), Majjhadese (Midlanders, or people of the Gangetic plain), Māgahe (i.e., Biharis), Aṃtavee (?), Kīre (Kashmiris), Ḍhakke (Punjabis), Seṃdhave (Sindhis), Mārue (Marwaris), Gujjare ([northern] Gujaratis), Lāḍe (Lāṭis [southern Gujaratis]), Mālave (Malwas), Kaṇṇāḍae (Kannadigas), Tāie (Tājiks, i.e., Persians), Kosalae (Kosalans, here apparently "Greater Kosala," i.e., Chattisgarh), Aṃdhe (Andhras), and Marahaṭṭhe (Marathas, Maharashtrians).

adaptations of the work, most notably the *Bṛhatkathāmañjarī* of Kṣemendra (Kashmir, c. 1050). How the *Great Tale* originally came to be written (as it was believed) in Paishachi is explained in the prologue. The story, familiar to every beginning Sanskrit student, contains many elements of relevance to our problematic. Guṇāḍhya, minister to the Sātavāhana emperor, wagers that the grammarian Śarvavarman will be unable to teach the king Sanskrit in six months as he has pledged to do (note how, in this later narrative tradition, the Sātavāhana conservatism regarding the use of Prakrit is coded as ignorance of Sanskrit); Guṇāḍhya himself is prepared to try to reduce the proverbial twelve years required to learn Sanskrit by only half. Śarvavarman, an important figure for all later non-Paninian grammarians (chapters 4.1, 9.4), knows how arduous is the task before him, and he throws himself on the mercy of Śiva's son Kārttikeya, also known as Kumāra. The god's inspiration enables him to compose the *Kātantra,* the *Brief System* (also called the *Kumāravyākaraṇa,* or Grammar of Kumāra).[54] This, as we have noted, was a stripped-down grammar for the new and expanding post-*vaidika* Sanskrit epoch of the early centuries C.E. (chapter 1.3), and by means of it Śarvavarman was able to achieve his purpose and win the wager. Guṇāḍhya had sworn, if defeated, to "observe a vow of silence in the three languages" and to "make use of Paishachi, and not Apabhramsha, Sanskrit, or Prakrit." He must therefore employ Paishachi when the time comes for him to publish in the world the *Great Tale* of the god Śiva.[55] The logic of the narrative rests entirely on a cultural convention that renders the idea of literature not written in Sanskrit, Prakrit, or Apabhramsha a bizarre, even demonic, anomaly.

A final example of the conceptual reality of the restriction on literary language and its functioning as a basic component of the self-understanding of creators of literature is provided by the *Saṃdeśarāsaka* (c. 1300). Abdul Rahman, the author of this messenger poem and one of the first Muslim poets to write in a South Asian literary language, migrated from the "Place of the uncultured *(mlecchadeśa)* in the West," where his father had been born, to Multan (in today's Pakistan) and the new cosmopolitan world (v. 3). He identifies himself as an Apabhramsha poet and makes it clear that he considered himself part of the lineage of those who "became poets in Apabhramsha, Sanskrit, Prakrit, and Paishachi" (1.4–6). To be sure, by the fourteenth

54. Also called *Kālāpa* or *Kalāpaka,* because it consists of a *kalāpa,* or four parts, but also later taken as associating the work with Kārttikeya via his peacock mount (*kalāpa* meaning also peacock's tail). On the names of the *Kātantra* see Lüders 1940: 717–18 (he takes it as originally the work of the Buddhist grammarian Kumāralāta; see chapter 4.1).

55. *Bṛhatkathāmañjarī* 1.3.46 and 51: *bhāṣātraye bhaviṣyāmi maunī . . . paiśācīm anapabhraṃśasaṃskṛtaprākṛtāṃ śritaḥ.* In Somadeva's *Kathāsaritsāgara,* a version of the *Bṛhatkathā* written also in Kashmir in the generation following Kṣemendra, the three languages renounced are Sanskrit, Prakrit, and language of Place *(deśabhāṣā)* (1.6.148), but Somadeva clearly recognizes the three literary languages in 5.129.

century such statements had become as much a *topos* of the literary system as the messenger-poem genre itself. Yet the language in which Abdul Rahman chose to write was literary Apabhramsha, and not his native language or the language of Multan.[56]

The choice from among the three primary literary languages was, for all theorists, largely determined by the genre in which one wrote. Particular forms of literature required particular linguistic vehicles—a tendency reproduced in early vernacularization, where different languages of Place were held to be suitable for different song genres (chapter 8.2), or for different deities (Avadhi for Rāma, for example, or Brajbhasha for Kṛṣṇa). Thus the *mahākāvya,* or courtly epic, and the *ākhyāyikā,* the dynastic prose-poem, were to be written only in Sanskrit; the *skandhaka* (also a courtly epic genre but differing from the *mahākāvya* in metrical organization) and the *gāthā* (a type of erotic verse) only in Prakrit, the *rāsaka* and *avaskandha* (two "pastoral" genres) only in Apabhramsha. No other language could be used as the "primary" code for such genres, and no secondary uses of language are to be found in them; they are counted as *śuddha,* "pure," or monoglot literary forms. Undoubtedly, some slippage can be found in the language-genre rule, which sometimes threatens to render it irrelevant. A *kathā* may be written in any of the three (or four) languages (and sometimes the others find place for secondary purposes, as in Uddyotana's work), and so can the independent lyric *(muktaka).*[57] But by and large the genre rule held firm. Whatever other factors may have conditioned the choice among the three literary languages, one that was unambiguously irrelevant during the first millennium—in the case of literature no less than in that of public inscription—was an author's religious affiliation. For reasons we do not yet fully understand, this long-term ecumenicism eventually did weaken along with the cosmopolitan formation itself, so much so that by the middle of the second millennium Apabhramsha and to a lesser degree Prakrit had become options available almost exclusively to Jains, whereas Brahmans began again to reassert their archaic monopolization of Sanskrit. But during the cosmopolitan epoch, one

56. The epigraphical record is also in accord on the triad of literary languages. Typical is a *praśasti* to Guhasena (*IA* 1881: 284), whose "mind was adept at creating literary texts composed in the three languages, Sanskrit, Prakrit, and Apabhramsha" (cf. Deshpande 1979: 60). The Tibetan account of four languages used by four Buddhist schools (Sanskrit by the Mūlasarvāstivādin; Prakrit by the Mahāsaṅghika; Apabhramsha by the Sammatīya; Paishachi by the Sthavira; see Lin 1949: 176–77) may well be modeled on that of Sanskrit literary theory (contrast Renou 1956: 89 n.). (Different is the story of the conversion of the four celestial kings, where the Buddha uses Sanskrit to address two, *drāviḍabhāṣā* the third, and *mlecchabhāṣā* the last, Lamotte 1976: 608–9.)

57. See Bhāmaha's *Kāvyālaṅkāra* 1.28 (perhaps read *saṃskṛtā prākṛtā ceti* in *pāda* c, with Vāḍhijaṅghāladeva on *KĀ* 1.38); *KĀ* 1.37–38, with Ratna there; *ŚP* pp. 725–27; Abhinavagupta on *Dhvanyāloka* 3.7.

chose a literary language far more often for aesthetic than for theological reasons.[58]

Yet what is central to the argument here is less this or that criterion for choosing among the literary languages than the restricted set itself of such languages from which the choice had to be made. When Bhāmaha and all later Sanskrit literary theorists asserted that *kāvya,* or literature *stricto sensu,* is written only in Sanskrit, Prakrit, or Apabhramsha, they meant what they said: only three languages were fit vehicles for literary expression, and local language was excluded. Their definition would be meaningless if all languages were thought to be suitable or even possible for literature—if, that is, "Prakrit" or "Apabhramsha" here were taken as referring generally to local language, like the sixteen languages mentioned by Uddyotana or the eighteen by Śāradātanaya or the fifty-six in Kannada country mentioned by Nāgavarma I at the end of the tenth century. It would be tantamount to stating the absurd and very un-Sanskritic tautology that literature is composed in language. It was precisely because the Sanskrit theoreticians meant what they said that their later vernacular compeers, like Śrīvijaya in ninth-century Mānyakheṭa, felt compelled to write the restriction out of their definitions of literature (chapter 9.2).

This strict and narrow interpretation of the three-language formula, so to call it, is corroborated by the entire literary history of the Sanskrit epoch. Generally speaking, literary production in the languages of Place began to manifest itself only in the last quarter of the millennium when the cosmopolitan epoch began to wane—indeed, their manifestation marks the most important sign of its decline (part 2). The apparent circularity here—that since Sanskrit and the other two languages define *kāvya* as such, *kāvya* can only exist in those languages—is not as vicious as it might first appear. The term *kāvya* (along with *kavitā* and so on) and its specific modes of expressivity would eventually be appropriated by vernacular writers, and when such *bhāṣākāvya* came into being, Sanskrit theorists would acknowledge it, if sometimes grudgingly. The first literary works in Old Gujarati that can be described as *kāvya* (though none seems to actually call itself this), such as the *Bhārateśvara Bāhubali Ghor,* appeared in the late twelfth century. And it was then, for the first time, that a cosmopolitan theorist in Gujarat, the Jain scholar and cleric Hemacandra (d. 1172), allowed for the possibility of producing a *mahākāvya* in the vernacular, what he called *grāmyabhāṣā*. As the very terminology suggests, a "courtly epic in the vulgar language" was something

58. See Pollock 2003: 61 ff. for details on the conditions of literary language choice, especially in relation to genre (Jules Bloch, I now find, also registered the genre constraint on language choice, and distinguished this from the determinants of "nationality and regionalism," 1965: 22); also p. 73 on the late-medieval revival among non-Jains, especially in Bengal, of a scholarly interest in Maharashtri.

that earlier would have been considered a fundamental contradiction in terms.[59]

Moreover, for almost the entire first millennium not just *kāvya* but any sort of nondocumentary text—that is, in written form—in a language other than Sanskrit, Prakrit, or Apabhramsha is rare. In the north, among some Buddhist communities, doctrinal texts were composed in other idioms in the course of the first millennium. A well-known *Dharmapada* exists in Gandhari, for example; Khotanese versions were produced of other scriptural and near-scriptural texts such as birth stories of the Buddha; there is also a northwest Prakrit *Milindapanha* from which the Pali version itself may have been translated. But in an important sense these kinds of religiophilosophical texts are irrelevant for the problem under discussion here, in part because such experiments so far as we know did not reproduce themselves in any sustained way, and, more important, because they did not participate in the cultural practice of *kāvya.* When Buddhists wanted to write *kāvya*—poets like Aśvaghoṣa, Āryaśūra, or Mātṛceta in the early centuries of the Common Era—they wrote in Sanskrit. In the south, the one exception regarding *bhāṣākāvya* in general and Buddhist literature in particular might be constituted by Tamil, but disentangling fact from fiction in Tamil literary history is complicated, and the more reliable the data (as in inscriptions), the more the Tamil case conforms with the general picture of literary South Asia (see chapters 3.1, 8.3, 10.1).

Whereas the discourse on literary languages is, accordingly, unequivocal in its restrictions and confirmed in its empirical reality, no rationale was ever offered by literary theorists. None of them explains what exactly qualifies a language for literary work. The very specification of limits—"Literature is written in A, B, and C," entailing "and not in X, Y, or Z"—implies some principle of selection. Perhaps this was self-evident and required no explicit discussion; in any case, the silence of the tradition forces us to work out for ourselves what constituted the qualification for literature. What in fact made these three languages alone eligible as vehicles for literary expression? The one distinctive feature shared by the three, and only these three, was their availability across region, ethnie, sect, and time. Both according to Indic conceptual schemes and in actual fact, none was tied to any particular place, people, creed, or era. All three escaped every spatial and social boundary; in some measure, both for these sociolinguistic reasons and thanks to the philological processes described below, they also escaped time itself, and with it the perceived mutability of so-called natural languages (which were, after

59. *Kāvyānuśāsana* 8.6, p. 449: *padyaṃ prāyaḥ saṃskṛtaprākṛtāpabhraṃśagrāmyabhāṣānibaddha[ṃ] . . . mahākāvyam.* On early Gujarati *kāvya* see further in chapter 10.1, and on Hemacandra's location at the threshold of the vernacular transformation and his response, chapter 10.2.

all, *apabhraṣṭa,* or "decayed" speech forms). To be qualified for literature, it seems, a language evidently had to be universally available—it had to be, in a word, cosmopolitan. And it had to be cosmopolitan because the political function to which it was tied was, as we shall see, cosmopolitan, too.

Once the archaic *vaidika* confines of Sanskrit were shattered, the language became vastly available—to Śakas, Kuṣāṇas, Buddhists, and others who had been excluded from or had long resisted participation in Sanskrit culture, as well as to royal courts across all of southern Asia (chapter 3.1). To what degree, however, does transcendence of social, spatial, and temporal limits apply to the case of Prakrit and Apabhramsha? Prakrit is a plural entity, as we have seen, with regional subtypes identified already from the time of Daṇḍin (Gaudi, Lati, and so on). These idioms, at some point in their prehistory, bore the deeper impress of regionality; their very names—which mean "relating to Gauḍa" (Bengal), to Lāṭa (southern Gujarat), and the like—indicate as much. Some of this regionality is reflected in the earliest Prakrit records, the inscriptions of Aśoka, where more localized linguistic features of Middle Indic are apparent: those that later grammarians and poets code as Lati or Magadhi can be found in Aśokan edicts placed, respectively, in places like Junāgaṛh in Gujarat and Pāṭaliputra in Bihar.[60] Moreover, some regions did continue, historically, to show preference for one or the other language. Literary texts in Apabhramsha were produced with greater frequency in what from the time of Daṇḍin was considered its birthplace, western India, than elsewhere in the subcontinent. Yet it is also clear that as part of the very process of becoming media for *kāvya,* the Prakrits early in the first millennium, and Apabhramsha not much later, were both transregionalized on the model of Sanskrit. However strong their local ties may have been at the start, these were quickly weakened and finally broken by the fifth or sixth century.

A major factor in this process was philology in the wide sense of the term. Both Prakrit and Apabhramsha came under the standardizing pressure of a growing scholarly apparatus—newly created grammars, dictionaries, metrical handbooks, dramaturgical treatises, and so forth—that thoroughly bears the stamp of Sanskrit. Instructive here is the earliest systematization of Maharashtri Prakrit, the *Prākṛtasūtra* (or *-prakāśa,* the Rules of Prakrit, or Light on Prakrit), a grammar composed in perhaps the third or fourth century by Vararuci (at least in its core form; chapters for the other Prakrits were added at a later date). This account derives Maharashtri by transformation rules from Sanskrit and is written in Sanskrit—two features that established the standard for later grammars, which continued to base them-

60. Bloch 1965: 16.

selves on Vararuci well into the second millennium.[61] Indeed, in thinking about this text, one of the leading Prakritists of an earlier generation was no doubt correct in her assessment that the language it described "did not run in the streets, but rather stayed demurely among the men of letters who had brought it into being," and that the grammar itself was composed above all to provide writers *of Sanskrit* with the means of composing Prakrit *gāthās*.[62] Of course, every literary language everywhere before modernity, and perhaps afterward, becomes a literary language precisely by leaving the streets of everyday communication and submitting to the new discipline of grammar, prosody, and rhetoric (as the history of vernacularization demonstrates, chapter 8.3). But what is especially significant with respect to the Prakrits is that this sort of discipline unhoused, displaced, and uprooted them, and soon "men of letters" who had no geographical connection whatever with Mahārāṣṭra or Śūrasena were cultivating Maharashtri and Shauraseni. This was as much the case with the early dynasties of southern India—the Kadambas of Kannada country, Pallavas in Tamil country, and Ikṣvākus, Cūṭus, and others in Andhra, who used Prakrit in their inscriptions—as it was with writers in the north like Vākpatirāja in eighth-century Kānyakubja, who used Maharashtri for his *skandhaka*, the *Gauḍavaho* (The Slaying of Gauḍa [King of Magadha]). Like Sanskrit, the Prakrits of *kāvya* texts were employed in firm accordance with the rules of the grammars that made them available for extraregional appropriation; the best students of the field have found them to be "unified and comparatively free from recognizable regional characteristics" despite the vast time-space context of their usage.[63]

At the level of ethnomethodology, too, it was precisely the grammaticization of certain Prakrits that made them *sādhu*, "correct," and thus endowed with an autonomous signifying power and accordingly fit for poetry. Early Mīmāṃsā, like other Sanskrit intellectual disciplines that share the same quasi-historical view of language development, viewed dialect *(apabhraṃśa)* as only indirectly expressive, that is, by means of the Sanskrit word it (somehow) called to mind: according to the standard example, dialectal *gavi* could signify "cow" only because it reminded the listener of the correct—Sanskrit—form, *gauḥ*.[64] For a writer like Kavikarṇapūra in late-sixteenth-century Ben-

61. Harivṛddha's lost grammar was one of the few actually written in Prakrit (Ratna on *KĀ* 1.33ff. cites him extensively; cf. Bhayani 1993: 162–66, who knows him only as a poet and prosodist). The prototype of Caṇḍa's grammar may also have been in Prakrit (Nitti-Dolci 1938: 209; von Hinüber 1986: 55).

62. Nitti-Dolci 1938: 8; 50.

63. See von Hinüber 1986: 66 for remarks on the unification of both the literary and inscriptional Prakrits.

64. The theorem is discussed in more detail in chapter 8.2; see also Pollock 2001b: 26ff. That Prakrit was grammaticized relatively early is suggested by the fact that a *deśīśāstra*, very pos-

gal, and no doubt for centuries before him, literary Prakrit could be considered correct speech *(sādhutva)* only because it was disciplined by grammar.[65]

As for Apabhramsha, associations with western India in general and Śvetāmbara Jainism in particular notwithstanding, it was used for literary production across the subcontinent for centuries: in the Deccan, for example, where around 970 at the Rāṣṭrakūṭa court Pupphayanta (Puṣpadanta) produced the *Mahāpurāṇa,* the first universal history in that language; or in Bengal, where the *Dohākośa,* an anthology of tantric Buddhist verse, was composed by Kānha and Saraha probably also in the tenth century. In the language of these and other texts produced in widely separated areas of the subcontinent—and if the many important works such as Caturmukha's *kāvya*s were available in more than fragmentary form, the argument would be even more compelling—scholars have concurred in finding an absence of regional variation and a linguistically "unlocalized" quality.[66] Although no substantial Apabhramsha philology survives from before the eleventh or twelfth century (Bhoja and Hemacandra), the transregionality revealed by the idiom of the texts themselves presupposes its existence.

Whether it was owing to philology or some other mechanism, however, Prakrit and Apabhramsha did succeed in slipping their local moorings and moving across space-time, on the model of Sanskrit. Even in the case of the shadowy Paishachi, with no texts in the language extant in India for centuries, if any ever were, a kind of cosmopolitan presence had to be constructed to accord with the dominant ideology of the transregionality of literary language. A late grammar composed about 1550 in Andhra Pradesh, the *Ṣaḍbhāṣācandrikā* (Moonlight of the Six Languages), describes the "regions" of the Paiśācas as including "Pāṇḍya country [in the heart of Tamilnadu], the "land of the Kekayas" [in Kashmir], Bāhlīka [in northern Afghanistan], Siṃha [Sindh], Nepāla, Kundala (north Karnataka), Sugheṣṇa [?], Bhoja [?, v.l. Bhoṭa, Tibet] and Gāndhāra [the region of Peshawar in today's Pakistan], and Haivakannojana [?]."[67]

Accordingly, what in the first instance qualified these few translocal codes for literary work was some sense that literature itself must be a translocal phenomenon for a translocal public. Writing at the court of his Cedi patron in Tripurī (in eastern Madhya Pradesh), the same Rājaśekhara who recounted the origins of the Primal Being of Literature and his journey through the

---

sibly a grammar, was attributed to an author mentioned in Hāla's *Sattasaī,* the anthology produced at the Sātavāhana court (Pischel 1965: 11).

65. *Alaṅkārakaustubha* p. 31.

66. Shackle 1993: 266, and Bhayani 1993: 294; see also Hardy 1994: 5, and Masica 1991: 53–5. I adduce the *Dohākośa* only as evidence of Apabhramsha's supraregionalism, not because the texts it contains were seen as *kāvya,* and I ignore here the long-standing disputes on whether its language is not Apabhramsha but really Bangla, Oriya, or Maithili.

67. *Ṣaḍbhāṣācandrikā* 1.29–30.

cosmopolitan sphere—the sort of journey that in fact made this sphere cosmopolitan in the first place (chapter 5.2)—explained how the ideal king's literary assembly should be configured:

> In the north of the king's hall are Sanskrit poets; a poet who commands a number of languages should be directed to sit in whatever place corresponds to the language in which he is most proficient, whereas the poet [equally] proficient in several languages may sit where he pleases. Prakrit poets sit in the east, Apabhramsha poets in the west, and Paishacha poets in the south.[68]

A hint of place of origin may still be lingering about them—Sanskrit as a northern language (as it would be regarded by Tamil poets), Apabhramsha in the (Jain) west, Paishachi in the inauspicious south—but these had all become cosmopolitan languages, which someone like Rājaśekhara himself in Tripurī could claim to have mastered (section 3 below). They alone could gain entry into literary space—and they occupied it fully, with no room left for any vernacular idiom.

While transregionality must therefore be acknowledged as an absolute criterion of literary capability, it is necessary at the same time to recognize the relative scale along which the cosmopolitan languages were ordered. No doubt mutually constitutive interactions from the first served to shape them as literary idioms, but in their mature forms of mid-first millennium, Prakrit and Apabhramsha were second-order codes on several counts. First, neither language ever enjoyed the vast diffusion that Sanskrit did; there is no evidence that they were used in any capacity in Southeast Asia. Second, neither Prakrit after the fourth century nor Apabhramsha at any time was permitted a role in articulating political discourse of any stripe. Third, despite the appearance of simplicity, currency, and popularity, both languages were learned languages and at least as dependent on the textbook as Sanskrit itself, if not more so. At a relatively early date, literary works in both Prakrit and Apabhramsha were equipped with *chāyā*s, Sanskrit translations, and in some cases they were eventually displaced by their Sanskrit renderings. Not only were Prakrit and Apabhramsha little naturalized in medieval literary culture, but the knowledge required to read and write them became increasingly scarce over time. Prakrit had a residual cultural character already in eighth-century Kānyakubja, where the court poet Vākpatirāja complained that no one any longer respected the language. The limit case is Paishachi, of course, whose single work, the *Bṛhatkathā,* was supplanted by Sanskrit adaptations from as early as the mid-sixth century (the first is ascribed to the Gaṅga king Durvinīta). Lastly, as literary idioms both Prakrit and Apabhramsha had highly restricted registers. They were by preference employed, at least in earlier epochs, to suggest rural simplicity and joyful vulgarity—all

68. *KM* pp. 54–55.

of course for courtly audiences. This makes for wonderful poetry, to be sure, but hardly provides a firm basis for an expanded literariness.[69]

All these notions find elaboration, but also some complication, in the literary treatises of King Bhoja of Dhārā, which provide the most systematic and detailed account of literary language in South Asian premodernity.

2.3 THE FINAL THEORY OF LITERARY LANGUAGE: BHOJA'S POETICS

The Pāramāra king Bhoja (r. 1011–55), whom we have already encountered in passing, was one of the most extraordinary figures in the history of literary culture in India. What makes him especially important in the present context is not his court or the legends that gathered around it (see chapter 4.2), though these defined Sanskrit civility for the later tradition, nor his major contributions to the Sanskrit canon in poetry and philosophy, but two exceptional literary-theoretical works: *Sarasvatīkaṇṭhābharaṇa* (Necklace of Sarasvatī, Goddess of Language) and *Śṛṅgāraprakāśa* (Light on Passion). These represent the most ambitious attempt that had yet been made (Rājaśekhara's incomplete oeuvre was an important precursor, chapter 5.2) to construct a cosmopolitan literary system as a totality, which Bhoja did by developing a complete taxonomy of the elements of literature and illustrating these categories with citations from the entire range of actually existing literature. Bhoja's system has sometimes been considered a departure, even a radical deviation, from earlier thinking (largely in view of his theory that the basic emotional register of literature is passion, as reflected in the name of the latter of his two books on poetics). This is erroneous. Bhoja's aesthetic theory, like his intellectual project as a whole, is an effort at reconstruction and rationalization, not revolution. His literary-critical works present a kind of *summa poeticae,* assembling and reordering the preceding seven or eight centuries of reflection on what literature was believed to be. Indeed, the very conservatism of his oeuvre may have been its undoing, for a new philosophical-religious aesthetics was being elaborated by Bhoja's contemporaries in Kashmir (Bhaṭṭa Nāyaka, Bhaṭṭa Tauta, and Abhinavagupta, among others) that was to transform Sanskrit literary theory fundamentally and per-

69. No study of *chāyā* as a genre is known to me. That Kṣemendra in his *Aucityavicāracarcā* glosses all Prakrit verses suggests that in eleventh-century Kashmir the language was no longer easily understood. The degree of corruption in manuscripts suggests widespread ignorance of Prakrit and Apabhramsha except among the truly learned. Sanskrit translations of Prakrit texts are especially prominent in the Jain tradition; a notable instance is the *Kuvalayamālākathā,* Ratnaprabhasūri's fourteenth-century version of Uddyotana's work. Vākpatirāja's protest is found in *Gauḍavaho* v. 95. On the Sanskrit adaptation of the *Bṛhatkathā,* see chapter 4.1 and n. 4. For Prakrit rusticity, see Tieken 1995.

manently. Bhoja represented the best and most influential of the past—and for that very reason, in the aftermath of the Kashmiri innovations, he would be largely forgotten.

It is precisely because Bhoja summarized the earlier history of literary thought at the moment when it was about to be exploded—not only by those Kashmiri theorists but also by the massive vernacularization of the subcontinent that was commencing everywhere—that his work is so valuable. A full account of this summation that would do justice to its complex architecture and arguments is impossible here.[70] It suffices to consider two extended passages, one from each of the two works, that are especially pertinent to an analysis of literature and the languages of literature as cosmopolitan practice. These are unique, if sometimes intricate, expositions and repay careful study.

The place of literature among the welter of forms of discourse in the world is considered in chapter 3 of the *Śṛṅgāraprakāśa,* which reviews the set of literary languages and genres (see appendix A.1 for the translation). To grasp the structural principles that distinguish the different realms of discourse identified here (those relating to "revelation," to "the seers," and to "the world") requires knowledge of a range of topics Bhoja addresses elsewhere in his analysis of the literary function. One is discursive prominence *(prādhānya):* whether the defining feature of a discourse is its actual wording (as in the case of revealed texts such as *mantra,* which do not have to be understood in order to be efficacious) or its meaning (as in the case of seers' texts, which can be reworded without loss) or both wording and meaning (as in the case of *kāvya,* as Bhāmaha had long ago defined it). Another is the nature of the intention *(vivakṣā)* underlying the discourse: in *kāvya* this is particularized *(viśiṣṭavivakṣā)* with respect to both word and meaning, in seers' texts it is pure and unequivocal *(vivakṣāmātra),* and in revealed texts it is nonexistent, since such texts, having no author, can have no authorial intention *(vaktur abhāvād vivakṣā nopapadyate).* A third issue concerns a more specific threefold division of the literary into modes of expressivity *(ukti),* whether "natural" and direct, "indirect" and troped, or "affective."[71] Making sense of the particular examples Bhoja has chosen—rather odd examples, after all—requires knowing something about his overall argument with respect to emotion and how it comes to be embodied in a literary text. Since Bhoja regards desire and passion as primary emotions underlying all others, he chooses passages, in all but a few cases, that deal with the agents and objects of these emotions. The Vedic *mantra* posits the mysterious microcosmic-macrocosmic equivalents *(upaniṣad)* where semen, the prime material sign

70. An initial attempt is made in Pollock 1998, 2001b.

71. *svabhāvokti, vakrokti, rasokti,* respectively. This three-part division is considered further in chapters 5.3 and 9.2. See also Pollock 2003: 48 ff. on *vivakṣā.*

of male desire, finds its place. The *brāhmaṇa* passage (of the *arthavāda* variety, which describes the value of a ritual act rather than commanding its performance) treats of the attainment of desire and the constitution of transcendent bliss; whereas the *smṛti* text has an injunctive character in describing women with reference to their place in a social order that prized hypergamy. The *purāṇa* verse, relating something that was believed to have actually happened, shows the demon Hiraṇyakaśipu looking lustfully at the different directions (which are feminine in grammatical gender) as he pursues his cosmic conquest. The *śāstra* text correlates certain characteristics of female sexuality with certain bodily signs, whereas the *kāvya* text, through the quintessentially literary trope of *śleṣa,* the bitextual figure (literally, "fusion" of two meanings), describes a man's longing for a woman he cannot have.

For an analysis of literary language as a category, however, we can plunge in *medias res.* First, the passage leaves no doubt that for Bhoja, as for the Sanskrit tradition at large, literature is a conceptually distinct and theoretically differentiated kind of language usage. Accordingly, when claims are made about what might or might not qualify as a language for literature, there is no ambiguity whatever about the communicative function at issue. Second, what constitutes difference within the three language species analyzed by Bhoja is significantly different for each. In the case of Sanskrit, it is genre or domain of employment. The discourse of *śāstra,* or systematic thought, differs from *mantra,* or liturgical formulas, and both differ from *kāvya* because each has a radically different intention and purpose (as Bhoja explains elsewhere). The Sanskrit language used in these genres, however, is not said to diverge in any way whatever. In fact, the examples selected (this is especially clear in Bhoja's Vedic choices) are linguistically indistinguishable from the language used for Sanskrit *kāvya.* If Sanskrit's discursive domains vary considerably, Sanskrit itself remains invariant across space and time; for Bhoja there is no regional or vernacular or popular Sanskrit, no new or old Sanskrit. Of course, he would have been familiar with the various distinctions in register that were commonly drawn: anomalies or archaisms had long been identified as *ārṣa* (sages' usage), whereas the distinction between *chandas,* the Veda, and *bhāṣā,* the language of scholarly learning, was as old as Pāṇini and based on linguistic criteria of differentiation. But in Bhoja's taxonomy Sanskrit is, generally speaking, absolutely uniform.[72]

Poles apart are the categories used to organize difference among the Prakrits: "pure," "defined," and "distorted." These seem to be Bhoja's own terms, and they are intriguing if somewhat obscure. They are not found elsewhere in Bhoja's work, nor do they map straightforwardly against the stan-

72. The same holds true for the chronologically earlier Ratnaśrījñāna (cited in chapter 1.1) and for the later *Vāgbhaṭālaṅkāra* (cited at n. 89). The Vedic register is treated in Bhoja's grammar (also named *Sarasvatīkaṇṭhābharaṇa,* composed 1042 C.E.), though in a separate chapter.

dard tripartition of linguistic phenomena (found first, as noted in section 2, in Bharata's *Nāṭyaśāstra*) that classifies Prakrit lexemes as "identical to" Sanskrit *(tatsama),* "derived from" Sanskrit *(tadbhava),* or irreducibly "of a Place" *(deśī);* quite to the contrary, Bhoja's *sahaja* or "pure" Prakrit comprises both *tatsama* and *deśī.*[73] The conceptual scheme at work here is a different one, apparently based on the nature/culture binary. Those forms of Prakrit that preserve in toto their *prakṛti,* or Sanskrit substance (one old etymology of *prākṛta,* as we have seen), as well as local forms would occupy the category of pure "nature"; Maharashtri and Shauraseni, by contrast, which constitute "defined"—in other words, philologized languages—and Magadhi and Paishachi, corruptions thereof, would fill the category of "culture." At all events, it is clear is that, in contrast to Sanskrit, the three categories of Prakrit refer not to genres but to linguistic distinctions. The languages are differentiated in their phonology, morphology, syntax, and lexicon, and their differences are ascribed—or at least this is implied by the names they are given—to their different regional origins (with of course the exception of the first, *saṃskṛtasama*).

Equally obscure are the principles by which the varieties of Apabhramsha are distinguished. But, in addition to their obvious linguistic differences, they refer, at least by nomenclature, to social status, with Bhoja's own Avanti placed unsurprisingly at the top. They are also shown to cover the geographical space of (northern) India, from west to east, and then south to at least the edge of the Deccan. In further contrast with Sanskrit, no distinctions are made by Bhoja among the Prakrits or Apabhramsha with respect to domains of usage: the examples he provides are solely poetry, Prakrit having lost all other functions by the time of Bhoja, and Apabhramsha never really having had many to lose.[74]

Most important, the now-familiar limit on languages included in the classification of literary codes is evident from the start of Bhoja's discussion. Not all of the wide variety of speech forms available in quotidian life come within the scope of his analysis, because obviously not all of them did or could func-

73. Some Jain authors understand *tadbhava* as "existing [eternally] in Sanskrit," eliding any suggestion of temporal change, see n. 38, and Kahrs 1992. Not everyone understood the word this way, however, certainly not Kannada grammarians (chapters 9.4, 10.2).

74. Prakrit grammatical and prosodical texts, as noted, were typically written in Sanskrit. It is curious, given the Jain presence at his court, that Bhoja ignores earlier Jain traditions of canonical and exegetical writing in Ardhamagadhi and Jain Maharashtri. Among contemporaneous *tāntrikas* Prakrit and even Apabhramsha were occasionally used in philosophical texts (e.g., in Abhinavagupta's *Tantrasāra;* cf. Hardy 1994 on *Yogīndu*). A discussion of the reasons for choosing Prakrit occurs in the twelfth-century Śaiva tantric *Mahārthamañjarī:* Sanskrit is obligatory only in discussing Vedic materials; in reflections on God and self, any language, however solecistic *(yatkiñcidbhāṣoparūṣita),* can be more than serviceable (pp. 185–86; I thank Whitney Cox for calling my attention to this work).

tion as literary-cultural media. We might be inclined to think that by Bhoja's time—remember that he was separated from Bhāmaha, the first systematizer, by nearly half a millennium—the triad of literary languages had become ossified convention, reproduced mechanically (the force of habit is so strong) and without reference to the real world, or, conversely, that the categories of Prakrit and Apabhramsha had grown so elastic as to embrace the entire spectrum of languages, cosmopolitan and noncosmopolitan, within the domain of *kāvya*. After all, vernacular *kāvya* would soon become a historical fact; indeed, in some places such as Karnataka and Tamil country it was already in existence.

Such an assumption would be false. The exclusion of regional languages from the conceptual map of permissible media for literary production was as much a fact for Bhoja in 1050 as it was a century later for Śāradātanaya in Maturai, who nowhere acknowledges the existence or even the possibility of Tamil *kāvya*. It is astonishing that while Bhoja reports on an Apabhramsha register in a place as distant from his home as Kashmir, he makes no mention of Kannada, which was in vigorous use for literary composition in the Karnataka of the Kalyāṇa Cāḷukyas, the polity bordering on Mālava to the south with which he, like his ancestors, had continuous and often belligerent relations.[75] If noncosmopolitan languages entered into the literary sphere at all—even the language that was spoken in the streets of his capital—it was, for Bhoja too, only in a second-order mimetic capacity.[76]

Bhoja argues this point out in his even more detailed analysis of literary language in *Sarasvatīkaṇṭhābharaṇa*. This (chronologically probably earlier) account is embedded in a larger problematic, the ornamentation *(alaṅkāra)* of literary discourse, which forms the central organizing principle behind Bhoja's conception of literariness. Ornamentation is said to consist of external, internal, and external-internal language properties. As the body is beautified by external attributes such as clothing or jewelry, by internal attributes such as clean teeth or manicured nails, and by attributes that may be said to function intermediately, such as perfume or cream, so literary lan-

75. On the Kalyāṇa Cāḷukyas see chapter 3.3. An intriguing reference to Bhoja's court is found in the *Karṇāṭakādambarī* of Nāgavarma (I?), who reports that Bhojarāja, in his admiration for the Kannada poem, made him a "gift suitable to the Lady of Poetry" (cf. *-kṛtivadhu* in *KRM* 2.1) consisting of horses "from Kalinga, Kamboja, and Balkh" (v. 96, p. 305). This almost certainly refers to Bhoja of Dhārā: what other Bhoja could have been called "lord of the earth" presiding over a "circle of learned men" in the first half of the eleventh century, the period in which most scholars place the *Karnāṭakādāmbarī*? Bhoja made grants to Brahmans from Karnataka (in 1021 to a "Karṇāṭa [Brahman] who emigrated from Śrīvāḍa"; in 1022 to a Brahman "who had come from the royal city Mānyakheṭa" (*CII* 7.2: 44 lines 17–18; 48 lines 14–15). Yet the improbability of a Kannada poet presenting his work at Bhoja's court, let alone his being sufficiently understood to be honored for the beauty of his work, remains high.

76. See the discussion of the *Rāulavela* in chapter 8.2.

guage is ornamented by three kinds of phenomena: (1) external properties of the word, which strictly concern the expression-forms, such as what Bhoja terms *gati*, the form appropriate for a work (verse, prose, or mixed), or *mārga/rīti*, the ways or paths characterized by the phonological, semantic, and syntactical construction of the utterance (see chapter 5.3); (2) internal properties, the pure figures of sense, such as natural description *(svabhāvokti)* or exemplification *(nidarśana)*; (3) properties that make use of both word and sense for their effect, such as simile (which requires use of a word such as "like") or, more obviously, bitextual poetry *(śleṣa)*. To the first of the external ornaments Bhoja gives the name *jāti*, or type of language (see appendix A.2 for the translation).

Bhoja again offers a fascinating exposition, inimitably his own, but complex enough to require substantial exegesis to make it intelligible in all its particulars. We would be wrong to refuse a priori to try and instead dismiss the discussion as a formally sophisticated but ontologically empty exercise in classification, driven by the structure of the classes themselves, with nothing real standing behind the structure.[77] In fact, Bhoja's distinctions reflect far more actuality than it may seem at first; one example is his theory of the Ways of literature (chapter 9.2). What he cites as actual in his illustrations typically was so.[78]

Bhoja's classification scheme once again leaves no doubt that for him there continued to operate the old and firmly limited conception of the restricted set of literary languages: Sanskrit, Prakrit (with three varieties), Apabhramsha, and Paishachi, all of them fully conceptualized as distinct from each other. Not only is this made clear throughout the passage (and stated explicitly in v. 16), but the taxonomy would otherwise make no sense. Consider the exclusive or uncommon type *(asādhāraṇī)* that Bhoja goes on to discuss, where a verse consists of one half-verse in one language and a second half-verse in another. He gives the example:

bhīṣmaproktāni vākyāni vidvadvaktreṣu śerate |
gose tiviñchiriñcholī tallaṃ tūhe vivallidā ||

The discourses Bhīṣma once gave now rest in the mouths of the learned
Like lotus pollen wafted about a small bank of a pond at dawn.

And then he comments, "Here the words in the first half of the verse are Sanskrit alone [i.e., they may not be read as Prakrit or any other language, in contrast to the "common" type], those in the second half are Prakrit alone.

77. This is the typical attitude even of his advocates; "indeed strange" is Raghavan's comment on Bhoja's conception of *alaṅkāra* (1978: 345), and the exasperation is typical (cf. chapter 5.3 n. 53).

78. At least half of his citations can be traced to real works, and the rest could probably be traced if we had his library (it was looted by Jayasiṃha of Gujarat, chapter 4.2).

This type is called 'uncommon' or 'exclusive' insofar as there is nothing in common with other languages."[79] Such a species could not even exist in the absence of a settled and formalized sense of what constitutes the precise boundaries of a given language. Thus, however true may be the "linguistic fact" that Sanskrit, Prakrit, and Apabhramsha are simply sets of points on a linguistic continuum, in the conceptual universe of medieval Indian thinkers they were completely discrete phenomena.

The restriction on the number of literary languages, and their individuation, fully confirm the evidence assembled so far. What the passage helps us understand, better than other available materials do, is how these were thought to have become literary languages in the first place—by virtue of their dominant function in a literary work—and how they related to and could be supplemented by other, subliterary languages. Bhoja is concerned not only with the choice of language in literary creation but with the sociology of language in relationship to literary mimesis. His typology of language is accordingly subsumed under the rubric "ornaments of sound": Language type *(jāti)* serves to ornament literature when it conforms to one or another aspect in the complex of properties termed appropriateness *(aucitya),* here referring to verisimilitude in respect to the social context being represented (*viṣaya,* v. 8), the character (v. 9), the topic (*vācya,* vv. 10–11), the historical setting (v. 15, a kind of historicism *avant la lettre*). With language type, Bhoja is concerned in the first instance with true representations in literature of the sociality of language usage. To be sure, this is something ultimately inseparable from a concern with real-life language usage itself, but that notion is implicit and less consequential here; at every step the question of literary representation has primacy. Thus, when we read that "the people of Lāṭa hear Prakrit gladly," this means that in representing a man from Lāṭa in a literary text one should show him speaking a western Prakrit. Similarly, in representing the epoch of the Sātavāhanas, one should show everyone speaking Maharashtri.

Only in an extended, subordinate sense does any of this carry implications for literary language choice. We need to keep this in mind when we read in Sanskrit literary theory that a poet should be "master of all languages" or "tell stories in all languages," as when Rājaśekhara advises writers on adopting languages for literature:

> For a poet who is independent, all languages are as much within his command as a single one—such is the view of Rājaśekhara. A given language is, more-

79. *SKĀ* 2.17, example 11 with following commentary. Ratneśvara notes (on *SKĀ* 2.17), "The linguistic features distinguished by the grammars of Pāṇini [on Sanskrit], Vararuci [on Prakrit], and others vary according to language type. Now, where only one sort of linguistic feature is found we have the 'pure' type. Where various features come together through a mixture of linguistic rules so as to be indistinguishable, as when water and milk are mixed, we have the 'common' type [that is, the verse can be read as one or another language via *tatsamas*]."

> over, adopted in virtue of [its prevalence in] a given region, as it is said, "The Gauḍas are devoted to Sanskrit, the people of Lāṭa are fond of Prakrit, the people of all Mālava, the Takkas [Ḍhakkas, Punjabis], and the Bhādānakas employ their own Apabhramsha, the people of Avanti, of Pāriyātra, and of Daśapura use Bhutabhasha [Paishachi]. The poet, however, who dwells in mid-Madhyadeśa is expert in all languages.

What the poet-theorist is concerned with here is precisely the mimetic usage of interest to Bhoja. And thus there is no inconsistency when elsewhere Rājaśekhara substantiates his claim to being an "expert in all languages" with a reference to the *four* literary languages.[80] The distinction between subordinate, imitative uses of languages and the principal, constitutive language of a literary text is implicit in the restatement of the old formula by the twelfth-century writer Vāgbhaṭa:

> There are the four languages *that may constitute the body* of a literary work: Sanskrit, the language of the heavenly beings, which is determinate [in its form] due to the sciences of language; Prakrit, which is multiform: born [of Sanskrit] [i.e., *tadbhava*], identical with it [i.e., *tatsama*], or of a Place *(deśī* or *deśya);* Apabhramsha, which is a pure form of language spoken in different regions; and Bhautika [Paishachi], which is said to be a language spoken by certain spirits *[bhūta]*.[81]

These precepts invite us to distinguish, and to read traditional accounts of literary language as distinguishing, between primary and secondary languages for literature. Primary languages were those that could serve as the foundation for a literary work, and were chosen for a given work on the basis of its genre. Secondary languages made occasional appearances according to the proprieties of sociological representation. It is especially in the direct discourse of drama that secondary, imitative language usage occurs (ruffians in the Sanskrit theater speak Magadhi, as gangsters in American-English the-

80. *Bālarāmāyaṇa* 1.11: *sarvabhāṣāvicakṣaṇaś ca sa evam āha,* and he lists them: the divine language, sweet Prakrit, lovely Apabhramsa, and the delightful Bhuta language. The preceding quote is *KM* 50.26 ff. Recall that four languages only are found in the body of his Primal Being of Literature (chapter 5.3).

81. *Vāgbhaṭālaṅkāra* 2.1–3 (my emphasis): *iti bhāṣāś catasro 'pi yānti kāvyasya kāyatām . . . apabhraṃśas tu yac chuddhaṃ tattaddeśeṣu bhāṣitam.* The same contrast seems to have been at work in the far earlier *NŚ* in what otherwise would seem to be a self-contradictory passage: "With respect to the Barbara, Kirāta, Āndhra, Draviḍa, and other peoples, one should not produce poetry in their vernaculars for the staging of drama. In the case of these peoples, and for Brahmans at a funeral dinner, the language to be used in drama is Shaurasena *[sic]*. Or, if preferred, languages of Place can be used by those who stage dramas, since poetry used in a drama can arise in various places" (*NŚ* [Bombay ed.] 17.44cd–45ab, 46cd–47ab: *na barbarakirātāndhradraviḍādyāsu jātiṣu | nāṭyayoge tu kartavyaṃ kāvyaṃ bhāṣāsamāśrayam || athavā chandataḥ kāryā deśabhāṣā[ḥ] prayoktṛbhiḥ | nānādeśasamutthaṃ hi kāvyaṃ bhavati nāṭake ||*

ater speak Brooklynese), which therefore Daṇḍin described as composed "in a mixture of all languages."[82] It occurs also in a few other literary works where reported speech is prominent, such as the *kathā*, or story, though in the Prakrit examples only, never the Sanskrit. Secondary language is thus actually an extraliterary factor, what Bakhtin, in the context of an analysis of literary language, calls a *thing*, which does not lie "on the *same* plane with the real language of the work."[83]

Thus, in view of the actual social differentiation in language use in premodern India as well as the mimetic principle that informed literariness—though both the sociolinguistics and the mimesis were treated by writers and thinkers in an entirely ideal and not empirical manner—literature is properly "ornamented" for Bhoja when the poet knows to use the language appropriate to a given narrative context. But only one of the three cosmopolitan languages may function as primary. A multilingual command of the secondary, imitative codes was admittedly part of the cosmopolitan poet's craft. Yet it is crucial to grasp that such multilingualism was itself transregional and thus in effect represented a kind of complement to the cosmopolitan practice evinced for the three main literary languages.

Around 1000, at a central Indian court that later, when the cosmopolitan order had waned, would be celebrated as the legendary embodiment of what Sanskrit literary culture once had been, the production of literature took place only in languages that had nothing in particular, and everything in general, to do with that court's location. To be sure, the locally specific was not entirely ignored; Bhoja was fully aware of the nature of the language of Place used in his realm—he names it Avanti—but for him it was to be employed, in literary-cultural terms, only in a thinglike way, when imitating a local speech-type. For him as for all his predecessors, the constitutive language of the literary text could only be Sanskrit or (with vastly decreasing frequency) Maharashtri Prakrit or Apabhramsha. These were all three subcontinental codes, bound to no people and no place, whose very names evoked not ethnic linkages but social and linguistic processes, and they were available for adoption across a virtually limitless space. Writers chose one or the other not on the basis of religious affiliation (all were ecumenical, with Buddhists as well as Brahmans writing Sanskrit, and Brahmans as well as Jains writing Apabhramsha) or native attachment (none bore the faintest trace of indigenism in the cosmopolitan epoch) but out of the requirements of the literary system itself, in view of the genre in which they were composing and the social order (courtly or rustic) that was thereby indexed. These were

82. *KĀ* 1.37: *nāṭakādi tu miśrakam.*
83. Bakhtin 1981: 287 (emphasis in the original).

the languages that defined literature as such. This remained as true for Bhoja as it had been for Bhāmaha five centuries earlier: "Literature . . . is composed in Sanskrit, Prakrit, and Apabhramsha." Period.

When the language of the gods entered the world of men, Sanskrit literati invented two closely related cultural forms, *kāvya* and *praśasti*. From the beginning, the languages in which *kāvya* could be composed were delimited in practice and, as the discourse on the language-substance of *kāvya* demonstrates, unambiguously conceptualized in theory as delimited. The ideas of language and literature that *kāvya* embodied, and the unbounded sociotextual community to which it spoke and among which it circulated, differed radically from those of the world in a state of vernacularization (chapters 8–10); indeed, they were the ideas and the community against which that world would eventually define itself. Much the same is true of *praśasti*. A glimpse has already been given of how, once Sanskrit became available for the enunciation of political will, it swiftly displaced every other code for the execution of this task. It is now necessary to chart the progress of this Sanskrit political discourse spatially, semantically, and pragmatically, which means charting at the same time the new conception of power and its supraregional domain of projection that made the cosmopolitan language the only possible language for its self-expression.

CHAPTER THREE

The World Conquest and Regime of the Cosmopolitan Style

3.1 INSCRIBING POLITICAL WILL IN SANSKRIT

The new political culture and cultural politics embodied in the public expression of power in Sanskrit spread across southern Asia with remarkable speed. Just to register this *digvijaya,* or conquest of the quarters—and the very unusual sort of conquest that it was—is to grasp something of the character and reality of the Sanskrit cosmopolis. Within a mere two centuries, in locales that ranged from Kashmir and Puruṣapura (Peshawar) in the foothills of the western Himalayas eastward to Champa (central Vietnam), Prambanam on the plains of central Java, and even beyond in the further islands of today's Indonesia, from the Kathmandu Valley in the north to the southernmost reaches of peninsular India and even, periodically, Sri Lanka, there arose a shared, Sanskrit way of speaking about and conceiving of the nature of political power. A number of intriguing questions are raised by this *digvijaya,* three of which are discussed in what follows. First, since the Sanskrit cosmopolitan style nowhere entered a linguistically empty space, complex interactions with local languages occurred. Considered carefully, these interactions reveal much about both the general character of the cultural-political identity of the cosmopolitan polity and the particular kind of tasks that Sanskrit—and never the vernacular—was empowered to execute, precisely as envisioned by the theory of literary language (chapter 2). Second, as the language of royal encomium, Sanskrit had aesthetic objectives that are immediately clear, though the political meanings generated by Sanskrit's unique expressive resources can be much harder to grasp. At the same time, Sanskrit political inscription could involve concrete negotiations of power, and this presents a third problem for analysis.

It is not necessary, even were it possible, to provide a complete survey of the institutionalization of the Sanskrit political idiom for the vast space-time of the cosmopolis.[1] Concentrating on a few exemplary cases will suffice to suggest the historical rhythm and spatial extent of the dissemination of Sanskrit, as well as the specific functions Sanskrit executed to the exclusion of other available codes. It makes sense to begin, however, with a brief account of the dramatic disappearance of Prakrit, since it both confirms several of the hypotheses about the social grounds of language choice framed earlier and allows us to glimpse the beginnings of the differentiation of language labor with respect to local language that was to become an essential feature of the Sanskrit cosmopolitan style across much of southern Asia.

The last sign of Prakrit in inscriptions in north India is in the hybrid Kuṣāṇa records of the Mathurā region.[2] No Prakrit whatever is to be found in royal inscriptions after the early fourth century, when Sanskrit entered history with an extraordinary, sudden éclat. In the south, the Kadambas of northwestern Karnataka, among the first historically attested dynasties of that region, continued to use Prakrit only up to the beginning of the fourth century. Two such inscriptions from the early fourth century record the gifting of a Brahman village to members of the Kauṇḍinya *gotta (gotra)* as "a place of the learned authorized by the four Vedas"—another telling example of the avoidance of Sanskrit (save for the benediction) in a public document, however *vaidika* and Sanskritic the environment might have been. The Kadamba overlord Mayūraśarman was still writing in Prakrit around 330–36, whereas the celebrated Tāḷagunda Pillar Inscription of the time of his great-great-grandson Śāntivarman (mid-fifth century) is composed in wonderful literary Sanskrit. It recounts how Mayūraśarman traveled to the Pallava capital, Kāñcīpuram, to pursue scriptural studies and describes his other *vaidika* accomplishments. This circumstance, given the prevailing analysis, has made the use of Prakrit in Mayūraśarman's actual extant records inexplicable to many scholars—though from what we have learned so far, we can see it makes perfect sense.[3]

The language practices of the Ikṣvākus, the ruling lineage of southeast Andhra that succeeded the Sātavāhana dynasty around 225 C.E. (and were themselves followed by the Pallavas within a couple of generations), are slightly asynchronous with respect to the disappearance of Prakrit, but they

1. For an exhaustive bibliographical survey see Salomon 1998.

2. Not relevant to this discussion are the later ornamental engravings of Prakrit poetry briefly in vogue in the educational environment of Bhoja's Dhārā (e.g., *EI* 8: 241–60).

3. The two early Prakrit inscriptions are found in *EC* 7: 251–52 (cf. also Sankaranarayanan 1994: 102–3). A date of 258 C.E. is ascribed to the Mayūraśarman record in *MAR* 1931: 50–60, but on shaky grounds (Gai places it between 300 and 400). Gai's edition of the dynasty's second extant record shows that it is virtually Sanskrit (*IEK* p. 61; contrast Sircar 1965–83, vol. 1: 473). On the puzzlement over Mayūraśarman's Prakrit, see *MAR* 1931: 57 n. 4. The Tāḷagunda inscription was first published by Bühler in *IA* 25: 29 ff.; see now *IEK* pp. 64 ff.

are instructive especially on the relationship between language and religious community. Of the Ikṣvākus' seventy-six extant records, the earliest forty are in Prakrit. Most of these come from Buddhist sites in Nāgārjunakoṇḍa, though a number celebrate the *vaidika* achievements of the dynasty.[4] These are followed by a set of Sanskrit epigraphs produced in the third generation during the reign of King Ehavala Śāntamūla; paleographically, they may be dated to the third or fourth century, so the language change may in fact be contemporaneous with Pallava developments.[5] For the remainder of its rule the dynasty reverted to Prakrit. The Sanskrit documents record the foundation and endowment of Śiva temples as well as the installation of a stone image of the Perfectly Awakened Buddha, providing yet further evidence not only that Buddhist inscriptions were not invariably issued in Prakrit but that Prakrit inscriptions were not invariably Buddhist.

Among the Vākāṭakas, who ruled over what is now eastern Maharashtra and southern Madhya Pradesh, the last Prakrit inscription (it is also the first copperplate grant, a new invention of this period) is found in the Bāsim plates of Vindhyaśakti II (c. 355). Although it is also the sole Prakrit record of the dynasty discovered so far, there is every reason to suppose that their earlier records would have been composed in Prakrit as well. As was true of the Sātavāhanas, Vākāṭaka royalty ranked among the preeminent Prakrit poets of the fourth and fifth centuries.[6] The plates provide an instructive finale to the historical transformation of public discourse while also offering one of the earliest examples of what was to become a key feature of the Sanskrit cultural order: the division of labor between Sanskrit and regional languages.[7] The introductory genealogical portion, not quite yet a *praśasti* yet still rhetorical in temper (as the crescendo of sacrificial accomplishments intimates) is written in Sanskrit:

> By order of the righteous great king of the Vākāṭakas, Vindhyaśakti, the son of Śrī Sarvasena the righteous great king, the grandson of Śrī Pravarasena the

4. See *EI* 31: 63, Caṃtamula is the performer of Vedic sacrifices *(agihota, agiṭhoma, asamedha)*, the donor of ten thousand cows *(gosatasahasa)*, etc. This record adorned a Buddhist *stūpa*.

5. The three Sanskrit epigraphs are found in *EI* 33: 149; 34: 19; 35: 12–13. See also Srinivasan and Sankaranarayanan 1979.

6. On the date of the Bāsim record see *CII* 5: vi. Vākāṭaka poets include Pravarasena II (*Setubandha*, c. 400), Sarvasena of the Vatsagulma branch (fragments of his *Harivijaya*, c. 330, have been collected in Kulkarni 1991 from Bhoja's works), and others whose verses are included in the *Gāhāsattasaī* (see *CII* 5: lvii).

7. The earliest instance of this division in the realm of Prakrit seems to be the step-well inscription mentioned in chapter 1 n. 58. This opens with a documentary portion in Prakrit, followed by a literary passage in Sanskrit commemorating the construction of a *śailaṃ . . . gṛham* of the *vṛṣṇīnāṃ pañcavīrāṇām*. Other contemporary documents found at the same site, including identifications of images of the gods, are in Prakrit (*EI* 24: 201, 204, 205). Note that inscriptions in the same place that are associated with the Śakas are in Sanskrit (*EI* 24: 206, 207).

righteous great king and performer of the *agniṣṭoma, āptoryāma, vājapeya, jyotiṣṭoma, bṛhaspatisava, sādyaska,* and—four times—the *aśvamedha,* the emperor, man of the Vṛṣṇivṛddha lineage, a son of [the goddess] Hāritī.

The business portion, on the other hand, detailing a grant of land to a group of Brahmans of an Atharvaveda community *(ādhivvaṇikacaraṇa),* is in Prakrit:

> We have now granted this village to the [Atharvavedins] in this village as a new gift which is to be enjoyed as long as the moon and the sun will endure . . . Half a share to Jivajja [i.e., Jivārya] of the Bhālandāyana lineage, to Ruddajja [Rudrārya] of the Kapiñjala lineage . . . It is to be exempt from the district police; from the purchase and digging of salt; from the [compulsory] gifts [to the king] of gold and grain. [8]

The grant ends with a benedictory phrase in Sanskrit *(siddhir astu).*

The record demonstrates once more, and unambiguously, that Sanskrit and Prakrit could inhabit the same cultural space, irrespective of religious affiliation, before Sanskrit's final victory in the political sphere. The prominence of Prakrit does not reflect ignorance of Sanskrit, and the supposed concomitance between Prakrit and Buddhism as against Sanskrit and Brahmanism is a chimera.[9] A more parsimonious, and historically more accurate, explanation is that the two idioms coexisted everywhere but had entirely separate discursive spheres from the start. By the early fourth century, as the Vākāṭaka record shows, these spheres had begun to intersect in new ways as Sanskrit emerged from its ritual sequestration to take on unprecedented expressive tasks in public, relegating Prakrit to the mundane documentary. Just this division of labor was to be replicated with respect to the languages of Place: Sanskrit would monopolize all ideational and expressive functions in inscriptional and other written discourse while assigning to regional languages the quotidian status and function they had in everyday life. This development has important implications for understanding not only premodern language interaction—neither bilingualism nor diglossia is in evidence here but rather that very different form of language domination that I have termed hyperglossia—but also the politics of culture and the culture of politics in Indian premodernity. Publicly inscribed political language is a sign with multiple and complex significations.

The tendencies in evidence in the Vākāṭaka plates, especially the new prominence given to Sanskrit in enunciating the political self-identification of rulership, the incipient literariness with which it executed that function, and the relegation of nonliterary, documentary tasks to other, quasi-local

8. The Prakrit portion is Mirashi's translation (*EI* 26: 154–55) slightly altered.

9. See Sircar in *EI* 34: 197–98. So, too, in Southeast Asia: if in Śrīvijaya the earliest inscription is in Old Malay and Buddhist (*JASB* 1935: 61), in Khmer country Buddhist inscriptions in Sanskrit are found from an early date (e.g., Vat Prey Vier, 664 C.E.).

codes, were to be reproduced throughout the entire subsequent history of Sanskrit inscriptional discourse across Asia. Exemplary is the case of the Pallavas of Tamil country.

The epigraphical remains of the Pallava dynasty enable us to follow developments of language in relation to power in a reasonably detailed and continuous fashion from the fourth until the early tenth century, when their dominions were largely absorbed by Cōḻa Āditya I around 910–15.[10] We briefly examined their earliest records in the course of analyzing language choice in the inaugural period of public writing (chapter 1.3). As we saw, the first four were in Prakrit, in accordance with the prevailing style; whereas they briefly identify the ruling overlord, none contains the least gesture toward the imaginative or the expressive—in short, the concerns of the *praśasti*. All of them, moreover, evince a generalized reluctance to employ Sanskrit in a this-worldly mode, however Brahmanical the religious context might have been and whatever the cost in linguistic correctness (recall how clumsy the Prakrit of these records has been judged).

A little after 400, four generations from the time of the first king to issue records, Śivaskandavarman (ruled c. 330–50)—thus at virtually the same moment similar changes happened elsewhere in south India—Prakrit was abandoned once and for all, and the inscriptional style of the Pallavas changed dramatically and permanently. Henceforth Pallava records are in textbook Sanskrit, and from the beginning they show the elements of what was becoming the standard *praśasti* style: the fixing of genealogical succession, the catalogue of kingly traits of the dynasty, and a eulogy of the ruling lord. To the eulogy is added the documentary account of the gift in question, its conditions, and the imprecations against violating them. Typical is the record of Vijayaskandavarman (III), where the expressive function of the *praśasti* inchoately manifests itself. Here the genealogy is traced back to the fourth generation and no further (something typical of many records and perhaps explained by the requirements of the *śrāddha,* or ancestral memorial, which invokes ancestors back to the third generation). Vijayaskandavarman's great-grandfather, the founder of the dynasty, is credited with performing the *aśvamedha* sacrifice; his grandfather is praised for his control of the "three powers," military, fiscal, and political, and for his capacity for "seizing kingship by his own heroic effort"; the king's father "won the blazing power of glory through victory in countless battles, and through this power subjected the circle of kings to his will." Vijayaskandavarman himself is described as "a man of character adorned with suitable conduct, a man true to his word, whose store of merit is increased day by day through gifts of land and gold and cows

10. Mahalingam assembled the Pallava inscriptions in chronological order *(IP)*. The supplementary volume containing inscriptions discovered since has yet to appear.

without number, who delights in obedience to gods and Brahmans, and who has gained true knowledge through the determination of the meaning of all the *śāstras*." The *praśasti* is followed by the details of the granting of a village to a Brahman and the standard imprecations against infringing upon it.[11]

The Pallava public text, with regard to the style of the prose *praśasti* at least, attained its final form at this point. The genealogy is composed in the art-prose *(gadyakāvya)* inaugurated in the Junagāṛh inscription five centuries earlier. Rudradāman's conspicuous nominalization and phonological density,

> *giriśikharatarutaṭāṭṭālakopatalpadvāraśaraṇocchrayavidhvaṃsinā yuganidhanasadṛśaparamaghoravegena vāyunā*

> a stormwind with an awesome force like the wind at the end of time leveled the hills, uprooted trees, and tore down embankments, turrets, towers, shelters

had now become the norm, along with dignified and rhetorically studied phraseology:

> *anekasamaralabdhavijayayaśaḥpratāpasya pratāpopanatarājamaṇḍalasya . . . 'nekagohiraṇyabhūmyādidānair aharahar abhivarddhamānadharmmasaṃcayasya devadvijaśuśrūṣābhiratasya sarvaśāstrārthanirṇṇayatatvajñasya*

> (Translated above: "won the blazing power of glory . . . "; "whose store of merit . . .")[12]

Like the style of the genealogy (which the Pallavas' competitors to the west, the Bādāmi Cāḷukyas, develop to perfection, section 3 below), its content would become formulaic across dynasties. There are, for example, characterological slots: the founder of the dynasty himself is typically credited with the achievement of great *vaidika* rites; one descendant masters the world of political practice with its three powers; another evinces personal resolve and bravery.[13] This is followed by the grant specifics, then by imprecations and the date.

All that remained to be added in later texts was the introductory invocation of the gods *(maṅgalācaraṇa)* in verse. This does not appear in Pallava records until the reign of Siṃhavarman III (c. 525–50) in a copperplate *praśasti,* as the text calls itself, composed by Medhāvin, one in a hereditary line of Pallava court praise-poets. With the appearance of this metrical *praśasti* (though no causal connection need be assumed) comes the first use of Tamil

11. *IP* 42 ff. = *EI* 15: 249–52 ("seizing kingship by his own heroic effort," *svavīryādhigatarājyasya,* pace Mahalingam in *IP* 35).

12. Sircar 1965–83, vol. 1: 176 ff. lines 6–7.

13. Any of these formulaic slots seems able to be filled by any member of the dynasty at any time. In the mid-sixth-century record of Kumāraviṣṇu (*IP* 62 ff.), the martial valor slot is filled by Skandavarman IV and the piety slot by Kumāraviṣṇu II. A similar recycling occurs in a record of Parameśvaravarman I of 687 (no. 45).

in Pallava records. Here we find the earliest example of a recurrent, even law-like phenomenon: the division of labor, evinced first in the Vākāṭaka grant, between cosmopolitan and vernacular language use, the one expressive and the other documentary, and the delay, often long-lasting, until the vernacular itself is elevated to do the work of *praśasti* (chapters 8.1, 10.1). For the first three centuries of Pallava rule, Tamil, the everyday language of their realm, was denied all political function. When it at last appeared in inscriptions, Tamil was wholly restricted to factual communication and would long remain so. Medhāvin's text shows this distribution of function with compelling force. It exploits all the phonic and semantic aesthesis of the Sanskrit language—combining at once the figure *śleṣa,* whose role in public poetry we will see to be central (section 2 below), with figures of sound—while detailing the specifics of the gift in a Tamil that, in comparison, is emphatically prosaic.

Medhāvin's *praśasti* begins with an invocation to the lordly *jinas*, sages, and gods, appropriately chosen in view of the fact that the recipient of the grant is a Jain monastic leader *(gaṇin).* This is followed by the genealogy of the Pallavas, which in this case starts with the creator god Brahmā. Siṃhavarman is born among the Pallava kings, "those whose lotus feet are as it were awakened by the light of the sunlike jewels on the heads of rival kings." Then his son is described in two bravura verses:

> Glorious Siṃhaviṣṇu could defeat the Lion[-form] of Viṣṇu / he defeated (the Telugu-Cōḻa king) Siṃhaviṣṇu; by his power he could conquer Arjuna with his bow. He ornamented his brilliant clan, and could destroy the bold in battle.
>
> Have not all the pure virtues of the ruling order—truthfulness, generosity, discipline—found a resting place in this magnanimous man as in no other? It was he who in his full power ravished the land of the Cōḻas, that Lady whose necklace is the Kāverī river, whose veil is the fields of paddy and sugarcane, whose lovely belt is the groves of areca nut and plantains.

In the Tamil portion of the grant that follows, King Siṃhaviṣṇu communicates an order to the *nāṭṭār,* the commune elders of the Perunagara-nāḍu, a subdivision of the Veṇkuṉṟk-kōṭṭam, informing them of the grant of the village Amancerkkahi plus another 16½ *paṭṭi* of land in the Dāmar village to the ascetic Vajranandi; additional conditions are noted and the grant's borders precisely described. "The eastern boundary is to the west of the jungle on the eastern side of the tank . . . and also of the garden of the toothbrush tree. Again, the southern boundary is to the north of the well belonging to Vēḷ Vaḍugan, and also of the jungle and of the boundary of the village Nīlapāḍi, and of the small waterlift of Virāṭan."[14]

14. The beginning of the inscription is damaged, and the Sanskrit portion is not always accurately printed in either *IP* 89 ff. or *TASSI* 1962: 41–83 (from which I take the translation of the Tamil portion, p. 82). The Sanskrit for the first verse runs: *śrīsiṃhaviṣṇur jitasiṃhaviṣṇuḥ*

To underscore the division of linguistic labor here and its discursive traits is to state the obvious for anyone who has read a single Indian charter, though it may be the very banality of the phenomenon that has prevented scholars from making much sense of it or even adequately recognizing it. It is an arresting fact that in six centuries of Pallava rule not a single inscription was produced in which Tamil does any work beyond recording the everyday—remitting taxes, specifying the boundaries of a land grant, and the like. While examples exist in earlier Pallava records of Sanskrit being used to document the everyday world—a function that would become increasingly rare wherever it could be relegated to the vernacular—none exists where the everyday language is allowed to do the work of Sanskrit in a *praśasti:* the literary work of interpreting and supplementing reality and revealing it in its truth.[15]

The changes found in the Pallavas' public discourse were part of a larger process that had commenced two centuries earlier and was virtually complete everywhere by the fifth. All across the subcontinent there came into existence, by a startling, nearly simultaneous set of transformations, a linguistically homogeneous and conceptually standardized form of Sanskrit political poetry.[16] Power in India now had a Sanskrit voice. And by a kind of premodern globalization—even Westernization—it would have a Sanskrit voice in much of the world to the east.

In the first centuries of the Common Era, one of the tipping points in the history of global exchange and cross-cultural contact, which saw also a dramatic expansion of trade between South Asia and the Roman empire, people in India began to develop relationships of new complexity and intensity with mainland and maritime Southeast Asia. It is unclear why such ties, comprising not only trade but also profound transculturation, did not develop in the lands to the north and west of India, where even older patterns of interaction had recently been intensified under Kuṣāṇa rule. But they did not, and western and central Asia would remain largely impervious to the spread of Sanskrit cosmopolitan culture (except of course in its Buddhist embodiment, which proved comparatively ephemeral). It is equally unclear why they did develop in the southeast. The scholarly models now on

---

balena jiṣṇur dhanuṣāpi jiṣṇum | *bhrājiṣṇuvaṃśaṃ svam alaṅkariṣṇuḥ nirākariṣṇus samareṣu dhṛṣṇūn* || I understand the second verse as follows: *satyatyāgavinītatādi vimalaṃ yasmin na labdhāspadaṃ vṛdaṃ kṣātraguṇaṃ samunnatamatau anyeṣv alabdhāspadam* | *yenāhāritarāṃ kaveratanayāhārāpi coḷāvaniś śāleyekṣuvaṇāṃśukā kramukarambhārāmasanmekhalā* || The hereditary position of *praśastikāra* is suggested by a Pallava grant issued two centuries later, which ends with the words "A descendant in the family of Medhāvin made the poetry of this *praśasti*" (*IP* 235).

15. One marginal exception to the documentary restriction of Tamil in Pallava grants is the account of the election of a new king, Nandivarman II, after the death of Parameśvara II around 730 (*IP* 325 ff.).

16. In the north of the subcontinent the documentary complement of the vernacular language was lacking, an apparent enigma considered in chapters 8.3 and 10.1.

offer that account for these happenings and the astonishing processes of culture-power change thereby set in motion—"one of the most impressive instances of large-scale acculturation in the history of the world," according to one authority—do more to prompt questions than to provide credible explanations.[17]

About the historical events themselves there seems to be a growing scholarly consensus. The new interactions and the migrations associated with them were almost certainly the doings of small groups of traders, adventurers, and religious professionals. There is no evidence for large-scale state initiatives (an eleventh-century Cōḻa adventure is the exception) or anything remotely resembling colonization. No ties of political subservience between these regions and the subcontinent are to be found, no forms of material dependency or exploitation, no demographically meaningful settlements of the subjects of any Indian polity, and certainly nothing resembling military conquest and occupation. Yet suddenly, from about the fourth century on, inscriptions written in Sanskrit began to appear with increasing frequency in the places now known as Burma, Thailand, Cambodia, Laos, Vietnam, Malaysia, and Indonesia. And though this style of political poetry died out rather quickly in Burma, it would continue far longer elsewhere (until the late thirteenth century in Cambodia, the mid-fifteenth century in Java).[18]

Just as murky as the causal grounds of the expansion of the cosmopolitan order of culture-power into Southeast Asia are the vector and dating of its dissemination. According to the now-conventional view, its provenance was the Coromandel coast during the period of Pallava dominion (and in the ninth and tenth centuries during the rule of the Pālas, through increased activity from the Bengal coastal regions). Though the assumption is reasonable geographically, it is made doubtful by, inter alia, the dating style, literary form, and paleography of the Southeast Asian Sanskrit records. From the start, records were dated in the Śaka era (beginning in 78 C.E.), a calendrical convention never once met with among the Pallavas, whose records use exclusively regnal years. It is among the Cāḷukyas of Bādāmi in today's Karnataka that the oldest continuous tradition of Śaka-era dating is found.[19]

17. The models in question, such as "Indianization," are discussed in chapter 14.1. The quotation is from Wheatley 1982: 28.

18. For Cambodia, *BEFEO* 25: 393 (a fifteenth-century date assigned to five undated records by Jenner 1982: 40, 52 seems improbable); for Java, see de Casparis 1991: 30.

19. See further on this in section 3. Their first record is dated *śakavarṣeṣu catuśśateṣu pañcaṣaṣṭiyuteṣu* ("when the Śaka years were four hundred and sixty-five," i.e., 543 C.E., *EI* 27: 9), a formula that bears comparison with the My-son Stele inscription from south Champa (Chhabra 1965: 51), *-uttareṣu caturṣu varṣaśateṣu śakānāṃ vyatīteṣu* ("after four hundred and . . . years of the Śakas had passed"; the lacuna prevents a more precise dating than between 479 and 577 C.E.). The fifth-century Funan records were also dated to the Śaka era (Coedès *BEFEO* 31: 8 and 1968: 36ff.). Others have taken the spread of the Śaka dating system to be co-

Formally, many early Southeast Asian texts typically include verse, as do Cāḷukya records, or even mixed verse and art-prose very much like the *campū* that would become the prized literary form in Karnataka.[20] For their part, the Pallavas never used verse (with the sole exception of the record of Medhāvin mentioned earlier). Paleography, too, makes it as easy to connect the early Khmer records with the Cāḷukyas as with the Pallavas.[21] All together, these data suggest a provenance for the transculturation process not on the southeast coast of India but rather the west-central coast, where Kadamba and then Cāḷukya power and culture were dominant. The period in question, after the fourth century, likewise tallies with the era of their political dominance.[22]

If much remains uncertain, then, about not only the material foundations but also the space-time matrix of the cosmopolitan transformation in Southeast Asia, there is nothing at all uncertain about its fact—and what a striking fact it is. All across mainland and maritime Southeast Asia, people who spoke radically different languages, such as Mon-Khmer and Malayo-Polynesian, and lived in vastly different cultural worlds adopted suddenly, widely, and long-lastingly a new language—along with the new political vision and literary aesthetic that were inseparable from it and unthinkable without it—for the production of what were often defining forms of political culture. In itself this is a remarkable development, but given the manner in

extensive with the spread of Cāḷukya power (Sircar 1965: 259, 264; 1965–83, vol. 2: 692–93; Nagaraju 1984: 72). For the Śaka era itself (or rather, the Śakas' two eras) see Bivar 1981.

20. Again the My-son Stele may be adduced. The *campū* form burst into prominence in tenth-century Karnataka in both Sanskrit (e.g., Trivikramabhaṭṭa, c. 915) and Kannada (e.g., Pampa, c. 940). See chapter 9.3.

21. All this makes a third-century date for the Vo-cahn inscription most improbable (pace Jacques 1991: 10 and Bhattacharya 1991: 6); Gaspardone's fifth-century dating was far more persuasive (1953: 477 ff.; so Dani 1963: 233). For the earliest dated Cambodian records, see *IdC* vol. 5: 17 (613), 20 (624). Paleography seems much less reliable for establishing the chronology of Southeast Asian inscriptions than it is usually taken to be. Thus, in Cambodia, the inscription of Guṇavarman (Sircar 1965–83, vol. 1: 511; Coedès *BEFEO* 31.1) has been dated to the mid-fifth century because of its "marked similarity" to that of the Pallava Uruvupalli grant (Chhabra 1965: 57; so Coedès). But aside from the fact that it has nothing in common with it either formally or discursively, some scholars have found its writing style identical to Pallava inscriptions from as late as the eighth century (Mahalingam, sixth chart, *IP* 1; similarly in Java the "Pallava-Grantha" script was unchanged between 400 and 750 [*CIJ:* 2]). Moreover, the first dated Cambodian records from the early seventh century show none of the discursive maturity of the putatively mid-fifth century text. To Kern's eyes, the earliest ones had a script "exactly" like that of the Cāḷukyas (cf. *ISC:* 12), see also Sircar 1965–83, vol. 1: 509 n., Nagaraju 1984 (less decided is Dani 1963: 230–32); for the conventional view, Bhattacharya 1991: 2.

22. Chinese sources on the history of fifth-century Cambodia (Coedès, previous note) mention a usurper named Kauṇḍinya, a clan name prominent in the records of the Kadambas (see section 1). A Kannada *Pañcatantra* may have made its way to Java (Sarkar 1970: 99; Durgasiṃha's was written in 1031, see chapter 9.2).

which it occurred—without the enforcement of military power, the pressure of an imperial administrative or legal apparatus, or the promptings of religious evangelism—it is one without obvious parallel in history, except indeed for South Asia itself. We can sense the character of the overall development by looking at the career of public Sanskrit in two regions, Khmer country and Java. If these two share a number of traits and conform broadly with the cosmopolitan paradigm as it was coming to be constituted in South Asia, the fate of the cosmopolitan order and the politics of vernacular culture differ markedly between them.

In Khmer lands the Sanskrit epigraphical habit grew continuously and dramatically, beginning with several sixth-century records thought to have been issued by the so-called Funan polity, the first of the more centralized political formations in the region that would come to express their political will in Sanskrit. A remarkable efflorescence occurred in the Angkor period, beginning in the late ninth century and reaching a high point in the tenth (when the grand inscriptions at Mebon [952] and Pre Rup [961] were composed).[23] And as the habit grew, so did the complexity and indeed the importance of the inscriptions themselves.

In general, the history of Cambodian inscriptional discourse corresponds closely to what we find in South Asia. Early inscriptions in Sanskrit, up to the time of the founding of the Angkor dynasty in the early ninth century, are brief if still fundamentally literary gestures. This was largely the case on the subcontinent, too, although longer *praśasti* texts became common earlier in the north (around the beginning of the fourth century) and somewhat later in the south (the Pallavas continued to produce simple records rather than public poems until the seventh century). One force for innovation in the discursive style of Southeast Asian inscriptions (as in dating and versification) is again likely to have been the Bādāmi Cāḷukyas and their successors, the Rāṣṭrakūṭas. Here political poetry, of which the Aihoḷe inscription of Ravikīrti is only the most famous of a number of examples (see section 3 below), achieves a dazzling complexity, especially in the records of the Rāṣṭrakūṭas Govinda III and Amoghavarṣa. Demonstrating a temporal and stylistic connection between Cāḷukya/Rāṣṭrakūṭa and Angkor poetry would require specialized study; for our purposes it suffices to show that between the ninth and thirteenth centuries, a very similar fascination with displaying in public the most sophisticated forms of political poetry seized the minds of royal elites in Khmer country exactly as it did in India.

The Cambodian records are thoroughly suffused with the idiom, intelli-

23. Of some 200 dated Cambodian records in Sanskrit, only about 40 (20 percent)—and of the approximately 225 undated Sanskrit records, only 75–80 (around 35 percent)—predate the founding of Angkor. Mebon and Pre Rup are published in *BEFEO* 25: 311 ff; and *IdC* vol. 1: 77 ff. (see also *BEFEO* 34: 770 ff.) respectively, and cf. Sharan 1981, and Bhattacharya 1991: 3.

gence, and political imagination found in the Sanskrit works of the subcontinent. Undoubtedly some local inflection is present from the beginning on both the religiopolitical and social planes. A Sanskritized Buddhism could be conjoined with royal eulogy in a combination not often found on the subcontinent.[24] Even more conspicuously divergent is the prominence of women, from the first verse of the first record of the time of Jayavarman (c. fifth century) to the very last, of 1293, which consists of a grand *praśasti* on the king's chief queen of a sort not found in India. A good example is the Mebon Inscription: it begins with a eulogy of Sarasvatī, followed by one of the king's maternal aunt (v. 10), then one of her daughter ("a second Lakṣmī to benefit the world, a noble coral tree of fame, [who] took birth from the milk ocean of that clan . . . a regal daughter of kings, whose fame was constantly sung by the celestial nymphs"). Such foregrounding is without obvious parallel in South Asia and can presumably be attributed to specific kinship structures in the region.[25]

Such localisms should not be exaggerated, however.[26] Inscriptional discourse at Angkor is thoroughly comparable to what one finds in India in terms of substance, form, and performative character. It is the self-presentation of royal elites composed in a Sanskrit that deploys, increasingly so over the centuries, all the rhetorical and formal resources of the most complex and sophisticated poetry, to say nothing of a virtually perfect orthography and grammar whose mastery shows not the least deterioration up to the moment of Angkor's decline. And it is publicly performed, so to speak, by being displayed in places of great symbolic importance, typically on pillars in royal or aristocratic temple confines. Yet another remarkable parallel with subcontinental cosmopolitan culture pertains to the status and function of the vernacular language in the Sanskrit epigraphs. Dated inscriptions in Khmer began to be produced at almost the same time as dated inscriptions in Sanskrit (early seventh century), indicating that vernacular literacy in Cambodia was fully mediated by Sanskrit literacy just as it typically was in South Asia (at least before the full engagement of the vernacularization process). The two languages had a completely unequal influence on each other, too: Khmer was massively in-

24. Rudravarman's record (Sircar 1965–83, vol. 1: 513–14) is probably mid-seventh century (or earlier, cf. Coedès in *BEFEO* 31: 9), thus necessitating a correction of Jacques 1991: 9. A striking Pāla example is discussed in section 2.

25. For Jayavarman see Sircar 1965–83, vol. 1: 509 ff. (no. 81); for the 1293 *praśasti, BEFEO* 25: 393 ff.; for Mebon, *BEFEO* 25: 309 ff. (cited are vv. 11–12; "took birth from the milk ocean of that clan," pace Finot). It is puzzling to read that "Our ability precisely to define the role of women in early Southeast Asian society is clouded by the epigraphic records . . . initiated by an élite who were emulating Indic culture. True to the Indian epics and religions that promoted male superiority and female dependency, there are infrequent references to women" (Tarling 1992: 190).

26. As they are by Wolters 1982: 91. See further in chapter 12.1.

vaded by Sanskrit at the lexical level from the earliest period, whereas Sanskrit remained untouched by Khmer (except for personal names, Khmer words never appear in Sanskrit). The asymmetrical cultural authority between the two languages is confirmed by precisely the hyperglossia found in southern India: Sanskrit is rarely used for the purely documentary, and Khmer never for the expressive.[27]

The presence of public Sanskrit in Khmer country during the thousand-year period from about the fifth century to the end of Angkor raises questions about cosmopolitan transculturation—about agents, audiences, and their purposes, and about the very shape of literary culture—even more insistently than the parallel process in southern India. First, who produced Sanskrit literary culture in Cambodia? Some ruling elites were of Indian origin, and Sanskrit learning may well have been passed down in the family. The first inscription of Yaśovarman (889 C.E.) describes one of his ancestors as "a Brahman who knew the Vedas and *vedāṅgas* and had achieved success in Āryadeśa."[28] But there is no reason to believe Sanskrit was not studied by the Khmer elites themselves, Indian ancestry or no (just as in the time of the Mughals, Indians, Iranian ancestry or no, mastered Persian). Until late in the Angkor period, Khmer princes were writing royal *praśastis*: Sūryakumāra and Vīrakumāra are identified in the epigraphs themselves as having composed the eulogies to their father, Jayavarman VII, in 1186–87.[29] Opportunities for learning were no doubt enhanced by the continual circulation of intellectuals back and forth to the subcontinent, as was clearly the case in the maritime regions: Śrīvijaya (on Sumatra) and the Buddhist university at Nālandā in Bodh Gayā (eastern Bihar) had close connections in the last centuries of the millennium; a ninth-century record from Java reports the "constant flow of people from Gurjaradeśa, bowed low with the devotion to the Buddha" (the presence in Java of Khmers, people from the Cōḻa realm, and others is also mentioned). Indian Brahmans were sometimes imported into Cambodia—for the lustration of the Khmer domain in the ninth century, for example—and Sanskrit poets from India were welcome guests at the Majapahit court in east Java as late as the fourteenth century.[30] Yet acknowledging the presence of literati from the subcontinent should not obscure the fact that, ultimately, Sanskrit

27. Nearly half of all Cambodian inscriptions are solely in Khmer, one-third are in Sanskrit alone, and a quarter use both languages. On the Sanskrit influence on Khmer see Pou 1991: 12 ff.; also Bhattacharya 1991: 6. The one exception to the resolutely documentary role of Khmer is the oath of fealty sworn to Sūryavarman II in 1011 (*BEFEO* 13.2:15–16).

28. *vedavedāṅgavid āryadeśe | labdhodayaḥ*, cf. *IK* no. 60, pp. 74 ff. v. 5.

29. *IK* nos. 177 and 178.

30. For the last three references see respectively *CIJ* vol. 1: 48 (x): *satatagurjaradeśasamāgataiḥ sugatabhaktibharapraṇatai[ḥ]*; de Casparis 1956: 195; and *IdC* vol. 4: 42 v. 14, noted by Wolters 1982: 91. In the Javanese *Deśawarṇana* (Majapahit, 1365; see also chapter 10.1), the poet mentions writing a Sanskrit *praśasti* (his word) for the king, and also notes that two Indian poets

literary culture became as much at home in Khmer country as it was in the Deccan. There is even reason to assume that a class of Khmer Brahmans evolved, since just such a class arose in Java and Bali.[31]

Second, why was Sanskrit used at all as a mode of political expression in the Khmer world? A partial answer can be provided by understanding the place of this mode of discourse in the emergent cosmopolitan formations (chapter 6.2), where Sanskrit with its aesthetic capacities and ideational associations served purposes radically different from those of local languages. Southeast Asian scholarship, for its part, seems largely uninterested in the problem.[32] Even the most accomplished regional histories, which raise large and important questions, are incurious about the language practices and rarely ask why or for whom Khmer people wrote in Sanskrit (whereas they often ask why the Vietnamese wrote in Chinese).[33] Most contemporary opinion has rejected the claim that Sanskrit was the "official language of the royal chancery," for which there seems to be no evidence beyond the inscriptions themselves (in fact, the same uncertainties hold for South Asia itself); on the contrary, everything suggests that the language used for the everyday functions of rule was Khmer. From this improbably pragmatic judgment, the pendulum has swung to an improbably idealist one: since the elite group that knew Sanskrit was too small to account for its use as a language of rule, we are told, and since the inscriptions are found generally on temple sites, the Sanskrit of the Khmer inscriptions must have had only one audience: the gods.[34] But this is incorrect, too. For one thing, we know absolutely nothing about the demographics of Sanskrit use in medieval Cambodia. For another, there certainly exist Sanskrit records that have nothing whatever to do "with the gods." An undated family poem, for instance, "tells of no foundation, no donation, and seems to have as its object simply to specify the extent of the family's property."[35] Moreover, the inscriptional poems themselves are nothing like prayers except in the initial verses of auspiciousness (*maṅgalācaraṇas*); and if these make the inscriptions prayer, all of Sanskrit literature would be a prayer. Inscriptional discourse in Cambodia had some other, political-cultural work to do. It makes claims about the political power of particular kings and notables, and it is directed to those for whom such knowl-

---

were present at court: one Buddhāditya from Kāñcīpuram, author of a long eulogy to the king, and a Mutali Sahṛdaya (Robson 1995: 93; cf. pp. 148–49).

31. On Khmer Brahmans, see de Casparis in Tarling 1992: 287.

32. Van Naerssen and de Jongh 1977, for example, are silent on the language question.

33. Wolters 1982: 74: the Vietnamese were appropriating the foe's language to defend an "independent status in the face of Chinese imperial pretensions," an argument not easy to make in the case of the Khmers' use of Sanskrit.

34. Jacques 1986: 328, critiquing Coedès's view on Sanskrit as a chancery language; cf. Jacques 1991: 12.

35. Coedès in *IC* vol. 5: 238.

edge is pertinent, the royal elite themselves. They are the "you" typically addressed in the opening invocation of such texts as beneficiaries of the appeal to divinity.[36] The fact that inscriptions are found at temples need signify no more than that the temple construction was also the occasion, or the temple itself a site, for the narrativization of the royal person's life. The discourse of the Cambodian *praśasti* is completely comparable to that found in copperplate and other kinds of inscriptions in India, which are clearly not addressed to gods.

Agents and audiences aside, the differences between Sanskrit and Khmer language practices are as obvious as their cultural asymmetry: the poetry of power in Cambodia was Sanskrit poetry, never Khmer. This can be formulated even more strongly: textualized literature, *kāvya,* up to the end of the Angkor formation was Sanskrit literature. No evidence whatever exists for Khmer literary production during the cosmopolitan epoch. This is stated not to deny to the Khmer the capacity for literary imagination but to bring to consciousness the cultural and political conditions under which the textualization of literature—the privilege of the expressive, nondocumentary inscription—becomes possible in history. Vernacularization is the subject of part 2 of this book, but it is worth signaling here this limit case: The character of Khmer language usage in the texts that are preserved, and the late historical development of Khmer literature (not before the sixteenth century), together suggest strongly that, in this particular world, the latter could not come into existence until Sanskrit literary culture itself came to an end.

The shape of that culture in the Khmer world presents yet another enigma. Remarkably, the political poetry in inscriptions is the only Sanskrit literature in Cambodia we have, and probably the only that ever existed. The Khmer world produced a Sanskrit literary practice that had fully mastered its philology and mythography; the Mebon and Pre Rup Inscriptions of the late tenth century demonstrate that the entire canon of Sanskrit poetry was studied, along with shastric texts from erotics to medicine. And the Sanskrit in Cambodian inscriptions is grammatically perfect across centuries. Yet this mastery issued in the production of not a single line of Sanskrit literature other than *praśasti* poetry. We find occasional reference to other kinds of Sanskrit textual production, but all of this material disappeared without a trace—assuming it ever existed.[37]

Thus in Khmer country—and this was typical of mainland Southeast Asia—Sanskrit was exclusively the cosmopolitan language of elite self-presentation:

36. See, e.g., *IC* vol. 5: 47; 239.10a; 251.11, 13, 15, 19.

37. A twelfth-century Cham king "supported his accession to the throne by writing a Sanskrit treatise said to resemble a *smṛti*" (Wolters 1982: 44); the Khmer king Yaśovarman I (c. 889–910) is supposed to have composed a new commentary on the *Mahābhāṣya, IK* no. 73b, p. 155 v. 13, though I do not derive that sense from the verse. Cf. Jacques 1991: 5.

only Sanskrit was employed for this purpose, and it seems to have been employed for no other. Sanskrit's career in the maritime regions, however, complements but also complicates this picture of cosmopolitan transculturation. Sanskrit inscriptions first appeared in Java in the early fifth century, concurrently with those on the mainland, Laos being among the earliest, but they continued to be produced with some frequency only through the ninth century, when the first inscriptions in Javanese were composed and, at the same time and not unrelatedly, the process of vernacularization was precociously inaugurated, first in an inscription of 824 (chapter 8.1, 3). From that point on, Sanskrit would be employed mainly in invocations and concluding verses; its use for serious public political expression was at an end (all told, only something like 250 inscriptions have been discovered). A brief Sanskrit revival did occur in the Majapahit period under Ādityavarman (fl. 1350), for reasons that are unclear, given that many documents remain unpublished. Sanskrit inscriptions were still being composed as late as 1447. In that year a copperplate record mostly in Javanese—the vernacular transformation was by now five centuries old—was issued in the name of the "supreme lord of all of Java" *(śrī sakalayawarājādhirājaparameśwara),* yet it includes an introduction of four verses in Sanskrit, showing that that language continued to be seriously cultivated as a courtly accomplishment.[38] As in the case of Khmer inscriptions, these Javanese texts are all royal records; inscriptional practice seems not to have extended outside the court—one significant difference from the Sanskrit cultural order in South Asia, where nonroyal records abound.[39]

The Sanskrit epigraphs produced in Java have much in common with the materials found elsewhere in the cosmopolitan world. They include *tāmraprasasti* (copperplate grants), *jayapatra* (edicts), and *praśasti* (as they often identify themselves). Many discursive features are familiar: grants record the date, the king's name and virtues, the specifications of the gift, and end with imprecations. And they transmit much of the familiar political-aesthetic idiom. An eighth-century inscription from the Malay Peninsula dramatically foregrounds the language and formal structures of Sanskrit poetry: It deploys all four principal metrical types *(samavṛtta, ardhasama-, viṣama-, jāti),* the rhetorical figures of high *kāvya* appear in profusion, and rare grammatical forms are paraded. Without invocation to any deity it begins its eulogy of King

38. V. 4: *sadmārtyavaktrakumudapravibodhanenduḥ duṣṭapravṛttitimiroṣṇakaropamānaḥ* | *satsv āgateṣv abhimukho 'vimukhaḥ khaleṣu lokeṣu nirmmalarucātulitas sukīrttyā* || (He is a moon to awaken the lotuses that are the faces of goodly men, a sun to drive away the darkness that is the behavior of the wicked. He is favorably inclined toward the good when they come before him and disinclined toward the bad. He is unmatched in the world for his fame, which sparkles brilliantly). The text is edited in Boechari 1985–86: 126–35; see generally de Casparis 1991: 46.

39. Several celebrated examples are described and translated in Pollock 1995b.

Viṣṇu[varman?] of the Śailendra lineage: He is a sun to destroy the darkness that is his foes, an autumn moon for all his brilliant royal glory, the very god of love incarnate; the moonlike fame arising from his good politics, discipline, bravery, charisma, learning, self-control, forbearance, composure, and liberality has eclipsed that of all other kings; he is the support of his own virtues and of other virtuous men. "Those whose hopes had been destroyed by the ring of flaming fire of poverty he restored to their state of well-being; as springtime is to mango trees, so the king is to the virtuous."[40]

As with the Khmer records, the Javanese Sanskrit inscriptions have certain distinctive features. Their bureaucratic jargon employs official titles, the majority of which are non-Sanskritic, suggesting a more complex negotiation between local and cosmopolitan political styles than was typical elsewhere. Harder to characterize is an aesthetic difference. Beginning with the very first records—undated memorials commemorating the footprints of a king and his elephant, including the fifth oldest, a verse inscribed on rock in praise of a near-by stream "with its clear, cool water as purifying as the Gaṅgā"—a certain local genius sets them apart. One inscription of 732 shows the standard opening (date; reference to the establishment of a *liṅgam* by the king; verses to Śiva, Brahmā, and Viṣṇu) but then offers a striking encomium *(māhātmya)* on "the incomparable island of Java *(dvīpavaraṃ yavākhyam atulam)*, rich in grain and goldmines, won by the gods with sacred mantras." We are told of a goodly king named Sanna who protected the earth according to *dharma* and ruled over his subjects affectionately as a father rules over his son. He died in course of time, and the world was helpless and grief-stricken. But there had been born from him, like another Mount Meru, a son named Sañjaya, who was the color of gold, with large arms and thighs, and tall, being "elevated by having his feet upon the [rival] kings who were the family mountains *(kulācala-)* situated on the earth." Respected by the learned, understanding the fine points of systematic thought *(śāstra)*, like Raghu he defeated numerous neighboring kings, and he now rules according to political wisdom *(nyāya)*. So long as he rules, people can sleep on the king's highway without fear of robbers; they gain *dharma, artha,* and *kāma.* "Surely the Kali Age is weeping ceaselessly, for there is no place here to take the impress of its limbs." This is nearly a textbook example of the Sanskrit *praśasti,* celebrating a universalistic political dominion, and the equally nonlocal cosmology and moral code that underwrite it. But the cadre in which this universalistic vision is embedded has a palpable, if elusive, local character.[41]

The date for the first use of Javanese in public documents for discursive

40. The Ligor Inscription (source of Coedès's discovery of the Śrīvijaya polity), is dated 775; published in Chhabra 1965: 26 ff.

41. *CIJ* vol. 1: 15 ff. (the line "like Raghu . . . " is corrupt). See p. 14 for the Gaṅgā reference and p. xix on the bureaucratic idiolect.

purposes (beyond the mere use of administrative technical terms) is 804, for the first Javanese *praśasti* 824, for the first versified literary inscription 856—thus some four centuries after the earliest Sanskrit records.[42] Thereafter, Javanese very quickly became the exclusive language of official texts; most of these are documentary and not expressive (usually recording the transfer of tax rights to religious institutions), and no major vernacular *praśasti* tradition was ever inaugurated. But around the same time, the mid-ninth century or a little later, we find an efflorescence of belles-lettres in Javanese without parallel in Southeast Asia until the rise of the Thai courtly literature of Ayutthaya. This was an entirely new literary culture—nothing indicates that a preexistent written literary tradition in Javanese had been displaced by Sanskrit—that constituted itself by completely absorbing and localizing the Sanskrit tradition (chapter 10.1). But, as in Khmer country, nothing suggests that the mastery of the cosmopolitan style, equally evident in the inscriptional *praśasti*s and in the new vernacular literature, led to the creation of a single Sanskrit text that would have been considered "literary" in accordance with prevailing local definitions.[43]

There are thus commonalities but also important and puzzling differences in the development of the new cultural-political order in the South and Southeast Asia sectors of the Sanskrit cosmopolis. Sanskrit in Java was primarily the vehicle for the enunciation of royal identification, as it was elsewhere. The Sanskrit public texts evince deep learning, and the language itself and its literary (though not always its aesthetic) features are untouched by local idiom and unaccompanied by any new noninscriptional poetry. Conversely, unlike virtually every other region where the vernacular was quickly literized under the influence of Sanskrit, Javanese was absent from public inscription for almost half a millennium. When it did come to be used for public records, it was exclusively for documentary purposes, as was the case elsewhere. But the habit of Sanskrit inscriptions more quickly became obsolete, in tandem with the emergence of a dynamic, Sanskritizing literature in Javanese—a development without parallel in Southeast Asia but stunningly similar to what is found in southern India (chapters 9, 10). Sanskrit began to die in Java the moment Javanese began to live, just as, five hundred years later in Cambodia, Khmer literature came into being only once Sanskrit has vanished.

Several points are worth restating in summation. First, it is astonishing how quickly—in hardly more than a century—the elements of a new cultural-

42. The record of 804 is published in *BEFEO* 46: 24ff. See further in chapter 8.1.

43. Cf. Sarkar 1970: 100; Zoetmulder 1974: 16. Other kinds of Sanskrit works were produced, such as *āgama* and ritual texts, though it is uncertain whether or not even these materials were imported (see in general Lévi 1933; Goudriaan and Hooykaas 1971; Nihom 1994). Sanskrit verses transmitted *pratīka*-like in Javanese texts cannot always be traced to mainland originals.

political form, a Sanskrit cosmopolitan way of political being, spread across southern Asia. No good explanations have been advanced to account for this transformation, and indeed, explanations are not ready to hand. We have seen that most of the usual factors in such large-scale change can be set aside at once. There was no event of conquest; no "Sanskrit" polity had conquered the subcontinent, let alone beyond. New universalist visions of power did arise at just this time (chapter 6.1), but none ever took on a presence real enough to effect such a transformation the way Romanization followed in the train of Roman legions (chapter 7). No religious revolution had taken place, and no new revelation was produced in Sanskrit to stimulate evangelism, nor did any transregional movement or institution even exist to propagate such a revolution, had one occurred. What transpired seems to have happened according to some cultural process of imitation and borrowing less familiar to us as causative than conquest or conversion, some impulse toward transculturation that made it sensible, even desirable, to adopt the new Sanskrit cultural-political style as an act of pure free will.

Second, the development of this style occurred at the cost of retarding or even arresting local literary traditions. An inverse relation of cultural power at some level where it intersected with political power obtained between Sanskrit and the vernaculars. When Sanskrit was superseded, it was precisely in combination with a new assertion of local literary language and local kinds of polity (chapters 9, 10). It is important to stress, however, the *literary* dimension of this asymmetry. Far from being proscribed in the documentary practices of the polity, the vernacular became obligatory, with Sanskrit increasingly and in the end completely excluded almost everywhere (north India, for complex reasons, excepted). Functioning as a language of record clearly meant functioning as an instrument of truth, and an enduring one (chapter 13.1). The actual practices of rule, too, must have always remained a matter of local speech. It is hardly an accident that we have little understanding of Sanskrit's role in the just-emerging documentary state of South Asia beyond its place in the aesthetic order. This is the case because we have no data—and we have no data because Sanskrit likely had no such role.[44]

Third, the cosmopolitan cultural gestalt generated by these transregional developments consisted of not just a shared language but a set of shared expressive practices and political representations, which points toward something like an aestheticization of power. If political will—in the form of a declaration of qualification to rule in consequence of history, identity, piety,

44. A work like the late-medieval *Lokaprakāśa* hardly proves that Sanskrit was the medium of governance in medieval Kashmir (Stein 1900, vol. 1: 130 n. 2). A remarkable set of documents from eighth-century Nepal shows that the language of record was the *deśabhāṣā,* though naturally not untouched by the Sanskrit lexicon (see Kölver and Śākya 1985, and chapter 8.1 and n. 20). The term "documentary state" is borrowed from Kivelson 1997: 640.

valor, intelligence, culture, civility, beauty, and an account of what that rule meant in terms of good works and heroic deeds—was to be expressed in a public text, it would henceforth and invariably have to be expressed in Sanskrit. To understand why this was so, we need to know something about how this expression worked.

3.2 THE SEMANTICS OF INSCRIPTIONAL DISCOURSE: THE POETICS OF POWER, MĀLAVA, 1141

It should be apparent by now how closely intertwined were the histories of *praśasti* and *kāvya*. Their beginnings as new kinds of nonliturgical, courtly, and even public language uses turn out, on sober assessment, to be more or less simultaneous. The theoretical restrictions on literary language spelled out so clearly in Sanskrit discourses on *kāvya* find their objective correlate in inscriptional practices, where the languages of Place were denied any literary function. That both *praśasti* and *kāvya* were practices located principally at political centers testifies to the consanguinity, in their structure and character, of culture and power in southern Asia in the first millennium. In addition, the expressive resources of which *praśasti* makes use corroborate its kinship with *kāvya,* for these are the sort employed when language begins to take itself seriously—that is, when it becomes literature. There are several points of disjunction, however, between the two cultural forms, and these need to be registered.

The first concerns a division of cultural labor that marked the production of inscriptional literature, and a corresponding discrepancy in the social location of the producers. Those who composed inscriptional political poetry are only rarely found to have also produced courtly literature, that is, textualized writing meant to be recited in the *sabhā,* the royal court, and to circulate thereafter among literati. The names of more than three hundred poets who composed inscriptional verses survive, but of these, it is possible to identify only a handful who are known—from their extant works, from being cited in anthologies or named elsewhere, or by their own declaration in an epigraph—to have also written literary texts. And of this handful only a very few are familiar to the literary historian: Trivikramabhaṭṭa at the court of Indrarāja III Rāṣṭrakūṭa (fl. 915), Cittapa in Bhoja's Dhārā a century later, Umāpatidhara at the Sena court in late-twelfth-century Bengal, and his contemporary Śrīpāla at the courts of Jayasiṃha and Kumārapāla in Aṇahilapāṭaka, Gujarat. Inscribed and textualized forms of literature seem to have belonged by and large to two separate social domains that rarely overlapped in the cosmopolitan epoch.[45]

45. The figures here are derived from Sternbach's collections (1980–85). Diskalkar 1961 speaks of eight hundred inscriptional poets (and he anticipates to some degree the socio-

Many authors of public poetry are clearly identifiable as men positioned in imperial service (and probably outside the literary salon), and this makes sense since they were composing texts that directly subserved the purposes of rulership. They ranged in social-political status from the least elevated clerks *(kāyastha)* to the highest officials. The latter include the *sāndhivigrahika,* the "peace and war official," who appears ubiquitously as *praśasti* writer from as early as the mid-fourth century (Hariṣeṇa at the court of the imperial Guptas); the *senāpati,* "master of the army," of the sort who composed an Angkor record of 1002; and royalty themselves, such as the Khmer princes Sūryakumāra and Vīrakumāra mentioned earlier.[46]

An equally curious fact about this political poetry is that, despite its profusion and its pervasion of the Indian cultural sphere—more correctly, its role in the creation of that sphere—the theoreticians of Sanskrit literature ignore it completely. *Praśasti* is never discussed in analyses of literary art in general or genre in particular, with two minor exceptions. Unsympathetic modern readers, who have judged inscriptional poets to be simple "versifiers" devoid of poetic inspiration and their verse to lack any literary merit, would argue that this theoretical neglect is further evidence that no one considered public poetry to be poetry at all—no one, perhaps, except the writers themselves.[47] We find them claiming literary status almost from the beginning of the Sanskrit cosmopolitan epoch, with Hariṣeṇa, who calls his Allahabad Pillar Inscription a *kāvya.* And it continues, from the Tāḷagunda Inscription (c. 455–470) of the Kadambas in today's Karnataka:

> In deference to the command of King Śāntivarman
> Kubja has written this, his own *kāvya,*
> upon the face of this rock,

to the Gwalior record of the Gurjara Pratīhāras of the mid-ninth century:

---

cultural distinction I draw here, though contrast his statement in 1960: 548). A very different relationship between inscriptional and textual literary production obtained in vernacular India (for Kannada examples see chapter 9).

46. For *kāyasthas* see e.g. *EI* 11: 20–25 (1128) or *EI* 12: 44–47 (c. 1350); for *sāndhivigrahikas,* e.g., *CII* 3: 204 (c. 375), *EI* 20: 105 (c. 1475). (A definition of the post of *sandhivigrahin* is given in the *Yaśastilakacampū* 3.250: "He reads out [documents], writes them, produces poetry [i.e., *praśasti*], interprets all scripts and languages, is adept at gauging the king's own standing and that of the enemy, a man of real talent.") The Angkor record of 1002 is printed in *IdC* V: 239.

47. E.g., Sternbach 1980, vol. 1: xxx. The *alaṅkāra* silence is broken only by Namisādhu (fl. 1069), who gives a definition in passing ("a *praśasti* is the description of a king's family on behalf of their glory *[yaśortham]*" on Rudraṭa's *Kāvyālaṅkāra* 16.36); Viśvanātha defines the *v[b]irudam* ("a praise poem for a king composed in verse and prose," *Sāhityadarpaṇa* 6.337) but has nothing further to say on the matter. In Java, the word "poet" is never found in inscriptions, which suggests to Zoetmulder that literature was not considered a "professional craft" in medieval Java (1974: 126–27).

Bālāditya, the single son of Bhaṭṭadhana . . .
who stands before King Bhojadeva like his own inner wisdom
[made manifest],
is the poet of this *praśasti,* which will last,
no less than the earth itself, to the end of the cosmic age;

and the Bilpaṅk epigraph of Śrīpāla in 1141:

Śrīpāla, emperor of poets and adopted kin
of King Siddharāja . . .
composed this superb *praśasti.*

As one late and anonymous *praśasti* writer said of his own verse, "This will be a source of inspiration for poets who [in future times] will read it"—and in fact many *praśasti*s continued to be read.[48]

Whatever may have been the sociological distance between inscriptional and textual poets, and whatever the conceptual distance between their productions in the minds of schoolmen, the writers of public records believed that what they were doing at least in part was creating poetry. The new and highly distinctive genre they developed, which found such great resonance across southern Asia, is striking in several respects. First, it fully exploits the aesthetic resources and expressive possibilities of the Sanskrit language. Second, it is the aesthetic dimension that constitutes the core purpose of the *praśasti,* often to the subordination or even exclusion of all other concerns—and to the incomprehension and irritation of fact-finding historians. Third, the genre and its aesthetic functions were restricted to Sanskrit, which enabled the *praśasti* writer to say and write things that were not yet sayable or at least not yet inscribable in any of the other languages of southern Asia. Sanskrit alone was authorized for figures of sense—of simile, metaphor, and a host of others but above all *śleṣa,* the capacity to express two significations simultaneously, which is one of the grandeurs of *praśasti* style and a unique achievement of Sanskrit culture, and yet another source of despair for those seeking to extract the historical kernel from the apparently dry husk of figuration (as also for translators, who have no choice but to do their work twice). Sanskrit alone was authorized for figures of sound, and, more important, for complex meters, which were one of the great cultural exports of Indian antiquity—"marvelous sounds," the early Chinese translators called them, searching for some way to describe a phenomenon absent in their own literature.[49] These semantic and phonic capacities radically separated the object of Sanskrit political discourse from the world of the everyday. This was

48. The texts are, respectively, from *CII* 3: 215; *EI* 8: 36, 18: 110, 40: 29; and *A Collection of Prakrit and Sanskrit Inscriptions [of Kattywar, etc.]* p. 87, v. 61. Evidence for the continued reading of epigraphs is discussed in chapters 3.3 and 6.2.

49. Mair and Mei 1991: 386–87.

so in part because the everyday world did not contain figures of sense and sound except randomly and below the threshold of intentional creation, but also because the everyday world was one of freehold conditions, tax exemptions, and other matters for which local language was the vehicle. It was no place for Sanskrit's unique communicative functions—interpretative complexity, ambiguity, polysemy, imagination, deep play, enchantment. It was these functions that were called upon to shape the expression of power, however surprising that might seem to the reader used to the prosaic discourse of present-day politics.

The domain of inscriptional aesthetics is thus effectively coextensive with the domain of Sanskrit literature, and any attempt to inventory the full range of literary resources deployed would mean writing a description of Sanskrit literariness as such. A more modest goal, and adequate to the purpose here, is to examine some of the expressive resources available to the *praśasti* poet and try to understand how these were put to use. A brief review of some representative if eclectically chosen materials are followed by a close look at one complete *praśasti* from twelfth-century Gujarat, a place and time of the Sanskrit cosmopolis of interest in other discussions in this book.

What impresses the contemporary reader most consistently and forcefully about the *praśasti* genre is the studied use of language per se. This is discourse on the political, after all, and it is meant to communicate some vision of power. But while political rhetoric has been both a practice and an object of study in the West from the time of the Sophists, nothing quite prepares us for what we find here. If as a genre *praśasti* can be said to be about anything, it is as much about exploring the capacities of the Sanskrit language for the production of praise as about the content of the praise itself. In the first instance, these capacities are tropological, since it is the system of figures of sense that constitutes Sanskrit literariness in its most elemental form (the very discipline of literary theory, *alaṅkāraśāstra,* draws its name from it). The entire range of figures accordingly finds application in inscriptions. But if these figures do seem in the first instance to turn language itself into an object for reflection, it is important to see that at the same time they are making new and compelling arguments about the nature of the political power that is their ultimate referent.

Notice first the simple simile *(upamā)*. Among the oldest Sanskrit inscriptions of Laos is one dating from the late fifth century, engraved on a ceremonial stele atop a sacred mountain west of the Mekong River. It was issued by one Devānīka (Army of the Gods), probably a Cham ruler, on the occasion of his inaugurating a reservoir named New Kurukṣetra. The record is composed in complex art-prose:

> He was anointed in the kingship by the grace of Śaṅkara, Nārāyaṇa, Pitāmaha [i.e., Śiva, Viṣṇu, and Brahmā] and the other gods. All of his deeds are infused

> with the good and beneficent efficacy acquired in his former births, and they transcend the human. He is like Yudhiṣṭhira in his dedication to the *dharma* of the good; like the king of the gods [Indra], in protecting his subjects; like Dhanaṃjaya [Arjuna] in conquering his foes; like Indradyumna in the number of sacrifices he has performed; like Śibi in the gifting of the great gifts; in his devotion to Brahmans like one who observes Brahmanical devotion to the blessed Great Being; like Kanakapāṇḍya in his adherence to political prudence; like the ocean in profundity, like Mount Meru in constancy.[50]

For the poet and his audience, what is evidently of principal importance about the career of Devānīka—we might even say, what is of actual *historical* importance—is not his defeat of the armies of Funan and the massive expansion of Champa power this victory appears to have made possible. Rather, it is the king's qualities of righteousness, guardianship, martial valor, piety, generosity, reverence, political wisdom, and emotional and moral distinction. Contemplated in themselves, such virtues are pure abstractions; it is only the narratives in which they are embodied that can bring them to life in the imagination. Hence the simile (technically a "garland of similes," *mālopamā*) that seeks to make Devānīka's grandeur comprehensible by comparing him with the celebrated heroes of the *Mahābhārata* and other lore.

This sort of figuration is ubiquitous in *praśasti* discourse, so much so that it sometimes seems to constitute the very heart of its purpose. When a seventh-century poet in Khmer country uses a poetic fantasy *(utprekṣā)* to represent a king as God's experiment in the totalization of virtue—"As if wanting to make available to view all the virtues of kings brought together in a single place, the Creator made this singular being on earth, King Rudravarman"—the king's unique qualification for rulership finds its formal correlate, in some sense even grounds its reality, in the capacity of *kāvya* for making that claim by means of troped language.[51] Similarly, when a poet in Mandasor (western Madhya Pradesh) in 530 uses a complex kind of metaphor to describe the historic defeat of the Hūṇa king Mihirakūla by King Yaśodharman:

> He who never suffered the indignity
> of bowing to anyone but Śiva; and who,
> because he was the one who held them by force,
> gave the Himālayas the reputation of being impassable—
> even he, Mihirakūla, was made to worship
> the feet of this king by the power of his arms,
> with offerings of flowers that fell from the crown
> of his head as he bent low, in pain,
> to do obeisance,

50. *BEFEO* 1956: 209 ff. "Kanakapāṇḍya" is obscure. See chapter 6.2 on the "New Kurukṣetra."
51. Sircar 1965–83, vol. 1: 513, v. 3.

it is as if the event has importance only to the degree it affords figures for a poetry of power.[52]

Other forms of rhetoric more complicated than simile, metaphor, and their congeners were developed for capturing more complex dimensions of power. How a more intimately fused kind of identification is rendered through the figure of *śleṣa* can be illustrated in a sequence of verses from a Pāla record of the early tenth century issued in the name of Nārāyaṇapāla (on the occasion of his granting a tax-free village to a group of Pāśupata Śaiva masters). The record includes descriptions of his ancestors, whose identity with various transcendent beings is communicated by one and the same string of words with two different meanings (something impossible to translate by a single word in English; thus "in the one . . . in the other"):

> May the leader of the world—He of Ten Powers [i.e., the Buddha], and King Gopāladeva—be ever victorious! With heart delighted by (in the one case) the Jewel of Compassion, (in the other) the most splendid gems *(kāruṇyaratna-),* the one showed amiable amity *(maitrī),* the other ever kept company with his beloved (queen) Maitrī. The filth of ignorance was washed away in the one by the clear waters of the stream of transcendent wisdom, in the other, by the stream of knowledge that informed him of (political) propriety *(samyaksambodhividyā).* The one overcame the assaults of Māra's servants, the other, the assaults of the lawless *(kāmakārin-),* and thereby the one gained everlasting quiescence, the other, continuous civil peace *(śānti).*
>
> From [Vākpāla] was born the victorious Jayapāla, who purified the earth with the very deeds of Upendra [the "younger brother of Indra," i.e., Viṣṇu]: He destroyed in battle the enemies of moral order [or, in the case of Indra, the enemies of Vedic sacrifice, *dharma*], and thereby brought the joys of world power *(bhuvanarājya)* to his elder brother Devapāla [King of the Gods, i.e., Indra].[53]

Here the unique expressive capabilities of Sanskrit poetry allow the poet to make statements about political power that could be made in no other way. Although it is possible, through punning, homonyms, and the like, to effect a *śleṣa* in any language, in Sanskrit it is elevated to an unparalleled high art form. Moreover, the history of this form suggests close, even constitutive, connections to the Sanskrit political sphere. Sustained use of bitextual poetry does not predate the Gupta period, when the Sanskrit cosmopolitan style crystallized; it was perfected by the poet Bāṇa at the mid-seventh-century court of Harṣavardhana of Kānyakubja, and from there—no doubt through the circulation of Bāṇa's *Harṣacarita* itself—was transmitted across the entire cosmopolitan space, profoundly influencing the way power enunciated

52. Sircar 1965–83, vol. 1: 419–20, v. 6.

53. *IA* 1886: 305–6 (generally following Hultzsch). Similar *śleṣa* verses open other Pāla grants, cf. e.g., Kielhorn in *EI* 4: 251 n.

itself in public.[54] In the instance before us, *śleṣa* induces, indeed compels, us to understand that the founder of the new spiritual order, the Buddha, and the founder of the Pāla dynasty and its new political order, Gopāladeva, are at once identical—the very stuff of language reveals their identity—and yet separate and different. Both achieved knowledge, but knowledge of different sorts, leading to different ends. Both made conquests, but again they were different: in the one case, conquest over the internal enemy, Desire, that lies at the root of rebirth; in the other, conquest over the external enemies of the polity. Both achieved peace, if different sorts of peace appropriate to their different spheres of action. The homology supplied by the substance of the Sanskrit language, whose words were thought to correspond by nature with their referents (the link is *autpattika,* "natural," chapter 1.1), allows us to grasp the transcendent Buddha and the terrestrial king together in a single cognitive moment—and yet keep them ontologically apart. The second verse even more clearly articulates the equivalence-with-difference of the human and superhuman realms: The younger prince secures *dharma,* as does the god Viṣṇu—the god with respect to *dharma*'s more archaic signification of Vedic sacrifice, the prince in the now-usual sense of the term as the generalized moral order. By protecting this order, the prince makes it possible for his elder brother (whose name, Devapāla, means Protector of the Gods) to achieve an unbounded sovereignty that constitutes the earthly analogue to the cosmic sovereignty Viṣṇu secures for *his* elder brother, Indra, Lord of the Gods. It is the power of the Sanskrit language in and of itself that permits this particular conception of political power—as an indissolubly interlocking of realms and persons—to come to expression.

To focus on figuration is obviously not to deny that inscriptional poets had other discursive objectives, including a factual referentiality that would be entirely familiar to a present-day reader. But what becomes abundantly clear by looking even randomly through the corpus of public poetry is that these other objectives were readily, even intentionally, downplayed in favor of an altogether different kind of expressive modality. What power does, however momentous—defeating a Hun king, for example—seems far less important than how power speaks; the particular exists only as vehicle, or occasion, or excuse, for the paradigmatic. The following verses, from a mid-ninth-century record of the Gurjara Pratīhāra overlord Bhoja are entirely typical of inscriptional poetry:

From [Vatsarāja] was born a son of great fame named Nāgabhaṭa—
it was said he was the Primal Being *(puruṣa)* himself who had been reborn.

54. On the history and character of *śleṣa* poetry see the definitive work of Bronner 1999; for an account of its role in the sculptural program of the Pallavas, Rabe 1997. The appeal of *śleṣa* for Khmer poets is massively in evidence in later inscriptions, e.g. *IdC* vol. 5: 244 ff.

And into this man's brilliance, like that of the divine Kumāra,
fell, mothlike, the kings of Āndhra, Sindh, Vidarbha, Kaliṅga.

Eager to ensure that good deeds founded upon the Vedas would flourish,
he collected taxes in accordance with Kshatriya law. And conquering
Cakrāyudha, who had made his base nature plain
by resorting to the enemy, he became eminent while remaining modest.

Other inscriptions offer information about the target of Nāgabhaṭa's conquest, Cakrāyudha, ruler of Kānyakubja. Were this not the case, the factual sense of the passage would be irrecoverable, since it is inseparable from, and ultimately and magically absorbed in, a mythic double-text concerning the Dwarf incarnation: the god Viṣṇu defeats the demon lord Bali by taking on the deceptive form of the Vāmana and then, as Trivikrama, God of Three Strides, expanding to encompass the universe. This deep text would have led the reader to understand another meaning for the second verse:

> He [could have] effected the binding of Bali by the brilliance of Kshatriya power, and thereby have far surpassed [Viṣṇu himself,] the God Armed with the Discus *(cakrāyudha)*, who had taken on a lowly stature [the Dwarf incarnation] in resorting to the foe [i.e., Bali], while he himself remained bowed [only] in modesty [unlike Viṣṇu's Trivikrama form].

And indeed, given that Nāgabhaṭa is himself represented as the Primal Being, it is by no means clear which constitutes the primary *(prakṛta, prastuta)* and which the secondary *(aprakṛta, aprastuta)* level of meaning here. One thing is not in doubt, however: the absorption of Kānyakubja into the Gurjara Pratīhāra sphere of power, however important a historical fact, is not the sole or even the primary referent in the mind of the writer.[55]

How such features of the rhetoric of power shaped political-historical discourse is visible throughout the corpus of inscriptions composed for Yaśovarman I. He was a principal figure in the formation of the new Angkor political order in the late ninth century, constructing the grand reservoir of Eastern Beray and the foundations of Yaśodharapura—with the hill of Phnom Bakheng, described as a new Mount Meru, at its center—which was to re-

55. Sircar 1965–83, vol. 2: 244, vv. 8–9; in the Sanskrit v. 9 runs as follows: *trayyāspadasya sukṛtasya samṛddhim icchur yaḥ kṣatradhāmavidhibaddhabaliprabandhaḥ* | *jitvā parāśrayakṛtasphuṭanīcabhāvaṃ cakrāyudhaṃ vinayanamravapur vyarājat* ||. That the factual can be wholly obscured by the mythic is shown in the "letterhead" of Vikramāditya VI issued from 1077–1123 (*EI* 12: 278 lines 88 ff. = 12: 153 lines 51 ff. etc.). In the *śleṣa* verse 50 ("This Cāḷukya-Rāma went off to search for the daughter of Janaka—his own beloved noble royalty—along with his brother, the son of Sumitrā, and accompanied by an army of monkeys. And at the seashore, from fear of the Many-Headed, came the king of Drāviḍa, dwelling place of the royalty belonging to Vibhīṣaṇa, who bowed low before him"), the mythic meaning has for us entirely occluded the factual except for the few obvious correlations, e.g., that a Cōḻa king declared himself to be Vikramāditya's vassal during some expedition to the south.

main the Khmer capital for the next half millennium. The preeminent concern of Yaśovarman's inscriptions, however, is not with the unique particulars of his exercise of power but with the general qualities of his kingliness. The Sanskrit rhetorical figures everywhere in use here, from simple simile, metaphor *(rūpaka)*, and hyperbole *(atiśayokti)* to more complex tropes such as apparent contradiction *(virodhābhāsa)* and inverted causality *(viṣama)*, not only represent this kingliness but in some sense actually create it.

In the first record of his reign, the contrarieties that kingliness comprises, which make it unlike anything in the quotidian world, can only be expressed by poetic contradiction: It is by bowing low and placing their heads on Yaśovarman's feet that vassal kings seek to raise themselves to eminent heights. The king, though apparently a singular being, is actually a multiple entity, for to wise men he is a guru; to women he is Kāma, god of love; to vassals he is the great king. He is at once skilled in battle and as handsome as the love god. His deeds make him equal to or even better than the gods: with his *dharma* ever increasing he uplifts the earth, and *adharma,* as if displaced by Viṣṇu, flees to the horizons; the Creator, thinking he has made another Śiva, is amazed at his own creation. In Yaśovarman's second inscription, the great majority of verses actually communicate nothing in particular except this poetry of power: Śrī, the goddess of royalty, may be generally fickle but never leaves Yaśovarman; Fate never obstructs his steps, for it is too afraid of him; his profundity must exceed even the ocean's since it is to the ocean that his enemies flee from him; he excels Kāma; he is like nothing so much as the Creator; he is a second Manu in very person. His intelligence and grandeur can be inferred from the fact that two divinities who never share the same dwelling—Lakṣmī, goddess of royalty and wealth, and Bhāratī, goddess of learning—both have taken up residence in him.[56] Such is the tenor of the public discourse of the man now regarded as Angkor's founder. He reigned for two decades, but his inscriptions are uninterested—not incapable, but uninterested—in telling us anything of a banal factual nature about this period. They have some other truth to establish, one that lies precisely in subordinating the constatation of local information to the imagination of the quasi-universal ideal, in the same way as the use of local language (here, Khmer) for the particulars of the grants was subordinated to the quasi-universal code of Sanskrit. The paradigmatic is the abstraction from the particular that enables fame to be eternal, and, given the ideology of its absolute

56. For Yaśovarman's first record, [Śaka Saṃvat] 811 (889 C.E.) marking the year of his accession, see *IK:* 74 ff., vv. 16, 17, 20, 24, 26; for his second record, *IK:* 81 ff., vv. 29–31, 33–35. The verse on Lakṣmī and Bhāratī is v. 3 from an undated inscription edited in *IdC* vol. 5: 92. On Yaśovarman's career in general see Coedès 1968: 111 ff., and Mabbett and Chandler 1995: 97–99 on his status as founder of Angkor.

unchangeability, Sanskrit is the one language in which the expression of eternal fame could remain eternal.

It is fame that forms the principle concern of *praśasti* discourse, and fame constitutes a core value of kingliness. There is no reason to doubt the sincerity of the Cāḷukya lord Pulakeśin II in 630, when he spoke, as many kings spoke, of "observing that the realm of transmigration has as little value as a reed, a bamboo shaft, a plantain tree; knowing that sense objects are as transient as the waves on the ocean, and that life itself is as impermanent as a water current trickling down the slope from the peak of a mountain"; while conversely "realizing that fame, gleaming like the autumn moon, has great rewards and is as permanent as the great elements, or atoms."[57]

The quest for fame found a material correlate in the victory pillar or stele upon which so much public poetry was engraved. In some ways the most magnificent of these is the very first (after Aśoka's *dharma*-monuments), the Allahabad Pillar of the second Gupta overlord, Samudragupta, the first major Sanskrit *praśasti* preserved to us after Rudradāman's some two centuries earlier. It stands as a wonder in stone—some thirty-five feet high—like the wonder in words that it bears; it presents a visual eulogy in its own right, to which the *praśasti* engraved upon it in fact refers. At the same time, it places the king's fame in the quasi-global context that the Sanskrit cultural order imagined for itself:

> This column is like an upraised arm of the earth pointing out [the way for] the fame of Samudragupta. For having pervaded the whole world by the great success obtained from his conquest of all the earth, it now has acquired a graceful, easy step for going hence to the abode of the Lord of the Thirty Gods.
>
> By his generosity, military prowess, tranquility, and command of the *śāstra*s
> his glory mounts on high, up and up, by this path and that,
> and purifies the three worlds like the white water of the Gaṅgā
> rushing down
> when released from the matted locks of Śiva, Lord of Beasts
> (Paśupati), that hold it in check.

The pillar "points out" the fame of Samudragupta by both its very presence and the *praśasti* that it bears, and it both physically and communicatively "points" fame's way toward heaven, where it will exist eternally, now that it has exhausted all the space available on earth. The comparison to the brilliant white Gaṅgā—fame is invariably white by poetic convention—hides a slight but telling inverted simile *(vyatirekālaṅkāra),* where the rank of the figure's source and target is reversed: the holy river, freed from the hair of Śiva, can only flow down to earth, whereas Samudragupta's glory, liberated

57. *EI* 27: 40, lines 24ff.

by his great deeds, ascends from the terrestrial domain and flows upward to heaven.[58]

The range of literary resources and thematics employed in the public poetry of the Sanskrit cosmopolis can best be indicated by looking at a single complete example in detail. A recently published inscription serves this purpose well on several counts. Dated 1141, it commemorates the restoration of a temple in Bilpaṅk, western Madhya Pradesh, dedicated to Virūpākṣa, the "Three-Eyed God" Śiva, on the part of Jayasiṃha Siddharāja, a Caulukya king who ruled in Gujarat in the early twelfth century (1093–1143). We have a second *praśasti* from Vaḍnagar (near ancient Valabhī) in Gujarat (1151) by the same poet, Śrīpāla (a textual as well inscriptional writer, whose poems however have been lost), and it is rare that multiple records of a single writer have been preserved.[59] Juxtaposing the two offers some insight into the competing claims of the aesthetic and typological over against the factual and historical in the creation of political poetry. The pragmatics of inscriptional discourse, or the effective power of poetry, is a complex question that will occupy us in the following section (3), and this text provides a good transition. The Caulukya lineage of Gujarat, in addition, was one of several that sought to share in the charismatic name of the Cāḷukya dynasty of Bādāmi, whose inscriptions are likewise examined in section 3. And last, twelfth-century Gujarat will be of interest to us in other contexts, especially in considering the history of political and grammatical correctness (chapter 4.2). The linkage between polity and grammar was one the most rulers acknowledged to some degree, though few strove so publicly as Jayasiṃha to actualize it. (See appendix A.3 for the translation.)

A central concern for many writers, as well as subjects, of *praśasti* almost from the beginning of inscriptional discourse (Aśoka and Rudradāman notably excepted) was to establish a truth of genealogy. For the Kalyāṇa Cāḷukyas of eleventh- and twelfth-century Karnataka, for example, we will see that promulgating a deep history of succession was an objective of demon-

58. *CII* 3: 203 ff. *ācakṣāṇa-:* "pointing," that is, directing his fame, as well as "pointing it out" (not, as per published translations, just "proclaiming" it). "Having pervaded . . . ": *sarvapṛthivīvijayajanitodayāvāptanikhilāvanītalam.* In the Mandasor *praśasti* of Yaśodharman, the conjunction of the rhetorical and physical embodiments of fame and their being eternalized by the praise-poem ("As if . . . to point the way to heaven above for the fame he has won by his own good deeds, this pillar has been erected by Yaśodharman . . . to last till the end of time," Sircar 1965–83, vol. 1: 420, v. 7) is so similar to the Allahabad Pillar Inscription that the poet may have read it (something not at all unlikely, see section 3).

59. E.g., the Vāsula who composed the Mandasor Inscription of Yaśodharman also wrote the Rīsthal Inscription (see Salomon 1989b); two inscriptions each of late-twelfth-century Kālacūri poets named Kumārapāla and Pṛthvīdhāra are known, and two of Sabhāpati II of Vijayanagara (Sternbach 1980, vol. 1 and 3 respectively s.v.); Nārāyaṇa Kavi wrote several *praśastis* of Rājendra Cōḷa (see Nagaswamy 1987: 11). For the Vaḍnagar *praśasti* see *EI* 1: 296 ff.

strably central importance (section 3 below). Yet Śrīpāla had only a very general interest in the matter, even treating it cavalierly. The Bilpaṅk version actually reverses the succession of two earlier kings, Vallabharāja and Durlabharāja, as transmitted in other, older texts and in the Vaḍnagar inscription, while including Nāgarāja, who is omitted altogether in Vaḍnagar. The same apparent indifference holds for historical factuality. Setting the record straight is a second major task of many *praśasti*s; the inscriptions of the Bādāmi Cāḷukyas of sixth- and seventh-century Karnataka to be examined shortly offer notable instances. Śrīpāla, however, omits most of the hard data of the Caulukya past; even the limited gestures toward the historically specific in the Vaḍnagar *praśasti* are absent. In the Vaḍnagar text, Mūlarāja is represented as seizing power from the then-ruling Cāpotkaṭa princes, the act that established the Caulukya dynasty in Gujarat; Cāmuṇḍarāja is credited with a victory against Sindh, Vallabharāja against Mālava, Durlabharāja against Lāṭa. All of that is lacking here, or is telescoped into the reign of Bhīma I. The only robust specificity concerns the poet's patron, Jayasiṃha himself (vv. 22 ff.)

The genealogical, like most other matters of fact, is manifestly of secondary importance to Śrīpāla. His objective is to give voice to what is enduring and charismatic about kingly power, and therefore to what is typological and paradigmatic and tied to no particular historical instantiation. The feat of destroying the Kali Age, with which Nāgarāja is credited in v. 10 here, is attributed to Karṇadeva in the Vaḍnagar record (v. 10); the sentiment expressed in reference to Cāmuṇḍarāja in v. 7 is assigned to Durlabharāja in the later record (v. 8: "Although expert in love he was unattainable to the wives of his enemies"); even the presumably nonfungible fact of divine incarnation in v. 15 here is transferred in the Vaḍnagar text to Jayasiṃha's successor, Kumārapāla (v. 14: "Because of his power his people recognized that he was Hari [i.e., Viṣṇu] descended from [heaven]"). All such traits can be distributed quite arbitrarily among the Caulukya rulers because they are traits of kingliness as such, out of time and out of place.

What Śrīpāla wants to communicate, and what he uses all the language resources at his command to communicate, is, first, the sheer power of a dynasty "that has set its foot upon this world" (v. 4). All other kings bow before them, polishing the Caulukyas' footstools with their turbans (v. 6). Other kings retreat in fear, abandoning their glorious palaces to the vermin (v. 9) as their queens flee to the forest, with nothing to adorn them ever again but wild red berries (v. 16). In order to win their subjects' loyalty (v. 12) kings do not just project military power, they also build temples and tender gifts to Brahmans, poets, and others (v. 20). Second, the poet wants to show that the philanthropy, the building projects, the battles, and the exaltation—practices familiar to us from across the landscape of the Sanskrit *praśasti*—are in the service of that single, overriding, even transcendent value: fame.

The pearl necklaces the king gifts to Brahmans become the white teeth in the broad smile of his fame (v. 20), the bleached bones of dead enemies are heaps of his brilliant white renown (v. 11). The conquered kings themselves, like so much stone quarried from their kingdoms and returned to them in transformed shape—the "uprooting and restoring" of kings being a thousand-year-old trope of imperial vassalage (see chapter 6.2)—are made into living pillars of glory proclaiming the universal power of Caulukya kingship (v. 19): the scars on their arms from wounds left by the king's sword are the lettering of his fame inscribed with perfect legibility, like the letters, "clear and distinct," that Gaṅgādhara the scribe has used to engrave the very inscription we are reading (v. 30).

Fame may be the product of concrete practices, but it is not something that exists concretely, like a temple or a victory pillar. It remains amorphous until embodied in some language; it remains unintelligible unless that language can speak in the figures of speech that explain to us the otherwise inexplicable; and it remains transient—which fame cannot be if it is true fame—if that language itself is transient. What fame requires, therefore, is a literary language of the gods. Let us be clear, too, about one additional fact: However much we may be inclined to abstract such an aesthetic of power from the workings and self-understanding of actual power, a *praśasti* like Śrīpāla's is the very expression of official culture. It is "at the behest of the king" himself that the text is engraved. Such works are as close as we can ever come to the public image rulers sought to have promulgated across the polity at large, and perhaps as clear a self-representation as ever occurred.

Trying to make sense of what inscriptional discourse aimed to achieve in the realm of meaning is especially important because that aim has long struck Western readers as odd in the extreme. This was the way power spoke at every royal court for a millennium or more all across the Sanskrit cosmopolis, and it spoke this way not because other discursive options, like the factual-referential or the vernacular, were unavailable but because they were thought to be unsuitable in many contexts. As announced by the very form of the *praśasti,* which became increasingly complex and learned over time—recall how the influence of such masters of *śleṣa* as Bāṇa grew over the centuries (and indeed, with equal vigor in the Deccan and Cambodia)—its preeminent goal was to make the real superreal, so to speak, by coding reality in the apparent impossibilities of poetic figuration. Since Sanskrit was used to enhance reality, it was excluded from expressing the everyday wherever in southern Asia the inchoate processes of vernacularization made local languages available. It was in those languages that the quotidian content of inscriptional discourse—which calls for the univocal and unequivocal, the very opposite of the polyvocal and equivocal style of figurative language—would come to be expressed. In southern Asia, therefore, the workly aspect of discourse was set off from the documentary by hard, unmistakable boundaries in a way altogether unknown in the theory or practice of modern European textuality. The different codes that Sanskrit public poets used, increasingly over time, to keep separate these two aspects were meant to bear distinct but related truths operative for related but distinctive worlds.

Viewed from this angle, the expressive and performative functions of the inscriptions must be seen to be as important as the informational and constative. This has not often been recognized, however. The skilled French philologists, for example, who edited the Southeast Asian Sanskrit inscriptions never ceased to complain of the sheer inanity of *praśasti* texts. "As poor in facts as they are rich in matters devoid of interest," "interminable panegyric," "virtually empty of historical materials," "the usual mythological bombast"—such are the cries of exasperation that recur whenever the epigraphical remains of Khmer country are discussed, and it would be easy to find parallels for India. While comments such as these paint a very misleading picture for much of the inscriptional record in Southeast as well as South Asia, it is unarguably the case that the concerns of the writers of public poetry were entirely different from those of their modern readers. What is arguable is why their concerns should be of no concern—or be empty or interminable or bombastic—to us. Poets took care beyond imagining to compose the great Cambodian Sanskrit inscriptions, the 218 complex *śleṣa* verses of Mebon, and the 198 verses of Pre Rup—indeed, to compose them so they fit the dimensions of a preselected stone surface—engrave them and prominently display them in temple or palace precincts. What other evidence do we need to take these poems seriously as cultural statements of significance?[60]

What, furthermore, are the facts and historical materials of which these texts are said to be devoid? If we assess them by the values of the conceptual scheme within which they were produced, the most important element is their very refusal of historical fact, since they seek to lift the lord they celebrate out of the flux of time and emancipate him from the constraints of place. We begin to understand them more richly the moment we begin to take their textuality as seriously as their composers did. Thus when we are told that "the veneer of Indian literary allusions in [Cambodian] inscriptions is no more than a metaphorizing of their situations and heroes and a comment on the quality of their scribes' education," we should ask: since when did metaphors lose their power or the education of the powerful become devoid of sociocultural significance?[61] Actually creating the fame and virtue of the king through a celebration of his virtue and fame—a textbook case of how to do things with words—is in great part what this textuality is meant to do; the metaphors of the texts were metaphors people lived by,

60. Finot in *BEFEO* 25: 289 and 309; Coedès in *IdC* vol. 5: 245 and 1968: xx. For the inference of the priority of stone to text, see Jacques 1991: 7–8.

61. Wolters 1979: 440.

and the education and cultural virtuosity they evince constituted a whole way of being.

Given the highly aestheticized, nonquotidian, even nonmundane uses of Sanskrit political discourse, it might be assumed that its concerns were not in fact political, or even (an argument noted earlier) that Sanskrit never did emerge entirely from its original archaic sphere of the numinous but simply extended that sphere to incorporate larger areas of social life. Such assumptions would be erroneous. Aesthetic objectives may have predominated, but this does not mean that those objectives were not political or that inscriptional discourse did not also advance claims about very concrete realities: territory, succession, royal prerogatives, or actual relations of political dominance. Indeed, these were often advanced, and with grave earnestness. Sanskrit *praśasti* discourse may have been expressive to its core, but what it expressed was, to its core, central to the domain of power.

3.3 THE PRAGMATICS OF INSCRIPTIONAL DISCOURSE: MAKING HISTORY, KALĀYṆA, 1008

The work of power in the Sanskrit *praśasti* was in part the work of the expressive and performative, executed by drawing on Sanskrit *kāvya*'s rich repertoire of formal and rhetorical devices to create and preserve the fame of the king. Yet dominant as this objective was, Sanskrit inscriptional discourse could have a decidedly pragmatic character as well. By this is meant not the straightforward materiality of the land boundaries or tax remissions that such records were primarily intended to specify or award: it was local language, not Sanskrit, that increasingly came to be used for such expression. The pragmatics of Sanskrit inscriptional discourse concerned the constitution of real-world power through, for example, asserting claims to rank or status. Reading the *praśasti* genre as a semantic order may not have prepared us for such purposes, but they were critically important to the epigraphic project across southern Asia.

By way of preface to a case study, let us consider again the records of Angkor. As we have seen, some readers, partly because of their understanding of the inscriptional discourse itself and partly because of their puzzlement over the communicative scope of Sanskrit in Cambodia, have taken these texts as purely metaphysical, messages directed to the gods alone. A set of one family's Sanskrit inscriptions from the period of Sūryavarman I (r. 1002–50), however, shows how mistaken this view is, for in these inscriptions it is possible to perceive real contestation over position and status within the Angkor bureaucracy. According to one recent assessment these texts are "historical genealogical inscriptions set up by hereditary official families for the purpose of recording their claims to property and rank throughout the previous two hundred years." The families in question "were intensely preoccupied with their prerogatives" and used any pretext, however trivial, to erect stele to establish their formal claims by listing the family's wealth.[62] That such epigraphs were considerably more than prayerful messages to the deities—that their messages (in this case, challenges to rival elites) were communicated to human beings and meant to be taken seriously—is further suggested by the repetition of the same record in various scripts on the same stele and by the painstaking care with which steles were sometimes faked.[63] That texts serving directly instrumental ends should have been composed in Sanskrit sharpens questions, already broached in the review of inscriptional semantics, about literacy, audiences, communication—and indeed the very status of belief in the power of public textuality as such to make these kinds of declarations.

It would be easy to adduce from all across the Sanskrit world instances of such promptings of power, intended to expand or emend the record of military conquest, for example, or to establish the history and status of family service (all of course local issues, the cosmopolitan idiom notwithstanding). But instead of exemplifying these in the eclectic manner suitable to a discussion of *praśasti* semantics, the specific and often highly local contests at issue in *praśasti* pragmatics call for the analysis of a single inscriptional corpus. Especially illuminating are the records of the Cāḷukyas of the Deccan. From the middle of the sixth century to perhaps as late as the seventeenth, families identifying themselves by this name or one of its many variants[64] ruled in the Indian subcontinent—from Veṅgi in coastal Andhra Pradesh and Vēmulavāḍa inland, westward to the royal complex of Bādāmi, Aihoḷe, and Paṭṭadakal in north-central Karnataka and Kalyāṇa (today's Bāsavakalyān, near Gulbarga and Bidar), and north to Aṇahilapāṭaka in Gujarat. Whether all the rulers who called themselves Cāḷukya were actually related, and if not, why they wished to be seen as related, are difficult questions, and answering them definitively would be a challenge linguistically, bibliographically, and historiographically: Records were issued not only in Sanskrit but also, with the onset of vernacularization after about 1000, in Kannada, Telugu, and Marathi (though curiously never in Gujarati). These are widely dispersed in the epigraphical literature, and countless documents from the later period remain unpublished. Moreover, distinguishing the reality of lineage affiliation from its mere representation poses serious problems.

62. Vickery 1985: 232.

63. For the repetition, see *IK* 60, 61; for the forgery, note the case already signaled by Coedès, *IC* vol. 5: 244 ff.

64. Including Cālukya, Caḷkya, Cāḷkya, Calikya, Calki, Caulukya, Solaṅki, Salki (inscription of Yuddhamalla, chapter 8.3), Saḷuki (inscription of Amoghavarṣa, chapter 9.1). These are probably distinctions without a difference, though Fleet took "Cāḷukya" to refer only to the "restored," i.e., Kalyāṇa, dynasty, "Caḷukya" only to the Bādāmi branch (*IA* 1890: 13).

Our aim here can be served by trying to make sense of the relationship between just two Cāḷukya ruling families: the one, based in Bādāmi, succeeded the Kadambas of the northwest of Karnataka to become the principal holders of power from about 500 to 750; the other, succeeding the Rāṣṭrakūṭas, established itself two hundred kilometers to the northeast at Kalyāṇa and ruled from 960 to 1200. These two dynasties present a relatively rare instance where the same—or rather, purportedly the same—ruling house regained power after a substantial interregnum. The question of their kinship may seem a narrow one, but it has much broader implications about the nature of the poetry of power in the Sanskrit epoch and the dynastic historiography, historical-political memory, and representations of the past that informed that poetry.

Only slowly over the course of the first century of their rule did the Bādāmi Cāḷukyas establish a coherent and stable lineage narrative and inscriptional style, and they did so by borrowing diverse elements from elsewhere. At the very beginning they appropriated much of their cultural idiom, indeed their very dynastic self-definition, from the Kadambas, the ruling family they had replaced. Their first copperplate grant, issued by Katti-Arasa, "King of the Sword" (Sanskritized as Kīrtivarman, c. 578), thirty-five years after the inaugural inscription of the dynasty, adopted wholesale the genealogical prelude of the Kadamba *praśasti* from a century earlier, which the Cāḷukyas were to preserve to the end of their rule. The conservation of genealogical energy in evidence here is a commonplace of rulership in India; the Kadambas themselves had borrowed from their predecessors, the Cūṭus and Vākāṭakas.[65] Other borrowings more intriguingly connect the Bādāmi Cāḷukyas with the western Kṣatrapas, such as their adoption of the Śaka era (they were the first dynasty to use this consistently) and some specific kinship terminology.[66] Why these Deccani kings should have chosen to date their records from the supposed commencement of Śaka rule in western India (which had ended 250 years earlier with the Śakas'

65. The formula runs: "Belonging to the Mānavya lineage, sons of the goddess Hārītī, meditating on Svāmi Mahāsena and the Mothers and consecrated in the kingship" (*EI* 28: 59ff.); its first occurrence in the Kadamba inscriptions is a record of Mṛgeśvaravarman, c. 450–75 (*IA* 7: 35). The Cūṭus on their coins and the Vākāṭakas in their grants similarly claimed descent from the goddess Hārītī.

66. Beginning with their first record, Pulakeśin I's inscription of Śaka 465 (583 B.C.E.). This is not quite "the earliest authentic instance of the use of the Śaka era in inscriptions" (Panchamukhi in *EI* 27: 5). Records of the Gurjara overlord Dadda II are dated Śaka 400 (*IA* 7: 61 ff.) and Śaka 407 (*JBBRAS* 10: 19ff.; cf. *IA* 12: 208; the first textual occurrence of the Śaka era is in the Jain *Lokavibhāga,* which dates itself to Śaka 380 [458 C.E.], cf. *EI* 27: 5). Cāḷukyas were to use the Śaka era until Vikramāditya VI inaugurated a Cāḷukya Vikrama era in 1075–76 C.E. (*EI* 12. 269ff.; *EI* 15: 348ff.), and Jayasiṃha of Gujarat established his own (Nagaraja Rao 1983: 123). The Śaka kinship term *sugṛhītanāmadheya* is used in reference to the Cāḷukya king Raṇarāga in an inscription of 602 (*IA* 19: 16). See Lévi 1904; also chapter 2.1.

defeat by the Guptas at Ujjayinī, c. 320),[67] or to adopt other aspects of their imperial style has never been explained. One answer may lie in the historical imitation and emulation of the sort that linked the Bādāmi Cāḷukyas to the Kadambas, which we will find elsewhere to be central to the concept and practice of southern Asian political self-identification (imperial imitation is discussed further in chapter 6.3). Here the homology would have been with the old and historic struggle between the Śakas and Sātavāhanas. If, as seems likely, the Pallavas came to frame themselves as the "virtual successors" to the Sātavāhanas (by adopting various cultural practices such as script), perhaps their "natural enemies" *(prakṛtyā śatravaḥ)*, as the Bādāmi Cāḷukyas described themselves, sought to constitute themselves as the Śakas reborn.[68]

Up to and beyond the reign of the great Pulakeśin II (r. c. 608–42), considerable variation is found in the form and content of Cāḷukya inscriptional discourse. A noticeable change took place around 658, when, a little more than a century after the first record, Vikramāditya I (r. 655–681) fixed the way the past was represented and established a paradigm of creative historiography that was maintained unchanged to the end of the Bādāmi dynasty.[69] The kind of variation found in earlier records suggests that inscriptional chroniclers did not make use of actual documents but instead had to rely on oral tradition. Alternatively, the standardization of the historical record may have been an innovation of the political culture of the age (it was in this era that the Pallava genealogy, too, was stabilized after some centuries of fluidity).[70] Cāḷukya inscriptional discourse now became the site for a marvelously adroit construction and interpretation of historical truth, as well as for an event-centered, chronologically punctilious narrative of that history—one, moreover, that was

67. Earlier and contemporary competitors like the Vākāṭakas and the Pallavas dated their records in regnal years, though they were aware of the Śaka era (a Pallava record produced in Bādāmi after the capture of the city is incised right up to a Cāḷukya inscription dated in the Śaka era, see *SII* vol. 11, pt. 1, line 7 = *IP* 35 ff.).

68. On Pallavas and Sātavāhanas, see Soundara Raman in Settar and Sontheimer 1982: 59–76, especially 64; Vikramāditya II's record of 742 (discussed later in this section) describes the family's natural enmity with the Pallavas. The Kālacūris of Broach, eventual successors to the Kṣatrapas, may have mediated the Śaka model for the Cāḷukyas. Soon after defeating the Kālacūris in 602 (*IA* 19: 17 line 11), the Cāḷukyas borrowed their writing style (Dani 1963: 178, 184) and elements of a political discourse (compare Pulakeśin II's record of 630, *EI* 27: 37 ff., with that of Buddharāja of 608, *EI* 12: 33 ff.; *CII* 4: 47 ff.).

69. The sole record of Ādityavarman, brother of Vikramāditya I, is undated (*JBBRAS* 16, p. 233 ff.) and his own dates are uncertain (cf. Ramesan 1962: 82), so this might be the first example of the "definitive form" of the Cāḷukya *praśasti* (at all events the first example is not the 612 record of Pulakeśin II, *IA* 6: 73 ff., pace Nilakantha Sastri in Yazdani 1960: 205).

70. The first copperplate record to display the final form of the genealogy (Brahmā, Aṅgiras, Bṛhaspati, Bharadvāja, Droṇa, Aśvatthāman, Pallava) dates from the reign of Parameśvaravarman I (r. 669–90; *IP* 152 ff.), the king who defeated Vikramāditya I and occupied Vātāpi (cf. *IP* liii ff.).

conducted in a brilliant prose style (in this trait harkening back to the art-prose of Rudradāman and Samudragupta). A new formal structure, which would henceforth remain unchanged, was also provided for this historical discourse, including opening with the celebrated invocatory verse at the start that frames the universalistic and salvific mission of kingly rule:

> Victory to the Boar Incarnation of Viṣṇu, shaking the ocean as it comes
> into view
> with the Earth resting at peace on the tip of its upraised right tusk.[71]

No longer do we see the merely formulaic gestures toward factuality typical of the earlier Bādāmi Cāḷukya documents, like the achievement slots noted earlier where historical reference functions as little more than ornamental epithet (Pulakeśin I "performed the *aśvamedha,*" Kīrtivarman "uprooted the Vanavāsis"). What is offered instead is an attempt at establishing a substantive narrative account of the dynasty. Vikramāditya II's record of 742 is exemplary of this new historical-political discourse. Notable is the mixture of the general with the particular, and of the referential with the expressive:

> Directly after his consecration as emperor over the entire world *(sakalabhuvanasāṃrājya)*—a self-choice marriage of Lakṣmī, goddess of royal power—he was infused with energy and made up his mind to destroy the Pallava, his natural enemies, who had stolen the luster of the former kings of his dynasty. Straightway he reached Turḍaka district, where he came face to face with the Pallava named Nandipotavarman, defeated him in battle, and put him to flight. He acquired the musical instruments . . . the battle standards; superior elephants, rutting, full grown, renowned; a treasure of rubies whose rays could destroy the darkness; and a treasure of gold it took many men to carry. He spared Kāñcī—hip-ornament on that lovely lady, the South—home of the Vessel-Born sage [Agastya]; he brought delight to the twice-born, the wretched, and those lacking a protector by his constant charity; he acquired great spiritual merit by returning vast treasures of gold to the stone temples built by Narasiṃhapota, like the Rājasiṃheśvara temple; he burned with the shooting flame of his power the Pāṇḍya, Coḷa, Keraḷa, Kaḷabhra, and other kings; and he planted the victory pillar of his fame, brilliant as the autumn moon, at the southern ocean, where waves boil at the shore glimmering with rays from the heaps of pearls released from the oysters struck and broken open by the trunks of the dolphinlike elephants shaken [by their fear of the ocean] . . . This King Vikramāditya, on the occasion of the winter solstice in his eighth regnal year, 664 years of the Śaka having elapsed, grants the village . . . [72]

71. The first instance of this verse is a record of Pulakeśin's second son, Vikramāditya, from 660 (*EI* 32: 175ff.).

72. *EI* 27: 125ff. (reading *chāyā* for *jaya* and *pratāpita* for *prasādhita* with the grants of Kīrtivarman II).

In this text, claims to universal rule—kingship over all the world, suzerainty over vague polities across southern India—are juxtaposed with a very specific account of the king's actions in a small part of that world, so specific as to include the names of the temples he benefited. These are self-consciously placed in a literary cadre where historical referentiality blends seamlessly with descriptive generalities familiar from the finest court poetry, such as Daṇḍin's late-seventh-century *Avantisundarī,* to which this *praśasti* bears close comparison.[73]

Though this particular combination of discursive features is not unknown elsewhere, in the Cāḷukyan case the larger historiographical process at work, specifically, the shape of the royal biography, is rather curious. The historical record for each king, as in the epigraph of Vikramāditya II, seems to have been established at the *beginning* of his reign, generally by memorializing a signal event of his youth or his accession to the kingship. In the case of Vijayāditya (r. 697–731), the narrative was determined at the very start of his rule and remained unchanged for the next thirty-five years. It was rare for a ruler to update his history except as a result of major achievements, as Vikramāditya I did following his capture of Kāñcīpuram in 671.[74] Once established, the record of a king would generally be transmitted by the successor intact, though sometimes microadjustments were made. In 682 Vinayāditya I rewrote the history of his father's recapture of imperial power, which had been interrupted by the Pallavas and their allies (the Trairājyapallava), only to have this revision rejected (or ignored) by his own son, Vijayāditya, in 697.[75]

The last copperplate grant issued by the Bādāmi Cāḷukya dynasty was that of Kīrtivarman II in 757 (though even before this date the Rāṣṭrakūṭas, who eventually displaced the Cāḷukyas, had begun to refer to their demise). More than two hundred years were to pass before the first dated copperplate of the Kalyāṇa Cāḷukyas was composed, a record of prince Satyāśraya from 974, though a few other documents of the family are available a little before this date. From their earliest records it is manifest that the cultural-political style of self-representation to which the new rulers in Kalyāṇa had access had nothing whatever in common with that of the Bādāmi branch.

73. The end of the *praśasti, kṣubhitakarimakaranihatasitaśuktimuktāphalaprakaramarīcivelākulodghūrṇamānārṇonidhānadakṣiṇārṇṇave,* may be compared with *Avantisundarī* p. 14 line 14, *taralataraṅgabhagnagarbhaśuktigarbhonmuktamuktāphaladalaśabalavālukena* ([He went a little further along the coast where] its sands were flecked with fragments of pearl released from oyster shells split open by the ceaseless action of the waves).

74. In a record of his sixteenth regnal year (*IA* 7: 219 ff.; a more correct version is *EI* 10: 100 ff. = Ramesan 1962: 46 ff.), the addition signaled by the *api ca* includes his victories over Narasiṃha, Mahendra, Īśvara, his taking of Kāñcī, and his defeat of Īśvarapotarāja.

75. For Vinayāditya's grant see Ramesan 1962: 58 ff.; for Vijayāditya's, *EI* 36: 313 ff. Trairājyapallava is probably "the confederacy of the three Pallava kingdoms" (so Sarma 1936: 40), rather than the Pāṇṭiya, Cōḻa, and Cēra kings (Panchamukhi in *EI* 22: 26 ff.).

At first the Kalyāṇa Cāḷukyas demonstrated no historical memory of or interest in the Bādāmi dynasty. Indeed, there is hardly any recollection at all of events prior to Ayyana, the father of Taila II, who is credited with restoring, or rather establishing, the lineage's power. Nor do the records evince the least concern with presenting the Kalyāṇa family as continuous with the Bādāmi line.[76] The extant records of Taila are concerned only with his own history: that he destroyed the Raṭṭas (that is, Rāṣṭrakūṭas), killed Muñja (king of the Paramāras of Mālava and uncle of Bhoja), took the head of Pāñcāla, and reigned twenty-four years in an era reckoned "from the year Śrīmukha."[77] In the same way, his son Satyāśraya reports only his own accomplishments in the records he issued. The standardized Bādāmi account, developed over a century or more, that had begun to function almost as a letterhead of the family had vanished without trace. An altogether new identity was asserted, one affiliated not with the solar dynasty of the Bādāmi branch but with the lunar dynasty (as in the case of the Veṅgi branch in coastal Andhra, which had split off from the Bādāmi lineage in the seventh century). The sole association with the older lineage, besides the opening invocation to the Boar incarnation of Viṣṇu and a representation of the old family crest of boar, sun, and moon, are the names themselves, personal ones such as "Satyāśraya" (which had been used by Pulakeśin II) and of course that of the lineage itself, "Cāḷukya," which stand out like dimly remembered formulas of a lost heroic language. The clearest sign of cultural discontinuity with the dynasty of two centuries earlier is the character of language used for some of the earliest Kalyāṇa records. This is Sanskrit, to be sure, but often a very faulty Sanskrit combining elements of Kannada and Marathi, a mélange of a sort completely unknown in the Bādāmi records and perhaps betokening the intensified vernacularization of the realm initiated a century earlier among the Rāṣṭrakūṭas (chapter 9). While the Kannada script of the period remained in common use, sometimes for the Sanskrit records a crude Nagari was employed. Equally notable, the dating (e.g., "from the year Śrīmukha") is according to a calendar system unrelated to the Śaka Saṃvatsara convention of the old Bādāmi clan.[78]

This is not to say that political memory in some form was not preserved at this period. If the public documents of the dynasty seem ignorant of or indifferent to the historical past and the imperial culture of old, the devel-

76. Gopal 1981: 26–28 considers the two dynastic lines to be continuous but offers no cogent argument in support.

77. See *IA* 21: 167 ff. (c. 974); and *EI* 4: 204 ff. (c. 982). It was Tailapa's beheading of Muñja (not the king of Pañcāla) that entered the historical record outside of Kalyāṇa (chapter 4.2).

78. In addition to Taila's record just mentioned, one of Yuvarāja Satyāśraya is dated Bhāva Saṃvatsara (c. 974) (*JHSB* 2: 214 ff.). Satyāśraya's record from one month later (*IA* 14: 140 ff.) is composed in very corrupt Sanskrit.

opment of a new form of textualized history shows that at some level the long-ago was being reconnected to the now, and already in the lifetime of Taila II. In Ranna's Kannada *Sāhasabhīmavijayam* (The Victory of the Bold Bhīma; also called *Gadāyuddham,* The Battle of the Clubs), a court epic written in honor of the heir apparent, Iṟivabeḍaṅga Satyāśraya, in 982, a decade or so after his father, Taila II, began to issue public records, the first genealogy is offered that connects the Bādāmi and Kalyāṇa Cāḷukyas, beginning with the "ancestors who were supreme lords in Ayōdyāpura *[sic]*."[79] Several features of Ranna's account merit comment. The assertion that the kings of this line originally reigned in "Ayodhyā" was a recently invented association that was to be elaborated on and standardized in later Kalyāṇa texts.[80] Ranna is aware of Pulakeśin I's *aśvamedha,* the principal act associated with him throughout Bādāmi Cāḷukya history; what is more astonishing, he knows "Maṃgalārṇa," that is, Maṅgaleśa. For reasons discussed below, this ruler had been dropped from the Bādāmi dynastic record centuries earlier, though the poet's knowledge extends only so far as his name. This sort of superficiality is true of the entire genealogy as Ranna presents it. Somehow, perhaps once again through an oral tradition, a *vaṃśāvalī,* or simple line of succession, of the earlier dynasty had been preserved. The quality of the historical memory here, as in all the contemporaneous Kalyāṇa documents, is in no way comparable to the earlier rich and detailed records of the Bādāmi era, and it is similarly unlike what was about to come. Admittedly, Ranna's purposes were contemporary and poetic, not genealogical and historical, yet it seems obvious he had little specific knowledge of these ancestors.

By the third generation there crystallized in Kalyāṇa a new order of poetry and polity. It was cosmopolitan insofar as it was reminiscent of and based

79. *Sāhasabhīmavijayam* 2.7 ff. (ed. Saṇṇayya and Rāmegauḍa pp. 18–19; ed. Kṛṣṇabhaṭṭa pp. 34–36). The lineage begins with Satyāśrayadēva, "also known as Viṣṇuvardhana," followed by Jayasiṃhadēva, "who was a lion to destroy the troops of elephants of the Rāṣṭrakūṭa," and then Raṇaraṅgasiṃha. Pulakeśidēva, the "supreme lord of the city of Vātāpi, who was consecrated for the horse-sacrifice ritual," comes next, then Kīrtivarmadēva, "who had the son Satyāśrayadēva the second, whereas the junior son was Maṃgaḷārṇa." There follows a straight list of the succession reasonably close to what we can establish from the Bādāmi records. The period of dynastic eclipse after Kīrtivarman II is filled in by Piriya Tailapa; Kundiya Bhīma, "who slew Mukundi"; Vikramādityadēva; Raṇaraṅgamalla Ayyana; Uttuṅgamalla Vikramāditya; and finally Taila II Āhavamalla, for whom alone the poem presents a substantial historical record. See also Narasimhachar in *IA* 40: 41–45; Gopal 1980: 31–39.

80. No evidence connects the Cāḷukyas to Ayodhyā before the reign of Satyāśraya around 974 (compare *JHSB* 2: 214 ff., Śrī Pṛthivīvallabha as overlord of Ayodhipur *[sic]*; a record of the following month still reads Kalyāṇapura, *IA* 14: 140 ff.); thereafter the link becomes standard (cf. *Vikramāṅkadevacarita* 1.62). The *Viṣṇupurāṇa* (4.14) shows how old is the trope that fifty-three kings of the Ikṣvāku dynasty reigned in Ayodhyā before moving south, where forty-eight members of the dynasty ruled (the numbers are different in later Cāḷukya records, see further in this section).

on the old imperial model, but it was profoundly committed to a new vernacularity in both culture and power. The precise nature of this culture, and the politics with which it was associated, will occupy us later (chapters 8, 9).[81] What is of immediate interest is the renewed concern with a more credible historical memory, and specifically with the practices and politics of historicality, that this new order in Kalyāṇa seems to have evinced.

When Vikramāditya V, grandson of Taila II, issued the first grant of his reign, the so-called Kauthem plates (named after the village in today's southern Maharashtra where they were found), in 1008–9 C.E., he dated it according to the old Śaka Saṃvat calendar (930).[82] This is the first hint of the thoroughgoing renovation—or re-creation—in historiographical style that distinguishes the Kauthem and later records from all previous documents of the dynasty, including Ranna's poem. Although as part of the new cultural order many documents, including *praśasti*s, were being issued in Kannada (chapter 9.1), the Kauthem record is composed in standard Sanskrit and high literary style, befitting the seriousness of its task, namely, setting right once and for all the historical relationship between the Kalyāṇa and Bādāmi Cāḷukyas. An analysis of the complete published epigraphical record reveals that the earlier history of the dynasty is systematically reproduced here. Many of the data derive from the standard copperplate format common from Vikramāditya I (fl. 655) onward—allusion is actually made to his records—and especially from Vijayāditya (fl. 697). But information was also taken from earlier Bādāmi materials, and from other, external and contemporaneous sources as well: Veṅgi Cāḷukya copperplates were consulted, and very probably one of Pulakeśin II's. But the most remarkable source of the Kauthem record—and there is not the shadow of a doubt that it was a source—is a celebrated *praśasti* that has so far gone unmentioned.

The first part of the Kauthem inscription begins in a predictable manner, with not only the standard Bādāmi invocation to the Boar incarnation but also the full "letterhead" of old (*samastabhuvanasaṃstūyamāna-mānavyasagotrāṇām,* etc.), reappearing for the first time after more than two centuries. As noted, this introductory portion is found in virtually every copperplate after Vikramāditya I, but Kauthem also contains striking details echoing earlier materials. For the first time since a 630 record of Pulakeśin II, the Cāḷukyas are said to be "favored by Kauśikī."[83] The names of two more an-

81. In chapters 4.3 and 8.2 a key text from the final years of the dynasty is discussed, the *Mānasollāsa* of Someśvara III (1131), a work vividly marked by the transitional nature of the cultural politics of the epoch.

82. *IA* 16: 15ff. (for the date see line 61). His father, Satyāśraya, was still ruling in 1007, defeating a Cōḻa king that year (*EI* 16: 74).

83. *IA* 16: 15ff., line 5; cf. *EI* 27: 37ff., line 5. Other resonances between Kauthem and earlier records include a description of the earth with her ocean-girdle "ornamented" *(makarika)*

cestors, Viṣṇuvardhana and Vijayāditya, have been added to the letterhead. The former had already been mentioned by Ranna as the actual founder of the dynasty though erroneously; no Viṣṇuvardhana is ever mentioned in any Bādāmi grant. The only persons of that name associated with the lineage are the younger brother of Pulakeśin II (also known as Kubja Viṣṇuvardhana Viṣamasiddha, "the hunchback Viṣṇuvardhana, who overcame his adversity"), who is credited with founding the Veṅgi branch of the dynasty, and his descendants. The insertion of Viṣṇuvardhana in the Kauthem grant was almost certainly an innovation borrowed (like several others) from records of the Andhra line.[84] The commencement of the Cāḷukya genealogy in the Kauthem record itself raises some interesting questions. Like Ranna's epic, Kauthem begins the lineage in Ayodhyā, where now it is specified that fifty-nine kings of the dynasty reigned there before moving south. Sixteen kings are said to have ruled in this southern dynasty—this agrees basically with the copperplate records—until it was "interrupted," *antarita,* a word harkening back to the earlier disruption of Cāḷukya hegemony after Pulakeśin II, which had been "interrupted by the three lords of earth" *(avanipatitritayāntarita-).*[85]

The next section of the plates demonstrates that there was far more to the historical research behind this document than can be explained by the writer's consulting contemporary records from the Andhra lineage or older ones from the Bādāmi clan. The plates show a style, a sequence of ideas, and references of a specific and consistent yet entirely different historical sort—references to events that are absent not only from all earlier Kalyāṇa documents but from the entire Bādāmi Cāḷukya dynastic record of the post-Pulakeśin era. These are available in only one other place: the great *praśasti* composed by the poet Ravikīrti in honor of Pulakeśin II and inscribed on the Meguṭi temple in Aihoḷe in 634.

The agreements between the plates and the *praśasti* are dense and unmistakable, comprising every feature from meter to trope to reference. Kauthem begins the Cāḷukya lineage with Jayasiṃhavallabha, just as the Aihoḷe inscription does, and the two use identical verse formulas. The stanza on Pulakeśin I and the founding of the capital Vātāpi (Bādāmi) agrees not only in point of meter *(āryā)* but in the specific figure used. One example of the numerous correspondences on significant dynastic events is the reference

---

with "elephantlike sea beasts *(karimakara)*" (lines 3–4)—rare terms not heard since the records of Pulakeśin II (631; *EI* 18: 257ff., line 50) and Vikramāditya II (742; *EI* 27: 125ff., line 50).

84. See the Veṅgi Cāḷukya copperplate of 946 C.E., *IA* 7: 15ff. (the phrase "favored by Kauśikī" appears here, too, line 2, as in most of their later grants). It is unclear which of the several Veṅgi Vijayādityas is meant. One issued the grant in 946 mentioned earlier in this chapter; another was the last of the dynasty to rule in Ayodhyā before moving south (see the record of Vīra Cōḷa, 1100; *SII* 1: 31ff.).

85. In a record of Vikramāditya I, *JBBRAS* 16: 236, line 15. On the "three lords of earth" (here *rājyatraya*), and on the Ayodhyā connection, see notes 75 and 80, this chapter.

in both texts to Kīrtivarman I as "destroyer of the Nalas, Mauryas, Kadambas." No other Bādāmi Cāḷukya document describes Kīrtivarman as anything more than the destroyer of "the Vanavāsis and others." The only identifiable source for Kauthem's specificity here is the Aihoḷe temple inscription.[86]

The connection between the two is further corroborated by the account of Maṅgaleśa. This king had disappeared from all Bādāmi records after Pulakeśin II, until he resurfaced some 350 years later as a mere name in Ranna's genealogy. Kauthem provides specific and detailed references to Maṅgaleśa's attack on Revatī island—an event unknown to any document save Aihoḷe—and more significant, to his dispute over the succession with his nephew, Pulakeśin II. Yet Vikramāditya V's *praśasti* poet does not just copy but rethinks and rewrites the historical record. Consider, first, verses 14 and 15 of the Aihoḷe inscription (in a literal translation):

> [Maṅgaleśa's] elder brother's son, named Pulekeśin, with a dignity like Nahuṣa's, was coveted by Lakṣmī (Goddess of Royalty). When he learned that his uncle was jealous of him because of this, Pulekeśin resolved to wander abroad as an exile. Maṅgaleśa, with his great capacity for applying the [three political powers] on all sides having been reduced—since [Pulakeśin] had appropriated [two of the powers,] political counsel and military energy—gave up, along with the effort to secure the kingdom for his own son, both his prosperous kingdom and his life.[87]

This is how Kauthem makes new history (lines 24–55):

> During the time that his elder brother's son, excellent though he was, was a boy and thus incapable of ruling, Maṅgalīśa *[sic]* bore the burden of the world on his own shoulders, and then made over the earth to Satyāśraya [Pulakeśin II] when he became a young man. For what member of the Cāḷukya dynasty would ever stray from the path of *dharma?*

About the historiographical process at work here—and "historiographical" seems to be the correct word—there can be little doubt. Just before the com-

86. The verse formula is *rājāsīj jaysiṃhavallabha iti khyātaḥ,* line 14 of Kauthem = line 3 of Aihoḷe (Jayasiṃhavallabha, by the way, is also mentioned in the Mahākūṭa Pillar Inscription of Maṅgaleśa, *IA* 19: 7–20, but no further parallels between that record and Kauthem are to be found). The *alaṅkāra* is the metaphor of the king as husband of the city (lines 17–18 *vātāpipurapatir* = lines 3–4, *ayāsīd vātāpipurivadhūvaratām*). For Kīrtivarman, lines 20–22 of Kauthem = line 4 of Aihoḷe.

87. *EI* 6: 9, trans. Kielhorn, slightly revised. "Good counsel and energy," *mantrotsāhaśakti.* The words are carefully chosen. Pulakeśin had to forego the third *śakti, prabhuśakti,* the power of the treasury and of his own army—both now controlled by his uncle—and rely on the other two, his sagacity *(mantra* = *jñāna)* and his energy. After regaining the kingship he came into possession of all three (v. 32). Maṅgaleśa had referred to himself as *śaktitrayasampannaḥ* (*IA* 7: 161 line 10; compare the Pallava record of Vijayaskandavarman cited in section 1, as well as *Arthaśāstra* 6.2.33).

mencement of his reign Vikramāditya V must have had Bādāmi Cāḷukya documents, especially copperplates, from three hundred years earlier collected and analyzed, along with more recent Veṅgi records.[88] It is clear that to do this he employed historians—again, what else to call a person who examines ancient documents with the intention of determining the truth, or a truth, of the past, having acquired the necessary philological and paleographic skills to do so?[89] Moreover, one must assume that the Kalyāṇa king went so far as to dispatch such a historian to travel the two hundred kilometers to the southwest in order to read the stone inscription at the celebrated Meguṭi temple in Aihoḷe.[90] Reestablishing the line between Bādāmi and Kalyāṇa, represented as seamlessly continuous in Kauthem and in all later copperplate grants of the Kalyāṇa dynasty, was clearly a matter of consequence to the newly established dynasty.[91]

The kind of historiographical project we encounter in the Kālyāṇa records implies something significant about the status of the polity—in premodern India no less than in Hegel's modern Europe—as a moral center that makes the very existence of historical narrative possible.[92] But there are humbler and in some ways more suggestive implications, too, about the kinds of political interests that may have mediated the transformation. It is no easy matter, at this distance in space and time, to specify precisely how the assertion of political power shaped the Kalyāṇa historiographical developments. One concrete condition of possibility that deserves mention is the struggle for dominion over the rich but dynastically unstable coastal area of Veṅgi between the deltas of the Kṛṣṇā and Godāvarī rivers in today's Andhra Pradesh.

88. The analysis was not always precise: Vikramāditya, for example, in the Kauthem plates, is called the son of Ādityavarman while earlier copperplates refer to him as elder brother.

89. A new, southern Nagari was used for writing Sanskrit in Kalyāṇa at this period; Bādāmi inscriptions were written in a Kannada-Telugu script that had been out of style for centuries; the script of the Veṅgi branch diverged widely from that of Bādāmi, and that of Kalyāṇa, too. The ability to read different scripts is specifically praised during this period (*EI* 12: 287; cf. *Vikramāṅkadevacarita* 3.17 [noted ad loc.], the king's skill *sarvāsu lipiṣu*); also *Mānasollāsa* cited in chapter 4.3.

90. Manuscript copies of these copperplate and lithic records (though not unknown) are unlikely to have been preserved from the Bādāmi dynasty three centuries earlier. Elsewhere kings are shown to read the genealogy of their family in temple inscriptions (Narasiṃha III of the Hoysaḷa dynasty in 1254 is described as examining a *vaṃśāvalī* in a Halebid temple composed early in the previous century, *EC* 5.1: xxvi). My analysis assumes that the seat of the dynasty was already in northeast Karnataka (Vikramāditya's father, Satyāśraya, is said to be reigning in "Kalyāṇapura" in *IA* 14: 140 ff.); the transfer from Mānyakheṭa is usually, though I believe erroneously, ascribed to Someśvara I (r. 1042–68).

91. The Kalyāṇa Cāḷukyas still had no clear sense of their genealogical history in the interval between the two dynasties. Kauthem gives only five names to fill in this period (c. 760–970), half as many as are recorded for almost the same extent of time (543–757) for the Bādāmi branch.

92. White 1987: 1–25, especially 12.

This contest began in 973, when the eastern Cāḷukya king Dānārṇava was killed in battle by the Telugu-Cōḻa chief Jaṭācōḻa Bhīma. Dānārṇava's two sons took refuge at the court of Rājarāja Cōḻa, who used the event as a pretext for asserting his claims on Veṅgi. The western Cāḷukyas also claimed the tract, which had in fact been politically consolidated first under the Bādāmi Cāḷukyas. (Recall that Viṣṇuvardhana, younger brother of Pulakeśin II, initiated Cāḷukya rule in the region, eventually achieving autonomy from Bādāmi, and Veṅgi continued to foster a powerful Kannada-speaking presence: this was, after all, the family seat of the pathbreaking Kannada writers of the tenth century, Pampa, Ponna, and Nāgavarma I [chapter 9].) Satyāśraya, father of Vikramāditya V, sought to gain control of the delta, launching an attack in 1005 in response to the assertion of control made by the Cōḻa king Rājarāja. In the following decades, the situation only deteriorated. A major battle was fought between the Cāḷukyas and Cōḻas in 1021 at Muyangi (Maski in today's Raichur district), and the reign of Someśvara (1044–68) was marked by constant war, as was that of his successor, Vikramāditya VI. It was only with the accession of Kulottuṅga Rājendra (r. 1070–1118), an eastern Cāḷukya prince but a Cōḻa by marriage, that Veṅgi was incorporated in the Cōḻa kingdom.[93] In 1076 the claims of Kulottuṅga as a descendant of both the older Cāḷukya line (through the eastern Cāḷukyas of Veṅgi) and the Cōḻas prevailed (however much sheer force of arms may have been the final arbiter). In 1008 it is probable that the same logic of descent and history operated, too. The claims of the Kalyāṇa branch, if its continuity with the Bādāmi line could be securely established, would far outweigh those of the Cōḻas under Rājarāja, who with no entitlement whatever had imposed administrative control on the region two years earlier.

The pragmatics of Cāḷukya inscriptional discourse thus comprise core questions of historical self-understanding, common to many other polities of the time.[94] This was not the simple history of "facts" so troubling to the editor of a standard history of the Deccan when he wrote, in reference to the inscriptions studied here, that "no useful purpose will be served by seeking to analyze such late and discordant traditions [as those of the Kalyāṇa Cāḷukyas] in any detail . . . Interesting as the beliefs cherished by the members of a historic dynasty for several generations, these puerile stories are of course of no value as factual history."[95] In actuality, we need to grasp that it

93. See Desai et al. 1970: 156–71; Nilakantha Sastri 1955: 178ff., especially p. 182. For Rājarāja's assertion of control, see *SII* 6, no. 102.

94. A comparable linkage was made between the Gaṅgas of Orissa and the western Gaṅgas of Karnataka for the first time in the twelfth-century records of Coḍagaṅga. The new founder of the dynasty became Vīrasiṃha, ruler of Kolāhala in Gaṅgavāḍi, eighty generations before Coḍagaṅga's father Vajrahasta (Berkemer 1993: 162–64; Schneibel 2000, chapter 1).

95. Nilakanta Sastri in Yazdani 1960: 206.

is not only the facts themselves that are of interest but also the interest in facts evinced by the historical actors. And that interest is embodied in the stories that such actors marshal facts to tell, as well as in the creation of facts (complementing the opposite tendency we saw in our study of inscriptional semantics, the intentional elision of all historical fact). What people believe is the case and what they want others to believe is the case are as important as what is the case.[96] Whether or not the Kalyāṇa dynasty had any real, *pāramārthika,* relationship to Bādāmi is of secondary importance here. For those making history in Kalyāṇa in 1008, one of the stories that the marshalling of facts served to tell was a pragmatic, *vyāvahārika,* truth concerning the dispute over which ruling lineage, Kalyāṇa Cāḷukya or Cōḻa, was the rightful successor to Bādāmi, and which had therefore the stronger claim to the rich delta of Veṅgi country. When Vikramāditya V asserted in 1008, "What member of the Cāḷukya dynasty would ever stray from the path of *dharma?*" he was making an argument in a dispute engaged not just on the battlefield but to a significant degree in the public documentary space of Sanskrit inscriptional discourse. And not just in inscriptional discourse but in virtually every other domain of Sanskrit culture as well, starting with the heart of that culture: grammar.

96. Contrast the positivist historiographical model of, e.g., Henige 1975.

CHAPTER FOUR

Sanskrit Culture as Courtly Practice

4.1 GRAMMATICAL AND POLITICAL CORRECTNESS: THE POLITICS OF GRAMMAR

The spread of a widely shared, largely uniform cosmopolitan style of Sanskrit inscriptional discourse would have been impossible without an equally vast circulation of the great *kāvya* exemplars of that style, accompanied by the philological instruments without which the very existence of such texts was unthinkable. The magnitude of the space through which Sanskrit *kāvya* circulated can be suggested by a few simple observations. The two great foundational texts of cosmopolitan Sanskrit culture, the *Mahābhārata* and *Rāmāyaṇa,* came to represent the basic common property of literary culture across southern Asia. The role of the *Mahābhārata* specifically in shaping the image of political space is discussed later (chapter 6.1). As for the *Rāmāyaṇa,* the history of its dissemination, and in the process its transformation, from Kashmir and Tibet to China and maritime Southeast Asia has been told often enough to need no repeating here, though those accounts do not always sufficiently stress the magnitude of this dissemination, which had no peers in premodernity. That the works of Kālidāsa, Bhāravi, Bāṇa, and Mayūra, among others—canonical authors in a quickly crystallizing canon—were assiduously studied by Khmer literati is fully evident in the inscriptional materials. Not only are the authors referred to by name but, more important, allusions to their work are scattered throughout the epigraphical corpus from an early date, suggesting how fully they were digested. The sixth-century science-poem *(śāstrakāvya)* of Bhaṭṭi, which marks an important advance in that genre of writing, occupied a position of cultural centrality in Java: its version—and not Vālmīki's—of the story of Prince Rāma may have formed the basis for the sculptural program that adorns the walls of the great temple complex at Prambanan in central Java, and it certainly provided the model for the ninth- or tenth-century *kakawin* that inaugurates Javanese vernacularization (chapter 10.1).[1]

Just as the *kāvyas* were studied everywhere throughout this domain, so were the texts of literary art *(alaṅkāraśāstra)*, metrics, lexicography, and related knowledge systems. Not only did these texts circulate throughout the cosmopolis with something like the status of precious cultural commodities; they came to provide a general framework within which a whole range of vernacular literary practices could be theorized, and it is in this context that we will revisit them in some detail in part 2. An example would be the career of a work like the *Kāvyādarśa*, the late-seventh-century treatise of Daṇḍin. Throughout the cosmopolis, and even beyond, this work was studied as the core text of literary theory and was continually readapted: in the Deccan, as the Kannada *Kavirājamārgam* (Way of the King of Poets), c. 875; in Sri Lanka, as the Sinhala *Siyabaslakara* (Sanskrit, *Svakīyabhāṣālaṅkāra* [Ornament of Our Own Language], mid- or late-ninth-century); in Tamilnadu, as the Tamil *Taṇṭiyalaṅkāra* (Literary Art of Daṇḍin), c. 1000; again in Sri Lanka, as Sangharakṣita's Pali *Subodhālaṅkāra* (Literary Art without Toil), c. 1200; as well as in Tibet, as translated by Sa-skya Paṇḍita and a disciple, around 1250. Ninth-century China also offers striking evidence of the enormous impact of Sanskrit: the introduction of complex patterns of tonal prosody—the critical transformation that made possible the Recent Style poetry of the high T'ang—was stimulated in part by the study of Daṇḍin and works of the same genre such as Bhāmaha's *Kāvyālaṅkāra*.[2] All this makes Daṇḍin's *Mirror* probably the most influential work on literary science in world history after Aristotle's *Poetics*.

An equally peripatetic account could be written of other components of Sanskrit literary science and philology, though the paper trail here is a little harder to follow. The vernacular intellectuals of southern India, Thailand, Cambodia, Java, and Bali took in Sanskrit metrics in a gulp, as they did Sanskrit lexicography (chapters 9, 10). In Java, interest in Sanskrit philological studies was intense and long-lasting, stretching from the Śailendra period (c. 800), when a Javanese adaptation of Amara's Sanskrit lexicon, the

1. On the *Rāmāyaṇa*'s Asian career most surveys (e.g., Raghavan 1980) only scratch the surface. A sophisticated if preliminary analysis of the poem in Southeast Asia is available in Collins 2003. Allusions to Kālidāsa's *Raghuvaṃśa* are found in Cambodian inscriptions from the seventh century (*ISC* 13, v. 6 = Ragh. 4.49, noticed first by Kielhorn *EI* 6: 4 n.) to the Pre Rup inscription of 961 (vv. 164, 199, 211, 290) and beyond (cf. Bhattacharya 1991: 2–4 and notes). Numerous other poets are mentioned, e.g., Bhāravi and Mayūra in an inscription of Yaśovarman (*IK* 104 ff., vv. 31 and 70 respectively). For Bhaṭṭi's poem in Java see Stutterheim 1925. The question of the exact textual sources for the Prambanan reliefs continues to occupy scholars, but the fact of their Indic origins cannot of course be contested. Doubts about the knowledge of Kālidāsa's work in Java (reviewed by Sarkar 1934: 224 ff.) were settled by Zoetmulder 1974: 307 ff. (an allusion to the *Raghuvaṃśa* appears in the earliest dated record, 732, cf. *CIJ*: 26 ff.).

2. Sanskrit rhetorical theory in China is explored in Mair and Mei 1991.

Amaramālā (Garland of Amara), was produced, to late-fifteenth-century Kaḍiri, where Tanakung composed the *Wṛttasañcaya* (Compendium of Meters). Tanakung used a wide variety of sources, not just (unsurprisingly) the *Piṅgalasūtra* (probably in the tenth-century recension made by Halāyudha) but also (surprisingly) the much-earlier *Nāṭyaśāstra* of Bharata. Influential, too, was Kedāra Bhaṭṭa's *Vṛttaratnākara* (Jewel Mine of Meters) of c. 1000—a work that, via its thirteenth-century Pali translation, *Vuttodaya*, would go on to play a defining role in seventeenth-century Ayutthaya, where it had a major impact on the creation of Thai poetry. It is in such instances of continuous and influential textual flows that we can gauge the extraordinary importance that Sanskrit cultural virtuosity held for poets, scholars, and their patrons throughout Asia and, equally important, the role that this virtuosity came to play in the constitution of cosmopolitan and, later, vernacular orders of culture and power.[3]

All that has just been described for *kāvya* itself and for its other ancillary practices is equally true of the knowledge system known as *vyākaraṇa*, language analysis or, more simply if less precisely, grammar. Indeed, it is truer of this discipline, since it carried cultural and political associations in premodern South Asia far more potent than any other form of knowledge. It therefore merits separate consideration.

Readers who know anything about Indian intellectual history are likely to know that the study of language was more highly developed in South Asia than anywhere else in the premodern world. From the archaic invocation to the Goddess of Speech (Vāk) in the *Ṛgveda* to the etymological speculation that lies at the heart of the sacerdotal thought of the *brāhmaṇas* to the grand synthesis of Pāṇini and the sophisticated tradition of exegesis that it stimulated, and in the many rival systems that sought to displace and surpass this tradition, premodern Indian thinkers were consumed by the desire to understand the mystery of human communication. And they had no peer in their explorations until, in one of the subtler ironies of Western intellectual history, Franz Bopp, William Dwight Whitney, Ferdinand de Saussure, Emile Benveniste, Leonard Bloomfield, and Noam Chomsky, learning both substantively and theoretically from Indian premodernity (being all of them Sanskritists or students of Sanskrit-knowing scholars), developed successively historical, structural, and transformational linguistics and, by these new forms of thought, invented some basic conceptual components of Western modernity itself.

3. On Sanskrit metrics in Java in general, see Zoetmulder 1974: 101 ff.; on the *Wṛttasañcaya* in particular, Kern 1920: 70, 73–77, 173–74; and especially Hunter 2001, which is definitive on the sources of the work (noting that Tanakung's knowledge of Sanskrit culture was gained at least in part in India). Halāyudha is discussed later in this section. The place of Indic metrics at the late-medieval Thai court is considered by Terwiel 1996; the depth of Sanskrit influence more generally is reviewed in Herbert and Milner 1989: 32.

The scholarly cultivation of language in premodern India, however, should not be seen—as it typically is seen—as a purely abstract intellectual discipline. No doubt Sanskrit grammar has enormous attraction for contemporary thought by reason of the marvelous architecture of its primary texts, the brilliance and complexity of the interpretive tradition devoted to it, and its underlying linguistic theory. But understanding the Indian care for language also depends, to a significant degree, on understanding the place of language care in the Indian social-moral order, and that in part means grasping its relationship to political power. To what extent and by what modalities Indian kings and courts cared about the correct use of language as codified in grammar and as manifested in literature, and the reasons they cared at all, are likewise central to our ability to comprehend the relationship of power to culture in premodernity. If thinkers in the West, on the threshold of modernity, were right to believe that "language has always been the companion of power," as the Castilian grammarian Antonio de Nebrija put in 1492, it is by no means clear that language has everywhere and always been the same kind of companion, so directly controlled and meekly subservient.

The categories found in Western representation about the linkage between grammatical and political correctness are hardly alien to the conceptual universe of the Sanskrit cosmopolis. On the contrary, these categories could easily be filled with Indic materials. The cultural-political problematic of correctness *(sādhutva)* itself is one generated from within the discourses and histories of grammars, the grammaticized language usage of *kāvya,* and the symbiotic ties of both grammar and *kāvya* with kings, courts, and larger polities. Moreover, as the elite's adoption of Sanskrit literary culture for the expression of political will shows, rulership and Sanskrit grammaticality and learning were more than merely associated; they were to some degree mutually constitutive. This is demonstrated by, among other things, the celebration of grammatical learning especially in kings, the royal patronage of such learning, and the competitive zeal among rulers everywhere to encourage grammatical creativity and adorn their courts with scholars who could exemplify it. On the other hand, the Indic categories and their embodiment in persons and texts followed a logic of their own, whose development we are able to trace over the entire space-time of the Sanskrit world. And we can trace a renewed development even later, too, once that world was coming to an end, for these ideas were of great consequentiality when concern for universal language and cosmocratic polity gave way to regionalized orders of culture-power. Understanding precisely what it meant to be politically and grammatically correct in the Sanskrit cosmopolis must be worked out from the empirical materials. It is only in following the development of South Asian representations that we learn to resist merely retrofitting onto India the peculiar linkages of Western modernity and can see what is different about the non-Western premodern.

No sooner had Sanskrit become the premier vehicle for the expression of royal will, displacing all other codes, than Sanskrit learning itself became an essential component of power. The figure of the learned king became quickly established, especially the king learned in Sanskrit philology (and we may with justice speak of "philology" since "grammar" is often found to be used metonymically, standing for knowledge of lexicology, prosody, and the like, including literature). In fact, the topos of the educated king can be found in *praśasti* discourse across the cosmopolis. A simple list of pertinent references is enough to demonstrate how the assertion of grammaticality, and with it literary skill, became virtually mandatory for the fully realized form of kingliness. It is not surprising that the first such allusion comes from the *praśasti* of the Kṣatrapa Rudradāman in Gujarat in 150, given the fashion that this particular text sets in other respects. The ruler describes himself as "one who has won wide fame by his theoretical and practical mastery and retention of the great knowledges, grammar, polity, music, systematic thought, and so on." In the mid-fourth century, Samudragupta, the second king of the imperial Gupta dynasty, is characterized in the *praśasti* engraved on the Allahabad Pillar as "master of the true meanings of the *śāstras*," a man of "truth-piercing learning," whose "way of poetry merits the closest study, and whose literary work puts to shame the creative powers of [other] poets." In a mid-sixth-century copperplate record of Durvinīta, a powerful lord of the western Gaṅgas in what is today southern Karnataka, the king is praised as the man who "composed the *Descent of Language* [now lost], and rewritten the [Paishachi] *Bṛhatkathā* [Great Tale] in the language of the gods." In Southeast Asia the same representation appears repeatedly. In Java, King Sañjaya is portrayed in an inscription of 732, noted in chapter 3.1, as "one who understood the finest points of the *śāstras*," whereas Jaya Indravarman I, in Champa around 970, is celebrated even more explicitly as an expert in Pāṇini's grammar and the *Kāśikā* (the late-eighth- or early-ninth-century commentary on Pāṇini). In Angkor in 1002, Sūryavarman I is beautifully eulogized as "one whose mind itself truly seemed a body that could move, with the *[Great] Commentary* [of Patañjali on Pāṇini's grammar] and the rest [of the grammatical treatises] for its feet, [the two kinds of] literature [prose and verse] for its hands, the six systems of philosophy for its senses, and *dharma* and the other *śāstras* for its head." A generation later, on the coast of Andhra country, Rājarājanarendra of the Veṅgi Cāḷukyas is described by the poet Nannaya as "lucid in thought, trained in the science of Kumāra [the *Kātantra* of Śarvavarman], a good Cāḷukya, luminous as the moon, [who] finds peace in studying the ancient texts."[4]

4. See respectively Sircar 1965–83, vol. 1: 179 *(śabdārthagāndhārvanyāyādyānāṃ vidyānāṃ mahatīnāṃ pāraṇadhāraṇavijñānaprayogāvāptavipulakīrti-); CII* 3: 212; *IWG* 82, 101 *(śabdāvatārakareṇa devabhāratīnibaddhabaḍḍhakathena);* Durvinīta here is also credited with a commentary on

We will have occasion later to explore how different was the logic of philology in the cosmopolitan epoch from what developed in the age of vernacularization, when a true epistemic revolution occurred (chapter 9.4). It is enough here to caution against falsely inferring from the above citations that such praise of royal personages derived from their capacity to set the standard for Sanskrit language excellence through the mastery of grammar and literature in the way that, in the case of Kannada, for example, Viṣṇuvardhana of the Hoysaḷa dynasty was described in 1117 as being "capable of making known all the rules of the science of language."[5] Rulers may have been thought to possess some natural capacity for realizing the linguistic norms of Sanskrit, but their own language practices were never believed to have *established* those norms; that conception was to be a new and distinctive feature of the vernacular epoch. In the Sanskrit thought world, normativity was always conceived of as preexistent to any actual instantiation: practices conformed to rules, while rules were never constituted out of practices.[6] Excellence in the command of the Sanskrit language was therefore something kings had to achieve through mastery of a theoretical body of material that already established that excellence, and all of them everywhere could achieve this to the same degree and in the same manner, assuming they were in possession of the right textual instruments. This attainment, as demonstrated by the references just cited, was one among other celebrated royal attributes and so was as essential to kingship as the martial power, political sagacity, physical beauty, fame, and glory that are repeatedly celebrated in the *praśasti* aesthetic.

Since it was theory that underlay the royal practice of grammatical correctness, which itself was seen as a component of political correctness, it stands to reason that power should have actively cared for grammar by sponsoring the production of grammatical texts and ensuring their continued study. The cultural-political relationship constituted thereby is a striking, if little studied, phenomenon. It may hardly have been recognized before Hartmut Scharfe offered the following insight in passing in his general survey of grammatical literature:

> A strong case can be made for the importance of princely patronage of grammatical studies. We can see three spurts of activity: in the 5th century A.D. (Candragomin, Bhartṛhari, Devanandin), the 11th to the 13th century A.D. (Kaiyaṭa, Bhoja, Hemacandra, Kramadīśvara, Anubhūtisvarūpa, Vopadeva, Puruṣottama,

---

the fifteenth chapter of Bhāravi's *Kirātārjunīya.* I see no grounds for Master's doubts about the meaning of this passage (1943: 36); *CIJ* vol. 1: 18 *(śāstrasūkṣmārthavedi-);* Majumdar 1974: 18; *IK:* 361 [= Sircar 1965–83, vol. 2: 710] (*bhāṣyādicaraṇā kāvyapāṇiḥ ṣaḍdarśanendriyā | yanmatiḥ dharmaśāstrādimastakā jaṅgamāyate* || [I read thus, for the printed *jaṅgamāyatā*]); for the Nannaya quotation see Narayana Rao and Shulman 2002: 57.

5. *śabdavidyāsamagralakṣaṇasuśikṣanum, EC* 5: 132.

6. See Pollock 1985.

> Trivikrama, Dāmodara) and in the 17th century A.D. (Bhaṭṭoji Dīkṣita and his school, Mārkaṇḍeya, Mīrzā Khān), which coincide with the Gupta dynasty, the prosperity of the Hindu kingdoms before the Muslim conquest and the height of the Mughal rule.[7]

This is a valuable observation even in the absence of any elaboration on the historical data (it is not immediately obvious, for example, what Bhaṭṭoji Dīkṣita and his school might have had to do with Mughal power, given that his patron was Veṅkaṭāppa Nāyaka, overlord of Ikkeri in western Karnataka), and no explanation offered at all for the "case," however strong it appears to be. But it is also slightly misleading if interpreted too narrowly: princely patronage was not just vaguely "important" to Sanskrit philology, and the history of the relationship between polity and philology was not just episodic, punctuated by spurts that nevertheless remain obscure in their origins and mysterious in their effects. On the contrary, royal power seems to have provided the essential precondition for the flourishing of the postliturgical philological tradition—as philology likewise provided a precondition for power—from the birth of the Sanskrit cosmopolitan order throughout its lifetime. And when that era waned, the paradigm of the power of grammar and the grammar of power as mutually constituting forces continued for the vernacular cultural-political formations that followed (chapters 9, 10) until modernity implanted a new kind of polity and a new understanding of language. Working out the exact times and places of this history is no easy matter, however, and it requires as precise an assessment as we can achieve.

For the earliest period of Sanskrit grammar the historical data are too thin to allow us to demonstrate the mutually constitutive relationship of grammar and power with much cogency. For what it is worth, the seventh-century Chinese pilgrim Xuangzang reported a legend regarding Pāṇini that shows the salience of the linkage for the tradition: on completing his grammar Pāṇini offered it to his king, who "treasured it very much and ordered that all people in the country should learn the book; one who could recite it fluently by heart would be rewarded with one thousand gold coins."[8] Matters take on at least slightly harder historical contours by the time of Patañjali's *Mahābhāṣya*. The evidence here is still slender but suggestive nonetheless, and extrapolating from later practices may allow us to illuminate some of its obscurities.

Earlier it was noted that the conventional dating of the *Mahābhāṣya* to c. 150 B.C.E. is not as unproblematic as some scholars think (chapter 2.1). It rests to a large degree on the authorship of the very few lines in the work that contain historical reference, and their interpretation. Two of the most important passages, both of them well-known and discussed for a century in

7. Scharfe 1977: 187.
8. Xuanzang, trans. Li Rongxi (1995: 80–81).

Indological scholarship, are the merest of passing references: "Here we conduct a sacrifice on behalf of Puṣyamitra," and "The Yavana besieged Sāketa [Ayodhyā]." Patañjali is usually understood to be speaking *in propria persona* in both passages and especially so in the second, *aruṇad yavanaḥ sāketam,* which is adduced to illustrate the rule that, in contrast to the perfect tense, the imperfect is to be used for events the speaker may have witnessed himself (no such additional probative force attaches to the first example, which simply illustrates a continuous present). Whether Patañjali here is citing earlier materials, precisely as the *Kāśikā* commentary would do in the ninth century by citing these instances from the *Mahābhāṣya* itself; whether the invader in question is not the Indo-Greek king Menander (which would imply a date of c. 150 B.C.E.) but instead the Śakayavana mentioned by Patañjali elsewhere, which would give a *terminus post quem* of the first century B.C.E. — these factors are important for absolute dating but not pertinent to our purpose here. What is relevant is that Patañjali—or the earlier grammarian he may have been citing—was seeking, in a very subtle way that virtually all later grammarians were to adopt, to identify himself, his patron, and the place where he worked. That location was obviously courtly, whether it was the court of the Śuṅga overlords (the dynasty to which Puṣyamitra belonged) who succeeded the Maurya kings or another court three centuries later.[9]

We remain to some degree in the realm of legend and conjecture with the next two important grammarians, the *bauddha* Kumāralāta and the *vaidika* Śarvavarman, but these legends and conjectures are nevertheless instructive regarding the linkage of grammar and power. Kumāralāta is known as a grammarian only through fragments of his work discovered in central Asia and brilliantly analyzed at the beginning of the century by Heinrich Lüders. Lüders had earlier recovered a literary text of Kumāralāta's (the so-called *Kalpanāmaṇḍitika*) and with persuasive arguments identified his oeuvre as created in the Kuṣāṇa realm in the second half of the second century C.E. The Kuṣāṇa emperor Kaniṣka appears in two of the tales in Kumāralāta's story collection, but no further evidence is available to determine just how close the grammarian's association with the court may have been.[10]

The grammarian Śarvavarman, author of the *Kātantra* (see chapter 1.2), is placed by legendary accounts at the Sātavāhana court in perhaps the second century. This location may receive some confirmation in a remark of

9. See *Mahābhāṣya* 3.2.123 (vol. 2: 123), and 3.2.111 (vol. 2: 119) respectively for the two quotations; the Śakayavana is mentioned in *Mahābhāṣya* vol. 1: 475.4. The convention of self-identification here, the "index fossil" *(Leitfossil),* was famously identified by Kielhorn in *IA* 7: 266–67 and elaborated by Liebich 1930: 264 ff. To their evidence may be added Dharmadāsa's *ajayaj jarto hūṇān,* "Jarta defeated the Huns" (*Candravyākaraṇavṛtti* 1.2.81), referring no doubt to his (otherwise unknown) patron; see later in this chapter for the examples from Hemacandra and Śākaṭāyana. On the *Kāśikā*'s practice in citing earlier materials see Scharfe 1976: 275.

10. Lüders 1979: 143.

Xuanzang's biographer, who reported that "recently a Brahman of southern India again shortened [Pāṇini's grammar] to twenty-five hundred stanzas for the king of South India." It is also certain that the *Kātantra* antedates Candragomin's work, which is reasonably securely dated to the mid-fifth century.[11] Legends and medieval reports, however, were somewhat unsettled by Lüders' demonstration of the intimate relationship between Kumāralāta's text and Śarvavarman's; the oldest manuscript fragments of the *Kātantra* have in fact been found in the remains of Buddhist monasteries in central Asia. The question of who borrowed from whom has yet to be settled, and the textual evidence of the grammars themselves is insufficient to decide the matter. Considering the question broadly, however, it makes far more cultural sense to assume that the *Kātantra* was adopted and expanded by the northern Buddhists than the other way around.

The *Kātantra* was an extraordinarily popular work that old legend links with divine revelation (chapter 2.2). Its sobriquet, *K[a]umāra,* sooner points toward its links with Kārttikeya Kumāra, son of Śiva, through whose inspiration it was produced, than to the Buddhist grammarian. With its radical simplification of the Paninian system and elimination of rules pertaining to Vedic forms, it was evidently intended to meet the new needs of Sanskrit usage outside the world of the Brahmanical liturgy more effectively than Pāṇini's work could. (The exclusivity, indeed, the *vaidika* sectarianism, with which the *Aṣṭādhyāyī* was guarded was often bemoaned by later inventors of new grammars, as shown in the Jain story of the origins of Hemacandra's grammar discussed below.) Of course, such an aim seems equally germane whether the grammar originated in the purely non-Vedic community of the Buddhists or in a court about to be transformed forever by a newly public Sanskrit after centuries of Prakrit use for all nonsacred culture. But it is precisely the *Kātantra*'s core project of desacralization that makes parts of Kumāralāta's text appear to be the additions of a borrower—such as the sections on *ārṣa,* or "seer's" usage, where the seer is the Buddha and the texts in which the usages in question occur are Buddhist Sanskrit canonical works. In addition, the *Kātantra* shows clear evidence of the author's training in Vedic *prātiśākhya* literature, which is less easily explained if we assume that the Buddhist Kumāralāta was its creator and Śarvavarman its adaptor.[12]

11. On Candragomin (or sometimes simply Candra) see below. Liebich placed the *Kātantra* in the first century C.E. (1930: 266). For Xuanzang's biography Li Rongxi 1995: 110 (the text adds, "but this version, though very popular in frontier and uncultivated countries, was never studied by the erudite scholars of India," Xuanzang himself having studied Pāṇini). Śarvavarman was familiar with Patañjali's work (Scharfe 1977: 163 note 8), and while Patañjali himself knew a *sūtra* text called *Kālāpaka* (on 4.2.65), this likely refers to a Vedic *śākhā* (cf. 4.3.101, vol. 2: 315 lines 13 ff.).

12. Little attention has been paid to the *Kātantra* since Liebich 1919 (see especially pp. 5 ff.) and Lüders (1940: 659–72). Two recent Indian editions adduce no new evidence, and

Moreover, study of the *Kātantra/Kumāra* was long cultivated in the south of India. We have already seen that the great Telugu poet Nannaya in eleventh-century Veṅgi described his patron, King Rājarājanarenda, as "trained in the science of Kumāra." Also remarkable is the number of southern grammarians, from the Jain Sanskrit grammarian Śākaṭāyana to the Kannada grammarian Nāgarvarma (II), who styled themselves Abhinavaśarvavarma(n), "the New Śarvavarma(n)." And this is to say nothing of the endowments for instruction in the *Kumāra* grammar found in inscriptions across southern India.[13] All this evidence is far more easily explained by accepting a south Indian origin, with later dissemination to the north, than by assuming (as Lüders did) that the work was appropriated from northern Buddhists. Indeed, such an appropriation would be something uncommon, perhaps even unexampled, in history and implausible in itself. Philology in premodern India—whether we are speaking of metrics, represented by such works as the *Chandaḥsūtra* ascribed to Piṅgala, or rhetoric, as synthesized in Daṇḍin's *Kāvyādarśa,* or indeed, the very idea of language analysis as such—seems typically to have originated in the *vaidika* world and to have spread thence to the Buddhists as well as to Jains and vernacular intellectuals, as is shown dramatically by the later Pali tradition *(Vuttodaya, Subodhālaṅkāra, Saddanīti).* It is hard to think of cases where the direction was reversed.[14] Even so, whether it was Śarvavarman or Kumāralāta who composed the original *Kātantra,* there is little doubt that the author was closely associated with a ruling power, whether in the south or in the north.

For the following centuries the history of the relationship between philology and polity—or at least, though this is hardly less pertinent, the history of representations about this relationship—is on somewhat firmer footing. The *Rājataraṅgiṇī* of Kalhaṇa, which, though completed around 1150, sought to assemble with as much care as possible the traditions of polity current in Kashmir from earlier periods, comments in a well-known (if partially corrupt) passage on the philological activities of King Jayāpīḍa of Kashmir (fl. 790):

---

both are ignorant of Lüders' work. Thieme 1971: 526 n. 1 judges the question of priority unanswerable.

13. Several are noted later in this section. It is thus incorrect to state that the *Kātantra* remained popular only in Kashmir, Nepal, and Bengal (Scharfe 1977: 162–63). Extant southern manuscripts are admittedly rare, but—to cite only one instance—five are available in the ancient Jain *jnānabhandar* in Moodabidri (these have yet to be taken into account for the history of the text).

14. Lüders 1940: 719 dates the grammar of Kumāralāta to the end of the third century and the *Kātantra* (as an adaptation of the former) to the fourth. This still finds endorsement in the specialist literature (e.g., Oberlies 1996: 269–70). The cases of Bhāmaha (in literary science) or Amara (in lexicography) might provide counterevidence to the claim that philology spread from the *vaidika* world outward if their primacy, let alone their Buddhist affiliations, could be more clearly established.

> Knowledge *(vidyā)* had utterly disappeared in this country, its very birthplace . . . But [the king] brought it down to earth once more . . . [and by so doing] made all men eager for it. Having had learned men brought from another country, the king made the *Mahābhāṣya* available once again in his own sphere of political power, after its [tradition of study] had been interrupted. He himself took instruction from a grammarian named Kṣīra[svāmin] and soon became celebrated among the learned as "Pandit Jayāpīḍa" . . . His fame as pandit so far exceeded his fame as king that the political errors [he afterward committed] did not cause it to fade in later ages.[15]

A second, parallel passage in Kalhaṇa recounts how earlier Abhimanyu (c. 450)

> became king and ruled unchallenged and fearless like a second Indra . . . He built a city that he greatly enriched, calling it after his own name, Abhimanyu Town, and crowned it [with a temple to] the god Śiva. A scholar named Candra, along with others, having then received a command from him with regard to the tradition of [grammatical] knowledge, made the *Mahābhāṣya* available [in Kashmir] and wrote his own grammar [i.e., the *Cāndravyākaraṇa*].

Much has been written about the wording and meaning of this second text, especially in connection with a celebrated passage in a much earlier work of grammatical philosophy, Bhartṛhari's *Vākyapadīya* (perhaps sixth century). This appears to recount how the *āgama*—here meaning the oral tradition of interpretation—of the *Mahābhāṣya* had been broken, preserved only in manuscripts extant in the south of India, and how Candra then revived the tradition by recovering it from the "mountain" (from a mountain ascetic, according to some, or from the holy mountain Śrīparvata or Śrīśaila in Telangana, according to one reading of an early gloss).[16] However the accounts of Bhartṛhari and Kalhaṇa are to be reconciled, clearly, for Kalhaṇa at least, the stories of the kings Abhimanyu and Jayāpīḍa are meant to be symmetrical as well as to convey a sense of the central place of royal patronage in the fostering of systematic Sanskrit knowledge, especially philological knowledge. They thus testify to the larger paradigm at work concerning the correlation of grammatical and political correctness. It is a matter of interest—and of some irony, in view of other narratives considered below—that the study of the greatest contribution to Sanskrit grammar after Pāṇini's own work should have had (or been thought to have had) so unstable a presence in the land of Śāradā, the very goddess of Sanskrit learning. Of course,

15. *Rājataraṅgiṇī* 4.486–91.

16. The *Vākyapadīya* passage is 2.485–86. The key verses in the *Rājataraṅgiṇī* translated here are these: *deśāntarād āgamayya vyācakṣāṇān kṣamāpatiḥ | prāvartayata vicchinnaṃ mahābhāṣyaṃ svamaṇḍale* || (4.488); *candrācāryādibhir labdhvādeśāṃ tasmāt tadāgame | pravartitaṃ mahābhāṣyaṃ svaṃ ca vyākaraṇaṃ kṛtam* || (1.176). The problematic second stanza, especially *pāda* b (printed here in emended form), has been exhaustively studied, along with the *Vākyapadīya* verses, in Aklujkar 1987 and 1991. On the date of Candragomin and related questions see Oberlies 1989: 11 ff.

one may assume that complaints concerning the decay of knowledge had by Kalhaṇa's day become something of a rhetorical commonplace: recall that Patañjali himself had bemoaned the deterioration of grammatical learning in his own time (chapter 1.1). Rhetoric is no less historical, real, and factual than the "real" facts of history, and the rhetorical celebration of the achievement of a king such as Abhimanyu in securing the revival of grammar, and with it a peculiarly valorized form of cosmopolitan culture, tells us something central about this culture's relationship to power. It was as much a royal obligation—or such is the clear implication of the *Rājataraṅgiṇī*—to ensure the stability and continuation of the grammatical order, and if necessary to import masters to accomplish this, as it was to ensure the political order through fair taxation and defense and the spiritual order through the construction and reconstruction of holy places. Indeed, as the story of Jayāpīḍa shows, expertise in grammatical learning was represented as a core component of kingly rule, one that, well developed, could even trump misrule (which, to read Kalhaṇa's account of the king's later depredations, was very considerable in the case of "Pandit" Jayāpīḍa).

A generation or two after Jayāpīḍa, a court of equal brilliance but quite different literary character came into being among the Rāṣṭrakūṭa dynasty in today's northeastern Karnataka. There is much to say about this multilingual, even experimental, culture-power formation (chapter 9), for it was here at the end of the ninth century that a new vernacularity first made itself manifest in the Deccan. Concurrently, however, the Rāṣṭrakūṭa court continued to assiduously cultivate the values of cosmopolitan culture. An example is provided by an important figure in the time of King Amoghavarṣa Nṛpatuṅga (c. 875), the grammarian Śākaṭāyana. He was one of those, perhaps the first, who styled himself the New Śarvavarman, intending thereby to affiliate himself with the non-Pāṇinian traditions of grammar and the scholarly innovations of the author of the *Kātantra* (whose topical exposition of grammatical subject matter Śākaṭāyana follows closely), as well as, no doubt, with Śarvavarman's cultural stature. Śākaṭāyana's *Śabdānuśāsana* (Instruction in Language) bears an autocommentary called *Amoghavṛtti,* named after his patron, whom he mentions in what by that time had become the obligatory illustration of the simple past tense: *adahad amoghavarṣo 'rātīn,* "Amoghavarṣa annihilated his enemies."[17]

A second representative of Sanskrit cultural-political values at the Rāṣṭrakūṭa court, belonging to the following generation, was Halāyudha. His *Kavirahasya* (The Poet's Secret) is an encomium of the Rāṣṭrakūṭa king Kṛṣṇa III (r. 939–67), "the king consecrated for imperial power *(sāmrājyadīkṣita)* over the land of the south," as he puts it (v. 6). At the same time the text illus-

17. *Śākaṭāyanavyākaraṇa* 4.3.208.

trates the morphology and semantics of every Sanskrit verbal root. Exemplary are the following two verses, which exhibit the six forms of the roots *grath* and *granth* and the four forms of the root *vid* (the verbal forms of these roots are in italics in the translation, in roman in the original) while describing the king's cultural attributes—or more precisely, the ideal cultural attributes of the cosmopolitan overlord:

> He *composes* (Prakrit) lyric poetry and constantly *writes* transcendently
> beautiful (Sanskrit) verses,
> he *makes* books in crystal-clear prose and *pens* plays,
> he *authors* commentaries on sacred and scientific texts and many other
> books,
> and his mind, pure and guileless by nature, *is confused* by nothing.
>
> He *knows* all the *śāstras* and yet no pride *is found* in him
> he *deliberates* on *dharma* in the company of good men, and *gains* honor
> among them.
>
> *gāthāṃ* grāthayati grathaty *aviratam ślokāṃś ca lokottarān*
> *gadyaṃ* granthayati *sphuṭārthalalitaṃ yo nāṭakaṃ* granthati ।
> grathnāti *śrutiśāstrayor vivaraṇaṃ granthān anekāṃś ca yaḥ*
> *svacchaṃ yasya manaḥ svabhāvasaralaṃ na* granthate *kutracit* ॥
>
> vetti *sarvāṇi śāstrāṇi garvo yasya na* vidyate ।
> vintte *dharmaṃ sadā sadbhis teṣu pūjāṃ ca* vindati ॥[18]

The *Kavirahasya* as a grammar doubling as a *praśasti* (or perhaps the reverse) is one of the earliest examples of what would become an important subgenre of Sanskrit literature. Halāyudha had something of a model before him in Bhaṭṭi's *Rāmāyaṇa* of the mid-seventh century. This science-poem, enormously popular, as we have seen, demonstrates the rules of language analysis and literary art in the course of telling the story of Rāma. The poet declares at the very end that he wrote the work "in Valabhī when Śrīdharasena was ruling," which suggests a courtly origin for the work, though so far as can be determined from the text itself the narrative was not specifically intended to map against the life of the ruling overlord and cannot easily be read that way. In what is perhaps the most sophisticated realization of the form of a science-poem, however, the late-twelfth-century *Dvyāśrayakāvya* (Double-Narrative Poem), the author, Hemacandra, illustrates the rules drawn from his own Sanskrit and Prakrit grammars while simultaneously relating by way of sustained *śleṣa* the history of his patrons, two kings of the Caulukya dynasty of Gujarat: Jayasiṃha Siddharāja (whose Bilpaṅk *praśasti* was discussed in chapter 3.2) and his successor, Kumārapāla. If for the purposes of analyzing the interrelationship between power and philology we widen the

18. *Kavirahasya* vv. 14, 49.

genre-domain of *śāstrakāvya* to include the illustration of not only grammatical but also rhetorical norms *(alaṅkāraśāstra)*, as the latter part of Bhaṭṭi's work in fact does, we perceive a vast field of scholarly poetic texts on kings and literary culture. Especially influential was the *Pratāparudrayaśobhūṣaṇa* (Ornament to the Fame of Pratāpa), a *praśasti* on a Kākyatīya king of late-fourteenth-century Andhra, that also exemplifies the full array of topics in the science of literary art (tropology, *rasa* theory, and so on). The genre was to live on in many vernacular embodiments, too, including Kavibhūṣaṇ's panegyric textbook to the Maratha king Śivājī, composed for the king's coronation in 1674.[19]

This brief survey of power and philology could easily be extended. Indeed, it seems possible to include almost every important intellectual who wrote on grammar in the Sanskrit cosmopolis, ending with Nārāyaṇa Bhaṭṭa, the great scholar of sixteenth-century Kerala who composed the *Prakriyāsarvasva* (The Sum Total of Grammatical Operations) at the insistence of the king of Ambalapuzha; Bhaṭṭoji Dīkṣita and his nephew Kauṇḍa Bhaṭṭa, both of them grammarians and philosophers of language who received patronage from the post-Vijayanagara *nāyaka* kings of Keladi in the seventeenth century; and, when the sun of Sanskrit cosmopolitanism had already set, Nāgeśa Bhaṭṭa (d. c. 1700), court philologist at the petty princedom of Śṛṅgaverapura in what is today eastern Uttar Pradesh.[20] And if in addition we include in the domain of philologists the scholars of literary science *(alaṅkāraśāstra)* who worked at royal courts, the list is long: from Daṇḍin (at the court of Śivaskandavarman Pallava in late-seventh-century Kāñcīpūram), Vāmana and Udbhaṭa (at the court of Jayāpīḍa of Kashmir, c. 800), and Ānandavardhana (at the court of Avantivarman, c. 850) to Viśvanātha (at the court of an unknown king of Kaliṅga), Śiṅgabhūpāla (himself a king of the Rēcarla dynasty in Telangana in today's Andhra Pradesh, c. 1330), Jagannātha (at the court of Shāh Jahān, c. 1650), and Viśveśvara (at the royal court of Almora, c. 1700). The list contains the name of virtually every important scholar in literary science save for those Kashmiris who, in the radically altered political conditions of the eleventh and twelfth centuries at the brink of the collapse of a creative Sanskrit literary culture, chose (or were forced) to avoid the court altogether.[21] This long list makes it obvious that Sanskrit literary culture was seriously nourished by the courtly elite, but it also suggests how far that elite felt called upon, perhaps even compelled, to provide such nourishment.

The rather vague data about the careers of philologists, and the perhaps

19. See Busch 1997.

20. See Kunjuni Raja 1980: 126; Dikshit 1982: 100.

21. Pollock 2001a: 397–400. The one tentative identification concerns Daṇḍin. Pace Lienhard (1984: 234–35) there is no reason to doubt that *Avantisundarī* is an authentic seventh-century text, and that its narrative proves the scholar's presence in the Pallava courtly milieu.

formulaic representations concerning the philological preoccupations of rulers, that are available in grammatical and rhetorical works can be made far more concrete and specific by glancing at the royal endowments aimed at supporting the reproduction of grammatical knowledge. No systematic inventory has ever been done of the massive evidence available for this in inscriptions. Yet princely benefactions made for the study of grammar and philological, literary, and philosophical knowledge generally—not just the support for purely *vaidika* knowledge that we find in the earliest land grants—are dramatically in evidence in the epigraphical record and evince a marked increase from about the tenth century on (whether this is an artifact of the chance preservation of records or in response to some actual changes in the cultural-political landscape remains unknown). Consider just Karnataka. In a remarkable inscription of Govinda IV of the Rāṣṭrakūṭa dynasty from 929, land is gifted to two hundred Brahmans in Puligeṟe in northwest Karnataka for the study of grammar (as well as political theory, literary criticism, history, logic, and, notably, commentary writing); a unique syllabus from a Kālamukha Śaiva college in Kōḍhimaṭha (in Shimoga district), described in a grant emanating from King Bijjaḷa of the Kāḷacūri lineage of Kalyāṇa in 1162, includes "analysis of the *Kaumāra* [i.e., *Kātantra*], *Pāṇinīya, Śākaṭāyanaśabdānuśāsana,* and other grammars"; and provision for training specifically in the *Kumāra* grammar is made by a benefaction in the same region in 1124. In Tamilnadu, the Cōḻa king Kulottuṅga (III) in 1235 donated some four hundred acres of land for the construction of what the epigraph calls a "hall for the analysis of the gift of grammar" *(vyākaraṇadānavyākhyānamaṇḍapa),* where students would also worship Mahādeva Śiva, the patron deity of grammar.[22]

Further amassing of data would only be redundant; the main point should be clear: that power's concern with grammar, and to a comparable degree grammar's concern with power, comprised a constitutive feature of the Sanskrit cosmopolitan order. A sense of just how vital a concern this was emerges, however, not from a review of patrons and benefactions but from an account of the dynamics of power and grammar in rival dominions in western India between 1000 and 1200, the last centuries of the Sanskrit cosmopolis's full, undiminished vigor.

22. Śiva's relationship to grammar merits a separate study. Note that the Sanskrit syllabary is traditionally transmitted according to the "*sūtra*s of Śiva," and stories of Pāṇini's revelation by Śiva's grace were known to Xuanzang (trans. Li Rongxi [1996: 80]). For the inscriptions see *EI* 13: 332 (the record of a donation to Brahmans for Brahmanical scholarship is in Kannada, in accordance with the increasing vernacularization of the region [see chapter 9, also 10.4 and n. 99], and offers a notable early example of *gadyakāvya*); *EC* 7; *SK* 102; *SII* 20: 105.20; *SITI* p. 501 (no. 518). Compare also Sankaranarayanan 1994. Grammar halls were common features of Cōḻa-era temples in Tamilnadu.

4.2 GRAMMATICAL AND POLITICAL CORRECTNESS: GRAMMAR ENVY

Sometime in the early 1100s, the celebrated Mahākāla temple in Ujjayinī (in today's Madhya Pradesh), the temple of Śiva in his form as the God of Great Time, was restored by a Paramāra king named Naravarman. To mark the event he inscribed there a long and impressive hymn to the deity. It is not so much the poem that arrests our attention, however, as what lies engraved below it: a *sarpabandha* (serpentine graph) used by students at the temple school for learning the Sanskrit alphabet (in the snake's body) and nominal and verbal endings (in the tail); and, to the left of the snake's head, the following verses (only partially legible here):

> This is the serpentine scimitar of language sounds of King Udayāditya. It is a badge to be worn on the chest of poets and kings.
>
> This unique magical sword belonging to the worshippers of Śiva, the kings Udayāditya and Naravarman, serves the *varṇasthiti,* the preservation of language sounds (and, social orders).[23]

These verses, or parts of them, and the accompanying grammatical chart are also found in the celebrated Bhojaśālā, or Hall of Bhoja, which functioned as school and literary center in the Paramāra capital city of Dhārā, as well as in a now-ruined temple outside the city. Naravarman, and the Paramāras more generally, clearly valued these verses as they valued the mastery of grammatical knowledge toward which they pointed. This impression is reinforced by the argument of the verses themselves, as well as their very wording. Grammar is a veritable weapon in the hands of a king, but one that works best when it is also in the hands of the *prajā,* the people of the realm. And what grammar preserves is not just language but sociality as such. This is powerfully enunciated in the second verse, in a manner unique to the genius of the Sanskrit language, by means of a *śleṣa:* the "preservation of language sounds" and the "preservation of social orders" are expressed by the same words, *varṇa-sthiti,* and so are ontologically linked by their semantic coreferentiality (we have seen the same core concept of Sanskrit culture at work in the identification of kings and gods in *praśasti*s, chapter 3.2). A king, the very self-conception of whose existence depended on the stability of the one—since the "regulation of social orders and life stages," as so many inscriptions put it (as did King Bhoja himself, cited below), was the most fun-

23. *CII* 7.2: 83 ff., vv 85–86: *udayādityadevasya varṇṇanāgakṛpāṇikā* | *kavīnāṃ ca nṛpāṇāṃ ca veṣo vakṣasi ropitaḥ* || *ekeyam udayādityanaravarmmamahībhujoḥ* | *maheśasvāminor varṇṇasthityai siddhāsiputrikā* [read *-pattrikā?*] || See p. 89 for another copy of the verses. The *śleṣa varṇasthiti* occurs first in *Harṣacarita* v. 13.

the other, knowledge of grammar. As their one signifier proves, the social and grammatical orders are related by their very nature.

Naravarman, the son of Udayāditya, was the author of hymns to the deities and praise-poems on the Paramāra family; he may even have composed the great Nagpur *praśasti* in 1104.[24] By these literary efforts he affiliated himself with a long line of poet-kings in the dynasty. A century and a half before him ruled King Muñja. Known by the sobriquet Vākpati, "Master of Speech," Muñja (or Utpala, as he was also named) was described by his own court poet, Dhanapāla, as the "ocean of all knowledge," and by Padmagupta, court poet to his younger brother and successor, Sindhurāja, as "the single shoot of the Wishing Vine of Sarasvatī, Goddess of Speech." This should not be taken—though it typically is taken—as yet more formulaic praise. A number of Muñja's memorable poems in Apabhramsha as well as in Sanskrit—he was one of the few poets outside of dramatists who can be said with certainty to have composed in both these cosmopolitan languages—are still extant, preserved in anthologies. When hostilities erupted between the Paramāras and the Kalyāṇa Cāḷukyas, Muñja was captured, jailed, hanged, and beheaded by Tailapa II, who "fixed his head on a pike in the courtyard" of his palace, "smearing it daily with curd as he nursed his rage." With the death of Muñja, a later poet said, "Sarasvatī lost her very home."[25] Muñja's nephew, and the elder brother of the Udayāditya mentioned earlier, was Bhoja.

Warrior, town planner, builder of irrigation works and more, as well as the most celebrated poet-king and philosopher-king of his time, and perhaps of any Indian time, Bhoja ruled over much of western India for more than forty years (1011–55) from his new imperial capital, Dhārā, in the region of Avantī in the country of Mālava, about one hundred kilometers southwest of Ujjayinī.[26] We get a far less vivid image of the man from his extant inscriptions, which are unexpectedly few in number (five copperplate grants survive all told) than from his remarkable writings, which span the range of San-

24. *CII* 7.2: 106 ff., v. 56: "[Naravarman] caused this temple to be made by Lakṣmīdhara [less likely: '[Naravarman], who bears the royal glory, caused . . . '], which is adorned with multiple *praśasti*s and hymns that he himself has composed" (cf. *CII* 7.2: 108 and *Paramāra Abhilekha:* 170).

25. See, respectively, *Tilakamañjarī* p. 5, v. 53; *Navasāhasāṅkacarita* 1.7; *Prabandhacintāmaṇi* pp. 22–25. It was noted in chapter 3.3 that in one of Taila's early inscriptions (*IA* 21: 167 ff., undated but c. 974 C.E.), Taila is said to have "slain Muñja and taken the head of Pañcāla." Perhaps Merutuṅga, author of *Prabandhacintāmaṇi,* conflated the events for dramatic effect. (On decapitating and displaying the head of an enemy king, see the Cōḻa instance in Nagaswamy 1987: 32 v. 14).

26. He is credited with the defeat of Turuṣkas at Dvārakā in 1001 C.E. in the *Śyāmalādaṇḍaka* (cited in *ŚP* [ed. Joyser] vol. 2: viii, and *Sarasvatīkaṇṭhābharaṇavyākaraṇa,* p. xiv, and cf. *CII* 7.2: 75 ff., and v. 19 of the inscription); his town-planning initiatives are described in his *Samaraṅganasūtradhāra* and embodied in *prabandha* tales of the building of the city of Dhārā; for his construction of a tank in Kashmir "with heaps of gold" see *Rājataraṅgiṇī* 7.190.

skrit disciplines. Bhoja was a poet of renown; one of his numerous works, the mixed prose-verse *Rāmāyaṇacampū,* quickly entered into the canon of Sanskrit classics in late-medieval India. A sixteenth-century commentator describes it thus: "This *campū* composition was written by King Bhoja. In the courtyard of his tongue Sarasvatī used to dance in ecstasy. And if mortals closely observe his speech, they too can become princes among poets." Bhoja was also a literary scholar whose vision of literature, expressed in his *Śṛṅgāraprakāśa,* was the most comprehensive India had ever seen (chapter 2.3). In the middle of this text, when offering an explanation of an invocation to Śiva he wrote at the beginning of the book, Bhoja shows us a glimpse of the political man reflecting on his kingly duties in the midst of his literary engagement. It remains one of the very few personal references in the dozens of works attributed to him:

> It is not just anyone who speaks this verse, but rather a very special man, a great lord [or, great devotee of the Lord] appointed by his elders to protect all the inherited realm. And it is he who hereby beseeches God to ensure—since God alone is capable of doing so—that while he is engaged in the composition of this book there should be no violation against the established order and practices of the social orders and life stages.[27]

Above all, Bhoja is remembered as the head of a fabled literary court and as a much-sought-after benefactor of poets. Bilhaṇa (fl. 1080), the most celebrated Kashmiri writer of the generation following Bhoja, who wandered across the cosmopolitan world in search of a just king and fit patron, speaks memorably of his regret that Bhoja had died before he could meet him:

> "Bhoja was a king with nothing in common with vicious overlords.
> How could you have failed to seek refuge with him? Now you are lost!"
> So the city of Dhārā seemed to speak to me, in sorrow,
> under the guise of doves moaning in the clefts of its high spires.[28]

Bhoja's name and fame would be emulated by princes for the next five hundred years: Kṛṣṇadevarāya, the great king of the Vijayanagara empire in the early sixteenth century, took as two of his titles Abhinavabhoja, "the New Bhoja," and Sakalakalābhoja, "Bhoja in All the Arts." Legends of correctness in *rājya* and *kāvya,* indeed, stories in which the literary text functions as a kind of political weapon, clustered around Bhoja more densely than around any other king in a world dense with narratives of polity and poetry. A dominant feature of these narratives concerns Bhoja's role as ultimate arbiter of grammatical correctness, rhetorical propriety, and literary good taste, all

27. *ŚP* p. 405 lines 10ff. (J 257.15ff.; for *pūrvajñaiḥ* read *pūrvajaiḥ; mahāmāheśvaraḥ,* v. l. *mahāmaheśvaraḥ*).

28. *Vikramāṅkadevacarita* 18.96 (conjecturing *hato 'si* for *hatāsmi*).

three being aspects of a single philological habit. Countless stories relate Bhoja's bountiful rewards for the perfect capping verse *(samasyā-pūrti,* or *-pūraṇa)* or the use of the *mot juste* (well-known among pandits even today is the tale of the gift of three *lakh*s of gold coins to a Brahman who used the rare word *jānudaghna,* "knee-high," to describe the water level of a river). He corrects the grammar in communications sent by other kings and exchanges verses and counterverses (*āryā*s and *pratyāryā*s) with rivals, such as Bhīma, king of the Gujarati Caulukyas, almost as acts of war.[29] It matters not a bit that these narratives are found in collections dating from three to five centuries after Bhoja's lifetime. The very longevity of the motif of a king's capacity for correct philological judgment serves to establish its historical importance. For philological judgment was not just that; it was a sign or, more justly, an index—given the ontological linkage just noted between the order of language and the order of society *(varṇasthiti)*—of correct political judgment. The political was thoroughly pervaded by the poetical and the philological—and above all by the grammatical.

Like so many other rulers, Bhoja is associated with an actual grammar, the *Sarasvatīkaṇṭhābharaṇa* (Necklace of the Goddess of Speech, the same name as was given to his first treatise on literary science [chapter 2.3] and, indeed, to his royal palace);[30] in this case, however, the king may well have composed the grammar himself. There is little doubt that the eight-chapter work—which, unlike earlier competitor-grammars such as those of Śarvavarman or Śākaṭāyana, includes a treatment of the Vedic register in its last chapter—was intended to supplant Pāṇini's *Aṣṭādhyāyī* (Eight Chapters). It employs many of the techniques of the classic text, sometimes quoting *sūtra*s from the *Aṣṭādhyāyī* itself, and incorporates many of the emendations offered by later writers, from Kātyāyana to the *Kāśikāvṛtti.* Later history shows, however, that this grand hope was nowhere fulfilled; as with Bhoja's literary treatises, it was only in south India, and only in a very few locales in south India, that the work was included in the grammar syllabus (it survives today in a small number of manuscripts). But indirectly its historical impact has been substantial.

Around 1140, less than a century after Bhoja's death, the Caulukya king of Gujarat, Jayasiṃha Siddharāja, marched against Bhoja's capital, perhaps

29. Bhoja corrects the grammar of King Kulacandra in *Purātanaprabandhasaṃgraha* no. 8 (also p. 21 paragraph 39). Bhoja and Bhīma exchange challenge verses in *Prabhāvakacarita* no. 18.14ff., with Bhoja eventually conceding ("How could one possibly conquer a region that produces such a poet as this?" Contrast no. 12 [37], and see also *Prabhandacintāmaṇi* p. 28, no. 45). In *Purātanaprabandhasaṃgraha* no. 11 (p. 20), King Gāṅgeya of Varanasi is released from Bhoja's captivity on the strength of a sophisticated verse composed by his court pandit Parimala. For *jānudaghna* see *Prabhandacintāmaṇi* p. 26 line 9 and *Bhojaprabandha* pp. 40–41 (and *Aṣṭādhyāyī* 5.2.37).

30. The Sarasvatīkaṇṭhābharaṇaprāsāda is mentioned in *Tilakamañjarī* p. 5; see also *CII* 7.2: 49 and n. 3.

the very campaign mentioned in the Bilpaṅk *praśasti* (chapter 3.3). There he was met by the sight of students in the Bhojaśālā studying the king's grammar night and day, an event that left a deep impression in his imagination. Whether it was on this campaign or another is unclear, but eventually Jayasiṃha sacked Dhārā, and among the loot he carried back to his capital Aṇahilapāṭaka was Bhoja's library, including the *Sarasvatīkaṇṭhābharaṇa* grammar.[31]

It was Bhoja's Sanskrit grammar that provided the impetus for, and was meant to be eclipsed by, the Sanskrit-Prakrit-Apabhramsha grammar of Hemacandra (1088–1172). This remarkable Jain spiritual master, besides being an intimate of King Jayasiṃha (who himself was a firm, even aggressive Śaiva) and the cleric responsible for the conversion to Jainism of Jayasiṃha's nephew and successor, Kumārapāla (r. 1143–73), was in many ways the very model of the universal intellectual of the late cosmopolitan epoch, and yet was awake to the emergent vernacularism (his theorization is discussed in chapter 10.2; his appreciation of the new "courtly epic in the vulgar language" was noted in chapter 2.2). It was at the express command of the king that Hemacandra composed his grammar, the *Siddhahemacandra,* as he tells us in a *praśasti* at the end of that work: "[King Śrī Siddharāja] was disturbed by the mass of prolix, unintelligible, and disorganized grammars and besought the sage Hemacandra to compose this grammar according to the proper rules. And an incomparable grammar it is." The patronage of King Siddharāja is not only reflected in the title of the grammar; it is, once again, coded in an illustration of the historical past verbal tense: "Siddharāja besieged Avantī" (5.2.8), thus commemorating the very event that brought Bhoja's library and his grammar to Hemacandra. All these matters are best related in a narrative contained in a fourteenth-century Jain story collection, Prabhācandra's *Prabhāvakacarita,* which largely supports the account coded in Hemacandra's grammar itself (see appendix A.4 for the translation).[32]

The many significations that grammatical correctness carried in the political environment of medieval India are encapsulated in this tale. While clearly retaining the numinous qualities associated with its legendary origins

31. On Jayasiṃha's visit to the Bhojaśālā, see *Prabhāvakacarita* pp. 156–157, 185 (and cf. *Śṛṅgāramañjarīkathā,* introduction, p. 10 n. 12). Bhoja's *Śṛṅgāraprakāśa* must have been among the looted books, for it is otherwise hard to explain how Hemacandra alone among the scholars of western India knew the text, from which he borrows heavily in his *Kāvyānuśāsana.*

32. Bühler long ago remarked on the grammar's corroboration of the *Prabhāvakacarita* narrative, namely, that the work is not only dedicated to Jayasiṃha but owes its existence to his demand (Bühler 1889: 183 ff., adducing other data to establish the historicity of the tale; he dates the actual composition of the grammar to about 1140, p. 185). The *Leitfossil* (on the *sūtra khyāte dṛśye*), in addition to *aruṇat siddharājo 'vantīṃ,* also includes *ajayat siddhaḥ saurāṣṭrān,* "Siddha conquered the people of Saurāṣṭra." For the *praśasti* see *Siddhahemacandra* after 8.4.448 ("prolix, unintelligible, and disorganized grammars," *ativistṛtadurāgamaviprakīrṇaśabdānuśāsana-;* cf. *saṃkīrṇa* in appendix A n. 6).

in the revelation of Śiva, and, accordingly, being stored in its most perfect form in the temple of the Goddess of Speech in the far-off land of Kashmir, from where Hemacandra acquired his supremely authoritative exemplars, grammar was at the same time clearly a precious cultural good, one that could be imported and whose very possession secured high prestige for its possessor. When Jayasiṃha insists on obtaining a new grammar, as Prabhācandra represents it in his tale, there is no implication whatever that this has to do with mere communicative efficacy, that a better understanding of the language makes for more effective rule or administration, as was the case in more or less contemporary Europe, where Nebrija (the celebrated example) contended that one purpose of his grammar was to facilitate the imposition of imperial law and rule. Such simplistic instrumentality does not apply to the knowledge of Sanskrit, which was never the language of rule in any quotidian sense of the term. There is even less cultural coherence in our supposing that Jayasiṃha sought a more cohesive political unity by means of a more cohesive linguistic unity, a linkage often asserted in European cultural-political theory and practice, most notably with the Pléiade and François I in mid-sixteenth-century France (chapter 11.3). The sphere and nature of Jayasiṃha's political project are entirely different. It is the vast Sanskrit cosmopolitan space that is his realm of concern, and the king spares no expense to reproduce the grammar and thereby ensure that it can circulate across this space—something unthinkable for any but the three languages of literature. The *Siddhahemacandra* was a grammar for the large world, not just for the smaller world of Gujarat where it was produced. Justification for the production of a new grammar is indeed sought in the critique of earlier works: Śarvavarman's *Kātantra* is too brief, Pāṇini's *Aṣṭādhyāyī* too closely associated with the Brahmans (according to the Jain narrative voice of the *Prabhāvakacarita,* speaking somewhat incongruously and ventriloquistlike through the Śaiva king Jayasiṃha). One real motivating force, however, is presented by the existence of a dominant grammar in the competitor polity of the Paramāras, and Jayasiṃha's primary objective is to supplant it and thereby, one assumes, appropriate the political charisma of the grammarian-king Bhoja. As Jayasiṃha himself declares, the new grammar is meant to confer royal glory upon the king, as it confers scholarly renown upon the grammarian—along with spiritual merit upon them both.

As we saw when considering the aesthetics of *praśasti* discourse, it was the glory of the king that was the preeminent concern of a literary composition in Sanskrit, not the particularities of the everyday world, for which the languages of Place increasingly came to be used. For only in a language dignified and stabilized by grammar—not in a lawless vernacular, unconstrained by predictable and universal grammatical norms and therefore in constant danger of degeneration—could the fame of the ruler receive permanent, even eternal expression: It is the Sanskrit poet who, according to the old trope, produces the "glory body" of the king, which remains on earth even after his mortal body has disappeared. The perfect language of textuality *(vāṅmaya)* functions as a stainless mirror continuing to reflect his glory image even when he himself is gone.[33]

Yet, as we can perceive in the account of the revival of grammatical knowledge in Kashmir under King Jayāpīḍa, and in the "serpentine scimitar of language sounds" of King Udayāditya, there is something more political and urgent to grammaticality than the somewhat abstract, distant, even transcendent quality of glory—something more deeply rooted and ramifying throughout the culture-power formation of the cosmopolis. In an important sense, the order of Sanskrit grammar—the same order that informs the most exquisite instantiation of grammatical language, namely, *kāvya,* and its specific political form, the *praśasti*—was a model or prototype of the moral, social, and political order: a just *(sādhu)* king was one who used and promoted the use of correct language *(sādhuśabda).* A similar logic was expressed by the seventh-century philosopher Kumārila in his critique of Buddhist language and thought: only by using a language whose form is true *(sat)* can one possibly speak the truth (*satya;* chapter 1.2). Indeed, the correlation in Sanskrit culture between good language and good action—especially dharmic, or ritual, action—is even older and more general: "The proper use of a single word, founded on grammar and known to be so, can grant one's wish in the world of heaven," runs an old proverb preserved in the *Mahābhāṣya,* which also warns us of the reverse: "A word corrupt in accent or phoneme improperly used not only does not transmit its sense but becomes a thunderbolt to destroy the sacrificer." As Bhoja states with lapidary simplicity, bad language leads to *adharma,* moral failure.[34]

The implications of the association between grammatical and political correctness are far-reaching. If the preservation of language sounds *(varṇa)* that grammar achieves was linked essentially to the preservation of the social orders *(varṇa),* and so to that of the polity at large, the obligation to maintain the order of language was no less than, and perhaps no different from, the obligation to maintain the political and spiritual order. This seems partly what Rājaśekhara, Bhoja's predecessor in the field of encyclopedic courtly poetics, is implying when he states, "If the king is a poet, everyone will be a poet" *(rājani kavau sarvo lokaḥ kaviḥ syāt).*[35] When the king is a true poet, when he

33. *Rājataraṅgiṇī* 1.45 and *KĀ* 1.5 and 1.3; compare *Vikramāṅkadevacarita* 1.26–27. "A king who has no poets can have no fame—how many kings have there been on earth whose names no one even knows? The fact that Rāvaṇa's fame is slight and Rāma's vast is evidence of the Ādikavi's power. Kings should never anger poets."

34. See *Mahābhāṣya* on 6.1.84 (5), Kielhorn vol. 3: 58, and Kielhorn vol. 1: 2; *ŚP* 473, *duṣprayuktaḥ punar adharmāya sampadyate* (cf. *KĀ* 1.6 for another formulation). The general point has been recognized by many scholars; see, for example, Deshpande 1985: 134.

35. *KM* p. 54 line 19.

successfully combines the primal form of culture with that of power, the whole world will successfully combine them, too—an idea that only seems to make sense if the order of Sanskrit poetry, and the grammar and literary sciences that underpin it, are somehow thought to recapitulate the order of the social and political world. Again, this equivalence comes about not through any simple instrumental application of philology but by some broader process of self-discipline and self-constraint. Power in the Sanskrit cosmopolis cared for language, without doubt, but in ways that no other cultural-political world has quite prepared us to understand.

4.3 LITERATURE AND KINGLY VIRTUOSITY

Sanskrit literature knew as wide a range of social sites for its production and consumption—from the village to the monastery to the private circle of aficionados—as any other premodern literature, but its primary location was undoubtedly always the court. The court was the source of both patronage and the glory *(yaśas)* conferred by the approbation of the learned—the former being pragmatically what kept the poet writing, the latter being what ultimately made writing worthwhile, at least for most poets. Thus it is surprising to register how little systematic and substantive work has been done on the courtly culture of Sanskrit, even though materials for doing so exist in abundance.[36] Much of the cultural hagiography of Bhoja mentioned earlier revolves around precisely this theme; a late work like Ballāla's *Bhojaprabandha* (Legends of Bhoja, c. 1600) looks back nostalgically at Bhoja's reign as the perfection of courtly literary life. (To demonstrate this ideality and as a kind of magical realist *avant la lettre,* Ballāla peopled Bhoja's court with poets from every historical epoch, from Kālidāsa to those of his own day.) And these accounts have already taught us something about the place of literature no less than that of philology in the Sanskrit cosmopolis at its high-water mark at the beginning of the second millennium. But something less singular and more general about the political sociality and intellectuality of literary culture—less concerned with particular persons than with institutions and, along with them, structures of understanding—may be captured by examining one of the few synthetic accounts of royal culture available from premodern India, the remarkable work on courtly practices titled *Mānasollāsa* (Mind's Delight), or sometimes *Abhilāṣitārthacintāmaṇi* (Wishing Gem of All Desires).

The *Mānasollāsa* is a mixed genre, part encyclopedia—the first in India, it would appear—and part "mirror for princes." It was composed in 1131 in Kalyāṇa during the reign of King Someśvara III, the last of the great lords of

36. Cf. Lienhard 1984: 16 ff.; Smith 1985: 87 ff.; Tieken 1992: 371 ff. I briefly explore some of these other social sites in Pollock 2003: 118–20, where an earlier version of this account of the *Mānasollāsa* appears.

the second Cāḷukya dynasty, probably by a court scholar but attributed to the king himself. In twelfth-century Karnataka the project of vernacularization was already well advanced (chapter 9), but while the Sanskrit encyclopedist importantly registers the transitional aspect of his cultural location—he provides some of the earliest textualizations we have of vernacular lyrics and showcases Kannada itself (see chapter 8.2)—his conceptual scheme is still of the cosmopolitan sort found in Bhoja. The work calls itself *jagadācāryapustaka,* "a book-teacher of the universal sphere [of practices]," and while its will-to-knowledge in every domain of human activity is indeed astonishing, what first and foremost interests the writer are the practices of lordly power. The book consists of five principal sections: the requirements for the acquisition of political power *(rājyaprāptikāraṇa);* the consolidation of power *(rājyasthirīkaraṇa);* the physical enjoyment of power *(rājyopabhoga);* the entertainments of intellectual delight *(pramoda[janaka-* or *-āpāyaka-]vinoda);* and the pleasures of sport *(sukhopapādikakrīḍā).* It is in the fourth section that *kāvya* comes in for consideration, in the subsections called *śāstravinoda,* "the entertainment of learned discourse," and *kathāvinoda,* "the entertainment of storytelling."[37]

The fourth section actually commences with the entertainment of weaponry *(śastravinoda).* Here the king himself comes forth to display his mastery of every conceivable weapon and the maneuvers associated with them. This is followed by the *śāstravinoda* subsection. Thereafter in succession are subsections on the skills of elephant drivers and horsemen, and on dueling, wrestling, cockfighting, hunting, and so on, ending with singing, instrumental music, dancing, storytelling, and the application of magical ointments. In some of these the king is a spectator; in others he is a participant. But in all of them he is centrally involved as connoisseur and critic.

The description of the *sabhā,* or cultural assembly, of the king at the start of the entertainments of intellectual delight section gives us a sense of not only who the participants and spectators for royal culture were but also the prominence among them of masters of verbal art. Included are, of course, courtiers *(sevaka),* ministers, princes, governors, vassals, but also scholars *(paṇḍita),* makers of poems *(kāvyakartṛ),* those skilled in languages of Place *(deśabhāṣāviśārada,* which notably constituted a separate and subordinate category of culture-makers within the cosmopolitan literary culture), reciters of literary texts *(pāṭhaka),* singers *(gāyaka),* epic reciters *(sūta),* genealogists *(māgadhabandins,* or "genealogists and reciters of praise-poems"), and last, the various women of the harem and courtesans.[38] The *śāstravinoda* section

37. These five parts are called *viṃśati,* "consisting of twenty," i.e., *adhyāyas* or chapters. I cite the work by *viṃśati* and *śloka,* as well as by volume and page number. For *jagadācāryapustaka,* see *Mānasollāsa* 1.10, vol. 1: 2; for *śāstravinoda,* 4.197 ff., vol. 2: 171 ff.; for *kathāvinoda,* 4.1406–32, vol. 3: 162–65.

38. *Mānasollāsa* 4.3–5, vol. 2: 155.

supplements (or sometimes replaces) these categories of courtiers with "accomplished poets, reciters, disputants and exegetes, and learned and wise men who know the *śāstra*" whom the king invites for his intellectual delight. These men are all "skilled in the arts of language, men of natural genius, practiced in the three precious knowledges [that is, grammar, hermeneutics *(mīmāṃsā)*, and logic], creators and interpreters *(utpādaka, bhāvajña)*, adept at versification and conversant with the principles of sweet poetry, and knowledgeable in all languages."[39]

The entertainment of *śāstra* begins with the king commanding the poets to "recite a lovely poem" and then himself reflecting on the poem's literary excellences and faults *(guṇān doṣān vicārayet)*. The boundaries of this reflection are clearly stated: "Words make up the body of a literary text, meaning is its life-breath, figures of speech its external form, aesthetic moods and feelings *(rasa, bhāva)* its movements, meter its gait, and grammaticality *(śabdavidyā)* its vital spot. In these does the beauty of the deity of literature consist."[40] Our own modern-day preference may be to downplay the metaphor of the "deity of literature," although the tenth-century poet Rājaśekhara speaks of a Primal Being of Literature, and the first great work of Kannada vernacularization similarly celebrates the Primal Being of the Literary Entity, while poets were routinely called Sārasvata, offspring of Sarasvatī, Goddess of Language.[41] Yet there is no question that the literary represented nothing remotely like the mere commodity it has become in modernity; it was a far more potent shaping force of culture and power. And its human makers participated fully in this force by creating new shapes of word and meaning: new shapes of words called meters, new shapes of meanings called tropes, new structures of signification called aesthetic feelings. What is most important, however, was preserving inviolate the literary deity's most vulnerable spots by correct use of language.

The *Mānasollāsa* next expands into a detailed account of the principles of literary knowledge that a royal connoisseur in late-twelfth-century central India was expected to possess and apply: the expression-forms *(guṇa)* of poetic language and the different kinds of "Paths" *(rīti)* of writing, the basic concepts and common varieties of meters, the major figures of speech, the features of the principal genres, and the components and operation of the primary aesthetic moods. The king listens to this talk about literature and reflects on the strengths and weaknesses of the poems he has heard recited.

39. "Reciters": read (with ms. A) *gamakān* (or *gamakīn*) for *gāyakān*. *Gamaka(i), vādin,* and *vāgmin* together constitute a triad peculiar to medieval (Karnataka?) courts. See for example *SII* 9.1: 92 (dated 1055 C.E.). "The principles of sweet poetry": read *madhurakāvya-* (for *madhurān*).

40. *Mānasollāsa* 4.197–206 (vol. 2: 171–72; *nānāprakṛtayaḥ* is obscure).

41. "Deity of literature," *kāvyadeva*. On Rājaśekhara's *kāvyapuruṣa,* see chapter 5.2; on the *Kavirājamārgam*'s *kāvyavastupuruṣa,* chapter 9.2; on the sons of Sarasvatī, Granoff 1995.

He then summons debaters, whom he zealously rouses to a disputation about the nature of singing, dancing, and music—which provides the encyclopedist an opportunity to set out the rudiments of inferential reasoning and debate strategies.[42]

The penultimate subsection—before the one containing the *camatkāravinoda,* or the entertainment of magical ointments and powders that render a person clear-sighted or invisible or enable him to walk on water—is the entertainment of storytelling *(kathāvinoda).* After the lord has completed his daily duties, dined, and rested, he should summon men to tell him stories about the deeds of heroes from the *Mahābhārata,* the *Rāmāyaṇa,* the *purāṇa*s, or the *Bṛhatkathā,* or from plays or courtly epics. The storytellers should be eloquent and cultured men, "who know the four languages"—that is, the standard three, Sanskrit, Prakrit, Apabhramsha, plus the newly elevated vernacular of the region, Kannada (see chapter 9.2)—who believe in the truth of the duties demanded by *dharma (āstikān dharmakāryeṣu),* men young in years but mature in intellect, who are veritable "axes to cut down the tree of sadness, fires to burn the tinder of despondency, moons to swell the ocean of passion, suns to open the lotuses of desire." The stories are recited solo or in groups of two or three or more. The solo reciter must be the best: He must be able to project his voice and should know the different *rāga*s, or melodies, since "he speaks *(vakti)* the story, with [occasional] singing unaccompanied by a rhythm instrument *(tāla).*" He must know grammar in all its details *(śabdaśāstraviśeṣajña),* must understand the principles (or truth, *tattva*) of the Vedas, and must have studied the various components of literary science *(sāhityeṣu kṛtaśrama).* He must know different scripts *(lipijña)*—that is, he recites from a written text, not from memory—and during recitation he must dissolve Sanskrit's often confusing euphonic combinations *(ślokān vakti padacchedaiḥ).* The recitation of Brahmanical Sanskrit stories is to be distinguished from the activity of the *sūta,* who recites stories in Prakrit languages, and that of the reciter of six-line verses in Kannada *(karṇāṭabhāṣā),* who should have a voice like that of a celestial singer.[43]

There are two points in the discourse of this unique document especially worth singling out in the context of the present discussion. First, the two sections examined here effectively exhaust what counted as literature *(kāvya, sāhitya)* before the wholesale vernacular transformation. *Kāvya* was a cosmopolitan practice, and the languages of Place—with the new exception of Kannada in its cosmopolitanized form—were excluded from the literary. Those languages are discussed, to be sure, by this "book-teacher of all practices," in a later subsection on entertainments devoted to the topic of singing (*gītavinoda, adhyāya* 16). The evidence and arguments raised there are ex-

42. *Mānasollāsa* 4.205–(404, misnumbered), vol. 2: 172–189.

43. *Mānasollāsa* 4.1406–32, vol. 3: 162–65.

amined in detail in chapter 8.2. For our present purposes we need only note that even if some elements of song were incorporated in storytelling, song itself was included neither in discourse *(śāstravinoda)* nor even in narrative *(kathāvinoda),* the two practices that constituted the general sphere of literary culture. It was something other—and its realm was vernacular.[44]

A second point, more directly pertinent to our argument, is that the practice of literary culture in the royal domain was above all an intellectual endeavor. It consisted of theoretically informed *(śāstrika)* reflection *(vicāra)* on normativity *(guṇa/doṣa)* and thus presupposed knowledge of the categories of literary analysis: *guṇa*s, or expression-forms; *mārga/rīti,* or the Ways/Paths of writing; *chandas,* or metrics; *alaṅkāra,* or tropology; and *rasa* and *bhāva,* or aesthetic moods and feelings. Without these there could be no analysis and accordingly no "intellectual delight." As something to be understood within the category of *śāstravinoda,* literature was part of a coherent discursive science, *śāstra,* yet it remained a *vinoda,* one "entertainment" among others. It was no more instrumental to power in any direct or overt way—no more concerned with the attainment or constitution of power—than the king's display of weaponry or his understanding of cockfighting. Literature was a central component of royal competence and distinction, of royal pleasure and civility, but not a weapon of power.

44. See chapter 8.2. Cf. the traditional verse: "Children understand song, beasts do, too, and even snakes. But the sweetness of literature . . . does the Great God himself truly understand?" (quoted by the glossator on *Rājataraṅgiṇī* ed. Stein 5.1, p. 72).

CHAPTER FIVE

The Map of Sanskrit Knowledge and the Discourse on the Ways of Literature

5.1 THE GEOCULTURAL MATRIX OF SANSKRIT KNOWLEDGE

When the scholar Hemacandra completed his grammar and presented it to King Jayasiṃha Siddharāja of Gujarat, the king had the book copied and distributed throughout the world—a world that was vast yet delimited in its vastness and completely named and known. The fact that a cosmopolitan grammar should have escaped its local confines in Aṇahilapāṭaka and circulated as far north as Nepal and as far south as Cōḻa country is in itself hardly surprising. After all, Sanskrit, like Prakrit and Apabhramsha (which are also analyzed in Hemacandra's grammar), was no language of Place and was quite capable of traveling far in the wider world. The travels of a grammar—its geographical dimensions—are something we Indologists typically reflect on as little as we reflect on a grammar's relationship to power. Nor do we normally think about how language and literature—to say nothing of culture in general—might be related to space, both concretely by their circuits of dissemination and conceptually by the complex process of producing what they appear only to represent. Nor, most important, do we often ask to what degree power might be informed by a sense of space or concerned with the cultural practices of people across space, though such issues appear to have been significant to Jayasiṃha himself. In actual fact, all the components in this dense network of forces—grammar, language, literature, and culture, as well as the society and polity to which these are symbiotically joined—have an irreducible dimension of spatiality. If we are to understand anything about the relationship between culture and power in South Asia before modernity, and specifically about that relationship within the problematic of cosmopolitanism and vernacularity, it is necessary to understand something about the history of the discursive organization of South Asian space.

This history is long and fascinating, though regrettably it has never been the object of a chronologically deep and systematic reconstruction. Such a reconstruction would have to depend entirely on textual materials. While graphic presentations of South Asia are available from a reasonably ancient period, these are often of the cosmological sort and very general and abstract. More representational diagrams than those found in the cosmographies were not known before the arrival of mapmakers from western and central Asia around the fifteenth century. Diverse explanations, none very convincing, have been offered for this lacuna in visual culture. It has been suggested that maps as we know them today may once have actually existed but they disappeared through the assaults of weather or war, though it hardly seems credible that *everything* could have been lost. Another view holds that popular literacy was negligible, while the literati able to produce such maps—and here "literati" is synonymous with the clerisy—had their gaze fixed upon eternity: "To those of a religious bent—which for many centuries probably included most learned persons—so mundane a task as preparing a seemingly accurate map of the finite terrestrial earth or a small segment of it could not have appeared particularly important."[1]

Yet just as literacy in premodern South Asia was almost certainly more widespread than what we might assume by extrapolating from contemporary statistics (consider, for instance, the unremarkable, even quotidian tone with which reading and writing are mentioned in literary texts),[2] so the literati were hardly the dreamy transcendentalists figured in the typical Orientalist account. They had their eyes firmly fixed on the ground beneath their feet. The various representations of space examined in this chapter, as well as the exquisitely detailed verbal maps in the land grants discussed earlier (chapter 3.1), unambiguously attest to this fact. The liturgical practices of those of a religious bent (both *vaidika* and *smārta*) affirm the same. If these practices often do reveal a propensity for space-time transcendence, they simultaneously turn exact spatial orientation into as basic an element of ritual as exact temporal orientation. Consider the formula for declaring the resolve *(saṃkalpa)* to perform a rite, which telescopically locates the actor within a framework at once global and local:

> [The sacrificer] should first recite the following: "Om! Here on this earth, on Jambūdvīpa, the Continent of the Jambū Tree, in Bhāratavarṣa, the Clime of the Descendants of Bharata, in Kumārikā Khaṇḍa, the Sector of the Virgin, in the field of Prajāpati, in such-and-such a place and such-and-such a spot"—depending on the specific place and spot in which the rite is held.[3]

1. Schwartzberg 1992, especially p. 329. A good Indological account is Sircar 1967.
2. See chapter 2.1, chapter 8, and Pollock 2003: 88 ff.
3. From the thirteenth-century Maharashtrian *dharmaśāstra* of Hemādri, the *Caturvargacintāmaṇi* (*Dharmakośa*, vol. 3 part 2: 1268). The time frame, too, is at once cosmic and ter-

Such ritual formulas closely parallel the structure of geographical understanding in various domains of worldly practice. This is clearly demonstrated by a land grant from almost the same time and place as the above text:

> In Jambūdvīpa, best of all continents, lies Bhāratavarṣa, most exalted of regions . . . In it is found Beḷvala [*sic*], native soil of the multitude of all tribes . . . In it lies the Nareyaṅgaḻ Twelve [an administrative grouping of villages], and therein lies the celebrated Brahman settlement *(agrahāra)* named Ittagi.[4]

So important, in fact, was the geographical mode of thought to Sanskrit literati that space not only became an object of knowledge to be fully organized in their discourse but, as we will see, wound up organizing discourse itself by providing a basic framework for structuring cultural knowledge.

If a systematic account of these rich materials remains a desideratum, we nevertheless understand enough at present to know that such an account would reveal a history of continual change. For one thing, the process by which larger conceptual spaces such as Jambūdvīpa or Bhāratavarṣa were constructed was gradual and halting. Older geotopes—such as those found in early Vedic texts, like Pañcanada, the "Land of the Five Rivers," or in later works, like Āryāvarta, the "Congregating Place of the Āryas"—may have been absorbed and displaced by newer ones, but they were never completely demoted as preeminent cultural-political frames of reference. The same process led to the expansion of such spaces. For the grammarian Patañjali around the beginning of the Common Era, Āryāvarta was bounded on the north by the Himālaya, on the south by Pāriyātra (the western Vindhyas), on the east by the Kālaka(ā) Forest (present-day Jharkhand), and on the west by Ādarśa (the Panjab between the Beas and Ravi rivers). For the Gupta king Samudragupta in the mid-fourth century (whose political space was radically different from that of Aśoka five centuries earlier), the eastern limit had become the Bay of Bengal (at Samataṭa), while for the poet Rājaśekhara around 920 (though he is echoing Manu and other earlier writers on *dharma*), the western limit had become the Indian Ocean.[5]

---

restrial: "Thereafter one must announce the time: 'During the second half of Brahmā's lifespan, in the cosmic age of the White Boar, in the Manu Interval of Vaivasvata, in the first quarter of the twenty-eighth *kaliyuga,* at such-and-such a year, when the sun is on its northern or southern course,' as appropriate; 'at such-and-such a season, month, lunar fortnight, lunar mansion, day, conjunction of stars, at the hour of Rudra, etc.,' as appropriate."

4. *EI* 13: 44, 53 (1112 C.E., northwest Karnataka). This specific reference is preceded, in vv. 7–14, by a description of the seven continents and oceans perhaps unique in the epigraphical record. Geographical descriptions that nest locales in ever lower-order categories are found in Karnataka epigraphy from about the twelfth century on. One grant from 1417 telescopes downward onto the locale *(viṣaya)* of Kāyikkaṇī from the outer ocean, the great island of Jambū, Mount Meru, "southern Bharata land," Āryākhaṇḍa, Tuludeśa, and so on (*KI* 1: 93).

5. *Mahābhāṣya* on 2.4.10 and 6.3.109; *CII* 3: 209 ff.; *KM* 93.17. On the shifting boundaries of Āryāvarta, see Deshpande 1993b: 83–107; for Ashokan and Gupta space, chapter 6.2.

We know, furthermore, that diverse models of geographical understanding were in play throughout premodern history. Even after such dominant supraregional concepts as Bhāratavarṣa came into being, they still had to contend with many archaic cosmologies stubbornly persisting from the mythic past.[6] These fantastic visions of space that piled cosmic spheres upon spheres to total seven, fourteen, or twenty-one—long a source of amusement to Western observers ("Ah, Sahib, after that it is turtles all the way down!")—seem to have coexisted easily with the more quotidian mental and verbal maps of the world through which people actually moved. Such visions clearly performed other cultural tasks that were complementary to and not in contradiction with worldly knowledge. Following yet another logic—different from the organization of worldly space and more concrete than the cosmic spaces—were the various geospheres generated by religious practices, such as pilgrimage circuits. The Śaiva world, for example, was a particular space marked out by the distribution across the subcontinent of those luminous aniconic symbols of the deity known as *jyotirliṅgas*.[7]

How these various endogenous spatial forms related to exogenous categories such as "Indikē" *(chōrē)* among the Greeks (as early as Herodotus), "India" among the Romans, or "al-Hind" among the Arabs also remains to be fully explored. The rich complexities of premodern nomenclature are matched by puzzling absences. There is, for example, no collective term, on the order of "Hellenismos," "Arabīya," or "Fārsīyat," for the culture that filled the subcontinent and spread far beyond its confines. The congruities and incongruities between the views from inside and outside, no less than among the various geographical schemata, left an impression on the traveler Xuanzang already in the seventh century: "In a careful study we find that Tianzhu is variously designated, causing much confusion and perplexity. Formerly it was called Shengdu, or Xiandou, but now we should name it Indu (India), according to the right pronunciation. The people of India use different names for their respective countries, while people of distant places with diverse customs generally designate the land that they admire as India."[8]

6. Kirfel 1959–74.

7. One *jyotirliṅga* map includes Somanātha (in Saurāṣṭra), Śrīśailam, Ujjayinī, Oṃkār, Kedāra "on the back of the Himālaya," Ḍākinī, Vārāṇasī, the Gautamī River, Citābhūmi, Dārukāvana, Setubandha, and Śivālaya (*Śivapurāṇa Koṭirudrasaṃhitā* 1.21 ff.; 68), though it is not clear that the Khmer might not have included themselves here (see chapter 6.1). On pilgrimage and geography Bhardwaj 1973 needs to be supplemented by research on medieval and non-Brahmanical accounts, such as the Jain *Vividhatīrthakalpa* (cf. Chojnacki 1995). The turtle story is told in Geertz 1973: 28.

8. Trans. Li Rongxi 1996: 49. Xuanzang adds that "Indu" means the moon (because sages shone on the country as the moon shines on all things). In what language did Xuanzang hear the word "Indu"? Greek "Indi[ka]" presumably vanished centuries earlier, and Arabic "Hind" was a century off.

Here Xuanzang flags for us yet another, and perhaps the most remarkable, aspect of geoconceptual change: Many places in premodern South Asia did not stay in place; toponyms moved around the subcontinent and across greater Asia, creating what to our eyes is a radically unfamiliar space, one far more open, more able to be replicated and even extended, than any known from elsewhere. As we will see, the conceptual order of Sanskrit geography in its mature form, focusing on Bhāratavarṣa, was uniform, stable, and, most significant of all, subcontinental, and this limit, once achieved, marked the boundary of geographical concern. But this was a boundary unlike any other. If in some important respects it excluded many spaces—even immense spaces of actual circulation relevant to the lives of people in medieval South Asia—the excluded often claimed inclusion by the very act of naming wherever they lived with the names of India. "India" was moveable and multiple.

The continuous transformation of relevant geographical frameworks, the coexistence of multiple cosmologies, the ambiguities of nomenclature, the mobility of place itself—all these together suggest the contingency of the process by which the mature form of the medieval geographical imagination hardened into the India that under conditions of colonial and nationalist modernity became somehow the authentic India. To explore that imagination, in the interests of understanding the cosmopolitan sphere against which vernacular worlds were eventually to constitute themselves, is accordingly not to authorize it nor to give substance to the cartographic paranoia of the nation-state. Rather, the point is to demonstrate both the instability of what imagination constructs and the possibilities thereby offered throughout history for conceiving of alternative modes of spatial belonging. This continuous changeability of geographical understanding informs the following examination of the final form this understanding acquired in the cosmopolitan epoch, which itself is meant as a preface to an account of the geocultural (and later, geopolitical) matrices of Sanskrit knowledge, of how the ways of knowing and the world that was the object of knowledge were informed by a cosmopolitan spatial idea and ideal.

The earliest statement of the mature or final shape of the Sanskrit geographical totality is found in a series of texts contained in the early *purāṇas* and exists in two recensions. The longer, which came to be appropriated by the *Mahābhārata* (6.10) and by Rājaśekhara (*Kāvyamīmāṃsā* chapter 17), is more recent and expands upon the older version, which for its part appears to have been derived from a single archetype.[9] The longer text existed already by the sixth or seventh century; the shorter likely antedates it by only a century or two.[10]

"To the north of the ocean and to the south of the Himālaya Mountains,

9. This is best represented in the *Garuḍapurāṇa* and *Śivapurāṇa*, see Kirfel 1931: 4–19.
10. The foundational work is Kirfel 1931.

extending for nine thousand *yojanas*," the archteype begins, "is Bhāratavarṣa [or Bharatavarṣa], where dwell the descendants of Bharata *(bhāratī saṃtati)*" (v. 1). It is the single *karmabhūmi,* the domain where action has post-terrestrial consequences (v. 2), the sole arena where the four stages of cosmic time *(yuga)* pertain (v. 16). There are nine sectors (*bhedas*, also called here *dvīpas*, islands or continents) of Bhāratavarṣa, "and the ninth is this one, surrounded by the sea, and a thousand *yojanas* in length from south to north" (v. 6). It is bounded by Kirāta people in the east, Yavanas in the west, Āndhras in the south, and Turuṣkas in the north (v. 7); and in the middle reside Brahmans, Kshatriyas, Vaishyas, and Shudras, each living according to their respective occupations: sacrifice, battle, commerce, and so on (v. 8). This ninth (pen-) insula of Bhāratavarṣa is the focal point of the text, which restricts itself in what follows to identifying the land's key topographical features: the seven "family mountains" that enclose it, from the Ṛkṣaparvata in Bengal to Malaya, the southernmost of the Western Ghats, and the dozen celebrated rivers that crisscross it, from the Śatadru in the Panjab to the Kāverī in the peninsula.[11]

There are points of obscurity in this earliest macroscopic description of southern Asia, as well as inconsistencies with later versions. The old puranic text divides Bhāratavarṣa into nine sectors that appear to be contiguous; only the ninth, later named Kumāri[kā], the Sector of the Virgin, is explicitly described as (largely) surrounded by the sea. Although Bhāratavarṣa itself is said to lie to the north of the ocean and the south of the Himālaya Mountains, the ninth sector occupies most of this space, containing as it does rivers that spring from the foothills of the Himālaya (like the Śatadru) as well as those in the far south such as the Kṛṣṇā and the Kāverī. It is only in Kumārī, too, that the four social orders are said to be found—all other sectors (or continents or islands) being inhabited by people born of the outermost order *(antyajajanāḥ)*[12]—this despite the fact that Bhāratavarṣa as a whole is earlier described as the "domain of karma," a notion typically linked with the social-moral regime of caste. In any event, these various social traits are all ascribed to Bhāratavarṣa itself in later representations: in Rājaśekhara's tenth-century geography (largely derived from subsequent puranic elaborations); Bhoja's eleventh-century *Bhuvanakośa,* "world-dictionary" or cos-

11. Manuscripts are equally divided between *bhārata-* and *bharata-*. (The ancestry of the Bharata in question is not mentioned here but is elsewhere much discussed. For Kālidāsa, he was the grandson of the sage Viśvāmitra; in the Ittagi inscription mentioned earlier he is the son of Ṛṣabha, and the descendant of Manu, *EI* 13: 44, vv. 7 ff.) "Kirāta" refers in a very general way to pastoral nomads; "Yavana" originally to Ionians and Greeks more generally, and later to Arabs (and, even later, Europeans); "Turuṣka" to Turkic peoples. A *yojana* is a vague term of distance, something like "league."

12. On those beings who dwell outside of Kumārikā, see the *Siddhāntaśiromaṇi* quoted in *Dharmakośa* vol. 3.2: 1268.

mography (in his *Samarāṅgaṇasūtradhāra* chapter 5); the (probably) twelfth-century political treatise *Bārhaspatyasūtra* (discussed in chapter 6.2); as well as the formulation of the ritual *saṃkalpa* cited earlier. Additional discrepancies are found in these accounts, however. In Bhoja's version, the world consists of seven great islands *(mahādvīpa),* conceived of as circles concentrically arranged, each surrounded by an ocean. In their very middle lies Jambūdvīpa, which in turn is made up of seven climes *(varṣa):* four to the north of Mount Meru, which is in the center, and three, including Bhārata, to the south. This Bhāratavarṣa, for its part, consists of nine sectors, the ninth being Kumārī. Each is a thousand *yojana*s long, and each is inaccessible to the others.[13] Together they extend from the southern ocean to the Himālaya, Kumārī accounting for the space between the southern ocean and Bindusaras in the Himālayas.[14]

Setting aside the intermittent fuzziness of detail in the puranic geography, we can perceive that the world of central concern to it does have considerable conceptual coherence. It is a limited domain, its margins marked by groups excluded from the *janapada*s, or people-places, that constitute the puranic world (v. 15—a passage not contained in the archetype and much expanded in the later version). To be sure, these were temporary exclusions along a rather rapidly shifting boundary of belonging; for instance, at the originary puranic moment the Āndhras are outside the ecumene and the Pārasikas (Persians) are inside (v. 15), whereas later, in the *Mahābhārata,* the Āndhras are normalized, so to speak.[15] While conceding such fluidity, we should note that for both the later representations and the puranic model on which they depend there remains always an inside and an outside. The border between the two is represented as a liminal zone, marking a transition to other lifeworlds where an altogether different physics of moral conduct prevails (with no retribution in future births for deeds done in this or past ones, for instance) along with an altogether different organization of time (with no fourfold division of cosmic ages with their entropic decline from the Kṛtayuga of perfection to the Kaliyuga of degradation). A different and threatening world abuts Bhāratavarṣa in the oldest puranic vision:

13. The longer puranic version shares the same vision, since it calls the nine island-continents "mutually inaccessible" (see Kirfel 1931: 35, v. 3d, compare p. 33 v. 1d; contrast his remark on p. 12).

14. See *Samarāṅgaṇasūtradhāra* chapter 5, especially vv. 8–11, 19–20, 57 ff., also *KM* 90.23–92.13. For Bhoja as for most classical accounts a substantial admixture of fantasy persists; each of the seven islands is surrounded by a different kind of sea: saltwater, ghee, curd, rum, and so on. Skepticism was already reported by Rājaśekhara a century earlier: "Some say there is only one kind of ocean, saltwater" (*KM* p. 91).

15. *Mahābhārata* 6.10.48. For Xuanzang (c. 640) Persia is no longer "in the domain of India" (trans. Li Rongxi 1996, p. 349).

"This island is continually beset at its borders by the uncultured."[16] With respect to differentiation from within, the expanded passage—as just noted, this is a later addition to the puranic text, perhaps linked with the cultural-political segmentation that intensified in the epoch of vernacularization (chapter 10.1)—divides up this interior space by a catalogue of human groupings that proceeds clockwise around the subcontinent, from the Kuru-Pāñcāla in the Midlands (just west of the Gaṅgā River), to the inhabitants of Kāmarūpa (Assam), from there to the southerners *(dākṣinātya),* and finally to the far west and the Pārasikas.

This primordial, puranic account of Indic space was very quickly and almost completely rationalized in the astronomical-cosmological encyclopedia of Varāhamihira, the *Bṛhatsaṃhitā.* Dating from the mid-sixth century and thus hardly much later than the puranic core text itself, the *Bṛhatsaṃhitā* offers a radically scaled-back geographical representation. Varāhamihira ignores the fabulous continents *(dvīpa)* lying outside of Bhāratavarṣa and restricts himself to a catalogue of what he calls the nine Places *(deśa)* of the subcontinental sphere. These are the central region (which contains inter alia Mathurā, Pāñcāla, Sāketa) and the eight cardinal points: the east (Magadha, Mithilā, Oḍra, etc.), southeast ([southern] Kośala, Kaliṅga, Vaṅga, etc.), south (the Kāverī River, Laṅkā, the Malaya Mountains, etc.), southwest (the land of the Pahlavas, Sindhusauvīras, Ānartas, etc.), west (the land of the Five Rivers), northwest (the land of the Tuṣāras and other little known peoples), north (Mount Kailāśa, and various mountain tribes), and northeast (again various mountain peoples). There are curious features in the *Bṛhatsaṃhitā*'s account as well: Vidarbha is somehow placed in the southeast, Bharukaccha apparently in the south, Kāśmīra in the northeast (not all of which can be reconciled by assuming that for Varāhamihira the east was true north). And the margins remain realms of teratology, inhabited by "Dog-Faced," "Horse-Faced," and "Tiger-Faced" peoples. Yet it is abundantly clear that Varāhamihira has in his head an ordered, demythologized map of Indic space, and this map became something of a baseline for subsequent representations: When the Uzbek polymath al-Bīrūnī studied the geography of al-Hind in the early eleventh century, Varāhamihira was still a major authority to be consulted.

There is of course nothing remarkable about people in premodern South Asia having a clear and accurate conception of the spatial organization of their world. What is remarkable is that the geographical template made available in embryonic form by the puranic text and reworked by Varāhamihira became the organizing logic of so much systematic Indian thought. To know the world in some of the most elementary aspects of its social, cultural, and

16. A verse from the *Vāyupurāṇa* (45.82) attached to the shorter recension. Such representations of borders, like those of restrictions concerning Sanskrit culture (see for example chapter 1.3), may more justly be taken as ideological atavisms than indices of a lived reality.

political domains meant, for the intellectual who wrote in Sanskrit, to know it as an immense, if specific, spatial order upon which those practices could be mapped. Here and in the next chapter we will look at some instances of all three domains, beginning with social properties.

At first glance, the sexual typology of the *Kāmasūtra* (perhaps third or fourth century) may seem an improbable source from which to draw, but in fact the text is entirely typical of the structure of social thinking in the Sanskrit world.[17] The taxonomy of sexual types is given in the second main section of the work, which deals with sexual intercourse, following a description of the kinds of physical traits and capacities, the desirability of forming matches among equals, and the appropriate kinds of embracing, kissing, scratching, and biting during lovemaking. (In accordance with the perspective typical of Sanskrit knowledge forms, the viewing subject is male and the object of sexual analysis is female.)[18]

> Sexual behavior with women should be in accordance with the prevailing attitudes *(sātmya)* of the region to which they belong. The women of Madhyadeśa are largely Ārya and thus insist on pure behavior; they dislike kissing and being marked by teeth or nails. The same is true for the women of Bāhlīka and of Avanti, but they are especially partial to intricate forms of lovemaking. Women of Mālava, as also Ābhīra women ["women of the lands of Śrīkaṇṭha, Kurukṣetra, etc."], have a predilection for embracing, kissing, and biting and scratching so long as they do not draw blood, and they can be brought to orgasm through spanking. The women from the Land of the Five Rivers are habituated to giving oral sex. The women of Aparānta and of Lāṭa have intense orgasms and moan softly and slowly. The women of Kośala and those of Strīrājya ["to the west of Vajravanta"] enjoy hard spanking and have vehement orgasms but prefer artificial devices. The women of Āndhra are delicate by nature, enjoy lovemaking, and have a predilection for impure acts and immoral behavior. The women of Mahārāṣṭra take pleasure in performing the sixty-four arts; they like talking dirty and crudely and are passionate in bed. The women of the City [Pātaliputra] do exactly the same, but only in strict privacy. Draviḍa women begin to release orgasmic fluids slowly even as they are massaged in foreplay. The women of Vanavāsi have moderate orgasms and permit all [the various kinds of physical acts]; they like to keep their bodies covered but will ridicule a man's [physical] shortcomings; they avoid men who are offensive, dirty-talking, and crude. The women of Gauḍa speak softly; their bodies are soft, too, and they are firm in their affections.[19]

17. The *Kāmasūtra* is later than the final recension of the *Arthaśāstra* (probably second century) and roughly contemporaneous with the early *purāṇas* (fourth or fifth century).

18. The commentator, Yaśodhara, does note that woman as subject is equally implied (2.5.20).

19. *Kāmasūtra* 2.5.20–33, pp. 287–90, with parenthetical reference to Yaśodhara. The regionalization of female characteristics is also found in the Old Hindi *Rāulavela* (discussed in chapter 8.2), cf. Bhayani 1994: xxxiv ff.

A passage like this invites speculation on many fronts, not least regarding the place of empiricism, or an image of empiricism, in Sanskrit systematic thought. The scientificity of the discourse here obviously depends on such empiricism, despite the fact that it is entirely imaginary. Its sole purpose is to show that nothing is beyond the reach of Sanskrit *śāstra;* everything everywhere, however intimate, is knowable and has become known. But especially worth highlighting in the present context is the role of the geocultural frame of reference itself in structuring this total social knowledge. Both the object of analysis—the practice and theory of sexuality—and the implied audience toward which this analysis is directed, are geographically organized, and this geography has limits, extending from Draviḍa country in peninsular India to Balkh in Afghanistan, and from Maharashtra to Bengal. Vātsyāyana does acknowledge alternative modes of comprehending sexual behavior and in fact ends his discussion with a qualification of the geocultural cognitive matrix: "[The teacher] Suvarṇanābha holds that personal predilections have more validity than those associated with region, and so he does not deal with regional sexual behavior. Moreover, in the course of time sexual behavior, dress, and forms of entertainment can pass from one region to another, and one has to be aware of this." Yet it is the geo-logical framework of understanding—where understanding a phenomenon, even a biological one, meant understanding it as spatially ordered, and understanding space itself meant understanding it as vastly transregional but not limitlessly so—that winds up dominating the *Kāmasūtra*'s categorization.

The same spirit that animates the *Kāmasūtra* finds expression in Sanskrit literary theory in the discourse on propriety *(aucitya).* Propriety came to function as a critical standard in literary judgment at a relatively early date, and by the time of its most complete exposition in the eleventh century it had become an all-embracing category of fitness, "the life force pervading the limbs of a literary text," in regulating the use of everything from particular preverbs, particles, and individual words (where propriety approximates finding *le mot juste*), to figures of speech, aesthetic moods *(rasa),* and the argument of the work as a whole.[20] The *Sāhityamīmāṃsā* (Inquiry into Literary Art), a handbook composed probably in south India in the fourteenth or fifteenth century, prescribes how literary description must harmonize with conventional regional characteristics:

> Among the people of Magadha [the women are to be described as having] heavy breasts; among the Kaliṅgas, beautiful eyes; among the Aṅgas, long arms; among the Vaṅgas, soft feet. The women of Kerala and Āndhra are to be described as having glossy curls, those of the Pañcālas, ruby lips. The navel is the feature to be described of the women of Lāṭa, the brilliant white teeth of the

20. See Kṣemendra's *Aucityavicāracarcā* vv. 8–10 in *Kṣemendralaghukāvyasaṃgraha.*

women of the south . . . Women of Dramila, Murala, tribal women, and those of Kāśikośala, the Pulindas, and the women of the south are generally to be depicted as dark, whereas the women of Bāhlīka, Mahārāṣṭra, Mālava, and the Pahlavas and others of the north are to be described as fair.[21]

The literary representation of the human female, no less than the analysis of women's sexual natures, is entirely space-contingent. Propriety is no abstraction; it is located, and located in a huge but particular world, one through which the bearers of Sanskrit culture actually moved. As will become clear, this locatedness, subsumed within a larger totality, is a fundamental dimension of the Sanskrit concept of literariness itself. We observed in the last chapter how an identical geocultural matrix conditioned the existence of cosmopolitan grammar in the description of the sphere of circulation of the *Siddhahemacandra:* "The text circulated and grew famous in all lands," from eastern Bihar to Assam, from Orissa to Sri Lanka, from Karnataka to Sindh and the land of the Persians beyond (appendix A.4).

One final example of the deployment of the geocultural matrix in Sanskrit thought relates to *saṅgīta,* a term that comprises song, music, and dance. In the twelfth-century *Bhāvaprakāśana,* whose discussion of languages was noted earlier (chapter 2.2), the author, Śāradātanaya, defines the two main sorts of dramatic dance forms, narrative and nonnarrative *(nṛtya* and *nṛtta),* and observes that in both cases the actor must employ the form according to the appropriate Path of Place *(deśa-rīti).* That is, in song, instrumental music, and dance, the local language and the gestures typical of the locale are to be used. "An actor must distinguish the different Places in order to understand their different Ways." These two terms, "Way" *(mārga)* and "Place" *(deśī, dēsi,* etc.), were to become central to the analysis of cosmopolitan and vernacular cultures, from the Ways of literary composition (see section 3 below) to the theorization of Place (chapter 10.2). What is of primary interest at present is Śāradātanaya's macrospatial framework of the analysis of cultural production. He begins his account of this macrospace with Bhāratavarṣa:

This region called Bhāratavarṣa is nine thousand *yojanas* in length, extending from "Rāma's Bridge" [Rāmeśvaram] to the Himālaya, and it is seven thousand *yojanas* in breadth from east to west. In the Kṛtayuga mortals dwell everywhere here in comfort, but in the Tretā and Dvāpara the cold causes them fear and they resort further and further south, 2250 *yojanas* in each *yuga,* until in the Kaliyuga they find themselves in this land. In the northern reaches, the demigods—*yakṣas, vidyādharas, siddhas, gandharvas*—and sages disport themselves with women. As for this fourth quarter of Bhāratavarṣa, the south, it is

21. *Sāhityamīmāṃsā* pp. 161–63 ("Pallava" is mistakenly given for "Pahlava"). The editor wrongly attributes the work to the twelfth-century scholar Maṅkhaka. A Viriñcimiśra is identified as author of a *Sāhityamīmāṃsā* by Lolla Lakṣmīdhara, court scholar for Kṛṣṇadevarāya c. 1520 (*Vijayanagara Sexcentenary Commemoration Volume,* p. 233), and this may well be the text before us.

> divided into sixty-four sectors with their different people-places (*janapada*): the Pāṇḍya, Kerala, Cōḷa, Sindhu, Siṃhala, Pāmara, Kaliṅga, Yavana, Mleccha, Pārasīka, Śaka, Gauḍa, Lāṭa, Vidarbha, Kāmarūpa, Andhra, Koṅkaṇa, Karṇāṭa, Suhma, Kāmbhoja, Hūṇa, Kārūśa, Gurjara, Saurāṣṭra, Mahārāṣṭra, Himmīra, Āvanti, Anūpaja, Aṅga, Vaṅga, Baṅgāla, Kāśīkośala, Maithila, Kirāta, Vardhrakāraṭṭa, Kuru, Pāñcāla, Kekaya, Auḍhra, Māgadha, Sauvīra, Daśārṇa, Magadha, Nepāla, Jain, Bāhlīka [read Vāhika], Pallava [read Pahlava], Kratha, Kaiśika, Śūrasena, Kājāna, Kārūśa, Yavana, Yadava [*sic*], Cakra, Kurava, Pārvatīya, Haimana, Kāśmīra, Maru, Keṅkāṇa, Nagna, Maṅkaṇa. These are the peoples that dwell between the Himālaya and the Bridge.[22]

Our concern here is not with attaching positive historical-geographical identities to the items in this list. They represent a mélange of archaic catalogue entries from the Sanskrit epics long since vanished from historical India (Kurus, Kekayas, Krathas, Kaiśikas); peoples of misty historical memory (Hūṇas, Śakas); grab-bag categories of the supposedly uncultured (Mlecchas, Yavanas) and what would now be called *ādivāsī*s, or tribal people (Pārvatīya, mountain people; Pāmara, pastoralists); peoples of the more recent puranic geography we have already encountered (Pahlavas, Śūrasenas); and peoples of everyday life (Koṅkaṇa, Karṇāṭa, Baṅgāla). What does claim our attention, rather than the presence or absence of historical identifiability, is the analytic framework used for examining artistic procedures, and the convictions about culture that underlie it: First, the world within which *saṅgīta* is practiced and theorized is conceived of—like the world of sexuality and the social propriety of literary representation—as large but limited, and this limit shapes both practice and theory. Second, the coherence of this world derives not from any conception of sacred space but from a set of interrelated cultural conceptions. Third, not only is this world knowable, it is known, and exhaustively so. And last, this world is Bhāratavarṣa, and Bhāratavarṣa only. Precisely these are the implications of the taxonomies of sexuality and sociality we have already examined. The same logic is at work in the discourse on literature itself, where the conception of an immense but finite and thereby bounded, if loosely bounded, realm of culture comes into sharper focus than anywhere else. The theorists of Sanskrit literature had a profound understanding of the relationship between literature and space, and they explored it in both mythic and shastric discourse.

5.2 POETRY MAN, POETICS WOMAN, AND THE BIRTH-SPACE OF LITERATURE

Sometime around 920, the poet-scholar who referred to himself by the patronymic Yāyāvarīya but is better known to us as Rājaśekhara abandoned

22. *Bhāvaprakāśana* 10.172, pp. 450–451.

the court of the Pratīhāra emperor Mahendrapāla of Kānyakubja, where he had been both poet and the king's guru, after an invasion of the capital that would mark the end of an imperial political order centered on that city. He returned to Tripurī (today a village near Jabalpur in Madhya Pradesh) and the court of the minor Cedi kings—Yuvarājadeva I was then reigning—where his father and grandfather had held important positions.[23] Here he began work on the first systematized conceptualization of literary culture as a whole, or at least as that whole exhibited itself at the highpoint of the Sanskrit cosmopolitan formation.

The title chosen for the text, *Kāvyamīmāṃsā* (Inquiry into Literature), aimed to establish intertextual ties with the great traditions of Vedic hermeneutics and thus constitutes a more assertive claim to cultural centrality than its English rendering may suggest.[24] The work was apparently to have comprised eighteen chapters, though only the first, "The Poet's Secret," is extant. Yet even in its truncated form the *Kāvyamīmaṃsā* is a singularly fascinating text. No other work of South Asian premodernity approaches it in breadth of vision of literary-cultural theory, and certainly no other is quite so idiosyncratic in its discursive practice. Bhoja in the following century shared Rājaśekhara's zeal for totalization, and his debt to the *Kāvyamīmāṃsā* is substantial (he cites it in *Śṛṅgāraprakāśa* forty times and alludes to it repeatedly). But Rājaśekhara differs from his later admirer both in purpose and temperament. Whereas Bhoja is acutely interested in grounding his literary theory in actually existing poetry, Rājaśekhara is less preoccupied with finding the telling proof-text (he rarely identifies a source), and is more often content to compose illustrations ad hoc. Despite the often luxuriant development of his exposition, Bhoja single-mindedly and systematically pursues his object—the analysis of literature at the level of word, sentence, meaning, expression-form, faults, figures, emotions, and so on—over the two thousand pages of the *Śṛṅgāraprakāśa,* offering conclusive judgments on centuries-long controversies over standard topics of literary theory. Rājaśekhara, by contrast, is far more inclined to invent such theory anew, in both style and substance.

In the same way that Rājaśekhara appropriates for literary theory an expository style that had never been used for it in the past (he adopts an older idiom of discourse, found in the *Arthaśāstra* to discuss the polity and in the *Kāmasūtra* to discuss the sexual body, in preference to the new scientificity that had come to mark literary theory elsewhere in the tenth century), so he also thematizes a whole range of topics that had never before been ex-

23. Mirashi in *CII* 4: clxxiv ff.

24. A renaissance in Pūrvamīmāṃsā occurred two or three centuries before Rājaśekhara (with the works of Kumārila and Prabhākara), and the system was also just then coming to be appropriated for literary science in Kashmir (McCrea 1997) and by writers like Bhoja (*ŚP* 337 ff., 476 ff.).

amined in a literary-shastric mode. These include the nature of poetic inspiration (chapter 4); modes of recitation (chapter 7); the lifeworld of the poet, including his daily routine, diversions, and even writing practices and the question of patronage (chapter 10); permissible and impermissible forms of literary quotation (chapters 11–13); poetic conventions (chapters 14–16); and divisions of space and time (chapters 17–18). He also asks, for the first time since Vālmīki's own charter myth-history in the "first poem" (see chapter 2.1) and the commencement of the *kāvya* tradition, how literature began. And he supplies the answer in an extended narrative that is as unique as the book in which it is found (see appendix A.5 for the translation).

Rājaśekhara's remarkable allegory takes its cue from the archaic cosmogony of the *Ṛgveda* (10.91). There, Puruṣa, the Primal Being, is produced (reciprocally) from a mysterious force named Virāṭ and, once born, spreads from one end of the earth to the other. He becomes the principal offering in the primeval sacrifice of the gods, and as he incorporates the world, the world and its four social orders are produced from him: the Brahmans are formed from his head, the Kshatriyas from his arms, the Vaishyas from his thighs, the Shudras from his feet, and from his other parts all other creatures and components of the terrestrial and celestial order. As many scholars have seen there is hierarchy among the orders thus produced, no doubt, but also complementarity. The functioning of the whole depends upon the functioning of all the components, which not only are distinct from one another and fully individuated but have each their own task to accomplish in the body politic (not yet a dead metaphor). What is more, the world-creating sacrifice of Puruṣa is a paradigm and is reenacted in every instance of earthly sacrifice, which is what sustains and reinvigorates the world.

This entire allegory we are invited to see at work in the case of Kāvyapuruṣa, Poetry Man, or the Primal Being of Literature. The literary comes into existence just as the world does. It is not coextensive with speech in substance, since obviously not all speech is *kāvya,* nor, for the same reason, is it coterminous with speech in time, something always already given in the world (*lokasiddha,* as the grammarians would say). As Rājaśekhara shows, *kāvya* is a new form of language altogether, arising through the formal structuring force of a new metrics (to be distinguished from the metrics familiar from and limited to scriptural texts).[25] And this new form has a precise beginning in time, at the moment when Vālmīki textualized as literature his very worldly, personal, and real emotional response to suffering. Just as Puruṣa embodies the sum total of the social world, so Kāvyapuruṣa embodies the sum total of the literary world: the *guṇas*, or expression-forms (including balance, clarity, forcefulness, and the like); figures of speech; metrical patterns; gen-

25. Compare *Uttararāmacarita* 2.5.1. How literature and scripture were thought to differ (Rājaśekhara himself is silent on the question) is discussed in chapter 2.3.

res; emotional modes; and, most important of all, languages. His mouth consists of Sanskrit, his arms of Prakrit (that is, Maharashtri), his groin of Apabhramsha, and his feet of Paishachi. Each language has a separate and well-defined identity and sphere of activity, and like the four social groups, the four languages are hierarchically ordered, each one necessary for constituting the whole of the culture body. Thus we learn here as unambiguously as anywhere that it is the cosmopolitan languages alone that qualify as languages for literature and so find a place in the embodiment of the Kāvyapuruṣa, whose own creation great poets recreate with every new composition, just as the cosmogonic sacrifice is recreated in every terrestrial sacrifice. The practice of literary culture presented here is without question a universal one: while the universe it constitutes may be finite, it is also final, so to speak, for no other exists outside it.

This finitude and finality are coded in what, for the purposes of the present discussion, is the most striking dimension of the allegory: its geocultural design. Rājaśekhara's entire literary-critical text, as well as much of his poetic oeuvre, is suffused with geographical thinking. In his drama *Bālarāmāyaṇa* he turns what had by his time become a tired, conventional *Rāmāyaṇa* scene—the return of Rāma and Sītā from the island of Laṅkā in the aerial chariot taken from the slain demon-king Rāvaṇa—into a veritable geography lesson. The entire penultimate chapter of the *Kāvyamīmāṃsā* is given over to analyzing the role of the geographical in literature, providing a sort of index to the spatial propriety to which writers must adhere when introducing specific places in their works (just as we find in the *Sāhityamīmāṃsā,* whose title discloses the influence of Rājaśekhara's text). At the end of the chapter the reader is advised to consult the author's *Bhuvanakośa,* or "Geographical Dictionary," a text that unfortunately has not been preserved. When Rājaśekhara discusses literary recitation (*pāṭha, KM* chapter 7), his mode of inquiry is again entirely spatial: he offers a survey of elocutionary styles extending from the Karnāṭas in the southwest, who recite everything, whatever the mood or style, with the same swagger *(sagarvam),* and the Drāviḍas in the southeast, who recite prose as well as verse in a singsong fashion *(geyagarbham),* to the Kāśmīrakas in the northwest, whose mode of recitation, great poets though they may be, is like a mouthful of bitter medicine to the ears, and to those in the Midlands, who inhabit the circle of Pāñcāla (the homeland of the author), "whose mode of reciting literature is like honey poured into the ears: their tone is what the style demands, their locution is complete, and they pause when the sense demands it." So, too, when he examines the linguistics of poetry: Vaidarbhas have a predilection for the analytic phrase, Gauḍas for compounding, southerners for secondary suffixes, and northerners for primary ones.[26]

26. See *Bālarāmāyaṇa,* 10.26–96; *KM* p. 34; 22.15ff; also Deshpande 1993b: 83–107.

The progress of Kāvyapuruṣa and his beloved Sāhityavidyā, "Poetics Woman," is a memorable product of just this geocultural vision. To be sure, Rājaśekhara is also concerned with making a point about the necessary relationship between literature and literary theory. Although Vidyā follows on the heels of Kāvya, she really can be said to lead him, for without knowledge of poetics literature is completely inert. As Rājaśekhara says elsewhere in his treatise, restating an older cultural axiom, "Literature depends on theory [and not the reverse], and therefore the poet must apply himself to theory first."[27] But again, what is especially important to register is the spatiality of Rājaśekhara's analysis. His account of literature and literary science takes the form of a lovers' pursuit—a kind of premodern bildungsroman, or even road movie—across the macrospace of Bhāratavarṣa in a *pratipradakṣiṇa,* or counterclockwise circumambulation, leading the couple from Gauḍa in the east to Pañcāla in the north, thence to what are today Gujarat, Rajasthan, and western Madhya Pradesh, and finally to the Deccan. As Sāhityavidyā pursues her beloved and slowly overcomes his resistance the two invent in each quarter of space the costumes for literary and dramatic representation *(pravṛtti),* the dance and musical modes *(vṛtti),* and the Paths of literature *(rīti).* Literariness and its theoretical knowledge, through their variable yet constitutive relationship, produce literature as a territorialized phenomenon, a cultural act that can be performed and conceptualized only within a specific spatial framework as described by the lovers' journey. This framework, like the languages that form the substance of literature, is at once constructed from the regional and represented as transregional by the very appropriation and accommodation of the regional in a single cosmopolitan conceptual scheme.

There is something marvelously idiosyncratic about Rājaśekhara's mind and mode of discourse, and the story of Poetry Man and Poetic Woman is a unique document in Sanskrit literary thought. But there is nothing in the least idiosyncratic about Rājaśekhara's conception of literature. His narrative style may be his own but what he expresses is, in every particular, a theoretical presupposition of Sanskrit culture as a whole.

5.3 THE WAYS OF LITERATURE: TRADITION, METHOD, AND STYLISTIC REGIONS

The elements of literary theory and culture in Rājaśekhara's story of Poetry Man and Poetics Woman did not arise ex nihilo any more than its geography did. There is a deep conceptual history to all these various components, though from their earliest appearance in shastric literature some uncertainty attends their analysis. Part of the problem stems from the synthesis of dra-

27. *KM* p. 2. On the theory-practice problem in general see Pollock 1985; on its place in early vernacularization see chapters 9.4 and 10.2 (and contrast 4.1)

maturgical and nondramaturgical literary theory that took place around the middle of the first millennium. This led to an appropriation of elements from the former—*vṛtti,* or mode, for example—for application to narrative or lyric poetry that has rightly been seen as ill-sorted. Studying the history of the critical lexicon of Sanskrit *kāvya* easily gives rise to the impression of a discourse run amok, with wildly irreconcilable understandings of categories and technical terms being juxtaposed, thanks to a pious conservatism that discarded nothing, not even the contradictory.[28] It is not easy to point to other taxonomies and analyses of features of literary language that are as complex in their subdivisions and as hard to grasp as a single coherent system of thought as those at issue in Rājaśekhara's myth.

That said, with respect to the category *mārga* (or *rīti*), a Way (or Path) of literary composition, it is possible to reconstruct an account that makes good sense and carries important implications for a history of the cosmopolitan cultural imagination. The details here can test the goodwill of the general reader: the Ways concern the minutiae of the language stuff of literature, the focus of the shastric discussion is narrow, and matters turn on fine points of linguistic or philological distinction. But in this case indeed *le bon Dieu est dans le détail,* and not just for the intellectual historian. Such matters were taken seriously by literati across Asia for centuries, and the stakes of such knowledge were high. We have seen how earnest were the politics of philology in premodern India. That lesson is reinforced when we consider how Recent Style poetry in T'ang China, the mastery of which even became obligatory for the civil service examination in the Sung, was created in part by innovations stimulated by the importation of Sanskrit poetic theory; how proficiency in the most complex Indic versification models was central to courtly training and cultural virtuosity in the Thai kingdom of Ayutthaya in the sixteenth century; how the ability to compose Tibetan poetry based on Daṇḍin's Sanskrit principles became a requirement of government service in seventeenth-century Tibet under the fifth Dalai Lama—all of which finds striking parallels in early modern Europe.[29] The intricacies of phonemic texture in a literary utterance, of degree of nominalization, of lexical choice may have become mere trivia in modernity. But we recover some sense of just proportion by registering the historical fact of their importance once upon a time and by realizing that in premodernity mastery of the Ways and the rest of the literary-critical discourse and practice was mastery of cultural virtuosity of a whole social world.

There is no space here to trace the development of the other regionalized components found in Rājaśekhara and elsewhere in Sanskrit literary the-

28. See for example Raghavan 1978: 184ff., especially 196.

29. Mair and Mei 1991; Terwiel 1996. I owe the Tibetan reference to Matthew Kapstein. European parallels are considered in chapter 11.

ory as we intend to do for the Ways. But it is worth mentioning that the geocultural matrix of knowledge described in section 1 also fundamentally conditioned the analysis of performative culture in Bharata's *Nāṭyaśāstra,* upon which Rājaśekhara drew. Fashion, or costume style *(pravṛtti),* is analyzed according to the familiar fourfold geographical division: Āvanti (i.e., western), Pāñcāla (northern), Dākṣiṇātya (southern), and Auḍhramāgadha (eastern). These first appear in Bharata's work in relation to an account of the ceremonial prelude of a dramatic performance *(pūrvaraṅga),* though the text is terse: "The ceremonial prelude should be done according to the Āvanti . . . [costume style]." Bharata's commentator, Abhinavagupta, explains: "Everyone associated with the production of the play about to be performed, from the director to the stage manager, is required to adopt the dress, idiom, gestures, and so on that conform with the regional style of the protagonist of the play."[30] The styles come in for discussion again later in the work, when the structure of the theater is described (*NŚ* chapter 13). Since characters with different regional traits are supposed to enter the stage from different doors intimating the direction of their provenance, the regional styles *(rīti)* naturally suggest themselves for treatment. Here, too, the *vṛtti*s, or dramaturgical modes, with which the styles are associated, are briefly discussed (though more fully in chapter 20). These are regionalized as well, but the regionalization is less mimetic, less concerned with representing something in the drama, than factual, believed to correspond to what people in the different regions of South Asia really preferred to watch in the theater. Again Abhinavagupta elaborates:

> There exists, to be sure, a fourfold division of the world: the south *(dakṣiṇāpatha),* the east *(pūrvadeśa),* the west *(paścimadeśa),* and the north *(uttarabhūmi).* Nor is this division [in the drama] arbitrary, since it may correspond to people's mental states *(cittavṛttibhedasaṃbhavāt).* For instance, the *kaiśikī* mode is found among the southerners because of the prevalence there of literary forms treating of love *(śṛṅgārapracuratayā).* Among westerners, including the people of Avanti, *kaiśikī* is also found, but also *sāttvatī* given the prevalence there of [Jain?] moral literature *(dharmaprādhānye).* In the east, both *bhāratī* and *ārabhaṭī* are used, in view of the prevalence of grandiloquent discourses. In the north country, although those same two modes are prevalent, people will tolerate love literature if only a little *kaiśikī* is used.[31]

A rather similar hesitation between representation and reality in the significance of literary components, which is to be observed in the case of lan-

30. *Abhinavabhāratī* on *NŚ* (ed. Kavi) 5.170ff.

31. *Abhinavabhāratī* on *NŚ* (ed. Madhusudan Shastri) vol. 2: 1128 (I read *āvantyasaṃgṛhīteṣu* for *āvanty eva saṃgṛhitā eṣu;* "grandiloquent discourses," *ghaṭāṭopavākyāḍambaraprādhānyāt,* uncertain; other obscurities must be ignored here). The general discussion of the *pravṛttis* is found in *NŚ* 13.37–58, of the *vṛttis* in *NŚ* chapter 20.

guage, too (chapter 2.2), marks the history of the interpretation of the Ways themselves.

It was only in the seventh century that the various stylistic options in literary composition came to be fully theorized, along with the other basic elements of literariness. *Mārga* (Way) was the earlier of the two terms used in this sense, supplemented by *rīti* (Path) at the end of the eighth century. The two words were used synonymously thereafter, though mutually exclusively: *mārga* was generally preferred in the south, and *rīti* in the north.[32] *Mārga,* the dominant and foundational term, functions metaphorically in Sanskrit discourse on three, or perhaps four, levels. First, it signifies a way or mode of practice that people have followed in the past—in short, tradition. The formulation found (perhaps for the first time) in the *dharmaśāstra* of Manu was to be repeated often: "One should go the way *(mārga)* of the good, since that is where one's father went and one's grandfathers. Going that way one comes to no harm." Similarly, "guarding the ways *(mārga)* codified in the *smṛtis*" (the scriptural texts on *dharma* that are "remembered") became something of a topos in inscriptional discourse. In reference to literary culture, *mārga* is often used with this connotation to refer to the tradition of poetry. Exemplary here is the introduction to the *Ādipurāṇa* of the Jain *ācārya* Jinasena (II), writing at the Rāṣṭrakūṭa court in northeast Karnataka in the mid-ninth century: "The way *(mārga)* of storytelling blazed by the *purāṇa* poets will be my route. What man would not wish to follow the way prepared by the ancients?" "We will strive to travel the way taken by the chief poets—what greater temerity in the world than this!" "It is thus the way illuminated by the great chief poets to which we aim to add our own illumination, to the best of our ability."[33]

Hardly to be separated from the idea of tradition is a second meaning of *mārga:* To "follow a way" implies not only a history of practice but also a procedure of practice—in fact, a "method," precisely what that English word etymologically signifies (from Greek *meth-odos,* "according to the way"). Expressions like "the way of knowledge" and "the way of devotion" *(jñānamārga, bhaktimārga)* became common around mid-millennium for expressing the different options in spiritual practice. *Mārga* in this sense found application in the practice of literature, too; the first extant instance may well be the Allahabad Pillar Inscription of Samudragupta, whose "way of poetry" *(sūkta-*

32. Kuntaka (early eleventh-century Kashmir, see below) uses *mārga* and *rīti* interchangeably. The contemporaneous Kannada writer Nāgavarma (II) uses both to show the double function of style, analyzed according to *guṇas* *(mārga)* or in relation to *rasa (rīti),* and discusses them in different sections of his book (see also chapter 9 n. 37).

33. *Ādipurāṇa* 1.31, 208, 209; *Manusmṛti* 4.178; the phrase "following the way of Manu" itself later becomes proverbial: *sakalasmṛtipraṇītamārgasamyakpālana* (carefully preserving the way promulgated by all the *smṛtis*) (*EI* 11: 82 line 13, a Sanskrit record of Dharasena of Valabhī, 571); *manumārggacaritar* (*EI* 15: 354, a Kannada inscription of 1098).

mārga) was said to "merit the closest study" (chapter 4.1). It was with this sense of *mārga* in mind, the writerly method of attaining poetic beauty or effect, that Yogeśvara, a startlingly original poet at the Pāla court in tenth-century Bengal, spoke of a group of writers each pursuing the way with a very distinctive voice:

> The way that Bhavabhūti opened up, that Bāṇa followed daily,
> and Kamalāyudha and Keśaṭa, too, without respite,
> that the dust of Vākpatirāja's feet purified—
> how skilled—and lucky, too—the writer able to discover it.[34]

Building on both these significations is a third sense that *mārga* acquired (and this is the only meaning *rīti* has in the theoretical context), referring to the modes of composition identified as regional according to the various conceptions of regionality examined below. An elementary discourse on regional variation in Sanskrit style had been in existence from the time of the *Mahābhāṣya;* Patañjali remarks on the tendency of southerners to make inordinate use of secondary suffixes, for example. Some five or six centuries later, in the introduction to Bāṇa's *Harṣacarita* (c. 640), something of this older conception, with a hint of the new, found expression: northern writers are said to have a predilection for double meaning *(śleṣa),* westerners for bare narrative *(arthamātra),* southerners for imaginative conceits *(utprekṣā),* and Gauḍa poets for phonic pyrotechnics *(akṣaraḍambara).*[35] The theory of the Ways hinted at here soon became more systematic and far-reaching, though its moment of ascendancy in critical discourse was admittedly rather brief, extending from the seventh to the tenth centuries. Yet if the idea of the Ways eventually lost its position of primacy in literary theory in favor of far more sophisticated, meaning-based categories, it retained enormous cultural-historical significance: It generated the contrastive binary *mārga/deśī,* "[Cosmopolitan] Way / [Vernacular] Place," that was used to conceptualize the process of vernacularization in much of South Asia during the second millennium.[36]

34. *Subhāṣitaratnakośa* 1733; see also Dharmakīrti's verse on rediscovering the way of literary creation (*SRK* 1729) and that of Vākpatirāja on going to the outer limit of the ways of earlier poets, where everything can appear brand new (*Gauḍavaho* vv. 84–85). In *KM* 11.6, the quick student of poetry works with a teacher in order "to hunt out the way of the poet" *(kavimārgaṃ mṛgayitum)* immediately, whereas other students first require remedial work.

35. *Harṣacarita* v. 7 (*arthamātra* seems close to the *svabhāvokti* attributed to the southern style, see below). For Patañjali's comment, *Mahābhāṣya* vol. 1: 8, line 8, *priyataddhitā dākṣiṇātyāḥ* (an idea later borrowed by Rājaśekhara, as noted earlier). On the *udīcya/prācya* (north/east) regional variation already in Pāṇini see chapter 1.2 and n. 54.

36. See chapter 10.2. A narrowing of the semantic range of *rīti* accompanies its diminished role in later intellectual history. Bhoja remarks: "The path *(panthāḥ)* in poetry made by the people of Vaidarbha, etc., is called *mārga.* It is (also) called *rīti* by derivation from the verbal

In addition to tradition, method, and mode, a fourth sense of the term *mārga* may be isolated, though it is somewhat more speculative and may be said to work at a sort of Heideggerian level of etymological determination. Given that the modes of composition in Sanskrit poetry are geographically coded, *mārga* as the term chosen to express them may carry some deep resonance with "marches" and "margins"—terms to which *mārga* may be etymologically related—meaning the regions with their accompanying borders of the world of literary culture.[37]

Important as the concept of the Ways is, previous scholarship has done little to clarify it. There is no good account of the basic differentiae at issue; key debates that the category stimulated (over the environmental determinants of cultural style, for example) have been ignored, and key metaquestions (like the significations and implications of this sort of regionalization for a putatively cosmopolitan culture) have been overlooked. All these levels of analysis can be addressed, however, if we pay close attention to what the Indian theorists actually say.

Although the discourse on the Ways begins for us with Bhāmaha in the middle of the seventh century, he critiques a concept that Daṇḍin a generation or so later (c. 680) inherits and fully accepts.[38] Since Daṇḍin reproduces this inheritance unproblematically, we may start with him. Daṇḍin acknowledges that the "Ways of literary language are multiple, and the differences among them subtle"—so subtle that Sarasvatī herself could not name them all, any more than we can put into words the difference between the kinds of sweetness in sugarcane, molasses, and treacle. Still, two types can be sharply differentiated: *vaidarbha* and *gauḍīya,* that is, "of Vidarbha"

---

root *rī* 'to go'" (*SKĀ* 2.27). Ratneśvara comments: "Composing words invested with *guṇa*s is *rīti.* Since poets intuitively understand that the commingling of expression-forms produces a veritable transubstantiation that sets literary discourse apart from everyday or scientific discourse, it is something 'sought' *(mṛgyate)* by them for all time, and is thus also called *mārga* . . . *Rīti* refers to the means [the Path] by which poets traditionally 'go' [in quest of fame]." Gopendra on Vāmana's *Kāvyālaṅkārasūtra* 1.2.6 understands: "(the Path) on which the expression-forms come together."

37. The evidence is unclear. Latin *margō, -inis,* Old High German *marka,* Irish *margan/mruig* (?), "border," "frontier" (perhaps "wild zone," where the antelope roams?) are nowhere in the Indo-European etymological literature connected with *mārga* or its etymon, *mṛga* (wild animal), yet in terms of historical phonology nothing seems to absolutely preclude the linkage. On "margins" see Derrida 1984: 97 and 1972.

38. Both likely depended on a lost common source. How the seventh-century theory of the Ways construes with Bharata's earlier *vāṅmārga*s, or ways of verbal mimesis *(vācikābhinaya)* (*NŚ* 24.49–51; Kāvyamālā ed. p. 273 f. is similar but not identical), remains unclear (see also Raghavan 1942: 177). Entirely unrelated are the dramaturgical narrative element called *mārga* ("telling the truth," a component of the *garbhasandhi,* see *Daśarūpaka* 1.38, *NŚ* 19.78 with Abhinava there), and the three (or four or six or twelve) *mārga*s that define certain rhythms in music, *NŚ* 31.8 ff.

(the area today often referred to as Berar and including parts of northern Karnataka and southern Maharashtra) and "of Gauḍa" (west Bengal); these he elsewhere and frequently refers to simply as "southern" and "northern" (or "eastern"), respectively. *Vaidarbha* is defined as "endowed with all the *guṇas*," or expression-forms—these are its very "life breaths"—whereas *gauḍīya* is characterized, generally speaking *(prāyaḥ),* by their inversion or absence *(viparyaya).*[39]

The *guṇas*, or properties of literary language usage (chapter 2.2), are explained in Rājaśekhara's story of Kāvyapuruṣa as follows:

(a) in phonology, features such as phonemic texture, or the harshness or mellowness measured by quantity of unvoiced or voiced stops, and their conjuncts

(b) in syntax, features such as the degree of nominalization

(c) in semantics or lexicon, features such as the relative predominance of those lexical items thought of as idiomatic and primary *(rūḍhi)* or those thought of as etymological and derivative *(yoga/yaugika)* (e.g., *padma,* "lotus," versus *paṅkaja,* "mud-born")

(d) in figuration, features such as the degree of metaphoricity

The best catalogue of these expression-forms is provided in Bhoja's *Śṛṅgāraprakāśa* in the context of an analysis of the various reactions *(anubhāva)* of characters in the literary text that contribute to the dominant emotional register *(rasa)* with which the different writing styles were increasingly being linked. Here the Paths (Bhoja uses the term *rīti* rather than *mārga*) are fourfold, with the new Ways of Pañcāla (the western Gangetic plains) and Lāṭa (southern Gujarat) being added to the two old Ways of Vidarbha and Gauḍa. These four are differentiated along the same four linguistic planes as in Rājaśekhara's account, with the addition of degree and type of alliteration:

(a) *Pāñcāla* shows moderate compounding, moderately harsh texture, occasional metaphoricity *(upacāra),* alliteration once in each quarter verse, and use of words in their conventionally restricted etymological signification *(yogarūḍhi);*

(b) *Gauḍīya* shows long compounds, harsh texture, extreme metaphoricity, repeated alliteration in each quarter verse, and repeated use of words in their conventionally restricted etymological signification *(yogarūḍhiparaṃparā);*

(c) *Vaidarbha* shows no compounding, very gentle texture, no metaphoricity, alliteration, and only rare use of words in their etymological signification *(yogavṛtti);*

39. The details are set forth in *KĀ* 1.40–102. For the use of "northern" and "southern" see 1.60, 80, 83, etc.; these terms are also preferred by the commentator Ratnaśrījñāna, who regards the geographical names as metonymical usage (see his commentary on 1.40).

(d) *Lāṭīya* shows a little compounding, rather gentle texture, no excessive metaphoricity, the type of alliteration that consists of repetition of the same word but with different reference *(lāṭīyānuprāsa)*, and the use of words simultaneously in both primary and etymological signification *(yaugikarūḍhi)*.[40]

All these factors are to some extent already present in Daṇḍin's extended discussion of the ten expression-forms (even in Bāṇa's; recall the feature of "phonic pyrotechnics" in reference to the Gauḍas, corresponding with Bhoja's "harsh texture"). Southern literature, according to this analytic, shows at their minimal degree the whole range of features—consonant clusters, compounding, words that signify only through etymological derivation, and figuration—whereas northern writing exhibits the maximal degree of all of these. The evaluative judgment implicit in defining northern writing as an inversion or even negation *(viparyaya)* of the qualities—or "virtues," another common sense of *guṇa*—that are fully realized in southern writing is made explicit elsewhere when Daṇḍin criticizes northern writing, emphasizing its "uneven" compositional texture (*vaiṣamya,* 1.50), flashiness (*dīpta,* 1.72), and pedantic overstatement (*atyukti,* 1.89, 92).[41]

In comparison with Daṇḍin's treatment of the Ways, Bhāmaha is brief, but a number of points he makes are important for our reconstruction:

Several authorities identify *vaidarbha* as something separate. Moreover, they say it is superior to the other even when the latter is eloquent [or true, *sadartha*]. Yet it is nothing but blind adherence to convention to draw a distinction between the two, as unthinking people do. One might argue that the phenomenon *vaidarbha* is [something real insofar as it is] derived from [the realm of] the Aśmaka dynasty [in the Deccan]. Be that as it may, the name could still be attributed arbitrarily [rather than deriving from inherent properties supposedly associated with the place]. If *vaidarbha* is simple in meaning, devoid of figuration, clear, straight, soft in phonological texture, and easy to listen to, it would differ only as song would differ. *Gauḍīya,* with its figuration, sophistication, sub-

40. *ŚP* 1048–52. Bhoja also touches on the Ways in chapter 10 *(ubhayālaṅkāra),* after his discussion of *jāti* (see chapter 2.3 and further below), which is his classification in *SKĀ* 2.27 ff. "Extreme metaphoricity" in (b): I conjecture *atyupacāravatī.* The reading printed, *nātyupacāravatī* (*ŚP* 1049), cannot be correct, since that is a characteristic of *lāṭīya* and clearly none is meant to be repeated; the reading is also contradicted by the example Bhoja gives here, which is one dense *aprastutapraśaṃsā* (compare *Kāvyālaṅkārasūtra* of Vāmana 4.3.4). For *yogavṛtti* in © Bhoja cites the example of the word *candraśekhara* from *Kumārasambhava* 5.58. The "alliteration" in (d) is technically *sthānānuprāsa* (see Ratneśvara on *SKĀ* 2.71); "the use of words simultaneously in both primary and etymological signification": *yaugikarūḍhi-.* I read thus for the editor's conjecture *yoga-* (p. 1052): the lexeme at issue (*Rāmacarita* 1.18) is *samaya,* "season"/ "[literary] convention" (in *pāda* c of this v. read *smṛta-* for *smita-;* see *SKĀ* 2.76 comm.).

41. Daṇḍin treats metaphorical usage under the *guṇa samādhi* (*KĀ* 1.93–100) but does not take it as a diagnostic of the Ways. On the contrary, he calls it the "sum and substance of literature," essential to all writers (1.100). On the other hand, he does characterize the northern Way as making particular use of figuration (1.50).

stance, learning, and orderliness, can be as excellent as *vaidarbha.* Language does not become beautiful merely by [employing the *vaidarbha* Way]; [literary] language requires the ornamentation of figuration [as is found in *gauḍīya*].[42]

The passage is not free of the textual and interpretive difficulties that obscure much of Bhāmaha's treatise, but the overall argument is not entirely dark. At the same time as Bhāmaha questions whether any ontological distinction can be drawn between the two Ways (neither of the terms *mārga* or *rīti* is actually used, just the geographical designations), he is certainly familiar with the characteristics that traditionally differentiated them and is evidently concerned with their proper employment. Thus the properties of the *vaidarbha* Way, if used to excess, bring the literary text perilously close to music, thereby barring it from the domain of literature altogether (like other Sanskrit theorists, Bhāmaha would have insisted that no art aspires toward the condition of music except music). Even more decisive are figures of speech: without them a text verges on the nonliterary. Thus untroped language, *svabhāvokti,* literally, natural description or even natural expression, is excluded from Bhāmaha's system even while he implicitly reckons it a property of *vaidarbha,* as it would explicitly be regarded by vernacular intellectuals in the coming centuries (chapter 9.2). In general, Bhāmaha's position seems contradictory, for he is eager at once to critique the idea that a hierarchy obtains between the two Ways and to argue that they do not really exist in the first place.[43]

A little more than a century after Daṇḍin, who invests the Ways with considerable importance but not primacy among the elements of literariness (*alaṅkāra,* or figuration, holds that position in his system), the Kashmiri Vāmana elevated the concept to a central place in literary thought. "The Path," he says (using his preferred term, *rīti*) "is to literature what the soul is to the body": just as painting has its substratum in the lines drawn on the canvas, so literature is founded on the Paths. The one innovation in Vāmana's account, besides the conceptual ascendancy of the category, is the addition of a third Path, that of Pañcāla, to *vaidarbha* and *gauḍīya,* the beginning of a proliferation that would produce the four Paths we have seen in Rājaśekhara

42. *Kāvyālaṅkāra* 1.31–36. I conjecture *-vaṃśād dhi* for *-vaṃśādi* in 33a. See Kirfel 1931: 47: *vaidarbhāḥ . . . | paurikā maulikāś caiva aśmakāḥ . . . || . . . dākṣiṇātyā tv amī deśāḥ.* There is no evidence of a work named *Aśmakavaṃśa,* to which some scholars believe this refers.

43. Ratnaśrījñāna (on *KĀ* 1.40 cited below) attacks Bhāmaha by name for his denial of the reality of the Ways. The Kannada writer Nāgavarma takes Bhāmaha's reference to "conventionality" as referring, not to the ontological reality of the north-south distinction, but to the view that one Way is superior to the other. He therefore states that both *mārga*s are said to be "expressive" *(saṃvādadoḷ . . . samārtha-)* and by *vibheda* means not simply "distinction" between the Ways but their (hierarchical) "opposition" (*Kāvyāvalōkanam sūtra* 522). On the complicated place of *svabhāvokti* in Daṇḍin's treatise see chapter 9 n. 39.

and Bhoja, and many more in later authors (see below). Curiously, however, Vāmana's theoretical prioritization is not matched by any new analytic insight. A Path remains for him "a particular arrangement of words," where particularity is generated by the various expression-forms (a list not much different from Daṇḍin's) that are discussed in detail in the course of his work. Like Daṇḍin, Vāmana describes *vaidarbha* as making use of all the expression-forms and defines the other Paths by their degree of lack of one or the other. Especially intriguing are Vāmana's examples: he illustrates *vaidarbha* with Kālidāsa's *Śākuntala* (2.6), a textbook example of *svabhāvokti,* natural description, and *gauḍīya* with Bhavabhūti's *Mahāvīracarita* (1.54), an exemplary instance of *vakrokti,* figuration. Even less than Bhāmaha does Vāmana explain the language principles implicit in his examples; nowhere are these two types of literary discourse thematized as analytical criteria of the Paths, despite their later significance.

When introducing the names of the Paths, Vāmana raises a question fundamental to the concept of regional styles that had already been broached by Bhāmaha (in his allusion to the southern dynasty) and that was to preoccupy later theorists: "Do such regional appellations imply that the very substances and qualities of literary texts come into being as a function of particular regions" the way the salt of Sindh (according to the commentator) differs from other types of salt? "No. The names mean only that these styles are found among the poets of those particular regions, Vidarbha and so on. That is, because these modes of composition, each in its own particular form, were discovered in the various regions by the poets living there, they were given those regional names. The regions as such, however, contribute nothing to the poems." Vāmana's explanation is hardly as compelling as his question and seems more than a little confused. It raises the red herring of a material determinant of the literary utterance while offering nothing to explain what does account for apparently regional styles among poets in various regions—what was it, after all, about particular regions that made it possible for their poets to discover certain styles? Vāmana seems to rest somewhere in the middle on the question of whether region is destiny: On the one hand, the different Paths are ontologically linked to different locales, being "perceived" or perhaps even "discovered" *(upalabdha-)* by people who lived there. On the other, they are a matter of autonomous artistic choice. Vāmana thus declares, invoking the older hierarchy among the Paths, that poets everywhere "should choose *vaidarbha* because of its full range of expression-forms, but not the others, where fewer are used."[44]

Vāmana's uncertainty about what determined the Ways and the actual nature of the regionality their regional names expressed was resolved, though

44. *Kāvyālaṅkārasūtra* and *Vṛtti* 1.2.6–22. On choice see *sūtra* 14; for the grounds of regional difference, *sūtra* 10.

in radically different fashions, by two thinkers located at opposite ends of both the Sanskrit cosmopolis and the historical process by which the cosmopolitan order gave way to something entirely new. One was Ratnaśrījñāna, a Sinhala Buddhist scholar who wrote at the Rāṣṭrakūṭa court of Kṛṣṇa III (r. 936–67).[45] It is in his commentary on the *Kāvyādarśa,* the oldest extant, that he gives expression to the idea of regional Sanskrit literature:

> The *vaidarbha* Way is a particular mode of composing literature that is defined by the use of aesthetic factors *(alaṅkāra)* relating to words themselves—that is, the ten expression-forms—and that is natural *(svābhāvika)* to southerners . . . Opposite to this is the mode of composing literature on the part of easterners designated the *gauḍīya* Way . . . [The existence of these two Ways] is a reality *(vāstavīya),* and their differentiation cannot be attributed, as Bhāmaha attributes it, to simpletons . . . But one might wonder, then, how it is that the *vaidarbha* Way may be observed among easterners, both in verse [and prose], no less than among southerners. Does this not make it as native *(nija)* to the former as it is to the latter? The answer is no, it does not. Even though it may be observed among the easterners, the southern Way is not native to them as it is to the southerners. Just because sandalwood may be observed elsewhere [than in Malaya] does not make it indigenous *(tajja)* to that other place. On the contrary, it remains indigenous to Malaya even if observed elsewhere. Thus, one may chance to observe the *vaidarbha* Way among easterners, but in reality it still belongs to Vidarbha, being congenital *(sahaja)* to southerners. One may likewise chance to observe the *gauḍīya* Way among southerners, but it remains something belonging to easterners because it is native to them. These two modes of composition, then, which differ in their natures *(prakṛti),* are designated as *vaidarbha* and *gauḍīya* by southerners and easterners because they are native to them—as in the case of the languages of Place *(deśabhāṣā)* . . . The presence of the *vaidarbha* Way among easterners is a result of their adopting a factitious character trait *(kṛtrimabhāva).*[46]

This is the strongest case made in Sanskrit intellectual history for true regionality in Sanskrit writing (and the evaluation of regional styles that it implies). It is no accident that it was made when and where it was, in the world of the late Rāṣṭrakūṭas, or that it is contained in a commentary on Daṇḍin (given the pivotal role Daṇḍin's work played in the vernacularization process then unfolding in the Deccan). We can capture the true significance of Ratna's position only when we come to understand how southern *vernacular* writers conceived of their language and the cultural-political project associated with the vernacularization process (chapter 9.2). His remains decidedly a minority

45. On Ratnaśrījñāna's date and location see Pollock 2005d.

46. Ratnaśrījñāna on *KĀ* 1.40; the last sentence is from his comment on 1.42. I read *dakṣiṇamārgo* (for *dakṣiṇamārgavat*) and silently correct the editor's misprints. "Both in verse [and prose]": *padyasādhāraṇa* is likely haplography for *gadyapadyasādhāraṇa.*

opinion, however, which thinkers from within the cosmopolitan horizon both contested on general theoretical grounds and neutralized by a very different assessment of the place of the Ways of writing in literary creation.

Almost contemporaneously with Ratnaśrījñāna there appeared the sharpest critique ever made of the notion that a writer of a given region is naturally constituted to reproduce a regional style. It was enunciated by a thinker of very original bent, Kuntaka of Kashmir (fl. 975), in a book, *Vakroktijīvita* (The Life Force of Literary Beauty), that is an exercise in extended literary analysis unique in medieval India. In one sense Kuntaka is animated by the spirit of Bhāmaha, but his grasp of the issues is much more fully developed:

> *Kārikā:* There are three Ways that form the means of literary creation, the gentle, the harsh, and the in-between.
>
> *Vṛtti:* There are three and only three Ways of literature, not two or four, just as there are only a certain number of musical notes. This finite number represents what competent people are actually able to perceive . . . The third Way constitutes a combination of the other two. . . .
>
> Now, there is considerable disagreement about the Ways. The earliest authorities spoke of three Paths, naming them *vaidarbha* and so on with reference to particular regions such as Vidarbha, and these Paths were arranged hierarchically from best to worst. Others said there were only two, *vaidarbha* and *gauḍīya*. Both views are groundless. If the differentiation of the Paths were based on differentiation of region, the former would be as numerous as the latter. Just because a literary creation is characterized by a certain Path does not mean it can be classified as a regional custom, like cross-cousin marriage. A regional custom rests entirely on traditional conduct; it never escapes the horizon of performative possibility *(śakyānuṣṭhānatā)* [in other words, it is something that one always, in principle, has the capacity to do]. Literary creation of that sort [i.e., that exhibits a certain Way], however, requiring as it does a whole set of causal factors like talent and so on, cannot be performed at will in the same way.
>
> Furthermore, one cannot argue that literary production [according to the *vaidarbha* Way, for example] is natural [to a southerner] in the way that certain beautiful sound components, timbre and the like, may be natural to the singing of a southerner. If this were so, it would be possible for anyone to produce a literary creation of that sort [that is, writing in the *vaidarbha* Way would be possible by virtue of one's being a Vaidarbhan]. Furthermore, whatever may be one's inborn talent, the whole set of acquired skills [necessary for literary creation], education and all the rest, do not vary region by region in any regular way. First, there are no grounds for positing such regular variation; [and second, there could in fact be irregular variation: a given trait we might expect to find in a given place] we may find not there but elsewhere.
>
> Again, it is senseless to differentiate the three Paths as best, average, and worst. When one is defining literature—"literature" being [stipulated as] something that stirs the hearts of sensitive readers—what would be the point

> in teaching those who cannot achieve something like the beauty of the *vaidarbha* Path to use Paths that are progressively inferior?[47] Moreover, those who offer these tenets would themselves surely deny [that they mean to offer negative advice, that is,] that they are talking about what to avoid. Nor is literature like a poor man's gift-giving, something that takes on value by the sheer fact of one's having done it to the best of one's ability.
>
> We would have no complaint if the point of having recourse to particular regions were simply to provide mere labels that asserted nothing *(nirvacanasamākhyā)* . . . The only sensible view is that different literary procedures such as these *(kāvyaprasthānabheda)* are a function of different literary sensibilities *(kavisvabhāvabhedanibandhanatva)*.[48]

Two key points in Kuntaka's critique, the denial of the environmental (or biological) determinism of culture and the hierarchy of literary styles, are closely related. The first criticism is no doubt driven principally by logic. If style were truly regional, there should be multiple styles, not just two or three, given the multiplicity of regions; and, more seriously, some relationship between biological nature and literary creation would have to be assumed, since what would it otherwise mean to relate style to geography in the first place? (Vāmana's simplistic denial clearly was no longer felt—if it ever was felt—to have any cogency.) No such relationship, however, can be defended, and in any event, the uniformity of Sanskrit cultural training ensures that such localism would everywhere be minimized. The implicit hierarchy of styles in Daṇḍin is meaningless for Kuntaka both in a discursive sense—why should the science of literature even bother with *gauḍīya* if it represents a failure to achieve beauty?—and also because the ontology that seems to underlie it is nonsensical. Style itself, however, is undoubtedly real, and is reducible to a few basic kinds. But these are of an abstract, nonlocalized sort—they have therefore been renamed "gentle," etc.—and are an effect of the sensibilities of the Sanskrit writer, which are underdetermined, or even wholly undetermined, by place.

Kuntaka's analysis is a perfect expression of the cosmopolitan consciousness of the Sanskrit intellectual, who perceived no fundamental variation in the nature of literariness across the immense space of the ecumene. Kashmir at the close of the first millennium was, in cultural-political terms, entirely different from the Deccan, insulated as it appears to have been from the kinds of regionalizing forces that shaped the literary theory of Ratnaśrījñāna. The realities of the language practices in the southern sector of the Sanskrit cosmopolis that underwrote the Ways of literature in the first place (chapter 9.2) would have been unintelligible to northern theorists, and the process of Kashmiri vernacularization that might have made it clear

47. The position of Vāmana, *Kāvyālaṅkārasūtra* 1.2.14–18.

48. *Vakroktijīvita* 1.24, pp. 40–41.

to them even in the absence of such practices was still centuries off. But there is a curious and slightly self-contradictory legacy to the kind of explication offered by Kuntaka, one shared by some earlier and most later writers. On the one hand, the Ways were retheorized in accordance with the mimetic and aesthetic underpinnings of Kuntaka's abstract schema—a given Way was now thought of as appropriate for a given literary mood or theme. On the other hand, the regionalized styles continued to proliferate in a way that would eventually make Kuntaka's reductio ad absurdum a reality.

The retheorization that contradicted the naturalizing interpretation represented by Ratnaśrījñāna actually began some time before Kuntaka. The literary scholar Rudraṭa (probably ninth century and probably not Kashmiri) includes the Paths under the aesthetic category of *anubhāva,* reaction, one of the components of the *rasa,* or dominant emotional state, that the literary text was thought to generate. The Ways of writing are folded into a classification of the responses that a character in various emotional situations might be expected to exhibit and are seen to function as a kind of mimetic of rhetoric or component of *rasa.* The *vaidarbha* and *pāñcāla* Paths are thus shown, very schematically, to be appropriate for the aesthetic emotions of "the erotic," "the piteous," "the fearful" and "the marvelous (or, uncanny)."[49] Perhaps the most elaborate analysis along these lines is provided by Bhoja. In his aesthetic theory reactions are categorized as "initiatives" or functions of mind, speech, heart or mood, and body *(manovāgbuddhiśarīrārambha)* prompted by the memory, desire, aversion, or will of a character who is responding to a particular person or event. Here the Ways are classified, along with costume and dramatic mode, as functions of mood *(buddhi)* and not speech *(vāk),* because the latter has to do with the content of the utterance, not its expression-forms.[50] The Ways, it should be noted, were never used or said to be used for imitating *regional difference* itself—an easterner was never supposed to be shown speaking in *gauḍīya* style—but only emotional difference: *gauḍīya* was appropriate for the heroic emotion and never for the erotic, while the reverse was the case for *vaidarbha.*

In Ānandavardhana's *Dhvanyāloka* (Light on Suggestion) of the mid-ninth-century this conception is taken to its limit. Here the Paths are emptied of all geocultural actuality and demoted to the status of a second-rate literary-critical analytic:

> The *vaidarbha, gauḍīya,* and *pāñcāla* Paths were made current [as analytic categories] by persons unable to give a clear idea of the true nature of poetry, for this true nature, which we have analyzed by using the concept of *dhvani* [sug-

49. *Kāvyālaṅkāra* of Rudraṭa 15.20. See also chapter 9.2, including n. 43.

50. Śāradātanaya follows Bhoja in including *rīti* under *buddhyārambhānubhāva* (*Bhāvaprakāśana* p. 9, 1.36, explicated p. 16, vv. 84ff.). See also *Sāhityadarpaṇa* p. 603: "Sometimes the Paths should differ by reason of what is appropriate to a given speaker."

gestion], manifested itself to them unclearly. Those who set forth the definitions of the Paths did have some slight, though indistinct, notion of the true nature of poetry. But as we have here demonstrated this nature clearly, any other explanation, as by means of the styles, becomes worthless.[51]

Like all other components of literary language in Ānanda's system, the Ways, along with the expression-forms that constitute them, have literary value—and so come in for analysis in isolating the "essence of literature" *(kāvyātma)*—only to the degree that they subserve the main goal of suggesting aestheticized emotions, the telos of literature. They are ultimately, as Abhinavagupta comments here, only a matter of *rasa.*

Yet paradoxically, even as the Ways of literature were being evacuated of any real regionality, they continued to multiply as if this were precisely what they signified. Whereas Daṇḍin and Bhāmaha began with *vaidarbha* and *gauḍīya,* the Ways of the south and north (or east), Vāmana added a third, *pāñcāla,* the Path of the (north-)central. Rudraṭa for his part had noticed a lacuna in the west and added *lāṭīya,* the Way of Lāṭa, or southern Gujarat. Bhoja added two more: *āvantika,* "relating to Avanti" (the area of Mālava), and *māgadha* (relating to Magadha, present-day Bihar). A few centuries later, Śāradātanaya observed that to the four main divisions of style known to him *(vaidarbha pāñcāla, lāṭīya,* and *gauḍīya)* could be added two more, the style of Saurāṣṭra, the Kathiawar peninsula in western Gujarat, and that of Drāviḍa country, peninsular India. Echoing Bhoja while actualizing Kuntaka's counterfactual he notes:

> The Paths are ways of composition belonging to particular regions, and thus bear the name of that region. In each particular Path there is a different degree of nominal composition, of phonological texture such as softness and the like, and a different order of metaphoricity/figuration *(upacāra),* and of alliteration. And this applies no less to Saurāṣṭra and Drāviḍa styles. Poets speak of four main types as a shorthand; there are an infinite number of styles deriving from the subdivisions of these, with variation in each and every writer according to his individual taste, and in each and every sentence. Scholars have actually identified 105 such Paths, but I forbear going into them for fear of unduly lengthening my book.[52]

Two centuries later still, Śiṅgabhūpāla, author of the *Rasārṇavasudhākara* (Moon over the Ocean of *Rasa,* c. 1330), repeating Śāradātanaya, argued that indeed, "the Paths are as many as there are different regions of the country," but added only one more to the list, a "mixed" *rīti* he calls *āndhra* (1.242).

51. *Dhvanyāloka* on 3.46 (Kashi ed. p. 517), slightly modifying the translation of Ingalls et al. 1991: 669.

52. *Bhāvaprakāśana* 1.84 ff., pp. 16–17 (ed. 1930 1.13 ff., p. 11). For Bhoja's list, see *SKĀ* 2.27 ff.

The propagation of ever new stylistic localizations during the period 1000–1500, in the teeth of ever more decisive arguments against their actual regionality, prompts us to pause and consider how to account for it. The contexts of this multiplication certainly suggest a cultural politics of a new sort. Every regional power seems to have felt called to represent its region on the cosmopolitan map of literary style—and precisely at the moment when the cosmopolitan order was everywhere on the point of ceding to a new vernacularity. For instance, the Śiṅgabhūpāla who added the *āndhra* style belonged to the Rēcarla dynasty that ruled in the area between the Vindhyas and Śrīśaila, in the heart of Telangana in today's Andhra Pradesh, in the epoch when *āndhra* was first being produced as a coherent regional representation (chapter 10.1). In the interests of this cultural politics, Ways were added even at the cost of intelligibility. It may be easy to ridicule Bhoja's classification—*āvantika* is defined "absurdly" as "not any one kind of *rīti* exactly, but something approaching all *rīti*s!"—but that does not help us grasp why he found it so important to expand the geographical world of literature that he would be willing to sacrifice taxonomical clarity. Its importance may have lain in the fact that Avanti, comprising the region between Vidarbha to its south and Lāṭa to its west, was beginning to take on a new kind of cultural-political definition in eleventh-century India—at least for the Paramāras and their king, Bhoja, whose realm was centered in Avanti and who (or whose immediate descendants) seem to have had the first faint stirrings of interest in the new vernacularity and its significations for a regional cultural politics.[53] Inclusion on a map of literary styles was clearly becoming a component of political self-representation, something that the central position of poets and literary scholars at royal courts, and the substantial literary and philological output of kings themselves, would lead us to expect. As significant as the regionalization itself, however, is its conceptual framework: for Bhoja, as for Rājaśekhara before him and Śiṅgabhūpāla after, regional self-understanding still had to be defined and established precisely within an overarching structure of some wider, cosmopolitan culture, even as—and perhaps precisely because—other forces of localization were beginning to make themselves felt.

The contradictions and tensions visible in the discourse on the Ways of Sanskrit literature find something of an objective correlate in the literary texts themselves. The very conception of a southern Way was likely to have made sense originally only given the linguistic sensibilities of southern-language poets writing in Sanskrit, something that can be perceived in southern vernacular literature (chapter 9.2). Traditional appreciations of actually existing poetry, too, suggest that regional style was, if not the consequence

53. I refer to the *Rāulavela* (Bhayani 1994), see chapter 8.2. The exasperation is Raghavan's (1978: 185).

of a fated regionality, at least a property that transcended any narrow correlation with aesthetic emotion. The obvious example here is Kālidāsa himself, who is celebrated in the poetic encomia as the very embodiment of *vaidarbha* literature and whose works evince close connections with Ujjayinī, Rāmtek (near Nasik), the Vākāṭakas, and other locales on the map of wider Vidarbha.[54]

We shouldn't carry this literary-cultural ecology or biology too far, however. Nothing suggests in the case of Bilhaṇa, a late-eleventh-century poet from Kashmir who describes himself as writing according to the *vaidarbha* Way ("a rain of nectar from a clear sky," "guarantor of literary beauty, something granted only the finest poets"), that anything was at work other than the aesthetic choice that his countryman Vāmana three centuries earlier urged poets to make (I say this in full awareness of the fact that the kingdom of his patron, Vikramāditya VI of Kalyāṇa, did indeed include part of Vidarbha).[55] This holds equally true for the *gauḍīya* Way. Attempts have been made to demonstrate the prevalence of a style of writing classifiable as *gauḍīya* in the inscriptional poetry of the Pālas and Senas, two ruling lineages in what is today Bengal, and therewith to discover an "indigenous" aesthetic. But the style of, say, Nārāyaṇapāla's record of c. 900 scarcely differs from what can be observed in the very first Sanskrit *praśasti* of all, Rudradāman's inscription at Junāgaṛh in the far west of India.[56] Moreover, it is perfectly clear to anyone who has read a page or two of Sanskrit poetry that the close correlation that Rudraṭa and Ānandavardhana saw between Ways and emotional registers was a matter of normal literary procedure. *Gauḍīya* style was regularly employed for the heroic and *vaidarbha* for the erotic—and obviously eastern poets did not write exclusively of war (and exclusively eastern poets) or southern poets exclusively of love (and exclusively southern poets).

The whole problematic of representation and reality in the history and traditional understanding of the Ways raises intriguing questions about the local understanding of local difference and forms of cultural identification during the cosmopolitan epoch. In this there is an interesting parallel with the history of the literary Prakrits and the shastric discourse on their characteristics. Like these dialects, the Ways may have begun their careers as loosely conceived regional modes of literary language. But the very act of conceptualizing and describing them in cosmopolitan literary theory made them universally available in the Sanskrit cultural order as potential modes of writing. A similar process occurred with the grammaticization of the

54. See *Avantisundarī* v. 15 on Kālidāsa; *Sūktimuktāvalī* v. 91 on Śīlābhaṭṭārikā ("expert in the *pāñcāla* Path") and v. 93 on Vijayāṅkā (after Kālidāsa she became "the dwelling place of *vaidarbha* language").

55. *Vikramāṅkadevacarita* 1. 9

56. Bhattacaryya 1981: 77 n.; 88. For the Nārāyaṇapāla grant see *IA* 15: 304ff.

Prakrits. This parallel in cultural phenomenology is further enhanced by the homology revealed when the Prakrits are mapped against the Sanskrit regionalized styles—Magadhi correlating with *gauḍīya,* Maharashtri with *vaidarbha,* Shauraseni with *pāñcāla*—which suggests something of a deep shared prehistory.[57]

What principally needs emphasizing, however, is the nature of the distinctions being drawn, or better, the kind of difference these distinctions make. On the discursive plane, what the category of the regional Ways most insistently communicates—and we should find no contradiction in this because the local actors never did—is the very cosmopolitanism of Sanskrit literature. This unification of literary language into a single if multiplex spatioconceptual framework is exactly what is imaginatively achieved in Rājaśekhara's account of the progress of Poetry Man and Poetics Woman. "Regional" differences are part of the repertoire of a global Sanskrit and thus constitute a sign precisely of Sanskrit's transregionality, indeed, its ubiquity: Its supposedly local colorings are in fact reproduced translocally and thereby offer an index of Sanskrit's pervasion of all local space. Put differently, *mārga* envisions the unity of Sanskrit literature as a genus with various regional species, just as in the *Kāmasūtra* regional species can be identified within the genus "woman."

It is just this singularity, implicit in *mārga* as a cosmopolitan rather than a truly regional cultural form, that would be rendered fully explicit when the Way became part of the new binary that would be foundational to the vernacular poetries that arose in the second millennium. Over against what came to be viewed as a unitary *mārga*—the tradition, method, mode, and vast zone of well-traveled, placeless Sanskrit culture—was constructed the *deśī,* the multiple cultural practices of Place, which do not travel but, by staying in place, create actual local difference according to a new and more grounded regionalization schema (chapter 10.2). By asserting the presence of real difference, the new binary subsumed all the older variations of the Sanskrit Ways under a unified totality, retrospectively demonstrating how homogeneous in fact the theoretical Sanskrit regionality was held to be.

The increasingly prominent geo-logic of Sanskrit knowledge forms throughout the first millennium is an arresting phenomenon with complex significations. Everything that came within their orbit, from sexual preferences to modes of literary recitation, was grasped as, or invested with, an identity ontologically linked to parts of a world. The world space thereby generated was itself at once huge but limited, definite but indistinct, bounded yet never

57. Note, however, that the theory of the Ways applies only to Sanskrit literature: there are no Ways of Prakrit or Apabhramsha. This is explicitly noted by the (undated) *Hṛdayaṅgama* commentary on *KĀ* 1.40: *gadyapadyātmakasya saṃskṛtasyaiva gauḍavaidarbhānusāreṇa viśeṣaṃ darśayitum āha astīti.*

sharply bordered. It could appear smaller in representation than the world in which Sanskrit texts actually circulated. The many regions of Southeast Asia that were home to one form or another of Sanskrit literary production from the fourth to the fourteenth century seem to be placed outside this realm. There was no literary Way of Sumatra, Laos, or Annam. Yet these places may in fact have been seen by their inhabitants not as Annam or Laos or Sumatra but as existing inside a Bhāratavarṣa (chapter 6.1). At the same time, the literary world space could be larger than the actual one: recall that the Pahlavas (Parthians or Persians) often found on the conceptual map of Sanskrit inclusivity though they remained largely off the factual map; so far as we know, no Sanskrit poetry was ever produced in Tabriz or Isfahan. Moreover, the various modalities of a thing's existence within this particular world exhausted the realm of possibility, and these modalities were themselves incidental to the essence of the thing. Thus literature was a phenomenon exclusively of Bhāratavarṣa—*kāvya* was Indian, however amorphous "India" itself may have been—and all its variations served only to foreground the essential monosubstance from which they varied. For the writers on the Ways of literature, as for Rājaśekhara's Poetry Man, regional difference related simply to style (the manner of practicing alliteration, recitation, gesture, or costume), not to substance (the culture of those acts themselves).

Again, this is not to assert that the vast area encompassed by the style borders of the Ways presented a Sanskrit literary sphere absolutely homogenous, whether linguistically, literarily, or culturally. Such a claim would be rash, though it is worth bearing in mind that the pedagogy of Sanskrit and the temper of its courtly participants did succeed in producing continuities and consistencies in literary practice across time and space that are truly astonishing. The main point is that by the doctrine of the Ways of literature a powerful and consequential idea of inclusion was promulgated within the conceptual horizon of the actors involved. Beyond all variation across space—or indeed, across time—beyond all factors of differentiation that in the end proved to be only instantiations of a higher-ordered unity, lay a larger organizing framework for cultural life, the *cosmopolitan* sphere. The texts are clear about this *cosmos;* what is harder to grasp is the vision of the *polis* that filled it.

CHAPTER SIX

Political Formations and Cultural Ethos

6.1 PRODUCTION AND REPRODUCTION OF EPIC SPACE

Our exploration of the complex relationship between literature and space began with a legendary account of the origin of Sanskrit literature and a literary-theoretical discourse on Sanskrit styles and their regional dimensions. Both perspectives are conditioned by a conceptual matrix fundamental to Sanskrit thought for ordering and explaining the diverse phenomena of culture and society as elements in a transregional network closely related to Sanskrit's own nonlocalized mode of existence. But there are other, literary linkages between literature and space. Narrative has an internal spatial logic, a "semiotic domain around which a plot coalesces and self-organizes," as one scholar puts it, though literature does not merely receive and reproduce this domain secondhand but helps to create it. In addition to literature's narrative mapping of a particular world, literary forms themselves are "place-bound" and have their "peculiar geometry . . . boundaries . . . and favorite routes."[1]

It is these two other properties—the space that has meaning for Sanskrit literature qua literature and the space of its literary forms—that now need to be addressed. It would be instructive to examine these for Sanskrit literary culture as a whole and to show the varieties of spatial logic present in premodern South Asia.[2] However, our focus here will be the Sanskrit *Mahābhārata:* investigating the space of literary content and the space of literary form in premodern India's most sustained and profound discourse on

1. Moretti 1998: 5.

2. For a preliminary analysis of Sanskrit literary culture in spatial terms see Pollock 2003: 102 ff.

power brings us into direct contact with a vision of cosmopolis as a political order that was as influential as any in shaping thought about and practice of polity during the first millennium. It is not often recognized just how significant a feature spatiality is for the *Mahābhārata,* both internally in the story it has to tell and externally in the kinds of literary-cultural practices that ensured the text's reproduction and promoted its circulation. Whatever other interests it may have, and there are many to be sure, the *Mahābhārata* seems especially concerned with creating a conceptual macrosphere of culture-power in the same way as its custodians were concerned with consolidating this sphere in the world of thought and action.

Everything about the *Mahābhārata,* from its history as a text to the history of its impact on South Asian culture, is huge and complex. There is little hard evidence about the origins of the work in its monumental form (eighteen books, and something on the order of a hundred thousand verses according to its own calculation). Even a cursory analysis of the manuscript data available in the critical edition reveals that the majority of the books were transmitted not orally but in reasonably stable form based on written archetypes. These cannot have come into being much before the beginning of the Common Era and are very likely of a much later date. This written transmission was vastly complicated by the fact that the text circulated as part of a living culture and grew and changed as dramatically as any living cultural phenomenon has ever done, producing a text-critical problem as large and intricate as any in world literature.

The genre to which the *Mahābhārata* belongs, and therefore the kinds of meanings traditional readers and listeners found in it, is not much easier to unravel than its textual history. It represents itself for the most part as *itihāsa,* an account of "they way things indeed were." However much modern scholarship may complicate the factuality of that record, many serious minds of medieval India concerned with telling the truth about the past took as Year One on their calendars the date of the war described by *Mahābhārata* and of the Kaliyuga that the war was believed to have inaugurated. Yet the *Mahābhārata* was not only *itihāsa,* it was also *kāvya.* For many later writers (as their encomia of poets show, and as Rājaśekhara's tale of Poetry Man confirms), Vyāsa, the supposed author of the *Mahābhārata,* was a poet second only to Vālmīki. Eventually the *Mahābhārata* came to also be viewed as a transcendently authoritative moral discourse; one ninth-century literary theorist conceived of the work as "moral discourse with the aura of literature." The last important medieval editor and commentator of the *Mahābhārata,* at the end of the seventeenth century, could thus say,

> To the objection that one should not comment on or recite the *Mahābhārata* as if it were a sacred text because it is a human creation . . . I respond: whether or not simpletons like us can find the Vedic sources from which the *Mahābhārata*

> is derived, it is derived from Vedic sources. The entire body of moral discourse remembered *(smṛti)* that was composed by Manu, Vyāsa, and the other omniscient seers is precisely like the Veda insofar as it is the enunciation of those who know the Veda. It should therefore be treated like scripture *(āgamayitavyam)* and commented upon and recited accordingly.[3]

Such different textual identities—history, poetry, moral law, and scripture—entailed for traditional readers and listeners quite different protocols of interpretation, and medieval Indian literary theory is unequivocal on the various kinds of meaning communicated by various textual types.[4] The additional complications that arise when the *Mahābhārata* (as also the *Rāmāyaṇa*) is subsumed under the European idea of epic, especially when epic is assessed within the context of modern European discourses on nation and novel, need separate analysis (chapter 14.2).

Of a complexity commensurate with its manuscript history and genre identity is the *Mahābhārata*'s very content. If the *Rāmāyaṇa* is rightly said to have become a veritable language for talking about the world, then the *Mahābhārata* became a veritable library of the world, for around the main narrative are piled high many volumes of lore and doctrine contributed by Indian thinkers and storytellers over centuries. The work famously celebrates its own encyclopedism, declaring near the start that "whatever exists in the world is to be found in the *Mahābhārata* and whatever is not there does not exist." Nonetheless, the text, over the course of tens of thousands of verses, never loses sight of the narrative core—the struggle between two sets of cousin-brothers for succession to rulership in the Kuru capital, Hastināpura—or of the central problematic upon which it is so adamantly insistent, the antinomy of political power:

> *arthasya puruṣo dāso dāsas tv artho na kasya cit* |
>
> Man is slave to power, but power is slave to no one.[5]

The dilemma of power—in the starkest terms, the need to destroy in order to preserve, to kill in order to live—becomes most poignant when those whom one must kill are one's own kin. That is why the *Mahābhārata* is the most harrowing of all premodern political narratives in the world: the *Iliad,* like the *Rāmāyaṇa,* is about a war far from home, the *Odyssey* about a postwar journey home, and the *Aeneid* about a war for a home. The *Mahābhārata* is about a war fought at home, and in any such war, both sides must lose.

3. Nīlakaṇṭha's commentary on the *Mahābhārata* p. 2, column 1.16; column 2. The *Bṛhatsaṃhitā* (c. 550), the Aihoḷe inscription (634), and the *Rājataraṅgiṇī* (c. 1150) all use a Kaliyuga dating system, among others, commencing (discrepantly) after the battle of Kurukṣetra. The *Mahābhārata* is *śāstrarūpe kāvyacchāyānvayini* in *Dhvanyāloka* 4.5, p. 530.

4. See chapter 2.3 and Pollock 2003: 48ff.

5. *MBh* 6.41.36; cf. vv. 51, 66, 77.

The spatial interests of the *Mahābhārata* exert the same kind of structuring force on the narrative as do its political interests, and this is so because the two are mutually constitutive: the political exists in space, and what exists in space is unavoidably related to the domain of power, whether as something inviting or something resisting incorporation. Thus the plotting of an epic geosphere, far from representing just another among the *Mahābhārata*'s myriad concerns, forms one of its central subjects. Power here is figured, in essence, as the command of space, however we are to understand the idea of command (and the difficulties of a satisfactory understanding should not be minimized), and the space to be controlled is thus a fundamental concern of power. The latter point merits particular scrutiny because it merited the *Mahābhārata*'s own scrutiny. Over and over the narrative maps a coherent supraregional domain, a zone within which political action was held to be operative and meaningful. In fact, such mapping presents itself at every important narrative juncture in the text—exemplifying in this something of Bakhtin's "chronotope," but with the chronotope's politics of space more clearly visible than Bakhtin himself may have understood.[6] Here are several key instances:

In preparation for his consecration as *cakravartin,* "wheel-turning emperor," the act that determines the course of the entire rest of the tale, Yudhiṣṭhira, the eldest of the Pāṇḍavas, sends out his four brothers to conquer "the four directions"—not "in the four directions" but the whole known world that had political meaning: Arjuna to the north, to defeat the people of Ānartta, the Kāśmīrakas, the Bāhlīkas, and others; Bhīma to the east, to defeat the people of Videha, Magadha, Aṅga, Vaṅga, and Tāmralipi; Sahadeva to the south, to defeat the people of Tripurā and Potana, plus the Pāṇḍyas, Drāviḍyas, Coḍrakeralas, and Andhras; and Nakula to the west, to defeat the kings of Marubhūmi, Mālava, and Pañcanada, as far as the Pahlavas.[7]

At the moment of greatest tension, on the eve of the war, Dhṛtarāṣṭra, the blind king who is uncle to the Pāṇḍavas and father of their rivals led by Duryodhana, muses in private with his confidant, Sañjaya. This scene has been preceded by a series of increasingly desperate and ultimately fruitless delegations sent by both sides in hopes of averting war, and the mustering of forces, which "has turned the whole orb of Jambūdvīpa, as far as the sun shines, into an armed camp." Dhṛtarāṣṭra believes catastrophe is inevitable, being convinced of the fact (however perplexed by it) that kings are always prepared to kill each other for possession of the earth: "O Sañjaya, these brave kings, who delight in war . . . are ready to give up their life for land . . . What virtues must this earth possess, Sañjaya! Speak to me of them." He asks about the different continents and in particular about Bhāratavarṣa—"object of my

6. Bakhtin 1981: 84–258.

7. *MBh* 2.23–29 (cf. 2.4).

son Duryodhana's craving, of the greed of the sons of Pāṇḍu, and of my own attachment"—and the regions and cities from which the countless soldiers have gathered for war. After describing the seven "family mountains" of Bhāratavarṣa, from Mahendra to Malaya, and the many great rivers from the Narmadā to the Kāverī, Sañjaya lists the multitude of *janapadas*, "people-places," beginning with the lands of the Kurus and Pāñcālas and proceeding in more or less clockwise order through a hundred or more locales, from Śūrasena, Kaliṅga, Kuntala, Kāśikośala, and Cedivatsa to the people-places of the south and west, ending with those of the Huṇas (Huns), Tukhāras (Tocharians), and Pahlavas (Parthians) in their mountain fastnesses.[8]

After the war, the Pāṇḍavas perform the horse sacrifice, thereby asserting their political authority over whatever space the sacrificial horse wanders through unchallenged. As a result the supralocal domain is plotted again, this time extending from Trigarta, Prāgyotiṣa, Maṇipūra, Magadha, Vaṅga, Cedi, Kāśī, Kosala, Āndhra, and Draviḍa across to Gokarṇa, Prabhāsa, Dvārakā, Pañcanada, and Gandhāra.

If the Pāṇḍavas' political power has now been confirmed, both the war and the new and meaner Kali Age it has inaugurated have sapped their strength and will: "Cursed be the law of power," they declare, "that has left us dead in life." They eventually renounce sovereignty and begin the *mahāprasthāna,* the Great Departure. They proceed first to the Lauhitya River (the Brahmaputra) in Bengal to the east, then "travel by way of the northern coast of the ocean to the southwest quarter," head for Dvārakā and thence to Mount Himavān, the great Sand Ocean, and Mount Meru. The journey is sketched in broad strokes, but the text takes care to note that the Pāṇḍavas, at the end of their "skein of journeys," have performed one last circumambulation of the earth for the possession of which they had earlier destroyed their family.[9]

Thus at every turning point of the main narrative—the royal consecration before the war, the survey of a world soon to be at war that is the very object of that war, the reaffirmation of dominion after the war, the ritual death march at the end of the story—the *Mahābhārata* continually insists on *placing* the action and thereby producing a specific macrospace, one with a uniformity, coherence, and salience that manifest themselves everywhere in the narrative. No doubt this space is sometimes rendered unfamiliar, confused, or exoticized. When the four brothers set out on their conquest in support

8. *MBh* 6.1.8; 6.5.3–5, 21; 6.9.1–2; 6.10.64–66 (reading *pahlava* for *pallava;* the *MBh*'s geography here is identical with that of the *Padmapurāṇa* 3.6–7, a version of the longer recension noted in chapter 5.1, see Kirfel 1931:3).

9. For the wanderings of the sacrificial horse see *MBh* 14.73–85; Yudhiṣṭhira's exclamation is found in 15.46.8; and reference to the brothers' final *prādakṣiṇya* in 17.1.44 and their course in 17.1.31–2.2.

of Yudhiṣṭhira's claim to sovereignty, Sahadeva conquers "Rome, Antioch, and a city of the Greeks" in the south beyond the land of the Tamils, which for its part is sometimes represented not just as the political domain of the Pāṇḍyas, Drāviḍas, and Coḍrakeralas but (if the names are to be taken literally) as the habitation of "One-Legged," "Camel-Eared," and other fantastic peoples.[10] But what should claim our attention above all is the very fact of the presence of this spatial representation in the *Mahābhārata,* not its precision according to later cartographic standards. There exists, the narrative insists, a recognizable geosphere where the *Mahābhārata*'s communicative medium, the Sanskrit language, and its message, the possibility as well as predicament of a sole royal power, have application. It is a space that has coherence, however blurred at the edges, and political content, however unrealizable the tragic tale shows it to be. The movements of the heroes are movements through a familiar world and rarely beyond it (they are always turned back from proceeding into the unfamiliar, as when Arjuna arrives at the northern reaches of Harivarṣa and the land of the Uttarakurus, where humans die if they enter and war cannot occur, 2.25.8 ff.). And this movement is typically inseparable from the political project they advance. One of the last images the work leaves on the mind's eye bears this double dimension: to abandon political power in the Great Departure is to sever one's ties to this macrospace, and to do that is to prepare for death.

The *Mahābhārata*'s narrative construction of a supraregional domain was complemented, or perhaps better, enacted, by a range of material-cultural practices relating to the text, including the spread and distribution of manuscripts, the creation of editions, and the various modes of popular dissemination. These practices accomplished two things at once. First, they reproduced narrated space by their location in and circulation through actual space, thereby investing the narrative with a new degree of actuality and cognizability. Second, they reasserted the symmetry of the political and cultural spheres, endowing the transregional cultural formation that found expression in Sanskrit with a political imagination of transregional scope.

The most obvious and concrete correlate between the fictional plotting of a macrospace and its factual reproduction lies in the diffusion of *Mahābhārata* manuscripts. It is striking how closely this followed the boundaries of the circuit represented in the narrative itself. Manuscripts of the work are found in Kashmir, Nepal, Bengal, Tamilnadu, Kerala, Maharashtra, Gujarat, western Panjab, and everywhere in between—but only there. Nothing suggests that there ever existed a central Asian or Burmese or Sri Lankan recension

10. *MBh* 2.28.49. "Roma" may refer to Constantinople (founded 324), but even then the location remains problematic. An expansion among southern manuscripts, at the point where the text describes the barbarous beings (found even in the sober Varāhamihira, see chapter 5.1), seeks to restore the civility of the southern region (see Reich 1998: 69).

of the *Mahābhārata*. Like other kinds of Sanskrit literature, the *Mahābhārata* no doubt did circulate across wider southern Asia from an early period. Manuscripts of the work were donated to temples in Cambodia as early as the sixth century, and individual verses were incorporated as quotations in a Javanese *kawi* text of about the tenth century. But in neither instance did these manuscripts ever become part of a tradition of textual reproduction, any more than there existed a tradition of primary creativity in *kāvya* beyond the inscriptional variety (an enigma of Sanskrit culture in Southeast Asia noted in chapter 3.1). The text was evidently studied and would eventually play a major role in the vernacularization process, especially in Java, but nothing indicates that it ever functioned as a component of a developing, productive literary culture that found expression in Sanskrit.

The *Mahābhārata* manuscripts are written in a wide variety of regional scripts. (That a truly transregional form of writing, Devanagari, would not come into wide use until the fourteenth or fifteenth century, at end of the cosmopolitan period, is only another of the wonderful incongruities of the Sanskrit cosmopolis.) Today we tend to think of these scripts as having been illegible outside their regions, but in fact there was far more intercommunication between them, at least among specialists, than can be assumed by the usual method of extrapolating from the conditions of modernity, under which an earlier "multiscriptism" (like an earlier multilingualism) has been much reduced. Manuscripts of the *Mahābhārata* written in Malayali (in the far southwest) and in Sharada (in the far northwest), the two scripts typically taken as the limit cases of cross-regional intelligibility, can easily be shown to have been mutually influential. Moreover, although manuscripts are classifiable into regional traditions, regionalism here pertains entirely to differences in local writing systems. No regionalization of any consequence, in point of dialect or in the particulars of material or social or even religious life, can be detected in any recension or version. To the degree that regional versions can be said to exist at all[11]—and the idea is not entirely modern but was known to editors in medieval times—they mark distinctions without differences. That is, while the text was undoubtedly expanded or contracted in one recension or another, this was unaccompanied by the least hint of localization. In short, the unmistakable impression given by hundreds of medieval manuscripts copied time and again for centuries on end is that the *Mahābhārata,* just like Sanskrit itself, existed in a quasi-universal transregional space and spoke across this space in an entirely homogeneous voice—until of course this voice became truly regional and new vernacular *Mahābhārata*s were created (chapter 10.1).

The transregional scope and character of the manuscript tradition were

11. Grünendahl 1993 importantly reconsiders the logic and reality of "regional versions" of the *MBh.* On regionality and recension see also Pollock 2003: 108 ff.

recapitulated in the great premodern editions of the *Mahābhārata* in both the locations of their production and the geocultural logic informing their text-critical procedures. There will later be occasion to note the ideological conjuncture of philology and nationalism that marked the *Mahābhārata* critical-edition project that began in Pune in the 1920s (chapter 14.2). But that was not the first time in South Asia that an edition of the *Mahābhārata* was deliberately created, albeit premodern editions differed markedly in critical method, social context, and cultural-political purpose from what was to come later.

There is a tendency, especially among scholars who deny the Pune critical edition any authenticity, to think of the so-called Nagari vulgate as a kind of natural formation, akin to an alluvial deposit at the mouth of the *Mahābhārata* tradition. It is of course nothing of the sort but, on the contrary, a conscious construction by Nīlakaṇṭha Caturdhara, a Maharashtrian Brahman who worked in Vārāṇasī in the last quarter of the seventeenth century. He tells us in his introduction that he gathered "many manuscripts from different regions and critically established the best readings." He did a substantial amount of editing in the process, since his text differs markedly from that of Devabodha, the earliest commentator whose work is extant, and who sometime in the eleventh century established a text affiliated with the Kashmiri tradition. The opening section of Devabodha's *Jñānadīpikā* (Light of Knowledge) makes no clear statement of critical methods, and it is not easy to infer what these may have been from the available portions of his work. But Nīlakaṇṭha's explicit acknowledgment of the transregional dissemination of manuscripts, and with it the tacit recognition that these are all versions of the same text and must be compared with each other to pierce through the darkness of ignorance and attain textual truth, are important markers of both a general theory of textuality as well as an understanding of this particular text's mode of being. Far from being peculiar to Nīlakaṇṭha, these beliefs were shared by every editor who cared to explain his method.[12]

Consider one edition prepared in late-medieval Bengal. In the introduction the editor, one Vidyāsāgara, intimates something about his method and something also of his conception of the *Mahābhārata* as a textual phenomenon. He describes the edition as based on "the traditional text of Gauḍa" *(gauḍīya-sāṃpradāyikā),* the "books of the Hogalavāḍa traditional text" *(hogalavāḍīya-*

12. The quotation is from Nīlakaṇṭha's commentary on the *Mahābhārata,* introduction, v. 6. On Nīlakaṇṭha see Minkowski forthcoming; on Devabodha, Sukthankar 1944: 274. An analysis of Devabodha's influential interpretive practice—the identification of the *tātpārya,* or essential purport, of every section of discourse (this would be imitated by later commentators for centuries, especially Arjunamiśra)—merits more study than De's few words (1944: ix).

saṃpradāyapustaka), and a version found in "books from the west" (*pāścātyapustaka*). Whatever these *saṃpradāyas*, or recensions, represented to the mind of the editor (they are nowhere further defined), they in fact possessed no true regional specificity aside from their currency in given regions—something shown to be true of virtually every work of Sanskrit literature that has been critically edited (which have regional recensions that nonetheless show no cultural regionality whatever). Vidyāsāgara identifies additional manuscripts, presumably not constituting *saṃpradāyas*, as Rāḍhīya, Vārendra, Kāmarūpīya, Maithila, Dokhaṇḍīya, and Rājagirīya. He also makes use of at least a dozen earlier commentaries, including Devabodha's (by then ancient) *Jñānadīpikā*, several of whose verses he borrows for his own introduction.[13]

We may well wonder whether such major initiatives as Vidyāsāgara's and Nīlakaṇṭha's could possibly have been executed or even conceived without substantial patronage. Both are silent on the question, but we know that in other cases the production of a new *Mahābhārata* edition was supported by royalty or other members of the elite. In the late fourteenth century, an annotated edition of the epic was prepared by Ānandapūrṇa Vidyāsāgara, the court scholar of Kāmadeva, overlord of the Kadambas of Gokarṇa and father-in-law of Harihara II, king of the recently founded Vijayanagara kingdom. A century later and at the other end of the subcontinent, Arjunamiśra prepared his annotated editions of both the *Mahābhārata* and its supplement, the *Harivaṃśa* (Dynasty of Hari), at the instance of one Satya Khāna (c. 1475), a powerful lord serving under the Pathan Sultans of Bengal and a patron of learning in Rajshahi.[14]

But in truth these data are relatively thin and do not help us grasp the most important point of all: what this intense philological activity meant in

13. Older commentators were therefore not only systematically studied, in Bengal at least, but the chronology of their succession was preserved in memory and was understood, one assumes, to represent a meaningful order. For a copy of the unique manuscript of Vidyāsāgara's *Jayakaumudī* I thank the curators of the Virendra Research Institute, Rajshahi. See also Bhattacharya 1944. The "Bengal recension" of the *MBh* is known from elsewhere (e.g., Nīlakaṇṭha on *MBh* 5.155.6, "Gauḍapāṭha"). Hogalavāḍa is likely Hāgalavāḍa, a feudatory chieftancy near present-day Bangalore founded in the mid-sixteenth century. Although not otherwise associated with a *MBh* textual tradition, the court (lower-caste Vīraśaiva converts) cultivated Sanskrit studies. For the historical lineage of *MBh* commentators, see the citation of Arjunamiśra in Sukthankar 1944: 267.

14. On Ānandapūrṇa see Raghavan 1939–40 and [1941]; Gode 1944 (however, Ānandapūrṇa Vidyāsāgara should be distinguished from the Vidyāsāgara mentioned in the previous paragraph; they are confused by Gode, among others); on Arjunamiśra, see Ghosh 1934–35; Gode 1935–36. Sukthankar refers to Anūpasiṃha (not a "Vārāṇasī notable" but *mahārāja* of Bikaner [r.1669–98], and a well-known bibliophile), as a patron of Nīlakaṇṭha (1944: 264 n.), but gives no further information. Minkowski 2002 notes that Nīlakaṇṭha mentions a patron (Anūpasiṃha) only once in all his works.

cultural-political terms. Arguably, the editorial efforts of Ānandapūrṇa may have been stimulated by the same neotraditionalist impulses that drove other Vijayanagara scholarly projects, such as the unprecedented edition of and commentary on the four Vedas prepared by Sāyaṇa-Mādhava in the generation before Ānandapūrṇa. A comparable stimulus, on a much smaller scale, may have been at work in the edition of book 12 of the *Mahābhārata* produced in Nepal in 1597. A normalized and scrupulously edited manuscript prepared at the behest of a Vaiṣṇava notable, the text was apparently intended for the use of the Malla kings in conjunction with the *pārāyaṇa,* or customary reading, of the work during consecration ceremonies (book 12 deals with, inter alia, the moral law of kings).[15] If we had anything like an adequate social history of literary patronage in medieval southern Asia, the list of known royal patrons materially involved in the production of editions of the Sanskrit *Mahābhārata* could without doubt be vastly expanded, given what we know concerning such patronage in the creation of vernacular *Mahābhāratas* from the later period—or indeed, what we know concerning the role of royal patrons in the dissemination of the *Mahābhārata* through sponsorship of popular oral performances. This performative aspect, the final component of the epic's supraregional diffusion that needs attention here, was perhaps more effective and vital than any other in ensuring that the transregional narrative achieved transregional impact.

Endowments or other forms of support for public recitation and exegesis of the *Mahābhārata* were provided by the ruling elite over a long period of premodern history. Although the epigraphical record on this topic, as elsewhere, awaits systematic study, even stray data-gathering reveals a remarkable level of royal involvement with the epic's reproduction across an immense space-time. In the realm of the Pallavas in southeast Tamilnadu, Parameśvaravarman I in 690 C.E. donated a village as a source of revenue to provide a temple with flowers, incense, water, and fire, and to pay for recitation of the *Bhārata.* A late-eleventh-century inscription from the Kottayam region of Kerala records that the annual income from a certain plot of paddy field was assigned to ensure the reading of the *Mahābhārata* in a Vaiṣṇava temple, while a charter of Madanapāla of Bengal (c. 1150) grants a village to a Campāhiṭṭīya Brahman as a fee for reciting the *Mahābhārata* to the chief queen, Citramatikādevī. Epigraphical evidence is easily supplemented by literary allusions. Bāṇa's *Kādambarī* (mid-seventh century), in what is clearly a reference to an everyday occurrence, describes a queen visiting the Mahākāla temple in Ujjayinī and hearing the *Mahābhārata* being read aloud. Similar references to kingly expertise in and concern with the epics is found in profusion from as early as the seventh century, when the Bādāmi Cāḷukya king

15. Jayapratāpamalladeva used the manuscript when reading the entire *parvan* over a two-week period in 1646 (Belvalkar 1966: xlv–vi.; Dunham 1991: 7).

Maṅgaleśa was described as "proficient in *Mānava, purāṇa, Rāmāyaṇa, Bhārata,* and *itihāsa,*" and as late as the eighteenth, when Śāhajī, king of Tancāvūr, invited to court a pandit "and listened to his exposition of the *Mahābhārata* day and night for three months."[16]

A conceptual supraregion of a particular shape and content was thus produced and continually reproduced across a real supraregion, not just narratively, in the very story the *Mahābhārata* tells, but also concretely, in the broad diffusion of manuscripts and the dispersed points of production for medieval annotated editions of the text, as well as culturally and linguistically, in both what the "regional" recensions say and how they say it. It was also demonstrated materially in the widespread existence of endowments for the continual performance and explication of the work. And most of this activity was promoted by the kinds of kings whose ideal types are the subject of the story. Given the relatively stable language and cultural content of the *Mahābhārata,* the megaspace recreated by textual dissemination and performance was a homogeneous one, where all regional differences were elided. And given the narrative substance and core concerns of the *Mahābhārata,* this space was projected above all as a political space, presupposing the transregional intelligibility and acceptability of a uniform logic of power and polity.

Moreover, the particular modalities of communication that marked the dissemination of the Sanskrit form of the work across all of South Asia without interruption for more than a millennium—oral performances on the basis of hand-written texts—constituted a method and a scale of inculcation of transregional political sensibilities probably without parallel in premodern world culture. The mode of understanding generated by this kind of dissemination was no doubt different from the conceptual-political effects induced by the print texts of modern mass culture, but it need not, by any means, have been less potent. And while no unitary collective subjectivity may have been evoked among listeners and readers by the narrative itself, nonetheless the text was for centuries reproduced everywhere in the very

16. *SII* 1: 150–51; *EI* 18: 340; *JASB* 69.1 (cf. Ghosh 1934–35, and Sukthankar 1944: 267 ff.; the commentator-editor Arjunamiśra was born into this same Brahman subcaste of Bengal four centuries later; and it was from his father, a professional reciter of the epic—"master of the *Bhārata,*" he calls him in his colophons, and "king of reciters," like their ancestor who had been gifted a village by the Pāla king—that he learned the text); *Kādambarī* p. 40 (see also Hemacandra's *Dvyāśrayakāvya* 6.6). A temple inscription from Sendalai (Tancāvūr district) reports an endowment in the form of land given to two brothers who were *Bharata[sic]*-expounders *(bharatappangu)* by Maravarman Sundara, the Pāṇṭiya king (*SII* 6: no. 12; undated, c. ninth century; see also *ARSIE* 1922 [1923] no. 546, another Pāṇṭiya grant for recitation of the *Mahābhārata* and *Rāmāyaṇa*). (I now find several of these references already available in Raghavan 1956: 505.) For Maṅgaleśa see *IA* 7: 161 ff., for Śāhajī, *Śāhendravilāsa* p. 19. Śāhajī's epic interests were paralleled, at the other end of India, by Jai Singh II of Jaipur (r. 1700–43), for whom the "contemplative speeches of Vyāsa" and "*itihāsas* like the *Bhārata*" were objects of constant attention (Horstmann 1994, adducing the *Īśvaravilāsamahākāvya,* a contemporary court poem).

world produced by the text itself, and every such actual place was thereby incorporated into the text's supralocal cosmopolitan conceptual space.

The text was also being read and performed, however, far away from the world apparently constructed by the text. This might be taken as an instance of how far the circulatory space of the Sanskrit cosmopolis exceeded its conceptual space. A more just, if less intuitive, understanding requires conceiving of South Asian space itself as exceeding its concrete landmass. What is so remarkable and deeply suggestive about the actual ways of being in the Sanskrit cosmopolis is that its conceptual space could be reproduced so easily and repeatedly in worlds located outside its apparent physical boundaries. As we saw, this was recognized clearly and explicitly as early as the seventh century: as Xuanzang put it, "People of distant places with diverse customs generally designate the land that they admire as India." Although it may not have engendered a tradition of textual reproduction in Java or Khmer country of the sort found across the subcontinent, the *Mahābhārata* was a decisive cultural force in both places: it was central to the development of *parwa* and *kakawin* literature in the one case, and in the other its narrative found frequent cultural expression in everything from conventional epigraphical allusions to plastic representations on bas reliefs on temple walls. The list of epic linkages in Southeast Asia could be vastly expanded. In what is today Laos, for example, a grant was made by an overlord named Somaśarman instituting "daily uninterrupted readings" of the *Mahābhārata* (which, in its "complete" form, was gifted to a temple along with manuscripts of the *Rāmāyaṇa* and *purāṇas*) at the very time that a Pallava king half a world away was establishing a similar endowment for the perpetual recitation of the text.[17] One effect of the geopolitical energies and associations of the epic in regions that were apparently excluded from the epic's space—at least according to a positivistic cartographic understanding—was to prompt them to reconfigure such a space of their own: if the epic did not include their worlds in Bhāratavarṣa, they would include Bhāratavarṣa in their worlds by wholesale toponymic transformation.

Thus across Southeast Asia a thorough-going reconstitution of the cognitive landscape occurred, where not only natural features like mountains and rivers but also regions and kingdoms were identified with names borrowed from the *Mahābhārata*. As late as the sixteenth century, in a description of the Javanese pilgrimage circuit titled the *Tantu Panngelaran,* the story is recounted how, at the origin of the island, the gods, having created men and women, moved Mount Meru from India to Java and took up their dwelling there. The Khmers, according to one compelling argument, saw themselves as living not in some overseas extension of India but inside an Indian world, one populated by the gods and heroes as depicted, above all, in the *Mahābhārata*. That

17. *ISC:* 30 (*IK:* 19): . . . *aśeṣaṃ bhārataṃ dadat* | *akṛtānvaham acchedyāṃ sa ca tadvācanāsthitim* ||

such a world was indeed recreated in Cambodia is richly demonstrated by the distribution throughout the country of the various "self-manifested signs" or "luminosity signs" *(svayaṃbhūliṅga, jyotirliṅga)* of the god Śiva, comparable to the twelve that plot out a kind of Śaiva space in the subcontinent; by the "new Kurukṣetra" that was founded, according to an inscription that cites verses from the epic itself, by King Devānīka in Vat Phu in the late fifth century and known to be in existence as late as the eleventh; and by the stunning half-mile-long frieze on the outer galleries of Angkor's main entrance, where panels narrating the great battle on the field of the Kurus are suggestively juxtaposed to those depicting the marching armies of Sūryavarman II. Not only was the reordering, or, more correctly, the epicizing, of Southeast Asian space common, it may have been directionally inflected. In Laos there appears to have been, in the west and east respectively, a Mālava and a Daśārṇa region—ancient toponyms in India for what are today Malwa and the region stretching east from Sagar district in Madhya Pradesh—while Champa to the east in what is now central Vietnam and Dvāravatī to the west on the Thai peninsula complement the epic's Campā in today's Bengal and Dvārakā in Gujarat.[18] A similar directionality could be found in central Java: Through the plains of Kedu, where the great monuments of Indo-Javanese culture are located, there ran a Gaṅgā River joining with a second river at a town called Prāgāwatī (Prayāgavatī). The plains are bounded by mountains, Himalaya-like, to the north; the great Buddhist shrine Borobodur was built in a place comparable in orientation to the Buddhist *stupa* of Barhut in central India; while to the far west there was a region known as Malaya (Malayu). As one of the most insightful of the early generation of Javanists put it, "There was intentional effort made to create in that part of Java . . . a replica of the Holy Land of India."[19] Clearly, space in the cosmopolitan sphere was infinitely fungible,

18. It is unclear what to make of the four traditional divisions of Champa: Amarāvatī (Quang Nam), Vijaya (Binh Dinh), Kauṭhāra (Nha Trang), and Pāṇḍurāṅga (Phan Rang), see Wheatley 1983: 396. On Java, see Lombard 1990: 13–14, who also cites Groslier 1979: 179 on Khmer country, and cf. Wolters 1979: 437–39 for the argument on the Khmers. For the twelve *jyotirliṅgas* see chapter 5.1 (the *svayaṃbhūliṅgas* are listed in a late commentary, cf. Gopinatha Rao 1971 2.1: 83 ff.); for Devānīka's inscription, see chapter 3.2. Some Chinese pilgrims, such as Yching (fl. 700) saw Pa-nan (Funan) as the southeast corner of Jambūdvīpa (Pelliot tr. *BEFEO* 3: 284; cf. de Casparis 1956: 185). Southeast Asian historical geography has been a magnet for sometimes eccentric interpreters of Ptolemaic toponyms with a curious lack of methodological candor. Among these G. E. Gerini is probably to be numbered, but his notion of the distribution of Southeast Asian regions in a similar "topographical order" to India, or "toponymic mimicry," retains interest (1909: 121). The most serious account since Coedès is Wheatley 1983, though a view of the whole is not easy to derive from his work.

19. Stutterheim 1939: 79–83. He might have also mentioned Java's Kalinga (and possibly its Madura) in the eastern part of the island, though we need (once more) to bear in mind how confused is the historical geography of early Java and how uncertain the identification of some of the toponyms.

with multiple exemplars of the same mountains, rivers, and regions. During the age of epic reproduction, geoculture possessed, in a real if quite unfamiliar sense, no singular "home" and "abroad," no hard inside and outside, no stable center and periphery, since home and inside and center could be recreated everywhere.

Concomitantly, and in an equally real if unfamiliar sense, India's own geography during the cosmopolitan period did not exist as we now think of it, nor as home, inside, and center, and so should no more be seen as the donor for these representations than the rest of the world should be seen as their recipient. India itself was a site under construction; what was taking place in Southeast Asia was occurring simultaneously in the subcontinent as well. In the far south, cities, regions, political zones, mountains, and rivers were being named for celebrated northern sites: Mathurā (Maturai), Pātaliputra, Mālava, Magadhaimaṇḍala (near Salem), Cedimaṇḍala (on the banks of the Penner), with a southern Kailāśa (Teṅkailās) in Kerala and Gaṅgā rivers seemingly everywhere. The Indianization of India itself at the level of geography was of a piece with virtually every other aspect of the growth of the Sanskrit cosmopolis, where similar cultural practices in everything from inscriptional eulogies to cosmocratic urban designs manifested themselves across the trans-region such that it is often impossible to say who was lender and who was borrower.[20]

In the regions to the north and west of the subcontinent a rather different situation presents itself. Certainly the *circulatory* space of the Sanskrit cosmopolis at different times in the history of the formation included large parts of western and central Asia: some of the oldest surviving manuscript fragments of Sanskrit literature have been found there (in what is now Xinjiang province of China, for example), and certainly texts of the Sanskrit knowledge systems, especially medicine, circulated across the region. But, as noted earlier, this area was never included in the conceptual space of the *Mahābhārata* and, correspondingly, was not in the zone of dissemination for its manuscripts. Instead, the region seems to have been slotted into the fantasy world of the "Northern Kurus" and the like; in addition, no toponymic transformation seems to have occurred there. The presence of limits to a quasi-universal cosmopolitan world are no simple thing to explain. The space into which the Sanskrit cosmopolitan order did not extend was occupied by early Persianate culture to the west, Tibetan and Chinese to the north and east. Historical parallels—such as the barrier formed by Greek culture against

20. Until toponymic duplication receives the detailed study it merits see Raghavan 1943, from which a number of my instances are taken. The recreation of Bhāratavarṣa in late-medieval Maharashtra in the pilgrimage circuits of the Mahānubhāvas, or the equation in Cōḻa records of the Gaṅgā and the Kāverī, may be pointing toward something rather different: the miniaturization of the cosmopolitan within the new vernacular worlds (chapters 9.3; 10.1, 3).

the expansion of the Latin cosmopolitan order in the eastern Mediterranean, certainly not beyond Mesopotamia (chapter 7.1)—suggest that, perhaps to the same degree that cosmopolitan cultures abhor and fill vacuums, they also seem to map out spheres of influence that do not overlap.

However much we may be persuaded of the coherence of epic space and its reproducibility in the cosmopolitan thought-world of premodern Asia, it is one thing to bring to light its shape or even to show that geocultural representations bore some conceptual political content, and another altogether to understand how that space related to the world in which real power was actually exercised.

6.2 POWER AND CULTURE IN A COSMOS

The conceptual space of the *Mahābhārata* is similar in its basic morphology to the realm created by the Ways of literary style, which underpins the various geocultural matrices of Sanskrit examined in chapter 5. Yet it crucially adds to those cultural forms a vision of the political in the widest sense of this term. The circuits repeatedly traced by the heroes generate a frame of reference in which the projection of power—the very goal of their progresses—takes on a new, more grounded intelligibility. The production of epic space at the same time engenders a new realm of belonging. As audiences would hear the recitation of the text all across the actual space of the narrative being recited they would hear themselves being included in that narrated space of power. Some more intimate sense of this larger political sphere, if only one of virtual belonging, would ineluctably have developed. At first sight we might be tempted to think of the space of the *Mahābhārata* as a merely conceptual domain, a pure *imaginaire,* rising like a bubble to the surface of epic discourse only to burst and disappear when the recitation of the discourse itself ended. However, the imaginary and the conceptual have a reality, and often a very consequential reality, of their own. Epic representations provided a template for structuring real political aspirations, or, what amounts to the same thing, the discursive understanding of political aspirations—how else do we know aspirations except through discourse?—among historical rulers across the space-time of the Sanskrit cosmopolis.

Obviously, literary representation was not the sole cause of the imperial vision in premodern India. In various forms this vision long antedated the Sanskrit cosmopolitan formation itself and was tied up with much larger, indeed Eurasia-wide, transformations in the idea and exercise of political power over the course of the second half of the first millennium B.C.E.[21] The oldest evidence both of the ambition of projecting transregional power and, equally important, of the shape of this transregion in the earlier period, is provided

21. See Pollock 2005a.

by the distribution of the Ashokan edicts. The space plotted by these inscriptional sites is notable for both what it does and what it does not contain. Except for a dense concentration in Brahmagiri, Gavimath, and other locales in central Karnataka (pointing toward Maurya interest in controlling the celebrated gold-producing region), most of the inscriptions are found in the Maurya core area and, remarkably, in the far northwest, today's Peshawar (Shahbazgarhi) and Kandahar in southern Afghanistan (ancient Arachosia). The limits of this physical distribution are echoed in the discourse of the inscriptions themselves: peninsular India is "beyond the borders" of Aśoka's domain, whereas Greeks and Iranians in the northwest are included. As for Bhāratavarṣa (to say nothing of "Indu," "al-Hind," or "India,"), it did not yet exist.[22]

On the eve of the consolidation of the Sanskrit cosmopolitan order, two Prakrit inscriptions charted out a similar kind of megaspace. The Nasik cave inscription, dated about 150 C.E., of Gautamī Bālaśrī, grandmother of the Sātavāhana overlord Puḷumāvi, describes in a kind of transregional geographic rapture the territory of her son, Satakarṇi: the regions called Asika (Ṛṣika), Asaka (Āśmaka), Mūlaka, Suraṭha (Surāṣṭra), Kukura, Aparānta, Anūpa, Vidarbha, and Ākarāvantika, and the mountain ranges named Vijha (Vindhya), Chavata (Ṛkṣavat), Pāriyātra, Sahya, Kṛṣṇagiri, Matsya, Siriṭana (Śrīstana), Malaya, Mahendra, Seṭagiri (Śreṣṭhagiri), and Cakoraparvata. This basically includes everything from the Western Ghats (Malaya) to the Eastern Ghats (Mahendra), and from Saurāṣṭra south to the Kṛṣṇā River in Andhra (Ṛṣika). Similarly, in the Hathigumpha cave inscription from perhaps the first century C.E., Khāravela of Kaliṅga describes how over the course of his reign he attacked the "western region" of Satakarṇi (of the Sātavāhanas), Ṛṣikanagara on the Kṛṣṇā, the Raṭhika and Bhojaka tribes (of the west), Gorathagiri and Rājagṛha (in Magadha)—an attack, he tells us, that forced the Yavana king then ruling in Mathurā to abandon that famous town. But we are then told something more: Khāravela made an expedition across "Bharadhavasa"—Bhāratavarṣa, the first appearance, it seems, of this term for the transregion in Indian epigraphy—and brought terror upon the kings of "the Northern Way" *(utarāpadha)* and the people of Magadha and Aṅga, as well as, in the south, the Pāṇṭiya realm. Aside from some discontinuity in the representation of space, the two inscriptions show unmistakably that an arena, vast but finite, within which political action made sense was on the point of amalgamating.[23]

22. "Everywhere within the conquered realm *(savata vijitamhi)* of the Beloved of the Gods, King Piyadasi, and among the people beyond the borders, the Cholas, the Pandyas, the Satiyaputras, the Keralaputras" (Hultzsch 1925: 28–29 [257–56 B.C.E.]). A convenient map of the distribution of the edicts is Schwartzberg ed. 1992, pl. IIIb5. For general remarks on the transformation of political-military space from the Maurya period onward see Ludden 1999: 64 ff.

23. *EI* 20: 72 ff. and Sircar 1965–83, vol. 1: 213 ff.; *EI* 8: 60 ff. and Sircar 1965–83, vol. 1: 203 ff.

Within a few centuries of these inscriptions the major historic transformation in the conceptual space of power in South Asia occurred. This fact can be observed most vividly in the mid-fourth-century Allahabad Pillar Inscription of Samudragupta, a foundational document of the self-expression of imperial polity in the Sanskrit cosmopolis not only for its aesthetics (chapter 3.2) but for its geopolitics. Like the Rudradāman epigraph, Samudragupta's record seeks added glory and ennoblement by associating itself with great kings of the past, having been engraved on a column bearing two Ashokan edicts. The pillar was appropriated in turn by the Mughal emperor Akbar, who moved it from Kauśāmbī to Allahabad, and by Akbar's son, Jahāngīr, and courtier, Bīrbal, who also left engravings. The monument thus embodies two millennia of Indian political charisma, less than but similar to the Junāgaṛh rock (chapter 1.3).

The dominant interest of the Allahabad Pillar record, overshadowing even the celebration of its own cultural refinement and that of the king, is to establish the spatial realm to which Gupta power pertained. This too is a concern shared with Rudradāman's inscription: recall the Śaka's boast that he "rules as lord of eastern and western Ākarāvantī, Anūpa country, Ānartta, Surāṣṭra, Śvabhra, Maru, Kaccha, Sindhusauvīra, Kukura, Aparānta, Niṣāda, and other areas gained by his valor." The geopolitical vision of Samudragupta, however, is grander and more coherent by an order of magnitude:

> [Samudragupta's] true magnificence combined with valor is illustrated by his first capturing and thereafter graciously releasing all the kings of the Southern Way *(dakṣiṇāpatha):* Mahendra of Kosala, Vyāghrarāja of Mahākāntāra, Maṇṭarāja of Kurāḷa, Mahendragiri of Piṣṭapura, Svāmidatta of Koṭṭura, Damana of Eraṇḍapalla, Viṣṇugopa of Kāñcī, Nīlarāja of Avamukta, Hastivarman of Veṅgī, Ugrasena of Pālakka, Kubera of Devarāṣṭra, and Dhanañjaya of Kusthalapuram . . . He exterminated many kings of Āryāvarta . . . [and reduced to tributary status] the frontier rulers *(pratyantanṛpati),* such as the lords of Samantaṭa, Ḍavāka, Kāmarūpa, Nepāla, and Kartṛpura, as well as the Mālavas, Ārjuneyas, Yaudheyas, Mādrakas, Ābhīras, Prārjunas, Sanakānīkas, Kākas, Kharaparikas, and others . . . [He was mollified] by various acts—the paying of homage, the offer of their daughters in marriage, and their petitioning for the right to rule their own districts and provinces—on the part of the Devaputra-Śāhi-Śāhānuśāhi, the Śaka Muruṇḍas, and all the lords residing in the islands, the Siṃhala and others.[24]

Several names of the regions and overlords Samudragupta conquered are unidentifiable, but many can be placed in the real world. The "kings of the Southern Way" probably represent the overlords and allies of what was earlier the domain of the Ikṣvākus and then of the ascendant Pallavas. Kosala,

24. *CII* 3: 203 ff. (translation modified; for the geographical identifications, pp. 13–31).

Mahākāntāra, and so on have been taken to refer, sequentially along a southern cline, to places in today's Orissa, Andhra Pradesh, and Tamilnadu (it is unclear whether this extends to the southwest). This *tour d'horizon* of the southern region is followed by, first, Āryāvarta, the north-central zone; then, in a sort of countercircumambulation of the quarters, the northeastern frontiers (Samantaṭa and Ḍavāka referring to areas in today's Bangladesh, Kāmarūpa to western Assam, Kartṛpuram to the Katyur Valley in Almora district); the west and northwest (Malwa, and so on); the far northwest (toward Kabul and the Oxus beyond), where the last of the Kuṣāṇas ("son of the gods," "king of kings") ruled; Surāṣṭra, where the last of the Śakas reigned; and, lastly, the subcontinental islands, including Sri Lanka. But again, rather than focusing on the exact correspondence of these place-names with spots on a present-day map, we are mainly concerned instead with the spatial morphology itself and its semiosis. What is being constituted here is a new conception of imperial sovereignty, one that is quasi-universal, seeking distant if not infinite projection within a geopolitical space that is bounded (there are both explicit and clearly implied "frontier" zones) and therefore intelligible. It can be termed a universal conquest—a "conquest of all the earth" *(sarvapṛthivīvijaya)* in the words of the inscription itself—because it exhausts the domain where the extension of a particular kind of political power has meaning.

Equally significant as the innovative quality of Samudragupta's discourse in rendering political space nearly symmetrical with the conceptual space of the Sanskrit cosmopolis is the extraordinary influence his inscription exerted, probably greater than any inscription in Indian history. This is owing to its having provided the model for the *digvijaya,* the conquest to the horizons, of King Raghu in the fourth chapter of Kālidāsa's *Raghuvaṃśa* (The Dynasty of Raghu):

> The conquering King Raghu set off from Ayodhyā east to Suhma and Vaṅga, where he planted his victory pillars on the islands in the Gangetic delta. He crossed the Kapiśā River and, guided by people of Utkala, he marched toward Kaliṅga "after imposing his violent power upon the head of King Mahendra." Leaving Kaliṅga, he made for the Kāverī River and, beyond that, to Mount Malaya, turning back east again to defeat the Pāṇḍya on the Tāmraparṇī River and then heading toward the Sahya Mountain Range in the west. Across the Muralā River he marched northwestward, conquering the Pārasikas and, further north, the Huns, Kambojas, and mountain tribes, the Kirāṭas and Utsavasaṅketas. Finally, he proceeded across the Lauhityā River to conquer the kings of the northeast in Prāgjyotiśas and Kāmarūpa.[25]

25. A summary of *Raghuvaṃśa* 4.28–85. Kamboja refers to an Iranian people of northern Afghanistan (cf. *JA* 1958: 45 ff.).

That Kālidāsa modeled his account of the legendary Raghu on Samudragupta's record has long been known,[26] but deeper connections than those so far identified can be found. Both Samudragupta and Raghu are represented as the third generation of their dynasty, both embody the powers of the world-guardians, both of them conquer and release their former foes, both reinstall them after dethroning them.[27] The pillars that Raghu plants at the Gaṅgā are a complement to the Allahabad inscription, believed to have originally been located at the Yamunā River. More important, even, than these shared features of kingly practice is the concordance in spatial imagination: Raghu covers the same territory as described by Samudragupta though he moves in the opposite direction: from eastern Uttar Pradesh to south-central Bengal to Orissa (Utkala) and Kaliṅga (Mahendra) and to Tamilnadu, but then on to Kerala (Malaya), and from there north to today's Afghanistan and Pakistan, and last to western and eastern Assam. Aside from geographical specificity, the image of a universal conquest is shared by both. As Kālidāsa says of Raghu, "His chariot of conquest would rest only at the furthest horizon."[28]

Thanks to Kālidāsa's appropriation—in itself a notable instance of the aestheticization of the political—the Samudragupta record was released from its immobilization in stone and set free for wide circulation. We have noted how the works of this great poet were assiduously studied across the cosmopolis, from Kashmir to Angkor and Java, and none more so than *Raghuvaṃśa*. This is no accident but rather a consequence and a sign of the political impulse that lay at the core of cosmopolitan Sanskrit culture. Along with the dissemination of the *Raghuvaṃśa* a new vision of the projection of power across an increasingly well-defined space—a space that might be located in various worlds in southern Asia—was disseminated throughout the cosmopolis and marked both literary and inscriptional discourse. One important example of the literary *digvijaya* is the account in Kalhaṇa's *Rājataraṅgiṇī* of the military expeditions of Lalitāditya Muktāpīḍa (c. 700–750), a universal overlord *(sārvabhauma)* who "adorned [all] Jambūdvīpa" and was utterly unlike the regional lords *(prādeśikeśvara)* of the common sort. The poet recounts the conquest of the quarters in due order: how Lalitāditya invaded Āryāvarta and defeated Yaśovarman of Kānyakubja; marched onward to the Bay of Bengal, to Kaliṅga, and south to Karnataka, the Kāverī River, Mount Malaya, and the nearby islands; then westwards and north to the Konkan, Dvārakā, and

26. See for example Ingalls 1976: 16 and n. 5 there.

27. Compare *Raghuvaṃśa* 4.43 with Allahabad line 20; *Raghuvaṃśa* 4.37 with Allahabad line 23. The topos of dethroning and reinstalling defeated kings is discussed further in what follows.

28. *Raghuvaṃśa* 3.5.

Avanti; thence into the Northern Way *(uttarāpatha)*, moving eastward from the country of the Kambojas toward the lands of the Tuhkhāras, Bhauṭṭas, Darads, and thence to Prāgjyotiṣa and finally Strīrājya, the "Kingdom of Women," and the land of the Uttarakurus.[29] The narrative very closely parallels the *Raghuvaṃśa* and, indeed, the various routes of circulation observed in the *Mahābhārata*. The additional detail in his account suggests that, like Kālidāsa, Kalhaṇa may have used a *praśasti* as a source—and perhaps one that was itself modeled on the *Raghuvaṃśa*.

There is certainly evidence that Kālidāsa's account fed back into the very inscriptional discourse that gave it birth, exerting its influence across the entire Sanskrit world within a few centuries of its composition. In the epigraphical accounts of their military undertakings, overlords in early-medieval Southeast Asia—Bhavavarman II in seventh-century Champa, Sañjaya in eighth-century Java—figure themselves as Raghu defeating his foes on all sides. Later kings and their inscriptional poets carry this emulation even further: Lakṣmadeva of the Paramāra dynasty of Mālava (1082–92) in one of his *praśasti*s closely follows Kālidāsa's reworking of Samudragupta's epigraph, down to the description of the war horses rolling on the banks of the Vaṅkṣu River, their withers stained with saffron.[30]

The political space of the epic actualized epigraphically by Samudragupta and literarily by Kālidāsa became a key component of Sanskrit political culture. In inscriptions this development is in evidence immediately after Samudragupta with his successor, Candragupta II (end of the fourth century), who had the following inscribed on the great iron pillar now at Mehrauli in Delhi:

> His fame was engraved on his arm by the sword as he stood in battle against the men of Vaṅga, he who could destroy assembled enemies when they attacked simply by facing them. He crossed the seven mouths of the Sindhu River and then defeated the Vāhlikas, and even today the southern ocean is perfumed by the breezes of his martial valor.

What is described here are the cardinal points on the map of Candragupta's power: Vaṅga (Orissa) in the east, Sindh in the west, Balkh (i.e., the Kuṣāṇas) in the north, and the southern ocean—the limits of the new vision of transregional political space.[31] While the shape of this space would remain largely stable in subsequent inscriptions, such exiguous presentation would quickly

29. *Rājataraṅgiṇī* 4.126–76.

30. *ISC* 13, vv. 6 and 7 = *Raghuvaṃśa* 4.49 and 54 (in both cases eliminating local Indian references to, respectively, the people of the Pāṇṭiyas and the women of Kerala); *CIJ*: 26 ff.; *CII* 7.2: 114, v. 54, cf. *Raghuvaṃśa* 4.67.

31. Or read "Vāhika" (for Vāhlika), i.e., Panjab (compare chapter 2 n. 47), *CII* 3: 259. On the spatial orientation see Sircar 1965–83, vol. 1: 284 n.

be replaced by far grander enunciations produced across the transregional cosmopolis.

In the century after Candragupta II, Yaśodharman of Mālava (r. c. 525–35) issued a record (noticed already in chapter 3.2) that not only alludes to the Samudragupta *praśasti* (it too reflexively comments on its being inscribed on a pillar) but also directly refers to the supersession of Gupta rule:

> Regions never possessed *(bhukta)* by the Gupta masters, though they showed their power in the course of their attack on all the earth *(sakalavasudhā)*, regions never penetrated by the command of the Hūṇa overlords, which could dislodge the crowns of kings . . . this man now possesses, scorning the environs of his own home.
>
> As far as the Lauhitya River, as far as Mount Mahendra, its foothills thick with palm trees, as far as Snow Mountain, its slopes embraced by the Gaṅgā, as far as the western ocean—all the lands are dappled with the rays from the gems on the crowns of the heads of his vassals as they bow to his feet, their pride in the power of their own arms destroyed.[32]

Yaśodharman too conceives of a now almost fixed transregional scale of power: from the Lauhitya River (the easternmost point reached by the Pāṇḍavas in their Great Departure) to Mahendra in today's Tamilnadu, the Himālaya in the north, and the Arabian Sea in the west. This is no mere empty space, however wild it may have been (he speaks of the "deserts, mountains, forests, ravines, and streams" he has conquered), but one that is truly an object of governance, which he claims to be the first to achieve.

The remarkable Aihoḷe inscription of the Bādāmi Cāḷukya king Pulakeśin II (634 C.E.), which as we saw stamped the self-definition of the recreated dynasty of the western Cāḷukyas at the millennium's end, conjoins local specificity with imperial grandeur to endow the latter with a powerful effect of the real. Pulakeśin is described as recovering the throne from his usurping uncle and then beginning his universal conquest: He first besieges Vanavāsi in the northwest and subdues the Gaṅga and Āḷupa lords in the south, thus seeking at the start to gain control of the greater part of what is today Karnataka. He proceeds to the Konkan and afterward conquers peoples up the northwest coast: the Lāṭas, Mālavas, and Gujaras. To the east rules Harṣa, king of Kānyakubja, who is defeated next, then the "three Mahārāṣṭrakas" with their ninety-nine thousand villages. Pulakeśin then rains terror on the people to the north and east in Kosala and Kaliṅga; obscures the splendor of the Pallavas in coastal Tamilnadu; and moves against the Cōḻas, Kēraḷas, and Pāṇṭiyas westward across the peninsula. At the end he returns home as a world conqueror:

32. Sircar 1965–83, vol. 1: 419, vv. 4–5. See also chapter 3.2 and n. 58 there.

> Endowed now with the three powers—energy, mastery, and good counsel—after conquering all the quarters, dismissing the lords of earth, and doing homage to gods and Brahmans, he entered Vātāpi and now rules this whole earth as if it were one city *(nagarīm ekām ivorvīm imām . . . śāsati),* its moat filled with the dark blue waters of the rolling ocean.[33]

Although its northernmost regions are here ignored, this political space is as literally *cosmo-politan*—the world governed as one city—as one can have. Yet paradoxically though suggestively, it is a finite cosmopolis, since the conquest of the quarters is arrested by the boundary of the seas. The references may be vaguely formulaic—the collocation "Cōḻas, Kēraḷas, and Pāṇṭiyas" antedates the record by centuries—but they are given focus and the appearance of reality by the juxtaposition of a kind of tactical factuality, such as the reference to the defeat of Harṣa.

From the world of the Pālas of Bengal comes a *praśasti* from the time of Nārāyaṇapāla (r. 875–932) written in honor of a Brahman family that had served for generations as royal advisers. The deeds of three of these men, Garga, Darbhapāṇi, and Kedāramiśra, are celebrated as follows:

> "Śakra is lord only of the eastern quarter, and even there the demons were able to defeat him. I made my master Dharma[pāla] king of all quarters." So [Garga] thought, and he laughed in derision at Bṛhaspati, counselor to the gods.
>
> It was thanks to Darbhapāṇi's political knowledge that King Devapāla made all the earth pay tribute, from the Father of Revā [Mount Vindhya], whose high-piled rocks are moistened with the madder of elephants, to the Father of Gaurī [Mount Himālaya], whose whiteness is intensified by beams from the moon on Śiva's crest, all the way to the two oceans, their waters reddened by the rising and setting of the sun.
>
> The lord of Gauḍa, having long paid homage to the wisdom of [Kedāramiśra], took possession of this footstool, the earth, with its tasseled border, the oceans, after annihilating the people of Utkala, humbling the Hūṇas, and humiliating the overlords of Drāviḍa and Gurjara.[34]

It is evidently essential that in the case of each ruler, Dharmapāla, Devapāla, and Nārāyaṇapāla, the supraregion of his dominion be enunciated, whether by mythic reference (the king of men exceeds the king of gods in his universality), by geographical reference (which naturalizes the dominion), or by a more strictly political reference (again, four peoples marking the four points of the political compass: the Hūṇas in the north, the people of Utkal in the east, the Drāviḍa in the south, and the Gurjaras in the west).

A last example from a *praśasti* from the court of the Gurjara Pratīhāras

33. *EI* 6: 5–7. For the topos "ruling the world as one city," see *Raghuvaṃśa* 1.30.

34. *EI* 2: 160–67, vv. 2, 5, 6; on Dharmapāla see also *EI* 18: 304–7, v. 15 and *EI* 4: 248, v. 6.

and dating to the second half of the ninth century celebrates an earlier king of the dynasty, Nāgabhaṭa:

> Of [Vatsarāja] was born a son of great fame named Nāgabhaṭa—people said he was the Primal Being himself. Into his princely power fell, like so many moths, the kings of Andhra, Sindha, Vidarbha, and Kaliṅga . . . He strove for the good of all humanity *(viśvajanīnavṛtteḥ),* and from the time of his youth his transcendent power revealed itself by forceful seizures of the forts of kings: those of Ānartta, Mālava, Kirāta, Turuṣka, Vatsa, Matsya, and others.[35]

Again, four points of a very particular compass function as the armature of imperial power: Andhra in the south, Sindh in the west, Vidarbha in the central region, and Kaliṅga in the east. If these had by this time primarily become placeholders for large regional spaces, they are once more given denser texture by specific reference to places in between: Ānartta in today's Gujarat, Matsya in central Rajasthan, Mālava to the east in Madhya Pradesh, Turuṣka in the far north, Vatsa centered on the city of Kauśāmbī on the Yamunā near Allahabad, with the Kirātas standing for pastoral nomads throughout this space. Real power, at this historical epoch, could be nothing less than this—but it would also be nothing more. At this point, too, an explicit universalist political ethos typically accompanied this spatiality: Everything Nāgabhaṭa did was for "the good of all humanity." Indeed, the dynasty insisted on affirming its universalist orientation; the family as a whole was "a place for refuge for the entire universe."[36]

The epigraphical texts thus enunciated a vision of a coherent space that extended *diganta,* "to the horizons"—though everyone knew there was, so to speak, space beyond the horizons—and represented the arena for a particular kind of political action. By this enunciation they not only discursively constructed the quasi universalism of the new Sanskrit cultural-political order but enacted it by their very ubiquity. The same claims being made in Mālava in the west were also being made in Aihoḷe in the south and in Bengal (by the Pālas) and in the north (by the Gurjara Pratīhāras), and often simultaneously, without apparent contradiction, however mutually exclusive the claims. "O Bhoja," begins a poem that may come from the king's own court (though it is preserved in a fourteenth-century story collection),

> the whole world of rulers is confounded with terror at the projection of your power: the Cauḍa [Cōḻa] lord enters the sea, and the Āndhra a cave; the Karṇāṭa foregoes his royal turban, the Gūrjara takes to the wilds, while Cedi trembles before your arms, and the great warrior king of Kānyakubja is hunched over with fear.

35. *EI* 18: 108, vv. 8, 11.

36. V. 4: *tadvaṃśe . . . trailokyarakṣāspade* (see also v. 6: *natasakalajagatvatsalo vatsarājaḥ,* "Vatsarāja was the beloved of the whole world, which bowed before him").

At almost the same moment that Bhoja's court poet was writing this verse, some five hundred kilometers to the south Someśvara I of the Kalyāṇa Cāḷukyas was being praised as

> destroyer of the pride of the powerful Cōḻa, the blazing submarine fire to the ocean that is the dynasty of Mālava [i.e., Bhoja's Paramāras], the wind to the clouds that are the kings of Aṅga, Vaṅga, Khaśa, Veṅgī, Pāṇḍya, Saurāṣṭra, Kērala, Nēpāḷa, Turuṣka, Cēra, Magadha.

Another five hundred kilometers to the southeast, Rājendra Cōḻa was being described as having

> sent the wheel of his authority and his tiger banner to every region; established his fame and charity in every land . . . rightfully worn his family crown of jewels while other kings wore on their heads his feet as a crown; and caused his scepter to sway over every land in Jambūdvīpa.[37]

This was a political culture, accordingly, where multiple universal sovereigns, like multiple Mount Merus, Gaṅgā Rivers, and fields of the Kurus, violated no principle of logic.

The quasi-universal dimension of power pervaded and shaped many other kinds of political practices and was explicitly thematized in more theoretical works. Consider for instance the composition of imperial armies. One Pāla-era record speaks of the earth sinking "under the weight of the infinite number of soldiers sent by the kings of all Jambūdvīpa, who have come to render service to the supreme king": they came from Gauḍa, Mālava, Khaśa, Hūṇa, Kulika, Karṇāṭa, and Lāṭa. A similar but denser description is found in a mid-tenth-century verse-prose poem, the *Yaśastilakacampū.* Here the Rāṣṭrakūṭa army is shown to be comprised of soldiers from the south *(dākṣiṇātya),* Dravida country *(drāmila),* the north *(auttarāpatha),* the Tirhut *(tairabhukta),* Gujarat *(gaurjara);* and elsewhere reference is made to contingents from the Himālaya, Malaya, Magadha, Madhyadeśa, and Māhīṣmatī.[38] The power that sustained transregional power was itself thought of as transregional.

Among shastric works that touch on the space of the political, two may be briefly noticed. The *Bārhaspatyasūtra,* pseudonymously attributed to the ancient sage Bṛhaspati in some incarnation or other, long enjoyed renown as a political handbook parallel and complementary to the *Arthaśāstra,* though

37. *Prabandhacintāmaṇi* p. 31 ("Kānyakubja" means literally "of the hunchback [son] of a virgin"); *EI* 15: 87 (1060 C.E.); *EC* 10: 87 (1072 C.E.).

38. *A* 25: 306, lines 27 and 36 (time of Nārāyaṇapāla, r. c. 875–932); *Yaśastilakacampū* pp. 461 ff. Note also the list of places sending ambassadors to visit the Rāṣṭrakūṭa king: Kerala, Cōḻa, Simhala, Śaka, Śrīmāla, Pañcāla, Aṅga, Kaliṅga, Vaṅga, Saindhava, Pāṇḍyadeśa, Kāśmīra, Nepāla, and Kauśala (468; vv. 247–49).

in its current form it is unlikely to antedate the twelfth century. The third chapter, after describing the necessary attainments of rulership (personal, political, moral, and religious), provides an account of what is clearly thought to be its essential geographical frame of reference:

> The earth is five million leagues in extent. It contains seven continents *(dvīpa)* and is surrounded by seven oceans . . . In the middle is the Land of Action *(karmabhūmi),* and in the middle of this land is the Rose Apple Tree of Mount Meru.[39] To the north is Mount Himavān; to the south the land extends nine thousand leagues. In the south lies Bhāratakhaṇḍa, and it is there that people's moral and immoral actions manifestly bear fruit. It is there that political governance [or, the "logic of legitimate force," *daṇḍanīti*] pertains, something to be studied by the people of Bhārata of all four social orders in the present and future as in the past. By this governance the blessed Sun attained power, the Wind, and all the gods, and mortals, too . . . It is a thousand leagues from Badarikā [in the Himalayas] to the Bridge [to Sri Lanka]. It is seven hundred leagues from Dvārakā [in Gujarat] to Puruṣottamaśālagrāma [Puri in Orissa].[40]

There is a vaster world beyond the cosmopolitan sphere, but it is largely unknown and has no relevance to Bhāratakhaṇḍa. The latter forms a coherent space, clearly conceived in its extent and more or less homogeneous in moral valence: it is, uniquely and as a whole, the place of moral action—a conception as old as the oldest connected description of this sphere in the puranic account (chapter 5.1); there is no division into good and bad regions (as in the *Yugapurāṇa,* composed on the eve of the cosmopolitan era, chapter 1.3).[41] Most important, it has now become the object of a coherent mode of rule. Thus governance as such has a specific spatial existence. Though it may also have a cosmic dimension—it is what enables the gods themselves to govern—its terrestrial location is in Bhāratakhaṇḍa and there alone.

Thus power no less than culture is spatially specific—and it is precisely this linkage that is made explicit in a text we turn to one last time, the *Kāvyamīmāṃsā* of Rājaśekhara. Sometime after returning to his hereditary position as court poet to the kings of the Kālacūri dynasty in Tripurī, Rājaśekhara wrote a drama celebrating the political power of his royal patrons, who ruled, as he put it, "in the entire region from where the Gaṅgā empties into the eastern sea to where the Narmadā empties into the western, from the Tāmraparṇī [Sri Lanka] in the southeast to the milk-ocean in

39. The reading here is uncertain.

40. *Bārhaspatyasūtra* 3.64–133. The editor dates the work no earlier than the sixth or seventh century, p. 17; it is probably not earlier than the twelfth if "Yādava" (3.105) refers to the Hoysaḷas of Karnataka or the Seünas of Maharashtra (likely given this location in the sequence). The text goes on to list the great realms *(mahāviṣaya),* subrealms *(upaviṣaya),* maritime kings, and mountain kings, all eighteen in number.

41. Also contrast Lotman 1990: 171–74 on medieval European literature.

the north." The Kālacūri kings adapted this and other comparable tropes of transregional dominion in their own epigraphs. In one grand *praśasti* composed in 980—its author says "it would have filled the poet Rājaśekhara himself with wonder"—the dynasty is described in insistently universalist terms:

> Kokalladeva . . . was like Indra on the orb of the earth that submitted to him . . . His valor . . . pervaded the circle of the three worlds *(tribhuvanavalaya)*. His forces were assembled for the conquest of the world *(bhuvanavijaya)* . . . Having conquered the whole earth, he planted two unique pillars [i.e., subordinated rulers], one in the quarter of sage Agastya [the south], King Kṛṣṇa [of the Rāṣṭrakūṭas], one in the quarter of Kubera [the north], King Bhojadeva [of the Pratīhāras].
>
> From [Mugdhatuṅga] was born Keyūravarṣa . . . He fulfilled the ardent desires of the minds of the women of Gauḍa, sported on the breasts of the ladies of Karṇāṭa even as a deer on a pleasure-hill, applied the ornamental mark to the forehead of the women of Lāṭa, enjoyed the pleasures of love with the women of Kāśmīra and the excellent songs of the women of Kaliṅga . . . Up to Kailāsa Mountain [in the north] . . . up to the excellent eastern mountain from where the luster of the sun rises and then up to the western lord of waters the valor of his armies caused unending pain to his enemies.[42]

It is in the context of such representations in the wider political culture that Rājaśekhara offered his observation on "universal" dominion. Most significant is the analogy he draws between the distribution of the Ways of literature that helped constitute the supralocal cosmopolitanism of Sanskrit as such and what he calls the *cakravartikṣetra,* or "imperial field." Some authorities argue that the fourfold categorization of the literary Ways (as belonging to Gauḍa in the east, Vidarbha in the south, Lāṭa in the west, and Pañcāla in the north) cannot be adequate to the innumerable literary regions of the Sanskrit world. "I would answer," says Rājaśekhara, "that although they may be countless, these regions can easily be conceived as the fourfold division [of a unity], in the same way that what is called the 'imperial field' is conceived as a unified whole, though of course its component regions are countless in respect of their specific properties." This imperial field he defines as "the thousand-mile-long region from Kumārīpura to Bindusaras. The man who conquers this is called the Wheel-Turning King."

Brief though this statement is, there may be no more suggestive instance of the perfect symmetry that existed between the space of Sanskrit culture and the space of power. And the representation of this space—from Kanyākumārī on the southernmost coast to the source of the Gaṅgā in the Himālayas—and the kind of power that fills it is one that Rājaśekhara, in the gathering

42. See *Viddhaśālabhañjikā* 4.21; *CII* 4: 210–11 and 217 (slightly modifying the translation of Mirashi); v. 85: *vismitakavirājaśekharastutyā.*

dusk of the cosmopolitan epoch, expresses by quoting the *Arthaśāstra*, a text composed some nine centuries earlier at the era's dawn.[43]

These citations from inscriptions and texts dating from the beginnings of the Sanskrit cosmopolitan period in the early centuries of the Common Era to its endings in the middle centuries of the second millennium, are the tip of a proverbial iceberg of geopolitical representation. Everywhere we look across the world of Sanskrit text production we discover the constant reiteration of a political transregionality, one almost completely settled in its contours by the middle of the first millennium. About the structure, stability, ubiquity, and cultural-political content of this transregionality there can be no doubt whatever. What still remains unclear is its relationship to the practices of rule.

The response offered by scholars to the kinds of declaration we have just surveyed has, with numbing consistency, been simply to impugn their veracity on the grounds of factuality. "More epic than historical," the editor of the Someśvara Cāḷukya record is quick to announce, expressing the commonsense view noted in the discussion of inscriptional aesthetics—a commonsense view with a long history, it turns out. Al-Bīrūnī, visiting India in the early eleventh century, declared in reference to the ninth-century Kashmiri king Muktāpīḍa, "According to their account he ruled over the whole world. But this is exactly what they say of most of their kings. However, they are incautious enough to assign to him a time not much anterior to our own time, which leads to their lie being found out."[44] It is no doubt true that the reality effects—the insistent specification of persons and places— so abundant in earlier records, such as Samudragupta's pillar inscription, became increasingly etiolated in later records, such that political discourse took on the vagueness and flatness of a literary topos. But the simplistic dichotomy between "historical" and "epic"—between the putatively concrete reality of political fact and the airy unreality of political fiction—that permits modern readers to empty the political discourse of transregionality of any significance whatever forecloses rather than expands the possibilities of interpretation by suppressing an all-important third mode of understanding. Here we grasp that fictions can themselves be social facts, that ideals are actually existing values, that imagination is information—and that, accordingly, the epic geomorphology of political aspiration may have exerted existential force not just on medieval thinkers and writers but on rulers, too.

To be sure, recognizing, as many scholars have done in other contexts, that representation comprises an important element of reality—it is at least an index of existing structures of what is desirable if not always possible—

43. *KM* pp. 9.27, 92.12; *Arthaśāstra* 9.1.18. Sircar 1960: 1 ff.

44. Cited by Stein, *Rājataraṅgiṇī* trans. p. 131 n. The view of the editor, L. D. Barnett, is found in *EI* 15: 86 n.

does not free us of the obligation of attempting to understand the concrete nature of the power that filled epic space. Just to pose these questions brings us to one of the most intractable problems of premodern Indian history: the structure and character of the imperial polity. It is intractable on every front in terms of categories, evidence, and interpretation.

When the concept of "empire" was used earlier in this study it was not without awareness that the term is notoriously resistant to coherent definition, and that, concomitantly, the way *rājya* actually worked in early India, and the political formations that embodied *rājya,* are very imperfectly understood. There is no reason to believe, for example, that there ever existed in India anything remotely comparable in any respect to the Roman *imperium* (chapter 7), though it is the Roman political order and its later incarnations in the West that have fundamentally shaped our notions of empire everywhere and of the deficiencies, even unreality, of formations that deviated from it. The bootstrapping required in trying to make sense of political lifeways that are unfamiliar and potentially incommensurable confronts us even more inescapably as we consider South Asia's vernacular epoch (chapter 10.3). When attempting to chart the features of empire, one gets the uncomfortable feeling that one is merely mapping artifacts produced by historians obliged to come up with categories for India's political past.[45]

Reinforcing the category problem is a data problem: the kinds of evidence available for making sense of early Indian empires. The primary reference point for any discussion of empire in first-millennium India is the Gupta formation (founded c. 320). But what data from the imperial Guptas themselves are actually available to us? The records issued in the name of the kings and queens of this dynasty, including seals, consist of a grand total of twenty-odd fragmentary documents and hardly more than 250 lines of printed text; from the founder of the lineage himself, Candragupta, we have nothing; from Samudragupta, only four records. Adding to these all the documents produced by those who directly or indirectly declared their subordination to the Guptas, we can double the number, and if we include two dozen recently published copperplate texts, another three hundred lines. All told perhaps a thousand lines of text (some of which are only partial or simply repeat genealogical information) constitute the entire direct textual basis of our knowledge of the nearly three centuries of Gupta imperial rule—thin gruel indeed, even if these calculations are off by a factor of two or three or more. And though materials of this kind for later polities may be richer, they are not necessarily more informative. Even with respect to Vijayanagara, the last great empire to have unified premodern southern India, the evidence leaves quite uncertain what

45. On classifying Indian political forms see the still-pertinent discussion in Fox 1977: xxiii. For the general problem of defining empire see Duverger 1980: 5–23, Morrison in Alcock et al. 2001: 1–9. Ideological constraints on Gupta historiography are considered in Lorenzen 1992.

"unification" may have meant, to what degree regions were actually incorporated, and how much central control Vijayanagara exercised. Scholars are not much better informed, in these respects, about a sixteenth-century polity than we are about that of the Guptas a millennium earlier—to say nothing of the Mauryas, who preceded the Guptas by six centuries.[46]

We are not primarily concerned here with the kinds of questions usually raised by students of early Indian political history: whether, for example, there was real bureaucratic centralization or only ritual hegemony in a virtual state, real conquest and domination or more ceremonialized kinds of subordination. Our interest is instead with cultural practices as these came to bear on forms of power, and what such practices may tell us about larger issues of political thought and action such as domination. Yet the relationship of culture to power can hardly be understood if we have no sense whatever of how power was embodied and how it worked. What general picture can we draw of the political sphere in South Asia from the time it entered into the historical record up to about the end of the first millennium?

There seems to be little doubt that while local forms of dominion must have varied widely, the favored mode of organizing, or aspiring to organize, political power in terms of space was large-scale and transregional. However difficult it may be to define this empire form in concrete terms, or to fill it with real content, it seems to have existed in southern Asia as a recognizable political type, its various embodiments sharing certain systemic features of political, social, and cultural behavior. Modernity's system of nation-states may be a useful analogy here. The structure of this system, which has arisen under the constraints of a capitalist world economy, produces a number of cultural effects: one cannot achieve the nation form without the elevation and standardization of a particular dialect in which the essence of the nation is thenceforth located, and in the same way a whole array of other cultural and political practices is isomorphically reproduced across polities. One can similarly isolate a premodern empire form, with its own distinctive repertory of practices—and in the creation and perpetuation of such a system, imitation and memory seem to have had no less important a role to play than in the reproduction of nations. The imperial form was successively recreated in South and Southeast Asia (and elsewhere, too), both synchronically, perhaps through what archaeologists sometimes call peer polity interaction or emu-

46. See Ramesh and Tewari (1990) for the recent copperplate finds. On Vijayanagara, see Sinopoli and Morrison 1995; Morrison (2000: 8–9) adds that disagreement about the nature of the empire may index the variability of the empire itself, as well as scholarly worry about variability. The weak evidentiary base of the later medieval period is discussed in chapter 10.3. The Indian situation is not of course unique; in the case of Byzantium, for instance, all the records of the central government, the provincial administration, and the Church have disappeared (Mango 1980: 6).

lation, and diachronically, through a process of historical memory. One line of remembering how to be imperial seems to have connected the Gupta and later imperial formations (such as the Rāṣṭrakūṭa) to the Kuṣāṇa-Śaka and thence to the Maurya almost as clearly as in Europe a line connected the Ottonian, Carolingian, and Roman formations, or, yet another line, the Byzantine and the Hellenic.[47] And just as the Ottoman, Safavid, and Mughal *saltānats* competed as universalist peer polities in the middle of the second millennium, so in the middle of the first, at the high-water mark of the imperial epoch in South Asia, did the Rāṣṭrakūṭas and Pālas, or Angkor and Champa.[48]

A review of some of the practices that created the empire form shows such continuities among imperial formations. Across the space-time of the Sanskrit cosmopolis we can perceive limited numbers of large-scale agrarian polities. These were so-called military-fiscal formations, where the exacting of tribute from local overlords, the gathering of taxes from large populations, the command of military resources, and the acquisition of women in matrimonial alliances could be and were exercised over vast, "multilingual," "multiethnic" populations (terms to be used with cautious sanitary quotes, since the social forms of consciousness [ethnicities] and the cultural practices [discursively unified languages] they imply did not yet exist in any conceptualized form). Political ceremonies such as the archaic horse sacrifice were resurrected to assert transregional claims of power, with kings like Dhanadeva of the Śuṅga dynasty or Pulakeśin I of the Cāḷukya, among countless others, imitating the ritual famously celebrated in book 15 of the *Mahābhārata*. Coinage recycled images and weights from empire to empire (Samudragupta imitating Kaniṣka imitating Augustus). The building or rebuilding of temples demonstrated imperial commitment to the present as well as the past of the community, as in the case of Jayasiṃha Siddharāja's reconstruction in Bilpaṅk (though for much of this world over much of this period temples seem to have been far less significant mediators of royal power than they were to become in Coḷa -era Tamilnadu or Gajapati-era Orissa, the two cases that

47. All of these are ultimately indebted, with important variations, to the Achaemenids, see chapter 1.3. The Guptas imitated the Kuṣāṇas (in their coinage, for example), and their founder appropriated the charismatic name of the old Mauryas. So also, the royal style of rule in early Vijayanagara borrowed broadly from the Hoysaḷas and perhaps the Bādāmi Cāḷukyas (Stein 1985: 33–35; 1989: 1, 111).

48. When the king of Java (i.e., at Kediri), the Yavana lord (i.e., the king of Annam), and the two kings of Champa (or the kings of the two Champas: Vijaya and Pāṇḍurāṅga) are said to devotedly supply water for the ablutions of Jayavarman VII (r. 1181–1218) at his consecration as king of Angkor (*IK:* 490 v. 166, cf. *BEFEO* 41: 255), both the ideal and the spatiality of the Sanskrit cosmopolis are being expressed. On empire and imitation more generally see Pollock 2005c; cf. also Duverger 1980: 21. On the nation form see Balibar 1991: 91. "Institutional isomorphism" in varied national settings is discussed in DiMaggio and Powell 1983; peer-polity interactions in Renfrew and Cherry 1986.

are often illegitimately generalized to all of premodern South Asia). The planting of victory pillars and other inscribed monuments far beyond the imperial core were meant to project an expansive territoriality. Such key cultural elements of *rājya* in India are famously described in yet another passage of that seminal document, the Allahabad Pillar Inscription (lines 20–24):

> He has favored all the kings of the south by releasing them after capture [to rule their own domains in subservience to him] . . . He has forcefully uprooted all the kings of Āryāvarta . . . and turned the kings of the forest regions into his servants . . . The border rulers [and others] he has made to gratify his awe-inspiring governance by paying all tribute, doing his bidding, coming before him to make obeisance . . . He has restored many kingly lines and kingships that have fallen [due to his power] . . . [The Kuṣāṇas, Śakas, and all island lords] have been made to serve him by various acts: presenting themselves to him, giving their daughters as gifts to him, requesting to be able to rule their own domains under the sign of the Garuḍa seal.

Many of these elements were consciously cultivated and reproduced as core values for centuries. Consider only the ideal of "uprooting" and "restoring" competitor kings—in other words, the creation of something like layered sovereignties. This can be traced from Rudradāman in second-century Gujarat to Govinda III in tenth-century Karnataka to Jayasiṃha Siddharāja in twelfth-century Gujarat.[49] The most decisive component of empire of this sort was extension in space. The ability to expand was presented axiomatically as unchecked by ecological, political, cultural, or other boundaries—as if the only limit was the fact, apparently never considered contradictory, that every assertion of universal dominion encountered competing assertions to universal dominion. Yet one can perceive a very peculiar shape to the universality of power in South Asia, one that becomes especially clear when contrasted with the vision of the *imperium romanum.* It was universality that knew its limits.

Far more accessible to us than the material repertory of the empire form is its cultural repertory. Here an increasingly important and ultimately dominant component (unavailable to the Mauryas or the Sātavāhanas) was a

49. See *bhraṣṭarājyapratiṣṭhāpaka* (Junāgaṛh inscription, line 12); *grahaṇamokṣānugraha, utsannarājavaṃśapratiṣṭhāpana, vijitānekanarapativibhavapratyarppaṇa* (Allahabhad Pillar Inscription, lines 20, 23, 26); *unmūlayan* [*sic leg.*] . . . *nṛpān* . . . *punaḥ punar atiṣṭhipat svapada eva* (*EI* 18: 245. 20–21, Govinda); *samutkhātāḥ pūrvaṃ tadanu nijarājyaṃ ca gamitāḥ* (*EI* 40: 29.17–18, Jayasiṃha). The idea may have been mediated by Kālidāsa, borrowing from Allahabad (e.g., *grahītapratimuktasya* . . . *mahendranāthasya, Raghuvaṃśa* 4.43, cf. *CII* 3: 33). Later commentators distinguish this *dharmavijayin,* or moral conqueror, from the *lobhavijayin,* the avaricious conqueror, who while seizing the land and power of a defeated king spares his life, and the *asuravijayin,* the demonic conqueror, who does not (Vallabha ed. Velankar, p. 93).

language of cosmopolitan stature, one that, in its very communicative capacities, was capable of embodying and transmitting transregional political aspiration. In Rome and in the *roma renovata* of Carolingian and Ottonian Europe this language was Latin, which, though in constant need of rehabilitation in the European Middle Ages, was retained and reinforced as a core component in the cultural and political understanding of polity (chapter 7.1). In West Asia from 1000 on it was New Persian, elevated by brilliant works of literary culture (especially one of the first, the *Shāh Nāmeh,* which worked as a kind of *Mahābhārata* for linking the new political formation of the Ghaznavids with an imagined Iranian imperial past) and rich bureaucratic idiom. These made New Persian the language that ruling elites from Sistān and Tabriz to Delhi would eventually adopt, regardless of what they spoke in the privacy of their bedrooms, if they hoped to fully realize the empire form. Similar in its cultural-political logic to Latin and Persian, as well as in its temporal and geographic spread, was Sanskrit.[50]

Though the features that constituted the power of Sanskrit—its various communicative capacities—and enabled it to do its cosmopolitan and imperial work have been addressed individually throughout this study, it is helpful to sum up the most important ones here. The first is undoubtedly the translocality that marked Sanskrit from a very early period. Claims to universal sovereignty would have been unintelligible if asserted in a *deśabhāṣā,* a language of Place; those languages were to become the medium of an altogether different—a regional—political conception (chapter 10.3). The second feature, closely related to the first, is Sanskrit's transethnicity, whereby such claims were not only intelligible but in a sense rational, since they comprised a view from everywhere in general and nowhere in particular. In both respects, Sanskrit showed itself as uniquely empowered for the empire form of premodernity. Its translocality was a matter of, so to speak, doing what comes naturally. Sanskrit was spread originally by what seems almost a process of cultural osmosis—the widely dispersed migrations of *vaidika* communities attested as early as the archaic period,[51] a trend intensified in the cosmopolitan epoch by the growing fashion of giving land grants to Brahmans (almost unattested before the third century C.E.) and endowments to Brahmanical schools and royal temples under Brahmanical control. And whereas once-local cosmopolitan languages, such as New Persian, may have attained transethnicity, they often retained a sense of tribal authenticity—something Sanskrit abandoned at an early date, if indeed it ever had it. Iran-

50. For the adoption of Persian by Mughals, which signaled conformity not in religious sentiment but in style of governance, see Alam 1998. On the *Shāh Nāmeh,* see Weryho 1986: 51 and Lazard 1993: 24 (both however burdened by teleology and anachronism).

51. Much labor has been devoted by Michael Witzel to charting this diffusion, see e.g., 1987; more generally, Ludden 1999: 79ff.

ian poets in the late medieval period saw other Persianate cultures as different or even aberrant.[52] By comparison, nothing, whether in linguistic substance, expressive style, or political imagination, differentiated the Sanskrit of the Paramāras from that of the Khmers.

A third dimension of Sanskrit's communicative capacity is its expressive power. This is primarily derived, not from its archaic liturgical associations—Buddhists, who numbered among the master poets of Sanskrit for a millennium, would have been entirely indifferent to such things—but rather from its aesthetic resources. These include Sanskrit's ability to make reality in a way more real by making it more noticeable, more complex, more beautiful thanks to the language's arsenal of formal and rhetorical attributes—the metrics and tropology that fascinated readers across the cosmopolis as well as the presence of a literary corpus offering successful exemplars of such linguistic alchemy. Neither of these resources was available to the languages of Place, which remained unelaborated and pre-aestheticized codes—precisely what documentary languages of deeds and contracts were supposed to remain—until they were transformed in the vernacular epoch. It was the very circulation of texts that helped produce the cosmopolis as such: courtly epics and histories, including such profoundly political visions as Kālidāsa's *Raghuvaṃśa* and Bāṇa's *Harṣacarita,* were studied across the Sanskrit world, as were textbooks on figures and metrics that regulated the production of beauty everywhere according to the same norms.

Fourth, Sanskrit was endowed, as every language of the empire form must be, with the dignity and stability conferred by grammar. Only in a code constrained by a set of norms and therefore escaping the danger of degeneration could important symbolic goods such as fame find enduring expression. But there is more to grammaticality than such quasi functionalism, something more firmly rooted in the Sanskrit tradition and revealing deep conceptual affinities between the orders of language discipline, literary aesthetics, and polity. If the order of Sanskrit poetry was the order of Sanskrit grammar, the latter was a model or prototype of the moral, social, and political order. We have seen how closely the history of grammar is related to the history of political culture (chapter 4.1, 2): The just man *(sādhu)*—above all, the just king—used and also promoted the use of correct language *(sādhuśabda).* Not only was Sanskrit therefore the appropriate vehicle for the expression of royal will, but Sanskrit learning itself became a component of kingliness. This idea found repeated expression in a centuries-long trope deployed by rulers, from Rudradāman in south Gujarat at the beginning of the millennium to Sūryavarman II in Khmer land at the end, who celebrated their Sanskrit learning, especially their grammatical learning, in public po-

52. The history of the concept *sabkh-i hindī,* the "Indian style," is discussed in Alam 2003: 177ff.

etry. When the king's grammar is correct, the king's politics are correct, and his rule will be as just as his words. The king who did not command the language of the gods could command the polity no better than a drunkard.[53]

With all these features Sanskrit cultural forms such as *kāvya* and *praśasti* were invested with a unique linguistic uniformity and stylistic coherence across the entire cosmopolis. Although naturally some local coloring would occasionally intrude—which would eventually come to full expression in the vernacular revolution—nonetheless, to participate in the cosmopolitan order meant precisely to occlude particulars of place as well as particulars of time. It is this very homogeneity, maintained across vast expanses and epochs, that makes it often impossible to localize or date a work of Sanskrit literature. And by the argument advanced here, it is precisely this impossibility that constituted Sanskrit's greatest attraction for those in quest of a universalist form of power, or seeking fame that transcended the limits of time and space.

As the form, style, and content of thousands of inscriptional as well as more strictly literary texts demonstrate unequivocally, both by education and in literary practice the Sanskrit poet participated in a transregional cultural sphere similar to that of his Latin peers on the western side of the hemisphere. Thus the poet Bilhaṇa, who in the middle of the eleventh century wandered in search of patronage from Kashmir to Gujarat and Mewar, and from Kānyakubja to Karnataka, could boast that "There is no village or country *(janapada)*, no capital city or forest region, no pleasure garden or school where learned and ignorant, young and old, male and female alike do not read my poems and shake with pleasure." He may have been exaggerating the accessibility of his work across social orders, but he was describing not just a possible world but the actual world for which Sanskrit poets and intellectuals had been writing for the preceding thousand years.[54]

A traveler through that world around the year 1000 would have seen, from the plain of Kedu in central Java to the basin of Tonlé Sap in Cambodia, from Gaṅgaikoṇḍacōḻapuram in Tamilnadu to Pravarapura in Kashmir and beyond, imperial polities that had so many features in common they would have seemed to constitute a single culture-power formation. Being so hard to perceive clearly in the data our account has largely ignored the material and social formations—the ranks and orders of dignity and worth that made up society; the corps of functionaries, scribes, and tax collectors who administered the polity; the organization of agricultural production and trade, for much of which a certain institutional isomorphism seems to have obtained

53. So *Rājataraṅgiṇī* 5.206 in reference to King Śaṅkaravarman (late ninth century). On the relationship between correct language and correct rule in Charlemagne's empire see Alcuin cited in chapter 11.1; in fifteenth-century Vietnam, chapter 12.2.

54. *Vikramāṅkadevacarita* 18.89.

across the cosmopolis.[55] Instead, stress has been laid on their common literary-cultural elements—which are at the same cultural-political elements—in part because these are what our data allow us to know but also and more important because it is these that created the cosmopolitan *mentalité*. They include the cultivation of a uniform idiom of Sanskrit, disciplined and dignified by grammar and lexically stable and therefore mutually intelligible to writers from Kashmir to Kalimantan; assiduous practice and mastery of the intricate codes and protocols of Sanskrit *kāvya* and *praśasti;* and the public presentation of stately poems in Sanskrit, engraved on the ubiquitous copperplates recording royal donations or on stone pillars looming up from gigantic architectural wonders. It was these texts that created a world like no other, inscribed from end to end and dense with cosmopolitan poetry; written not by "Indian" (let alone "Hindu") poets but by Sanskrit poets, they engendered a world, or world within a world, without difference.

There was thus undoubtedly a concrete reality to the Sanskrit cosmopolis—it is no mere illusion of the historian's retrospective gaze—this vast ecumene extending across a third of Eurasia over the course of a millennium or more, in which scholars, religious professionals, courtiers, and rulers everywhere shared a broad "communality of outlook" and could perceive "ubiquitous signs" of their beliefs.[56] By the criteria of modernity, it was a formation of a very peculiar sort to be sure, a species of shared life entirely different in genesis and character from that produced by common subjecthood or fealty to a central power. It was an immense community without factitious political unity, a community without a unique center, or, better put, one with centers everywhere—with multiple Gaṅgā Rivers and Mount Merus—and circumferences nowhere. It was, however, primarily a symbolic network, one created by the presence of a similar kind of discourse in a similar language deploying similar idioms and styles to make similar claims about the nature and aesthetics of political rule: about kingly virtue and learning, the *dharma* of governance, and the peculiar universality of dominion in a world of plural universalities.

The nature of the interactions of culture and power in the Sanskrit cosmopolis and the relation of both to the social order with its various forms of identity (caste, lineage, sect, and the like) are far too complex for any one author to hope to theorize completely afresh. Yet the explanations currently on offer are hardly adequate. For example, to see Sanskrit culture in relation to imperial power as an instrument of legitimation, let alone of ideological mystification, albeit the unchallenged scholarly view, is entirely

55. Lombard 1990: 11.

56. Wolters 1982: 43–44. There is no little irony in the fact that descriptions framed by Wolters here (and Lombard above) to capture what they felt was something uniquely Southeast Asian are entirely applicable to South Asia. See chapter 14.1 and n. 22 there.

anachronistic (see chapter 13.3). Imperial politics might become more intelligible and coherent when understood as, to some extent, an aesthetic practice; the poetry of politics that erected the very foundation of the cosmopolitan order certainly seems to be a far more appropriate role to assign to Sanskrit discourse than any manipulative function it may be thought to have exercised. Admittedly, to speak of aesthetic practice may be thought only to restate the question of the political in premodern South Asia, not to answer it. But this is so only because the understanding of the "aestheticization of the political" at our disposal is too narrow. Somehow the concept must be freed from the now-dominant interpretations between which it is caught: the Scylla of Walter Benjamin's total state, where "the introduction of aesthetics into political life" is invariably linked to fascism and war, and the Charybdis of Clifford Geertz's theater state, where "spectacle was what the state was for," its central task therefore being not so much ruling as merely displaying "the dominant themes of high culture."[57]

There was once a way of being political—or so the Indic material seems to suggest—that derived in some measure from the forms of expressivity and style that it deployed, from the cultural commitments it produced and helped to reproduce, and from the moral values from which these commitments sprang. Equally important, these commitments and forms were to all appearances accepted voluntarily rather than coerced. They were compatible with continued adherence to local forms and commitments, however inadequate these may have been judged for the universalist political order, so that they would flourish only once that order was replaced by something different. And they accordingly entailed a politics that were more voluntaristic than seems possible to those who unhistorically homogenize all variants of premodern power. How diverse the nature of power in premodernity actually was, and how diverse its possible relationships with culture will become clearer if we analyze an influential source of much homogenizing thinking, one that has provided for many observers the paradigm of empire and for the cosmopolitan possibility itself: the *imperium romanum.*

57. Benjamin 1969: 241; Geertz cited in Wheatley 1983: 423. This is discussed further in chapter 11.2.

CHAPTER SEVEN

A European Countercosmopolis

7.1 *LATINITAS*

We can gain a sharper sense of the peculiar nature of the cultural order that Sanskrit helped to create, and the kind of political order for which it was cultivated, if we consider both from an explicitly comparative perspective. There is a natural tendency, exhibited even (or especially) in social and cultural theory, to generalize familiar forms of life and experience as universal tendencies and common sense. Comparison offers an antidote to this by demonstrating the actual particularity of these apparent universalisms. Among those forms of life and experience, Latin literary culture and the Roman political formation, as well as their later histories in medieval Europe, have a special salience for our analysis. Both in themselves and for their contribution to the world against which modernity has defined itself, Latinity and the Roman Empire have importantly shaped contemporary conceptions of language, literature, transculturation, and the supraregional political form.

Other world regions might be deemed just as suitable for our purpose as the Latinate. Juxtaposing the cultural and political processes of Sinicization with those of the Sanskrit cosmopolis would be enormously valuable, most pointedly with regard to places like Champa and Dai-Viet, where the two great alternatives in premodern Asian globalization met toe to toe. But it will become clear in part 2 that in the most consequential later phase of the story told here, that of vernacularization, the East Asian parallel breaks down, or at least a very different historical trajectory manifests itself. In Vietnam, to continue with that case, regional individuation in the cultural-political sphere was asserted hesitantly in the late medieval period but then arrested, and vernacularization was consummated only under the vastly changed circumstances of colonialism. The same holds true for almost the entire periphery of the Middle Kingdom, Japan excepted. In China itself, vernacularization in the full sense of the term used here never occurred (only something more like popularization, as in the vernacular novel), and as a consequence there never arose a "flourishing literary tradition" in Cantonese, Taiwanese, or Shanghaiese.[1] The civilizational orders of the premodern world, whether Latinate, Hellenic, Sinic, or other, are of interest to a study of the Sanskrit cosmopolis not only per se but for the kinds of processes that led to their displacement by other orders of culture and polity—and it is these that are most clearly demonstrated in the Latin and later European cases.

The brief review that is called for of Latin literary culture and its political formation—which aims to assess, in a word, how *latinitas*[2] and *imperium* compare with the *kāvya* and *rājya* of the Sanskrit world—can be presented most effectively by a broad consideration of four constituent features: the history and character of Latin as a cosmopolitan language, the beginnings of literature and its place in Roman society at the time of its beginnings, the processes of globalization and transculturation known as Romanization, and the style and work of the empire form.

Basic to a comparative assessment of the career of Latin as a cosmopolitan language is, first, the fact that we are able to observe it *become* such a language and identify the specific conditions of this becoming, both in its initial phase and in its later revivifications. How Latin developed, very slowly and over the course of many centuries, from a local idiom spoken in the lower Tiber Valley into a supraregional language constitutes, as a distinguished student of the subject put it, "one of the surprises of history."[3] It may have been surprising that this happened at all, but there is little surprise regarding how it did happen: through an intimate and unambiguous dependence on a military-political project, first republican, later imperial, and then later Christian. Latin traveled where it did as a language of conquest: first, as the language of a conquest state, initially Roman but later Carolingian and Ottonian; second, as the language of a missionizing and eventually conquest church.

A second important comparative fact about the history of Latin is that for the first three or four centuries of its cosmopolitan career, the language stood in a relation of pronounced cultural inequality with Greek. Greek shaped the development of Latin in the formative years of its literary culture while also constituting a barrier to Latin's advance in the eastern Mediterranean. In view of its subordination to Greek and the dramatic beginnings of its literary life (to which we turn momentarily), Latin itself embodies important

1. Mair 1994: 730 (a statement in some tension with the overall thrust and title of his article).

2. On *latinitas* ("'Latinness' . . . and especially the literary style that marked the high literature of Rome and those who sought to perpetuate it"), see Bloomer 1997: 1–2.

3. So for example Hammond 1976: 39.

features of a "cosmopolitan vernacular," that is, a vernacular aspiring to cultural dominance through the appropriation of features of a superposed language (a subject more fully explored in chapters 9.3, 10.1). The key difference, of course, is that Latin actually became cosmopolitan instead of simply aspiring to that status. Perhaps it was partly owing to this transformation into a language of high culture on the Greek model that Latin literary speech *(sermo artificialis* or *sublimis)* gradually grew more distant from everyday language (the so-called *sermo vulgaris* or *humilis,* "popular" or "earth-bound" speech), so far as we can say anything certain about this latter register.[4] This seems to have been a simple, even mechanical, consequence of literarization and the self-elevation from the quotidian code that literary language strives to attain in most times and places—or at least in India and Europe before modernity—in order to constitute itself precisely as literary.

Starting in the fifth or sixth century, Latin's distance from the everyday increased for entirely other reasons. In accordance with the process of historical imitation at work in shaping the empire form of medieval Europe (what one scholar has called the "nostalgia of ecumenism"),[5] Latin was adopted as the sole medium of political and literary expression among Frankish kings and their descendants for some four centuries. The political imaginary of the Carolingian court around 800 was filled with visions of *roma renovata,* and Latin naturally became a basic component of that worldview. By that period also, the spoken forms of the language had so diverged from the written that it was difficult for speakers to recognize the everyday medium of communication as "Latin." The gulf that had opened between spoken and written Latin (the latter now named, with increasing propriety, the *sermo scholasticus*) was acknowledged by both the court and the Church. Around 780 Charlemagne summoned the great scholar Alcuin from York, and the various treatises he wrote over the next few decades (*De orthographia,* On Spelling; *De litteris colendibus,* On the Care of Learning) sought to promulgate a new, supposedly more authentic and certainly non-Romance pronunciation of Latin—precisely the sort that would have been preserved by nonnative speakers (Alcuin was a Northumbrian). At the same time, the Council of Tours (813) required the translation of sermons into what had long since emerged as the early Romance vernaculars (see chapter 11.1). Similar reforms were made during the so-called Ottonian renaissance two centuries later, when the conception of a *translatio imperii* (transfer of power) once more necessitated a *translatio studii* (transfer of learning) and thus a revivification of Latin. Language was indeed the *compañera* of empire in the West, and continuously so for almost two millennia before Nebrija declared it to be so. In both Carolingian and Ottonian Europe, literary and even doc-

4. See Herman 2000; still useful is Auerbach 1965: 25–66.

5. Nicolet 1991: 33.

umentary production in regional languages was long discouraged in favor of an imperial-language textuality increasingly unfamiliar to the court, to say nothing of its distance from the speech of everyday life.[6]

The sociolinguistic biography of Sanskrit was entirely different. The historical record does not enable us to attribute to it any local roots at all. Whereas some regional languages such as New Persian achieved transregionality through merit, and others such as Latin had it thrust upon them through military conquests, Sanskrit seems to have almost been born transregional; it was at home everywhere—and perhaps, in a sense, at home nowhere. In respect to everyday discourse Sanskrit was, from a very early date—indeed probably from its very beginnings—marked by distance and distinction. In general its relationship with actual local speech types was hyperglossic, as it has here been named, something to which the distance between Latin and its "earth-bound" register, a classic diglossic situation, bears no comparison. For all that, or perhaps precisely as a consequence, at no period before modernity do we find for Sanskrit the kind of widespread deterioration from the literary norm observable in the Latin of ninth-century or twelfth-century France and Germany (which is not to deny that there were always inexpert writers of Sanskrit). Moreover, Sanskrit was disseminated by a process that, if admittedly obscure, can nowhere be identified with the sort of military-political, or later, military-religious, project that we find impelling the dissemination of Latin.

In its general morphology the literary culture of the Latin world was conditioned by the history of the language itself. In this it shows considerable divergence from Sanskrit, albeit the two demonstrate substantial similarity in their later development. To understand the phenomenon of the literary in the Latinate world we need to grasp the fact that Latin literature, like Sanskrit literature, began, though it remains unclear how comparable are the circumstances of these two beginnings. There can be no doubt about the fact of invention in the case of Latin, so long as we are clear about what was being invented. As already noted, the theoretical problem of beginnings in general and literary beginnings in particular will be addressed in greater detail later, since it is fundamental to the question of vernacularization (chapter 8.1). For now it is enough to note that, however we wish to conceive of literature—as a universally or only a locally defined imaginative use of expressive, workly language; as an absolute or a relative phenomenon—literature was, in both the Latin and Sanskrit worlds, something committed to writing. And in Rome, the creation of written texts conforming to an already dominant local definition of literature—or what can be taken as literature in some universal sense of the term—commenced at a particular moment.

"Our knowledge of a literature written in Latin," according to a recent

6. For medieval cultural-political developments see Banniard 1995 and Contreni 1995.

standard account, "begins abruptly in 240 B.C." with the work of Livius Andronicus, a freed Greek slave from what is today Taranto in southeast Italy. Some three centuries of historical Roman existence prior to this, which were marked by such attainments as codified laws, have left no trace of "artistic composition" and only scraps of text evincing "linguistic satisfaction and emphatic solemnity" (these terms doing duty for a stipulative definition of literature that is lacking in the account). Even the few indications of oral heroic tales are wholly inconclusive and do little to establish a prehistory of an epic or another expressive verbal art. Evidence for literature prior to 240 B.C.E., the account concludes, is so meager as to suggest a purely "practical culture." Indeed, evidence of writing itself before this period is meager in the extreme, and Latin literature no doubt "begins" in one sense by the application of writing to expressive language. But a second condition is set by the presence of a superposed Greek literary culture. Andronicus produced a translation from Homer's *Odyssey* and adapted Hellenic drama, and at the same time created a specifically poetic language that would influence later Latin poetry. His use of precocious archaisms, the replacement of Greek divinities by Roman ones (as in the opening invocation of his *Odyssey*, where an ancient water deity, Camena, takes the place of Musa), and perhaps most important, his use of the Italic saturnian meter, can without difficulty be taken as enhancing the project of localization and authentication.[7]

One scholar of general literary culture who clearly grasped the importance of the historic rupture that occurred in mid-third-century Rome was Mikhail Bakhtin. As he puts it in his own peculiar idiom: "The purely national Latin genres, conceived under monoglottic conditions, fell into decay and did not achieve the level of literary expression." Put in the terms used in this book, pre-Hellenic forms of Latin aesthetic expression, existing in the absence of a superposed cultural formation, never attained the state of inscription. But what is important about the beginning of Latin literature, in addition to the sheer fact that it did begin—and "with a sideways glance" at Greece, as Bakhtin expresses it, with misleading understatement—are the circumstances under which this beginning occurred. And here neither Bakhtin nor the standard account just cited is very instructive. Bakhtin con-

7. See Kenney and Clausen 1982: 53–58; cf. Gruen 1990: 82 and Goldberg 1995: 46 (for both scholars, the "conscious" invention of "literature" in the third century is an established fact). Nothing is offered in Conte 1994: 13–27 (largely a restatement of Kenney and Clausen) to support the claim that the "existence of a long prehistory" is "necessarily presupposed by the abrupt 'creation' of a national literature in the days of Andronicus" (p. 27, the mechanical response to cultural innovation; the presupposition is entirely unnecessary). Reflection on how "literature" is to be stipulated, as it must be if claims about its beginnings are to be made, is oddly lacking in the secondary scholarship, though see now Habinek 1998. Although writing is of the essence of literature, the most recent major work on writing and literacy in antiquity is oblique on the matter (Harris 1989, cf. p. 158).

ceives of the transformation as nothing more than a language question, the problem of bilingualism: "From start to finish, the creative literary consciousness of the Romans functioned against the background of the Greek language and Greek forms." The standard account hesitatingly suggests that the Hellenization of Latin may have been an expression of a new cultural tendency analogized from the Hellenization of other languages and literatures, of which the Septuagint Bible (late second century B.C.E.) is a strong example. More recently, scholars have sought to relate the invention of Latin literature to the victory of the First Punic War (264–41), Rome's growing hegemony in the western Mediterranean, and its evolving imperial self-understanding. Whatever the truth of this last argument for positivistic history—and there is admittedly something monocausal and reductive about it—it does enjoy ethnohistorical authority: the connection was one that later Romans themselves made. The second-century scholar Gellius wrote that at the time when peace was made with the Carthaginians ("Phoenicians"), the poet Livius Andronicus "taught Rome to make literature."[8]

In the case of Sanskrit, too, a radical break in the history of culture was effected by the invention of an altogether new form of textualized expression, in this case, what would come to be called *kāvya*. The circumstances under which this invention occurred—or under which processes already under way were consolidated—must have been shaped by a variety of factors, as we have seen, not the least being the invention of writing itself in the middle of the third century B.C.E., around the time written Latin first became common. One social factor that has seemed salient for our analysis is the presence of ruler lineages recently immigrated from western and central Asia who not only patronized a new Sanskrit literature but may themselves have been poets, as, for example, Rudradāman represents himself to be (chapters 1.3, 2.1). Here we find a potentially significant parallel with the cultural agents who invented Latin literature. Not only was Livius Greek, but the two great poets who succeeded him were neither Roman nor native speakers of Latin: Naevius (d. 204 B.C.E.), who came from the area of today's Naples, and Ennius (d. 169 B.C.E.) from Calabria on the southeast coast, were Oscan-speaking Hellenized Italians.[9] As the Sanskrit cosmopolis shows so strikingly

8. For his remarks on Latin literary beginnings see Bakhtin 1981: 61. Gellius 17.21.42 is cited in Gruen 1990: 82, n. 10. The *Cambridge Ancient History* relates the cultural invention to "the stimulus of the Hannibalic War and the national feeling it provoked" (Astin et al. 1989: 429) but does not argue the matter out (or justify "national," compare chapter 11 n. 36). See again Habinek 1998, who places the invention of literature in the context of a Roman identity crisis as its power grew, and more generally Gruen 1990: 79–123.

9. See Gruen 1990: 97 n. 129, citing Gellius for the fact that Ennius took pride in being trilingual, in Oscan, Greek, and Latin, and p. 119, n. 196 on Suetonius (who calls Andronicus and Ennius *semigraeci*).

as well, there existed no cultural agents who were not always already transcultured (see chapter 14.1).

Another parallel or possible connection is intriguing but difficult to establish: Was the new employment of written Sanskrit as a prestige language for the creation of workly texts a reaction to superposed cultural forms then manifesting themselves for the first time on the eastern frontier of the Hellenic world, just as literature written in Latin was a response to the same cultural phenomena on the western frontier? Some evidence suggests the possibility. A Greek theater was then in existence in what is today northern Afghanistan (Ai Khanoum); bilingual intellectuals translated Aśokan edicts into literary Greek in the mid-third century B.C.E., while interactions among Hellenic and South Asian sculptors produced the unprecedented sculpture of Gandhāra; four centuries later, in 149–50 C.E.—squarely in the middle of the reign of Rudradāman—a scholar with the title Yavaneśvara (Lord of the Greeks) prepared a Sanskrit prose translation of a Greek work (probably from Alexandria) on the casting of horoscopes, which with another (lost) Greek text formed the basis of the Indian developments in the art of horoscopy until the introduction of Islamic ideas a millennium later; a portion of *Mānasāraśilpaśāstra,* a work on architecture of approximately the sixth century, was adapted from Vitruvius ("a parallel almost down to every detail"); the cult of the important south Indian and Sri Lankan goddess Pattinī and that of Isis have recently been shown to be closely linked by cultural transmission.[10] Nineteenth-century Indology sought to demonstrate just this sort of dependency, speculating for example that the *Rāmāyaṇa* must have been translated from Homer and Sanskrit drama adapted from Athenian exemplars (comparable to Livius Andronicus's Latin adaptations, though the parallel seems never to have been drawn). Such questions are certainly not in themselves illicit so long as they are free of the arrogant presuppositions of superior donor-cultures and inferior receiver-cultures that often underwrote this kind of inquiry in the past. More positively viewed, these questions can stimulate exploration of the continuous circulation (rather than "diffusion") of cultural goods that we know marks all of cultural history. Recall that the Greek epic cycle itself did not emerge fully armed from Zeus's head but contained substantial Mesopotamian elements.

10. See Schlumberger and Bernard 1965; Benveniste 1964; Pingree 1978: 3–5 (Yavaneśvara as someone "exercising some sort of authority over Greeks settled in the domains of the Western Kshatrapas in those areas of India later known as Gujarat, Mālwā, and Rajasthan"; on *Mānasāra* see Goetz 1959: 178 (his words are quoted in the text); on Pattinī, Fynes 1993. Peter Green has argued against any "genuine literary interpenetration between Greek and other cultures" (1990: 316), but the absence of word-for-word translation that he seems to have in mind is largely a modern invention and can hardly be used as an argument.

Until more data become available to decide the matter, it remains an open question whether or not India and Rome participated at the eastern and western frontier, respectively, in the same system of literary-cultural circulation. But whatever may be the brute facts of Sanskrit literary beginnings, cultural memory in South Asia has acknowledged nothing superposed to Sanskrit either in its origins or in its later history. This is the first in a number of stark contrasts with Rome. Rome's cultural debt to Greece was the source of continuous, anxious literary reflection verging on shame; Cicero's defensiveness, for example, about the use of Latin for philosophical discourse when previously only Greek had been used (and which prefigures the vernacular anxiety we meet in the early-modern European treatises) has no parallel in the Sanskrit world.[11] Another striking dissimilarity is the fact that Sanskrit literary culture, until a very late period (Vijayanagara), was never harnessed to a political project in so direct and instrumental a way as we find in both republican and imperial Rome.[12] Naevius, the second major poet after Andronicus, composed a now-lost epic combining Rome's prehistory (Aeneas's settling in Latium) with contemporary triumph (the First Punic War) and told an even more archaic tale of political origins in his work on Romulus and Remus. The historicist project of empire intensified further with Ennius, who turned the *klea andrōn,* the glorious acts of men of the Greek epic, into the *maxuma facta patrum,* the deeds of the empire-building Roman ancestors, in his *Annales* and so claimed for himself the title *homerus redivivus* (according to some, his being a Pythagorean gave him an additional reason for the assertion). And this is to say nothing of the supreme example of imperial poetry, Vergil's *Aeneid.* The whole conceptual universe of Sanskrit, its placelessness and universalism, strongly discouraged such productions, though they were not entirely unknown; something like Kālidāsa's *Raghuvaṃśa* might qualify as a counterexample, though as an allegory of the imperial Guptas, even when it borrows directly from their records (as in the Allahabad inscription), its touch is so light as to be all but imperceptible.

In Latin's later history, however, as it became increasingly severed from its Roman roots, its historicism and localization—and indeed, its engagement with the real—became ever more attenuated. Servius, the most important commentator on Vergil in late antiquity, already referred to a "law of poetic art" prohibiting treatment of historical matters openly. It was in part this tendency that prompted the Romance philologist Erich Auerbach to characterize medieval Latin as a "purely artificial language written according to ancient models and often degenerating into a kind of pedantic puzzle . . .

11. See *De finibus* 1. Du Bellay in the mid-sixteenth century alludes to Cicero (see chapter 10.2).

12. See Pollock 2001a: 400–404.

incapable of expressing the life of the times." Recent scholarship rightly argues that Auerbach's evaluation ignores the fact that some literatures do not aim to express the life of the times, indifferent as they are to any simple mimetic enterprise.[13] This in fact seems to be especially the case with many cosmopolitan languages, which seek transcendence of time in the same degree they achieve transcendence of space, and which accordingly invite special attention to their expressive capacities as the element that makes them different from quotidian local idioms and preferable for certain kinds of cultural work. Given these objectives, their avoidance of the everyday real, even when it is readily accessible in parallel—say, vernacular—aesthetic contexts, is clearly a choice and not a failure. What remains unclear, however, is whether these tendencies suffice to explain the complexities of the history of political historicism in the two literatures in question: how the political acted as midwife at the birth of Latin literature but was more and more marginalized in its later rebirths, and how it was excluded from the Sanskrit cosmopolis at its commencement only to gain admittance at its culmination.

Another remarkable disparity lies in the fact that explicit care for language, in the Roman grammarian as in the Roman overlord, seems to have never attained the conceptual coherence and centrality it acquired in southern Asia. Grammar was a relatively late intellectual enterprise in classical antiquity, and it was a consequence of, and always remained a component of, forensic rhetoric, or the arts of public persuasion (though Servius, Cassiodorus, and others in the fifth and sixth centuries would enunciate a homology between grammatical and political rule and discipline). Rulers, for their part, were more often patrons than producers of literature; few Roman emperors are credited with poetic creativity. Although the topos of the *rex doctus,* the learned king, makes its appearance in late antiquity, literacy among the nobility was exceptional and came to be reckoned as pertinent to kingly virtue only much later, it seems: in the time of Charlemagne, when the powers of grammar and *imperium* first became continuous and the ideal emperor was first represented as both soldier and scholar.[14]

As for the poets themselves, they had always cared deeply about language discipline—*latinitas* was from the beginning a virtue of the writer—and as a result, a transregional normativity in grammaticality, metric, genre, and the rest was widely cultivated. In the universalization of a set of standards for literary language, Latin cosmopolitanism bears striking similarities to its Sanskrit counterpart. Consider this suggestive description:

13. See Irvine 1994: 135 on Servius; Auerbach 1965: 121–23; and Godman 1987: 7–8, who cites the Auerbach passage.

14. Irvine 1994: 306 (see also p. 13 on earlier Roman representations). The war accounts of Julius Caesar and Augustus's *Res Gestae* are a set apart. On the topos of the *rex doctus,* see Godman 1987: 25–27; on aristocratic illiteracy, See 1985: 35–36.

> The leading features of the literary culture of the later Roman Empire are its conservatism, its uniformity, and its widespread geographical diffusion . . . Based on the same classics and an identical technique, the education system produced a literary culture which was . . . completely uniform; there were no regional schools of literature. Whether he lived and wrote in Gaul, Africa, or Illyricum, in Thrace, Cappadocia or Egypt, the training of every aspirant to literary fame was identical, and the exemplars which he strove to emulate the same. This uniform culture was, moreover, remarkably widely diffused.[15]

Because of this standardization of training and diffusion Horace could boast of readers of his work in Dacia (Romania) and on the Black Sea; Martial could claim that his work circulated as far as Britannia, and that in Vienne on the Rhone men young and old, and girls as well, were reading his epigrams—precisely the sort of boast and claim we have seen the Sanskrit poet Bilhaṇa making a millennium later. Although Latin certainly varied over its cosmopolitan space in its spoken registers, it was not perceived to do so by grammarians largely because variation was minimal across its textual registers. "In texts of all kinds, literary, technical, and all others," according to a leading authority on vulgar Latin, "the written Latin of the first five or six centuries C.E. looks as if it were territorially homogeneous, even in its 'vulgar' registers. It is only in later texts, of the seventh and eighth centuries, that we are able to see in the texts geographical differences that seem to be the precursors of similar differences in the subsequent Romance languages." As its ties to living speech weakened, *latinitas* was increasingly regarded as a changeless and (in a Hegelian sense) virtually self-identical phenomenon; the unconcern with prescriptive grammar in late antiquity gave way, not unexpectedly, in Carolingian times to the intellectual preeminence of grammatical thought.[16]

Comparable at least in its effects, though deriving from a more profoundly theorized vision of human existence and language, was the Sanskrit grammarian's sense of his language's historical existence as a "panchronistic flatland."[17] What in the early period may have been encountered as dialectal or regional variation and described as difference was transformed by the beginning of the first millennium (in Patañjali) into prescriptive option. The archaic epochal distinction between sacral and nonsacral language found in Pāṇini's grammar (*chandas,* "Verse," or the Veda, and *bhāṣā,* the learned

15. Jones 1964: 1008; see also Millar 1996: 9–10.

16. References to Martial's claims are found in Veyne 1994: 365, and Harris 1989: 227, who also cites Horace, p. 224. Roman indifference to systematic grammar was inherited from the Greeks, whose sudden interest in this "new subject" during the second century B.C.E. seems to have been stimulated by competition with a new cosmopolitan language, Latin (Swain 1996: 40). On late-imperial grammarians cf. Kaster 1988: 50ff.; for the medieval period Contreni 1995: 729–30. "Vulgar Latin" textuality is discussed in Herman 2000: 117.

17. Deshpande 1985: 124.

"discourse" used for scholastic discussion and disciplines of the Veda) lived on in medieval India only in the term *ārṣa,* the "language of the seers," a euphemism for justifying solecisms. Concomitantly, no grammarian or literary scholar during the cosmopolitan period ever conceived of Sanskrit as changing according to geographical location the way the so-called regional Prakrits were thought to change in their phonology, morphology, and lexicon. On the contrary, we find what might be called a "*panchoristic* flatland" too—where no variation is found across space—which was a basic component of Sanskrit language ideology. Recall how the tenth-century thinker Ratnaśrījñāna put it: "Whereas the Prakrits are multiform, Sanskrit is uniform."[18] To return to a question raised at the start of this account, a variety of Sanskrits, perhaps even what we might want to designate as "vernacular Sanskrits," admittedly existed in spoken and certain written registers, but their use for the production of *kāvya* and *praśasti* was completely restricted; the "conservatism" and "uniformity" of Latin literary culture were as characteristic of Sanskrit as its "widespread geographical diffusion."[19]

The parallels adduced so far suggest that in many of its components cosmopolitan literary culture was something replicable across the ancient world. But with respect to the processes of transculturation—the degree of compulsion to conform to the new culture, say, or the tolerance of diversity—radically different modes can be observed in the Latin and Sanskrit worlds. The ways in which and the reasons why peoples throughout Eurasia adopted unfamiliar cultural practices and thereby fundamentally reshaped their lifeworlds and histories are questions critically important to a history of culture and power before modernity, especially when viewed comparatively. And yet one cannot tell this from reviewing the scholarly literature on the subject. It is astonishing how little the process has been studied for either side of the world, but the lack is especially curious in the case of Romanization. Although central to the creation of a supraregional culture and polity in the premodern West, one contributing to the very conceptualization of "Europe" and "Western civilization," Romanization has only recently and tentatively become the object of serious study. Not so long ago a leading historian of the Roman Empire, contemplating the history of scholarship on what the "choice" to Romanize signified, declared that "there seems to have been no scholarly attention paid to anything but the symptoms" of Romanization and that in one "richly informed" work "there are only two or three lines devoted to the motives for cultural change; and I recall noth-

18. Commentary on *KĀ* 1.33: *ekaprakāraṃ saṃskṛtaṃ prākṛtaṃ tv anekaprakāram.* See chapter 1.1.

19. On "vernacular Sanskrit" see chapter 1.3. It is not clear to me that scholars are always fully awake to some of these distinctions (cf. Deshpande 1993b: 38–40).

ing more than that in all my reading."[20] While studies of the acceptance of Roman political and economic practices by conquered peoples have proliferated over the past decade—archaeology in particular, with its interest in urbanization, trade, agricultural development, and the like, has become increasingly interested in Romanization[21]—it is hard to find anything that would make this statement less true today for the most dramatic instance of transculturation: the history of literary culture. The fact is, if one wrote literature at all in the Roman Empire, one wrote in Latin.[22] Nowhere in the vast expanse from Mauretania and Lusitania in the west to Dacia and Syria in the east was literature ever produced in a local language (even the production of non-Latin inscriptions, as shown below, becomes increasingly rare), and what this absence meant, and how it may have meant differently across the Roman world, are basic questions that have rarely been raised.

We may not have any strong models for the adoption of Sanskrit culture either, but what we do know suggests how little the process had in common with Romanization. Nowhere do we see the conqueror's prestige providing the catalyst for cultural change, since nowhere in the expansion of the Sanskrit cultural order can we point to military conquest. Nowhere can we demonstrate that there was bureaucratic compulsion to adopt Sanskrit as there often was to adopt Latin, given the place of Roman law in the administration of the provinces. Whatever the status of *dharma* in the Sanskrit cosmopolitan conceptual order, practical law remained resolutely local (exemplary here, if at the end of the cosmopolitan epoch, is the localization of *dharmaśāstra* in Thailand as *thammasat*). The supposedly built-in afflictions of Sanskrit culture—caste, patriarchy, Brahmanical power, and the like—are hard to demonstrate as necessary concomitants of the cosmopolitan package. The Khmers, who, to judge from the spectacular political poetry they composed, were full participants in the Sanskrit cosmopolis, developed nothing on the order of the caste practices found in India and were blithely indifferent to Indian gender inequality.[23] Nor do we find in the Sanskrit cosmopolis anything comparable to the influence exerted by a core culture in a center-periphery world-system relationship that we find in Rome. There was no actual center to the cosmopolis, only a conceptual center—and precisely for this reason it was one that could be and was replicated in many dif-

20. MacMullen 1990: 60 and n. 33. An important earlier essay is Brunt 1990: 267–81 (originally written 1976).

21. For Romanization as an archaeological problematic see Blagg and Millett 1990, and more recently Woolf 1998.

22. In the eastern empire, Latin had to contend with another transregional language, Greek, which was to have its own complex interactions with Slavic vernaculars in the later Byzantine Empire (Sevcenko 1991).

23. Notwithstanding assertions about gender to the contrary on the part of some Southeast Asian historians (chapter 3.1 and n. 25 there). For the question of caste, see Mabbett 1977.

ferent places. The progressive Sanskrit transculturation eastward was not a matter of much interest to the Indian mainland—neither an object of political ambition nor a source of cultural hubris—if we are to judge from the paucity of references in Sanskrit literary texts or geocultural knowledge systems to the world of Southeast Asia.

It is in the modes of interaction with local culture, however, given the unidirectional transculturation that Romanization seems to have represented, that the differences between Latin and Sanskrit appear the most pronounced. This is above all visible in the fate of local languages. In Italy itself, and later in the western provinces of Gaul and Iberia, the same combination of military conquest and administrative co-optation of the native elites engendered profound and lasting transformations of local cultural systems. By the end of the first century B.C.E., all the languages of Italy other than Latin (including Oscan, Umbrian, and Etruscan) had disappeared from the inscriptional record; they had no continuing documentary, let alone literary, existence. A similar fate awaited the regional languages of the larger Roman world. While many of these apparently first became literized under the influence of Latin (the rest under the influence of Greek), they did not long preserve a written existence.

The Celtic languages of Gaul and those of the Iberian peninsula, the languages of North Africa including Punic (Phoenician) and Libyan, and most of those of the Roman Near East—all of these may have maintained an oral vitality for some centuries after Roman conquest, but they did not become, or perhaps were not permitted to become, part of literary culture of any sort and all eventually died out (Greek of course excepted). It is not because the literary works in Oscan, Umbrian, or Libyan of the Oscan- or Umbrian- or Libyan-speaking poets Naevius, Ennius, Plautus, and Terence have all vanished that we have not a scrap of literature in their native language; it is because none was ever produced. Thus while it may be true that Latin "define[d] a civilization without filling it" insofar as nobody outside the core areas spoke that language at home, it is writing that counts in civilization, and Latin defined writing and wrote the rest out of the record.[24] As Pliny the Elder (d. 79 C.E.) put it, Italy was "chosen by the power of the gods . . . to gather together the scattered realms and to . . . unite the discordant wild tongues of so many peoples into a common speech so they might understand each other,

24. The quotation is from MacMullen 1990: 32. On the disappearance of the languages of Italy, see Brunt 1990: 276–79; on Celtic and Celto-Iberic, MacMullen 1990: 62, 293 nn. 14, 17, and 294 n. 24; Blagg and Millett 1990: 231; Drinkwater and Vertet 1992: 25; for North African languages Millar 1968; on the eastern provinces Millar 1993 passim. See also Harris, 1989: 175–85. Our concern here is not with the survival of local languages as such (of which there is clear evidence in many places) but with literary culture; nor with the low rates of literacy outside the Roman world but with the fact that local languages were never allowed—as they were from Karnataka to Java—to enter the record of the literate.

and to give civilization *(humanitas)* to mankind, in short to become the homeland of every people in the entire world."[25]

It is probably prudent to hesitate before drawing too negative a conclusion from so complicated an epigraphical and literary record. Yet there is no doubt that the expansion of the borders of Latinity and the reduction of language diversity that followed were in fact viewed throughout history as closely linked with the expansion of the political borders of Latium. And this view would have consequences of its own for those who sought to imitate Rome. To many vernacular literati of the High Renaissance, for example, the historical model of cultural politics they found in Rome was one they strove to apply in the crystallizing nation-states. Thus a counselor to Louis XII wrote in the early sixteenth century, "What did the people and the Roman princes do when they ruled as monarchs over the world and sought to perpetuate their rule and make it eternal? The most sure and certain means they found was to magnify, enrich, and elevate their language, Latin . . . and afterward, to teach it to the lands and provinces and peoples they had conquered." In fact, the author was only echoing an ancient conviction found already in Augustine, for whom Rome "imposed its language upon the subject peoples at the same time as it imposed its political yoke."[26] These are, to be sure, expressions of observers from thought worlds quite distant and different from those of late-Republican and imperial Rome, and they almost certainly misinterpreted as policy what may have been instead the unintentional outcomes of process. Other kinds of evidence—from Galicia, for example, with respect to Celtic religious practices over a three-hundred-year period—suggest toleration or at worst indifference. But the fact remains that the expansion of Latin was accompanied by a stunning eradication of local language, and the observation that Romanization represented "a sort of decapitation of the conquered culture" seems apposite.[27]

The southern Asia case is as different in the domain of culture as we will see it to be in the exercise of power. Instead of being effectively proscribed, local language everywhere achieved written expression first through the mediation of Sanskrit and thereby embarked on the path that lead ultimately to Sanskrit's supersession. To be sure, literacy in local languages would be confined to the realm of the documentary and excluded from that of the expressive for centuries. But this was only because the literary function was coterminous with the political, and the political, given the supraregional ideal that informed it, was reserved exclusively for the supraregional code of San-

25. *Historia naturalis* 3.39, cited in Woolf 1998: 57.

26. Claude de Seysell cited in Derrida 1984: 98; Augustine (*De civitate dei* 19.7) cited in Dagron 1969: 24.

27. MacMullen 1990: 62 and 32. Cf. Nicols 1987 on Galicia, though contrast Blagg and Millett 1990: 220ff. on the suppression of the Druids.

skrit. The subliterary domain in which local languages were first and most vigorously put to work across much of southern Asia—specifying the boundaries of a deed or the precise conditions of a gift and its disposition—nonetheless retained substantial cultural significance. That such use as a language of record hardly renders a code culturally inferior is shown again by the contrast with later developments in the West, where Latin did not cede its documentary primacy until the late medieval period, since it was, or was thought to be, the sole eternally invariant language. In southern Asia, on the other hand, the terms of land grants and donations were also meant to be binding "as long as the sun and moon shall last"—the formula that closes so many of these documents—yet apparently no contradiction was felt in using the languages of Place, changeable though they were thought to be, to express these terms (see further in chapter 13.1).

The linguistic symbiosis of Sanskrit and local language in India is a complex topic not easily summarized, but there was certainly a history of convergence between them, both in phonology and lexicon. This history was continuous and began when Sanskrit began, for it is visible already in the oldest stratum of the Vedic corpus. (Southeast Asia offers an important contrast here, since, as epigraphy shows, the entire flow of influence was one way; as we have seen, Sanskrit may have massively invaded Khmer, to take that example, but it remained entirely impervious to any reciprocal influence.) Perhaps a more suggestive index of Sanskrit's relation to local styles of culture is the remarkable adaptability of the Sanskrit graphic sign itself, a "substitutability" that made it unique among the various "immense communities" of premodernity.[28] Latin carried the Roman script with it wherever it went and tolerated no fundamental deviation from the metropolitan style for centuries to follow (no later development, of uncial, minuscule, or anything else, ever constituted a cognitive break). And the script was indivisible from the literature: Vergil could have written the opening words of the *Aeneid, arma virumque cano,* only in a single alphabet, and from then on the words would be written only in that alphabet. In southern Asia, no writing system was ever so determinative of Sanskrit (until, ironically, Devanagari attained this status just as the cosmopolitan era was waning). Whereas early Brahmi script ultimately shaped all regional alphabets in South Asia and many in Southeast Asia (Burmese, Lao, Thai, Khmer, and probably Javanese), that script tolerated modification, often profound modification, wherever it traveled. Through this process, which appears to have occurred more or less synchronously across the Sanskrit world, scripts quickly began to assert a regional individuality in accordance with local aesthetic sensibilities, so much so that by the eighth century one self-same cosmopolitan language, undeviating in

28. Anderson 1983: 20–25.

its literary incarnation, was being written in a range of alphabets almost totally distinct from each other and indecipherable without specialized study.[29] Kālidāsa could have written the opening words of the *Raghuvaṃśa, vāgarthau iva saṃpṛktau,* in Javanese, Thai, or Sinhala script, in the Grantha script of Tamil country or the Śāradā script of Kashmir. Perhaps no better sign than the graphic sign itself shows how clearly one could be in the Sanskrit cosmopolis and simultaneously remain at home.

7.2 *IMPERIUM ROMANUM*

All the dissimilarities in cultural modalities just discussed—in language ideology, practices of literary culture, and transculturation processes—ultimately cannot be dissociated from the profound differences in the orders of political power of which Latin and Sanskrit were the expressive instruments. One of the most serious conceptual impediments to understanding the specific character of what is usually called "empire" in southern Asia results, as suggested earlier, from the fact that our ideas of premodern transregional political formations have been shaped by Western exemplars in general and by the historical construction of the Roman Empire in particular.[30] But *imperium,* to the degree that we can take its measure against the very imperfect image we are able to form of the southern Asian *rājya,* appears to have constituted a radically incommensurate political formation. At the same time, our image of the Roman Empire, archetypal though it may be, is also far from perfect. Even specialists disagree on its character as a structure of governance—this is something that seems to lie entirely in the eye of the scholarly beholder. Thus Francophone scholars are prone (perhaps unsurprisingly) to perceive a far more standardized and bureaucratic structure than Anglo-Saxon scholars, who stress (perhaps unsurprisingly) the limited aims of the empire, such as peacekeeping and taxation—or rather, peacekeeping in the service of taxation—and find a more passive and very much undermanned form of rule.[31]

It is undoubtedly hazardous to take sides where the experts themselves differ, but to the observer looking across from South Asia, the Roman Empire does appear to have striven for and achieved a degree of centralization and strong governance for which concrete parallels in premodern India (the ideal visions of Kauṭilya aside) are hard to find. Rome's bureaucrats and mil-

29. Dani 1963 remains the only detailed survey of the development of regional scripts, though he ignores all cultural questions. On Java, see de Casparis 1975: 28 ff.; 1979. Regionalization of graphic as well as linguistic identities is considered briefly in part 2 of this book. On professional "multiscriptism" see chapter 3.3 and n. 89 there.

30. This point is well made by Woolf 2001, esp. pp. 311 ff. On the problem of historical language more generally see Ricoeur 1965: 27.

31. Contrast for example Nicolet 1991: 130 ff. and Lendon 1997: 2 ff. on the census.

itary apparatus, spread across an immense territory, seem to have exercised control over everything from garrisons to the standardization of legal forms, currency, and weights and measures. To impose its will the Roman state employed coercion (far more than persuasion); taxation and the enumeration of its subjects for purposes of taxation (six million were counted in 48 C.E.); widespread use of uniform legal practices; and, on occasion, techniques of active Romanization, uneven but real, in cultural and political behavior, with a selective awarding of the coveted status of citizen that was designed to incorporate elites of the periphery. Equally important is the fact that there was indeed a periphery. The development of cartographic representation under conditions of imperial governance in the Roman world contrasts strongly with what we find in South Asia, where such mapping appears to have been completely nonexistent despite the presence of densely detailed and complex representations of space—a contrast hardly to be dissociated from differences in the exercise of military power.[32] That the *imperium* also knew exactly where the outside was—knew its own spatial form, so to put it—is shown very concretely by Hadrian's Wall in northern Britain, designed as a twelve-foot-high, ten-foot-thick, seventy-five-mile-long barrier to "separate the Romans from the barbarians." There was a single and irreproducible center, too—no toponymic mimicry here, the sole and anomalous exception being the creation of "Renewed Rome" *(roma renovata)* with the founding of Constantinople in the fifth century.[33]

All these features of empire—the coercion, the state apparatus, the metropole-hinterland relationship—find expression in a remarkable document from imperial Rome, "The Accomplishments of the Divine Augustus," which was engraved on bronze pillars set before the emperor's mausoleum sometime after his death in 14 C.E. The tablets have long since vanished, but the text is known from copies distributed to the various temples dedicated to the Divine Augustus across the empire (at Ancyra, Apollonia, Pergamon, Antioch, and very likely elsewhere). Even a brief selection points up crucial differences over against the practices of the Sanskrit cosmopolitan order:

> 1. The achievements of the Divine Augustus by which he brought the world [lit., the circle of the lands] under the empire of the Roman people *(quibus orbem terrarum imperio populi Romani subiecit)* . . . 3. I undertook many civil and foreign wars by land and sea throughout the world, and as victor I spared the lives of all citizens who asked for mercy. When foreign peoples could safely be pardoned I preferred to preserve rather than to exterminate them . . . 26. I extended the

32. See Nicolet 1991, especially 95, on the development of imperial Roman maps; contrast chapter 5.1.

33. Imperial control and the uniformity of instruments of governance are discussed in general in Brunt 1990 (contrast Woolf 2001: 311); Sherwin-White 1973: 200 ff. deals with citizenship as reward. For Hadrian's Wall, see *De vita hadriani* of Aelius Spartianus 11.1.

> territory of all those provinces of the Roman people on whose borders lay peoples not subject to our government . . . At my command and under my auspices two armies were led almost at the same time into Ethiopia and Arabia Felix; vast enemy forces of both peoples were cut down in battle and many towns captured. 27. I added Egypt to the empire of the Roman people. Greater Armenia I might have made a province after its king, Artaxes, had been killed, but I preferred, following the model set by our ancestors, to hand over that kingdom to Tigranes, son of King Artavasdes . . . 28. I founded colonies of soldiers in Africa, Sicily, Macedonia, both Spanish provinces, Achaea, Asia, Syria, Gallia Narbonensis and Pisidia . . . 30. The Pannonian peoples, whom the army of the Roman people never approached before I was the leading citizen, were conquered . . . the Dacian peoples [were compelled] to submit to the commands of the Roman people . . . 32. The following kings sought refuge with me as suppliants: Tiridates, King of Parthia, and later Phraates, son of King Phraates; Artavasdes, King of the Medes; Artaxares, King of the Adiabeni; Dumnobellaunus and Tincommius, Kings of the Britons; Maelo, King of the Sugambri.[34]

The Roman imperial order was not about expanding the center to the periphery—as so often occurred, however unprogrammatically, in the symbolic political practices of southern Asia—but about incorporating the periphery into the single Roman center. If some Romans (the Stoics) may have thought of themselves as *kosmou politai,* citizens of the world (though the phrase is Greek and was never translated into Latin), this seems partly owing to the Romans' ability to transform the *kosmos* into their *polis,* or rather—as the poet Ovid put it on the eve of Augustus's eastern campaign—to transform the *(ingens) orbis* into their *urbs,* the vast world into their own city. Pulakeśin II, we recall, ruled the "whole earth as if it were one city," expanding the city to the world, as it were, rather than the reverse, while the very concept of "subjecting the world to the power" of one people is nowhere at any time attested in the Sanskrit cosmopolis. Indeed, the very idea of ethnicized power—the *populus romanus* of whom Augustus was the "leading citizen"—and its construction as a unitary political subject is entirely absent from the southern Asia cosmopolitan order. The kind of sentiments used to describe this subject—typical is Cornelius Nepos's *Life of Hannibal* (c. 50 B.C.E.): "No one doubts that the Roman people *(populus)* are superior in virtue to all peoples *(gentes)* . . . that they take precedence over all peoples *(nationes)* in courage"—are equally foreign, having never been enunciated in reference to any political collectivity in premodern South Asia.[35]

34. Trans. Brunt and Moore 1967: 19ff. A good analysis is provided in Nicolet 1991: 15ff., especially 20.

35. Nepos, *Hannibal* 1. On Ovid's *ingens orbis in urbe fuit* (and *romanae spatium est urbis et orbis idem,* cited below) see Nicolet 1991: 33, 114, and Rochette 1997. On the Romans as an ethnic-political community see Woolf 2001: 316.

Absent from cosmopolitan southern Asia is the kind of sentiment Augustus expressed in declaring, "When foreign peoples could safely be pardoned I preferred to preserve rather than to exterminate them" (para. 3)—words written, as one scholar put it, to make known to foreign peoples Rome's "powers of collective life and death."[36] Absent, too, is its complement, the political demonology attached to peoples who could not easily be incorporated, such as the Parthians, Rome's eastern enemies. Contrast for a moment the very different practices in these two universalist orders at the point where they nearly met in western Asia in the early centuries of the millennium. Here Rome sought to contain if not destroy the region's inhabitants—the *parthos feroces*, the murderous Parthians, as Horace referred to them[37]—while at exactly the same time groups akin (if distantly) to the Parthians, the Śakas as well as the Kuṣāṇas, were migrating into the southern Asian subcontinent to a far different destiny. The Śakas contributed to the creation of the great cosmopolitan cultural order by producing the first royal public inscriptions that made use of the Sanskrit language and, according to some scholars, by stimulating the invention of new genres of Sanskrit literature (chapter 2.1); the Kuṣāṇas patronized new and highly influential forms of Sanskrit Buddhist culture, especially a Sanskrit Buddhist literature—the great poet Aśvaghoṣa was very likely associated with the court of Kaniṣka in the mid-second century—and established a remarkable transregional political order that would link South and central Asia.[38]

The practices of empire in the two worlds were as different as their principles. No imperial formation arising in the Sanskrit cosmopolis ever stationed troops to rule over conquered territories. No populations were ever enumerated. No uniform code of law was ever enforced anywhere across caste groupings, let alone everywhere in an imperial polity. No evidence indicates that transculturation was ever the route to imperial advancement in the bureaucracy or military. Even more dramatic differences are to be seen in the domain of political theology. Evidence for the providential character of the Roman state—the belief that it was universal and willed by the gods—is abundant in Latin literature and is a constituent of Roman thinking from the end of the third century B.C.E. on. That no full political theology may ever have been elaborated does not mean that the sentiments of poets and thinkers were merely court flattery. When Cicero later wrote that it was "by the will of the gods that we have overcome all peoples and nations," he was expressing

36. Veyne 1994: 348–50; he also cites and discusses Augustus's *Res gestae* 3.2 on pp. 353–54.

37. See Hardie 1997: 46–56, who calls attention to the long afterlife of the images created here.

38. The demonology I have described for late medieval India (Pollock 1993b) seems to have few if any explicit predecessors in the cosmopolitan era.

an idea long and widely resonant in the minds of Romans—there is no reason not to take him at his word.[39]

The providential nature of the empire was not just a heavenly mandate; it was actually embodied in the notion that the emperor was divine. The temples throughout the empire in which copies of Augustus's *Res gestae* were placed were dedicated to his worship, and cities competed keenly for the honor to build them. Historians who address the important if vexed question of the cult of the emperor typically speak of a Roman strategy of deploying the emperor's divinity and the imperial cult—the subject of annual celebration "in every city and province and army camp of the empire"—for the purposes of legitimation of the political order and the consolidation and pacification of the populace.[40] Whether or not such notions as strategic deployment and political legitimation are entirely apposite and not anachronistic even in the Roman context may be questioned; for southern Asia it is doubtful that such practices can be said to have ever occurred or that the very concepts are even relevant (chapter 13.3).

Indeed, once we learn to look free from the prejudgments derived from Roman and later European experience that tend to obscure our vision, there is no cogent evidence that any remotely comparable instrumentality was attached to the numinous status of the overlord in Sanskrit cosmopolities. Here is perhaps the most surprising difference from Rome, given the lingering Orientalist presuppositions of premodern Indians as priest-ridden and religion-besotted. To be sure, kings in India were constructed as "consubstantial god-men," as I once called them, but the logic and political effects of this construction were, I suggest, entirely different from what was found at Rome. In his inscriptions Samudragupta may be said to be "equal" to the divine guardians of the four directions (no mere rhetoric here, since it was old doctrine that the king in his very being was an amalgam of "shares" of these lordly powers). He may be equated with Puruṣa, the Primal Being (like other kings, as we have seen in chapter 3.2). His very status as a man may be discounted: "He is a human being only insofar as he performs the rites and conventions of the world—he is [in fact] a god whose residence is this world." However, the king seems to equal the Primal Being only in his practical functioning—"because of the prosperity of the good and the destruction of the bad" that he brings about—not because of his religious centrality. Indeed, he himself is a worshipper, the "supreme devotee of Bhagavān [Viṣṇu]."[41]

39. For evidence on the providential state and its interpretation see Momigliano 1987: 144; Brunt 1978: 162, 165 addresses the universality and divine order of the empire (perhaps forgetting the Achaemenid ancestry of the ideas, see Pollock 2005a).

40. On the imperial cult see Sherwin-White 1973: 402–8; the quote is from Woolf 2001: 321. See also Lendon 1997: 168–72.

41. *CII* 3: 228 and 203 ff. especially 24. The king as god-man in the Indian epic is discussed in Pollock 1991: 15–54. Something of the bivalence in attitude here is captured by Somade-

Whatever the complexities of such political-theological positions and views, three points can be made with reasonable certainty: First, if the Indian king was widely, perhaps invariably, viewed as a god-man, and if his icon might be displayed in temples—like the icons of the Pallavas in the Vaikuṇṭhaperumal temple in seventh-century Kāñcīpuram—he was never the center of a royal cult and never the object of religious worship.[42] Second, the supreme deity was irrelevant as a source of royal authority. A talismanic presence or apotropaic force? Yes, without doubt—from Viṣṇu in the fourth-century world of the Guptas (whose seal was marked with Garuḍa, the eagle of Viṣṇu) to Virūpākṣa in sixteenth-century Vijayanagara. But a granter of heavenly mandate, a justifier of rule, a transcendent real-estate agent awarding parcels of land? Never, not for Samudragupta nor for anyone in South Asia who followed after. Last, and concomitantly, the king's transcendent god was never the god of a political *ethnie.* Many royal cities in India indeed had their divine myths of foundation (as late as Vijayanagara, 1340), and virtually every dynasty claimed divine origin. But no one, ruler or people, ever claimed anywhere at any time that God had chosen them or given them a land or provided them with guidance or enabled them to conquer other peoples and lands.

We approach the core of this large contrast between the two cosmopolitan formations when comparing their two "foundational fictions," whose opening words have been quoted earlier and which offer the most concentrated expressions of their respective thought worlds. At the beginning of the *Aeneid,* Vergil "sings of arms and the man," the flight from Troy to Italy, the origins of the Latin people *(genus latinum),* the high walls of Rome, and *imperium sine fine,* power without limit. In his *Raghuvaṃśa,* Kālidāsa bows down to the mother and father of the universe, who are "fused together like a word and its meaning," in order that he might more deeply understand word and meaning when he tells the story of a universalistic political power—*diganta rājya,* power as far as the horizons—and the dynasty of the mythopoetic Raghus. Two visions of "cosmo-politan" order are offered here, and they differ profoundly.

First, consider the character of the *polis* each one projects: The one is comprised of a particular people whose historical origins are of fundamental concern to the narrative of the poem and who are clearly placed in time and

vasūri in his treatise of political theory, the *Nītivākyāmṛta* (tenth century, Karnataka): "The king is a supreme divine power *(paramaṃ daivatam),* he bows to no one—except to his gurus (*gurujanebhyaḥ,* i.e., parents and teachers)" (5.70; see also chapter 10 n. 87).

42. Or at least not until the seventeenth-century, if we accept the recent analysis of Nāyaka kingship in Narayana Rao et al. 1992. The statements holds true even for the *devarāja* cult instituted by Jayavarman II of the Khmers in the early ninth century; see Mabbett and Chandler 1995: 90 and Jacques 1994: 8.

space. The other is centered not on a particular people but on a lineage of mythic status (the *sūryavaṃśa* or solar dynasty) so inclusive that half the kings of India could, and did, claim descent from it, while the place (Ayodhyā), if a real piece of land in eastern Uttar Pradesh, could just as easily be conceived of as located in central Thailand (Ayutthaya, whose kings traced their lineage, at least nominally, to the solar kings, especially Rāma). Second, observe how different are the frames of reference for the *cosmos* as it is meaningful for human life: In the one case, it is the city of Rome expanded to embrace the whole world—again as Ovid put it: "The land of other nations has a fixed boundary, but the space of the city of Rome is the space of the world"—complete with its high walls of the sort Hadrian and other emperors were later to replicate elsewhere in the empire. And the expansion of the frame happened by the will of God: indeed, the divine proclamation was later made openly in the *Aeneid* ("I have granted empire without end," declares Jupiter) and to a fully ethnicized political community ("Romans, masters of the world, the people of the toga"). In the other, the frame is instead "all that moves with life" *(jagat),* where the father and mother of the universe choose no one people for rule over others, and where, in historical fact, no ruler ever proclaimed his identity in ethnic terms. Last, note how markedly different are the conceptions of the relationship between culture and power in the cosmopolis. In the one case, literature works as a verbal instrument for celebrating power: the *Aeneid* is clearly mapped against the imperial present and the text is virtually addressed to Augustus. In the other, literature is a celebration of the power of the verbal instrument itself; accordingly, the historical present of the imperial Guptas shows through the veil of allegory only on the rarest of occasions.[43]

This brief exercise in comparative cosmopolitanism is intended to point up how variable are the ways in which culture and power have related to each other—through language, literary practices, transculturation, political order—in the empire forms of premodernity. There has been, it would seem, not just one cosmopolitanism in history but several, and this fact will be of considerable importance when we ask (as we do later in this book) about the uses of such historical comparativism for future cultural and political practices. Furthermore, many of these same distinctions are visible in the regional worlds that superseded the cosmopolitan formations, and having identified them will help us make better sense of the very different paths these worlds followed in the course of the vernacular millennium.

43. See *Aeneid* 1.1 ff., 279, 282; *Raghuvaṃśa* 1.1; Ovid *Fasti* 2.684.

PART TWO

The Vernacular Millennium

CHAPTER EIGHT

Beginnings, Textualization, Superposition

8.1 LITERARY NEWNESS ENTERS THE WORLD

It is obvious that we cannot analyze the history of vernacularization—the term used here for the literary and political promotion of local language—or even observe it taking place, without knowing precisely what it is we are trying to observe and analyze. If we are concerned with the transition from quasi-universal to more regional ways of being in the spheres of culture and power, we will pay attention to, among other things, the ways people began to produce texts that were local rather than translocal in body and spirit—in their language and spheres of circulation as well as in their content. In the history of texts, we will be interested in understanding both the beginning of vernacular textuality as such and the major points of transition between types of textuality. We have seen that the dominant contemporary typology, largely congruent with premodern South Asian conceptions, distinguished two sorts of language use: the documentary (or informational, constative, contentual) and the workly (or imaginative, performative, expressive). The latter, given its role in representing and constituting cultural worlds as well as in enunciating political power, has particular relevance for our problematic. But vernacularization has to be examined initially as a double moment: when local language for the first time came to be written down for documentary purposes, and when it was first textualized for the workly tasks—the task of culture done by literature and the task of power done by political discourse—already defined by the cosmopolitan culture, whose authority the vernacular sought to supplement and eventually to supplant. It is crucial to register that such moments are rarely simultaneous. A time lag between them, often very substantial, is usual, and the literary silence that fills this empty space has something important to tell us.

None of these categories—localization, textualization, literarization—is uncomplicated. Equally vexing and even more fundamental is the problem of commencement itself. In what sense can it be claimed, let alone determined, that vernacularization actually began? The very idea of a beginning is beset by enigmas; it raises complicated issues in historiography, and even in epistemology, ontology, and ideology. All beginnings have an aura of the provisional, since in principle some earlier instance might always be found. This suspicion of imposture can mislead us into believing that beginnings do not really exist, that some predecessor of our first text, and some predecessor of that predecessor, ever await discovery. There is even a certain philosophical grounding to this suspicion. A dominant form of Indian thought known as Sāṃkhya (no less than certain strands of Western scholastic philosophy) holds that a beginning is, ontologically speaking, unthinkable. According to the "doctrine of preexistent effects" *(satkāryavāda),* nothing can be produced that does not already exist latently in its cause (as the European schoolmen put it, *ex nihilo nihil fit*). Beginnings start to fade into infinity.[1]

This often-unexamined conviction about the obscurity of beginnings is coupled in literary historiography with the peculiar belief that literary traditions follow a developmental cycle, with all the biologism implicit in that phrase. Thus the argument is often made that the earliest texts in a literary tradition that display any formal or other kind of mastery cannot, for that very reason, be the first. Literary mastery for many scholars must presuppose a long prehistory of failure. But this is an idea borrowed unreflectively from other areas of culture. The history of painting, at least according to some objectivist accounts, may be represented, like that of science, as a history of a certain kind of progress; the "systematic conquest of the appearances of things" is something at which artists obviously got better and better, both in South Asia and in Europe. But the history of literature is not that of realist painting.[2] Nothing compels us to accept the analogy with artisanal experiment and growth of expertise, let alone with the growth of children or plants. On the contrary, the development model works neither positive-historically nor ethnohistorically for literature. It cannot accommodate the many literary traditions that seem to have begun with mastery (again, in some objectivist sense) and is entirely contradicted by representations across literary traditions of the untranscendable preeminence of all "first poems."

1. So the novelist Ian McEwan: "There are always antecedent causes. A beginning is an artifice, and what recommends one over another is how much sense it makes of what follows" (1998: 17–18).

2. Though some great literary critics have thought so, including Auerbach (cited in Gallagher and Greenblatt 2000: 212–13). On the history of European painting see Danto 1987: 70.

Conceptual and cognitive problems of an even more complicating nature also plague beginnings. Producers of culture can believe they are making a new beginning when in the eyes of others they are not. Or they may suppose they are simply reproducing the old when other eyes see clearly that they are making it new. ("How can we possibly imagine anything novel?" said a tenth-century Indian logician as he proceeded to change the history of his discipline.) Beginnings are often nothing but what inventors of traditions, whether modern or premodern, choose to turn into beginnings. They may remember selectively, erasing one beginning in favor of another; or they may deny the possibility of beginning altogether. The delusion of autochthony and primevality is what enables traditions (like nations) to constitute themselves. Or a cultural beginning might mark only the beginning of what a tradition has chosen to preserve—here "beginning" means more narrowly only successful beginning. For some brands of historiography, both Orientalist and postcolonial, beginnings are conceptually permissible only in colonialism, which in India plays the role both historically and historiographically that modernity plays in European cultural history. For Orientalism, Indian culture and power before colonialism had no history because nothing ever happened. Colonial critique, for its part, derives its power largely from the assumption—less often the demonstration—of the sharp discontinuity and new beginning in power and culture that colonialism uniquely wrought. Similar beginnings are ex hypothesi excluded for precoloniality, which therefore once more is left without a history. To this can be added a certain antihistoricism common even to those sympathetic to the study of precolonial Indian culture. This stems in part from a European aesthetic that locates the most important feature of literature in its capacity to transcend the moment of its genesis and in part from the serious claims of Sanskrit (and broader South Asian) normativity, whereby history can be escaped by the poet's cleaving to eternal standards of language and literary practices. Thus the Tamilist is just as prone to view Tamil literature as a "simultaneous order" rather than a historical one as the Sanskritist is to reassert the "timeless nature" of *kāvya*.[3]

Beyond the conceptual, cognitive, ideological, and antihistoricist or aestheticist baggage that encumbers the very concept of a beginning are more basic categorical and discursive difficulties. If we say that "Gujarati literature begins in the late twelfth century with the narrative poem *Bhārateśvara*

3. So Zvelebil 1974: 2, and Lienhard 1984: 48, 52. A full-dress analysis of beginnings must exist but I have yet to find it. Brief but important reservations are found in Bloch 1993: 53–57 (he speaks of the *idole* or even *démon des origines, obsession embryogénique*). Said 1975 raises none of the questions of interest here. The tenth-century logician is Jayanta Bhaṭṭa (*Nyāyamañjarī* introduction v. 8).

Bāhubali Ghor," or that "Maithili literature begins with Vidyāpati's collection of lyrics in the mid-fourteenth century," what assures us that the former is not the last work of Apabhramsha or that the latter is not in fact composed in Bangla (both positions that have been defended)? Just as imprecise as language categories are cultural categories such as "literature," "poem," or "lyric." A genre cannot be said to have a beginning in literary history until one has decided what that genre is—a decision often implicitly bound up with assumptions about when it began. Accounts of the origins of the European novel offer a good example.

However vexatious these enigmas appear, none is fatal to the historiography of vernacularization in South Asia. In fact, a number of them form the substance of a historical analysis of the phenomenon itself. How categories of culture were created through the vernacularization process, why the memory of one textual beginning was erased in favor of another, and why this text rather than that was selected by a tradition to be preserved as primal—these are some of the very elements of vernacularization at work. The representations of beginnings within literary traditions themselves, how people thought they had made history with literature, and most important, what they believed literature to be (the content they poured into a category that a modern reader would recognize as expressive and workly) and even what they believed language to be—these are components of the history of vernacularization as critical as any brute facts we can recover. From this perspective, what producers of Kannada workly texts counted as Kannada literature is itself a historical truth—a *vyāvahārika sat* or *certum*—that linguists or literary historians may be right to challenge but cannot ignore.

We encountered the problem of beginnings also with regard to cosmopolitan literary culture. Many scholars assume *kāvya* to reach back into the mists of prehistory—a view made doubtful, however, by the history of Sanskrit culture through the first millennium B.C.E. and its radical transformations from the early centuries C.E. Indian tradition itself is unanimous in its belief that *kāvya* could begin: the *Vālmīki Rāmāyaṇa* claims to have begun it, and poets as early as 150 C.E. concurred. Further testimony to the local truth of this literary beginning and of the very possibility of literary beginnings is provided by vernacular literary cultures, many of which take the account of Vālmīki's firstness as a charter and locate their own beginnings in moments of locally derivative epic discourse. The beginning of Latin literature in the last decades of the third century B.C.E., again through appropriating an epic voice, would seem to be an accepted fact. Regarding Persian literature, the first lines of New Persian poetry were composed (an innovation that the *Tārikh-i Sistān* makes clear was in response to the superposed model of the Arabic panegyric) in Sistān a little after the middle of the ninth century—or so some scholars have argued. But getting clear on these questions is no easy thing. It is therefore unsurprising that such core questions as how literary newness, especially vernacular newness, enters the world, and when and under what circumstances of social or political or aesthetic change this occurs are not often posed.[4]

What needs to be critically probed is the proposition that at certain times and places a language comes to be deployed in certain new ways, as never before in its history, for making certain kinds of texts that we call literary because their inventors in their own ways called them so. For reasons clarified below, the texts in question are taken here to be written uses of language for expressive purposes that came into being by emulation of superposed models of literature. Whatever may have occurred earlier, in the world of orality, is neither recoverable nor relevant to the history of such vernacular inauguration. Like a formal or genre feature (the *tripadī* meter, the mixed prose-verse *campū,* blank verse, the novel), a tradition as such ("Kannada" literature, "French" literature) also begins. No significant historical or conceptual factors differentiate such beginnings from each other, aside from the fact that the creation of traditions as such requires more sensitive theorization and more careful definition than a form or genre. No more than a form or a genre is a literary tradition always already existent, and nowhere, therefore, has literature been coeval with its language, not even with its written form. The histories of vernacular languages in South Asia demonstrate this unequivocally, not least by the temporal gap mentioned earlier that separates the moment of literization, or the attainment of literacy, from the moment of literarization, or the attainment of literature—a gap that is often chronologically appreciable and always historically significant.

Earlier we analyzed the Sanskrit cultural axiom that literature could be made only in a restricted set of languages—Sanskrit, (Maharashtri) Prakrit, and Apabhramsha (chapter 2.2, 3). That is, only these could furnish the "body" of the literary text, with other languages permitted to appear only in a mimetic role when the imitation of regional speech was required (and this was rare enough). All three languages are distinguished by their cosmopolitan spatiality, the distinction that qualified them for the literary task in the first place. In the case of the political discourse called *praśasti,* whose creation was concurrent with that of *kāvya,* the set was narrowed to Sanskrit. From the moment Sanskrit became the language of political discourse at the beginning of the first millennium, everywhere permanently supplanting Prakrit, it remained the sole such language across all of southern Asia until

4. Any volume in Gonda 1973 ff. may be examined as evidence of the silence or confusion or both on vernacularization as a process. For Sanskrit beginnings see chapter 2.1; for Latin, chapter 7.1; for New Persian Lazard 1993: 24, 21 (it is a measure of the power of nationalist ideology and its quest for antiquity and continuity that the very possibility of commencement is paradoxically denied: "it is the *same Persian language* at three stages of its history: Old Persian . . . Pahlavi . . . and New Persian" [emphasis added]).

about the beginning of the second millennium. Thus literature and the discourse of politics both, like the political practice to which they were tied, could only be conceived of as a translocal phenomenon. When the regional languages first began to attain written form, starting in the latter half of the first millennium generally speaking, they were used exclusively as documentary idioms; it was only around the turn of the millennium that they came to be transformed into codes for political expression and, more or less simultaneously, for literature. Before that moment of transformation, the existence of many vernacular languages could be conceptually registered, even in texts that promulgated the restrictive triad of literary languages, but they were never regarded as potential media for composing literate workly texts. On the contrary, they were located outside the sphere of literary culture, in the realm of the oral, specifically, the sung (*gīta, gītā, gīti, gāna,* etc.).

The reality of the Sanskrit axiom of literary-language exclusion and its implications for the early history of vernacularity are confirmed by various kinds of hard and soft data: the inscriptional record, where we can actually observe the hesitancy regarding the literization of the vernacular, to say nothing of its literarization; later Sanskrit works of literary criticism and royal encyclopedias, which reassert the old cultural norms on the eve of the vernacular revolution; and traditional accounts of the history of vernacular writing, which demonstrate resistance to the old norms. We will review the inscriptional record first in order to examine the historical reality of commencement, though this review is brief and selective (additional detail is found in chapters 9 and 10). While nomenclature like "Kannada" or "Gujarati" has to be used to refer to the languages, the linguistic, conceptual, and even cognitive boundaries that underwrite such terminology must have been blurry until vernacularization itself was well underway and the work of sharpening language differences through the production of corpora of literary texts had begun. We begin with some reasonably transparent cases before turning to the more complex.

The south Indian language we now call Kannada had no presence whatever in the inscribed documents of the early Karnataka polities until the end of the fifth century, when it was first committed to writing, possibly among the Kadambas. It remained altogether mute thereafter in the political record to the end of the Bādāmi Cāḷukya period in the mid-eighth century; the merest scraps of short Kannada documents, amid a sea of Sanskrit records, are found from before the ninth century. Only in the latter half of the ninth and the beginning of the tenth centuries, in the last three or four generations of rule of the Rāṣṭrakūṭas of Mānyakheṭa, did Kannada begin to be used more widely for documentary purposes, and eventually for articulating the political-expressive. With this development began the marginalization of Sanskrit as a code of political discourse that would lead to its virtual displacement among the Kalyāṇa Cāḷukyas to the north and the Hoysaḷas to the south (c. 1000–

1300). It was during the reign of the later Rāṣṭrakūṭas, too, that Kannada was first theorized as a vernacular literary medium and Kannada *kāvya* entered securely into positive history as well as the historical memory of Kannadiga poets themselves.[5]

The history of Telugu closely follows that of Kannada. Telugu entered the epigraphical record around the end of the sixth century, thus almost simultaneously with Kannada. It remained a language of very modest and entirely documentary usage for the following three centuries. Around the same time that Kannada first came to be employed for expressive purposes, Telugu intellectuals began to experiment with the vernacular as a literary language. It may have been Jains and Śaivas in the southwest region of Rāyalasīma who first made what one scholar has called the "momentous experiment" of vernacularization with workly inscriptions of the mid-ninth century. But the writers of the southwest were almost certainly participating in the same transformation in literary practices that in the late ninth and early tenth centuries led courtly intellectuals to the north and east, among the Veṅgi Cāḷukyas and their feudatories, to begin to replace Sanskrit with Telugu for political discourse in inscriptions.[6] Similar to the idiom of this discourse is the first *kāvya* in Telugu, produced at the Veṅgī Cāḷukya court around 1050.

In the polities of today's Maharashtra, Sanskrit alone was used in the inscriptional record from the mid-fourth century, which marked the end of the Prakrit period among the Vākāṭakas. By the late eighth century Marathi had acquired something of a linguistic identity, being listed among the sixteen spoken languages in Uddyotanasūri's *Kuvalayamālā* (see chapter 2.1, 2), yet it was not until two centuries later that the language found written form. When in the late tenth century Cāmuṇḍarāya, the Gaṅga minister and literary scholar, completed construction of the Bāhubali Gōmaṭeśvara colossus at Śravaṇabeḷgoḷa, he signed the foot of the statue with the words "Cāmuṇḍarāya made this" in three languages and four scripts: Kannada (Kannada characters), Tamil (Grantha and Vattelutu), and Marathi (Nagari).[7] Within a generation, a couple of Marathi epigraphs of an entirely documentary sort were composed.[8] It was not before the late thirteenth and early fourteenth centuries that the first expressive political discourse appeared in

5. A case-study of Kannada is provided in chapter 9.

6. Pertinent Rāyalasīma inscriptions include *ETI:* no. 86 (c. 850, Guntur district) and no. 82 (c. 850, Nellore district); a pertinent eastern Cāḷukya inscription is *ETI:* no. 87 (c. 892–922, Nalgonda district); the record of Yuddhamalla is discussed below. It is Nagaraju 1995 who speaks of the "momentous experiment" of Telugu vernacularization.

7. *EC* 2: 159–60, nos. 272, 273, 276 (the Marathi reads *śrī cāvuṇḍarājēṃ karaviyalēṃ*). Tulpule 1979: 313 thus needs modest emendation.

8. Tulpule 1963: 1–14 (a stone inscription of 1012 recording a grant of a minister of the Śilāhāra dynasty; a copperplate of 1060, the first in Marathi, on a transaction between two Brahmans).

Marathi, from the domain of the Yādava dynasty (900–1300) in northern Maharashtra. The first evidence of written Marathi literature is the biography of a spiritual master produced a little earlier. Again the time lags are remarkable: two centuries or more separate the (at least nominal) recognition of Marathi as a separate language (779) from its first use in a documentary context (983), while another two to three passed before it was employed for expressive purposes both literary (1278) and political (1305).[9]

For the first four to five centuries of their written existence, then, Marathi, Telugu, and Kannada produced not a single text of culture or power that we could identify as expressive, imaginative, workly—or, more accurately put, nothing that anyone in medieval India would have called *kāvya* or *praśasti*. The languages were all silent, literarily as well as politically. (Nothing whatever indicates the existence of earlier vernacular *praśasti*s, or explains why, if they had once existed, they should have all been lost when Sanskrit examples have been preserved in abundance from all across these regions.) Such vernacular invisibility over the very long term was the rule rather than the exception in the world of cosmopolitan Sanskrit. This fact—and its correlative, that vernacularization was not a necessary process but entirely elective and conditional—is demonstrated by the history of Tulu, the language of coastal Karnataka, which had no literary or even documentary existence until as late as the nineteenth century (and even since then, its written uses have remained highly circumscribed), or that of Konkani, a language of Goa and southern coastal Maharashtra, which was rarely if ever used even for documentary purposes until the modern period.[10] In neither case has evidence of substantial earlier vernacularization been lost; rather, it was never produced in the first place.

Far more complex is the case of Tamil, both intrinsically and because of the complications of ethnohistorical narratives (chapter 10.1). We saw that the Pallavas of Kāñcīpuram made no use whatever of Tamil in their records for the first two and a half centuries of their rule (chapter 3.1), something especially curious given that the literization of Tamil had long preceded the dynasty. In fact, some of the oldest writings in the subcontinent are Tamil Brahmi cave inscriptions, dated tentatively to the last two centuries B.C.E.[11] When Tamil finally appeared in Pallava public writing in the middle of the

9. The 1305 inscription of Brahmadevarāṇe is discussed in section 3, and Mhāibhaṭa's *Līlācaritra* (1278) is considered in chapter 10.1.

10. This does not imply illiteracy in either region, for Sanskrit literacy was common. The predecessor of modern Malayalam script is often called Tulu-Malayalam, being widely shared among the Brahmans of Tulunadu and north Kerala. But it was never used to literize Tulu itself.

11. These inscriptions are all prosaic graffiti; some record royal gifts, one mentions the succession of Cēra rulers. See Mahadevan 1970, especially 13–14 (Mahadevan 2003 appeared too late to make effective use of here). Sātavāhana coins were also inscribed in Tamil and Telugu (Ray 1986: 44).

sixth century, the language discharged exclusively documentary tasks, and this remained the case to the end of the dynasty. For the six hundred years of their existence, with very few exceptions, the Pallavas never spoke literarily in Tamil in their public records.[12] The discursive division of language labor found among the Pallavas between a workly Sanskrit and a documentary Tamil also applies generally to the corpus of inscriptions of the Pallavas' successors, the Cōḻas, in their earliest period, before the dramatic transformation of the vernacular epoch commenced. No systematic collection of the Cōḻa inscriptional record has ever been published, but it seems clear that Tamil was not used for expressing more than prosaic content, and certainly not for composing anything comparable to Sanskrit *praśasti,* for the first two centuries or so of the dynasty. This situation changed modestly during the reign of Rājarāja I (r. 985–1014), but the inscriptions of his successors (Rājendra, for example, in a record of 1025, and Rājādhirāja, in one of 1046) offer evidence of a dramatically new expressive political discourse in Tamil that had come into existence by the mid-eleventh century.[13]

A structurally similar development, though following a slightly different timeline, is found among the Pāṇṭiyas (600–1300), who ruled in what would be represented in later history—in part via legends promoted by the Pāṇṭiyas themselves—as the site of the prehistoric *caṅkam,* or literary "academy," and the heartland of Tamil literary culture, namely, the region of Maturai in the peninsular south (it is prominently identified in the earliest representations as the "region of pure Tamil," chapter 10.1). The history of this dynasty (or dynasties) is confusing, as is their epigraphical record, for which again, no systematic collection exists. Some of the Tamil Brahmi documents just mentioned are associated with the Pāṇṭiyas, but these are few and followed by a half-millennium gap. With the reconstitution of the dynasty under Kaḍuṅgōṉ in the early seventh century Sanskrit inscriptions began to appear, but Tamil came to be used for expressive purposes only later, perhaps first in an eighth-century charter.[14] To be sure, this was almost two centuries earlier than Kannada or Telugu, but it was also as much as eight centuries after Tamil

12. Aestheticized inscriptions are sometimes found within Pallava domains, as in the two singular verses engraved on a c. eighth-century temple in Tañcāvūr district (*EI* 13: 134ff., especially pp. 143, 148). Being completely untouched by Sanskrit in idiom and discursive style, these present a picture of literary-political inscription very different from what was to come. They may have been unique experiments, with no prehistory and no future. According to Zvelebil 1992: 126, an inscription from Pūlāṅkuṟicci shows that "by 500 A.D. at the latest, polished literary Tamil as we know it from ancient texts was used—perhaps with slight alterations—in inscriptions, too." The inscription is undated and still, it seems, unpublished.

13. For Rājarāja I see *SII* 3: 14–15 or *EI* 22: 245–46; Rājendra, *SII* 1: 95–99 and *SII* 2.1: 105–9; Rājādhirāja, *SII* 3.1: 51–58.

14. The record of Cēntaṉ, discussed in section 3. Note that *SII* 14, the volume of Pāṇṭiya records, begins with a *Sanskrit* inscription of 770.

was first committed to writing. The reorientation of cultural politics in the case of both the Cōḻas and the Pāṇṭiyas correlated with important innovations in the literary-cultural sphere (chapter 10.1). The uncommonly obscure prehistory of Tamil literature makes it less easy to argue that these represent the kind of literary beginnings that are elsewhere copresent with the commencement of vernacular political discourse. But there is no doubt that for many centuries Tamil was, if not mute, then certainly not loquacious in the domain of the political-expressive, until in the last several centuries of the millennium it began to speak with an altogether new and confident voice.

Almost equally hard to trace is the vernacular transformation in the north.[15] Yet the overall picture is not entirely dark, and what we see broadly conforms to the historical shape of developments identified for central and peninsular India. From west Panjab to Gujarat, from Kashmir to Nepal, and across the central plains to Orissa, Bengal, and Assam, local language was wholly excluded from the inscriptional record of political power in the early medieval period. Not only did Gujarati and Gwaliyari, Oriya and Bangla, do no aesthetic work, they did not speak at all in the public domain of the polity until the thirteenth or fourteenth century at the earliest, notwithstanding in some cases a long prehistory of literization.[16]

In the speech area of Gwaliyari (the name is not consistently used in the region itself), one of the earliest inscribed texts is a five-line document on a pillar of a Gwalior temple describing how King Bīraṃmadeva (or Bīram Dev) underwrote the construction of the edifice in 1405. It is not much in itself, to be sure, but its time and place are rightly seen as symptomatic of an important change that was in the offing. It can hardly be coincidental that this first known public use of the vernacular in the region came only a generation before the poet Viṣṇudās wrote the first *kāvya* in the Gwaliyari language in 1435.[17] The vernacular voice began to speak expressively in the political domain elsewhere in north India around the same time. One of the earliest workly inscriptions in Gujarati is a record from Meḍapāṭa (Mewar, Rajasthan) composed by the court poet of a Sisodia king named Rājamalla in 1489. A fuller discussion of this record is offered in section 3 below, but its broader implications may be noted here. The vernacular *praśasti* in Gu-

15. See especially the chapters by McGregor and Yashaschandra (McGregor 2003, Yashaschandra 2003) in Pollock ed. 2003.

16. Prior to the fifteenth century, vernacularity did begin to penetrate the business portions of northern inscriptions in nondramatic but still significant ways; the number of unattested "Sanskrit" words in a Pāla grant of the ninth century suggests just this kind of infiltration, see Kielhorn in *EI* 4: 245.

17. For the Ambikādevī temple inscription see Dvivedi 1972: 51, who notes that Viṣṇudās's patron, Ḍūṃgarendra Siṃha, did continue to issue inscriptions in Sanskrit. Viṣṇudās's *Mahābhārata* is discussed in chapter 10.1 (see also chapter 8.2). The important work Dvivedi 1955 came to my attention too late to be of much use here.

jarati, as in other north Indian languages generally, was a phenomenon of the later medieval period, although the language had a considerably longer prehistory. When at last it was produced, it bore the deep impress of Sanskrit, yet it could be felt without contradiction as a language of Place, which is what it names itself in the record. It was not much earlier than this inaugural manifestation of Gujarati inscriptional expressivity that *kāvya* began to be written in the language: texts like the *Bhārateśvara Bāhubali Ghor* (a Jain *rāso,* or heroic narrative) and the *Vasantavilāsa* (Sport of Spring, a *phāgu,* or cycle of lyrics) first appeared around the thirteenth century.[18]

The historical dynamic of vernacularization is perfectly illustrated in the case of Newari, the Tibeto-Burmese language spoken in the Kathmandu Valley of Nepal. Newari long antedated the advent there of Nepali, the language of Gorkhālī immigrants of the late medieval period that, after the final defeat of the Mallas in 1768, was in a position to become the language of the modern nation-state. Legal documents preserved in a Buddhist monastery in Pāṭaṇ show that by the tenth century Newari was regularly employed in commercial transactions, deeds of sale, mortgages, and certificates of donation. In these nonpublic records we see the same pattern of language specialization found in other spheres of communication in the cosmopolitan public world and maintained in the later epigraphic record: Sanskrit is employed for the framework of the documents and their "general principles," as the editors call them, whereas the business specifics are given in Newari. The vernacular was entirely absent from inscriptional discourse until the fourteenth century, around the time the Malla dynasty consolidated its power; it was then employed exclusively for pragmatic ends, with Sanskrit continuing to dominate. Not until the seventeenth century—that is, some seven hundred years after the language was first literized for pragmatic functions—did political and literary writing appear in Newari (exemplary is a 1655 inscription of Jayapratāpamalla discussed further in section 3). This political discourse was complemented by a remarkable, intensive production of workly texts, especially courtly dramas directly authored by kings such as Siddhinarasiṃha of Pāṭaṇ (1619–61) and Jagatprakāśamalla of Bhaktapur (fl. 1644–73), and the first Newari *kāvya.*[19]

18. The former text has been dated to 1170 on internal evidence; the *Vasantavilāsa* is probably fourteenth century (Brown 1962: 6).

19. For the Pāṭaṇ documents see the superb edition of Kölver and Śākya 1985. Earlier textualized materials in Newari include a royal genealogy, the *Gopālarājavaṃśāvali,* that dates from the late fourteenth century, translations of Sanskrit scientific materials, and a bilingual text of the *Hitopadeśa* in a manuscript dated 1360. General accounts of the literary history of Newari are Malla 1982: 35, 60–64, and Lienhard 1974, esp. 18, 151–52. Brinkhaus 1987 discusses the earliest full-scale Newari drama (between 1666 and 1672), calling attention to the use of Newari for songs in Sanskrit/Prakrit dramas in fifteenth-century Nepal as preparatory to what I have called "primary" literary production (chapter 2.3).

Vernacularization in Nepal shows some unusual complications, however, or more justly put, shows in pronounced form complications that are often obscured elsewhere. Simultaneously with the rise of a new literature in Newari came a resurgence, unprecedented elsewhere, of political inscription in Sanskrit, which had diminished dramatically with the end of the Licchavi dynasty in the ninth century. In addition, other regional languages such as Maithili were also cultivated at the seventeenth-century Nepal courts, where they experienced a sustained period of literary efflorescence. Nepali entered the mix, too, in the late-medieval period. Literized considerably later than Newari (in the early fourteenth century) it was used exclusively for documentary inscriptional purposes until the seventeenth century, when, apparently at the prompting of Newar kings, it was promoted in the public inscriptional domain for purposes that approached the expressive. The literary career of Nepali did not commence in earnest, however, until the eighteenth century—some five hundred years after its literization—and the first productions, in a manner typical of the vernacularization process, were adaptations from the Sanskrit.

The trends we have seen thus far are corroborated in Java and Khmer country (chapter 3.1). Though found in written form almost contemporaneously with the appearance of Sanskrit in the seventh century, Khmer was used only for pragmatic purposes until the end of the Angkor polity in the fourteenth century. Literary texts in the vernacular seem to not antedate the seventeenth century, a full millennium or more after Khmer was first literized.[20] In Java we find an entirely different situation but one strikingly similar to that in South Asia both in chronology and in the pattern of cultural change. Although Sanskrit inscriptions are extant from at least the fourth century and were produced for the next five hundred years, Javanese is almost completely absent in the epigraphical record. Only in the early ninth century—some four to five centuries after the first epigraphs—did documentary charters in the vernacular begin to appear. These were quickly followed by expressive records (the first dated one is 824) and then by an astonishing vernacular literary output, with an array of texts unparalleled in Southeast Asia but bearing the closest comparison with Kannada, Telugu, Brajbhasha, and other Indic traditions.[21]

With regard to any one of these languages—which are themselves only

20. The first poetic text in a Khmer inscription is dated 1701, though a manuscript work in Khmer verse (indeed, the oldest extant), the *Lpoek Aṅgar Vatt*, the "Poem of Angkor Vat," is dated 1620 (Khing 1990: 24–59). The one shred of earlier Khmer verse is a four-line strophe in mixed Sanskrit-Khmer dated Śaka 896 (974 C.E.) (*JA* 1914: 637–44 [= Coedès nos. 173, 174]).

21. For the beginning of inscriptional Javanese (804) see Zoetmulder 1974: 3; de Casparis 1975: 31 (who notes that literization may have occurred earlier, on the evidence of the Dinoyo grant of 760 C.E.). The Kayumvungan record (824) contains fourteen lines of Sanskrit verse followed by the first *praśasti* in Javanese; for another of 862, see *CIJ* 64 ff. and 171 ff.

parts of the vast world of southern Asian literary cultures—it is no easy matter to determine the precise inception of its existence in writing and the rise of its political and literary expressivity, or to chart and understand the time gap between these two moments, let alone to configure their disparate chronologies into a single sensible narrative. Yet this does not mean that literization and literarization were not historical processes or that certain broad tendencies cannot be perceived. In virtually every case, an interval, often substantial, separated the moment a language was first attested as an individuated code and medium of pragmatic communication from the moment a vernacular political discourse was produced in public inscription. More or less simultaneously with the latter development—at all events, close enough in time to posit a causal linkage—the vernacular came to be used for the composition of expressive texts. Through their idiom and imagination, both political and literary texts show unequivocally that they were modeled on Sanskrit, though modeled with highly distinctive regional differences that disclose complex negotiations with the cosmopolitan literary idiom in everything from vocabulary to thematics. In addition, if vernacular writing everywhere at first complemented Sanskrit, in most places it eventually replaced it, signaling a moment of profound transition in the history of Indian culture. And since the site of so much of this cultural production was the royal court, with both inscriptional and literary discourse participating in the same dynamic of political-cultural localization, vernacularization signaled as well a moment of profound transition in the history of power. A temporal shape to these transformations can also be discerned. In its initial stages, vernacularization was a southern Indian innovation of the last quarter of the first millennium; by a complicated process (discussed in chapter 12.2) it became a characteristic of most regional polities by the middle of the second.

No sooner do we try to make such sense of these data than we meet the skeptic's objections regarding beginnings mentioned earlier: that they are factual positivities, to be shunned in a world where no factual positivity exists outside the texts that make them such; that they require conceptual objects like unified languages ("Marathi") and cultural practices ("literature") that are indefinable or nonindigenous or nonpremodern or only a gradual invention of European modernity that cannot be retrofitted onto South Asian premodernity; that every beginning is only the earliest survivor, that surely predecessors must have once existed that have been lost through natural selection, change in cultural fashion, or other vicissitude; that the "filter of tradition" makes us misconstrue the earliest preserved texts as radical discontinuities rather than as the chance preservations they are;[22] that variation in the speech norms of the vernaculars, faster than any in the cosmopolitan language, must have impeded understanding in later generations

22. See Schieffer 1985: 88 ff., and compare Zink 1992: 89.

and led to the loss of earlier vernacular literature; and last, that traditions are in any case sites of willful forgetting, that they are invented by medieval hegemons or their modern-day epigones by suppressing one beginning in favor of another, and that latter-day scholars are often duped into acquiescing to such machinations—a clear demonstration of how dubious the whole affair of beginnings really is, a fool's game.

Some of these objections are clearly valid. Narratives of beginnings in premodernity are admittedly no more innocent than they are in nationalist literary history, and cases can easily be found where one beginning was suppressed even as another was affirmed. When a fourteenth-century Kannada writer names the mid-tenth-century poet Pampa as the *ādikavi,* or primal poet, he is not only commenting on Pampa's impact on Kannada literary history but also ignoring at least a century of earlier work. When Narasiṃha Mahetā, the fifteenth-century devotional poet of Gujarat, came to be considered the *ādikavi* in modern Gujarati literary history (in Narmad's *Kavicaritra,* Lives of the Poets, 1866), three centuries of notable literary production were dismissed in the interests of a new, more regional variety. Such developments can be found in many places in premodern South Asia.[23] Yet most of the objections just catalogued to charting a history of vernacularization pose problems more of detail than of foundations, whereas most of the basic reservations about beginnings cannot withstand serious scrutiny.

One such assumption, endlessly repeated and never examined, is that vast amounts of literature everywhere must have preexisted the earliest surviving texts but have unaccountably vanished without a trace: five hundred years of Marathi literature, seven hundred years of Newari literature—a thousand years of Khmer literature, which George Coedès held was destroyed in "the one long series of disastrous wars" that is the history of Cambodia. When the Javanist P. J. Zoetmulder expressed doubts about the existence of this Khmer literature at any time during the Sanskrit cosmopolitan period, pointing to the preservation of vernacular literary texts in Java under conditions not dissimilar to what Coedès believed accounted for the disappearance of such texts in Cambodia, he was hinting at an analysis that accords far better with what we actually do know, namely, that a language could and did exist—easily and vigorously and sometimes even knowledgeably—as a communicative medium and even as a conceptual category while remaining wholly excluded from the sphere of written imaginative or political text production.[24] Nowhere is the history of expressive, workly texts of literature and political discourse found to be coextensive with the history of a language. Literary silence

23. See chapter 10.4 on the second vernacular revolution. On the elevation of Narasiṃha to the status of first poet, see Yashaschandra 2003: 587 ff.

24. Zoetmulder 1974: 17 (though he backtracks on p. 50), who cites Coedès. The same arguments might apply to western Europe: the tradition that preserved the Goliardic Latin poets

is real, and it can be broken; and when it is broken, something truly consequential in history is taking place.

When we observe the breaking of this silence in Telugu in the ninth century by the inscriptional poets of Rāyalasīma and the courtly poets of the Veṅgi Cāḷukyas; in Marathi in the thirteenth century by Mhāibhaṭa, Jñāndev, and other poet-philosophers in or around the Yādava court with their own inscriptional writers; in Newari in the seventeenth century by the royal playwrights and makers of vernacular *praśasti*s in Bhaktapur and Pāṭaṇ—we are encountering the same kinds of literary beginnings found in the cosmopolitan worlds of a millennium earlier: in Sanskrit with the *Vālmīki Rāmāyaṇa* and the exemplary new *praśasti* literature signaled by the work of the Kṣatrapa overlord Rudradāman, and in Rome with Livius Andronicus's Latin adaptations of Homer and Greek drama after a centuries-long literary void. These kinds of beginnings are found in later European history, too, in the twelfth century when intellectuals at the Anglo-Norman court invented French literature and the troubadours at southern French courts created a new poetry in Occitan, or two centuries later when Dante and his immediate predecessors began to produce a Florentine literature. The same kind of rupture in the historical continuum, if on a smaller scale, is seen in genre innovations: in the creation of the Gujarati novel in 1866 with *Karaṇaghelo* by Nandaśaṅkar Mehta, of the Gothic novel in 1764 with Walpole's *Castle of Otranto,* and of Spanish drama on December 24, 1492 with Juan del Encina's performance at the court of the Duke of Alba.[25]

The historical beginnings of vernacular traditions are beginnings in the strong sense of breaking with the past to produce not just something innovative in genre or style but a whole new cultural modality, a new way of being in the world. The calendrical identifications of the break are not offered here as absolute truths. In some instances the accounts I give—of this historical moment or that particular actor—are probably mistaken or will someday be shown to be mistaken. Inscriptions can indeed be destroyed and manuscripts can vanish (though hardly centuries of inscriptions and manuscripts), and heirs of the traditions in which such ruptures occurred did sometimes conceal or revise them. But absolute temporal precision is a secondary issue, high though the stakes have sometimes been, especially in nationalist discourse.[26] More significant is the general proposition that at certain points

---

would have preserved pre-twelfth-century French poetry, had there been any, much as early-medieval Irish poetry was preserved under comparable circumstances.

25. For the Spanish theater, Gumbrecht 1988: 37.

26. The nationalist politics of beginnings is illustrated in the controversy over the *chanson de geste* (Bloch 1989 and 1990). In South Asia, attempts to affiliate a *bhāṣā* with the oldest possible linguistic stratum is a hallmark of nationalist literary history. Bangla is often taken to begin with the tenth-century Apabhramsha *caryāpada*s—texts also claimed by Oriya and Maithili.

in history people actively transformed the structures of culture (and concomitantly of power) in their world, and that they knew full well they were doing so, sometimes recording the event by commemorating a primal poet or producing an ethnohistorical genealogy of poets that posits an absolute beginning of a tradition. Of course we know that forms of Telugu had been used long before the experiments of the tenth-century Andhra literati, that forms of Marathi existed before the works of the Vārkarī and Mahānubhāv spiritual masters, that there was Latin before the productions of the Greek- and Oscan-speaking innovators, and French before the activities of the creative intellectuals at the court of Henry I. But with the Norman courtiers, with Ennius and Naevius and Livius, with Jñāneśvar and Mhāibhaṭa, and with the Telugu poets in Veṅgi and Rāyalasīma a momentous literary-historical inauguration is marked. We have the evidence to see these acts of vernacularization actually happening. What we need to analyze more precisely are the specific factors that made them possible.

Two decisive steps were taken, and these were historically, and necessarily, related. First, poets asserted local literary culture by acquiring—or sometimes seizing—the privilege of writing expressively after centuries of exclusion. In some cases this exclusion was the result of asymmetries of social privilege. More often it was connected with the fact already noted, that the literary and the political functions, closely correlated, were regarded as necessarily transregional in their idiom and their aspiration. Second, vernacular poets achieved literary expressivity by appropriating and domesticating models of literary-language use from superposed cultural formations. Literization, or writing the vernacular, does not on its own inaugurate the process of vernacularization; it must be combined with literarization, the creation of new literary discourse (and often, though not always, with its congener, political discourse). Making literature as such, and as something distinct from anything else—to say nothing of making history with literature—requires writing it down. But writing literarily can only emerge out of a matrix of other preexisting and dominant literatures. These two factors and the various claims associated with them are examined in the following two sections.

8.2 FROM LANGUAGE TO TEXT

Just as the inscriptional record demonstrates that the vernaculars were from the first excluded from the literary function as typified in the literary subgenre of political praise-poetry, so a range of softer evidence confirms the cultural axiom that *kāvya* was a cosmopolitan cultural practice presupposing the use of cosmopolitan language. Two texts introduced earlier are particularly illuminating here. Both were written in the late twelfth century, when the vernacular transformation was everywhere coming into evidence and the older mentality of cosmopolitanism was consequently being thrown into high relief.

We can be brisk with the *Bhāvaprakāśana* of Śāradātanaya, already discussed in connection with the geocultural matrix of Sanskrit culture and the prevernacular accounting of literary languages (chapters 5.1 and 2.2). That Śāradātanaya was fully aware of the multiplicity of spoken languages actually existing in the Sanskrit cosmopolis is clear from the list he supplies. Although his catalogue of eighteen languages differs to some extent from those familiar from Buddhist and Jain traditions (as well as from other, longer lists such as one in Kannada that gives fifty-six, chapter 9.4), these are fully and distinctly individuated codes for Śāradātanaya—as they were for the late-eighth-century writer Uddyotanasūri, who supplies yet another grouping and set of instances (chapter 2.2). At the same time, Śāradātanaya makes clear what Uddyotana leaves implicit. The earlier author, who wrote in Maharashtri Prakrit with occasional mimetic use of other languages, fully acknowledged and indeed practiced the axiom that literature is an enterprise for cosmopolitan languages, and thus none of the sixteen regional idioms he refers to were, or could be, codes for *kāvya*. According to Śāradātanaya, however, the eighteen languages by which the various people of the sixty-four regions of Bhāratavarṣa communicate with each other "are everywhere known as uncultured *(mleccha)*. Musical compositions are however produced in them in the various regions, which the learned call 'local' *(deśī)* or 'localized' *(deśika)*." By contrast, the languages used for drama, and by extension for literature as such, are the familiar restricted set: Sanskrit, the forms of Prakrit, and Apabhramsha.[27]

No doubt some vagueness attaches to several of these regional language categories; the number eighteen, long consecrated in Sanskrit thought (however unclear its origins in application to language), must willy-nilly be filled up. Yet the main point for our discussion is unambiguous: the cosmopolitan intellectual's old conviction that literature as such is composed only in cosmopolitan languages. Sanskrit above all but also Prakrit and Apabhramsha was still being reasserted as late as the twelfth century. Even in drama, regionalized identities were still not to be represented by actually existing local idioms such as Marathi but rather by the grammaticized and thus translocal (and entirely bookish) Prakrits, such as Shauraseni. By contrast, the world of the "uncultured," that is, of the uncourtly and noncosmopolitan languages of Place, was subliterary: a domain of the sung, the unwritten, the oral.

27. *Bhāvaprakāśana* 10.172–77, pp. 452–53 (see chapter 2.2). The eighteen culture areas are Dramiḍa, Kannaḍa, Āndhra, Hūṇa, Himmīra, Siṃhala, Pallava [*sic;* read Pahlava], Yavana, Jaina, Pārvatīya, Pāmara, Kaṣa [Nepal], Vardhrakas, Kāmboja, Śaka, Nagna, Vākaṭa, and Koṅkaṇa. Some of these are obscure. "Jaina" might signify a form of Gujarati; it is unclear what specifically Vardhraka, Kāmboja, Śaka, and Nagna mean in terms of language practice. "Musical compositions are however produced in them in various regions," *tattaddeśeṣu saṅgītaṃ tattadbhāṣābhir anvitam.*

The picture we get from the *Bhāvaprakāśana*'s brief list is reinforced by the remarkable discussion of vernacular language and its cultural functions in the contemporaneous *Mānasollāsa,* the great royal encyclopedia composed by King Someśvara in northern Karnataka in 1131 (its account of *kāvya* as a courtly practice was examined in chapter 4.3). Some elements of song were no doubt incorporated in storytelling, but song itself, *gīta* or *gīti,* is not discussed by Someśvara in his chapters on *kāvya,* which, as we saw, are located in the sections named "the entertainment of learned discourse" *(śāstravinoda)* and "the entertainment of storytelling" *(kathāvinoda).* Instead, song is differentiated from literature by being treated as an entertainment in its own right *(gītavinoda).* It is only here, in relation to song, that the vernacular languages enter into discussion for the author of the *Mānasollāsa.* And when it comes to song, all that has been shown to constitute the literary, from the Ways of writing to figures of speech to grammaticality—in brief, the special "unity of word and meaning" that defined *kāvya* from at least the time of Bhāmaha in the seventh century—no longer applies.

This does not mean that song was an untheorized activity; far from it. Nothing in old India was untheorized. Someśvara's chapter on *gītavinoda* is a detailed inventory and taxonomy of melody, rhythm, prosody, and so on, as well as an authorization of their uses—thus including everything that typically goes into the making of "theory" in Sanskrit culture. Moreover, the text avers, unlike unaccomplished singers, who do not understand the words of a song, the best singers are indeed knowledgeable in grammar, figures of speech, the arts in general, and the theory of singing in particular.[28] Among a singer's primary attainments—and what distinguishes him most fundamentally from the poets and storytellers—is his expertise in the languages of Place: he is *deśabhāṣāviśārada.* The text states this connection between song and language of Place unequivocally:

> From the *Sāmaveda* first derived sounds *(svara);* from sounds, notes *(grāma);* from notes, scales *(jāti);* from scales, the determination of melody *(rāganirṇaya);* from melody were derived [or: related to melody are] the spoken languages *(bhāṣā);* from them, the dialects *(vibhāṣā);* and from them, the local codes *(antarabhāṣikā).*[29]

Since the languages of Place were thus intimately linked to melody and rhythm, the choice of a language of Place was similarly closely connected with genre, as we will see momentarily.

28. *Mānasollāsa* 4.18, vol. 3: 2; 4.20–21, vol. 3: 3.

29. *Mānasollāsa* 4.120–21, vol. 3: 12; for *deśabhāṣāviśārada* see 4.22, vol. 3: 3. If the vernacular was reserved for song, naturally not all song was reserved for the vernacular (cf. *Viṣṇudharmottarapurāṇa* 3.2.10–11: "Song is twofold: Sanskrit or Prakrit. A third variety is *apabhraṣṭa,* but it is limitless; because of the various regional languages, no limit can be put upon it").

After describing melody the chapter proceeds, by way of a discussion of their metrical organization, to provide examples of an array of songs (*prabandhas*, "compositions") in the languages of Place.[30] Determining with certitude which languages are being represented is not always easy. For one thing, except for naming Kannada *(karṇāṭā bhāṣā)* and Gujarati *(lāṭī)* (besides of course Sanskrit, Prakrit, and Apabhramsha), the text is silent about language identities. This is not surprising, for it is in part through *literary* production and other, related stable forms of elaboration that languages are unified and conceptually and discursively constituted as such in the first place. A second impediment is the serious corruption to which the non-Sanskrit materials throughout the work have been exposed in the course of manuscript transmission. The gradual loss in the later medieval period of the polyglot knowledge that the text suggests was once deep and extensive may be a sign of the increased "incommunication" that vernacularity brings in its wake.[31] Despite these obstacles, several of the languages exemplified by the *Mānasollāsa* can be identified as forms of Avadhi, Bangla or Oriya, Lati, Madhyadeshiya, Magadhi, and Marathi.[32]

A notable feature of the *Mānasollāsa*'s conception of the crystallizing vernaculars is their restriction to particular genres or social contexts. Some kinds of compositions, such as the *ṣaṭpadī* (six-measure), are to be sung only in Kannada (v. 289), others only in Gujarati. Some are to be sung in mixed language, like the *haṃsapada* (perhaps a waddling "goose's step"), the first half of which is in Sanskrit, the second half in a language of Place (vv. 321, 323). The *śukasārikā* (parrot-mynah), a question-answer song, is half in Kannada and half in Gujarati (vv. 329–30). The *vicitra* (harlequin) composition is a polyglot genre describing the Ten Avatars of Viṣṇu, the example offered proceeding from Kannada and Marathi to Madhyadeshiya, Bangla, and then Sanskrit (v. 339).[33] Some genres, such as the *paddhaḍī,* can be in any language (vv. 316, 318). Someśvara summarizes his discussion as follows:

> This wide variety of worldly compositions *(prabandhā laukikāḥ)* are to be sung at feasts and at various functions. The three-measure *(tripadī)* [in Kannada, v. 280] on a theme of frustrated love is typically sung while threshing by those plying the tools. The six-measure (*ṣaṭpadī*) [in Kannada] is used in tales *(kathā),* the *dhavala* [in Apabhramsha] at weddings; the auspicious *(maṅgala)* is to be sung at festivals, and the *caryā* [in Bangla or Oriya; v. 380] is to be sung by spir-

30. The description of melody is found in *Mānasollāsa* 4.123–98, vol. 3: 12–20.

31. On "incommunication" and its history, whereby multilingual capacities in premodernity were eroded by the monolingualization of modernity, see Kaviraj 1992b: 26.

32. See Bhayani 1993: 297–309 (Madhyadeshiya, or language of the Midlands, is Bhayani's term). My debt to Bhayani's work is obvious throughout the following discussion.

33. The reference in Entwistle and Mallison 1994: 63 (citing Mallison 1986: 25 n. 68) presumably refers to this passage (thus read 1131 for 1113).

> itual adepts. The *ovī* is sung at threshing time by women in Maharashtra; the *caccarī* [in Apabhramsha[34], v. 302–3] at the Holi festival, and the *rāhaḍī* when a warrior is described [cf. v. 419]. The *danti* is to be sung by cowherds in their own languages. So much for the different domains of songs . . . The rules governing these compositions in terms of rhythm, language, *rāga,* tones, *pāṭa* (?), and key notes *(tenaka)* have to be followed in singing and must not be broken. Breaking the rules produces faults and the violation of norms. For all other compositions [where] there is no restriction as to language I have adduced illustrations in Sanskrit only for purposes of instruction.[35]

On the evidence of this remarkable document several inferences about the history of South Asian vernacularization, not easily harmonized with each other, suggest themselves. The most obvious, which gains probability when measured against the discourse on *kāvya* (chapter 2.2, 3) and the other data adduced from the history of inscriptions and Sanskrit cultural theory, is that for this particular observer at a powerful court in the mid-twelfth-century Deccan the world of vernacular culture was still largely untouched by the production of literature. Marathi, Gujarati, and the other languages of Place remained excluded from the courtly practice of *kāvya* and were of concern to the author only in the domain of song. As in early vernacular Europe, and in accordance with an older language-genre model obtaining in the South Asian cosmopolitan world (where Maharashtri Prakrit was used for *gāthā,* or pastoral poetry, for example, and Sanskrit for *ākhyāyikā,* or dynastic prose poems, chapter 2.2), there was a division of genre labor among languages: the *caryā* was sung only in Bangla/Oriya, the *ovī* only in Marathi. Later, in the era of high vernacularization, however, all languages of Place would seek to perform most varieties of literary work, as was the case also in vernacular Europe after the energies of nationalism had begun narrowing language choice.[36]

The one exception to Someśvara's exclusion of the vernaculars from the literary function is constituted by Kannada, the language of the king's own realm, which for some three centuries had been the object of sustained literary cultivation. The fact that even while promoting his local idiom in this fashion Someśvara should have retained the mentality of the cosmopolitan intellectual—he is credited with a Sanskrit *mahākāvya,* the *Vikramāṅkābhyudaya,* in honor of his celebrated father Vikramāditya VI, an imitation of Bil-

34. The text identifies the language of the *caccarī* as *prākṛtabhāṣā,* though it is clearly Apabhramsha. This attractive *caccarī* song ("[In the spring], farmers recite the poems of the King, sing them according to meter and rhythm," etc.) has been brilliantly restored by Bhayani.

35. *Mānasollāsa* 4.550–58, vol. 3: 81–82.

36. On language and genre in early India see chapter 2 n. 58; for late-medieval Europe, Armstrong 1982: 269 (Castilian was used for solemn prose, Galician-Portuguese for lyrics, Norman for didactic works).

haṇa's *Vikramāṅkadevacarita* of c. 1080—by no means represents a contradiction at this epoch of the vernacular revolution. On the contrary, it was precisely such an orientation that led to the synthesis of registers that lies at the heart of early Kannada literature (chapter 9.3).[37] The same ecumenical impulse seems to have prompted Someśvara to record and define the full range of cultural practices—albeit as subliterary practices for him—from across India, from Bihar and Orissa to Maharashtra and Gujarat. The king clearly meant to show that he knew the whole world of culture and the character and proper place of each item within it, that he was indeed a true cosmopolitan of the vernaculars.

Equally important as the *Mānasollāsa*'s discussion of the restriction of *kāvya* to the three traditional literary languages (along with the author's own newly enhanced vernacular) are the textualizations it provides of the vernacular songs. In fact, these passages represent some of the oldest examples of written poetry in a number of north Indian languages, which is otherwise exceedingly rare at this period and for several centuries to come. How marginal to literary culture the local codes were held to be is suggested by the character of the few additional vernacular textualizations we have, where they invariably supply, not the body of the text, but a secondary, mimetic feature. This is the case with the *bhāṣācitra,* or polyglot, genre found in Sanskrit literature, as is illustrated by the following verse preserved in an anthology prepared at the court of the Śākambharī Chauhans in 1363, and attributed to one Śrikaṇṭhapaṇḍita (Sanskrit words are italicized; words in various languages other than Sanskrit are in roman):

> *nūnaṃ* bādala chāi kheha pasarī *niḥśrāṇaśabdaḥ kharaḥ*
> *śatruṃ* pāḍi luṭāli toḍi hanisauṁ *evaṃ bhaṇanty udbhaṭāḥ* |
> jhūṭe *garva* bharāmaghāli *sahasā* re kanta mere kahe
> *kaṇṭhe* pāga *niveśa* jāha *śaraṇaṃ śrīmalladevaṃ prabhum* ||

> Clouds are gathering and covering the sky, the herds of asses are braying harshly. The soldiers cry out, "Let us kill the enemy, strike him, despoil him, cut him down." "My friend," said one to me, "is it not better to give up this false pride at once, remove your headgear and place it at your throat, and take refuge with Lord Śrīmalladeva?"[38]

In this praise-poem to the otherwise unknown king Śrīmalladeva, which is quoting the words of the terrified soldiers under attack from his army, the

37. See chapter 9. The notable exclusion of Tamil and Telugu from Someśvara's survey may reflect continuing hostilities that had long marked Cāḷukya-Cōḻa relations (see especially chapter 3.3).

38. *Śārṅgadharapaddhati* no. 555 (p. 87; the translation in *pāda* c is uncertain), cited in Chaudhuri 1954: 9, who suggests that the later mixed-language poems of Mughal court poets like Rahīm (fl. 1600) were a continuation of this tradition.

vernacular serves purely imitative ends. It is in this same analytic framework that we should place one of the earliest written works of a north Indian vernacular, the so-called *Rāulavela* (Court Diversion), which has been preserved in an inscription from Dhārā (no more precisely datable than 1050–1300). This work, which reports a series of conversations by courtly personnel and courtesans, seems to be, not so much a vernacular poem, but a late Apabhramsha one that cites vernacular speech forms characteristic of the different regions represented. Here again, the vernacular functions as an imitative code rather than as the primary vehicle of a literary composition—precisely what we would expect given the literary theory of Bhoja, overlord of the city where the *Rāulavela* was produced.[39]

What excluded the languages of Place from the domain of *kāvya,* or at least constituted a symptom of their exclusion, was the fact that *kāvya*'s characteristic form, the written expressive text, was for the majority of vernaculars a cultural anomaly as late as the twelfth century. Epigraphical history demonstrates that many vernaculars attained written embodiment only hesitantly and, even having done so, functioned first and for long thereafter only in the documentary sphere. This situation persisted until texts such as Someśvara's began to demonstrate the possibility, if only at the boundary of the literary, of making the languages of Place speak expressively in script.

Scholars have paid insufficient attention to the fact that the history of what was constituted as the literary in South Asia was profoundly shaped by written textuality—and that this alone makes it possible for us to know this history. Indeed, these are two reasons why in the present work literary *writing* as a literary-cultural and sociocultural phenomenon—not just a cognitive or technological one—is taken as an essential factor in the development of literature. Since, unlike orality, written textuality as a discrete problem in the history of South Asian literary cultures has never been an object of sustained reflection, every aspect of it remains to be studied. Consider just how enormous is the space-time map covered by the progression of literary writing for the different regional languages of southern Asia. Leaving aside the historiographically convoluted case of Tamil, this development spanned at least three-quarters of a millennium, from around the late eighth or early ninth century, when Kannada (and Javanese and Sinhala) attained literary embodiment of a sort that entered into circulation, to the fourteenth and fifteenth centuries, when an astonishingly intense interest in the textualization of the vernacular seized the minds of northern Indian poets, prompting them to write literature in, for example, Assamese (Mādhava Kandalī, c. 1350), Bangla (Caṇḍidāsa c. 1350), Hindavi (Dāūd 1379), Gwaliyari (Viṣṇudās 1435), and Oriya (Baḷarāmadāsa c. 1450). The size of this map, along with certain

39. On the *Rāulavela* see Bhayani 1994, and cf. McGregor 1984: 7–8 and n. 21. Bhoja's theory of literary language is analyzed in chapter 2.3.

linguistic and ideological factors, makes historicizing the development of literary writing in the vernaculars even more difficult for South Asia than for Europe. Some of the key issues in this development might be clarified by juxtaposing the vernacular with the Sanskrit tradition, where so much of the cultural paradigm for premodern South Asia was defined and with which the vernaculars sought at once continuity and discontinuity.

We have seen how the development of Sanskrit *kāvya* was inseparable from writing (chapter 2.1). The prelude to the *Rāmāyaṇa*, the first poem, could foreground the work's oral origin and transmission only because the new mode of literacy made it possible to conceptually grasp orality as such in the first place. In its structure and complexity the *kāvya* of the post-*Rāmāyaṇa* period is unthinkable without literacy, and it was without a doubt always preserved through literate and not oral transmission. Orality undoubtedly remained central to the performance of *kāvya*, but it was oral performance of a written text, read out from the script when not memorized outright. Such evidence concerning the place of writing in Sanskrit literary culture may not itself answer the many questions pertaining to the creation of vernacular literatures, but it helps us figure out the right questions to ask. What does literization do to create literature? What transformations does it bring about in a text qua text in terms of internal organization, structure of exposition, or degree of novelty?[40] Does a performative vocality continue to manifest itself in written texts?[41] How did poets and scholars in different regional traditions think and write about writing itself? How did they conceptualize what can or should be written, or think about what writing does to change a composition? Was the text committed to writing considered a form of culture different from the one that is not written? (Sanskrit critics give no indication they believed an illiterate Sanskrit poetry was possible, even while fully appreciating the fact that Sanskrit poetry was something orally performed and often memorized.) How, in short, did India's traditions distinguish between what is and is not written—or better, between what exists only when it is performed and what continues to exist afterward because it has attained written form?

It is important to take note of the social dimension of writing in addition to its impact on texts. In South Asia, as often elsewhere, vernacular literary writing (though hardly vernacular writing as such) was sometimes seen as a social resource, subject to control or even hoarding, or as a privilege that could be granted or denied.[42] Writing down a workly text is not only a mode of authorization; it opens up the possibility of dissemination and offers a

40. See Godzich 1994: 79 on the textual consequences of different technologies of the word.

41. See Zumthor 1987.

42. A recent survey (Martin 1994) is curiously silent about the role of writing and social power in the vernacular transformation.

promise, however illusory, of permanence. Authorization, like dissemination and permanence, presupposes the authority and interest of a sociotextual group. Writing is also a form of recognition that the knowledge contained in the language is worthy of preservation, first through the initial act of inscription but also through recopying. All these different factors had central bearing on the capacity of vernacular literature to achieve the breakthrough to literarization.

Despite the fact that these same factors characterized writing in the Sanskrit cosmopolis, an ideology of pure orality nevertheless long continued to assert itself in certain aspects of Sanskrit learning (chapter 2.1). What is noteworthy, and especially pertinent to our discussion, is how this ideology—the phonocentric episteme of Sanskrit, to name it grandiosely—was gradually rejected in the case of the vernaculars. It is striking to register how often and how self-consciously early vernacular texts acknowledge their written existence. Pampa, the tenth-century Kannada writer, promises strength and wealth and other benefits to all "who undertake to read out, and hear, and write [i.e., copy]" his poem, and he complains that the composition of a poetaster "is only a waste of the hands of the copyists, a waste of the pure palm leaves." His successor in the fifteenth century, Kumāravyāsa (Vyāsa the Younger), vows, at the moment he begins to compose his own *Bhārata,* never to arrest his stylus as it races over the palm-leaf page; and he shows Vaiśaṃpāyana, on the verge of recounting the original *Mahābhārata* to Janamejaya, receiving from Vyāsa a book of the poem, which he consecrates with fragrant powders and unhusked grain and from which he then reads aloud. At the start of his Gwaliyari *Mahābhārata,* Viṣṇudās honors the thirty gods, bows his head to Vyāsa, and assures his audience that "If a man reads and appreciates my work, it will remove his sins, and no illness or stain will be there to be seen." At the end of the work, hearing the poem is contrasted with reading it: "He who listens to this work gains the merit of bathing in the Gaṅgā, he who reads it, the good fortune of dharmic acts." And if Sarasvatī, the goddess of learning and literature, who watches over Viṣṇudās's efforts, continues to strum the traditional *vīnā,* her bracelets jingling to mark the rhythm—something that suggests the continuing importance of the auditory experience—she is now shown to hold a book in her hand even while she plays.[43]

43. See *VAV* 14.65: *bhāratakathāsaṃbaṃdhamaṃ bājesal* | *baresal kēḷal oḍarcuvaṃge;* 1.12: *barepakā ṟara kaigaḷa kēḍu, nuṇṇanappaḷakada kēḍu* (*aḷaka* is the cadjan leaf). For Kumāravyāsa see *Karṇāṭabhāratakathāmañjarī* 1.15; 2.8–9 *(koṭṭanu . . . pustakava . . . vitatapustakavanu sugandhākṣateyoḷ arcisi).* The late-tenth-century Kannada poet Ranna got his poem *Gadāyuddha* "corrected" by the Daṇḍanāyaka Kēsi; the verb used is *tirdu,* which here must refer to written emendation (*Sāhasabhīmavijayam* 1.51). For Viṣṇudās, see *Mahābhārata,* respectively, "Ādiparvan" *doha* 3: *paṛhata gunata pātaka harai rogu kalaṃka na disa;* "Svargārohaṇa" (p. 182), *jo ra sune tihi gaṅgā asnānu* | *yo ra paṛhaiṃ tihi dharamu kalyān;* "Ādiparvan" *caupāī* 17: *kara kaṃkana sohahi tālīna* | *pustaka pāni bajāvai vīna* || McGregor 2003: 918, has also noted the importance of this last im-

How prominent writing became in vernacular traditions even in the domain of noncourtly devotional poetry (where the song form might seem more in keeping with the performative context of worship) can be seen in a verse attributed to the fourteenth-century poet Janabāī of Maharashtra:

> Cidānanda Bābā wrote down the words of the verses Jñāneśvar spoke.
> Sopān wrote the words of Nivṛtti, and Jñāndev wrote the sayings of Muktai.
> The one who wrote for Caṅga was Śam the smith, and Kecār was writing the words of Paramānanda.
> What Pūrṇānanda said, Paramānanda wrote . . .
> The one for Savata the gardener was Kaśiba Gurav. Vāsudev was the scribe *(kaita)* of Kūrma.
> Ananta Bhaṭṭ wrote-down-the-verses *(abhyaṅga)* of Cokhamela, and thus Pāṇḍurāṅga wrote down those of Nāma's Jani.[44]

The verse constructs a scribal as well as a spiritual lineage, celebrating the centrality and novelty of a new vernacular literacy (and at the same time showing how widespread across the social orders was the desire to acquire it). The creation of a text in memorable language was no longer simply an oral event, and memorization no longer the preferred mode of storage; writing had become so important that the writer merited mention along with the author. No doubt the commitment to oral performance was maintained, and to oral knowledge as the preeminent form, but the act of writing was now both in fact and in perception a sine qua non of the vernacularization process: not only had languages of Place come to be used for purposes beyond the documentary but that usage was now concretized in a text-artifact.

These few allusions could easily be multiplied to show that literacy was constitutive of vernacularization as a historical process and, what is more, that literacy often took on a cultural and conceptual importance radically at odds with Sanskrit's nostalgic valorization of orality. Something of this complex transformation is suggested by the history of the word *akṣara,* "phoneme" or "syllable," as it migrated from Sanskrit to Kannada (in its *tadbhava,* or derived, form, *akkara*). In the Sanskrit tradition the term had long been associated with the notion that the language is both fundamentally phonocentric as well as eternal and uncreated (*autpattika,* as theorized by Mīmāṃsā), as suggested by its usual etymology: "that which does not decay" *(a-kṣara). Akṣara* also came to connote the Sound par excellence, the primal Sanskrit utterance *oṃ.* Thus when Kṛṣṇa in the *Bhagavadgītā* asserts his greatness by declaring that "Among words I am the single *akṣara*" (10.25), he is identify-

age. The literary culture of medieval Java is likewise literate through and through (Zoetmulder 1974: 126 ff., 137–38, 153, et passim; Robson 1983: 310–12).

44. *Śrī Nāmdev Gāthā* 1970, app. a, "Janabāīce Abhaṅga" section, p. 983, song 408. I thank Christian Novetzke for this reference and for permitting me to cite his translation.

ing himself with this irreducible and eternal core of language. By the tenth century in Karnataka, however, the term had come to predominantly signify written letters, the knowledge of writing, and literacy-based knowledge in general. Inscriptions offer such usages as the "handwriting [signature] of Bhummayya" (*bhummayyanakkaram;* 890), or the "handwriting of Ayyappa Dēva" (*ayyappa dēvanakkara,* 977), while the poet Pampa speaks of the "letters that Fate writes upon the forehead *(nosaloḷ baredakkaram ā vidhātranā),* and Ranna (993) of "the words of the daughter of the sun . . . that shone as brightly as writing carved in stone" *(dinakarasutāvacanam . . . kaṇḍarisi kalloḷiṭṭa akkaramum eṃbinegam esadapudu). Akkarigas* were men who knew letters, and inscriptions detail emoluments to those who made their living by reason of their command of literacy *(akkarigavṛtti),* that is, grammarians. When Pampa describes the greatness of the people of Vanavāsi, in the Kannada heartland, and lays stress on their talent for literacy,

> *cāgada bhōgadakkarada gēyada goṭṭiyalaṃpinimpuga-* |
> *lgāgaram āda mānasar e mānasar . . .* ||

> The people who were a true source for producing the sweetness of charity, enjoyments, letters, song, literary gatherings, and satisfaction—were real people indeed,

or when he speaks of "the gatherings of the lettered, the good words of learned men" *(akkaragoṭṭiyuṃ cadurarolpātuṃ),* the new equivalence of learning and literacy is unmistakable.[45] It was, accordingly, no longer just the *vāgmin,* the "master of speech," who was held to embody learning, as had been the case in the Sanskrit world (chapter 2.1); the "man of letters" now embodied it, too.

This inversion of the semantic field of *akṣara* was no minor semantic anomaly; it represents a significant conceptual transvaluation emerging from within the vernacular domain. Although the instability and changeability of the languages of Place were rarely thematized in South Asia to the same degree as in Europe (where writers feared their vernacular work would become unintelligible within a few generations), the dominant language ideology in India persisting to the very eve of colonialism generally reckoned all vernacular language to be *apabhraṣṭa,* corrupted dialect. Among Sanskrit theorists the vernacular was held not only to result from speaker incompetence but to be incapable of encoding real knowledge. We have seen how this idea took full shape in the seventh century when Kumārila drew a strong correlation between discourse that is true and language that is correct and true,

45. *VAV* 4.29 (on Vanavāsi) and *EI* 20: 68 (a grant of Vikramāditya V, 1012) first aroused my curiosity concerning new meanings of *akṣara.* For the other references cited see *akkara, akkaragoṭṭi* s.v. in *Kannada Nighaṇṭu* (Venkatasubbiah 1975–90).

that is, Sanskritic (chapter 1.2). Even before his time, the argument was standard in scholastic circles that *apabhraṣṭa* language communicates meaning only by reminding the listener of the original, predialectal word from which the *apabhraṣṭa* word was presumed to have been corrupted. Thus the word *akkara* itself, ex hypothesi, could only signify by somehow evoking the "real" word, *akṣara*. As late as the seventeenth century, Sanskrit intellectuals were arguing that the capacity of vernacular literary texts *(bhāṣāprabandha)* to communicate meaning was due "only either to the illusion that they are expressive in themselves, or to the latent presence of the grammatically correct [Sanskrit] words that they suggest."[46] There is thus an interesting irony in the fact that a key descriptor of the eternal and changeless nature of the Sanskrit language, the "changeless syllable" itself, should come to be applied to the ephemeral and changeable vernacular, albeit a vernacular seeking—perhaps precisely because it was a vernacular seeking—to arrest its changeability by writing.

In linguistic terms, the breakthrough to writing in the languages of Place seems to have been an unproblematic occurrence in most of southern Asia.[47] In some regions it occurred more or less simultaneously with the first appearance of Sanskrit writing and was entirely mediated by Sanskrit. But it was not at all a foregone conclusion that mere literization would lead to literarization, the creation of expressive texts in the languages of Place. Writing was indeed a necessary precondition of literariness in the process of vernacularization—this is sufficiently suggested by the prominence of the writer in the verse of Janabāī or the centrality of books and reading in the poems of Pampa and Viṣṇudās. But vernacular literariness was not a necessary consequence of writing; as the time lag evident in the inscriptional record demonstrates, it was a highly contingent development, and when it occurred it constituted a breach in the habitual order of culture and power.

On the formal plane, vernacular literarization presented a challenge in the development of everything from metrics to style and genres. Yet it presented an even greater challenge in the realm of culture-power. The focal point of one dimension of this complex, namely political power, was of course the polity, and the transformation of conceptions of governance that produced vernacularization and were in turn reproduced by it will be examined

46. See further in Pollock 2001b: 26ff.; Houben 1996, Cardona 1999. Not all Sanskrit thinkers conceded the incapacity of dialectal forms. One grammarian argues that the injunction to use "correct language" cannot be made solely for the purpose of achieving communicative efficacy since this efficacy is no less present "in *apabhraṃśa* language used by Drāmilakas [i.e., Tamilians]" than in Sanskrit. Rather, scripture declares that the use of *apabhraṃśa* produces hindrances to spiritual attainments (Vṛṣabha on *Vākyapadīya* 1.129, p. 210).

47. I must entirely pass over issues such as the development of vernacular syllabaries, though the ease with which this occurred in southern Asian contrasts with the situation in medieval Europe (chapter 11 n. 7).

in chapter 10. In other domains of culture-power vernacularization was no less a contested act; indeed, expressive literacy in the vernacular—not mere literacy as such—was often represented as an audacious defiance of the established order. This was not at its core a religiously motivated challenge, as is usually assumed, nor was it necessarily demotic, though both demotic and religious associations were sometimes present. These points can be briefly illustrated by several accounts of vernacular defiance from around the middle of the second millennium, beginning with two narratives transmitted by the Marathi biographer Mahīpati (c. 1715–90). One concerns Eknāth, a Brahman poet-scholar of the late sixteenth century, the other, Tukarām, a Shudra poet of the early seventeenth.

Tukarām, according to Mahīpati's account, had a divine vision one night and thereafter performed hymns of praise *(kīrtana)* to the god Viṣṇu and composed "pleasing and inspired poems" that delighted the people and increased Tukarām's reputation. Evil-minded Brahmans were enraged by this and decided "to tie in a cloth all his manuscripts of poetry and throw them into the water." "You teach principles contrary to religion and lead people to accept devotion *(bhakti),*" they said. "That language of yours is Marathi and therefore impure. It should never be heard." They seized the manuscripts of his metrical compositions called *abhaṅg*s, weighted them with stones, and sank them in the river Indrāyanī, declaring, "If within thirteen days the Life of the World [Viṣṇu] takes them out dry, only then shall we pay them honor." Tuka appealed to his god: "You appeared to me in a dream and ordered and inspired me, ignorant as I was, to write. Why have you brought this calamity on me? It was by your command that I composed these disjointed, misshapen verses; now is it your wish that I should sink these verses into the water?" After thirteen days Tuka's manuscripts were seen floating on the surface of the river, unharmed. In thankful praise he composed seven *abhaṅg*s, all filled with the literary emotion of compassion.

Structurally similar is the story of Eknāth of Pratiṣṭhāna (Paithan) in Maharashtra. "Good and pious people" besought him to write in Marathi a poetic version of the *Bhāgavatapurāṇa,* the central religious-literary work of medieval Vaishnavism. The "great poet," who confessed himself to be "without devotion, without knowledge, unstudied in the *śāstra*s, unread in the Vedas," received "poetic inspiration" by the gift of his guru's blessing. Two chapters of his Marathi version of the eleventh book of the *Bhāgavata* were taken to Vārāṇasī and read out, "with their pleasing style," to some disciples of the leader of a powerful monastic order, who feared that the vernacular *(prākṛta)* text would cause the Sanskrit original to be superseded, "for then no one would care to read the Sanskrit." Summoned to Vārāṇasī to answer for his "improprieties," Eknāth eventually won over the abbot, but other scholars remained hostile and seizing the vernacular text, threw it into the Gaṅgā. Miraculously, the river "lifted up both her arms and caught the book in her hands." All the Brahmans of Vārāṇasī then worshipped the work with due rites and prepared copies of it by their own hand.[48]

Tukarām's work consists largely of confessional-devotional lyrics; Eknāth's carries on a tradition of philosophical poetry in Marathi begun with Jñāneśar's literary reworking of the *Bhagavadgītā*. Admittedly both tales emphasize Sanskrit's claims to religious authority and to a unique communicative capacity for transmitting certain kinds of truth, which the Marathi works were implicitly challenging. But equally important is the stress placed on the aestheticized use of the vernacular and the questionable legitimacy of employing written Marathi for that purpose. It was Tukarām's temerity in putting his poems in writing that provoked the reaction of the traditional literati. And when he defended his use of Marathi—three centuries after the grand declaration of Jñāneśvar that he would make "the blessed era of holy knowledge come to the city of Marathi" (discussed further in chapter 10.1)—he was defending the right not just to sing let alone to speak the vernacular but to write it. As for Tuka's own poetry, it is pervaded by images of literary composition that seem unthinkable for a poet ignorant of writing.[49]

It is this aesthetic handling of the vernacular that is everywhere foregrounded in Mahīpati's accounts. These are texts composed by "master poets" through "poetic inspiration" in a "pleasing style of literary language" and aiming toward a "literary emotional effect," as for example the "compassionate" mood. It is even suggested that Tuka's poems were threatened with destruction at least in part because of their aesthetic shortcomings ("I composed these disjointed, misshapen verses," he confesses).[50] Even given the constraints of religious privilege, it seems improbable that the mere act of inscription of Tukarām's and Eknāth's texts would have prompted the kind of response they did legendarily had they not had such pretensions to the culturally elevated status of literature. It was as much for "writing poetry" in

48. Two versions of the Tukarām tale (here combined) are found in Mahīpati's *Bhaktavijaya* 52: 247–83 (tr. Abbott and Godbole 1934: 289–91, slightly modified here); and *Bhaktilīlāmṛta* 35: 29–152 (tr. Abbott 1930: 202–14, where Tuka's oppressor is named Rāmeśvara Bhaṭṭa of Vagholi, whom he tries to mollify by reciting a hymn to Viṣṇu, "[putting] his gracious words in poetic form"). For Eknāth see *Bhaktilīlāmṛta* 21: 30–202; 22: 1–44 (tr. Abbot 1927: 172–93); "for then no one would care to read the Sanskrit," *maga saṃskṛta koṇī na vācitī* [21: 51]).

49. See for example Chitre ed. 1990: 71, *lekhile kavitva māje sahaja bol;* p. 65, *karī āvaḍī vacane | pāladūni kṣaṇe kṣaṇe.* Generally Tukarām speaks of "making poetry" (cf. p. 63, *karu kavitva kāya nāhī ātā lāj*).

50. The references to the literary are to *Bhaktalīlāmṛta* 21: 61 *(kavīśvara)* and 146 *(kavitva);* 35: 45 *(kavitva bole prasāda vacana); Bhaktavijaya* 52: 254 *(rasāḷa kavitva prāsādika); Bhaktalīlāmṛta* 35: 152 (*karuṇā[-rasa]*) and 56 *(abadda vāṃkuḍeṃ vadaloṃ kāhīṃ).* It is in keeping with the last point that his poetry refers repeatedly to the literary challenge before him ("Have I utterly lost my hold on reality / To imagine myself writing poetry," is a common sentiment in Tuka's oeuvre; tr. Chitre 1991: 5–6).

the vernacular as for the fact that it was poetry on the theme of "ultimate reality" *(kavitva kelem̐ paramārtha lekhan)* that Tukarām was attacked by the Brahmans.[51] What rendered Eknāth's writing of literature so socially problematic was likewise its vernacularity. After all, Eknāth was a Brahman; and while Tukarām was a Shudra (though reportedly a landed Shudra), his subalternity might hardly have mattered if—ironic as this may seem—he had been writing literature in Sanskrit. Kālidāsa himself, who according to persistent legend was a low-caste man inspired by the deity to write, and his many non-Brahman successors—like the potter Ghroṇa, who in Rājaśekhara's eyes wrote Sanskrit poetry "rendered pure by the Goddess of Speech" (chapter 1.1)—would have served as precedents.

That it was less the expression of religious sentiment than the production of written literary work in the vernacular, with all its implications for the broader literary culture, that constituted a large portion of this historic defiance is demonstrated by other versions of the drowned-manuscript motif outside of Maharashtra. According to a seventeenth-century hagiography, the Brajbhasha poet and Puṣṭimārg adept Nanddās (fl. 1570, thus a contemporary of Eknāth) "sang" the tenth book of the *Bhāgavata* "in vernacular verse." When the Brahman reciters of lore and *Bhāgavata* exegetes of Mathurā learned of this, they besought Viṭṭhalnāth, Nanddās's spiritual preceptor, saying, "Our livelihood will disappear as a result of this vernacular *Bhāgavata*." In accordance with his guru's command Nanddās consigned the entire book, except for the *rāslīlā* section, to the Yamunā.[52] In this account the dispute concerns not the authorization to speak of the spiritual in the vernacular, something hardly in short supply in the Puṣṭimārg community at the end of the sixteenth century (though many of the vernacular works appeared only after the death [1530] of the founder, Vallabha, whose own writings were exclusively in Sanskrit). It concerns instead written vernacular literariness, an innovation that threatened an old economy of literary-cultural power based on Sanskrit and a whole class of bilingual intermediaries. Once again, writing is shown to be pivotal: Nanddās might "sing" his vernacular poem at the moment of its creation, but its very existence depended on writing: when he drowns the text-artifact, the text itself drowns, too.

Vernacular assertion, writing, literature, cultural power, and the economy of cultural production are motifs complexly combined in two final examples I wish to cite, one from Bengal, the other from Andhra. The Bangla *Caitanyacaritāmṛta* (The Nectar of the Life of Caitanya), the preeminent poetical

51. *Bhaktalīlāmṛta* 35: 69.

52. *Vārtā* 4 in Gupta 1947: 146 ("sang in vernacular verse," *bhāṣāchandoṃ meṃ gāi*). For directing me to this text I thank Stuart McGregor, who reports that other hagiographies provide other explanations for the fate of Nanddās's vernacular text (on the surviving fragment of which see McGregor 1971: 491).

biography—and decidedly literary biography—of the theologian and mystic Caitanya (d. 1533), was completed by Kṛṣṇadāsa probably around 1600. According to a later account, Caitanya appeared to the poet in a dream and told him, "Describe these things in a book." When the author replied, "It is not in my power to write a book," he was told, "Take hope; Caitanya will enter into you and write." The resulting poem, however, provoked the wrath of the custodians of the Caitanya tradition, especially Jīva Gosvāmin. Outraged that the text was composed in Bangla and worried that it would eclipse the Sanskrit literary and theological works of the Gosvāmins, Jīva flung the manuscript into the river—where it floated unharmed. The *Caitanyacaritāmṛta* was the last in a long series of Bangla-language biographies of the spiritual master. It appeared at least a century after the upsurge of vernacular writing in the Bengal region, it was written by a man steeped in Sanskrit culture, and the text itself offers a very different account of its origins. Yet the old narrative of vernacular rejection and reaffirmation was clearly felt to be applicable—and indeed, it does seem particularly apposite in this case, since there is an unmistakable boldness about the *Caitanyacaritāmṛta,* in its metrical form and linguistic register and in the fact that it actually translates into Bangla much of the Sanskrit it cites. It sought, or could be perceived as seeking, a high vernacular idiom meant not just to parallel the cosmopolitan but to replace it, thereby pointedly challenging the dominant cultural order.[53]

Telugu traditions concerning Śrīnāthuḍu, the premier poet of late fourteenth-century Andhra and author of works that are altogether this-worldly in character (*Bhīmeśvaravilāsamu,* for example, or *Śṛṅgāranaiṣadhamu;* see chapter 10.1), similarly demonstrate that at its core the problematic of writing and culture-power was more about social than religious interactions. A story still told by oral poets regarding the inscription of Śrīnāthuḍu's epic text, the *Palnāṭivīrabhāgavatamu,* reverses the perspective of the topos while preserving its fundamental significations: At the command of the god Cennakēśava, who appeared to him in a dream, Śrīnātha composed a poem about the heroes of Palnāḍu, dictating it to seven scribes over two months. When later the poet recommenced his dissolute life, the god laid a curse on him that his work would come into the hands of untouchables. Distraught at the prospect, Śrīnātha threw the manuscript of his poem into the river—from where men from two low-caste communities, the Māla and Mādiga, retrieved it.[54] Although

53. The tales are from the *Vivartavilāsa* and *Amṛtasārāvalī,* see Dimock 1966: 84–85. In the *Caitanyacaritāmṛta* (trans. Dimock and Stewart) the author is prompted by Kṛṣṇa to write (1.8.45–79). Stewart 1994: 235–37 discusses the text's vernacularity, and Dimock and Stewart 1999: 37–38 its literariness. The text abounds in *alaṅkāra*s but uses only *deśi* meters, not *vṛtta*s, in contrast to other cosmopolitan-vernacular texts. It is also one of few Bangla texts to elicit a Sanskrit commentary.

54. Narayana Rao 1986: 153–54.

the vernacular poem may have been composed orally (to all appearances like the actual oral epic, the *Palnāṭikathā*, of which it is a literary reworking), it was clearly understood to exist in some essential way only in its written version: in that form alone could it be destroyed or seized by others.[55] Equally important is the social logic of the Śrīnātha narrative. Its ironic reversal suggests—and here there is indeed a demotic dimension—that the power of writing and the literature that writing made possible could come into the possession of the lowest of vernacular communities only by accident.

As for Śrīnātha's dream, like those of Kṛṣṇadāsa and Tukarām, it presents another powerfully suggestive motif in tales of vernacular beginnings. The decision to make the vernacular speak literarily is so fraught that it can require the direct intervention of a power beyond that of the dominant cultural order: the power of a divine being. Only thus could the king of Vijayanagara himself, Kṛṣṇadēvarāya, be empowered to write his remarkable poem, the *Āmuktamālyadā*, in Telugu in 1517. In the introduction, a god comes to the author in a dream—a god significantly localized as "the Great Viṣṇu of Andhra"—and announces:

> You astounded us with honeyed poems in the language of the gods . . .
> Is Telugu beyond you? Make a book in Telugu
> now, for my delight.
> Why Telugu? You might ask.
> This is the Telugu land.
> I am the lord of Telugu.
> There is nothing sweeter . . .
> Don't you know?
> Among all the languages of the land,
> Telugu is best.[56]

If the king is to compose a poem in Telugu, and not just compose it but write it down in a book—and especially if it is literature that attempts to offer, as the *Āmuktamālyadā* does, a total vision of governance—he needs less the inspiration of the god than his authorization, and a sort of authorization he might never have needed for the creation of political literature in the language of the gods. The same is true across the social spectrum, from Kshatriyas like Kṛsṇadēva to Brahmans like Śrīnāthudu, Eknāth, and Kṛṣṇadāsa to Shudras like Tukarām. For traditional communities, even as late as the

55. This is precisely the implication of the tale of the lost medieval Tamil Śaiva hymns: when these vanished and were "forgotten" until rediscovered in the Cidambaram temple in the eleventh century, it was the texts themselves that disappeared along with their text-embodiment. See Buck and Paramasivam 1997: 10ff. (and cf. Zvelebil 1973); Shulman 1988: 111–14.

56. *Āmuktamālyadā* 1–13, 15, tr. Narayana Rao 1995: 24. When the late-sixteenth-century poet Keśavdās decides to write the tale of Rāma in (Braj)bhasha, the primal poet Vālmīki appears to him in a dream-vision (*Rāmacandracandrikā* 1.7ff.; see Busch 2003: 96–97).

seventeenth century, to write vernacular literature was almost to turn the cultural world upside down. This aporia at vernacular beginnings and the divine intervention necessary to overcome it will confront us again when we consider Europe and the story of the first English poet, Cædmon (chapter 10.1).

The tales of defiance offered in the vernacular literature itself, along with the strictures on vernacular literary textualization reproduced theoretically in texts like the *Bhāvaprakāśana* and pragmatically in texts like *Mānasollāsa,* represent all the data we have at present for understanding the sociology and ideology of vernacular literacy and literature in premodern India. A properly critical history of literary cultures in South Asian premodernity is only slowly coming within our reach. It will require much greater clarity about the particular social and political factors that determined what might and might not be committed to writing and, more important, which languages were permitted to make literature and which were literarily silenced. For these questions our premodern data may to some degree be supplemented by the work of students of contemporary orality.

Especially instructive is the study of Telugu martial narratives by V. Narayana Rao. Central to his analysis of contemporary epics and the long-term history of their literization (the creation of what he calls "secondary" epics) is the social and aesthetic power of writing itself. His vivid account of the dynamics of the transition to manuscript culture helps us gauge how important writing was for the history of literary vernacularization. "Writing and the materials of writing, like palm leaves," he explains,

> have an almost magical, authoritative significance in oral societies . . . In India, traditional people worship books as deities. People . . . pick up books or paper which they have accidentally hit with their feet and bring them close to their eyes to ask the goddess of knowledge (Sarasvatī) to forgive them for the sin of disrespecting her. For a folk singer, accordingly, the palm-leaf text is worthy of worship. It is also a means of legitimizing his oral text . . . His knowledge [is not] self-validating . . . A performance not based on a text, nor authored by a great sage, is a *pukkiṭi purāṇam,* a merely oral story.[57]

We should be cautious in extrapolating backward from present-day Andhra to Tukarām's seventeenth-century Maharashtra, Viṣṇudās's fifteenth-century Gwalior, or Pampa's tenth-century Karnataka, let alone in thinking of this vast period as one seamless cultural weave. Yet anyone who knows India knows how true is the description of the power of the written text given

57. Narayana Rao 1986: 152 (in view of the tales discussed earlier, rivers probably do not represent "the flowing of oral tradition," p. 155). This assessment is confirmed elsewhere in the same volume by accounts of the "official temple manuscript" present during Tamil bow song performances (p. 176) and of performances of the Maṇikkuṟavaṉ (p. 256).

above. (Indeed, that in India despised manuscripts are destroyed by immersion, a holy act, and rarely burned as in Europe has to do with just this aura of the written word.) There is justification, too, to extend with prudence into earlier vernacular worlds the account that Narayana Rao goes on to provide of the literization of Telugu oral epics. He shows, first, that inscription itself was the procedure for authorizing and authenticating the knowledge of an oral composition and, second, that constituting value through the very medium used to communicate it was reinforced by the pseudonymous attribution of authorship to higher-caste poets, as in the tale of Śrīnātha, and by the renaming of the text with a cosmopolitan accent: thus the simple *Palnāṭikathā,* "Tale of Palnāṭi," was recast as the *Palnāṭivīrabhāgavatamu,* "The Great Vaiṣṇava Epic of the Hero Palnāṭi." Of a piece with these two factors yet even more consequential is a third: literization produced complex textual transformations of narrative and style (such as framing a text with the poet's biography and a statement of his intention in writing the work) that anticipated those of modern editors and printers.

None of this should be taken to suggest that the rise of manuscript culture in India, whether diachronically or synchronically viewed, entailed a clean and permanent break between the oral and the written. To the contrary, the ongoing interaction of the oral and the literate constitutes one of the most remarkable and unique features of Indian literary culture. If oral compositions could be literized, literized compositions could also return to oral circulation, and the interplay between oral and literate composition and transcription could become dizzyingly complex.[58] Then, too, what contemporary field research can tell us is limited: there are often major differences, both cognitive and cultural, between the transcription of an oral performance as an aid to memory or in order to preserve it and the choice to write literature in the languages of Place (even when, as the tale of Śrīnātha shows, the literate poet dictates and leaves the actual inscription to scribes). Clearly, for the vernacular worlds of medieval India, writing was not simply "writing down"; it was a completely different mode of making culture. A number of features at every level of literary culture distinguish written vernacular texts from those produced in a world completely ignorant of writing.

First, a new and unmistakable stability as well as clear limits on modification accrue to the literary text in manuscript culture.[59] Although few manuscripts of Pampa's or Viṣṇudās's *Mahābhārata* now survive, the variants clearly indicate a transmission that in both cases was exclusively literate—copying from one manuscript to another—precisely as was the case for San-

58. See for example Blackburn and Ramanujan 1986: 4–5.

59. At least texts of continuous works. Even in the Sanskrit tradition the effects of oral performance on discontinuous *muktaka* texts such as Bhartṛhari's *śatakas* have been substantial (Pollock 2003: 91).

skrit *kāvya*. This is true even for a poem like Tulsīdās's *Rāmcaritmānas*, perhaps the single most revealing example of the special relationship between oral and written in premodern India. The work of a literate poet produced in written form, the *Mānas* was disseminated far more widely on the lips of wandering performers than on palm leaves. Yet its manuscripts reveal a history of textual transmission that was astonishingly stable and entirely literate, with none of the kind of formulaic variation familiar from oral traditions elsewhere.[60] Second, the formal features exhibited in oral compositions (formulaic expressions, repetition, and other elements noted in relation to the *Palnāṭivīrabhāgavatamu*) are vastly attenuated in literate literature, and written texts also make use of a substantially different set of genres.[61] Third, and as a consequence of the first two properties, a very different status of authorship, whether real or presumed, attaches to a written text. Only authors of written works are included in the canons constructed in ethnohistorical accounts of literature; the oral poet stands entirely outside of history.[62] Fourth, the fact of inscription entails a new spatiotemporal distance between literary production and consumption, between author and reader; an unprecedented consultability of the text, and a host of other features related to cognitive reception and narrative (the rise of the omniscient narrator, for example, is linked to the disappearance of the oral performer). Last, there is an increase in the social asymmetry between textual and nontextual culture—between cultures of face-to-face intimacy and cultures mysteriously mediated by material stuff, even if the medium is something as familiar as the palm leaf or birch bark used for manuscripts in India. It is this asymmetry, and the cosmopolitan culture that long occupied the higher pole in the relationship, that vernacularization challenged by the act of literary writing. And it did so by localizing features of the cosmopolitan literary culture whose very lack in the languages of Place had constituted their inferiority in the first instance.

The history of literary cultures is not inherently continuous, then, broken only by breaks in our archival record and changing only through the quasi-biological process of language change itself. There are true caesuras, and among the most consequential factors are the technological—writing—and the sociocultural—the authority of superposed models discussed in the following section. Before literacy, people may well make "history" of a "lit-

60. Lutgendorf 1991: 9, 117, 11–31, and 141. Especially important on transmission history is Chaubhe 1967: 40–45.

61. On textualization in relation to oral epics in India, see Honko 1998. This work suggests that a more compelling question than identifying individuality (so Martin 1994: 159 on the *jongleurs*) is determining why such material was written down at all, when it was written, and how the oral work is thereby transformed.

62. The literary-historical canons of Kannada and Sanskrit are discussed in chapter 9.2.

erary" kind by using language orally in unprecedented ways. But such oral culture is not only unknowable in its historicity, it is excluded from the literary history made by committing texts to writing. The written not only ceases to be oral in a formal sense; it morphs into a completely new entity. It is no redundancy to say that a literary work does not exist until it becomes literate. Moreover, it is not just the textual consequences of the technology of literacy but also access to this technology and its social acceptability that are shaping forces in the history of literary cultures.

8.3 THERE IS NO PARTHENOGENESIS IN CULTURE

As we have seen, writing as such was a necessary but not a sufficient condition for the inauguration of vernacular literary culture in South Asia, and the transformation of written language into expressive discourse that marked that inauguration was usually separated from the moment of literization, often by centuries. When the transformation did occur, it was through the emulation of superposed models of the literary; no literary culture, indeed, probably no element of culture, is ever entirely self-generated. This last claim can be explored along three parallel routes: by reassessing the common but mistaken notion that literary writing in the vernacular is somehow natural in a way that writing in a cosmopolitan language is not; by reviewing the cosmopolitan conception of the literary as a stable category that fundamentally shaped local cultural expectation and action in the early second millennium; and by exemplifying these general observations with a few instances of early vernacular literarization offered in the epigraphic record.

A distinction between "mother tongue" and "father tongue" is frequently drawn in the analysis of South Asian cultures.[63] This dichotomy is meant to mark vernacular codes as innate, intimate, natural, and artless forms of expression more or less untouched by cultural prescription or normativity, and cosmopolitan languages as exogenous, remote, learned, and learnéd. This contrast—analogous to the old anthropological distinction between "little" and "great" traditions—presupposes that literary creation in the languages of Place is intended as an escape from, and actually does escape from, the realm of power that constrains writing in the elite, dominant, hegemonic, even colonial *Kultursprachen*. In the early South Asian sphere, this meant Sanskrit above all, but later also Persian and English.

Much of this vocabulary and many of the concepts it underwrites are borrowed from elsewhere and are ill-suited to the South Asian context. Notions like "natural" in reference to language, often coupled with "historical" or "living," have been used in the West to distinguish vernacular languages from

63. The distinction was popularized by A. K. Ramanujan (e.g, 1999: 449 [an essay originally written in 1989]).

"artificial" and "formal" languages—French, say, in contrast to Latin.[64] Yet "naturalness" is itself a component of a vernacular language ideology produced in early-modern Europe. Found in several of the anxiety-laden "defenses of the vernacular" written from the fifteenth to the seventeenth centuries (chapter 10.2), the ideology of naturalness takes on heightened value in the domain of literary expression in Romanticism. Wordsworth's "Preface to Lyrical Ballads" (1800) famously enunciated this view when it promised to give its readers "the language really used by men"; even more forcefully formulated was Coleridge's description of Wordsworth's poetry ("To William Wordsworth," 1807) as "a sweet continuous lay" of Truth that was "not learnt, but native, her own natural notes."

Moreover, a cultural as well as a historical mistranslation is at work here. The expression "mother tongue" was current in no Indian lexicon before European expansion (Kannada *tāyinuḍi,* "mother speech" is a modern calque, like other comparable Indian expressions). Moreover, the very applicability of the phenomenon behind the figure—based on assumptions about a singular first language acquired in childhood—has often been challenged for the South Asian context, where, however counterintuitive this may seem to the Western observer, some speakers are known to possess multiple first-language capacities.[65] The historical mistranslation is even more instructive. As applied in the South Asian context, the dichotomy effaces the very distinction it was first devised to capture along with an important insight regarding the elements of power, authority, and control that govern literary writing as such, whether vernacular or cosmopolitan. The belief that language use in literature could ever be natural was already in dispute when Henry David Thoreau first used the distinction in English to contrast the spoken and written forms of one and the same language: "There is a memorable interval between the spoken and the written language . . . . The one is commonly transitory, a sound, a tongue, a dialect merely, almost brutish, and we learn it unconsciously, like the brutes, of our mothers. The other is the maturity and experience of that; if that is our mother tongue, this is our father tongue, a reserved and select expression, too significant to be heard by the ear, which we must be born again in order to speak."[66] To write, Thoreau implies, especially to write literarily, in no matter which language, is to enter a new context of power—even, perhaps, patriarchal power—beyond that of speech. And in this new context of literacy, especially its highest form, lit-

64. For "natural" and the other descriptors in relation to French, see Derrida 1984: 92, 95.

65. Khubchandani 1983: 9. On the gendered metaphor itself see also Ramaswamy 1997: 15 ff.; the representation "mother tongue" is masterfully historicized in Spitzer 1948; Skutnabb-Kangas and Phillipson 1989 provide a contemporary academic perspective.

66. See Thoreau 1995 (1854): 98. I say "in English" because the vernacular as *materna lingua* (and Latin as *sermo patrius*) appears in the early twelfth century (Spitzer 1948: 15 ff.).

erary literacy, every language comes to be invested with unfamiliar and ever more stridently articulated rules of usage. The very capacity to exercise the skill to write literarily is a sign not only of privilege and authority but also of disciplined subordination to norms and constraints. Asserting this capacity is a theme powerfully present in the narratives of vernacularity in Tukarām and others. And what made the assertion in those cases an actual defiance was the enactment in the vernacular of the very norms and constraints of literary Sanskrit that centuries of denial had seemed to render impossible.

The ideology of the naturalness of vernacular literariness was not entirely unknown in premodern South Asia. Regional-language writers, principally those who promoted the second, or "regional," vernacular revolution (chapter 10.4), commonly asserted that their access to *kāvyaśakti,* the talent or inspiration to create literature, was either wholly unmediated by learning and training or, what amounts to the same thing, was conferred by a god. In fact, the trope of intellectual self-depreciation (recall Eknāth's confession of being "without knowledge, unstudied in the *śāstras*") had become so trite by the seventeenth century that Akho, a celebrated Gujarati poet of the period, ridiculed it as completely disingenuous: "Such poets . . . tell us at the beginning of their works, 'We are ignorant of the units of prosody and we don't bring in your figures of speech, having not mastered them.' Through such sniveling disclaimers, they merely establish their self-importance and beg for our pity."[67] In addition, we occasionally meet with the idea that forms of language, if not as singular as contemporary notions of mother tongue, are comparably native *(nija).* The tenth-century literary scholar Ratnaśrījñāna argued that "the Ways of literature are as native as one's [singular] language of Place" (chapter 5.3). Both representations are interesting above all for what they misrepresent: vernacularization is inaugurated when a language of Place is in fact *denaturalized* so as to become literary, and this results from the direct mediation of superposed models of what counts as literature. In most of the South Asian cases before the middle of the second millennium, this meant the superposed model of Sanskrit, whose well-defined character and historical power make the categorical problem of specifying what counts as literature in the process of vernacularization far less bedeviling in India than it has become in Western modernity.

It is perfectly true, from the viewpoint of *pāramārthika sat,* that anything can be literature, since it is not an ontological category but a pragmatic decision. It is also true that the idea of "literature" that Europe brought to India in the late eighteenth century mediates our understanding of the pre-

67. Tr. Yashaschandra 2003: 578 n. One of the earliest disclaimers is Basavaṇṇa's "I don't know anything like time-beats and metre" (tr. Ramanujan 1973, p. 82, no. 494); see also Viṣṇudās's statement quoted in chapter 10.1, and of course Tulsī's (Lutgendorf 1991: 8).

colonial past.[68] And lastly it is true that definitions of the literary in India are saturated with local content: just as one person's history is another's myth, or one person's science another's magic, so what constitutes the literary, and whether there even is a literary, must always in the first instance be a local decision, for change in and contention over the literary occur locally, too. For all these reasons no stipulative definition from whatever source would seem to be of much use; in fact, literary history is largely a history of the continual redefinition or reconstruction of what people have taken the literary to be.

Yet little of this helps us to understand *vyāvahārika sat*—what writers in the vernacular epoch thought they were doing when they turned expressive language into text-artifacts—or to understand the salient fact that nonconventionalist, in fact fundamentally essentialist thinking about literature affected the way people both wrote and read in premodern South Asia. We need to investigate such essentialism from within, both its powerful historical pressures and the resistances to them. The story of South Asian literary culture in part concerns the ongoing confrontation with and contestation of this internal colonization of the field of the literary.

In premodern India at certain times and places people demonstrably began to make and do things with texts that had little in common with earlier kinds of texts and practices. In the case of Sanskrit, this meant producing and using texts that had nothing to do with the archaic liturgical domain (chapter 2). To these new texts various names were given, but ultimately the term *kāvya* and, later and more metadiscursively, *sāhitya* came to predominate. What precisely defines *kāvya* was long a matter of debate, but it was a debate of details, held on the common ground of an old and widespread consensus. It is this older consensus that Bhoja invoked when he said, "People traditionally define literature *(kāvya)* as the 'unity' *(sāhitya)* of word and meaning" (chapter 2.3). Other language uses were characterized by the predominance of one or the other: the wording (in the case of the Vedas) or the meaning (in the case of the *purāṇa*s and *śāstra*s). Literature, however, was a unique form of discourse in which what is said joins with how it is said in an indissoluble unity.

Thus two closely related discursive traits of *sāhityaśāstra,* the science of the literary, need to be kept in mind. First, literature was universally and unambiguously understood to be a phenomenon radically different from all other forms of textuality. Second, theory was both required and able to specify exactly what this difference is (the story of Poetics Woman, beloved of Poetry Man, intimated just this idea, chapter 5.2). If debate about the precise nature of the literary was intense, there was no debate about the fact that

68. Noted by many, e.g., Dharwadker 1993.

it was amenable to conceptualization and description. The very soul of *kāvya* could be inspected and exemplified, and these examples, along with the tradition of discourse that ordered and explained them, modeled a singularly influential form of culture that occupied the entire conceptual domain of aestheticized language use.

Any new vernacular literature, accordingly, had to acknowledge and come to terms with the superposed model established in the cosmopolitan tradition for everything from lexicon and versification to figures, genres, and themes. A few illustrations, drawn from the early epigraphical record from across southern Asia, should suffice to demonstrate some of the ways in which this conformity was achieved. The examples show how, in general, the languages of Place began to put aside the old oral idiom and to speak instead a new *cosmopolitan vernacular,* that synthetic register of an emergent regional literary language that localizes the full spectrum of expressive qualities of the superposed cosmopolitan code.

The verses contained in an undated (perhaps eighth century) charter of the Pāṇṭiya king Cēntaṉ are apparently one of the earliest instances of an aestheticized public political discourse in Tamil. Presenting the Tamil words in roman font shows graphically the effects of superposition at the most intimate levels of language use:

> pāṇḍya*kulamaṇipradīpaṇ* āy *prādurbhāv*añcheydu
> *vikram*aṅgaḷāl araiśaḍakki maṟaṅkeḍuttaṟam perukki |
> *agrahāram* pala cheyd*aparimitam* āgiya *hiraṇyagarbha-*
> *gōsahasratulābhār*attu *mahādān*aṅgaḷāṟ *kali*kaḍindu ||

> He was a jewel lamp to the Pāṇṭiya family [in which] he was born.
> By his prowess he subdued kings, destroyed wickedness, and increased goodness.
> Brahman freeholds he created without limit, and performed many Great Offerings, such as the Golden Embryo,
> Gift of a Thousand Cows, Self-Weighing against Gold, acts by which he chastised the Kali Age.[69]

This is clearly no longer the language or the discursive style that was used for boundary measurements and tax exemptions in the earlier Pallava grants (chapter 3.1); it is the language and style of Sanskrit political poetry gradually being domesticated to the ways of the Tamil world. In addition to the fusion of transregional and regional languages, a number of the topoi familiar from Sanskrit *praśasti* discourse—the troped beauty of the king ("jewel lamp"), his martial valor, moral perfection, and generosity—reappear here in local garb. It is the lord's personal attainments, along with his ritual disci-

69. *EI* 38: 27 ff., tr. Krishnan and preserving his transliteration (the meter is unknown to me). The dating of the grant is made problematic by obscurities in the succession of Pāṇṭiya kings.

pline, that invest with authority and efficacy the endowments that underwrite his kingliness. The grandeur of such accomplishments requires the commensurate grandeur of a cosmopolitan idiom, made palpable by the fact that a good half of the lexemes are Sanskrit. Of a piece with this sort of Pāṇṭiya innovation were developments in Cōḻa political discourse beginning with the reign of Rājarāja I (r. 985–1014). Here we find side by side with the Sanskrit *praśasti* (which is often retained) the *meykkīrtti,* an account of "true fame" or "personal fame," a new public literary-political genre that details the genealogy and achievements of a king along with mention of his *biruḍas*, or titles. The expressive character of this discourse, like its distance from the documentary function, is apparent from the start and becomes increasingly so among the grand productions of Rājarāja's successors. The *meykkīrtti* is marked throughout by a cosmopolitan-vernacular idiom embodied in the term itself, which offers a blending of Tamil *(mey)* and Sanskrit *(kīrti)* that epitomizes the larger cultural (and political) synthesis under way.[70]

Something of the cultural energy of this cosmopolitan-vernacular idiom in Tamil country spread, at a later date, beyond the political and literary domain to become employed in exegetical prose by the theologians of Teṅkalai (southern) Vaishnavism in the twelfth and thirteenth centuries, its perceived hybridity expressed in the new name it acquired: *maṇipravāla* (literally, pearl and coral).[71] But two features about the origin of this style in Tamil country need to be made clear: first, it lay altogether outside the sphere of religion (in addition to the evidence of political poetry, it was theorized first in a courtly grammar of the eleventh century, the *Vīracōḻiyam* [see chapter 10.2]); second, it was not unique to Tamil. *Maṇipravāla* embodied the very process of localization of the Sanskrit universal, in both political discourse and literature, that was occurring across southern Asia from this moment on, with the vernacular at first supplementing Sanskrit and later taking on an ever-increasing proportion as vernacularization gained power and confidence.

A comparable but more richly suggestive vernacular transformation commenced in the Telugu tradition a century or two after this Pāṇṭiya record. Especially instructive is a record issued by the eastern Cāḷukya prince Yuddhamalla sometime between about 890 and 950. A few stanzas (in *madhyāk-*

70. The abbreviated definition of *meykkīrtti* is from the *Madras Tamil Lexicon* s.v., adapting the *Paṉṉirupāṭṭiyal* v. 311 (I owe the reference to the late Norman Cutler). Prior to the Cōḻa period we find other terms, or none: thus a Tamil *praśasti* (so called in the text itself) is preceded by a Sanskrit *praśasti* (so called in the text) in a Pāṇṭiya record of perhaps the eighth century (*EI* 17: 291–309). In *SII* 3: 441 ff., issued by Rājasiṃha III in his sixteenth year (i.e., early tenth century), the Sanskrit *praśasti* (so named, v. 38) is followed by a prose Tamil text containing a highly developed *meykkīrtti* (though not so named).

71. The term appears not to be used widely by medieval Vaiṣṇavas themselves. Alternative interpretations are offered in Freeman 1998; see also chapter 9.2. A useful short history of *maṇipravāla* in Tamil religious culture is Venkatachari 1978.

kara, a moraic verse form) from the opening of this text give a good idea of what it meant to invent a Telugu vernacular political discourse (Telugu words are in roman):

nṛpāṃkusātyantavatsala satyatriṇētra
*vistaraśrīyuddhamall*uṇḍ*anavadyavikhyātakīrtti* ।
*prastutarājāśray*uṇḍu *sakalavastusamēt*uṇḍu *rājasalkibhūvallabh*uṇḍartti ॥
paragaṃga bejavādaṃ gomarasvāmiki *bhakt*uṇḍai guḍiyu ।
*nirupamamati nṛpadhām*uṇḍa etticce negidīrcce maṭhaṃbu ॥

A goad to kings, deeply affectionate [to his subjects], the Three-Eyed God [Śiva] in truth [or, in truthfulness], a man of vast royal glory is Yuddhamalla, whose fame is widespread and irreproachable.
The refuge of illustrious kings, the ornament of the three worlds, endowed with all precious things, beloved of the earth of the Salki [Cāḷukya] kings, [who] with pleasure
Built along the Gaṅgā in Bejavāḍa a temple to Gomarasvāmi, since he was his devotee,
And erected a seminary—this man of peerless intelligence and royal grandeur.[72]

On display here are a language and a register for which Telugu had never before been the vehicle; the idiom and lexicon are those of the Sanskrit *praśasti.* All the traits of lordliness and their peculiar literary formulations in the Sanskrit tradition are applied to Yuddhamalla: warrior violence coupled with parental affection, the particular kind of divinity whose ontology can only be expressed through the literary metaphor, royal charisma *(śrī)* and fame *(kīrti)* that are established by the very illocutionary force of naming them, hierarchical superiority, assertive public generosity, intelligence. The language shows throughout how greedily the vernacular was appropriating the cosmopolitan—without a knowledge of Sanskrit the text would be almost unintelligible—even while gesturing constantly toward the local. It now energizes the Sanskrit with vernacular verbals (e.g., *uṇḍu*), now preserves what seems almost an affectionate indigenizing *tadbhava* "Gomarasāmi" (in place of "Kumārasvāmin," which, with some metrical adjustment, could have been substituted). Equally noteworthy here, if modest and subtle, is the localization of the geocultural matrix, which would everywhere be found at work in the creation of the cosmopolitan vernacular: "along the Gaṅgā in Bejavāḍa" unobtrusively identifies the Kṛṣṇā River, on whose bank the town of Vijayavāḍa is located, with a core cosmopolitan symbol.[73]

A sense of the new expressivity in Marathi is offered by the first workly political text, an inscription of 1305 issued by one Brahmadevarāṇe, "pleni-

72. *EI* 15: 150–59, tr. Pantulu.

73. The many records of which the Yuddhamalla document is representative show that the *deśī* qualities and "chaste Telugu" some have seen in the early Telugu epigraphs (Nagaraju 1995) are an illusion.

potentary *(sarvādhikāri)* who subsists off the lotus feet of the Yādava king, Rāmacandra, the wheel-turning king of vast power." It contains several fragmentary verses in *ovī* meter, preceded by a prose passage describing the reconstruction of an earlier "self-manifested" temple in the town of Velāpur (Marathi words and morphemes are in roman):

> . . . yāpurī *puṇya* joḍīleṃ *kīrtti pātalā* to *gāḍha* vāṣeyā vāṣāṇi jaida *kiṃ varṇo mahimā gajāgajadhurā brahmena* tayā *seva*kute.
>
> paiṃ *kīrtivilāsu* kālu galilā satreṃ *dhvaje* lāgalāṃ ।
> *cau* < . . . > dhiṃ cālata bhītarī *dvijavarī*ṃ *o* < . . . > vālilā *suravar*iṃ
> *gaganī*ṃ *varṇik*iṃ gāyilā vaṭaiā hā *bhavatu devatā* ।
> *vaṭesvarā pujā* < . . . > *janma* < . . . > nāhi *hṛdayā* kīru < . . . >
> kumārukājā ।
>
> . . . In this way, he acquired merit and attained fame. How can the greatness of his victory, which has been praised in profound words, be described? Brahma[-devarāṇe], the most excellent one, by the service he has rendered,
>
> without doubt, to his own great glory, he has swallowed [all-devouring] Time itself. His flag has been planted for a long time. Four Brahmans have walked in and done worship to him; the gods in the sky have sung his praises in verse. Vaṭaiā [Vaṭeśvara] is his god, his deity. Worship of Vaṭeśvara is his life's greatest deed. Truly he [has] not [done this] for the sake of a son.[74]

Much of the argument of this text is unclear, but what is most salient about it is not: that an argument is being made, and in a newly expressive language. No longer was the vernacular used simply to report an act and record a state of affairs ("In the year *Śaka* 982 . . . two charters regarding the town of Sthitipuri were deposited with Mālavabhaṭṭa by the village assembly . . . Further, one hundred and twenty seven gold pieces were deposited with Dāvodara for the maintenance of the assembly. This deed was witnessed by . . . ").[75] It is now directed toward producing an act, a speech act, and changing states of affairs, affairs of the imagination. As was so often the case in the cosmopolitan cultural order, the reader or listener is meant to be persuaded of the fame and grandeur of the patron. And as in the overdetermined world of Sanskrit-style *praśasti,* this fame and grandeur must be named by the poet, who succeeds in augmenting them by the very admission that he is defeated in the attempt. All this is the expressive province of *kāvya.*

The first workly political inscriptions in Java appeared even earlier than their mid-ninth-century peers in Kannada and Telugu. The first versified epigraph is a remarkable record from 856 that exhibits full control of the panoply of quantitative meters (*vasantatilakā* is used in the selection that

74. Tulpule 1963: 248–55. I thank Anne Feldhaus for her help with this uncertain text.
75. *EI* 38: 121–24 (dated 1060 C.E.)

follows), which are adapted only with considerable difficulty to the Javanese language, as well as the figures of sense and especially sound that characterize Sanskrit *kāvya.* The work is remarkable for what in Sanskrit is termed the quality of *citra,* or brilliance (it is replete with *yamakas*, *prahelikās*, and the like). Indeed, the text exemplifies the true autotelic nature of *kāvya,* where the real subject of the poem is the poetic use of language itself. Only one strophe is needed to demonstrate all this (Javanese words and morphemes are in roman):

tlas maṅkan*oparata* sang *prabhu jāti* ning rat
rājya [*sic*] karatwanasiliḥ taṅanān inangsö |
dyaḥ *lokapāla* ra*nujāmata lokapāla*
*swasth*ang *prajā sacaturāśrama wipramukhya* ||

After these [deeds], the king Jātiningrat [Birth of the World] resigned; the kingship and the court were handed over to his successor: Dyaḥ Lokapāla [Guardian of the World], who was equal to a younger brother of the [divine] Lokapāla; free were his subjects, divided into the four *āśramas* with the Brahmans at the head.[76]

Viewed from within the paradigm of vernacularization, the localization of the cosmopolitan aesthetic here looks very familiar indeed, though this should not mislead us into ignoring or underestimating the mastery and genius involved in wedding the two in this particular case (see further in chapter 10.1).

From south India and Southeast Asia we turn briefly to the west and north. The presence of the cosmopolitan idiom made itself visible with particular insistence in the first literary inscriptions of what is now called Gujarat-Rajasthan. Among the oldest is the Mewar *praśasti* of 1489 mentioned earlier. Near the end of a bravura performance in Sanskrit the poet declares, in the metapragmatic mode still necessary for announcing the unprecedented vernacular experiment, "In accordance with the king's command we now write down a few lines in our language of Place [here, Old Gujarati], which is readily understandable to those unskilled in the language of the gods." Here is a sample of what he writes (Gujarati words are in roman):

tiriyā *putra dvāparadharmmāvatāra vidvajjanadainyadavadahanadāvānala pīrojakhānamānamarddana rājavṛntaparamācārya śrī mokalendra* huā . . .

He had a son, Śrī Mokalendra, an incarnation of the *dharma* of the Dvāpara Age, a forest fire to burn the thickets of despair of the learned, one who crushed

76. De Casparis 1956: 280–330; pp. 312 and 318 (this Lokapāla would be remembered half a millennium later, in a grant issued by Hayam Wuruk in 1367, as an incarnation of Wiṣṇu come to earth; see Worsley 1991: 184). De Casparis notes the text's chronological primacy but not the cultural-historical significance of its being written in Javanese rather than Sanskrit—another example of looking directly at emergent vernacularity without seeing it (cf. chapter 9 n. 7).

> the pride of Pīrojakhāna [Firoz Shah] and was the supreme teacher of the hosts of kings . . .[77]

One may indeed wonder whether the occasional use of a vernacular pronoun *(tiriyā)* or finite form *(huā),* like the use of the Telugu verbal in the earlier example, sufficed to render more intelligible such complex art-prose for those unskilled in the language of the gods. But this is only to point to a question that is omnipresent in the analysis of the social realities of vernacular literariness: Could vernacularization have truly been directed toward facilitating communication, as many scholars believe—and as the introduction to this example itself suggests—when that goal is so clearly defeated in the very act of trying to achieve it? Or was vernacularization seeking some other cultural-political value less amenable to functionalist explanation?

Something of just this nonfunctionalist, aesthetic component is suggested by a final example from seventeenth-century political discourse in Newari. Although Newari may never have assumed as autonomous a role in political expression as what can be found elsewhere, it did begin to assert itself in a new way that offered an appropriate complement to the innovative literary production noted earlier. One inscription (1655) of Jayapratāpamalla, who in the best cultural fashion of the Sanskrit cosmopolis styled himself *kavīndra,* king of poets, opens with a prodigious compound some four hundred syllables in length (slightly abbreviated in the following selection; Newari words are in roman):

> *ripumuṇḍamaṇḍalakhaṇḍanapracaṇḍakāṇḍamaṇḍitakodaṇḍālaṅkṛtabhujadaṇḍadānasantānasammānitaguṇigaṇagīyamānānavadyagadyapadyādivividhakāvyakaraṇacāturīdhurīṇasatatakṛtamīmāṃsānyāyapātañjalavedāntavaiśeṣikavyākaraṇakāvyakoṣālaṅkārādisakalaśāstrānuśaraṇasugatamatavinoditāntaṣkaraṇaśitikaṇṭhabhālanayanasamutthabālavahnibhasmībhūtasmarasmaraṇānutsukakaraṇasundaraśrīśrīśrīpaśupatipādapāthojaparāgarāgitaśrīmanmāneśvarīṣṭadevatāvaralabdhaprasādadedīpyamānaravikulatilakahanūmaddhvajanepāleśvaramahārājādhirājabhupakesariśrīśrīkavīndrajayapratāpamalladevena* thama thva *śloka* ciṅāv *stotra* yāṅāv thva *sāhāsana* rohosa coskāva taysa juro.

> His arm adorned with a bow furnished with an arrow furious in destroying the mobs of his lowly foes; honored for his constant charity; foremost in the skill of making literature of different kinds, whether prose or verse, faultless literature eulogized by the crowds of connoisseurs; constantly taking refuge in all the *śāstras*—hermeneutics, logic, yoga, Vedānta, cosmology, grammar, litera-

77. *A Collection of Prakrit and Sanskrit Inscriptions* p. 123 (for *rājavṛnta* read *rājavṛnda*). The Sanskrit introduction runs: *gīrvāṇavāṇyām avicakṣaṇair narais sukhāvaseyāni vacāṃsi kānicit*| *sadeśabhāṣām* [read: *svadeśabhāṣām*] *anusṛtya bhūpater anujñayā lekhapathaṃ nayāmahe*|| For the Gujarati genealogy see p. 123. In Madhyadeshiya, *praśasti* remains unaccountably rare and the documentary function is primary. Typical is a record of Mahmūd Shāh II of Malwa (1513 C.E.) on remission of taxes, with an opening formula in Sanskrit (*EI* 15: 291–93).

> ture, lexicography, rhetoric; his heart delighting in the doctrine of the Buddha; ornament of the Solar dynasty ablaze with the grace derived from a boon from his Chosen Deity, the glorious Māneśvarī, who herself is rouged by red pollen from the lotus-feet of the thrice-glorious Śiva Paśupati, so handsome a god as to satisfy the longing coming from calling to mind the God of Love, who himself had been burned to ashes by a small flame shooting forth from the forehead eye of Śiva; the banner of Hanumān; the king of Nepal, the king of kings, the twice-glorious king of poets, Jayapratāpamalla himself composed these verses, made the hymn of praise, caused it to be written as an inscription on stone, and put it in place.

There follows another mighty Sanskrit compound that leads into the genealogy of the Koch Bihar kings (their succession is marked with Newari possessives), the end of the text reverting to vernacular documentation of the temple the king and his queen built on the Cowtail Mountain. Every topos of kingship coupled with every trope of literary Sanskrit is found in this remarkable record. Perhaps no more eloquent, or extreme, example of the attempt to be local while remaining assertively global can be found in the realm of vernacular language practice in South Asia.[78]

A wholly Sanskritic definition of the literary, as a very specific way of using language in written form, was fully present to the minds of medieval vernacular literati, and it had a decisive role to play in the history of regional literatures. Yet the principle in operation here may not be peculiar to that time and place. On the contrary, we may be seeing here a strong tendency with wider application, perhaps even a law: it is only in response to a superposed and prestigious form of preexistent literature that a new vernacular literature develops. The intellectuals of ninth- and tenth-century Karnataka, Andhra, and Java who invented Kannada and Telugu and Javanese literature did so now in emulation of, now in competition with, now in antagonism toward the example of Sanskrit. But no different is the case of Dante in fourteenth-century Florence—his guide into the world of the vernacular, Vergil, was the preeminent poet of a superposed Latinity—and countless of his peers across medieval Europe. This is not to say that emulation and invention of this sort took place only in the vernacular millennium and not before or after; witness Livius and Homer, or Nandaśaṅkar Mehta and Walter Scott. Nor was it the only historical dynamic at work in the transformation of the vernacular world: the rise of the "regional vernacular" can be taken as rejection

78. *IA* 9: 163 ff. (I thank Bronwen Bledsoe for pointing me toward the inscription and translating the Newari portion). On Jayapratāpamalla's ceremonial recitation of the Sanskrit *Mahābhārata* at his coronation, see chapter 6 n. 15. Public political discourse in Nepali has a very similar history (see the text from Kathmandu issued by the same Jayapratāpamalla in 1670 in Clark 1957: 167–72, who suggests that *bhākhā (bhāṣā)* at this period refers to Nepali and *deśabhākhā* to Newari, p. 187); also Hutt 1988: 77–95.

of the cosmopolitan-vernacular aesthetic and, perhaps, the politics with which it was associated (chapter 10.4). But in premodern South Asia it was the notion of literary language that Sanskrit had defined, along with the literacy of literature, that everywhere underpinned the vernacular transformation. There, and elsewhere too, it was only in the presence of a dominant transregional cultural formation that the alternative cultural world produced by vernacular literature could become an alternative. And only by appropriating the signs of superposition in everything from vocabulary to aesthetics could it become a world, a self-adequate literary culture according to the prevailing scale.

What precisely is dominant in a "dominant" cultural formation? What constitutes the prestige of "prestige" languages? Why are the dominant and the prestigious seized upon by a subposed formation? When and where and how are they seized? Such questions lead inevitably to the problem of power and the theorization of the vernacular polity. The purpose of framing the hypothesis of superposition is to make a historical point about vernacularity without which such theorization cannot be initiated. We can't even know to ask what makes the creation of literature possible and desirable for a given social or political world until we realize that literatures are indeed created. The historiographical problem of identifying those creative beginnings is assuredly complex, even where traditions did not actively strive to complicate them still more (as happened in Tamil). Yet the complexity of the problem does not render it incoherent. Rather, it prompts us to look harder to grasp the principles in play. One formulation worth careful consideration was offered by Antonio Gramsci, as skilled a theorist of culture-power as any, when he argued that there is no parthenogenesis in language—or, by implication, in cultural history: Language does not merely "produce other language," it does not change simply by reacting upon itself. Instead, "innovations occur through the interference of different cultures"—these different cultures being themselves, of course, subject to the very same processes in a kind of unbroken chain of borrowings—and these moments of innovation and the agents responsible for them are in principle subject to historical specification.[79] We find no more powerful illustration of this formulation, and no arena of greater historical precision, than the creation of the regional world of Kannada.

79. Gramsci 1991: 178.

CHAPTER NINE

Creating a Regional World: The Case of Kannada

9.1 VERNACULARIZATION AND POLITICAL INSCRIPTION

Few local literary cultures of premodernity anywhere permit us to follow the history and reconstruct the meanings of vernacularization with quite the same precision as is possible for Kannada, the language of what is now the southern union state of Karnataka. We can chart the shifts in cosmopolitan and vernacular cultural production without interruption from about the fifth century on, based on texts that are for the most part securely datable—an almost unparalleled antiquity and chronological transparency. Much of the data is the hard evidence of epigraphs, and their quantity is breathtaking. The region must be one of the most densely inscribed pieces of real estate in the world, with more than twenty-five thousand records (poems, charters, genealogies, donations, contracts) issued mainly by the courts of kings and their vassals.[1] Added to this are textualized works representing some of the earliest vernacular literature in the subcontinent to which dates can confidently be assigned. Among these is the first text in South Asia—perhaps anywhere—that self-consciously theorizes the relationship between vernacular and cosmopolitan ways of literary practice, the *Kavirājamārgam* (c. 875).

It is true that as many as half of the extant epigraphs of Karnataka remain unpublished, and that many early works have been lost. But the search for inscriptions has been intensive, and the picture of the epigraphical history of Kannada has not changed appreciably in a century. As for texts, we know a good deal about what is no longer extant, whereas much of what the Kan-

1. But also by village communities (see *SSS* introduction on the *vīragal*, or commemorative hero-stone inscription). Some 14,000 inscriptions from the eight districts of the Mysore princely state alone were published in *Epigraphia Carnatica* (1886–1919).

nada tradition, from the moment it became a tradition, considered important we actually do possess. Thus the formulations made in what follows about the historical development of Kannada rest on a foundation available for no other vernacular culture. What is more, we can locate much of this cultural transformation with reasonable precision within the political sphere. This conjuncture does not enable us to unravel all of the complexities of premodern Indian polity, but it does point toward important developments bearing on an understanding of the history of power and culture that would otherwise remain obscure.

All these aspects of Kannada-language textuality—its antiquity, density, historicity, and sociology—place the issue of vernacular beginnings in a sharp light, and they confirm trends that reveal themselves elsewhere in southern Asia. We can more or less watch the literization of the language occur, and we can observe the gradual process by which the idiom is transformed from a documentary to a workly instrument for both political and literary discourse. The asynchrony of the commencement of writing and the commencement of literature is as perspicuous and dramatic here as anywhere, so too the context within which literary and political expressivity began. Since the question of how vernacularity played itself out in the political domain is central to the theme of this book, the history of Kannada's use as a political code must be carefully reconstructed before considering the long-term negotiation between cosmopolitan and vernacular in literary production and its larger significations.

One of the facts established by intensive epigraphical searching is that the literization of Kannada began in earnest—becoming something more than casual graffiti and entering into cultural and political history—no earlier than the start of the sixth century. For nearly three-quarters of a millennium before that point, all written materials in the region—inscriptions as well as literary, philosophical, and religious texts—were composed in Sanskrit or Prakrit. All ruling lineages expressed their political will first in Prakrit (beginning with Ashokan edicts in the mid-third century B.C.E.) and then, in the dramatic shift recounted earlier (chapter 3.1), exclusively in Sanskrit. Only slowly and tentatively did Kannada come into use for the documentary—though not as yet the literary—portion of inscriptions.

In northern Kannada country the Kadambas, successors of the Sātavāhanas and their feudatories, the Cūṭukula Śātakarṇis, exercised power from the early fourth century until the beginning of the seventh. By the ninth century at the latest, their core area centered on Vanavāsi was considered the home of the prestige dialect that was to become the standard for literary Kannada. Yet for the entire life of the dynasty its political language, after a short-lived initial experiment with Prakrit, was almost exclusively Sanskrit. Aside from a four-line document found at the village of Halmiḍi, undated but assigned now to about 500 and thus representing the first extant instance of inscribed Kannada, two brief records constitute the sole exceptions to the Kadambas' vernacular silence. The first Kannada epigraph after Halmiḍi was issued sometime between 575 and 580 by Maṅgaleśa, a ruler of the successor lineage, the Bādāmi Cāḷukyas (chapter 3.3). This was just the time of Medhāvin's Pallava Tamil record (chapter 3.1), and the Kannada vernacular project is equally undeveloped and prosaic:

> Hail! May he incur the guilt of the five great sins and be buried in the seventh hell who injures the gift that has been made at the rate of half a *visa* to the garland makers who work for the god Lañjigesara, which is the gift to the stone house [i.e., cave] of glorious Maṅgalīśa, the beloved of the earth.[2]

And, like the Tamil of the Pallavas, it would remain undeveloped for the life of the dynasty, even while the Cāḷukyas' Sanskrit epigraphs are models of the cosmopolitan political style (chapter 3.3).

From the time of these Cāḷukyas the cultural politics of language in Karnataka kingdoms can be followed with increasing clarity, and it conforms to the pattern found elsewhere in the subcontinent. The percentage of inscriptions issued by or within the sphere of royal power that are wholly or partially in Kannada relative to those wholly in Sanskrit rose steadily as dynasty followed dynasty, the ninth-century Rāṣṭrakūṭas marking a turning point. The proportion of records in Sanskrit shrank from about 80 percent in the period 741–819 (the approximate level of the Bādāmi Cāḷukyas) to 15 percent in the period 819–974 (of the 180 records extant from the reign of Kṛṣṇa III, r. 939–96, only ten are in Sanskrit). For the succeeding dynasty, the Kalyāṇa Cāḷukyas, nearly 90 percent of epigraphs are in Kannada—a nearly complete reversal within the space of three centuries.[3]

The shift to Kannada as the primary language of expressive political discourse—and no longer merely a secondary language of counting, measuring, particularizing, and sanctioning—began late in the reign of Nṛpatuṅga Amoghavarṣa (c. 875), the Rāṣṭrakūṭa king at whose court literary vernacularity was first theorized, and gathered momentum during the time of Kṛṣṇa III (c. 940).[4] A record from each will repay closer examination. Among the

2. *IA* 10: 60. The Halmiḍi inscription (*MAR* 1936: 72 ff.) has been reconsidered in Venkatachala Sastry 1999 and Gai 1991. For the two additional Kadamba Kannada epigraphs see *CKI* 106, 163 (both probably sixth or seventh century). The rudimentary style of Maṅgaleśa's inscription reappears in the third extant Kannada grant, that of the Cāḷukya king Vijayāditya, sometime between 696 and 734 (*IA* 10: 103–4). The brief versified inscription in *IA* 10: 61 is distinctively expressive but undatable. On the nonpolitical Śravaṇabeḷgoḷa verses see later in this chapter.

3. The Kannada/Sanskrit ratios for the Bādāmi Cāḷukyas are 30/89; for the Rāṣṭrakūṭa 7/37 for the years 741–819, 80/14 for 819–974; for Kalyāṇa Cāḷukyas, 205/25 (figures based on Naik's survey of 1948 and Gopal 1994: 429–65, and sharing their limitations). If the calculations are rough, the tendencies are unmistakable and corroborated by developments elsewhere.

4. Two documentary texts from earlier in the century (including the first Kannada copperplate, 804) are important precursors (*EI* 33: 327–32; *EC* 8: 5; *Kannaḍaśāsanasaṃpada*, pp. 5–6).

first public inscriptions attempting to make Kannada do the work of cosmopolitan Sanskrit is one issued by Amoghavarṣa in 872 in connection with the renewal of a tax remission granted to a Brahman community in the days of the Cāḷukya kings. In two verses the fifty Brahmans are praised for their Sanskrit learning and *vaidika* respectability (Kannada words and morphemes are in roman):

> *śruti*yoḷ *viśrutaviśvasmṛti*yoḷ *vyākaraṇakāvyanāṭakatarkka-* |
> *sthiti*yoḷ *sarvāgama*doḷ *caturmukhapratim*ar ayvadiṃbar *vipr*ar ||
>
> modaloḷ sisūḷ ahāḻaṃ *viditaśrīsaḷukirājya*doḷ paḍedu *mahā-* |
> *sadamalasarvakratu*gaḷan*udārataramā*ge bēlva *viprōttam*aran ||[5]

> These fifty Brahmans are like the Four-Faced [Brahmā] himself in [their command of] scriptures orally transmitted, and all the celebrated scriptures remembered, in the principles of grammar, *kāvya,* drama, logic, in all texts of systematic knowledge.
>
> Having summoned those great Brahmans of Sisūḷahāḻaṃ [Sisuvaṉa Halli], which was obtained long ago during the renowned kingship of the Śrī Saḷuki, a great dwelling place where the oblations are given liberally in all auspicious sacrifices, [the king . . .][6]

Though seemingly a slight gesture, this inscription has considerable historical significance, for it exhibits the first impulses of what were to become major vernacular forces. Brahmans, the beneficiaries of royal largesse, are here eulogized not in the language that underwrote their prestige but in a new idiom that sought to appropriate that prestige, in part by the very claim, here instantiated, of its capacity for rendering their praise and in part by the form—the cosmopolitan vernacular form—in which it does this. The agent of this cultural transformation was the royal court, which was clearly choosing to express its political will in Kannada after centuries of Sanskrit monopolization. Furthermore, the document evinces a trend confirmed time and again by the Kannada material: political vernacularization not only did not exclude the Brahman community, it had nothing to do with religious identity at all.

In the mid-tenth century, Kṛṣṇa III, after achieving a notable military victory (killing a Cōḻa prince at Takkōla, taking both Kāñcī and Tañcāvūr, and decimating Cōḻa power, according to his inscriptions), embarked on a looting expedition to the north. There in 964 he defeated Sīyaka Harṣa of the

5. The meter, called *kanda,* is derived from the Prakrit *khandhaa* (Sanskrit *skandhaka,* an *āryagīti*). It gave its name to the genre of courtly epic, the *skandhaka* (*KĀ* 1.37), exemplified in Pravarasena's fifth-century *Setubandha.* For vernacular philologists the second-consonant rhyme *(prāsa)* here distinguishes courtly Kannada from Sanskrit (see section 4).

6. *SII* 11.1.10 (using the text as reprinted in *SSS* pp. 5–7).

Paramāra family of Malwa (the grandfather of Bhoja). Kṛṣṇa commemorated the event with a *praśasti,* the first of that genre in Kannada. The text commences in prose, with the normal grandiloquent prelude (*paramabhaṭṭāraka paramēśvara śrīprithvīvallabha mahārājādhirāja,* "Supreme master, supreme lord, glorious beloved of earth, great king of kings") followed by a list of the king's titles *(biruḍa)* whose form carefully but firmly localizes the discourse (Kannada words and morphemes are in roman):

> nallara maruḷan ānevedeṃgaṃ calake nallātaṃ *vairiviḷāsaṃ madagajamallaṃ parāṃganāputraṃ* gaṃḍa*mārtaṇḍan akālavarṣaṃ nṛpatuṅgaṃ* kaccegam *śrīmat*-kannara*dēvam.*
>
> He who bewitches beloved couples (with his good qualities), who is endowed with the beauty of a war elephant, a good man in his firmness, who sports with enemies and wrestles with wild elephants, a son to wives of other men, a sun to heroes, who rains down blessings even out of season, the summit of kings, one girdled with courage [or, conqueror of Kāñcī], glorious Kannaradeva.[7]

A good portion of the critical cultural-political work of this text gets done at the microlevel of linguistic form. The first three titles (*nallara maruḷan,* etc.) are Kannada, the next three Sanskrit (*vairiviḷāsam,* etc.), the seventh *(gaṃḍa-mārtaṇḍan)* a combination of the two (of the sort that would be increasingly disallowed by grammarians as an *arisamāsa,* or "compound of hostiles," except when used in a royal title such as this), the next two fully Sanskrit, the last two almost wholly Kannada (*kann-ara* is a vernacular calque, via Prakrit *kaṇha* and Kannada *arasa,* on *kṛṣṇarāja*). It may seem far-fetched to see conscious calculation in this style, but in fact the kind of careful balancing we find here between globalizing and localizing registers would become a preoccupation in both the theory and the practice of Kannada literature and philology. It is no surprise that it should make itself felt in the core practice of royal naming at the very inauguration of the vernacular political turn. As the *praśasti*'s narrative continues, it nuances motifs of the earlier cosmopolitan political discourse. The theme of the epithet "son to the wives of other men"—one who regards married women as mothers and therefore sexually unavailable—is developed by three of the four verses that follow. The metaphor references the king's magnanimity in allowing his defeated enemies to keep their wives and, by implication, their power of governance (a variation on the long-lived topos of uprooting enemy kings and restoring them to tributary status, chapter 6.2). The one verse standing outside this thematic offers a precedent for the king's military prowess: "The Pāṇṭiya who

7. *EI* 19: 289. The editor is unaccountably silent about the text's significance as the first Kannada *praśasti* (cf. line 36), though he usefully notes its translation of Sanskrit political idiom (p. 288). See also Desai et al. 1970: 138–42.

conquered in the *Bhārata* war and earned the name of one who knows a single throne with Indra, his clan / the Cōḻa uprooted root and branch—and root and branch did [Kṛṣṇa] Ānevedeṅga uproot his." For some centuries it had been a boast of the Pāṇṭiya dynasty of Tamil country to have participated in the epic war (yet further evidence of the presence of *Mahābhārata*'s historicity in the eyes of premodern rulers).[8] The glory derived from this genealogy was passed on to their conqueror, and to their conqueror's conqueror, the scarce resource of epic political charisma recirculating in uninterrupted continuity. But something has changed here. The charismatic claims are now being made in an idiom neither the Cōḻa nor the Pāṇṭiya were likely to have understood (Tamil and Kannada having increasingly become mutually unintelligible) or even read (recall the palpably different scripts for Kannada and Tamil that Cāmuṇḍarāya used to sign the Bāhubali statue in 983). The *praśasti*'s language is designed for a narrower, more local audience who wanted to hear and see the cosmopolitan language of polity in a local embodiment. The very boast of uprooting the enemy is now translated from the Sanskrit, *kṛtvā caulānvayonmūlanam,* into Kannada, *cōḻana bēraṃ bērinde kiḻtan.* For the record as a whole, form has acquired its own content: tacking back and forth between the vernacular near and the cosmopolitan far, and the vivid sense of commensurability this modulation generates, are the objective correlates of a much larger politics of culture.

An identical history marks the use of the vernacular in political discourse in the south, where the Gaṅga dynasty held power from the end of the fourth century to the end of the tenth. These rulers entered epigraphical history in Sanskrit and inscribed not a single word of Kannada until the late sixth century. A purely documentary role for Kannada in these texts continued even in the first *versified* Kannada inscriptions the Gaṅga kings issued in the eighth century. These later inscriptions, the versification notwithstanding, record the facts of contracts or deeds as we find in documentary texts everywhere ("The headmen of Toḷḷa village, the fortunate seventy-six chief men, have been full witnesses to the grant made by the king"). Not until the late ninth century did a Gaṅga ruler—King Eṟeyappa, c. 890—use Kannada for more than factual content, but when he did so it was dramatic (Kannada words and morphemes are in roman):

> *samastabhuvanavinutagaṅgakuḷangaganānirmmaḷatārāpatijaḷadhijaḷavipuḷavaḷaya-mēkhaḷākalāpālaṃkṛtyaiḷādhipatyalakṣmīsvayaṃvṛtapatitāvadādyagaṇitaguṇagaṇa-vibhūṣaṇavibhūṣitavibhūti śrīmad*eṟeyapparasar pagevarellaman *niḥkṣatram*māḍi gaṅgavāḍitombhattārusāsiramuman *ekacchatracchā*yeyoḷ āluttam iḻdu.

8. See chapter 6.1. Pāṇṭiya claims about their role in the *Bhārata* war (*EI* 19: 290 n.) arguably stimulated the precocious vernacularization of the text in their realm (chapter 10.1 and n. 7).

> The spotless moon in the sky that is the Gaṅga lineage, whose praises are sung throughout the world; the husband chosen by Lakṣmī herself, goddess of royalty, for lordship over earth as far as the vast circle of the waters of the ocean that form her ornamental belt; one whose power is adorned with adornments—masses of virtues—such as these, which cannot be counted: this glorious King Eṟeyappa stripped all his enemies of political power and ruled in the shade of a single royal parasol over the Gaṅgavāḍi 96,000.[9]

This is unprecedented vernacularity, entirely new in lexicon, style, and mode of representation. It is powerfully infused with Sanskrit idiom and grandiloquence (a single compound consisting of twenty-eight words precedes the king's name), however much these are tempered by the predominantly Kannada idiom that follows. It is also rich with universalist political imagery (signaled by the reference to lordship to the ends of the oceans), however much this stands in tension with the localization of rule to the political sphere of the Gaṅgas and the specific revenue structure by which their villages *(pāḍi)* were organized. But the key point for the argument here is that not until the end of the ninth century was such vernacularity beginning to be heard in the public political arena in southern Kannada country.

Even this cursory account discloses several fundamental features of the vernacularization process. First, we see once again a gulf between literization and literarization. Something on the order of four centuries separated the earliest written Kannada documents of the late fifth century from the discourse, literarily self-conscious in both form and content, of the Kannada *praśasti* text produced in the late ninth. That this is a real gulf in time and no mere artifact of the evidence that chanced to survive is validated by other histories (discussed later) relating to inscriptional poetry outside the political sphere, the production of the earliest textualized literature in Kannada, the crystallization of literary culture more generally, and the ethnohistorical memory of the literary tradition itself. Nothing justifies the assumption that earlier inscriptional literature disappeared, let alone disappeared in such quantity as to weaken the inference that something new and significant had occurred in this region near the end of the millennium.

Second, we find a correlation between vernacular innovation and a reconfiguration of the culture-power order. As a vernacular political discourse was consolidated, Sanskrit began to yield its place as a cosmopolitan language, fading to almost complete insignificance before the flourishing of Kannada productions in polities like that of the Hoysaḷas (c. 1000–1300). This was a gradual shift, of course; Sanskrit would retain some efficacy in the public do-

9. *EI* 1: 350, tr. Fleet (slightly emended). For the *kanda* verse of the eighth-century record, see *IWG:* 254 lines 19–21 (cf. also pp. 274 and xxxvi), and for the late-sixth-century record, p. 104. Versified but wholly documentary inscriptions are found in northern Karnataka as well, notably in a Rāṣṭrakūṭa text of 918 C.E. (*IA* 12: 223).

main, as witnessed in the continuing importance of the Sanskrit genealogical statement for the early Cāḷukyas of Kalyāṇa (chapter 3.3), or even later, in the patronage of Sanskrit court poets on equal footing with their vernacular peers, as with Bilhaṇa at the court of Vikramāditya VI (c. 1080). Nor did developments after the fourteenth century plot a rectilinear decline. The Vijayanagara empire (1340–1565), though centered in northern Karnataka, saw a dramatic decrease in the production of expressive political inscription in Kannada (also in Telugu and Tamil), while a Sanskrit imperial idiom modestly reasserted itself.[10] At all events, the late ninth century unquestionably marked a moment of transition when Kannada increasingly came to function as the primary code of political communication. And concomitant with the crystallizing of a Kannada language region by the very production of such royal documents (just as neighboring Marathi, Tamil, and Telugu regions were forming due to similar productions in those languages), the political formations themselves gradually took on the character of vernacular polities (chapter 10.3).

A third feature of vernacularization toward which the inscriptional history points is the creation of a wider regional-language literary culture, arising symbiotically with the new political discourse. In the vernacular epoch, as in the cosmopolitan, *praśasti* and *kāvya* were co-conceived, both conceptually and institutionally, with the court functioning as engine for the stimulation of literary production of a textualized sort, if now vernacular production.[11] A few experiments in literary textualization may be datable to a generation or two before the transformation that is signaled in the records of Amoghavarṣa and Eṟeyappa. (As we will see, there is no reason to believe that centuries of earlier Kannada literary texts vanished without trace while an explosion of writing, with major creative and philological works succeeding each other decade by decade, should have been preserved from the tenth century on.) Besides the sheer quantity of new texts, which were now constituting tradition rather than random experimentation, works began to be produced that evince a self-awareness of both the very fact and the meaning of the fact of producing literature in Kannada. Whatever may have occurred

10. Aside from *praśastis*, Sanskrit's proportion in the total documentary output of the court remained more or less what it had been among the Kalyāṇa Cāḷukyas. Less than 7 percent of inscriptions issued by or mentioning the Vijayanagara emperor are in Sanskrit; at no time does Sanskrit account for more than 10 percent of the total production of public documents (see also chapter 10.3). Post-Vijayanagara *nāyaka* polities seem completely indifferent to the earlier cultural-political self-assertion in Kannada (as the *Keladi Arasa Śāsanasamputa*, passim, demonstrates).

11. Expressive epigraphs from outside the court exist as well. The first such datable text (929) is a lovely poem on the town of Puligeṟe (*EI* 13: 326 ff.). Jain epitaphs at Śravaṇabeḷgoḷa (e.g., *EC* 2: 70 nos. 25, 86, 98) exhibit the same cosmopolitan vernacular style as the *praśastis*, but they are all undated. (The wild guesses of the first editor, e.g., *EC* 9: 21 [Citradurga 43]: "Date? About 500 A.D.," continue to find acceptance, see Sivarudrappa 1974: 67).

earlier, a new cultural practice and consciousness marked the late ninth century as a true inauguration—the moment when an aesthetics of vernacular power began to produce a new power of vernacular aesthetics.

9.2 THE WAY OF THE KING OF POETS AND THE PLACES OF POETRY

The text that announced the new vernacular aesthetics is the *Kavirājamārgam,* "The Way of the King of Poets," written probably near the end of the reign of Nṛpatuṅga Amoghavarṣa, and no doubt in Mānyakheṭa, his new capital city in northeastern Karnataka. In fact, the *Mārgam* may have been the first text in world culture to theorize a vernacular poetics. It shows itself to be vitally aware of the normative claims of a transregional cultural order and a readiness to conform to its demands even while developing strategies for negotiating difference from it in order to both equal and displace it. The work must thus be central to any analysis of the process of vernacularization.[12]

The Rāṣṭrakūṭa court of the ninth century was as remarkable for its still-brilliant Sanskrit culture as for its dynamic literary experimentation in a variety of languages. It was there that Jains turn decisively to Sanskrit for the production of their universal histories, as witnessed in the *Ādipurāṇa* (837) of Jinasena II (Amoghavarṣa's spiritual preceptor); there, too, the first full-scale grammatical analysis of Sanskrit by a Jain was produced, the *Śabdānuśāsana* of Śākaṭāyana (chapter 4.1). An important literary current in Apabhramsha also found expression at Mānyakheṭa, displaying itself most powerfully two generations after Amoghavarṣa in the work of Puṣpadanta (fl. 950), the first to use the language for a Jain poetic history.[13] But the truly decisive innovation occurred in Kannada. The *Mārgam,* which aims at defining what it means to do a *kavi*'s work in the Kannada language, consolidated a recently invented idea of what this work was and thereby laid the foundations for the vernacular revolution.

The *Mārgam* to some degree tempers its own claim to innovation by the predecessors it cites. In a way that prefigures and embodies the conceptual

12. The Tamil *Tolkāppiyam* is probably earlier (see chapter 10.1), but its main binary is not cosmopolitan/vernacular but standard/nonstandard: *centamil/ [koṭuntamil],* or straight Tamil / [crooked Tamil] (Zvelebil 1992: 134–36). Scholarship on the *KRM* in the West is inversely proportional to the text's historical significance (five brief articles, nothing in the last half-century). No translation exists in any Western (or Indian) language.

13. Jinasena's *Ādipurāṇa* (based on the lost *Vāgarthasaṃgraha,* Upadhye 1983: 231–35), later called *Mahāpurāṇa* with the addition of Guṇabhadra's work (c. 898). Note also Asaga's *Vardhamānacarita* (853), the first Sanskrit biography of Mahāvīra. The one work actually ascribed to Amoghavarṣa is the Sanskrit philosophical hymn *Praśnottararatnamālikā.* Prakrit literary production (cf. Altekar 1960b: 412) is unsurprisingly absent; as inscriptional history shows, it had become a residual or even archaic cultural feature, see chapter 2.2.

project of the work as a whole, in the prologue the author salutes first Bāṇa, the greatest of the Sanskrit prose stylists, and then praises the Kannada prose writers Vimalōdaya, Nāgārjuna, Jayabandhu, and Durvinīta (vv. 1.25–29). Similarly, a list of the most "vaunted [Sanskrit] poets, who made possible the creation of great poetry" (Guṇasūri [unknown], Nārāyaṇa [author of the *Veṇisaṃhāra*], Bhāravi, Kālidāsa, and Māgha) is followed by a catalogue of the best Kannada writers of verse—Paramaśrīvijaya, Kavīśvara, Paṇḍitacandra, Lōkapāla—whose "preeminent exposition of [all] the components of literature has become the model *(lakṣya)* of poetry forevermore." About most of the Kannada writers we know next to nothing, but there is no reason not to assume that all of them were close in time to the date of the text—or even members of Amoghavarṣa's own literary circle.[14] This is actually so in the case of (Parama-)Śrīvijaya, who had a major hand in the composition of the *Mārgam* itself.

That vernacular literature was indeed a new venture is strengthened by the *Mārgam*'s acknowledgment of the difficulties of locating literary models for its prescriptive project. The author confesses he is forced to "beg for scraps" of Kannada literature like a mendicant:

> Both Sanskrit and Prakrit are available according to one's wish for composing literature with refinement, since to be sure there are already available both literary models and norms *(lakṣya, lakṣaṇa)* in great abundance for each of the two. But the discourse I will present requires begging scraps *(tirikoṟegoṇdu)* [of Kannada literature] to make it intelligible, and it is extremely difficult for anyone to do in the case of Kannada [given the absence of models and norms] the way the ancient teachers [of Sanskrit and Prakrit did].[15]

On the other hand, the *Mārgam* recognizes a *paḻagannaḍa,* "old Kannada," with some kind of aestheticized functions, the continued use of which the work is expressly intended to prohibit. It is clear that the text seeks to not only legislate a new cosmopolitan variety of the vernacular but to disallow other sorts of poetries:

> Thinking that well-established poems [from the past] themselves ever provide the only source of norms for poetry, men lacking the power of theory *(āgama)* compose [literature today] misusing old Kannada even while knowing full well that it no longer meets [the aesthetic standard] of Place. Archaic Kannada

14. *KRM* vv. 1. 31–32 ("preeminent exposition . . . ," *niratiśayavastuvistaraviracane lakṣyaṃ tadādya kāvyakkeṃduṃ,* perhaps referring to the eighteen *kathāvastu*s). Some of these names are uncertain. Paṇḍita and Candra may be separate writers; that Paramaśrīvijaya refers to a single individual is shown by the final verse in the work. For Kavīśvara see Upadhye 1983: 231–35. Nothing supports identifying Durvinīta with the mid-sixth-century Gaṅga king (whose records celebrate his Sanskrit scholarship, chapter 4.1 and n. 4), let alone Nāgārjuna with the Buddhist philosopher of the third century (so Sivarudrappa 1974: 70).

15. *KRM* 1.41–42.

> composed in the following way . . . is appropriate only for the poetic practices of those olden times. They are altogether tasteless in terms of [the aesthetic standard] of Place. [Using that language today] is like wanting to make love with an old woman.[16]

It is not easy to grasp the real implications of this passage. What is being excluded from the new literature is a register that was very likely oral, and it most certainly had come to be viewed as unrefined and uncourtly. From the work as a whole it is obvious that the literary language the *Mārgam* sought to promote over against this *paḻagannaḍa* was, and was understood to be, a radically different idiom, a cosmopolitan vernacular of the very sort that was just then making its first appearance in the realm of public political discourse.

The newness of the new literary language is corroborated by other, locally constructed forms of chronological evidence, which merit a brief review here. These ethnohistorical representations are significant in themselves no less than for their positive historicization. For among the beginnings most meaningful for cultural history are those that participants in the culture themselves marked as beginnings, the memories of the past they chose to preserve and, precisely through such choices, to make historically consequential. One form for such memory in South Asian literary culture is, as we saw earlier (chapter 2.1), the eulogy of past poets *(kavipraśaṃsā)*. Kannada writers adopted the convention quickly, at the virtual commencement of their literary history. Such eulogies are a prime mechanism of canonization, and it is the canon that allows a tradition to come into being. The *Mārgam*'s catalogue of models, the prototype of these literary eulogies, represents the impulse to construct just such a tradition, however precociously.[17]

Several praise-poems written in the three centuries following the *Mārgam* give us a good sense of the history, canon, and cultural position of Kannada literature as the writers themselves understood them. Important examples are offered by the *Karṇāṭaka Pañcatantram* (1031, the first such eulogy available after the *Mārgam*)[18] of Durgasiṃha, minister of state *(sāndhivigrahika)* at the court of Jagadekamalla I of the Kalyāṇa Cāḷukyas; the *[Vīra]vardhamānapurāṇam* of Nāgavarma II, scholar of Kannada grammar, rhetoric, and lexicography (also at the court of Jagadekamalla); the *Anantanāthapurāṇam* of Janna (1230), court poet to the Hoysaḷa king Vīraballāḷa; and the *Śabdamaṇidarpaṇam* of the grammarian Kēśirāja (1260), also at the Hoysaḷa court. The first of these offers the paradigmatic case.

Durgasiṃha prefaces the eulogies of Kannada authors with a chronolog-

16. *KRM* 1.48–50. "Composed in the following way": hereafter follows a series of vocables that have defied exegesis.

17. No comprehensive study of the *kavipraśaṃsā* exists for Kannada literary history.

18. Pampa's *Ādipurāṇa* contains only a list of spiritual teachers (in imitation of Jinasena's text); the *VAV* has none, and Ranna mentions only Sanskrit poets (*Gadāyuddham* 1.8–9).

ically ordered list of the great poets of the cosmopolitan world, beginning with Vālmīki and Vyāsa, whereby Kannada is positioned in reference to the global literary order, and to that order alone. No writers of other traditions are listed because no authority accrues to a vernacular from affiliation with other vernaculars. After providing an almost perfect chronology of a thousand years of Sanskrit literature up to Rājaśekhara in the early tenth century, the Sanskrit list concludes with Daṇḍin, the seventh-century author of the *Kāvyādarśa*.[19] For reasons discussed later, this is meant to facilitate the transition to Śrīvijaya, who is placed at the start of the Kannada canon and to whom the *Kavirājamārgam* is here ascribed. "His *Kavimārgam* became a looking glass and a hand-torch for the minds of the poets who contemplate it." The list continues in chronological order, ending with the great poets of the mid-tenth century, Ponna and Pampa.[20] A similar procedure is followed by Nāgavarma, who likewise begins with Śrīvijaya and continues in chronological order down to the great triumvirate of Ponna, Pampa, and Ranna. Janna follows an even more precise historical sequence, while concentrating on poets closer to himself in time (and beginning not with Śrīvijaya but with the late-tenth-century poet Guṇavarma). The one exception is the grammarian Kēśirāja, but he has a different agenda: not so much to praise poets as to identify the poets who will serve as his models. Virtually all on his list are found on the other lists, and none is demonstrably earlier than Śrīvijaya.[21]

The evidence is thus unequivocal, and the implications significant. All authors of Kannada praise-poems viewed the commencement of Kannada literary chronology the same way that Sanskrit writers regarded the commencement of the Sanskrit: as a rupture in time, a moment of discontinuity, when something new began. Although no one would be awarded the title "primal poet" *(ādikavi)* in Kannada until the fourteenth century, when

19. The Sanskrit list continues, after Vyāsa, with Viṣṇugupta (supposed author of the *Pañcatantra*) and the sole Paishachi writer, Guṇādhya, and then proceeds to the masters of *kāvya* and *kāvyaśāstra:* Vararuci, Kālidāsa, Harṣa and Bāṇa, Mayūra, Nārāyaṇa, Dhanañjaya (author of the *Rāghavapāṇḍavīya*), Vāmana, Bhallaṭa, Bhāmaha, Bhīma (?), Bhavabhūti, Bhāravi, Bhaṭṭasrī (?), and Māgha. After Rājaśekhara is added the undatable Kāmandaka *[sic]*, author of the celebrated *nītiśāstra*.

20. *Karṇāṭakapañcatantram* 1.22–27. Listed are: Śrīvijaya; the author of the *Mālatīmādhavam* (i.e., Kannamayya); Asaga (author of the [lost] *Karṇāṭakumārasambhavam* and the Sanskrit *Vardhamānacaritam* [extant], latter half of the ninth century); Manasija (undatable); Candrabhaṭṭa (end of the tenth century); Ponna (patronized by King Kṛṣṇa III, r. 939–67); Pampa (first work dated 942); and Gajāṅkuśa (identical with Gajaga, c. 1000).

21. See Nāgavarma, *Vīravardhamānapurāṇam* 1.2–8 (a second, abbreviated canon appears in 1.27); Janna, *Anantanāthapurāṇam* 1.35 (cited also in Puttappa 1988: 90); Kēśirāja, *Śabdamaṇidarpaṇam* 1.5. On the dates of a number of poets mentioned in these lists see Venkatachala Sastry in Nayak and Venkatachala Sastry 1974, vols. 3 and 4; especially vol. 3: 348 (Asaga), 355 (Guṇanandi), 652–57 (Kannamayya), 658 (Manasija), 660 (Candrabhaṭṭa), 665 (Gajāṅkuśa), and 670 (Nāgadēva).

Pampa was so consecrated (and he remained primal poet from that point on),[22] there is little question that in the minds of writers like Durgasiṃha and Nāgavarma the *Mārgam* and its redactor (or author), Śrīvijaya, occupied a comparable position. What is especially important is that in none of these lists, from as early as 1031, can we perceive any literary-historical memory reaching back before the ninth century. And this starting point finds further confirmation in the actual practices of reading and quoting. What constitute the historically significant texts of Kannada literature in the praise-poems of Nāgavarma's literary work are the same that are meaningful to him in his works on grammar and rhetoric. Here he names no poet earlier than Pampa (942) and cites none, so far as we are able to tell, earlier than Guṇavarma (900).[23] Whether or not workly uses of the Kannada language that were textually inscribed—that is, Kannada literature—had in fact existed before the time of the *Mārgam,* they made no history, since later poets had no memory whatever of them. If we are to take the representations of the working writers in the early second millennium seriously, as a true index of effective literary history, then we must conclude that to their minds their vernacular tradition was an astonishingly recent invention.[24]

In fact, the arrival of literary newness into the Kannada world is precisely what explains the existence of a work like the *Mārgam,* for the task it sets itself is to puzzle through the complex interactions between a mature, long-dominant cosmopolitan literary culture and an emergent culture of Place. In this respect, it is a text to set beside Dante's *De vulgari eloquentia* (c. 1300; see chapter 11.2, 3). There are in fact intriguing cultural-political parallels between the *Mārgam* and the *Eloquentia,* but also some signal differences. At the micro level, unlike Dante's work, the *Mārgam* did not aim to produce a unified language for the court and courtly culture at large from among competing dialects; the standardization of Kannada (and the term "standardization" is neither imprecise nor anachronistic) was effected by far more inconspicuous processes of homogenization quickly consolidated by grammars. Instead, the goal of the *Mārgam* was to produce a language qualified for normatively defined literature. At the macro level, the *Mārgam* had a relationship to political theory and practice far less transparent than the *Eloquentia,* which sought explicitly to give voice to a cultural program for a Holy Roman Empire that Dante fervently longed to see revived. Nonetheless the *Mārgam*'s sociopolitical location carries important implications of its own. How we are

22. Pampa's primacy is found first in the *Dharmanāthapurāṇa* (1410) *(Kannaḍa Nighaṇṭu* s.v. *ādikavi).*

23. For the citations in Nāgavarma see *Kāvyāvalōkanam* pp. lx ff. Among the poets Kēśirāja cites as authorities none antedates the ninth century (*ŚMD,* ed. Venkatachala Sastry 1994: 3–5).

24. One of the few scholars who acknowledges this possibility is Chidananda Murthy 1978: 252.

to interpret these, and in precisely what ways the culture-power vision of the *Mārgam* is to be distinguished from its European counterparts, are questions that bear centrally on the theorization of vernacularity in South Asia.

If there is no uncertainty about the location of the *Mārgam*—the court of Amoghavarṣa Nṛpatuṅga of the Rāṣṭrakūṭa dynasty, whose brilliance in understanding both poetry and polity the text celebrates throughout—the identity of its author has been the object of controversy. It seems probable the work was a joint production. While the later tradition viewed Śrīvijaya as the principal author, and he is mentioned prominently in the text itself, he must have been redacting the cultural theory formulated by his patron-king: he is often described in the *Mārgam* itself as having written "in conformity with the views of Atiśayadhavala" (the "One of Pure White Fame," i.e., Nṛpatuṅga), and his work as having been "approved by the supreme king Nṛpatuṅga." In fact, it is evident throughout that the "Way of the King of Poets" is conceived of as the Way of Nṛpatuṅga alone. "Only the wise, those prepared to follow the route of the correct Way of King Nṛpatuṅga, will be able to approach without hazard the ashram of literature, which is unapproachable except by this route."[25]

Just as significant as location and authorship is the text's relationship to its cosmopolitan models. It is by no means going too far to say that the work—as its very title shows—would have been unintelligible to any reader without serious knowledge of Sanskrit. It seems paradoxical that a vernacular revolution was inaugurated and effected in large part by appropriating from the target of revolt. Yet this fact, like the *Mārgam*'s dependence on the tradition of Sanskrit poetics of the previous two centuries—Bhāmaha's *Kāvyālaṅkāra* and especially Daṇḍin's *Kāvyādarśa*—is entirely representative of the cosmopolitan-vernacular project that vernacular intellectuals at the end of the first millennium were attempting to carry out.

Earlier we saw how the circulation of texts on Sanskrit poetics like Daṇḍin's was a major factor in the creation of the Sanskrit cosmopolis in first-millennium Asia, as well as an important indicator of the mode of existence of this cosmopolitan order and the aesthetic values it embodied (chapter 4). At the same time, such theory provided a conceptual framework within which emergent literatures of Place could be conceptualized everywhere from ninth-century Sri Lanka to thirteenth-century Tibet and fifteenth-century Thailand. Precisely the same route was taken in the subcontinent itself—another good example of the Indianization of India—and nowhere earlier or more consequentially than in Kannada country. Here, too, the *Kāvyādarśa* played a critical role. Its place in shaping the discourse of the *Mārgam* was accom-

25. On Śrīvijaya, see *KRM* 1.150, 2.55, prose after 2.155; on Nṛpatuṅga, 1.44, 147; the title *kavirāja* had been claimed by kings from at least the time of Samudragupta (chapter 4.1). For a brief discussion of authorship see Srikantia 1983 (1933): 852–59.

panied, and no doubt even made possible, by an intensive reengagement with the Sanskrit original on the part of scholars in the region. The evidence for this reengagement comes from a generation or two after Nṛpatuṅga and Śrīvijaya, but it was undoubtedly the fruit of longer-termed trends, or perhaps a response to the *Mārgam*'s own appropriation of Daṇḍin's work. The earliest extant commentary on Daṇḍin, that of the Sinhala Buddhist Ratnaśrījñāna, was almost certainly produced at the court of the Rāṣṭrakūṭa king Kṛṣṇa III during the middle decades of the tenth century. From the same time and place came a second gloss by Vādijaṅghāla (a sobriquet meaning "swiftest debater"). This scholar is to be identified with the Vādighaṅghaḷa Bhaṭṭa described in a tenth-century Gaṅga grant as an "expert in the exegesis of the science of literature" as well as a "political theorist influential in shaping the thinking of Kṛṣṇa [III], who by following his advice, systematic and sound both for the present and for the future, has been enabled to conquer the quarters."[26] The third oldest commentary, that of Taruṇavācaspati, was composed at the Hoysaḷa court in the late twelfth century. Daṇḍin clearly spoke with special force to Deccani intellectuals. The reason for this seems to lie in the possibilities his theory offered for conceiving of literature as an actually regionalized cultural practice, and thus for reconceptualizing the cosmopolitan Ways of literature themselves. The basis for such an interpretation of Daṇḍin's theory lies, as we will see, in its historical origins.

Although nowhere naming its Sanskrit models, the *Mārgam* fully recapitulates the structure of Daṇḍin's work (in some ways even functioning as our oldest commentary on the text), while at the same time appropriating much of the substance of Bhāmaha's *Kāvyālaṅkāra*.[27] The text first defines literature and then describes the potential shortcomings *(doṣa)* in language usage that detract from literature and those expression-forms *(guṇa)* that enhance it (chapter 1); next, figures of sound are catalogued (chapter 2), and then figures of sense (chapter 3). In addition to its structural similarity to Daṇḍin's work, the *Mārgam* adapts perhaps two hundred of the illustrative verses, and a number of those that define figures and prescribe more general literary procedures, from Sanskrit antecedents.[28] The work is not a translation of the Sanskrit, however, though it is sometimes erroneously described as such. Translation as we normally conceive of it—rendering a

26. *MAR* 1921: plate X, 8 ff., lines 168–69: *niravadyasāhityavidyāvyākhyānanipuṇa-; sakalarājavidyāpratipādanapratibuddhabodhaprabodhitavallabharāja- . . . tadātvāyatisughaṭamantrakramopadeśānuṣṭhānavaśīkṛtākhiladigaṅganā- . . . kṛṣṇarājadeva-*. On Ratnaśrījñāna and Vādijaṅghāla see Pollock 2005d; also chapter 5 n. 44.

27. The *KRM* refers to its sources simply as "the old poets" (e.g., 2.51) and the like. Two centuries later Nāgavarma shows no reluctance to name his sources: Vāmana, Rudraṭa, Bhāmaha, and Daṇḍin (*Kāvyāvalōkanam* v. 961).

28. See the appendices to both the Madras edition and that of Seetaramaiah (1968).

text from a language the unintended reader does not understand into a language he does—makes no cultural sense in this world. There is little doubt that Kannada literacy at this period was always mediated by Sanskrit literacy. But more than this, the *Mārgam* has a totally different agenda from that of its Sanskrit models. The work is precisely an exercise in the localization of global poetics, a kind of experiment in literary self-fashioning that proceeds by charting sameness, without which there could not be *literature* as defined by the governing model, while striving to establish difference, without which there cannot be *Kannada* literature.

Difference is marked not only by the set of features that are included and how they are included but also by the set of features that are excluded and have to be so. Thus, a verse from Bhāmaha on the value of literature and the fame that it can bring the writer is faithfully reproduced. But it is followed by others that rewrite Bhāmaha's definition of poetry, which had been so influential in the Sanskrit tradition: "Literature is word and meaning united . . . It is twofold in being either prose or verse, and threefold in being composed in Sanskrit, Prakrit, or Apabhramsha." The *Mārgam* turns this into the following:

> Literature consists in the Ways of well-turned expression, generated by an intention of the poet *(kavibhāvakṛta-)* and distinguished by a variety of language properties. It is a construction of particularized words, in which are found rhetorical figures bringing to light a variety of meanings.
>
> According to the thought of the Moon of the World of Men [Nṛpatuṅga], there ever belongs to the Primal Being of the Literary Entity two portions with many components: supreme ornamentation and body.
>
> And of these two, according to the pronouncement of the One of Pure White Fame, the "body" is defined in the literary tradition of the usages of the great poets as twofold: prose and verse.[29]

The first verse highlights the key role of the Ways, which we consider below, and recapitulates Bhāmaha's division of word and meaning. The second corresponds to nothing in Bhāmaha but rather adapts Daṇḍin, framing the distinction between the language-body and its trope-ornaments that governs the rest of the treatise.[30] Most important, the restriction on languages that had been constitutive of the cosmopolitan order necessarily had to be omit-

29. *KRM* 1.22–24; see 1.20–21 and Bhāmaha, *Kāvyālaṅkāra* 1.2, 8.

30. See *KĀ* 1.10. Primal Being of the Literary Entity, *kāvyavastupuruṣa;* cf. the *Mānasollāsa*'s "deity of literature" (*kāvyadeva,* see chapter 4.3) and Rājaśekhara's Primal Being of Literature, or Poetry Man (*kāvyapuruṣa,* see chapter 5.2). Elsewhere in the *Mārgam* and in early Kannada literary theory, the literary text is typically represented as feminine: *kṛtivadhu, kṛtinārī, kṛtisati* (*KRM* ed. Seetha Ramiah p. 182).

ted. This would not have been so, incidentally, had the categories "Prakrit" or "Apabhramsha" encompassed Kannada in the conceptual world of Kannada speakers. They clearly did not.[31]

The double procedure of demonstrating cosmopolitan identity and constituting vernacular distinction finds clear expression in one of the *Mārgam*'s most suggestive analytical moves, though one that has long puzzled Kannada scholars. This is the appropriation of one of the core concepts of Sanskrit poetics as the work's organizing logic as well as its very name: *mārga* or the "Way" of literature. We have seen that variety in styles had become a defining trait of Sanskrit literariness by the ninth century and that it was conceptualized as plural and regional. There was thought to be an eastern way (of Gauḍa, or Bengal) as well as a southern (of Vidarbha, or Berar), and later a northern (of Pañcāla, or the Gangetic plain) and a western (of Lāṭa, or southern Gujarat), with others added in the following centuries (chapter 5.3). What differentiated these regional ways of making Sanskrit literature was the use of expression-forms—phonological, semantic, and syntactical—as well as the density of rhetorical figures in the poetic text. Daṇḍin had famously defined southern literature as endowed with all the expression-forms, with northern (or eastern) poetry characterized by their inversion (or absence). On the discursive plane, the primary implication of this taxonomy was the very cosmopolitanism of Sanskrit literature: its regional differences were matters of style only, not substance, and thus a measure of Sanskrit's very transregionality, its pervasion of all local spaces—Sanskrit poetry was ubiquitous. Ubiquitous, too, was Sanskrit theory, which for half a millennium had set the rules of the literary game. The new vernacular intellectuals were obliged to come to terms with both.

At first glance, the discourse on the Ways in Kannada seems a wholesale borrowing from the Sanskrit tradition. The *Mārgam* introduces the term *mārga* in its broader connotation of literary method or even literature itself—*sūktamārga,* "the Ways of well-turned expression"—hearkening back to a phrase used since Samudragupta half a millennium earlier. "Literary work of the great Way" is the supreme use of language, in all its formal and aesthetic complexity:

> The man who understands language can communicate with others, disclosing to them the thoughts that he intended. Wiser than he is the man who can communicate much meaning in brief compass.
>
> Wiser still is the man who knows how to make his words enter into [and] unite with meter. More learned than all these is the man who without hindrance can produce works of the great Way.[32]

31. For a rare reference to Kannada as Prakrit see the eighth-century inscription in *KI* 3, lines 9–10 (and cf. Yazdani 1960: 240).

32. *KRM* 1.15–16. "Works of the great Way," *mahādhvakṛtigaḷ.*

Accordingly, in other contexts *mārga* is contrasted with "flawed" poetry (*duṣya*, e.g., 2.7–8). Such usage is perfectly intelligible, and quite unremarkable. What has confused, even astonished scholars is the *Mārgam*'s adopting the notion of the regional Ways for differentiating *Kannada* poetry itself:

> It is impossible fully to comprehend the procedures of the Ways and reach a conclusion about the multiplicity of their options. Having considered the rules on words of the earlier [Sanskrit] *śāstras*, I will say a little with respect to Kannada so that the matter in general may be clear . . .
>
> Poets arise in a world without beginning and thus are infinite in number; of infinite kinds, too, are their individualized expressions, and so the Way exists in infinite variety . . .
>
> But to the best of my ability I will briefly discuss the distinction—their differences perceived by the old [Sanskrit] writers who considered the matter—between the two excellent Ways, the northern and the southern, in the manner that I understand it . . .
>
> Of these two the southern Way has ten varieties, according to the [ten expression-forms] . . .
>
> The northern Way has varieties differentiated by the presence of the inverse of these properties.[33]

This general exposition is followed by an exhaustive illustration of every property, taken from the discussion of expression-forms in Daṇḍin and Bhāmaha, which the author concludes are foundational to Kannada poetics:

> Whatever the words [used in a literary text], they will enhance the virtue of Kannada by [conforming to] the distinctions related to the usages of the two Ways described here. Let the learned come to clarity herein in accordance with the procedures that are followed and ascertained as alternative modes, with the help of the illustrations given below, by the One Endowed with Consistent Political Wisdom [Nṛpatuṅga].[34]

What the *Mārgam* appears to have done, in brief, is to graft the very discourse that made Sanskrit cosmopolitan onto the local world of Kannada.

Modern Kannada scholars have found the very postulate here not just irrelevant to actual Kannada poetry but worse, incoherent. No advance has been made since the great philologist R. Narasimhacharya impatiently dismissed the discussion as entirely misdirected: "northern" and "southern" in Kannada poetics refer merely to the "schools or styles in Sanskrit"; there is

33. *KRM* 2.46, 49, 51, 54, 55. "Rules on words," reading *padavidhi-* (with Seetha Ramiah); "presence of the inverse," *viparyayavṛtti.*

34. *KRM* 2.101. "One Endowed with Consistent Political Wisdom," *nītinirantara.*

no evidence that anything comparable existed in Kannada.[35] Though the judgment offers no help in understanding what the *Mārgam* may have intended by using the doctrine of the Ways to analyze Kannada literature, it does reveal how irrelevant to a local literary culture the doctrine has seemed to modern scholars. The two *mārgas*, meant to reaffirm the limitless expansion of Sanskrit literature precisely by identifying all the quasi-regional varieties it can possess, have been incongruously pasted onto the unequivocally limited sphere of Kannada. Thus the category *mārga* appears to capture nothing of the actual character of Kannada literature and to fit only to the degree that the vernacular enacted a kind of precolonial mimicry of the dominant cultural formation.

The *Mārgam* emerged from the center of one of the most powerful polities in ninth-century India, and this fact, if not a general principle of hermeneutic charity, should invite us to ponder seriously what it may have meant to deploy the talk of global Sanskrit in representing a vernacular-language poetics. Metadiscursively it might be argued that faced with exclusion from the transregionality of Sanskrit and refusing to be caught in the brackets of the local, the *Mārgam* was seeking to remap the cosmopolitan Way onto the local world of Karnataka. It therefore had to speak of a northern and a southern style of Kannada poetry—the domain of Kannada had to be shown to embrace a north and a south, to constitute a regional world unto itself—whether or not such a division corresponded to any actually existing forms of literature.[36] In a word, if the local was to participate in the world of the literary, a world defined by supraregional languages, it had to evince its translocal capacities.

Such an analysis may capture something of the cultural-political impulse at work in the *Mārgam,* and other evidence seems to corroborate it. But another rationale, equally significant if somewhat more complicated, underpins it. Consider first how the *Mārgam* differs from and supplements its Sanskrit models. It renames the Ways as "north" and "south"—the categories *gauḍīya* and *vaidarbha* being of course impossible for Kannada—and thereby relaxes the narrowly spatial implications of the taxonomy.[37] Second, it introduces a distinction that from the vantage point of standard Sanskrit po-

35. Narasimhacharya 1934: 121–22.

36. The differentiation does not refer to a dialectal division between north and south in Old Kannada: the same literary idiom was used by poets at the Gaṅga court in the south and at the Cāḷukya court in the north (like the unified literary language of the troubadour poets, chapter 10.1). The *Kannaḍa Nighaṇṭu,* s.v. *uttaramārga,* mistakenly glosses it by *uttarakannaḍa* (north Karnataka/Kannada).

37. Recall that Daṇḍin's tenth-century Rāṣṭrakūṭa commentator uses "north" and "south" by preference (chapter 5 n. 39). The eleventh-century Kannada writer Nāgavarma (II), who treats the question in his *Kāvyāvalōkanam,* favors "north" and "south" in his discussion of *mārga* (e.g., *sūtra* 124) but uses *vaidarbha* and so on in connection with *rīti* and *rasa* (vv. 781 ff.).

etics seems odd enough to constitute a category error: it differentiates the Ways according to the two main divisions of Sanskrit rhetorical practice, *vakrōkti* and *svabhāvōkti,* indirect and direct (or "natural") expression:

> Two Ways, accordingly, came into prominence, and with them two different forms of expression, based on a regular concomitance *(niyati):* on the one hand, indirectness *(vakra),* on the other, directness *(svabhāva).*
>
> Direct narration *(svabhāvākhyānam)* is an invariable characteristic of expression found in the southern Way. The use of well-known indirectness of expression *(pratītavakrōkti),* of which there are many varieties, is found in the celebrated northern Way.[38]

It is no longer so much the mere presence or absence (or "inversion") of the expression-forms as such that differentiates the Ways, as in the Sanskrit tradition. Instead, "southern" poetry is now represented as an expression devoid of tropes and that accordingly foregrounds the phonological and other linguistic properties of literary expression itself; "northern" poetry, by contrast, relies more on figures of speech (the "many varieties" referred to in the *Mārgam* passage just quoted). Such a dichotomy is for the most part unarticulated in the Sanskrit tradition, but in fact it helps to make the whole of Sanskrit's discourse on styles finally intelligible.

Only faint hints at these distinctions can be found prior to the *Mārgam.* Bhāmaha had noted, without elaboration, that the *gauḍīya* Way is troped *(alaṅkāravad)* and *vaidarbha* untroped *(avakrokti)* as well as endowed with expression-forms (including the use of primary rather than etymologically derived lexemes, a stylistic feature termed *prasāda*). For Daṇḍin, too, *gauḍīya* is troped, and when he declares that "all of literature is differentiated into two [main categories]: direct expression and indirect expression," he is likely pointing, if rather vaguely, to the same distinction.[39] The problem is fully thematized only much later, in Bhoja's *Śṛṅgāraprakāśa.* There are three "sources of beauty in literature," Bhoja observes: indirect expression *(vakrokti),* direct expression *(svabhāvokti),* and the expression of emotion *(rasokti).* "Indirect expression is when prominence is given to tropes, simile, and the rest; direct expression, when prominence is given to expression-forms." How far Bhoja's correlation—of expression-forms and thus *vaidarbha* (or southern) style with direct expression, and *gauḍīya* (or northern) with tropes—has been judged to deviate from the Sanskrit understanding of the categories is evident from

38. *KRM* 2.52–53.

39. *Kāvyālaṅkāra* 1.34–35; *KĀ* 1.50, 2.360. Daṇḍin agrees with both the *KRM* and the *ŚP,* but he confusingly lists *svabhāvokti* among figures of speech. At all events, he clearly knew a conception of literature in which direct description and figural indirection formed two fundamentally different styles. Similarly, Vāmana adduces precisely apt illustrations though nowhere explicating the principles in play (chapter 5.3).

the words of his own editor, who found it completely unintelligible. In the light of the *Mārgam,* it becomes clear.[40]

The logic of both the *Mārgam*'s argument and the examples it cites produces a geography of Kannada styles that perfectly embodies the options available to the vernacular poet in the Sanskrit cosmopolis. The analyses just examined, coupled with the distinctions detailed in Bhoja's earlier account (chapter 2.3), enable us to reduce the Ways to their essentials and see that they comprise real alternatives in vernacular aesthetic practice:

(a) "Southern" Kannada literature focalizes the stuff of language itself and accordingly employs figuratively unadorned description; "northern" Kannada literature, by contrast, focalizes tropes (the feature represented by Sanskrit theorists as differences in the degree of metaphoricity).

(b) Among the most distinctive of expression-forms is minimal degree of nominal compounding shown in southern Kannada literature; northern literature shows an abundance of compounds *(ojas).*

(c) Southern Kannada literature is marked by the prevalence of Kannada *(dēsi)* words, the analogue of primary lexemes (*rūḍha,* "conventional," "idiomatic") in the Sanskrit tradition; northern literature is marked by the prevalence of unmodified Sanskrit loans (*samasaṃskṛta* [= *tatsama* in other traditions]), the analogue of derivative or etymological *(yaugika)* lexemes in Sanskrit.[41]

Thus, far from using categories irrelevant to, let alone incommensurate with, the analysis of Kannada, the *Mārgam* is identifying and counterposing the two modes of writing that constituted the fundamental cultural choices for Kannada, indeed, for all South Asian vernacular literatures. The northern and southern types of Kannada literature prefigured what were very soon to be named *mārga* and *deśī* (Kannada *dēsi*), the aesthetic "of the Way" and

40. *ŚP* p. 678, cf. *SKĀ* 5.8. Bhoja's grasp of the matter may be explained by the southern orientation of his work (manuscripts of his *ŚP* were preserved only there; on the possible presence at his court of the author of the *Karṇāṭakakādambarī,* see chapter 2.3 and n. 75). The judgment on deviation is found in Raghavan 1963: 136–37. Bhoja's *rasokti/svabhāvokti/vakrokti* tripartition is echoed in a near contemporary text from Kashmir, the *Vakroktijīvita,* pp. 98, 134.

41. On the prevalence of metaphoricity *(upacāra)* outside the southern style, see the discussion of Rājaśekhara and Bhoja in chapter 5.2, 3. The illustrations of the two Ways provided in *KRM* 2.60, 62 can be distinguished on the basis of *svabhāvōkti* (southern) and *vakrōkti* (northern, the *śleṣa ku[-]valayam* and other figures); similarly in 2.110, the first half shows *svabhāvōkti,* being untroped, the second shows *vakrōkti,* being one long *rūpakasamāsa.* The same logic holds for the *Kāvyāvalōkanam* and its illustrations (vv. 501 ff.), which indicate the same understanding. On the role of *yoga* and *rūḍhi* in *gauḍīya* and *vaidarbha* styles, see chapter 5.3. The *KRM*'s intricate discourse elsewhere (the north/south morphological distinctions described in 2.102–11) resists interpretation.

"of Place" (chapter 10.2). In addition to this deeper logic, the *Mārgam*'s discussion is important for the telling irony it reveals in the dialectic of cosmopolitan and vernacular literary practices in history. The source of this organizing taxonomy of Sanskrit poetry seems to lie not in anything to do with the nature of Sanskrit poetry as such but rather in the inclinations of southern poets—Tamil-born poets like Daṇḍin himself, who helped establish the Ways as authentic options—to write Sanskrit in conformity with the sensibilities of the southern languages—sensibilities eventually made visible by the production of literature and literary theory in the vernacular.[42] When vernacularization was fully initiated at the end of the first millennium in Karnataka, the styles that southern writers had already theorized for Sanskrit were far more naturally *retheorized* for languages like Kannada, where direct description, noncompounding, use of primary (*deśī*, or non-Sanskrit) lexemes, and a range of other properties such as moderate second-syllable alliteration were actual and active components, as any passage of early Kannada poetry demonstrates. The *Mārgam*'s "south" thereby became southern and vernacular India, contrasted with and distinguished from a "north" that was northern and Sanskritic India—less separate spaces than complementary aesthetics. *Deśī* was not yet, and would not for a long time become, a way of expressing an oppositional mode of identification.[43]

The larger principle to extract from this apparently narrow and admittedly complex case concerns the mutually constitutive interaction of the local and the global. This is something that, once we learn to look, we can find time and again in the production of literature across southern Asia. Just as the cosmopolitan was constituted through cultural flows from the vernacular—the origin of the Ways was being thematized by Sanskrit writers such as Rājaśekhara (chapter 5.2, 3) almost contemporaneously with the *Mārgam*—so the vernacular constructed itself by appropriating from the cosmopolitan, though without always registering that reappropriation was actually at work.[44]

The *Mārgam* has a range of other discursive projects it seeks to advance

42. Recall that Daṇḍin's earliest commentator understands *svabhāvokti* as the mode of expression "natural" to southern poets and accordingly regards the different Ways as "inborn," "native," "proper" to the poets of the particular regions (see chapter 5.3).

43. Chapter 10.4. Although in Tamil "north" *(vaḍaga)* can itself connote Sanskritic, in Kannada neither *baḍaga* nor *uttara* ever seems to bear this meaning. The choice between styles in the *KRM* is not yet conceptualized as wholly independent of other aesthetic considerations. In accordance with Rudraṭa's innovation, the Ways even in the *KRM* are tied to emotional registers (*KRM* 2.98 ff. expands Rudraṭa's *Kāvyālaṅkāra* 15.20, see chapter 5.3). The *Kāvyāvalōkanam* also links the "Paths" with *rasa* (chapter 4 is titled *rītikramarasanirūpaṇādhikaraṇam*).

44. In a parallel process of intertextuality Potana, a fifteenth-century Telugu poet, appropriated and localized in his *Bhāgavatamu* the tenth-century Sanskrit courtly *Bhāgavatam,* which itself had appropriated the Tamil songs of the Āḷvārs (Shulman 1993, especially pp. 155–56).

in the domain of vernacularity. The most obvious is its quest to establish Kannada literature as a conceptual entity worthy of descriptive and prescriptive treatment. The text itself is an enactment of this objective, for it constitutes Kannada as a language of systematic knowledge—even science—in the very act of constructing it as a language of literature. Another purpose is to discipline usage and thereby to invest Kannada with the stability and dignity required of a literary language. Related to this is a third major concern: charting Kannada divergences over against cosmopolitan Sanskrit in everything from genres to the nature of "pure Kannada" words *(accagannaḍa)* and the permissible forms of their combination with Sanskrit words in nominal compounds. These features of language ideology (two of which are examined further in section 4 below) mark the beginnings of a vernacular philology that would be vigorously developed in the following centuries and that testifies to the programmatic transformation in cultural consciousness and practice that vernacularization represented.

The last of the *Mārgam*'s objectives that merits discussion is perhaps the most salient of all for a consideration of poetry and polity at the beginning of the second millennium: the concern with placing Kannada literary culture in space and defining the collectivity that participates in this culture. The text constructs a geocultural sphere radically discontinuous with the fundamentally supraregional, or better, preregional, spheres that functioned as matrices of Sanskrit thought (chapter 5.1). And this new sphere has a concreteness of a sort never attained (and never intended) in the Sanskrit discourse on *mārga*. The crucial move in this construction is made early on in the text and serves to frame the discussion that follows. After juxtaposing to the old canon of Sanskrit masters the new masters of Kannada (1.31–32) and briefly noting literary genres unique to Kannada,[45] the text answers the implicit question of where this new canon and the untranslatable genres it contains have pertinence:

> Between the Kāverī and the Gōdāvarī rivers is that culture-land *(nāḍu)* in Kannaḍa, a well-known people-place *(janapada)*, an illustrious, outstanding political realm *(viṣaya)* within the circle of the earth.
>
> And even within this, there is a culture-land between Kisuvoḷal, the renowned great city of Kopaṇa, Puligeṟe, and Oṃkuṃda, a place praised by good people. It is there, should one wish to know, that is found the very heartland of Kannaḍa *(kannaḍada tiruḷ)*.[46]

45. "Not in use for all languages but in Kannada alone are the *cattāṇa* and the *bedaṇḍe*" (1.33–35). A much-disputed passage, but Kittel's "That in Kannaḍa which (according to the opinion of some) is wholly insufficient with regard to (its) words" (Kittel 1903: 386) seems impossible.

46. *KRM* 1.36–37.

The broader significance of the conceptual category "culture-land," which grounds the idea of region in this time and place, will be considered later (chapter 12.1). Here let us just note that although the *Mārgam* itself is uninterested in establishing or even alluding to the political coherence of this cultural place, despite its growing isomorphism with the domain of power in late Rāṣṭrakūṭa and Kalyāṇa Cāḷukya times (chapter 10.3), it seems obvious that in the verses just cited the various technical terms—culture-land *(nāḍu)*, people-place *(janapada)*, and political realm *(viṣaya)*—are fully intended to be overlapping.[47]

The northern and southern boundaries by which the *Mārgam* first broadly defines the relevant region (which is meant to include what is today southern Maharashtra but exclude the expanse to the east in Andhra Pradesh and northern Tamilnadu) mark a space that hearkens back to the older, puranic geographical representations (chapter 5.1): "The most beautiful country on earth is south of the Vindhya Mountains and north of the Sahya Mountains [= Western Ghats]."[48] That older conception is hopelessly vague, to be sure—and that is just the point we need to register. It is precisely the hazy vision of geoculture in the era before vernacularization that was to be rendered ever more distinct in the *Mārgam* and in the texts, both literary and political, that followed.

That the author of the *Mārgam* should have any interest at all in identifying a relevant geography for the literary culture to which the text belongs is arresting, given the long-dominant paradigm of the unbounded circulation of Sanskrit. This geographical interest was in fact brand-new, as was the understanding of literary culture it reflects: the whole apparatus of literary knowledge that the work assembles is meant for a particular world, and for that world alone. And it has application to only a particular people-place. In fact, it is specifically, even exclusively, participation in this literary culture alone—and not what we now think of as ethnicity—that endows the inhabitants of this culture-region with conceptual coherence:

> People in that culture-land *(nāḍavargaḷ)* are able to both speak in full awareness of what is seemly and reflect in full awareness of what has been spoken. By nature they are clever, and even without intensive reading *(kuṟitōdadeyam)* they are proficient in the usages of literature.

47. *Nāḍu* of course has a range of significations. It can be used to refer to a small group of villages (e.g., Kundaranāḍu), or a bigger area, like Banavāsenāḍu (for the Banavāse twelve thousand, which could also be referred to as *viṣaya* or a *deśa*, rather as medieval European political discourse used *civitas*, *regnum*, and *provincia* almost interchangeably). See Mulay 1972: 41 ff. The term *mahānāḍu* seems used only in reference to guilds (see chapter 12.2).

48. Kirfel 1931: p. 43 v. 32. For "south of the Vindhya mountains," a variant gives "where the Gōdāvarī is."

> Moreover, even common men, without conscious intention, are all knowledgeable each about his own language practices. Even small children are adept at communicating their discrimination, and even the mute what they wish to express.[49]

Unlike the rootless and placeless cosmopolitan language, whose very name bespeaks unconcern with any particular local habitation (recall that *saṃskṛta* means "the refined," "the grammatically analyzable," and, as a resonance from an archaic period, "the sacramental"), here place and language have become fully homonymic, as they would in most of the other vernacular worlds coming into being in the following centuries. Kannada is the language of Kannaḍa ("Karṇāṭa[ka]" in Sanskritized form), the "culture-land *(naḍa* < *nāḍu)* of the black soil *(kar)*."[50] Such naming offers yet further acknowledgment that the circulatory sphere of the *Mārgam*'s literary culture had nothing in common with the limitless space of the great Ways of Sanskrit.

In contrast to the relatively indistinct if circumscribed *nāḍu* of Kannada between the Kaveri and Godavari, the more narrowly conceived "culture-land" located within it is specified precisely. By an auspicious circumambulation from northeast to northwest the text maps a rectangular area between the Malaprabhā and Tuṅgabhadra rivers with Kisuvoḷal (more commonly known today by its ancient sobriquet, Paṭṭadakal) to the northeast, Kopaṇa (Koppala or Kopananagara, just to the north of Hampi-Vijayanagara) to the east, Puligeṟe (today's Lakshmeshvar) to the south, and Oṃkuṃda (Okkuda in Belgaum district) in the west.[51] This smaller zone, too, like the larger space within which it is located, would increasingly find mention outside the *Mārgam,* confirming both the cultural significance of the literary representation the text offers and the reality of the zone for the practices of the polity.

The fact that the *Mārgam* was demarcating a region that actual producers of literary culture took as meaningful is shown by the repeated references to the "heartland of Kannada" by the first generations of vernacular poets. Around 950 Pampa described his work as "sweet poetry with the power of order and [composed] in the native Kannada language of the heartland *(sājada tiruḷa kannaḍadoḷ),* Puligeṟe, which is known as the place resplendent with kings." In his eleventh-century work Nāgavarma praises "the great poet Ranna" for having "won brilliant fame with his *Ajitajinēśvaracaritam,* elaborating it in the Kannada of the heartland *(tiruḷa kannaḍadoḷ),*" while Ranna himself at the end of the tenth century had declared that the true "Kannada

49. *KRM* 1.38–39.

50. That *kannaḍa* was understood as a *tadbhava* of *karṇāṭa* is certified by Kēśirāja (Kittel 1894, s.v. *kan* 2). On the etymology see also Barnett in *EI* 12: 145. Master has suggested instead *karunāḍu* or "high country" (1928: 175). See also Venkatachala Sastry 1997: 42–68.

51. On Oṃkuṃda see Seetha Ramiah (1975: 188); the identification is uncertain.

of the heartland *(tiruḷa kannaḍam)*" is the Kannada of the Puligeṟe region.[52] Dating to exactly the same epoch are the first indications of a new political-administrative coherence applied to the same area. To celebrate a historic defeat of the Cōḻa army about 950, the Rāṣṭrakūṭa overlord Kṛṣṇa III granted a vast tract of land to his vassal the Gaṅga king Būtuga II, which in addition to the province of Banavāsi consisted of four districts: Beḷvola, Puligeṟe, Kisukāḍu, and Bāgenāḍu. The first contains Oṃkuṃda, the second Puligeṟe itself, the third Kisuvoḷal—three key points on the map of the Kannada heartland.[53] It was at this point, too, that epigraphical discourse first began to link the concepts of the two greater and lesser *nāḍus* that constitute the *Mārgam*'s literary-culture region of Kannada, situating them in relationship to the vaster transregional space. A Kannada inscription of 930 eulogizes Kūntaḷadeśa, another old and vague designation of Kannada-speaking lands but at this period more distinctly mapped in relationship to both Jambūdvīpa, the inhabited world, and Bharatakhāṇḍa, the subcontinent: "In the circle of the land of Bharata is a perfect ornament, the region of Kūntaḷa, and a very gem in this realm is the people-place of Purikara [Puligeṟe], the Two Six-Hundred [administrative unit]."[54] If the name "Kūntaḷa" is archaic, it is something altogether new to find its inhabitants simultaneously identifying themselves in relationship to both a core region and a larger totality.

How clearly the politics of vernacular poetry surfaced at the linguistic level, in the choice of a dialect for literary elevation, is shown by the fact that it was the ritual and political core of the Bādāmi Cāḷukyas, the ruling lineage displaced by the Rāṣṭrakūṭas a century before the *Mārgam* was composed, that constituted the "heartland of Kannada." The extraordinary concentration in this zone of the earliest free-standing stone-built temples in India, for which the Cāḷukya dynasty is justly celebrated, testifies eloquently to its centrality for the rulers.[55] It was undoubtedly the political status of the region—of Puligeṟe, "the place resplendent with kings," as Ranna calls it, and of Paṭṭadakal, literally, the "Stone of the Turban" (i.e., the site of the coronation ritual)—that secured for its dialect the sanction of royal prestige and thereby primacy in Kannada literary culture. This primacy was claimed even before that culture came into existence, which occurred long after the demise of the Cāḷukya rulers and extending over a region far wider than they ever controlled. Why it was not among the Cāḷukyas in Puligeṟe but instead among

52. *VAV* 14.58; *Vīravardhamānapurāṇam* 1.9; *Sāhasabhīmavijayam* 1.42 (he refers to the Puligeṟe region by the administrative name, the "Two Six-Hundred Kannaḍa country").

53. *EI* 2: 170 ff.

54. *EI* 13: 311, lines 24–25. For some general remarks on the new geographical practice, see Naik 1948: 32. This formula may have been adapted from the much older Brahmanical custom of the *saṃkalpa* (chapter 5.1). On Kūntaḷadeśa see Venkatachala Sastry 1997: 69–75.

55. See Michell 2002.

the Rāṣṭrakūṭas in Mānyakheṭa, 250 kilometers to the northeast, that Kannada literature was inaugurated is no easy question to answer.[56] But there is no uncertainty about the *Mārgam*'s discourse and the texts produced in its wake. The new literary language was created at the end of the first millennium by drawing on long-term associations of political charisma present in the adopted dialect. Its creators were members of a highly self-aware courtly elite who sought above all to define a way of cultural being over against the cosmopolitan dominant. They were fully conscious that the literature they produced had relevance in a world far smaller than the limitless space of the Sanskrit they sought to supplement and eventually supplant. Yet as this literature developed, the place in which it operated was newly emplaced, so to speak, and took on ever clearer conceptual contours for the practices and culture and power.

9.3 LOCALIZING THE UNIVERSAL POLITICAL: *PAMPA BHĀRATAM*

No text in Kannada makes clearer how the aesthetic and cultural-political theorization at the heart of the *Kavirājamārgam* was actualized by court poets than the first extant literary work in Kannada, Pampa's *Bhāratam,* also titled the *Vikramārjunavijayam* (Arjuna's Victory of Power, c. 950). Pampa belonged to what seems to have been a family of Kannadiga Brahmans who had emigrated to coastal Andhra Pradesh when the Bādāmi Cāḷukyas established a collateral ruling lineage in the region of Veṅgi in the seventh century. Pampa (in broad accord with the new geoscopic vision) thus describes his natal village: "Within the land bordered by the Malaya Mountains [of Kerala] and the Himalayas is the *maṇḍaḷa* of Beṅgi [Veṅgi], where a singular place is found, forever beautiful, far-famed by the name of Veṃgipaḻu." He ultimately sought service as a military man under Arikēsari II, a member of yet another Cāḷukya lineage with its base in the town of Vēmulavāḍa (or Lēmulavāḍa) in today's Karimnagar district of Andhra Pradesh. For his adherence to the "proprieties of the millet" *(jōḷada pāḻi),* that is, his obligations to his master in war (for which payment was traditionally made in grain), he was rewarded with a grant of property (an *agrahāra*) lovingly described in the poem. He may also have worked as an inscriptional poet for his patron.[57]

Pampa's career marks a moment of dramatic intensification in the pro-

56. The complexity is compounded by the view that the Rāṣṭrakūṭas may have emigrated from southern Gujarat as late as the last few decades of the eighth century, Nṛpatuṅga being the first to make his home in Karnataka (Ramesh in Gopal 1994: 34–37, on thin evidence).

57. *VAV* 14.40. The (Sanskrit) Karimnagar Inscription of the mid-tenth century (Krishnarao 1932, Venkata Ramanayya 1953: 82 ff.) and the *VAV*'s introductory *praśasti* have striking parallels. The Kurkyāl Inscription of Pampa's brother Jinavallabha (edited and discussed in Venkatachala Sastry 1979: 23–32) mentions the land-grant village (Dharmapuram) awarded to the poet.

duction of vernacular literary culture in the Deccan. Major writers of the era include Ponna, "emperor-poet" *(kavicakravarti)* at the court of Kṛṣṇa III of the Rāṣṭrakūṭas, and, in the next generation, Ranna, honored with the same title, at the court of Tailapa II and his son, Iṟivabeḍaṅga Satyāśraya, of the Kalyāṇa Cāḷukyas. From these authors, as from Pampa, are preserved substantial amounts of poetry. It is notable that all three continued a tradition, begun around the time of the *Mārgam,* of producing work in two major literary genres, one political, *laukika* (this-worldly), based on the Sanskrit *Mahābhārata* or *Rāmāyaṇa,* and the other religious, *āgamika* (scriptural), based on (usually) Jain moral tales.[58] The significance for us of the *laukika* genre lies, first, in its revealing the shaping role of the political in vernacular literary production in Karnataka (pervading the *Mārgam* and announced every time a precept on writing is ascribed to "the One Endowed with Consistent Political Wisdom") and, second, in its illuminating the very particular ways, the epic ways, in which the political had begun to be vernacularized.

The processes of vernacularization in Pampa's work are intricate and merit analysis at every level but especially those of linguistic register, theme—comprising both the narrative and its political subtext—and spatialization, something inseparable from the theme chosen. First, on the plane of register, it is remarkable how Pampa strives to realize the *Mārgam*'s cosmopolitan-vernacular ideal. Indeed, the poet's enduring influence in the Kannada literary tradition lies in some measure in his success in devising a local idiom grand enough to compete with Sanskrit on the terms Sanskrit had set, an achievement only made possible by a strategic appropriation of Sanskrit that would mark the idiom of classical Kannada henceforth. Pampa is very clear about his concern to mediate the aesthetic of Place with that of the Way, to negotiate a certain cultural difference even while declaring an affiliation with a superposed cultural order. He announces this intention at the start of his work, and it remains throughout the text's stylistic preoccupation:

> In its imagination [a poem] must be new, and the texture of the composition must be supple. Thus constituted, the composition must partake of the idiom of Place *(dēsiyoḷ puguvudu)* and at the same time must penetrate into the idiom of the Way *(mārgadoḷ taḷvudu).* In this way it becomes truly beautiful—as beautiful as a tender mango tree in springtime, drooping under the heavy weight of flowers and new shoots, and crowded with bees, and with the cuckoo singing, and only the cuckoo.[59]

Here the binary of Way and Place, reworking the *Mārgam*'s northern and southern Ways, is enunciated apparently for the first time in Kannada literature. Equally significant, the complementary opposition of the indirect style

58. See chapter 10 n. 96.
59. *VAV* 1.8.

of tropes (*vakrōkti*) in the aesthetic of the Way, and the direct style (*svabhāvōkti*) in the aesthetic of Place, which underwrote in part the *Mārgam*'s north-south differentiation, is echoed by Pampa at the end of his work:

> Enveloped with fame, pervaded by a single intention, [now] joined with tropes (*alaṃkṛti*), [now] constructed in the style of Place—a poem that can be said to have all this, and to show narrative mastery (*vastuvidye*), is a true poem. These are features passed down from of old, without which nothing can be a poem. The *Complete Bhāratam* (*samastabhāratam*) as well as the great work, the *Ādipurāṇam*, trample underfoot all other poetry of the past.[60]

The calculation of the relative weight of the local and translocal found at work in the *Mārgam* was thus hardly a matter of mere theory. Its project was on full display in the poets' literary procedures. It was Pampa's success in crafting the most accomplished form of the cosmopolitan vernacular that prompted one critic in the next generation to praise his poetry (with an echo of the *Mārgam*) as "captivating in the Way of poets matured in both Ways of composition."[61]

At the second level, that of theme, Pampa was to have an equally profound influence on the literature that followed by reason of both his inspired choice of prototype and the ways in which he transformed this prototype in his art. Pampa conceived of his *Vikramārjunavijayam* as the first "complete" vernacular version of the *Mahābhārata*, and he makes it clear that in vernacularizing the Sanskrit epic he was not intending to produce a demotic or popular work. On the contrary, the poem was solicited by court literati:

> The learned (*paṇḍitar*) felt that no great poet in the past had properly composed the complete *Bhāratam*—an unprecedented thing—without damaging the body of the tale while suggesting its magnitude, and that this was something only Pampa could do. And so they gathered together and besought [me]; and so I undertook to compose this work.[62]

Pampa may not have been entirely accurate in this assessment of his vernacular innovation. A version of the Sanskrit epic had been written in Tamil at the court of a Pallava king a century earlier, though we have it only in fragmentary form and it may never in fact have been completed.[63] Nor, perhaps, does the story of the invitation of the literati at the commencement of the poem fully harmonize with what we learn at its end: that it was his patron,

60. *VAV* 14.59; cf. 5.64. The *Ādipurāṇam* is Pampa's second (and one *āgamika*) work.

61. Durgasiṃha, *Karṇāṭakapañcatantram* 1.26.

62. *VAV* 1.11.

63. The Tamil tradition is confusing. Peruntēvaṉār's Tamil adaptation, the *Pārataveṇpā*, appears to have been produced at the Pallava court of Nandivarman III (r. c. 830–52); a Pāṇṭiya version may have been composed around the same time. See further on in this chapter.

King Arikēsari, who urged him to compose the complete *Bhāratam* as a historical narrative about himself:

> Arikēsari with affection sent a messenger and gave much [wealth] to [Pampa]: he sought to have his own fame established in the world by asking him to compose a historical tale *(itihāsakathā)* in this fashion.
>
> This great poem is as sanctified *(śrauta)* as the Gaṅgā River for him. And [yet] without any assistance, I composed it then within a year, that it might be said to have been born from the illustrious lineage of great poets.
>
> The complete *Bhāratam* that was manifested thus—it was not just any king who capably and with affection had it composed, and not just any talented poet who composed it. If someone were to patronize it, it would be you alone who could; if someone were to compose it so that your noble fame should last, it would be Pampa alone who could. What other poets are there on earth such capable composers, what other kings such capable patrons?[64]

Whether first or not, whether generated from the community of the learned or by royal fiat, with his local epicization Pampa performed a primal act of Kannada vernacularity of a sort that would repeatedly be attempted elsewhere in the vernacular millennium (chapter 10.1). At issue everywhere was the literary exaltation of the vernacular, but there were cultural-political aims too in most localizations of the *Mahābhārata.* This was eminently so for Pampa. He had a large political design in view, one that formed a perfect correlate at the thematic level with the aesthetic mediation between Way and Place that marks the linguistic organization of the work. Yet his design recovers its deeper significance only if we remember the one he took from his model.

Earlier we sought to gauge the role of the Sanskrit *Mahābhārata* in the production of the ideal of transregional power and in the "imaginary institution" of India itself (chapter 6.1). One important feature of the work, intimately related to both these effects, is its territorial vision: the subcontinent as a whole, and as a limit, is its core frame of reference. Like most grand epics but more so, the *Mahābhārata* is obsessed with mapping out a world relevant to its political vision and to the space within which that vision was to be realized. Accordingly, the multiple mappings simultaneously constitute an expression, even an enactment, of political power. The heroes' wanderings in exile, their conquest of the quarters prior to declaring universal sovereignty, and so on, down to their last funereal circuit when they renounce the world of power in despair for the slaughter they caused to win it—all these acts continually reproduce and reinforce the image of a vast yet

64. *VAV* 14.51–53.

bounded sphere of political reference. To a premodern audience this sphere may have appeared vague and hazily bounded; in some important sense its places may not even have been the same as the places of the same names that are now marked with cartographic precision by latitudinal and longitudinal coordinates. But the conceptual sphere constituted an ideal totality of sorts, the *cakravartikṣetra,* or imperial field, that finds mention in books of political wisdom as well as treatises of literature (chapter 6.2). It is this epic space, and the politics that filled it, that Pampa sought to redefine in his vernacularized version.

Pampa often refers to his poem as a *samastabhāratam,* with *samasta* having three important meanings: He attempted to reproduce the "whole" of the main narrative of the Sanskrit poem though in "compressed" form, without reproducing the proverbial hundred thousand verses of the original. But he also wanted his epic to be understood as a "composite" narrative: the poem's patron and his family, along with his overlord, enemies, and region, are explicitly identified with the heroes, allies, antagonists, and world of the Sanskrit epic—or rather, as Pampa puts it (in verses cited in what follows), to make his patron the standard of comparison for the epic hero, thus reversing the traditional relationship between the source and the target of a simile. To be sure, like Kālidāsa, Pampa is no simple allegorist, and his touch is light—how light is shown by the fact that scholars remain uncertain of the historical original behind the principal fictional antagonist.[65] But his directions to the reader are clear enough. He not only opens the poem with Arikēsari's genealogy and closes it with an account of the king's great deeds and his coronation, but he makes an explicit declaration of his intention at the beginning of his work:

> [Some poets] make comparison [of a contemporary king] and, by making him the hero [of their poem], elevate him to the eminence of kings of old, even when he is not a man who possesses the virtues worthy of a vast canopy of fame. Given that King [Arikēsari], Ocean of Virtues *(guṇārṇava),* surpasses in goodness even the noble kings of old, it is a desirable goal for me to introduce this man into this story by comparing Arjuna to him.
>
> . . . He is the man I have made the hero of this story, and, comparing the celebrated Arjuna to him, I have taken up the main structure of this story so as to compose [this poem] in all sincerity.[66]

A telling point about local invention in general can be made on the basis of this kind of allegorization, which poets after Pampa would use repeatedly.

65. On the likely equivalence of Kakkala (or Karkala)—on whom see later in this chapter—with Duryodhana see Gopal 1994: 162. In his great work Thimmappayya assumes rather too mechanical an allegory (Thimmappayya 1977: 145–203).

66. *VAV* 1.14, 51.

Kannada scholars invariably identify the allegorical mode used here with the Sanskrit figure *samāsokti,* the "trope of abbreviation" (which consists of characterizing the target implicitly while referring only to the source). But no Sanskrit rhetorician would ever have used this term to describe a structural feature of an entire narrative. To apply it to Pampa's *Bhāratam* is therefore to assimilate him to a nonexistent cosmopolitan tradition and so diminish what may very well have been a vernacular innovation.[67]

At critical junctures in the poem, the story of the Vēmulavāḍa Cāḷukyas' political fortunes, with Arikēsari assuming the position and power of primary vassal as the structure of Rāṣṭrakūṭa power began to fray, is skillfully permitted to push through the veil of the myth-epic. A good example of such strategic disclosure, and of the character of the double narrative itself, is offered by a passage whose location at the center of the poem marks it as pivotal. In anticipation of the cataclysmic battle, the sons of Dhṛtarāṣṭra, Arjuna's enemies, are describing the hero's deeds—his pride in fighting the great god Śiva and acquiring magic weapons, his valor in defeating demons, the grandeur of his sharing the throne of Indra, king of gods. Here "Indra" could just as well stand for Indra III Rāṣṭrakūṭa, Arikēsari's maternal uncle, just as "gods" could equally signify kings—brilliant examples of the kind of *śleṣas* that had marked cosmopolitan discourse for centuries (chapter 3.2). At this very point the discourse glides seamlessly into an account of the poet's royal patron: how Arikēsari defeats the usurping Rāṣṭrakūṭa prince, Govindarāja, and restores to power the rightful ruler, Amoghavarṣa III, and in doing so constitutes himself as paramount overlord in Kannada country in the middle of the tenth century:

> The majesty of this Ocean of Virtues; the greatness he possesses, like that of the ocean, for those who take refuge with him, holding his ground, shielding and saving King Vijayāditya, that Forehead Ornament of the Cāḷukya family, when Govindarāja [IV Rāṣṭrakūṭa] was enraged with him; the heroism of this Crest-Jewel of Vassals, who attacked and conquered again the vassals who came in battalions on orders of the supreme emperor Gojjega [Govindarāja]; the strength of the arms of this Arikēsari, who restored imperial power *(sakalasāmrājya-)* to King Baddega [Amoghavarṣa III Rāṣṭrakūṭa]—who had come to him trusting in him—after destroying the overweening king [Govindarāja], who

67. On *samāsōkti* see Thimmappayya 1977: 147–49, and for its standard definition in Sanskrit, *Kuvalayānanda* vv. 60 ff. The mixed prose-verse literary form of the *campū* may have been a Kannada invention (beginning with Guṇavarma, c. 900, whose now-lost work is known through citation). Although the Prakrit *saṃkīrṇakathā,* such as the *Kuvalayamālā,* has certain affinities with the Kannada examples, it shares little of their grandeur, especially in its prose passages. Ratnaśrījñāna's naming Āryaśūra's *Jātakamālā* a *campū* (*KĀ* 1.31) seems more a matter of sectarian pride than genre affiliation. It is not a coincidence that the first undisputed Sanskrit example, the *Nalacampū* of Trivikramabhaṭṭa (fl. 915), was composed at the court of Indrarāja III Rāṣṭrakūṭa.

> had taken a stand in opposition, and who all alone put to flight the great hero Bappu, the younger brother of [the enemy] Kakkala.[68]

The historical details—how in the final decades before the collapse of Rāṣṭrakūṭa rule real power had shifted further to the east to a lineage calling itself Cāḷukya and based in the town of Vēmulavāḍa in today's western Andhra (only to be seized around 973 by yet another Cāḷukya family further north, see chapter 3.3)—are not what sustains our attention in such a passage. It is instead the cultural form Pampa invented to communicate these details. He refashioned in the vernacular a Sanskrit epic discourse on power and thereby reenvisioned the old transregional political order for another, very different kind of world.

In full accord with this political re-visioning is the new spatialization of Pampa's poem. At this third level of negotiation with the cosmopolitan prototype, the text's geographical imagination is adjusted to the new narrative project. The "City of the Elephant," Hastinapura, which is home to the Bhārata clan in the Sanskrit epic, becomes Vēmulavāḍa. The grand circumambulation of the quarters of the subcontinent that is repeatedly deployed to organize the action of the epic becomes a circuit of the central Deccan. The rivers from which the waters are collected for the hero's coronation ritual at the end of the work even include a stream in the Kannada heartland of Banavāsi, described in one of the poet's most justly cherished passages.[69] What Pampa has done is shrink the great Clime of the Descendants of Bharata *(bhāratavarṣa)* to a Kannada regional world and narrow the vision of political power to the space in which it appears to have actually operated in the late tenth century. The *Mārgam*'s *kannaḍada nāḍu,* the "culture-land in Kannaḍa," is now the all-important political and aesthetic framework. This third literary modality, providing local analogies for transregional points of reference, is an exact spatial equivalent to what occurs at the level of narrative with the realist localization of the myth-epic's political discourse and at the level of linguistic form with the creation of a cosmopolitan-vernacular literary language.

It is in the context of this cultural-political achievement that we need to understand Pampa's important claim at the end of his work—in the very last verse, before the rewards of reading *(phalaśruti),* the list of the poem's moral exempla, and the colophon—regarding the ethical and political instruction of the community for which he has written his *Bhāratam:* "In view of this apposite [re]composition of the celebrated work of Vyāsamuni, and in view of his production of his expansive poems of Place *(dēsi),* is it for nothing that [Pampa] has become known as 'Teacher of the Culture-Land *(nāḍu)*'?"[70] The

68. *VAV* 9.52 prose.
69. *VAV* 1.51 ff., 4.26 ff., 14.31 with Narasimhachar's note (in *Pampabhāratadīpike*) ad loc.
70. *VAV* 14.62. *nāḍovaja* is a *tadbhava* of *nāḍu-upādhyāya.*

land to which Pampa transmits a new political vision is here projected as a kind of whole—by no means coextensive with what is today the union state of Karnataka but overlapping with parts of it—marked out intelligibly in conceptual space, though far less precisely in geographical space than the juridical-political needs of the modern Indian national state require. And an audience is conceived to exist for the poet's art and instruction—or better put, an audience is summoned into being by the poet's art and instruction—who would learn a new vision of polity, a vernacular epic vision in what was a new and differently relevant regional world.

Pampa's *Vikramārjunavijayam* was the first in a series of localizations of the superposed epic tradition in Kannada country. Within a couple of generations Ranna produced his *Sāhasabhīmavijayam,* providing a comparable double-narrative poem for the Kalyāṇa Cāḷukya court.[71] Still other Karnataka *Mahābhāratas* reproduced such localizations, in the service of what seem to have been new or different cultural-political projects. These include the *Karṇāṭabhāratakathāmañjarī* (The Essence of the Bhārata Story in Kannada) of Kumāravyāsa (1419–46, an exact contemporary of the Gwaliyari *Mahābhārata* poet Viṣṇudās, chapter 10.1) and the *Jaiminibhāratam* of Lakṣmīśa (c. 1520–85). Neither pursues precisely the same aims as Pampa's *Bhāratam.* The hero of Kumāravyāsa's work, for example, is the god Viṣṇu himself, though now Viṣṇu in localized form—Vīranārāyaṇa of Gadag, the poet's native town in northern Karnataka. The invocation throughout the book of "Gadugina Vīranārāyaṇa" thus generates its own quite unmistakable form of regionalization. More important still, it was texts like Kumāravyāsa's and Lakṣmīśa's that took the impulse of epic vernacularization out of the royal court and, through oral performance (on the basis of written texts) in villages across the Kannada-speaking world, actualized the vast sociotextual community that existed in Pampa's work only *in potentia* as a projection of his literary idiom, narrative of power, and geographical vision.[72] Yet, absent Pampa's various achievements—his aesthetic, political, and territorial vernacularizations—this community of readers, listeners, and cultural subjects might not have come to be at all.

9.4 A NEW PHILOLOGY: FROM NORM-BOUND PRACTICE TO PRACTICE-BOUND NORM

The *Kavirājamārgam* went some way in establishing the groundwork for a systematic reflection on and disciplinary organization of literary Kannada. The

71. See *Sāhasabhīmavijayam* 1.31: "The great poet Ranna has composed this *Gadāyuddham* comparing the King Satyāśraya Pṛthivīvallabha to the son of the Wind [Bhīma]."

72. Over 150 manuscripts of Kumāravyāsa dating from the mid-sixteenth century onward are extant; for Pampa's *Bhārata* we have only four. Kumāravyāsa's familiarity with Pampa is dis-

philologization attested first in the *Mārgam* is not only precocious but, with respect to other literary cultures of southern India, both autonomous and uncommon. Kannada grammatical science originated in complete independence from Tamil, the only tradition of comparable antiquity.[73] By the same token, Kannada philology seems to have exerted little influence on its neighbors. Marathi, notwithstanding the Kannada example at its doorstep, was grammaticized first by nineteenth-century missionaries. Even so, the history of south Indian philology, to say nothing of its comparative history, is still very much in its infancy in the West, and many questions concerning the wider conversations among Deccani and peninsular intellectuals that may have taken place during the early centuries of vernacularization remain, not only unanswered, but even unasked.

Although the *Mārgam* refrains from a systematic study of grammar, prosody, or lexicon (given the parameters established by its Sanskrit models), it touches on all three areas, broaching a number of topics that both because of their importance to the cosmopolitan vernacular and because it is the *Mārgam* that broached them, would continue to be addressed by grammarians, metricians, and lexicographers for centuries to come. More important than the specific problematics the *Mārgam* bequeaths, however, is the metadiscursive framework within which it situates them. It bears repeating that what everywhere conditions the *Mārgam*'s exposition is the specification of Kannada distinction, and this distinction is constituted against the backdrop of the Sanskrit philological episteme—defining what language, especially the language of literary culture, is supposed to be. Every feature of the literary in Kannada is marked by a calculation of how the local responds to the seemingly ever-present global. Equally consequential is what the local had to do, philologically speaking, in order to respond at all.

Various features of that dominant episteme have been noted already, but a brief summary may be useful. Fundamental was the transcendent authority from which philological knowledge was supposed to derive. Sanskrit grammatical traditions often associated knowledge of the language with an episode of divine revelation, a sacral relationship perpetuated in temple endowments for the study of grammar (chapter 4.1). While revelation is called upon to authorize cultural (and often political) practices in many

cussed in Nayak and Venkatachala Sastry 1974, vol. 5: 661 ff. There is no scholarship on the Kannada *Jaiminibhāratam* in the West; its reception history and relation to the Telugu version (c. 1450–80) await clarification even in Kannada scholarship.

73. The first datable Tamil grammar, the *Vīracōḻiyam*, was not produced until the early eleventh century (on the *Tolkāppiyam*, see chapter 10 n. 39); the Telugu *Āndhraśabdacintāmaṇi*, long ascribed to the eleventh-century poet Nannaya, is now viewed as a mid-seventeenth-century work (chapter 10 n. 38). Linkages between the *Śabdamaṇidarpaṇam* and the Tamil *Naṉṉūl*, and between *Karṇāṭakabhāṣābhūṣaṇa* and *Āndhraśabdacintāmaṇi*, remain to be explored.

parts of the world, the Sanskrit tradition perfected the argument for the transcendence of its own authority and the primacy of its changeless linguistic organization, from which all other languages could mark their difference only as deviation and corruption. In accordance with this ideologeme, forms of Sanskrit philological thought were held to communicate a priori norms unaffected by history. Sanskrit grammar, accordingly, never proceeds by way of literary exemplification: literature does not authorize grammar, but instead, grammar authorizes literature.[74] This was the consensus even among Sanskrit literary theorists: "Words and meanings endowed with expression-forms and without faults"—so begins the most famous definition of *kāvya* in Indian history (Mammaṭa's *Kāvyaprakāśa,* Light on Literature, c. 1050). To express the matter in Sanskrit terms, the *lakṣaṇa,* or norm, always precedes the *lakṣya,* its embodiment. When explaining this very binary, introduced in the definition of language analysis *(lakṣyalakṣaṇe vyākaraṇam),* the grammarian Patañjali dismisses the role of instantiations: "From the rules themselves people can grasp the words [that instantiate them]."[75] The grammatical norms were regarded as eternal largely because the practices that, conceptually at least, formed the primary object of Sanskrit grammatical inquiry, namely, those of the Veda, were considered timeless, even authorless.[76]

As a result, a philology in the service of a cosmopolitan vernacular was compelled first of all to secure some kind of authority to establish norms, discipline, and stability. This was all the more necessary given its object. After all, a vernacular was a language whose very essence, according to prevailing representations, consisted of abnormality, indiscipline, instability, and untruth. Here is how the *Mārgam* addresses the issue:

> Among all herds of animals wild and domesticated, and flocks of birds, there have been forever countless languages produced each for its own species. In the same way, there exists innately among men the uncultured use of languages.
>
> How can unlearned, common people know how to judge that one usage is good and another bad? Their behavior is indifferent, just as herds of animals will indifferently eat grass or grain or fodder.
>
> Therefore, one must completely master theory. The man who has not first studied for himself the earlier literary compositions cannot possibly either possess knowledge with respect to words or attain beauty in a literary work.

74. Thus literature was often produced to illustrate grammar (see chapter 4.1). In Patañjali's *Mahābhāṣya,* literary works are rarely cited and never as standards of usage or proof texts (chapter 2.1). Literary usage does not become authoritative for Sanskrit grammar until perhaps the seventeenth century (*Prakriyāsarvasva,* Scharfe 1977: 174 n.).

75. *sūtrata eva śabdān pratipadyante, Mahābhāṣya* vol. 1: 12.15 ff.

76. See chapters 1.1 and 4.1, and Pollock 1985, 1989, 1997.

> Even a dimwit can derive some knowledge straightaway by instruction from a teacher—but there will be no real strength in his expression. Are not male and female parrots able to repeat immediately what they have learned?[77]

While recognizing the multiplicity of languages and acknowledging a certain inborn linguistic competence, the *Mārgam* is unwilling, in conformity with the dominant paradigm, to grant literary status to raw practice; correct usage must be knowledgeable usage. But in the languages of Place there exists no divine grammar by which usage can be judged correct in the first place. If knowledgeability derives from mastery of some kind of theory *(āgama),* this in turn is shown to be intimately, if paradoxically, dependent on antecedent *literary* practices that have achieved some kind of canonicity (hence the centrality, to the *Mārgam* and later philological works, of the encomia of past poets). The circularity implicit here, as well as the criteria of excellence, are questions passed over in silence.

The founding of grammatical norms on literary practices in the vernacular world (it is present in Tamil, Telugu, and elsewhere, too, chapter 10.1) represents a radical break with earlier thought. An entirely new model of cultural authority had to be constructed, and a new legislative power generated. These were the aims behind the *Mārgam*'s project of theorizing, constituting, justifying, and safeguarding Kannada difference in every area of literary form. Consider for a moment the discussion of the selection of lexical items. The first chapter of the *Mārgam* closes with a statement encapsulating its general view:

> Words should enter [into a poem] in accordance with the thought [of the poet] and should not be permitted to counteract it. The beauty of the language of the culture-land [must be maintained] in the [use of] Kannada words *(nāḷnuḍiya beḍaṃgu kannaḍada mātinol).* Propriety must be observed for Sanskrit words in due measure, and no stumbling over [Sanskrit] words with their harsh phonemes should be permitted. The composition thereby achieves sweetness and becomes strong, growing forth like the sprout of a vine. Such is the Way of the One Endowed with Consistent Political Wisdom.[78]

This admonition for solicitous attention to proportionality in the quantity of vernacular and cosmopolitan words—the issue that underpins the many forms of what, as we have seen, would elsewhere be called *maṇipravāla*[79]—finds specific application in the structure of compounds, a topic treated meticulously by later grammarians under the rubric *arisamāsa,* "compound of hostiles":

77. *KRM* 1.7–10.

78. *KRM* 1.149.

79. The same issue was addressed in Renaissance defenses of poetry (chapter 11.3, especially n. 31).

> One should form compounds in the Kannada language with the awareness that, if there is to be an intermixture of Sanskrit loan words *(samasaṃskṛta-)*, this must be done judiciously. Such is the Way enunciated by those conversant with theory.
>
> If however one intentionally decides to join in compound-expressions [the aforementioned] Sanskrit and Kannada words without understanding [the conditions of their combinability], the poem will be aesthetically displeasing *(virasam)*, as when mixing drops of buttermilk with boiling milk.[80]

A variety of other formal properties, beyond lexical choice and nominalization, required a defense of the local on the part of the *Mārgam*. One example from the domain of metrics is the apparent violation of caesura. In the Kannada realization of cosmopolitan verse forms (both Sanskrit and Prakrit), the particular rhythmic sensibilities of Kannada required, from an early date, ignoring word-boundary pauses within and over the metrical line (and sometimes at the half-stanza). Examples are found in some of the oldest poems in the language, like the Śravaṇabeḷgoḷa epigraphs. The *Mārgam* needed to justify and defend local practice and did so by appealing again to a new vernacular authority: "Earlier teachers *(ācārya)* explain this 'fault,' so to call it, as a virtue in Kannada; in fact, they prefer it. They violate caesura on the grounds that it is superfluous, since in its stead is placed an initial alliteration that segments [the line] *(khaṃḍaprāsa)*, and argue that this is in accordance with the aesthetic of Place *(dēsi)*."[81]

All these fine points in the balance of Kannada and Sanskrit are likely to seem mere empty scholasticism to present-day readers. But a fairer evaluation takes note of the importance given to such issues in the framing of theory by vernacular intellectuals everywhere—not just at the royal courts of India but across the greater part of Asia for a thousand years, and in vernacularizing Europe too (chapter 11.2)—who freighted them with large cultural-political significance. The preservation of a proportionate distinctiveness in such things as lexicon, nominalization, and the structure and selection of meters was a core value in the practice of vernacularity; this is transparent in Pampa, whose opening verses echo the *Mārgam* and whose poetry throughout enacts its prescriptions. Such fastidious negotiation between the cosmopolitan and vernacular in theory and practice occurred at the most intimate levels of discourse. It is noteable that, while the technical vocabulary of the *Mārgam* for discussing metrics, lexicon, and the rest is almost exclusively Sanskritic (a tendency that continues unchecked in the entire later tradition), their aesthetic impact is usually described in a vernacular idiom. In the passage cited earlier, highly Sanskritized language pertaining to sys-

80. *KRM* 1.51, 58.
81. *KRM* 1.75.

tematic thought is complemented by *dēsi* words for beauty *(beḍaṅgu)* or force of expression *(nuḍivalme)*.[82] It is as if the localization of the imaginative and the aesthetic, in the face of the globalization of the informational and the conceptual, had become part of the common sense of vernacularity—as if it were possible, at the start of the vernacular epoch, to be local only in feeling the world but not in knowing it.

Given the powerful model of Sanskrit philology, with its full apparatus of grammars, dictionaries, treatises on the arts of literature (especially poetics and versification), and commentaries galore, a comparable set of instruments for disciplining and dignifying a language of Place was clearly essential if vernacularization was to be successful. The philological works of Kannada, which grew out of a theory of vernacular aesthetics as presented in texts like the *Mārgam* and embodied in poems like Pampa's, not only shared the project of ensuring the cultural-political elevation of Kannada but, like the Sanskrit texts to which they looked, were almost without exception the products of courtly activity. This imposing body of scholarship deserves a monograph of its own, for though it has some parallels in other south Indian vernacular cultures, none seems to have been as insistent on the production and defense of literary difference, or perhaps as accomplished in its scientific achievement. (The only component absent from the philological repertory of Kannada is commentaries on literary works, something especially puzzling in the Indian context.) Here only a few key texts can be noticed, to give a sense of the larger development, before we look in more detail at the masterpiece of Kannada philology, the *Śabdamaṇidarpaṇam.* While acknowledging that the god of vernacular philology most definitely lies in the details, this review concentrates on major themes and tendencies in the process by which Kannada was confirmed as a cosmopolitan vernacular while keeping in view the political orders in which this process was embedded.

In the late tenth century, two new forms were developed for Kannada philology: the lexicon and the metrical treatise. The first dictionary, only fragmentarily preserved, is the so-called *Rannanighaṇṭu* (c. 990), ascribed to Ranna, "emperor-poet" to the kings of the Kalyāṇa Cāḷukya dynasty. We cannot get a very precise sense of the text's scope from the extant portion, but in addition to offering synonyms of rare Kannada words by way of the local lexeme *(dēsi)* or Sanskrit derivative *(tadbhava),* it supplies definitions in Sanskrit for what in some cases are everyday Kannada words. This suggests that its objective was disciplinary ennoblement, that it aimed to provide the appurtenances of scholarship, whether practical or not, without which the ver-

82. *KRM* 1.9–10. So also in the eulogies to poets. Janna praises Guṇavarma for his clever language *(jāṇṇuḍi),* Pampa for his sweetness *(iṃpu),* Ponna for the quality of his thought *(bage)* (*Anantanāthapurāṇam* of Janna 1.35). Compare Robson 1983: 312 on the Javanese *kalangwan.*

nacular could not be literary.[83] It is perhaps just this tendency that was strengthened in the great Sanskrit-Kannada lexicons that followed Ranna, such as Nāgavarma's *Abhidhānavastukōśa* (c. 1040) and Maṅgarāja's *Abhinavābhidhānam* (1398). In their conceptual organization these works were wholly dependent on the models of Sanskrit lexicographers, as Nāgavarma acknowledges by citing his predecessors.[84] Their main purpose was to make available to writers of Kannada poetry as wide a range as possible of Sanskrit vocables and their synonyms. Whether the rise of this genre of lexicon was connected with a deterioration of Sanskrit competence among Kannada literati is unclear; the evidence of long-term change in linguistic knowledge is not easy to interpret. While the later history of lexicography is decidedly Kannada-centric, with a half-dozen dictionaries produced between 1400 and 1700 that define *dēsi* and *tadbhava* words to serve the reader of Kannada literature, the target idiom in use is often the far more Sanskritized form. At all events, one thing is as unambiguous in the history of Kannada lexicography as it is in Kannada literature: while Sanskrit had fully penetrated the language, it nevertheless was always perceived as something other than local.[85]

Around the time Ranna was taking the first steps in Kannada lexicography, Nāgavarma completed the first treatise on Kannada metrics, the *Chandōmbudhi* (Ocean of Meters). Among the more intricate prosopographical problems of early Kannada literary culture is sorting out the different Nāgavarmas; there may have been as many as five in the first few centuries. According to scholarly consensus, the author of the *Chandōmbudhi,* normally identified as Nāgavarma I, was a Brahman of the Kauṇḍinya *gotra* and a descendant of settlers in the very village of Veṅgi where Pampa's father was born. He eventually relocated to Kannada land and became a client of Rakkasa, younger brother and later successor to Rāchamalla, the Gaṅga king who ruled in the last quarter of the tenth century. Nāgavarma tells us that he "learned from the learned" and wrote for them a treatise, a work "flowing with the nine *rasas*, new in diction, in which the ways of Place have become a thing of beauty," a text he knows full well to be an innovation, "an unprecedented work."[86]

83. The extant portion actually begins: *kuḷir ene śaityam,* "The [Kannada word] *kuḷir* means [Sanskrit] *śaitya* [cold]"; similarly v. 5, "*beḷaku* means *dīpa* [lamp]"; v. 6, *baḷi* means *vaṃśa* [bamboo/lineage]."

84. Amarasiṃha, Bhāguri, Śāśvata, and Halāyudha.

85. On Kannada lexicons see Nayak and Venkatachala Sastry 1974, vol. 3: 733–35; Venkatachala Sastry 1992.

86. *Chandōmbudhi* v. 12 [4] (the name of the village is Veṅgipaḷu); vv. 27–28. See also *Kāvyāvalōkanam,* ed. Narasimhachar 1967: 14–15. Krishnabhatta's edition restores the opening verses (in praise of Śrī, Śiva, Vināyaka, Durgā, the Sun, and Bhāratī) suppressed by Kittel. Nāgavarma refers to the learned in v. 8 [2] *(ballar)* and his work as *apūrvam āge kṛtiyam* (v. 8

Tenth-century Karnataka was in fact a time and place of remarkable creativity in metrics across the board, a discipline of decisive importance for literary art and one that, as formulated in India, had enormous repute throughout Asia. The first known commentary on the ancient Sanskrit *Chandaḥsūtra* of Piṅgala (perhaps along with much of the section on nonsacred meters in the *Chandaḥsūtra*) was written by Halāyudha, the Sanskrit lexicographer who provided a model for later Kannada dictionaries and whose grammatical *śāstrakāvya, Kavirahasya* (The Poet's Secret) we noticed earlier.[87] One of the earliest synthetic accounts of Sanskrit *kāvya* metrics was produced by Jayakīrti in the *Chandonuśāsana* (c. 1000), which includes a substantial section on Kannada meters.[88] Although it is impossible for us to reconstruct the conversation between Sanskrit and Kannada metricians, Jayakīrti's work suggests that it was very likely two-way. And yet the discursive universe was entirely Sanskritic. The whole structure of Nāgavarma's exposition, for instance, with respect to basic vocabulary, foundational concepts, techniques of scansion (*guru, laghu, pāda,* the eight *gaṇa*s, and so on) would be familiar to students of Sanskrit prosody, even though it is Kannada that Nāgavarma is characterizing within this borrowed apparatus and upon which his eye is fixed. Second-consonant rhyme *(prāsa),* for example, is explained not as such but as differentiating Kannada from Sanskrit (vv. 31 ff.; it is something essential for Kannada, without which poetry in the language is unable to achieve beauty, v. 50). But it is the larger framework of Nāgavarma's exposition of the metrical types that shows most clearly how the relationship of cosmopolitan and local forms was addressed in vernacular theorization.

Nāgavarma argues that a wide range of meters, arising from the cosmopolitan languages, are universally available to languages of Place. A long-misunderstood passage at the beginning of his formal exposition makes this clear:

ademṭemḍoḍe saṃskṛtaṃ prākṛtam apabhraṃśaṃ paiśācikam emba mūṟuvare bhāṣegaḷoḷ puṭṭuva [draviḍāndhrakarṇāṭakādiṣaṭpancāsat] sarvaviṣayabhāṣājātigaḷ akkuṃ.

If one were to ask, [we would say that] there are species of meter common to all the languages [of the fifty-six dominions, Drāviḍa, Āndhra, Karṇātaka, and so on]. These metrical species have arisen from the three languages, Sanskrit, Prakrit, and Apabhramsha, and from the "half" language, Paishachi.[89]

---

[2]) and *aśeṣavidvadjanahitamam* (v. 29 [Kittel 11 differs]). "In which the ways of Place . . . ," *dēsiye dēsevettudem . . . prabandhamam* (v. 11 [16]).

87. Chapter 4.1. Halāyudha's commentary on the *Chandaḥsūtra* was written at the court of Muñja of the Paramāras, where the metrician emigrated perhaps in consequence of the weakening of Rāṣṭrakūṭa power with the death of his patron, Kṛṣṇa III.

88. Velankar 1949: 37–38.

89. See *Chandōmbudhi* p. 10 in the edition of Krishnabhatta (the bracketed portion is available in a number of mss.).

It is not that the fifty-six languages themselves have arisen from the cosmopolitan languages, as all scholars who have dealt with the passage have suggested ("daughter languages," according to Ferdinand Kittel).[90] No Kannada grammarian or scholar of any other philological discipline, while fully acknowledging the limits of the vernacular relative to the transregional presence of Sanskrit, Prakrit, and Apabhramsha, ever conceived of Kannada as having evolved from some other language (let alone used the language of kinship to describe this). Rather, Nāgavarma's point is that all literary languages make use of the cosmopolitan metrical forms, and these he proceeds to describe: the fixed syllabic meters *(akṣaragaṇa)* and certain moraic meters with or without fixed cadences *(mātrāchandas, mātrāgaṇachandas)* (chapters 2–4). It is these structures that are borrowed directly from "both languages," Sanskrit and Prakrit, and are common to "the languages of all realms" (*sarvaviṣayabhāṣā-*, chapter 1, v. 44 [70]). Sharply to be distinguished from these, however, are the meters specific to the vernacular world, those "species belonging to the [language of the] Karṇāṭaka region" (*karṇāṭakaviṣaya[bhāṣā]-jāti,* which he describes in chapter 5). If the vernacular knows its place, it also knows its prerogatives.

Instructive as these early works on lexicography and metrics are, the supreme achievement of Kannada philology is unquestionably grammar. It is here that all the powerful tendencies driving forward the process of vernacularization converged in a remarkable synthesis. The quest for specification of the vernacular particular from within the dominating Sanskrit epistemological universal, the search for discipline in the supposedly lawless dialectal and a new authority upon which this discipline could be founded, the role of the royal court as the social site par excellence for the production of systematic vernacular knowledge—this entire culture-power complex of vernacularity found its most condensed expression in Kannada grammar.

The *Kavirājamārgam* laid the groundwork for a philological science in Kannada, including grammatical science, and did so from a location at the center of the Rāṣṭrakūṭa court. The same symbiosis of grammar and power remained everywhere in evidence in the Kannada world in the centuries following the *Mārgam.* The actual grammatical organization of Kannada began with two texts of the early eleventh century. One, the *Kāvyāvalōkanam* (Light on Literature), is a literary treatise written in Kannada and very similar in conception to the *Mārgam* except that its first chapter, known as the

90. *Chandōmbudhi* ed. Kittel prose section 67, p. 22; cf. p. 21 for "daughter languages." Rice translated: "Born in the three and a half languages . . . are the Dravida (Tamil), Andhra (Telugu), Karnataka (Kannada) and others" (*Karṇāṭakabhāṣābhūṣaṇam,* p. iv); so Master: "There will be the fifty-six varieties of language, Tamil, Telugu, and Kanarese, etc., which originate from the three and a half languages" (1943: 44). The correct analysis of this passage I owe to T. V. Venkatachala Sastry.

"Śabdasmṛti" (Tradition of Words), comprises a brief systematic exposition of the rudiments of grammar. The other, the *Karṇāṭakabhāṣābhūṣaṇa* (Ornament of the Kannada Language), is a full grammar written in Sanskrit. The author of both works is Nāgavarma (II)—distinguished from his namesakes by the sobriquet Kavitāguṇōdaya (Source of Literary Excellence) that appears in the colophons of his works. This Nāgavarma held the post of *kaṭakopādhyāya,* "teacher of the *kaṭaka,*" at the court of Jayasiṃha Jagadekamalla I of the Kalyāṇa Cāḷukya dynasty (r. 1015–42).[91] The next significant work—and one of the greatest vernacular grammars of the premodern world—is the *Śabdamaṇidarpaṇam* (Jeweled Mirror of Language, henceforth *Darpaṇa*). This was written by Kēśirāja in 1260 at the Yādava (that is, Hoysaḷa) court, where he too was a teacher of the *kaṭaka,* as he proclaims at the end of his book:

> The *Śabdamaṇidarpaṇam* of the noble Yādavakaṭakācārya Kēśava will endure as long as the sun and moon, Mount Meru and the ocean, spreading far and wide.[92]

Whatever the precise meaning of the title *kaṭakopādhyāya* (or *kaṭakācārya,* as Kēśirāja writes it; perhaps "head teacher of the royal capital"), it was evidently a position central to court culture and one that its occupants were proud to advertise. That grammarians so often held the post makes it clear, too, that, like lexicography, metrics, and literature itself, vernacular grammar—as the history of its Sanskrit counterpart would lead us to expect—was an enterprise underwritten by political elites and courtly intellectuals.

As an epistemological object Kannada grammar, too, was profoundly shaped by its Sanskrit model: the last premodern grammar of the language (Bhaṭṭa Akalaṅka Deva's *Karṇāṭaśabdānuśāsana,* 1604), like the first *(Karṇāṭakabhāṣābhūṣaṇa),* was written in Sanskrit. And yet a tension may everywhere be felt as this exogenous casing, capacious and flexible though it may be, is stretched over a language built to totally different specifications that con-

91. On the evidence of Nāgavarma's recently discovered *campū,* the *Vīravardhamānapurāṇa,* which is dated to 1042. In *Anantanāthapurāṇam* (1230) Janna refers to Kavitāguṇōdaya Nāgavarma as Jagadekamalla's *kaṭakopādhyāya.* (The second half of Janna's verse refers to "the *kaṭakopādhyāya* of the present day" under the Hoysaḷa king Narasiṃha II [r. 1220–35], i.e., Sumanōbāṇa, the teacher of Janna (and father-in-law of Mallikārjuna, see the following note). Nāgavarma II is also author of the *Abhidhānavastukōśa* referred to earlier.

92. *ŚMD* v. 341. He attributes the same title to his maternal grandfather: "I am the poet Kēśava, the glorious grandson of Sumanōbāṇa, who was a poet and *kaṭakācārya* of the Yādavas; and the son of Cidānanda Mallikārjuna, supreme master of *yoga*" (v. 2). Mallikārjuna was a literary anthologist and *praśasti* poet; his grand eulogy of the Hoysaḷavaṃśa is carved on the walls of the Mallikārjuna temple in Basarāḷu, *EC* 7: 211 ff. nos. 29 and 30, dated 1234 and 1237); his *Sūktisudhārṇava,* prepared for the Hoysaḷa king Vīrasōmēśvara (r. 1234–54) (see 1.24 and colophon) is the foremost anthology of early Kannada literature.

stantly threatened to escape its enclosure. The points of deviation that result from this misfit are as significant as the points of convergence. Let us examine the latter first.

The most striking fact is that the structure of the grammatical exposition is entirely Sanskrit-derived. Consider the formal organization in the eleventh-century Kannada-language "Śabdasmṛti." Its six sections concern, respectively: technical terminology *(saṃjñā),* euphonic combination *(sandhi),* the noun *(nāma),* nominal compounding *(samāsa),* the secondary derivative *(taddhita),* and the verb *(ākhyāta).* This very closely resembles the structure of Śarvavarman's *Kātantra,* though Nāgavarma adds a section on technical terms, absent in the *Kātantra,* and eliminates the case relation *(kāraka)* section that the ancient grammar included. Indeed, it was clearly in tribute to Nāgavarma's skill in having adapted this grammar to Kannada that he was adorned with the title "The New Śarvavarma" *(abhinavaśarvavarma),* just as it was clearly in tribute to Śarvavarman's own post-Vedic, this-worldly understanding of Sanskrit grammar that his work (and not Pāṇini's) was chosen as the model for vernacularization in the first place.[93] Precisely the same structure is preserved in the *Darpaṇa,* too, though it is enlarged to include the verbal root *(dhātu),* the secondary derivative from Sanskrit (here termed *apabhraṃśa*), and the indeclinable *(avyaya).*

Not only the structure of Kannada grammar is derived from Sanskrit, so is the entire technical vocabulary for the description of Kannada grammatical phenomena. The *Darpaṇa* uses *kriyā* for verbal action; *bhūta, bhaviṣyat, saṃprati* for past, future, and present tense; *prathama[puruṣa], madhya, uttama* for third, second, and first persons of the verb; *kāraka* for case relations; *vibhakti* for case ending; *ekavacana* and so on for number; *guṇavacana* for adjective; *sarvanāma* for pronoun; *bhāvavacana* for abstract noun. And for those instances where Kannada possesses a grammatical function unavailable in Sanskrit, Sanskrit terminology is invented. Thus *gamakasamāsa* is used to refer to certain kinds of so-called consecutive compounds unknown to Sanskrit or not considered compounds (though sometimes resembling the *aluksamāsa*), while *liṅga* is used to refer to nominal themes, including declinable verbal bases. That the eyes for which this work was intended sometimes seem to be predominantly Sanskritic is suggested by explanations such as the one provided for the dual number: "Although dual morphemes do not exist in Kannada, the dual can be inferred from the context" (*sūtra* 94). The evidence from lexicography for the pervasion of the vernacular by Sanskrit during

93. *Kāvyāvalōkanam* 4.23, and *Anantanāthapurāṇam* 1.34, where Nāgavarma is called "a present-day Śarvavarma" (*idānīṃtanaśarvavarma;* recall the similar title given to Śākaṭāyana two centuries earlier). On the Sanskrit grammarian Śarvavarman see chapter 4.1. Thirty-four of the 280 *sūtras* of the *Bhāṣābhūṣaṇa* (and 17 of the 97 *sūtras* of the "Śabdasmṛti") are borrowed or translated from the *Kātantra* (Kulli 1984: 41).

this period is further confirmed in the Sanskrit glosses that Kēśirāja provides for his list of roots, as well as in his final chapter on "obscure usages" *(gūḍhapadaprayogam)* of earlier writers, which are again defined by Sanskrit terms.

Yet if the discursive foundations of the grammar are wholly appropriated from Sanskrit, its conceptual orientation, as the example of the dual number or the *gamakasamāsa* shows, is, on the contrary, to constitute its object by way of a range of differentia from Sanskrit—in phonology, *sandhi,* syntax, vocabulary, and the rest. The premodern grammarians of Kannada fully understood that their object of analysis was an order of language different from the one whose analytical tools they adopted in order to describe it, and that therefore a tension between the two was inherent. They never maintained that the language was a derivative of Sanskrit, any more than the lexicographers and metricians did. Nor did they consider it a Prakrit (let alone an Apabhramsha), in contrast to some north Indian regional languages (Gujarati, for example, was conceived of as such by its poets as late as the eighteenth century).[94] No grammarian ever adopted the diagnostic model available from earlier Prakrit grammars for deriving the forms of Kannada by transfer rules from Sanskrit. The one exception to the otherwise consistent picture of Kannada autonomy is found in the analysis of *tadbhava* words, but to understand this requires a more general account of the grammarians' conception of the Kannada lexicon.

The *Darpaṇa* analyzes the vocabulary of Kannada according to four categories: *dēśīya,* "words of Place," often also termed *accagannaḍa,* "pure Kannada"; *apabhraṃśa* or *tadbhava,* "corrupted words," that is to say, those derived from Sanskrit or Prakrit; *samasaṃskṛta,* "words equal with Sanskrit," borrowed directly with virtually no phonological change (called *tatsama* in Sanskrit philology); and *tatsama,* twenty-one vocables (*maṇi, mañca,* etc.) that Kannada and Sanskrit share though the question of provenance is undecidable.[95] It is only for the *apabhraṃśa / tadbhava* lexemes that we encounter the use of transformational phonological rules that seem to presuppose the primacy of Sanskrit. But Kēśirāja presents these lexemes at once as "*tadbhava*s of Sanskrit" *(sakkadada tadbhavaṃgaḷ)* and as "Kannada [words] that have arisen for [i.e., in place of] Sanskrit" *(saṃskṛtakke puṭṭida kannaḍa).* Indeed, his purpose is anything but to fetishize their Sanskrit origins. Quite the opposite, such words provide precisely a way to *avoid* the use of Sanskrit: "For those who want to employ pure Kannada *(accagannaḍam)* with unadulterated expres-

94. So for the seventeenth-century Gujarati poet Akho (Yashaschandra 2003: 581). I know no reference to Kannada as Prakrit except the inscription noted in n. 31 of this chapter and a fragmentary record of 700 (*IA* 10: 60; whether the language in question is Kannada may be doubted).

95. Neither Kēśirāja nor any other Kannada grammarian ever put the matter just this way, however. The words in the *tatsama* category are all clearly Dravidian in origin.

sion *(cokkaḷikeyim)* without resorting to Sanskrit, *apabhraṃśa* words provide a handy treasury. They are permitted to form compounds with *dēśīya* words."[96] The analysis of *tadbhava* and *dēśīya* words is meant to help frame Kannada's stringent rules on nominalization (one of them is given in the above *sūtra*), which serve to index the heterogeneity of Kannada and Sanskrit: unlike the two other classes of words, the *tadbhava* and *dēśīya* (along with the twenty-one *tatsamas*), which can freely compound with each other, Sanskrit cannot enter into compounds with "pure Kannada words" except in such rare circumstances as archaisms and lists of courtly titles *(biruḍa)*. Other such combinations, as we saw in the *Mārgam* too, are considered "conflicted" or "hostile" compounds.[97]

The concern, found throughout the *Darpaṇa,* with specifying what makes Kannada different is consolidated at the end of the text in a memorial verse that seeks to identify nine factors, in everything from phonology, *sandhi,* and syntax to lexicon and prosody, that make up "the uniqueness of Kannada":

> Compounds that are intelligible [even though they do not conform to the rules of Sanskrit compounding] *(gamakasamāsa);* the phonemes /ḻ/ *[ṟaḷa],* /ṟ/ *[śakaṭarepha],* /ḷ/ *[kuḷa],* and /ḷ/ *[kṣaḷa];* harmonious *sandhi* [not exceeding two phonemes]; locative absolutes that are appropriate [to Kannada, i.e., even given the absence of strictly locative forms]; vocables that are identical to Sanskrit [but used with slight phonological change] *(samasaṃskṛta);* v/m and h/p functioning as allophones [as they do not in Sanskrit]; the ban on using Sanskrit indeclinables as nominal themes; the fact that [certain] conjunct consonants are prosodically weak [as they are not in Sanskrit]; and "violation" of caesura.[98]

The verse may be an interpolation, since nowhere in the text does Kēśirāja use the phrase *sati saptami* (locative absolute) or discuss the syntactic structure as such (though absolute constructions certainly do exist in Kannada), or examine caesura violation.[99] Yet manuscripts show that the verse is old

96. *ŚMD sūtra* 314.

97. The strictures on compounds of incompatibles such as *mukhatāvare* (in contrast to *mukhapadma*) are found at *ŚMD sūtra* 185 (especially the *prayoga*), cf. 90 *prayoga* (where *KRM* 1.59 is also cited). On *tadbhavas* see also *ŚMD* 266–67 and *vṛtti; tatsama* is described in 312, *samasaṃskṛta* in 90. From the analysis in the *ŚMD* one may deduce that, for Jains of the Kannada grammatical tradition (including Kēśirāja), *tadbhava* did not mean "existing [eternally] in that [i.e., Sanskrit]," pace Kahrs 1992, especially p. 245; nor were such words considered *prākṛta* "only insofar as they are not subject to the regularizing rules that govern the eternally existing forms of Sanskrit." Implicit in the *ŚMD,* as the preference for the term *apabhraṃśa* shows, is a conception of temporal change; also, the rule-boundedness of *tadbhava* derivation is obvious in Kēśirāja's exposition.

98. *ŚMD sūtra* 342.

99. If I understand correctly, the verse seems to get a few things wrong. The phoneme /ḷ/ called *kṣaḷa,* for example, which in Kannada represents Sanskrit /l/, is not in fact included among

and, in its attempt to specify not only the principal Kannada distinctions but the difference those distinctions make, it expresses what premodern readers are likely to have felt about the grammar's procedures and Kannada's very character. If Kannada was constructed as a conceptual object from the perspective of a Sanskrit that defined literary language, the construction was nevertheless intended to demonstrate heterogeneity and not homogeneity, indeed, to forge a grammatical weapon from the materials offered by Sanskrit in order to preserve the local particular by distancing itself from Sanskrit—and from other south Indian languages, too. Although a number of the linguistic features distinguishing Kannada from Sanskrit are of course common to other Dravidian languages, nowhere does Kēśirāja comment on what Kannada shares with Tamil or Telugu, only on how it relates, differentially, to Sanskrit.

The *Darpaṇa*'s treatment of *tadbhava/apabhraṃśa* words, which specifies and organizes a wide range of sound changes, is a notable if imperfect attempt to find lawlike processes in the apparently lawless phonological behavior of "dialectal" or "corrupted" words. It also raises a set of critical questions about the method of vernacular philology as such. When Kēśirāja explains at the beginning of his chapter on *apabhraṃśa* words that their proper use depends on the observation of norms *(lakṣaṇa)* and due regard for idiom *(lōkarūḍhi)*,[100] he is clearly directing attention toward the search for regulation and the basis of normativity presupposed by regulation. It was the challenge of precisely this search that had helped to consolidate the new method initiated by the *Mārgam* four centuries earlier and thus to bring about the complete inversion in the relationship between literature and grammatical theory, summarized earlier in this chapter, that had dominated the Indian thought world for a millennium.

It is, however, in the Kannadiga grammarians' empiricist procedures that the startling discontinuity effected by the quest for vernacular normativity is most dramatically revealed. This is evident as early as the first Kannada-language grammatical work, the "Śabdasmṛti," where literary examples are cited repeatedly.[101] But the real force of the vernacular reversal in the vector of grammatical authority is felt in the *Darpaṇa*. It is not just in reference to domains beyond the descriptive reach of the grammar, like the possible

the five phonemes of Place belonging to "pure Kannada" that Kēśirāja introduces when describing the phonological differences between Kannada and Sanskrit (these five are /ṟ/, /ḻ/, /ḷ/ [the kuḷa], /e/, and /o/). Rather it is one of the ten that are peculiar to Sanskrit (along with vocalic /r/ and /l/ both light and heavy, palatal and retroflex /s/, the three types of *visarga;* see *sūtra*s 29, 43).

100. *ŚMD sūtra* 266: *īkṣisi śikṣāsūtrada lakṣaṇamaṃ lōkarūḍhi kiḍadavol.*

101. In the same author's Sanskrit-language *Karṇāṭakabhāṣābhūṣaṇa,* quotations are comparatively few (cf. Nayak and Venkatachala Sastry 1974, vol. 3: 718 and n. 509; a seventeenth-century commentary on the work, however, cites profusely).

meanings of roots and verbal themes, that the reader is advised to come to a determination after consulting the works of those who have achieved exemplary status (*lakṣyasiddhiviḍiduvan aṟidu, sūtra* 262); for every feature under discussion, however straightforward it may be (*sandhi,* for example, or case terminations) and however undisputed the grammarian's judgment, a basis in literary usage must be provided. The text opens with an invocation of the great poets of previous generations who are to be Kēśirāja's authorities:

> The expert Way *(sumārgam)* of Gajaga, Guṇanandi, Manasija, Asaga, Candrabhaṭṭa, Guṇavarma, Śrīvijaya, Honna [= Ponna], Hampa [= Pampa], Sujanōttaṃsa—these provide the illustrative instances *(lakṣya)* in this work.[102]

Indeed, the *Darpaṇa* is as much an anthology of poetry as it is a grammar. Some twenty poets and thirty different works are cited, and virtually every rule is illustrated with quotations. At the same time, some of the proof texts cited may be Kēśirāja's own; after all, he proudly declares his status as a poet at the beginning of the text, and he ends with an account of his literary productivity. The ultimate source of normativity, therefore—and here we are at a conceptual boundary at the farthest remove from Sanskrit—can in fact be discovered in the poet-grammarian himself. We can let Kēśirāja speak here for himself: "Wherever he proceeds is the Way; however he undertakes to plant his step is the proper stance. What is inexplicable to Kēśava? . . . He alone is master of language norms in the world." [103]

The consequence of the imposition of norms through the new authority claimed by those in possession of literary excellence—including kings, like Viṣṇuvardhana of the Hoysaḷas in 1117, who himself was "capable of teaching the rules of grammar" (chapter 4.1)—was to produce a literary language of great conservatism and uniformity. By the middle of the thirteenth century, when Kēśirāja wrote, the Kannada language had begun to change dramatically. At the most basic level, the distinctive phoneme /ḻ/ *(ṟaḷa)* had already become obsolete and indistinguishable from the /ṟ/. Even though the grammarian shows himself to be fully aware of this change by allowing the phonemes to function as rhyming consonants, he insists on preserving their individuality. (The great phoneme shift from /p/ to /h/, however, was already too far advanced to be reversed; Kēśirāja actually writes Hampa instead of Pampa.)[104] As for uniformity, whereas undoubtedly a vast variety of dialects of caste and status must have been in use, only a small amount of what is apparently dialectal variation is permitted in the grammar (such as optional lengthening of /a/ in the genitive or in the accusative or before -*vōl*).

102. *ŚMD* v. 5.

103. *ŚMD* 338: *naḍedude mārgaṃ padaviḍal oḍarisidude bhaṅgi kēśavaṅgariduṇṭe* . . . | . . . *tān e lōkadoḷ lākṣaṇikam* || See also *sūtra* 2 and for his works *sūtra* 339.

104. See *sūtra* 170 (the shift was already flagged in the *Bhāṣābhūṣaṇa, sūtra* 115).

In fact, in addtion to the *Darpaṇa* itself, the literary works upon which it is based by and large promulgate a literary Kannada that had become a regional, supradialectal code. Poets and intellectuals at the southern courts of the Gaṅgas and Hoysaḷas wrote according to the same linguistic norms as their northern peers. Thus Ranna, before releasing his Kannada *campū, Sāhasabhīmavijayam,* which he composed for a king at the northernmost Karnataka court of the Cāḷukyas, could easily have his work "evaluated by the leading men in the metropolis of the king of the Gaṅgas," in the southernmost Kannada kingdom.[105]

Some four centuries after first committing the Kannada language to written form, Kannada intellectuals had embarked on a course of ever-accelerating literarization, a process fully visible in the epigraphical record, whereby a whole new set of texts and practices was brought into being. The *Kavirājamārgam* appropriated the discourse of the cosmopolitan Ways for the vernacular sphere in what turns out to have been the reappropriation of a very old, and southern, contribution to the discourse of cultural cosmopolitanism itself. It described the elementary forms of a vernacular philology and established Kannada as a language of science even as it demonstrated that it could function as a language of literature. Moreover, the *Mārgam* turned space into place by mapping out the domain within which the new literature would circulate, and it projected something of a community of readers and listeners. All these concerns were elaborated and refined in the centuries after the composition of the *Mārgam* by a wide range of new developments: the local epicization of Kannada polity by Pampa and the localization of the Sanskrit literary global through an array of poets and poems it has hardly been possible even to mention here,[106] the maturation of an ennobling philology in texts on metrics like *Chandōmbudhi,* and the continuing refinement of grammar from the *Karṇāṭakabhāṣābhūṣaṇa* to the *Śabdamaṇidarpaṇam.* Asserting at once the regionality of Kannada and its literary value by associating the discourse on the language closely with that of Sanskrit, emplacing or replacing the placeless Sanskrit (in matters of lexicon, meter, theme) while articulating what was thereby marked as Kannada distinctiveness—all these discourses helped to produce a quintessential cosmopolitan vernacularism. Though this vernacularism may seem to refer more often to a new aesthetic and cultural sense of being than to a new social or political world, it was certainly made possible only by new and very particular social and political conditions.

105. *Sāhasabhīmavijayam* 1.40: *doreyaṟiva vastupuruṣar | parikisi belemāḍe gaṅgamaṃḍalacakrī- || śvarakaṭakottamanāyaka-.*

106. These include such works as the *Karṇāṭakakumārasaṃbhavam* of Asaga in the late ninth century and the *Karṇāṭakamālatīmādhavam* of Kannamayya in the eleventh (both lost), Nāgavarma's *Karṇāṭakakādambarī* in the eleventh, and Durgasiṃha's *Kārṇāṭakapañcatantram* in the twelfth.

If the *Kavirājamārgam* and all the great works that followed in its wake give us a vivid sense of the discursive and literary strategies by which a high-culture vernacular is produced, how are we to make sense of the historical conditions, the time and place, that allowed this transformation? Why did vernacular poets starting in the ninth century renounce not just a potential but an actual translocal, quasi-global audience of Sanskrit and for the first time begin to speak locally? Why did vernacular intellectuals at some of the most powerful courts in India choose to constitute their language as a new cognitive object and target of normative management? What, historically speaking, was the political content of the new cultural forms they were all creating? How were these forms shaped by, and how in turn did they help to shape, the polities to which they make constant reference and from the very centers of which they emerged?

These questions are hard enough to answer for the Kannada world alone, but any serious attempt would also have to take into account the larger environment in which identical changes were occurring. The vernacular transformation for which Kannada provides so dramatic an instance was a pan-Indian, quasi-global phenomenon; new literatures were about to be called into existence nearly everywhere. Of course there is no reason to believe that all instances of vernacularization share a single logic and can be subsumed under a single explanatory model. But this is something we cannot know prior to reconstructing something of its macrohistory.

CHAPTER TEN

Vernacular Poetries and Polities in Southern Asia

10.1 THE COSMOPOLITAN VERNACULARIZATION OF SOUTH AND SOUTHEAST ASIA

Processes of literary-cultural transformation exactly like those found in the Kannada-speaking world are in evidence across much of southern Asia for a period of some five centuries beginning a little before 1000. Given so vast a domain with local complexities everywhere, and few comprehensive accounts existing for any one language let alone for the entire southern Asian world, only the general shape of this vernacular revolution can be sketched out here, with a few especially representative or complex instances examined more closely. Several features discernible in many instances (not, of course, all) will serve as focal points: the place of the superposed tradition with respect to the key components of literary textuality (lexicon, metric, theme, genre, and so on) and the ways in which it was appropriated and localized; the geocultural sphere of literary communication and how this presented itself as an object of explicit representation, something that can be called literary territorialization; and the relationship between vernacular literary production and the royal court and, accordingly, the degree to which power concerned itself with the stimulation of vernacular culture and the significance of this concern for understanding the transformed vision of political life.

It makes sense to start this sketch with the regions contiguous to Kannada country. In the Telugu-speaking areas, vernacular intellectuals began experimenting with Telugu in epigraphical culture in the ninth and tenth centuries (chapter 8.1), but none of this material inaugurated a tradition of reproduction or entered into circulation. It was in the coastal regions of Andhra under the patronage of the Cāḷukyas of Veṅgi in the eleventh century, modestly prefigured by the tenth-century inscription of Prince Yuddhamalla (chapter 8.3), that vernacularization began in earnest. As seems almost predictable, given the history of Kannada vernacularization, the first of these significant vernacular texts was the *Mahābhāratamu,* an adaptation of the Sanskrit epic by Nannaya Bhaṭṭa (c. 1050). Nannaya's text was composed according to the formal requirements of Sanskrit literature and in a new cosmopolitan idiom that would remain the dominant literary register in Telugu for the next seven hundred years. The cosmopolitan enhancement of the language in its transformation from the documentary to the literary is easily traceable in the epigraphical record.[1] Nannaya's masterpiece was followed by a surge of vernacular literary production in every way comparable to what we find in Kannada. The philological apparatus was somewhat slower in developing, however, if the first Telugu grammar, the *Āndhraśabdacintāmaṇi* (Wishing Stone of the Language of Andhra), though ascribed to Nannaya himself, is in fact to be dated to the seventeenth century (chapter 9.2.) The first reference to a geographical entity called Andhra is found in the fourteenth-century *Bhīmakhaṇḍamu* of Śrīnāthuḍu, court poet to the vassals of the Kākatīya kings on the eve of their slow capitulation to the Khaljī Sultanate (1309–22). Here the Gōdāvarī delta is represented as "the very heart of the land of Āndhra, its seven rivers like seven veins of nectar running from the center of a lotus." A contemporary of Śrīnātha effectively gives expression to all three historical innovations at once—the newness of the vernacular invention, its production of place, and the dynamic cultural politics of the courts—when he declares (making use of the binary that was to become a cornerstone of vernacular theory, as we will see in section 2 below), "Earlier, there was poetry in Sanskrit, called *mārga* / The Cāḷukya kings and many others caused poetry to be born / in Telugu and fixed it in place, as *desi,* in the Andhra land."[2]

Marathi, virtually unliterized until the tenth century, first appeared in royal charters in the eleventh; over the course of the next two centuries, the number of epigraphs employing the language grew by a factor of ten, but all of these records are resolutely and unmistakably documentary. The first expressive inscriptions date from the end of the thirteenth century and the court, or the ambit of the court, of the Yādavas, who ruled from their center in Devagiri from the late ninth century until 1318, when they were subjugated by the Delhi Sultanate. Some sense of this new inscriptional discourse was provided in the discussion of Brahmadevarāṇe's record of 1305 (chapter 8.3). It was around the same time, amidst the swiftly changing political

1. From 900 to 1100 the number of Sanskrit loan words in Telugu nearly doubled (*ETI,* especially p. cix).

2. Nannecōḍuḍu, *Kumārasambhavamu* 1.21, tr. Narayana Rao and Shulman 2002: 69. All these data undercut the hypotheses of Nagaraju 1995, especially that distance from the court was a precondition for Telugu vernacularization.

conditions of late-thirteenth- and early-fourteenth-century Maharashtra, that the inaugural literary texts in Marathi were produced. These are, in the first instance—and anomalously, given patterns elsewhere—works by members of two religious communities, the Mahānubhāvas and the Vārkarīs. The former movement was founded by Cakradhara, whose spiritual biography is narrated in the *Līḷācaritra* of Mhāibhaṭa (1278). Despite the sect's apparent anti-Brahmanism and hostility to Sanskrit (Cakradhara's immediate successor, Nāgadev Bhaṭobāsa, was not only instrumental in committing the master's words to writing but refused to allow them to be translated into Sanskrit), one of the more important texts in this tradition is the *Gadyarāja* (King of Art Prose) by a Brahman author named Hayagarva (Hayagrīva). Written around 1320, this work is a version of the Kṛṣṇa legend adapted from the *Bhāgavatapurāṇa,* composed in a heavily Sanskritized register and, despite its name, in the Sanskrit meters of high literature.[3] Among the Vārkarīs the most important text is the *Jñāneśvarī* (c. 1290), a poem framed as a commentary on the *Bhagavadgītā.* The work is remarkable not least for showing how aware the early vernacular intellectuals were of the novelty of their enterprise, how assertive about the challenge they were mounting, and how defensive about their temerity in making the language of Place speak literarily. The author, the poet-scholar Jñāneśvar, aimed to have "the blessed era of holy knowledge come to the city of Marathi," so that both his "language of Place and Sanskrit may display their beauty on the self-same throne of the *Gītā.*" And he asserted, "Although my language may be Marathi, it will surpass nectar"; "if my Marathi version of the original Sanskrit *[Bhagavadgītā]* is read carefully, with a clear understanding of its meaning, no one could say which is the original." Such metapragmatic announcements, modulated by the defensiveness of one fully aware of the historic importance of his innovation, are to be found across the vernacularizing world, wherever literary newness was being created.[4]

It was also with the Yādavas of Devagiri that the word "Maratha" *(marhāṭe),* which had earlier been a territorial/linguistic term, was first closely associated. Equally significant is the new territorialization of religious practices seen in the self-consciously regionalized pilgrimage circuit created by the Mahānubhāvas within the Marathi-speaking realm. Cakradhara himself had commanded his followers: "Do not go to the Kannada country or the Telugu coun-

3. Raeside 1989, especially pp. xvi–xxxiii (it is called *gadya* although versified because the verses are unrhymed, unlike those used by later vernacular poets). On Mahānubhāva literature in general see Tulpule 1979: 316 ff. especially p. 325. The philosophical prose work *Vivekasindhu* is now dated to the end of the thirteenth century (Tulpule 1979: 316).

4. See respectively *Jñāneśvarī* 12.16, 10.45, 6.14, 10.43. For the at once assertive and defensive vernacular, cf. Somanātha's Telugu *Basavapurāṇa* (c. 1300): "Let it not be said that these words are nothing but Telugu. Rather, look at them as equal to the Vedas" (tr. Narayana Rao 1990: 6).

try. Stay in Maharashtra"—evidence of the degree to which certain new kinds of culture boundaries had begun to crystallize. Later writers of this religious order took pains not just to define this domain by providing a variety of mappings (blurry though such precartographic mappings must be) but also to demonstrate that staying home came at little cost to the pilgrim: the greater number of India's shrines and sacred sites and holy cities were shown to be already located in Maharashtra by the same sort of toponymic mimicry found in peninsular India and Southeast Asia (6.1): they represented Paithan as Kāśī, Ṛddhipur as Dvāravatī, and the Godāvarī River as the Gaṅgā itself.[5]

Tamil country, as noted several times earlier, presents a more complex and contested history of literary culture than anywhere else in South Asia. Yet here, too, there is little doubt that major transformations of literary culture occurred in the centuries just before and after the beginning of the second millennium. The element of complexity is introduced by a unique, and uniquely obscure, vernacular literary prehistory. This includes a corpus of courtly literature, purportedly from the *caṅkam,* or literary "academy," of the first centuries C.E. (a dating that would be clearly anomalous in South Asian literary history), that gradually disappeared from the historical record—almost completely so by the mid-second millennium—until rediscovered at the end of the nineteenth century, as well as noncourtly hymns of Śaiva and Vaiṣṇava spiritual masters typically dated to the seventh or eighth centuries that were lost and rediscovered only at the beginning of the second millennium. Opaque as this early history may be, what seems beyond dispute is the role of the ascendant dynasties at the end of the first millennium C.E. in reconstituting Tamil literature and the cosmopolitan-vernacular dimension of this literary transformation. Several key events of this period suggest this strongly.

It was around the ninth century, in the inscriptional record of the Pāṇṭiyas, that the legend of the *caṅkam* first took on a certain fixity. Understood less literally, the legend would appear to be substituting an older beginning for what may have been the innovations of vernacular intellectuals, especially Buddhist and Jain, in the just-preceding centuries. In the eleventh century, under the aegis of Rājarāja Cōḻa, the *bhakti* poems of the *Tēvāram* were said to have been assembled—after being rediscovered in the great temple at Cidambaram—and incorporated into the newly formalized temple liturgies. Whatever the historicity of this tale, what is noteworthy is how it insists on the text-artifactual—rather than the oral—existence of the vernacular works in question (see chapter 8.2). A model for such anthologizing or canonizing activity among the Śaivas, as well as for the political patronage that under-

5. For the hypothesis that Marathi had become the "state language" of the Yādavas, see Deshpande 1979: 69. On the ethnonym *marhāṭe* see Feldhaus and Tulpule 1992: 94. The new pilgrimage circuit is discussed in Feldhaus 1986, who cites Cakradhara (p. 535).

wrote it, may have been provided by the work of Nāthamuni, who half a century earlier performed the same service for the Vaiṣṇava materials in the *Divyaprabandham* (Heavenly Works). Around the same time a surge of Tamil commentarial writing on the Sanskrit model, embracing both literary and scholarly works, found expression. The new vernacularization in political expression that can be traced to this period was fully in keeping with such developments. As we have seen, the language by which political power had expressed itself in Tamil country for much of the first millennium, even in the realm of the Pāṇṭiyas, the legendary site of the *caṅkam*, was Sanskrit.[6] This began to change in the eighth or ninth century, with records such as those of the Pāṇṭiya king Cēntaṉ discussed earlier, and even more dramatically in the Cōḻa realm from around 1000 with the invention of the Tamil *meykkīrtti* and the ornate historiographical records of Rājarāja I and his successors (chapter 8.1, 3). These innovations in the last quarter of the first millennium were linked to broader trends in the Tamil literary sphere as a whole.

We have noted that a fragmentarily preserved, perhaps never completed, Tamil adaptation of the *Mahābhārata* by Peruntēvaṉār, the *Pāratavenpā* (The *Bhārata* in Veṇpā Meter), can be placed at the Pallava court of Nandivarman III in the mid-ninth century, which would make it the first vernacularization of the epic in South Asia.[7] With the production of Kampaṉ's grand adaptation of the second Sanskrit epic, the *Rāmāyaṇa*, in the later Cōḻa period (perhaps mid-twelfth century, though the date is much disputed), the idiom no less than the theme of which suggest a vernacularization of the cosmopolitan aesthetic, a new epoch of Tamil literature appears to have commenced. Royal patronage now began to show a decided preference for Tamil as opposed to Sanskrit literature, which had still enjoyed patronage at the beginning of Cōḻa rule (evidenced by, for instance, the *Rājajrājavijaya* and the *Rājarājanāṭaka*, both lost).

Equally as striking as the production of new literature in Tamil in the last two centuries of the first millennium was the philologization of the language (considered briefly in section 2). In addition, commentaries on such culturally central Tamil texts as the *Tirukkuṟaḷ* were beginning to reread the Tamil literary past through Sanskrit rhetorical categories. Indeed, the critical vocabulary of literary and linguistic analysis came to be deeply colored by Sanskrit, though determining precisely when this occurred is tied up with

6. For the *caṅkam* inscription see *SII* 3: 454. Sivathamby 1986: 36–45 emphasizes the role of the Pāṇṭiyas in stimulating the legend of the *caṅkam*. The work on early Tamil literary history by Tieken (2001), proposing a radically revised chronology, appeared too late to be fully assessed here.

7. Prepared at the instance of the Pāṇṭiya kings (see chapter 9 n. 8), though its date is uncertain. See *SII* 3: 454; Aiyangar 1933: 71 ff., and Zvelebil 1974: 130, 143, who refers to a third version produced under Kulōttuṅka in the twelfth century (lost) and the better-known later text of Villiputūr Āḻvār (early fifteenth century).

the Tamil tradition's thorny problems of dating. Not the least of the localizations was the term *kāvya* itself *(kāppiyam)*, along with its specific subspecies (such as *aimperuṅkāppiyaṅkaḷ* = *pañcamahākāvya*, the "five [principal] courtly epics"). Among other genre and text-structural terms perhaps most significant was the binary *ilakkaṇam* and *ilakkiyam* (rule and instance). The provenance of this category was the Sanskrit grammatical tradition—the terms *lakṣaṇa* and *lakṣya* are first attested in a supplementary rule of the grammar by Kātyāyana about the second century B.C.E.—but it was put to work in the vernacular Tamil tradition in far more fundamental ways, to signify, respectively, grammar and literature as such.[8]

The literary and literary-critical cosmopolitanization of the Tamil vernacular was complemented by a territorialization of Tamil cultural space more explicit than any heretofor. A notable example occurs in a Tamil commentary written around the turn of the millennium. Remarking on a traditional verse that defines the genre "preface" as including information on the author's name and his school, the commentator observes that the "boundaries" of the text—that is, its circulatory space—is also a topic to be dealt with in a preface, and he proceeds to describe the bounds of his primary text:

> By boundary we mean that each book pertains to a certain geographical area. What are this book's boundaries, you ask? They are the Vēṅkaṭam mountains in the north, Cape Kumari in the south, and the ocean on the east and west. This we know because Kākkaippāṭiṉiyār and Tolkāppiyaṉār have said, "In the north and the south, the west and the east, / Vēṅkaṭam, Kumari, and the sweet-water seas: / the range of a book lies within these four bounds / when one expounds with clarity," and, "Northern Vēṅkaṭam and southern Kumari: / in between / is the good world where people speak Tamil."[9]

A more precise regionalization in a somewhat later text offers the first literary territorialization effected through a mapping of the "region of pure Tamil" language *(centamiḻnilam)*: "To the north of the river Vaikai (on whose banks is situated the city of Maturai), to the south of the river Marutam, to

8. On the *Vīracōḻiyam* see section 2 of this chapter. Gros 1994 discusses the *Tirukkuṟaḷ* commentaries. The literary-cultural terminology includes *pirapantam (prabandha)*, *kāṇṭam (kāṇḍa)*, *atikāram (adhikāra)*, *peruṇkāppiyam (mahākāvya)*, and *carukkam (sarga)*. The *vārttika* of Kātyāyana (14: *lakṣyalakṣaṇe vyākaraṇam*) is found in *Mahābhāṣya* vol. 1: 12. Zvelebil's argument on Tamil's unique "metalanguage" (1992: 128 n. 113) is confused, especially when what he goes on to discuss as a basic dichotomy "originating in protoliterate or even preliterate Tamil civilization" is *ilakkaṇam* and *ilakkiyam*. Elsewhere he suggests that the terms were indeed borrowed, but from Prakrit/Pali, not from Sanskrit (p. 143 n. 35), though neither language ever uses either term as a binary or in the technical sense.

9. Nakkīraṉār on *Kaḷaviyal* or *Akapporuḷ*, as translated by Buck and Paramasivam 1997: 3 (the second verse Nakkīraṉār quotes from Paṉampāraṉār's preface to *Tolkāppiyam*). The commentary mystifies its own history by placing itself in the *caṅkam* age. Its true date is probably a little before the beginning of the second millennium (Buck and Paramasivam 1997: xi).

the east of Karuvūr, to the west of Maruvūr."[10] And, as elsewhere, we find in Tamil country the recreation of cosmopolitan space, with Maturai, for example, duplicating Mathurā, and the Kāverī the Gaṅgā (which one Cōḻa king is said to have actually brought "to his own country," in order thereby to "attain royal grandeur").[11]

One last southern example to be considered is Sri Lanka, which differs in some important ways from the cultural regions just described.[12] For one thing, documentary Sinhala was literized much earlier than any of the languages discussed so far, Tamil excepted (donative inscriptions in Sinhala were issued as early as the second century B.C.E.), and for another, expressive uses of the vernacular are found in graffiti dated as early as the fifth century. Moreover, medieval Sri Lanka participated in a second cosmopolitan cultural formation, that of Pali and southern Buddhism. Sanskrit may never have occupied a dominant position in aesthetic or political expression, though important *kāvya* in the language was produced there and power did sometimes express itself in Sanskrit as late as the mid-ninth century.[13] Yet Sanskrit was a shaping force behind the scenes in Sri Lanka and elsewhere in the Pali world. When, around the beginning of the second millennium, Pali became a medium for the production of a new cosmopolitan cultural order in Burma, Thailand, Cambodia, and Laos, it was in part thanks to the acceptance of Sanskrit literary forms in which Pali intellectuals had finally acquiesced—above all *kāvya* and its philological knowledge (especially grammar and metrics)—after more than a millennium of what seems to have been stubborn and self-conscious resistance to Sanskrit's cultural project.[14]

Despite this complicated prehistory and the twofold movement, the transformations that occurred in Sinhala literary culture around the start of the second millennium bear a strong resemblance to developments elsewhere. The rise of Sanskrit-style praise-poetry is one such innovation. The register of this poetry may differ from the examples found on the mainland, since

10. From Iḷampūraṇar's commentary on the *Tolkāppiyam.* Later scholiasts, as noted by Zvelebil (whose translation I use), elaborate on and extend the area (1992: 136). Maruvūrpakkam, or Maruvūrpaṭṭiṉam, seems to be the name for an area proximate to the city of Kāviripūmpaṭṭiṉam, the erstwhile capital of the *caṅkam* period Cōḻas and the setting for the first book of the *Cilappātikaram;* Karuvūr is another name for Vañci, the Cēra capital on the west coast. No river Marutam is known to me. The *Naṉṉūl* also provides a map of its domain of application.

11. See *EI* 25: 258 vv. 32–35; the Gaṅgā and political power are associated in a 1037 record of Rājendra (Nagaswamy 1987: 32 v. 17). For the toponymic duplication see chapter 6.1.

12. Fundamental here is Hallisey 2003.

13. There is no reason to doubt the Sri Lanka origins of Kumāradāsa's fifth century *Jānakīharaṇa.* For Sanskrit in inscriptions see *EZ* 1: 1–9 (the record is in an early form of Nagari).

14. See generally Collins 1998: 63–72, and, on the history and character of Pali *kāvya,* Collins 2003. The philological works include the *Saddanīti,* the Pali grammar composed in Pagan in 1194, and the twelfth-century prosody handbook *Vuttodaya* (chapter 4.1).

direct Sanskrit loan words *(tatsama)* are absent and the lexicon has a far more indigenized character, given that Sanskrit had long been mediated through Pali. But the very deployment of the vernacular in the political arena—earlier inscriptions had been in prosaic Pali—constitutes an entirely comparable irruption of the new. In its themes, too, this political discourse is essentially indistinguishable from what we encounter everywhere else: fame, virtue, martial valor, and the continuing quasi-universalist political claims—in 930 King Siri Saṅgbo (Śrī Saṅgabodhi) of the Okāva (Ikṣvāku) dynasty "reduced the other Kshatriya families of the whole of Dambadiv (Jambūdvīpa) to the position of vassals"—were now coded in a language that could not be, and was perfectly well known not to be, universally understood.[15] Dramatic and unprecedented changes occurred in the domain of literature as well. Vernacular writers began to carefully select and adapt formal and thematic features of Sanskrit poetry; exemplary here is the *Kavsiḷumiṇa* (*Kāvyacuḍāmaṇi,* Crest Jewel of Poetry) of King Parākramabāhu II (c. 1250), a poem deeply imbued with Sanskrit literary ideals.

It is from this period, too (first under Kassappa IV, r. 898–914, and more decisively under Parākramabāhu I, r. 1153–86), when the island attained something approaching political unification, that the earliest literary representations are found of a newly coherent geocultural space. The same Siri Saṅgbo could now be described as the "forehead ornament of the island of Sri Lanka" *(sirilakdivaṭ talāṭik),* while detailed personifications of the island as a beautiful woman began to appear, first in a tenth-century Pali commentary on the *Mahāvaṃsa* and again in a twelfth-century Sinhala poem, the *Pūjāvaliya.* Some scholars also suggest that it was at this time that the term "Sinhala" first acquired more noticeable if still somewhat vague connotations of a wider political community, no longer referring, as it had earlier, merely to ruling lineages.[16]

The literary-cultural transformations visible in southern India extended throughout the Sanskrit cosmopolitan sphere of mainland and maritime Southeast Asia. Here Java has special claim on our attention, given the dramatic example it provides. In the early ninth century, after a silence of more than four hundred years, Javanese became the exclusive language of official documents. The same period marks the appearance of the first expressive inscription, a text that fully evinces the cosmopolitan-vernacular style (chapter 8.3)—but not only style: the epigraph tells of a king, Rakai Pikatan (he was to be the subject of the first Javanese literary text as well) who "possessed the knowledge, difficult to acquire, of *dharma* and *adharma*" *(durlabha* weruḥ niṅ *adharmmādharmma).* This king, who bore the sobriquet "Birth of

15. *EZ* 3: 138–48 (the phrase cited is on pp. 139–40).

16. *EZ* 6: 16; for the geographical representations see Walters 1993, and Hallisey 1994; on "Sinhala," Gunawardhana 1990, Rogers 1994.

the World," understood full well the universalistic political ideal, but he deployed it in the most particularized of ways, to "protect the land of Java righteously" (mang*rakṣa bhūmi* ri jaw*ārjawa*). No other idiom than the cosmopolitanized vernacular could have articulated such a sentiment in a manner that marries content so seamlessly to form. And at precisely this same moment, when Javanese seized the place of Sanskrit in the domain of royal inscription, vernacular poets began to produce a grand new literature, the very designation of which, *kakawin* (derived from *kāvya*), embodied the new synthesis it represented.

This extraordinary efflorescence of courtly texts began tentatively in the old polities on the plains of central Java, then more assertively, beginning in the eleventh century, in the new courts to the east (Kaḍiri, Singhasāri, Majapahit), and it continued with great vigor for the next four to five hundred years. This is a vast body of texts, comprised of the *parwa* (Sanskrit *parvan*), also known as *wawachan* (*vacana*), and *kakawin* genres, the latter composed in the idiom known as *kawi* (*kavi*) and using Sanskrit meters. The corpus comprises a *Mahābhārata* in its *itihāsa* form (a prose adaptation studded with direct citation from the Sanskrit original), and *kāvya* versions of both the *Rāmāyaṇa* and the *Mahābhārata*, as well as numerous courtly adaptations of epic tales. As a whole, Javanese offers a paradigm case of the appropriations, negotiations, and compromises achieved by a cosmopolitan-vernacular literary culture. And it bears close comparison to the cultures of southern India in respect to language, philologization, literary form and style, and, most unexpectedly, the localized and allegorized representations of political power and its geocultural expositions.[17]

About the Sanskritization of the Javanese literary idiom, it is enough to remark that as many as one third of the lexical items were borrowed without phonological change from Sanskrit *(tatsama)*. A lexicographical concern to organize this literary language was in evidence early on, assuming a date in the Śailendra period for the *Amaramālā,* which employs the model of the (approximately) fifth-century Sanskrit lexicon of Amara. Especially notable is the wholesale adoption of the complex quantitative Sanskrit meters and their adaptation to an entirely different linguistic medium, accompanied by a sophisticated prosodic science (as embodied in the fifteenth-century *Wṛttasañcaya,* Compendium of Meters) inspired by Sanskrit prototypes.[18]

17. For the Javanese *Mahābhārata* see Phalgunadi 1990 [–1997]; the *pratīka*-like Sanskrit quotations are discussed in Zoetmulder 1974: 89–92. On the *Rāmāyaṇa kakawin* see n. 19 for this chapter. Similar transformations have been noted in other cultural spheres: in architecture, for example, the cosmic cosmopolitan style of Borobudur and Prambanan gave way to a "new autochthonism" (Zoetmulder 1974: 26); see also Robson 1983: 296.

18. See chapter 4.1. The Sanskritized register of Old Javanese is discussed in Zoetmulder 1974: 8 ff. New synonymical dictionaries citing Old Javanese poetry available from the early

Most pertinent for a theorization of the new literary culture is the *kakawin* itself. This genre, invented in perhaps the mid-ninth century, consists largely of courtly adaptations of Sanskrit epic narratives that in their structure, inspiration, degree of innovation, and measured fidelity to the original are indistinguishable from the *campūs* that made their first appearance at the same period in the Deccan. The genre commences with a vernacularization of Sanskrit's primal poem, the *Rāmāyaṇa,* via the seventh-century *śāstrakāvya* of Bhaṭṭi (chapter 4.1), a choice that announces the learned character of the *kakawin* genre. It is indicative of the narrative and aesthetic independence of vernacularization in Java that the final 44 percent of the text, according to one careful estimate, corresponds to nothing in the *Bhaṭṭikāyva.* Courtly *kāvya* materials continued to be appropriated from Sanskrit throughout the history of the genre. A good illustration is the *Sumanasāntaka* (Death by a Flower) of Monaguṇa (c. 1200), in which the poet, as he tells us himself, rendered Kālidāsa's *Raghuvaṃśa* "into the vernacular in *kakawin* form" (*pinrākṛta,* literally Prakritized), a Javanization of subject matter no less than of language, and—returning us to the context of power that was fundamental to the genre of *kakawin*—"offered it to his king as a gift of holy water."[19]

Compared to its vernacular cousins from mainland India, the *kakawin* shows rather less interest in the detailed production of place. The *Bhāratayuddha,* written in eastern Java in 1157, contains not a single specific reference to a Javanese locale. Yet *kakawins* are otherwise wholly localized aesthetic objects, and "Java" as a reference point seems omnipresent; in many texts the story takes place in India, but it is an India transported to Java (like Angkor with its Mount Meru, or Thailand with its Ayutthaya).[20] A fully articulated geocultural interest is evinced, however, by the *Deśawarṇana* (Description of the Place, 1365). Its subject is no epic theme but the journeys of King Rājasanagara (better known as Hayam Wuruk, ruler of Majapahit in East Java, 1350–89) across his realm. The very raison d'être of the poem lies in the mapping of vernacular place, a linking of sites within a clearly conceptualized, narrativized space. This is produced both implicitly in the circuit of the king's journeys as well as explicitly in various subnarratives, including one that tells how Java had once been divided into two parts but has now become united, "with a king of the whole country . . . to be a sign that the king is vic-

colonial period may have a precolonial genealogy in the *Amaramālā* (see also Gonda 1973: 185 and n. 40). On the *Wṛttasañcaya,* see chapter 4.1 and n. 3. Grammatical texts are late, and an *alaṅkāraśāstra* is altogether lacking.

19. For the *Rāmāyaṇa kakawin* see Hooykaas 1958, and Uhlenbeck 1975: 212; on the *kakawin*'s relationship to Sanskrit sources, Zoetmulder 1974: 26 ff., and 307–9 for the *Sumanasāntaka.*

20. For subtle references constantly calling the reader back home see Zoetmulder 1974: 187–88.

torious over the whole world as a sovereign ruler."[21] Again the strain of the old cosmopolitan universalism can be heard, but it has been remodulated for a smaller, regional world, that of Java alone—an apt illustration of the political ethos that underwrote the vernacular transformation.

Like the great south Indian vernacular *campūs*, the major *kakawins* are epic allegories of local political power—or rather, they are allegory-*like*, since the royal patron and the epic hero he represents are ontologically linked.[22] The very first Javanese literary text, the *Rāmāyaṇa kakawin*, can plausibly be interpreted as the victory of King Rakai Pikatan (Rāma) over Bālaputra (Rāvaṇa), last of the Śailendra kings of Java. (It might even be viewed as the victory of Shaivism over Buddhism; in the inscribed poem about Rakai Pikatan discussed above, the battle of Kumbhayoni, another name for Pikatan, against Bālaputra is equated with Śiva's attack against Tripura.) Later examples of such double narratives abound, indicating that *kakawin* was the literary form par excellence for the exploration and aestheticization of the vernacular political. Precisely as in the case of South Asia, the conceptual universe of medieval Java was permeated by persons and symbols and categories drawn from the Sanskrit epics. And precisely as we find in vernacular versions of the epic from places like Vēmulavāḍa in Karnataka or Gwalior in Bundelkhand (see below), the Javanese version represents multilayered interactions between cosmopolitan and local forms of political, moral, and aesthetic consciousness. We see this at work even at the level of lexicon: Sanskrit was used to constitute the domain of the *kakasatriya* (Kshatriya) code and a transcendent ethic, while Javanese was used for the domain of the family, the sexual, the affective—and the actively political.[23]

In north India, the dramatic multiplication of possible codes for making literary and political statements, which in south India, Sri Lanka, and Southeast Asia took place between approximately 900 and 1300, occurred at a somewhat later date and under very different conditions of political and cultural change. In fact, here a historical problem of great complexity confronts

21. *Deśawarṇana* 68.5, p. 75, tr. Robson. Cf. 83.2: "The land of Java has become more and more renowned for its purifying power in the world: It is only India [Jambūdvīpa] and Java that are noted for their excellence as fine places . . . And so constantly all kinds of people come from other countries in countless numbers—see: India [Jambūdvīpa], Cambodia, China, Annam, Champa, the Carnatic, and so on, Gaur [Gauḍa] and Siam are their places of origin" (83.2, 4 p. 85). Recall the 1447 record issued in the name of the "supreme lord of all of Java" (*śrī sakalayawarājādhirājaparameśwara;* chapter 3.1).

22. The true name of the courtly epic genre may be not *kakawin* (meaning simply "stanza") but *palambang*, which may have signified something close to allegory (Robson 1983: 299ff.).

23. Worsley 1991 offers a reading of the fourteenth-century *Arjunawijaya* in this spirit. For Kumbhayoni's defeat of Bālaputra, see de Casparis 1956: 297 and 290 (where however the connection with the *Rāmāyaṇa kakawin* is not made). Day 1996 discusses the *Bhāratayuddha* in the context of twelfth-century politics.

us, and only a very provisional account of some key moments and routes of vernacularization can be indicated by way of a preface to a more detailed consideration of one case where the now-familiar pattern at least partially asserted itself.

While the individuation of a number of northern Indian regional languages is evident as early as the last quarter of the first millennium, some of the earliest known instances of their literization are those contained in Someśvara's encyclopedia of 1130 (chapter 8.2). Here songs in a range of languages, including forms of Gujarati, Bangla or Oriya, and Madhyadeshiya, were textualized perhaps for the first time. It was only at the end of the twelfth century that the first Gujarati literary texts (the *Bāhubali Ghor rāsos*) were written, and only in the middle of the fourteenth that poets in the Maithili region began to produce their first literary texts. For other languages of Place, including those now called Assamese, Bangla, Oriya, and Newari, the breakthrough to literary writing occurred at an uneven pace between the fourteenth and the early seventeenth centuries. Although the early picture as a whole is very murky, by any reckoning the refashioning of the north Indian *bhāṣās* for literary culture happened far later than for those in the south, and this time differential raises puzzling questions. While the vernacularization process is evidently contingent on a range of social, political, and cultural factors, in the north a certain constraint may have been imposed by the genetic relationship between the cosmopolitan and vernacular codes. Did north Indian languages develop a mode of coexistence with Sanskrit that obscured their vernacular potential in a way impossible for the languages of south India and Southeast Asia? Parallels with the literary-cultural transformation of western Europe suggests that such a hypothesis may be worth considering.

Very much like Kannada and other Sanskrit-distant Dravidian languages of south India, Latin-distant Germanic languages such as Old English developed vernacular literary cultures on the cosmopolitan model as early as the beginning of the ninth century. By contrast, like Sanskrit-near Indo-Aryan languages of north India, Latin-near Romance languages such as Florentine required as much as five centuries more to do so (chapter 11.1). When we descend from such broad analogies and try to understand the specific language features and cultural mechanisms that might have contributed to these differential developments, no good theories exist for South Asia. Scholars of early Romance, for their part, have come to see the vernacularization process as a conceptual or cognitive event no less than a linguistic one. Until around 800, as the ways of spoken Latin steadily changed among the populace at large, the language that continued to be written as Latin was read forth in church or at court as early Romance. Then, as now, spelling was far more conservative than speech, and the necessary phonological and even morphological transformations that turn Latin into the Romance languages would have been made unconsciously as lectors enunciated the text according to their local speech habits. In Britain or Ireland, by contrast, such public readers, who spoke vernaculars genetically unrelated to Latin, preserved what they considered the correct pronunciation of the learned language. At the same time they acted on their perception of language difference by producing far earlier script vernaculars than was the case for what eventually became French, Spanish, and Italian. It was just such clerics, like Alcuin (chapter 7.1), who helped initiate the Latin language reforms when he arrived from Britain at the Carolingian court. They pronounced Latin in accordance with the written text, letter by letter *(literatim)*, which rendered it unintelligible to Romance-speaking listeners, and among the latter a cognitive transformation ensued. What they had hitherto been speaking, they realized, was no longer in fact Latin, the standard in which they had continued to write, but something new: Français, for example, or Castellano. It was this realization that led to the orthographic and other practical and conceptual innovations (to transmit the "new" language more transparently) without which vernacularization cannot occur.

This constellation of factors in its entirety was of course absent in South Asia, but a few of its elements were present, and these might help explain the highly discrepant rates of vernacularization in south and north India. Is it possible to argue that for some audiences in the north who swam in the wide sea of Sanskrit (and Apabhramsha) culture, Sanskrit (or Apabhramsha) was to some degree vernacularized in public performance until such time as the distance between the written and the pronounced became too obvious to ignore and the process for resolving the contradiction became too evident to overlook—with the result that the oral vernaculars themselves were fully literized and thereby made available to literary culture as new codes for expressive writing?[24]

This model minimizes knowledgeable agency when such agency is massively in evidence elsewhere in South Asian vernacularization, and it presupposes an erosion of the communicative competence in Sanskrit (or Apabhramsha) for which we have little evidence. Still, it may help explain why it was precisely those in the north who did not swim in the Indic sea—that is, Muslim literati from at least the fourteenth century on—and worked with different literary-cultural models, who seem to have been the first to literize and literarize the languages of the Midlands (which they named Hindavi, Hindvi, or Hindui,

24. On the origins of the Romance vernacular as a cognitive breakthrough see Wright 1991, 1997 (supported by Banniard 1992; though cf. Banniard 1995, especially p. 704). Italian provides an even stronger example of the vernacular realization of a classical language, a circumstance to which the retardation of full, orthographic vernacularization has been traced by Kristeller 1984: 10. There is no evidence one way or the other that Sanskrit or Apabhramsha texts were ever performatively realized in phonologically or morphologically vernacularized modes, while the Church's pressure for language reform leading to the recognition of the vernacular development has of course no parallel in South Asia.

"Indian language," and which local people called simply *bhāṣā* or *bhākhā*, "speech," or sometimes, with more regional specificity, Madhyadeshiya, Gwaliyari, or the like). These literati were primarily writers associated with Sufi lineages, such as Bābā Farīd (d. 1265) or Maulānā Dāūd of Jaunpur, whose *Candāyan* (dated 1379) marked the beginning of a literary tradition that, as one scholar recently described it, "had come into being with startling suddenness."[25] Even earlier vernacular experimentation is ascribed to South Asian Persianate poets, like the Ghaznavid court poet Masʿūd Saʿd Salmān Lāhorī (1046–1121) and Amīr Ḳhusrau (1253–1325) at the court of the Delhi Sultanate.[26] The process of vernacularization, especially among the Sufis, has typically been explained by a functionalist argument based on the supposed need of a familiar idiom for inculcating Islam among the Hindu masses. More recently, however, scholars have convincingly emphasized the suitability of the vernacular to the Sufi aesthetic—mystical-ecstatic, extra-Quranic, even domestic and feminine. For those who did swim in the Indic sea the early literization of Hindavi may also have been hindered by the general disapproval with which noncosmopolitan literary inscription was regarded by traditional custodians of literacy in Hindu communities, a theme so prominent in tales of vernacular inauguration (chapter 8.2). Very different was the attitude to vernacular inscription that prevailed among Muslim literati; no doubt shaped initially by newly flourishing Persianate literary practices, this attitude might then have been generalized across the wider literary culture.[27]

However the commencement of north Indian vernacularization and the time lag vis-à-vis the south are to be explained, outside the Sufi ambit it was the royal courts in the power shadow of the Sultanate that took the lead in producing complex literate vernacular culture, characterized by extended literary works and eventually (by the seventeenth century) philological treatises. (To be sure, influential nonliterate vernacular compositions were produced outside the court—such as those by Kabīr, Nāth yogis, and others—but these were the sort of materials that Someśvara would have classified as song.) Mid-fifteenth-century Gwalior under the Tomars provides a telling instance, though it may be a precocious exception rather than the rule for

25. Shackle 1993 (the *Farīd Bāṇī* may however date from the fifteenth century); McGregor 2003: 914ff.

26. On Salmān's putative Hindavi *dīvān* (ascribed to him by a thirteenth-century literary history), see Sharma 2000: 161; on Ḳhusrau, McGregor 1984: 24–26, and Faruqi 2003: 805.

27. Shackle rightly observes that examples of non-Muslim vernacular literature in early north India are remarkably few (1993: 282). On vernacularization and proselytization, see Eaton 1974. Phukan 1999 emphasizes the role of the vernacular in the ecstatic practice of the *samāʿ*; see also Shackle 1993: 270 and 274, and Asani 2003: 632–33. The Hindu resistance to vernacular textualization gives added weight to Dāūd's statement that he wrote the *Candāyan* in the "Turaki," or Perso-Arabic, script under his teacher's guidance (and then "sang it in Hindavi"); see McGregor 2003: 915, who notes that, although the *Candāyan* may have circulated orally as well, it was transmitted in written form from the outset.

the Midland's culture until some centuries later. We noted earlier the evidence, albeit slender, provided by an inscription of 1405 for political expression in the vernacular and the inference some have drawn about the use of Gwaliyari as a language of state among the Tomars.[28] In the following generations were produced the first literary texts that attempt to recreate the cosmopolitan world of Sanskrit in local form, while the court patronage, or at least the productivity, of Sanskrit writers began to wane.[29] The key poet here, as noted earlier, was Viṣṇudās, whose Gwaliyari *Mahābhārata* (also called *Pāṃḍucarita, Bhāratha,* and *Mahābhāratakathā*) was composed in 1435. This was a period of considerable political uncertainty in northern India: The sack of Delhi by Temür in 1398 and the breakup of the Sultanate opened up new opportunities for political self-expression on the part of Hindu princes. Indeed, Gwalior itself had been seized by the Tomars in the power vacuum left by the invasion (it would be reconquered only a century later), and in particular the year 1435 (pointedly noted in the poem itself, *Ādiparvan caupāī* v. 34) was a perilous moment for Viṣṇudās's patron, Ḍūṅgendra Siṃha Tomar (r. 1425–54) in his struggle with Muḥammad Khaljī of Mandu. Once again, vernacularization commenced with the localization of the *Mahābhārata,* redeploying old subject matter in a way relevant to the people of contemporary Gwalior in terms of their culture and its relationship to the past, their present political circumstances, and not least, their new relationship to a literary language of Place.[30]

Three aspects of Viṣṇudās's martial narrative deserve mention here. First, the author's repeated allusions to the literate and vernacular character of the text he is producing point toward the originality of his undertaking; neither feature would be openly announced were neither a novelty. Second, he emphasizes that his setting is a courtly one, and his audience learned, who would be expected to read his poem as well as hear it recited (chapter 8.1). And last, the poem as a whole is at once a localization of the epic and an epicization of the local. Like the *kakawin* and the *campū,* Viṣṇudās's work

28. That the language was contemporaneously known as Gwaliyari is shown by an "Eight Language" poem of the time (the other seven mentioned are Gujari, Marahatthi, Karnati, Dakina, Sindhu, Parasi, and Tilangi [i.e., Telugu]; see Dvivedi [1972]: 14–15). Viṣṇudās's language retains elements of Apabhramsha (note that his chief characters are called Dudiṣṭilu and Jirjodhana). On Hindavi as the semiofficial language of the Lodīs and the Sūr Sultāns see Alam 1998: 319 and n. and 325.

29. During the reign of Ḍūṅgendra Siṃha, Viṣṇudās's patron, not a single Sanskrit text was produced under the sponsorship of the king, his ministers, or even the Jain laity (Dvivedi, *Mahābhārata [Pāṇḍavacarita]* pp. 50–51), whereas the previous generation had produced such works as Nayacandrasūri's *Hammīramahākāvya.* The other writer of renown in Gwalior at the time was the Apabhramsha poet Raïdhū, though he was not patronized by the court.

30. The characterization is in part that of McGregor 1999. See also Dvivedi [1972]: 142 ff. On the historical moment more generally see Jackson 1999: 321 ff. The text dates itself to Saṃvat 1492 [1434–35 C.E.] in vv. 34–35.

is a double narrative: his patron is equated with the epic hero Bhīma (as in Ranna's *Sāhasabhīmavijayam,* chapter 9.3), into whose lunar lineage the king was born. Here is how the poet introduces his work:

> *Doha:* . . . I will tell [or vernacularize, *bhākhaũ*] the *Bhāratha,* in the hopes of gaining eternal, immortal power *[sidhi].* (v. 2)
>
> *Caupāī:* . . . the court *(sabhā)* will be delighted hearing this famous tale, the calamity of the Kauravas and Pāṃḍavas. (v. 10)
>
> . . . The king had summoned the poet [Viṣṇu] Dāsa, (v. 35)
>
> he, the very axle of the Tauvars [Tomars], of the Pāṃḍu lineage himself, the king, Dauṃgar Singh, the great hero, (v. 36)
>
> [Who], given the strength of his arms, no one can doubt is Bhīma himself . . . (v. 37)
>
> "Tell, O poet Dāsa, having placed inspiration in your heart, the true tale of the Kauravas and Paṃḍavas . . . " (v. 39)
>
> "I have learned only a little of the *Bhārathu,* the ancient tale *(purāṇa).* I have no knowledge of metrics or other literary principles. [But] O god [i.e., Dauṃgar Singh], listen single-mindedly. I now tell the *Bhārathu,* with full exposition." (v. 41)[31]

A separate study would be needed to show how far this identification between patron and hero has shaped Viṣṇudās's narrative, and to make sense of the specifics of its historical reference.[32] But the cosmopolitan-vernacular norms (sometimes mediated through Apabhramsha) toward which Viṣṇudās aspires throughout his work are clear enough. The one element lacking is the production of vernacular place, a distinctive deficiency in vernacular poetry in the Midlands but one that seems to accord with other tendencies—toward dialectal and political fragmentation, for example—in the development of culture-power in the area,.[33]

Considered all together, these cases from across southern Asia demonstrate, first, that the development of written literature in the languages of Place was hard to imagine without the model of Sanskrit, and, second, that the appropriation of this model was marked, formally and thematically, by sophisticated and variable modes of synthesis. A paradigm instance at the level of form is offered by the history of metrics. Sanskrit verse forms, and often those of Prakrit and Apabhramsha, were successfully incorporated while local song prosodies were also retained and increasingly theorized.

31. *Mahābhārata* pp. 3–5.

32. In the "Sabhāparvan" Jarāsandha's death and the wrestling scene loom large, as does the presence of Bhīma in "Virāṭa." As in Java and Karnataka, overt allegorical identification is avoided.

33. McGregor 1984: 35.

With equal ease Kannada writers employed the grand Sanskrit syllabic meters, the Prakrit *khandhaa,* and the local *ragaḷe.* Cosmopolitan verse experiments may have been fewer in Marathi (though sometimes spectacular, as in the *Gadyarāja*), and less frequent in Gwaliyari (the trope of vernacular ignorance of Sanskrit metrics has some purchase in Viṣṇudās and, aside from some later experiments by Keśavdās, Sanskrit metrics would never catch on) and Bangla (in the *Caitanyacaritāmṛta, deśī* meters predominate), whereas the Javanese *kakawin* absorbed Sanskrit versification in toto.[34] At the level of theme, Sanskrit literature inaugurated vernacular traditions almost everywhere. Whether or not they could claim chronological firstness, most "primal" poets, from Pampa in tenth-century Karnataka to Eḻutacchan in sixteenth-century Kerala, were consecrated as primal by their choice of theme, which was almost invariably epic. Epic vernacularization occurred so frequently—witness Europe at the same period (chapter 11.1), and indeed Rome from the beginning of Latin literature (chapter 7.1)—that it must been seen an essential strategy in the development of an emergent literary culture. To the vernacular epics of Peruntēvaṉār in Tamil, Pampa and Ranna in Kannada, Nannaya and Tikkana in Telugu, the poet of the *Rāmāyaṇa* in Javanese, and Viṣṇudās in Gwaliyari could be added a wide array of others, including, in Assamese, Harivara Vipra's *Jaiminibhārata* and Mādhava Kandalī's *Rāmāyaṇa,* both from the mid-fourteenth century, and, in Oriya a century later, Śaraḷadās's adaptation of the *Mahābhārata* and Baḷarāmadāsa's of the *Rāmāyaṇa.*[35]

One of the more important meanings of such epics was precisely the fact of their being epics in languages of Place, their demonstration of the "literary capability" of the vernacular code.[36] But they also had cultural-political aims corresponding to those of the primary epic itself, albeit for worlds smaller by an order of magnitude. This correlates closely with the fact that vernacularization was typically initiated and promoted from the center of the polity, at the court of the ruling lord. Because "literature" in South Asia also comprised workly political discourse, the literary vernacularization of the court entailed the court's political vernacularization; the king's repre-

34. In Brajbhasha the situation is more complicated. Cosmopolitan-vernacular experiments were less common after Keśavdās (Busch 2003, chapter 4), and local or Apabhramsha-derived metrics largely prevailed in practice. Thai, where a Sanskrit-Pali metric predominates, provides a telling counterexample.

35. The epicization of language, space, and political order through the *Mahābhārata* was shadowed by vernacular *Rāmāyaṇas,* often evincing a different political project. There was not always overlap. In the Kannada world, a vernacular *Rāmāyaṇa* tradition had little presence.

36. For the idea of *Literaturfähigkeit,* a term of R. Schieffer's, see chapter 11.1 and n. 4. Agamben makes a similar point in a similar context: "A work's material content cannot be separated from its truth content and the language in which a work is written cannot be irrelevant to the work's material content" (1999a: 47).

sentation as epicized hero was an effect on the literary-narrative plane of a growing localization of political imagination and practice. An important component of this was the literary production of place. In vernacular narratives, the boundless universalizing Sanskrit tale was refitted onto the perceptible, traversable, indeed governable world of regional political practice. Newly miniaturized literary chronotopes were reproduced in the distribution of the epigraphical documents of political rule, as well as in the circulation routes of the actual manuscripts of the literary texts. Like manuscripts of the Sanskrit *Mahābhārata,* those of the epic in the vernacular moved through the very space they narrated, and only through that space.[37]

Both the literary character and the courtly location of vernacular texts demonstrate that in many cases the cultures of Place were intended to at once replicate and replace the global order of Sanskrit (although this was not true in all cases; Sufi poets, for example, had other agendas). By appropriating Sanskrit models for literary expressivity and sometimes for political discourse; by remapping epic spaces onto local places; and by evoking, through the very practice of vernacular culture, new sociotextual communities to inhabit these new vernacular places and to produce and reproduce themselves through reading and hearing those new vernacular texts—in all these ways the literati of southern Asia at the start of the second millennium introduced an entirely new cultural formation. Before trying to make objective sense of this formation as an order of power as well as of culture, it will be helpful to see how Indian thinkers conceptualized the new regionality they were beginning to practice.

10.2 REGION AND REASON

Like their peers in the Kannada world, vernacular intellectuals elsewhere sought to conceptualize the spreading revolution in literary culture and, in particular, to make sense of the new practices in reference to the dominant models against which they were defining themselves. To employ for the production of literary and political texts languages that those models had long and actively excluded from the domain of expressivity and imagination, characterizing them as rustic, solecistic, and incapable of direct communication, required a new disciplinary focus as well as a new discourse on the local. These were developed above all in grammar and lexicography, where a newly theorized and even ennobled category termed *deśi* (*deśī, deśya, dēsi, dēse,* etc.), or the practices of Place, came into being, along with or dependent upon a new understanding of the sources of cultural authority. As in the case of literature and political expression, this new vernacular philology was typically the project of court elites.

37. See chapters 8.3, 9.3, and 6.1.

Most remarkable and sophisticated of all these philological initiatives were the new grammaticizations of the vernacular, often conjoined with poetics. The history of these developments in Kannada has been examined in some detail (chapter 9.2, 4). For Telugu, Kētana in the thirteenth century produced the *Āndhrabhāṣābhūṣaṇamu* (Ornament of the Speech of Andhra), but far more celebrated is the *Āndhraśabdacintāmaṇi.* Long ascribed to the mid-eleventh-century poet Nannaya, scholarly opinion today is divided about the history of this work. Yet the tradition long ago made its decision about where and when and by whom the grammaticization of Telugu should have occurred. This is captured in a verse about Nannaya's originality that has circulated for centuries: "Praise to him, teacher of poets, who first enunciated the grammar of the language of Andhra." The author credited with the invention of Telugu literature with his vernacularization of the *Mahābhārata* must at the same time have invented the authoritative norms for the language of literature—or so the logic of the cosmopolitan vernacular requires (chapter 9.4). And like the *Karṇāṭakabhāṣābhūṣaṇa,* the mid-eleventh-century Kannada grammar of Nāgavarma II, it did so in Sanskrit and in *sūtra* style, conceptualizing its objects of analysis in full accord with Sanskrit grammatical categories.[38]

At about the same time that Nannaya was inventing—or assumed by a later tradition to be inventing—Telugu philology, a parallel process was under way in Tamil country. The *Vīracōḻiyakārikai* (Treatise for King Vīracōḻa) was composed by Puttamittiraṉ (Buddhamitra), "the lord of Poṉpaṟṟi" and probably a vassal of Vīrarājendra Cōḻa (r. 1063–69). It is the "pure Tamil spoken by the Cōḻa king, Vīrarācentiraṉ" that forms the subject of the work. Like the (apparently) archaic *Tolkāppiyam,* with which it is clearly familiar, the *Vīracōḻiyam* examines both grammar and literature, but in a way far more profoundly influenced by Sanskrit grammatical terminology and theory and Sanskrit rhetorical science. Explicitly making use of the old rules of grammar sanctioned by "northern texts" (*vaṭanūl,* that is, Sanskrit), along with the literary science of Daṇḍin's *Mirror* (whose author is named), it signals an appropriation of Sanskrit analytic categories unprecedented in Tamil (it is here that we find the earliest use of the term *maṇipravāla* to refer to the register that permits the inclusion of inflected Sanskrit words in Tamil poetry). And by identifying the *vaidarbha* Way with Tamil, the *Vīracōḻiyam* implicitly affiliates itself with what many saw as the preeminent form of the cosmopolitan idiom. Additional philological work in Tamil, including a complete new

38. The oft-quoted (Sanskrit!) verse runs: *vācām āndhramayīnāṃ yaḥ pravaktā prathamo 'bhavat* | *ācāryaṃ taṃ kavīndrāṇāṃ vande vāganuśāsanam* || (cited in Narasimhacharya 1934: 10). For arguments attributing the work to Appakavi, the mid-seventeenth-century poet who wrote the principal Telugu commentary on the text, see Narayana Rao 2003: 386–88. A comparative study of Nāgavarma's *Bhāṣābhūṣaṇam* and Kētana's remains a desideratum.

grammar, the *Naṉṉūl* by Pavaṇanti, who wrote under the patronage of a Gaṅga king in the early thirteenth century, and a full translation of the *Mirror* somewhat earlier (the *Taṇṭiyalaṅkāra*, rendered with more fidelity to the original than other versions), complete the development of a deluxe toolbox for the creation of the new vernacular.[39]

Comparable theorizations of the vernacular among the political elites were taking place from one end of the Sanskrit cosmopolis to the other. In Sri Lanka a full philological apparatus was developed. Daṇḍin's *Mirror* was once again adapted, under the title *Siyabaslakara* (Sanskrit *Svakīyabhāṣālaṅkāra*, Ornament of Our Own Language), perhaps as early as the mid-ninth century (at the court of King Sena I, r. 846–66).[40] A new grammatical and poetical treatise was composed in the thirteenth century, the *Sidatsaṅgarāva* (*Siddhāntasaṃgraha*, Compendium of Principles), partly mediated through the Tamil model of the *Vīracōḻiyam* but clearly indebted to Sanskrit (as well as Sanskrit-influenced Pali) sources, as was the fifteenth-century lexicon of Sinhala, Sanskrit, and Pali, the *Ruvanmala*. In Tibet, a remarkable transformation began in the first half of the thirteenth century under the influence of Sa-skya Paṇḍita (1182–1251), whose summary of cosmopolitan learning, *The Scholar's Gate*, comprises a grammatical analysis of Tibetan inspired by the Sanskrit model of Pāṇini. Daṇḍin's *Mirror* was translated yet again as well as other Sanskrit philological works, including the fifth-century Sanskrit lexicon, the *Amarakośa*, rendered into Tibetan in the thirteenth century. Interest in disciplining Tibetan on the part of political leaders (the "clerical potentates") was well established at this period and would continue with vigor into the following centuries.[41]

As even this brief overview shows, with the exception of Tibet and Java, vernacular philologization was initially a south Indian enterprise. North India followed suit eventually but along quite specific and much narrower routes. The single most arresting fact about developments in the north is that no grammaticization whatsoever was produced: none of the languages

39. While the *Tolkāppiyam* is often dated to the early centuries of the first millennium, one sober assessment places it a few centuries before the appearance of its first commentaries in the thirteenth century (Swamy 1975). On the *Vīracōḻiyakārikai* see especially Monius 1997: 189, 202 (the claim that the work is "a self-consciously Buddhist statement on the nature of Tamil" does not seem to be sustained by the evidence). Scholarship on *Naṉṉūl* outside of Tamil is thin (Scharfe 1977: 183, Zvelebil 1975: 192–93); the new translation (Sripati 1995) is unhelpful.

40. The Sinhala adaptation omits the global-local stylistic distinctions of the Ways prominent in the Kannada version. For the possible identification of Ruvan-mī, author of the paraphrase *(sannaya)* that accompanies the *Siyabaslakara* and perhaps of the work itself, with Ratnaśrījñāna, commentator on the *KĀ*, see Pollock 2005d.

41. For Sri Lanka, see Scharfe 1977: 195 and again Hallisey 2003; for Tibet, Verhagen 1992: 377 ff. (correlating grammatical activity with the dominance of a centralized political power) and 1996; Gold 2003 on Sa-skya Paṇḍita; and more generally Kapstein 2003.

of Place—Assamese, Bangla, Gujarati, the varieties of Madhyadeshiya—had a written grammar until the colonial period. Even in Maharashtra, where Sanskrit grammatical studies achieved uncommon brilliance (with Vopadeva in the fourteenth century, Rāmacandra Dīkṣīta in the sixteenth, and Bhaṭṭoji Dīkṣīta and Kauṇḍa Bhaṭṭa in the seventeenth), the Marathi language itself was entirely ignored; a single exception is a short list of Marathi case endings included in the language manual of a Mahānubhāva scholar of the fourteenth century.[42] This absence may be a function of the conceptual haziness of the Sanskrit-near languages, also reflected in the fact that several had no stable name (for instance, though the name "Brajbhasha" was not unknown before the modern period, in its place we more often find simply *bhākhā/bhāṣā* in premodern texts). That said, there was no doubt a philological elaboration of these languages that we simply do not know about. We are only beginning to understand how significant was the process of philologization at the level of lexicography and poetics (though not in grammar) for Brajbhasha's development, from the late sixteenth century, as a courtly vernacular or even cosmopolitan surrogate. And evidence for a pretheoretical, pragmatic grammaticization of northern vernaculars is provided by the increasingly standardized forms of the literary language through the late medieval period, such as some scholars have found to be the case with fourteenth-century Gujarati.[43]

It is not the mere presence of new philologies but their methods and related cognitive processes that signal the depth of the vernacular transformation of culture. It is true that in the early centuries of vernacularization the grammars themselves were sometimes composed in Sanskrit, and in virtually all cases the conceptual framework for grammatizing the vernaculars was Sanskritic (so that notions such as *kāraka,* case relation, were used where they had little linguistic propriety). With respect to method, however, we find everywhere the profound difference from the cosmopolitan episteme that we encountered in Kannada (chapter 9.4). The ancient if seemingly counterintuitive Sanskrit axiom that "practice follows theory" *(prayogasya śāstrapūrvatva)* had been tenable given the conviction that coherent and true knowledge *(śāstra)* is eternal and therefore can never be invented but only (re)discovered. This notion, and the correlative relationship between rule and instance, were turned upside down in the vernacular project, since its theorization was

42. The absence of precolonial grammaticization in north India is unstudied. Bhatia 1987: 9–15 surveys what little has been done for Hindi. The fourteenth-century *Pañcavārttika* of Bhīṣmācārya is not a Marathi "grammar" (Pandharipande 1997: xl); the only section applicable to Marathi is a morphological list (M. Deshpande, personal communication). On the north-south European homologies see chapter 12.1 and section 1 of this chapter.

43. On Brajbhasha see Busch 2003, especially chapters 3 and 4; on the unity of early Gujarati, Yashaschandra 2003: 573.

manifestly new and the source of its authority fundamentally problematic. Vernacular philology everywhere, not just in Kannada, was compelled to derive its authority from literary models. Tamil grammars are explicit about the matter, succinctly inverting the age-old Sanskrit view: "Literature yields grammar just as oil is obtained from sesame seed. There is no grammar without literature, just as there is no oil without sesame seed," "The rules of grammar are uttered after the study of earlier literature has taken place."[44]

The procedure (however circular) of establishing rules inductively from normative instances rather than deducing practice from rules had long marked the Prakrit and Apabhramsha traditions. In the eighth book of his *Siddhahemaśabdānuśāsanam,* which conceived of itself as the summation of all earlier grammars (chapter 4.2), the twelfth-century scholar Hemacandra validates the rules for Prakrit and Apabhramsha by adducing literary proof texts (he does this frequently for Prakrit and consistently for Apabhramsha); but for Sanskrit he cites none, in keeping with the practice of earlier grammarians.[45] At the microscopic level of analysis a similar conception is in play, as in his discussion of words that cannot be analyzed by base and stem, according to normal Sanskrit procedures. These include Prakrit words (*tatsama*s and *tadbhava*s, loans and derivatives, respectively, from Sanskrit) as well as what Hemacandra calls *bhāṣāśabda,* or *deśī* words. With respect to the latter he notes, "If these words have not been used by earlier poets they should not be employed if they are hard to understand. Instead, synonyms should be substituted for them."[46] The key point here, in brief, is that writers of *deśī* or local language were hereby being empowered to authorize correct usage; it was not correct language itself—the perfect language of the gods forever preexisting human practice—that authorized their usage, as had been the case for earlier cosmopolitan writers.[47] Whereas Hemacandra thus seems to

44. See Zvelebil 1992: 131–32, citing *Akattiyam* and *Naṉṉūl* respectively. I say "seemingly counterintuitive" because for many contemporary thinkers all perception is theory-laden.

45. See Cirantanamuni 1981: 1–35 (Prakrit); 36–85 (Apabhramsha). For Prakrit, literary illustrations are typically cited in the subcommentary (the *Nyāsa*) for Apabhramsha, directly in the *vṛtti* (the *Prakāśikā*); the significance, if any, of this procedure is unclear. The Prakrit works include celebrated (though unnamed) texts like the *Sattasaī, Setubandha, Karpūramañjarī, Paümacariya, Vasudevahiṇḍī,* and *Gauḍavaho* (see Vaidya in his edition of the *Prakrit Grammar of Hemacandra,* p. 206); the Apabhramsha texts are all anonymous, and while most are almost certainly real citations, at least four were composed by Hemacandra himself (cf. Alsdorf 1937: 72–73).

46. The example offered (in Sanskrit) is *kuśala* for *kṛṣṭa* in the sense of learned or skilled (*Siddhahemacandraśabdānuśāsana* 8.2.174).

47. See chapter 9.4. Three centuries later Appayya Dīkṣita stated this explicitly (with respect to Prakrit at least): the decision as to correct usage of Prakrit words is made on the basis of not only grammatical rules but also "the actual practices of those familiar with poetry *(kāvyajñalokavyavahārāt)* . . . Thus even though not taught in the grammar [a given usage is correct] if it conforms with the practices of those trained in [Prakrit] poetry *(kāvyābhiyuktavyavahāra-)*" (*Prākṛtamaṇidīpā,* p. 2).

appreciate, with some methodological reflexivity, the emergence of local theorization in grammar with its countervailing epistemology, his other philological writings show how the cosmopolitan mentality persisted even as the practices of Place were being systematically conceptualized. Hemacandra lived at a moment in intellectual history—at the threshold of the vernacular epoch—before the *deśī* had in fact become local. This seeming paradox, and the evolving historical semantics of the word *deśī,* can be seen in Hemacandra's vernacular lexicon, the *Deśīnāmamālā* (Dictionary of the Words of Place, c. 1150), a work whose very existence testifies to the growing prominence of localized culture in theoretical reflection. Hemacandra had his finger on the pulse of the impending vernacular transformation—recall that he was the first to allow the possibility of a "vulgar courtly epic"—and yet he had still a prevernacular understanding, so to put it, of the project he had taken in hand.[48]

Hemacandra opens his *Dictionary* with the declaration that "The *deśī* is hard to collect, by and large, and once collected it is hard to understand. But in this book the master Hemacandra collects and analyzes it." Much that is developed in his subsequent exposition is embedded in this opening statement. The feminine noun *deśī* here is not an adjective (modifying an understood *bhāṣā*) but rather a noun meaning something like "[a cultural practice] of Place." Later we are told that by *deśī* is meant "theorizations of Place" *(deśīśāstrāṇi,* v. 2), whereas the adjectival form, *deśya* or *deśaja,* refers to words themselves.[49] It is important to grasp what Hemacandra implies in his prologue. The "practices of Place" (which for later thinkers, as we will see, included everything from language to dance movements and melodies) are not necessarily available in an unmediated way, as if they were somehow natural and instinctive rather than cultural and learned; quite the contrary, *deśī* is "hard to understand." And if this seems surprising to us—after all, what is more familiar than the words of one's own place?—Hemacandra is echoing a conviction widespread throughout earlier South Asian literary cultures. Consider the once-influential (and now almost wholly forgotten) Prakrit work *Līlāvaī* of Koūhala (c. 800). This romance begins with a request from the author's mistress for a story. When her lover protests that he has no such skill, she asserts her indifference to artistry: "Any words that clearly communicate meaning are good; what care we for rules? So tell me a tale in Prakrit, which simple women love to hear—but don't use too many *deśī* words,

48. On Hemacandra's view of *grāmyabhāṣā mahākāvya* see chapter 2.2 and n. 59. He mentions predecessors for his grammar (e.g., *Deśīnāmamālā* p. 13) but none is extant (Dhanapāla's *Pāiyalacchī* [973] treats lexemes of Place sparingly). It is unclear what we are to make of the *deśīśāstras* later ascribed to authors included in the *Sattasaī* (Pischel 1965: 11).

49. See for example *Deśīnāmamālā* p. 1, opening verse; the previous citation is from p. 1, *vṛtti* on the opening verse.

so that it's easy to understand."[50] In fact, as Hemacandra affirms, *deśī* requires scholarly attention:

> After carefully examining all the available theorizations of Place we undertook this task in order to help others—that is, to save people sinking down in the mud of language solecisms whether because the words had not been properly defined, their orthography had remained indeterminate, their meanings could not be harmonized with earlier authorities, or simply because [these earlier theorizations] blindly followed convention in their definitions and spellings.[51]

Evidently, using "words of Place" was not doing what comes naturally. Throughout the dictionary Hemacandra shows that research is essential for the correct usage of *deśī*. In one passage he notes that a word (which he gives as *ayataṃcitam* in the sense of "amassed") is read by some differently (as *avaacciaṃ*):

> Whose orthography is correct and whose is wrong we cannot decide [a priori] since *deśī* [by definition] follows no hard and fast rules. Since the spelling cannot be determined in the absence of an analysis of base, stem, and so on, the only sure way for us to proceed is by founding our judgment on the preponderance of written usage.[52]

Note that the problems Hemacandra faced, which he frequently identified as solecism *(apabhraṣṭa)*, derived from variations in *spelling;* it is often a *lipi-doṣa,* or fault in (ortho)graphy, on the part of earlier writers that prompts his intervention. Cearly for Hemacandra, *deśī* was not only not unmediated, natural, or easy, it was not even oral.

What are these words of Place that require scholarly intervention and study for proper usage? "They are not simply the words used in particular places," says Hemacandra,

> such as Maharashtra, Vidarbha, among the Ābhīras, and so on. If that were what was meant [by *deśī*], it would be an impossible task to collect these words even over an entire lifetime. What we mean by the word *deśī* is instead [the lexicon of] a specific language, namely, Prakrit, such as is used from time immemorial. "Even (Brahmā) Vācaspati, the Lord of Speech himself, does not possess the skill to collect all the words that are used in all regions, not if he had a thousand cosmic cycles to try."[53]

50. *Līlāvaī* vv. 40–41: *pavirala-desi-sulakkham.*

51. *Deśīnāmamālā* 1.2 *vṛtti,* (omitting *pratīka*s), p. 2: *niḥśeṣadeśīśāstrāṇāṃ . . . pariśīlanena . . . prādurbhūtaṃ kvacid arthāsamarpakatvena kvacid varṇānupūrvīniścayābhāvena kvacit pūrvadeśī-visaṃvādena kvacid gatānugatikatānibaddhaśabdārthatayā,* etc.

52. *Deśīnāmamālā* 1.47 *vṛtti,* p. 25: *tatra keṣāṃ lipibhramaḥ keṣāṃ neti na vidmo niyāmakābhāvāt. varṇānupūrvīvijñānaṃ tu prakṛtyādivibhāgam antareṇāśakyakriyam. bahutarapustakaprāmāṇyāc ca niyate vartmani pravṛttāḥ sma.*

53. *Deśīnāmamālā* 1.4 *vṛtti,* p. 3. Words used "in particular places such as Maharashtra" and so on had already been noted in his grammar; see below.

Words of Place, accordingly, are restricted to two types: The first is lexemes that cannot be generated by the transformational rules concerning base, suffix, and so on taught in Hemacandra's grammar. (Such words are elsewhere said to be "preformed" or given *[siddha]* and "to be understood in everyday communication" *[lokataḥ]*, yet they are not merely current speech items but words that have been admitted into the literary language.) The second is lexemes that can be so generated but have a different primary meaning from what is assigned to them in their "original" form, that is, in Sanskrit dictionaries.[54] A fundamental assumption of the dictionary, unspoken perhaps because it is self-evident, is that any word used in Sanskrit ceases ipso facto to be *deśī*. But the practical impossibility of knowing everything written in Sanskrit carries the theoretical impossibility of validating any word as truly *deśī*. Scholars, in fact, have pointed to the many items included in Hemacandra's dictionary that are easily derivable from Sanskrit by the rules he supplies in his own grammar, or are used in Sanskrit in the very sense Hemacandra assigns to them as *deśī*, or are found exclusively in regional languages and therefore, on Hemacandra's own stated principle of lexical domains, should have been excluded from his dictionary.[55]

More consequential than these methodological difficulties, however, is the startling definition of the very project of the *Deśīnāmamālā:* to assemble a dictionary of words of Place that are not, in fact, thought of as located in any given place. Instead, they are forever embedded in the eternal language stuff of Prakrit though not derivable from it; that is, they are not amenable to analysis in the way that obvious derivatives, *tadbhavas*, are. Many of the words examined are entirely unrelated to Prakrit in any conventional understanding of the term—some are Kannada, Telugu, Tamil, Persian, or Arabic—and yet this unrelatedness is nowhere recognized. Such apparent oversight makes sense only within a cosmopolitan conceptual scheme of the sort adopted in Hemacandra's grammar. As he takes care to remind readers at the beginning of his dictionary (and as we will recall from chapter 2.2), his text is concerned exclusively with those languages, all of them transregional, that had been recognized for the preceding millennium as the sole literary codes (Sanskrit, Maharashtri, Shauraseni, Magadhi, Paishachi—including its

54. For example *mahānaṭa*, "great dancer," which according to Hemacandra has the specific *deśī* meaning of Hara (Śiva) (1.3 *vṛtti*, p. 4).

55. So already Bühler (cited in *Deśīnāmamālā*, introduction, pp. 4, 8). Hemacandra does often exercise fine discrimination: thus he distinguishes *akka* (masculine, in the sense of envoy) and *akkā* (feminine, in the sense of sister) as *deśī*, being found in Kannada and other Dravidian languages, from *akkā* in the sense of mother, said to be found in Sanskrit and therefore not *deśī* (1.6, p. 5). *Siddhahemacandra* 8.2.174 refers to "words such as *āhittha* [angry, confused], *lallaka* [frightening], and so on that exist as preformed *(siddha)* in places like Maharashtra and Vidarbha" and which "are to be understood from everyday usage." They thus intermittently come within the purview of his grammar but are not pertinent to his lexicon.

even more obscure subvariety, Culikapaishachi—and Apabhramsha). Accordingly, *deśī* words can only be treated if viewed as part of this lexicon of the cosmopolitan literary. As Hemacandra says, they are not *tatsamas*, lexemes "identical with that [Sanskrit]," which therefore would have been covered in the rules described in books 1–7 of his grammar; nor are they *tadbhavas*, those "arising from that [Sanskrit]," which are described in book 8. "Neither [category] applies to *deśya* [words]," which thus have to be included in a "modest appendix" at the end of the grammar, which is precisely what the *Deśīnāmamālā* supplies.[56]

As late as the end of the twelfth century, then, a cosmopolitan intellectual of western India was still able to view the literary local as wholly subsumable under, and capable of being conceptualized only within, a global cultural formation. It does not of course follow that for all the preceding centuries the identification of regions as distinct zones of cultural practice was entirely absent, only that it was inconsequential. While the epic world was nominally regionalized, culture was both represented and textualized as absolutely homogeneous; the Bengali recension of the Sanskrit *Mahābhārata* reveals no Bengali Sanskrit style, the Malayali recension no Malayali cultural practice. If ancient grammarians recognized regional variations in Sanskrit usage, these never constituted anything like dialectal divisions. In the theory of *vaidika dharma,* too, variation across space was acknowledged *(deśadharma)* but in the last analysis brought under a superordinate category of universal moral obligation.[57] In all these aspects of the cosmopolitan thought world, the region had no cultural, let alone social or political, salience.

Around the time Hemacandra was writing, however, vernacular intellectuals were beginning to completely alter the rules of the cultural theory game. Regional-language grammarians reconceptualized *deśī* as a fundamentally local language feature; in the *Śabdamaṇidarpaṇam,* the word is used interchangeably with *accagannaḍa,* "pure Kannada." The same sharper differentiation of the cultures of Place from the culture of placeless Sanskrit was

56. *Siddhahemacandra* 8.1: "The grammatical analysis of Prakrit, which follows that of Sanskrit, comprises a set of rules relating to Prakrit in its two types of origin from Sanskrit: (1) as preformed *(siddha),*" here meaning the *tatsama* form that is identical with Sanskrit, "and (2) as subject to transformation operations *(sādhyamāna),*" i.e., the *tadbhava* form, which is "derived from Sanskrit" (or, "exists eternally in Sanskrit," see chapter 2.3 and n. 73). The dictionary is called an appendix to the grammar in *Deśīnāmamālā* 8.77 *vṛtti,* p. 345. Persian words include *bandho* (*banda,* servant), and Arabic words, *karālī* (*khilāl,* toothpick), though none is expressly identified as either.

57. References to the (very moderate) linguistic regionalization in Pāṇini and Patañjali are provided in chapters 1.2 and 5.3. On epic recensions see chapter 6.1. For most *mīmāṃsakas*, *deśadharma* is, strictly speaking, a misnomer: a truly dharmic practice is by definition universally obligatory for everyone in the *vaidika* social world; any regionalization of dharma practice is based on pure error *(bhrānti;* see *Mīmāṃsāsūtra* 1.3.15 ff., the *holākādhikaraṇa).* For a broader consideration of the question, see Wezler 1985, especially p. 12.

elsewhere being made by means of a new binary: *mārga-deśī,* the practices of the great Way and of particular Places. *Mārga,* the key word for literary practices that adhered to the quasi-universal norms of the Sanskrit world (chapter 5.3), was transformed into the counterpositive that made regionality as such conceptually intelligible and *deśī* truly local. Not only a new semantics but also a new episteme of cultural regionality is sedimented in the history of the *mārga-deśī* distinction. This history has yet to be traced, or the connections between literary and broader cultural discourses clearly mapped out. Yet the available data, especially on music and dance, suggest how intensive and extensive the conversation must have been, around the turn of the millennium, on the relationship between local and translocal lifeways.

In music, the *mārga-deśī* distinction—"the only important [one] of this type in the evolution of Indian musical style"—accompanied the expansion of musical resources near the end of the first millennium, which in turn prompted the new theoretical focus on the *deśī* repertoire and the codification and rationalization of traditions of Place that eventually supplanted those of the Way.[58] The system of five *mārgatālas*, "rhythms of the Way," known to the Sanskrit *Nāṭyaśāstra* was elaborately supplemented by a system of 120 *deśītālas* in Śārṅgadeva's *Saṅgītaratnākara* (Jewel Mine of Music), a text composed at the Maharashtrian court of the Yādava king Siṃhaṇa around 1240 (thus in the generation preceding the spectacular vernacular efflorescence of Jñāneśvar, Mhāibhaṭa, and others). Similarly, the ancient system of *grāmarāgas*, scale melodies, now assimilated melodies of Place *(deśīrāga).*[59] In the appropriately named *Bṛhaddeśī* (The Great [Treatise on] Practices of Place; tenth century), the first musicological text to employ the binary, the two terms are used to set not only the supralocal against the local but rule-boundedness against freer form.[60] The latter notion is restated in the fifteenth-century *Saṅgītadarpaṇa* (Mirror of Performance): *mārga saṅgīta* was instituted by Śiva (Druhiṇa) and performed in his presence by Bharata, and it bestows spiritual liberation, whereas *deśī saṅgīta* is popular *(lokānurañjana)* and is performed in a given place *(deśa)* in the style *(rīti)* of that place.[61] If *mārga* was derived from the theoretical enunciation of the *Nāṭyaśāstra,* it was in keeping with the archaic cosmopolitan model of the priority of theory over practice that it should depend on earlier institutions as well as enunciations. The "Way" in music thus connoted cultural practices that were Sanskrit in

58. Rowell 1992: 12, 208; cf. 192–93.

59. Rowell 1992: 208; Nijenhuis 1977; 1974: 62 ff. on *mārgatāla* (see *Nāṭyaśāstra* 31.8 ff.).

60. The opening of the text is corrupt, but this seems the clear implication. The work was in all likelihood composed by a Kannadiga. Its pseudonymous author, the legendary sage Mataṅga, is closely associated with Kiṣkindhā (Hampi in northern Karnataka); more important, the work deals extensively with Kannada prosodical forms (*Bṛhaddeśī* 3.86–4.87).

61. *Saṅgītadarpaṇa* 1.3–6; see 1.21 ff. Also Kumbha's *Saṅgītarāja* 3.3–4 (p. 21). Nijenhuis 1977: 5–6 denies that early *mārga* music was exclusively "religious" (see Raghavan 1963: 585).

origin and invariant—and now religious as well, given that the *laukika*, or worldly, character of Sanskrit, a function of the cross-community appeal of cosmopolitan culture, had begun to retreat to the narrower world of Brahmanical society as the vernacular millennium advanced. By contrast, *deśī* implied not only locally variable, decidedly popular, and nontranscendental musical practices but irregular, improvisational, even pretheoretical practices—until, of course, they were themselves captured by the cosmopolitan rationality in which all these works (and they are mostly Sanskrit works, after all) still participated: the *deśī* not only could be but had to be subjected to the discipline of cultural theorization in the new vernacular world.

In dance theory, too, from the end of the tenth century onward, the *mārga-deśī* distinction became the logic that structured the knowledge form as a whole. The *Nṛttaratnāvalī* of Jāyasenāpati (1254) defines *mārga* as derived from the *veda* on *nāṭya* (that is, the *Nāṭyaśāstra*), "sought out" *(mārgita)* by the great sages of the past, and practiced by notables *(santaḥ)*. *Deśī*, by contrast, is linked to the pleasure of people in their various places:

> Like an experienced courtesan pampered by kings, *deśī* seduces sophisticated men with a taste for different places by means of its various charming traits, such as accord with particular languages, dress styles, and ornaments. As a general rule, kings love what is new, and so, to please my king, all the new dances now being invented, dances of Place, which are so called from their being practiced in different places, will now be described—dance, that is, of the present day, since dance of the past derives from *śāstra*, and dance of the future cannot as yet be described.[62]

A number of themes already noticed are usefully summarized here: the novelty of local practices becoming objects of scholarly attention; the special beauty with which they were now being invested over against more archaic cosmopolitan forms precisely by reason of their heterogeneity; the grounding of local culture in theory rather than conceptualizing it as something invented in practice; and the centrality of the royal court in stimulating interest in the textualization and eventual theorization of such local forms. Like *deśī* music, *deśī* dance was now being cosmopolitanized. Local dance features

62. *Nṛttaratnāvalī* 5.2–5 ("all the new dances now being invented," *yad yad utpādyate navam* || *nṛttam*). For the *mārga-deśī* distinction see 1.52, 54. Jāyasena was elephant commander for Kākatīya Gaṇapati of Āndhra (himself described as "skilled in discriminating between *mārga* and *deśī*," 5.10) and a junior contemporary of Śārṅgadhara (whose *Saṅgītaratnākara* Jāyasena hoped to overshadow, just as his patron sought to overshadow the Yādava patron of Śārṅgadhara; see Raghavan's introduction, pp. 9, 74). The *mārga-deśī* distinction in dance was introduced in the *Daśarūpaka* (1.9; late-tenth-century Dhārā) to differentiate movement that "relates to emotion," or dance-drama *(nṛtya)*, from movement that "relates to rhythm and tempo," or nonrepresentational dance *(nṛtta)*. So Jāyasena (1.50ff.): his first four chapters deal with *mārga/nṛtya*, the remaining with *deśī/nṛtta*.

were by and large given Sanskrit (and not Telugu) names by Jāyasenāpati, and his codification in Sanskrit of these local phenomena was meant to make them accessible to a supralocal world.

It is in the domain of literature, and above all in the literary theory of southern intellectuals, however, that the rationality and regionality of region found their clearest expression. Here alone, in fact, *deśī* achieved full conceptualization. As we have seen, when *mārga* began its career as a technical term in the Sanskrit discourse on literature, it functioned first as a multiple and expansive category for identifying "regional" styles of a single unified cultural substance, *kāvya,* across cosmopolitan space (chapter 5.3); no one ever postulated regionalized Sanskrits for the production of literature, unlike the nominally regionalized Prakrits or the actually regionalized languages of Place. Given the cosmopolitan nature of *kāvya,* it is unsurprising that the distinction between *mārga* and *deśī* is found nowhere in Sanskrit poetics: literature cannot be local in the thought world Sanskrit defines. It was southern intellectuals, first in the Kannada-speaking world, who redeployed the term *mārga* to describe the Ways of *vernacular* writing. For the *Kavirājamārgam* the northern and southern Way meant the vernacular's Sanskritized and localized registers respectively (chapter 9.2); the term *deśī* appears infrequently and never as an antonym to *mārga.* The dichotomous usage was invented by poets a few generations later; Pampa may have been the first to use it in reference to the localized and Sanskritized registers: "[This *Bhāratam*] must partake of the idiom of Place *(dēsi)* and at the same time must penetrate into the idiom of the Way *(mārga)*." From that point on, the binary would be used in this sense repeatedly, as in Ranna's courtly epic of c. 1000: "The celebrated *rasa*s being made attractive to the mind, *mārga* used fittingly, *dēse* making the poem attractive—thus composed does a poem become useful to a king." Moreover, the semantic field of *dēsi (dēse,* or *desi,* or *deśī)* became at once descriptive and evaluative. The vernacular was not only "placed" over against the placeless universal but was superior to it: *dēsi* connotes the "fit," the truly "beautiful."[63]

Elsewhere in the Deccan a similar development occurred. In Telugu literary culture, for example, *mārga* and *deśī* were first used in the tenth and eleventh centuries to refer to Sanskrit and Telugu, respectively, as separate linguistic codes. It was perhaps in the work of the fourteenth-century poet

63. Pampa speaks of "the full beauty *(dēsiyan)* of springtime flowers"; a *dēsikāṟti* is a beautiful woman for Aggaḷa in his early twelfth-century *Candraprabhapurāṇam;* a *dēsigāṟa* is a maker of the beautiful, an artist, for Kumāravyāsa (see *Kannaḍanighaṇṭu* s.v. *dēsikāṟti* and *dēsigāṟa*). For uses of *dēsi/dēse* in this sense already in the *Kavirājamārgam* see *KRM* 1.50, 75. Pampa's verse is *VAV* 2.17; Ranna's is *Sāhasabhīmavijayam* 1.36. On the parallel transformation in Europe (e.g., Dante's *nobilior est vulgaris*), see chapter 11.2.

Śrīnāthuḍu that the terms were first used to signify Sanskritized and localized registers of the vernacular itself. Developments in the north, again, were more obscure, and little historical scholarship exists to clarify matters. It thus remains to be determined just how old is the application of the term *rīti* in the sense of the cosmopolitan vernacular, a usage that crystallized at the end of the sixteenth century among Brajbhasha writers like Keśavdās. Recall that *rīti* had been employed as an alternative to *mārga* in the writings of northern theorists from the time of Vāmana of Kashmir (c. 800), and when the influential early-twentieth-century historian of Hindi literature Rāmcandra Śukla named the epoch of the cosmopolitan vernacular *rītikāl,* the Age of the Path, he may have been hearing a long echo of the term in the rhetorical (and musicological) tradition.[64]

Not everywhere, of course, nor consistently were literary phenomena rethought according to the new cosmopolitan-vernacular distinction, and care must be taken to respect the epistemological differences deriving from the varieties of historical experience. Just as the interaction of a language of Place with transregional Sanskrit signaled by the *mārga-deśī* categories must not be conflated with such faceless oppositions as standardized/nonstandardized, classical/folk, high/low, so it must not be assimilated uncritically to categories of altogether different provenance. In Tamil country, for instance, although the *mārga-deśī* binary was by no means unknown (again, its detailed history remains to be written), the main burden of conceptualizing literature seems to have been borne by other categories, such as *centamiḻ* and *kuṭuntamiḻ* (correct and colloquial Tamil), which antedate *mārga-deśī.*[65] And in Kerala beginning in the late fourteenth century yet another category, or indeed language, *maṇipravāḷa,* functioned as the principal rubric under which varieties of the cosmopolitan style were identified.[66]

When *mārga* came to be complemented by the term *deśī,* the hitherto linguistically homogeneous and only stylistically regionalized literature in Sanskrit was reconceptualized, perhaps more clearly than ever, as a pan-Indian

64. For Telugu see Narayana Rao 1990: 5–6, and 2003, especially 424–27. Śukla 1988: 161–67 does not explain his terminology, but he seems to be the only begetter (Busch 2003, chapter 2). Keśavdās, like later writers in Brajbhasha, uses *rīti* only in the sense of "method" (e.g., *rasarīti, Kavipriyā* 13.5.1, *Rasikapriyā* 16.16; Allison Busch, personal communication; see also McGregor 1984: 126). Neither *mārga* nor *deśī* in the technical sense appears in his work. On *rīti* in music theory, vaguely linked with *mārga,* see Rowell 1992: 317.

65. *Mārga* does not "correspond" to Tamil *cenmal* (straight, beautiful; in fact, generally connoting un-Sanskritized), and *deśī* has nothing to do with the nonliterate or with the "crooked" or dialectal (pace Zvelebil 1992: 132–33).

66. The starting point is the *Līlātilaka,* a Sanskrit-language grammar that theorizes a new literary Malayalam out of a code impregnated by Sanskrit and conceptually undifferentiated from Tamil (Freeman 1998, 2003: 448 ff.). See also chapter 8.3.

singular through juxtaposition with the emergent heterogeneous regionalisms. And *kāvya,* literature as a cultural form fashioned so as to be intelligible everywhere and at all times, gave way to literatures written in codes locked in Place and no longer fully meaningful or even intelligible elsewhere. From this point on, as the cosmopolitan world of Sanskrit slowly disintegrated, the category *mārga* ceased to have a role to play in either the conceptual or the substantive history of South Asia, except in its new meaning as the cosmopolitan form of the vernacular itself. As for the category *deśī,* only the first phase in its long history has been sketched here. Of no little significance is the reemergence of the term as "(swa)deshi" in the late-colonial and postcolonial periods as a new antonym to "Western." Just as the multiple Ways of Sanskrit became singularized under pressure from the multiple Places that were newly vernacularizing, so under pressure from Western modernity the multiplicity of southern Asian places achieved a new and different kind of conceptual unification.

Equally noteworthy are the historical semantics of *deśī* in relation to the culture-power complex, especially in contrast to the biologism of "nation" in Europe, but there is occasion to think through the implications of this contrast later (chapter 12.1). What claims our attention at once is the actual relationship between the newly conceptualized cultures of Place and the political orders in which this conceptual work was produced and by which it was sustained.

10.3 VERNACULAR POLITIES

The vernacular transformation of literary and political communication in southern Asia is something we can see, measure, and know. Looked at from the outside (once we know how to look), it worked in ways that are almost entirely transparent; looked at from the inside, it produced in many instances its own local theorizations. Far more obscure is the transformation of the political orders that with few exceptions (the most notable being Bengal) stimulated and sustained the cultural change. From Kalyāṇa in Karnataka to Kaḍiri in Java the role of the royal court in sponsoring the vernacular revolution is indisputable, yet the nature of polity itself remains elusive. For Sanskrit cosmopolitanism, which was neither impelled by political expansion nor stimulated by religious revolution, we saw that none of the common historical explanations for premodern transculturation makes much sense; the process had a different, unfamiliar cultural logic behind it. Perhaps the same holds true for the vernacular political order that superseded it.

Not only can we say that no scholarly account of South Asian polity during the vernacular millennium enjoys any kind of wide consensus, but the two dominant models, the so-called segmentary and the feudal, give radically different, even irreconcilable assessments of the political and moral economies.[67] The one point of agreement seems to be that for the period between 1000 and 1500, the South Asian "state"—if that is even the right term—is rather hard to find. The segmentary model envisions a hierarchically parcellated authority with a form of benign hegemony at the center that is intermittent and almost exclusively ritual—a state virtually without politics, the "prepolitical" India that Weberians often speak of (with unfavorable comparison to China). The feudal model posits an exploitative state that withers away under enormous transfers of wealth to an increasingly powerful landed nobility. Both accounts seem largely concerned, to the exclusion of many other matters of social-theoretical or cultural-theoretical interest, with how much central coercion and incorporation may be said to have existed.

For the interested nonspecialist reading through this scholarship it is difficult to get any lively sense of what the state in premodern (or rather pre-Mughal) South Asia actually was, beyond a structure for organizing and embodying a very limited set of practices. Among these it would seem necessary to include the building of capital cities and, increasingly in some places, temples; the gifting of land to Brahman, Jain, and other communities and the endowing of religious institutions; the granting of revenue income to loyal military men and the extraction of taxes; the undertaking of expeditions of conquest, or at least of raiding and looting; and the attempt to perpetuate a structure of power by ensuring its transfer through the patriline. Most of these practices show substantial continuity over a very long term, though in any given instance the whole assemblage—the state—seems to have been a pretty fragile affair. Few ruler lineages endured for more than two to three centuries—a veritable law of political entropy that applies ubiquitously to the Cōḻas, Kalyāṇa Cāḷukyas (making their claim to continuity with their Bādāmi namesakes all the more dubious, chapter 3.3), Yādavas, Hoysaḷas, Gajapatis, Senas, and even to the newer ruler lineages such as the Ghaznavids and Khaljīs and the last great imperial formations before colonialism, the Vijayanagara and Mughal empires.

By and large, the literature on the medieval Indian polity has produced an image both hazy and gray. The haziness is a consequence again of our sadly impoverished data. We have seen how desperate the situation is with respect to the Guptas (chapter 6.2), but things are scarcely better for polities more recent by a millennium. For the comparatively well-documented Cōḻa realm fundamentally contradictory assessments reign in contemporary scholarship; where Burton Stein saw segmentation, for example, others have seen massive centralization.[68] From before the Mughal period, aside from

67. The essays collected in Kulke 1995 summarize some current debates and demonstrate the conceptual disarray. See also the judicious remarks in Ludden 1999: 69 ff.

68. On the Cōḻas, see Stein 1980. The strongest case for bureaucratic centralization is made in the works of Karashima and his colleagues, beginning with Karashima 1984.

inscriptions, we possess scarcely any documentary sources for any South Asian polities: no chancery accounts, no records of legal or judicial proceedings, no correspondence of political elites, virtually not a single intact capital city. Although the Rāṣṭrakūṭas were among the most powerful political formations of first-millennium India, not one state-minted coin has been preserved and not one structure is still standing in its once-grand capital, Mānyakheṭa—in fact, it is an index of the quality of our sources that scholars are even unsure where the city was located.[69] For this and other reasons, few polities have been studied in detail synchronically, and fewer still longitudinally, with respect to any features beyond questions of dynastic succession, relations with other polities, and methods of extraction of wealth and rule. It is almost impossible to get any sense of what polities were actually for or what it meant to live as a subject of the Cāḷukya overlords of twelfth-century Kalyāṇa or the Tomars of fifteenth-century Gwalior. Change across this space seems as difficult to identify as change across time, and so, as if in despair, scholars narrow the scope of their inquiry to ever smaller features on the political (especially political-economic) landscape.

As for the grayness of the image, this results from the kinds of questions that have been asked of the medieval polity and the kinds that have not. The former generally pertain to administration, bureaucracy, and economy; the latter, the discursive and cultural dimensions of the polity, how its participants may have conceived of it, and how culture, above all, literary culture, may have worked to enunciate and represent it. Language and literature are notable for their near-total absence from scholarship on the medieval polity—this despite the fact that, in terms of the evidence actually extant, they constitute some of its principal concerns.[70] In short, many aspects of premodern Indian forms of rule that might be of interest to contemporary political and cultural theory are almost entirely dark to us.

Yet a further difficulty in understanding the nature of the polities in this period—in addition to the problem of bad data and the indifference to asking the kind of questions the available data encourage us to ask—is a conceptual problem not dissimilar to the one encountered in the case of empire: our models of nonimperial political orders (such as the feudal) are largely those of medieval and early-modern Europe, and the challenge of how to think beyond these to what may be unfamiliar conceptions and uses

69. Altekar (1960b: 46) and Desai et al. (1970: 142) place it in eastern Maharashtra (130 km. southeast of Sholapur); others (rightly, I believe) in present-day Sadem *taluk*, Gulbarga district (cf. Gopal 1994: 37, 41), though almost nothing is found there there that points toward the site's imperial past.

70. Culture is not discussed in Kulke 1995 or in its most important predecessor, Fox 1977. The preoccupations in the field are represented in Karashima 1992: emergence of new groups of landholding elites, techniques of resource extraction, etc. (Talbott 2001 appeared too late to be taken fully into account here.) Few important medieval sites have been excavated.

of power, including its relationship to culture, is a serious one. In the present discussion, therefore, the approach to the issue of polity is both partial and provisional; the focus is on those questions about political formations that the history of literary culture not only enables but compels us to ask, and the challenge is to ask these in a way that, terminologically at least, does not short-circuit the possibility of learning something different from what the history of European forms has already taught us to expect.

One significant new development in the nature of power that becomes clearly visible around the beginning of the second millennium, albeit one difficult to demonstrate with real precision, concerns geopolity. Both generating and generated by the practices and representations in literary culture, which were themselves prompted and promoted by court elites, this development comprised three elements we have repeatedly encountered: the production of political texts in languages of Place; their distribution within—and thereby their creation or corroboration of—new vernacularly bounded domains; and the articulation in literary texts of new and more coherent images of these domains. What these and other kinds of evidence indicate is the gradual displacement of the centuries-old aspiration for universal imperium, both the grand representation and its highly varied realizations (chapter 6.2), in favor of something unmistakably different: a narrowing of the acceptable or practicable scope for the projection of power and the implementation of actual rule. Lasting dominion was no longer sought far beyond the core region, which in some places seems to have undergone greater consolidation through conquest of the hinterlands, more intense bureaucratization, and the establishment of more fixed royal centers (Mānyakheṭa, Kalyāṇa, Veṅgi, Warangal, Tañcāvūr/Gaṅgaikondacōḻapuram, Devagiri, Dvārasamudra, Gwalior, and so on). Political power, however this protean concept is to be defined, may have remained distributed if not fragmented among numerous ruling lineages. Yet often the expanded central zone achieved a certain symmetry with the literary-language areas being newly generated by the production of political and expressive texts and their circulation in copperplate and manuscript form. A good example is Tamil country under the Cōḻas.

In an early but suggestive essay Stein examined the production of political regionality in the premodern Tamil world.[71] He agrees with the argument that has been offered here, that new regional orders of polity (which he calls cultural subregions) first became identifiable throughout much of India by the twelfth century. Neither here nor elsewhere in his writings is Stein concerned to address the macrohistorical questions raised by this new manifestation of regionality; his interest lies only in the mechanisms by which it was produced in Tamil land. Yet even given these self-imposed limits, his obser-

71. Stein 1977: 20.

vations have wider application, especially the distinction drawn between "circulatory" (or functional) and "cognitive" (or formal) regions. The former are constituted by the actual movement of people through space; the latter are produced through linguistic criteria and the representation of place in textual remains. For much of history, according to Stein, these two kinds of regions did not coincide, but by the thirteenth century, under the Cōḻa overlords, circulatory space attained a certain isomorphism with cognitive region; a much closer fit now obtained "between the conception of a *Tamilakam* covering a substantial part of peninsular India and the actual movement of quite ordinary people within that larger, cognitive region."[72]

In terms of Stein's then-developing theory of segmentary power, this circulatory region marked the limits of Cōḻa ritual hegemony rather than actual governance, a question that can be bracketed here for the moment. Whether the order was hegemonic or governmental, what is most notable is that, for Stein, the principal mechanism for constituting its circulatory sphere was not the armed force of the state or its political administrators but the new cosmopolitan-vernacular literary textuality of Cōḻa dynastic inscriptions, which the military and the political elite disseminated across the region. Regionalization is no mere artifact of our texts; on the contrary, Stein argues, it was the text-artifacts themselves that by their very presence and idiom, as well as their circulation and representations, produced in the minds and bodies of people the reality of the images they transmitted. They both articulated in their discourse and produced by their diffusion a new cultural-political space, one that excluded even as it included. (Though Stein does not note this, the Cōḻa kings were not interested in inscriptionally marking areas outside this region as part of their space, even if such areas sustained a clear Tamil political and cultural presence: in southern Kerala, for example, Tamil-language Cōḻa epigraphs are rare, and they are never found in the central or northern parts of the region.)[73] Finally, in addition to the media component of functional circulation, Stein calls attention to the role in this whole process of the Brahman literati, those specialists in cultural theory, systematic pedagogy, and liturgies defining ultimate social distinction: it was the creation of Brahman settlements in every community as well as canonical temples and seminaries that helped create "a macroregion of distinctive and homogeneous cultural quality."[74]

72. Stein 1977.

73. Narayanan 1996: 60 (I thank Rich Freeman for this reference).

74. Stein 1977: 17. Stein does not register the fact that the notion of conceptual space itself was new, mutually constitutive with the new circulatory practices, and supplanting an older, hazy, and larger notion of Tamilakam (as represented in the eighth-century [?] *Cilappatikāram*). And he exaggerates its "moral" dimension: if pertinent to some cultural-political zones (like Maharashtra with its regional pilgrimage circuit), it was irrelevant to others (the culture-land

Stein's account, which finds further support in the transformations of Tamil literary culture described in section 1 of this chapter, corroborates explicitly and implicitly the key factors in the cultural-political change identified here: cultivation of the cosmopolitan vernacular for political texts, new definitions and practices of culture-space, and the court's formative interest in the production of vernacularity. Elite literati everywhere now dressed the language of polity in local clothes and thereby began to redefine, in the most practical terms, the relationship between culture and power. They conceived of their vernacular realms as limited, and familiarly so: the world of Tamil was now restricted "to the north of the river Vaikai (on whose banks is situated the city of Maturai), to the south of the river Marutam, to the east of Karuvūr, to the west of Maruvūr"; the Gōdāvarī delta became "the very heart of the land of Āndhra, its seven rivers like seven veins of nectar running from the center of a lotus"; the "land of Kannaḍa, a well-known people-place," was securely placed "between the Kāvērī and the Gōdāvarī rivers," and its prestige idiom was even more particularly localized; "Lady Lanka" became a whole that could be described in all its parts. However variable the degree of their specificity, such representations of vernacular places began to appear with increasing frequency across southern Asia, and they were filled with political content.

What underlay such changes, and why they took place when they did, are questions Stein does not raise, and if a generation later we know enough to pose them sharply, we are still far from providing convincing answers. A review of the "hard" historical background of vernacularization is offered later (chapter 12.2), but we still require a cogent hypothesis about the causal linkage between, on the one hand, cognitive regions and the language practices that constituted them and, on the other, the political practices that produced circulatory regions. In other words, what kind of relation did cultural regionalization bear to the creation of regionalized polity?

The decision among court intellectuals to abandon the global language of Sanskrit and speak locally in their literary and political texts inaugurated a determinate literary-cultural dynamic. Vernacular language choice, within the context of Sanskrit cultural norms and activities, entailed a commitment to a range of disciplinary language practices (grammaticization, for example) and technologies for reproduction (writing) that constituted the vernacular as a separate literary code. In prediscursive life there existed not languages but only language-continua, and along such a continuum, what in later discourse came to be named, say, Kannada imperceptibly merged into what was later called Telugu. In such a world, Kannada and Telugu should not even be regarded as pregiven points on a spectrum; the eventual seg-

of Kannada). In Tamil country, the sacred geography of the Śaiva Nāyannārs was epiphenomenal to their circulation through space and never coherently enunciated (Spencer 1970).

mentation of that continuum was an effect of, among other things, literary vernacularization itself. The resultant language boundedness has a logic akin to that of spatial boundedness, though each has its specific instrumentalities. The former (pertaining to Stein's conceptual domain) deploys grammars, dictionaries, and literary texts to discipline and purify but above all to define and exclude. The latter (pertaining to Stein's circulatory domain) uses related cultural-political practices such as the distribution of royal inscriptions to divide homogeneous space. The unification of vernacular language not only partakes of the logic of the unification of a new type of political place, it is historically copresent with it.

Thus, the segmentation of linguistic continua and homogeneous space into vernacular languages and heterogeneous places represents a cultural act, not a natural fact. These spatial divisions are not givens, and yet they are not, for all that, unreal. The dichotomy some draw between the natural and the social in theorizing regionality seems too reductive to accommodate the premodern Indian data.[75] The production of vernacular places may be a social, historically contingent phenomenon, but it is also clearly not something constituted by sheer representation alone. Such places were brought into existence by the literary-language practices of vernacular writers and corroborated by the inscriptional-material practices—textual signs of material transactions such as land gifting—of ruling lineages. Thus, the distribution pattern of Kannada inscriptions issued by the Kannada-speaking Cāḷukyas (who also issued Marathi inscriptions on their western periphery) or of Marathi inscriptions by the Marathi-speaking Yādavas (who also issued Kannada inscriptions on their eastern periphery) may signify not so much accommodation to natural language areas as the ongoing reproduction of a division of vernacular locations that these real practices themselves had recently helped to create.[76]

In the early second millennium, the language-literary-culture area, vague though it undoubtedly was everywhere, nonetheless had begun to constitute something like a limit of political practice. And everywhere across the political landscape the contrast being made between the earlier imperial and post-imperial formations was evident. To put this in the simplest comparative terms, unlike the ancient Sātavāhanas, neither the later Rāṣṭrakūṭas nor even more obviously their successors, the Cāḷukyas of Kalyāṇa, sought to secure and maintain overlordship from coastal Maharashtra through Ujjayinī to Āndhra and the northern Tamil coast. On the contrary, the political domain of the Cāḷukyas came more and more to approximate the culture-region as described in the principal Kannada literary texts discussed earlier.[77] The Caulukyas of

75. E.g., Bourdieu 1991a: 221.

76. See the find-spot maps in Naik 1948 (after p. 128) and Tulpule 1963: 47. For Andhra, Talbot 2001: 36.

77. See chapter 9, and compare Gopal 1981: 386.

Pāṭaṇ in Gujarat and the Yādavas of Devagiri in Maharashtra, unlike the imperial Śakas and Kuṣāṇas around the beginning of the Common Era or the later Gurjara Pratīhāras, did not aim to extend their power infinitely but sought more limited domains of authority and control within the newly visible Gujarati and Marathi vernacular zones (vaguely separated somewhere around the Tapti River). Similar kinds of new constraints were evident elsewhere, as in the domain of the Gaṅga-Gajapatis: their sphere of governance seems to have increasingly sought symmetry with the domain of Oriya, in contrast to the unbounded imperial enterprise of Khāravela a thousand years earlier.[78]

To be sure, these newly crystallizing vernacular places should not be thought of as bounded territories on the model of modern nation-states, whether in thirteenth-century Tamil country as described by Stein or anywhere else in South Asia. Before modernity, boundaries of both power and language—and language boundaries both real and conceptual—often remained broad and messy. Ruling lineages were also, in some cases, more mobile than at first they may appear.[79] Yet the vernacular area was beginning to mark a perimeter of political enterprise in Tamil country, the Deccan, and elsewhere, and was operationalized as such in royal communicative practices—as find-spot maps of local-language inscriptions demonstrate—and in royal representations. The Hoysaḷas offer a textbook case.

The Hoysaḷa dynasty of Karnataka entered the historical record decisively at the end of the eleventh century with the inscriptions of King Vinayāditya. From then until the disappearance of the family as a political power in the mid-fourteenth century (according to the law of dynastic entropy), the limits of their geopolitical sphere were articulated clearly, consistently, and even insistently in their public records. From his base in Śaśakapura (in today's Kadur district) Vinayāditya is represented as ruling all the lands "bounded by the Koṅkaṇ, Āḷvakheḍa, Bayalanāḍu, Talakāḍ, and Sāvimale"—boundaries repeated in the inscriptions of his grandson Ballāḷa (1101). The identification of several of these toponyms is uncertain, but some are clarified in the inscriptions of Ballāḷa's brother and successor, Viṣṇuvardhana, who in 1117 described the extent of his domain as follows:

78. The discourse on Oḍradeśa became more clearly defined in the fourteenth century, when the *Utkalamāhātyma* first described its four centers: Koṇārka, Ekāmra, Virajā, and Puruṣottama (Puri). Simultaneously, the political practices of the ruling dynasties became more concentrated in this area. The work of Kulke is central here, e.g., 1993 (cf. also Schneibel 2000).

79. About forty such lineages existed in the subcontinent at the beginning of the second millennium. Whereas some were not necessarily tied to given territories (witness the Karṇāṭa kings who migrated to rule in Mithila and Bengal from around 1000 until ousted by the Tughluqs in the fourteenth century), Chattopadhyaya is right to speak in other cases of "lineage areas," e.g., Gaṅgavāḍi, as being "integrated as administrative units to form supralocal power" (elsewhere a parcelization among unrelated lineages could be represented as a unified territory, Gurjaradeśa; see Chattopadhyaya 1995a: 217–20).

> By relying on the strength of his arms he guarded the earth bounded on the east by the lower ghat of Naṅgali, on the south by Koṅgu, Cēram, and Anamale, on the west by the Bārakanūr and other ghats of Koṅkaṇa, on the north by Sāvimale.

In 1140 near the end of his reign Viṣṇuvardhana provided a list of the provinces "united under the single umbrella" of his rule, corresponding to the area extending from the southern Mysore plateau, north as far as present-day Belgaum, and eastward as far as Hampi between the Kṛṣṇā and Tuṅgabhadra rivers. In later records, such as those of Viṣṇuvardhana's son Narasiṃha in 1143 and Narasiṃha II in 1228, although the urban core had shifted to Dvārasamudra, these boundaries reappear with only slight variation. When all this information is collated, a zone emerges that is bounded by the present-day Kolar district in the east, the Coimbatore and Salem districts in the south (Koṅgu), the Koṅkaṇ and the ghats in the west, and the Kṛṣṇā River in the north. Lastly, in a record of 1237 from the reign of Vīrasōmēśvara (the one composed by his court poet Cidānanda Mallikārjuna, chapter 9.4), the king, "emperor of the south" *(dakṣiṇācakravarti)*, is said to have had "incorporated in the book of accounts" a dominion whose limits were Kāñcī in the east, Vēḷāpura in the west, the Kṛṣṇā in the north, and Bayalanāḍu in the south. The north-south limits remained the same, as apparently had the western boundary, but the Hoysaḷa power sphere was now represented as having stretched further eastward.[80]

Several features of the new vernacular political order are revealed in these documents. First, over the course of some three centuries the Hoysaḷas represented their political power as contained within boundaries. Not only was this representation remarkably stable over the entire period, but the boundaries themselves and the conception of political territoriality they constituted had nothing whatever fuzzy about them. The demarcated zone conformed to a large degree with a Kannada culture region, one produced and continuously reproduced by the physical distribution and discursive content of the representations themselves. Political power was not extended beyond the Kṛṣṇā northwestwards into Marathi-speaking areas, nor northeastwards into Telugu land, nor beyond Kolar into Tamil country (the southern zone, to some degree, excepted), nor beyond the ghats into Kerala. It is true that Viṣṇuvardhana in the 1130s could continue to claim victory over an epic ar-

80. See Rice in *EC* (1st ed.) 5.1: xii–xiii and n. (the unknown Sāvimale is to be located somewhere around the Kṛṣṇā River). The epigraphs referred to here are, in order: *EC* 4: Ng. 32; *EC* 5: Bl. 199; *EC* 5: Bl. 58; *EC* 5: Ak. 18 (included are the Gaṅgavāḍi Ninety-six Thousand, the Banavase Twelve Thousand, the Palasige Twelve Thousand, and the "two [that make] Six Hundreds" (i.e., Beḷvola 300 and Puligeṟe 300; see Dikshit 1964: 28); *EC* 5: Ak. 55; *EC* 5: Cn. 204 (the slight variations are : Naṅgali in the east, Vikrameśvara in the south, Āḷvarakheḍa in the west, the Heddore [or Perddore] River in the north); *EC* 7: 215, lines 7–9 (the verse is corrupt).

ray of capitals and kingdoms across the Sanskrit cosmopolis: Aṅga, Kuntala, Kāñcī, Madhura, Mālava, Cēra, Kērala, Nolamba, Kadamba, Kaliṅga, Vaṅga, Baṅgāla, Varāla, Cōḻa, Khasa, Barbbara, Oḍḍaha, Kach, Sinhala, Nēpala. And in 1173 Narasiṃha could still be described—according to an ancient patriarchal trope figuring political domination as sexual domination—as

> a great swan sporting in the lake of the women of Āndhra, a sun to the lotus faces of the women of Sinhala, a golden belt to the waists of Karṇāṭa women, a musk ornament on the cheeks of the women of Lāṭa, saffron paste on the gobletlike breasts of Cōḻa women, a moon to the water-lily eyes of Gauḍa women, a wave on the [river] that is the beauty of Baṅgāla girls, a bee to the lotus faces of the women of Mālava.[81]

Yet by now, the occasional spectacular looting expedition aside, this was a truly symbolic discourse, evacuated of all real aspiration to universal dominion.[82] Its continuing appeal derived from the cultural nostalgia for a cosmopolitan order, of which the most apposite communicative correlate was the magnificent Kannada inscriptional form in which it was promulgated—itself a supreme example of the cosmopolitan vernacular style (this is illustrated in the preceding citation's extended "garland of metaphors"). Real political power now openly acknowledged new and narrower constraints of a geocultural sort in a way that previously had never, or never so insistently, been the case. And this limited domain showed full self-awareness about its place in the world: the Hoysaḷanāḍu, or culture-land of Hoysaḷa power, "a land that milks out every wish," was placed in Kuntaladeśa, which is in the land of Bharata, Bhāratavarṣa itself being found to the south of Mēru in the midst of Jambūdvīpa, sealed about by the ocean.[83] Power, like language and literary culture, was no longer cosmic or universal, but sharply de-fined and firmly em-placed.

The new interaction between language or culture area and political region apparent in documents like those from the Hoysaḷa court was shaped by the complex dialectic sketched out earlier. Such areas are never natural but are created. Here they were created in part by the distribution of vernacular texts (suggesting at the same time a widely understood, almost standard literary language), the very process that contributed to the production of the political region, as the Cōḻa case shows. Evident in the particular kinds of mapping produced by the new practices of literary and political culture is a re-visioning of political dominion as a regionalized practice. Accordingly,

81. For the citations see *EC* 5: xiv n., and p. 128; xix.

82. Bayly reads the *cakravarti* claims of later kings far too literally as militating against regionalism (1998: 26–27).

83. *EC* 5: 475 (Cn. 197 dated 1233). For this telescopic style of geography, see chapters 5.1, 9.1.

even if the precise nature of the state in its institutional structure continues to elude us—whether it was segmentary, feudal, or other—it may be possible to perceive in this coproduction of literary-cultural and political space the coming-into-being of something no less important for the history of political orders in South Asia. Short of leaving this something a conceptual blank—"some yet unspecified 'medieval Indian social formation,'" or "the medieval Indian system"—we may inch closer to the truth if we designate it the "vernacular polity," thereby acknowledging at least one identifiable factor that was important in shaping it.[84]

It goes without saying that the trend toward vernacular polity was not everywhere uniform or rectilinear. Some scholars speak of "imperial projects" or imperial "reflections" in tenth-century Sri Lanka or thirteenth-century Java, or even "imperial polities" at the very time and place I perceive new vernacularizations of political culture. We have seen that various nostalgic representations of empire of the old sort continued into the early centuries of the second millennium (analogous to the claims to sovereignty within a territory that in late-medieval Europe were still expressed in the idiom of Roman *imperium*). We might also find more convergence among the different scholarly positions if "imperial" were more narrowly specified—perhaps indeed as the cosmopolitan vernacular at the level of political practice.[85] Yet elsewhere during the vernacular millennium in southern Asia entirely different political developments do confront us, a sort of coexistence of historically distinct modes of political production. In Khmer country, a prevernacular and universalist polity maintained itself up to the fourteenth century, while in the subcontinent itself are found periodic attempts to reactualize the imperial ideal, most dramatically in Vijayanagara during a two-hundred-year period ending in 1565. Yet even here are distinctive features that suggest the force of the new vernacular political and cultural-political orders. In its forms of political communication, for example, Vijayanagara scarcely resembled an empire of the older sort. Its multiple vernacular character was projected with high visibility, with inscriptions issued in the languages of the different areas that came under Vijayanagara sway (save Marathi and unliterized idioms like Tulu, Koḍagu, and Konkani) and distributed in a way that dramatically illustrates the communicative regionalization of

84. The citations are from Stein and Habib (cited in Kulke ed. 1995: 16). Kulke notes that "what was new [at the beginning of the second millennium] was the dense network of mutual dependency which linked the centre and its enlarged core area to a hitherto unknown degree" (1995: 255). The regional mappings in literary and political texts pointed to here corroborate the implied *deśī* integration.

85. Regarding Sri Lanka see Walters 2000; for Java, Day and Reynolds 2000: 7. Kulke calls the medieval political orders "imperial polities" but never explains why or precisely how they differ from the "mighty empires" that preceded them (1995: 242–62). Compare also Inden 1990: 228 ff. For late-medieval European political language see Black 1992: 111, 113.

the late-medieval Indian world.[86] This offers striking confirmation of the political acknowledgment that vernacular language had become at least a basic condition of practical rule, too, if not of the theory of rule. Nonetheless, as in contemporaneous Europe, where the transformation of the political landscape in the post-Ottonian world and the development of more limited forms of political order had become irreversible, despite the creation of new empires (Austro-Hungarian) or new-style transnational conquest states (Napoleonic France), the historical trend in southern Asia toward vernacular political formations was everywhere manifest and the age of empire decidedly past—until new competitors for power (Tughluqs, Lodīs, Mughals) gradually began to change the rules of the political game for many regions.

If language, place, and power were becoming mutually constitutive through the representations and circulation of vernacular texts, what seems anomalous is the actual role of the royal court. Although it was the primary agent in the creation of the vernacular polity, the court as such rarely came to direct expression. No text, even of courtly origins, shows explicit concern with the political-cultural coherence of the locale it creates. Despite the growing symmetry between conceptual realm and actual sphere of rule among the Rāṣṭrakūṭas and Cāḷukyas, under whose auspices many of the Kannada texts enunciating that realm were produced, no Kannada literary or documentary text openly proclaims a *Kannada* political project. The political as an overt enterprise of a culture-territory remains unspoken, and nothing remotely like a "Kannada nation" ever found expression. Indeed, an ethnolinguistic-political category of that sort would have been unintelligible.

Moreover, no text in the period overtly offers a new conceptualization of polity in accord with the new realities of rule. Consider the political discourse accompanying the dramatic vernacularization of political space in late-tenth-century Karnataka. In 960, Somadevasūri, a Jain abbot and intellectual celebrated as the author of a major Jain moral narrative, the *Yaśastilakacampū,* wrote in Sanskrit a manual of political philosophy called *Nītivākyāmṛta* (Immortal Precepts of Political Wisdom). Somadeva was an intimate of the Cāḷukya court of Vēmulavāḍa during the very years Pampa was writing his local epic; he almost certainly had access to the court of the Cāḷukyas' over-

86. In what are now the Karnataka districts of Shimoga, Hassan, Mandya, north and south Kannara, Dharwar, and Chikkamagalur, inscriptions are found almost exclusively in Kannada; so also (though the data set is smaller) in the northwestern districts of Bijapur, Belgaum, Bidar, and Coorg. In the eastern border districts of Bellary, Chitradurga, Kolar, Raichur, and Tumkur more than two-thirds of the inscriptions are in Kannada, with a quarter in Telugu (by contrast, the number of Telugu inscriptions in today's Andhra Pradesh district of Anantapur rises to 50 percent). In the southeast border district of Mysore, the vast number of inscriptions are in Kannada, with Tamil constituting less than 10 percent (percentages are based on the corpus collected in *Vijayanagara Inscriptions*).

lords, the Rāṣṭrakūṭas. Contemporary evidence also shows that men like Somadeva actively participated in the formulation of royal policy: Vādijanghāla, the Jain scholar who commented on Daṇḍin's *Kāvyādarśa,* is celebrated in a contemporary document as a political adviser to Kṛṣṇa III (chapter 9.2). Whatever other interest Somadeva's treatise may hold, two features immediately attract our attention: For one thing, nothing whatever in the doctrines of political action it enshrines marks the *Nītivākyāmṛta* as Jain; the text unequivocally demonstrates how fully insulated the discourse of statecraft was from the philosophical, theological, and spiritual doctrines of the religions of the period. More important, there is nothing substantively new, let alone vernacular, in Somadeva's text; as the very title implies, the principles of statecraft were thought to exist out of time. Much of the work is borrowed whole cloth from treatises as old as the first or second century. Clearly no political-structural let alone epistemic changes of the intervening millennium impeded such borrowing, and nothing in the old material was seen as out of date. In fact, the *Nītivākyāmṛta* was still held in esteem in political circles five centuries later under the much-changed social and political circumstances of the Vijayanagara empire. In the same way, the most important work of political thought in the Vijayanagara world, the fourth chapter of King Kṛṣṇadēvarāya's Telugu courtly epic, the *Āmuktamālyadā* (contemporary with, if radically different from, another important early vernacular text of political thought, Machiavelli's *Prince,* 1515), was derived from the *Śukranītisāra,* an archaic vision of polity composed perhaps a thousand years earlier.[87] Governance, or the understanding of governance, had attained a kind of equilibrium, arguably a kind of perfection, where "stasis" could be acknowledged as a value and a mark of civilizational achievement. The problem of governance, it was evidently believed, had been solved long ago. The precepts necessary for its success were "immortal"; they would never age and never change.

The contrast between the spectacular invention of vernacular literary production and its new cultural and geocultural discourse, and the absence of any commensurate new political discourse, may strike us as paradoxical. But this should not be taken as signaling a conceptual delinkage of culture and power. What it does signal, instead, is the unfamiliar nature of this linkage and of the political processes thereby implied, for nothing can be clearer than the interest Indian rulers had in both the cultural creation of vernac-

87. Mastery of the *Nītivākyāmṛta* is celebrated in a *praśasti* to Lakṣmīdhara, minister to the Vijayanagara emperor Devarāya, dated 1411 (cf. *SII* 4: 267; reprinted in *SSS* p. 162). Kṛṣṇadevarāya's text awaits serious analysis (work under way by Narayana Rao and others may change our assessment), but for the present see *Vijayanagara Sexcentenary Commemoration Volume* (1936), p. 188, and Sarasvati 1925. Somadeva, too, cites *Śukranītisāra,* as well as *Bṛhaspatisūtra,* Bhāguri, Nārada, Gautama, and *Arthaśāstra.* Such citations are not like Dante adducing Vergil in *De monarchia;* the earlier political theorists provide Somadeva with precepts for action, not just proof texts.

ular places—however much it may have been South Asian poets who created them—and their political actualization. Equally unfamiliar conceptions of peoplehood, indeed, an absence of peoples from the constitution of vernacular regions and polities, will again strike us paradoxical (chapter 12.1). Yet it is, of course, only the peculiar histories of power, culture, and ethnicity in the West that render the Indian experience unfamiliar and paradoxical, and the explanation of the nature of the vernacular polity, if inevitably prestructured for us by these histories, should not be reduced to them.

Taken together, the complexity and diversity in the real functioning of the state, in the creation, actualization, and interrelationship of culture region and power region, and in the dynamism of cultural theory and the stasis of political theory suggest that a unified understanding and an adequate explanation of vernacular polity remains very much a goal of future research. What alone seems to connect all the instances we have examined is the sense—obscure yet perhaps vital—that at the level of power, as at the level of culture, everybody was going local, just as earlier they had gone global.

10.4 RELIGION AND VERNACULARIZATION

If the vernacular polity created in southern Asia during the first five centuries of the second millennium remains obscure as a structure for exercising power, there is no doubt that the vernacularization project was initiated (in many cases) and promoted and practiced (in most cases) by those who exercised such power. This judgment is based on overwhelming evidence, only a sample of which can be presented here; it is, however, completely at odds with scholarly opinion, which holds that religious consciousness and especially the religious movement now called devotionalism *(bhakti)* constituted the engine of the vernacular revolution. A leading political theorist in contemporary South Asia can certainly be forgiven for reporting what is after all the unchallenged consensus that the "gradual separation of [the] emerging literatures [of the vernacular languages] from the high Sanskrit tradition" is to be traced to "religious developments" hostile to the Sanskrit tradition, against which the vernacular literatures made an "undeclared revolution": "The origin of vernacular languages appears to be intimately linked to an internal conceptual rebellion within classical Brahmanical Hinduism."[88]

To categorically deny any role of religious sentiment in the creation of culture obviously makes no more sense for South Asia than for anywhere else. Some linkage between language choice and religious identity has long been in evidence in South Asia. The resistance of early Buddhism to redact-

88. Kaviraj 1992a: 1–39, 1992b: 25–65. See also Tharu and Lalitha 1991–93, vol. 1: 57 and Feldhaus 1986: 532, a list that is easily extended.

ing the words of the Buddha in Sanskrit is one example (chapter 1.1); the long-cultivated preference of Jains for the eastern Prakrit dialect believed to have been that of Mahāvīra, the founder of the faith, is another. Yet the religious dimension has been much exaggerated. For one thing, no invariable concomitance can in fact be established between religion and literary-language use: Buddhists and Jains produced *kāvya* in Sanskrit with as much zeal and mastery as Brahmans produced *kāvya* in Prakrit and Apabhramsha. For another, Brahmans were as prominent in the vernacular revolution as non-Brahmans; indeed they often helped initiate it (Mādhava Kandalī in fourteenth-century Assam and Viṣṇudās in fifteenth-century Gwalior are two in a very long list). More decisive than religious affiliation as a factor in the literary language choice was the literary system as such, especially the requirements of genre and aesthetic register. Then again, Sanskrit itself was hardly unconnected with *bhakti*. From a relatively early date much devotional literature was written in the language—everything from short lyrics like the *Mukundamālā* of Kulaśekhara (tenth century?) to the most influential work of them all, the *Bhāgavatapurāṇa* (tenth century). And conversely, a good deal of *bhakti* literature in vernaculars such as Brajbhasha was self-confessedly derived or even translated from Brahmanical Sanskrit works.[89]

The standard interpretation, then, of the relationship of religion and vernacularization, especially the *bhakti* axiom, rests on a foundation of both general and particular imprecision. We seem to have been misled by yet another Protestant presupposition—and ironically one dubious for its own sphere (chapter 11.1)—about the role of the Reformation in the growth of vernacular languages.[90] In addition, substantial and long-term primary evidence, such as that supplied by the development of Kannada, demonstrates positively that the general consensus is erroneous. These data also suggest, more broadly, that a religious transformation of vernacular culture and consciousness, where it does occur, is typically secondary to, and only made possible or necessary by, a foregoing political transformation.

According to textbook accounts, the origins of Kannada literary culture lie in the aim, as an earlier scholar put it, of being "loyal to the precept of the founder of [the Jain] faith that the vernacular should be used for preaching to the masses." Kannada is thus supposed to have first been adopted for the creation of written literature by Jain religious professionals in adherence to the commandment of Mahāvīra (d. [traditionally] 527 B.C.E.) that the *jainadharma* be propagated in the languages of Place rather than Sanskrit.

89. The *aṣṭachāps* of the Puṣṭimārg appropriated Sanskrit hymnal models, as the Vaiṣṇava hagiographies explicitly report (see the *Caurāsī Vaiṣṇavan kī Vārtā, prasaṅga* 5, on Sūr's imitation of Viṭṭhalnātha's Sanskrit verse, and the discussion in Taylor 1997, chapter 3).

90. For a discussion of such presuppositions in Buddhist studies see Schopen 1997: 1 ff.

There are serious problems with this account, however, including the inconvenient fact noted earlier that no such precept exists in Jain scripture; indeed, it may even have been invented by modern scholarship, through a series of circular assumptions from the existence of Jain vernacular literature itself and false analogies with the Buddhist example.[91] Even if such a precept had been in force in popular sentiment, many mysteries remain. Why did it take more than a thousand years for the requisite loyalty to reveal itself in literary production in the Kannada-speaking region, where Jains had lived since the third or fourth century B.C.E. (it took even longer in Gujarat, the very center of Śvetāmbara culture)? Why, in contrast to Buddhist practice in north India (and central and east Asia), did the vernacular precept never lead to the production of versions of the Jain canon in local languages, if indeed proselytization was part of the goal (Jain Ardhamagadhi, the canonical language, would have been no more intelligible to Kannada audiences than Sanskrit)? And why at precisely the time and place that literature in the vernaclar at long last manifested itself in the Kannada world did leading Jain intellectuals (such as Jinasena, or Guṇabhadra, who wrote the Sanskrit *Mahāpurāṇa* in the ninth century at or near Mānyakheṭa), whose loyalty one assumes to have been beyond doubt, begin to use *Sanskrit* rather than Kannada for their *āgamika kāvya,* or scripture-inspired didactic poetry? Many Jain writers also preferred Sanskrit for their moral tales written according to the norms of *laukika kāvya,* or worldly poetry, as they called it. Somadevasūri and his *Yaśastilakacampū* (959) were mentioned earlier; a similar situation prevailed to the north, where the Jain poet-scholar Dhanapāla, living in the Paramāra domain, completed his Sanskrit *Tilakamañjarī* around 1000. And when not opting for Sanskrit they often preferred Prakrit (Uddyotanasūri among countless others) and not the vernacular. Equally important, the primary audience for many early vernacular works was not even Jain. In his *Sāhasabhīmavijayam* (c. 1000), Ranna is unambiguous about the religious affiliation of his first reader (and hero of the work), Iṟivabeḍaṅga Satyāśraya: he is an ardent Śaiva.[92]

Not only is there nothing to show that vernacularization was driven principally by Jain, Buddhist, or *bhakti* imperatives of religious popularization, vernacularization was not, to begin with, "popular" in any meaningful sense of the word. The assumption that, as one leading authority has put it, "the whole point of using the vernacular instead of Sanskrit or Persian was popular intelligibility," is for many traditions, and most certainly Kannada, just as mistaken, if just as widely believed, as the correlation of vernaculariza-

91. Only faintly relevant is a text that tells how Mahāvīra's speech was miraculously received in the vernaculars (Dundas 1996: 141). For the textbook account see Altekar 1960a: 314.

92. *Gadāyuddham* 1.21: *haracaraṇakamalabhṛṃgaṃ . . . iṟivabeḍaṅgaṃ.*

tion and anti-Brahman religious insurgency.[93] The purpose of popular communication can hardly have been served by a literature like that of Old Kannada (or Gujarati or Telugu or Javanese), whose very intelligibility presupposed a solid grounding in Sanskrit lexicon, syntax, metrics, and rhetoric. This is in fact even truer of Kannada works of *scriptural* inspiration, which show a statistically measurable increase in the use of Sanskrit vocabulary over the *laukika* poems themselves. Put another way: since we cannot accurately gauge how widely intelligible Sanskrit itself may have been, the only fair assessment, in view of the actual character of Old Kannada, is that demotic communication cannot possibly have been its aim. In the Kannada case, as we saw, Pampa makes it clear that he was writing for erudite readers, "the learned *(paṇḍitar)*," and we can hear the same claim echoing through this corpus of literature.[94]

A number of the earlier Kannada poets were Jains, to be sure, but many of these were either first-generation Jains or so-called Jain Brahmans (the latter a group apparently peculiar to or at least prominent among the Digambara laity of Karnataka) who retained decisive sympathies for their *vaidika* past.[95] Moreover, early Kannada literature often has little or nothing to do with Jainism as such. If many poets composed Jain moral histories, they also composed courtly myth-epics derived from Brahmanical, not Jain, epic traditions. In fact, it was the convention for poets of Jain heritage to compose in both genres from the very beginning of the literary tradition as we know it.[96] Aside from these kinds of works, a range of texts such as the *Karṇāṭapañcatantram* (1031) and *Karṇāṭakādambarī* (1030), to say nothing of the *Kavirājamārgam* itself, supply evidence enough of an audience and a literary culture for whom religious identity was only secondary. The *Mārgam* in particular explicitly promotes a literary sphere—or rather, the literary court that

93. Masica 1991: 59. For the north Indian vernaculars the statement is not sustained by the materials adduced in the present work (chapters 8.3 and 10.1); for the Dravidian languages it is patently false.

94. *VAV* 1.11, see chapter 9.3. The work's manuscript history, which shows no trace of oral variants, corroborates that the work circulated through literate networks.

95. Examples include the Gaṅga minister and general Cāmuṇḍarāya (fl. 975, the son of a "Brahmakṣatriya family" (*Cāmuṇḍarāyapurāṇam* 1.20 prose); Nāgavarma II (fl. 1040), "born of the heavenly coral tree arising in the ocean of Brahmans" (*Kāvyāvalōkanam* vv. 960 and 964); and Pampa, who refers to himself as a "god on earth" and to his Vedic heritage (*VAV* 14.48, 14.49). This seems to be the case outside Karnataka, too (cf. Dhanapāla's genealogy in *Tilakamañjarī* 1.53, where he calls himself a *vipra*).

96. The double focus is found across the centuries: Asaga wrote the *laukika Karṇāṭakumārasaṃbhavam* (lost) and the *āgamika Vardhamānapurāṇam* (still in Sanskrit); Guṇavarma, the *Śūdrakam* and the *Harivaṃśapurāṇam* (both lost); Ponna, the *Bhuvanaikarāmābhyudayam* (lost) and the *Śāntipurāṇam;* Ranna, the *Sāhasabhīmavijayam* and the *Ajitapurāṇam.* Pampa clearly juxtaposes his *Vikramārjunavijayam* as a *laukika* text to his *jināgama* text, the *Ādipurāṇam* (*VAV* 14.60). See also chapter 9.2.

was the entryway to such a sphere—in which participation was dependent on a cultural virtuosity that may have acknowledged, yet self-consciously transcended, religious particularisms:

> Anyone who betakes himself to the great Nṛpatuṅga and becomes a member of his literary circle *(sabhā)* must be devoted to the fine understanding of all worldly *(laukika)* matters, as well as [Jain] scriptural *(sāmāyika)* and eminent *vaidika* matters. He must be adorned with distinguished utterances, analyses, and arts relating to the knowledge of literature *(sāhita,* Sanskrit *sāhitya).* He must have exceptional insight and highly skilled conduct and be entirely clear-thinking, fully analyzing each and every definition and example [of poetry].
>
> Only a man empowered by his familiarity both with [theoretical] learning *(śruta)*—if you bother to consider the matter—and always with the practices *(prayoga)* of the greatest poets will be honored by the members of the court of [Amoghavarṣa] Atiśayadhavala, the King of Pure White Fame.
>
> How will the man who is not well versed in grammar, literature, drama, everyday practices *(lōka),* the arts, religious tenets *(samayam),* as well as in the various forms of rhetoric—how will he ever gain entrance to the city of [Amoghavarṣa] Vivekabṛhaspati, the God of Discrimination?[97]

Recall, too, the early vernacular textualizations of Someśvara's *Mānasollāsa,* the royal encyclopedia from twelfth-century Karnataka (chapter 7.2): if many of these are Vaiṣṇava hymns, the author is explicit that their vernacularity is by no means primarily determined by their religious dimension:

> Out of devotion to Bhagavān Viṣṇu, I have sung his praises in these compositions. But there is no invariant rule for these to be directed only to Viṣṇu.
>
> One can praise Viṣṇu or Śiva or Brahmā or the Sun or Gaṇeśa or Bhairava or Kṣetrapāla (Śiva);
>
> Devī or Sarasvatī or Gaurī or Lakṣmī or Caṇḍī or any other deity. One can praise a king or the heir apparent or a person endowed with great powers; a queen or princess or beloved woman.
>
> Indeed, a singer may sing at his own sweet will, wherever his mind may lead him.

This acknowledgment is preceded by Someśvara's summary of a number of the regional-language songs he has described in detail, on which he comments: "This wide variety of *worldly* compositions are to be sung at feasts and at various functions."[98]

If we still had all the Kannada literature produced in the formative period,

97. *KRM* 3.219–20; 1.5, 6.

98. *Mānasollāsa* vol. 3: 82, vv. 559–63 (in v. 559 I conjecture *na tv eṣu* for *tattveṣu*); also chapter 8.2. The fact that royal praise-poems could be composed in the languages of Place is illus-

the supposed correlation between vernacularization and religion would very likely look even more insignificant than the remnants of this archive make it appear today. This is precisely the sense one gets from examining the epigraphical record, too; in the social history of Kannada vernacularization revealed here religious affiliations constituted a condition of no discernible consequence. Numerous grants were made by non-Jains to non-Jains for the study of traditions of learning that are most decidedly non-Jain—and yet this discursive world was thoroughly suffused with Kannada.[99] The same applies for one of the earliest versified Kannada inscriptions (that on the Brahmans of Sisūḷahāḻam, chapter 9.1) and, in fact, for the very first Kannada inscription of all, the Halmiḍi record, which begins with a benedictory verse addressed to Viṣṇu and commemorates a man famed for his munificence in bestowing ritual victims for many sacrifices—hardly the product of a Jain cultural environment.

For the Kannada tradition, then, the widely assumed correlation between religious imperatives in general—to say nothing of the "conceptual rebellion" of *bhakti* in particular—and the crystallization of the vernacular is completely unwarranted. And it is unwarranted for many South Asian vernacular literary cultures. Not only do early texts frequently not support the hypothesis of vernacularization as an anti-Brahmanical religious revolt, they fundamentally contradict it. An inaugural work of Assamese literature, Mādhava Kandalī's *Rāmāyaṇa* of 1350, was produced by a *paṇḍit* calling himself "king of poets" writing at the command of a king and striving for the aesthetic and emotional register *(rasa)* of *kāvya*. The work carries not a hint of devotionalism; in fact Mādhava declares: "The story is not a divine revelation, it is a worldly tale" *(devavāṇī nuhi iṭo laukika he kathā)*. And it was precisely in order "to make up for the earlier poem's total lack of devotional sentiment" that a later poet rewrote Mādhava's poem.[100] At the western end of the Sanskrit cosmopolis, none of the earliest texts (of the thirteenth or fourteenth century) in Gujarati—such as the *Bhārateśvar Bāhubali Ghor* (a vernacular literarization of a traditionally didactic narrative, the Bāhubali episode of the *Ādipurāṇa*), let alone the erotic *Vasantavilāsa* (Springtime Diversion)—show any trace of a conceptual religious rebellion or the new

trated in the *Mānasollāsa,* where examples of the *aḍillā,* vv. 268(+ *maḍillā?*)–71, and the *mātṛkā,* vv. 311–14, are in praise of Someśvara himself.

99. A Kannada inscription of 930 describes two Brahman generals, both *somayājins*, and their good works on behalf of the Brahmans of an *agrahāram* "matured in faultless Vedic knowledge" (*EI* 13: 326 ff.). A bilingual epigraph of 1098, which is divided evenly between Sanskrit and Kannada verse, offers eulogies on the minister Sōmēśvara Bhaṭṭa, a Ṛgvedin Brahman, and his king, Vikramāditya VI; when Sōmēśvara's virtues are extolled, including those relating to his recitation of the Veda, the language used is Kannada (*EI* 15: 348 ff.). See also *EI* 20: 64 ff., 15: 85 ff., 12: 278 ff.

100. Smith 1988: 27–28, 35–36.

devotionalism. In the Midlands, the oeuvre of Viṣṇudās evinces no particular concern with *bhakti* either: if any echo of *bhakti* can be said to be present, it is remarkably muted.[101] At the easternmost end, in the courtly *kakawin*s in Javanese, and in southern India beyond the Kannada-speaking area, whether in eleventh-century Telugu texts (such as Nannaya's *Mahābhārata*), thirteenth-century Sinhala works (such as the *Kavsiḷumiṇa* of King Parākramabāhu II), or fourteenth-century Malayali compositions (courtesan works like the *Vaiśikatantram* [The Libertine's Rulebook] and the *Accicaritam* triad constitute some of the earliest textualized Malayali materials), the process of vernacularization was entirely untouched by religious concerns. With respect to Tamil, the later *bhakti* poetry cannot be said to have inaugurated vernacular literary culture if the standard dating of the *caṅkam* corpus is even remotely correct. And at all events, the cosmopolitan-vernacular transformation of Tamil from the beginning of the second millennium is largely analogous, ideologically, to the other cases. Whatever the place of Buddhism in Tamil literary texts like the *Cilappatikāram* or philological texts like the *Vīracōḻiyam,* these cannot be connected to the kinds of religious resistance central to the reigning scholarly consensus. Seen in this light, the exceptions (the Mahānubhāva hagiographies and Vārkarī poetic commentaries in Marathi, or the course of vernacularization in Bengal, to the degree this can be reconstructed from the meager remains) seem to be just that, exceptions.

In north India, if some languages of Place were used outside the court for devotional literature from an early date, they were also used, and even earlier, outside the Hindu sphere altogether, among Sufi orders for their esoteric practices, and so cannot be connected with any vernacular insurgence. As we have seen, key works include the *Farīd-bāṇī* (no later than the end of the fifteenth century), an early corpus of poems in western Hindavi (or Punjabi or Siraiki or Multani), and, in the east, Dāūd's *Candāyan* (1379), a so-called romance (*premākhyān*), in eastern Hindavi (Avadhi). If these texts emerged from a cultural-political matrix different from that of most other cases of South Asian vernacularization, they seem to have developed a literary language adopted by later writers who more closely conformed to the standard model. In any case, neither work had much if anything to do with popular communication or religious proselytizing.[102]

Religion was largely irrelevant to the origins of South Asian vernacularization in part because, according to a very old and defining conception formulated by Bhoja around the beginning of the vernacular millennium, "the

101. McGregor 1999.

102. See n. 27, this chapter. Levtzion 1996 offers a macrohistorical argument on Islamic vernacularization. Similarly in central Asia, the literarization of Turki at fifteenth-century Timurid courts was stimulated by social and aesthetic processes devoid of religious concerns (see Dale 1996: 646).

art of literature is nonsectarian."[103] But it was also irrelevant because vernacularization was a courtly project, and the court itself, as a functioning political institution, was largely unconcerned with religious differences. This perhaps surprising claim is confirmed by, among other things, the history of religiophilosophical change and political response during the several centuries around the beginning of the second millennium.

These centuries were a time of astonishing intellectual ferment, marked by attempts at fundamentally reconceptualizing the self and its identities, which were variously deconstructed, rendered contingent, or reconstructed. Developments in Karnataka are again especially instructive. A radical monism, enunciated in the eighth century and associated with philosopher Śaṅkara, was systematized and elaborated in the following centuries by Sanskrit intellectuals at the Śṛṅgeri monastery in the far west of the region. Based on older conceptions of the self, this system argued, with new discursive rigor, for a radical metaphysical erasure of all difference—of all contingent identities—and a fundamental unity of being. Beginning in the early twelfth century, two major variations on this conception developed. The first, originating in Tamil country but strongly present in southern Karnataka, was the "qualified monism" of the Śrīvaiṣṇavas. In their theology a kind of personal individuality of the self was maintained, the individual souls constituting the body of God, while sociologically they extrapolated the Advaitins' abstract monism toward a kind of social equality. The second was a dualistic revision—restoring real selves who are ontologically different from the deity, real identities, new doctrines of predestination and election, and, for some of its history at least, a reassertion of caste privilege—formulated by Madhva (d. 1317) in coastal Karnataka. Through all this extraordinary change Jain religious professionals and their temples and places of learning continued to thrive, although occasionally their rivalry with other religious orders, like the rivalry of these orders with each other, could turn violent and their places of worship could be appropriated by other groups.[104]

The contrast between all this intellectual ferment, at once social-theoretical, philosophical, theological, and spiritual, and the continuity of political practices is remarkable. It is hard to detect any consequences for the structure and functioning of polity from such utterly incommensurate systems of belief and religiosity, with their irreconcilable disagreements about the self and its destiny after death and, accordingly, about how to act in the world. If King Nṛpatuṅga (d. 880) was in fact a Jain, his religious affiliation left no mark

103. *ŚP* 398.10–11: *sāhitasya sarvapārṣadatvāt* (the sense is clear from the context; Ratneśvara on *SKĀ* 3.3 too narrowly glosses with *nānādarśanarītyupajīvanam ucitam*).

104. On twelfth-century Vaiṣṇava temple reforms in Tamilnadu, see Stein 1980: 233. For the position of Jains, see the (perhaps overly roseate) account of Saletore 1938: especially 286 ff. (contrast the inscription from Magadi *taluk* [Bangalore], of 1386, *EC* 2: 285–87).

on the Rāṣṭrakūṭa political order, which differed in no way from that of his successor five generations later, Kṛṣṇa III (d. 967), a Śaiva. In no discernible way did the Hoysaḷa kingdom of southern Karnataka change as a functioning political institution when King Biṭṭideva (Viṣṇuvardhana) converted (or is thought to have converted) to Shrivaishnavism around 1100. A similar conclusion can be drawn for polities beyond the Deccan. Much of what is today eastern India was ruled for some four centuries (until the early twelfth) by the Pālas, a dynasty that richly patronized Mahāyāna and Vajrayāna (Tantric) Buddhism. To the west in present-day Gujarat, King Kumārapāla converted to Jainism in 1160, an event of enormous significance if measured by the number of Jain literary accounts it inspired. Yet it is hard to identify in Gujarat or Bengal any political consequeces of these very distinctive, or very new, religious identities. In Vijayanagara, to cite a last case, royal grants were awarded indiscriminately to centers of learning and worship associated with the Mādhva, Śrīvaiṣṇava, and Jain orders according to this or that king's predilections, but these carried no implications for the nature of imperial rule; all of these disciplinary orders typically enjoyed substantial and even-handed patronage. Some scholars may detect here a military-political policy of ecumenicism; it is just as reasonable to conclude that religious distinctions were simply irrelevant to the exercise of power. There was no specifically Śaiva or Vaiṣṇava political practice, no specifically Jain political philosophy (as Somadevasūri's political tract shows), no specifically Mahāyāna theory of political power. The disconnect between religion and rule was far more fundamental than contemporary scholarship acknowledges—and far more fundamental than in late medieval and early modern Europe. It is, in short, a serious misreading to claim that for the premodern period "the essentials of Indian politics can never be grasped without an understanding of religion."[105]

This is not to say that the new religious movements that arose at a later date did not have a substantial impact on literary cultures and their regionalization of cultural life. The point is to try to gauge these consequences with greater historical and theoretical precision. The hypothesis that the new religious consciousness in general, and devotionalism in particular, constituted the very basis of vernacularization as such in South Asia makes it more difficult to understand the later religiocultural transformations that did in

105. Guha 1997: 47. The denial of "a 'divorce' of religion and politics" typically assumes that politics, *artha*, was "encompassed" by universalist *dharma* (Wink 1986: 16–17), a notion based on the ahistorical work of Louis Dumont and Jan Heesterman that mistakes a sociopolitical theory for what variously came to count as "religion" before modernity. On a putative Mahāyāna theory to "disprove the omnipresence of the [Western] logic of power," see Wallerstein et al. 1996: 56–57. The Pālas, the preeminent "Mahāyāna" kings of India, evince nothing specifically Buddhist in their political practice (and they patronized Shaivism as intensely as any Śaiva king, as *IA* 1886: 306, 38–39 [Nārāyaṇapāla], and *IA* 14: 140 [Mahīpāla] suffice to demonstrate).

fact occur. In addition to their powerful social challenges, which carried implications for a potentially radically different kind of polity, movements such as Virashaivism in south India or *nirguṇa* (abstract) devotional traditions in north India (from about the sixteenth century on) contested on the plane of literary culture precisely the idiom and values of cosmopolitan vernacularism. A more detailed account of the later history of vernacularization would show that for some parts of India we can speak of *two* vernacular revolutions: one that was cosmopolitan in its register and divorced from religion, and another that might best be termed regional, both for its anti-Sanskritic, *deśī* idiom and for its close linkages with religious communities that developed distinctively regionalized characters. The second revolution is unthinkable without the first, and might well be seen as a kind of counterrevolution. Developments in Karnataka in the twelfth and thirteenth centuries and Gujarat in the fifteenth provide good examples.

The creation of a cosmopolitan vernacular synthesizing the perceived contradiction between the regional and supraregional produced its own new contradictions, and in response to these, yet more local forms of culture were often created. In Karnataka, a certain *ressentiment* against the cosmopolitan vernacular was already in evidence by the early twelfth century. In his collection of Jain stories, the *Dharmāmṛta* (1112), Nayasēna insisted that if one is going to write Kannada one should write pure Kannada *(suddagannaḍa)*, and if one wants to use Sanskrit one should write pure Sanskrit; one does not mix ghee and oil, or string a necklace of smooth pearls (that is, Kannada words) interspersed with rough and biting peppercorns (that is, Sanskrit). The thirteenth-century poet Āṃḍayya in his *Kabbigara Kāva* (The Love-God/Protector of Poets) experimented with producing a literary register wholly purged of Sanskrit loans, a phenomenon of linguistic cleansing that can be found, with varying local motivations, across literary cultures.[106] At the more pragmatic level of inscriptional practice, some cosmopolitan vernaculars eventually came to occupy the higher pole of a vernacular diglossic situation, analogous to the earlier hyperglossic relation of Sanskrit to the languages of Place. In Kannada this occurred as early as the Iṭṭage inscription of 1112: here the *praśasti* portion of the record employs Old Kannada, whereas the business portion is composed in what scholars now term Medieval Kannada.[107] This new division of dialect labor, which would eventu-

106. On Sanskrit and Kannada see *Dharmāmṛtam* 1.41–42. A very similar critique is found in Brahmaśiva's *Samayaparīkṣe.* Examples of linguistic cleansing elsewhere include the eleventh-century Persian *Shāh Nāmeh,* which sought to minimize Arabic words, and the works of the nineteenth-century writer Charles Doughty, who sought to minimize Latinate ones.

107. *EI* 13: 37ff. (with Barnett's note). It is unclear how far the newness of Medieval Kannada (*naḍugannaḍa,* a modern term) was perceptible to those who invented it as a script language.

ally become common, points also to the new social significance of a non-cosmopolitan Kannada, which was just about to make itself known in the most explosive way.

The new sociality of this more localized Kannada came to manifestation in the cultural production of the Vīraśaivas. In what without anachronism can be described as a revolutionary movement in both culture and power, these "militant" or "heroic" Śaivas appeared in northeastern Karnataka at the end of the twelfth century under the leadership of a loosely knit group of spiritual adepts and political elites. At the start, the social and political project of the movement was self-consciously anti-Brahman and anticaste, and, more broadly speaking, counterhegemonic and even antinomic; their leader, Basava (1132–86), may have inspired or even led an insurrection against the regional overlord in the name of low-castes and untouchables. Although many historical questions persist regarding the true character of this project, the transformation in vernacular literary culture it effected is not open to dispute.

Three dimensions of this transformation are especially noteworthy in light of our earlier findings. First, the Vīraśaivas employed a register for cultural communication that was radically different from the idiom of the cosmopolitan vernacular. This reflected no simple historical evolution of the language—the high idiom would continue to be used for literary composition for centuries to come (indeed, it is the language described in Akalaṅka Deva's grammar of 1604). It was instead an attempt to replace the cosmopolitan idiom with one far more regionalized in everything from lexicon to syntax. Second, they employed a totally new literary form, or better, an antiform—unversified simple prose—that they called *vacana,* or plain speech. The *dēsi* quality of language was thus wedded to a consciously decultured form of composition. To be sure, the anti-aestheticism of the *vacana* should not be exaggerated. Though it is nonmetrical, any number of recognizable rhetorical and other workly strategies common to *kāvya* are put to use. Moreover, Basava himself declared his consanguinity with the greatest representatives of cosmopolitan literary culture, albeit with the most Śaiva dimension of that culture, when he wrote, "They say I have no kith and kin / but I am Bāṇa's, I am Mayūra's, / I am Kālidāsa's. / My elder uncle Kakkayya and Cennayya my younger uncle / kissed me and held me, / O Kūḍalasaṃgayyā."[108] Nonetheless, South Asia had not seen anything quite like this, an almost postliterary form of literature. Third, in addition to innovations in language and form, the authors of the *vacanas*—often men and women of profound cosmopolitan learning, typified by Allama Prabhu (fl. 1175)—

108. *vinagārū illa vinagārū illavembaru / bāṇanava nānu mayūranava nānu / kāḷidāsanava nānu,* etc. (ed. Deveerappa 1967: 115). The trope is common in Vīraśaiva poetry (cf. e.g., *EC* 7: 558); the poets mentioned were popularly celebrated for their acts of extreme devotion to Śiva.

resisted what had by now become the entirely normal practice of authorly inscription: with rare exception *vacanas* were never committed to writing by the producers themselves; in fact, few textualizations were made before the fifteenth century.[109] The *vacanakāras* may thus be said to have attempted at once to retrieve a certain authenticity of orality and to undo a centuries-long cultivation of vernacular literacy.

It is impossible to separate these transformations in the idea, form, and nature of literature from the frontal assault the Vīraśaivas at their origin waged on the political, social, and spiritual orders of the elites. This topic cannot be explored further here, but it should be noted that this assault and the Vīraśaivas' new standards of culture certainly contributed to the demise of Kannada cosmopolitan vernacularity. As a component of political culture, the cosmopolitan vernacular was virtually dead by the later Vijayanagara period, during which no significant literature was produced at court, though works wholly or partly in the idiom would continue to be written into the modern period.[110]

The second vernacular revolution as it occurred in fifteenth-century Gujarat is equally instructive. Gujarati vernacular culture commenced in the late twelfth or early thirteenth century, and for the following two hundred years and more the idiom employed was not just learned but exuberantly erudite. The language was the high cosmopolitan vernacular, and the themes were typically the grand old tales from Jain and Brahmanical lore and epic but also adaptations from the Sanskrit prose *kāvya* tradition (as in the *Pṛthivīcandracarita* of 1422 and Bhālaṇ's adaptation of Bāṇa's Sanskrit prose masterpiece, the *Kādambarī*, c. 1500) using metrical forms that privileged cosmopolitan over *deśī*. All this changed dramatically with the Vaiṣṇava devotional poet Narasiṃha Mahetā (c. 1414–80). Although a Nāgara Brahman fully equipped with the Sanskrit culture of that caste group, he renounced both the social and the aesthetic forms in which he had been trained. Legend tells of his very personal relationship to the deity, however unspiritual the matters in which this relationship exhibited itself (the god's help with letters of credit, dowry, and the marriage of his son). In addition to merchants, Narasiṃha's socioliterary sphere included the untouchables (Ḍheḍha), who invited the poet to sing among them, to his lasting infamy in the eyes of his fellow Brahmans. Like the Kannada *vacanakāras*, Narasiṃha seems to have refused to commit his compositions to writing; no evidence is available of any manuscript tradition for almost two centuries after his death.

109. The role of the Viraktas, an ascetic order, in textualizing and narrativizing this material in fifteenth-century Vijayanagara is the subject of a University of Chicago dissertation by Prithividatta Chandrashobhi currently in progress.

110. On the paradoxical position of courtly Kannada in Vijayanagara, see Pollock 2001a: 400ff.

The newness that entered the world of Gujarati culture with Narasiṃha—including the kinds of themes that marked his (sacred) biography, the social worlds in which he chose to move, the idiom of his poetry, and perhaps even some of its forms (if the *prabhātiyuṃ,* or lyrical morning prayer, was not Narasiṃha's invention it certainly became indissociably linked to him)—would be fully registered in the consciousness of the literary tradition. This is signaled by the fact that by the mid-nineteenth century Narasiṃha had come to occupy the undisputed position of primal poet *(ādikavi)* in the vernacular (chapter 8.1). Narasiṃha's was a new firstness, a second one created centuries after a very different, cosmopolitan-vernacular literary beginning.[111]

Important features in the histories of the Kannada and Gujarati literary cultures were paralleled in many other regions. In Assam, a cosmopolitan and worldly literature represented by Mādhava Kandalī was followed within two centuries by a fervid Vaiṣṇava *bhakti* culture promulgated by Śaṅkaradeva, also a Brahman (there are other parallels here to the Kannada world, such as the eventual Sanskritization of the anti-Sanskrit tradition). Such was also the case with many of the *bhakti* poets of the fifteenth and sixteenth centuries in north India, such as Kabīr and Dādū, where resistance at the social and the literary levels was combined, leading to the complex question of the textual constitution of essentially authorless texts, an issue never encountered for the cosmopolitan vernaculars.[112] In Java, too, the cosmopolitan vernacular *kakawin* was superseded by the radically indigenized *kidung,* which rejected the *kakawin*'s Sanskritized meters, lexicon, themes, and, to some degree it seems, even its literacy and social habitus in favor of the local, the oral, and the noncourtly. There were certainly divergences from this pattern of secondary revolution; the regional-vernacular challenge driven by new forms of religious consciousness was by no means uniform across South Asia. In Telugu, cosmopolitan vernacularity was never seriously interrupted, the high style maintaining its vitality into the early modern period. And with regard to Brajbhasha, subsequent to the *bhakti* innovations the cosmopolitan vernacular was spectacularly *reinforced* by the poets of *rītikāl* from the end of the sixteenth century until the coming of European modernity.

Vernacularization in South Asia was a transformation in ideas and practices that were at once both deeply political and deeply aesthetic, much the same as the transformation that marked the cosmopolitan epoch, though in service of a new regime of culture and power that is still imperfectly understood. What does seem certain, however, is that in most instances reli-

111. Mallison 1986; Yashaschandra 2003, especially pp. 583 ff. Mallison seems fully justified in assuming the absence of a literate tradition of transmission for the poet's work until the seventeenth century (p. 34). Such was the case with Kabīr (manuscripts of whose works first appeared some 150 years after his death) and, as we have seen, with the *vacanakāras*.

112. On the problem of authorship in *bhakti* poetry see Hawley 1988.

gion was irrelevant to this transformation, and only became relevant as a later reaction, in the process I have called regional vernacularization. Here, not only was the idiom of the dominant literary culture rejected, along with many of its core features (themes, genres, patronage structures, even authorship and textualization), in favor of precosmopolitan values, but religious identities themselves showed a strong trend toward regionalization. Virashaivism, at its birth rippling out across northern Karnataka, eastern Maharashtra, and western Andhra Pradesh, became progressively almost exclusively a Kannadiga phenomenon in the following centuries. The Mādhvas, despite the image promulgated in hagiographies of Madhva as a spiritual *digvijayin*, or universal conqueror, changed from a religiophilosophical movement receptive to conversion to a Brahmanical subcaste of the Kannada region. Shrivaishnavism, despite a lingering presence at historical sites of memory outside Tamil country such as Melkote in Karnataka, became a phenomenon of the Tamil-speaking sphere. In Maharashtra, the Mahānubhāva and Vārkarī movements never developed communities beyond the region but instead reinforced regionality by such things as a new pilgrimage circuit with explicit restrictions on transregional circulation. A Vaishnavism with distinctive Bangla inflections—even if spiritually based in Mathurā and promulgated by masters like the Goswamis hailing from the Deccan—came into being in the sixteenth century, inspired by the charismatic figure of Kṛṣṇa Caitanya (d. 1533). Comparable in its regionality is the Vaishnavism peculiar to what is now western Rajasthan-Gujarat, the Puṣṭimārga of Vallabha (d. 1530); even earlier, Narasiṃha's verse was seen to have a particular Gujarati regional component: "The *bhakta* Narasī has purified the land of Gurjaras," says the *Bhaktamālā,* a late-sixteenth-century collection of hagiographies.[113] The new vernacularism, then—noncosmopolitan, regional, *deśī* in outlook—combined a different, local way of poetry making with a different, local way of spiritual being.

Allusion has been made in the course of this chapter to contemporaneous events in western Europe that show remarkable parallels with the wave of vernacularization that swept over South Asia in the first half of the second millennium. Examining these in greater detail will help us determine whether the various complexities of the South Asian case can be illuminated by crosscultural comparison.

113. Cited in Mallison 1986: 21, who notes the insistence in that work that Gujarat had not been Vaiṣṇava before Narasiṃha. Indeed, the dominant religious forces had been Jain and Śaiva.

CHAPTER ELEVEN

Europe Vernacularized

11.1 LITERACY AND LITERATURE

To an outside observer, the vernacularization of Europe as a literary-cultural process in itself and, even more so, in relation to political processes appears to be one of the great understudied topics of Western history. The editor of a recent edition of the *Oxford History of Medieval Europe,* while observing that a major factor in "the new diversity" that marked the late Middle Ages was "the exploitation of a variety of languages in important writings," confesses himself at a loss to explain the development itself; the origins of the vernacular turn are for him as "mysterious" as its results are "obvious and spectacular." A historian of communication in the medieval world complains that the whole question of the relationship between oral culture and literate vernacular literature needs rethinking; while a new edition of the standard work on the transition to written culture in late-medieval England records the same puzzle in a different formulation: "[So] much remains speculative about the beginnings of writing down vernacular languages in Europe. The hardest question to answer precisely is why a growing number of patrons and writers in the twelfth century ceased to be satisfied with Latin as the medium of writing and experimented with 'Romance' and 'French' instead."[1]

That the problem should seem so mysterious and the answers so speculative must stem in some measure from the fact that European vernacularization has apparently never been studied synthetically, as a unified problem meriting comparative historical analysis in its own right, let alone as a question with social or political ramifications of potential importance for social

1. See respectively Holmes 1992: 327–28; Richter 1994: 357; Clanchy 1993: 218.

theory.[2] Nor is it surprising, given our ignorance about the major issues, that a number of minor but consequential ones remain obscure as well—not least, who did what and when they did it. We are left to follow our party affiliations, so to speak, when trying to adjudicate among the different social-historical analyses. Antonio Gramsci, one of the few writers to have thought clearly and carefully about vernacularization as a cultural-political problematic, offers one strong formulation from the perspective of progressive pre–World War II internationalism. Vernacularization, he believes, came from the "national-popular" below: the vernaculars were raised up "against Latinizing 'mandarinism'" and came to be written down "when the people regain[ed] importance." This position should by no means be taken to represent a political man's lack of scholarship, for it is close to the view of the greatest comparative Romance scholar of the period, Erich Auerbach, for whom the manifestation of vernacular literature marks a "liberation from clerical Latin culture" and a popular if not populist impulse. E. R. Curtius, by contrast, representative of a conservative intelligentsia searching for a usable European past amidst the rubble of World War II, is convinced that vernacularization derived from re-Latinized elites above: "Without this Latin background, the vernacular literatures of the Middle Ages are incomprehensible." For value-neutral centrists of the present, who subscribe to a kind of cultural naturalism (chapter 13.1), agency disappears altogether: people do not actively choose to create literary script vernaculars under dynamically changing political conditions; instead, these just "emerge."[3]

So large and intricate a subject as the history of European vernacularization, especially when framed as a problematic—the conjuncture of specific forms of culture and power—that is itself insufficiently synthesized in specialist scholarship, requires a book of its own and knowledge far deeper than an Indianist could possibly possess. All that can reasonably be done here is to sketch some basic features—as least those that appear basic to a nonspecialist—that may have some bearing on the issues of South Asian vernacularization. These features include, first, the problem of literary beginnings and the role of a superposed literary formation, in this case Latin, in the creation of vernacular cultures (comprising the nature and place of literacy, the elaboration of demotic language, the definitions of literature, and the pro-

2. For western Europe, a range of works chart the cosmopolitan-vernacular dialectic in literature (e.g., Jones-Davies 1991) and in scientific discourse (e.g., Chartier and Corsi 1996). But I find none that investigates the culture-power problematic over time, across polities, and in depth.

3. Gramsci 1991: 188, 168; see also pp. 226–34 on the "bourgeois-popular" vernacular in its conflict with "aristocratic-feudal" Latinity; Auerbach 1995: 216; Curtius 1990: viii and 383–88; Bartlett 1993: 198. Contrast Kristeller cited in n. 34, this chapter, and Derrida 1984: 97. Godman 1987: 8–9 describes Auerbach's position (so Bakhtin 1984: 465 ff.; it remains a tenet of "liberal nationalism," as in Kymlicka 1999: 71).

duction of philological appurtenances appropriate to literary culture, such as lexicons and grammars); second, the anxiety of creating new vernacular literary cultures; and third, the relationship, if any, between these cultural developments and the institutions of political power of the late medieval world in which they occurred. We can best proceed by examining a few exemplary cases that have benefited from the attention of recent scholarship.

As in South Asia, the nature, control, and dissemination of literacy crucially affected the creation of vernacular European literary cultures; and, as in South Asia, literacy in western Europe had a specific history, inflected by factors peculiar to that world. We noticed earlier how Roman imperial practices led to the near-total elimination of regional languages (Celtic, Punic, and so on) from the inscriptional record of North Africa and western Europe (chapter 7.1); as a result, from around the beginning of the Common Era literacy as such in the western Mediterranean always meant *Latin* literacy. The very term *litterae* signified not just letters but Latin letters, in the same way that *grammatica* meant the grammar of written Latin, indeed, the Latin language itself, for vernacular intellectuals as late as Dante. Accordingly, in the very episteme inherited from the cosmopolitan literary culture of antiquity, "vernacular letters (or literacy, or literization)," to say nothing of "vernacular grammar" or "vernacular literature," constituted a virtual contradiction in terms—until it was remembered, by vernacularizing writers like Joachim Du Bellay in the sixteenth century, that Latin itself had once been a vernacular (section 2 below).

The place of literacy in the medieval world is a topic of extensive, sophisticated ongoing research that is challenging long-held opinions about how widespread was the cultural darkness of the post-imperium "Dark Ages." There remains little doubt, however, that the critical and distinctive determinant in the history of medieval literacy lies in the Church's control of literary culture for most of the first millennium after the fall of Rome and into the thirteenth century. This means that, in addition to such obvious if complicated technical problems as adapting the Latin alphabet to non-Latinate phonologies, there are substantial ideological issues that impinge on our understanding of the history of vernacular literacy. Decisions as to what might or might not be committed to writing, for example, were made within the shadow of the Church and its religious values. The limits of what was thought to be worthy of inscription and diffusion—in the useful terminology of one scholar, what was *literaturfähig*, or capable of literary existence—were very narrow even through the Carolingian period. Moreover, in the self-understanding of the clergy, the production and reproduction of texts were a form of monastic, even ascetic, practice, and writing as such was intimately bound up with religious education and custom, all of which tended to favor the copying of religious materials in Latin. Add to this a certain Christian unease in taking pleasure in "literature"—basically, any non-Christian textuality—perceptible already in the works of the early Church fathers and still consequential at the end of the millennium. Thus, despite some evidence of interest at Charlemagne's court in the literization of Germanic heroic narratives, vernacular poetry was largely ignored if not repudiated. As the cleric Alcuin famously put it (albeit while addressing what should be read and heard in a monastery), "What has Ingeld to do with Christ?" Besides these ideological matters concerning the norms and practices of the Church, other, material factors also played a role in constraining vernacular literary production. One was the simple cost of parchment. The paper revolution in Europe, by way of Muslim Spain, would begin only in the twelfth or thirteenth century. (In India, by contrast, palm leaf and birch bark were everywhere and continuously available and were often preferred even after paper became common in the later medieval period.)[4]

Two closely related problems for vernacularization follow from this state of affairs: one pertains to the authorization of the vernacular for the creation of literature and the degree of its self-confidence, so to speak, given the added weight of the Latin tradition; the other pertains to the transition from oral to written culture. The former comes to expression itself in the complex anxieties of vernacular intellectuals that are examined in section 2. The latter merits consideration first, since it is not only fundamental but especially thorny, given that the breakthrough to vernacular literacy occurred in a world where the vernacular was by definition oral and the written by definition Latin.

As was true in the sphere of Sanskrit culture, vernacular writing systems in Europe were by and large adaptations from the cosmopolitan (Latin in the West, Greek in the influence zone of Byzantium). Here, however, their development was largely dependent on clerics and their churchly projects, while in the Sanskrit cosmopolis the first instances of vernacular literization were documents of political transactions, durable deeds, records of endowments. The dates of vernacular inscription vary widely across western Europe, and the circumstances under which it occurred are just as variable. Britain experienced several moments: an initial vernacular literacy was erased by Danish invasions at the end of the eighth century, to be resuscitated, or reinvented, by King Alfred in the ninth. Iceland in some ways presents a model instance of the entire process in telescoped fashion: vernacular literary culture was absent until the twelfth century when missionaries developed a local writing system, and within two centuries a notable and relatively large body of literature and philology (especially phonology) had been created. In Romance Europe

4. On medieval literacy, see McKitterick 1990, Doane and Pasternack 1991; on *litteratus* Grundmann 1958 and Irvine 1994: 2 ff. The religious and material constraints on medieval literary culture are discussed in Schieffer 1985 (who uses the term *literaturfähig* for what was thought to be worthy of committing to writing and of diffusion, p. 72). Alcuin is cited in Irvine 1994: 332 (Ingeld is a hero of Germanic legend).

we can point to specific moments of breakthrough for the documentary vernacular and the literary vernacular, such as in Castile, where we know with uncommon precision that the first occurred in 1206, the second in 1207 (see section 3). What is becoming increasingly clear from recent research on primeval moments of vernacularization is that new literary cultures were created by intentional acts of writing; the image of a gradual, almost accidental textualization of poetry composed orally by poets utterly unfamiliar with literate—that is, cosmopolitan—culture seems to be largely an illusion.

New studies suggest that a range of inaugural works of vernacular European literature were produced from within a literate world but one still bearing the memory of orality. The popular view of Cædmon (fl. 680) as the very model of the Anglo-Saxon oral singer—an illiterate cowherd filled with a divine afflatus, pouring forth his full heart in profuse strains of unpremeditated art—is far from likely to have been the case. In fact, one scholar has persuasively characterized him as an "exemplum of grammatical culture." The world of written textuality is constitutive not only of the account of Cædmon's literary invention in Bede's *Historia ecclesiastica gentis Anglorum* (Ecclesiastical History of the English People, 731–32) but of Cædmon's primal poem itself, which constructs a "written image of orality." Cædmon exercises his divine gift by listening to holy writ as it is read out to him and then transforming this into verse—which in turn, according to Bede, was "so delightful to hear, that even his teachers wrote down the words from his lips and learnt them." Moreover, the verse he composed essentially belongs to the genre of interpretive glosses on scriptural texts. Whereas such glosses may have a formulaic quality to them, and Cædmon himself may have been unable to read, his poetry was not an entirely preliterate oral composition; on the contrary, it is unthinkable in the absence of a literate literary culture. Similar arguments have been adduced to prove that *Beowulf* represents a series of oral songs subjected to literization and redaction within a monastic (specifically, an aristocratic monastic) environment. The texts of the *chansons de geste* as well—and here a century-long dispute seems to have finally been resolved—far from being the consequence of a gradual literization of folk culture, represent primary literate products on the part of court literati of the twelfth and thirteenth centuries. Like the prologue of Vālmīki's *Rāmāyaṇa* (chapter 2.1), these works have been seen as "staging" an oral communicative situation with a comparable, almost wistful retrospection; the character of orality in the texts themselves is artificial (except insofar as it mimics the oral practices that really did once exist, and often continued to exist).[5] Everywhere, and quite predictably, the new literary vernacular felt compelled by a common if unacknowledged law of technological preservation to present itself as a continuation of the ar-

5. See Irvine 1994: 431–35 on Cædmon; Sorrell 1992 on *Beowulf;* Gumbrecht 1983, especially 168, on the *chansons de geste* (an idea that goes back to Bédier).

chaic oral—the way in India rock-cut cave temples preserved the now-nonfunctional pillars of their wooden predecessors and the first books printed in the nineteenth century preserved the shape, including representations of the string-holes, of their palm-leaf antecedents.

One should not of course draw too sharp a line between orality and literacy in Europe any more than in South Asia. Long after the transition to vernacular literacy, oral performance features continued to inform the textualization of early French literature. The case of the Occitan lyrics of the twelfth and thirteenth centuries is particularly complex, reflecting the dynamism of the moment when orality was being subsumed under a new culture of vernacular literacy. No one any longer seriously doubts that the troubadour poets were literati in the old sense: they knew Latin and some had read the works of Ovid and other classical poets, whom they actually cited on occasion and who in general formed an important frame of reference for their lyrics. At first they appear to have composed in a semi-oral mode—without inscription perhaps (at least no manuscripts from the twelfth century are extant) yet in a complex, nonextemporaneous way uncharacteristic of primary orality. Entire poems in fixed form may have been mentally fashioned for later inscription (perhaps in the manner reported for the twentieth-century Russian poet Osip Mandelstam, or for the Telugu poet Śrīnāthuḍu, chapter 8.2), while taking on something of a life of their own when diffused in oral performance by the *jongleurs,* thus generating the kind of textual variation that has been called *mouvance.* Within a couple of generations, however, the troubadours were committing their works to writing; by the thirteenth century a powerful compulsion to fix Occitan poetry in written form showed itself everywhere, and an identical process seems to have been activated wherever troubadour poetry spread, in northern France, Germany, Italy, and Iberia. Thus literacy—in a rather different form from what we find in Cædmon and others, but literacy nonetheless—provided a basic condition of possibility for Occitan cultural production from the start; indeed, in an obvious way, it marked the start.[6]

If literacy accompanied Christianity wherever it went (as earlier it had accompanied Romanization), the cultural and cognitive obstacles to the transition to a specifically vernacular literacy were still substantial. In part these derived, as just noted, from the clergy's control of literacy and from the

6. Bond 1995: 239 notes that "the significance of the conjunction in time, space, and social class of the spread of literacy and the appearance of the troubadour lyric has barely been raised with regard to the question of origins"; a question that pertains not only to the sudden rise but also to the sudden preservation of the poetry. See Paden 1995 and 1983: 87ff., and Ferrante 1982 especially on troubadour learning and grammar as discipline; Zumthor 1987 on *mouvance* and oral elements embedded in the early French and Occitan literary texts. For Mandelstam's oral composition see Mandelstam 1970: 269; 184ff.

Church's definition of what materials were appropriate for literization, but they also derived in part from the continuing domination of Latin models of cultural superiority, whereby to write literature meant to write Latin. Thus the speciation of Romance itself was retarded for a number of specific reasons (that of the various Romance languages was even later). One of these was the difficulty of establishing vernacular orthographies in a world where orthographical exactitude on a phonographic-alphabetic principle had come to be invested with both religious and political significance (a valuation that was to be intensified by the Reformation). Alcuin spoke to the latter concern from a location at the center of Charlemagne's court when he declared, "All uses of the written word in the king's realm must display or preserve the king's dignity, and only correct [i.e., classicizing] Latinity is worthy of texts produced in the king's realm." Another impediment was the natural habit—and recent scholarship suggests strongly that it was a habit—of reading Latin texts aloud, especially during the sermon, in a *vernacular* way, until the Carolingian language reforms of the ninth century required reading *literatim,* "letter by letter" (this reform applied in France, at least; in Italy a vernacularized pronunciation of Latin was to persist for some four more centuries).[7] For these reasons, literized literatures did not appear in any density until the twelfth century; the few texts from before that period were isolated experiments that never engendered a continuing vernacular literary practice. Though some early materials doubtlessly disappeared, Europeanists have come to realize that loss is an altogether insufficient explanation for what one scholar has characterized as the "meager corpus of vernacular literature in the continental West before c. 1100."[8]

The disparity in the pace of vernacularization for the Romance and Germanic (the Latin-near and Latin-distant) languages is one familiar in South Asia, as noted earlier, where Indo-Aryan and Dravidian (the Sanskrit-near and Sanskrit-distant) show a similar difference. In fact, the time frames here are remarkably close. Whereas the production of literature in Gujarati and Madhyadeshiya began in the twelfth and the fifteenth century respectively, precisely like French and Spanish, Tamil and Kannada had developed fully outfitted vernacular literary cultures by the end of the ninth century, as was the case in Ireland and England. This is not to claim that the linguistic grounds for these historical developments were the same in both cases. (If

7. Creating vernacular alphabets was far more problematic in Europe than in South Asia. See Wright 1996; Lodge 1993: 107; See 1983: 55. Alcuin is cited in Irvine 1994: 308. Giard 1989: 217 ff. charts some later developments and comments on the tension in the Reformation between orthographic reformers, who sought to make God's Word transparent to the simple Christian, and conservative philologists, who sought to preserve etymology. The hypothesis of writing Latin and reading it aloud as vernacular is discussed in chapter 10.1.

8. Richter 1994: 232.

some of the arguments mentioned in chapter 10.1 are accurate, written Germanic had to have a new form whereas Romance could long be written as Latin; whether such a situation might have obtained in South Asia is unclear.) But there are a range of remarkable homologies in the developments in these two worlds. Let us first look at Britain, where vernacularization had major consequences beyond its own narrow domain.

Tentative written vernacular gestures had been made in England prior to the ninth century, but these were modest and, as noted, were for the most part obliterated during the Danish invasions. The end of the ninth century, however, witnessed a moment of dramatic inauguration in the history of vernacularization, both in terms of the quality of intentionality and quantity of production, and by reason of the fact that English texts then written entered into a secure tradition of reproduction that would last at least into the twelfth century. The vernacular was made the object of discursive enhancement through an intensive, state-directed program of translation under King Alfred (r. 871–99) that included English versions of both ecclesiastical texts (such as Augustine's *Soliloquies* and other works of the Church fathers) and philosophical texts (such as Boethius's *Consolation*). Although vernacularization was obviously meant to serve primarily spiritual ends, the first major textualizations of poetry were also produced at this time, including *Beowulf* (1000), while several landmark historical and juridical texts were also composed. The authorization and magnification of the vernacular effected by the translation program were complemented in the tenth century by the beginnings of a philological tradition, including Ælfric's English preface and glosses on his Latin *Grammatica* (995), which invented a new English metalanguage for linguistic description, and a range of other glossarial and encyclopedic works.[9]

The justification for such vernacularization that Alfred offered (in the celebrated "Preface" to his translation c. 880 of Pope Gregory's seventh-century *Pastoral Care*) was the erosion of competence in Latin. Yet this argument seems to stand in tension, if not in contradiction, with the nature of the new vernacular literary culture itself, which was wholly modeled on Latin and only possible through the efforts of bilingual intellectuals mediating the textualization of English through Latin. The resultant texts themselves presuppose, according to one recent study, a "larger network of Latin texts and textuality for their very articulation and intelligibility." It was the "authority and cultural purpose of both insular and continental *grammatica*" that Alfred appropriated "for a new, distinctively English grammatical culture."[10]

9. For earlier traditions of literacy see Lerer 1991. Helpful is Irvine 1994: 405–60; see especially 413–14 on Ælfric. English would not receive a systematic grammatical description until the sixteenth century (Machan 1991: 233).

10. Irvine 1994: 415.

More particularly, it was on the cultural and political model of Latinity available in Carolingian Europe (which was originally advanced by Anglo-Saxons anyway) that English vernacularization was promoted, and for political purposes that Alfred well understood. As shown by the predominance of translation over other kinds of literary production, Latin was viewed as the source of the new culture, but not by that fact its superior. Alfred's explicit argument that Latin itself had once been a vehicle for translation (from Greek) was intended to assert the newly empowered vernacular's equality with the cosmopolitan code. In addition to the literarization of the vernacular, Alfred projected both a new sociotextual community in the very act of translating Latin religious texts "into that language we can all understand," as the "Preface" puts it, and also a new territorial sphere in which this language has communicative efficacy: Angelcynn—not just England but also, importantly, the English—where the Humber and the Thames no longer marked other kingdoms, was now endowed with a new unity of place, language, and people.[11] No better illustration of the basic processes of the vernacularization dynamic is available than ninth- and tenth-century England—except perhaps for ninth- and tenth-century Karnataka. Through the initiative of court elites, the styles, genres, literariness, language discipline, and other "textual values" of a superposed cultural formation were appropriated and domesticated for the production of literary and political texts without precedent. These texts then entered into a tradition of reproduction, and by their very circulation and geocultural idiom increasingly came to articulate a new vernacular world.

The literarization of the vernacular languages on the Continent presents us with another situation strikingly comparable to that of southern Asia. Here, too, in many instances we can observe a significant time lag—testifying to actual impediments to or even hesitations about vernacular literariness—between the moment of the vernacular's initial speciation in the documentary practices of the political elites and the moment when it was employed for creating a vernacular literature meant to rival the superposed Latin. Nothing illustrates this quite so well as the history of what we now call French.

It is almost common knowledge that the first documentary use of Romance was in the Oaths of Strasbourg (in connection with a dispute among the sons of Charlemagne over Lotharingia, today's Alsace-Lorraine), which were drawn up in 842 and recorded at a later date in Nithard's Latin history. What is not often recognized, however, is that this originary moment

11. On Alfred's translation program see especially Irvine 1994: 421; he also notes how through the redeployment of the phrase *utraque lingua,* "both [written] languages," originally applied to Latin and Greek, English was permitted to attain the authorized and even canonical status of Latin (417). Davis 1998: 614–20 calls attention to the new territorialization of ninth-century literary culture.

was followed by two and a half centuries of almost complete silence for the vernacular literary voice—just as happened with Marathi and a number of other South Asian languages of Place. As one literary historian has sensibly concluded, the mere existence of *la langue romane* was not sufficient cause for it to become a language of culture (that is, a language of literature), and "nothing ensured that it would then become such a language; or more exactly, nothing ensured that it would ever be committed to writing."[12] The failure to achieve literization is a very real historical possibility: in South Asia, as we have seen, it occurred with Tulu, for example, and Konkani.

The observations just cited stand in conflict with the widespread belief, applied to French no less than to other literary cultures, in an infinitely receding temporal horizon of vernacular literature. This is grounded on various presuppositions, usually unexamined, such as the unreality of beginnings, the essential coextensiveness of language and literature, and the presumption that earlier and less successful prototypes must have paved the way for the high artistry of supposedly inaugural masterpieces. Consider the following formulation on beginnings in a recent French literary history: "Although debates about the origins of French literature are often confined to the few hagiographic texts that were actually copied before the Crusade . . . in a very real sense there were no discrete origins, since it appears that the oral literature of France came into being along with the French language as it developed out of popular Latin."[13] The first assumption here, that something oral is to be considered "literature" without further specification, is as misleading as the second, that when this "oral literature" existed there also existed what could be called "French literature," "the French language," and indeed "France." To challenge such assertions is not to raise a mere nominalist quibble. We cannot grasp the history of vernacularization at all if we fail to grasp the roles of, on the one hand, the breakthrough to literacy and, on the other, the production of expressive textuality according to the norms of the superposed literary culture. There are similar conceptual problems in hypostatizing "French literature" even though it was discursively created only centuries later, in representing "French" as preexistent to textualization rather than produced through it, and in ascribing to it boundaries any less factitious and constructed than those of the nation-state.[14] If we hold that a literature is forever copresent with a language ("the oral literature of France

12. Zink 1992: 15. Banniard also observes that for clear bilingualism to have emerged in France a written form was required "whose conception was difficult and whose necessity was far from obvious"; "written forms and conventions of Romance did not really become widely used until the emergence of a desire to create a Romance literature" (1995: 707). On the Oaths and their many emblematic problems (both philological and ideological), see Bloch 1989.

13. Duggan 1989: 20.

14. For a linguistic view of the matter with respect to French, see Wright 1991. For recent work on how beliefs about what constitute real languages (and that they exist naturally in the

came into being along with the French language"), we cannot even raise questions about the choice of "French" as a vehicle of literature instead of Latin or any other idiom, or about the nature of this "literature," let alone more pointed questions about the specific sociocultural factors that restricted early textualizations to hagiographies or that fueled the sudden proliferation of textualizations of oral songs after the First Crusade.

What did alter the situation, enabling *la langue romane*, or Old French, not merely to exist but to become a language of culture, was the conquering Normans' encounter with the literary culture of England, the body of deeply rooted Old English as well as Anglo-Latin poetry whose genesis we have already described. It was through the emulation of that culture that "French literature"—expressive texts in a code understood to be different from other codes and given a new name in acknowledgment of that fact—began its life. And it indeed *began*, suddenly emerging, as David Howlett puts it in his recent study, "fully formed, mature, brilliant, with hardly a trace of false starts or hesitations or earlier experiments." All the earliest extant texts in every genre of Old French literature, literate in every sense and many of them based on Old English models, were Insular productions, created in twelfth-century Anglo-Norman England—and these were the first. "It is difficult to believe," Howlett argues, confronting head-on the skepticism over vernacular beginnings, "that in the cultural centre of Western Europe . . . a Continental Old French literature once existed but disappeared with hardly a trace among extant manuscripts, with hardly a reference to the fact that it ever existed, and yet an extensive and varied Franco-Latin literature from the same time and place survived." A far more reasonable assumption is that no such corpus did exist, that it was only in the twelfth century that the French vernacular was transformed, with astonishing abruptness, into a language of political record and courtly literature. Howlett deserves a full hearing:

> The Francophones were drawn into a remarkable Insular culture which confronted them for the first time with the idea and the fact of an extensive and glorious vernacular literature . . . Many desired roots in the English past as well as a place in the Francophone present. It was only the encounters of Francophones with Insular literary traditions in both Latin and English that allowed the emergence of a mature literature in French, fully formed at its very beginnings . . . a sudden issue of imaginative cultural engineering.[15]

Such imaginative cultural engineering, once we acknowledge its possibility, can be found in evidence repeatedly—from the invention of Latin literature

world) construe with forms of social domination, see Woolard and Schieffelin 1994: 63 (unsurprisingly restricted to colonial encounters).

15. Howlett 1996: 165–66.

in Republican Rome around 240 B.C.E. (chapter 7.1) to the invention of Gwaliyari literature in Tomar Bundelkhand in 1435 (chapter 10.1)

Also part of a wider pattern is the political sociology of French vernacularization. Courtiers and clerics at the court of King Henry I were central to the process, and it was the coming into being of this newly literate aristocratic lay public that provided the context for the subsequent creation of literature in French on the Continent. There, in the north, the warrior aristocracy patronized the written *chansons de geste* from around 1100 (when one poet, perhaps named Turold, composed the literate *Chanson de Roland*). Almost simultaneously in the south, the same class underwrote the creation of a courtly culture that defined itself by a new aesthetic and a linguistically unified—or at least supradialectal—Occitan and produced a new literature with the lyrics of Guillem de Peiteus (1071–1127) and his followers. This, too, is something most scholars now regard as an abrupt invention (which seems to some to have arisen "as if from nothing"); Dante thought so too, two centuries later, as indeed did the troubadours themselves; at least they evince no literary memory of poets before Guillem. Assessments of this Occitan poetry in recent scholarship suggest that it was an unqualified expression of the kind of cosmopolitan-vernacular impulse we have seen across southern Asia: it strove to combine a "lyric drive" that was oral, vernacular, secular, and courtly with a "poetic drive," or better, a literary drive, that had hitherto been literate, Latin, sacred, and church-schoolish.[16] An epistemological as well as political context of the sort we have also seen before conditioned the philologization of French, a vast problem we can only glance at (and briefly return to in chapter 11.3). The first systematic grammaticizations of French, which date to the mid-fourteenth century and were produced at the court of Anglo-Norman England, include John Barton's *Donat françois* (before 1409). This work was modeled on the Latin grammar of the fourth-century scholar Donatus, which influenced the conceptualization of vernacular language systems even where (as in morphology) the Latin paradigm was entirely incompatible[17]—precisely as Sanskrit philology offered a grammatical model and terminology that were adopted even where the local materials, such as Kannada phonology or Marathi morphology, had to be shoehorned in.

Visible across the world of vernacularization was yet another important factor noticed at various points in South Asian history: literary-cultural, and perhaps even peer-polity, emulation. In south India, Telugu poets of the

16. On the origins of the Provençal lyric, see Bond 1995, especially p. 250. Wolff 1982: 99 remarks on the elimination of dialectal particularities in the troubadour poetry; compare the unification of early literary Kannada by the eleventh century (chapter 9.2, 4) and Gujarati by the fourteenth (chapter 10.2).

17. Lusignan 1986: 95, 111 ff. (pp. 113–14 on the morphological retrofitting).

eleventh century were likely responding to the model of Kannada poets of the tenth, just as Kannada, Sinhala, and Tamil philologists produced vernacular versions of Daṇḍin's Sanskrit *Mirror of Literature* and Śarvavarman's Sanskrit *Brief System* of grammar, with a widely shared sense that this was what everyone should be doing. Similarly, the production of Assamese, Bangla, and Oriya adaptations from the Sanskrit *Rāmāyaṇa* in northern India during the fourteenth and fifteenth centuries has about it a distinct air of imitation and competition.[18] In Britain, it was the presence of a powerful model in English writing, both expressive as well as documentary, that suggested to the Normans the possibility of creating something comparable in their own vernacular; this new model of a literature in French led in turn to the invention of expressive textuality elsewhere on the Continent.[19]

Emulation of neighbor literary cultures as well as sharp beginnings are visible in other instances of vernacularization in western Europe. Especially pertinent in this connection are the arguments concerning the creation of the *Poema de mio Cid* offered by the late Colin Smith. He takes issue with both the traditionalists and the oralists, as he calls them, the former supposing a long period of literary development—of which, however, we have no record whatever—and the latter believing that the early Spanish epic was oral and the surviving manuscripts are records of actual improvised (or memorized) performances. For the traditionalists authorship seems to be infinitely deferred, whereas for the oralists it is an unintelligible category; neither suffices to explain the appearance of a work like the *Poema de mio Cid*. For Smith, there is little to sustain belief in the existence of a "fully vernacular epic" in Spain before the appearance of the *Cid* sometime in the first decade of the thirteenth century (just as there is little that invites such an assumption for France before about 1100, the time of the Oxford manuscript of the *Chanson de Roland*). The *Cid* was "the first epic to be composed in Castilian" and "did not depend on any precedent or existing tradition of epic verse in Castilian or other Peninsular language or dialect." And it was a written text, composed by an author who knew Latin (quite certainly) and French (very probably): his models for vernacular literarization were the French *chanson de geste*, *Roland* in particular, and, to some degree, classical rhetoric and the newly revived Roman legal studies. The circumstances surrounding the writing of the *Cid*—the creation of the literary work under the sign of a superposed culture, the invention of a new cosmopolitan vernacular register, the employment of writ-

18. The historical relationship among Mādhava Kandalī's Assamese *Rāmāyaṇa* (mid-fourteenth century) and Kṛttibās's Bangla and Baḷarāmadās's Oriya versions (both late-fifteenth century) remains to be explored. Smith 1988 is concerned largely with thematic questions.

19. Roger Wright (personal communication) suggests that this kind of imitation may account for the profusion of Latin writing in ninth-century Córdoba as an attempt to emulate the Islamic literary culture of the time.

ing for the first time and in a way that distances the work from preexistent oral culture, and the implementation of these changes with an eye clearly directed to parallel developments in other regional traditions—makes early-thirteenth-century Iberia in general and the poet of the *Cid* in particular a compelling instance of vernacular inauguration.[20]

The model of vernacularization developed here from the Germanic and Romance language materials of Insular and western-continental Europe has application in other regional worlds as well. A last example is drawn from the history of literary culture in Hungarian, which perfectly exemplifies the principal features already encountered: cosmopolitan superposition, vernacular beginnings, and political contextuality. Speakers of Hungarian lived in a purely oral world preceding King Stephen I's conversion to (Roman) Christianity in 1000. Nothing of this oral pagan culture found textualization prior to what has been described as its "ruthless extermination" in the following centuries; in fact, literate vernacular culture was nonexistent aside from a stray funeral sermon (c. 1200) or hymn (a "Lament of Mary," c. 1300). Literary production in these early centuries made use exclusively of Latin, most significantly the so-called Chronicles of Hungary (thirteenth and fourteenth centuries) and the first lyric poetry in the mid-fifteenth, that of Janus Pannonius (who seems to have seen no contradiction in using the ancient language of Rome to articulate his credo, "Look around and do not forget to be a true son of the present"). Two events combined to alter this situation fundamentally: the Reformation (recall that Martin Luther's *Theses* were posted in 1517) and the victory of the Ottomans at Mohács in 1526. A *Four Gospels* in Hungarian appeared in 1536, an event that did much to advance the supersession of Latin not just for sacred writing but for all forms of literary production (here at least the Protestant presupposition holds). The philological disciplining of the language followed quickly: the first Hungarian dictionary was produced in 1536, the first grammar in 1539. It may be hard to decide which of the two events, religious reform or political threat, functioned as the main catalyst for this philologization, but the appearance of a vernacular history of Hungary (1575), the historical poems of Tinódi at the end of the century, and the lyrics of Bálint Balassi (d. 1594; his most important work, "In Praise of Frontierlands" was described recently as a tribute to the soldiers "who fought the Turks daily on the borderlands of Christendom and Islam") leave little doubt that the new political realities contributed centrally to the vernacularization process.[21]

The difficulties of historicizing the vernacularization of Europe—of

20. Smith 1983: 9, 216, 1, cf. 181 ff.; for his insistence on writing, see pp. 74, 190. Not everyone of course agrees with Smith's interpretation (Wright 1994, especially chapters 19–20).

21. See Czigány 1984 (on Balassi see p. 50, on Christianization p. 16), whom I follow for this brief sketch, while seeking to avoid the predictable eternalism in his account (e.g., p. 43).

grasping the fact of beginnings, the role of writing, the meaning and place of superposed models in the creation of literature—are clearly substantial. Yet there is no doubt that the early centuries of the second millennium witnessed in Europe what can only be described as a vernacular revolution, one that followed a time line closely approximating the analogous process in South Asia. There is no doubt, either, that the phenomenon proceeded across the whole of western Europe in something like a wave of emulative advance: late-first-millennium vernacularity in England influenced the creation of a new Anglo-Norman and then a continental French literature in the eleventh and twelfth centuries, which influenced the vernacularization of Iberia, while simultaneously southern France developed an extraordinary new literature that prompted imitation and stimulated vernacularization from Italy to northern Germany. In the languages we now call French, Spanish, German, and Hungarian it was no longer a matter of one-off experiments in vernacular literization—here a German biography of Christ (the *Heliand*, 830), there a French saint's hymn (the *Sequence of St. Eulalie*, 881–2) or a Hungarian funeral sermon (the *Halotti Beszéd*, 1200), virtually all transpositions of, or deeply informed by, Latin religious works. This was the commencement of whole literary traditions—intentional, reflexive, memorialized, circulating, continually reproduced, and philologized. The entire process, moreover, was one whose novelty and very commencement were fully apparent to the agents involved. This is shown not only by the vernacular anxieties examined below (section 2) but by the explicit historicist assessment of early writers. When, for example, in the *De vulgari eloquentia* Dante speaks of writers like Peire d'Alvernha (fl. 1150) as the first to use the vernacular for poetry (*in ea primitus poetati sunt*, X.2), or when Petrarch writes to Boccaccio (around 1350) that "Latin is of course the nobler *(altior)* language, in both prose and poetry, but for that very reason it has been so developed by earlier writers that neither we nor anyone else can add much of anything to it. The vernacular, on the other hand, has only recently been discovered *[(vulgaris) inventus ad huc recens]*. It has been mishandled by many and tended by only a few; rough as it is, it could be much beautified and enriched, I am sure," they may be taken as speaking for all vernacular writers in the early centuries of the millennium, who were fully conscious of the cultural-political transformation in which they were participating.[22]

Like Dante's or Petrarch's statement, the historical sketches we have just given testify in their different ways to the continuing dominance of Latin literacy and literature and the central role of the cosmopolitan code in the vernacularization process. There is no question that the vernacular literary

22. *De vulgari eloquentia* book 1 chapter 10; Machan 1991: 233 (whose translation is modified here on the basis of Petrarca 1965: 879). For Petrarch, literary Tuscan was a learned language; his notes for his vernacular poems are in Latin.

cultures of Europe, precisely like those of South Asia, not only borrowed from the cosmopolitan but also contributed to it: think only of the adoption of stress accent and rhyme from the vernaculars in some later Latin (as indeed in some later Sanskrit). The cosmopolitan, it bears repeating, can logically be nothing but a higher-order synthesis or generalization of local practices, though its homogenizing force is such that it rarely leaves behind historical traces to demonstrate this fact. Yet as a fully formed cosmopolitan culture when the vernacular epoch commenced, Latin (like Sanskrit) shaped the revolution far more profoundly than it was shaped by it. Vernacular literacy everywhere in Europe for centuries to come not only presupposed and was mediated by Latin literacy (being able to read and write the vernacular without being able to read and write Latin must have been a rarity), but the very sense of what literature meant as a cultural form was taken from Latin. E. R. Curtius was thus largely correct to characterize the beginnings of French literature in the eleventh-century *Song of St. Alexis* as a "well-considered composition of a scholarly poet who knew the devices of rhetoric and had read Virgil." The same is no less the case with the Anglo-Norman poets, the poets of Occitan lyrics, the twelfth-century German *Minnesängers*, the author of the Castilian *Cid,* to say nothing of Dante and the other literary pioneers in Florentine. All of them, as one recent restatement of Curtius puts it (if perhaps too strongly) "are subsequent and secondary phenomena" to be analyzed "in terms of the primacy of Latin."[23]

To attempt, as vernacular intellectuals attempted, to displace the most powerful literary-cultural force in European history—the sole model of linguistic permanence, grammatical discipline, aesthetic depth and weight, artistic excellence, and authorizing tradition—must have seemed a stunning act of defiance. What this effort certainly revealed was a deep-seated anxiety about the vernacular's very capacity for literary creation.

11.2 VERNACULAR ANXIETY

It is wholly in keeping with the historical character of a vernacular culture, which must define itself and make good its claim to speak at all, let alone to speak the truth, that its authorization should sometimes be ascribed to a transcendent power. And such divine ascriptions are perhaps the best indicator of the anxiety provoked by the act of seeking vernacular literariness within

23. Godman in Curtius 1990: 650 (who also cites Curtius). On the mediation of vernacular literacy by Latin literacy in twelfth- and thirteenth-century Germany see Palmer 1993: 7. (Note that Dante states he entered into Latin through the vernacular but is silent about literacy, *Il Convivio* 1.13.) Cerquiglini seems the odd man out (1999: 20). No comprehensive account of European vernacularization in relationship to Latin seems to be available (as of 1990, Gröber's *Grundriss* of 1902 was "still the only survey that extends as far as 1350," Godman 1990: 607).

the power shadow of a cosmopolitan formation. In South Asia the felt need for the direct command of a god to underwrite vernacular literature persisted long into the second millennium; we saw this to be so in Maharashtra and Andhra even in the fifteenth, sixteenth, and seventeenth centuries, when Tukarām, Śrīnātha, Kṛṣṇadevarāya—Shudra, Brahman, and even king—all needed to receive a divine commandment in a dream to be able to write in the vernacular, despite three or more centuries of ongoing vernacularization. Indeed, the same was true in the erstwhile vernacular tradition of Latin itself: Horace describes how Romulus, the demigod founder of Rome, appeared to him in a dream and forbade him to "join the vast ranks" of those who wrote poetry in Greek.[24]

The origin story of English poetry illustrates a similar exigency. Bede writes of Cædmon, whose role in the literate culture's image of vanished orality we have already noted, that "having lived in a secular habit till he was well advanced in years, [he] had never learned anything of versifying"—presumably implying that only those who had some religious education and therefore knew Latin could create verse. For Cædmon to undertake the vernacular composition of poetry required divine intervention. One night, a being appeared to him in a dream and commanded him to sing. Cædmon did so, though against his will—and the result was English poetry. The next day he recited his creation to "many learned men," who realized he had been visited by the grace of God. What he versified, as we noted earlier, was a recitation from scripture, a literate text in Latin. He adapted—or interpreted, glossed, or complemented—it in English: "He soon after put the same into poetical expressions . . . in English, which was his native language," an accomplishment Bede further vindicates by confessing himself unable to successfully translate its "dignity and beauty" back into Latin. The dream thus defends the use of English, among the literati in particular ("even his teachers wrote down the words from his lips and learnt them"), for whom only Latin—plus ideally at least Hebrew and Greek, the languages inscribed on the Cross—had been considered appropriate for making verse in praise of God. Cædmon's tale also leaves no doubt that vernacularization could occur only in dependence on the cosmopolitan Latin tradition.[25]

The themes of vernacular anxiety only just discernible in the Cædmon tale—the inferiority of the local language in general over against the cosmopolitan, particularly its morphological and semantic changeability and instability, its supposed lexical deficiency, its lack of "dignity," and the absence of a tradition of great exemplars—would be produced across European traditions for centuries, demonstrating how very slow in coming was the ver-

24. Horace, *Satires* 1.10.31 ff. Note that Du Bellay recalls Horace's dream (Du Bellay 1948: 188; see later in this section).

25. Colgrave and Mynors, ed. 1969, book 4, chapter 24, pp. 415–17; See 1985: 13, 54; 1983.

nacular's success in acquiring literary-cultural self-confidence. Three moments in this long history, examined here in decreasing detail—the first comprising the literary-critical works of Dante that inaugurated Italian literature, the latter two, vernacular "defenses" in French and English—give us a sense not only of the persistence of the sentiment but also of the arguments used to contest it and their connection with larger developments in the spheres of literary culture and cultural politics.

A key text in the vernacularization not only of Italy (given that it is located near the commencement of that tradition) but of Europe as a whole (given that its key themes reverberated in France, England, and elsewhere into the seventeenth century) is Dante's *De vulgari eloquentia* (On Vernacular Eloquence, c. 1300). It is puzzling that such a theorization was produced first for a Latin-near language, when we might have expected it for the Latin-distant English or German (as in South Asia, where the first such treatises were written for the Sanskrit-distant Kannada and Tamil), and we return to the problem further (chapter 12.1). It is even more puzzling that the defense of the vernacular was made not in the vernacular itself (as again in Kannada and Tamil) but in Latin. But these are just two in a series of inversions, reversals, and ironies that mark Dante's classic statement.

One vital aspect of Dante's project is captured in its title: to offer arguments for the ennoblement of vernacular language in its *written* form (to which the term *eloquentia* refers in medieval Latin). The treatise begins by celebrating the vernacular's domestic and natural character: it is acquired without rule and unmediated by thought; the rule-bound cosmopolitan language is, by comparison, secondary and artificial (1.1). Indeed, for Dante, *nobilior est vulgaris* (1.4), an astonishing transvaluation of cultural values, but one that is ironically self-limiting because, at that historical juncture, it could be expressed only in Latin and not in the vernacular. Furthermore, not only is the vernacular nobler than the cosmopolitan; in its nonliterary state it can actually boast of a greater antiquity: Dante regards Latin as a deliberate and comparatively recent creation, intended to enable communication across time thanks to its grammatical invariability (1.9). But another more obvious ironical reversal looms for the domesticity and naturalness of the vernacular: Dante's treatise itself attempts to reduce nature to culture—the domestic and local to the courtly and translocal. The vernacular will be truly elevated to the level of literary competence only when its naturalness is defeated and the irregular, haphazard, and accidental nature of vernacular composition, as Dante describes it, is disciplined and controlled.

Such regulation and normativity are precisely what Dante's scientific account of the vernacular aims to secure. In addition, it seeks to create from the fourteen dialects of "Italian" (*vulgare Latium,* itself part of a tripartite *ydioma,* referring to the languages of the "Yspani, Franci et Latini") a single "illustrious" or courtly vernacular that will encompass all these different forms;

this can be achieved only by turning away from the maternal dialect (2.14). The qualifications that Dante invokes in determining the courtly vernacular are multiple: one dialect is too crude, one too harsh and masculinizing, another too soft and feminizing; one is insufficiently courtly and too local *(non curialia sed municipalia),* another too foreign by reason of admixture of alien elements (it no longer has *puras loquelas,* pure speech items). The one illustrious vernacular will be a language that is common to all people of Latium, or Ytalie, but unique to none (16.4 *hec nullius civitatis Ytalie propria sunt, et in omnibus comunia sunt*). (Dante conceptualizes and describes this domain [1.10], as indeed he presents the language map of the rest of Europe [1.8], with the geocultural interest and clarity typical of the vernacularizing intellectual.) This vernacular will achieve distinction through linguistic centrality, social elevation, political presence, and literary history—with "literary" clearly defined according to cosmopolitan norms as workly textuality, a capacity ascribed so defensively to the vernacular that others must have doubted it could apply at all. But such a crystallization will only happen through discipline in the fine points of literary technique and through cosmopolitan emulation:

> I frequently called those who write verse in the vernacular "poets"; and this presumptuous expression is beyond question justifiable, since they are most certainly poets, if we understand poetry aright: that is, as nothing other than a verbal invention composed according to the rules of rhetoric and music (*fictio rethorica musicaque poita* [i.e., tropology and metrics]). Yet they differ from the great poets, that is, those who obey the rules [i.e., the Latin poets], since those great ones wrote their poetry in a language, and with a technique, governed by rules *(sermone et arte regulari),* whereas these write at random *(casu)* . . . Thus it comes about that, the more closely we try to imitate the great poets, the more correctly we write poetry.[26]

An equally remarkable defense—this time in the vernacular—is found in the first book of the *Il Convivio,* Dante's autocommentary on his *canzoni.* Here the problem confronting the author is the defense of, not literary production in the vernacular, but rather scholarly production. The objective of the first book of the *Convivio* is to argue out why the commentary that follows is written in Italian, not in Latin, the language of learning. (The *Eloquentia*'s reasoned defense of the literary vernacular, on the other hand, could only be set forth in the language of reason, Latin.) Dante's rationale is powerful and dramatic, and again, apparently unprecedented. The performative argument—a self-exemplifying vernacular discourse on vernacular discourse, precisely as in the *Kavirājamārgam*—is already a compelling one.

26. *De vulgari eloquentia* 2.4, tr. Botterill (who notes "'the rules' are those of Latin, and the poets who follow them . . . are those of the classical Latin tradition," p. 97).

Others are discursive: For one thing, since the *canzoni* are composed in the vernacular, if the exposition were in Latin, with its greater nobility (note the ambivalence here), virtue, beauty, incorruptibility, and eternality—all virtues lacking in the corruptible, unstable vernacular—the roles of sovereign text and servile commentary would be reversed. For another, the reasons that prompted some contemptible men of Italy to denigrate the vernacular are all false (they blindly follow the learned crowd, they seek to blame their tools for their poor skills, and so on). But the most powerful argument of all is emotional: one has a "natural love for one's native speech," Dante asserts in the fifth chapter—and for perhaps the first time in the history of European thought. This bare assertion, however, hardly prepares us for the intensity of chapters 12 and 13. There he proclaims his love for his native language as the closest of friendships, both intrinsic, since the vernacular is the first language to enter his mind, and extrinsic, since through it "one is connected to one's relatives, fellow citizens, and one's own people." The vernacular is the cause both of one's own being (one's parents conversed and so united through the vernacular) and of being good, since it is the entryway into learning (albeit Latin learning). In fact, everything that engenders and strengthens any true friendship works to strengthen Dante's friendship with the vernacular, such that "Not simply love but the most perfect love is what I ought to have, and do have, for [my vernacular language]."[27]

Many of the themes of vernacular self-assertion that we have seen in South Asia are assembled in these two remarkable treatises: the geocultural frame of reference of the vernacularization project, the catalyst that literature represents in the larger cultural transformation of this frame, the limiting condition presented by the cosmopolitan tradition both in the definitions and practices of literature it offers as well as in its grammatical and other philological forms of discipline. But there are European particulars too, above all, the emotional link to the vernacular as one of friendship, loyalty, even love. We can detect a certain *ressentiment* in Dante's assertiveness. He describes vernacular writing at the inaugural moment as almost accidental *(casu)* given the undisciplined nature of the medium in use. If it is to become a vehicle for literature—an unambiguous, well-articulated category inherited from the Latin tradition, *fictio rethorica musicaque poita* (Dante here cites *magister noster Oratius,* our master Horace)—and for the discourse of the courtly world that produces literature and is in turn reproduced by it, mastery of the superposed models and of grammar and poetics *(sermone et arte)* must be attained. The natural, local, plebeian, unruly vernacular must become artful, translocal, courtly, and disciplined (*illustre, cardinale, aulicum, curiale,* 16.6)—it must become, in short, cosmopolitan.

27. Dante, *Il Convivio* 1.10.5; 1.13.10 (tr. Lansing).

All these themes were restated with renewed energy in the sixteenth century, when the defense of vernacular literature became a veritable subgenre in European writing.[28] It may seem curious that the most powerful cases of vernacular anxiety were presented at this point, some three or more centuries after the turn to local literary language across western Europe. In part this may reflect a continuing uncertainty about the very possibility of a vernacular's survival. Thus Montaigne could acknowleddge in 1585 that he wrote his collection of essays in French because it was meant "for a limited number of people and for a limited number of years. If it had been a subject destined to last, I would have had to commit it to a more stable language [i.e., Latin]." And he adds, "Given the continual variation which our language has undergone up to the present time, who can expect its present form to be still in use in fifty years' time? It slips away from our hands day by day and in the course of my lifetime it has changed by half."[29] Yet a more cogent explanation for the rise of the defense genre may be the historical moment, for these texts appeared when a new form of polity, one defined in part by a new relationship between language and power, was coming into existence.

Joachim Du Bellay's defense from mid-century France and Sir Philip Sidney's celebrated English treatise from the following generation are exemplary of the whole genre. These works are distinguished from *De vulgari eloquentia* (which Du Bellay certainly knew) in several ways. Whereas Dante wrote his principal treatise on the vernacular in Latin, the later works (like the *Convivio,* though without either Du Bellay or Sidney being aware of the text) aim to demonstrate in their very practice the vernacular discursive competence they preach; they are at once constative and performative texts. There is also far greater hostility toward the superposed tradition of Latinity than one finds in Dante's works, and a far more transparent political agenda. These latter two features are no doubt closely related: a new and more classicized, cosmopolitanized vernacular was being created in service of a new and more territorially expansive national-imperial project.

In *La deffence et illustration de la langue francoyse* (1549), Du Bellay, a member of the circle of literati known as the Pléiade and a counselor of King François I, conceived of the vernacular as requiring not just elevation *(illustration),* in view of what he saw as its earlier humble rusticity, but also defense because it was seen as vulnerable, even under attack: the same natural law

28. On Castilian, for example, see Darbord 1991: 63–65, and more generally Ferguson 1983 (whose psychoanalytic framework of interpretation I cannot accept, my chapter subtitle notwithstanding). I know no work that compares Du Bellay and Dante, though Du Bellay's debt to Speroni's *Dialogo delle lingue* (1542), and Speroni's to Dante, are well known.

29. Montaigne, "De la vanité," *Essaies* 3.9 (partially cited in Lodge 1993: 129). The sentiment was still being expressed a century later (Fumaroli 1984: 142–43); the topos is as old as Dante, *Convivio* 5.4.7.

that commands us to defend our birthplace obliges us to defend the dignity of our language (2.12). Notions of *dignité* and *honneur,* however vigorously they may have stimulated earlier vernacularization processes, are here brought into the very center of the discussion. Languages are no longer to be hierarchized on the basis of their genealogies, a conception still alive for Dante; instead, they are by nature equal. Their virtues result from the desire and will of mortal beings with their varying degrees of *artifice* and *industrie,* and all that distinguishes these languages along a scale of value are the quality of the literature produced in them by such labor and skill, and the literary-cultural discipline of being more carefully *reiglées* (1.1 [a term of Dante's, 2.4]; 1.10). The absence of neither morphological complexity nor quantitative metrics as such betokens inferiority; there is enough evidence testifying to the talents of the French (above all, their possession of what no classical culture ever had: printing and artillery, 2.9).

Latin nonetheless remains a spirit to be exorcised from French literary culture, having recently experienced a return from the dead, as it were, thanks to the humanists, in France no less than in Italy. Du Bellay seeks to do this by presenting Latin as itself a vernacular that succeeded by learning from Greek; and in just the same way French, like it or not, must learn from Latin. He does not wholly ignore the pre-sixteenth-century French literary past (if he underestimates its debt to Latinity): some great works were produced (*Roman de la Rose,* for example), and they remain a source for enriching the lexicon of literary French. But Latin is now the self-conscious model, and not only for literature but also for the relationship of literary culture to polity. The day of *rondeaux, vyrelaiz, chantz royaulx* is past; it is now time for a new classicism, for vernacular epics and historical chronicles, and for *doctrine* and *erudition* (2.3, 4), the scientification of the sort the *Deffence* itself proceeds to offer with respect to lexicon, rhyme, prosody, and the like, and in the absence of which a self-conscious cosmopolitan vernacular cannot exist.[30] The purpose of all these works is to dignify the language so as to add to the honor of France (2.5). The final chapter is actually subtitled "Exhortation aux francoys d'ecrire en leur Langue: aveques les louanges de la France" (Exhortation to the French to write in their language: along with praises of France), indicating how indissolubly joined vernacularity and polity had become for Du Bellay: his aim was to produce a "Gallic Hercules" who would "draw the nations after him by their ears with a chain attached to his tongue." Again Latin provides the perfect model, since the glory of the Romans lay no less in the expansion of their language than in the expansion of their borders.[31]

30. On the *Deffence* as a repudiation of the older vernacular past see Fumaroli 1992: 926 ff.

31. Du Bellay 1948: 197, 183. For his colleague Ronsard, balance was required ("I want to advise you again," he wrote to a young poet, "not to overdo Latin, like our predecessors, who

Du Bellay's call for a studied classicization of the vernacular was part of a much broader cultural and political movement, and what the age demanded. French literature moved from Rabelais in the 1530s to the first classical *tragédie* and *comédie* in 1552–53 to writers like Montaigne and Aubigné at century's end (Latin was not killed in the process, however; Du Bellay himself continued to write in it). In England at nearly the same moment the conquest of the vernacular must have seemed wholly assured. The mid-sixteenth century saw an extraordinary proliferation of literary texts. More's *Utopia*, written first in Latin in 1516, was available in English by 1551. And the efflorescence of lyric poetry from Thomas Wyatt, Henry Howard, and others, followed by the beginnings of Elizabethan drama and eventually works like Edmund Spenser's *Faerie Queen* (1590), is a story too well known to need retelling here. Yet worry about possessing "a kingdome of our own language" continued to unsettle English intellectuals quite visibly at mid-century.[32] It is this worry that Sir Philip Sidney seems to be addressing in his *Apology for Poesie* (written in 1583; published posthumously in 1595).

As the title declares, the purpose of the work is to argue in defense of imaginative literature as such, not of the particular language in which it happens to be written. Yet traces of the old vernacular anxiety persist. When Sidney analyzes "diction," for example, or the "outside" of poetry, he asserts his preference for plain English and his aversion to "hony-flowing matron eloquence," and "farre fetched words, that many seeme Monsters, but must seeme strangers to any poore English Man"— his aversion, in other words, to outlandish and alien Latinisms (what from an Indian perspective might be called the *bhāṣā* poet's fear and loathing of the *tatsama*). And if plain-spoken English poets sometimes go awry, it is not the fault of their language, he defensively asserts, for "we may bend to the right use both of matter and manner: whereto our language giveth us great occasion, being, indeed, capable of any excellent exercising of it":

> I know some will say [English] is a mingled language. And why not so much the better, taking the best of both the other? Another will say it wanteth Grammer. Nay truly, it hath that prayse, that it wanteth not Grammer: for Grammer it might have, but it needes it not; beeing so easie of it selfe, and so void of those cumbersome differences of Cases, Genders, Moodes, and Tenses, which I think was a peece of the Tower of Babylon's curse, that a man should be put to schoole to learne his mother-tongue.[33]

---

quite recklessly adopted an infinite number of foreign words from the Romans. For there are perfectly good words in our own language," Ronsard 1993: vol. 2, 1187).

32. See Helgerson 1992, especially pp. 1–18, and chapter 3 for the "chorographic" developments that accompany the victory of the vernacular.

33. Sidney 1997: 125, 127.

Several important if somewhat contradictory claims are made at once here. Like Du Bellay, Sidney is eager to declare his vernacular the equal of any other in the world, but he must specifically deny the relevance of its historical origins. These origins are now understood within the new conceptual scheme of biology, which supplants the old quasi-historicist one of Babel. Languages (naturally implying Old English and Norman French) are thought of as originally pure stocks that can interbreed. The mixing of languages, however, unlike that of peoples perhaps (or horses, which provide the *Apology* with its opening trope), does not necessarily diminish their expressive capacity: the offspring can preserve the good qualities of both parents and even be greater than either. The absence of grammatical regulation—the eternal scandal of the vernaculars—is now represented as virtue rather than vice: the complex morphology of Greek and Latin is not the golden armor that preserved them from harm but mere baggage, and the very ease of learning that resulted when English disencumbered itself of such weight is a sign of its excellence. Nobody needs to go to school to learn one's mother tongue except those still doing penance for a prehistoric sin.

The tensions in the text are not unlike those in Dante and Du Bellay, and need not detain us long. It is obviously inconsistent to argue so artfully for an artless English; Sidney did not learn the rhetorical, high courtly style of the *Apology* at his mother's knee. Moreover, by the very production of a text that puts the mother tongue to school Sidney undermines his own argument, just as earlier Dante unwittingly forced his "natural" vernacular—precisely the quality that made it preferable to Latin—to become as cultured as Latin (and just as Thoreau several centuries later would turn the gentle mother tongue into the stern father tongue with the rod of philology in hand, chapter 8.3). And clearly biology and Babel cannot both be right on the origins of language difference. More important than these unavoidable contradictions is the new self-confidence in evidence here with which the vernacular was now beginning to speak. This was the result not only of three centuries of "defense" and an even longer period of "illustration," but also of the vernacular's status as the voice of a new vernacular state. What cured vernacular anxiety was power.

11.3 A NEW CULTURAL POLITICS

It should be apparent from the materials assembled thus far that the vernacular revolution in Europe was unthinkable without the central stimulus provided by the increasingly powerful royal courts of the later Middle Ages and Renaissance. The *idée reçu* of an official Latin counterposed to a popular vernacular, or indeed, of a vernacular lay spirit of *il popolo* fighting a Latin churchly authority—a belief long cherished even by keen students of the age like Bakhtin and Gramsci—is contradicted by the substantial evidence of clerical interests in the vernaculars to say nothing of the demotic popularity of Latin as demonstrated by the works of the Goliards, the Archpoet, and others. So also, the image of a democratic vernacularism fighting the forces of a Latinate feudalism is contradicted by the feudal promotion of the vernaculars and, in Italy at least, the cultivation of Latin in the free republics.[34] The cases we have examined, with the exception of sixteenth-century Hungary, where the notorious instability of the court after 1300 may have been what retarded the turn toward regional-language literary production, show that vernacularization was a core concern of court intellectuals and elites, precisely as it was in southern Asia.

This is not to say that any one political logic attaches to vernacularization—that it is always and everywhere an exclusively centralizing political logic, for instance—or that the political is related to it monocausally. A range of other factors, including class, gender, and professional identity, undoubtedly contributed, too. It has been argued, for example, that the new vernacular prose historiography developed in thirteenth-century northern France was patronized by feudal aristocrats to counter the centripetal forces of the French monarchy; and that at the Anglo-Norman court it was above all the women who demanded vernacular literary texts as a consequence of the (supposed) inadequacy of their Latin learning.[35] Whatever the particular modulations, however, vernacularity across Europe was to become a characteristic and consequential element in the practice of rulership and governance. Signs of its strategic deployment in the interests of a political principle can be observed from the very beginning of the vernacular millennium, becoming ever more distinct over time. A glance at a few cases we have already noticed—England in the ninth century, Castile in the thirteenth, Tuscany in the fourteenth, and France in the fifteenth and sixteenth—suffice to demonstrate this.

It was noted earlier that in late-first-millennium England, vernacularization was a project clearly and straightforwardly directed by the court in the interests of the political community. With the accession of Alfred in 871, and especially after the recapture of London in 886 from the Danes, which politically united all of England outside Danelaw, the project was powerfully accelerated, and English became for the first time an official language of the state. Although the court was certainly concerned with the enhancement of learning in the interests of spiritual betterment, the political objective was indissociable from it. While the greater part of literary production was straight translation of Latin works, two key political texts constituted an important ex-

34. As P. O. Kristeller reminds us, 1965: 122.

35. Marcia Colish (in conversation) called some of these instances to my attention (for the first see Spiegel 1993). Women's access to Latin varied from place to place (Mathilda of England was evidently well educated, Bond 1995: 246). Gender as a factor in vernacularization varies, too, across cultures. If prominent in Japanese, it is irrelevant for Kannada and Telugu.

ception: the *Anglo-Saxon Chronicles* (890) and a law code, both of which were assembled partly from earlier materials (some of them possibly vernacular) under Alfred's supervision from his capital at Winchester. These two bodies of text—the sort that would figure prominently in the creation of new vernacular cultural politics in Alfonsine Castile and elsewhere—equipped the vernacular polity with a deep history and a clear sense of its legal status, both of which were required in view of the imperial model that Alfred sought to emulate and supplant: that of Charlemagne, whose own genealogy and legal status were constantly put in evidence. In everything from Alfred's biography—which Asser (893) closely modeled on Einhard's Latin biography of Charlemagne (825) while recoding it for vernacular culture and polity—to the unification of the Anglo-Saxon kings (around 880), scholars have found evidence of a cultural-political program on the Carolingian model but expressing a new local cultural self-consciousness. If earlier it had been the responsibility of Christian rulers like Charlemagne to render Latin literary culture an "image of *imperium* and *auctoritas,*" it now became their responsibility to mandate this rendering in the vernacular. The *renovatio* of Roman culture and power on the Continent thus inspired the invention of an Insular culture and power. In short, within the context of the long-term and varying relationship between grammar and political power, where for almost a millennium the care for Latin had been intimately linked with the care for *imperium,* the new vernacular literary culture of the England of Alfred and his successors can hardly be understood except as tied to a new mentality and new modes of identification that had an unmistakable political resonance.[36]

No less dramatic and unambiguous an instance of the court's political management of the vernacular occurred in thirteenth-century Castile. It has recently been demonstrated with great precision that at the start of that century court functionaries for the first time began to write intentionally in the vernacular for political purposes. The inaugural instance, a treaty between Castile and Leon, is extant and can be dated to Palm Sunday, 1206. Drawn up in the Castile chancery, the document would have appeared revolutionary in that context, if not heretical: the archbishop was in charge of the chancery ex officio, Romance was still largely denied validity in its written form, and the reform of spelling (in the service of vernacularization) bordered on sin.[37] From that point on, however, despite periodic interruptions

36. Though to call this a "national identity and ideology" *tout court* (Irvine 1994: 14; 415 ff.; cf. Davis 1998) is problematic (see the arguments in chapter 14.2). References in this paragraph are to See 1983: 50 ff. and Irvine 1994: 416–18 and 13–14. On Alfred's directive (found in the "Preface," Irvine 1994: 419) that young free men must develop competence in vernacular literacy (so the new law code would be accessible to them), see Lerer 1991.

37. Wright 1996 describes the struggle between Latin and Castilian proponents in the chancery and the simultaneous development of political and literary texts (for the treaty itself,

in the first decades, vernacular political culture, and with it literary culture, developed with an extraordinary intensity—for example, it was in the year following the treaty document that the one manuscript of the *Cid* was prepared. Central to the consolidation of this process were the innovations at the court of Alfonso X el Sabio ("the Learned," r. 1252–82).

The meaning and memory of the historic break that Alfonso's reign signaled—and "break" is more appropriate than "renaissance," the usual descriptor, since textual vernacularity was being generated, not regenerated—were recorded two centuries later when Antonio de Nebrija remarked in the celebrated preface to his grammar of Castilian (1492) that it was at Alfonso's court that Castilian first "began to shows its powers." Castilian has all the marks of a cosmopolitan-vernacular idiom, but in this case one shaped not only by Latin (in particular Roman jurisprudence) but also by Arabic culture, which was now being translated into Castilian rather than Latin as earlier. Castilian was cultivated across the full spectrum of text genres, both political and literary; vernacularization in the two spheres was clearly regarded as mutually supporting, and chancery and scriptorium as united. The use of the vernacular for all state documents except international diplomacy became a matter of royal policy. Well-known is the remarkable Castilian redaction of the laws of the realm, the *Siete partidas* (Seven Divisions [of Law]), which sought to extend royal control over all judicial and legislative activities. Of a piece with the vernacularization of law was the creation of a Castilian historiography that sought to narrate the past of both the local geopolitical space (*Estoria de Espanna* [The Chronicle of Spain]) and the world as a whole (*General Estoria* [The General Chronicle]), both left incomplete at Alfonso X's death in 1282. Although the vernacularization of political communication had commenced under Alfonso VII (d. 1214), these grand prose works had no predecessors; the history of Spain commissioned by el Sabio's father, for example, was in Latin (written by the archbishop of Toledo). Instead, they were born, as one scholar puts it—once again using a trope that figures forth astonishment at the invention of the literate vernacular—"full-fledged like Minerva, with Alfonso assuming the role of Jupiter." Elsewhere in his literary-cultural production Alfonso observed, and perhaps helped to invent, the more pluralistic genre-language convention noted earlier, so that, for example, his *Cantigas* are composed in what has been described as troubadour-Galician. But the impetus given to the creation of unified culture in both the literary and the political domain was unprecedented and irreversible, and it maps closely against Alfonso's peninsular political objectives: his desire to unify all forms of knowledge and the Castilian language

Wright 2000). A decree of 1214 mandates the use of Castilian in royal communications (Smith 2000).

is analogous to his quest for the political centralization of Castile, "dominating everything, centralizing everything around himself."[38]

The politics of Dante's vernacular project are complicated, and the interpretive problems resist easy summary. *De vulgari eloquentia,* especially read in conjunction with his political tract, *De monarchia,* has elicited totally divergent interpretations even in specialist literature. A political scientist, for example, argues that the two tracts—and thus the very notions of culture and power—represent parallel and nonintersecting concerns for Dante, whereas a literary historian insists that Dante's political, linguistic, and aesthetic theories are thoroughly intertwined and grounded in "national" thought of a decidedly modernist cast. What is not in dispute is the geocultural framework of Dante's *vulgare illustre,* while the fact that the language is meant to be *curiale* and *aulicum*—related to a court and a palace—leaves no doubt about the political context he had in mind. Yet the kind of polity Dante conceived of as home to this literary culture is far less distinct. In fact, as he himself shows, there was a decided tension in his thinking: in response to the question what good is the creation of a courtly vernacular to Italy when there is no Italian court, he answers, "We have a court, though in the body it is scattered" (*De vulgari eloquentia* 1.18). The larger political goal Dante envisaged was the unification of Italy within a reconstituted Holy Roman Empire. How exactly the illustrious vernacular was meant to function in this Germanic kind of political formation is obscure in the text, but Dante leaves little doubt that it was for this new imperium that the language was intended. Or perhaps this is less obscurity than unfamiliarity, of a moment in European political-cultural history when the absolute symmetry of ethnic state and language had not yet become common sense.[39]

The sudden emergence of courtly literature in French in Norman England was part of a larger transformation that included the beginnings of the creation of a French documentary state (albeit one never as rich as that of thirteenth-century Castile). The first written laws in French appeared soon after the conquest, in 1069 and 1080, the first charter in 1140, and while Latin was far from being displaced as a language of state, French came to be used more and more for the business of the polity. Political ends have been discerned as well in the first systematic grammatical description of French (mid-fourteenth century England): it was likely prompted by a perception

38. Socarras cited in Burns 1990: 11. For Alfonso see Smith 2000, and Burns 1990, especially 1–18, 90–108 (chancery-scriptorium), 141–58 (historiography), 183–84 (law); the citation on the origins of Alfonsine prose is from p. 38. For the genre-language convention see the earlier discussion in chapter 8.2 and n. 36. See Nebrija 1946: 8 for his quotation.

39. The discrepant views on Dante's cultural politics are Breuilly 1994: 4 and Garber 1989: 12–13. Perhaps the best capsule account of Dante's treatise "as an act of national-cultural politics (in the sense that 'nations' had at that time and in Dante)" is Gramsci (1991: 187–88).

of ruling elites on the eve of the Hundred Years' War that they needed to know French and demonstrate a certain Frenchness to strengthen their claims on northern France. In southern France, by contrast, while the earliest grammaticization of Occitan (indeed, the first of any Romance language) the *Razos de trobar* (Account of Composition) by the Catalan Raimon Vidal (c. 1200), was likewise composed outside Occitan country—or better put, in an area that (after the battle of Muret in 1213 when Provence ceased to be ruled from Catalonia) was being politically created as outside Occitania—the project's objective was pedagogical rather than political. Rather different circumstances surrounded one of the last such Occitan literary treatises, the *Leys d'amors* (Laws of Love), written in Toulouse around 1330 in an attempt to resuscitate the troubadour tradition and Occitan literary culture as such after the Albigensian Crusade had effectively annihilated both. Whatever the differences in the political motivations of vernacularization in northern and southern France, there is broad agreement on the fact that it was largely a consequence of the desires and needs of a "new aristocratic laity" with new cultural norms, where literacy was no longer an exception but rather a royal virtue.[40]

Yet the vernacular's route to domination was by no means direct. True enough, in the Île-de-France itself, the oeuvre of Chrétien de Troyes offered a powerful example of a new imaginative literature at the end of the twelfth century, and a milestone in political-discursive French was marked by a new vernacular historiography, almost contemporaneous with Alfonso's and based in part on translations from the Latin, the *Roman des rois* (Romance of the Kings, 1274, prepared at the royal abbey of Saint-Denis for Philip III) and the *Grandes chroniques de France,* of which the *Roman* forms the core. Still, such eloquent testimony to the achievements of the vernacular and to its political patronage notwithstanding, the felt need to wage its defense clearly remained. We have seen that as late as the sixteenth century writers like Montaigne were haunted by a sense of the vernacular's instability and its uncertain future. At the same time they understood full well how critical political power was to its survival. Montaigne himself, in a passage cited earlier, goes on to make the point succinctly in a wonderful metaphor available only then, on the threshold of capitalism: it is the responsibility of good literature to try to "nail down" the vernacular in hopes of keeping it from changing, but

40. See Howlett 1996, especially 1, 22, 162–66. Zink 1992: 91, 101 refers to the courtly context of continental French literary production; see also Banniard (1995: 707 and note 48), whom I quote in the text. For southern France, see in general Akehurst and Davis 1995, and in particular Bond's contribution, p. 250. The grammaticization of French is discussed in Lusignan 1986: 91–127; cf. Giard 1989 (and cf. Wright 1994: 243 on the newly conceptualized geocultural separation of Catalonia and Occitania after 1213). See comments on changes in the very conception of kingly culture in the first centuries of the second millennium (1985: 38).

its credit—its trustworthiness and authority as well as solvency—will necessarily follow "the fortune of our state."[41]

It is in Du Bellay's *Deffence* that the linkage between politics and the vernacular was first argued out explicitly: in due time, he declares, when France takes up the reins of imperial rule *(monarchie),* its language will spring from the ground and grow to great heights (1.3). The relationship between language and political power is mutually constitutive for Du Bellay: *monarchie* requires a great vernacular literature if it is to achieve its ends, whereas a literature requires a *monarchie* if it is to flourish at all. And he provides historical grounds for this claim: it was King François I who made it possible for the French language to advance. "Our language was crude and vulgar, but he rendered it elegant"; through a royally sponsored series of translations, philosophers, historians, orators, and poets have learned to speak French. Du Bellay's main worry is whether François at his death might have taken French—that is, the court's support of French as the language of state—with him to his grave.[42]

Two decades after the *Deffence,* Du Bellay's colleague Pierre Ronsard published an epitome of French poetic practices (1565) that everywhere reveals his close reading of Du Bellay's treatise yet advances beyond it precisely in articulating the new cultural politics. Ronsard urges the young poet to whom his work is addressed to choose among the dialects of "our France" for the creation of his poetry. In the past, the rulers of provinces may have "desired the extreme honor of their subjects' writing in the language of their native country"—"for princes, in imitation of the Romans, should be as eager to extend the boundaries of the language of their countries *(pays)* as the bounds of their realms *(seigneurie)*." But today, with France under one king, everyone speaks the courtly language; that is, the language of literature is now French, but a French that exhibits its supralocal presence by its capacity to accept, indeed to invite, the provincialisms of a Gascony or a Lyon. No doubt Ronsard is alluding to Du Bellay himself (who had died a few years earlier) when he praises "those of the moderns who have during the last fifteen years illuminated *(illustré)* our literature, now justly proud in this glorious achievement. Happy demigods, they who cultivate their own earth, nor strive after another, from which they could only return thankless and unhappy, unrecompensed, unhonored. The first to dare abandon the ancient Greek and Roman languages for the greater glory of their own truly must be good sons, not ungrateful citizens; worthy to be signalized in a public statue."[43] The cultivation of the cosmopolitan vernacular is not only a project of literary culture; it is a central concern, or should be a central concern, of civil society and the state.

41. Montaigne 1962: 961.

42. *Deffence* 1.3–4.

43. Ronsard 1950: 998–1000. A translation of the *Abrégé* is available in Richter 1989.

Du Bellay and Ronsard seem to be far less fawning courtiers than newly empowered vernacular intellectuals whose vision had been deeply stamped by recent political history, above all by the language policies of François I (r. 1515–47). It was at the instance of this king that a series of laws were promulgated that supply essential background for understanding the political moment of the *Deffence* and of the Pléiade's work in general. These include the Ordinance of Villers-Cotterêts (1539), the most important juridical act of the king's reign and one that did much to ensure the victory of the vernacular. Among its many remarkable provisions for the reform of the state's administrative and judicial procedures is the requirement that all civil and criminal judgments, in fact all procedures of the courts and all its documents, "be pronounced and registered and made over to the parties in the French mother tongue." In part, as the Ordinance itself makes clear, this was a response to the growing incomprehension of Latin; yet it was also acknowledgment that a single courtly idiom could and did have application across the domain of France, including by then Occitania, as the Ordinance itself specified. Villers-Cotterêts thus effects a double erasure—of superordinate Latin and of subordinate regional vernaculars—in the interest principally of administrative efficiency. The death of François and the ensuing uncertainty of the outcome of his cultural politics (and the poet's own fortunes) may have induced Du Bellay's melancholy. Be that as it may, clearly in France too, as in Iberia and Britain and increasingly everywhere in western and central Europe, there would be no turning back from the transition now under way. The vernacular polity was now unquestionably taking on the contours of the nation-state of modernity.[44]

44. See further on the relationship of the "Ordonnance" and the *Deffence* in Dubu 1991, and Lodge 1993: 127, and for later cultural-political developments, Fumaroli 1983. Similar (if even earlier) edicts were issued to ensure the use of German in Silesia, of Czech in Bohemia, and of English in Wales (Bartlett 1993: 214, 220).

CHAPTER TWELVE

Comparative and Connective Vernacularization

12.1 EUROPEAN PARTICULARISM AND INDIAN DIFFERENCE

Brief and selective as it is, the foregoing sketch of some key moments in the historical transformation of literary culture and power in western Europe should suffice to point up some of the extraordinary parallels with contemporaneous developments in southern Asia. The great innovation that was to enduringly change these two worlds occurred during the first five centuries of the second millennium, and it shows a remarkably consistent morphology. (Other apparent moments of vernacularization outside of this time period are either problematic in their history, as in Tamil country in the early first millennium, or entirely divergent in their literary-cultural character, as in Ireland during the same period.) One way to understand this series of transformative events is through a comparative-historical approach, which focuses on the morphology and analyzes it along a more or less ideal-typical grid. Another is the connective-historical, which concentrates on the chronology and inquires whether there were linkages between the two societies within the same time frame.[1] We will take each approach in turn.

The gradual dissolution of the universalist Latin order, which had been sustained for more than a millennium under Roman and then Christian *imperium,* was marked by a concomitant creation of new, self-consciously regionalized forms of literary production and political communication. Alfred's England at the end of the ninth century was a model early instance of the creation of a vernacular literature and the beginnings of a vernacular documentary state under the direct guidance of the royal court. Many of the processes at work

1. The distinction between comparative and connective history, drawn first by Karen Wigen, is discussed (and so characterized) in Lieberman 1997: 451.

there—translation, adaptation, philologization, documentation—remind us strongly of what was occurring at precisely the same epoch in the Kannada-speaking areas of the Deccan. It was this English vernacular literary culture that in the late eleventh century provided the model for Norman literati. Thereupon, partly in imitation of earlier vernacularizations, partly as an independent response to comparable historical forces, the production of new script vernaculars proceeded, from the early twelfth to the sixteenth centuries, in what we saw was a wave of advance across western Europe, from England to northern France, and again, from Occitania, Catalonia, and Castile to northern Italy and southern Germany. In all these places, a new written vernacular form was being invented, with Latinate learning everywhere mediating the invention while Latin models of literature provided a framework for the development of new forms of imaginative expression.

Over the same period, vernacularization in southern Asia radiated out to encompass nearly the entire Sanskrit cosmopolitan space from Gujarat to Java. Here, too, we can often perceive the impulse toward literary-cultural emulation—among southern Indian courts from the tenth to the twelfth centuries (Kannada and Telugu) and eastern Indian courts from the fourteenth to the fifteenth (Oriya and Assamese)—though sometimes we find what appear to be rather more independent responses to similar historical forces (as in Kerala in the fourteenth century or Nepal in the seventeenth). It was predominantly Sanskrit knowledge and texts that underwrote the literization of the vernaculars and many of their most dramatic inaugural—or what came to be regarded as inaugural—productions. Foremost among these were the new epics (especially *Mahābhāratas*) that appeared in a veritable flood, outfitted with new local forms and embodying a distinctively local aesthetic. Something similar occurred in Europe, too, with the creation of new heroic narratives like *Le chanson de Roland* and the *Poema de mio Cid,* which gave way two centuries later to the more self-consciously classicized vernacular epic, such as Camões's *Lusíadas* or Tasso's *Gerusalemme liberata.* Between the two types, as if showing the way from the one to the other, stood Dante's Vergil.[2] Not only epics were being adapted, however, but many other genres of cosmopolitan literature. One literary event that suggests how deep are the structural homologies between European and Indian vernacularization, and how nearly synchronous, is the 1251 translation into Castilian of the Arabic *Kalila wa Dimna,* the celebrated "mirror for princes." The Arabic itself had been translated much earlier (via the Persian) from a Sanskrit original, which was in turn rendered into Kannada by Durgasiṃha in 1031 at the Kalyāṇa Cāḷukya court.

In both Europe and South Asia a gradual vernacularization of political

2. For an account of this literary history see Quint 1993.

processes can be clearly observed as well, most distinctly in the domain of documentary text production but also in the increasingly sharper definitions of geocultural landscapes in historiographical, philological, epic-narrative, and related forms of literary-cultural discourse. This has been illustrated so far only in the case of early Angelcynn, but it would be easy to do the same for many other times and places from the beginning of the epoch of vernacularization. When the troubadour poet Peire Vidal wrote, "With my breath I draw toward me the air I feel coming from Provence; everything from there moves me," and, more famously, when the Minnesanger Walther von der Vogelweide wrote, "To many a land I've paid a call / On the best my eyes I've gladly laid / . . . But it's German worth that transcends them all. / From the Elbe to the Rhine / and then back as far as Hungary / women dwell that far outshine / all that in the world my eyes could see," both poets were in an important sense *producing* a Provence and a Germany in a way that was impossible prior to vernacular literarization.[3]

The vernacularization of Europe was accompanied by a pronounced ambivalence toward a cosmopolitan order that simultaneously enabled the vernacular to speak literarily yet constrained it—the ambiguity being marked by centuries of appropriations from, imitations of, and defenses against Latin and its domination of literary culture. Vernacular paranoia was sometimes a response to a real threat. Educated Latinists and churchmen were often hostile to the idea of a vernacular scholarly and literary culture: in 1210 the University of Paris ordered the burning of works on theology in the vernacular.[4] A spirit of vernacular distrust and defiance is visible in South Asia, too, sometimes manifested as direct attack on Sanskrit, as in the case of certain Kannada literati of the twelfth and thirteenth centuries (chapter 10.4) or the Hindi religious poet Kabīr in the fifteenth, who famously contrasted the stagnant well water of Sanskrit with the fresh running currents of the vernacular. Here too, the paranoia was based on a real threat—of drowning, however, rather than burning (chapter 8.2). But far more often the defense of the vernacular in South Asia took a positive and reasoned spirit whereby language equality was not just asserted but demonstrated by theorization of a localized poetics that could meet the standard of the cosmo-

3. "Ab l'alen tir vas me l'aire / Qu'ieu sen venir de Proensa; / Tot quant es de lai m'agensa" (cited in Akehurst and Davis 1995: 24); "Ich han lande vil gesehen / unde nam der besten gerne war: / [übel müeze mir geschehen, / kunde ich ie min herze bringen dar / daz im wol gevallen / wolde fremde site. / nu waz hülfe mich, ob ich unrehte strite?/] tiuschiu zuht gat vor in allen. / Von der Elbe unz an den Rin / und her wider unz an Ungerlant / mugen wol die besten sin, / die ich in der werlte han erkant" (*Preislied* vv. 3–4, Maurer 1972: 80–82, slightly modifying the old translation of Zeydel and Morgan).

4. Zink 1992: 59. Wright 1996 offers a case study of Latin hostility to Romance in the person of Ximénz de Rada, Archbishop of Toledo.

politan order. This can be observed across the vernacular epoch, from the ninth-century *Kavirājamārgam* for Kannada and *Siyabaslakara* for Sinhala to the *Bhāṣābhūṣaṇ* (Ornament of the Vernacular) for Brajbhasha, a mid-seventeenth-century work composed by Jasvant Siṃh, king of Marwar, and modeled on a variety of Sanskrit texts, in particular an eleventh-century Sanskrit rhetoric, the *Candrāloka* of Jayadeva. If in both worlds the vernacular was equally felt to be in need of "ornamentation" or "illustration," the vernacularity of the Indian philological projects, very much in contrast with the importunate assertiveness of Dante or Du Bellay, was rarely argued out; except in its title, the *Bhāṣābhūṣaṇ* is silent about its purposes.[5] Even at this point in the history of courtly Brajbhasha, it all seems to have gone without saying.

In the sphere of grammar, greater linguistic distance from the cosmopolitan language—a more pronounced sense of difference and relative "alienation" from the superposed dominant that made philological definition of the regional language cognitively easier and perhaps more necessary—seems to have conditioned developments in South Asia and Europe in comparable ways. Thus it was in ninth-century England under King Alfred that one of the earliest grammatical cultures was promoted, providing the background for Ælfric's English *Grammatica* a century later (995), and it was in mid-twelfth-century Iceland that the first Scandinavian phonology was produced (the *First Grammatical Treatise*). A Castilian grammar, by contrast, did not appear until the very end of the fifteenth century (Nebrija's *Gramatica Castellana* in 1492), and an Italian grammar not until the beginning of the sixteenth (Fortunio's *Regole* in 1516). Similarly, although Kannada and Tamil (and perhaps Telugu) were grammaticized by the middle of the eleventh century, no north Indian vernacular was the object of any kind of linguistic analysis prior to European expansion. Latin models (whether Donatus or Priscian) powerfully shaped both English and Romance grammars, the latter in particular straining to squeeze their materials into Latinate paradigms, precisely as Sanskrit norms influenced precolonial grammars of the south Indian languages. (Vernacular grammarians seem to have tried to minimize this misfit by affiliating themselves with Śarvavarman's non-Vedic *Brief System* rather than Pāṇini's *Eight Chapters*, but this affiliation only provided justification for the grammaticization of nonsacral language; the basic incompatibility of linguistic systems remained.) A more general European vernacular theorization was developed unexpectedly first in Italy, the Latin-nearest region, while in South Asia it was initiated where we would expect it, in the Sanskrit-distant domain of Kannada at the inaugural moment of vernacularization. However,

5. The exception is v. 209: "I have written this modern work *(grantha navīna)* for the kind of person / Who is scholarly, skilled in the vernacular *(bhāṣānipuna)*, and clever with literary arts" (cited in Busch 2003, chapter 4).

Italy conforms to expectations in being one of the last areas to develop a script vernacular, and Latin-distant England in being one of the first.[6]

Although it has not been possible here to explore the grammatical materials concretely and examine the actual linguistic mechanisms at work, except for Kannada (chapter 9.4), the parallels in a broad array of microprocesses are equally astonishing. The more obvious include the widespread replacement of quantitative metrics by a prosody based on stress-accent and end-rhyme in Romance and north Indian *bhāṣā*s (with transitional experiments around the late twelfth century in both Latin and Sanskrit by, respectively, the Goliards and Jayadeva in the *Gītagovinda*). Less obvious but no less important is the highly regulated, almost statistically calibrated judgment on lexical choice among global and local possibilities, something that pertains across both regions even though in Europe no typology comparable to the Indic distinctions *tatsama, tadbhava,* and *deśī* was ever developed for conceptualizing this choice.[7] Again, the different genealogical relations that different vernaculars, "primary" or "derivative," bore to Latin—what Gramsci refers to as Latin's "molecular" influence on the former and "massive" influence on the latter—had consequences that need to be kept in mind here, precisely as in the case of Sanskrit.[8] There are some dissimilarities, too, at this level of comparison: the problems, both technical and ideological, encountered in establishing vernacular alphabets in Europe, for example, seem never to have arisen in India. The Indo-Europe parallel works at the level of macroprocesses, too, such as the asynchrony we have noted between north and south vernacularization, whereby, to speak generally and in gross language-family terms, Germanic Europe and Dravidian India may be contrasted with Romance Europe and Indo-Aryan north India in both the pace and the nature of their vernacularizing processes.

6. The unanticipated priority of Italian in vernacular theorization is noticed also by Apel 1980: 104. For Ælfric's *Grammatica* ("a close adaptation of the *Excerptiones de Prisciano*") and the development of an English metalanguage capable of explaining Latin (noted in chapter 11.1), see Irvine 1994: 413. On the Icelandic phonology, developed in the generation after the first literization (in the *Book of the Icelanders,* 1122–33), see Haugen 1972; on the methodological relationship between Latin and early French grammars, Lusignan 1986: 114. Regarding the late appearance of Italian grammar, Agamben notes that "Only the appearance of Latin as a dead language allowed the vernacular to be transformed into a grammatical language"—Latin's grammar-derived immortality having been compromised when the Quattrocento humanists had to resurrect it and thereby recognized its corruptibility (1999a: 43–61, p. 55 for the quote).

7. Perhaps this deficiency accounts for Bakhtin's erroneous view—erroneous certainly for India but also I think for Europe—that internal dialogization of discourse in the "poetic genres" "does not enter into the work's 'aesthetic object'"; the language "is a unitary and singular Ptolemaic world outside of which nothing else exists and nothing else is needed" (Bakhtin 1981: 285 ff.)

8. Gramsci 1991: 178.

The pervasive cosmopolitan influence on grammar, philology, and cultural theory more broadly conceived is symptomatic of the far-reaching dominance that both Latin and Sanskrit would continue to exercise in the intellectual sphere. In neither realm did the vernacular revolution extinguish the cosmopolitan knowledge formation. Information, whether philosophical, scientific, or theological, was less susceptible to vernacularization than imagination. (Furthermore, imaginative literature too would continue to be produced in Latin and Sanskrit, entropically and in a more or less nostalgic spirit, up to the threshold of modernity.) In the domain of philosophy, Latin remained dominant in England and France until the latter half of the seventeenth century. The first important work in English, Bacon's *Advancement of Learning*, was published in 1605; the first in French, Descartes' *Discours de la méthode*, in 1637 (though both were translated soon afterward into Latin). The vernacularization of systematic knowledge never occurred to the same degree in India, and Sanskrit would remain dominant among Hindu scholars for another two centuries, until those who had read Bacon and Descartes—the European colonialists—contributed to its final displacement in the nineteenth century.[9]

This remarkable set of parallels serves more to index the pressures that cosmopolitan cultures continued to exert than to point up the particularities of vernacularization. The latter reveal themselves more clearly when we chart instead the differences that mark the European and South Asian experiences. This enables us quickly to perceive that however similar in their lineaments the two historical transformations appear to be, the conceptual foundations of vernacularization, its social and political uses, and thus its meanings to the participants are often radically different in the two cases. Neither should be taken as constituting the paradigm of historical development of human societies against which the other is to be reckoned a deviation or deficiency. Instead, their differences provide the materials for rethinking the models that currently do inform our theories of culture and power.

One startling and unanticipated contrast between South Asia and Europe pertains to the affective conditions for vernacularization. It was earlier noted (chapter 8.3) that nowhere in South Asia before colonialism did the emotive and naturalizing trope "mother tongue" find expression. Nowhere do we hear a discourse of friendship or love toward the vernacular; there is nothing comparable to what Dante called the "natural love of one's own speech," or to the passion the *Convivio* exhibits on the question of vernacular attachments. Think only of how language naming in South Asia serves to remove the vernaculars from the realm of tribal affections and affiliations characteristic of European language appellations. The cosmopolitan codes of India were named for language-specific processes of grammaticality—

9. For details see Pollock 2005c.

Apabhramsha (decayed), Prakrit (natural), Sanskrit (perfected). The names for the vernaculars, for their part, seem as a rule to abstract them from the domain of the group and locate them in what seem almost ecospheres. If we take seriously the term for the vernacular, *deśa-bhāṣā,* "language of Place," then we must conclude it was far more often region that made a language (and a people) than the reverse. "Kannada" thus betokens the language of the "cultivated land of black soil"; Malayalam that of the "sandalwood mountains"; Dakani that of "the south"; Brajbhasha that of the place of Kṛṣṇa's birth; Gwaliyari, Bundeli, Sindhi, and so on the languages of those places. In Europe, by contrast, language names reflect facts of biology and ethnology and so belong to peoples, like French, the language of the Franks, or English, that of the Angles. It is no accident that in its historical semantics the term *deśī,* the cultural practices of Place, which was used to reference the new culture-power complex of the vernacular millennium in southern Asia, should contrast so dramatically with the trope of biological descent used in Europe (e.g., *natus,* "[in]born," yielding "native," and ultimately "nation").

Related to the matter of nomenclature is the widespread production in European discourse of the High Middle Ages, once literary vernacularization was fully engaged, of what have been called ethnic origin-paradigms or *mythomoteurs,* what Max Weber called ethnic fictions. These may be seen as a logical corollary of the prevalent belief—as the epigram of a tenth-century Christian poet has it, starkly contrasting with the Indian view—that "a language makes a people" *(gentem lingua facit).* The more the vernaculars took on conceptual and terminological unity and reality, as a direct consequence of literization and subsequent employment in literature, the more this ideological linkage between language and ethnicity stimulated a genealogical passion. No synthetic account of these myth elements appears to exist; taken as an ensemble, however, the late medieval speculations on the Greek sources of the Spanish language, the Germanic-Frankish sources of French, the Celtic-British sources of English, the Etruscan or even Aramaic sources of Italian—and more, the new historical origin tales tracing the French to the Trojans (end of the twelfth century) or the Scots to the Scythians (1320)—suggest that some widely shared and formative cultural-political conception was in operation. (This *topos* may have been borrowed from the ethnic fiction of the Romans themselves, who from the beginning of the imperial period sought a noble line of descent in the heroes exiled from Troy, as if expansion of empire were simply returning home.) To these may be added the connected historical accounts of kingdoms and peoples that emerged at a very early date in the vernacular epoch. Several have already been mentioned, such as the *Anglo-Saxon Chronicles* (end of the first millennium), the Alfonsine *Estoria de Espanna* (c. 1270), and the *Grandes chroniques de France* (late 1300s). Their ethnopolitical idiom is expressed as clearly as anywhere in the earliest among them, the tenth-century *Battle of Brunanburh* (incorporated in the *Anglo-Saxon Chronicles*). Athelstan's victory over the Danes is recounted: "Never before this / was there greater slaughter on this island / . . . since the Angles and Saxons / came upon these shores from the east, / sought Britain over the broad sea, / proud war-makers, overcame the Welsh, / the glorious nobles, to obtain the homeland." What all these discourses share is a concern with origins, purity of descent, and exclusion of mixture, as well as a sense of historical necessity and a growing conception of peoples as the subject of history—and therefore, perhaps inevitably, of peoples and languages in competition. By the sixteenth century, the struggle for preeminence among the vernaculars—Italian over French, French over English—had become as prominent a part of the intellectual landscape as the dispute among the disciplines in the medieval universities.[10]

The concerns of vernacular intellectuals in India were entirely different. It is true that only a fraction of the tens of thousands of texts composed by premodern Indian writers in dozens of languages have been read by modern scholars. But nowhere in the texts they have read is it possible to point to a discourse that links language, identity, and polity; in other words, nowhere does ethnicity—which for purposes of this discussion we may define as the political salience of kin group sentiment—find even faint expression. It is equally impossible to locate evidence in South Asia for the linkage of blood and tongue so common in medieval Europe, or for cultures as associations restricted by so-called primordial ties. In the case of Karnataka, "people of the *nāḍu,*" and even "Kannadiga" may have been created through literary representation, but at no time in the Kannada world—or anywhere else in South Asia that I can see—is it possible to perceive the production of "fictive ethnicity," where "the frontiers of kinship dissolve" and a new "circle of extended kinship" comprising "the people" comes into existence.[11] No doubt social forces such as caste endogamy, despite important challenges

10. On the *Ursprungsparadigmen* as speculation on language origins, see Garber 1989: 36; on *mythomoteurs,* Armstrong 1982: 129ff., and cf. Giard 1989: 221; for a more general political perspective, Black 1992: 111, Reynolds 1983 and 1997: 250–331. The tenth-century Christian poet is cited by Bartlett 1993: 198; see, more generally, Schulze 1996: 108. Analyses of three of the cases of ethnogenesis mentioned are provided in Czigány 1984: 20–22 (Hungary), Garber 1993 (Germany), and Brown 1998 (France; for its direct political instrumentality, Reynolds 1997: 282). Note Brown's discussion of the work of the *grands rhétoriqueurs* of early-sixteenth-century France, such as *Illustrations de Gaule et singularitez de Troye* (1510), where Francus, the son of Hector, is projected as the progenitor of the French people—a discourse that now occurs in French rather than the Latin that was common in earlier texts. On competition among languages and peoples, see Giard 1989: 210.

11. Balibar 1991: 93ff, especially p. 96.

throughout history like that of the Vīraśaivas, worked against integrative ethnicity. But whatever the reason, narratives of ethnicity and histories of ethnic origins of the sort that obsessed late-medieval Europe did not exist in any form in South Asia before the modern period.

Moreover, the choice of literary language was indeed a choice in South Asia even in the vernacular epoch and was never seen as the result of biological destiny, while vernacularization itself was most certainly not the "gradual, unself-conscious, pragmatic, not to say haphazard development" that some have seen in the European case (though even for Europe the characterization is dubious).[12] Speakers of Konkani or Tulu or Kodagu could and did choose Kannada for their expressive texts, and this was a pattern that repeated itself throughout southern Asia. To participate in an Indian vernacular literary culture was not at the same time to claim affiliation to a religious community of narrow construction or a kinship group of consanguineous necessity. And these literary cultures themselves demonstrated little concern for the "uniqueness" of "national character" that, though first postulated by Herder in the early nineteenth century, has been the fixation of European societies throughout the vernacular millennium. On the contrary, all appear to have striven for a kind of equivalence among themselves in part precisely by their attempts to approximate Sanskrit cosmopolitanism. The South Asian vernacular turn was not a quest for authenticity, nor was it informed by any kind of vision, historicist or other, of the unity of the folk. In fact, we find no explicit discourses whatever on the origins of peoples, dynastic lineages excepted. (Lineage histories do figure prominently in courtly vernacular works, though even here the genealogy of rulership was homogenized into the two lineages, "lunar" and "solar," that were prevalent across cosmopolitan space.) We find no remotely comparable discourse on vernacular language origins either. One is hard-pressed to identify a single instance of the propagation of shared group memories or narratives of common descent.

At the level of language ideology, a profound contrast pertains to the attitude toward language multiplicity in Christian Europe and in southern Asia. In the former, multilinguality was long tainted with the guilt of diversity: Babel marks an original sin, and European cultural politics over much of the vernacular millennium can arguably be interpreted as expiation of this sin through a project of reduction and hence of purification. Throughout the fourteenth and fifteenth centuries, as a recent survey shows, conquerors attempted to suppress this language or that (English at the hands of the French, for example, or Polish at the hands of the Teutonic Knights), and subjected peoples were forced to adopt this language (Polish speakers German) or were prohibited from using that one (English

12. Anderson 1983: 45.

speakers Irish). This attitude persisted into modernity, becoming more deeply informed by a political principle. For the Jacobin Abbé Gregoire in 1794, France was still "at the Tower of Babel," and bringing men closer to the truth demanded a common language and the "eradication of dialects."[13] In South Asia, although forms of will-to-power in the realm of language, and even narratives of language decay, are certainly to be found, no one ever mythologized the need to purify—let alone actually sought to purify—original sins of diversity through a program of eradication. Diversity was not a sign of divine wrath, nor was multilinguality a crime that demanded punishment. And if in practice vernacularization did lead eventually to the erosion of multilingual capabilities, along with the rise of incommunication, it was never explicitly or implicitly promoted in opposition to other languages. On the contrary, the image of Someśvara of Kalyāṇa in 1131, at his court in the heartland of Kannada culture, listening to songs in a half-dozen languages from Avadhi to Oriya, suggests even a kind of cosmopolitanization of the literary vernaculars for which early European parallels, even inexact—for example, Charles V's celebrated multilinguism (Spanish for speaking with God, Italian with women, French with men, and German with his horse)—are not easy to find.

Whatever else may have played a part in the revolution in European literary culture—certainly political elites were everywhere a driving force (other factors are considered in section 2 below)—the religious element appears to have always contributed. In fact, there seems to be an overdetermination of literary vernacularization by religious vernacularization. It was translations, adaptations, and imitations from Latin religious literature that often signaled the beginning of the vernacular turn. This is the case in what we now call French: starting with the *Sequence of St. Eulalie* in 881, all of the (relatively few) literary texts preserved to the end of eleventh century are religious poetry (saints' lives, miracle stories, prayers in verse, edifying tales). The same dynamic of religious translation and adaptation holds true for German, beginning with the *Heliand* in the ninth century and reaching a high-water mark in the sixteenth century with Luther's Bible. Evidently in the early centuries the place of religion in vernacularization had much to do with the Church's monopoly on literacy and its definition of what was worth committing to writing, as well as the role of missionizing and the uses of reading in that venture. But a larger confluence of communicative, social, and political factors eventually made itself felt, including the growing decay of Latin competence already in evidence by the ninth century (most dramatically and explicitly announced in King Alfred's vernacular writings), the desire for easier access to

13. On Gregoire's policy of *écraser les patois,* see Grillo 1989: 24; more generally, Certeau et al. 1975, and Bell 1995. For the fourteenth- and fifteenth-century materials, see Bartlett 1993: 202–3.

religious knowledge and simplification of religious practices, and the assertions of religious individuality on the part of European rulers.[14]

In the South Asian case there is no reason to believe that Sanskrit communicative competence diminished to any appreciable extent anywhere, even including Southeast Asia (with the exception of Cambodia after the Angkor polity). This was certainly the case for south India during the entire period considered here (800–1500), and it seems to have been largely true for north India as well. Undoubtedly Sanskrit literary culture in the north was challenged by various new or newly intensified sociopolitical developments from about the twelfth to the fifteenth century, such as civil chaos in Kashmir, or disruptions in traditional patronage networks in places like Kānyakubja and Vārāṇasī during the consolidation of the Sultanate. But no evidence points to a widespread decline in Sanskrit proficiency, and in fact the efflorescence of Sanskrit science and scholarship in the succeeding period suggests just the opposite. Italy in the fourteenth and fifteenth centuries, on the other hand, may present a typical case where the loss of Latin learning among a section of the nobility and bourgeoisie prompted both the translation of Latin texts into the vernacular and the creation of a body of vernacular literature.[15] The pioneering vernacular intellectuals in southern Asia, however, did not choose Kannada, Gujarati, or Javanese because they could not write in Sanskrit, or because audiences could no longer read or comprehend Sanskrit—and certainly not because they were at last paying heed to some archaic religious injunction to use the vernacular for proselytization. They had other, less instrumental purposes in mind, and less familiar but evidently meaningful values such as vernacular distinction and aesthetic difference.

It is precisely in the area of religion, especially religion in conjunction with political power, that things look so unexpectedly different. In comparison with western Europe, religion in South Asia was largely irrelevant to the history of vernacularization. Consider for a moment a small but telling contrast in the semantics of the term "region." The Kannada term *nāḍu,* "area" or "locale" (from the verb *naḍu,* "to fix firmly in the ground," "to make an establishment"), which played an important role in the construction of a vernacular polity in the Kannada-speaking Deccan, has as an antonym *kāḍu,* uncultivated forest.[16] The operative metaphor involved in this concept of re-

14. The relationship between Latin competence and vernacularization is more complicated than this suggests. In Norman England, for example, Latin experienced its greatest efflorescence precisely at the time French literature was being invented.

15. Kristeller 1984.

16. As noted in chapter 9.2, *nāḍu* is embedded in the very name "Kar-ṇāṭa[ka]" and in this shows itself to be rather different from the Tamil *nāḍu*s (autonomous peasant microregions, Stein 1980). Yet a distinction similar to the one in Kannada is found in Tamil in the later me-

gion evokes human labor and (agri)cultural transformation; counterposed to the places of the social world were the spaces of the natural world. When the poet Pampa claimed the title "Teacher of the *nāḍu*" by his literary achievement, he had in mind a cultural as much as a political place, a regional world that one teaches, or cultivates, as well as rules, and that exists as much through literary circulation as through dominion. The semantics of political place in Latinate Europe contrast markedly: although the English word "culture" itself still bears an ancient resonance of labor on the land (from Latin *colo*, to till, cultivate), the term for region, *regio*, bespeaks a religious act of the *rex* that produces what it decrees.[17] In these two worlds the power to turn space into place, and the concomitant significance of place, was embodied in radically different forms of social agency.

Doubts were raised earlier about the dominant view that religious sentiment was the driving force in primary, cosmopolitan vernacularization in southern Asia (chapter 10.4). In the majority of cases—from Assamese and Gujarati to Kannada, Malayalam, and Telugu—literary production in the vernacular was from the beginning, and at least up to the onset of what I have called regional vernacularism, as much or more concerned with the terrestrial than with the transcendent. In fact, this dimension of the cosmopolitan vernacular, and the *laukika*, "this-worldly," cultural and political values it represented, may have been part of what the regional-vernacular revolution was targeting. Evidence for this terrestrial orientation lies in the fact that Indian vernacularization showed little concern with making religious texts more widely available. In contrast to the European case, the most important or certainly the most sacrosanct Sanskrit scriptures, with the exception of the *Bhāgavatapurāṇa* (see chapter 8.2), were left untranslated. (The regional-vernacular movement produced its own scriptures to supplement or replace the Sanskrit ones in worship, prayer, and song: the Kannada Śaiva *vacana* that sought to establish a sort of counteraesthetic, Marathi hagiographies that themselves quickly became sacred texts, Bangla Vaiṣṇava lyrics and biographies of the religious reformer Caitanya.) Moreover, religious pluralism rather than individualism was generally characteristic of medieval rulership (a rare exception being Tamil country under the Cōḻas, c. 1000–1200, when

---

dieval period; see Ludden 1999: 148 ff., who also comments on the disintegration of the intelligibility of the binary during the agricultural expansion of the early modern period, when under new regimes of reclamation *kāḍu* took on the meaning of dry but cultivable land.

17. Bourdieu 1991a: 221. In other respects the spatial lexicon of Latin and the western European languages is permeated with images of military violence: "province," from *vincere*, to conquer; "district," from *distringere*, to restrain [offenders], etc. (see also Foucault 1980), unlike that of Sanskrit or Dravidian, which envisions space as an object of enjoyment, when not sheer geometry: *āhāra* (from *āhṛ*, to obtain a livelihood); *bhukti* or *bhoga* (*bhuj*, to enjoy), *bhāga* (*bhaj*, to share), *deśa* (*dik*, direction), *maṇḍala* (circle), *nāḍu*, *rāṣṭra* (*rāj*, to shine, rule), *viṣaya* (sphere, domain), etc. (see also Mulay 1972).

an assertive Shaivism held sway). Perhaps there is no more eloquent contrast between the South Asian and European vernacular worlds than that offered by Vijayanagara in the fifteenth century and first half of the sixteenth and that of the Holy Roman Empire after the Religious Peace of Augsburg in 1555: The Vijayanagara polity showed an egalitarianism in its patronage of religious communities as thorough as the indifference to religion it showed in its actual political practice (chapter 10.4). In Europe, the principle of *cuius regio, eius religio* held sway, by which every ruler, from Electors to local lords, was empowered to dictate the religious denomination of his territory. There is no question that the vernacular millennium in South Asia witnessed a dramatic regionalization of religious cultures, but a top-down determination of this process was not even a possibility on any Indian conceptual map.[18]

A final and crucial difference, possibly related to the highly marked status of linguistic diversity, concerns the long and explicit linkage in much of the West between power and language as ethnically conceived (according to the dynamic previous described). If the vernaculars often sought to recreate both the cosmopolitan culture and the empire form at the regional level (through the development of a classical idiom, the production of vernacular epics, and the like), this was never conceptualized as a cosmopolitan project. Instead, culture and power came to be conjoined in a way that, though rare before the second millennium—the linkage of the two in the Latin-Christian concept of *translatio studii et imperii* was only distantly comparable[19]—would eventually take on the character of normalcy. This conjunction was found across the landscape of Europe from at least the start of the fourteenth century (when Dante was still showing ambivalence about it, chapter 11.3). Wenceslas II in 1300 was offered the crown of Poland on the grounds that "it is fitting that those who do not differ much in speaking the Slavic language enjoy the rule of a single prince."[20] Whatever its original meanings may have been, the threat that Jeremiah has God make to the people of Israel—"I shall impose upon you a people whose language you shall not know" (Jer 5:15)—had become for Nicole Oresme, the early-fourteenth-century scholar and councilor of Charles V of France, a proof text for rejecting transnational imperial government: "And that is therefore something as contrary to nature as if a man should rule over a people who do not understand his mother tongue."[21] It is

18. On the principle *cuius regio,* see Schulze 1996: 130. For the symmetry of religion and polity in European thought more generally compare Tocqueville, "A côté de chaque religion se trouve une opinion politique qui, par affinité, lui est jointe. Laissez l'esprit humain suivre sa tendance, et il réglera d'une manière uniforme la société politique et la cité divine; il cherchera, si j'ose le dire, à harmoniser la terre avec le ciel" (1963: 168).

19. An interesting discussion of this concept is offered in Kermode 1975.

20. Bartlett 1993: 202–3.

21. And he enunciates this in French, not Latin: "Et pour ce est ce une chose aussi comme hors nature que un homme regne sus gent qui ne entendent son maternel langage" (cited in

clearly only a step from Oresme's discourse to the beginning of the "thin simplifications" represented by the Ordinance of Villers-Cotterêts two centuries later and its requirement that the "French mother tongue" be used exclusively in all judicial and administrative proceedings.[22]

The demand for a new symmetry between regional power and regional language raised by Oresme and fulfilled by François I was to be echoed time and again in the coming centuries. Lorenzo de' Medici, while still dismayed that his mother tongue was "somehow lowly and despicable," realized that it was "world events" that made languages great, and he encouraged his young countrymen to work toward strengthening Florentine political power by writing in the regional language of Tuscany. A generation later, Antonio de Nebrija argued out the relationship between vernacular language and power most explicitly in the dedicatory letter to Queen Isabel of his grammar of Castilian on the eve of what would turn out to be the most remarkable exemplification of the doctrine, Spanish colonialism.[23] The linkage found institutionalized expression from the sixteenth century on with the establishment of academies for the purification and disciplining of vernaculars: Accademia della Crusca in 1582—encoding the ideology of pure and impure language in its very name (*crusca* signifying chaff)—and the Académie française in 1635.

No Indian text before modernity, whether political or grammatical, even acknowledges any conjuncture of these two elements. Nor did the concern with language purity ever find institutional embodiment, whether in the political or the civil sphere. Nonetheless, just as South Asian poets held language discipline to be the highest virtue in literary culture, so South Asian rulers regarded the vernacular and its development with the utmost seriousness. Clearly something very different was in play in this world: power was obviously concerned with culture in vernacular India, as it had been in cosmopolitan India, but in some way no longer intuitively comprehensible to us.

The appropriation of a scaled-down version of imperial literary culture

---

Lusignan 1986: 111, who makes the larger argument that political decisions of the French kings marked every important stage in the development of the French language in the fourteenth and fifteenth centuries, p. 187). On language prohibition, extermination, and politics see Bartlett 1993: 202–3 (where the envoys to Wenceslas II are cited).

22. Elsewhere the shift to the vernacular in judicial and administrative contexts happened for different reasons. In Italy, vernacular language came to be used for great numbers of court and chancery documents without state mandate by the fifteenth century (Kristeller 1984: 19). On the "thin simplifications" of the modern state, Scott 1999.

23. Medici 1991: 103–14; Painter 1993: 68; and more generally Jones-Davies 1991: 153–67. To argue that Nebrija's efforts to *reduzir en artificio* the Castilian language "proceed from his vivid desire to see uniformity imposed, in the interest of conquest" (Paden 1983: 71; see also Joseph 1987: 46) seems overly teleological. A likelier explanation may be found in his vocation as professor of Latin at the University of Salamanca.

in a newly regionalized world produced a cosmopolitan vernacularism in southern Asia, but one without, it seems, the "vernacular mobilization" that the history of Western culture-power insists on as its necessary sociopolitical correlate.[24] It may simply be that at present we do not have the history or the social science to understand what other ends beyond such mobilization might have been or still are available or possible. Assessing the empirical data of the vernacular and its cosmopolitan complement for rethinking that social-science theory will occupy us in the last part of this book. What we do and do not know about its historical conditions of possibility we can address at once.

12.2 A HARD HISTORY OF THE VERNACULAR MILLENNIUM

Is it possible to understand the gradual abandonment of transregional in favor of regional languages for the creation of literary and political texts, along with the transformations in polity this choice both reflected and reproduced, as a connected Eurasian historical phenomenon? Can we identify a credible existing account, or provide a new one, to explain such transformations as a unified spatiotemporal process connecting Java to England from the beginning of the second millennium through the following three or four centuries, by which time the basic structures of vernacular literary cultures were set in place? This would be a very tall order in itself. No less difficult are the theoretical questions such an account would have to address, concerning among other things the relationship between culture and power, and whether the variations in outcome—emergent political orders ranging in character from vernacular polities in some places to national states in others—can be brought under a single historical explanation.

No explanation seemed required for the consolidation of the empire form of polity and culture across this same space during the first millennium. This is so because both India and Rome had inherited their imperial models from Achaemenid Persia, and though they radically modified this model, each in its own way, empire was seen as the way things were even before the cosmopolitan epoch commenced.[25] On the other hand, the radical transformation of this world and the consolidation of entirely new regionalized culture-power formations demand some kind of causal account. This is even more the case when we add to the fact of the breakup of the old order the striking simultaneity, relatively speaking, of comparable events across Eurasia, and the density of the homologies, in everything from the microinteraction between cosmopolitan and vernacular registers and ideologies of philologization to

24. Smith 1990: 184; see the further reflections in chapter 14.2.
25. See Pollock 2005a.

the macroproduction of newly localized geospheres in literary texts and the growth of vernacular documentary states. And by causal account I mean an explanation based on human action. There is far too much evidence of agency in general and cultural-political choice in particular—visible in the often substantial time lag between inaugural inscription and the commencement of literary vernacularization, for example, or in the anxiety of vernacular intellectuals before the decision to write locally—to ascribe vernacularization to simple, let alone highly synchronized, evolution. (The very proposition that culture "evolves" is open to question, see chapter 13.1.) Nor can we rest content with positing some second-millennium Axial Age where analogous changes in culture and consciousness—or changes defined so broadly as to appear analogous—showed themselves everywhere and simultaneously for no particular reason.[26]

Even assuming that the multifarious instances adduced so far have been convincingly construed as kindred phenomena, constituting a coherent and unified conceptual object, the very idea that one grand historical explanation could tie them all together must seem preposterous, notwithstanding the genre of popular world history that discovers monocausal explanations in ecology, technology, or whatever. The understandable antipathy of the scholarly age, except among some biologists of language and culture, for such unified theories and totalizing explanations undoubtedly places constraints on us, as does abiding theoretical uncertainty concerning the very mechanisms of change, once simplistic materialist models are discarded. More serious problems are raised by the uncertainty about key developments in the historical period itself, especially in southern Asia from about 900 to 1200, or even up to 1500. Much of our most significant positive data for this period comes in fact from the products of vernacularization themselves, and clearly that process cannot easily be called upon to explain itself (even here no hypotheses are on offer, beyond the dubious premise of religious reaction). Structures of economy and polity have been far less studied, and the evidence for studying them is thin. All this may explain if not justify the fact that major new scholarly projects have effectively written the epoch of vernacular commencement out of what counts in Indian history.[27] If, by contrast, European historiography shows fewer areas of darkness, the problem of literary culture in relation to social and political power seems to have been ignored in the grand works of synthesis. We now know a great deal about the

26. This is not to belittle the contributions made by the best Axial Age scholarship (e.g., Eisenstadt 1989) toward our understanding of civilizational formations. But the Axial Age itself is far too diffuse and shapeless and unmotivated a phenomenon to admit of any good historical explanation.

27. The *Cambridge Economic History of India* begins in 1200; the *New Cambridge History of India* commences with Vijayanagara a century later.

lineage of the absolutist state and the history of the civilizing process, but rarely in the impressive body of scholarship of which these thematics are representative are the language and literary medium of such political and social processes described or analyzed.[28]

In view of these obstacles, it seems sensible here to attempt no more than a brief overview of some Eurasia-wide trends that might have created conditions under which the new vernacular choices in culture and power made better sense than the cosmopolitan choices of the past. This review assumes throughout the cogency of various components of a particular theory of cultural change, especially in relation to other kinds of change, which are more directly argued out in part 3.

The first of several striking temporal conjunctures between Eurasia-wide developments around the beginning of the second millennium and the commencement and intensification of vernacularization relates to the global integration of trade and commerce. Originating in the eighth century and intensifying through the eleventh, what has been described as a new world system came into being that eventually linked Bruges in western Europe to Hangchow in eastern China through intermediary nodes in South Asia such as Cambay and Cochin, creating a vast network of material exchange far more intense than anything previously known, including the Silk Road network of the first millennium. This international trade economy reached its climax by 1350 and began to disintegrate after 1400 under a series of major disruptions that produced a worldwide recession. Among these, the most significant sociopolitical upheaval was the Ming Rebellion and China's subsequent isolation from central Asia; most prominent among environmental disruptions was the Black Death (which however spared South Asia). The Indian subcontinent was fully integrated into both the West Asian and East Asian circuits. It profited greatly from the export of spices and finished cloth, with a balance of trade that would remain in its favor throughout the period. And like the rest of the world system, India experienced at its high point a powerful resurgence of urbanization and, accordingly, a stabilization of the various political centers mentioned throughout this study.[29]

Trade may not have played so direct a role for the agrarian communities of the central Deccan, where vernacularization was most intense during these centuries, as it did for southern Gujarat, Kerala, or the Coromandel coast,

28. In both Anderson 1974 and Elias 1994 the silence on the vernacular revolution is complete, as it is in the synthetic account of late-medieval Asian societies offered by Chaudhuri 1990.

29. See Abu-Lughod 1989 (especially pp. 268 ff.), from which much of this paragraph derives, and 1993. Kulke refers to "the resurgence of trade and urbanism around A.D. 1000," and as the title of his collection *(The State in India: 1000–1700)* shows, he takes this a key point of periodization, yet the date's significance is scarcely discussed let alone linked with wider Eurasian phenomena (Kulke, ed. 1995: 13; cf. 226 n.).

although the Rāṣṭrakūṭas' rise to power might be related to the upsurge in west-coast trade following the Arab conquest of Sindh in the eighth century, which marked the start of the new world system in the Indian Ocean. To be sure, there is evidence of the growing importance of overseas merchant guilds from the region. One such association from Karnataka, the Five Hundred Masters of the Ayyavoḷe, was established near the beginning of the vernacular transformation and continued until the fourteenth century, participating with increasing reach throughout this period in the great international trading circuit. Through its periodic meetings (called the gathering of "the Great Nāḍu"), Ayyavoḷe seems to have constituted a translocal social formation of a regionally coherent kind. Equally important, it declared its cultural commitments in a set of remarkable inscriptions in courtly literary Kannada.[30] Even more important than the simple increase of trade was the impact of these worldwide economic developments on agricultural production. With the commencement of the age of vernacularization an expansion of agrarian territories began simultaneously all across Eurasia. In South Asia in particular, scholars now regard this as a moment of historic significance, when the interactive expansion of agricultural and dynastic territories produced the basis for all the major agrarian regions of the subcontinent. Indeed, the epoch up to the end of the thirteenth century has been called the "crucial formative period for agrarian history in the subcontinent."[31]

If the economic history of the age of vernacularization is becoming increasingly clear, the causal relationship of these material changes to the cultural transformations themselves is far from self-evident. Scholars of the precapitalist world system rarely concern themselves with cultural change, and few cogent hypotheses are available even for Europe. One recent study, while correctly dating the key developments in the differentiation of the Romance languages to the period 1000–1300, is unable to offer any convincing argument linking economic growth or political regionalization and centralization with developments in literary culture. Instead, vernacularization is seen as a functional response to a new need "to keep in touch throughout large regions," while the terminological identification of the new vernaculars, especially those that were "culturally and politically important," is vaguely ascribed to the changes in the "fabric of society."[32] And indeed, it is not easy to move beyond this vagueness. There is, for example, no obvious reason why urbanization and material abundance, whether in Karnataka or Tuscany, should require *vernacular* expression in either literary or political texts. A causal conjuncture between new wealth and new culture-power formations

30. The guild is discussed in Abraham 1988, especially pp. 45 ff.; the *mahānāḍu* in Dikshit 1973.

31. Ludden 1999: 77 ff.

32. Janson 1991: 23.

may readily be assumed, but why should these formations turn out to be regionalized—or, more surprising, aristocratic rather than mercantile, as the works of Pampa, the troubadours, and so many others show they were? (By contrast, the Indian-Buddhist literary culture of the earlier Silk Road age was mercantile and Sanskritic.)

The expanding global economy of the early second millennium with its impact on the formation of states and regional cultures may well have constituted a "second, medieval revolution,"[33] but any explanation based on this revolution must account for the fact that regionalization and vernacularization began in earnest in some places, such as Karnataka, in the ninth century, before this system was fully formed, and in many other places, such as the Hindi heartland, no earlier than the fifteenth century (in Nepal and Cambodia, even later), long after it was disrupted. (Moreover, some scholars implicitly question the system's historical importance: in Southeast Asia, many areas of which participated fully in the world trading network, the truly consequential material developments, in commerce, urbanization, and the like took place in the fifteenth century, again long after the network had disintegrated.)[34] The precise contribution, then, of a newly flourishing trade network and an expanding agricultural sector to the origins and crystallization of the vernacularizing process remains obscure, and we may again be observing a case of concomitance rather than causality.

Moreover, a theory of cultural change based on the late-medieval world system certainly cannot account for the very different developments for literary culture in East Asia. While the region was an essential component of that system, with the sole exception of Japan there was a complete absence of vernacularization in the sense in which the term is used throughout this book. It is true that in Vietnam in the fourteenth or fifteenth century a demotic script was developed (*chū' nōm,* an adaptation of Chinese characters for the writing of Vietnamese sounds) by means of which Vietnamese literature was able to present itself in a non-Chinese form for the first time. The significance of this cultural-political move at the time may have been greater than it now appears, for it took place in a world where, as one scholar put it, the standardization of writing, like the standardization of wagon axles, was a metaphor for good government. And it occurred at a watershed moment in intellectual-political history when a localization of Chinese cultural materials, along with a nostalgic indigenization, was evident in a number of domains. Yet in terms of inau-

33. Ludden 1994: 9–10.

34. The polities of eastern Java (Kaḍiri, Singhasāri, Majapahit), for their part, seem to show a new kind of economic organization—mixed agricultural-maritime—but it is unclear what other kinds of social or political transformations took place in the so-called post-*pralaya* period, when the central plains were abandoned for the east. Lieberman 1993; 1997: 449 ff., and Reid 1990 place the critical moment of discontinuity in the fifteenth century.

gurating a new cultural politics, this innovation essentially died on the vine. The full vernacularization of Vietnam—like that of Korea, despite the development there too of a demotic writing system in the mid-fifteenth century owing to King Sejong's reforms—would be the project of a derivative modernity. Indeed, the breakthrough to vernacularization was absent throughout the Chinese world, including in China itself. There the maturation of a written "vernacular Sinitic" would not occur until the May Fourth Movement of 1919; for the preceding millennium, "the amount of unadulterated writing in the other vernacular Sinitic topolects and languages is so pathetically small as to be virtually nonexistent."[35] What was determinative in East Asia was obviously not economic change but the specific character of the imperial polity, its language politics, and its neo-Confucian ideology.

The period 1000–1400 saw not only the consolidation of a great precapitalist world system and the expansion of agriculture throughout Eurasia but also the rise of new nomadic empires, like that of the Saljuq Turks in the eleventh century and that of the Mongols in the thirteenth, based in and radiating out from central Asia to southwest Asia and central Europe. It may be questioned whether defining the entire epoch by the rise of these political formations, as various new periodizations of Eurasian history invite us to do, is fully warranted.[36] It is nonetheless true that the existence of these empires did much to secure the new transregional trade system. But their historic impact might have extended even further. Although the evidence (and the argument) is not entirely clear, the new spatial identities of Europe and South Asia may have owed something to the nomads' Eurasia-wide migrations during the early part of the vernacular millennium. To be sure, the two regions differed sharply in their ability to deal with the nomadic migrations: Western Europe succeeded in excluding them precisely at the time when South Asia became most open to their advances, culminating in the establishment around 1300 of a powerful new conquest state in the north of the subcontinent, the Delhi Sultanate, by Turkic tribes (Khaljīs, Tughluqs, and others). Yet some scholars have detected in response to these migrations a "parcelization of space" in both Europe and South Asia, producing mutually exclusive units of territory governed by ever more uniform political orders (who often adopted the superior war technology, especially cavalry, from the nomadic peoples in order to consolidate their rule).[37] This characterization fits well with the image of culture-power projected in the texts of the vernacular epoch, with their new, spatially limited polities and liter-

35. Mair 1994: 707, 725, 730 (his argument regarding Buddhist missionizing and vernacularization [see especially p. 722], however, is erroneous for southern Asia). For Vietnam, see Wolters 1988: 27, vii, 31–32, and Nguyen The Anh 1996: 113–39.

36. See for example Bentley 1996: 766–68.

37. Gommans 1998, especially 132–22.

ary cultures of Place that unified the language of the region and textualized, so to speak, the region of the language through new representations of territorial coherence. But once again, whereas the outcomes are comparable, the proximate causal factors—the nomads' defeat on the one hand, and their success on the other—are diametrically opposed. Also left unaccounted for in this explanation is the vernacularization of Southeast Asia, where no direct role can be ascribed to pastoral nomadism for the vernacular innovations of tenth-century Java or fourteenth-century Thailand.

To speak of the world system and of the rise of nomadic empires as these impinged on South Asia leads inevitably to consideration of the expansion of Islam as a factor in global change during this period. That the first three or four centuries of the second millennium constituted a major watershed in South Asian history is of course undoubted, but this historical fact has typically been conceptualized in religious terms as "the rise of Muslim power"; the new system of trade and the expansion and consolidation of agrarian regions have only recently come to be appreciated as shaping forces operating entirely outside the confines of religion. For a variety of intellectual and political reasons—many of them good reasons—there is a palpable reluctance among contemporary scholars to regard Islam itself as a substantialized agent of historical change (there is a preference instead to ascribe agency to particular trader groups or nomadic peoples who happened to be Muslim) or to think of its advent as either defining an age over against the archaizing Hindu and the modernizing colonial or as a universal solvent for all tough historiographical questions concerning late medieval South Asia. Undoubtedly the expanding nomadic empires and global trading networks were fostered as much by non-Muslims (such as the Mongols) as they were by the recently converted Turkic tribes (Ghaznavids, Ghorids, Khaljīs, and others) who were to transform South Asia. Yet it is also undoubted that there did occur an expansive movement of peoples under the ideology of Islam—a movement, as one authority has it, consisting of "well-executed military maneuvers directed by a central command . . . undertaken for quite rational purpose . . . [and] driven by powerful religious forces"—that to some degree coincided with the vernacular revolution in western Europe and southern Asia.[38] What the expansion of Islam may have contributed to the conditions of vernacular possibility therefore merits consideration here, however brief the narrative must be and however inexpert the narrator.

38. The quotations are from Eaton 1993: 10–11; his discussion on pp. 8 ff. usefully reviews the historiography of Arab conquests. Ludden 1994 shows the ambivalence about the role of Islam in explaining large-scale political and cultural change in South Asia: on the one hand the "second medieval revolution" is shown to be tied up with Muslim power (pp. 9–10 and 15), and, on the other, it is denied that the "rise of Muslim power" should function as the "one overarching theme" (p. 10).

Interactions with the carriers of Islam actually commenced in Europe and South Asia with striking simultaneity in the year 711, when Arab and Berber armies under the Umayyad dynasty of Baghdad took Gibraltar and, half a world away, Arab forces from Iraq rode into Sindh. The conquest of the western Mediterranean has been credited with profound and enduring consequences. Perhaps the first scholar to argue this out was Henri Pirenne in the early decades of the last century. His general thesis regarding the economic history of Europe, which, broadly stated, posits a retardation of the Mediterranean economy through what he believed was Arab obstruction of trade routes, enabling the rise of northern Europe ("Without Mohammad," he said famously, "Charlemagne would have been inconceivable"), has recently been reexamined and seriously questioned. But Pirenne's arguments regarding literary-cultural history have been ignored, though they retain considerable interest.

As Pirenne rightly points out, peoples moving into Europe in previous centuries, such as the Germanic tribes in the fourth and fifth, were assimilated into the culture of "Romania" (by a kind of "Romanization" described in chapter 7). In this respect, the eighth-century conquest was unprecedented. There was no such assimilation; instead a complete redirection of culture occurred, "a profound transformation where language was concerned." Much of what Pirenne goes on to assert can no longer be accepted in full. Although it is true, and importantly true, that Arabic eventually replaced Latin in North Africa, Pirenne was wrong to believe that an educated clergy and Latin disappeared from Spain after the conquest: ninth-century Córdoba knew a vibrant and literate clerical culture, that of the Mozarabs, whose extant writings fill several volumes. Latin did not suddenly "cease to be spoken about the year 800," and people were not "beginning to speak Spanish." In Francia, Latin as a spoken language had long been changing (as all spoken languages change), but it continued to be spoken as Romance, which was not conceptually constituted as different from Latin until the Carolingian spelling reforms of the early ninth century described earlier. The decay of Latin literary culture—something perhaps not unconnected with the decline of city life in the Mediterranean—had already been remarked upon by Gregory of Tours at the end of the sixth century, long before the Arab conquests. As for Spanish (or rather, Castellano), it would not even be created for another six centuries (and Español not until the sixteenth century). If it is largely true that "by the most curious reversal of affairs, which affords the most striking proof of the rupture effected by Islam, the North in Europe [between the Seine and the Weser] replaced the South both as a literary and as a political centre," traditions of Latin textuality nevertheless remained strong in the south. And at all events, the Arab conquests in the western Mediterranean were only one aspect of a vast movement of peoples in medieval Europe, including Vikings from the north and Slavs and Magyars from the east, who left in their wake widespread disruption of educational institutions in England, France, and Spain. All that said, Pirenne is pointing toward something consequential about these historical events in relation to the course and character of vernacularization. If the actual linguistic processes were more complex than he realized, the emergent Islamic states do appear to have constituted a new and powerful stimulus to language and literary-cultural development.[39]

It seems reasonably clear that the initial stages of vernacularization in northern Europe, occurring in King Alfred's England, had nothing directly to do with the expansion of Islam on its western frontier. In southern Europe, by contrast, the great moments of vernacularization, such as continental French and Occitan in the twelfth century and Castilian in the thirteenth, took place in an environment significantly marked by interactions with Muslim cultural-political formations in both the western and eastern Mediterranean, most powerfully during the Crusades. Some scholars have pointed to the general upsurge in vernacular textualization at just this period, especially of the *chansons de geste.* These poems, while addressing a range of local issues such as family prosperity and honor, explicitly thematize the Christian wars against the Saracens. Many of the songs in the important cycle *La geste du roi* (twelfth century), for example, have to do with Charlemagne's battles against the infidel, which have been said to embody the ideal of the Crusades.[40] The composition of the Oxford version of the *Chanson de Roland* is now generally dated to about 1100 (though it looks back imaginatively three centuries) and is closely connected with the spirit of the First Crusade (1095–99), strong echoes of which may be heard in the text (not least line 1014: *Paien [Sarrazins] unt tort / e chrestiens unt dreit,* "The pagans [Saracens] are wrong, and the Christians are right").

In Spain, the Reconquista, which ended around 1250, conditioned the environment within which the kings of Castile, especially Alfonso X, created Castilian as a language of culture and polity. *Poema de mio Cid,* the inaugural vernacular literary text, was shaped by much the same historical circumstance as the *chansons de geste*—including prominently, again, the Crusades. As one recent study describes it, "The example of Castile's great command in battle against the Moors was modernised and held up, very much in the way that the example of Charlemagne and Roland, campaigners against the Moslems of Spain, was held up by 'Turoldus' [putative author of the *Chanson de Roland*] for the French of about 1100, as the barons and armies sought recruits to hold Syria and Palestine against the Moslems." The only surviving written version of the *Poema de mio Cid,* dated to 1207 as we have seen (chapter 11.3), appeared one year after a papal bull was issued to encour-

39. Pirenne 1958: 274–78. I am aware of no good critique of the Pirenne thesis on literary culture; for the economic thesis, see Hodges and Whitehouse 1983, and Havighurst 1976.

40. Zink 1992: 78, cf. 78–87. On increased textualization, see Duggan 1989: 20.

age Christians to unite against the Muslims of Spain; arguably, the textualization of the poem was somehow connected with the recruitment of soldiers to the Christian armies fighting the Muslim south.[41]

Such facts, though the tip of yet another iceberg, are still only one dimension of a complicated picture of political and cultural interaction: Muslims had also served among the forces of Christian kings (in Leon, for example), and vice versa; the *Cid* is anything but an anti-Muslim tract; the splendor of Alfonso's cultural world resulted in part from his eagerness to recreate something of the glory of the Córdoba caliphate and from his appropriation of Islamic learning through translation; a number of features of Occitan literary culture, some argue convincingly, are unimaginable without literary communication with Arabic poetry.[42] Leaving aside the Church itself—which was no small influence, of course—nothing here suggests an attitude of hostility toward Muslims qua Muslims. Aside from the documented cultural influences, it seems hazardous to suggest any role for Islam in relation to western European vernacularization beyond the possibility that it contributed to a political and communicative context within which speaking literarily from a regional position—a position in Place—seemed somehow more urgent than speaking from a cosmopolitan location. Just this impulse appears to have been at work in later developments in central Europe, where Hungarian literati first produced a vernacular literary culture in response to Ottoman hegemony in the sixteenth century. The new cultural-political realities of the early second millennium seem to have elicited a multiple and hence vernacular response, rather than a unified and hence Latin one.

In South Asia, too, vernacularization in its inaugural stages developed without any direct connection with the expansion of Islam on its eastern frontier. Like England, Tamil and Kannada had well-developed literary cultures of Place by the end of the first millennium. Moreover, the effects of the Arab conquest of Sindh were of a rather different order from what occurred in the western Mediterranean. While the economic impact turned out to be substantial, especially in bringing the region into denser networks of exchange than had previously been the case (in particular by mediating the transfer of South Asian crop species to the West), Arab political power was largely confined to Sindh and seems to have had little measurable cultural impact. It would be another three centuries, around the year 1000, before vastly more transformative encounters took place with competitors for power from central Asia, leading to the establishment of the Sultanate of Delhi. The events of these later centuries did have cultural consequences in northern India that bring them into closer comparison with developments in southern Europe.

To be sure, not all of these consequences were related to the problem of

41. Smith 1983: 96–99.

42. On the last point, see Menocal 1987.

vernacularization. In South Asia, as to a lesser extent in Europe, the very presence of Islam seems on occasion—and in some tension to the regionalization of consciousness so often described here—to have prompted new constructions of *transregional* identities among cosmopolitan literati. The term "Hindu," for example, was used for the first time in fourteenth-century Sanskrit inscriptions as a (contrastive) self-identification in response to the presence of Turkic power. Similarly, it was in reference to Charles Martel's defeat of the Arabs at Tours and Poitiers in 732 that the term "Europeans" *(Europenses)* was first employed by an anonymous Latin chronicler of Córdoba; thereafter, "Europe" was frequently used in reference to Charlemagne.[43] The cosmopolitan culture that underwrote this new (and assuredly very superficial) transregional collective identity in South Asia was undoubtedly eroding in some areas in the north, though not necessarily in consequence of these political events. In Kashmir, for example, the production of most major forms of Sanskrit court poetry ceased after the twelfth century, but this seems to have resulted from internal processes of civic disintegration unrelated to the central Asian powers, whose control over the Kashmir Valley was not consolidated until the fifteenth century, and who in fact sought thereafter, with only mixed success, to revitalize Sanskrit culture.[44]

With the collapse of some important urban sites of cosmopolitan learning in the Midlands, such as Kānyakubja at the end of the twelfth century, the center of Sanskrit culture might well be said to have shifted southward to the sphere of the Vijayanagara empire from the late fourteenth century on, in a way not unlike the northward shift of Latin culture in the ninth century to Aachen. Few areas in northern India after the fourteenth century, aside from what had become the new frontier zone of Mithilā on the Nepal border, seem to have shown quite the same vitality of Sanskrit literary production as earlier until a revival set in during the early Mughal period—a decline hardly surprising given the widespread enfeeblement of the court culture that was required to sustain it. But the fate of Sanskrit literature and learning more broadly construed remains for north India a matter of scholarly disagreement and requires more intensive empirical study than it has yet received. There is little reason to believe that the reproduction of *paṇḍita* lineages, the real educational infrastructure of Sanskrit culture, was disrupted seriously enough to create a vacuum for the development of vernacular literary cultures. But of course, such cultures in India typically did not grow in a vacuum. Those who invented them were poets trained, and deeply trained, in Sanskrit. There was thus nothing in India analogous to the weakening of the Latin education system (assuming that did in fact occur), or to the various renaissances this weakening brought in its wake.

43. Talbott 1995: 700; See 1985: 42.
44. Pollock 2001a: 395–400.

While the impact of these events on vernacular literary cultures also awaits in-depth research, it may well have been substantial. It is only from the late thirteenth century at the earliest that evidence is found for literary production in any of the north Indian vernaculars; what we do not know, again, is exactly how this development relates to the social and political events of the epoch. There are dramatic instances of vernacularization largely contemporaneous with the expansion of Sultanate power and that actually remark on its presence, such as in Maharashtra. Reverberations of the rise of the new political powers, quite like those in the *chansons de geste,* may be heard in a wide variety of early north Indian vernacular works. These are sometimes very explicit and hostile, as in one early western Rajasthani text, the *Kānhaḍadeprabandha* of Padmanābha (1455), which purports to describe the events of Mahmud of Ghazni's sack of the great Śiva temple at Somnath in Gujarat four centuries earlier. Again, sometimes they are very muted, as in the vernacular *Rāmāyaṇas*, whose composition around the periphery of the Sultanate seems almost to shadow the Sultanate's expansion.[45] These cases, however, may once again mark only historical coincidence rather than consequence.

Possibly more consequential for the development of north Indian vernacular culture than any hostile interactions were the literary compositions that Muslim literati produced in Indian languages of Place. Scholars are only beginning to explore the wider influence of this literature, but it appears to have extended far beyond the audiences, courtly or Sufi, to which it was originally directed. The formative contribution to vernacular culture of these new immigrants would be remarkably analogous to the innovative role of the Śakas in the crystallization of cosmopolitan culture a millennium earlier (chapter 1.3)—and just as remarkably discrepant with European historical experience (including earlier experience, see chapter 7.2). The absence of Muslim participation in the nascent vernacular cultures of France or Iberia becomes especially striking and suggestive when measured against its presence in Hindavi, Kannada, or Tamil. There are indications that this aesthetic accommodation or convergence began as early as the eleventh century with Masʿūd Saʿd Salmān Lāhorī; it was certainly part of the oeuvre of Amīr Ḵhusrau in the early fourteenth century and of the collection of Bābā Farīd's texts a little later. At all events, the great Hindavi Sufi works of the late fourteenth and the fifteenth centuries, including Dāūd's *Candāyan* and Jāyasī's *Padmāvat,* did not go unnoticed by non-Muslim communities of readers and listeners, as the many non-Sufi adaptations indicate. There is little evidence, by con-

45. Pollock 1993b: 286–87 (alterity may not always be what it seems, of course: the patron of the Bangla *Rāmāyaṇa,* for example, was a Muslim, Rukannuddīn Bārbak Śāh, 1459–74; see Smith 1988: 38). The character of the political-military environment of early Marathi vernacularization is suggested by a passage from the *Smṛtisthala* translated in Feldhaus and Tulpule 1992: 92 ff.

trast, of active cross-community literary communication during this epoch in other areas, such as Gujarat or Andhra. At least we do not know at present whether the Gujri poetry of Shaiḵh Bahā ud-Dīn Bājan (d. 1506), for example, was read outside the Muslim community, or whether Dakani poetry found any resonance among Telugu writers.[46] It is uncertain whether the near-total absence of scholarship on such literary intercommunication—the legacy, it would seem, of a modern communalization of literary history and scholarship—is the cause of our ignorance or a consequence of the fact that this intercommunication did not take place.

The expansion of Islam on its western and eastern frontiers may accordingly supply an additional piece in the complicated puzzle of historicizing the vernacular millennium, though it also adds new complexities of its own. In some cases the consolidation of vernacular cultural-political orders may have been connected with the presence of the new competitors for power. War may have made vernacular polities as much as the vernacular polities seem to have made war.[47] Other kinds of interactions with Islamicate cultures suggest that more strictly literary processes were at work: emulation of and appropriation from literati who provided fresh forms and themes, as in twelfth- and thirteenth-century Sicily and Occitania, or who first demonstrated, as in fourteenth-century Avadh, the very possibility of vernacular literacy (part of a general civilizational tendency toward localizing Arabic literary modes), much as the imitation of eroding imperial formations had helped make possible the English and Kannada vernacular worlds three centuries earlier.

The precise weight of the contribution of globalizing Islam cannot easily be calculated because it was only one component of other, larger-scale forces at work in the same period—above all, the new world network of trade that enriched both South Asia and Europe and helped make possible the burgeoning development of agricultural regions and urbanization. All these Eurasia-wide factors may well have conditioned, in ways that await adequate clarification, the development of vernacular literary cultures. But the conceptual and political variations found in the outcomes of the vernacularization process—like the variations in the imperial political and cultural formations that preceded them and upon whose foundations they were built—show that people in western Europe and southern Asia reacted very differently to these forces. In these differences lie profound implications for political and cultural theory.

46. The works of certain religious poets such as Qāẓi Qādan in Sindhi or Bullhe Shāh in Panjabi were more amenable to circulation (see Asani 2003: 615 ff.).

47. I here adapt a phrase of Charles Tilly's (1975: 42).

PART THREE

Theory and Practice of Culture and Power

CHAPTER THIRTEEN

Actually Existing Theory and Its Discontents

13.1 NATURAL HISTORIES OF CULTURE-POWER

If the passing of the so-called master narratives that have shaped modern ways of knowing the world—accounts based on belief in the progress of scientific reason, for example, or human emancipation—is partly a result of discontent with their apparent claims to a monopoly on truth or their rigid laws of developmentalism, there is no little irony in the fact that they are being replaced, in some instances, by what might be called cultural naturalism as the explanatory model of change in the history of culture and power. To be sure, theories linking cultural change and biological evolution have a lineage reaching back into the nineteenth century; the confrontation between the scientization of culture and the resistance to the perceived political consequences of such scientization—especially the differentiation of cultures into more or less evolved—has a legacy almost as old as Darwin himself.[1] A steady increase in reformulations of the doctrine has recently become noticeable nevertheless, and whether these are directly articulated or simply implicit in the protocols of interpretation, they offer serious challenges to the explanatory frameworks commonly used in the humanities and social sciences. In such reformulations, focus on the practices of everyday actors knowledgeably engaged in social action, such as choosing among different forms of cultural or political practice under specific historical conditions, cedes place to causal models derived either from the natural sciences, especially evolutionary biology and ecology, or from the study of technological change, which itself is often combined with evolutionism. The turn to

1. See Fracchia and Lewontin 1999. The issue of *History and Theory* in which their article appears is titled "The Return of Science: Evolutionary Ideas and History."

cultural naturalism is especially common (and perhaps not unexpectedly so) in explaining large-scale transformations—the cosmopolitan transformation of the world, or its later vernacularization, would be perfect candidates. And here cultural naturalism carries considerably more stultifying political consequences than the projection of inequality inherent in the older Darwinian model.

In literary studies, a new kind of cultural history has been offered that maps literary-cultural change against what is seen as the evolutionary tempo of physics and technology. Technological change, such as printing, is here conceived of as the sole locus of human evolution as it now exists, as well as the driving force behind both cultural change (such as "new communications situations") and ideational change (such as new collective mental structures). While few scholars are likely to accept this entire package, many adopt one component or another. Perhaps nowhere in contemporary thought does this explanatory model find more powerful expression than in the systems-theory sociology of Niklas Luhmann. Here a similar evolutionism to what we encounter in the literary theory just described (which in fact was adapted from Luhmann) is extended to social change at large and over the long term. Techniques of "communication dissemination" (speech, writing, print) are thus correlated with forms of "social-system differentiation" (segmentary, stratified, functional) across the historical spectrum. This pair, communications media and system differentiation, constitute in their interplay the core of culture-power change. This change happens, so it seems, through a kind of autopoiesis or, more simply put, through the internal dynamics of the system itself.[2]

There is no denying that innovation in the material technologies of literary culture played a pivotal role in the transformations charted in this book. It was precisely because of the reproducibility offered by the new manuscript culture, or so I have argued, that Sanskrit *kāvya,* and likewise Latin literature, took on their peculiar character. While admittedly remaining a cultural form that was fully realized only in public performance, *kāvya* was created through the power of writing. And as textual criticism makes clear, large-scale works were from the first preserved and circulated exclusively in a written and hence more or less stable embodiment, and not in an oral and hence widely variable one. As for vernacularization, the factor that allowed it to exist

2. On technology and cultural change, see Gumbrecht 1988: 19ff. An evolutionary model of literary history has recently been proposed in Moretti 2004 (though this fits poorly with the "deliberate human effort" he cites on p. 54). I must forgo here any discussion of memetics, its relevance to my problematic notwithstanding. My brief remarks on Luhmann are based on Luhmann's 1985 essay (cf. Gumbrecht's discussion, 1988: 20); I make no claim to having come to grips with his complex, at times impenetrable, oeuvre (especially Luhmann 1995 and 1998). Parallels between systems analysis and structuralism are explored in Holub 1994, who also comments on the deep antihumanism of both social theories.

at all as a historical event, both for the primary actors involved and for us later observers, and that rendered the prevernacular past prevernacular, was again writing—or more precisely, what I have called literization and literarization, which can both be thought of as at once material and social phenomena. A world of local oral poetry of course existed long before and continued to exist long after the vernacular revolution, but it was now separated both in sociological and aesthetic terms from the world of vernacularity (it was retroactively constituted as a world of "song," not of literature; chapters 2.2, 8.2). A similar analysis of communication dissemination helps explain the nature of empire as well as of vernacular polity: the character of both was indissolubly linked to the rise of new documentary practices, and both derived a significant portion of their reality from the respectively wider and narrower spatial distribution and discursive character of Sanskrit inscriptions and inscriptions in languages of Place.

To some extent, then, developments in communications media and social-political "function differentiation" are indeed pertinent to an analysis of culture-power in South Asia's past. But it is also essential to realize that these developments cannot in any sensible way be characterized as natural or evolutionary. On the contrary, what we encounter everywhere is strategic choice, or strategic resistance. Whether or not vernacular languages may be said in some sense to have "evolved"—whether or not they are as much biological as social phenomena, whether or not there will ultimately be found a language organ or grammar gene—vernacularization itself, as the process has been understood here, was a cultural-political decision and often a fraught one. It entailed abandoning a cosmopolitan code and radically transforming local language practices in accordance with the expressive norms of that dominant model, and it meant applying to those practices a certain technology, writing, that had never previously been applied to them.

This sort of decisionism, or culture-making in consequence of deliberate choice, marks all instances of vernacularization, though it is not of course unique to vernacularization as such; it marks cosmopolitanization, too, for here people consciously abandon intimate, seemingly innate cultural practices in favor of new and learned ones. Buddhists of the early period (and if we are to believe the Vinaya account, discussed in chapter 1.2, the Buddha himself), having decided to eschew Sanskrit for their oral scriptural texts, chose to revoke that decision around the beginning of the Common Era, under what appear to have been radically new political conditions introduced by the Kuṣāṇa empire. The very act of permitting Sanskrit to speak openly in the everyday world was itself a decision (on the part of the Śakas, among others) made against the backdrop of centuries of its public silence. My contention about this silence is not just an argument from silence, so to say; it is demonstrable from the mid-third century B.C.E., when the voice of polity was a Prakrit voice, but it is inferable even earlier from the hieratic-scholastic seclusion in which the Sanskrit language was held. Even as poets eventually decided to shatter this seclusion and produce expressive and other nonsacral texts in Sanskrit and, equally important, to commit them to writing, participants in many other areas of Sanskrit culture reasserted archaic practices of orality and exclusivity. Some, like Kumārila, the seventh-century Mīmāṃsā theorist, redoubled their insistence that learning the Veda from a concrete text-artifact—"by means contrary to reason, such as from a written text"—could never achieve the efficacy of the Veda learned in the authorized way, "by repeating what has been pronounced by the mouth of the guru."[3] It is especially when juxtaposed to such conceptions, moreover, that the first public inscription of political poetry in Sanskrit recovers the element of audacity, even scandalousness, that made history. The cultural-political act of the Śaka prince Rudradāman in the middle of the second century—which, if not actually inaugurating a new communications model, at the very least affirmed its acceptability and perceived efficacy in dramatic fashion—must accordingly be seen, like all the others, as a choice. It was contingent on events and circumstances, to be sure, but by no means was it merely a consequence of the availability of a technology. During the four centuries or more of literacy and public inscription prior to Rudradāman, no one—for the reasons that have been offered in chapter 1, or, if those are incorrect, then for some other, better ones—made the choice he made.

The history of literary language provides a good test of the naturalistic, evolutionary paradigm of cultural development that Luhmann conceptualizes so powerfully but that many accept as common sense without necessarily knowing his ideas. Students of South Asian and of European languages alike often imagine language change as occurring completely unmotivated by human interests, like the budding of trees in spring. Scholars tend to explain the Prakrits as evolving in a parallel (that is, sociolinguistically distinct) track with Sanskrit out of Vedic (or out of Sanskrit itself, if they have entered far enough into the Indian grammatical worldview); or Apabhramsha as evolving out of the Prakrits; or the north Indian languages of Place as evolving out of Apabhramsha; or Kannada, Telugu, or Malayalam as evolving out of "proto-Dravidian" as best attested in the *caṅkam* literature of Old Tamil. (Similar models can be postulated for European languages, with French, Italian, Portuguese, and Spanish thought of as evolving out of Latin, and Dutch, English, and German as evolving out of Germanic.) All this language evolution is thought to occur if not so much according to a formal Darwinian notion of natural selection and adaptation to environmental factors yet still phylogenetically, like one life-form from another. It is of course no accident

3. See chapter 2 n. 23.

that the two models of biological and cultural change are so closely associated: they emerged from the same matrix of late-eighteenth-century European empiricism, when language (like life itself) for the first time attained historicality—albeit a history devoid of intentional action.[4]

This image cannot be completely wrong. There is no question that language change has something mysterious about it, which is why it has preoccupied some very good minds for a very long time, and also why nonspecialists enter into the matter with some trepidation. There is also no question that its complexity cannot be accounted for by any monocausal model. Some change does seem entirely unmotivated: the postpositions in Hindi that replaced the morphological complexities of Old Indo-Aryan, or the *p*→*h* sound change in medieval Kannada, were no one's decision or invention. And if we look through the widest-angle lens of cultural and political change at the historical-philosophical question of structure and agency, it is no doubt generally true, as Marx wrote in the *Eighteenth Brumaire,* almost too famously to quote, that "men make their own history, but they do not make it as they please; they do not make it under self-selected circumstances, but under circumstances existing already, given and transmitted from the past." Yet the evidence available from premodern South Asia suggests that some other principle, not encompassed by a mechanistic evolutionary paradigm, was involved in the observable transformations of many features of language change—lexicon, orthography, and others—and indeed, in the constitution and development of literary cultures generally speaking. In fact, such evidence as this goes some distance in helping us decide among the various hypotheses seeking to account for large-scale language change.

A useful restatement of the general problem and of the competing hypotheses devised to account for it, insofar as these hypotheses may be tested in South Asia, has been provided by the linguist Hans Hock. According to Hock, given variables are selected for generalization "as socially significant as a marker of group identification" on grounds that, from a linguistic perspective, appear to be wholly arbitrary. In fact, the process of language change is best seen as governed by social factors that are nonlinguistic, though these factors may often be difficult to specify: "Because in most 'post-mortem' analyses of linguistic change it is not possible to recover the social conditions which gave rise to it, we are in most cases dealing with an explanation only in principle: While the actual social determinants of the change may escape us, we can be quite certain that there was some such determinant."[5]

These determinants are not further specified by Hock, nor are any ex-

4. See for example Foucault 1970: 263–302.

5. Hock 1986: 648, 655. To extrapolate this Labovian prestige model to a world that is as distant as possible from Labov's New York City in the 1970s of course requires further argument.

amples provided of what might constitute social motivation. From among the determinants and motivations suggested in the foregoing pages of this book, three are worth considering here. First, in the constellation of language practices in which new immigrants to South Asia in the early centuries of the first millennium appear to have been positioning themselves, Sanskrit continued to occupy the place it had held for many earlier centuries: the language of the sacral sphere. Both the documentary and the expressive domains of the court, by contrast, were Prakritic (we know the Sātavāhana case best, and it is unequivocal), and it was in conjunction with the transference, to all appearances a dramatic transference, of Sanskrit from the sacral sphere to the world of political and literary practice that the Sanskrit cosmopolitan formation came into being. Second, certain non-*vaidika* religious communities, for their part, had long embodied other additional "social determinants," as indicated by the early avoidance of Sanskrit among Jains and Buddhists that eventually and completely yielded to the attractions of the new cultural order. Third, early-second-millennium courts sought to recapitulate the imperial aesthetic of the Sanskrit cosmopolis at the regional level, thereby producing a cosmopolitan-vernacular style in both literature and polity as a fundamental strategy of cultural individuation if not political self-identification.

It is this last moment that provides us with the most powerful evidence both for the voluntarism that underpins literary-cultural change in South Asia and for its nonlinguistic, social-historical determinants. We have repeatedly observed how, despite the fact that local language was literized wherever and whenever Sanskrit spread, vernacular literarization often followed only after a hiatus of centuries, in some instances as many as four (in the case of Marathi) or seven (in the case of Newari) or even ten (in the case of Khmer). Intervals of this magnitude—no mere artifact of preservation, since Sanskrit inscriptional materials from the same period have been preserved in abundance—are clearly not amenable to an explanatory model based on technological-evolutionary rhythms but rather point toward other kinds of constraints and opportunities for vernacular expression that are themselves various and complex, applying to Shudras (Tukarām) no less than to kings (Kṛṣṇadevarāya) and Brahmans (Eknāth, Śrīnāthuḍu, Nanddās) (chapter 8.2). For the materials of South Asian literary culture, mechanistic models make little sense; we find neither the kind of linkage that systems-theory imagines nor the kind of mechanical necessity that cultural evolutionism implies. Not only do people seem to have made cultural decisions with complete indifference to the logic of evolutionary efficiency, but technology, communication, and society clearly have far less orderly interrelations than any one formula could capture. Moreover, this history is everywhere sufficiently discontinuous and episodic to be only explainable as differential choices of cultural-political actors in response to differential cultural-political circumstances.

What we are seeing here is not an unwilled, blind, predetermined development of language, which branches out into vernacular diversity or converges into cosmopolitan unity the way a tree branches out or streams converge into the main current. The very conceptual scheme of evolution transferred from biology to language is wholly inadequate to the evidence of vernacularization and cosmopolitanization. For one thing, "acquired characteristics" in language obviously can be, and are constantly being, transmitted. For another, whereas some aspects of language change may vindicate the evolution metaphor—phonological and morphological mutation do seem to be random and to proceed according to some mechanical law; isolation of varieties does seem to lead to differentiation—a great deal of language change, as just observed, is entirely intentional.[6] People are not compelled to vernacularize—to develop alphabets and orthographies and written literature in local language—by evolutionary forces through some immanent program or directionality. They have reasons for doing so, however difficult it may sometimes be for us later observers to specify or understand them. The appropriate model, then, seems to be not the blind watchmaker, since users of language do not necessarily think they are constructing a long-term grand design called a language (it is only for the historical linguist that language is an intentional object), but, on the contrary, the sighted handyman, who knowledgeably puts things together in order to achieve immediate pragmatic ends. The history of cosmopolitan and vernacular language in South Asia is the history of people making choices about the use of phonemes, lexemes, registers, themes, genres, whole languages—or rather what through such choices thereby become "whole languages"—to achieve specific expressive and political ends. Even if we think of cosmopolitanization and vernacularization as class categories rather than events, the metaphor of evolution, let alone its logic, has no discernible place. To echo Vico once again: Human history, unlike natural history, has been created by human beings, and precisely for that reason it is something they can hope to know.[7]

Whether or not human linguistic diversity as such is a "fatality," at least with respect to the melancholy consequences for political orders that Benedict Anderson intended with this characterization, is a question that will concern us in the following chapter.[8] Aside from the interesting fact that even

6. More explicit discussions must exist of the limits to the biological metaphor than I have been able to find (one balanced assessment is McMahon 1994: 315–40). A good historical demonstration of its inapplicability is the work of Wright, e.g., 1991. The critical issue of intentionality is mentioned only once, in passing, in Fracchia and Lewontin's critique of cultural evolution (1999: 72).

7. Indian traditions are divided here. Mīmāṃsakas, who posited language as natural and eternal, would dispute Vico; Buddhists, who took it as social and conventional, would not.

8. Anderson 1983: 41 ff., especially 46.

in this least biblical of scholarly voices may still be heard the guilt of Babel—the sin of diversity and the perceived need to expiate difference that has haunted Western thinking about language and culture for centuries, but that India has never known—this statement is not, at least by one fair construction, quite true: diversity is not destined but produced. Just as only homogenous, empty space exists until it is segmented and differentiated and filled by the creation of those cognitive entities we call places, so Language—not languages—exists in a spectrumlike continuum and is only segmented and differentiated when languages become objects to be known and named and distinguished from one other. And among the most decisive practices whereby a language comes to be known, named, and distinguished from others is the production of literature. However much one may insist that even prior to their conceptual construction and discursive elaboration individual languages do exist in some real and fated sense, there is nothing whatever fated, unself-conscious, haphazard, or even gradual about the development of literary-language diversity. As is made clear at every turn in the history of literary cultures in South Asia, as also in Europe, diversity is something willed—and willed long before "nineteenth-century dynasts" were first "confronted with the rise of hostile popular linguistic-nationalism," as Anderson believes. And this is so because literature itself is willed.

Thus the vernacular literary languages we have studied here did not "emerge" like buds or butterflies at their fated biogenetic moment, whether through a natural process of linguistic evolution or a complementary process of linguistic decay on the part of cosmopolitan languages. They were made by acts of knowledgeable choice. Yet not many scholars seem willing to acknowledge the possibility that literary-cultural actors in the past chose to be vernacular, or cosmopolitan for that matter; and those who are willing seem to have done very little with the idea. One of the few clear acknowledgments comes from Mikhail Bakhtin (who states the matter with the customary humility of Western universalist theory): "The actively literary linguistic consciousness at all times and everywhere (that is, in all epochs of literature historically available to us) . . . finds itself inevitably facing the necessity of *having to choose a language*."[9] Yet what Bakhtin never seems to spell out, at least in adequately detailed historical terms for specific languages in the everyday sense (by "language" he often seems to mean socio-ideological registers), is what is at stake in this choice—what else in the social and political world is being chosen when a language-for-literature is chosen. For it is one thing to recognize that literary-language diversity is willed and quite another to specify the historical factors that go to shape the exercise of this will. If we examine the theoretical frameworks on offer that do try to provide such specification, more-

9. Bakhtin 1981: 295 (emphasis in the original).

over, we soon find that none of them is entirely adequate to the evidence of premodern South Asia. This is so, in part, because of false extrapolations made from European history about the place of language in society.

13.2 PRIMORDIALISM, LINGUISM, ETHNICITY, AND OTHER UNWARRANTED GENERALIZATIONS

There are a number of basic conceptions, derived from Western experience, about language as a social fact that seem problematic in light of the data on culture and power in South Asia gathered in these pages. Like so many of the big-ticket questions we are examining, these conceptions have been the object of extended reflection in social theory for a long time. It is possible to address only a few of the major issues and positions here.

Foremost among these conceptions is the conviction that language is a core factor, or even *the* core factor, in social-group identification, one that focalizes the group's emotional energy to a peculiar or even unique degree. Indeed, one might even say that for much social theory, language is assumed to be the object of a kind of cultural-political cathexis. There has certainly been enough in the history of European vernacularization to justify this assessment. Recall only the kind of desire and intense longing that Dante brought to the matter of language when he spoke in impassioned terms of "the natural love for one's own speech": "Not simply love but the most perfect love is what I ought to have, and do have, for [my vernacular]." One could follow the trail of this affective attraction, tinged by a certain anxious defensiveness, for the next half-millennium, to the point when (around 1920, on the eve of events that would prove him so tragically wrong) the German-Jewish philosopher Franz Rosenzweig could describe his attachment to his language as "thicker than blood." Even Antonio Gramsci was making a "national-popular" rather than a Whorfian observation when he wrote: "Every language is an integral conception of the world and not simply a piece of clothing that can fit indifferently as form over any content." These individual expressions of language devotion have been replicated, as we would expect, for social groups as a whole—here phylogeny recapitulates ontogeny—at least from the time of Herder, whose formulation of language with regard to the *Volksgeist* in 1784 is probably too familiar to need citing: "The best culture of a people cannot be expressed through a foreign language; it thrives on the soil of a nation most beautifully, and, I may say, it thrives only by means of the nation's inherited and inheritable dialect. With language is created the heart of a people."[10]

10. For Dante see chapter 10.2; Rosenzweig is cited in Klemperer 1987: 6; Gramsci 1991: 226. The most convenient source for Herder's *Materials for the Philosophy of the History of Mankind* is the online "Modern History Sourcebook," http://www.fordham.edu/halsall/mod/1784herder-mankind.html.

It is therefore also not unexpected that modern social theory has appropriated a view that sees "native language" as the fundamental feature of human existence. This is a conviction shared across the disciplinary and indeed political spectrum. The philosopher Charles Taylor is representative of a contemporary scholarly consensus when he asserts not only that language is the "essential viable and indispensable pole of identification" but that this identification is primeval and stands outside of history.[11] The centrality of language in the construction of social group identity was given particular prominence in social theory by the anthropologist Clifford Geertz in the early 1960s in an essay that effectively introduced the term "primordial" into discussions of national sentiment. Here Geertz borrowed from Edward Shils's idea of primordialism as comprising certain first-order "givens" of social life such as kinship or religious custom, which are invested by actors with a sense of deep historical continuity, in contrast to second-order civic sentiments of belonging such as loyalty to guild or party. Geertz confidently linked primordialism to language as one of those givens of social existence, possessing as he thought it does an "ineffable" power to coerce behavior: language attachment can function, or can be made to function, as a central component of social action. This kind of primordialism with respect to language Geertz termed "linguism," and he devoted particular attention to analysis of the phenomenon in India, where "for some yet to be adequately explained reasons" the phenomenon was "particularly intense." We should note that for Geertz primordialism is an analytical concept employed to make a sociological claim, namely, that actors behave as if "congruities of blood, speech, custom" have an "overpowering coerciveness in and of themselves." He does not employ it to make the ontological claim that such congruities are in fact real. The distinction saves the sociological value of the category in itself but does not necessarily save the conclusion that Geertz draws (again with the usual theoretical modesty), that "for virtually every person, in every society, at almost all times" such attachments are present.[12] At least it does not save the conclusion so far as linguism in India is concerned.

The empirical data Geertz found in India and upon which he based his theory about the particularly intense degree of linguism there were derived from a series of developments, indeed, political turmoil and sometimes violent social upheavals, related to the reorganization of union states on the basis of language in the mid-1950s. The process had begun already in 1921 when the Indian National Congress decided to order its regional activities according to "linguistic provinces"; eventually, the creation of language-based

11. Cited in Birnbaum 1996: 39. A salutary corrective with respect to the need for historical thinking is Appiah 1994, especially p. 156.

12. Shils 1957; Geertz 1963, on "linguism," pp. 110–13. I am not sure that Eller and Coughlan 1993 catch the distinction between the two types of claims.

states was added as a plank to the Congress's elector platform. Between 1956 and 1971 twenty-one such states were created in the union, with strong agitation accompanying the process everywhere. The elevation of Hindi to the status of national language sparked an even more dramatic and violent backlash, marked by self-immolations in Madras State in 1964–65. These developments did not come from nowhere, to be sure; we have seen how very tight was the premodern linkage, unfamiliar though it often appeared in its dynamics, among language, culture, and power. Yet the truly salient attitudes in both the political reorganization of states and the affective response to it—attitudes toward language purity, exclusivity, and singularity when coupled with bureaucratic rationality—were of entirely recent stamp and largely exogenous origin (something of which Indian nationalists were themselves largely unaware).[13] The data Geertz took as empirical evidence corroborating his theory of language in society, making it valid everywhere and at all times (India being the best test case), had in fact been produced by Western modernity. The epistemic paradox here has been demonstrated often in the history of Orientalism, where colonial theory discovered in the archaic East only what colonial power confected in the first place. Viewed from a slightly different angle, linguism may be seen as an element of modernity creating the very past modernity claims to overcome. The supposed irrational attachment to language of nonmodern minds, rather than impeding the development of the modern state, may lie at the very heart of modernity's project.[14]

The main dispute about primordialism among scholars nowadays, whether regarding language sentiment in particular or community belonging more generally, focuses on its ontology: Do primordial ties have deep reality or only surface facticity? Are they an ancient inheritance of sentiment and memory or a recent product of the manipulative practices of nationalist movements? The dominant view of political scientists, historians, and anthropologists is decidedly in favor of the constructivist account that perhaps Max Weber first offered: primordial sentiment with respect to linguism (not his term, of course) is generated through the "cultural work" of elites, producing a "belief in the exclusiveness of [a] language community" that comes to seize the masses through the democratization of culture.[15] There is unfortunately more wishful thinking than historical substance in this view, which

13. Washbrook 1991; Ramaswamy 1997, especially 244ff. My summary of the states-reorganization history has benefited from Ayres 2004: 194–241, which discusses the support of Ambedkar and the opposition—based on nonhistorical, purely national-integrationist arguments—of Nehru.

14. See Appadurai 1996: 146.

15. Weber is quoted in Stargardt 1995: 99; for the anthropological viewpoint, Appadurai 1996: 148.

surely derives from the (always unspoken) conviction that we can only change and defeat what has been newly invented. How elites are actually able to enforce a belief in language exclusivity on a blank-slate collective mind, or why the tradition of invention in the case of such beliefs should be so long and so successful, are questions we will not come much closer to answering by ever more insistent reiterations of the constructivist position. What should be, though rarely is, challenged in the first place is the underlying assumption that language or any other kind of primordial sentiment, whether real or factitious, is the transhistorical phenomenon Geertz took it to be. The fact is, the affective attachment that produces linguism—or that can be deployed to produce the illusion of linguism—and all the associated varieties of social-political belonging based on language are not universal features of human existence at all. There is no evidence whatever for linguism in South Asia before modernity, since all the various factors were absent that conjoined to produce the phenomenon in Europe over the course of the vernacular millennium (and perhaps beginning already in the era of Latinity) and that were universalized thence in both cultural theory and political practice.

Observe first how the sentimental attachment to language that is ubiquitous in Europe is incommensurable with anything we know about premodern South Asia. Not only did no notion of mother tongue exist, but even for the contemporary period South Asian sociolinguists have been able to speak confidently, if paradoxically to the modern ear, of a "plurality of mother tongues" for a single individual (chapter 8.3). Incommensurable, too, are the attitudes toward, and practices in the face of, language diversity. We have seen how multilinguality was viewed as punishment for the sin of human pride at Babel, for which penance was sought through coercive political action, either explicitly in the attempts to "eradicate the dialects" during the French Revolution and beyond, or implicitly by language proscriptions and attempts at eradication throughout the medieval and early-modern periods (chapter 12.1). But the trope of the curse of multilinguality lives on as a powerful theme in even the most sophisticated European cultural theory. The French symbolist poet Stéphane Mallarmé spoke of language as "imperfect due to its very plurality"; and the great German philosopher and critic Walter Benjamin, when proclaiming that "the history of a redeemed humanity is the only universal history," held that redemption presupposes, or rather is, some universal language that would put an end to the Babelic confusion.[16]

This Western linguistic monism, at once very peculiar and completely symptomatic, would have been utterly unintelligible in the thought world of premodern South Asia. If the progress of Latin around the beginning of the Common Era entailed the reduction of linguistic diversity across the west-

16. For Mallarmé, see Hollier 1995: 235; for Benjamin, Agamben 1999b: 48–61.

ern Mediterranean world, the progress of Sanskrit entailed the literization of a vast range of vernaculars in southern Asia (chapter 7.1). Nowhere in the texts of premodern South Asia do we find the least hint of despair at the proliferation of languages, whether eighteen (Śāradātanaya), fifty-six (Nāgavarma), or whatever canonical number happened to be in vogue. Moreover, if rulers undoubtedly coordinated practices of power with practices of culture, as in the language boundaries they observed when issuing inscriptions, the kind of multilingual vernacular court in evidence in twelfth-century Karnataka was never viewed as exceptional (chapter 8.2). Although local language in South Asia did remain literarily silent for centuries, given the understanding that quasi-universal political power required a language of quasi-universal extension, it was everywhere enabled to function as a language of record—to be used, for example, in inscriptions detailing the terms of a temple endowment, a mortgage, or a deed meant to last "as long as the sun and moon." This right to *record,* a function of central cultural significance, would continue to be denied even to French and German as late as the fifteenth century.[17] In the Latin world, the vernacular, unsystematized by grammar, was viewed as unstable and mutable in the way Latin was not, and hence as unsuited for the expression of perduring truth required of a language of record. The proliferation of vernacular grammars in India, at least in the south, may presumably have tempered the fear of mutability. But this was certainly not the case in Nepal, Khmer country, or Java, where local languages of record flourished in the absence of grammaticization, and where, accordingly, some other kind of openness must have been in play.

In addition to the fact that the primary grounds for cathexis on one's native language (as mother tongue or biological property) were absent, and celebration rather than condemnation of language diversity is everywhere in evidence—think only of Uddyotanasūri's cheerful reportage of the Babel of Vijayapura (noted in chapter 2.2)—there is also no reason to believe that language ever functioned in premodern South Asia as a component of ethnicity, as this phenomenon is understood in modern social science. Indeed, the very constitution of peoplehood through kinship, group solidarity, and common culture, especially language—however self-evident a feature of European history—is very hard to demonstrate for any period of South Asian history before modernity and seems just another fallacious universalization of a Western particular.[18] *Bhāṣā,* "speech, language," nowhere

17. Clanchy 1993: 197 ff., especially p. 223, and Irvine 1994: 331–32, who draws a contrast with England in the ninth and tenth centuries.

18. When the authors of a new work on ethnicity open their book with the assertion that "Though the term 'ethnicity' is recent, the sense of kinship, group solidarity, and common culture to which it refers is as old as the historical record" (Hutchinson and Smith 1996: 3), they are assuming precisely what stands in need of demonstration.

connoted a "people," as did *lingua* or *Zung* or *jazyk* in late-medieval Latin or German or Slavic.[19] Languages were typically named, not after peoples, but after ecological features or regions, whether real or mythic. People were simply bearers of language, they were not defined by language. As Śāradātanaya put it in the twelfth century, the eighteen languages by which the people in the sixty-four regions of Bhāratavarṣa communicated with each other were "named after a few from among these regions: the bearers of these languages are the people of Dramiḍa, Kannaḍa, Āndhra . . ." (chapter 8.2). Languages never made peoples, and were never linked with particular kin groups in narratives of vernacular beginnings.

Indeed, no such narratives existed, and it is here, in the absence of discourses on the historical origins of peoples, that we find a distinction from European history that makes a very large difference. Of course accounts, often satirical, of local variation in everything from styles of elocution to styles of sexuality are hardly unknown—in fact, the discursive regime of the Sanskrit cosmopolitan cultural order is built atop precisely such regional differentiation (chapter 2.1, 5). And people were sometimes said to be of places and to use languages of Place: Karṇāṭas were of Karṇāṭa and used Kannada, Drāviḍas were of Draviḍa and spoke Dravida, and so on. But we do not actually know, through positive data, that people in such regions ever thought of themselves as constituting groups united through language and place; they most certainly never constituted themselves as communities of common descent, with horizontal solidarities and narratives of shared memories. Far more salient for a historical political anthropology are caste and subcaste groups. These cross-cut putative peoples both externally (what is a Brahman in terms of "ethnic" affiliation?) and internally (how would Lingayats, Vokkaligas, Kurubas, or any of the numerous subcastes have been thought to constitute a "Karṇāṭa people" in the fifteenth century?). And they do so to such an extent that the very idea of peoplehood is rendered virtually meaningless for premodern India (vague categories such as the archaic *ārya* had no political salience during our period), and fictive ethnicity—of the sort mentioned earlier (chapter 12.1) as a necessary condition for the production of "the people"—a thing impossible to produce.

This silence is eloquent, and radically at odds with the noise of the ethnogenesis narratives of vernacularizing Europe, the historical origin myths found everywhere that trace the French back to the Trojans, the Hungarians to the Huns, and everyone else to someone else. Not only do we find in premodern South Asia nothing comparable to such narratives but we find nothing like the European chronicles and histories of kingdoms and peoples, let alone the full-dress historical narratives into which these discourses of

19. Bartlett 1993: 201.

languages and peoples eventually morphed, such as the *Anglo-Saxon Chronicles* or the *Grandes chroniques de France.* In India, the great regional narratives are those of kings and places, such as Kalhaṇa's Sanskrit *Rājataraṅgiṇī,* c. 1150, or of saints and places, such as Cēkkiḻār's Tamil *Periyapurāṇam,* c. 1150. Last, we find nothing comparable to the inevitable if melancholy pendant to all this narrative: the European discourses on competition for the preeminence of languages and peoples, the "battle of the vernaculars" in the vacuum left by Latin, which became especially intense in the sixteenth century.[20] Thus if we accept current scholarly opinion on the elements required for constituting an ethnic community—principally, a common proper name, a myth of common ancestry, shared memories of a common past, and a sense of solidarity—we are forced to conclude that ethnicity as the term is presently understood in social science was hardly prevalent in premodern South Asia, if it can be said to have existed at all.[21]

Language was never the "indispensable pole of identification" in South Asia before modernity made it such. Neither Weber's "'ethnic' connotation . . . created by the language group," nor vernacular attachment and anxiety, nor the fear of language diversity, nor even self-conscious ethnogenesis, along with ethnolinguistic competition, ethnic boundaries, and all the rest, seem to constitute the indispensable, ineluctable features of the human condition they are too often and too facilely assumed to be.[22] Vernacularization in South Asia, and its cosmopolitan antecedents, while structurally so similar to their European analogues, seem to have followed some entirely different logic of culture-power.

13.3 LEGITIMATION, IDEOLOGY, AND RELATED FUNCTIONALISMS

Unwarranted generalizations based on European particulars pertain not only to the sociality of language but also to the place of culture as such in relation to power. In fact, social theory on this subject presents problems that

20. See Giard 1989: 210.

21. Things may have begun to change under the new social and political conditions of the early modern period. In the *bakhar* of the eighteenth-century Marathas, Sumit Guha finds a discourse of what he calls ethnic pride (Guha 2004); the military labor markets of the Mughal period may have incubated comparable developments in the north (Kolff 1990). Gordon considers the critical period for the rise of the Maratha ethnonym to be 1400–1600, and the key condition to be the military service of Marathi-speaking units, though the evidence for this is thin (1994: 193 ff.; see also chapter 10.1 and n. 5 for the use of the term *marhāṭe*). For the constituents of ethnicity see Hutchinson and Smith 1996: 6–7. Verdery 1994 also contrasts the malleability of ethnicities of the [nonmodern] non-West with their peculiar fixity in western Europe, and rightly identifies as decisive the kinds and histories of state-making involved.

22. Typical is Gellner's tacit assumption that ethnic boundaries are presupposed rather than produced (1983: 1).

are perhaps even more insuperable. Not the least of these is that the dominant explanations offered for the transculturation of polity and politicization of culture in premodern South Asia are shot through with a functionalism that is both anachronistic and conceptually flawed. Social practices and mental processes that are in fact specific to the circumstances of one thin slice of human history, and whose import even there is uncertain, are often blithely assumed to have ubiquitous and transhistorical force. The model of culture and power that provides the core logic of these explanations, moreover, has come in for serious critique in Western social theory itself. That theory takes many forms, though all versions basically concur that it is the contribution of cultural features to the operation of a social or political system that constitutes their principal significance. I want to look briefly at three of these explanatory models, along an ascending curve of functionalist complexity: communication, socialization, and legitimation, or better, ideology, of which legitimation as usually conceptualized is only a subtype. Much of the material the following critique draws upon concerns transculturation processes in Southeast Asia, since these put the puzzling nature of cultural appropriation in an especially stark light. The Indianization of India itself is ordinarily not understood as such in the first place and so is rarely thought to need explanation—people were just being themselves, after all—but even there, when an explanation is offered, it is generally functionalist.

The weakest argument, and the most quickly dismissed, explains the role of Sanskrit across much of the cosmopolis but especially in Southeast Asia as driven by practical interregional communication needs. Unfortunately, there is no direct evidence that Sanskrit was ever used to fulfill these needs outside of certain scholastic and liturgical environments. There are undoubtedly some real enigmas here, such as Sanskrit's massive invasion of the Javanese lexicon (upward of 40 percent, and penetrating to the most quotidian level), but these enigmas may be open to other kinds of solutions.[23] If any Indian language can be said to have functioned as, or contributed to, a Southeast Asian koiné it is far more likely to have been Tamil.[24]

A second, slightly more robust form of this communicative functionalism is exemplified in the sociolinguistic arguments for the turn to Sanskrit among

23. It remains undeterminable whether the transformation of Javanese resulted from direct contact or from indirect contact in the form of intensive reading (Zoetmulder 1974: 15). A strong parallel is modern literary Russian, where liturgical mediation accounts for the prevalence of Church Slavonic (Sevcenko 1991: 14). In India itself, Persian was never a widely spoken idiom but left substantial traces in demotic speech.

24. The communication model I am questioning is Filliozat 1977: 405. Consider the number of Tamil words in Malay, which came about through trade and commerce (Filliozat 1977: 401–2; some of what are taken to be Tamil words sedimented in Southeast Asian languages could, of course, be Kannada; see chapter 3.1 for a possible western Indian provenance of early Southeast Asian transculturation). The koiné of the region was probably Malay (Tarling 1992: 114).

north Indian Buddhists in the early centuries of the Common Era, as well as in the religious arguments for vernacularization. The adoption of Sanskrit by Buddhists after centuries of resistance is often explained by its being "the language of learning" or possessing "technical precision." We are never told why, after five centuries, it suddenly became necessary or desirable for Buddhists to begin to participate in such learning, or indeed why the precision of the local languages of Buddhism (Gandhari, Tocharian, and so on), which had often been vehicles for liturgy, metaphysical doctrine, and moral discourse, had suddenly failed. The fact that the cosmopolitan transformation of Sanskrit occurred concomitantly with the consolidation of Kuṣāṇa power, however, suggests, if not a clear cause, at least a clear context for the momentous change, and one fully in keeping with the abundant evidence over a very long term of a specific kind of politicization of literary culture in premodern South Asia. Even stronger objections can be made to the proposition that the vernacularization was propelled by religion. In the case of Kannada, we saw that this still unchallenged belief derives from the assumption that vernacular writers were being loyal to Jain precept in using local language for "preaching to the masses" (chapter 10.4). This explanation bumps up against several inconvenient facts, however: no such explicit precept can be found in Jainism, and even if it were, twelve centuries is a rather long time to have waited to show it loyalty; Jain clerics began to use Sanskrit to a far greater degree than ever before during the very period when they began to use Kannada; the vernacular they developed would have been incomprehensible to any "masses," or at least masses unschooled in the fine points of Sanskrit language and style. Vernacularization in Karnataka, and in many other places in southern Asia, was conditioned not by religion but by the rise of a new political order. That the point of production of vernacular literature was the royal court suggests that a less familiar kind of social practice was at work than can be understood through communicative functionalism. If this was so, a less familiar kind of theory may be required to explain it.

A subset of social functionalism is the argument of status enhancement or social mobility known as "Sanskritization." As a descriptive term in linguistics, the idea is benign enough—but largely because it has no intellectual content. It means to merely point to a set of almost mechanical processes whereby languages qua sound-and-form systems aspired to the condition of Sanskrit. It does not explain, and makes no pretence of wanting to explain, what this aspiration meant for language as a symbolic or social system. Consider again the Buddhists of north India in the centuries around the beginning of the Common Era. We know they Sanskritized their dialects in linguistic terms, but no very cogent explanations of why they wanted to do so are on offer. When we are told that this came from a "desire to emulate the practices of the Brahman communities," we have again to wonder why this desire was so late in coming, and why it arose when it did. As this last argument demonstrates, the concept of Sanskritization—usually understood as referring to the universalization of Brahmanical lifeways (especially diet) and thoughtways (especially hierarchy) among lower-caste and tribal groups—has another weakness: it appears subject to no historical contingencies whatever. Sanskritization is presented either as completely random or as a ceaseless process, without beginning or end, everywhere available to explain transculturation, as if Sanskrit culture were a higher form of life toward which lower forms inevitably aspire.[25] What is worse, the supporting analysis is typically restricted to the domain of caste and ritual, or else carries implications from this domain. The concept has so constrained the field of inquiry that it is now possible to find serious historical scholarship based on the contrast between Sanskritization as a process effected through the medium of "religious culture" and Islamicization as inhabiting the domain of "secular" culture."[26] The relations of culture and power so central to the choice to affiliate with the Sanskrit cosmopolitan order are entirely occluded; rarely is the general matter of cultural production even raised, let alone the specific question of what it meant to address a supralocal as opposed to a local audience in terms of either the sociality of the process or the aesthetics of the product. Emptied thus of both agency and the historical social worlds within which agency operated, the concept of Sanskritization ignores most of the critical aspects of the transculturation process; it has become a hindrance rather than a help to critical inquiry in the domain of literary-cultural change. Perhaps we should expect no more, however, for one can sift through the much deeper scholarship on Latinity (Romanization) and vernacularity and be equally disappointed.

More complex functionalist conceptions confront us when we leave the realm of communication and socialization for that of mental formations. The strongest version here is that specific application of ideas to the social-political world known as "ideology," a large genus of which "legitimation" is one species. Both of these concepts may be seen as particular instances of a more general tendency to explain thought and culture exclusively by the functions they execute in the domains of social or political power. In trying to make sense of the cultural transformation of southern Asia, especially in the cosmopolitan period, this sort of instrumental logic rules unchallenged. Consider just one analysis of the cultural history of Southeast Asia, which contrasts the very

25. See for example Srinivas 1989: 56–72; Staal 1963. The quotation is from Salomon 2001: 250. The concept is alive and well in social analysis: In trying to make sense of the differential development of low-caste political consciousness in modern India, Jaffrelot (2000) contrasts what he sees as "ethnicization" among south Indian castes with the more traditionalizing accommodation to dominant norms—Sanskritization—in the north.

26. Wagoner 1996: 872.

different selection of "items from the cultural repertoire of ancient India" made by the people of Khmer country and of Pagan in the first millennium. A universalized vision of authority made sense to the Khmers because, situated as they were in the lower Mekong basin, they were relatively protected from threats from outsiders. Achievement was measured less "by the moral quality of the ruler than by the amoral power of the god whom the ruler worshipped." Accordingly, Khmer kings "learned to justify their authority by placing it in a universal context of devotion that could fully absorb the religious aspirations and compel the loyalty of their followers." To those in Pagan, such a vision made no sense; it was "too catholic, too indiscriminate, and too amoral for the political and intellectual process that evolved in the Irrawaddy basin." Here Buddhism provided a clearer program for moral action and for vindicating one's place in society by the demonstration of merit. The choice of items in the Indian cultural repertory was thus entirely a consequence of their instrumental role in the execution of predefined types of political and moral will that themselves seem almost environmental epiphenomena.[27]

It is entirely understandable to want to figure out why the appeal of Sanskrit cosmopolitan culture varied as it did across the polities of premodern southern Asia. Why in fact did ruling elites in Khmer country adopt it with such fervor and people in Pagan largely ignore it? The characterization of the options just cited seems unobjectionable, even elegant. But the explanation assumes that people have political and moral needs they fill by choosing items in the marketplace of political and moral ideas, and that they do so in a way as apparently unthinking as what Edmund Leach suggests for his famous "Hill People," whose animism seems as much a simple function of ecology and economy as the Buddhism of his "Valley People"—no room for value commitments here.[28] Yet isn't it possible that people conceive of political and moral needs in the first place through such visions as Brahmanism and Buddhism, that these are not instruments for filling needs but might in fact create them, and that their appearance in one place and not in another is a consequence of entirely contingent factors, such as the presence or absence of certain itinerant religious professionals? Moreover, the functionalist argument distinguishing Pagan from Angkor, and Buddhist functions from Brahmanical functions, falters, as such explanations generally do falter, on its inability to account for different outcomes of the same inputs.[29]

27. Tarling 1992: 157–64 (an otherwise useful survey).

28. Leach 1960.

29. A simple example: the Black Death brought about a labor shortage that in Europe "strengthened the hands of workers and yeomen and decisively ended the remnants of serfdom. In contrast, similar die-offs in Egypt had no such effect; there was a change in regimes at the top, but the new set of Mamluk rulers never reduced their pressures on the peasants" (Abu-Lughod 1993: 87).

We find forms of Buddhism and Brahmanism coexisting, commingling, and competing in the same place at the same time for patronage in ninth-century Java—and indeed in Angkor itself.

The logic of instrumental reason is central to the argument that in premodern southern Asia, cultural systems across the board were "needed" for political "legitimation." Though this constitutes the principal explanatory maneuver, repeated mechanically ad infinitum, it is an explanation that itself seems to have never been explained, let alone critiqued and defended. A work like the *Cambridge History of Southeast Asia*—chosen again in part because transculturation in Southeast Asia was so dramatic, complex, and, evidently for some observers, disturbing (chapter 14.1)—offers evidence at every step. "Indian cultural symbols" allowed Cham leaders to "mobilize local populations," for example, and enabled "aspiring leaders" in central Java "to acquire a superior legitimacy that would distinguish them from the others and enable them to prevail."[30]

The *Cambridge History* is being singled out not as an example of some unusually impoverished theoretical approach but as a representative of academic consensus. One leading scholar of the past generation in the field of Southeast Asian studies regarded the entire process of what he called the acculturation of the region in just this way: Southeast Asians were "relatively advanced" at the beginning of the Common Era, and "came to realize the value of Indian concepts as a means of legitimizing their political status, and possibly, of stratifying their subjects. To achieve this end they summoned to their courts Brahmans skilled in protocol and ritual" leading to "the whole exceedingly complex ceremonial of Indian court life."[31] And the theoretical model extends beyond Southeast Asia. Most historians of premodern South Asia conceive of the place of culture in the medieval Indian polity exclusively in such terms, at every level of practice: The crystallization of Tamil literature took place in a period that saw "the rise of regional dynasties which legitimized themselves with reference to an indigenous culture." The demand for the appropriation of agricultural surplus "required new forms of religio-political legitimation." It was a task incumbent preeminently on Brahmans to "create such legitimation"; there was an "urgent necessity" to raise the status of rulers "in order to legitimize the claim to a regular system of imposts." A dizzying array of almost Ptolemaic epicycles—"vertical legitimization" and "horizontal legitimization"—is added to account for this. The same Brahmans came to mainland Southeast Asia "in order to legitimize the new status and wealth of these chiefs," something for which "obviously there existed a tremendous need," which "obviously no other traditional institution was

30. Tarling 1992: 254, 205–6. This is a fortiori the case in earlier scholarship, e.g., Naerssen and de Jongh 1977: 41 and passim.

31. Wheatley 1961: 186.

able to provide." "Obviously in both [South India and Southeast Asia] there had existed the same or at least similar socio-political needs for a new type of legitimation."[32]

Unfortunately, nothing in these assertions can be taken as obvious in the least, however often they might be repeated. On the contrary, nothing compels us to believe that legitimation, or its higher-order form, ideology—two key components in the social analysis of capitalist modernity—have anything like the salience in noncapitalist nonmodernity that scholars have attributed to them. This is not of course a claim that goes without saying; it needs to be argued out, from the historical nature of legitimation and ideology themselves. The stakes of this argument are rather high, after all, since what is at issue are the different, potentially radically different, relationships over time of culture to power and the theoretical implications of this difference; for it is culture that produces meaning, and legitimation is a form of meaning. Difficult questions are involved, and I make no pretense of doing more here than simply registering a number of doubts and hesitations.

Whatever the prehistory of legitimation theory (it arguably derives from the crisis of post-Napoleonic constitutional monarchies), in the sphere of social theory it was made into a core component of the analysis of power by Weber. There is no need to go into detail on the three sorts of legitimacy claims and the kinds of authority these claims sustain (rational claims produce legal authority, while traditional and charismatic claims produce traditional and charismatic kinds of authority), nor to critique the analysis of "traditional authority." That it is based on "age-old rules and powers" and requires obedience from the traditional status of rulers is hardly news, though the place of "impersonal duty" rather than "personal loyalty" may be far greater in early South Asia than Weber allowed. What is problematic is the notion that such power requires, or indeed can even be the object of, a process of legitimation.

Aside from the historical specificity and cultural limits of its radically constitutive notion of law *(lex)*, and the function of law in relationship to a political formation, in its most fundamental (English) sense "legitimation" signifies transforming something that is "false" into something that is "true"—a bastard son into a legal heir, for example. Such a transformation, however, presupposes a moment of discontinuity, so to put it, a potential lack in the antecedent state of affairs, which one proceeds to fix. Weber himself explained that such a moment does indeed exist: "Custom, personal advantage, purely affectual or ideal (value-rational) motives of solidarity do not form a sufficiently viable basis for a given domination; a further element is normally added: the belief in legitimacy." Besides the apparent contradic-

32. Tieken 2003: 278; Kulke, ed. 1995: 237–40; 1990: 20–21, 30, cf. 22.

tion with what he proceeds to argue (that legitimacy or the legitimation of traditional domination rests on custom, "everyday belief in the sanctity of immemorial traditions"), there is an apparent anachronism: Weber seems to be looking at the past from a location of modern disenchantment and extending back into time the separation of structures and beliefs characteristic of modernity. To put this in Weberian terms, he is unhistorically transposing to the precapitalist world the instrumental rationality of capitalism that functions as a defining principle of modern political life. What leads us to believe that in precapitalism the concept of legitimacy/legitimation exists at all, if according to Weber's own thesis there is no location outside the lifeworld for a rationality directed exclusively toward ends to operate separately from a rationality directed to values regardless of cost? Legitimacy/legitimation must be understood, again according to Weber, as something that "functions basically as a subjective-internal supplement"—that is, something supplied by the instrumental rationality of capitalist modernity—"to a given public order."[33] Why, accordingly, should we hold that pre- or noncapitalist power "needs" culture to effect its own legitimation?

Weber himself believed he was providing only a possible typology of relations of power, and one that at any event would have to be tested and likely modified in the face of new empirical data.[34] The concession to the possibility of theoretical revision required by new historical materials has never been much appreciated by some students of Weber, however; conjecture has since hardened into conviction, and it has proven impossible to find any sustained critique of legitimation from within historical sociology. One thinker who has been troubled by all this, though less from a historical perspective than from the more unlocated vantage point of philosophy, is Paul Ricoeur. He rightly if somewhat obliquely links the problem of legitimacy/legitimation to that of ideology in general. For Ricoeur, ideology, itself a notoriously slippery concept, is something that "occurs in the gap between a system of authority's claim to legitimacy and our response in terms of belief . . . Ideology functions to add a certain surplus-value to our belief in order that our belief may meet the requirements of the authority's claim."[35] Legitimation, too, is a process that works through a cultivation of belief, the adding of "surplus-value," but only in the context of a conflict of belief. It is here that, for Ricoeur, the problems start for the world of pre- or nonmodernity. Can we even speak of ideologies, Ricoeur fairly asks, "of non-

33. Weber 1978, vol. 1: 56 and 63; "Types of Legitimate Domination" is found on pp. 212–83.

34. "The usefulness of the above classification [of ideal types of legitimate domination] can only be judged by its results in promoting systematic analysis . . . The idea that the whole of concrete historical reality can be exhausted in the conceptual scheme about to be developed is as far from the author's thoughts as anything could be" (Weber 1978, vol. 1: 216; see also p. 263).

35. Ricoeur 1986: 183.

modern cultures, cultures which have not entered the process . . . [of] the collapse of universal agreement? I think that integration without confrontation is pre-ideological . . . Ideology arises not on the collapse of the ritual dimension but from the open conflictual situation of modernity."[36] If the world of nonmodernity is pre-ideological, and if legitimation is indissolubly linked with ideology, then Weber's typology of "legitimate domination" and thus of the function of legitimation—and with it the reduction of culture to a pure logic of power—cannot be assumed to be transhistorically applicable.

There are admittedly weak links in the preceding argument. The lesser of the two major problems is the ideological dimension of legitimation itself. This, Ricoeur suggests, is something one has to read into rather than out of Weber, since the concept of ideology is missing from Weber's chapters on legitimacy. But the answer seems to be supplied by Weber's own statement regarding power's cultivation of belief: that every system of domination "attempts to establish and to cultivate the belief in its legitimacy."[37] I return to this issue, at least in its cognitive dimension, shortly. The greater problem lies in taking premodernity as pre-ideological. Ricoeur by no means stands alone in the view that ideology in the strong sense—that is, false consciousness, misrecognition, discourse of false necessity, and the like (for which alone we should reserve the name "ideology" and thus not diminish its analytic precision by letting it do double-duty for any "idea-system")—is a quintessentially modern phenomenon. This is not necessarily the case, however, for the reason he offers, in reliance on Karl Mannheim, that premodernity is pre-ideological because "universal agreement" had not yet collapsed. It is patently false, for South Asia at least, that before the coming of colonial modernity there existed a single, unified, unblurred vision of either power or culture. Early Buddhism affected a far-reaching disenchantment of the world in terms of the *doxa* that characterized everyday social practices, preeminently the practices of sacrificial ritual and the social differentiation known as caste (chapter 1.2), and equally searching critiques were offered repeatedly over the course of the following millennium (by the Vīraśaivas among others). But there are other, better grounds for thinking that ideology in the strong form may make little sense for premodern southern Asia; many scholars have come to realize this implicitly, though few have sought to clearly specify these implications.

Let us take an argument from the economic sphere. Under the regime of capital, certain kinds of economic exchange become deeply mysterious as surplus labor (to keep for the moment with the classical theory) is surreptitiously extracted from workers and the real conditions of their existence

36. Ricoeur 1986: 259–61.
37. Weber 1978, vol. 1: 213; Ricoeur 1986: 183, 202.

come to be hidden from them—and mysterious they must become if those conditions are to be perpetuated. The idea that workers are free to sell their labor under capitalism, for example, can be viewed as part of a systematic distortion of the reality that they are free to do nothing of the sort: they either sell it or die. How necessary or meaningful, one must ask, would any such core ideological function be in the world before capitalism, where the conditions of economic exchange are entirely transparent?[38] A related way to conceive of the specificity of ideology to modernity is put forward by the political theorist Claude Lefort. Ideology arises in the world of modernity in order to efface the new historicity—the new openness and indeterminacy—of the social world under capitalism and to "legitimate" its order. "Ideology is the sequence of representations which have the function of re-establishing the dimension of a society 'without history' at the very heart of historical society." It is not hard to see the difficulties of applying this definition of ideology to a "cool" society like precapitalist South Asia—and this is a claim we can make without thereby committing ourselves to any nonsensical notions of utter stasis. Lefort also points up the tension between the competing, conflictual interests of capital and labor in modernity, but he focuses on the formal freedoms conferred on the individual that make coercion by the state an infrequent option. What is needed to explain the coherence of such a society despite such inherent pressures toward instability is, among other things, ideological control.[39] With no such limit placed on coercion in premodernity by constitutionally guaranteed freedom, ideology has in fact no raison d'être at all.

Such views on the place of modernity in the creation of ideology are complemented by more pragmatic reflections on the sociology of contemporary peasant life in Southeast Asia. Here good theoretical and historical reasons are offered for concluding that the entire concept of ideology as we have always understood it—as a discourse that reproduces domination—is "simply irrelevant" for domination in agrarian societies. The hegemonic deployment of discourse in fact does not exist in this world; the dominated pretend to believe but in fact do not.[40] Invoking the idea of hegemony leads us of course to Gramsci, whose views on the historicality of the concept should be registered here though they recapitulate some ideas already mentioned. For Gramsci, hegemony is linked constitutively to the domain of public life that he names civil society, which is relatively independent of state controls. In developed capitalist polities, legitimacy rests on a fairly stable "equilib-

38. See Abercrombie et al. 1990, where however the argument is not extended to precapitalism.

39. Lefort 1986: 181–236 (such at least is the argument I take from this dense but important essay). The sentence cited is on p. 201.

40. Scott 1990: 70–107, especially p. 87.

rium of hegemonic and coercive institutions." This Gramsci contrasts with an older type of state that lacks such a vital reciprocity with civil society: "In the ancient and medieval state alike, centralization, whether political-territorial or social . . . was minimal. The state was, in a certain sense, a mechanical bloc of social groups . . . The modern state substitutes for the mechanical bloc of social groups their subordination to the active hegemony of the directive and dominant group." On this account, hegemony could not function in premodernity for the simple reason that the arena in which by definition it does function, namely civil society, did not even exist.[41]

One may therefore agree with Ranajit Guha—that in "pre-capitalist politics . . . dominance neither solicits nor acquires hegemony," making no attempt "to integrate or assimilate [subjugated populations] into a hegemonic ruling culture"—but only up to a point. For the grounds for agreement is either a position Guha dismisses (that in general there is no historical situation in which politics is not always-already an element of culture), or one that he ignores (that hegemony is a phenomenon peculiar to capitalist modernity). It is certainly not the position he accepts: that premodern polity in South Asia was pure despotism, functioning entirely through dominance ("fear") and hence able to forego all attempts at manufacturing consent. This image of precapitalist power is pure invention—in fact, it is standard-issue Orientalism.[42] Political power is just the capacity to achieve outcomes; it is not *inevitably* linked with conflict and is not *necessarily* oppressive. Certainly there is substantial evidence in premodern South and Southeast Asia to support this point. In short, it is not a known fact but simply a mechanical application of a theorem extrapolated from capitalism—and here is a third example to add to the unwarranted generalizations of Weber, Bakhtin, Geertz, and others—to say that "the history of all hitherto existing societies is the history of class struggle."[43]

Even more pointed objections to ideology in general and legitimation in particular have been expressed in contemporary sociological theory. For one thing, the proposition that culture legitimates power can be seen as simply another functionalist explanation. We can read this from the record of the

41. Gramsci 1971: 54.

42. Guha 1997: 72, 63, 92; see pp. 63–65, where the author bases his views of South Asian despotism on such accomplished historians of precapitalist politics as Montesquieu and Voltaire. To conclude from a normative text like the *Dharmaśāstra* of Manu that in premodern India "force and fear are the fundamental principles of politics" (p. 30) is like treating Mill's *On Liberty* as an account of the actual practices of British liberalism.

43. Note that Engels (in the 1888 edition of the *Manifesto*) restricted "history" here to "written history," since the new study of prehistory revealed the existence of primitive communism. Such openness to empirically driven theoretical revision is less in evidence among some later Marxists (as it is among some Weberians). On power and achieving outcomes, see Giddens 1984: 257.

concept's deployment in historical-sociological analysis: the extraction of surplus, as we saw, "required new forms of religio-political legitimation"; there existed an "urgent necessity" to raise the status of rulers "in order to legitimize the claim to a regular system of imposts"; "a tremendous need of additional legitimation" of their new status and wealth was felt on the part of Southeast Asian chiefs. Legitimation theory is thus open to the wider critique of functionalism, offered perhaps most effectively by the sociologist Anthony Giddens. He argues, with greater subtlety than selective quotation can suggest, that social systems "have no 'needs'"; "not even the most deeply sedimented institutional features of societies come about, persist, or disappear because those societies need them to do so. They come about *historically,* as a result of concrete conditions that have in every case to be directly analyzed; the same holds for their persistence or their dissolution."[44] A critique of legitimation per se I find nowhere explicitly offered in Giddens's oeuvre, but one can be elaborated with the conceptual resources he offers, which address cognitive processes at a deeper level than we have probed to this point.

As already suggested, legitimation implies the attempt, through the application of ideas or acts, to make a political or other phenomenon appear to conform to a set of norms when ex hypothesi it may not. Such a theory of action is vulnerable to various criticisms. It rests either on a model of consensual rational choice that is largely belied by experience, or on what is almost a conspiracy theory of politics: "legitimation" suggests a knowledgeability on the part of rulers that is unavailable to people at large, who are therefore cultural dopes and dupes, since they are induced to believe in ideas opposed to their interests that rulers know to be such.[45] Moreover, from what vantage point, in a world of continuous political practices—that is, in the world of premodernity—would it be possible even to perceive the asymmetry between political fact and political norm? In the historical experience of a tenth-century Indian, there had always been kings who had always exercised power in a given way. No one had ever experienced anything else; no standard of comparison existed for doubting the inevitability of kingship, which accordingly approximated a natural law. Of course rulers could be just or unjust, true heirs or false, but there is no reason whatever to assume they cared let alone needed to secure the assent of their subjects one way or

44. Giddens 1981: 18.

45. Bourdieu proposes another cognitive model when he argues that to attain efficacy, symbolic capital or power must be recognized as legitimate, though it is the outside observer who raises the question of legitimacy. It "does not arise as such for the dominated"; "the answer that the dominated give to it in practice appears as an answer only to those who raise the question" (Bourdieu 1990: 112). But one may well ask whether legitimation can explain the workings of a social system if no one involved in the system knows or grasps anything about legitimation at any level of consciousness.

the other. In such circumstances, the process of legitimation would seem not only cognitively redundant but virtually unthinkable.[46] Then again, as Giddens might ask, what area of "normative commitment" is in fact being addressed by legitimation? After all, there are large domains of routinized social life that are not "directly motivated." In other words, why bother? Lastly—and here he is joined by a number of recent thinkers such as those cited earlier—many scholars assume subaltern people to be far more enmeshed in consensual ideologies than they may actually be. Indeed, some have argued cogently that legitimation (or ideology), if it does anything at all, is far likelier to be a means of building *ruling class* consensus.[47]

We have seen everywhere in this book that culture was centrally important to power both during the period of the Sanskrit cosmopolitan order and during the vernacular millennium. All the critical innovations in the aestheticization of language and its philologization came from the stimulus offered by court patronage. Sanskrit virtuosity was a core component of cosmopolitan power from the time of Rudradāman and Samudragupta to the last kings of Angkor, and Kannada virtuosity had a similar centrality for Rāṣṭrakūṭa kings in ninth-century Karnataka, and Tamil virtuosity for Cōḷa kings in twelfth-century Tamilnadu. No doubt basic issues of self-understanding and the truth of one's place in a genealogy of charisma were encoded in discourse, whether cosmopolitan or vernacular, as in the case of the Cāḷukyas of Kalyāṇa (chapter 3.3) or the Hoysaḷas of Dvārasamudra (chapter 10.3), but there is little reason to hold that such discourse was intended to "add a certain surplus-value" to the beliefs of those subject to domination. A sociocultural theory designed to account for one world does not necessarily account for another, especially one that, by every measurement we can employ, was so radically different.

How, then, do we make sense of the discourse of power as it is offered in the texts of cosmopolitan and vernacular culture in southern Asia? To deny that its function was the legitimation of power does not entail denying that the putative agent of legitimation, the polity, possessed no power worth legitimating in the first place, had legitimation been an option. In other words, our denial of modern social theories of power places us under no obligation to accept only a ritual (segmentary) or theater state model for Indic polities and assume that power existed only to serve rites or pomp, that symbol and ceremony were not embellishments of the state but "what the state was for."[48] Indian polities were more substantial, more powerful, than the-

46. See Scott 1990: 75.

47. Giddens 1981: 67. The argument against the efficacy of consensual ideologies in the case of dominated communities is developed in Scott 1990. Abercrombie et al. 1980, 1990 argue for their role in promoting ruling-class solidarity.

48. This view is fully elaborated in Geertz 1980; see also chapter 6.2.

ater or ritual. They stimulated agricultural production, promoted trade, endowed educational institutions, built temples and other monuments, and made war. And if we argue, as much of our data invites us to do, that culture was concerned with the aestheticization of power, it does not mean that an aesthetic is all that power was. Our concern throughout has been with *vyāvahārika sat,* the subjective horizon of the actors involved. From within that horizon it is not so very hard to imagine an attitude toward culture according to which it played an authentic, unquestioned role in the ennoblement of political life—an attitude whereby care for language was not a sham or a show but a core value of what it meant to be just and good, whereby good literature was a moral component of good and just governance—cosmopolitan literature of cosmopolitan governance, and vernacular literature of vernacular governance.[49]

Denying the applicability of the concept of legitimation, it goes without saying, does not mean denying that very cruel and very consequential discourses of power existed in the world of South Asian premodernity.[50] Moreover, resisting the assumption a priori that premodern culture always and ever fulfilled a legitimation function does not mean resisting a priori the assumption that culture had a defining relationship to power. There is in principle no contradiction between finding domination and the discourses of domination in the domain of everyday social relations, or preserving for culture a role in the constitution of political life, and challenging the view that power deployed culture for mystifying or effacing the contingency of the political sphere, or harnessed culture to governance and control the way the ideology theory posits for capitalist modernity.

The notion of legitimation, along with Sanskritization, ethnicity, linguism, and cultural naturalism, are not the only obstacles that modern Western theory places in the way of understanding premodern India. Two other analytical frameworks are even more obstructive: the one that frames India as the civilization it always was and that other that frames it as the nation it never could be.

49. See chapter 4; also Pollock 2001c. For a succinct account of the intellectual history of the notion of the "aesthetic state," see Jay 1992, and for a comprehensive analysis, Chytry 1989.
50. See for example Pollock 1990.

CHAPTER FOURTEEN

Indigenism and Other Culture-Power Concepts of Modernity

14.1 CIVILIZATIONALISM, OR INDIGENISM WITH TOO LITTLE HISTORY

One particular mode of theorizing and explaining culture implicitly rejects, or is entirely indifferent to, both culture's evolutionary development and its purely instrumental contribution to power. Instead, culture is viewed as something just there, and as ever self-identical. It is considered outside the flux of time, whether natural or political, or else endowed with so deep a history as to appear forever beyond time. And its stance in relationship to power is presumed to be almost one of consanguinity, certainly not that of an object to be deployed at the will of power.

There are various discursive embodiments of this conception of culture in general and especially in relation to power, but two are especially pertinent to our larger problem of the cosmopolitan and the vernacular as historical forms of life. Both derive from a more basic idea about human existence, one not specific to any particular type of social or political structure, which we can call simply indigenism, or autochthony. The first locus, at one end of the scale of forms and constituting the largest cultural structure of all, is what since the mid-nineteenth century (and not before) has been called a civilization, the cultural discourse concerning which I will call civilizationalism. The second, at the other end of the scale, combines autochthony and the cultural essence of civilization with the (supposedly) smallest complete unit of culture and power to produce what is termed a nation, its discursive modality being nationalism. These are not of course entirely equivalent entities: civilizationalism is routinely thought of as a conceptual or analytic object, whereas nationalism is at once a category of analysis and a category of practice.[1] Na-

1. This useful distinction is Bourdieu's; see Brubaker and Cooper 2000: 4.

tionalism is an active force, and the nation is something to be achieved, unlike civilizationalism, which summons us to no action, or a civilization, which is not something anyone ever sets out to build. Yet both civilizationism and nationalism are expressions of a far more deep-seated and widespread understanding of culture-power than either evolutionism or social-scientific functionalism. And in the case of nationalism, this understanding has been specifically restricted, in the most recent assessments, to the era of modernity.

Civilizationalism and nationalism and their antipodal if complementary orientations to historical grounding, along with the indigenism that underlies both discourses, form core topics in European intellectual and political history as well as intellectual and political practice. In their vastness and complexity they are no less unwieldy than the other questions addressed earlier, and applying to them an even remotely adequate analysis is no less of a challenge. Yet like the others, they are too important to our theme to ignore, since they are the conceptual categories into which cosmopolitan and vernacular orders of culture-power are typically (if tacitly) slotted in the contemporary thought world. Once again, our approach is to isolate some key themes and tendencies and focus on some representative positions, concentrating on the evidence offered by literary culture.

We have seen how a concern with narrating the origins of peoples and placing them securely in time and space (the so-called *Ursprungsparadigmen*, *mythomoteurs*, and ethnic fictions examined in chapter 12.1) preoccupied most of the nascent literary cultures and polities in late-medieval Europe. Tracing the metastasis of this conceptual scheme into modernity would require a careful assessment of, above all, early-nineteenth-century indigenism, especially as expressed most famously in the tracts of German idealists such as J. G. Herder and J. G. Fichte. More relevant perhaps as an introduction to the presuppositions of modern civilizationalism and nationalism as categories of analysis and practice, respectively, is the transmutation of these ideas in certain strands of modern philosophical discourse. Paradigmatic here, both for the arguments it offers and for their political payout, is the work of Martin Heidegger. Heidegger is notoriously complicated, and easily distorted by a cursory review. Yet the vernacular aboriginality that seems to be woven into his most basic ontology is worth registering, alongside the fundamental ways in which the materials of Indian premodernity contradict it.

In two of his brief but influential post–World War II essays, Heidegger seeks to provide further grounding for his notion of the fundamental mode of "Being-there," or human existence. Like all his work, these writings do not yield up their secrets easily, and interpretations vary. In "Building Dwelling Thinking" (1951), one of his aims seems to be to discover, by way of an etymological analysis of the language that speaks these terms, the true nature of what it means to *be in place*. The first two words of the title present themselves to our everyday understanding as contrastive: not every building is a place for dwelling, for instance, even if building is usually necessary for dwelling. Yet if we submit ourselves, as Heidegger calls upon us to do, to the regime of the language in which they are articulated—since "man acts as though *he* were the shaper and master of language" yet "in fact *language* remains the master of man"—we will be shown the truth, the "real meaning," of these terms. "To build" *(bauen)* in Old English and Old High German means "to dwell" and is cognate with "to be" (as in *[Ich] bin, [Du] bist*). In some archaic and absolute sense, then, being itself must be coextensive with building and cultivating residence in a place. It is such located dwelling that accordingly constitutes the "basic character of human being."[2] This ontological linkage between dwelling and being, which is vindicated by the "highest and everywhere the first" court of appeal, namely language, can be correlated with Heidegger's explicit analysis of rootedness in the 1955 "Memorial Address." In the course of critiquing modernity and technology and the anomie they produce, Heidegger stops to ask, "What is happening here? . . . Answer: the rootedness, the autochthony, of man is threatened today at its core." His great worry is whether man's work in the future can still be expected "to thrive in the fertile ground of a homeland," or instead, "will everything now fall into the clutches of planning and calculation?"[3]

David Harvey, who has recently called attention to these essays, offers what I think is a fair gloss on their broader implications. For Heidegger, constructing a place must entail "the recovery of roots," and so a viable homeland. There alone can culture in general and art in particular flourish, for experience "becomes incommunicable beyond certain bounds precisely because authentic art and genuine aesthetic sense can spring only out of strong rootedness in place."[4] The deep anticosmopolitanism that finds expression in these essays of Heidegger was basic doctrine to conservative thought through much of the previous century (and we will see in the epilogue to this book how oppositional thinkers like Gramsci sought to contest it). But what above all Heidegger's tortured analysis of language and the meanings thought to inhabit language primevally and eternally succeeds in demonstrating is, not transcendental and transhistorical truth, but what some have called the "constructed certitude" of the countermodern.[5] Even less charitably construed, it represents another spurious generalization of a European datum—and perhaps not a concrete datum but only an imaginary one at that. For the etymon on which Heidegger bases this small but by no means trivial part of his argument is found in Sanskrit, too, where it does not bear

2. Heidegger 1971: 145–61.
3. Heidegger 1966: 48–49.
4. Harvey 1993: 14.
5. Beck 1997: 62–70.

out his logic. "Dwelling" and "being" are not wholly unrelated to each other in the conceptual world of the Sanskrit cosmopolitan, since "being" (or "becoming," the Sanskrit root *bhū*) is related to *bhavana,* "a dwelling." But more important is the fact that the etymon is also related not to any particular place but to the world as a whole, *bhuvana.*[6] Place was irrelevant in a cultural-political formation that saw itself as existing everywhere in general and nowhere in particular. Perhaps language does not speak a singular truth after all, whether of autochthony or anything else, but only multiple truths that have their different historical logics.[7] The specific difficulties of his analysis aside, Heidegger is a key witness in giving voice, at the most rarified level of European thought, to a widely shared conviction about the inevitability of cultural ways of being. These stand outside history, inscribed in the very stuff of human language and consciousness. And perhaps far from being a reaction to modernity, Heidegger's philosophization of the rootedness of human being may be one of modernity's basic modes of self-understanding.

There is more to say about this specific question when we consider the role of indigenism, identity formation, and related forces in the thought world of contemporary nationalism. The tendency to conceive of culture as a primeval entity connected with being in a place and as existing before and standing outside the vagaries of historical process, operates at the macrolevel of analysis, too, since the idea of the indigenous, if more often implicit than expressed, has powerfully shaped the discourse on civilizations. "Civilization" is the name commonly given to what are in fact the cosmopolitan culture-power orders discussed in the first part of this book: societies that were organized according to the empire form and that produced cultural coherence by means of the great transregional languages and literatures. More than this, civilization is the culture-power formation often implicitly contrasted with the nation, which for its part is the putative ideal form of vernacular culture-power. Curiously, like nations, civilizations are also usually held to comprise closed, stable sets of practices, which (unlike the case of nations) can be imposed upon other closed and stable sets, that is, civilizations that are weaker or stronger, or—borrowing from cultural naturalism, the first conceptual scheme we analyzed (chapter 13.1)—less or more "evolved."

The history of the treatment of such civilizational questions is, once again, especially instructive in Southeast Asian studies with regard to the transculturation process that was once termed Indianization (or Hinduization). Here too it quickly becomes clear that the deployment of civilizationalist discourse, besides recuperating basic presuppositions about indigenism, is no more separable from the larger historical-political contexts in which it occurs than is

6. The Sanskrit root *bhū* = OHG *būwan,* etc.

7. The logic, in Heidegger's case, is the one of radical conservative politics, which provided the motor for his understanding of ontology no less than that of etymology (Bourdieu 1991b).

the deployment of nationalist discourse, though civilizationalism's purchase on political action may be more attenuated. To an outsider looking in at the field of Southeast Asian studies, the history of the civilization problem appears to fall into two major phases of conceptualization.[8] The first is what we may think of as the colonial-European and Indian-chauvinist stage. Here civilizations are thought of as unequal, or civilization itself (in the singular, as connoting the civilizing process, or progress) is viewed as unevenly distributed over the world. It is rather like a scarce resource, though one that moves in the reverse direction insofar as it is something not extracted but implanted. The view of the great civilizational orders as preexistent cornucopias of elements that are then disseminated, sporelike, across time and space was in fact long a dominant view promulgated by anthropology, the science of culture, where it was known as the diffusionist model. For one of its more celebrated proponents, Alfred Kroeber, diffusionism tells the story of always already powerful and complete civilizations conferring their gifts upon "retarded or primitive cultures."[9]

In the first stage of the transculturation analysis of Southeast Asia, this conferral was intimately linked with colonialist presuppositions. On the European side, the Indianization of Asia was seen as an antecedent to its own contemporary imperial project; on the Indian side, it was taken as a consoling reminder of India's own triumphant colonial past in the face of a humiliating colonized present. One of the typical Indian voices here is that of the historian R. C. Majumdar, who conceived of the growth of the Sanskrit cosmopolis as colonization by a master race, with "Indian colonists" confronting "local people [who] were almost semi-savages" but who were all thoroughly transformed as "Indian social and religious ideas were deeply implanted in the soil." For it is almost a "universal law," he adds, "that when an inferior civilization comes in contact with a superior one, it gradually tends to be merged into the latter."[10] The source of such thinking, and probably of the specific construction itself, was entirely European. The French art historian Alfred Foucher had argued in the 1930s that the Indianization of Southeast Asia was a matter not simply of influence but of "real colonization, in the full sense of the word."[11] French Orientalists evidently viewed what they interpreted as premodern colonization by Indians as a forerunner of their own well-known *mission civilisatrice;* George Coedès actually spoke in terms of the "civilizing

8. An instructive parallel is offered by the place of Byzantium in the historical imagination of Russia and the Soviet Union (Sevcenko 1991, chapter 9).

9. Kroeber 1952, especially p. 392: "In the main, these backward cultures depend [on] and derive from the great ones."

10. Majumdar 1944: 23. The colonial discourse long antedates him; see Mookerji 1914: 128 ff.

11. Cited in Chakravarti 1978–80, vol. 1: viii.

activity of India." To the idea of a shared colonial objective was eventually added, in the case of the Dutch in Indonesia, an element of racialization. The cultural transformation of Java, in both the modern and the premodern periods, was thus said to be the work of "Aryans"—that is, Indians and Dutch—punctuated by a somber Muslim interregnum.[12] As we have seen in the first part of this study, however, there is no evidence whatever for the thesis of colonization in any acceptable sense of the term. The transculturation of Southeast Asia was the work of traders, adventurers, and itinerant religious entrepreneurs. There was no Indian military presence let alone conquest, no political subordination or material exploitation, no demographically significant settlement of Indians, no "empire-by-accident," no conquering of half the world whether intentionally or "in a fit of absence of mind." As for the idea of a racially superior class of culture-founders *(Kulturstifter),* the idea is about as credible as the knowledge form of race science *(Rassenkunde)* that produced it. The Aryan discourse was deployed by the Dutch purely for its then politically useful anti-Islamic resonance.

In the second phase of research on the region, after World War II, the assertion of deep, even aboriginal civilizationalism came to expression. From this point on, the whole object of the study of Southeast Asia was to be, no longer what was brought into the region—"Southeast Asia as a receptacle for external influences"—but rather the continuity and specificity of "native" culture itself, "the cultural distinctiveness of Southeast Asia both as a whole and in its parts."[13] This new emphasis on recuperating some degree of cultural individuality and authenticity, indeed, some precolonial culture as such, apart from the Sanskrit cosmopolitan sort, found some of its more sophisticated formulation in the work of O. W. Wolters, notably in his writings on the Khmer, and in that of Denys Lombard, the historian of Java.

Besides offering masterful analyses of what is, linguistically and historically, often exceedingly complex material, Wolters's scholarship is uncommon in its attempt to assess in an open and critical (and not just antiquarian) spirit the place of Indian cultural flows in mainland Southeast Asian history. His principal monograph begins by putting in place an interpretive framework, echoed by others since, that governs the whole of his ensuing cultural analysis: "Indianization," he maintains, did not introduce "an entirely new chapter in the region's history" but instead simply "brought ancient and persisting indigenous beliefs into sharper focus." In the domain of political power, for example, the process did not create an altogether new form but only served to make possible "a heightened perception of the overlord's superior prowess" via his ascetic or heroic achievement and his relationship

12. Coedès 1968: xvi; compare Day and Reynolds 2000: 4. On Java, Lombard 1990: 12. I now see that George Spencer (cited in Abu-Lughod 1989: 288) also noted the parallel.

13. Reid 1990: 1.

with the god Śiva's divine authority consequent on that achievement. It is entirely false, therefore, to believe "that Southeast Asian peoples could graduate to statehood only with the assistance of Indian influence."[14]

Yet for the key conceptions that underwrote many Southeast Asian polities in the historical period and that Wolters goes on to discuss, such as universalist sovereignty and the ruler's intimate relationship or identity with a supreme god through *bhakti*, there is a lot of Indian evidence but, so far as I can see, none from non-Indian Southeast Asia. Indeed, it is from the *Sanskrit* evidence that Wolters derives much of his interpretation of Southeast Asian kingship and political systems more generally, despite the conceptual framework of his argument, which grants primacy to continuity with "ancient and persisting indigenous beliefs." A case in point: the symbology of quasi-universal sovereignty in Khmer country was never enunciated in any language other than Sanskrit; the use of Khmer was scrupulously restricted to the specification of material details. It is very hard, for the Sanskritist at least, to identify the slightest Cambodian inflection in the Sanskrit inscriptions Wolters analyzes beyond the occasional localism with respect to gender relations or sectarian practices (chapter 3.1). This is entirely expected, of course, since a principal function of the Sanskrit discourse was to efface local difference in favor of the transregional standard. Moreover, an argument about prehistoric features is just as unfalsifiable as the more general one that represents Indianization as a mere catalyst for the manifestation of preexistent cultural ideas, or as a vehicle for preexistent practices, given how little is known of the nature of political power in Khmer country in the earlier period.

More problematic areas of interpretation appear when we probe deeper. The assumption that a historical thought world can be separated from the historical language in which it is embodied—that Sanskrit in Cambodian inscriptions could have been expressing non-Sanskrit notions, "prehistoric features"—is very hard to justify or even to comprehend. Like many other scholars, Wolters was inclined to take Indian literary allusions in inscriptions as mere veneer, decoration, and metaphorization. But if we did not already suspect as much, recent scholarship such as that of George Lakoff and others is there to affirm that metaphors are not mere figures of speech but primary ways of perceiving the world and, moreover, that if metaphor universally structures everyday conceptual systems, much metaphorical thinking is culture- and language-specific. Similarly, when Wolters tells us that everything that had no connection with "personal cults and the accompanying perception of zones of holiness" had "nothing to do with the Khmers' sense of being in the Hindu world," we might want to reserve judgment on whether there were in fact significant areas of Khmer life unconnected with zones of holiness

14. Wolters 1982: 10–11, 13.

and power. Rather than seeing the process of Indianization as merely foregrounding the indigenous, as "something which depended on a Southeast Asian capacity for making sense of what was 'foreign' and unfamiliar in terms of what was already familiar," it may be just as reasonable to reverse the equation: Indianization could have meant learning to see what was local and familiar from an entirely unwonted, macroscopic perspective—in effect, to create something new, something that had never been there before.[15] Nor is it clear that the basic assumption of indigenism in play here should even be granted in the first place. The foreign does not become such until civilizationalist thinking makes it so. Prior to that, the "foreign" is simply a cultural element circulating in the vast world, its origins undecidable and very likely irrelevant to the people who proceeded to make use of it.

Similar claims of indigenous primacy are made in Denys Lombard's assessment of the transculturation of Java. He presents the picture of a "Southeast Asian culture" (notably in the singular) arising during the first millennium and providing the region with "solid geohistorical foundations": the "heart of Java" beat for almost a millennium "according to the same rhythm as that of Angkor and Pagan, and then Sukhotai." But Lombard is unwilling to allow any role for extraregional flows in shaping this culture. Like Wolters, he asserts that Sanskrit as used in Java "refers to realities that are properly Javanese." Again, this is to rely on a curious theory of culture that sees reality as constituted prior to and independent of language, and on a cultural logic that posits a primeval, unitary, self-identical Javaneseness over which Sanskrit is wrapped like so much packaging. Lombard is of course right to insist that understanding the Sanskrit and Sanskrit-inspired texts of Java requires placing them in a Javanese social world. But this is true of every text everywhere; there is no Sanskrit text in India that can be understood without being placed in a *cadre local,* however much the text may have sought—as many Sanskrit texts sought—to escape it. And to be sure, the authors of the *kakawin*s may with some justice be seen as standing in the same relation to Sanskrit as Corneille and Racine did to the Greek and Latin authors of classical antiquity. But if the analogy is meant to imply superficiality, irrelevance, inauthenticity, or insincerity, it is entirely misleading. It would then capture nothing to help us actually understand, whether for first-millennium cosmopolitan-imperial Southeast Asia or for seventeenth-century vernacular-national Europe, the role cultural models played, how transculturation worked, or why literature was the privileged form for mediating political self-identification.[16]

The conceptual framework shaping the scholarship of these leading historians of Southeast Asian culture and thought was itself shaped by a civi-

15. Wolters 1982: 65, 91 ff; 1979: 440; 1994: 13.
16. Lombard 1990: 13–14.

lizationalist indigenism with its roots as deeply sunk into the political realities of its time as was the first, colonialist phase of research. It was a framework generated by decolonization and new state-building, and so it is hardly surprising that historical scholarship discovered what it was looking for: the autonomous culture that the newly autonomous region required—a region whose long and independent history would demonstrate that no one's assistance was needed for graduating to statehood. The conceptual problems in the interpretative framework are graver than this etiology suggests, however. They comprise a failure to see culture rather as a historical process, but as a unitary, self-sufficient, ever-pregiven thing; a failure to grasp the "indigenous" as anything more than the moment on a time line prior to the particular transformation one is studying and falsely generalized across history or, better put, as the point prior to which it proves impossible to historicize the acquisition of the cultural trait in question. What the history of transculturation at work in the Sanskrit cosmopolis demonstrates every step of the way, however, is that all culture is really transculture. Indigenism is to the history of culture what creationism is to the history of the cosmos.[17]

Whatever the accuracy of my genealogy of civilizationalist thinking in the case of Southeast Asia studies, there is no doubt that in the minds of the strategic planners of post–Cold War America civilizations have taken on hard, inflexible, and perfected shapes they never previously had, precisely the sort that civilizationalism demands. No longer are they processes of continuous historical transformation; they have become completely closed and static systems, and understanding these systems, their unchanging and eternal character and political proclivities, is presently central to the development of U.S. foreign policy. The bitter fruit of civilizationism has now been born in the cartoonish account, midwived by the schematic thinking and reductivism of Oswald Spengler and Arnold Toynbee, found in the work of Samuel Huntington. Here civilizations are not changeable objects in the minds of people participating in changeable relations of culture and power but frozen, thing-like entities that by their very nature clash—ignorant armies in the night indeed—and, in this shallow vision, become very much part of the turbid ebb and flow of human misery.[18]

17. While recognizing the serious historical problems with "indigenism" ("What is the cut-off year for being 'indigenous' if everyone immigrated at some point?"), John Bowen makes a case for a strategic use of indigenist discourse: when, for example, the issue "has to do with the power of states to displace vulnerable people—whether their ancestors got there first is not really what is important" (paper presented to the Regional Worlds Conference, University of Chicago, May 1996). But other arguments, drawn from political economy for example, could be equally effective and less spurious.

18. See Huntington 1996, and for one critique among dozens, Hannerz 1999. The agonistic trope appears already in Kroeber (the Pacific war was the "clash" of Occidental and Oriental civilizations, 1952: 381). The Comparative Civilizations Project at the University of Chicago,

Even outside the security-state paradigm, in purportedly post-area-studies scholarship on globalization, for example, civilizationalism continues to shape the analysis. Consider two representative essays, one a general statement on globalization, another a study of the historical globalizing process in nineteenth-century East Asia, Polynesia, and the Pacific Northwest. In the first, where an effort is made to resist endorsing the process of universal homogenization by a "pretheoretical commitment to global heterogeneity," we are told how "each distinctive civilization possesses as part of its symbolic heritage a conception of the world as a whole" that shapes its "orientations to the world as a whole and [its] forms of participation . . . in the global-human circumstance."[19] The second essay critiques the interpretation of the globalization-localization problematic as "a physics of proportionate relationships between economic 'impacts' and cultural 'reactions.' The specific effects of the global-material forces depend on the various ways they are mediated in local cultural schemes." Civilizations exist in a global flow of material exchange but do not respond to that exchange in a mechanistic and uniform manner. Instead, "indigenous peoples" variously "integrate their experience of the world system in . . . their own system of the world."[20]

For the first author, civilizations are clearly still regarded as natural kinds, each possessing a single, unified worldview and a single heritage whose distinctiveness is now under threat for the first time in history. But not only is such a characterization grossly inaccurate, it is not even entirely intelligible. What possible "conception of the world as a whole" could be said to characterize "Indian civilization," which has witnessed struggles over conceptions of the world of the most incommensurable and irreconcilable sort for three millennia? More important, when permitted to underwrite today's practice of area studies, such a representation of uniformity and singularity tends to produce what it purports to merely characterize. The pedagogical outcomes of this practice cannot be elaborated on here; suffice it to say that all that could negate the Huntington vision of the civilizations of South and Southeast Asia in the first millennium (or those of Central and South Asia in the second, or of West and South Asia in the first millennium B.C.E.)—all that in fact unified these regions to the degree that little except later nomenclature created distinctions among them—cannot be studied within the typical institutional structures of American universities. Civilizationalism permits study only of what divided them, or rather, thanks to the very ignorance propagated by civilizationist institutional structures, what can be imagined to have done so.

---

initiated by Robert Redfield in the early 1950s, was something of a counterdiscourse to the neocolonial objectives of the United States (Sartori 1998).

19. Robertson 1992: 130–33.

20. Sahlins 1988: 4–5.

For the second author, too, while he strongly argues against the standard image of the local as inert wax for the developmental imprint of the global, local cultural schemes and systems of the world of indigenous peoples are still a priori, given and permanent. Manchu emperors of the eighteenth century seem to belong to much the same system as Ch'in Shih Huang-ti of the third century B.C.E. But local systems are never stable; they are constantly and often radically changing in direct response to wider cultural flows. Recall one instance mentioned earlier from the history of the transregional circulation of Sanskrit literary theory: literary culture was important to the Chinese system of the world for centuries; the ability to compose Recent Style poetry was required to pass the civil service examination from the Sung period onward. But we now know that some defining features of this poetry were developed in the T'ang by the importation of Sanskrit literary theory, one of the more important cultural luxury items disseminated across an Asian network of premodern globalization.[21]

To avoid evacuating all process and thereby immobilizing human activity into the static form of the indigenous, deeper historical probing is needed. This would show that all indigenous cultures have been produced through exchange in the course of long-term translocal interaction; their "systems of the world" are at once products of the world system and, equally important, the sources of inputs that produced that system in the first place. It is accordingly erroneous to think of "local cultural schemes" or "little traditions" as either local or little. Wherever we look, we find them defining, or rather creating, themselves through participation in vaster processes and interactions. And by the same token, it is erroneous to think of a civilization, or a "great tradition," as a unitary entity of whatever size. Indeed, a stable singularity called "Indian culture," so often conjured up by Southeast Asian indigenists, never existed. What did exist was only a range of cultural and political codes and acts, many recently developed (Sanskrit *kāvya,* public inscriptions, free-standing temple building, quasi-universalist political imagery, land-grants to Brahmanical communities, and so on) and undoubtedly generated out of various local practices. The history of this generative process often escapes our grasp, or is recoverable only with the greatest effort. Only gradually did all these practices coalesce into something like a cosmopolitan unity, one that was both "at home" and "abroad" across this entire space. Not only is "Indianization" something of a empty signifier, since no unitary force ever existed to produce the process except in the trivial sense that the subcontinent provided one important source of new cultural flows to southern and eastern Asia; not only is it a crude sort of teleology, erroneously presupposing as cause what was only produced as effect; but equally

21. Mair and Mei 1991, especially p. 461; see also chapter 4.1. Sahlins's remarks on China are found in 1988: 22.

remarkable, and almost always overlooked, is the fact that the Indianization of Southeast Asia was concurrent with, and no different from, the Indianization of India itself.

It is thus one of the ironies of Wolters's generally persuasive overall analysis, which he offers in the hope of contributing to the creation of a "genuinely Southeast Asian history," that what he describes for Khmer country actually applies unconditionally to India as well. The Hinduism Wolters wants to put in scare quotes to argue that all Khmer "Hinduism" actually echoed "pre-Hindu beliefs" has to be put in scare quotes for India, too; the image of a stratum of elites who "in different centres could perceive ubiquitous signs of its beliefs" and shared "a broadly based communality of outlook," the primacy of the "now" and the openness to the new, the mobility and transferability of the cosmic center, the "relaxed sense of power"—all this makes as much sense in the Indian context as it does in the Southeast Asian.[22]

The same critical praise can be offered of Lombard's learned appreciation of Javanese transculturation. There is no reason to believe that the *mentalité* of the *kakawin* poets in respect to their Sanskrit models, whatever it may have been, was any different from that of the regional-language poets of India itself, Pampa, Nannaya, Kampaṉ, Tulsīdās, and others. All these poets, too, were no less Indianized than the Javanese *kawi*s; at the same time they helped to propel the process of Indianization. The complex dialectic at work here is one we have seen well illustrated in the domain of literary theory. The Sanskrit poetics that helped transform Chinese poetry was itself generated out of a complex interaction with local aesthetic norms of the mid-first millennium (chapter 9.2). Over the following centuries, writers from Karnataka, Sri Lanka, Tamil country, Tibet, and beyond used this now-global discourse, in which the original local inputs had been entirely effaced, to fashion, or refashion, a new vernacular poetics.

The same logic holds true outside the realm of literary culture. Take Lombard's vision of cosmic Southeast Asian polities: their social organization, courts, administrative apparatus, and above all the grand agrarian cities geometrically planned in orientation to the cardinal points and set within imaginary geographies that, with the local mountains, rivers, and springs, recapitulated the geography of Bhāratavarṣa; the urban structures "freighted with cosmic symbolism, helping one to visualize the order of things"[23]—all this can be said to apply equally to much of the subcontinent. The chronol-

22. Wolters 1982: 43–44; 1979: 435; 1994. This holds true even for such specific tropes as noted in Wolters 1994: 7 in reference to Erlangga: When his poet says that Erlangga distributed booty among his soldiers and "took away only the glory for himself," he may well have been alluding to Kālidāsa's Raghu, who gives away in the Viśvajit sacrifice all that he conquered in his *digvijaya,* since "the good acquire only to bestow" (*Raghuvaṃśa* 4.84; see chapter 6.2).

23. Lombard 1990: 11. For a Graeco-Latin parallel see Millar et al. 1966: 9–10.

ogy of the invention of many of the new cultural and political practices under discussion here is often far too complex to enable us to identify the source of any one of them, and where we can follow the path of borrowing, the source can sometimes be identified in Southeast Asia itself, and not in India.[24] Indeed, some scholars hypothesize that south India and Southeast Asia stood in a relationship not of primacy and imitation but of "cultural convergence," both of them responding to the same social-political or cultural stimuli in the same ways.[25] Stunning evidence in support of this hypothesis is provided by the virtually simultaneous rise, in the ninth and tenth centuries, of the vernacular *kāyva* in the Deccan and the *kakawin* in Java (chapter 9.1).

There is of course no special deficiency—or excess—in South and Southeast Asia that renders civilizationalism empty and indigenism spurious as concepts. Elsewhere in the world of premodernity we can perceive the same dynamic historicity of cultural change neutralized by the same static historiography, the same messiness of civilizations managed by the same tidiness of civilizationalism, the same flow of culture immobilized in the same tidal pool of cultural indigenism. The Indianization of Southeast Asia was possible only because Indianism in India itself was coming into being through new cultural inputs from the West: the public display of royal inscriptions that began with Aśoka in the third century B.C.E., as well as his very idiom of rule, were borrowings from Achaemenid Persia; political inscription in Sanskrit began at the court of Śaka newcomers from western Asia. We have seen that an Indian called the "Lord of the Greeks" invented Indian astrology by translating a Hellenistic horoscopy into Sanskrit in the mid-second century (the greater part of the Indian doctrine of omens and portents was likewise borrowed, from Mesopotamia), and that the author of the *Mānasāra,* a sixth-century Sanskrit work on architecture, adapted Vetruvius. Had we the eyes to see them, we might discover that Greeks and Romans left other traces of their literatures in the subcontinent as common as the *denarii* horded in Arikamedu in Tamilnadu and the shards embedded in the alluvium of the Bay of Bengal that bear "the names of craftsmen whose kilns lay on the outskirts of Arezzo."[26] But Romanization itself—if we can use that term here for South Asia—was, in turn, made possible only because its principle components, foremost among them Latin literary culture, were then being newly invented by imports from non-Romans: the innovations of Greek- or Oscan- or Umbrian- or Libyan-speaking poets such as Livius, Naevius and Ennius, Plautus, and Terence. We could trace the circulation of vernacular

24. The *dharmacakra* motif of Dvāravatī (eastern Thailand), which has its origins in Khmer country (as opposed to Gupta India) is a modest case in point (Brown 1996).

25. See Kulke 1990: 22 ff., 26.

26. Wheeler 1954: 150. See further on these borrowings in chapter 7.1.

cultural forms as easily as we can that of their cosmopolitan predecessors. Indeed, we have already seen that Insular French literature is unthinkable without its Anglo-Saxon antecedents, and that the earliest Castilian literature depends to some degree on the continental French that borrowed from the Insular; similarly, the innovations of Sicilian and Occitan poetry bore the impress of Arabic poetry and provided stimulus for new literary inventions in Italy and Germany.

In fact, from such a perspective, something like "Westernization" can be seen as a permanent and global phenomenon. In a real sense different areas have functioned as Wests for different Easts at different periods of history. These were Wests not only geographically but often in terms of a self-declared superiority in political and economic power, rationality, and degree of "civilization." England could be said to be France's West in the seventeenth century when the notion of French national identity arose as a direct consequence of the invention of the idea of the nation in England; France was Germany's West in the nineteenth when Germans reactively defined their *Kultur* in direct contrast to France's *civilization;* Germany was Russia's West at the start of the twentieth, when Prussian bureaucrats were summoned to refashion the Czarist state—a state eventually destroyed through an ideology supplied by two nineteenth-century compatriots. In similar ways Iran functioned as India's West not only in the Achaemenid and Sasanian periods but equally dramatically in the sixteenth and seventeenth centuries when immigrant poets and painters from the Safavid realm helped shape Indo-Persian culture. Besides being the West to much of mainland and maritime Southeast Asia, India was sometimes perceived as China's West—think of the classic Chinese text *Journey to the West,* which describes the quest for Indian Buddhist culture on the part of the Chinese pilgrim Xuanzang. Throughout much of their history, China was Japan's West. And ancient Egypt was Greece's, Greece was Troy's, and ultimately Rome, in an important sense, was Greece's. And last, America became the West's West—until Japan, for a while at least, became America's own.

Nor is there anything unique about Westernization: one could perform a similar geo-cultural-historical operation for "Easternization," with Lydia and Phrygia functioning as Greece's East around the beginning of the first millennium B.C.E., Greece as Rome's East in the third through first centuries B.C.E. (Hellenization), "Germany" as "France's" East in the sixth through ninth centuries C.E. (Germanicization), France as England's East in the eleventh through fourteenth (Normanization), and India as central Asia's from the second to the tenth (Buddhicization).

The point of this exercise should now be clear. From whatever vantage point we look, if we are prepared to look historically, civilizations reveal themselves to be processes and not things. And as processes they ultimately have no boundaries; people are constantly receiving and passing on cultural goods.

No form of culture can therefore ever be "indigenous"; that term, it bears repeating, is only the name we give to what exhausts our capacity for historicization. When taken as anything more than this, the idea inhibits our perceiving that all cultures participate in what are ultimately global networks of begging, borrowing, and stealing, imitating and emulating—all the while constructing themselves precisely by sublating this history and affirming a specious autogenesis. From the processual perspective, "culture" or "civilization" (as in "Indian Civilization 101") becomes nothing but an arbitrary moment illegitimately generalized, a freeze frame in a film taken for the whole story. Each of these moments is in fact only an instance of exchange, an entrepôt, a site for reprocessing cultural goods that are always already someone else's.[27]

This circulatory character of culture is never countenanced in indigenist thought (or never at least by recipients, only by donors). In civilizationalism it is simply lost in a haze of general historical amnesia. In the vernacular variety of civilizationalism, namely nationalism, it is actively buried in a surfeit of history.

14.2 NATIONALISM, OR INDIGENISM WITH TOO MUCH HISTORY

Nationalism, as I have argued at the beginning of this chapter, comprises a particular relation between culture and power that in many respects constitutes a conceptual complement to civilizationalism. If civilizations evince the most complex expression of this relationship, nations evince the least, being predicated on a one-to-one correspondence between the two phenomena. If civilizations are the framework in which cosmopolitan languages and imperial forms of polity have typically been conceptualized, nations are supposed to be the site of vernacular culture and the power of the sovereign state—or more precisely put, since nation and nationalism are a category of practice as well as a theory of that practice, the social form that explains their very genesis. Indeed, the only theoretical understandings obtaining in the social sciences concerning the conditions and logic of vernacularization assign to it the decisive role in the formation of the nation: vernacularization without the nation implies a world of culture without power, or a world where power is nothing but culture. Like civilizationalism but even more so, nationalism operates with indigenist presuppositions, and it is likewise thor-

27. On the "local-globals" that we all are, see Latour 1993: 122; see also Braudel 1980: 203, who raises the important question: what do cultures refuse to borrow? Other scholars have made similar points (usually asserted out of goodwill rather than argued with historical evidence) about both the jerry-built constructedness of civilizations (e.g., Hannerz 1991: 127) and the translocal production of "local" cultures (e.g., Pred 1995: 1074ff.)

oughly enmeshed in the production and reproduction of political power. However, unlike civilizationalism, which ignores or even occludes the messy historical origins of its object, nationalism seeks its roots in history—and the deeper they can be sunk, the better.

The specific modern Western notion of "nation" pertained to a specific modern Western phenomenon until the time when this concept and its form were exported from the West to the rest of the world. The "derivative discourse" account of this process on offer in the case of Indian nationalism can hardly be disputed once the terms of that account are granted.[28] What is disputable is whether the terms should be granted in the first place. Hesitating to do so does not mean fatuously searching for an Indian or Kannadiga or other nation before nationalism (like representing King Alfred's project of the ninth century, or even Augustus's nine centuries earlier, anachronistically as one of national identity and ideology). It means instead asking, among other things, whether standard explanations for the emergence of the culture-power complex today called nation are adequate to the evidence actually adduced, especially the role attributed to language and literature in the theorization of the nation. It means inquiring whether these explanations are the only way to make sense of the relationship of culture and power in the course of their development in the vernacular millennium, as various theoretical accounts insist, or whether the realm of historical possibility is wider than such theory acknowledges. Last, it means determining whether in South Asia the kind of nation brought into being in modernity took the specific form it did because of the specific histories of South Asia. Reviewing the fit, or misfit, of theories of European modernity over against South Asian premodernity is meant to help us better understand the particularity of the latter but also to test apparent certitudes that draw their strength in part from differences more often assumed than demonstrated.

One of the more intractable problems of this entire enterprise is the tangled history of the very concept, which can hardly be ignored when attempting to assess the adequacy of its theorization. The understanding of "nation" in the early nineteenth century, when its most consequential enunciation was being offered in European discourse, diverges radically from more recent thinking, where the term has been drastically and narrowly redefined to produce a virtually new category of both analysis and practice. Yet the historical-conceptual gaps between these moments are not often recognized, let alone bridged. The depth of this divergence emerges with particular clarity when we contrast the recent conceptualization with that of G. W. F. Hegel, who was the most important thinker to link the political form of the nation with a specific literary-cultural form. The story line here, in a

28. See Chatterjee 1986a.

word, is that, from the standpoint of European thought, India had once been but then, somehow, abruptly ceased to be a nation. And this is a story worth reconstructing.

Again, whether or not my reconstruction of this history is valid, everyone agrees that the modern European idea of the nation that interested Indian intellectuals at the end of the nineteenth century was something new to them—as it was new, generally speaking, to Europeans themselves. (That colonialism was the precondition for this "official nationalism" to take hold in India, as is so often asserted in contemporary scholarship, is of course true, but it is the truth of a tautology: that Western-style modernity was a precondition for Western-style modernity.) To understand how this newness related to all that came before, as a conceptual problem on the one hand and a practical one on the other, has been an important task for scholars and political actors alike. Because he combined both personas, Gramsci was able to grasp a number of the key questions better than most. The general problem of the surplus of history that invests the nation with its supposedly primeval and continuous existence—the conundrum of "old societies and new states," as it was called (with terminological fastidiousness) in the 1950s—is one that Gramsci formulated memorably in the case of Italy as "the paradox of a very young and a very old country at the same time (like Lao-tse born at the age of eighty)." He rightly perceived that the mentality at work here was located in a "rhetorical prejudice (originating in literature), according to which the Italian nation has always existed, from ancient Rome to the present day." Emphasizing again the role of literary culture in this process, he argued that "the preconception that Italy has always been a nation complicates its entire history and requires anti-historical intellectual acrobatics." "History [i.e., historiography] was political propaganda, it aimed to create national unity—that is, the nation—from the outside and against tradition, by basing itself on literature. It was a *wish,* not a must based on already existing conditions." The nation, moreover, had only a literary-cultural status, it was "more a rhetorical . . . entity than a felt cultural reality, existing at most for the intellectual and ruling elites but not for the people."[29]

Gramsci's insights are suggestive to students of South Asian culture-power structures in underscoring the complicated genealogy of the nation, identifying literary culture as the arena within which this genealogy is most powerfully enunciated, and emphasizing the very limited sphere in which the conceptual object produced by this culture circulates. Yet he is still giving us only the easy part. Like the critics of primordialism, he succeeds in asking all the right questions but offers no help in answering them. How are we in fact to comprehend the new child's paradoxical old age, or assess the relationships

29. Gramsci 1991: 167, 201, 256–57, 198 (a valuable exegesis, though with other emphases, is offered in Kaviraj 1992a: 9).

that do exist between past and present in the making of the modern nation, or grasp why people should believe they exist at all? How can we explain why this prejudice should be rhetorical in the first place, and why literary culture, of all things, should be the prime site for the elaboration of these relationships? And finally, how should we account for the fact that so few people (the "elites") could make so many perceive so purely rhetorical an entity as real?

Once again, it is possible to examine only a few of the big problems that confront us here. Two in particular that have been central to theorizing the European nation and to framing the questions that troubled Gramsci are also central to this book. The first, in the domain of language, is the process of vernacularization. The second, in the domain of literature, is what might be called epicization and novelization, that is, the politicization of epic and novel in actual practice and, more particularly, the place that theory has accorded to each in the narrative constitution of the nation. The explanatory role of vernacular language can be quickly surveyed, given that much of this material is familiar. Epicization and novelization require more attention, since some key materials have never been given the prominence they deserve.

However much they may diverge on other matters, the two works that continue to exert the greatest influence on both theories of nationalism and cultural studies more broadly, Ernest Gellner's *Nations and Nationalism* and Benedict Anderson's *Imagined Communities,* agree on one thing at least: that cultural-cognitive processes play a primary role in the generation of the nation. More specifically, both view language, especially the creation of standardized literary language, as a fundamental mechanism in the production not only of national consciousness but of the necessary precondition of this consciousness, the homogenization of identity, whether through pedagogical or literary processes.

According to Gellner's well-known thesis, a decisive feature of nationalism is located in the shifting boundaries of what he identifies as literary and nonliterary cultures. In agrarian, or "agro-literate," societies, a wide gap existed between rulers and ruled; the former participated in high literary cultures typically larger than any polity, the latter in low nonliterary cultures typically smaller than any. High literary cultures are those that made use of the transethnic and transpolitical idioms, like Latin or Arabic, associated with a faith and a church—what Anderson calls the "sacred languages" that linked "classical" or "sacred" communities, such as Christendom and Ummah Islam. These are described by Gellner as mysterious, inaccessible liturgical codes, which elites, in order to enhance the barrier and deepen the chasm between clerisy and laity, sought to distinguish even further from the demotic by incomprehensible pronunciations or arcane scripts. Local cultures, by contrast, remained unwritten and "invisible." The implications Gellner draws from this situation are large indeed: "Perhaps the central, most important fact about agro-literate society is this: almost everything in it militates against the definition of political units in terms of cultural boundaries . . . One might put it this way: of the two potential partners, culture and power, destined for each other according to nationalist theory, neither has much inclination for the other in the conditions prevailing in the agrarian age." (Although Gellner leaves "culture" deliberately undertheorized throughout, he makes it clear that "an at least provisionally acceptable criterion of culture might be language.") Thus the factors determining political boundaries "are totally distinct from those determining cultural limits," and any correspondence of a dynastic state with a language and a culture occurred only "by accident." All this can change under only one condition, industrialization. This produces a demand for a mobile, hence egalitarian, hence educated workforce and, concomitantly, a need for standardized literary language—something developed by either the generalization of high literary culture or the elevation of low culture (or, in the terms used in this book, the latter's literization and literarization). It is the state that creates, or recreates, such culture, whereby a coincidence of the units of power and culture—the nation-state and its ideology, nationalism—is generated.[30]

Although it remains the most widely accepted explanation of the origins of European nationalism,[31] Gellner's model has been challenged on various points; the deeper social history of language and literary culture in South Asia (and indeed, in Europe) offered here complicates it still further. We will consider some of these criticisms to Gellner later in the chapter, as well as to the claims (also widely accepted) made by Anderson. One argument symptomatic of a larger difficulty is Anderson's thesis (though the genealogy of his idea is long) regarding the specific place of literature, literary genres, and literary representation in producing the "rhetorical prejudice" that Gramsci identified as fundamental to nationalism. Although Gramsci does not elaborate on the cultural mechanisms at work, he no doubt has in mind the practice of literary historiography, for undoubtedly it was this form of rhetoric, not just in Italy but across nineteenth- and twentieth-century Europe, that most effectively produced the prejudice of the antiquity of the nation. In fact, it is precisely this conviction that makes it impossible for the nationalist literary historian to admit that vernacular literatures have a beginning, for if the nation extends back in time immemorially, so must its imaginative self-expression.[32]

30. Gellner 1983: 11–12, 39, 50, 141 ff.; p. 43 for the definition of culture.

31. See Hall 1998.

32. The "very close association between Romantic (mostly linguistic) nationalism and the rise of modern organized literary history" was noted as long ago as Wellek and Warren's *Theory of Literature* in 1942 (cited in Hollier 1995: 236). It is no coincidence that an important nationalist of the Risorgimento, Francesco de Sanctis, was at the same time author of a well-known (though not in fact primordialist) history of Italian literature (1870).

The relationship between literature and nation has been theorized far beyond the autochthony that informs the discourse of literary historiography, as something at once more fundamental and more widely diffused throughout the literary system. A concrete linkage between the two was posited in philosophical discourse before European literary historiography was even invented, having been argued, if not first at least most consequentially, by Hegel in the 1820s, when he portrayed the "epic" as the sort of text that seeks to communicate the "national story." During the years when Gramsci was reflecting on the nature of nationalism's rhetorical prejudice, notable developments in literary theory, particularly genre theory, severed the epic-nation linkage that Hegel had forged, though without replacing it. Georg Lukács and Mikhail Bakhtin contrasted the moral economy of epic and "novel," thereby rendering the epic irrelevant for communicating the story of what was now understood, at least by implication, to be a very different nation from what Hegel had in mind. Two generations later these ideas were supplemented and revised, most influentially by Anderson, in the now-dominant theory that sees the novel as historically coeval with the nation as such and so constituting the fundamental literary form in which the nation attains representation and tells its story—novelization entailing the novelty of the nation, so to put it, its "astonishing youth" now thematized for the first time. This is a complex chapter in European intellectual history but important enough to our purposes here to try to summarize.

As one of the early theorists of the exceptionalism of the European nation-state, Hegel occupies an important place in understanding the relationship between the literary and the national at a period in European history when the very concepts were taking on their modern significations. This aspect of his work seems not to have received much discussion in contemporary debates, although it raises interesting questions. Some of these are related to the lexicon of Hegel's exposition, and so we need to be attentive to his original texts at every step. One of these is his *Lectures on Aesthetics* (1817–29; published 1835–38). Here it is the "epic proper" that forms the core of the national narrative. The term "epic," he explains, refers to the "absolutely first books" possessed by every "great and important nation" *(jede grosse und bedeutende Nation):* the Greeks and Romans, the Persians, the Hebrews and Arabs (whose Old Testament and Qur'an emphasize the religious dimension of life), the Indians, and, later, the Germanic and Romanic peoples (*Nibelungenlied, Edda, Cid,* and the like)—texts that Hegel stresses are "actual epic materials that pertain to *national* medieval concerns, deeds, and characters" *(echt epischen Stoffe, die noch schlechthin nationale mittelalterliche Interessen, Taten und Charaktere in sich fassen).* Such works, which display to our eyes the "individual spirits of each nation," are central because they treat of events connected with the total world of a nation and epoch, and in them "the spirit that is originary to [the nation] finds expression." "The content and form of epic proper are the entire world-outlook and objective manifestation of a people's spirit *(Volksgeist)* presented in its self-objectifying shape as an actual event." Epics express "the affairs of an entire nation" *(die Sache der ganzen Nation)*, the "national condition" *(Nationalzustand)*, "the viewpoint of a national spirit" *(die Anschauung eines nationalen Geistes)*. And, albeit originating in the *Urzeit* of a people as their absolutely first books, such epics remain permanently valid for them so long as "the factual characteristics have an inner connection with those really substantive aspects and tendencies of the nation's existence." This vital connection between the "factual" and the "national substance of spiritual consciousness" *(die nationale Substanz des geistigen Bewusstseins)* applies, for example, to the indigenous geography that belongs to nationality (*[die] einheimische Geographie [die] zur Nationalität [gehört]*). However, the enduring life of an epic—its capacity to produce continuing effects—suffers if the "link between this more recent past and the original starting-point have been altogether snapped," as occurred, for example, in the case of the Germanic epic, the *Nibelungenlied*.[33]

As we can observe, nothing in Hegel's usage of *Nation* is ambiguous. The term bears no obvious premodern meaning—as in, say, the idiom of the medieval church councils, where the word referred to a country's elite. And this makes it difficult not to conclude that Hegel's understanding of the concept is radically at odds with what we find in Gellner and other recent thinkers.[34] If Hegel, like Gellner, finds a primary mode of the nation's existence to lie in language and literature (though Hegel includes without distinction epics written in the cosmopolitan languages like Persian and Sanskrit and those in the vernacular languages like Spanish and French), *Nation* clearly had for him an entirely different historical character, or rather, a non- or trans-historical character. For Hegel, a precociously nationalized intellectual himself, *Nation* is clearly a primeval entity, antedating and shaping even the absolutely first books that discursively construct it. In this he was entirely typical of the age; for Marx, too, capitalist modernity, far from inventing nations, simply compels them to introduce "what it calls civilization into their midst, that is, to become bourgeois."[35] Hegel's vision was typical of a later age as well: it differs from Heidegger's ontologically primal being-in-place only insofar as it regarded such being as self-evident, needing no

33. Hegel 1975: 331, 404, 336, 338, 345, 346 (I generally adopt, though sometimes adapt, the translation of Knox). Hegel does not ask whether the break with its epic past was linked with the fate of the German nation, or whether the resultant weakness was that of a *Kulturnation* faced with the task of transforming into a *Staatsnation*.

34. For the usage of the Church councils, see Greenfield 1996: 7 ff.

35. Marx and Engels 1981: 30: "sie zwingt [alle Nationen], die sogenannte Zivilisation bei sich selbst einzuführen, d.h. Bourgeois zu werden."

philosophical vindication. And indeed, his view hardly differs from the civilizationalism of today's prophets of clash, for whom "Hindu," "Confucian," and other civilizations are eternal and unchanging configurations of culture.

It might be assumed that the concept of *Nation* in Hegel refers to what is now often called a civilization (the Marx-Engels passage of course complicates this terminological confusion still further). However, in his usage the term comprises the emergent nations of modern Europe, such as Spain, which were unlikely to have been viewed as constituting separate civilizations. Moreover, there is a distinction among these nations of a sort not usually drawn in differentiating civilizations that brings them close to what is meant by "nation" in the contemporary idiom. If the epic can underwrite the nation, not all nations are equally capable of being thus underwritten, and it is the absence of the *state,* or rather the reason for its absence, that explains why. For Hegel, the state is, famously, the production of a reality in accordance with right and law, and many "nations may have passed a long life before arriving at this their destination," even if "during this period, they may have attained considerable culture in some directions." India has not yet arrived. While the recent discovery of the kinship of Sanskrit and German, "a great discovery in history—as of a new world" proved conclusively for Hegel "the diffusion of those nations from Asia as a center," what impressed him more was the radically "dissimilar development of what had been originally related" in terms of state-building.[36] In the *Lectures* we are invited to connect this political history with Hegel's evaluation of the literary aesthetics of the national story in non-Western epics, in particular, the "Oriental epic" (the aesthetics are a symptom of the failure of the state, of course, rather than the cause). The Oriental epic has as its "center" "the symbolic type," which in the case of the Indian epic is "incapable of the prosaic circumspection of the intellect" (Indians are *geistige Pflanzennaturen,* beings that are plantlike in their mentality) and, concomitantly, deficient in the "prose of history" wherein the state finds its true expression. The *Mahābhārata* and *Rāmāyaṇa* (which Hegel knew intimately through his association with the Sanskritist Franz Bopp in Berlin) explain to us "the entire outlook of the Indians," not only "in its whole splendor and magnificence" but also "in its confusion, fantastic flabbiness and lack of real truth."[37] Those whose texts lack real truth may have a nation but cannot have a state, in the sense of a self-consciously historical polity created in accordance with right and law. As for the novel, the literary form that was in the course of attaining unchallenged cultural dominance during the very period Hegel was writing, its role is not remotely like that of the epic. It is merely the "modern bourgeois epic," and, like the

36. Hegel 1956: 59–60.

37. Hegel 1975: 394 (on the symbolic type); 396 (on the Indian epic).

bourgeoisie itself, it fails as an art form to produce the immediate unity of the individual and the general.[38]

It was not, however, Hegel's vision of epic nations, with or without the crowning achievement of the state, but the contrast between epic and novel that interested literary theorists in the first half of the twentieth century. This contrast functioned as something of a fulcrum to leverage a number of important cultural-historical issues, and the work it has done is typified in the cultural-critical theories of Lukács and Bakhtin. For Lukács, writing in the immediate aftermath of the First World War and its ethical chaos, the problem of moral values in literature looms larger than the relationship between literary and political forms. Indeed, what centrally distinguishes epic from novel is the status of the community's ethical coherence, "whether the general civilization is an integrated or a problematic one" (one may well ask whether Lukács's use of the term "civilization" signals an indifference at this period of European history to the question of polity and poetry). Building largely on Hegel, though ignoring the framework of the nation that shaped Hegel's exposition, Lukács also sees the novel as a form of epic, but the epic "of an age in which the extensive totality of life is no longer directly given, in which the immanence of meaning in life has become a problem." The true epic, by contrast, is the literary form of an integrated civilization, in which values are pregiven and heroes, as a consequence, do not agonize over what to do. The novel is a form that literature takes in a "degraded society" and is therefore the story of the search for value, for "restored epic fullness."[39] To put this in another idiom: epic is the genre of the certitudes and mechanical solidarities of *Gemeinschaft*, while the novel is the genre of the rising ambiguities and organic solidarities of *Gesellschaft*.

Closely related to Lukács's vision of the old epic's moral plenitude (though apparently ignorant of it) is the conception of epic distance found in Bakhtin. The place of literary genres in relation to forms of polity is not overtly thematized here, either. Where Bakhtin does attempt to situate the novel in relation to the national problematic he is unclear and at times demonstrably in error: scholars have increasingly come to see that his conception of the novel as a form that decenters national cultures—through the stimulation of "social polyphony"—cannot be sustained. His contrast between epic and novel, however, continues to find resonance.[40] Bakhtin tries

38. Hegel 1975: 392.

39. Lukács 1971: 27, 56; cf. also Bennett 1990: 93.

40. I know of no sustained critique of Bakhtin's theory of the counternationalism of the novel; for now see Moretti 1998: 45 n. and references there. Bakhtin's ideas on epic and novel have also been called into question for Russian literary history (Griffiths and Rabinowitz 1990: 1–39). But his large generalizations retain heuristic power.

to isolate among other things those discursive features that specifically mark off the genre of novel from that of epic (which for Bakhtin is by definition Western—how far had the global reach of cultural analysis in Hegel contracted in a mere century). The most important of these features are located in the new presence in the novel of the *present* itself. Borrowing from Goethe and Schiller a distinction between the "absolute past" of the epic and the "absolute present" of the drama, Bakhtin argues that the epic is, for every audience, a world irremediably completed, one to which no bridge can afford passage. "The epic world is constructed in the zone of an absolute distanced image, beyond the sphere of possible contact with the developing, incomplete and therefore re-thinking and re-evaluating present"; it is "finished and closed like a circle." "Contemporaneity as such" can never become an object of representation for the epic, since its temporality is hierarchized, distant, and valorized in its distance. In contrast, the novel, unlike other forms of literature, has from the beginning been "structured not in the distanced image of the absolute past but in the zone of direct contact with inconclusive present-day reality."[41]

When these two conceptions of the novel—as the genre of contemporaneity and as the genre of modernity's moral indeterminacy—were wedded to a renewed commitment to a kind of Hegelian understanding of the relation of culture and power, the reigning interpretation of the genesis and character of the novel was produced. I say "a kind of Hegelian understanding," since the renewed concern with the poetics of power produced something Hegel would probably have found incomprehensible: the nation—not the nation-state but the nation, since there are communally imagined nations without states—was now conceived of as a historically new phenomenon, both existentially and cognitively. For Anderson and his followers, the novel is the preeminent cultural form that gives expression to this phenomenon and does so totally, in its substantive, formal, and technological aspects.

Substantively, the novel is the genre that narrates the national (or newly nationalized) community, "'re-presenting' the *kind* of imagined community that is the nation," as Anderson phrases it. According to one leading literary historian, the novel is the "new symbolic form" that the nation "needed . . . in order to be understood"—given its demand for an unfamiliar, obscure species of loyalty and its "wider, more abstract, more enigmatic dominion." For other critics, the novel not only accompanies but also enables the rise of the nation by "objectifying the 'one, yet many' of national life"; the novel satisfies a "national longing for form." And in one of the more extreme extrapolations of this postulate to "third-world" literature, if there exists no

41. Bakhtin 1981 (original 1938): 17, 19, 38.

novel there exists no nation; if a new nation comes into being, every novel that comes into being with it in turn functions as "national allegory."[42] Formally, the novel correlates with the nation through a number of internal and external features. It does so internally along both axes of the spatiotemporal plane: first, through a narrative temporality that fits the time of modernity—where every moment is a transition to something new in an ever-developing progress—something that makes it an exact analogue for the nation (and a disanalogue for the premodern "sacred community," with its cosmological fullness of time); second, through a narrative spatiality, whereby the novel (often through what Anderson calls a "skein of literary journeys" or "looping sojourns") wrests its fictional space from other, prenational geographical matrices and forms the national fictional space so as to become the true symbolic form of the nation.[43] Externally, the novel correlates with the nation through the standardized—now national—vernacular languages in which novels are written. Last, with respect to technology, innovations contemporaneous in origin with the novel (and with the newspaper, the new documentary form of national literary culture), above all, "print-capitalism," provide the material engine whereby the form of the national imaginary is able to achieve its true *national* extension. The new possibility for textual dissemination offered by print, the generalized literacy connected with it, and the new market economy of reading escape premodernity's constraints on communication whereby earlier literary (as well as literary-historical) representations remained an affair, as Gramsci puts it, "existing at most for the intellectual and ruling elites but not for the people."

Any account of so complicated a set of theories on literary and political forms spanning two centuries, especially one so compressed as this, will no doubt be inaccurate in places. But in addition there are ambiguities internal to the theories themselves. Only consider the understanding of "novel." Whereas according to Lukács's account the genre is specific to the early modern and subsequent periods in Europe, Bakhtin's conceptualization is idiosyncratic. At one moment he relates the novel to the particular character of certain nineteenth-century Russian narratives; at another it has a much more expansive history starting as far back as the Manippean satire; at yet another it bears an even more capacious signification, both because "novelization" for Bakhtin means counterdominant writing as such, and because "novel" is the "ever-becoming" genre and hence ex hypothesi indeterminate. The inability to frame a workable definition of "novel" and other genres, including of course "epic" (Hegel's generalities notwithstanding, it is not obvious what in literary terms unites the *Aeneid,* Qur'an, and *Nibelungenlied*) is not

42. See respectively Anderson 1983, especially p. 30; Moretti 1998: 17; Brennan 1990: 49; Jameson 1986. Not all these assertions are sustained by adequate evidence.

43. This is the formulation of Moretti 1998: 53, 45; see also Anderson 1983: 32 ff., and 105.

peculiar to Lukács and Bakhtin but is so widespread that some scholars have deemed the sociology of literature, which aims to link "genre dominants" with "social dominants," a discredited intellectual project.[44]

The same difficulty clearly attaches to the use of "nation," though here the issue is not only one of historical semantics; there are notorious conceptual difficulties as well. More candid historians throw up their hands at trying to frame a normative definition. Even to restate polemically a definition that problematizes definition itself—to suggest that "a nation is a group of people who use the vocabulary of nationality as if they could really isolate what it meant"—fails to go far enough; what, after all, is "*the* vocabulary"?[45] And it goes without saying that definitional problems have their consequences: what people understand by "epic," "novel," and "nation" fundamentally affects their historical accounts of "epic" and the rest, though the serious ambiguities involved rarely seem to give anyone much pause.

Granting all these difficulties, the pragmatist could still answer that we are not dealing here with positivities; that it is immaterial whether the novel really was invented with the invention of the capitalist nation, or whether a wide range of narrative and other differences can be found in the forms of European writing that people have termed epic (*Epopöe, épique,* etc.) and novel (*Roman, roman,* etc.). What is material is the fact that at a particular moment in history people began to call certain forms of literature "novels" and did certain things with them, and still call them so and do certain similar things with them; in the same way, people began to call certain social formations "nations" and did certain things with them, and still do. What a nation really is, apart from such representations and uses, is indeterminable—in fact, apart from them it may be nothing.

Yet a stronger critique of the European discourse, beyond its terminological imprecision is possible, and has its place. To assess the history and character of Western theories about the history and character of the nation—epicization, novelization, their correlation with political forms, and the nature of those forms themselves—is important, and not just because these theories pretend to know the world better and to claim universal explanatory validity. The very object of analysis, the nation itself, has similarly sought universality almost as a substantialized agent in itself, and in thereby setting the rules of the game it has predetermined the outcome of theory's claim. Whatever the truth of the history of its constitution, the nation has been disseminated across the globe and its adoption has been enforced everywhere ("*The* origin and spread of nationalism," Anderson's subtitle, exemplifies the implicit singularity and universality of both the analysis and its object). If

44. Bennett 1990: 107. On the instability in premodern South Asia of the genre I call here "epic" see chapter 6.1 and Pollock 2003: 59–60.

45. The first citation comes from Hobsbawm 1990: 5; the second, from Dickie 1991: 191.

these theories are self-contradictory and not entirely adequate even for explaining the development of European cultural and political orders, let alone South Asian premodernity, critique may disclose alternative realities and possibilities that vanished unachieved when European nationalism swept all before it. Theories of nations do not of themselves produce nations and their violence, of course, and critique will not undo them. But such theories purport to describe their necessary conditions of enablement, and it is this sense of necessity that bears on future action, and so merits critical attention.

There is already a substantial body of literature objecting to Gellner's and Anderson's functionalist accounts of the place of culture in nationalism. Gellner's specific hypothesis linking language, education, industrialization, and nationalism has been critiqued both from a comparative perspective (by scholars of East Asia, who have pointed to the standardized and standardizing systems of education in Korea and Vietnam in contexts devoid of vernacularization, let alone industrialization) and historically (by scholars of European nationalism, who have found indubitable forms of "nation-building" preceding industrialization).[46] The language history that supplies the ground of Gellner's general hypothesis is even more vulnerable to criticism. The model is entirely innocent of the complexity of literary-cultural formations present in the agro-literate world itself and their very particular histories, nor can it successfully integrate the evidence of the vernacular millennium, whether in South Asia or in Europe, in its historical depth and causal relationship to political and social change. The history of Sanskrit (which Gellner and Anderson both may certainly be forgiven for ignoring) shows that other kinds of cultural-political formations have been available in history beyond the "sacred community" linked by the language of a church or a faith. Sanskrit in the cosmopolitan period was never exclusively associated with any one faith or singular scripture, was never the vehicle of new revelation or a church, and was in no way restricted to other-worldly uses; to the contrary, at the beginning of the Common Era, Sanskrit became the instrument for an entirely new poetics of power (to say nothing of other forms of worldly knowledge) that would continue to be produced for ten centuries or more.

More tellingly, the simple dichotomy between transregional ecumene and invisible local vernacular before modernity that forms the bedrock of Gellner's thesis crumbles once we realize that the most significant steps in the production of unified (or unifying) vernacular literary cultures were first taken, dramatically and across medieval Eurasia, from within the heart of agro-literate societies themselves in the course of the first half of the second

46. Tønnesson and Antlöv 1996: 6; Hroch 1996, especially p. 85. For Greenfield, nationalism was generated in the seventeenth century by social-structural processes set in motion by a constrained aristocracy (Greenfield 1996). Others insist on seeing European nationalism as contingent upon colonialism (Segal and Handler 1992).

millennium. Completely undisturbed by historical facts in the formulation of his theory, Gellner alludes to the actual development of literary cultures only once when asking, counterfactually, what might have happened had industrialization begun "during the High Middle Ages, before the development of vernacular literatures and the emergence of what was eventually destined to become the basis of the various national high cultures?"[47] But "the development" did begin, and "what was eventually destined" did emerge, precisely in the High Middle Ages. Northern Romance, specifically the dialect of the Île de France that would eventually come to be called French, was being used extensively for literary production by the middle of the twelfth century and for the production of administrative texts by the thirteenth. It effectively attained its majority by the sixteenth—after the High Middle Ages had ended, of course, but long before the appearance of anything that can fairly be termed industrialization—when it became the sole vehicle of law and the primary language of the leading writers of the day. And its "disadvantaged cousins," the dialects of Gascony, Limousin, and so on, had "lost caste" or were doing so even before the beginning of the print revolution that, according to Anderson, was responsible for their demotion.[48] The vernacular revolution was a complex historical event, to be sure, and its material foundations as we have seen are not easily identified; no doubt it is to be linked in some way to the mercantile, agricultural, and urban transformation of the period (chapter 12.2). At all events, the transition central to Gellner's thesis, whereby "high culture," the object of literization, codification, and pedagogy, became a matter of "desperate concern" to rulers—as it did to Lorenzo de' Medici in 1470, or François I in 1540— in fact commenced long before the industrialization that Gellner assumed was its primary determining factor. The transition was also well before any appreciable impact of the print-capitalism that is supposed to have first "'assemble[d]' related vernaculars" into unitary and codified literary languages. The literary cultures produced in South Asia during the period 1000–1500 show in many instances (Kannada, Telugu, and Gujarati are examples) various signs of the philological regulation and unification, and even something approaching the standardization, that many scholars in addition to Anderson too readily believe to have been a project of European modernity in association with print technology.[49]

47. Gellner 1983: 78–79. As Nairn memorably puts it, history for Gellner "tends to be the mildly annoying stuff which happens between one sociological model and another" (1996: 275).

48. Anderson 1983: 45.

49. The same holds, of course, for Sanskrit, a quintessentially standardized language. Even the most accomplished linguists assert that print "mediates the very process of linguistic standardization," Silverstein 2000: 132–33, though his definition of standardization (p. 121) fits Sanskrit if it fits anything. See also chapter 1.3 and n. 51.

More significant still are the signs of a convergence of boundaries of culture and power in the agro-literate world that is theoretically impossible in Gellner's model. The conjuncture is reasonably clear, if only as a representation, from the earliest stages of European vernacularization (the discourse on Angelcynn in Alfred, for example, or Ytalia in Dante). It has even more distinct contours in South Asia, where from Maharashtra and Karnataka to Sri Lanka and Java vernacularization was accompanied by the production of new and often precise literary representations of political place. But there is far more going on here than representation. Vernacular polities initiated cultural-political practices (to which find-spot maps of inscriptions bear eloquent testimony) that tended to reproduce then-crystallizing language regions as administrative regions, or perhaps helped produce such regions in the first place. In twelfth-century Tamil country, circulatory and conceptual spaces were brought into a palpable symmetry by the distribution of documents produced by Cōḻa rulers. The nature of the political boundaries, the logic of the literary spatiality, and their significance for the production of a felt reality of belonging all need further clarification, but there can be little doubt that such reality was produced. And although it may be difficult to make sense of the political principle at work in this new convergence, it was almost invariably a project of the royal court, and thus it is certain that a political principle was always at work.

These considerations make it hard to agree with Gellner that "no-one, or almost no-one, has an interest in promoting cultural homogeneity" in agro-literate society, or that it would be "absurd" to link local culture with a political principal before modernity.[50] An additional irony shadows one of his principal cases: "Islamic civilization" is taken as a paradigmatic agro-literary sphere entirely impervious to the impulse toward vernacularization, but the facts show quite the opposite. Like the Sanskrit cosmopolitan order, wherever Islamicate culture traveled it enabled what was often the initial literarization of many local cultures. In India this occurred by the fourteenth century with the rise of the great Sufi allegorical romances in Avadhi.[51]

Like the history of language, the ideas and practices of literary culture in premodern South Asia, both cosmopolitan and vernacular, raise serious doubts about the necessary conditions postulated for the genesis of the European nation. In some cases comparable practices produced noncomparable outcomes; dissimilar contents can be found in similar forms, and similar contents in dissimilar forms, rendering suspect many of the causal

50. Gellner 1991: 130; 1983: 46–48, 10–12. Tønnesson and Antlöv err in claiming that "religious factors have played much the same divisive role that vernacular languages have played in Europe." Asians have indeed "not just pirated European models," but not for the reasons they give (1996: 23–24).

51. Gellner 1983: 75 ff. Contrast Levtzion 1996, and see chapter 10.1.

correlations asserted. This can be shown by a brief assessment of the South Asian materials for a critique of Western theory on the epic and novel and their relationship to the forms of power in general and the genesis of nationalism in particular. The textual traditions that arose around the *Mahābhārata*, in particular, enable us to explore the various themes raised in this literary theory: moral economy, conceptual distance, space and geography, and dissemination and communication.

Whether Lukács's contrast—between the epic as the literary form of an integrated civilization and the modern novel as that of a world where meaning is no longer immanent in life—holds even for European literary history may be questioned. But it certainly makes no sense whatever for South Asia. If the Sanskrit epic can be said to be about any one thing, it is about the contested nature of social and political values. The *Mahābhārata* offers perhaps the most sustained study in world literature of the undecidability of conflicting moral claims—what the text itself repeatedly calls the "subtlety" of the moral order—and this was something often noted by premodern Indian readers. For an influential ninth-century thinker, what the epic chiefly addresses is the collapse of social value: "[The *Mahābhārata*'s] purpose as a whole is the production of despair with social life."[52] This is an interpretation of epic not as social fullness but as social abyss, of power not as perfected but as unperfectable since, as Vyāsa says, it is "slave to no man."

Perhaps in part because of this always unperfected character of the epic in South Asia, the epic past was never viewed as absolutely passed, as irreversibly complete; it was never felt, through Bakhtin's "hierachized temporality," to be situated at some immeasurable distance from the present. The history of its reproduction and reception suggests, dramatically to the contrary, that the epic in southern Asia was never believed to be *over* at all; it continued to be rethought and rewritten for centuries and even today has lost little of its vitality. Bakhtin may be pardoned for the flaws in his theory, however, since the capacity of a work such as the *Mahābhārata* to articulate the present is unlike any found elsewhere. Western epic did die long ago and can experience only parodic revivification; James Joyce's *Ulysses* is the paradigm case in modernity, but a certain parodic dimension attaches to early-modern works such as the *Gerusalemme Liberata* or the *Lusíads*. Indian epics, on the other hand, have been constantly and earnestly relived. Not only has "contemporaneity as such" always been an object of representation, but "the zone of direct contact with inconclusive present-day reality" seems almost of necessity to have been epicized. Epic reiteration inaugurated vernacular literary cultures across southern Asia, and this nowhere constituted a simple process of translation within the narrow limits known to contem-

52. *Dhvanyāloka* of Ānandavardhana p. 570 (on 4.5).

porary practices: the epics were updated, localized, and imaginatively reenacted. Recall only Pampa's Kannada *Mahābhārata,* where the hero Arjuna is explicitly equated with the poet's patron, King Arikēsari, or Ranna's, where the soon-to-be-overlord Iṟivabeḍaṅga Satyāśraya is said to *become* Bhīma. There are countless instances of epicization, in a vast array of literary and performance genres, with greater or lesser degrees of explicit presentism across the entire landscape of literary history in South and Southeast Asia up to the present.[53] This differs profoundly from the discontinuity in national significance that Hegel observed in 1820 in the case of the Germanic epic: "To try to impress on our civilization today that this is something which should claim our own deep native sympathy and must be something national for *us,* is an attempt, however often ventured, which means overvaluing these partly misshapen and barbaric ideas and completely misconceiving the sense of spirit of our own present."[54] The novel filled the "sympathy" gap left by the death of the European epic, a gap never experienced in South Asia.

That a past epic like the *Mahābhārata* can serve transhistorically as a medium for processing every historical present—and can do so in spite of its moral indeterminacy, or perhaps precisely because of it—may raise few serious theoretical problems for us. This, after all, is what makes a classic a classic. Less easily accommodated is the logic of Indian literary spatiality, or the chronotope as we might call it after Bakhtin, considered in reference to the spatial domain of the Indian political. We saw that the novel is held to be the form par excellence for narrating the national space; at the cognitive level this space can even be said to exist largely through such narration, complemented and reinforced by a new documentary form, the modern map. For theorists of nationalism, the vision of space in question—the nation as a "bounded sovereignty," as Anderson puts it, with inherently limited though somewhat elastic borders—is entirely new and specific to modern thought, and fundamentally different from the ideas and practices of space in premodernity. A recent exposition of this idea charts the emergence of a national territorial representation in modern Siam, where the "geo-body of the nation" was seen as purely an effect of modern geographical knowledge. "Nationhood was literally 'formed' by the demarcation of its body" through modern cartography. The types of spatial representation that existed in premodern Siam (three-world cosmographic maps, pilgrimage maps, and the like) were always expressed in nonpolitical, "non-secular" terms.[55] For Ander-

53. This theme is explored with respect to *Rāmāyaṇa* traditions in Pollock 1993b, and in Richman 1991 and 2001.

54. Hegel 1975: 403.

55. Thongchai Winichakul 1996 (a convenient summary of his 1994 monograph). Edmund Leach had of course much earlier, if very generally, signaled the modernity of frontiers, e.g., of "Burma" (Leach 1960).

son and his followers, as for Gellner, it is the nation that for the first time politicized space.

It is not proved, however, that these claims, whether about the novelistic or cartographic narration of the nation or about the politicization of space generally, derive from true incommensurabilities of geographical understanding and their cultural and political consequences, or instead, from different technologies of representation coupled with different conceptions of governance. Boundaries after all were omnipresent in premodernity; just think of Roman practices of space concretized by Hadrian's Wall in Britain or the northern *limes,* the fortified barrier stretching from Koblenz to the Danube (along with a clear enumeration of the contents of this space through the census). Premodern boundaries may often have been "thicker" than the Roman—frontiers rather than borders, in the parlance of political geographers—precisely because thin boundaries could not easily be measured, represented, or policed. But neither were thin borders a conceptual blank in premodernity, certainly not for South Asians. The borders of a royally endowed Brahman settlement were described with extreme precision because they entailed important material distinctions: land on this side of the border was to belong to this person or group; it was to be immune from taxes or royal jurisdiction in a way that land on the other side was not. The language-cum-administration regions of the vernacular polity had limits, too, never knife-edge thin, to be sure, but not because such limits were cognitively unavailable. Rather, they were simply not essential to the particular conceptions of power in play, which nonetheless were conceptions of power. No in-depth account of border practices exists for premodern South Asia but the evidence is there to be assembled, and this suggests that the strong formulation of radical conceptual difference invariably drawn by theorists of nationalism may well be overdrawn. Indeed, even in early-modern Siam, when King Chulalongkorn disputed with the French over the eastern bank of the Mekong, the fact that the "multiple submission" of this area "had long been recognized by the Siamese" is arguably at least as relevant to the formation of the geo-body as the fact that it eventually could be translated into the graphic representation of modern cartography.[56]

"Each genre possesses its own space, then—and each space its own genre": this is nowhere truer than in premodern South Asia, whether the genre in question is the product of *śāstra* or *kāvya,* information or imagination.[57] Sanskrit discourse across a wide range of knowledge systems was regulated by geocultural matrices; the literary system itself was theorized on the basis of geographical zones plotted across a knowable, even familiar, this-worldly—and decidedly not "non-secular"—space. In the epic, an organized concep-

56. Thongchai Winichakul 1996: 80.

57. Moretti 1998: 35. On genres of literary space in Sanskrit see Pollock 2003: 103 ff.

tion of space fundamentally structures the narrative from beginning to end, and a veritable "skein of literary journeys" incessantly made across the same spatial vastness serves to unify the many locales into a single locus. To claim, then, as it is so often claimed, that "the geographical unity of India is . . . a creation of the British mapping of their empire" is as historically shallow as it is conceptually naïve.[58] One unanticipated, even counterintuitive feature of the epic space, but central to the theorization of the premodern cosmopolitan sphere, is the fact that it was universally reproducible: Mathurā was found in the south of the subcontinent (Maturai) as well as in the north, Mālava and Daśārṇa in the west and east of Laos as well as in west and the east of Madhya Pradesh, Kurukṣetra in Khmer country as well as in the Midlands, Mount Meru in Java as well as in the Himalayas, and the Gaṅgā River seemingly everywhere. Sometimes these were viewed as reproductions—the "New Kurukṣetra"—but much more often it was just Meru or Mālava or Mathurā, the *same place* simply, not even re-placed.

Epic space was not only organized (by the sixth century it had taken on a firm shape that it retained from that point on with few major revisions), intelligible, literarily encoded, and replicable across the cosmopolis; it also possessed some political coherence embodied in the ideal of the "imperial field." And it was shrinkable as this ideal began to shrink. Even as the epic chronotope underwrote the conceptualization of the transregional culture-power sphere, it simultaneously and correlatively functioned as a template for the regional countersphere. Pampa in his *Bhāratam* reduced the world of the Sanskrit epic to fit the new political space of the tenth-century Deccan. His text's formulation in the conceptual shadow of the Sanskrit epic is as vitally important for the theorization of such regional space as the fact of replicability is for the theorization of cosmopolitan space. It is uncertain whether or not Gellner's assertions are true (or even fully comprehensible) regarding the "pre-modern, pre-rational visions" of "not properly united, but hierarchically related sub-worlds" against which he measures the newness of the nation, which is an "internally unitary world" without "special realms." But there is little in premodern South Asia to sustain, and much to contradict, his belief that "almost everything" in the premodern world militated against defining political units by cultural boundaries. This is not to deny that developments in Europe itself had a historical specificity that may be captured in these formulations, but rather that the generalization from this specificity to everywhere else may need to be rethought.

Although variously coherent visions of polity, both cosmopolitan and vernacular, may have thus been sustained in South Asia by carefully crafted forms of literature, can it be claimed that such visions were made known to

58. Edney 1997: 16, cf. also 3, 9, 335 (cf. Biggs 1999 on late-medieval France and England).

sufficient numbers of the subjects of those polities to render them historically meaningful, "a felt cultural reality" and not a mere dream for "the intellectual and ruling elites but not for the people"? The cognitive actualization of new political spaces, produced in part through the texts of literary culture, and with it the possibility that culture in premodernity could function beyond the circle of court literati as a political principle—one with a specific rationality of its own, not assimilable to that of capitalism and nationalism—depends on the potential for communicative diffusion. It was to address this need for such diffusion that the notion of print-capitalism was elaborated in theorizing the modern nation-state. But the effects of print are often exaggerated by theorists, precisely to create a contrast with the supposed communication deficiencies of premodernity. The true watershed in the history of communicative media, in India at least, was the invention not of print-capitalism but of script-mercantilism of the sort found in both Sanskrit and vernacular cultures. This manuscript culture was enormously productive and efficient. It has been estimated that over thirty million manuscripts are still extant (eight million in Rajasthan alone), along with many hundreds of thousands of inscriptions—a mere fraction of what once must have been available.[59] This script-mercantilism involved professional scribes and patrons who purchased their wares as well as nonprofessionals who copied manuscripts for personal use or for family members or teachers. (Recall how King Jayasiṃha spent 300,000 coins to have Hemacandra's grammar reproduced, so that the text "circulated and grew famous in all lands" from Assam to Sri Lanka to Sindh.) Continuing oral performance practices, their reproducibility enhanced by comparatively stable text-artifacts, magnified the impact of script-mercantilism to produce a dissemination of the culture-power ideas of the Indian epics greater than anything achievable through print-capitalism.

Like its impact on dissemination, the effect of print on textuality itself is also often overstated. Those who know something of the history of the critical edition of the Sanskrit *Mahābhārata* begun in Pune after the First World War are often too quick to suppose it an example of modernity's reductive textual episteme at work in a world previously so enchanting in its chaotic orality. Undoubtedly the Pune project represented an instance of a powerful ideological conjuncture of philology and nationalism of the kind clearly visible a generation earlier in Europe, in the Franco-Prussian war of philology around the Frankish epos; it seems hardly accidental that the project should have been organized in the region that a few years later (1925) gave

59. The estimate comes from the Indira Gandhi National Centre for the Arts. For all of Greek literature, classical, Hellenistic, and Byzantine, some thirty thousand manuscripts are extant—which the Indic materials thus exceed by a factor of a thousand (Christopher Minkowski, in conversation).

birth to the neo-Hindu rationalist movement.[60] The nation-state then gestating in the womb of the colonial order certainly required an ancient birth certificate in modern printed form. But the Pune project was not the first time in South Asia that an edition of the *Mahābhārata* was deliberately created, and indeed, in no way did it mark the beginning of a textual-critical approach to the work.

The greater part of the epic had been transmitted in a reasonably stable written mode (admittedly with massive expansions) from at least the fifth century, and some measure of editorial work accompanied this transmission everywhere. We alluded earlier to such work in eleventh-century Kashmir (Devabodha), fourteenth-century Goa (Vidyāsāgara), fifteenth-century Bengal (Arjunamiśra), seventeenth-century Varanasi (Nīlakaṇṭha), and a few other places, but it is certain that there were many more attempts to bring logical order to the written tradition of the text—not the order of a Lachmann or even a Bedier, but an order specific to its own epistemic world (chapter 6.1). The manuscripts that formed the basis for these editions of the *Mahābhārata,* and the new ones that were generated from them in turn, circulated in large numbers across the entire cosmopolitan space. If the unmediated impact of these manuscripts would still have to be considered limited due to constraints on literacy, the numerous endowments we noted for public recitation instituted by rulers everywhere assured wide promulgation of the epic. All this holds true for the vernacular epics as well. In Kannada country Kumāravyāsa's *Karṇāṭabhāratakathāmañjarī* and the *Jaiminibhāratam* are still extant in hundreds of manuscripts; more important, these works were broadcast via oral performance into every village in the region on the basis of these written texts (the present-day loudspeaker recitations heard each summer across Kerala of Eḻuttacchan's *Rāmāyaṇa* recapitulate much older performance practices). A class of professional, often hereditary, performers and exegetes of both cosmopolitan and vernacular epics—men like Arjunamiśra or the two itinerant reciters of Kampaṉ's *Rāmāyaṇa* mentioned in a fourteenth-century inscription from western Tamilnadu—were active across southern Asia for centuries on end and constituted a vast network of propagation.[61]

If there is truth to the idea that no Indian hears the *Mahābhārata* for the first time, as A. K. Ramanujan once put it, this is due to, and further evidence

60. On the Pune edition, see van der Veer 2001: 116–33. Bloch 1986 and 1990 discusses the growth of German and French national philologies in relation to the Frankish epos. On "Hindutva," see the epilogue.

61. On Arjunamiśra, see chapter 6.1. The reference to the two reciters of Kampaṉ, themselves sons of a reciter, is found in a Kannada inscription (*EC* rev. vol. 8, Hassan no. 89, dated 1377–78): *kaṃbada rāmāyaṇada nārāyaṇana makkaḷu rāmāyaṇada rāmapanu lakṣmaṇanu* . . . , literally, "sons of [the] Nārāyaṇa of the *Kampaṉ Rāmāyaṇa,* both Rāmapa and Lakṣmaṇa of the *Rāmāyaṇa.*"

of, the vitality and ubiquity of this network. One need not by any means assent to Nehru's nationalist subtext (or to his simplistic valorization of "history") to appreciate the historical significance of what he observed during a political tour of the country in the 1930s:

> The old epics of India, the *Ramayana* and the *Mahabharata* and other books, in popular translations and paraphrases, were widely known among the masses, and every incident and story and moral in them was engraved on the popular mind and gave a richness and content to it. Illiterate villagers would know hundreds of verses by heart, and their conversation would be full of reference to them or to some story with a moral, enshrined in some old classic . . . I realized that even the illiterate peasant had a picture gallery in his mind, though this was largely drawn from myth and tradition and epic heroes and heroines, and only very little from history. Nevertheless it was vivid enough.[62]

Constant oral reiteration, enabled by manuscript culture, achieved in premodernity what print itself has failed to achieve in still largely rural South Asia: the production of coherent mass representations of the geography of power no less than of the ontology of power.[63] The cosmopolitan spaces and vernacular places of a South Asian cultural-political order—Bhāratavarṣa (the Clime of the Descendants of Bharata), Kannaḍanāḍu (the culture-land of Kannada), and others—were insistently detailed in the epic narratives themselves, concretely plotted out by the circulation of epic manuscripts, and publicized intensively and extensively through epic oral performance, each epic in its own transregional or regional zone. This makes it hard to accept, for South Asia at least, a whole range of scholarly assertions: that only the modern map can have brought such geo-bodies to life in the imagination and made discourse about them sensible;[64] that belief in the premodern existence of regions constitutes "a curious misreading" of the past since the "sense of region and nation emerged together through parallel self-definitions" in modernity, and upon this recognition depends any understanding of "the distinctive, layered character of Indianness"; that it was only "subjection to British rule" that brought about some higher-order identification among "the many different highly compartmentalized communities of South Asia." It is not obvious what evidence underlies such assertions, all of them repeated as self-evident truths, nor what purpose they serve other than to impede an understanding of "the distinctive, layered character of Indianness."[65]

Let us now try to bring some order to the threads of these complicated

62. Ramanujan 1999: 162–63; Nehru 1946: 56.

63. Guha 1985: 106–7.

64. Thongchai Winichakul 1996: 76.

65. See, respectively, Tønnesson and Antlöv 1996: 18, and Khilnani 1998: 153 for what is in fact ubiquitous dogma; for Chatterjee (1993: 95 ff.), "country *(deś)* and realm *(rājatva)*" are recent colonial imports; for Ahmad (1992: 260; cf. also 256, 264), the *Mahābhārata*'s role in

issues about culture and power as enunciated in the European theory of the nation, especially in relation to their incongruence with the history of culture and power in premodern South Asia, and see what conclusions can be drawn for an understanding of both entities and, equally important, for a theory of theory and a regrounding of practice.

First, many of the elements held to distinguish the modern novel from the archaic epic can be found in premodern South Asian texts. Of course profound differences exist between the genres: like the novel, Indian epics can be "structured in the zone of direct contact with inconclusive present-day reality," yet instead of intensifying the inconclusiveness of reality through a dialogical proliferation of meaning, as the modern novel may be said to do, the Indian texts, both vernacular and cosmopolitan, aim to take what is inconclusive and, so to speak, conclude it. Nonetheless, the South Asian combination of characteristics suggests that the novel per se may not have the exclusive relationship with the conceptual properties said to define the nation that standard theorization claims. It is not necessarily the case that epic action is situated at an inaccessible remove or describes a world of perfect moral order, or that it is incapable of bearing moral ambiguity, marked by cosmological temporal plenitude, or composed in a remote archaic language. The novel is not necessarily the sole site for exploring the tensions of the present in a demotic idiom; it does not have a singular connection with the production of coherent political space and is not the only vehicle for expressing the one-yet-many of complex polity.

Second, if the theory of the novel, at least in some of its major formulations, does not identify criteria adequate to differentiate its object from other literary forms—and the fact that these forms are not Western is exactly why this inadequacy is not only not irrelevant but precisely to the point—we are not authorized to draw from it the large conclusions about the nation or modernity that this differentiation was intended to ground. From this perspective, too, the scandalous absence of an autonomous development of the novel in South Asia, which was a source of worry to Indian nationalists as great as the scandalous absence of a Chinese epic for historians of Chinese literary culture, can hardly have the cultural-political import it is normally assumed to have. According to Hegel's more restricted definition, the novel is simply the "bourgeois epic," and so its peculiar development in South Asia only correlates with the peculiar development of a bourgeois class with its particular story to tell.[66] It becomes less interesting, then, to correlate novel with nation, and nonnovel with nonnation, than to ask why the discourse on

creating this cultural-political *imaginaire* is an effect of a modernist and communalist remaking of the past.

66. "The Indian 'renaissance' had no historical links with the revolutionary mission of a progressive bourgeoisie seeking to create a nation in its own image" (Chatterjee 1986: 28).

political community in India so long remained epic, and to try to understand the kinds of community that epic came to articulate.

Third, if the criticisms expressed earlier have any cogency, then the historical logic of some of the more influential theories of the nation becomes not only unpersuasive in its own sphere of application but dubious in view of what happened outside of Europe. Not all agro-literate polities were sacred communities, their languages were not always mysterious nor their scripts arcane, they did not invariably serve to render local language invisible. The invention of vernacular literary culture was not necessarily a consequence of industrialization. Print-capitalism was not necessarily the instrument required to assemble and unify vernacular languages, and it was not always an effective, let alone the sole, instrument for the supralocal dissemination of cultural-political ideas of supralocal community.

The disruption of modern European cultural-political theory by premodern South Asian cultural-political practice raises a number of hard questions for both areas of investigation. If we follow Hegel, do such features as "indigenous geography" in the Indian epic belong, in any useful sense, to *Nationalität* as Hegel understood it? Such was the conviction, predictably, of modern Indian nationalists who in the struggle against colonialism sought a deep history of national autonomy.[67] And if so, what are the implications of this conjunction and, indeed, of Hegel's equation of epic and nation more broadly? If premodern India represented, if not a Hegelian nation-state, at least a Hegelian nation at the very moment "nation" was being theorized and practiced in the West, what does this imply for a differential history of the European idea of the nation? When and why did the non-West lose its nationality in the eyes of Western knowledge? What happened to make it possible in 1963 to describe India (in E. M. Forster's gently mocking image) as "waddling in at this late hour to take her seat among the nations," or in 1984 to frame such breezy collocations as "Nigeria, India and Indonesia" when pronouncing on "the rise to prominence of some Third World states which clearly cannot be termed 'nations,'" or in 1993 to claim that "[the Congress Party] attempted to turn an old civilization into a nation"?[68] It is even more important to ask whether students of the history of culture-power can move completely beyond this formulation of the problematic and think autonomously about premodern and postmodern South Asian polit-

67. Representative is Mookerji 1914.

68. Geertz 1963: 139; Smith 1986: 7; and cf. Lewis and Wigen 1997: 8 ("That we elect to call such internally divided countries as India, Nigeria, or even Switzerland nation-states shows a determined desire to will uniformity out of diversity"; only "very few countries" qualify for being nation-states "in the strict sense of the term," since they somehow constitute a "basic unit of the human community"); Varshney 1993: 242 (a view not peculiar to modern Indian political thought; so the oft-cited Lucian Pye: "the fundamental problem in China's modernization is that China is really a civilization pretending to be a nation-state," 1992: 1162).

ical practices when modern Western practices are not only in our heads but have been theorized precisely in opposition to their supposedly archaic Asian antecedents—antecedents only imperfectly understood at that. If so, is it possible to grasp and understand specific and unfamiliar political forms, in particular a copresence or complementarity of political forms, that are not the European subnation or nation or civilization but are forms with cultural-political logics of their own?

A plea for conceptual and practical autonomy does not entail arguing, as some have done, that new hybrid categories should be invented for India, a "civilizational nation," for example.[69] It is indeed interesting and important to ask why in India (as in China) a political entity can now be found that differs so significantly from western Europe with its multiple states, and to explore the historical contingencies that made nation-states of France and England but not of Tamilnadu and Maharashtra. Yet the idea of "civilizational nation" (to say nothing of "protonation")[70] commits us to too many of the theoretical assumptions that have been challenged in the course of this chapter—assumptions that need to be resisted even if it sometimes seems like ever more arduous bootstrapping is required to grasp the non-Western, non-modern, nonnational. For this means forcing oneself to set aside the conceptual objects and interpretive apparatus constituted by Western modernity and nationalism without having much of anything else to put in their place.

A good example of this predicament is offered by the theorization of vernacularization. Literary-cultural processes entirely comparable to those of Europe occurred in premodern South Asia, yet the political outcomes were altogether different. Vernacularization, however, is viewed as so central a component of nationalism as to have been accorded its own structural slot under what has been designated "vernacular mobilization" (chapter 12.1). It cannot, it seems, be conceptualized as anything but national and thus loaded with all the baggage (the instrumentalization of culture as ideology, personhood as ethnic subject) that accompanies nationalism. The functionalist and teleological thinking that such models encourage—vernacular literary cultures are destined to operate as they do in the early modern European nation, this end explains their function, and if they do not have this function they cannot have any other, they are "invisible"—rules out in advance alternative theoretical possibilities about how culture and power can relate. Thus for one scholar of nationalist thought, to create a modern nation compatriots "must be turned into co-nationals through a process of mobilization into the vernacular culture"; this alone permits the "old-new culture" to become a base for the political and cultural competition of modernity. This may well appear to be true for the always already nationalized world of West-

69. Tønnesson and Antlöv 1996: 29, cf. 23.
70. See the problematic theorization in Hobsbawm 1990: 46–79.

ern modernity. But for premodern South Asia—where power was clearly concerned with culture and played a central role in the genesis of vernacularization though it never became an element of political mobilization—we have no obvious reason to accept either option of the dichotomous conclusion: the one the author draws himself, that the "old culture" of nonmodernity "had no other end beyond itself," or the one drawn by teleologists and primordialists, who are invariably predisposed to conceive of developments like vernacularization as signs of the nation before nationalism.[71]

Here once again the conceptual-terminological trap discloses itself. It seems impossible for the contemporary observer to even imagine a different constellation of culture-power—with a different understanding of the relationship and competing claims of the local and the global, of what constitutes community and how community relates to language, of what it means for people to be in place and for power to be in place—than what has been bequeathed to us by a historically very peculiar, temporally very thin, and spatially very narrow slice of human history. To question the dominant models explaining the place of culture in the creation of nineteenth-century European nationalism is not to demand inclusion of premodern South Asia by suggesting that the Sanskrit epic communicated a European *Nationalität* or that the processes of southern Asian vernacularization in any instance expressed the same political "desperation" as nineteenth-century Europe, even less that they are to be taken as national-cultural processes in their own right. On the contrary, the point of assessing the causal models developed to explain Western developments is to raise the question whether the logic of culture—both vernacularization and cosmopolitanism—must invariably be concomitant with the logic of power as we know it in the political forms, nation and empire, respectively, of particular moments in Western history. The theory developed from that history fails to help us understand, and even impedes us from seeing, what did happen elsewhere and how that might differ from what eventually produced the peculiar combination of culture and power in the modern world called the nation-state.

There is reason to doubt that culture is always and everywhere produced for the sheer legitimation of power, or for no social reason whatever but simply in the course of natural evolution. Language choice may not always and everywhere be an expression of ethnic identity, and peoples are not always constructed through deep historical narratives. Ethnicity itself, as normally conceived, may not always and everywhere even exist. Literature, the site where nations and regions and peoples insist on locating their real, continuous,

71. Smith 1990: 184. What filled the lacuna of "ethnic" (i.e., linguistic) mobilization in South Asia was not, however, mobilization on religious grounds, at least not before the modern period (pace Tønnesson and Antlöv 1996: 24, who again exaggerate the place of religion as far as premodern India goes).

primeval selves, may actually begin, and may do so by a process of continuous give and take from contiguous literatures. Present-day understandings of civilization may be based on indigenist conceptions that are unhistorical and reductive, while conceptions of the nation may be linked with views of culture in general that are anachronistic and simplistically functionalist.

In sum, there are serious problems in using off-the-rack Western theory to understand South Asian premodernity, and they in turn call that theory into question. If we are prepared to acknowledge the methodological fallacy of positing motives for action prior to determining those motives from the empirical materials, and if we can develop an openness to being surprised by the possible strangeness of the past, then we need to go back to the drawing board in trying to theorize the meanings of cosmopolitan and vernacular in South Asia before modernity. If the lexicon of the discourses on culture-power in the West is limited by the presuppositions of the nationalist and capitalist modernity it embeds, then a new semantics of culture-power is necessary, with different, more open presuppositions.[72]

This is not just a scholastic matter, whether of literary-critical vocabularies, political-science categories, or historical enigmas such as the absence of an autonomous development of Asian nationalism. It is instead a matter of resisting the prejudgments that such vocabularies entail, the categorizations that limit alternative possibilities, and the historical judgments based on accepting the terms of an argument that are inapplicable in the first place. Such resistance is not mere mischief-making. It is rather an attempt to recover and understand forms of culture and power that may counter the logic of nationalism and capitalism, and perhaps thereby help us escape into possibilities that will seem less utopian the more they are shown to have once been actualized. If we are to reach a different theory of theory for the future, one that grounds a different future practice, we need a new past and better ways to make sense of it.

72. If we are to unthink monological determinations of Western knowledge and recuperate some role for experiences and perspectives of the non-West (Wallerstein et al. 1996: 56 ff.), our work has to be grounded in history and philology and not in wishful thinking (cf. chapter 10.4 and n. 105).

Epilogue

From Cosmopolitan-or-Vernacular to Cosmopolitan-and-Vernacular

Few things seem as natural as the multiplicity of vernacular languages used for making sense of life through texts—that is, for making literature. And few things seem as unnatural as their gradual disappearance in the present, especially from the pressures exerted by globalizing English. Literary-language loss is in fact often viewed as part of a more general reduction of diversity in a cultural ecosystem, a loss considered as dangerous as the reduction of biological diversity, to which—in another instance of cultural naturalization—it is often compared. Today's homogenization of culture, of which language loss is one aspect, seems without precedent in human history, at least for the scope, speed, and manner in which such change is taking place.

Yet as this book has sought to demonstrate, the sense of what is natural needs two important qualifications. First, the vernacular cultural orders that seem to be threatened everywhere were themselves created over time. These are not the primeval lifeways of autochthons; like the Spartoi of Thebes, "the sown people" born from the dragon teeth planted by Cadmus, autochthons do not exist outside of their own mythical self-representation. Second, by the very fact of their creation, the new vernacular cultures themselves replaced a range of much older practices that affiliated their users to a global space rather than to a local place. And it is only now, when the millennium-long vernacular epoch is coming to an end, that this past can be seen as a whole—the grand transformations from the old cosmopolitan to the new vernacular order, and from the vernacular to the new and far more disquieting global order of the present day—and so can be drawn upon for understanding that long history of culture and power. Very different cosmopolitan and vernacular practices have existed in the past, and the histories of these practices and the choices they embodied have something to tell us about possible future choices in the face of what often seems to be the desperate alternatives available: a national vernacularity dressed in the frayed period costume of violent revanchism and bent on preserving difference at all costs, and a clear-cutting, strip-mining unipolar globalism bent at all costs on obliterating it.

The language of the gods had a history in the world of men more complicated than any one scholar or book can capture with real adequacy; even summarizing here the findings of that attempt is a challenge. What will be most useful is to briefly review the larger shape of the cosmopolitan and vernacular orders of culture-power in their most salient comparative features. This will be especially helpful for drawing out the implications of their histories, similarities, and differences for a reconstruction of theory and practice and the ways these get produced, as critiqued in the third part of the book. Given my reconstructive aim, the relevance of long-term and comparative historical analysis of literary and political practices, as well as the meaningfulness of past choices to future ones, need to be clarified. I try to do this at the end of this epilogue by reflecting on, first, certain tendencies in contemporary Euro-American thought to rehabilitate an indigenist vernacularism from the left, and then some postcolonial arguments that offer possible escape routes from the dilemmas seen in the various cosmopolitan-vernacular conflicts that closed out the second millennium and have opened the third.

It may be helpful to start by restating why I have proceeded as I have done in this account. Four points of method have been central. First, my intention has been to think about culture and power as action as much as idea, deed as much as declaration. This lets us see that some people in the past have been able to be cosmopolitan or vernacular without directly professing either, perhaps even finding it impossible to justify either one rationally. By contrast, in the attempt to vindicate cosmopolitanism or vernacularism, the very production of a discourse on the universal or the particular has often entailed objectification and abstraction, along with their associated political imperatives, such that the cosmopolitan took on the character of compulsion, and the vernacular, that of inevitability.

Second, the specific practices I have privileged here, because they have been privileged in the historical experience of South Asia, are those of literary culture, or how people do things with texts—expressive, discursive, or political texts. The terms "cosmopolitan" and "vernacular" have largely been taken as modes of literary (and intellectual and political) communication directed toward two audiences whom lay actors know full well to be different: the one unbounded and potentially infinite in extension, the other practically finite and bounded by other finite audiences, with whom, through the very dynamic of vernacularization, relations of ever-increasing incommunication come into being. It has seemed easiest to think of the distinction here, in communicative capacity and concerns, as that between a language that travels well and one that does not.

Texts and doing things with texts may seem a long way from the desperate choices mentioned above. And yet literary communication has importantly shaped the social and political sensibilities that make such choices possible. Literature constitutes an especially sensitive gauge of sentiments of belonging; creating or experiencing literature that is meant for a large world or a small place is a tacit declaration of one's affiliation with that world or place. The production and circulation of literary texts, accordingly, are not like the production and circulation of material things. The universalization of particular technologies, or the particularization of universal ones, that characterizes a dominant form of contemporary globalization carries no hint of belonging; the practices of literary culture, by contrast, are practices of attachment.[1]

Third, it has been important for me to understand the language of the gods in the world of men, and the cosmopolitan and vernacular formations it helped shape, not only historically but also comparatively, in order to make the analysis of cosmopolitanism itself more cosmopolitan and to expand the range of vernacular particulars from which richer generalizations can be made. The practices of literary communication that actualized these modes of belonging in southern Asia and western Europe show remarkable chronological and formal symmetries, but profound differences, too, in both the mentalities and the modalities of social and political action to which the new communicative practices related and which they underwrote. These differences are consequential both for modern theory, which they disrupt, and for modern practices, which they open up.

The refusal to reify the cosmopolitan or the vernacular by foregrounding doctrines while ignoring doings needs to be matched by a refusal to fill either category in advance with any particular social or political content. The book throughout has striven to demonstrate how variable this content has been in the past, and so may yet be in the future. That said, it is no easy thing to think outside of modern categories. The very particular and privileged mode of political identity in "cosmopolitan," for example, undercuts its own logic of universality, while the very particular and unprivileged mode of social identity in "vernacular" is crippled by its own specificity. The historical semantics of our categories have harried us at every step, from "epic" and "empire" to "novel" and "nation."

The fourth and last point of method touches on the very purpose of historical reconstruction. A deep archaeology of culture and power seems useless in a world such as ours where history usually means last week's news, and

1. See Robertson 1992: 102.

in an academy where historical thinking has lost its innocence to ideology critique, discourse analysis, or—worst predator of all—boredom. But the problem of why we should want historical knowledge has a degree of urgency directly proportionate to our awareness of the fact that the past is always written from a location in the present. And in the present case the urgency is maximal, since the questions of local and global culture, power, community, and the rest are matters not only of the past but also of the future—matters of choices yet to be made about self and other, freedom and necessity, even war and peace. In the face of such challenges, it is unhelpful to say, as a writer on the history of liberty recently said, that our historiographical purpose should be simply to "uncover the often neglected riches of our intellectual heritage and display them once more to view," holding ourselves "aloof from enthusiasm and indignation alike."[2] This sentiment of dispassion does not become more possible or true the more it is invoked, as it has often been invoked since Tacitus first gave expression to it. Our enthusiasm and indignation shape our argument whether we like it or not—one can hardly doubt that the neo-Roman theory of positive freedom that the historian has so valuably reconstructed is the theory he prefers. And they do more to undermine historical argument the more they are suppressed.

We must come clean about our purposes, and the more modest these purposes are, the better. There is nothing very problematic or theoretically interesting about examining the past to see how people have acted and trying to understand which acts had bad consequences and which had good ones. We do this even though we know that the historical knowledge derived from such an examination carries no guarantee that better practices will follow. A history of cosmopolitan and vernacular orders of culture-power should therefore seek, enthusiastically and indignantly, to compare past choices, when there have been choices, in order to inform future ones—doing history cannot and should not be separated from making history. Those choices will always be responses to conditions of power and culture that are far more complex than any single account can hope to capture, and for that reason often seem to elude any intentional and knowledgeable action. But if intentions and knowledge count, then good intentions are better than bad ones, and knowledge better than ignorance. Śaṅkara, the eighth-century Indian thinker, put it with unarguable simplicity: "Two persons may perform the same act, both the one who understands and the one who does not. But understanding and ignorance are different, and what one performs with understanding becomes far stronger than what one performs in ignorance."[3]

❖ ❖ ❖

2. Skinner 1998: 118.

3. Commentary on *Cāndogya Upaniṣad* 1.1.10.

The world of Sanskrit that came into being a little before the Common Era and the world of Latin that arose almost simultaneously were remarkably similar. After centuries of both discursive and geographical limitation, the two languages embarked on an extraordinary career of expressive elaboration and spatial dissemination. Their near-concurrent development as written codes for what in both worlds was conceptualized as this-worldly *(laukika, saeculare)* communication occurred after centuries of restriction to liturgical, magical, and generally supramundane (and largely oral) textuality. In addition, both quickly achieved unprecedented diffusion across what in both worlds was seen as virtually a global space. As poets from Gujarat to Java were writing Sanskrit, so poets from Spain to Mesopotamia were writing Latin. This universality pertained to substance as well as to extension. Both worlds evinced a similar style of cultural discipline, discernible in the cultivation of language and in the mastery of the canon of literature and systematic thought. Sanskrit and Latin alike were, in a very literal sense, written to be readable across both space and time—and read indeed they were. And they produced a sense of belonging that affiliated readers to each other across vast space and time.

With these practices of culture, however, the parallels between the two types of cosmopolitanism end. In respect to power they differed as radically as the historical experiences that produced them. Recall for a moment the question of terminology. In contrast to the West, with its political category *imperium romanum* and literary and cultural category *latinitas,* there was no self-generated descriptor for either the political or the cultural sphere that Sanskrit created and inhabited. The fact that Sanskrit never sought to conceptualize its own universality is indeed entirely consistent with its historical character as a cultural-political formation, an alternative form of cosmopolitanism in which "here" was not made "everywhere," but remained "nowhere in particular." Indissociable from the semantics of these two culture-power orders were their specific pragmatics. Latin traveled where it did as the language of a conquest state, and wherever it traveled—Iberia, North Africa, the Near East—it obliterated the languages it found. The Sanskrit cosmopolis was also created by movement, of course, though not the movements of conquerors. The coercion, co-optation, juridical control, even persuasion of the *imperium romanum* were nowhere in evidence in the Sanskrit cosmopolis; those who participated in Sanskrit culture chose to do so, and could choose to do so. Far from proscribing local script vernaculars, Sanskrit mediated their creation everywhere it traveled and often at the very moment it arrived. To be sure, these languages were confined to the realm of the documentary for many centuries, but only because the literary function was coterminous with the political function, and the sphere of the political in the cosmopolitan epoch, by definition always "extending to the horizons," was the exclusive preserve of a Sanskrit that likewise acknowledged no boundaries but those same horizons.

Unlike the *imperium romanum,* the space of Sanskrit culture and the power that culture articulated were never demarcated in any concrete fashion: the populations that inhabited it were never enumerated, standardization of legal practices was nowhere attempted beyond a vague conception of moral order to which power was universally expected to profess its commitment. Sanskrit cosmopolitanism never carried particularistic religious notions like those that marked the recreated cosmopolitan forms of Charlemagne and Otto. Buddhists, Jains, Śaivas, and Vaiṣṇavas all wrote more or less similar poetry and engaged in identical political practices. Sanskrit cosmopolitanism was not about absorbing the periphery into the center but turning the periphery itself into a center, not about taking the whole world into our city *(ingens orbis in urbe fuit)* but taking our city into the whole world *(nagarīm ekām ivorvīm imām . . . śāsati).* Sanskrit cosmopolitanism duplicated locations everywhere; it was a world of all centers and no circumferences, with golden Mount Merus and purifying river Gaṅgās appearing ubiquitously.

We have thus two forms of cosmopolitanism—not a European comprehensive universalism and a narrow Asian particularism.[4] While the practices of culture that helped to generate them were remarkably similar, the practices of power with which they were associated were radically different. And if the two cosmopolitanisms were both capable of transcending the local and stimulating feelings of living in a larger world, their modalities were profoundly different: the one coercive, the other voluntaristic.

The broad symmetries that permit comparison between *kāvya* and *rājya* and *latinitas* and *imperium romanum* are even more in evidence in the vernacular formations that superseded them. Here we have seen an astonishing range of parallels pertaining to the profound and wholly active transformation that occurred in the practices of both literary culture and political power, which formed at once the narrative substance and real-world context of so much of the literature in question. Yet like the two models of cosmopolitanism they replaced, the vernacular formations also show irreducible, and highly instructive, differences.

A coherent constellation of cultural and political features manifests itself in the vernacularization of southern Asia. The literization of local codes was nowhere simultaneous with their literarization; the interval between the two moments lasted in some cases five centuries or more. The dominance of Sanskrit in literary and political text production was ended by a conscious challenge from vernacular intellectuals beginning in south India around the ninth century, with the process everywhere more or less complete by the end of the sixteenth. Literary production consisted to a large degree of texts derived from cosmopolitan genres and appropriating many of their formal fea-

4. As T. S. Eliot, in his own provincial way, thought of Vergil (Kermode 1975: 22–23).

tures. A new aesthetic of Place, *deśī,* moderated these borrowings by balancing them with local forms, while new projects of spatiality—vernacular chronotopes that plotted out the domain of vernacular culture, putting culture in place for the first time, "the culture-land of Kannada," "the heart of the land of Andhra," "beautiful Lady Lanka"—began to find expression in literary texts. The primary impetus for vernacularization in most cases was provided by ruling elites, who were increasingly turning to the vernacular as the language of political communication, too.

In western Europe, vernacularization began in earnest in late-ninth-century England, where the Latinate literary culture of the Carolingian empire provided the consciously adapted model. Insular vernacular culture was quickly imitated by Anglo-Norman elites, which led to the creation of a Continental French literary culture soon thereafter. In Occitania, Castile, Florence, and beyond, vernacularization spread like wildfire. Perhaps the quintessential moment was at the end of the process, at the court of François I in the mid-sixteenth century, where writers of the Pléiade saw themselves as charged with the task of securing the triumph of the vernacular at the same time as new forms of language governmentality were being instituted by the French court.

With the creation of the cosmopolitan vernacular, the new reading communities, and the new visions of vernacular political space, once again the parallels between the two worlds end. The divergences are equally remarkable and can be found at every level of the vernacularization process: language ideology, including the sources and moral status of language diversity; the correlation between language and community; the linkage between vernacular language and political power.

While care for language was as intense in southern Asia as anywhere in the world, no southern Asian writer before the colonial period ever represented this care through an emotional attachment to language. The vernaculars were languages of Place, not facts of the biology of ethnicized peoples, and the ecocultural zone that made a language was not a region of birth, a *natio.* No discourses exist in southern Asia on the origins of languages or peoples, like the myths of languages and peoples, transmogrifying into chronicles and histories of kingdoms and peoples, that can fairly be called an obsession in medieval Europe. No writer in southern Asia ever linked political power with linguistic particularism as did Wenceslas II of Bohemia in the fourteenth century, Lorenzo de' Medici in Florence a century later, and Du Bellay in Paris a century later still. No language in southern Asia ever became the target of direct royal regulation; sanctions were never imposed requiring the use of one and prohibiting the use of another. At the time when episodes of vernacular extermination were occurring in Europe, kings in Karnataka were issuing royal records in Kannada for the core of their culture-power *deśa,* in Telugu for the eastern sector, and in Marathi for the western, and in their courts these kings were entertained with songs in these languages as well as Avadhi, Bihari, Bangla, Oriya, and Madhyadeshiya—producing, in fact, a virtual cosmopolitanism of the vernaculars.

What from developments in Europe might be taken as basic constituents of the vernacularization process are entirely absent from the historical experience of southern Asia. Language was most certainly of interest to court elites in southern Asia but the logic of their cultural politics was as incommensurable with that of their European contemporaries as the logic of their cosmocratic predecessors had been with that of their Latin counterparts. The nascent nation-states of Europe everywhere evinced a correlation between people, power, and culture; the vernacular polities of southern Asia instead made possible a cultural accommodation to the conditions of a realm of power on the part of those who entered it. If power had begun to express itself in the languages of Place, it never made that language instrumental to its own self-conception let alone to the existence of the citizen-subject. Just as there had been two different cosmopolitanisms, two different ways of being in the great space of culture-power—a compulsory cosmopolitanism and a voluntary one—so there were two different vernacularities, two different ways of being in the small place of culture-power—a vernacularity of necessity and one of accommodation.

❖ ❖ ❖

The shortcomings in the above account in point of method and conception are not hard to identify. Methodologically, the attempt to see the forest and not just the trees makes schematic reduction impossible to avoid. Conceptually, too much stress is placed on distinctions, creating a largely demonic West over against a largely angelic East, in the interest of redressing the historical imbalance. Yet this historical reconstruction does claim a certain reality. Cosmopolitan and vernacular have been real alternatives in Asia no less than in Europe; in both regions power has had as much inclination for culture as culture for power; in both, culture and power were everywhere and always produced by deliberate choices and conscious practices. Still, however comparable may have been the basic conditions of possibility across the Eurasian world during the 1,500-year period under discussion, promoting certain cultural and political changes of a comparable sort, the differences in the resultant formations were deep and irreducible. Clearly, the possibilities for making history were very various.

If attempting to know the past is difficult, and no less so than the theoretical and metatheoretical challenges this attempt must confront, equally difficult is the metapractical question why we want to know it at all. Can historical knowledge open up a domain of alternative possibilities at a time when the choices of culture-power before us seem all bad and the dilemmas intolerable, yet apparently inevitable? Cosmopolitanism and vernacularism in their contemporary Western forms—American-style globalization and ethnonationalism—is one such domain of bad options. It is hard not to see their most deformed developments in the confrontations between NATO and Serbia that closed out one century of confrontation and between the United States and Afghanistan and Iraq that opened another. No simple formula can capture the complexity of these confrontations, but it may not be too far wrong to see them as pitting a threatened and at times irrational vernacularity against a new and terrible kind of imperial cosmopolitanism.

India, for its part, is hardly immune now to bad choices. The worst at present is the choice between a vernacularity mobilized along the most fragile fault lines of region, religion, and caste, and the grotesque mutation of the toxins of postcolonial *ressentiment* and modernity known as Hindutva, or Hindu nationalism. The very names of the groups that make up the institutional complex of Hindutva—including the Bharatiya Janata Party (Indian People's Party) and its ideological wing, the Vishwa Hindu Parishad (World Hindu Council)—bespeak what had never been spoken before, postulating in the one case a single Indian "peoplehood" *(janata)*, in the other, Hinduism as an aggressive universalism. What is immediately clear from the history we have followed in the course of this book is that Hindutva is a perversion of India's great cosmopolitan past, while the many new subnational movements (as in Assam and elsewhere) represent an entirely new, militant vernacularism, indeed, a kind of Heideggerization of Indian life.

In thinking about the kinds of choices between the cosmopolitan and vernacular that are now available—mostly bad and bitter and sad choices—in relation to the historical past we have just surveyed, it may help to put them into a more familiar idiom by way of two brief texts Antonio Gramsci produced in the early 1930s concerning the vernacular-national and cosmopolitan-universalist problematics. Gramsci's reflections on the large questions of literary culture and political power over the long history of the West are uncommon, innovative, and passionate, however unsuccessful he may have been in developing a coherent position about the competing claims of the cosmopolitan and the vernacular either as cultural or political values. The two small texts to be considered meditate, in their own way, on these problems.

The first of these concerns the relationship between the particular and the universal in literature. Serious people—André Gide is mentioned—believe writers are able to serve the general interest only to the degree that the work they produce is more particular. Gide himself had originally developed this idea within a purely aestheticist paradigm: one cannot promote the universal or any other good without the perfection of "artistic power, however defined," and the latter always comes from and depends on the particular. The particular, however, for many in the 1920s, was precisely the national. The question accordingly raised here is whether being particular itself is necessarily a function of being national, as many conservative intellectuals insisted, including those who in 1919 asked in a public manifesto, "Is it not by nationalizing itself that a literature takes on a more universal signification, a more humanly general interest? . . . Is it not profound error to believe that one can work on behalf of European culture through a denationalized literature?"[5]

Here is not the place to pursue in any detail the arguments against this position, Heideggerian *avant la lettre.* One could certainly suggest that being rooted in a place is not what makes a "genuine" work of art flourish; rather, certain works create, or help to create, that sense of rootedness, which a posteriori consecrates those works as "genuine"—such surely is the logic taught by a history of literature that produced and canonized first the rootless Kālidāsa and then the rooted Pampa. What interests us in these reflections on the literary particular, beyond the genealogy of the idea and its remarkable implications in modern Europe—that the particular is the real general and that nationalism may "equivocate" as the true universalism—is the answer Gramsci gestures toward by noting the radical difference, as he emphatically puts it, between two modalities of particularity: *being* particular and *preaching* particularism. To express this in the terms used in this book: while vernacularity is essential for art and for life, we can and must distinguish between a vernacularity of necessity and one of accommodation, and strive somehow to achieve the latter.

In the second text, a brief comment on the past and future of the idea of the Italian nation-state, Gramsci raises the question of the universal while pursuing the same basic problem just mentioned, wondering now whether the forces that produced the unification of Italy must also inevitably produce a militaristic nationalism. He argues that such nationalism is antihistorical: "It is, in reality, contrary to all the Italian traditions, first Roman and then Catholic," which he tells us are cosmopolitan. But then, as if sensing the incompleteness of his answer, he asks the far more important question whether a new type of cosmopolitanism may ever be possible, beyond "nationalism and militaristic imperialism: Not the citizen of the world as *civis romanus* or as Catholic but as a producer of civilization."[6] In other words, is it possible to be universal without preaching universalism?

The tension between the particular and the universal, the vernacular and the cosmopolitan, the local and the global—not all precisely the same phenomena, to be sure, but now inextricably linked—has lost little of its urgency since Gramsci's day. It shows itself to be as pressing and intractable as ever, with new and more complex versions of vernacularity developing in response to what is perceived as cosmopolitanism in its ugly-American embodiment.

5. Gramsci 1991: 260–61 (a summary of and comment on an article by Julien Benda).
6. Gramsci 1991: 246–47.

To get a sense of where we stand now, let us look briefly at two recent attempts by accomplished thinkers, inheritors of one of the historical types of vernacularism and cosmopolitanism whose genesis has been traced in the course of this book, to rehabilitate the national vernacular under a liberal or progressive guise, one by stressing culture, the other, power. By way of conclusion we can then ask whether any response to this new indigenism is available in a postcolonialism that may still bear the impress or stored energy—whatever may be the right metaphor—of those other, and very different, cosmopolitan and vernacular histories.

In a recent work on multicultural citizenship, the Canadian philosopher Will Kymlicka introduces the idea of a "societal culture" that provides its members "with meaningful ways of life across the full range of human activities . . . encompassing both public and private spheres." Societal cultures, which turn out to differ little from national cultures, constitute the true basis of freedom. The congeries of practices termed societal cultures "did not always exist" but were produced from, among other factors, the new elevation of the vernacular (explained following the Gellnerian model). Yet in the author's treatment this assemblage has somehow been able to escape the historicity of the nineteenth-century moment of its genesis. Vernacular cultures are simply there as givens; they demand unequivocally to be accommodated precisely as they are, unquestioned about their present let alone historical constitution. They are the only "meaningful context of choice for people" and worth preserving at all costs. Violations of the space of vernacular cultures, accordingly—through open borders, for example—would be disastrous since "people's own national community would be overrun by settlers from other cultures"; they would as a result be unable "to ensure their survival as a distinct national culture." "Most people" (somehow the author knows most people) "would rather be free and equal within their own nation . . . than be free and equal citizens of the world, if this means they are less likely to be able to live and work in their own language and culture." A necessary vernacularism if there ever was one.[7]

A less openly ethnocultural defense of vernacular nationalism is offered by the Scottish scholar Tom Nairn, who approaches the problem through the domain of the political. The breakup of Soviet socialism, Nairn says, buried the old internationalism of promoting working-class solidarity to counteract capitalism and nationalism. In its place has come "internationality," the bland but dangerous homogenization of the world whose very effect is to produce local, often violent, resistance. The way forward now must be through, and not outside, nationalism, and of course through capitalism. All that is left for internationalists to decide is "what sort of nationalists they

7. Kymlicka 1995: 76, 80, 93 (Kymlicka 1999 now argues not for liberal nationalism but for "multination federation"). A strong critique of Kymlicka is offered in Waldron 1995: 93–119.

will become." As the 1919 intellectuals would have phrased it, the only way to be universal now is to be national. As for the dangers? Well, "are the fragmentation and anarchy really so bad?" These words were written two years into the siege of Sarajevo, five years into the struggle in Kashmir, ten years into the movement for Tamil Eelam—with Rwanda one year away, Chechnya two, Srebrenica three, and the renewed Intifada and response in Israel-Palestine four. Of course these are not identical situations—and not all twentieth-century horrors, many far worse than these, can be subsumed under the extreme vernacular mobilization of nationalism. Yet each of these recent cases seems poised in its own way on the particularistic, vernacular brink, the "Ethnic Abyss," that seems increasingly resistant to Nairn's denial that "here is no abyss, in the hysterical-liberal sense."[8]

Kymlicka and Nairn are representative of many contemporary thinkers (not just small-country nationalists but proponents of multiculturalism, identity politics, and so forth) for whom vernacularity stands outside of history—except to the degree that history demonstrates its necessity (which it does continually)—and constitutes an essential component of human existence. The conservation of vernacular culture and the acquisition of vernacular polity, now coterminous with nationalism, is a categorical imperative in the face of a universalism seen only as mandatory. Such a vision of the present and future is a distillate, or so it seems arguable, of convictions about autochthony reproduced throughout the history of European vernacularization under an old pressure from compulsory cosmopolitanism.

To these views we may juxtapose the perspective of those who have inherited, if not always with clear awareness of the fact, the very different traditions of the South Asian cosmopolitanism and vernacularism detailed in this book. These are legatees, in addition, of the world's longest and most fraught engagement with globalization in its harshest form, European colonialism. The rich inventory of strong formulations about particulars and universals, especially Asian particulars and Western universals, found among these intellectuals is something one may again and reasonably take to be a kind of sedimentation of historical experience—without thereby endorsing an iron determinism—though it is no straightforward matter to assess its value. Surely getting beaten up all the time by the schoolyard bully has a way of focusing the mind on violence more than is the case for kids who have been left in peace. And while such historical experience does not convert automatically into an advantage for thought or practice, it clearly encourages a propensity for thinking. We may not be wrong to suppose, therefore, that these two powerful formative experiences—a long encounter with autonomously produced cosmopolitan and vernacular practices, followed by firsthand knowl-

8. Nairn 1996; the texts quoted are on pp. 274–76.

edge of the new and heteronymous cosmopolitanism of colonialism and its consequence, an ossified vernacularism—have inclined some thinkers to search harder, not for a unified theory of transcendence but for "cracks in the master discourses" and, more important, for practices that overcome the dichotomous thinking that marks our current impasse.[9]

It is from within the world of these intellectuals that some of the more compelling suggestions are being offered on ways to address the desperate choices imposed by capitalist modernity.[10] Might it be possible to transcend the dichotomies of modernizing (and homogenizing) cosmopolitanism and traditionalizing (and rigidifying) vernacularism by understanding that the new must be made precisely through attachment to the old, and by recognizing that only such an attachment enables one to grasp what in the past can and must be changed? Take as one example the seemingly irreconcilable alternatives of the universalist discourse of the liberal state—where secularism demands the submergence of religious difference in a homogeneous juridical order—and the historical particularities of a given community's ways of life (understanding that these are in fact historical): might this irreconcilability yield to a strategic politics that seeks to institute such a transformation from within communities themselves (whether Muslim, Vaiṣṇava, Maratha, or other), while resisting demands for liberalization or democratization that are official, top-down, imposed from the outside? In other words, affective attachment to old structures of belonging offered by vernacular particulars must precede any effective transformation through new cosmopolitan universals. Care must be in evidence: the desire to preserve even as the structure is changed.[11] Analogously, the choice between the global and the local, whether in the production of culture or in the organization of power, may find some kind of resolution in the blunt refusal to choose between the alternatives, a refusal that can be performed in practice whatever the difficulty in articulating it in theory.

Indeed, such practices can actually exist without necessarily being theorized. The Sanskrit cosmopolis offers just such an instance—another apparent anomaly of India, itself the "strangest of all possible anomalies," as Macaulay phrased the unintended compliment.[12] Indeed, such anomalies may be precisely what is needed in a world of almost nomologically reenacted violence between the localisms and globalism of modernity: the anomaly of a universalism that does not stand in contradiction with cultural or political particularism or preach its own necessity, that knows its limits and yet has centers everywhere and circumferences nowhere; the anomaly of a ver-

9. The phrase is Dipesh Chakrabarty's, in conversation.
10. See for example Chatterjee 1997; Nagaraj 1998; Chakrabarty 2000.
11. Chatterjee puts several of these ideas well (1997: 261–62 and 280–85).
12. Cited in Khilnani 1998: 16.

nacularism with multiple mother tongues, free of longing for language origins and people origins, and free of the conjuncture and exclusivity of language-people-place. Exhuming these anomalies as future potentialities, by decivilizing and denationalizing the Indian past where they were once lived realities, is something that might be achieved by a seriously historical account of Sanskrit in the world, one seeking not a return to roots but a "coming-to-terms with our 'routes,'" an unsentimental and nondefensive history, and one that is not merely, pointlessly erudite.[13]

Might not the historical reality of such anomalies, with their different cultural-political logic where middle terms were not excluded, suggest the possibility of making the future one of And rather than Either/Or? The proclamation has the ring of a slogan, and a utopian slogan at that. And it does not mechanically yield policy outcomes, either, that would be capable of directly adjudicating today's most pressing questions of the cosmopolitan and vernacular—the minority cultural rights that we must support, for instance, or the ethnochauvinist politics that we must resist.[14] Yet the proposal to seek And is worth entertaining as a life practice, and it derives some pragmatic sustenance from an awareness of the varied cosmopolitan and vernacular possibilities that were available before modernity—the once-existent *topoi* from which utopianism can take hope, those real places and real practices of the past that show how malleable are the iron laws of culture and power. To know that some people in the past could be universal and particular in their practices of culture and power without making their particularity ineluctable or their universalism compulsory is to know that better cosmopolitan and vernacular practices are at least conceivable, and perhaps even—in a way those people themselves may never have fully achieved—eventually reconcilable.

13. Hall 1996: 4; Gramsci 1991: 170.

14. In fact the formulation is taken from a German sociologist whose argument is not a precipitate of comparable historical experience but derives instead from an abstract model of risk theory (Beck 1997).

Appendix A

A.1 BHOJA'S THEORY OF LITERARY LANGUAGE (FROM THE *ŚṚṄGĀRAPRAKĀŚA*)

A group of words with unitary meaning constitutes a unit of discourse *(vākyam)*. There are three species of such units: Sanskrit, Prakrit, and Apabhramsha.

Sanskrit units of discourse are of three types: relating to revelation *(śrauta)*, relating to the seers *(ārṣa)*, and relating to the world *(laukika)*. Those relating to revelation have two subdivisions: *mantra* (liturgical formulas) and *brāhmaṇa* (liturgical commandments and explanations). The following is an example of *mantra:*

> That very thing is fire, wind, the sun, the moon,
> it is semen, nectar, *brahma,* water, Prajāpati.

The following is an example of *brāhmaṇa:*

> When one is healthy and prosperous among men, overlord of others, endowed to the full with all human pleasures—that constitutes man's highest bliss.

Those units of discourse relating to the seers are of two types: *smṛti* (revealed texts remembered) and *purāṇa* (accounts of the past). An example of *smṛti* is the following:

> Only a Shudra woman can be the wife of a Shudra man. She can be the wife of a Vaishya man, as can a Vaishya woman. These two can be the wife of a king [Kshatriya], as can a Kshatriya woman, and any of the three can be the wife of a Brahman, as can a Brahman woman.

An example of a *purāṇa* is the following:

> There lived a demon named Hiraṇyakaśipu, and the gods were so beside themselves with fear of him that they would make obeisance to any direction where the demon happened to look askance.

Those units of discourse relating to the world have two subdivisions: *kāvya* (literature) and *śāstra* (systematic thought). An example of *kāvya* is the following:

> Who would not be driven mad
> with thirst by these lips of yours?
> With their coral color/shadelessness *(vidrumacchāyā)*
> they are like a path right through the desert.

An example of *śāstra* is the following:

> A woman whose eye is bright white and long-lashed will have a love temple like fresh churned butter.

A Prakrit unit of discourse can be one of three types: pure *(sahaja),* defined *(lakṣita),* and distorted *(śliṣṭa).* Pure is twofold, either identical with Sanskrit *(saṃskṛtasama)* or of a Place *(deśya).* An example of the first is: *sarale sāhasarāgaṃ parihara* etc., (O simple girl, give over this reckless desire . . .);[1] an example of the second is: *vippa api āpu* etc.[text unclear].[2] Defined is twofold, either of Mahārāṣṭra or of Śaurasena. An example of the former is: *ṇamaha avaḍhḍhiatuṅgaṃ* etc. (Pay homage to Him who is lofty without having been elevated . . .); an example of the latter is: [example missing]. Distorted is either of Paiśāca or of Māgadha. An example of the former is: *panamata panaappakuvia-* etc. (Pay homage to [Rudra whose image falls on Gaurī's toenails] as she sulks in jealousy . . .); an example of the latter is: *hadamāṇuśamaṃśabhoyaṇaṃ* etc. (Feasting on the flesh of men fallen in battle . . .).

Apabhramsha is threefold: highest, middle, and lowest (literally, youngest). The highest is that of Avanti, Lāṭa, and environs. The middle is that of the Ābhīras, the Gūrjaras, and environs. The lowest is that of the Kāśmīras, Paurastyas (easterners) and environs.[3]

1. The phonology allows the passage to be read as either Sanskrit or Maharashtri Prakrit. On the literary function of this type of Prakrit, see *SKĀ* 2.17 prose.

2. Here nothing can be read as Sanskrit, though the sentence does not consist exclusively of *deśī* words (e.g., *parihasanteī*). The passage is corrupt, however; see Kulkarni 1989: 44.

3. *ŚP* 165.15 ff. See Raghavan's edition of the *ŚP* for the sources of quotations in this passage that could be traced. The Apabhramsha illustrations, with a couple of exceptions, are corrupt beyond repair (see Bhayani in Kulkarni 1989: app. 1 pp. 2–3). It is nonetheless clear that all the examples are poetry, and most are love lyrics.

A.2 BHOJA'S THEORY OF ORNAMENTATION (FROM THE *SARASVATĪKAṆṬHĀBHARAṆA*)

(2.5) There are twenty-four types of ornaments of the word, which will now be defined and exemplified.

(6) The first is the category that is itself called "type," i.e., the species of language *(bhāratī)* used in a text, Sanskrit and the rest. Language type functions as an ornament of speech *(vāk)* by reason of its being employed in a way appropriate to the subject matter and other aspects of the work.

(7) ["With reference to appropriateness in general,"] some people [should be shown to] speak only in Sanskrit, some only in Prakrit, some in an idiom "common to" two languages *(sādhāraṇī)*, and so on [see vv. 17 ff.], some in the language of the uncultured *(mlecchabhāṣā)*.

(8) ["With reference to appropriateness in respect to communicative situation or place,"] the language of the uncultured is not [to be shown as] used at sacrificial rites, one should not [show anyone] speaking anything but Prakrit to women; nor "mixed" language (*saṃkīrṇa* [see vv. 17 ff.]) to high-born people, nor Sanskrit to the uneducated.

(9) ["With reference to appropriateness in respect to character type,"] gods, ["sages, kings"] and so on [should be shown to] speak Sanskrit; *kinnaras* and other demigods Prakrit; *piśācas* and other terrestrial spirits Paishachi, and low castes Magadhi.

(10) ["With reference to appropriateness in respect to content,"] Sanskrit alone is to be used for writing about certain subjects, Prakrit alone for others, and Apabhramsha alone for yet others.

(11) One subject may most appropriately be represented in Paishachi, Shauraseni, or Magadhi; some may lend themselves to two or three languages, some to all [six] of them.

(12) ["With reference to appropriateness in respect to the occasion,"] presenting to literary gatherings *(goṣṭhī)* stories *(kathā)* where either Sanskrit or languages of Place *(deśabhāṣā)* are used to excess does not bring one much esteem in the world.

(13) ["With reference to regional predilections,"] the people of Lāṭa hear Prakrit gladly and disdain Sanskrit. The Gūrjaras take delight in their own Apabhramsha as in no other ["and therefore both should be shown in dramas or narratives using these languages"].

(14) ["As for the Gauḍa there is a proverb":] "I tell you, Brahman, either a Gauḍa, to preserve his status, must avoid Prakrit literature altogether, or the language itself would have to change"

(15) ["With reference to appropriateness in respect to historical epoch,"] who during the reign of Āḍhyarāja ["that is, Sātavāhana"] did not speak Prakrit? Who did not speak Sanskrit in the time of Śrīsāhasāṅka ["that is, Vikramāditya"]?

(16) Heavenly speech ["Sanskrit"] is worthy to hear; the best Prakrit is mellifluous by nature, Apabhramsha is lovely, Paishachi can be used to compose enchanting literature; the language of the people who dwell in Mathurā ["Shauraseni"] and that of the people of Magadha are appealing to the clever. He who can compose in them all is the most successful, the very king, of poets.

Now, authorities hold that language type has six varieties: pure, common (*sādhāraṇī*), combined (*miśrā*), mixed (*saṃkīrṇā*), exclusive (*nānyagāminī* [i.e., not common]), and degenerate. All six languages have all six varieties of ornamentation.[4]

A.3 ŚRĪPĀLA'S BILPAṄK *PRAŚASTI* OF KING JAYASIṂHA SIDDHARĀJA

Oṃ! Homage to Śiva!
(1) May the God whom eight-eyed Brahmā ever bears in mind
and twelve-eyed Kumāra holds in devotion,
to whom thousand-eyed Indra bows and the King of Serpents,
with twice so many eyes, offers hymns of praise—
may this Virūpākṣa, God of the Three Eyes,
the target of ten thousand eyes of lovely women filled with love,
quickly destroy all the bad karma of good men.
(2) Hail to the God Virūpākṣa, whose half-body the glorious
Goddess adorns:
when Kāma, god of the flower bow, his own body burned
by the flame from Virūpākṣa's forehead eye,
entered the Goddess's large left eye, a pool of the drink of
immortality,

4. *SKĀ* 2.5–17 (a much abbreviated version of this discussion is found in *ŚP* 577–78). Bracketed additions in quotation marks comprise the remarks of the commentators Ratneśvara and Bhaṭṭa Narasiṃha; bracketed additions without quotation marks are my clarifications. In v. 2.6 c Bhaṭṭa Narasiṃha correctly reads *sārthaucityādibhir* (for *sā tv aucityādibhir*). "In the language of the uncultured": Transcriptions of languages from outside the Indo-Aryan and Dravidian worlds are singularly rare. In Prakrit texts, I find only Uddyotana's Tājik Persian (noted in chapter 8.1), and none whatever in Sanskrit (in the *Lalitavigraharāja* of Somadeva, written in 1153, the two central-Asian Turuṣkas introduced at the beginning of act 4 speak Magadhi). "To preserve his status," *svādhikārājihāsayā* (in the *KM*, from which Bhoja probably borrowed the proverb, the reading of the printed editions is *svādhikārajihāsayā*, p. 33.27, as it is in *ŚP* 607); "Prakrit literature," *gāthā*. The context of the proverb in *KM* is the claim that "people to the east of Vārāṇasī, the people of Magadha and so on, recite Sanskrit literature beautifully but have no talent for Prakrit." Verse 13 is borrowed from *Kāmasūtra* 1.4, and v. 16 is adapted (rewriting *pāda* c to add Shauraseni and Magadhi) from Rājaśekhara's *Bālarāmāyaṇa* 1.11. In v. 16 a I read *prakṛtamadhurā prākṛtadhurā* (for *prakṛtamadhurāḥ prākṛtadhurāḥ*).

as if on the bank he left his bow on her half
of the body, under the guise of her brow.
(3) "It was through your power that Rāma, son of Jamadagni,
destroyed all Kshatriyas. You must therefore now create
someone to protect me!" So Earth begged the moon-crested god
when the law of the fishes had come to prevail,
and then and there, in an instant, he created a single hero
from the water in the ritual vessel *(culuka)* for his evening twilight
worship.
(4) This king was named Culukya, and from him sprang
the great dynasty that has set its foot upon this world
and enjoyed to its heart's content the rewards
of the pious acts of legions of Brahmans.
(5) Among them was a king named Śrīmūlarāja,
famed for his virtues, the very abode
of the sciences of statecraft, a ruler
whose courage was beyond reproach.
(6) His footstool was marked by a line where the turbans
of his border vassals had rubbed it smooth;
it seemed a four-posted reception hall
built to welcome his new bride, Fame.
(7) His son, Cāmuṇḍarāja, was a great lover and a man of purity:
he constantly sought the company of the goddesses of royalty
of the enemy circle of kings he violently destroyed
while keeping his distance from their wives.
(8) From him was born king Vallabharāja,
who with his virtues/ropes *(guṇa)* captured the good,
and with his delightful ways/battles *(raṇa),* the wives of his foes.
(9) His kinsman Durlabharāja next took up the earth
with an arm that by its forceful grasp
equaled the tusk of the great-tusked cosmic Boar.
On the palaces in the cities of enemy kings
woodworms carved what seemed like rows of letters
capable of publishing abroad his enormous fame.
(10) His younger brother, born at an auspicious hour,
was Śrī Nāgarāja, who conquered the king of kings,
and by his righteousness all but ended the *kaliyuga,* and thus achieved
success in the other world and in the eyes of other men.
(11) His son was Śrī Bhīmadeva, a king whose fame
even today shines brightly in all directions,
as if it had taken shape in the mounds of white bones
of the heroic armies of his enemies.

(12) The great tree of his heroism was lush
with the flower of his subjects' loyalty, for he watered it well:
with the blood that poured from the severed fingers of the King of Sindhu,
with the tears cried by the women of Lāṭa
tinged with saffron from their cheeks, with the floods
wept by the army of the king of Mālava when cut down by his sword.
(13) His son, Śrī Karṇadeva, was the very forehead ornament of kings:
from slapping the heads of his war elephants in rut
his hand was always colored a deep vermilion
that stained the backs of enemy kings as they bowed before him—
and it looked at the same time like Kamalā, Red Lotus Goddess of Power,
making the gesture of stability.
(14) Pleased by repeated sacrifices performed by priests
richly rewarded by the king's gifts, Indra invited him to heaven,
and the king agreed to go, but only after anointing
his son, Śrī Jayasiṃhadeva, into the kingship.
(15) "The Primal Person himself has come as avatar
to earth! Śiva, Foe of Andhaka, will bestow on him
perfection of alchemy that will make him overlord
over perfected beings. He will delight
in bold action unassisted and will perform
miraculous deeds at a moment's notice."
Such predications men of higher knowledge
made about this king at the very hour of his birth.
(16) The beautiful wives of overlords who were his enemies
he reduced to living in mountain caves,
and the garlands of red *guñja* berries on their breasts—
their only companions in forest exile—appeared
liked wreaths of sparks from the fire of his anger.
(17) The king was ornamented with every art *(kalā),* like the moon with digits *(kalā);*
as the moon bears a full disc *(pūrṇamaṇḍala),* so he bore
a full circle of vassals *(pūrṇamaṇḍala).*
The only trait of the moon the king lacks is its stain.
(18) That this king manifests himself
in all the imaginings of lovely women,
in their wishes, pronouncements, visions, in the paintings
that they paint in sport, in what they see in their dreams
must signal the perfection of his multiform magic powers.

(19) First uprooted, then reestablished in their kingships,
distinctly inscribed with thousands of scars from wounds
left by the work of his sword—in every direction
kings are transformed into living pillars of glory
that proclaim the victory of this world conqueror,
who is ready to protect all who bow their head to him.
(20) It seems to laugh with all the pearl necklaces
in the houses of the Brahmans; it seems to sing
with the buzzing bees drunk on the fragrant smell
of must from the elephants gifted to his court poets;
it almost dances with the motions of the flags
upon the countless temples he has built:
thus his fame seems to take pleasure
as it teaches other kings the holy rite of generosity.
(21) Prime factor in his success in war,
source of the wealth of untold blessings,
doubly perfected is his alchemy *(rasa)*,
the one called quicksilver liquid, and the other named the taste
for heroism.
(22) He has restored to respect what had fallen into disrespect,
the city of Avantī that had lost its protection;
and though hard even for him to do, he has rebuilt Dhārā.
He destroyed enemy fortresses and emptied the country
of Mālava of the people of Mālava.
Not just in name, clearly, is he "master of political power."
(23) When in good will he toured the land of Mālava,
conquered by the power of his arms, he came upon
the god Virūpākṣa indecorously housed
in a ruined temple. He paid worship and had a vision of the god
illuminated by the light from the crescent moon in His hair,
by the fire from His forehead eye, by the glow
from the jewels in the heads of the snakes on His chest.
(24) Then, in devotion to the Supreme Lord
he had a temple built, with a towering summit,
high as a mountain, and a place
where lovely birds come soaring in their play.
(25) This temple has been given a rich and ruddy glow
with all its golden finials and pennants, and almost embodies
the reverence the golden king of mountains
has for Śiva, God of the Mountain, and Gauri, the Mountain's
Daughter.
(26) The many rich temple services
offered in worship

by Siddharāja
have brought a beneficent gleam even to the eye
of Virūpākṣa, God of the Three Eyes.
(27) So long as Mount Himālaya
adorns the sea-girt earth,
so long may this worshipful temple
of Virūpākṣa give delight.
(28) Śrīpāla, emperor of poets, adopted kinsman
of King Siddharāja, who in a single day
once produced a masterpiece of literature,
composed this praiseworthy poem of praise *(praśasti)*.
(29–30) Śrī Jinabhadrācārya, also known
as Rājavallabha, a master of literature,
first among the pious, and foremost of Jain sages,
had this poem engraved, at the behest of King Siddhapati,
by the Brahman Gaṅgādhara,
whose letters are clear and distinct.

In the year [of Vikramāditya] 1198, Āṣāḍha śudi 1 [Saturday, June 7, 1141][5]

A.4 THE ORIGINS OF HEMACANDRA'S GRAMMAR (FROM PRABHĀCANDRA'S *PRABHĀVAKACARITA*)

Once upon a time Siddharāja conquered the political sphere of Mālava . . . One day, those in charge of the library books taken from Avantī were dis-

5. *EI* 40: 27 ff.; a second transcription is found in Singh 1991 (the Vaḍnagar *praśasti* referred to below is edited in *EI* 1: 296 ff.). In v. 2 the correct reading has been perceived by Singh: *yadarddhe bhrūvyājāt taṭa* (for: *yadardhenduvyājāt tata*); v. 9: "tusk": I read *daṃṣṭrām* (for *daṃṣṭrā*). The marks of the woodworms are meant to suggest that the palaces have been abandoned; v. 10: "who conquered the king of kings" is obscure; one might expect "who conquered Nāgarāja, king of serpents," in supporting the earth (though the facsimile of the stone itself clearly has *rājarāja*). As *dvidhā* shows, *paraloka* is meant to be taken in two senses here. In v. 13 the correct reading is *pṛṣṭam arañjayat* (for *pṛṣṭasaraṃ jayad*). For the image of Śrī leaving her lotus and taking up residence in the lotuslike hand of the monarch, see the nearly contemporary textualized *praśasti* of Udayaprabha, the *Sukṛtakīrtikallolinī* vv. 34 and 43. On royal alchemy see *Mānasollāsa* 2.l, vol. 1, pp. 29 ff. (it was presumably these magical practices that gave Siddharāja control over spirits such as Barabaraka, who assisted him in his Mālava campaign, see *Sukṛtasaṃkīrtana* of Arisiṃha p. 67 and *Purātanaprabandhasaṃgraha* pp. 23 ff.). In v. 19: neither *avatūlaiḥ (EI)* nor *avabhūlaiḥ* (Singh) makes sense to me. Regarding v. 21: in Vaḍnagar v. 11, Jayasiṃha "relieved the burden of debt of the world by means of his alchemy" *(siddharasa-)*. In v. 22: I conjecture *kārayan* (for *kāraṇam/dhāraṇaṃ*); v. 23: cf. Vaḍnagar v. 11: *bhaktyākṛṣṭavitīrṇadarśanaśivaḥ*, "to whom Śiva, drawn by his devotion, granted a vision of himself." In v. 30: "behest," *niropataḥ*, unattested in Sanskrit but compare *ṇirova* in Prakrit, and *niropa* in Old Marathi and Kannada. The final *pāda* of the *gīti* here is lacking three *mātrās*.

playing them, when the king caught sight of a textbook. The Master asked what it was and they informed him, "This is Bhoja's grammar; it is the science of language now current in the world. For the king of Mālava, the crest-jewel of scholars, composed texts on grammar, rhetoric, astrology, logic, medicine, politics, alchemy, architecture, arithmetic, augury, metaphysics, dreams, and the interpretation of bodily marks; books that explain signs and portents, and the very crest-jewels of astronomical investigations; an exposition of the nature of revenue, a work on prices called *Meghamālā*." The king replied, "Is there in our library no such fundamental grammatical text? How can it be that there is no such learned individual in all the land of Gujarat [capable of composing such a work]?" To a man, all the scholars turned their eyes toward Hemacandra. Then, with great devotion and deference, the king besought the lord: "Produce a grammatical text and fulfill my dreams, great seer. None but you can do it. At the present time, the abbreviated Kalāpaka [= *Kātantra*] text is current; but it provides no acceptable guide to the formation of words. The Paninian text is a 'limb of the Veda,' according to the Brahmans, and they arrogantly resent [others using it]—why bother with those dimwits? It would mean glory for me and renown for you, best of sages, and spiritual merit, if you were to make a new grammar for the benefit of all the world." Hemacandra listened and then replied, "What you say serves only to remind me of a task [I already had in view]. But there exist eight grammars in written form, and they are to be found, without doubt, only in the library of [the temple of] Śrī Bhāratī, Goddess of Speech. Let Your Majesty have his men bring those manuscripts from the land of Kashmir, so that I can properly compose my grammatical textbook."

Hearing his words, the king at once dispatched his high officials to the heart of the land of the Goddess of Speech. They reached the Goddess in the city of Pravara [= Srinagar], and having paid homage with obeisance, they praised her with recitations and eulogies. And gratified, she spoke aloud and directed her functionaries: "Śrī Hemacandra the Śvetāmbara possesses the wealth of my grace. He is, as it were, a second form of me. For his sake, make over to his emissaries the collection of books, and send them on their way." The ministers of the Goddess, accordingly, showed the emissaries proper honor and made over the books to [their leader] Utsāhapaṇḍita and sent him [and the others] on their way.

Soon they made their way back to their town, filled with the grace of the Goddess and fairly tingling with joy beyond measure. Those who had been addressed by the Goddess told the king everything—about the great honor she had shown to lord Hemacandra, and how gratified she was by his firm devotion. When he heard this, the king was overjoyed and said, "Blessed is this realm of mine—and I myself—where so accomplished a scholar resides."

Now, Hema[candra]sūri, having examined the collection of grammars, made a new, glorious, miraculous text known as the *Siddhahaima*. It was eight chapters in length, comprising thirty-two quarter sections, containing an appendix on irregular formations *(uṇādi)*, gender, and a list of verbal roots. It consisted of *sūtras* and an excellent commentary thereon, a dictionary of nouns, and a synonym lexicon. It was the very crest-jewel of grammatical texts and [came to be] held in esteem by scholars everywhere. The voluminous grammars that had existed in earliest times were impossible to read in full, even in an entire lifetime, and hence were actually an impediment to fulfilling the three life goals; they were confused, riddled with faults, or unintelligible in places. Hence scholars of today take this grammar as their standard. At the end of every quarter section is a single verse describing the lineage of kings starting with Mūlarāja [founder of the Gujarati Caulukya dynasty], with a tetrad of verses at the very end of the book [counting as a single verse]. This constitutes a wonderful *praśasti* of thirty-five verses composed by the attentive [Hemacandra]. It was read aloud by preeminent scholars in the presence of the king. The king spent 300,000 coins to have the book copied in the course of a year. At the king's command, officials from every department zealously summoned three hundred scribes and showed hospitality to them. The books were copied, and one set was given to the most energetic scholar of each and every school of thought.

The text circulated and grew famous in all lands: Aṅga, Vaṅga, Kaliṅga, Lāṭa, Karṇāṭa, Kuṃkaṇa, Mahārāṣṭra, Surāṣṭra, Vatsa, Kaccha, Mālava, Sindhu-Sauvīra, Nepāla, Pārasīka, Muraṇḍa, Gaṅgāpāra, Haridvāra, Kāśi, Cedi, Gayā, Kurukṣetra, Kānyakubja, Gauḍa, Śrīkāmarūpa, Sapādalakṣavat, Jālandhara, central Khaśa, Simhala, Mahābodha, Cauḍa [Cōḻa], Mālavakaiśika. Twenty copies along with explanations were sent by the king with great gratitude to the Kashmiris, and the text was deposited in their library. Everyone takes care of what they value highly; how much more would the Goddess [cherish Hemacandra's grammar]?

There was a brilliant clerk by the name of Kākala, who was a student of the eight grammars, a scholar to outstrip the King of Divine Serpents himself [Patañjali]. Lord [Hemacandra] straightway made him the teacher of the text, since he could grasp its true meaning at a glance and expound it. And every month on the fifth day of the lunar fortnight, called "The Day of Knowledge" *(jñānapañcamī)*, he would hold an examination, and the king would adorn with ornaments all who were successful. To those who became proficient in the text the king awarded fine shawls, golden jewelry, soft chairs, and parasols.[6]

6. *Hemacandrasūricaritam, Prabhāvakacarita* no. 22: 185.10 ff.; vv. 73 ff.; "textbook," *lakṣaṇapustakam;* "metaphysics," or "omens," *adhyātma-;* "a work on price called *Meghamālā*," the text is uncertain here; "fundamental [grammatical] text," *śāstrapaddhati;* "eight grammars": there

A.5 THE INVENTION OF *KĀVYA* (FROM RĀJAŚEKHARA'S *KĀVYAMĪMĀṂSĀ*)

I once heard from my teacher the following ancient and auspicious tale:

Once upon a time, the students of Dhiṣaṇa [Bṛhaspati] put a question to him in the course of their lessons: "You said that your own guru was Kāvyapuruṣa, "Poetry Man," the son of Sarasvatī, Goddess of Speech. Who was he?" Bṛhaspati answered them as follows:

Long ago Sarasvatī performed ascetic penances on Snowy Mountain, in the hope she might give birth to a son. Viriñca [Brahmā] was pleased by this, and said to her, "I will create a son for you." And in due course she gave birth to Poetry Man. No sooner was he born than he paid homage at her feet and spoke the following metrical speech:

All the universe is made of language
and objects are its magic transformation.
Here am I, mother, your transformation, Poetry
incarnate, I who now clasp your feet.

The Goddess, seeing the stamp of versification—something previously unique to the language of the Veda *(āmnāya)*—now present in the realm of everyday speech *(bhāṣā),* embraced him with joy and whispered to him, "Child, inventor of metrical speech, you surpass even me, your mother and the mother of all that is made of language. How true what people say, that to be outdone by one's own son is like having a second. Before your birth, the learned knew only prose, not verse. Today, metrical speech, which you have discovered on your own *(upajña),* begins its life. What praises you deserve. Your body consists of words and meanings, your mouth consists of Sanskrit, your arms of Prakrit, your groin of Apabhramsha, your feet of Paishachi,

---

seems to be no traditional list, only six are mentioned in a Kannada Jain inscription of 1053 (*EI* 16: 55): *Cāndra, Kātantra, Jainendra, Śabdānuśāsana* [of Śākaṭāyana], *Pāṇini,* and *Aindra,* though perhaps the *Sārasvata* and the Prakrit grammar of Vararuci were meant to be added (note that rival grammars were often studied simultaneously, though one doubts comparatively, see the Beḷgami inscription in the Kōḍimaṭha, *EC* (ed. Rice), vol. 7: 129–132 and 190–93); "in written form," *pustakāni;* "recitations and eulogies," *pāṭhanastavaiḥ;* "those who had been addressed," *-uditāḥ,* or read *-ditam,* "everything that had been said"; "gender," probably read *riṅkat;* "in earliest times," *ādau;* "confused," *saṃkīrṇa-,* compare *viprakīrṇa-* in the *praśasti* verse at the end of the *Siddhahemacandra.* The author of the story has little sense of Kashmir, geographically or intellectually. Note that the Śāradā temple is not in the capital but some three days journey outside. (Stein 1900, vol. 2: 286 remarks with some justice on the exaggeration in this account of the greatness of Sanskrit learning in Kashmir, though in fact the generation of scholars of the mid-twelfth century, which included Ruyyaka, Maṅkha, and Kalhaṇa, was quite brilliant, see Pollock 2001a.) On the other hand, Prabhācandra's understanding of Hemacandra's extensive use of earlier grammars is correct, indeed, understated. Kielhorn identified at least fifteen different sources.

your chest of mixed language. You are balanced, clear, sweet, noble, and forceful. Your speech is brilliant utterance, your soul aesthetic feeling, your hair the different meters, your wit question-answer poems, riddles, and the like, while alliteration, simile, and the other figures of speech adorn you. The Veda itself, which gives voice to things to come, has praised you thus:

Four horns he has, three feet, two heads, seven hands;
thrice-bound he roars; a great god
who has entered the mortal world.

Powerful being though you may really be, pretend you are not so now, and take on the ways of a child."

With this, she placed him on the couchlike bench of a large boulder under a tree and went to bathe in the heavenly Gaṅgā. At that very moment, the great sage Uśanas, who had come out to gather fuel and *kuśa* grass, found the child lying overcome by heat in the noonday sun. Wondering who might be the parent of this unprotected child, he brought him to his own ashram. When after a moment Sārasvateya revived, he bestowed on him metrical speech. And then suddenly Uśanas proclaimed, to the astonishment of all those present:

Day after day the poets milk her,
yet she is never milked dry!
May Sarasvatī, dairy cow of poetry,
be ever present in our hearts.

Then Uśanas taught that knowledge to his students. From that time on wise men have referred to Uśanas as Kavi ["wise one"], and it is by way of allusion to him that poets are designated *kavi* in everyday usage. This word for poet is derived from the verbal root *kav,* which literally means "to describe," and "poetry" *(kāvya)* means literally "the object [produced by the poet]." The compound "Poetry Man," for its part, is used figuratively *(bhaktyā)* in reference to Sārasvateya because he is none other than poetry itself.

The Goddess of Speech soon returned, and failing to find her son, she wept from the very depths of her heart. Now, Vālmīki, the best of sages, happened to be passing by. Humbly he told her what had happened and showed the Blessed Goddess the ashram of the son of Bhṛgu. With her breasts moist with milk she embraced her son and kissed him on the head; and out of good will toward Vālmīki, the son of Pracetas, she secretly made over metrical language to him, too. Later, after she had dismissed him, he came upon the sight of a young crane crying mournfully for his mate, whom a Niṣāda hunter had killed. And filled with grief *(śoka),* the poet uttered this first verse *(śloka),* in a voice of mournful wailing:

May you never find fulfilment in all your living years, Niṣāda,
for killing one of these cranes in the act of making love.

Then the Goddess, with divine vision, granted a secret power to this very verse: any poet who should recite it first, this one verse, before reciting any other, would become a son to Sarasvatī herself. For his part, the great sage, from whom this utterance first emerged, composed the history *(itihāsa)* called the *Rāmāyaṇa*. Dvaipāyana, reciting the same verse first and by reason of its power, composed the collection *(saṃhitā)* of one hundred thousand verses called the *[Mahā]Bhārata*.

Now, some time later, when two distinguished Brahman sages were having a dispute about *śruti*, the Self-Existent God [Brahmā], ever diplomatic, referred the question to Sarasvatī for judgment. Hearing of the goings on, her son was ready to accompany her, but she refused to allow him. "For one like you who has not received permission from Parameṣṭhin, Brahmā Who Stands on High" she said, "the voyage to His world can be perilous," and so turning him back, she set out on her own. Poetry Man stalked off in anger, and when he did, his best friend, Kumāra, began to cry and scream. "Be still, Kumāra, my child," Gaurī said to him, "I'll put a stop to this." And she fell to thinking. "The only bond that holds people back is love. I will create a special woman to keep Sarasvatī's son in thrall." She then gave birth to Sāhityavidyā, "Poetics Woman." And she instructed her as follows, "This is your lawful husband, who has stalked off in anger. Follow him and bring him back. And you sages who are present, perfected in the science of literary art, go sing the deeds of these two, Poetry and Poetics. This will prove to be a treasure-store of literature for you." The blessed Bhavānī fell silent, and they all set out as directed.

They all went first to the east, where are found the peoples called the Aṅgas, Vaṅgas, Suhmas, Brahmas, Puṇḍras, and so on. As the daughter of Umā tried to entice Poetry Man she put on different kinds of dress in the different regions, and this was imitated by the women of the various places. In that first place the costume *(pravṛtti)* was called Auḍramāgadhī and was praised by the sages as follows:

Woven necklaces on chests wet with sandalwood paste,
scarves kissing the parted hair, a glimpse of the breasts,
bodies the hue of *dūrvā* grass from their use of aloe—
may such costume ever regale the women of Gauḍa.

And the men of that country also adopted the attire Sārasvateya himself happened to be wearing, and it became the male costume specific to Oḍra and Magadha. As for the dance and music-making and so on that she performed, that became the *bhāratī* mode *(vṛtti)*, and the sages praised it as they had done earlier. And what he spoke when as yet not under her thrall, incomparable though she was—verses dense with compounds and alliteration, and filled with repeated use of words in their conventionally restricted etymological signification *(yoga[rūḍhi]paramparā)*—that became known as the Path *(rīti)* of Gauḍa. And the sages praised it as they had done earlier. In due course I (Rājaśekhara) shall discuss the nature of *vṛtti* and *rīti.*

Next he went north to the country of Pañcāla, where are found the peoples called the Pāñcālas, the Śūrasenas, the Hāstināpuras, the Kāśmīrakas, the Vāhīkas, the Bāhlīkas, the Pāhlaveyas, and so on. As the daughter of Umā tried to entice Poetry Man it went as before. Her costume there was called the central Pāñcāla and was praised by the sages as follows:

Cheeks with flashing sparkles of dangling earrings,
bright necklaces gently swinging hanging down to the midriff,
garments billowing out from hips to ankles—
pay homage to the costume of the women of Kānyakubja.

This time Sārasvateya's interest was piqued. As before, the men of that country also adopted the attire he was wearing then. As for the partial dance, vocal and instrumental music and graceful gesture *(vilāsa)* that she displayed, that became the *sāttvatī* mode, and because it had sinuous movements it was also called the *ārabhaṭī.* The sages gave praise as they had done earlier. And what Sārasvateya spoke when partly in her thrall, incomparable though she was—verses with partial compounds and modest alliteration, and filled with metaphorical expressions *(upacāra)*—that became known as the Path of Pañcāla.

Next he went west to the country of Avanti, where are found the peoples called the Āvantis, Vaidiśas, Surāṣṭras, Mālavas, Arbudas, Bhṛgukacchas, and so on. As the daughter of Umā tried to entice Poetry Man it went as before. Her costume there was called the Āvanti—it is midway between the central Pāñcāla and the southern costume. Accordingly, too, there are two modes there, the *sāttvatī* of the north and the *kaiśikī* of the south. And it was praised by the sages as follows:

The men and women wear the costume of Pañcāla,
and that of the south—may they all find pleasure in it!
The recitation and gestures, too, of men and women
in the land of Avanti combine both Paths.

Next he reached the southern region, where are found the peoples called the Malayas, the Mekalas, Kuntalas, Keralas, Pālamañjaras, Mahārāṣṭras, Gaṅgas, Kaliṅgas, and so on. As the daughter of Umā tried to entice Poetry Man it went as before. Her costume there was called the Southern. And it was praised by the sages as follows:

Coiffeur of braided hair curly down to the root,
foreheads marked with fragrant saffron powder,
the knot of skirts made tight by tucking at the waist—
long live the costume of the women of Kerala.

This time Sārasvateya fell deeply in love with her. As before, the men of that country also adopted the attire he was wearing then. As for the complex dance, vocal and instrumental music, and graceful gesture she manifested, that became the *kaiśikī* mode. The sages gave praise as they had done earlier. And what Sārasvateya spoke when altogether enthralled by her—verses with moderate alliteration and no compounds, and only [rare] use of words in their etymological signification *(yogavṛtti)*—became known as the Path of Vidarbha. And the sages praised it as they had done earlier.

Now "costume" *(pravṛtti)* refers to an order of arrangement of clothing, "mode" *(vṛtti)* to an order of arrangement of bodily movements, and "path" *(rīti)*, to an order of arrangement of words. Teachers have argued that a fourfold categorization of costumes and modes cannot be fully adequate to the countless number of regions. In Yāyāvarīya's view, these regions, though countless, are easily conceived of as a fourfold division, in the same way that what is called the "Imperial Field" *(cakravartikṣetra)* is conceived as a unified whole, though of course its component regions are countless in respect of their specificities. That is to say, the Imperial Field extends north a thousand *yojana*s from the South Sea onward [to Bindusaras, the source of the Gaṅgā], and there these costumes are worn. Beyond dwell divine beings, but they should be represented as wearing the costume of whatever place they visit, though in their own region they do as they like. Those who live on other continents, similarly, follow the costume and mode of their places. The "paths," which are only three [and not four], will be discussed below.

In the country of Vidarbha there is a city called Vatsagulma, where the God of Love often comes to play. There the son of Sarasvatī married the daughter of Umā by the love-marriage rite of the *gandharva*s. The bride and groom in due course left that place and, enjoying themselves in the different regions on the way, returned to the Snowy Mountain, where Gaurī and Sarasvatī, now kin by marriage, were dwelling. The young couple did obeisance to them, and their mothers gave them their blessing and had them take up their dwellings, in the form of imagination, in the minds of poets.

By their creation of this pair they have made a heavenly world for poets, a place where poets, while continuing to dwell in the mortal world with a body made of poetry, may rejoice for all ages with a body divine.

Thus Self-Existent Brahmā
created Poetry Man.

And the poet who understands the division here
will rejoice in this world and the world beyond.[7]

7. *KM* pp. 5–10. I read *anupreṣitaś ca* for *anuprekṣitaś ca* (p. 7.7), and conjecture *kāvyaṃ karmaṇi* for *kāvyakarmaṇo* (7.1) and *pratibhāmayena* for *pratibhāvamayena* (p. 10.10). My emendation here, *yogarūḍhiparaṃparāgarbham* for *yogavṛtti-* (p. 8.14), is certified by *ŚP* 1050 (= Mysore ed p. 681); an example of the category "conventionally restricted etymological" usage would be the quasi kenning "oblation-bearer" for fire. For *yogavṛtti* we would expect *rūḍhivṛtti,* but compare chapter 5.3. *Yoga* and *rūḍhi* are differentiating factors in *gauḍa* and *vaidarbha* styles from the time of Daṇḍin, as is clear from his analysis of *prasāda* (*KĀ* 1.45–46), though the terms themselves are not used in the *KĀ*. The use of "metaphorical expressions" (*upacāra,* e.g., "the bed tells of her sorrow") is not symmetrical with the traits of the other Paths, but in the adaptation of the passage by Bhoja, the degree of metaphoricity in the other Paths is catalogued as well (see chapter 5.3). The verse at the beginning, "Four horns," etc., is *ṚV* 4.58.3; *Mahābhāṣya* vol. 1: 3 explains the riddle (the four horns are the four parts of speech, the three feet the three temporal aspects, etc.). The "mixed language" of Kāvyapuruṣa's chest is not a fifth category but rather echoes Daṇḍin's *saṃkīrṇabhāṣā,* the mixture of the three or four literary languages in a polyglot genre like drama (chapter 2.2). On the "Imperial Field," mentioned also in *KM* 92.10 ff., see chapter 6.1. Vatsagulma is the ancient name of Bāsim (Madhya Pradesh), the find-spot of the important Vākāṭaka inscription discussed in chapter 1.3. The "division" mentioned in the last line refers presumably to the division of labor between "Poetry Man" and "Poetics Woman" (so the modern Sanskrit commentary of Madhusudana Mishra).

Appendix B

B.1 APPROXIMATE DATES OF PRINCIPAL DYNASTIES

Achaemenids 550–330 B.C.E.
Mauryas 320–150 B.C.E.
Śakas 100 B.C.E.–400 C.E.
Kuṣāṇas 100 B.C.E.–400 C.E.
Sātavāhanas 225 B.C.E.–250 C.E.
Ikṣvākus 225 C.E.–300
Vākāṭakas 250–500
Kadambas 300–600
Guptas 320–550
Pallavas 300–900
Gaṅgas 400–1000
Bādāmi Cāḷukyas 500–750
Veṅgi Cāḷukyas 625–1075
Pāṇṭiyas 600–1300
Gurjara Pratīhāras 725–950
Pālas 750–1200
Rāṣṭrakūṭas 750–975
Cōḻas 900–1200
Yādavas of Devagiri 900–1300
Angkor 900–1400
Kalyāṇa Cāḷukyas 960–1200
Caulukyas of Gujarat 1000–1300
Hoysaḷas 1000–1300
Kākatīyas 1100–1400
Vijayanagara 1340–1565

B.2 NAMES OF IMPORTANT PEOPLES AND PLACES WITH THEIR APPROXIMATE MODERN EQUIVALENTS OR LOCATIONS

Ābhīra: people of eastern Gujarat
Aihoḷe: town in Karnataka
Aṇahilapāṭaka: Patan, Gujarat
Ānart[t]a: northern Gujarat
Aṅga: eastern Bihar
Aparānta: coastal Gujarat and parts of Maharashtra
Arbuda: Mount Abu, Rajasthan

Avanti: western Madhya Pradesh, often specifically the city of Ujjain

Ayodhyā (Sāketa): Ayodhya, Uttar Pradesh

Bādāmi (Vātāpi): town in Karnataka

Bāhlīka: Bactria, Balkh

Bharukaccha (also Bhṛgukaccha): Broach, Gujarat

Bhauṭṭa: Tibetan

Bilpaṅk: Ratlam district, Madhya Pradesh

Cedi: southern Madhya Pradesh

Cedivatsa: Jabalpur region near the Narmada

Devagiri: Daulatabad, Maharashtra

Dhārā: Dhar, Madhya Pradesh

Dramila, Draviḍa: Tamilnadu

Dvārakā: town on the Kathiawar coast

Dvārasamudra: Halebid, Karnataka

Ekāmra: Bhubaneshvar, Orissa

Gandhāra: region of northwest Pakistan

Gaṅgāpāra: area in northern Bihar

Gauḍa: west Bengal

Gokarṇa: town on the south Karnataka coast

Hampi (also, Kiṣkindhā): town in northern Karnataka

Haridvāra: Hardwar, Uttar Pradesh

Hūṇas: people of the far northwest

Kaccha: Kutch, Gujarat

Kaliṅga: central coastal Orissa

Kalyāṇa: Basavakalyan, Karnataka

Kāmarūpa: Assam

Kamboja: northern Afghanistan

Kāñcī(puram): city in Tamilnadu

Kānyakubja: Kanauj, Uttar Pradesh

Karuvūr (also, Vañci): Perur, Kerala

Kāśī: Varanasi, Uttar Pradesh

Kāśikośala: Chattisgarh

Kāṭiāwāḍ (also, S[a]urāṣṭra): peninsular Gujarat

Kauśāmbī: Kosam, Uttar Pradesh

Kauṭāra (also, Vo-cahn): town in Cambodia

Khambhāt: Cambay, Gujarat

Khaśa: southern Kashmir

Kisuvoḷal (also, Paṭṭadakal): town in Karnataka

Kośala: eastern Uttar Pradesh

Koṅkaṇa: the Konkan

Kuntala: northern Karnataka

Kurukṣetra: region in Haryana (also, Vat Phu region, Cambodia)

Lāṭa: southern Gujarat

Lauhitya: Brahmaputra river

Madhyadeśa: western and central Gangetic plain

Magadha: southern Bihar

Mahābodha: probably Bodhagaya

Mahendra: the Eastern Ghats

Māhīṣmatī: Maheshvar, southern Madhya Pradesh
Maithilā: of northern Bihar
Mālava: Malwa, central Madhya Pradesh
Mālavakaiśika: possibly eastern Madhya Pradesh
Malaya: the Western Ghats
Mānyakheṭa: Malkhed, Karnataka
Marubhūmi: the Thar desert
Mekala: the Maikal range
Murala: northern Karnataka
Muraṇḍa: Taxila region
Oḍra: Orissa
Oṃkuṃda: Okkuda, Karnataka
Pahlavas, Pāhlaveyas: Parthians
Pañcāla: western Uttar Pradesh
Pañcanada: Panjab
Pārasīka: Persia, Persian
Pāṭaliputra: Patna
Paṭṭadakal: see Kisuvoḷal
Pot[h]ana: region north of Hyderabad
Prabhāsa (also known as Somanātha): town on the Kathiawar coast
Prāgjyotiṣa: Gauhati, western Assam
Pratiṣṭhāna: Paithan, Maharashtra
Pravarapura: Srinagar, Kashmir
Puligeṟe: Lakshmeshvar, Karnataka
Puṇḍra: northern Bengal
Puruṣapura: Peshwar, Pakistan
Puruṣottama(śālagrāma): Puri, Orissa
Rāḍhīya: of Burdwan in west Bengal
Rājagirīya: of southern Bihar
Sapādalakṣavat: Ajmer region of Rajasthan
Saurāṣṭra: see Kāṭiāwāḍ
Sindhu(-Sauvīra): Sindh
Somanātha: see Prabhāsa
Śrīkāmarūpa: see Kāmarūpa
Śrīmāla; Bhinmal, Rajasthan
Śrīśaila: hill in Telangana, Andhra Pradesh
Śrīvijaya: Palembang, Sumatra
Suhma: Gangetic delta
Śūrasena: Mathura region, Uttar Pradesh
Tāmralipi: south Bengal coast
Trigarta: area in Himachal Pradesh
Tripurī/Tripurā: city in central Madhya Pradesh
Tuṣāras: Tocharians
Ujjayinī: Ujjain, Madhya Pradesh
Utkala: Orissa
Vāhīkas: people of the Panjab
Valabhī: Vala, Gujarat
Vanavāsi (Banavase): Banavasi, town and region in western Karnataka
Vañci: see Karuvūr
Vaṅga: central-southern Bengal
Vārāṇasī: see Kāśī
Vārendra: of east Bengal
Vatsa: Allahabad region, Uttar Pradesh
Vatsagulma: Basim, Maharashtra

Vēmulavāḍa: Lemulavada, Andhra Pradesh

Vidarbha: Berar

Videha: Mithila region, northern Bihar

Vidiśa (Vaidiśa, of Vidiśa): Bhopal

Vijayavāḍa: Bejavada, Andhra Pradesh

Virajā: Jajpur, Orissa

Vo-cahn: see Kauṭāra

PUBLICATION HISTORY

Some of the materials in this book were first sketched out in the following lectures and publications. I am deeply grateful to the various audiences for their spirited engagement with my ideas.

"Axialism and Empire." In *Axial Civilizations and World History,* edited by Johann Arnason et al. Leiden: E.J. Brill: 2005. Originally presented as a paper to the Conference on Axial-Age Transformations, European University Institute, Florence, December, 2001.

Viśvātmaka Deśabhāṣe. Translated by Akshara K.V. Heggodu (Karnaṭaka): Akshara Prakashana, 2003.

"Cosmopolitan and Vernacular in History." In *Cosmopolitanism,* edited by Carol Breckenridge et al. Durham: Duke University Press, 2002. Originally presented as a lecture to the Workshop on Cosmopolitanisms, University of Chicago, May, 1999; presented again in modified form at the Center for Cultural Studies, University of California, Santa Cruz, February, 2001, and the Max-Weber-Kolleg für Kultur- und Sozialwissenschaftliche Studien, Universität Erfurt, Erfurt, Germany, June 2001.

"The Cosmopolitan Vernacular." *Journal of Asian Studies.* 57.1 (1998): 6–37. A preliminary version of this paper, entitled "Three Local Cultures in the Sanskrit Cosmopolis," was presented at the 1995 meeting of the Association for Asian Studies, Washington, D.C.

"India in the Vernacular Millennium: Literary Culture and Polity, 1000–1500." In "Early Modernities," edited by S. N. Eisenstadt et al., special issue, *Daedalus* 127.3 (1998): 41–74. Originally presented as "The World in Vernacularization: Language, Community, and Polity in India, 900–1500," to the conference From Empires to Nations and States: Collective Identity, Public Sphere, and Political Order in Early Modernity, Swedish Collegium for Advanced Study in the Social Sciences,

Uppsala, June 1996. Also presented in modified form as a lecture at Harvard University, Cambridge, Massachusetts, May 1997, and at the École des haute études en sciences sociales, Paris, April 1998.

"The Sanskrit Cosmopolis, A.D. 300–1300: Transculturation, Vernacularization, and the Question of Ideology." In *Ideology and Status of Sanskrit: Contributions to the History of the Sanskrit Language,* edited by Jan E. M Houben. Leiden: E. J. Brill. 1996.

"Introductory Note" and "Literary History, Indian History, World History." In "Literary History, Region, and Nation in South Asia," edited by Sheldon Pollock, special issue, *Social Scientist* 23.10–12 (1995): 1–7, 112–42. Also presented as lectures at the Central University, Hyderabad, December 1993.

"Making History: Kalyāṇi, A.D. 1008." In *M. S. Nagaraja Rao Felicitation Volume.* Bangalore: n.p., 1995.

"Writing before the Nation." Paper presented at the conference South Asian Cultural Studies and the Subject of Representation, Joint Committee on South Asia, American Council of Learned Societies/Social Science Research Council, Durham, February 1993; presented in a somewhat modified form and entitled "Postcolonial Reading and Precolonial Writing in India: The Problem of the Culture-Nation" at the conference Dimensions of Ethnic and Cultural Nationalism in Asia, cosponsored by the University of Wisconsin-Milwaukee/Marquette University Center for International Studies and the *Journal of Asian Studies,* February 1993.

"The Language of the Gods in the World of Men: Reflections on Sanskrit in History." Inaugural lecture, University of Chicago, February 1990.

BIBLIOGRAPHY

ABBREVIATIONS

AA	*Artibus Asiae*
ABORI	*Annals of the Bhandarkar Oriental Research Institute*
AHR	*American Historical Review*
AiS	*Asian Survey*
AJP	*American Journal of Philology*
AK	*Archiv für Kulturgeschichte*
AL	*Anthropological Linguistics*
AmA	*American Anthropologist*
AORM	*Annals of Oriental Research* (Madras)
ARA	*Annual Review of Anthropology*
ARSIE	*Annual Report on South Indian Epigraphy*
ARSS	*Actes de la recherche en sciences sociales*
AS	*Abhilekhasaṃgraha*
AS/ÉA	*Asiatische Studien / Études asiatiques*
ASI A/R	*Archaeological Survey of India, Annual Reports*
ASR	*American Sociological Review*
BCH	*Bulletin de correspondance hellénique*
BEFEO	*Bulletin de l'école française d'extrême-orient*
BEI	*Bulletin d'études indiennes*

BI	*Barhut Inscriptions*
BJS	*British Journal of Sociology*
BSOAS	*Bulletin of the School of Oriental and African Studies*
BTLV	*Bijdragen tot de Taal-, Land- en Volkenkunde*
CA	*Current Anthropology*
CC	*Cultural Critique*
CI	*Critical Inquiry*
CII	*Corpus Inscriptionum Indicarum*
CIJ	*Corpus of the Inscriptions of Java*
CKI	*Corpus of Kadamba Inscriptions*
ClI	*Classics Ireland*
CQ	*China Quarterly*
CSSAAME	*Comparative Studies in South Asia, Africa, and the Middle East*
CSSH	*Comparative Studies in Society and History*
CW	*Classical World*
EC	*Epigraphia Carnatica*
EI	*Epigraphia Indica*
EJCS	*European Journal of Cultural Studies*
EJP	*European Journal of Philosophy*
EPW	*Economic and Political Weekly*
ERS	*Ethnic and Racial Studies*
ETI	*Early Telugu Inscriptions*
EW	*East and West*
EZ	*Epigraphia Zeylonica*
HEI	*History of European Ideas*
HT	*History and Theory*
HW	*History Workshop*
IA	*Indian Antiquary*
IAN	*Inscriptions of Ancient Nepal*
IC	*Indian Culture*
IdC	*Inscriptions du Cambodge*
IEK	*Inscriptions of the Early Kadambas*
IESHR	*Indian Economic and Social History Review*

IHQ	*Indian Historical Quarterly*
IIJ	*Indo-Iranian Journal*
IJDL	*International Journal of Dravidian Linguistics*
IK	*Inscriptions of Kambuja*
IP	*Inscriptions of the Pallavas*
ISC	*Inscriptions sanscrites du Cambodge*
IWG	*Inscriptions of the Western Gaṅgas*
JA	*Journal asiatique*
JAAS	*Journal of Asian and African Studies*
JAHRS	*Journal of the Andhra Historical Research Society*
JAOS	*Journal of the American Oriental Society*
JAS	*Journal of Asian Studies*
JASB	*Journal of the Asiatic Society of Bengal*
JBBRAS	*Journal of the Bombay Branch of the Royal Asiatic Society*
JESHO	*Journal of the Economic and Social History of the Orient*
JESI	*Journal of the Epigraphical Society of India*
JHSB	*Journal of the Historical Society of Bombay*
JIABS	*Journal of the International Association of Buddhist Studies*
JIH	*Journal of Indian History*
JIP	*Journal of Indian Philosophy*
JMEMS	*Journal of Medieval and Early Modern Studies*
JOI	*Journal of the Oriental Institute* (Baroda)
JORM	*Journal of Oriental Research, Madras*
JRAS	*Journal of the Royal Asiatic Society*
JRS	*Journal of Ritual Studies*
JSEAS	*Journal of Southeast Asian Studies*
JWH	*Journal of World History*
KĀ	*Kāvyādarśa*
KI	*Karnatak Inscriptions*
KM	*Kāvyamīmāṃsā*
KRM	*Kavirājamārgam*
MAR	*Mysore Archaeological Report*
MAS	*Modern Asian Studies*
MBh	*Mahābhārata*

MHJ	*Medieval History Journal*
NGC	*New German Critique*
NLH	*New Library History*
NLR	*New Left Review*
NŚ	*Nāṭyaśāstra*
OT	*Oral Traditions*
PBA	*Proceedings of the British Academy*
PMS	*Pūrvamīmāṃsāsūtra*
PO	*Poona Orientalist*
PT	*Political Theory*
QJMS	*Quarterly Journal of the Mythic Society*
Raghu	*Raghuvaṃśa*
Rām	*Rāmāyaṇa of Vālmīki*
RH	*Revue historique*
RP	*Romance Philology*
RR	*Romanic Review*
RS/SI	*Recherches sémiotiques / Semiotic Inquiry*
ṚV	*Ṛgveda*
SA	*South Asia*
SII	*South Indian Inscriptions*
SITI	*South Indian Temple Inscriptions*
SKĀ	*Sarasvatīkaṇṭhābharaṇa*
ŚMD	*Śabdamaṇidarpaṇam*
SO	*Studia Orientalia*
ŚP	*Śṛṅgāraprakāśa*
SRK	*Subhāṣitaratnakośa*
SSI	*Social Science Information*
SSS	*Śāsana Sāhitya Sañcaya*
ST	*Social Text*
STII	*Studien zur Indologie und Iranistik*
TASSI	*Transactions of the Archaeological Society of South India*
TITLV	*Tijdschrift voor Indische Taal-, Land- En Volkenkunde*
TS	*Theory and Society*
VAV	*Vikramārjunavijayam*

WZKSA	*Wiener Zeitschrift für die Kunde des Südasiens*
ZDA	*Zeitschrift für deutsches Altertum*
ZDMG	*Zeitschrift der deutschen morgenländischen Gesellschaft*
ZVS	*Zeitschrift für vergleichende Sprachforschung*

PRIMARY SOURCES IN SOUTH ASIAN LANGUAGES

Abhidharmakośa of Vasubandhu. Edited by Dwarikadas Sastri. 2 vols. Varanasi: Bauddha Bharati, 1970–73.

Abhilekhasaṃgraha. Edited by Gautamavajra Vajracarya and Mahesaraja Pant. Kathmandu: Samsodhan Mandal, [1964?].

Adhvaramīmāṃsākutūhalavṛtti of Vāsudeva Dīkṣita. Edited by P. N. Pattabhirama Sastry. 3 vols. New Delhi: Lal Bahadur Shastri Vidyapeeth, 1968–69.

Ādipurāṇa of Jinasena. Edited by Pannalal Jain. 2 vols. 4th ed. New Delhi: Bharatiya Jnanapith, 1993.

Alaṅkārakaustubha of Kavikarṇapūra. Edited by Sivaprasad Bhattacaryya. Rajshahi: Varendra Research Society, 1926.

Amarakośa. See *Nāmaliṅgānuśāsana.*

Anantanāthapurāṇam of Janna. Edited by E. C. Devirappa and M. C. Padmanabhasarma. Mysore: Kannada Adhyayana Samsthe, 1972.

Āpastambadharmasūtra. Edited by A. Chinnaswami Sastry. Varanasi: Chowkhamba Sanskrit Series Office, 1932.

Arthaśāstra of Kauṭilya. Edited by R. P. Kangle. 3 vols. 2d ed. Bombay: University of Bombay, 1969.

Avantisundarī of Daṇḍin. Edited by Suranand Kunjan Pillai. Trivandrum: Government Press, 1954.

Bālarāmāyaṇa of Rājaśekhara. Edited by Gangasagara Raya. Varanasi: Caukhamba Surbharata Prakasana, 1984.

Bārhaspatyasūtra. Edited by F. W. Thomas. Lahore: Moti Lal Banarsi Dass, 1921.

Bhaktavijaya of Mahīpati. Edited by Visvanatha Kesava Phadake. Pune: Yasavanta Praksana, 1974.

Bhaktilīlāmṛta of Mahīpati. Edited by Damodar Samvalaram et al. Bombay: Induprakash Press, 1935.

Bhāvaprakāśana of Śāradātanaya. Edited by Madan Mohan Agrawal. Mathura: Usha Agrawal, 1978; also Yadugiri Yatiraja Swami and K. S. Ramaswami Sastri (Baroda: Oriental Institute, 1930).

Bhojaprabandha of Ballāla. Edited by Kasinath Pandurang Parab. 2d ed. Bombay: Nirnaya Sagar Press, 1904.

Bṛhaddeśī of Mataṅga. Edited by R. Sathyanarayana. Hampi: Kannada University, 1998 (Kannada script); also Prem Lata Sharma (New Delhi: Indira Gandhi Centre of the Arts, 1992-).

Buddhacarita of Aśvaghoṣa. Edited by E. H. Johnston. 2 vols. Calcutta: Baptist Mission Press, 1935–36.

Chandōmbudhi of Nāgavarma. Edited by Kukkila Krishnabhatta. Mysore: D. V. K.

Murthy, 1975; also F. Kittel (Mangalore: Basel Mission Book and Tract Depository, 1875), reprint, New Delhi, 1988.

A Collection of Prakrit and Sanskrit Inscriptions [of Kattywar, etc.]. No editor. Introduction by Peter Peterson. Bhavnagar: State Printing Press, [c. 1896].

Corpus of the Inscriptions of Java. Edited by Himansu Bhusan Sarkar. 2 vols. Calcutta: Mukhopadhyay, 1971.

Corpus of Kadamba Inscriptions. Vol. 1. Edited by B. R. Gopal. Sirsi: Kadamba Institute of Cultural Studies, 1985.

Daśarūpaka of Dhanaṃjaya with the *Avaloka* of Dhanika and the *Laghuṭīkā* of Bhaṭṭanṛsiṃha. Edited by T. Venkatacharya. Madras: Adyar Library and Research Centre, 1969.

Deśīnāmamālā of Hemacandra. Edited by R. Pischel. 2d ed. Bhandarkar Oriental Research Institute, 1938.

Dharmakośa. Vol. 3, pt. 2: *Saṃskārakāṇḍa.* Edited by Laxmanshastri Joshi. Wai: Prajnapathasala Mandala, 1938.

Dharmāmṛtam of Nayasēna. Edited by R. Shama Sastri. Mysore: University of Mysore, 1924.

Dhvanyāloka of Ānandavardhana with the *Locana* of Abhinavagupta. Edited by Pattabhirama Sastry. Varanasi: Chowkhamba Sanskrit Series Office, 1940; also K. Krishnamoorthy (Dharwar: Karnatak University Press, 1974).

Dvyāśrayamahākāvya of Hemacandrasūri. No editor. Vava, Banasakantha: Sri Vava Jaina Svetambara Murtipujaka Sangha, [1986].

Early Telugu Inscriptions. Edited by Budharaju Radhakrishna. Hyderabad: Andhra Pradesh Sahitya Akademi, 1971.

Epigraphia Carnatika. Edited by H. M. Nayak et al. Mysore: Kannada Adhyayana Samsthe, 1972-; for vols. 9–17, the 1st ed. Mysore, 1886–1919, has been used.

Gadāyuddham. See *Sāhasabhīmavijayam.*

Gauḍavaho of Vākpatirāja. Edited by N. G. Suru. Ahmedabad: Prakrit Text Society, 1975.

Harṣacarita of Bāṇa. Edited by Kasinath Pandurang Parab. Bombay: Nirnaya Sagar Press, 1938.

Inscriptions du Cambodge. Vols. 1, 4, and 5. Edited by Georges Coedès. Paris: Boccard, 1953.

Inscriptions of Ancient Nepal. Edited and translated by D. R. Regmi. New Delhi: Abhinav Publications, 1983.

Inscriptions of the Early Kadambas. Edited by G. S. Gai. New Delhi: Indian Council of Historical Research, 1996.

Inscriptions of Kambuja. Edited by R. C. Majumdar. Calcutta: Asiatic Society, 1953.

Inscriptions of the Maukharis, Later Guptas, Puspabhutis, and Yasovarman of Kanauj. Edited by Kiran Kumar Thaplyal. New Delhi: Indian Council of Historical Research, 1985.

Inscriptions of the Pallavas. Edited by T. V. Mahalingam. New Delhi: Agam Prakashan, Indian Council of Historical Research, 1988.

Inscriptions of the Western Gaṅgas. Edited by K. V. Ramesh. New Delhi: Agam Prakashan, Indian Council of Historical Research, 1984.

Inscriptions sanscrites du Cambodge. Edited by M. A. Barth. Paris: Imprimerie nationale, 1885.

Jayakaumudī (Commentary on the *Mahābhārata*) of Vidyāsāgara. Unnumbered MS, Virendra Research Institute, Rajshahi.

Jñānadīpikā of Devabodha. *Bhīṣmaparvan,* edited by S. K. Belvalkar. Pune: Bhandarkar Oriental Research Institute, 1947; *Sabhāparvan,* edited by R. D. Karmarkar. Pune: Bhandarkar Oriental Research Insititute, 1949.

Kādambarī of Bāṇa Bhaṭṭa. Edited by P. L. Vaidya. Pune: Oriental Book Agency, 1939.

Kāmasūtra of Vātsyāyana. Edited by Devadatta Shastri. Varanasi: Chowkhamba Sanskrit Series Office, 1964.

Kannaḍa Nighaṇṭu. Edited by G. Venkatasubbiah and N. Basavaradhya. 5 vols. Bangalore: Kannada Sahitya Parishad, 1970–95.

Kannaḍaśāsanasaṃpadam. Edited by Rudrayya Chandrayya Hirematha and M. M. Kalburgi. Dharwar: Karnataka University Press, 1968.

Karṇāṭabhāratakathāmañjarī of Kumāravyāsa. Edited by Venkatesa Iyengar [Masti]. Mysore: Prasaranga, University of Mysore, 1974.

Karnatak Inscriptions. Vol. 1. Edited by R. S. Panchmukhi. Dharwar: Kannada Research Office, 1941.

Karṇāṭakabhāṣābhūṣaṇam of Nāgavarman. Edited by R. Narasimhachar. Mysore: Sarada Mandira, 1975 (original edition included in the *Kāvyāvalōkanam,* Mysore, 1902); also Lewis Rice (Bangalore: Mysore Government Press, 1884), reprint, New Delhi, 1985.

Karṇāṭakakādambarī of Nāgavarma. Edited by N. Anantharangachar. Mysore: Usha Sahitya Male, 1973.

Karṇāṭakapañcatantram of Durgasiṃha. Edited by C. P. Krishnakumar. Bangalore: Government of Karnataka, 1994.

Kavirahasya of Halāyudha. Edited by Ludwig Heller. Greifswald: Julius Abel, 1900.

Kavirājamārgam. Edited by M. V. Seetha Ramiah. Bangalore: Karnataka Sangha, 1968; reprint, Bangalore, 1994; also M. V. Seetha Ramiah, rev. ed. (Mysore: D. V. K. Murthy, 1975); A. Venkata Rao and H. Sesha Aiyangar, 2d ed. (University of Madras [Kannada Series], 1973); K. Krishnamoorthy (Bangalore: IBH, 1983).

Kāvyādarśa of Daṇḍin. Edited by D. T. Tatacharya. Tirupati: Shrinivas Press, 1936.

Kāvyalakṣaṇa [= *Kāvyādarśa*] of Daṇḍin. Edited by A. Thakur and Upendra Jha. Darbhanga: Mithila Institute, 1957.

Kāvyālaṅkāra of Bhāmaha. Edited by B. N. Sarma and Baldeva Upadhyaya. Varanasi: Chowkhamba Sanskrit Series Office, 1928; also Ramana Kumara Sarma (Delhi: Vidyanidhi Prakasana, 1994).

Kāvyālaṅkāra of Rudraṭa. Edited by Durgaprasad and Wasudev Laksman Shastri Panshikar. Bombay: Nirnaya Sagar Press, 1928.

Kāvyālaṅkārasūtra and *Vṛtti* of Vāmana. Edited by Ratna Gopal Bhatta. Varanasi: Vidya Vilas Press, 1908.

Kāvyamīmāṃsā of Rājaśekhara. Edited by C. D. Dalal et al. 3d ed. Baroda: Oriental Institute, 1934; also Madhusudhana Misra (Varanasi: Chowkhamba Sanskrit Series Office, 1931–34).

Kāvyānuśāsana of Hemacandra. Edited by Rasiklal C. Parikh and V. M. Kulkarni. 2d ed. Bombay: Sri Mahavira Jaina Vidyalaya, 1964.

Kāvyāvalōkanam. Edited by R. Narasimhachar. 3d ed. Mysore: University of Mysore, 1967.

Keladi Arasara Śāsanasaṃputa. Edited by Keladi Venkatesa Joyisa. Gadag: Virasaiva Adhyayanasamsthe, Srijagadguru Tontadarya Samsthanamatha, 1991.

Kṣemendralaghukāvyasaṃgraha. Edited by E. V. V. Raghavacharya and D. G. Padhye. Hyderabad: Sanskrit Academy, Osmania University, 1961.

Kuvalayamālā of Uddyotanasūri. Edited by A. N. Upadhye. Bombay: Bharatiya Vidya Bhavan, 1959; reprint, Palitan (Surat), n.d.

Līlāvaī of Koūhala. Edited by A. N. Upadhye. Bombay: Bharatiya Vidya Bhavan, 1966.

Mahābhārata. Edited by V. S. Sukthankar et al., 19 vols. Pune: Bhandarkar Oriental Research Institute, 1933–71.

Mahâbhârata with the commentary of Nīlakanṭha. Edited by Ramachandrashastri Kinjawadekar. 6 vols. Pune: Chitrashala Press, 1929–33.

Mahābhārata (Pāṇḍavacarita) of Viṣṇudās. Edited by H. N. Dvivedi. Gwalior: Vidyamandir Prakasan, 1973.

Mahābhāṣya of Patañjali. Edited by Franz Kielhorn. 3 vols. 3d ed. Pune: Bhandarkar Oriental Research Institute, 1962–72.

Maharashtratila Kahi Tamrapata va Silalekha. Edited by Vishnu Bhikaji Kolte. Bombay: Maharashtra Rajya Sahitya ani Samskrti Mandala, 1987.

Mahārthamañjarī of Maheśvarānanda. Edited by Vrajavallabha Dviveda. Varanasi: Sanskrit University, 1972.

Mānasollāsa of King Someśvara. Edited by G. K. Shrigondekar. 3 vols. Baroda: Oriental Institute, 1925–61.

Mīmāṃsādarśanam. Edited by K. V. Abhyankar and G. Joshi. 5 vols. Pune: Anandashrama Press, 1970. (*Śābarabhāṣya* and *Tantravārttika* are cited by page and line number, Jaimini by *sūtra* number.)

Nāmaliṅgānuśāsana of Amarasiṃha. Edited by Krishnaji Govind Oka. Pune: D. G. Khandekar, 1913.

Nāṭyaśāstra of Bharata. Edited by Madhusudan Shastri. 2 vols. Varanasi: Banaras Hindu University, 1971–81; also Sivadatta and Kasinath Pandurang Parab (Bombay: Nirnaya Sagar Press, 1894); M. R. Kavi et al. (Baroda: Oriental Institute, 1926–92).

Navasāhasāṅkadevacarita of Padmagupta. Edited by V. S. Islampurkar. Bombay, Government Central Book Depot, 1895.

Nītivākyāmṛta of Somadevasūri. Edited by Sundarlal Sastri. Varanasi: Sastri, 1976.

Nṛttaratnāvali of Jaya Senapati. Edited by V. Raghavan. Madras: Government Oriental Manuscripts Library, 1965.

Nyāyadarśana. Edited by Amarendramohan Tarkatirtha. Calcutta: Metropolitan Printing and Publishing House, 1936–44.

Nyāyarakṣāmaṇi of Appayya Diksita. Edited by S. R. Krishnamurthi Sastri et al. Secunderabad: Srimad Appayya Deeksthitendra Granthavali Prakasana Samithi, 1971.

Nyāyasudhā of Someśvarabhaṭṭa. Edited by Mukunda Shastri. Varanasi: Chowkhamba, 1909.

Pampa Bhāratam emba Vikramārjunavijayam. Edited by Venkatanaranappa. Mysore: University of Mysore Press, 1926; reprint, Bangalore, 1990.

Pampabhāratadīpike. Edited by R. Narasimhachar. Mysore: University of Mysore Press, 1971.

Paramāra Abhilekha. Edited by A. C. Mittal. Ahmedabad: L. D. Institute, 1979.

Prabandhacintāmaṇi of Merutuṅga. Edited by Jinavijaya. Santaniketan: Singhi Jain Jnanapitha, 1933.

Prabhāvakacarita of Prabhācandrācārya. Edited by Jinavijaya Muni. Ahmedabad: Sanchalaka-Singhi Jaina Granthamala, 1940.

Prakrit Grammar of Hemacandra. Edited by P. L. Vaidya. Rev. ed. Pune: Bhandarkar Oriental Research Institute, 1980.

Prākṛtacandrikā of Śrīśeṣakṛṣṇa. Edited by Prabhakara Jha. Varanasi: Bharatiya Vidya Prakashana, 1969.

Prākṛtamaṇidīpā of Appayya Dīkṣita. Edited by T. T. Srinivasagopalacharya. Mysore: University of Mysore, 1953.

Prākṛtasarvasva of Mārkaṇḍeya. Edited by Krishna Chandra Acharya. Ahmedabad: Prakrit Text Society, 1968.

Pramāṇavārttika of Dharmakīrti. Edited by Raniero Gnoli. Rome: Instituto italiano per il medio ed estremo oriente, 1960.

Purātanaprabandhasaṃgraha. Edited by Jinavijaya. Calcutta: Abhisthata-Singhi Jaina Jnanapitha, 1936.

Puruṣaparīkṣā of Vidyāpati. Edited by Kalidasa Shastri. Bombay: Nirnaya Sagar Press, 1881 (Śaka 1803).

Pūrvottaramīmāṃsāvādanakṣatramālā of Appayya Dīkṣita. Edited by Vaidyanatha Sastri. Srirangam: Vani Vilas Press, 1912.

Raghuvaṃśa of Kālidāsa. Edited by Rewa Prasad Dwivedi. Delhi: Sahitya Akademi, 1993; also H. D. Velankar (Bombay: Nirnaya Sagar Press, 1948).

Rājataraṅgiṇī of Kalhaṇa. Edited by M. A. Stein. Bombay: Education Society's Press, 1892; reprint, Delhi, 1960.

Rannanighaṇṭu of Ranna. Edited by M. M. Kalaburgi. In *Mārga: Saṃśodhana Prabandhagaḷa Sankalan*. Bangalore: Naresh and Company, 1988.

Rasārṇavasudhākara of Śiṅgabhūpāla. Edited by Ganapati Shastri. Trivandrum: Government Press, 1916.

Śabdamaṇidarpaṇam of Kēśirāja. Edited by T. V. Venkatachala Sastry. Bangalore: Kannada Sahitya Parishad, 1994; also A. Shanker Kedilaya (Madras: University of Madras, 1973).

Saddanīti of Aggavaṃsa. Edited by Helmer Smith. Lund: C. W. K. Gleerup, 1928–66.

Sāhasabhīmavijayam (Gadāyuddham) of Ranna. Edited by B. S. Saṇṇayya and Rāmegauḍa. Mysore: Prasaranga, 1985; also K. V. Kṛṣṇabhaṭṭa (Mysore: Geetha Book House, 1973).

Śāhendravilāsa of Śrīdharaveṅkaṭeśvara. Edited by V. Raghavan. Tiruchi: Kalyan Press, 1952.

Sāhityadarpaṇa of Viśvanātha. Edited by Durgaprasad. Bombay: Nirnaya Sagar Press, 1922.

Sāhityamīmāṃsā of Maṅkhaka. Edited by Gopinath Sastri. Varanasi: Sampurnanand Sanskrit University, 1984.

Śākaṭāyana-vyākaraṇaṃ svopajnā-amoghavṛttisamalaṅkṛtam. Edited by Sambhunatha Tripathi. Delhi: Bharatiya Jnanapitha Prakasana, 1971.

Samaraṅgaṇasūtradhāra of Bhoja. Edited by T. Ganapati Sastri. Baroda: Central Library, 1924.

Saṅgītadarpaṇa of Dāmodara. Edited by K. Vasudeva Sastri. Tanjore: S. Gopalan, 1952.

Saṅgītarāja of Mahārāṇa Kumbha. Edited by Premlata Sharma. Varanasi: Banaras Hindu University Press, 1963.

Sarasvatīkaṇṭhābharaṇālaṅkāra of Bhoja. Edited by Biswanath Bhattacharya. Varanasi: Banaras Hindu University, 1979.

Sarasvatīkaṇṭhābharaṇālaṅkāravyākhyā of Bhaṭṭanarasiṃha. Ms. MT 2499, Governmental Oriental Manuscript Library, Madras.

Sarasvatīkaṇṭhābharaṇa[vyākaraṇa] of Bhoja. Edited by T. R. Chintamani Dikshit. Madras: University of Madras, 1937.

Śāsana Sāhitya Sañcaya. Edited by A. M. Annegeri and M. Mallari. Dharwar: Kannada Samsodhana Samsthe, 1961.

Śāstradīpikā of Pārthasārathi Miśra. Edited by Dharmadatta Jha. Varanasi: Krishnadas Academy, 1988.

Śāstrasiddhāntaleśasaṃgraha of Appayya Dīkṣita. Edited by S. R. Krishnamurti Sastri. Secundarabad: Srimad-Appayya-Diksithendra-Granthavali Prakasana-Simiti, 1973.

Shaḍbhāṣācandrikā [sic] of Lakṣmīdhara. Edited K. P. Trivedi. Bombay: Government Central Press, 1916.

Siddhahemacandraśabdānuśāsana. Vol. 1. Edited by Vijayalavanyasuri. Bombay: Srirajanagarastha Jainagranthaprakasakasabha, V. S. 2007 (1950).

South Indian Temple Inscriptions. Vol. 1. Edited by T. N. Subrahmaniam. Madras: Government Oriental Manuscripts Library, 1953.

Śrīkaṇṭhacarita of Maṅkha. Edited by Durgaprasad and Kasinath Pandurang Parab. Bombay: Nirnaya Sagar Press, 1887.

Śṛṅgāramañjarīkathā of Bhoja. Edited by Kalpalata K. Munshi. Bombay: Bharatiya Vidya Bhavan, 1959.

Śṛṅgāraprakāśa of Bhoja. Edited by V. Raghavan. Cambridge: Harvard University Press, 1998- (pp. 917 ff. are cited from the forthcoming vol. 2); also G. R. Joyser (Mysore: Coronation Press, 1955–[69]).

Subhāṣitaratnakośa of Vidyākara. Edited by D. D. Kosambi and V. V. Gokhale. Cambridge: Harvard University Press, 1957.

Śūdracintāmaṇi of Śeṣa Kṛṣṇa. Edited by Gopi Nath Kaviraj. Varanasi: Vidya Vilas Press, 1933.

Sukṛtakīrtikallolinī of Udayaprabha. Edited by Punyavijaya. Bombay: Bharatiya Vidya Bhavan, 1961.

Sūktimuktāvalī of Jalhaṇa. Edited by Embar Krishnamacharya. Baroda: Gaekwad Oriental Series, 1938.

Tantravārttika of Kumārila. See *Mīmāṃsādarśanam*.

Tilakamañjarī of Dhanapāla. Edited by N. M. Kansara. Ahmedabad: L. D. Institute of Indology, 1991.

Vacanas of Basavanna. Edited by H. Deveerappa. Translated by L. M. A. Menezes and S. M. Angadi. Sirigere: Annana Balaga, 1967.

Vāgbhaṭālaṅkāra of Vāgbhaṭa. Edited by Sivadatta and Kasinath Pandurang Parab. Bombay: Nirnaya Sagar Press, 1895.

Vakroktijīvita of Kuntaka. Edited by K. Krishnamoorthy. Dharwar: Karnatak University Press, 1977.

Vākyapadīya of Bhartṛhari. Kāṇḍa 1. Edited by K. A. Subramania Iyer. Pune: Deccan College, 1966.

Vardhamānapurāṇam of Nāgavarma. Edited by B. S. Sannayya. Mysore: Kannada Adhyayana Samsthe, 1974.

Viddhaśālabhañjikā of Rājaśekhara. Edited by Jivananda Vidyasagara. Calcutta: Sarasvati Press, 1883.

Vijayanagara Inscriptions. Edited by B.R. Gopal. 4 vols. Mysore: Directorate of Archaeology and Museums, Government of Karnataka, 1985-.
Vikramāṅkadevacarita of Bilhaṇa. Edited by V. S. Bharadwaj. 3 vols. Varanasi: Samskrit Sahitya Research Committee of the Banaras Hindu University, 1958.
Vikramārjunavijayam. See *Pampa Bhāratam*.
Vinayapiṭakam. Edited by Hermann Oldenberg. London: Pali Text Society, 1879–83.
Vīravardhamānapurāṇam. See *Vardhamānapurāṇam*.
Viṣṇudharmottarapurāṇa. Bombay: Srivenkatesvara Steam Press, n.d.; reprint, Delhi, 1985.
Viṣṇupurāṇa. Bombay: Srivenkatesvara Steam Press, 1910; reprint, Delhi, 1984.
Yaśastilakacampū of Somadevasūri. Edited by Sivadatta and Kasinath Pandurang Parab. Bombay: Nirnaya Sagar Press, 1901.

PRIMARY SOURCES IN EUROPEAN LANGUAGES AND SECONDARY SOURCES

Abbott, Justin E. 1930. *Tukaram: Translation from Mahipati's Bhaktalilamrita*. [Pune]: Scottish Mission Industries.
———. 1927. *Eknath: A Translation from the Bhaktalilamarita*. Pune: Scottish Mission Industries.
Abbott, Justin E., and N. R. Godbole. 1934. *Stories of Indian Saints: An English Translation of Mahipati's Marathi Bhaktavijaya*. Pune: Aryabhusan Press.
Abercrombie, Nicholas et al., eds. 1990. *Dominant Ideologies*. London: Unwin Hyman.
———. 1980. *The Dominant Ideology Thesis*. London: Allen and Unwin.
Abraham, Meera. 1988. *Two Medieval Merchant Guilds of South India*. Delhi: Manohar.
Abu-Lughod, Janet. 1993. "The World System in the Thirteenth Century: Dead-End or Precursor?" In *Islamic and European Expansion: The Forging of a Global Order*, edited by M. Adas. Philadelphia: Temple University Press.
———. 1989. *Before European Hegemony: The World System* A.D. 1250–1350. New York: Oxford University Press.
Adas, Michael, ed. 1993. *Islamic and European Expansion: The Forging of a Global Order*. Philadelphia: Temple University Press.
Agamben, Giorgio. 1999a. *The End of the Poem*. Stanford: Stanford University Press.
———. 1999b. *Potentialities: Collected Essays in Philosophy*. Stanford: Stanford University Press.
Agrawal, V. S. 1963. *India as Known to Pāṇini*. 2d ed. Varanasi: Prithvi Prakashan.
Ahmad, Aijaz. 1992. *In Theory: Classes, Nations, Literatures*. London: Verso.
Aiyangar, S. Krishnaswami. 1933. "The Tamil Sangam in a Pāṇḍyan Charter." *IHQ* 9: 63–75.
Akehurst, F. R. P., and Judith M. Davis, eds. 1995. *A Handbook of the Troubadours*. Berkeley: University of California Press.
Aklujkar, Ashok. 1991. "Interpreting *Vākyapadīya* 2.486 Historically (part 3)." In *Pāṇinian Studies: Professor S. D. Joshi Felicitation Volume*, edited by Madhav Deshpande and Saroja Bhate. Ann Arbor: University of Michigan Center for South and Southeast Asian Studies.
———. 1987. "Rājataraṅgiṇī 1.176." In *Ancient Indian History, Philosophy and Culture:*

Essays in Memory of Professor Radhagovinda Basak Vidyāvācaspati, edited by Pratap Bandyopadhyaya and Manabendu Banerjee. Calcutta: Sanskrit Pustak Bhandar.

Alam, Muzaffar. 2003. "The Culture and Politics of Persian in Pre-Colonial Hindustan." In *Literary Cultures in History: Reconstructions from South Asia,* edited by Sheldon Pollock. Berkeley: University of California Press.

———. 1998. "The Pursuit of Persian Language in Mughal Politics." *MAS* 32.2: 317–49.

Alcock, S., et al., eds. 2001. *Empires.* Cambridge: Cambridge University Press.

Ali, Daud. 2000. "Royal Eulogy as World History: Rethinking Copper-Plate Inscriptions in Cola India." In *Querying the Medieval: Texts and the History of Practices in South Asia,* edited by Ronald Inden. New York: Oxford University Press.

Alsdorf, Ludwig. 1974. "Die Entstehung der neuindischen Sprachen." In *Kleine Schriften,* edited by A. Wezler. Wiesbaden: Steiner.

———. 1937. *Apabhraṃśa-Studien.* Leipzig: Deutsche Morgenländische Gesellschaft.

Altekar, Anant Sadashiv. 1960a. "The Rāshtrakūtas." In *Early History of the Deccan,* edited by G. Yazdani. London: Oxford University Press.

———.1960b. *Rāshṭrakūṭas and Their Times.* Pune: Oriental Book Agency.

Anderson, Benedict. R. O'G. 1992. "The New World Disorder." *NLR* 193: 3–13.

———. 1991. *Language and Power: Exploring Political Cultures in Indonesia.* Ithaca: Cornell University Press.

———. 1983. *Imagined Communities: Reflections on the Origin and Spread of Nationalism.* London: Verso.

Anderson, Perry. 1992. *A Zone of Engagement.* London: Verso.

———. 1974. *Lineages of the Absolutist State.* London: Verso.

Apel, Karl-Otto. 1980. *Die Idee der Sprache in der Tradition des Humanismus von Dante bis Vico.* 3d ed. Bonn: Bouvier.

Appadurai, Arjun. 1999. "Globalization and the Rush to History." Sawyer Seminar lecture. New York, Columbia University.

———. 1996. *Modernity at Large: Cultural Dimensions of Globalization.* Minneapolis: University of Minnesota Press.

Appiah, Kwame Anthony. 1994. "Identity, Authenticity, Survival." In Charles Taylor, *Multiculturalism: Examining the Politics of Recognition,* edited by Amy Gutman. Princeton: Princeton University Press.

———. 1991. "Is the Post- in Postmodernism the Post- in Postcolonial?" *CI* 17.2: 336–57.

Armstrong, J. 1982. *Nations before Nationalism.* Chapel Hill: University of North Carolina Press.

Asani, Ali S. 2003. "At the Crossroads of Indic and Iranian Civilizations: Sindhi Literary Culture." In *Literary Cultures in History: Reconstructions from South Asia,* edited by Sheldon Pollock. Berkeley: University of California Press.

Assmann, Jan. 1997. *Moses the Egyptian: The Memory of Egypt in Western Monotheism.* Cambridge: Harvard University Press.

Astin, A. E., et al., eds. 1989. *The Cambridge Ancient History.* Vol. 8: *Rome and the Mediterranean to 133 BC.* Cambridge: Cambridge University Press.

Auerbach, Erich. 1967. *Gesammelte Aufsätze zur romanischen Philologie.* Bern and Munich: Francke.

———. 1965. *Literary Language and Its Public in Latin Antiquity and in the Middle Ages.* Princeton: Princeton University Press.

Aung-Thwin, Michael. 1995. "The 'Classical' in Southeast Asia: The Present in the Past." *JSEAS* 26.1: 75–91.
Austin, J. L. 1962. *How to Do Things with Words.* Cambridge: Harvard University Press.
Ayres, Alyssa. 2004. "Speaking Like a State: Nationalism, Language, and the Case of Pakistan." PhD. diss., University of Chicago.
Bakhtin, M. M. 1984. *Rabelais and His World.* Bloomington: Indiana University Press.
———. 1981. *The Dialogic Imagination: Four Essays.* Austin: University of Texas Press.
Balakrishnan, Gopal, ed. 1996. *Mapping the Nation.* London: Verso.
Balibar, Etienne. 1991. "The Nation Form: History and Ideology." In *Race, Nation, Class,* by Etienne Balibar and Immanuel Wallerstein. London: Verso.
Banniard, Michel. 1995. "Language and Communication in Carolingian Europe." In *The New Cambridge Medieval History,* vol. 2, edited by Rosamund McKitterick. Cambridge: Cambridge University Press.
———. 1992. *Viva voce: Communcation écrite et communication orale du VIe au IXe siècle en Occident latin.* Paris: Études Augustiniennes.
Bansat-Boudon, Lyn. 1992. *Poétique du théâtre indien: Lectures du Nāṭyaśāstra.* Paris: École française d'extrême orient.
Barthes, Roland. 1986. *The Rustle of Language.* New York: Hill and Wang.
Bartlett, Robert. 1993. *The Making of Europe: Conquest, Colonization, and Cultural Change, 950–1350.* Princeton: Princeton University Press.
Bauman, Richard, and Charles L. Briggs. 1990. "Poets and Performance as Critical Perspectives on Language and Social Life." *ARA* 19: 59–88.
Bayly, C. A. 1998. *Origins of Nationality in South Asia: Patriotism and Ethical Government in the Making of Modern India.* Delhi: Oxford University Press.
Beck, Ulrich. 1997. *The Reinvention of Politics: Rethinking Modernity in the Global Social Order.* Oxford: Polity Press.
Bell, David A. 1995. "Lingua Populi, Lingua Dei: Language, Religion, and the Origins of French Revolutionary Nationalism." *AHR* 100.5: 1403–37.
Belvalkar, Sripad Krishna, ed. 1966. *The Śāntiparvan: Introduction.* Pune: Bhandarkar Oriental Research Institute.
Benjamin, Walter. 1969. *Illuminations.* New York: Schocken.
Bennett, Tony. 1990. *Outside Literature.* London: Routledge.
Bentley, J. H. 1996. "Cross-Cultural Interaction and Periodization in World History." *AHR* 101.3: 749–70.
Benveniste, Émile. 1964. "Édits d'Asoka en traduction grecque." *JA* 252: 137–57.
Berkemer, Georg. 1993. *Little Kingdoms in Kalinga: Ideologie, Legitimation und Politik Regionaler Elite.* Stuttgart: Steiner.
Bhandarkar, R. G. 1933. *Collected Works.* Vol. 1. Pune: Bhandarkar Oriental Research Institute.
Bhardwaj, Surinder Mohan. 1973. *Hindu Places of Pilgrimage in India: A Study in Cultural Geography.* Berkeley: University of California Press.
Bhatia, Tej K. 1987. *A History of the Hindi Grammatical Tradition: Hindi-Hindustani Grammar, Grammarians, History and Problems.* Leiden: E. J. Brill.
Bhattacharya, Dinesh Chandra. 1944. "Vidyāsāgara's Commentary on the Mahābhārata." *ABORI* 25: 99–102.
Bhattacharya, Kamaleswar. 1991. *Recherches sur le vocabulaire des inscriptions sanskrites du Cambodge.* Paris: École française d'extrême-orient.

Bhattacharyya, Sivaprasad. 1981. *Studies in Indian Poetics.* Calcutta: Firma KLM.

Bhayani, Harivallabh Chunilal. 1994. *Rāulavela of Roḍa.* Ahmedabad: Parshva Prakashan.

———. 1993. *Indological Studies: Literary and Performing Arts, Prakrit, and Apabhramsa Studies.* Ahmedabad: Parshva Prakashan.

———. 1988. *Studies in Desya Prakrit.* Ahmedabad: Kalikala Sarvajna Sri Hemacandracarya Navam Janma Satabdi Smrti Siksan Samskar Nidhi.

Biggs, Michael. 1999. "Putting the State on the Map: Cartography, Territory, and European State Formation." *CSSH* 41.2: 374–411.

Birnbaum, Pierre. 1996. "From Multiculturalism to Nationalism." *PT* 24.1: 33–45.

Bivar, A. D. H. 1981. "The 'Vikrama' Era." In "Monumentum Georg Morgenstierne." Special issue, *Acta Iranica* 21. Leiden: E. J. Brill.

Black, Antony. 1992. *Political Thought in Europe, 1250–1450.* Cambridge: Cambridge University Press.

Blackburn, Stuart H., and A. K. Ramanujan, eds. 1986. *Another Harmony: New Essays on the Folklore of India.* Berkeley: University of California Press.

Blagg, Thomas, and Martin Millett, eds. 1990. *The Early Roman Empire in the West.* Oxford: Oxbow Books.

Bloch, Jules. 1965. *Indo-Aryan from the Vedas to Modern Times.* Paris: Adrien-Maisonneuve.

———. 1911. "Sur quelques transcriptions de noms indiens dans le Périple de la mer Erythrée." In *Mélanges d'indianisme Sylvain Lévi.* Paris: E. Leroux.

Bloch, Marc. 1993. *Apologie pour l'histoire, ou Métier d'historien.* Paris: Armand Colin.

Bloch, R. Howard. 1990. "New Philology and Old French." *Speculum* 65: 38–58.

———. 1989. "The First Document and the Birth of Medieval Studies." In *A New History of French Literature,* edited by Denis Hollier. Cambridge: Harvard University Press.

———. 1986. "Naturalism, Nationalism, Medievalism." *RR* 76: 341–60.

Bloomer, W. Martin. 1997. *Latinity and Literary Society at Rome.* Philadelphia: University of Pennsylvania Press.

Boechari, 1985–86. *Prasasti Koleksi Museum Nasional.* Jilid 1. [Jakarta: n.p.].

Bond, Gerald A. 1995. "Origins." In *A Handbook of the Troubadours,* edited by F. R. P. Akehurst and Judith M. Davis. Berkeley: University of California Press.

Bose, M. 1970. *Classical Indian Dancing: A Glossary.* Calcutta: General Printer and Publishers.

Bourdieu, Pierre. 1991a. *Language and Symbolic Power.* Cambridge: Harvard University Press.

———. 1991b. *The Political Ontology of Martin Heidegger.* Stanford: Stanford University Press.

———. 1990. "Reading, Readers, the Literate, Literature." In *In Other Words: Essays towards a Reflexive Sociology.* Stanford: Stanford University Press.

———. 1980. "L'identité et la représentation: Éléments pour une réflexion critique sur l'idée de région." *ARSS* 35: 63–72.

———. 1977a. "The Economy of Linguistic Exchanges." *SSI* 16.6: 645–68.

———. 1977b. *Outline of a Theory of Practice.* Cambridge: Cambridge University Press.

Bourdieu, Pierre, and Loïc J. D. Wacquant. 1992. *An Invitation to Reflexive Sociology.* Chicago: University of Chicago Press.

Bowen, John, and Roger Peterson, eds. 1999. *Critical Comparisons in Politics and Culture.* Cambridge: Cambridge University Press.

Braudel, Fernand. 1980. *On History*. Chicago: University of Chicago Press.
Breckenridge, Carol, and Peter van der Veer, eds. 1993. *Orientalism and the Postcolonial Predicament*. Philadelphia: University of Pennsylvania Press.
Brennan, Timothy. 1990. "The National Longing for Form." In *Nation and Narration*, edited by Homi K. Bhabha. London and New York: Routledge.
Breton, Roland J-L. 1997. *Atlas of the Languages and Ethnic Communities of South Asia*. Beverly Hills and New Delhi: Sage.
Breuilly, John. 1994. *Nationalism and the State*. 2d ed. Chicago: University of Chicago Press.
Brinkhaus, Horst. 1987. *Jagatprakāśamallas Mūladevaśaśidevavyākhyānanāṭaka: Das älteste bekannte vollständigüberlieferte Newari-Drama*. Stuttgart: F. Steiner Verlag Wiesbaden.
Bronkhorst, Johannes. 2001. "The Origin of Mīmāṃsā as a School of Thought." *SO* 94: 83–104.
———. 1983. "Pāṇinian Grammar in the Post-Patañjali Period." *JIP* 11.4: 357–412.
Bronner, Yigal. 1999. "Poetry at Its Extreme: The Theory and Practice of Śleṣa in Indian Culture." Ph.D. diss., University of Chicago.
Brough, John. 1980. "Sakāya Niruttiyā: Cauld kale het." *Abhandlungen der Akademie der Wissenschaften, Göttingen, Philologisch-historische Klasse* 117: 35–42.
———. 1954. "The Language of the Buddhist Sanskrit Texts." *BSOAS* 16: 351–75.
Brown. E. 1998. "The Trojan Origins of the French: The Commencement of a Myth's Demise, 1450–1520." In *Medieval Europeans: Studies in Ethnic Identity and National Perspectives in Medieval Europe*, edited by Alfred P. Smyth. London: MacMillan.
Brown, Robert L. 1996. *The Dvaravati Wheels of the Law and the Indianization of Southeast Asia*. Leiden: E.J. Brill.
Brown, W. Norman. 1962. *The Vasanta Vilāsa*. New Haven: American Oriental Society.
Brubaker, Rogers, and Frederick Cooper. 2000. "Beyond Identity." *TS* 29: 1–47.
Brunt, P.A. 1990. *Roman Imperial Themes*. Oxford: Clarendon Press.
———. 1978. "Laus Imperii." In *Imperialism in the Ancient World*, edited by P. Garnsey and C. R. Whittaker. Cambridge: Cambridge University Press.
Brunt, P.A., and J. M. Moore, tr. 1967. *Res gestae divi Augusti: The Achievements of the Divine Augustus; with an Introduction and Commentary*. London: Oxford University Press.
Buck, David C., and K. Paramasivam. 1997. *The Study of Stolen Love*. Atlanta: Scholars Press.
Bühler, Georg. 1890. "Die indischen Inschriften und das Alter der indischen Kunstpoesie." *Sitzungsberichte der philosophisch-historischen Classe der Kaiserlichen Akademie der Wissenschaften zu Wien* 122.11: 1–97.
———. 1889. *Über das Leben des Jaina Mönches Hemacandra*. Denkschriften der kaiserlicken Akademie der Wissenschaften, philosophisch-historische Klasse, no. 37. Vienna: Akademie der Wissenschaften.
Burns, Robert I., ed. 1990. *Emperor of Culture: Alfonso X the Learned of Castile and His Thirteenth-Century Renaissance*. Philadelphia: University of Pennsylvania Press.
Busch, Allison. 2003. "The Courtly Vernacular: The Transformation of Braj Literary Culture 1590–1675." Ph.D. diss., University of Chicago.
———. 1997. "Kavibhūṣaṇ." Paper presented at the Annual Conference on South Asia, Madison, University of Wisconsin.
Caillat, C. ed. 1989. *Dialectes dans les Littératures indo-aryennes*. Paris: Collège de France.

Cardona, George. 1999. "Approaching the Vākyapadīya." *JAOS* 119.1: 88–125.

———. 1988. *Pāṇini: His Work and Its Traditions.* Vol. 1. Delhi: Motilal Banarsidass.

———. 1978. "Still Again on the History of the *Mahābhāṣya.*" *ABORI* 58–59: 79–99.

Casanova, Pascale. 1999. *La Republique des lettres.* Paris: Seuil.

Casparis, J. G., de, ed. 1991. *Sanskrit outside India.* Vol. 7 of *Panels of the Seventh World Sanskrit Conference.* Leiden: E. J. Brill.

———. 1979. "Palaeography as an Auxiliary Discipline in Research on Early South East Asia." In *Early South East Asia: Essays in Archaeology, History and Historical Geography,* edited by R. B. Smith and W. Watson. New York and Kuala Lumpur: Oxford University Press.

———. 1975. *Indonesian Palaeography.* Leiden and Köln: E. J. Brill.

———. 1956. *Selected Inscriptions from the 7th to the 9th century A.D.* Prasasti Indonesia 2. Bandung: Masa Baru.

Cerquiglini, Bernard. 1999. *In Praise of the Variant: A Critical History of Philology.* Baltimore: Johns Hopkins. (Orig. French ed., 1989.)

Certeau, Michel de. 1975. *L'Écriture de l'histoire.* Paris: Gallimard.

Certeau, Michel de, et al. 1975. *Une politique de la langue: La Révolution française et les patois; l'enquête de Grégoire.* Paris: Gallimard.

Chakrabarty, Dipesh. 2000. *Provincializing Europe.* Princeton: Princeton University Press.

Chakravarti, Adhir. 1978–80. *The Sdok Kak Thoṃ Inscription.* 2 vols. Calcutta: Sanskrit College.

Chartier, Roger, and Pietro Corsi. 1996. *Sciences et langues en Europe.* Paris: Ecole des hautes études en sciences sociales.

Chatterjee, Partha. 1997. *A Possible India: Essays in Political Criticism.* Delhi: Oxford University Press.

———. 1993. *The Nation and Its Fragments.* Princeton: Princeton University Press.

———. 1986a. *Nationalist Thought and the Colonial World: A Derivative Discourse?* London: Zed.

———. 1986b. "Transferring a Political Theory: Early Nationalist Thought in India." *EPW* 221.3: 120–28.

Chattopadhyaya, Brajadulal. 1995a. "Political Processes and the Structure of Polity in Early Medieval India." In *The State in India: 1000–1700,* edited by Hermann Kulke. Delhi: Oxford University Press.

———. 1995b. "State and Economy in North India: Fourth Century to Twelfth Century." In *Recent Perspectives of Early Indian History,* edited by Romila Thapar. Delhi: Oxford University Press.

Chaubhe, Sambhunarayan. 1967. *Mānas Anuśīlan.* Varanasi: Nagari Pracarini Sabha. (V. S. 2024)

Chaudhuri, Jatindrabimal. 1954. *Khān Khānān Abdur Rahim (1557–1630 A.D.) and Contemporary Sanskrit Learning (1551–1650 A.D.).* Calcutta: J. B. Chaudhuri.

Chaudhuri, K. N. 1990. *Asia before Europe: Economy and Civilisation of the Indian Ocean from the Rise of Islam to 1750.* Cambridge: Cambridge University Press.

Chhabra, Bahadur Chand. 1965. *Expansion of Indo-Aryan Culture during Pallava Rule, as Evidenced by Inscriptions.* Delhi: Munshi Ram Manohar Lal.

Chidananda Murti, M. 1978. "Kannada Language and Literature during the Chalukyas of Bādāmi (c. 540–750 A.D.)." In *The Chalukyas of Bādāmi: Seminar Papers,* edited by M. S. Nagaraja Rao. Bangalore: The Mythic Society.

Chitre, Dilip Purusottam, tr. 1991. *Says Tuka: Selected Poetry of Tukaram.* Delhi: Penguin Books.

———. 1990. *Punhā Tukarām.* Pune: S. K. Belvalkar.

Chojnacki, Christine. 1995. *Vividhatīrthakalpaḥ: Regards sur le lieu saint Jaina.* Pondichery: Institut français de Pondichery, École française d'extrême-orient.

Chytry, Josef. 1989. *The Aesthetic State: A Quest in Modern German Thought.* Berkeley: University of California Press.

Cirantanamuni. 1981. *Dodhakavṛtti.* Bombay: Jaina Dharmika Tattvavijnana Pathasala.

Clanchy, M. T. 1993. *From Memory to Written Record: England 1066–1307.* 2d ed. Oxford: Blackwell.

Clark, T. W. 1957. "The Rānī Pokhrī Inscription, Kāṭhmāṇḍu." *BSOAS* 20: 167–87.

Coedès, G. 1968. *The Indianized States of Southeast Asia.* Honolulu: University Press of Hawaii.

Colgrave, Bertram, and R. A. B. Mynors, eds. 1969. *Bede's Ecclesiastical History of the English People.* Oxford: Clarendon Press.

Collins, Steven. Forthcoming. "Déjà vu All Over Again: *Sakāya niruttiyā* and Translation in Pali Texts." *JAOS.*

———. 2003. "What is Literature in Pali?" In *Literary Cultures in History: Reconstructions from South Asia,* edited by Sheldon Pollock. Berkeley: University of California Press.

———. 1998. *Nirvana and Other Buddhist Felicities.* Cambridge: Cambridge University Press.

Conte, Gian Biagio. 1994. *Latin Literature: A History.* Baltimore: Johns Hopkins University Press.

Contreni, John J. 1995. "The Carolingian Renaissance: Education and Literary Culture." In *The New Cambridge Medieval History,* vol. 2, edited by Rosamund McKitterick. Cambridge: Cambridge University Press.

Curtius, Ernst Robert. 1990. *European Literature and the Latin Middle Ages.* With an epilogue by Peter Godman. Princeton: Princeton University Press.

Czigány, Lóránt. 1984. *The Oxford History of Hungarian Literature: From the Earliest Times to the Present.* Oxford: Clarendon Press.

Dagron, Gilbert. 1969. "Aux origines de la civilisation byzantine: Langue de culture et langue d'état." *RH* 241: 23–56.

Dale, Stephen F. 1996. "The Poetry and Autobiography of the *Bābur-nāma.*" *JAS* 55.3: 635–64.

Damsteegt, Th. 1989. "The Pre-Kuśāna and Kuśāna Inscriptions and the Supercession of Prākrit by Sanskrit in North India." In *Mathurā: The Cultural Heritage,* edited by Doris Meth Srinivasan. New Delhi: American Institute of Indian Studies.

———. 1978. *Epigraphical Hybrid Sanskrit, Its Rise, Spread, Characteristics, and Relationship to Buddhist Hybrid Sanskrit.* Leiden: E. J. Brill.

Dani, A. H. 1963. *Indian Palaeography.* Oxford: Clarendon Press.

Dann, Otto, ed. 1986. *Nationalismus in vorindustrieller Zeit.* Munich: Oldenbourg.

Dante Alighieri. 1996. *De vulgari eloquentia.* Translated and edited by Steven Botterill. Cambridge: Cambridge University Press.

———. 1964. *Il Convivio.* Translated by Richard Lansing. Edited by G. Busnelli et al. 2 vols. New York: Garland, 1990.

Danto, Arthur. 1987. *State of the Art.* New York: Prentiss Hall.

Darbord, Michel. 1991. "La langue et l'empire dans l'humanisme espagnol." In *Langues et nations au temps de la renaissance,* edited by M. T. Jones-Davies. Paris: Editions Klincksieck.

Davis, Kathleen. 1998. "National Writing in the Ninth Century: A Reminder for Postcolonial Thinking about the Nation." *JMEMS* 28.3: 611–37.

Day, Tony. 1996. "War and Death as Domestic Bliss: Locating the Dominant in the Old Javanese Bharatayuddha." Paper presented at the Annual Meeting of the Association for Asian Studies, Honolulu, April.

Day, Tony, and Craig Reynolds. 2000. "Cosmologies, Truth Regimes, and the State in Southeast Asia." *MAS* 34.1: 1–55.

De, S. K., ed. 1944. *The Jñānadīpikā Mahābhārata-tātparya-ṭīkā of Devabodhācārya on the Udyogaparvan of the Mahābhārata.* Bombay: Bharatiya Vidya Bhavan.

Derrett, J. Duncan. M. 1957. *The Hoysaḷas: A Medieval Indian Royal Family.* Madras: Oxford University Press.

Derrida, Jacques. 1992. *Acts of Literature.* Edited by Derek Atridge. London: Routledge.

———. 1984. "Languages and Institutions of Philosophy." *RS/SI* 4.2: 91–154.

———. 1972. *Marges de la philosophie.* Paris: Minuit.

Desai, P. B., et al. 1970. *A History of Karnataka.* Dharwar: Kannada Research Institute.

Deshpande, Madhav. 1993a. "The Changing Notion of *Śiṣṭa* from Patañjali to Bhartṛhari." *AS/ÉA* 47.1: 95–133.

———. 1993b. *Sanskrit and Prakrit.* Delhi: Motilal Banarsidass.

———. 1992. "Sociolinguistic Parameters of Pāṇini's Sanskrit." In *Vidyā-vratin Professor A. M. Ghatage Felicitation Volume,* edited by V. N. Jha. Delhi: Sri Satguru.

———. 1985. "Historical Change and the Theology of Eternal Sanskrit." *ZVS* 98: 122–49.

———. 1979. *Sociolinguistic Attitudes in India.* Ann Arbor: Karoma.

Deveerappa, H., ed. 1967. *Vacanas of Basavaṇṇa.* Translated by L. M. A. Menezes and S. M. Angadi. Sirigere: Annana Balaga.

Dharwadker, Vinay. 1993. "Orientalism and the Study of Indian Literatures." In *Orientalism and the Postcolonial Predicament,* edited by Carol Breckenridge and Peter van der Veer. Philadelphia: University of Pennsylvania Press.

Dickie, John. 1991. "Review of Hobsbawm *1989.*" *HW* 31: 189–92.

Digby, Simon. 2004. "Before Timur Came: Provincialization of the Delhi Sultanate Through the Fourteenth Century." *JESHO* 47,3: 298–356.

Dikshit, G. S., ed. 1982. *Studies in Keladi History.* Bangalore: The Mythic Society.

———. 1973. "Mahanadu." In *Śrīkaṇṭhikā: Dr S. Srikantha Sastri Felicitation Volume.* Mysore: Geetha Book House.

———. 1964. *Local Self-Government in Mediaeval Karnataka.* Dharwar: Karnatak University.

DiMaggio, P. J., and W. Powell. 1983. "The Iron Cage Revisited: Institutional Isomorphism and Collective Rationality in Organizational Fields." *ASR* 48: 147–60.

Dimock, Edward C. 1966. *The Place of the Hidden Moon: Erotic Mysticism in the Vaiṣṇava-Sahajīya Cult of Bengal.* Chicago: University of Chicago Press.

Dimock, Edward C., and Tony Stewart. 1999. *Caitanyacaritāmṛta of Kṛṣṇadāsa Kavirāj.* Cambridge: Harvard University Press.

Dirks, Nicholas. 2001. *Castes of Mind: Colonialism and the Making of Modern India.* Princeton: Princeton University Press.

———., ed. 1998. *In Near Ruins: Cultural Theory at the End of the Century.* Minneapolis: University of Minnesota Press.

———. 1992. "Castes of Mind." *Representations* 37: 56–78.

Diskalkar, D. B. 1961. "Sanskrit Poets Who Were Authors of Both Inscriptions and Literary Works." *PO* 26: 1–54.

———. 1960. "Qualifications and Subjects of Study of Inscriptional Poets." *JIH* 38.2: 547–65.

———. 1957. "Classification of Indian Epigraphical Records." *JIH* 35: 177–220.

Doane, A. N., and Carol Braun Pasternack, eds. 1991. *Vox Intexta: Orality and Textuality in the Middle Ages.* Madison: University of Wisconsin, 1991.

Drinkwater, J., and H. Vertet. 1992. "'Opportunity' or 'Opposition' in Roman Gaul?" In *Current Research on the Romanization of the Western Provinces,* edited by Mark Wood and Francisco Queiroga. Oxford: BAR.

Duara, Prasenjit. 1995. *Rescuing History from the Nation: Questioning Narratives of Modern China.* Chicago: University of Chicago Press.

Du Bellay, Joachim. 1948. *La deffence et illustration de la langue francoyse.* Edited by Henri Chamard. Paris: Didier.

Dubu, Jean. 1991. "De l'Ordonnance de Villers-Cotterêts à la Deffence et Illustration de la Language françoise: Affirmation politique et Revendication littéraire." In *Langues et nations au temps de la renaissance,* edited by M. T. Jones-Davies. Paris: Editions Klincksieck.

Duggan, Joseph. J. 1989. "The Epic." In *A New History of French Literature,* edited by Denis Hollier. Cambridge: Harvard University Press.

Dundas, Paul. 1996. "Jain Attitudes towards the Sanskrit Language." In *Ideology and Status of Sanskrit: Contributions to the History of the Sanskrit Language,* edited by Jan E. B. Houben. Leiden: E. J. Brill.

Dunham, John. 1991. "Manuscripts Used in the Critical Edition of the *Mahābhārata:* A Survey and Discussion." In *Essays on the Mahābhārata,* edited by Arvind Sharma. Leiden: E. J. Brill.

Duverger, Maurice. 1980. *Le Concept d'Empire.* Paris: Presses universitaires de France.

Dvivedi, Hariharanivas. 1955. *Madhyadeśīyabhāṣā (Gvāliyārī).* Gwalior: Navaprabhat Press.

Dvivedi, Radhe Shyam. [1972]. *Hindī Bhāṣā aur Sāhitya meṃ Gvāliyar Kṣetra kā Yogdān.* Gwalior: Kailash Pustak Sadan.

Eagleton, Terry. 1983. *Literary Theory: An Introduction.* Oxford: Blackwell.

Eaton, Richard. 1993. "Islamic History as Global History." In *Islamic and European Expansion: The Forging of a Global Order,* edited by Michael Adas. Philadelphia: Temple University Press.

———. 1974. "Sūfi Folk Literature and the Expansion of Indian Islam." *History of Religions* 14.2: 117–27.

Eco, Umberto. 1996. *The Search for the Perfect Language.* Oxford: Blackwell.

Edgerton, Franklin. 1953. *Buddhist Hybrid Sanskrit Grammar and Dictionary.* Vol. 1: *Grammar.* New Haven: Yale University Press.

Edney, Matthew H. 1997. *Mapping an Empire: The Geographical Construction of British India, 1765–1843*. Chicago: University of Chicago Press.

Eisenstadt, S. N., ed. 1989. *The Origins and Diversity of Axial Age Civilizations*. New York: State University of New York Press.

Elias, Norbert. 1994. *The Civilizing Process*. Oxford: Blackwell.

———. 1987. "The Retreat of Sociologists into the Present." In *Modern German Sociology*, edited by Volker Meja et. al. New York: Columbia University Press.

Eller, Jack David, and Reed M. Coughlan. 1993. "The Poverty of Primordialism: The Demystification of Ethnic Attachments." *ERS* 16.2: 183–202.

Emeneau, Murray. 1974. "The Indian Linguistic Area Revisited." In "Contact and Convergence in South Asian Languages," edited by F. C. Southworth and M. L. Apte. Special issue, *IJDL* 1–3: 92–134.

———. 1966. "The Dialects of Old Indo-Aryan." In *Ancient Indo-European Dialects*, edited by H. Birnbaum and J. Puhvel. Berkeley: University of California Press.

Entwistle, Alan W., and Françoise Mallison, eds. 1994. *Studies in South Asian Devotional Literature: Research Papers, 1988–91*. New Delhi: Manohar; Paris: École française d'extrême-orient.

Falk, Harry. 1993. *Schrift im alten Indien: Ein Forschungsbericht mit Anmerkungen*. Tübingen: Gunter Narr.

———. 1991. "Kunstdichtung in den Höhlen von Rāmgarh." *AS/ÉA* 45.2: 257–76.

———. 1988. "Goodies for India: Literacy, Orality, and Vedic Culture." In *Erscheinungsformen kultureller Prozesse*, edited by Wolfgang Raible. Tübingen: Gunter Narr.

Faruqi, Shamsur Rahman. 2003. "A Long History of Urdu Literary Culture, Part 1: Naming and Placing a Literary Culture." In *Literary Cultures in History: Reconstructions from South Asia*, edited by Sheldon Pollock. Berkeley: University of California Press.

Fasold, Ralph. 1984. *The Sociolinguistics of Society*. Oxford: Blackwell.

Feldhaus, Anne. 1986. "Maharashtra as a Holy Land: A Sectarian Tradition." *BSOAS* 49.3: 532–48.

Feldhaus, Anne, and Shankar Gopal Tulpule. 1992. *In the Absence of God: The Early Years of an Indian Sect*. Honolulu: University of Hawaii Press.

Ferguson, Margaret. 1983. *Trials of Desire: Renaissance Defenses of Poetry*. New Haven: Yale University Press.

Ferrante, Joan. 1982. "Was Vernacular Poetic Practice a Response to Latin Language Theory?" *RP* 35: 586–600.

Filliozat, Jean. 1977. "Le Sanskrit et le Pāli en Asie du sud-est." *Comptes rendus, Académie des Inscriptions et Belles-lettres:* 398–406.

Foucault, Michel. 1980. "Questions on Geography." In *Power/Knowledge*, edited by Colin Gordon. New York: Pantheon Books.

———.1970. *The Order of Things*. New York: Random House.

Fowden, Garth. 1993. *Empire to Commonwealth: Consequences of Monotheism in Late Antiquity*. Princeton: Princeton University Press.

Fox, Richard G., ed. 1977. *Realm and Region in Traditional India*. Durham: Duke University, Program in Comparative Studies on Southern Asia.

Fracchia, Joseph, and R. C. Lewontin. 1999. "Does Culture Evolve?" *HT* 38.4: 52–78.

Frauwallner, E. 1960. "Sprachtheorie und Philosophie im Mahābhāṣya des Patañjali." *WZKSA* 4: 92–118.

Freeman, J. Richardson. 2003. "Genre and Society: The Literary Culture of Premodern Kerala." In *Literary Cultures in History: Reconstructions from South Asia,* edited by Sheldon Pollock. Berkeley: University of California Press.

———. 1998. "Rubies and Coral: The Lapidary Crafting of a Language for Kerala." *JAS* 57.1: 38–65.

Fumaroli, Marc. 1994. *L'âge de l'éloquence.* 2d ed. Paris: Albin Michel.

———. 1992. "Le génie de la langue française." In *Les lieux de mémoire,* vol. 3, edited by Pierra Nora. Paris: Gallimard.

———. 1984. "L'apologetique de la langue française classique." *Rhetorica* 2.2: 139–61.

———. 1983. "Rhetoric, Politics, and Society: From Italian Ciceronianism to French Classicism." In *Renaissance Eloquence: Studies in the Theory and Practice of Renaissance Rhetoric,* edited by James J. Murphy. Berkeley: University of California Press.

Fussman, Gérard. 1988. "Documents épigraphiques kouchans (V)." *BEFEO* 77: 5–25.

———. 1982a. "Documents épigraphiques kouchans (III)." *BEFEO* 71: 1–46.

———. 1982b. "Pouvoir central et régions dans l'Inde ancienne: Le problème de l'empire maurya." *Annales ESC* 4 (July-August): 621–47.

———. 1980a. "Nouvelles Inscriptions Śaka." *BEFEO* 67: 1–43.

———. 1980b. "Review of Damsteegt 1978." *JA* 268: 420–26.

Fynes, R. C. C. 1993. "Isis and Pattinī: The Transmission of a Religious Idea from Roman Egypt to India." *JRAS* 3d series 3: 377–91.

Gai, G. S. 1991. "Halmidi Inscription of Kākustha Bhaṭṭāra: A Fresh Study." *JESI* 17: 111–16.

———, ed. 1965. *Bombay-Karnatak Inscriptions.* Vol. 4. Delhi: Manager of Publications.

Gallagher, Catherine, and Stephen Greenblatt. 2000. *Practicing New Historicism.* Chicago: University of Chicago Press.

Garber, Jörn. 1993. "Vom universalen zum endogenen Nationalismus: Die Idee der Nation im deutschen Spätmittelalter und in der frühen Neuzeit." In *Dichter und ihre Nation,* edited by Helmut Scheuer. Frankfurt: Suhrkamp.

Garber, Klaus, ed. 1989. *Nation und Literatur im Europa der frühen Neuzeit.* Tübingen: Max Niemeyer Verlag.

Gaspardone, Emile. 1953. "La plus ancienne inscription d'Indochine." *JA* 241: 477–85.

Geertz, Clifford. 1980. *Negara: The Theatre State in Nineteenth-Century Bali.* Princeton: Princeton University Press.

———. 1973. *The Interpretation of Cultures: Selected Essays.* New York: Basic Books.

———. 1963. "The Integrative Revolution: Primordial Sentiments and Civil Politics in the New States." In *Old Societies and New States: The Quest for Modernity in Asia and Africa,* edited by Clifford Geertz. Glencoe, IL: The Free Press.

Gellner, Ernest. 1991. "Nationalism and Politics in Eastern Europe." *NLR* 189: 127–34.

———. 1983. *Nations and Nationalism.* Oxford: Blackwell.

Gerini, G. E. 1909. *Researches on Ptolemy's Geography of Eastern Asia.* London: Royal Asiatic Society, Royal Geographical Society.

Gerow, Edwin. 1977. *Indian Poetics.* Vol. 5, fasc. 3 of *A History of Indian Literature,* edited by Jan Gonda. Wiesbaden: Harrassowitz.

Ghosal, S. N. 1956. "Controversy over the Significance of Apabhramsa." *JASB* 22.1: 23–37.

Ghosh, Jogendra Chandra. 1934–35. "Arjuna Miśra." *IC* 1: 706–10.

Giard, Luce. 1989. "L'entrée en lice des vernaculaires." In *Histoire des idées linguis-*

tiques, edited by Sylvain Auroux, vol. 2: *Le développement de la grammaire occidentale.* Liége, Bruxelles: Mardaga.

Giddens, Anthony. 1990. *The Consequences of Modernity.* Stanford: Stanford University Press.

———. 1984. *The Constitution of Society: Outline of a Theory of Structuration.* Berkeley: University of California Press.

———. 1981. *A Contemporary Critique of Historical Materialism.* Berkeley: University of California Press.

Gode, P. K. 1944. "New Light on the Chronology of the Commentators of the Mahābhārata." *ABORI* 25: 103–8.

———. 1942. "Nīlakaṇṭha Caturdhara." *ABORI* 23: 146–57.

———. 1935–36. "Arjuna Miśra." *IC* 2: 141–47.

Godman, Peter. 1987. *Poets and Emperors: Frankish Politics and Carolingian Poetry.* Oxford: Clarendon Press.

Godzich, Wlad. 1994. *The Culture of Literacy.* Cambridge: Harvard University Press.

Goetz, Hermann. 1959. "Imperial Rome and the Genesis of Classical Indian Art." *EW* 10: 153–81, 261–68.

Gold, Jonathan C. 2003. "Intellectual Gatekeeper: Sa-Skya Paṇḍita Envisions the Ideal Scholar." Ph.D. diss., University of Chicago.

Goldberg, Sander M. 1995. *Epic in Republican Rome.* New York: Oxford University Press.

Goldman, Robert, tr. and ed. 1984. *The Rāmāyaṇa of Vālmīki: An Epic of Ancient India.* Vol. 1: *Bālakāṇḍa.* Princeton: Princeton University Press.

Gombrich, Richard. 1996. *How Buddhism Began: The Conditional Genesis of the Early Teachings.* London: Athlone Press.

———. 1990. "When the Mahāyāna Began." In *The Buddhist Forum,* edited by Tadeusz Skorupski, vol. 1, *Seminar Papers 1987–88.* New Delhi: Heritage Publishers.

Gommans, Jos. 1998. "The Eurasian Frontier after the First Millennium A.D.: Reflections along the Fringe of Time and Space." *MHJ* 1.1: 125–44.

Gonda, Jan, ed. 1973-. *A History of Indian Literature.* 10 vols. Wiesbaden: Harrassowitz.

Gonda, Jan. 1973. *Sanskrit in Indonesia.* 2d ed. New Delhi: International Academy of Indian Culture.

Gopal, B. R., ed. 1994. *The Rāṣṭrakūṭas of Malked.* Mysore: Geetha Book House, on behalf of the Mythic Society, Bangalore.

———. 1992. "Dakṣiṇa Bhāratada Eraḍu Pramukha Vibhinna Samājagaḷu." In *Māna. H. M. Nayaka Abhinandana Grantha,* edited by S. L. Bhyrappa et al. Mysore: Geetha Book House, 1992.

———. 1986. "Two Dominant Societies of South India—Karnataka and Tamil Nadu: A Study in Contrast." In *Proceedings of the Thirty-Second International Congress for Asian and North African Studies: Hamburg, 25th–30th August 1986,* edited by Albrecht Wezler and Ernest Hammerschmidt. *ZDMG* supplement 9. Stuttgart: Steiner.

———. 1981. *The Chalukyas of Kalyana and the Kalachuris.* Dharwad: Karnatak University Press.

———. 1980. "Gadāyuddha Mattu Itihāsa." In *Rannakavikāvyavimarśa.* Mysore: Kannada Sahitya Parisat.

Gopal, B. R., and N. S. Tharanatha, eds. 1996. *Kadambas: Their History and Culture.* Mysore: Directorate of Archaeology & Museums.

Gopinatha Rao, T.A. 1971. *Elements of Hindu Iconography.* 2 vols. in 4. Varanasi: Indological Book House. (Orig. pub. 1914–16.)

Gordon, Stewart. 1994. *Marathas, Marauders, and State Formation in Eighteenth-Century India.* Delhi: Oxford University Press.

Goudriaan, Teun, and C. Hookyaas. 1971. *Stuti and Stava.* Amsterdam: North Holland Publishing Co.

Gramsci, Antonio. 1991. *Selections from Cultural Writings.* Edited by David Forgacs and Geoffrey Nowell-Smith. Cambridge: Harvard University Press.

———. 1971. *Selections from the Prison Notebooks of Antonio Gramsci.* New York: International Publishers.

Granoff, Phyllis. 1995. "Sarasvatī's Sons: Biographies of Poets in Medieval India." *AS / ÉA* 49.2: 351–76.

———. 1992. "Buddhaghosa's Penance and Siddhasena's Crime: Indian Attitudes Towards Language." In *From Benares to Beijing: Festschrift for Dr. Jan Yün-Hua,* edited by K. Shinohara and G. Schopen. Oakville. Ontario: Mosaic Press.

Green, Peter. 1990. *Alexander to Actium.* Berkeley: University of California Press.

Greenfield, Liah. 1996. "Nationalism and Modernity." *Social Research* 63.1: 3–40.

Grierson, George Abraham. 1927. *Linguistic Survey of India.* Vol. 1, pt. 1: *Introductory.* Calcutta: Government of India Central Publication Branch.

Griffiths, Frederick T., and Stanley J. Rabinowitz. 1990. *Novel Epics: Gogol, Dostoevsky, and National Narrative.* Evanston, IL: Northwestern University Press.

Grillo, R. D. 1989. *Dominant Languages: Language and Hierarchy in Britain and France.* Cambridge: Cambridge University Press.

Gros, François. 1994. "Cinq fois cinq vingt-cinq: Autour des commentaires du livre de l'amour de Tiruvalluvar." In *Genres litteraires en Inde,* edited by Nalini Balbir. Paris: Presses de la Sorbonne nouvelle.

Groslier, Bernard. 1979. "La cité hydraulique angkorienne: Exploitation ou Surexploitation du sol?" *BEFEO* 66: 161–202.

———. 1973. "Pour une géographie historique du Cambodge." *Les Cahiers d'Outre-Mer* 104: 337–79.

Gruen, Erich S. 1990. "Poetry and Politics: The Beginnings of Latin Literature." In *Studies in Greek Culture and Roman Policy.* Leiden: E.J. Brill.

Grundmann, H. "Litteratus/illitteratus: Der Wandel einer Bildungsnorm von Altertum zum Mittelalter." *AK* 40: 1–65.

Grünendahl, Reinhold. 1993. "Zur Klassifizierung von Mahābhārata-Handschriften." In *Studien zur Indologie und Buddhismuskunde,* edited by Reinhold Grünendahl et al. Bonn: Indica et Tibetica Verlag.

Guha, Ranajit. 1997. *Dominance without Hegemony: History and Power in Colonial India.* Cambridge: Harvard University Press.

———. 1985. "Nationalism Reduced to 'Official Nationalism.'" *Asian Studies Review* 9: 103–8.

Guha, Sumit. 2004. "Transitions and Translations: Regional Power and Vernacular Identity in the Dakhan, 1500–1800." In *CSSAAME* 24.2: 23–31.

Gumbrecht, Hans-Ulrich. 1988. "Beginn von 'Literatur'/Abschied vom Körper?" In *Der Ursprung von Literatur: Medien, Rollen, Kommunikationssituationen zwischen 1450 und 1650,* edited by Gisela Smolka-Koerdt et al. Munich: Wilhelm Fink.

———. 1983. "Schriftlichkeit in mündlicher Kultur." In *Schrift und Gedächtnis: Beiträge zur Archäologie der literarischen Kommunikation,* edited by Aleida Assmann et al. Munich: Wilhelm Fink.

Gunawardana, R. A. L. 1990. "People of the Lion." In *Sri Lanka: History and the Roots of Conflict,* edited by Jonathan Spencer. London and New York: Routledge.

Gupta, Akhil, and James Ferguson. 1992. "Beyond 'Culture': Space, Identity, and the Politics of Difference." *CA* 7: 6–23.

Gupta, Dindayal. 1947. *Aṣṭachāp aur Vallabhasampradāya.* Allahabad: Hindi Sahitya Sammelan.

Habinek, Thomas. 1998. *The Politics of Latin Literature: Writing, Identity, and Empire in Ancient Rome.* Princeton: Princeton University Press.

Haksar, A. N. D., ed. 1995. "Sanskrit Literature." Special issue of *Indian Horizons* 44.4.

Hall, John, ed. 1998. *The State of the Nation: Ernest Gellner and the Theory of Nationalism.* Cambridge: Cambridge University Press.

Hall, Stuart. 1996. "Who Needs 'Identity'?" In *Questions of Cultural Identity,* edited by Stuart Hall and Paul de Gay. London: Sage.

Hallisey, Charles. 2003. "Works and Persons in Sinhala Literary Culture." In *Literary Cultures in History: Reconstructions from South Asia,* edited by Sheldon Pollock. Berkeley: University of California Press.

———. 1994. "The Cultural Politics of Medieval Sinhala Poetry." Paper delivered at the Workshop on Language, Literature, and Empire, University of Chicago.

Hammond, Mason. 1976. *Latin: A Historical and Linguistic Handbook.* Cambridge: Harvard University Press.

Hanks, William F. 1996. *Language and Communicative Practices.* Boulder: Westview.

Hannerz, Ulf. 1999. "Reflections on Varieties of Culturespeak." *EJCS* 2.3: 393–407.

Hardie, Philip, 1997. "Fifth-Century Athenian and Augustan Images of the Barbarian Other." *ClI* 4: 46–56.

Hardy, Friedhelm. 1994. "Creative Corruption: Some Comments on Apabhraṃśa Literature, Particularly Yogīndu." In *Studies in South Asian Devotional Literature: Research Papers, 1988–91,* edited by Alan W. Entwistle and Françoise Mallison. New Delhi: Manohar; Paris: École française d'extrême-orient.

Harris, William. 1989. *Ancient Literacy.* Cambridge: Harvard University Press.

Hartmann, Jens-Uwe. 1988. *Neue Aśvaghoṣa- und Mātṛceṭa-Fragmente aus Ostturkistan.* Nachrichten der Akademie der Wissenschaften, philologisch-historische Klasse, no. 2. Göttingen: Vandenhoeck and Ruprecht.

Harvey, David. 1993. "From Space to Place and Back Again: Reflections on the Condition of Postmodernity." In *Making the Futures: Local Cultures, Global Change,* edited by Jon Bird et al. London: Routledge.

Haugen, Einar. 1972. *First Grammatical Treatise: The Earliest Germanic Phonology.* 2d rev. ed. London: Longman.

Havelock, Eric A. 1963. *Preface to Plato.* Cambridge: The Belknap Press of Harvard University Press.

Havighurst, Alfred F., ed. 1976. *The Pirenne Thesis: Analysis, Criticism, and Revision.* Rev. ed. Lexington, MA: Heath.

Hawley, John Stratton. 1988. "Author and Authority in the Bhakti Poetry of North India." *JAS* 47.2: 269–90.

Hegel, G. W. F. 1975. *Aesthetics: Lectures on Fine Art.* Translated by M. Knox. Oxford:

Clarendon Press. (Original German ed. *Vorlesungen über die Ästhetik.* 2 vols. Frankfurt/Main: Suhrkamp, 1970).
———.1956. *Philosophy of History.* New York: Dover.
Heidegger, Martin. 1971. *Poetry, Language, Thought.* New York: Harper and Row.
———. 1966. *Discourse on Thinking.* New York: Harper and Row.
———. 1960. *Der Ursprung des Kunstwerkes.* Stuttgart: Reclam.
Heine, Heinrich. 1964. "Aphorismen und Fragmente." In *Sämtliche Werke,* vol. 14. Munich: Kindler.
Helgerson, Richard. 1992. *Forms of Nationhood: The Elizabethan Writing of England.* Chicago: University of Chicago Press.
Hélias, Pierre Jakez. 1978. *The Horse of Pride: Life in a Breton Village.* New Haven: Yale University Press.
Henige, David. 1975. "Some Phantom Dynasties of Early and Medieval India: Epigraphic Evidence and the Abhorrence of a Vacuum." *BSOAS* 38: 525–49.
Herbert, Patricia, and Anthony Milner. 1989. *South-East Asia: Languages and Literatures, a Select Guide.* Honolulu: University of Hawaii Press.
Herman, Jósef. 2000. *Vulgar Latin.* Translated Roger Wright. University Park: Pennsylvania State University Press.
Hinüber, Oskar von. 1986. *Das Ältere Mittelindisch im Überblick.* Vienna: Der Österreichischen Akademie der Wissenschaften.
———. 1985. "Pāli and Paiśācī as Variants of Buddhist Middle Indic." *BEI* 3: 61–77.
———. 1983. "Die Älteste Literatursprache des Buddhismus." *Saeculum* 34.1: 1–9.
Hobsbawm, E.J. 1990. *Nations and Nationalism since 1780: Programme, Myth, Reality.* Cambridge: Cambridge University Press.
Hock, Hans. 1996. "Pre-ṛgvedic Convergence between Indo-Aryan and Dravidian? A Survey of the Issues and Controversies." In *Ideology and Status of Sanskrit: Contributions to the History of the Sanskrit Language,* edited by Jan E. M. Houben. Leiden: E.J. Brill.
———. 1986. *Principles of Historical Linguistics.* Berlin: de Gruyter.
Hodges, R., and D. Whitehouse. 1983. *Mohammed, Charlemagne, and the Origins of Europe: Archaeology and the Pirenne Thesis.* Ithaca: Cornell University Press.
Hollier, Denis. 1995. "Literature as a Dead Language." In *The Uses of Literary History,* edited by Marshall Brown. Durham and London: Duke University Press.
———, ed. 1989. *A New History of French Literature.* Cambridge: Harvard University Press.
Holmes, George, ed. 1992. *The Oxford History of Medieval Europe.* New York: Oxford University Press.
Holub, Robert. 1994. "Luhmann's Progeny: Systems Theory and Literary Studies in the Post-Wall Era." *NGC* 61: 143–59.
Honko, Lauri. 1998. *Textualising the Siri Epic.* Folklore Fellows Communications, vol. 118, no. 264. Helsinki: Suomalainen Tiedeakatemia/Academia Scientiarum Fennica.
Hooykaas. C. 1958. "The Old Javanese Rāmāyaṇa: An Exemplary Kakawin as to Form and Content." *Verhandelingen der koninklijke Nederlandse Akademie van Wetenschappen, Afd. Letterkunde,* n.r. 65.1.
Hopkins, A. G., ed. 2002. *Globalization in World History.* New York: Norton.

Horstmann, Monika. 1994. "Govinddevjī of Vrindaban and Jaipur." In *Studies in South Asian Devotional Literature: Research Papers, 1988–91,* edited by Alan W. Entwistle and Françoise Mallison. New Delhi: Manohar; Paris: École française d'extrême-orient.

Houben, Jan E. M., ed. 1996. *Ideology and Status of Sanskrit: Contributions to the History of the Sanskrit Language.* Leiden: E. J. Brill.

———. 1996. "Socio-linguistic Attitudes Reflected in the Work of Bhartṛhari and Later Grammarians." In *Ideology and Status of Sanskrit: Contributions to the History of the Sanskrit Language,* edited by Jan E. M. Houben. Leiden: E. J. Brill.

Howlett, David. 1996. *The English Origins of Old French Literature.* Dublin: Four Courts Press.

Hroch, Miroslav. 1996. "From National Movement to the Fully-Formed Nation: The Nation-Building Process in Europe." In *Mapping the Nation,* edited by Gopal Balakrishnan. London: Verso.

Hultzsch, Eugen, ed. 1925. *Inscriptions of Asoka.* Vol. 1 of *Corpus inscriptionum indicarum.* New Delhi: Archaeological Survey of India.

Hunter, Thomas M., Jr. 2001. "Wṛttasañcaya Reconsidered." *BTLV* 157.1: 65–96.

Huntington, Samuel. 1996. *The Clash of Civilizations and the Remaking of World Order.* New York: Simon and Schuster.

Hutchinson, John, and Anthony D. Smith, eds. 1996. *Ethnicity.* Oxford: Oxford University Press.

Hutt, Michael. 1988. *Nepali: A National Language and Its Literature.* New Delhi: Sterling Publishers; London: School of Oriental and African Studies.

Inden, Ronald., ed. 2000. *Querying the Medieval: Texts and the History of Practices in South Asia.* New York: Oxford University Press.

———. 1990. *Imagining India.* Oxford: Blackwell.

Ingalls, Daniel H. H., et al., tr. 1991. *The Dhvanyāloka of Ānandavardhana with the Locana of Abhinavagupta.* Cambridge: Harvard University Press.

———. 1976. "Kālidāsa and the Attitudes of the Golden Age." *JAOS* 96.1: 15–26.

Irvine, Martin. 1994. *The Making of Textual Culture: "Grammatica" and Literary Theory, 350–1100.* Cambridge: Cambridge University Press.

Jackson, Peter. 1999. *The Delhi Sultanate: A Political and Military History.* Cambridge: Cambridge University Press.

Jacob, Judith M. 1996. *The Traditional Literature of Cambodia: A Preliminary Guide.* New York: Oxford University Press.

Jacques, Claude. 1994. "Les Kamrateṅ Jagat dans l'ancien Cambodge." In *Recherches nouvelles sur le Cambodge,* edited by F. Bizot. Paris: École française d'extrême-orient.

———. 1991. "The Use of Sanskrit in the Khmer and Cham Inscriptions." In *Sanskrit outside India,* vol. 7 of *Panels of the Seventh World Sanskrit Conference,* edited by J. G. de Casparis. Leiden: E. J. Brill.

———. 1986. "Economic Activities in Khmer and Cham Lands." In *Southeast Asia in the 9th to 14th Centuries,* edited by D. G. Hall and A. C. Milner. Singapore: Institute of Southeast Asian Studies; Canberra: Australian National University, Research School of Pacific Studies.

Jaffrelot, Christophe. 2000. "Sanskritization vs. Ethnicization in India: Changing Identities and Caste Politics before Mandal." *AiS* 40.5: 756–66.

Jameson, Fredric. 1986. "Third World Literature in the Era of Multinational Corporations." *ST* 15: 65–88.

Janson, Tore. 1991. "Language Change and Metalinguistic Change: Latin to Romance and Other Cases." In *Latin and the Romance Languages in the Early Middle Ages,* edited by Roger Wright and Rosamund McKitterick. London: Routledge.

Jay, Martin. 1992. "'The Aesthetic Ideology' as Ideology; or, What Does It Mean to Aestheticize Politics?" *CC* 21: 41–61.

Jenner, Philip N. 1982. *A Chronological Inventory of the Inscriptions of Cambodia.* 2d rev. ed. Honolulu: University of Hawaii, Center for Asian and Pacific Studies.

Jha, Amiteshwar, and Dilip Rajgor. 1992. *Studies in the Coinage of the Western Ksatrapas.* Nashik: Indian Institute of Research in Numismatic Studies.

Jones, A. H. M. 1964. *The Later Roman Empire.* Oxford: Clarendon Press.

Jones-Davies, M. T., ed. 1991. *Langues et nations au temps de la renaissance.* Paris: Editions Klincksieck.

Joseph, John Earl. 1987. *Eloquence and Power: The Rise of Language Standards and Standard Languages.* New York: Blackwell.

Kahrs, Eivind G. 1992. "What is a Tadbhava Word?" *IIJ* 35: 225–49.

Kane, P. V. 1962–75. *History of Dharmaśāstra.* 5 vols. Pune: Bhandarkar Oriental Research Institute.

Kapstein, Matthew T. 2003. "The Indian Literary Imagination in Tibet." In *Literary Cultures in History: Reconstructions from South Asia,* edited by Sheldon Pollock. Berkeley: University of California Press.

———. 2001. *Reason's Traces.* Somerville, MA: Wisdom Publications.

Karashima, Noboru. 1992. *Towards a New Formation: South Indian Society under Vijayanagar Rule.* Delhi: Oxford University Press.

———. 1984. *South Indian History and Society: Studies from Inscriptions, A.D. 850–1800.* Delhi: Oxford University Press.

Kaster, Robert A. 1988. *Guardians of Language: The Grammarian and Society in Late Antiquity.* Berkeley: University of California Press.

Kaviraj, Sudipta. 1992a. "The Imaginary Institution of India." In *Subaltern Studies VII: Writings on South Asian History and Society,* edited by Partha Chatterjee and Gyanendra Pandey. Delhi: Oxford University Press.

———. 1992b. "Writing, Speaking, Being: Language and the Historical Formation of Identities in India." In *Nationalstaat und Sprachkonflikt in Süd- und Südostasien,* edited by Dagmar Hellmann-Rajanayagam and Dietmar Rothermund. Stuttgart: Steiner.

Kedilaya, A. Shanker, tr. 1963–77. *Śabdamaṇidarpaṇam. AORM* 18: 1–29; 19: 30–55; 20: 56–75; 21: 1–41, 117–40; 22: 141–272; 23: 273–344; 24: 345–418; 26: 419–34; 27: 435–60.

Kenney, E. J., and W. V. Clausen, eds. 1982. *The Cambridge History of Classical Literature.* Vol. 2: *Latin Literature.* Cambridge: Cambridge University Press.

Kermode, Frank. 1975. *The Classic: Literary Images of Permanence and Change.* New York: Viking Press.

Kern, H. 1920. "Wṛtta-Sañcaya: Oudjav. leerdicht over versbow." In *Verspreide Geschriften,* vol. 9. 's-Gravenhage: Martinus Nijhoff. (Orig. pub. 1875.)

Khilnani, Sunil. 1998. *The Idea of India.* New York: Farrar, Straus, Giroux.

Khing, Hoc Dy. 1990. *Contribution à l'histoire de la littérature khmère.* Vol. 1: *Littérature de l'époque "classique" (xv*[e]*–xix*[e] *siècles).* Paris: Editions l'Harmattan.

Khubchandani, L. M. 1983. *Plural Languages, Plural Cultures: Communication, Identity, and Sociopolitical Change in Contemporary India.* Honolulu: University of Hawaii Press.
Kielhorn, Franz. 1889. "Quotations in the *Mahābhāṣya* and the *Kāśikā-Vṛtti.*" *IA:* 326–27 (= *Kleine Schriften,* Wiesbaden: Steiner, 1969, vol. 1: 187–88).
Kirfel, Willibald. 1959–74. *Symbolik des Hinduismus, des Buddhismus, und des Jinismus.* 2 vols. Stuttgart: A. Hiersemann.
———. 1931. *Bhāratavarṣa (Indien): Textgeschichtliche Darstellung zweier geographischen Purāṇa-Texte nebst Übersetzung.* Stuttgart: Kohlhammer.
Kittel, Ferdinand. 1903. *A Grammar of the Kannada Language in English.* Mangalore: Basel Mission Book and Tract Depository.
———. 1894. *Kannada-English Dictionary.* Mangalore: Basel Mission Book and Tract Depository.
Kivelson, Valerie. 1997. "Merciful Father, Impersonal State: Russian Autocracy in Comparative Perspective." *MAS* 31.3: 635–63.
Klemperer, Victor. 1987. *LTI: Notizbuch eines Philologen.* Leipzig: Reclam.
Kloss, Heinz. 1976. "Abstandsprachen und Ausbausprachen." In *Zur Theorie des Dialekts,* edited by Joachim Goeschel et al. *Zeitschrift für Dialektologie und Linguistik,* Beiheft n.f. 16.
———. 1967. "'Abstand Languages' and 'Ausbau Languages.'" *AL* 9.7: 29–41.
Kolff, D. H. A. 1990. *Naukar, Rajput, and Sepoy: The Ethnohistory of the Military Labour Market of Hindustan, 1450–1850.* Cambridge: Cambridge University Press.
Kölver, Bernhard, and Hemrāj Śākya. 1985. *Documents from the Rudravarṇa-Mahāvihāra, Pāṭan.* Vol. 1: *Sales and Mortgages.* Sankt Augustin: VGH Wissenschaftsverlag.
Krishna, Sankaran. 1994. "Cartographic Anxiety: Mapping the Body Politic in India." *Alternatives* 19.4: 507–21.
Krishnarao, Bhavaraj V. 1932. "Ve(Le)mulvada Inscription of Arikesarin II." *JAHRS* 6.3–4: 169–92.
Kristeller, Paul Oskar. 1984. "Latein und Vulgärsprache im Italien des 14. und 15. Jahrhunderts." *Deutsches Dante-Jahrbuch* 59: 7–35.
———. 1965. "The Origin and Development of the Language of Italian Prose." In *Renaissance Thought,* vol. 2. New York: Harper and Row.
Kroeber, Alfred. 1952. "The Ancient Oikoumenē As a Historic Culture Aggregate." In *The Nature of Culture.* Chicago: University of Chicago Press. (Orig. pub. 1946.)
Kulkarni, V. M. 1991. *Sarvasena's Harivijaya.* Ahmedabad: L. D. Institute.
———. 1989. *Prakrit Verses in Sanskrit Works on Poetics.* Delhi: Bhogilal Leherchand Institute of Indology.
Kulke, Hermann. 1995. "The Early and the Imperial Kingdom: A Processural Model of Integrative State Formation in Early Medieval India." In *The State in India: 1000–1700,* edited by Hermann Kulke. Delhi: Oxford University Press.
———, ed. 1995. *The State in India: 1000–1700.* Delhi: Oxford University Press.
———. 1993. *Kings and Cults: State Formation and Legitimation in India and Southeast Asia.* Delhi: Manohar.
———. 1990. "Indian Colonies, Indianization or Cultural Convergence: Reflections on the Changing Image of India's Role in South-East Asia." *Semaian* 3: 8–32.
Kulke, Hermann, and Dietmar Rothermund. 1986. *A History of India.* Totowan, NJ: Barnes and Noble.
———, eds. 1985. *Regionale Tradition in Südasien.* Stuttgart: Steiner.

Kulli, J. S. 1984. "Kannada Grammars and Sanskrit Tradition." *IJDL* 13.1: 40–47.
Kymlicka, Will. 1999. "Cosmopolitanism, Nation-States, and Minority Nationalism." *EJP* 7.1: 65–88.
———. 1995. *Multicultural Citizenship*. Oxford: Clarendon Press.
LaCapra, Dominick. 1983. *Rethinking Intellectual History: Texts, Contexts, Language*. Ithaca: Cornell University Press.
Lamotte, Etienne. 1976. *Histoire du buddhisme indien, des origines à l'ère śaka*. Louvain-la-Neuve: Université de Louvain, Institut orientaliste.
Latour, Bruno. 1993. *We Have Never Been Modern*. Cambridge: Harvard University Press.
Lazard, Gilbert. 1993. *The Origins of Literary Persian*. Bethesda, MD: Foundation for Iranian Studies.
Leach, E. R. 1960. "The Frontiers of 'Burma'." *CSSH* 3.1: 49–73.
Lefort, Claude. 1986. *The Political Forms of Modern Society: Bureaucracy, Democracy, Totalitarianism*. Oxford: Blackwell.
Lendon, J. E. 1997. *Empire of Honour: The Art of Government in the Roman World*. Oxford: Clarendon Press; New York: Oxford University Press.
Lerer, Seth. 1991. *Literacy and Power in Anglo-Saxon Literature*. Lincoln: University of Nebraska Press.
Lévi, Sylvain. 1933. *Sanskrit Texts from Bali*. Baroda: Oriental Institute.
———. 1904. "On Some Terms Employed in the Inscriptions of the Kshatrapas." *IA*: 163–74.
Levtzion, Nehemia. 1996. "Restructuring Sufi Brotherhoods, Rural and Vernacular Islam." Paper presented to the Conference on Collective Identities, Public Sphere and Political Order, Uppsala. An abbreviated version published as "The Dynamics of Sufi Brotherhoods," in *The Public Sphere in Muslim Societies*, edited by M. Hoexter et al. (Albany: State University of New York Press, 2002).
Lewis, Martin W, and Kären E. Wigen. 1997. *The Myth of Continents: A Critique of Metageography*. Berkeley: University of California Press.
Li Rongxi, tr. 1996. *The Great Tang Dynasty Record of the Western Regions*. Berkeley: Numata Center for Buddhist Translation and Research.
———. 1995. *A Biography of the Tripiṭaka Master of the Great Ci'en Monastery of the Great Tang Dynasty*. Berkeley: Numata Center for Buddhist Translation and Research.
Lieberman, Victor, ed. 1997. "The Eurasian Context of the Early Modern History of Mainland South East Asia, 1400–1800." *MAS* 31.3.
———. 1993. "Local Integration and Eurasian Analogies: Structuring Southeast Asian History, c. 1350–c. 1830." *MAS* 27.3: 475–572.
Liebich, Bruno. 1930. *Kṣīrataraṅgiṇī: Kṣīrasvāmin's Kommentar zu Pāṇini's Dhātupāṭha*. Breslau: M. & H. Marcus.
———. 1919. *Das Kātantra*. Vol. 1 of *Zur Einführung in die indische einheimische Sprachwissenschaft*. Sitzungsberichte der Heidelberger Akademie der Wissenschaften, no. 4. Heidelberg: C. Winter.
Lienhard, Siegfried. 1984. *A History of Classical Poetry: Sanskrit—Pali—Prakrit*. Vol. 3, fasc. 1 of *History of Indian Literature*, edited by Jan Gonda. Wiesbaden: Harrassowitz.
———. 1974. *Nevārīgītimañjarī: Religious and Secular Poetry of the Nevars of the Kathmandu Valley*. Stockholm: Almqvist and Wiksell.
Lin Li-kouang. 1949. *L'aide-memoire de la vraie loi*. Paris: Adrien-Maisonneuve.

Lodge, R. Anthony. 1993. *French from Dialect to Standard.* London and New York: Routledge.

Lohuizen-De Leeuw, J. E. van. 1949. *The "Scythian" Period.* Leiden: E. J. Brill.

Lombard, Denys. 1990. *Le Carrefour javanais, essai d'histoire globale.* Vol. 3: *L'héritage des royaumes concentriques.* Paris: Éditions de l'école des hautes études en sciences sociales.

Lorenzen, David. 1992. "Historians and the Gupta Empire." In *Reappraising Gupta History: For S. R. Goyal,* edited by B. Ch. Chhabra et al. New Delhi: Aditya Prakashan.

Lotman, Yurij. 1990. *Universe of the Mind: A Semiotic Theory of Culture.* Bloomington: Indiana University Press.

Lotman, Yurij, and B. A. Uspensky. 1978. "On the Semiotic Mechanism of Culture." *NLH* 9: 211–32.

Ludden, David. 1999. *An Agrarian History of South Asia.* Vol. 3, pt. 3 of *The New Cambridge History of India.* Cambridge: Cambridge University Press.

———. 1994. "History outside Civilization and the Mobility of South Asia." *SA* 17.1: 1–23.

Lüders, Heinrich. 1979. *Bruchstücke der Kalpanāmaṇḍitikā des Kumāralāta.* Wiesbaden: Steiner. (Orig. pub. 1926.)

———. 1940. *Philologica Indica.* Göttingen: Vandenhoeck and Ruprecht.

Luhmann, Niklas. 1998. *Observations on Modernity.* Stanford: Stanford University Press.

———. 1995. *Social Systems.* Stanford: Stanford University Press.

———. 1985. "Das Problem der Epochenbildung und die Evolutionstheorie." In *Epochenstrukturen und Epochenschwellen im Diskurs der Literatur- und Sprachhistorie,* edited by H. U. Gumbrecht and U. Link-Heer. Frankfurt: Suhrkamp.

Lukács, Georg. 1971. *The Theory of the Novel.* Cambridge: MIT Press. (Orig. pub. 1920.)

Lusignan, Serge. 1986. *Parler vulgairement: Les intellectuels et la langue française aux XIIIe et XIVe siècles.* Paris: Vrin.

Lutgendorf, Philip. 1991. *The Life of a Text: Performing the Rāmcaritmānas of Tulsīdās.* Berkeley: University of California Press.

Mabbett, Ian. 1977. "Varṇas in Angkor and the Indian Caste System." *JAS* 36.3: 429–42.

Mabbett, Ian, and David Chandler. 1995. *The Khmers.* Oxford: Blackwell.

Machan, Tim William. 1991. "Editing, Orality, and Late Middle English Texts." In *Vox Intexta: Orality and Textuality in the Middle Ages,* edited by A. N. Doane and Carol Braun Pasternack. Madison: University of Wisconsin, 1991.

MacMullen, Ramsay, 1990. *Changes in the Roman Empire: Essays in the Ordinary.* Princeton: Princeton University Press.

Mahadevan, Iravatham. 2003. *Early Tamil Epigraphy from the Earliest Times to the Sixth Century A.D.* Cambridge: Harvard University Press.

———. 1970. *Tamil-Brahmi Inscriptions.* Madras: State Department of Archaeology, Government of Tamilnadu.

Mair, Victor H. 1994. "Buddhism and the Rise of the Written Vernacular in East Asia: The Making of National Languages." *JAS* 53: 707–51.

Mair, Victor H., and Tsu-Lin Mei. 1991. "The Sanskrit Origins of Recent Style Prosody." *Harvard Journal of Asiatic Studies* 51.2: 375–470.

Majumdar, R. C. 1974. *Study of Sanskrit in South-East Asia.* Calcutta: Sanskrit College.

———. 1944. *Hindu Colonies in the Far East.* Calcutta: General Printers.

Malamoud, Charles. 1997. "Noirceur de l'écriture: Remarques sur un thème littéraire de l'Inde ancienne." In *Paroles à dire, paroles à écrire,* edited by Viviane Alleton. Paris: Éditions de l'école des hautes études en sciences sociales.

Malla, Kamal Prakash. 1982. *Classical Newari Literature: A Sketch.* Kathmandu: Educational Enterprise.

Mallison, Françoise. 1986. *Au point du jour: Les Prabhātīyam de Narasiṃha Maheta: Poète et saint vishnouite du Gujaret (XVe siècle).* Paris: Ecole française d'extrême-orient.

Mandelstam, Nadezhda. 1970. *Hope against Hope: A Memoire.* New York: Atheneum.

Mango, Cyril. 1980. *Byzantium: The Empire of New Rome.* New York: Charles Scribner's Sons.

Martin, Henri-Jean. 1994. *The History and Power of Writing.* Chicago: University of Chicago Press.

Marx, Karl, and Friedrich Engels. 1981. *Ausgewählte Schriften in Zwei Bänden.* Vol. 1. Berlin: Dietz Verlag.

Masica, Colin. 1991. *The Indo-Aryan Languages.* Cambridge: Cambridge University Press.

Master, Alfred. 1949–51. "Gleanings from the Kuvalayamālā Kahā I: Three Fragments and Specimens of the Eighteen Desabhāsās," and "II: Specimens of Prose Apabhraṃśa and Middle Indian Mixed with Sanskrit." *BSOAS* 13: 410–15 and 1004–16.

———. 1943. "The Mysterious Paiśācī." *JRAS:* 34–45, 217–33.

———. 1928. "Mahārāṣṭra and Kannaḍa." *IA* 57: 174–76.

Maurer, Friedrich, ed. 1972. *Walther von der Vogelweide: Die Lieder.* München: Fink.

McCrea, Lawrence. 1997. "The Teleology of Poetry in Medieval Kashmir." Ph.D. diss., University of Chicago.

McEwan, Ian. 1998. *Enduring Love.* London: Vintage.

McGregor, Stuart. 2003. "The Progress of Hindi, Part 1: The Development of a Transregional Idiom." In *Literary Cultures in History: Reconstructions from South Asia,* edited by Sheldon Pollock. Berkeley: University of California Press.

———.1999. "Viṣṇudās (AD 15c) and his Rāmāyaṇa-kathā." In *Studies in Early Modern Indo-Aryan Languages, Literature, and Culture,* edited by Alan Entwistle and Carol Salomon. Delhi: Manohar.

———. 1984. *Hindi Literature from Its Beginnings to the Nineteenth Century.* Vol. 8, fasc. 6 of *A History of Indian Literature,* edited by Jan Gonda. Wiesbaden: Harrassowitz.

———. 1971. "Some Manuscripts Containing Nanddās's Version of the Prabodhacandrodaya Drama." *JAOS* 91.4: 487–93.

McKitterick, Rosamund, ed. 1995. *The New Cambridge Medieval History.* Vol. 2. Cambridge: Cambridge University Press.

———, ed. 1990. *The Use of Literacy in Early Mediaeval Europe.* Cambridge: Cambridge University Press.

———. 1989. *The Carolingians and the Written Word.* Cambridge: Cambridge University Press.

McMahon, April M. S. 1994. *Understanding Language Change.* Cambridge: Cambridge University Press.

Medici, Lorenzo de'. 1991. *Selected Poems and Prose.* Edited by Jon Thiem. Translated by Jon Thiem et al. University Park: Pennsylvania State University Press.

Mehendale, M. A. 1948. *Historical Grammar of Inscriptional Prakrits.* Pune: Deccan College, Postgraduate and Research Institute.

Mehta, Pratap Bhanu. 2000. "Cosmopolitanism and the Circle of Reason." *PT* 28.5: 619–39.

Menocal, Maria Rosa. 1987. *The Arabic Role in Medieval Literary History: A Forgotten Heritage.* Philadelphia: University of Pennsylvania Press.

Michell, George. 2002. *Pattadakal.* New Delhi: Oxford University Press.

Millar, Fergus. 1993. *The Roman Near East, 31 B.C.– A.D. 337.* Cambridge: Harvard University Press.

———. 1968. "Local Cultures in the Roman Empire: Libyan, Punic and Latin in Roman Africa." *Journal of Roman Studies* 58: 126–34.

Millar, Fergus, et al., eds. 1966. *The Roman Empire and Its Neighbours.* London: Weidenfeld and Nicolson.

Minkowski, Christopher. Forthcoming. "Nīlakaṇṭha's Vedic Readings in the *Harivaṃśa* Commentary." In *Proceedings of the Third Dubrovnik Conference on the Sanskrit Epics and Purāṇas,* edited by Petteri Koskikallio.

———. 2002. "Nīlakaṇṭha Caturdhara's *Mantrakāśīkhaṇḍa.*" *JAOS* 122.2: 329–44.

Mirashi, V. V. 1981. *The History and Inscriptions of the Sātavāhanas and the Western Kshatrapas.* Bombay: Maharasthra State Board for Literature and Culture.

Mishra, Kameshwar Nath, ed. 1993. *Aspects of Buddhist Sanskrit.* Saranath, Varanasi: Central Institute of Higher Tibetan Studies.

Mitchiner, John. 1986. *The Yuga Purāṇa.* Calcutta: Asiatic Society of Bengal.

Mitra, Rajendralala. 1878. *Buddha Gaya: The Great Buddhist Temple.* Reprint, Delhi, 1972.

Momigliano, Arnaldo. 1987. "The Disadvantages of Monotheism for a Universal State." In *On Pagans, Jews, and Christians.* Middletown, CT: Wesleyan University Press.

Monius, Anne E. 1997. "In Search of "Tamil Buddhism": Language, Literary Culture, and Religious Community in Tamil-Speaking South India." Ph.D. diss., Harvard University.

Montaigne, Michel de. 1962. *Oeuvres complètes.* Edited by Albert Thibaudet and Maurice Rat. Paris: Gallimard. Translated by Donald Frame: Stanford: Stanford University Press, 1958.

Mookerji, Radhakumud. 1914. *The Fundamental Unity of India (from Hindu Sources).* London: Longmans, Green and Co.

Moretti, Franco. 2004. "Graphs, Maps, Trees: Abstract Models for Literary History—3." *NLR* 28: 43–63.

———. 1998. *Atlas of the European Novel 1800–1900.* London and New York: Verso.

Morrison, Kathleen. 2000. "Coercion, Resistance and Hierarchy: Local Processes and Imperial Strategies in 14th-16th-Century South India." In *Empires,* edited by S. Alcock et al. Cambridge: Cambridge University Press.

Mulay, Sumati. 1972. *Studies in the Historical and Cultural Geography and Ethnography of the Deccan.* Pune: Deccan College.

Müller, F. Max. 1882. *India: What Can It Teach Us?* New York: U. S. Book Company.

Naerssen, F. H. van, and R. C. de Jongh. 1977. *The Economic and Administrative History of Early Indonesia.* Leiden and Köln: E. J. Brill.

Nagaraj, D. R. 1998. "Introduction." In *Exiled at Home,* by Ashis Nandy. Delhi: Oxford University Press.

Nagaraja Rao, M. S., ed. 1983. *The Chālukyas of Kalyāṇi.* Bangalore: The Mythic Society.

———. 1978. *The Chalukyas of Bādāmi: Seminar Papers.* Bangalore: The Mythic Society.

Nagaraju, S. 1995. "Emergence of Regional Identity and Beginnings of Vernacular Literature: A Case Study of Telugu." In "Literary History, Region, and Nation in South India," edited by Sheldon Pollock. Special issue, *Social Scientist* 23.10–12: 8–23.

———. 1984. "The Palaeography of the Earliest Inscriptions of Burma, Thailand, Cambodia, and Vietnam." In *Svasti Sri: Dr. B. Ch. Chhabra Felicitation Volume,* edited by K. V. Ramesh et al. Delhi: Agam.

Nagaswamy, R. 1987. "Archaeological Finds in South India: Esālam Bronzes and Copper-Plates." *BEFEO* 76: 1–51.

Naik, A. V. 1948. "Inscriptions of the Deccan: An Epigraphical Survey (circa 300 B.C.—1300 A.D.)." *Bulletin of the Deccan College Research Institute* 9: 1–160.

Nairn, Tom. 1996. "Internationalism and the Second Coming." In *Mapping the Nation,* edited by Gopal Balakrishnan. London: Verso. (Orig. pub. 1993.)

Narasimhacharya, R. 1940. *History of Kannada Literature.* Mysore: Wesley Press and Publishing House.

———. 1934. *History of Kannada Language.* Mysore: University of Mysore.

Narayana Rao, V. 2003. "Multiple Literary Cultures in Telugu: Court, Temple, and Public." In *Literary Cultures in History: Reconstructions from South Asia,* edited by Sheldon Pollock. Berkeley: University of California Press.

———. 1995. "Coconut and Honey: Sanskrit and Telugu in Medieval Andhra." In "Literary History, Region, and Nation," edited by Sheldon Pollock. Special issue, *Social Scientist* 23.10–12, 24–40.

———, tr. 1990. *Śiva's Warriors.* Princeton: Princeton University Press.

———. 1986. "Six Telugu Folk Epics." In *Another Harmony: New Essays on the Folklore of India,* edited by Stuart H. Blackburn and A. K. Ramanujan. Berkeley: University of California Press.

Narayana Rao, V., and David Shulman, trs. 2002. *Classical Telugu Poetry: An Anthology.* Berkeley: University of California Press.

Narayana Rao, V., et al. 1992. *Symbols of Substance: Court and State in Nāyaka Period Tamil Nadu.* Delhi: Oxford University Press.

Narayanan, M. G. S. 1996. *Perumals of Kerala.* Calicut: n.p.

Nayak, H. M., and T. V. Venkatachala Sastry, eds. 1974-. *Kannaḍa Adhyayana Saṃstheya Kannaḍa Sāhitya Caritre.* 5 vols. Mysore: Kannada Adhyayana Samsthe, University of Mysore Press.

Nebrija, Antonio de. 1946. *Gramatica Castellana.* Madrid: Edición de la Junta del Centenario.

Nehru, Jawaharlal. 1946. *The Discovery of India.* New York: The John Day Company.

Newman, John. 1988. "Buddhist Sanskrit in the Kālacakra Tantra." *JIABS* 11: 123–40.

Nguyen The Anh. 1996. "Le Vietnam." In *Initiation à la Peninsule indochinoise.* Paris: L'Harmattan.

Nicolet, Claude. 1991. *Space, Geography, and Politics in the Early Roman Empire.* Ann Arbor: University of Michigan Press.

Nicols, John. 1987. "Indigenous Culture and the Process of Romanization in Iberian Galicia." *AJP* 108: 129–51.

Nihom, Max. 1994. *Studies in Indian and Indo-Indonesian Tantrism: The Kuñjakarṇadharmakathana and the Yoga Tantra.* Vienna: de Nobili.

Nijenhuis, Emmie te. 1977. *Musicological Literature.* Vol. 6, fasc. 1 of *A History of Indian Literature,* edited by Jan Gonda. Wiesbaden: Harrassowitz.

———. 1974. *Indian Music: History and Structure.* Leiden and Köln. E. J. Brill.

Nilakanta Sastri, K. A. 1972. *The Pāṇḍyan Kingdom: From the Earliest Times to the Sixteenth Century.* Madras: Swathi Publications.

———. 1955. *The Cōḻas.* 2d ed. Madras: University of Madras.

Nitti-Dolci, Luigia. 1938. *Les grammairiens prakrits.* Paris: Adrien-Maisonneuve.

Norman, K. R. 1993. "Theravāda Buddhism and Brahmanical Hinduism: Brahmanical Terms in a Buddhist Guise." In *Collected Papers,* vol. 4, 271–80. Oxford: The Pali Text Society. (Orig. pub. 1991.)

———. 1988. "The Origin of Pali and Its Position among the Indo-European Languages." *Journal of Pali and Buddhist Studies* 1: 1–27 (= *Collected Papers,* vol. 3, 225–43).

———. 1980. "The Dialects in which the Buddha Preached." In *Die Sprache der ältesten buddhistischen Überlieferung,* edited by Heinz Bechert. Göttingen: Van den Hoeck and Ruprecht.

———. 1979. Review of *Epigraphical Hybrid Sanskrit. Lingua* 48: 291–94.

Nyíri, J. C. 1996. "Zum Funktionswandel der Geisteswissenschaften im Zeitalter der Post-Literalität." In *Zukunftsaspekte der Geisteswissenschaften: Vier Vorträge,* edited by Bernhard Fabian. Hildesheim, Zürich, and New York: Olms-Weidmann.

Oberlies, Thomas. 1996. "Das zeitliche und ideengeschichtliche Verhältnis der Cāndra-Vṛtti zu anderen V(ai)yākaraṇas (Studien zum Cāndravyākaraṇa III)." *STII* 20: 265–317.

———. 1989. *Studien zum Cāndravyākaraṇa.* Stuttgart: Steiner.

Paden, William. 1995. "Manuscripts." In *A Handbook of the Troubadours,* edited by F. R. P. Akehurst and Judith M. Davis. Berkeley: University of California Press.

———. 1983. "Europe from Latin to Vernacular." In *Performance of Literature in Historical Perspective,* edited by D. W. Thompson. Lanham: University Press of America.

Painter, Douglas M. 1993. "Humanist Insights and the Vernacular in Sixteenth-Century France." *HEI* 16: 67–73.

Palmer, Nigel F. 1993. *German Literary Culture in the Twelfth and Thirteenth Centuries.* Oxford: Clarendon Press.

Pancamukhi, R. S. 1941. *Karnatak Inscriptions.* Dharwar: Kannada Research Institute.

Pandharipande, Rajeshwari. 1997. *Marathi.* London, New York: Routledge, 1997.

Panikkar, K. N., ed. 1999. *The Concerned Indian's Guide to Communalism.* New Delhi: Penguin.

Parpola, Asko. 1981, 1994. "On the Formation of the Mīmāṃsā and the Problems concerning Jaimini." Parts 1 and 2. *WZKSA* 25: 145–77; *WZKSA* 38: 293–308.

Patterson, Lee. 1990. "Literary History." In *Critical Terms for Literary Study,* edited by Frank Lentricchia. Chicago: University of Chicago Press.

Perkins, David, ed. 1991. *Theoretical Issues in Literary History.* Cambridge: Harvard University Press.

Petrarca, Francesco. 1965. *Francisci Petrarchae operum.* Reprint. Ridgewood, NJ: Gregg Press. (Orig. pub. Basel, 1554).

Phalgunadi, I. Gusti Putu. 1990[–97]. *Indonesian Mahābhārata.* Delhi: International Academy of Indian Culture and Aditya Prakashan.

Phukan, Shantanu. 1999. "Through a Persian Prism: Hindi and Padmavat in the Mughal Imagination." Ph.D. diss., University of Chicago.

Pingree, David. 1978. *The Yavanajātaka.* Vol. 1. Cambridge: Harvard University Press.
Pirenne, Henri. 1958. *Mohammed and Charlemagne.* London: Allen and Unwin. (Orig. French ed. pub. 1939).
Pischel, Richard. 1965. *Comparative Grammar of the Prākṛt Languages.* Delhi: Motilal Banarsidass. (Orig. German ed. pub. 1900.)
Pollock, Sheldon. 2005a. "Axialism and Empire." In *Axial Civilizations and World History,* edited by Johann Arnason et al. Leiden: E. J. Brill.
———. 2005b. "Empire and Imitation." In *Lessons of Empire,* edited by Craig Calhoun et al. New York: New Press.
———. 2005c. "The Languages of Science in Early-Modern India." In *Contributions to Indian and Cross-Cultural Studies: Volume in Commemoration of Wilhelm Halbfass,* edited by K. Preisendanz. Vienna: Akademie der Wissenschaften.
———. 2005d. "Ratnaśrījñāna." In *Encycopaedia of Indian Wisdom: Dr. Satya Vrat Shastri Felicitation Volume.* Delhi: Bharatiya Vidya Prakashan.
———. 2004. "The Meaning of *Dharma* and the Relationship of the Two Mīmāṃsās: Appayya Dīkṣita's 'Discourse on the Refutation of a Unified Knowledge-System of Pūrvamīmāṃsā and Uttaramīmāṃsā.' In "Dharma," edited by Patrick Olivelle. Special issue, *JIP* 32: 769–811.
———, ed. 2003. *Literary Cultures in History: Reconstructions from South Asia.* Berkeley: University of California Press.
———. 2003. "Sanskrit Literary Culture From the Inside Out." In *Literary Cultures in History: Reconstructions from South Asia,* edited by Sheldon Pollock. Berkeley: University of California Press.
———. 2002. "Introduction: Cosmopolitanisms." In *Cosmopolitanism,* edited by Carol Breckenridge et al. Durham: Duke University Press.
———. 2001a. "The Death of Sanskrit." *CSSH* 43.2: 392–426.
———. 2001b. "The New Intellectuals in Seventeenth-Century India." *IESHR* 38.1: 3–31.
———. 2001c. "The Social Aesthetic and Sanskrit Literary Theory." *JIP* 29: 197–229.
———. 1998a. "Bhoja's *Śṛṅgāraprakāśa* and the Problem of Rasa: A Historical Introduction and Translation." *AS/ÉA* 70.1: 117–92.
———. 1998b. "India in the Vernacular Millennium: Literary Culture and Polity, 1000–1500." In "Early Modernities," edited by S. N. Eisenstadt et al. *Daedalus* 127.3: 41–74.
———. 1997. "'Tradition' as 'Revelation': Śruti, Smṛti, and the Sanskrit Discourse of Power." In *Lex et Litterae: Essays on Ancient Indian Law and Literature in Honour of Oscar Botto,* edited by S. Lienhard and I. Piovano. Turin: Edizioni dell'Orso. Corrected reprint in: *Boundaries, Dynamics and Construction of Traditions in South Asia,* edited by Federico Squarcini (Florence: Florence University Press, 2005).
———. 1995a. "In Praise of Poets: On the History and Function of the *Kavipraśaṃsā.*" In *Ānandabhāratī: Dr. K. Krishnamoorthy Felicitation Volume.* Mysore: DVK Murthy.
———. 1995b. "Public Poetry in Sanskrit." In "Sanskrit Literature," edited by A. N. D. Haksar. Special issue, *Indian Horizons* 44.4.
———, ed. 1995. "Literary History, Region, and Nation in South Asia." Special issue, *Social Scientist* 23.10–12.
———. 1993a. "Deep Orientalism? Notes on Sanskrit and Power beyond the Raj."

In *Orientalism and the Postcolonial Predicament,* edited by Carol Breckenridge and Peter van der Veer. Philadelphia: University of Pennsylvania Press.

———. 1993b. "*Rāmāyaṇa* and Political Imagination in India." *JAS* 52.2: 261–97.

———, tr. and ed. 1991. *The Rāmāyaṇa of Vālmīki: An Epic of Ancient India.* Vol. 3: *Araṇyakāṇḍa.* Princeton: Princeton University Press.

———. 1990. "From Discourse of Ritual to Discourse of Power in Sanskrit Culture." *JRS* 4.2: 291–320.

———. 1989. "Playing by the Rules: *Śāstra* and Sanskrit Literature." In *The Śāstric Tradition in the Indian Arts,* edited by A.-L. Dallapiccola and S. Zingel-Avé Lallemant. Wiesbaden: Steiner.

———, tr. and ed. 1986. *The Rāmāyaṇa of Vālmīki, An Epic of Ancient India.* Vol. 2: *Ayodhyākāṇḍa.* Princeton: Princeton University Press.

———. 1985. "The Theory of Practice and the Practice of Theory in Indian Intellectual History." *JAOS* 105: 499–519.

———. 1984. "The *Rāmāyaṇa* Text and the Critical Edition." In *The Vālmīki Rāmāyaṇa,* vol. 1, *Bālakāṇḍa,* translated and edited by Robert Goldman. Princeton: Princeton University Press.

Pou, Saveros. 1991. "Sanskrit, Pali and Khmero-Pali in Cambodia." In *Sanskrit outside India,* vol. 7 of *Panels of the Seventh World Sanskrit Conference,* edited by J. G. de Casparis. Leiden: E. J. Brill.

Pred, Allan. 1995. "Out of Bounds and Undisciplined: Social Inquiry and the Current Moment of Danger." *Social Research* 62.4: 1065–91.

Prinz, W. 1911. "Bhāṣā-wörter in Nīlakaṇṭha's Bhāratabhāvadīpā und in anderen Sanskritkommentaren." *ZVS* 44: 69–109.

Puttappa, K. V., ed. 1988. *Kannaḍa Kaipiḍi.* Mysore: University of Mysore Press.

Pye, L. 1992. "Social Science Theories in Search of Chinese Realities." *CQ* 132: 1161–70.

Quint, David. 1993. *Epic and Empire.* Princeton: Princeton University Press.

Rabe, Michael. 1997. "The Māmallapuram Praśasti: A Panegyric in Figures." *AA* 62.3–4: 189–240.

Raeside, Ian. 1989. *Gadyarāja: A Fourteenth-Century Marathi Version of the Kṛṣṇa Legend.* Bombay: Popular Prakashan; London: School of Oriental and African Studies, University of London.

Raghavan, V., ed. 1980. *The Ramayana Tradition in Asia.* Delhi: Sahitya Akademi.

———. 1978. *Bhoja's Śṛṅgāraprakāśa.* 3d ed. Madras: Punarvasu.

———. 1963. *Bhoja's Śṛṅgāraprakāśa.* 2d ed., Madras: Punarvasu.

———. 1956. "Methods of Popular Religious Instruction in South India." In *The Cultural Heritage of India,* edited by Haridas Bhattacharyya, vol. 4, 2d ed. Calcutta: Ramakrishna Mission Institute of Culture.

———. 1943. "Bodhi and Visnupada in N.-W. India and Toponymic Duplication." *The Indian Geographical Journal* 18.2: 98–104.

———. 1942. *Studies on Some Concepts of the Alaṃkāra Śāstra.* Adyar: Adyar Library.

———. [1941]. "Notes on Some Mahābhārata Commentaries." In *A Volume of Studies in Indology Presented to P. V. Kane,* edited by S. J. Katre and P. V. Gode. Pune: Oriental Book Agency.

———. 1939–40. "The Date and Works of Ānandapūrṇa Vidyāsāgara" *AORM* 4.1: 1–5.

Raja, K. Kunjunni. 1980. *The Contribution of Kerala to Sanskrit Literature.* Madras: University of Madras.
Raman, K. V. 1973. "Recent Discoveries in Pandyan History." In *Journal of Indian History Golden Jubilee Volume,* edited by T. K. Ravindran. Trivandrum: University of Kerala.
Ramanujan, A. K. 1999. *The Collected Essays of A. K. Ramanujan.* New Delhi: Oxford University Press.
———. 1973. *Speaking of Shiva.* Harmondsworth: Penguin.
Ramaswamy, Sumathi. 1997. *Passions of the Tongue: Language and Devotion in Tamil India 1891–1970.* Berkeley: University of California Press.
Ramesan, N. 1962. *Copper Plate Inscriptions of Andhra Pradesh Government Museum, Hyderabad.* Vol. 1. Hyderabad: Government of Andhra Pradesh.
Ramesh, K. V., and S. P. Tewari, eds. 1990. *A Copper-Plate Hoard of the Gupta Period from Bagh, Madhya Pradesh.* New Delhi: Archaeological Survey of India.
Rapson, E. J. 1897. *Indian Coins.* Strassburg, K. J. Trubner.
Rau, Wilhelm. 1985. *Die vedischen Zitate im Vyākaraṇa-Mahābhāṣya.* Stuttgart: Franz Steiner.
Ray, Himanshu. 1986. *Monastery and Guild: Commerce under the Satavahanas.* Delhi: Oxford University Press.
Reich, Tamar. 1998. "A Battlefield of a Text: Inner-Textual Interpretation in the Sanskrit Mahābhārata." Ph.D. diss., University of Chicago.
Reid, Anthony. 1990. "An 'Age of Commerce' in Southeast Asian History." *MAS* 24.1: 1–30.
Renfrew, C., and J. Cherry, eds. 1986. *Peer Polity Interaction and Socio-Political Change.* Cambridge: Cambridge University Press.
Renou, Louis. 1957. "Introduction générale." In *Altindische Grammatik,* by Jakob Wackernagel. Göttingen: Vandenhoeck and Ruprecht.
———. 1956. *Histoire de la langue sanskrite.* Lyon: Editions IAC.
———. 1942. *Terminologie grammaticale du sanskrit.* Paris: É. Champion.
Renou, Louis, and Jean Filliozat. 1947. *L'Inde classique.* Vol. 1. Paris: Payot.
Reynolds, Craig J. 1995. "A New Look at Old Southeast Asia." *JAS* 54.2: 419–46.
Reynolds, Susan. 1997. *Kingdoms and Communities in Western Europe 900–1300.* 2d ed. Oxford: Clarendon Press.
———. 1983. "Medieval *Origines Gentium* and the Community of the Realm." *History* 68: 375–90.
Richman, Paula, ed. 2001. *Questioning Ramayanas.* Berkeley: University of California Press.
———, ed. 1991. *Many Ramayanas.* Berkeley: University of California Press.
Richter, David. 1989. *The Critical Tradition.* New York: St. Martin's Press.
Richter, Michael. 1994. *The Formation of the Medieval West: Studies in the Oral Culture of the Barbarians.* London: St. Martins.
Ricoeur, Paul. 1986. *Lectures on Ideology and Utopia,* edited by George Taylor. New York: Columbia University Press.
———. 1965. *History and Truth.* Evanston: Northwestern University Press.
Robertson, Roland. 1992. *Globalization: Social Theory and Global Culture.* London: Sage.
Robson, S. O., tr. 1995. *Deśawarṇana by Mpu Prapañca.* Leiden: KITLV Press.

———. 1983. "Kakawin Reconsidered: Toward a Theory of Old Javanese Poetics." *BTLV* 139: 291–319.

Rocher, Ludo. 1994. *Orality and Textuality in the Indian Context.* Sino-Platonic Papers, no. 49. Philadelphia: Dept. of Asian Art and Middle Eastern Studies, Univ. of Pennsylvania.

Rochette, Bruno. 1997. "Vrbis-Orbis." *Latomus* 56.3: 551–53.

Rogers, John D. 1994. "Post-Orientalism and the Interpretation of Premodern and Modern Political Identities: The Case of Sri Lanka." *JAS* 53.1: 10–23.

Ronsard, Pierre de. 1993–94. *Oeuvres complètes.* Edited by Jean Céard et al. 2 vols. Paris: Gallimard.

Rowell, Lewis. 1992. *Music and Musical Thought in Early India.* Chicago: University of Chicago Press.

Saberwal, Satish. 1991. "Segmentation and Literacy." *EPW* 26: 723–38.

Sachau, Edward C., tr. 1910. *Alberuni's India.* London: Kegan Paul, Trench, Trübner and Co.

Sahlins, Marshall. 1988. "Cosmologies of Capitalism: The Trans-Pacific Sector of the World System." *Proceedings of the British Academy* 74: 1–51.

Said, Edward. 1975. *Beginnings: Intention and Method.* New York: Basic Books.

Saletore, Bhasker Anand. 1938. *Mediaeval Jainism, with Special Reference to the Vijayanagara Empire.* Bombay: Karnatak Publishing House.

Salomon, Richard. 2001. "'Gandhari Hybrid Sanskrit': New Sources for the Study of the Sanskritization of Buddhist Literature." *IIJ* 44.3: 241–52.

———. 1998. *Indian Epigraphy.* Delhi: Munshiram Manoharlal.

———. 1997. "On Drawing Socio-Linguistic Distinctions in Old Indo-Aryan: The Question of Kṣatriya Sanskrit and Related Problems." In *The Indo-Aryans of Ancient South Asia,* edited by G. Erdosy. Delhi: Munshiram Manoharlal.

———. 1995. "On the Origin of the Early Indian Scripts." *JAOS* 115.2: 271–79.

———. 1989a. "Linguistic Variability in post-Vedic Sanskrit." In *Dialectes dans les Littératures indo-aryennes,* edited by C. Caillat. Paris: Collège de France.

———. 1989b. "New Inscriptional Evidence for the History of the Aulikaras of Mandasor." *IIJ* 32: 1–36.

Salomon, Richard, and Gregory Schopen. 1984. "The Indravarman (Avaca) Casket Inscription Reconsidered." *JIABS* 7.1: 107–23.

Sankaranarayanan, S. 1994. "Sanskrit Education in Ancient Karnataka (Epigraphical Survey)." *Brahmavidya* 58: 100–124.

Sarasvati, A. Rangasvami. 1925. "Political Maxims of the Emperor-Poet, Krishnadeva Raya." *JIH* 4: 61–88.

Sarkar, Himansu Bhusan. 1970. *Some Contribution[s] of India to the Ancient Civilisation of Indonesia and Malaysia.* Calcutta: Punthi Pustak.

———. 1934. *Indian Influences on the Literature of Java and Bali.* Calcutta: Greater India Society.

Sarma, Somasekhara. 1936. "The Māyalūr Plates of Vinayāditya. *JORM* 10: 27–46.

Sartori, Andrew. 1998. "Comparative Civilizations and Political Imagination of Postwar America." *Positions* 6.1: 33–65.

Scharfe, Hartmut. 1977. *Grammatical Literature.* Vol. 5, fasc. 2 of *A History of Indian Literature,* edited by Jan Gonda. Wiesbaden: Harrassowitz.

———. 1976. "Second 'Index Fossil' of Sanskrit Grammarians." *JAOS* 96: 274–77.

Schieffer, Rudolf. 1985. "Über soziale und kulturelle Voraussetzungen der frühmittelalterlichen Literatur." In *Neues Handbuch der Literaturwissenschaft,* edited by Klaus von See, vol. 6, *Europäisches Frühmittelalter.* Wiesbaden: Aula-Verlag.
Schlumberger, Daniel, and Paul Bernard. 1965. "Ai Khanoum." *BCH* 89: 590–657.
Schneibel, Jeffery. 2000. "The Production of Jagannātha." Ph.D. diss., University of Chicago.
Schopen, Gregory. 1997. *Bones, Stones, and Buddhist Monks: Collected Papers on the Archaeology, Epigraphy, and Texts of Monastic Buddhism in India.* Honolulu: University of Hawaii Press.
Schulze, Hagen. 1996. *States, Nations and Nationalism. From the Middle Ages to the Present.* Oxford: Blackwell. (Orig. German ed. pub. 1994.)
Schwartzberg, Joseph. 1992. "Introduction to South Asian Cartography." In *History of Cartography.* Vol. 2, bk 1. Edited by J. B. Harley and David Woodward. Chicago: University of Chicago Press.
———, ed. 1992. *A Historical Atlas of South Asia.* 2d impr. Oxford: Oxford University Press.
Scott, James. 1999. *Seeing Like a State: How Certain Schemes to Improve the Human Condition Have Failed.* New Haven: Yale University Press.
———. 1990. *Domination and the Arts of Resistance: Hidden Transcripts.* New Haven: Yale University Press.
See, Klaus von. 1985. "Das Frühmittelalter als Epoche der europäischen Literaturgeschichte." In *Neues Handbuch der Literaturwissenschaft,* edited by Klaus von See, vol. 6, *Europäisches Frühmittelalter.* Wiesbaden: Aula-Verlag.
———. 1983. "Caedmon u. Mohammed." *ZDA* 112: 225–33.
Segal, Daniel A., and Richard Handler. 1992. "How European is Nationalism?" *Social Analysis* 32: 1–15.
Segal, Jeffrey, ed. 1993. *International Journal of the Sociology of Language* 99. Special issue on koinés.
Settar, S., and Gunther D. Sontheimer, eds. 1982. *Memorial Stones: A Study of Their Origin, Significance, and Variety.* Dharwad: Karnataka University, Institute of Indian Art History; New Delhi: South Asia Institute, University of Heidelberg.
Sevcenko, Ihor., ed. 1991. *Byzantium and the Slavs in Letters and Culture.* Cambridge: Harvard Ukrainian Research Institute; Napoli: Instituto universitario orientale.
Shackle, Christopher. 1993. "Early Vernacular Poetry in the Indus Valley: Its Contexts and its Character." In *Islam and Indian Regions,* vol. 1, edited by A.-L. Dallapiccola and Stephanie Zingel-Avé Lallemant. Stuttgart: Steiner.
Shaffer, L. 1994. "Southernization: Economic, Medical, and Literary Developments in Southern Asia." *JWH* 5.1: 1–21.
Shapiro, Marianne. 1990. *De vulgari eloquentia: Dante's Book of Exile.* Lincoln: University of Nebraska Press.
Shapiro, Michael C., and Harold F. Schiffman. 1983. *Language and Society in South Asia.* New Delhi: Motilal Banarsidass.
Sharan, Mahesh Kumar. 1981. *Select Cambodi[a]n Inscriptions: The Mebon and Pre Rup Inscriptions of Rajendra Varman II.* Delhi: S. N. Publications.
Sharma, Sunil. 2000. *Persian Poetry at the Indian Frontier.* New Delhi: Permanent Black.
Sherwin-White, A. N. 1973. *Roman Citizenship.* 2d ed. Oxford: Clarendon Press.
Shils, Edward. 1957. "Primordial, Personal, Sacred and Civil Ties." *BJS* 8: 130–45.

Shrinivasan, M. S. 1989. *The Cohesive Role of Sanskritization and Other Essays*. Delhi: Oxford University Press.

Shulman, David. 1993. "Remaking a Purāṇa: The Rescue of Gajendra in Potana's Telugu *Mahābhāgavatamu*." In *Purāṇa Perennis: Reciprocity and Transformation in Hindu and Jain Texts,* edited by Wendy Doniger. Albany: State University of New York Press.

———. 1988. "Sage, Poet, and Hidden Wisdom in Medieval India." In *Cultural Traditions and Worlds of Knowledge: Explorations in the Sociology of Knowledge,* edited by S. N. Eisenstadt and I. F. Silver. Greenwich, CT, and London: JAI Press.

Sider, Robert D. 1980. "Credo quia absurdum?" *CW* 73: 417–19.

Sidney, Sir Philip. 1997. *Defence of Poesie, Astrophil and Stella and Other Writings*. Edited by Elizabeth Porges Watson. London: Dent.

Silverstein, Michael. 2000. "Worfianism and the Linguistic Imagination of Reality." In *Regimes of Language: Ideologies, Polities, and Identities,* edited by Paul V. Kroskrity. Sante Fe: School of American Research Press.

Silverstein, Michael, and Greg Urban, eds. 1996. *Natural Histories of Discourse*. Chicago: University of Chicago Press.

Singh, A. K., ed. 1991. "Virūpākṣa Temple Inscription of Jayasiṃha Siddharāja, Year 1198." *Purātan* 8: 61–64.

Sinopoli, Carla M., and Kathleen Morrison. 1995. "Dimensions of Imperial Control: The Vijayanagara Capital." *AmA* 97.1: 83–96.

Sircar, D. C. 1965–83. *Select Inscriptions Bearing on Indian History and Civilization*. Vol. 1. 2d ed. Calcutta: Calcutta University; vol. 2, Delhi: Motilal Banarsidass.

———. 1967. *Cosmography and Geography in Early Indian Literature*. Calcutta: Indian Studies: Past & Present.

———. 1965. *Indian Epigraphy*. Delhi: Motilal Banarsidass.

———. 1960. *Studies in the Geography of Ancient and Medieval India*. Delhi: Motilal Banarsidass.

———. 1939a. "Date of Patañjali's Mahābhāṣya." *IHQ* 15: 15–20.

———. 1939b. "Inscriptional Evidences Relating to the Development of Classical Sanskrit." *IHQ* 15: 38–46.

———. 1939c. *Successors to the Sātavāhanas*. Calcutta: Calcutta University Press.

———. 1937–38. "Kāvya Style in Inscriptions of the Successors of the Sātavāhanas." *IC* 4: 240–47.

Sitaraman, B., et al. 1976. "A List of the Tamil Inscriptions of the Chola Dynasty." *JAAS* 11: 87–180.

Sivarudrappa, G. S., ed. 1974-. *Samagra Kannaḍa Sāhitya Caritre*. Bangalore: Centre of Kannada Studies.

Sivathamby, Karthigesu [Karttikecu Civattampi]. 1986. *Literary History in Tamil: A Historiographical Analysis*. Thanjavur: Tamil University

Skinner, Quentin. 1998. *Liberty before Liberalism*. Cambridge: Cambridge University Press.

Skutnabb-Kangas, Tove, and Robert Phillipson. 1989. "'Mother Tongue': The Theoretical and Sociopolitical Construction of a Concept." In *Status and Function of Languages and Language Varieties,* edited by Ulrich Ammon. Berlin, New York: de Gruyter.

Smith, Anthony D. 1991. *National Identity*. Reno, Las Vegas, and London: University of Nevada Press.

———. 1990. "Towards a Global Culture?" In *Global Culture: Nationalism, Globalization and Modernity*, edited by Mike Featherstone. London: Sage.

———. 1986. *The Ethnic Origins of Nations*. Oxford: Basil Blackwell.

Smith, Colin. 2000. "The Vernacular." In *The New Cambridge Medieval History*, vol. 5, edited by David Abulafia. Cambridge: Cambridge University Press.

———. 1983. *The Making of the Poema de mio Cid*. Cambridge: Cambridge University Press.

Smith, David. 1985. *Ratnākara's Haravijaya: An Introduction to the Sanskrit Court Epic*. Delhi: Oxford University Press.

Smith, W. L. 1988. *Rāmāyaṇa Traditions in Eastern India*. Stockholm: University of Stockholm, Department of Indology.

Smyth, Alfred P., ed. 1998. *Medieval Europeans: Studies in Ethnic Identity and National Perspectives in Medieval Europe*. London: MacMillan.

Snell, Rupert. 1991. *The Hindi Classical Tradition: A Braj Bhāṣā Reader*. London: University of London, School of Oriental and African Studies.

Sorrell, Paul. 1992. "Oral Poetry and *Beowulf*." *OT* 7.1: 28–65.

Spencer, George W. 1970. "The Sacred Geography of the Tamil Shaivite Hymns." *Numen* 17.3: 232–44.

Spiegel, Gabrielle M. 1993. *Romancing the Past: The Rise of Vernacular Prose Historiography in Thirteenth-Century France*. Berkeley: University of California Press.

Spitzer, Leo. 1948. "Muttersprache und Muttererziehung." In *Essays in Historical Semantics*. New York: Russell and Russell.

Srikantia, B. M. 1983. "Karnataka Kavirajamargam (Review of A. Venkata Rao and H. Shesha Aiyangar, eds., *Kavirajamargam*)." In *Śrī Sāhitya: Complete Works of Professor B. M. Srikantia*. Mysore: University of Mysore, Institute of Kannada Studies. Orig. pub. in *QJMS* 23.3 (1933).

Srinivas, M. N. 1989. "A Note on Sanskritization and Westernization." In *The Cohesive Role of Sanskritization and Other Essays*. Delhi and New York: Oxford University Press. (Orig. pub. 1956.)

Srinivasan, Doris Meth, ed. 1989. *Mathurā: The Cultural Heritage*. New Delhi: American Institute of Indian Studies.

Srinivasan, P. R., and S. Sankaranarayanan. 1979. *Inscriptions of the Ikshvāku Period*. Hyderabad: Government of Andhra Pradesh.

Sripati, Muthu Krishna, tr. 1995. *Nannul: A Perceptive and Comprehensive Translation in English*. Madurai: n.p.

Staal, J. Frits. 1963. "Sanskrit and Sanskritization." *JAS* 22.3: 261–75.

Stargardt, Nicholas. 1995. "Origins of the Constructivist Theory of the Nation." In *Notions of Nationalism*, edited by Sukumar Periwal. Budapest, London, and New York: Central European University Press.

Stein, Burton. 1989. *Vijayanagara*. Vol. 1, pt. 2 of *The New Cambridge History of India*. Cambridge: Cambridge University Press.

———. 1985. "Reapproaching Vijayanagara." In *Studies of South India: An Anthology of Recent Research and Scholarship*, edited by Robert E. Frykenberg and Pauline Kolenda. Madras and New Delhi: New Era/AIIS.

———. 1980. *Peasant State and Society in South India*. Delhi: Oxford University Press.

———. 1977. "Circulation and the Historical Geography of Tamil Country." *JAS* 37.1: 7–26.

Stein, M. A. 1900. *Kalhaṇa's Rājataraṅgiṇī.* 2 vols. Westminster: A. Constable. Reprint, Delhi, 1989.

Sternbach, Ludwik. 1980–85. *Poésie sanskrite dans les Anthologies et les Inscriptions.* 3 vols. Paris: Institut de civilisation indienne.

Stewart, Tony. 1994. "One Text from Many: *Caitanyacaritāmṛta* as 'Classic' and 'Commentary.'" In *According to Tradition: Hagiographical Writing in India,* edited by W. M. Callewaert and Rupert Snell. Wiesbaden: Harrassowitz.

Stutterheim, Willem Frederik. 1939. "Note on Cultural Relations between South-India and Java." TITLV 79: 73–84.

———. 1925. *Rāma-legenden und Rāma-reliefs in Indonesien.* 2 vols. Munich: G. Müller.

Śukla, Rāmcandra. 1988. *Hindī Sāhitya kā Itihās.* Varanasi: Nagari Pracarini Sabha. (Orig. pub. 1929.)

Sukthankar, V. S. 1944. *Sukthankar Memorial Edition.* Edited by P. K. Gode. Pune: Memorial Committee.

Supomo, S. 1993. *Bhāratayuddha: An Old Javanese Poem and Its Indian Sources.* New Delhi: International Academy of Indian Culture and Aditya Prakashan.

Swain, Simon. 1996. *Hellenism and Empire: Language, Classicism, and Power in the Greek World A.D.* 50–250. Oxford: Clarendon Press.

Swamy, B. G. L. 1975. "The Date of the Tolkāppiyam: A Retrospect." In *Silver Jubilee Volume, AORM* 25: 292–317.

Tagare, Ganesh Vasudev. 1948. *Historical Grammar of Apabhraṃśa.* Pune: Deccan College.

Talbott, Cynthia. 2001. *Precolonial India in Practice: Society, Region, and Identity in Medieval Andhra.* Delhi: Oxford University Press.

———. 1995. "Inscribing the Self, Inscribing the Other: Hindu-Muslim Identities in Pre-Colonial India." *CSSH* 37.4: 692–722.

Tambaiah, Stanley. 1976. *World Conqueror and World Renouncer.* Cambridge: Cambridge University Press.

Tarling, Nicholas, ed. 1992. *The Cambridge History of Southeast Asia.* Vol. 1: *From Early Times to c. 1800.* Cambridge: Cambridge University Press.

Taylor, Woodman Lyon. 1997. "Visual Culture in Performative Practice: The Aesthetics, Politics, and Poetics of Visuality in Liturgical Practices of the Vallabha Sampradaya Hindu Community at Kota." Ph.D. diss., University of Chicago.

Terwiel, B. J. 1996. "The Introduction of Indian Prosody among the Thais." In *Ideology and Status of Sanskrit: Contributions to the History of the Sanskrit Language,* edited by Jan E. M. Houben. Leiden: E. J. Brill.

Tharu, Susie, and K. Lalitha. 1991–93. *Women Writing in India, 600 B.C.* to the Present. 2 vols. New York: The Feminist Press at the City University of New York.

Thieme, Paul. 1982. "Meaning and Form of the 'Grammar' of Pāṇini." *STII* 8/9: 3–34.

———. 1971. *Kleine Schriften.* Wiesbaden: Steiner.

Thimmappayya, M. 1977. *Nāḍoja Pampa.* 2d ed. Mysore: Geetha Book House.

Thongchai Winichakul. 1996. "Maps and the Form of the Geobody of Siam." In *Asian Forms of the Nation,* edited by Stein Tønnesson and Hans Antlöv. London: Curzon Press.

———. 1994. *Siam Mapped: A History of the Geo-Body of a Nation.* Honolulu: University of Hawaii Press.

Thoreau, Henry David. 1995. *Walden.* Edited by Walter Harding. New York: Houghton Mifflin. (Orig. pub. 1854.)

Tieken, Herman. 2003. "Old Tamil Caṅkam Literature and the So-called Caṅkam Period." *IESHR* 40.3: 247–78.

———. 2001. *Kāvya in South India: Old Tamil Caṅkam Poetry.* Gronigen: Egbert Forsten.

———. 1995. "Prākṛt Poetry: Hāla's Sattasaī." In "Sanskrit Literature," edited by A. N. D. Haksar. Special issue, *Indian Horizons* 44.4.

———. 1993. "The So-Called Trivandrum Plays Attributed to Bhāsa." *WZKSA* 37: 5–44.

———. 1992. "Hāla's *Sattasaī* as a Source of Pseudo-desi Words." *BEI* 10: 221–67.

Tilly, Charles, ed. 1975. *The Formation of National States in Western Europe.* Princeton: Princeton University Press.

Tocqueville, A. de. 1963. *De la Démocratie en Amérique.* Paris: Union generale d'editions. (Orig. pub. 1835.)

Tønnesson, Stein, and Hans Antlöv, eds. 1996. *Asian Forms of the Nation.* London: Curzon Press.

Tulpule, Shankar Gopal. 1979. *Classical Marāṭhī Literature: From the Beginning to A.D. 1818.* Wiesbaden: Harrassowitz.

———. 1963. *Prācīna Marāthi Korīva Lekha.* Pune: Pune Vidyapith Prakashan.

Uhlenbeck, E. M. 1975. "De interpretatie van de Oud-Javaanse Ramayana-kakawin: Enige algemene beschouwingen en gezichtspunten." *BTLV* 131.2–3: 195–213.

Upadhye, A. N. 1983. *Papers.* Mysore: University of Mysore.

———. 1965. "Languages and Dialects Used in the Kuvalayamālā." *JOI* 14: 317–25.

van der Veer, Peter. 2001. *Imperial Encounters: Religion and Modernity in India and Britain.* Princeton: Princeton University Press.

Varshney, Ashutosh. 1993. "Contested Meanings: Hindu Nationalism, India's National Identity, and the Politics of Anxiety." *Daedalus* 122.3: 227–62.

Velankar, H. D. 1949. *Jayadāman.* Bombay: Haritosha Samiti.

Venkata Ramanayya, N. 1953. *The Chalukyas of L(V)emulavada.* Hyderabad: Archaeological Department, Government of Hyderabad.

Venkatachala Sastry, T. V. 1999. "Halmiḍi Śāsanada Artha." In *Śāstriya,* vol. 1. Bangalore: Sapna Book House. (Orig. pub. 1972).

———. 1997. *Namma Karṇāṭaka.* 2d ed. Bangalore: Kannada Sahitya Parisat.

———. 1992. "A Historical Survey of Dictionaries Sanskrit and Kannada." *Arts Journal* (University of Mysore) 54: 163–76.

———. 1979. *Śabdārthavihāra.* Mysore: Aparna Prakashan.

Venkatachari, K. K. A. 1978. *The Maṇipravāla Literature of the Śrīvaiṣṇava Ācāryas.* Bombay: Ananthacharya Research Institute.

Verdery, Katherine. 1994. "Ethnicity, Nationalism, and State-Making." In *The Anthropology of Ethnicity,* edited by Hans Vermeulen and Cora Govers. Amsterdam: Het Spinhuis.

Verhagen, Peter C. 1996. "Tibetan Expertise in Sanskrit Grammar: Ideology, Status and other Extra Linguistic Factors." In *Ideology and Status of Sanskrit: Contributions to the History of the Sanskrit Language,* edited by Jan E. M. Houben. Leiden: E. J. Brill.

———. 1992. "'Royal' Patronage of Sanskrit Grammatical Studies in Tibet." In *Ritual, State and History in South Asia: Essays in Honour of J. C. Heesterman,* edited by A. W. van der Hoek et al. Leiden: E. J. Brill.

Verpoorten, Jean-Marie. 1987. "Le Droit de l'Adhyayana selon la Mīmāṃsā." *IIJ* 30: 23–30.

Veyne, Paul. 1994. "Humanitas: Romans and Non-Romans." In *The Romans,* edited by Andrea Giardina. Chicago: University of Chicago Press.

Vickery, Michael. 1985. "The Reign of Sūryavarman I and Royal Factionalism at Angkor." *JSEAS* 16.2: 226–44.

Vijayanagara Sexcentenary Commemoration Volume. 1936. Dharwar: Vijayanagara Empire Sexcentenary Association.

Vogel, Claus. 1979. *Indian Lexicography.* Vol. 5, fasc. 4 of *A History of Indian Literature,* edited by Jan Gonda. Wiesbaden: Harrassowitz.

Wagoner, Philip. 1996. "'Sultan among Hindu Kings': Dress, Titles, and the Islamicization of Hindu Culture at Vijayanagara." *JAS* 55.4: 851–80.

———. 1993. *Tidings of the King: A Translation and Ethnohistorical Analysis of the Rāyavācakamu.* Honolulu: University of Hawaii Press.

Waldron, Jeremy. 1995. "Minority Cultures and the Cosmopolitan Alternative" In *The Rights of Minority Communities,* edited by W. Kymlicka. Oxford: Oxford University Press.

Wallerstein, Immanuel, et al. 1996. *Open the Social Sciences: Report of the Gulbenkian Commission on the Restructuring of the Social Sciences.* Stanford: Stanford University Press.

———. 1991. *Geopolitics and Geoculture: Essays on the Changing World-System.* Cambridge: Cambridge University Press.

Walters, Jonathan S. 2000. " Buddhist History: The Sri Lankan Pali Vamsas and Their Community." In *Querying the Medieval: Texts and the History of Practices in South Asia,* edited by Ronald Inden. New York: Oxford University Press.

———. 1993. "Lovely Lady Lanka: A Tenth-Century Depiction." *The Sri Lanka Journal of the Humanities* 19.1–2: 45–56.

Warder, A. K. 1972. *Indian Kāvya Literature.* Vol. 1: *Literary Criticism.* Delhi: Motilal Banarsidass.

Washbrook, David. 1991. "'To Each a Language of His Own': Language, Culture and Society in Colonial India." In *Language, History and Class,* edited by Penelope J. Corfield. Oxford: Blackwell.

Weber, Max. 1978. *Economy and Society.* 2 vols. Berkeley: University of California Press.

Weryho, Jan W. 1986. "The Persian Language and Shia as Nationalist Symbols: A Historical Survey." *Canadian Review of Studies in Nationalism* 13.1: 49–55.

Wezler, A. 1985. "Dharma und Deśadharma." In *Regionale Tradition in Südasien,* edited by Hermann Kulke and Dietmar Rothermund. Stuttgart: Steiner.

Wheatley, Paul. 1983. *Nāgara and Commandery: Origins of the Southeast Asian Urban Traditions.* Research Paper nos. 207–8. Chicago: University of Chicago, Department of Geography.

———. 1982. "Presidential Address: India beyond the Ganges—Desultory Reflections on the Origins of Civilization in Southeast Asia." *JAS* 42.1: 13–28.

———. 1961. *The Golden Khersonese: Studies in the Historical Geography of the Malay Peninsula before* A.D. 1500. Kuala Lumpur: University of Malaya Press.

Wheeler, Mortimer. 1954. *Rome beyond the Imperial Frontiers.* London: G. Bell and Sons.

White, Hayden. 1987. *The Content of the Form: Narrative Discourse and Historical Representation.* Baltimore: Johns Hopkins University Press.

Whittaker, C. R. 1994. *Frontiers of the Roman Empire. A Social and Economic Study.* Baltimore: Johns Hopkins University Press.

Wink, André. 1997. *Al-Hind: The Making of the Indo-Islamic World.* Vol. 2: *The Slave Kings and the Islamic Conquest, 11th–13th Centuries.* Leiden: E. J. Brill.

———. 1986. *Land and Sovereignty in India: Agrarian Society and Politics under the Eighteenth-Century Maratha Svarājya*. Cambridge: Cambridge University Press.

Witzel, Michael. 1987. "On the Localisation of Vedic Texts and Schools." In *India and the Ancient World: History, Trade and Culture before* A.D. 650. edited by G. Pollet. Leuven: Department Oriëntalistiek.

Wolff, Philippe. 1982. *Les Origines linguistiques de l'Europe occidentale*. 2d ed. Toulouse: Association des Publications de l'Université de Toulouse-le Mirail.

Wolters, O. W. 1994. "Southeast Asia as a Southeast Asian Field of Study." *Indonesia* 58 (October): 1–17.

———. 1988. *Two Essays on Dai-Viet in the Fourteenth Century*. New Haven: Council on Southeast Asia Studies, Yale Southeast Asia Studies.

———. 1982. *History, Culture, and Region in Southeast Asian Perspectives*. Singapore: Institute of Southeast Asian Studies.

———. 1979. "Khmer 'Hinduism' in the Seventh Century." In *Early South East Asia: Essays in Archaeology, History, and Historical Geography*, edited by R. B. Smith and W. Watson. New York and Kuala Lumpur: Oxford University Press.

Woolard, Kathryn A., and Bambi B. Schieffelin. 1994. "Language Ideology." *ARA* 23: 55–82.

Woolf, Greg. 2001. "Inventing Empire in Ancient Rome." In *Empires*, edited by S. Alcock et al. Cambridge: Cambridge University Press.

———. 1998. *Becoming Roman: The Origins of Provincial Civilization in Gaul*. Cambridge and New York: Cambridge University Press.

Worsley, P. J. 1991. "Mpu Tantular's Kakawin Arjunawijaya and Conceptions of Kingship in Fourteenth-Century Java." In *Variation, Transformation, and Meaning: Studies on Indonesian Literatures in Honour of A. Teeuw*, edited by J. J. Ras and S. O. Robson. Leiden: KITLV Press.

Wright, Roger. 2000. *El Trabado de Cabreros (1206): Estudio sociofilológico de una reforma ortográfica*. London: Queen Mary and Westfield College.

———. 1997. "Linguistic Standardization in the Middle Ages in the Iberian Peninsula: Advantages and Disadvantages." In *De Mot En Mot: Aspects of Medieval Linguistics: Essays in Honour of William Rothwell*, edited by Steward Gregory and David Trotter. Cardiff: University of Wales Press.

———. 1996. "Latin and Romance in the Castilian Chancery (1180–1230)." *Bulletin of Hispanic Studies* (Liverpool) 73: 115–28.

———. 1994. *Early Ibero-Romance*. Newark and Delaware: Juan de la Cuesta Monographs.

———. 1991. "The Conceptual Distinction between Latin and Romance: Invention or Evolution?" In *Latin and the Romance Languages in the Early Middle Ages*, edited by Roger Wright and Rosamund McKitterick. London: Routledge.

Wright, Roger, and Rosamund McKitterick, eds. 1991. *Latin and the Romance Languages in the Early Middle Ages*. London: Routledge.

Yashaschandra, Sitanshu. 2003. "From Hemacandra to *Hind Svarāj*: Region and Power in Gujarati Literary Culture." In *Literary Cultures in History: Reconstructions from South Asia*, edited by Sheldon Pollock. Berkeley: University of California Press.

Yazdani, G., ed. 1960. *Early History of the Deccan*. London: Oxford University Press.

Zink, Michel. 1992. *Littérature française du moyen age*. Paris: Presses universitaires de France.

Zoetmulder, P.J. 1974. *Kalangwan: A Survey of Old Javanese Literature.* The Hague: Martinus Nijhoff.

Zumthor, Paul. 1987. *La lettre et la voix: De la "littérature" médievale.* Paris: Seuile.

Zvelebil, Kamil. 1992. *Companion Studies to the History of Tamil Literature.* Leiden: E.J. Brill.

———. 1975. *Tamil Literature.* Leiden: E.J. Brill.

———. 1974. *Tamil Literature.* Vol. 10, fasc. 1 of *A History of Indian literature,* edited by Jan Gonda. Wiesbaden: Harrassowitz.

———. 1973. "The Earliest Account of the Tamil Academies." *IIJ* 16: 109–35.

INDEX

Aachen, 492
Abdul Rahman, 97–98; *Saṃdeśarāsaka*, 97
Abercrombie, Nicholas, 523n47
Abhimanyu (king), 172
Abhinavagupta (philosopher), 91n38; on *dhvani*, 218; on *kāvya* and Veda, 76; on literary languages, 93–94n47; philosophical-religious aesthetics of, 105; on *pravṛtti*, 206
Ābhīras, 70, 92
Abstandsprachen, 24n24
Accademia della Crusca, 481
accagannaḍa (pure Kannada), 374–75, 405–6
Accicaritam, 429
"Accomplishments of the Divine Augustus, The" (Roman document), 275–78
Achaemenid Persia, 59, 482, 537
adhikāra, 53, 71
ādikavi (primal poet), 296, 341–42, 435
Āditya I (Cōḷa king), 119
Ādityavarman (king), 130, 151n68
Advaitins, 430
Ælfric, *Grammatica*, 444, 471
āgama (oral tradition), 132n43, 172, 366
Agamben, Giorgio, 396n36, 472n6
āgamika (scriptural), 357
āgamika kāvya (spiritual poetry), 425
agro-literate society, 542–43, 551–53, 562
Aihoḷe inscription, 125, 157–59, 225, 243–44
Akalaṅka Deva, 433; *Karṇāṭaśabdānuśana*, 372
Akbar (Mughal emperor), 239
Akho (Gujarati poet), 320, 374n94
ākhyāyikā (dynastic prose-poem), 86, 98, 302
akṣara ("phoneme"/"syllable"), history of, 307–9
akṣaraḍambara (phonic pyrotechnics), 208, 211
alaṅkāra (figuration): Bhoja on, 109–10, 110n77, 583–84; Daṇḍin and, 212; *kāvya* and, 76; literary theory and, 89–90; *mārga* and, 212, 214
alaṅkāraśāstra (literary theory): Bhāmaha and, 90; Bhaṭṭi and, 175; dramaturgical/nondrammaturgical synthesized in, 204–5; influence of, 163; lateness of, *kāvya* and, 89–90; literary language choice in, 111–12; *praśasti* and, 135, 135n47, 137; propriety categorized in, 198–99; Rājaśekhara on, 201–4
Alcuin of York, 392, 440, 443; *De litteris colendibus*, 261; *De orthographia*, 261
Alfonso VII (king of Spain), 463
Alfonso X (king of Spain), 463–64, 490; *Cantigas*, 463
Alfred (English king), 440, 444–45, 461–62, 468, 471, 553

Allahabad Pillar Inscription: cultural elements of *rājya* in, 253; educated king topos in, 166; "historical" vs. "epic" and, 249; influence of, 144n58, 240–41, 243; as *kāvya*, 135; *mārga* in, 207–8; political goals of, 143–44; power spatialized in, 239–40
Allama Prabhu, 433–34
allegory, 360–62, 388
Almora, 175
Altekar, Anant Sadashiv, 412n69
Amara, 163–64, 171n14
Amarakośa (Sanskrit dictionary), 92, 399
Amaramālā (Javanese dictionary), 163–64, 388, 389n18
Amaru (king), 36
Āṃḍayya (poet), *Kabbigara Kāva*, 432
Amoghavarṣa (Rāṣṭrakūṭa king), 338; emigration to Karnataka, 356n56; Kannada vernacularization and, 332–33, 339; *Kavirājamārgam* and, 343; *praśasti* of, 125; *Praśnottararatnamālikā*, 338n13; religious affiliation of, 430–31
Ānandapūrṇa Vidyāsāgara, 231, 231n14, 232
Ānandavardhana (literary scholar), 175, 220; *Dhvanyāloka*, 217–18, 225n3
an-atta, 52
Anderson, Benedict: critique of, 550–51; on linguistic diversity, 503–4; on nation and politicized space, 555–56; on novel and nationalism, 544, 548–49; on print revolution and language loss, 552; on rhetorical prejudice, 543; work: *Imagined Communities*
āndhra (mixed *rīti*), 218–19
Andhra, 380–81, 453, 494
āndhras, 194, 195
Andronicus, Livius. *See* Livius Andronicus, Lucius
Angelcynn, 470, 553
Angkor dynasty: educated king topos in, 166; empire form recreated in, 252; epicizing of space in, 235; founding of, 125n23, 141–42; ideological view of, 515–16; *praśasti* poets in, 135; Sanskrit cosmopolis and, 16; Sanskrit inscriptions in, 125–27, 125n23, 148–49; vernacularization and, 294
Anglo-Latin poetry, 447
Anglo-Norman literature, 451, 452
Anglo-Saxon Chronicles, 462, 474–75, 511
Antlöv, Hans, 553n50, 564n71
anubhāva (reaction), 217
apabhraṃśa: Apabhramsha vs., 95, 95n51; communicative efficacy of, 309n46; definition of, 92; Kēśirāja on, 374–75, 375n97; Mīmāṃsā and, 102
Apabhramsha: *apabhraṃśa* vs., 95, 95n51; Bangla and, 297n26; Bhoja's taxonomy of, 108–9, 110–11, 582; as cosmopolitan language, 104; definition of, 91–92; grammar and ritual in, 46n17; grammatical/prosodical texts in, 401n45; grammaticization of, 101, 103, 401; Jainism and, 103, 113, 338; *kathāvinoda* and, 187; as *kāvya* language, 13, 26, 90, 92, 93–98, 98n56, 101, 103, 113, 287–88, 299, 424; language-naming and, 474; literary genre rules for, 98–100; naturalistic view of development of, 500; qualifications for *kāvya*, 100–104; Rājaśekhara on origins of, 203; Sanskrit vs., 13–14; as second-order code, 104–4, 105n69; vernacularization and, 395; in Viṣṇudās *Mahābhārata*, 394n28, 395
Apabhramsha literature, 178, 394n29
apabhraṣṭa language, 46n17, 100–101, 300n29, 308–9
Apel, Karl-Otto, 472n6
Appadurai, Arjun, 10n17
Appayya Dīkṣita, 51n30, 401n47
Arabic language, 432n106
Arabs, 192, 489–91; literary culture of, 463, 469, 491
Archpoet, 461
Ardhamagadhi (Jain canonic language), 44n15, 55, 94, 108n74
ardhasama meter, 130
Arikēsari II, 356, 359–62, 555
arisamāsa (compound of hostiles), 366–67
aristocracy, European: literacy and, 448; nationalism and, 551n46; vernacular polities and, 465
Arjunamiśra (commentator), 230n12, 231, 233n16
ārṣa (sages' usage), 52n31, 107, 170, 269, 581
arthamātra (narrative), 208
Arthaśāstra, 201, 246–47, 249
ārya (meter), 52, 157
Āryas (Sanskrit speech community), 40

Āryaśūra, *Jātakamālā*, 361n67
Āryāvarta, 58, 70n60, 191
Asaga: *Karṇāṭakumārasaṃbhavam*, 426n96; *Vardhamānacarita*, 59, 338n13, 426n96
Aśmaka dynasty, 211
Aśoka (Maurya overlord): Allahabad Pillar Inscription and, 239; Greek translations of, 265; influence on inscriptional discourse, 59–60, 537; Persian influence on, 59, 537; Prakrit edicts of, 59–60, 68, 101, 537; Prakrit edicts of, dissemination of, 237–38, 238n22; supposed hostility to Sanskrit, 61
Assamese language, 304, 391, 396, 400
Assamese literature, 428
Asser, 462
Aṣṭādhyāyī (Pāṇini): later competing grammars and, 170, 180, 182; regional variation in, 66n54; sacral vs. nonsacral language in, 45–47, 268–69
Aśvaghoṣa, 59, 70, 77, 277
atiśayokti (hyperbole), 142
Aubigné, Théodore Agrippa d', 459
aucitya (propriety), 76, 111, 198–99
Aucityavicāracarcā (Kṣemendra), 105n69
Auerbach, Erich, 266–67, 438
Augsburg, Religious Peace of (1555), 480
Augustine (saint), 272; *Soliloquies*, 444
Augustus (Roman emperor), 275–78
Ausbau (elaboration), 24n24
autochthony, 34, 388n17, 525, 527. *See also* indigenism
autpattika, 47, 52, 53, 140, 307
Avadhi, 553
Avanti, 108, 113, 218, 219
āvantika (Avanti style), 218, 219
Avantivarman (king), 175
avaskandha ("pastoral" genre), 98
Axial Age, 483, 483n26
Ayodhyā, 60, 155, 155n80, 157, 280
Ayres, Alyssa, 507n13
Ayutthaya literary culture, 132, 164, 205, 280
Ayyana (king), 154
Ayyavoḷe, Five Hundred Masters of the, 485

Bacon, Francis, *Advancement of Learning*, 472
Bādāmi Cāḷukya dynasty: influence on Southeast Asia, 125; inscriptional discourse and lineage narrative of, 120, 144–45, 149–53; Kalyāṇa Cāḷukyas and, 154, 156–59, 159n89, 411; Kannada inscriptions in, 288, 331–32; Kannada/Sanskrit ratios in, 332n3; Kannada use of, 355; power of, spatialized, 243–44; *praśasti* and, 125; Śaka-era dating and, 123–24
Bādari (scholar), 41, 41n3
Bāhubali Gōmateśvara colossus (Śravaṇabeḷgoḷa), 289
Bakhtin, Mikhail, 472n7; chronotope of, 226, 555; on epic distance, 32, 547; epic/novel contrasted by, 544, 547–48, 547n40, 549–50; on hierachized temporaltiy, 554; on language choice, 504; on Latin/Greek relationship, 263–64; Latin/vernacular dichotomy and, 460; on secondary language, 113; on unified langugage, 23
Baḷarāmadāsa, 304, 396
Balassi, Bálint, "In Praise of Frontierlands," 450
Bali, 163
Ballāla, *Bhojaprabandha*, 184
Bāṇa, 77; influence of, 146; *Kavirājamārgam* and, 339; Khmer study of, 162; on *mārga*, 211; *śleṣa* and, 139–40, 146; vernacular adaptations of, 434; works: *Harṣacarita*, 85n28, 139, 208, 255; *Kādambarī*, 232, 434
Bangla language, 297n26, 399–400
Bangla literary culture: cosmopolitan verse experiments in, 396; genre restrictions in, 302; literization/literarization asynchrony in, 292, 391; Muslim patronage in, 493n45; regional vernacularization in, 479; vernacular textualization in, 304, 312–13
Banniard, Michel, 446n12
Bārhaspatyasūtra, 195, 246–47, 247n40
Barton, John, *Donat françois*, 448
Basava, 433
Battle of Brunanburh, 475
Bede the Venerable (saint), 453; *Historia ecclesiastica gentis Anglorum*, 441
Bengal, 228, 232, 559
Bengali, 405
Benjamin, Walter, 36, 258, 508
Benveniste, Emile, 164
Beowulf, 441, 444
Bhagavadgītā, 307–8, 311, 382
Bhāgavatapurāṇa, 310–11, 312, 351n44, 382, 424, 479
Bhaktamālā (hagiography collection), 436

Bhaktapur, 297
bhakti (devotionalism): poems, 383; regional vernacularization and, 435–36; Sanskrit and, 424; Southeast Asian rulers and, 531; vernacularization and, 428–29
Bhālāṇ, 434
Bhāmaha: *alaṅkāraśāstra* and, 89–91; Bhoja and, 109; criticism of, 212n43; influence of, 343, 344–46, 344n27; *Kavirājamārgam* and, 345–46, 347; *kāvya* language and, 90, 99, 114; on *mārga*, 209, 211–12, 212n43, 218, 349; philology and, 171n14; on regional Ways, 213; works: *Kāvyālaṅkāra*, 89–90, 163, 343, 344–46; *Prākṛtaprakāśa* commentary, 56n36
Bhandarkar, R. G., 88–89, 89n35
Bharata, 93–94, 209n38. See also *Nāṭyaśāstra*
Bhāratakhaṇḍa, 17, 247
Bhāratam (Pampa). See *Vikramārjunavijayam*
Bhāratavarṣa: epic narratives of, 560; first use of, 238; *kāvya* localized in, 222; language-naming in, 510; literary science localized in, 204; recreation of, 236n20, 536; regional idioms of, 299, 299n27; Sanskrit geocultural matrix and, 191, 192–96, 199–200; Southeast Asian epic linkages to, 234–36; vernacular polities and, 419
Bhārata war, 335
Bhāratayuddha, 389
Bhārateśvara Bāhubali Ghor, 99, 285–86, 293, 391, 428
Bharatiya Janata Party (Indian People's Party), 575
Bhāravi, 162, 163n1, 339
Bhartṛhari (philosopher), 82, 83, 172, 316n59
Bhartṛmeṇṭha, 81
bhāṣā (speech): *chandaḥ* vs., 46, 54n33, 66, 107, 268–69; definition of, 46, 46n19; ethnicity and, 509–10; nationalism and, 297n26
bhāṣācitra (polyglot genre), 303
bhāṣākāvya, 99–100
Bhāsa plays, 81
bhāṣāśabda (*deśī* words), 401
Bhatia, Tej K., 400n42
Bhaṭṭa Nāyaka, 105
Bhaṭṭa Tauta, 105
Bhaṭṭi, 162–63, 174, 175; *Bhaṭṭikāvya*, 389
Bhaṭṭoji Dīkṣita, 168, 175, 400
bhāva, 95, 188
Bhavabhūti, *Mahāvīracarita*, 213
Bhavavarman II (Champa overlord), 242
Bhīma (Gujarati king), 180, 180n29
Bhīṣmācārya, *Pañcavārttika*, 400n42
Bhoja (Gurjara Pratīhāra overlord), 140–41
Bhoja (king), 14, 76, 83n22, 87, 87n32; on *alaṅkāra*, 109–10, 583–84; on *anubhāva*, 217; conservatism of, 105–6; cosmography of, 194–95, 195n14; court of, 109n75, 134, 179, 245–46; cultural hagiography of, 184; emulation of, 179, 181, 182; grammatical/political relationship and, 177–78, 179–80, 180n29; influence of, 218; inscriptions of, 178; Jain language choices and, 108n74; on literary languages, 91, 93n45, 107–14, 304; literary taxonomy of, 105, 106–7, 106n71; looting of library of, 180–81, 181n31; on *mārga/rīti*, 208–9n36, 218, 219; as poet, 178–79; regionalization in, 219; on religion and literature, 429–30; as ruler, 178, 178n26; significance of, 105–6; works: *Bhuvanakośa*, 194–95, 203; *Samarāṅgaṇasūtradhāra*, 194–95, 195n14; *Sarasvatīkaṇṭhābharaṇa*, 105, 109–14, 180, 181, 583–84. See also *Śṛṅgāraprakāśa*
Bhojaśālā (Dhāra), 177, 181
bhujaṅgavijṛmbhita meter, 69n58
Bhutabhasha. *See* Paishachi
Bilhaṇa (Kashmiri poet), 179, 220, 256, 268, 337; *Vikramāṅkadevacarita*, 183n33, 302–3
bilingualism, 264, 446n12
Bilpaṅk, 252; epigraph, 136, 144–46, 181, 584–88
Bīrbal (Mughal courtier), 239
al-Bīrūnī (Uzbek polymath), 196, 249
Black Death, 484
Bloch, Jules, 99n58, 285n3
Bloomfield, Leonard, 164
Boccaccio, Giovanni, 451
Boethius, *Consolation*, 444
Bond, Gerald A., 442n6
Bopp, Franz, 164, 546
Borobodur shrine (Java), 235, 388n17
Bourdieu, Pierre, 52, 522n45
bourgeoisie, 545, 546–47, 561–62
Bowen, John, 533n17

Brahmadevarāṇe, 324, 381
Brahman (caste), 41; Buddhism and, 57–58; grammar vs. ritual and, 46; Jainism and, 426, 426n95; Kannada vernacularization and, 333; Khmer importation of, 127–28; language choices of, 113; legitimation theory and, 516–17; origins of, 202; regional vernacularization and, 434; Sanskrit monopolization by, 98; spatialization of, 194, 556; Tamil political regionality and, 414; vernacularization and, 310–12, 424
brāhmaṇa, 107, 164, 581
Brahmanism: Buddhism vs., 515–16; "resurgence of," 74, 74n69; Sanskrit and, 28–29, 118; vernacularization as rebellion against, 423. See also *vaidika* culture
Brahmaśiva, *Samayaparīkṣe*, 432n106
Brahmi script, 59, 273, 290, 291
Brajbhasha: *bhakti* and, 424, 435; as cosmopolitan vernacular, 471; cosmopolitan-vernacular experiments in, 396n34; Keśavdās and, 314n56, 396n34, 409, 409n64; language-naming and, 400, 474; literary beginnings in, 314n56; *rīti* and, 409, 409n64
Bṛhaspati (sage), 246
Bṛhatkathā: Bhoja and, 93n45; Kashmiri version of, 97n55; origins of, 96–97; Paishachi and, 92–93, 96–97; Sanskrit adaptations of, 104, 166
Brinkhaus, Horst, 293n19
Brough, John, 54n33
Bruges (Belgium), 484
bubonic plague, 484
Buddha, 54–55, 54n33, 100, 140
Buddhāditya (poet), 128n30
Buddhaghosa, 58
Buddhajīva of Kashmir, 54n33
buddhi (mood), 217
Buddhism: Brahman converts in, 58; Brahmanism vs., 515–16; ideology and, 519; *Kātantra* and, 170; language as social convention in, 503n7; language choices of, 55–56, 65, 92, 100, 423–24; literacy and, 82n19; literary language in, 98n56; Pali and, 386; patronage of, 431, 431n105; philology and, 171; Prakrit and, 117, 118; precosmopolitan Sanskrit and, 40–41; Sanskrit geocultural matrix and, 235; Sanskritized, 126, 513; Sanskrit rejected by, 51–56, 61, 502; Sanskrit use of, 56–59, 66, 72–73, 100, 101, 113, 513; *vaidika* cultural order transvalued by, 51–56, 52n31; vernacularization and, 383, 486
Buddhist Hybrid Sanskrit, 56, 66, 486
Buddhist literature: *kāvya*, 424; Kuṣāṇa patronage of, 277; languages used for, 100, 103, 486; mercantile nature of, 486; palm-leaf fragments of, 86
buddhyārambhānubhāva, 217n50
Bühler, Georg, 79n11, 181n32
Bundeli language, 474
Bundelkhand, 448
Burma, 123, 228, 386
Byzantium, 251n46, 270n22, 440, 529n8

Cædmon, 441, 453
Caitanya (theologian/mystic), 436, 479; *Caitanyacaritāmṛta*, 312–13, 396
Cakradhara, 382–83
cakravartikṣetra (imperial field), 248, 360
Cakrāyudha (Kānyakubja ruler), 141
Cāḷukyas: Ayodhyā linked to, 155n80, 157; inscriptional discourse and lineage narrative of, 149–61, 151n68; name variants of, 149, 149n64; Old Kannada and, 348n36; political/cultural domain of, 416–17; Śaka era and, 150n66. *See also* Bādāmi Cāḷukya; Caulukyas of Gujarat; Kalyāṇa Cāḷukya; Veṅgi Cāḷukya *dynasties*
Cāḷukya Vikrama era (1075–76), 150n66
Cambodia: disappearance of vernacular texts in, 296–97; epicizing of space in, 234–35; *Mahābhārata* manuscripts in, 229; Pali cosmopolitan formation in, 386; Sanskrit inscriptions in, 25, 123, 124n21, 125–30, 125n23, 147, 148–49, 531; Sanskrit linguistic influence in, 478; Sanskrit literary influence in, 163; trade and vernacularization in, 486. *See also* Angkor dynasty; Khmer *entries*
Cambridge Ancient History, 264n8
Cambridge History of Southeast Asia, 516
Camões, Luis de, *Lusíades*, 469, 554
campū (prose-verse narrative): influence of, in Southeast Asia, 124; *Jātakamālā* as, 361n67; *kakawin* and, 389; in Karnataka, 124, 124n20; Viṣṇudās *Mahābhārata* and, 394–95; as written *kāvya*, 86

Cāmuṇḍarāja (king), 145, 289
Cāmunṇḍarāya (Gaṅga minister), 426n95
Caṇḍa, 102n61
Caṇḍidāsa, 304
Candragomin, 170, 172
Candragupta (Maurya king), 68
Candragupta II (Gupta king), 242–43, 250
caṅkam (literary academy), 291, 383–84, 384n6, 386n10
caṅkam literature, 500
capitalism: cosmopolitanism/vernacularism dichotomy and, 579; European vernacularization and, 465–66; legitimation theory and, 517–18, 519–21; nation-state and, 251; novel and, 549; premodern empire form compared to, 251–52; print-capitalism, 548, 549, 552, 558, 562; vernacularization and, 577; Western culture-power ideology and, 33–36, 565
Cardona, George, 45–46n17, 81n15
Carolingian Europe, 261–62, 392, 439–40, 445, 573
caryā (song genre), 301–2
caryāpadas, 297n26
Casparis, J. G. de, 326n76
Cassiodorus, 267
caste system: Buddhism and, 519; ethnicity narrative and, 510, 514n25; ideology and, 519; precosmopolitan Sanskrit and, 40–44; Sanskritization and, 514; vernacularization and, 502
Castile, 441, 452, 461, 462–64, 469
Castilian language, 449–50, 463–64, 471, 481n23, 489, 490
Castilian literary culture, 538, 573
Catalonia, 469
Catholic Church, 392n24; Latin monopolized by, 28–29; literary culture controlled by, 439–40, 442–43, 477–78; multilingualism and, 476–77
Caturmukha, 103
Caulukyas of Gujarat (dynasty), 144–46, 174, 180–81, 416–17
Cēkkiḻār, *Periyapurāṇam*, 511
Celtic languages, 271, 272
Cēntaṉ (Pāṇṭiya king), 322, 384
Champa: educated king topos in, 166; empire form recreated in, 252; epicizing of space in, 235; Sanskrit cosmopolis and, 14, 115; Sanskrit inscriptions in, 137–38; Sinicization vs. Sanskriticization in, 259–60; traditional divisions of, 235n19
chandaḥ (verse): *bhāṣā* vs., 46, 54n33, 66, 107, 268–69; kingliness and expertise in, 188
chanson de geste, 297n26, 441, 448, 449, 490
Chanson de Roland (attr. Turold), 448, 449, 469
Charlemagne: Alcuin and, 261, 443; European vernacularization and, 439–40, 462; "Europe" used in conjunction with, 492; Islam and, 489, 490, 492; and Latin, spoken vs. written, 261; as learned king, 267
Charles V (French king), 477, 480–81
Chattopadhyaya, Brajadulal, 417n79
chāyā (Sanskrit translation), 104–5, 105n69
China: as civilizational nation, 562n68; global trade/commerce and, 484; peripheral vernacularization and, 259–60, 486–87; Sanskrit cosmopolis and, 236; Sanskrit literary influence in, 163, 205, 535
Chinese language, 21, 128, 128n33
Ch'in Shih Huang-ti, 535
Chomsky, Noam, 164
Chrétien de Troyes, 465
Christianization, 10. *See also* Catholic Church
chronotopes, 226, 397, 555, 557, 573
Chulalongkorn (Siamese king), 556
Cicero, Marcus Tullius, 266, 277–78
Cid, Poema de mio, 449–50, 452, 463, 469, 490–91
Cilappatikāram, 386n10, 429
citra (brilliance), 326
Cittapa (*praśasti* poet), 134
civilizationalism: civilizations as processes and, 538–39; current impact of, 533–34, 533–34n18; Heidegger and, 546; Southeast Asian transculturation process and, 528–32, 535–38; Western power-culture ideology and, 9–10, 34–36, 525–28
Clausen, W. V., 263n7
Coedès, George, 296, 529–30
coins, Prakrit vs. Sanskrit on, 74n70
Cōḻa dynasty: Cāḷukya lineage narratives and, 160–61; contradictory scholarship on, 411–12, 411n68; cosmopolitan miniaturization and, 236n20; influence of, in Java, 127; length of rule, 411; political

regionality in, 413–14; political space in, 553; Śaiva influence in, 479–80; Tamil virtuosity and, 523; vernacularization in, 291–92, 323, 383–84
Coleridge, Samuel Taylor, "To William Wordsworth," 319
Colish, Marcia, 461n35
Collins, Steven, 54n33
colonialism: beginnings and, 285; civilizationalism and, 529–30; cosmopolitanism/vernacularism dichotomy and, 578; India as "prepolitical" before, 6, 285; language ideology before, 308; nationalism and, 541, 551n46; power-culture practices and, 35
Comparative Civilizations Project (University of Chicago), 533–34n18
copperplate inscriptions: Bādāmi Cāḷukya, 150–51, 151n68, 153; of Bhoja, 178; Gupta, 250; Javanese, 130–31; Kannada, 332n4; Kauthem plates, 156–59, 159n90; manuscript copies of, 159n90; Marathi, 289n8; political significance of, 14, 59–60, 257; Prakrit, 63–64, 64n49, 117–18; Sanskrit, 156–59, 166, 257; Tamil, 120–22; vernacular polities and, 413
Córdoba (Spain), 449n19, 489, 491
Coromandel coast, 484
cosmography, 194–95, 195n14
cosmology, 192, 193
cosmopolitanism, 10–11; European vs. Sanskrit vernacularization and, 30; *kāvya* language qualifications and, 101; literary analysis and, 90; literary beginnings and, 286–87; spheres of influence of, 236–37; vernacular anxiety and, 452–60; vernacularization and, 451–52; vernacular literature and, 6–7
cosmopolitanism/vernacularism dichotomy: current impact of, 567–68; as either/or choice, 35, 574–79; research methods, 568–70; resolution of, 579–80; theoretical problems of, 19–20
cosmopolitan vernacular, 343; Dante on, 456; definition of, 26, 322; *deśabhāṣā* and, 322–29; displacement of, 29; epoch of (*rītikāl*), 409; European vernacularization and, 466–67, 573–74; European vs. South Asian, 470–71, 481–82; in India, south vs. north, 390–95; Kannada as, 368; *Kavirājamārgam* and, 26–27, 357–58, 362, 364–65; Latin vs. Sanskrit as, 260–61; regional vernacularization vs., 432–36, 432n106; in South Asia, 380–87; in Southeast Asia, 387–90; Tamil political regionality and, 414–15; vernacular anxiety and, 456
courtly culture: European vernacularization and, 460–67; grammar envy in, 177–84; grammatical/political correctness and, 162–76; literature and kingliness in, 184–88; vernacularization and, 410, 430, 573–74. *See also* grammatical/political correctness; kings/kingliness; *specific dynasty*; *specific king*
court patronage, 231n14; cultural/political significance of, 231–33; empire form and, 256; epic space and, 232–33; grammatical/political correctness and, 15, 167–68, 175–76; literature and, 184; Muslims and, 493n45; religion and, 431, 431n105, 480; script-mercantilism and, 558; significance of, 523; vernacularization and, 337, 380–81, 384
Crusades, 447, 465, 490
cuius regio, eius religio, 480
cultural naturalism, 34, 438, 497–505, 527
culture, definition of, 2
culturism, 33
Curtius, E. R., 438, 452
Cūṭu dynasty, 102, 150

Dadda II (Gurjara overlord), 150n66
Dādū, 435
Dai-Viet, 259–60
Dakani language, 474
Dakshinatya Prakrit, 55–56, 56n36
dakṣiṇa, 52n31, 63
Damsteegt, Th., 72n66
Dānārṇava (Cāḷukya king), 160
dance theory, 199–200, 407–8, 407n62
Daṇḍin: commentaries on, 348n37, 351n42; dissemination/influence of, 163, 205, 344n27; grammatical/political relationship and, 175; hierarchy of styles in, 216; *Kavirājamārgam* and, 341, 345–46, 347; on language as speech, 82, 83; on literary languages, 90–93, 113; on *mārga*, 209–10, 211, 211n41, 212, 218, 349; on *svabhāvokti*, 349n39; works: *Avantisundarī*, 152. See also *Kāvyādarśa*
Dani, A. H., 274n29

Dante Alighieri, 460; cultural/political boundaries in, 553; Florentine literary beginnings and, 297; language and identity in, 505; Latin superposition and, 328; Occitan literary culture and, 448; works: *Il Convivio*, 455–56, 457, 473; *De monarchia*, 464; *De vulgari eloquentia*, 342, 451, 454–55, 457, 464
Darwin, Charles, 497, 500
Daśarūpaka, 407n62
Dāūd, 304, 393; *Candāyan*, 393n27, 429, 493
Deccan: Apabhramsha use in, 103, 108; Cāḷukya inscriptions in, 149–50, 160–61; epic vernacularization in, 362, 389; European vernacularization compared with, 468–69; influence of Daṇḍin in, 163, 214, 344; literary genre rules in, 302; philological history in, 364; regional vernacularization in, 408–9, 478–79; Sātavāhanas and, 62; *śleṣa* masters in, 146; trade and vernacularization in, 484; *vaidarbha* in, 211; vernacularization in, 173, 214, 356–57; vernacular *kāvya* in, 537; vernacular polity in, 417
Delhi Sultanate, 487, 491, 493
deśabhāṣā (languages of Place): Abhinavagupta on, 93–94n47; Bharata on, 93; ethnicity narrative and, 510; first *kāvya* in, 292; genre restrictions on, 93, 299–302; grammar and, 366; language-naming and, 474; literarization of, 309–10, 391; literary exclusion of, 187, 298–304; literary production in, 99; literization of, 309; *mārga* and, 214; mimetic usages of, 96; naturalistic view of development of, 500; political texts in, 413, 427–28n98; Sanskrit geocultural matrix and, 199–200, 299, 299n27; Sanskrit interaction with, 118, 133n44, 272–74; Sanskrit metrics and, 370–71; Uddyotanasūri on, 96, 96n53
deśadharma, 405
Desai, P. B., 412n69
Deśawarṇana, 127–28n30, 389–90, 390n21
Descartes, René, *Discours de la méthode*, 472
dēsi (local lexeme), 368–69, 374–75
deśī (practice of Place): cosmopolitanism and, 22; European vs. Sanskrit vernacularization and, 472; in Kannada literature, 350–51; language-naming and, 474; *mārga* vs., 12, 208, 221, 357–58, 359, 405–10, 407n62; Prakrit and, 108; regional vernacularization and, 433, 436, 573; Sanskrit geocultural matrix and, 199; Sanskrit philology and, 401–5; *vacana*s and, 433; vernacular philology and, 397, 405–10; vernacular polities and, 420n84
deśīśāstra, 102–3n64
Devabodha, 230n12; *Jñānadīpikā*, 230, 231
Devanagari, 229, 273
Devānīka (Cham ruler), 137–38
Devapāla, 244
dhamma, 51
Dhanadeva (king), 60, 252
Dhanapāla (Jain poet/lexicographer), 87n32, 178; *Tilakamañjarī*, 87, 425
Dhārā (Mālava capital), 177, 178, 178n26, 181
dharma, 40–41; Buddhist redefinition of, 51–52; *deśī* and, 405; as sacrifice, 51n30, 140; Sanskrit texts, 66; *vaidika* liturgy, preservation of, 71
Dharmadāsa, 169n9
Dharmapada, 100
Dharmapāla, 244
dharmaśāstra, 270
Ḍheḍa (caste), 434
dhvani (suggestion), 76, 217–18
dialects, 65n52
dictionaries: European vernacular, 450; Javanese/Sanskrit, 388–89n18; Kannada, 368–69, 370; memorization of, 82; Prakrit/Apabramsha, 101; Sanskrit, 82, 92, 399; vernacular, 402–5, 405n56, 416
diganta rājya, 31, 279–80
digvijaya (conquest of the quarters), 115, 240–41
Diskalkar, D. B., 134–35n45
Dohākośa (Buddhist anthology), 103
domination, 35–36
Donatus, 448
doṣa, 90, 188, 344
Doughty, Charles, 432n106
Drāviḍa, 218
Dravidian languages, 443, 472, 479n17
dṛśyakāvya (drama), 84
Du Bellay, Joachim, 439, 458–59n31, 460, 573; *La deffence et illustration de la langue francoyse*, 457–59, 466–67

Dumont, Louis, 431n105
Ḍūṅgendra Siṃha, 394, 394n29
Durgasiṃha (Cāḷukya poet), 340–41, 342, 469; *Karṇāṭakapañcatantram*, 340
Durlabharāja (king), 145
Durvinīta (Gaṅga king), 104, 166, 339
Dvivedi, Hariharanivas, 292n17

East Asian literary cultures, 486–87
Eaton, Richard, 488n38
economism, 33
ecumenicism, 98–99, 113
Edgerton, Franklin, 54n33
Ehavala Śantamūla (king), 117
Einhard (biographer), 462
Eknāth (Brahman poet-scholar), 310–12, 502
Eliot, George, 18
Eḷuttacchan, *Rāmāyaṇa* adaptation of, 559
Emeneau, Murray, 65n52
empire/empire form: cultural repertory of, 253–56; displacement of, 413; early Indian, 250–51; *imperium romanum* vs. Sanskrit cosmopolis, 267, 274–80, 571–72; intellectual, 6; material repertory of, 251–53; medieval political orders as, 420n85; politicization and, 31; Sanskrit communicative capacity and, 254–56; Sanskrit geocultural matrix and, 237–59; spatialization of, 242–46; vernacular polities vs., 420–21; vernacular recreations of, 480
empiricism, 198
Encina, Juan del, 297
Engels, Friedrich, 521n43, 546
England: Danish invasions of, 440, 444; Latin pronunciation in, 392; Roman spatialization in, 275, 280, 556
England, Anglo-Norman: French grammaticization in, 464–65; French literary beginnings in, 297, 447–48, 451, 573; Latin primacy in, 452; literary emulation in, 451, 573; women and vernacularization in, 461
English language: grammaticization of, 471; Latin texts translated into, 445, 445n11; naturalness and, 318, 319, 319n66; Old English, 391, 447
English literary culture: cosmopolitan order and, 391, 468–69; emulation and, 449, 451, 494; ethnic fictions in, 474; French grammaticization and, 448; Islam and, 490; Latin influence on, 444–45, 472, 478n14; literacy and, 440, 444; Norman conquest and, 447; South Asian vernaculars compared with, 468–69; vernacular anxiety and, 453, 459–60; vernacular polities and, 461, 461–62, 464–65
Ennius, 264, 271, 298, 537; *Annales*, 266
epic, 547n40; community and, 547; as national stories, 544–47, 545n33, 554–58; novel vs., 544, 547–50, 561–62; vernacularization of, 395–97, 469. See also *Mahābhārata* entries; *Rāmāyaṇa* entries; *specific epic*
epic discourse, 32
epic distance, 547–48
epicization, 235, 542, 555
epic space: Bakhtin on, 547–48; European vs. Sanskrit vernacularization and, 470; nationalism and, 556–58; in Pampa *Mahābhārata*, 359–63; production of, 226–28; reproduction of, 228–37, 557; Sanskrit geocultural matrix and, 226–37; in Sanskrit inscriptions, 242–46, 249–50; in Southeast Asia, 234–36
Erlangga, 536n22
Estoria de Espanna, 463
ethnicity: European ethnic fictions, 474–75, 510–11, 526; European vs. Sanskrit vernacularization and, 474–76, 509–11; in Marathi literary culture, 511n21; theoretical problems of, 564; Western power-culture ideology and, 34
ethnicization, 514n25
ethnonationalism, 575
eulogies, 368n82
Eurasia: empire form in, 237; Sanskrit cosmopolis and, 257; transculturation in, 269–70, 551; vernacularization in, 551–52
Eurasia, European/South Asian interaction in: global trade/commerce, 484–87; Islam and, 488–94; nomadic empires and, 487–88; significance of, 30, 482–84
Europe: first use of term, 492; Latin as cosmopolitan language in, 254, 261–62; linguism in, 508; literacy in, 82–83; literary beginnings in, 286, 296–97n24, 297; modernity and cultural history of, 285; paper revolution in, 440; South Asian polities and, 412–13

Europe, vernacularization of: anxiety provoked by, 451, 452–60, 470; Catholic Church and, 439–40; classicization in, 459; competition in, 475; as defiance, 452; emulation in, 448–52, 573; epic space in, 470; epic vernacularization, 396; ethnic fictions in, 474–75, 510–11, 526; features of, 438–39, 450; gender and, 461, 461n35; global trade/commerce and, 484, 485, 494; grammaticization and, 460, 471–73; historiographical problems of, 450–51, 460–61; indigenism and, 526–28; Islam and, 488–91; language-naming and, 474; language/power linkage in, 480–81; Latin and, 444–45, 445n11, 448, 451–52; Latin-near vs. Latin-distant, 391–92; literacy and, 439–48, 469–70; literary beginnings in, 440–48; as literary-cultural process, understudy of, 437–38, 438n2; multilingualism and, 476–77, 508; naturalness and, 319; nomadic empires and, 487; orality and, 440–42; orthography in, 443, 443n7; pace of, 451, 469, 573; political motivations of, 460–67; political space and, 479, 479n17; problems of, 440; religion and, 477–78, 480, 480n18; Romance vs. Germanic languages, 443–50; significance of, 19. *See also* vernacularization, European vs. South Asian
evolutionism, 497–505, 498n2, 527

Farīd-bāṇī, 429
feudalism, 460–61
Fichte, Johann Gottlieb, 526
Filliozat, Jean, 512n24
Five Hundred Masters of the Ayyavoḷe, 485
Florentine language/literature, 297, 391, 573. *See also* Italian language; Italian literary culture
Forster, E. M., 562
Fortunio, Gian Francesco, *Regole*, 471
Foucher, Alfred, 529
Four Gospels, 450
Fracchia, Joseph, 503n6
France, 446n12
François I (French king), 182, 457, 466–67, 481, 552, 573
Frauwallner, E., 81n15
French language, 21, 392; grammaticization of, 448, 465; naturalistic view of development of, 500; in Norman England, 464–65; Old French, 446, 447; right to record in, 509
French literary culture: Anglo-Saxon influence on, 538; beginnings of, 297, 298, 452, 573; classicization in, 459; dialect and, 448n16; ethnic fictions in, 474; Islam and, 493; language/power linkage in, 480–81, 480–81n21; Latin influence on, 451, 472, 489; multilingualism in, 477; in Norman England, 464–65; orality vs. literacy in, 442, 442n6; vernacular anxiety in, 457–59, 470; vernacularization of, 446–49; vernacular polities in, 461, 465–67. *See also* Occitan literary culture
French Revolution, 508
Funan, 235n19
Funan records, 123n19
functionalism, 511–16, 522

Gadāyuddham (Ranna). See *Sāhasabhīmavijayam*
gadyakāvya, 68, 120
Gajapatis, 411
Galicia, 272
Gandhāra, 14, 265
Gandhari language, 55, 56n38, 57, 94n47, 100
Gaṅga dynasty, 160n94, 335–36, 348n36, 378
Gaṅgā River, 16, 246, 257
Gāṅgeya (Varanasi king), 180n29
Gaspardone, Emile, 124n21
gāthā, 98, 102, 302
gati, 110
Gaudi (Prakrit dialect), 91, 101
gauḍīya (northern style): Ānandavardhana on, 217–18; Bhāmaha on, 211–12; Bhoja on, 210–11; definition of, 209–10; Kannada and, 348n37; in *Kavirājamārgam*, 346–51; Kuntaka on, 215–16; Magadhi mapped against, 221; Ratnaśrījñāna on, 214; in Sanskrit literature, 220; Vāmana on, 213. See also *mārga*
Gaul, 271
Gautamī Bālaśrī, 238
Geertz, Clifford, 14, 258, 506–7
Gellner, Ernest, 542–43, 545, 551–53, 552n47, 556, 557; *Nations and Nationalism*, 542

General Estoria, 463
geography, Sanskrit, 189–200
Gerini, G. E., 235n19
Germanic epics, 440, 555
Germanic languages, 391, 443–44, 472
Germanic tribes, 489
German language, 500, 509
Germany, 451, 452, 469, 545n33
Geste du roi, La (song cycle), 490
Ghaznavids, 254, 393, 411, 488
Ghorids, 488
Ghronṇa (poet), 43, 312
Giddens, Anthony, 8, 522–23
Gide, André, 575–76
gīta (song), 300
globalization: civilizationalism and, 534; contemporary, 1, 10, 10n17, 251, 534, 567–68, 575; language loss caused by, 567–68; during vernacular millennium, 484–87, 494
Goa, 559
Goliards, 461, 472
Gombrich, Richard, 82n19
Gopāladeva (Pāla founder), 140
Gopālarājavaṃśāvali, 293n19
Gopendra, 209n36
Gordon, Stewart, 511n21
Goswamis, 436
Govinda III (Rāṣṭrakūṭa king), 125, 253
Govinda IV (Rāṣṭrakūṭa king), 176
grammar(s): cosmopolitan, 189; dissemination of, 189; European vernacular, 448; European vs. Sanskrit vernacularization and, 471–73; Kannada, 371–77; literacy and, 82; order of, as moral/social/political prototype, 183; Pali, 386n14; possession of, as prestige, 177–84; power-culture relationship and, 15, 27, 144; Prakrit, 101–3; Prakrit vs. Sanskrit and, 66n53; as *praśasti*, 173–74; precosmopolitan Sanskrit and, 39, 44–49, 45–46n17; purpose of, 47, 47n20; Śiva and, 176n22; sociality preserved by, 177–78; standardization of, 101–3; vernacular, 364n73, 381, 384–85; vernacular norms of, 366–67. *See also specific language*
grammatica, 439
grammatical/political correctness: educated king topos and, 166–67; empire form and, 255–56; historical linkage of, 168–76; implications of, 183–84; *kāvya* and, 162–64; Latin vs. Sanskrit, 267; patronage and, 167–68, 175–76; prestige associated with, 15, 177–84; in Sanskrit cosmopolis, 165, 184
Gramsci, Antonio, 527; on hegemony, 520–21; on Latin/vernacular opposition, 438, 460, 472; on linguistic innovations, 329; on nationalism and literary culture, 505, 541–42, 576; on particular vs. universal, 575–76; on rhetorical prejudice, 543; on textual dissemination, 549
grāmyabhāṣā, 99–100
Grandes chroniques de France, 465, 474, 511
Grantha script, 289
granthastha, 82
Greek language: European ethnic fictions regarding, 474; influence of, 88–89, 268n16, 458; Latin vs., 21, 260–61, 263–64, 270n22; as prototype, 65n51; Sanskrit texts translated into, 265; vernacular literization and, 440
Greek literary culture, 263–64, 265, 297
Greek philosophy, 53–54
Greeks: cosmopolitan space and, 236–37; Roman cultural debt to, 266; South Asia as categorized by, 192; South Asian interaction with, 265
Greenfield, Liah, 551n46
Green, Peter, 265n10
Gregoire, Abbé, 477
Gregory I (pope), *Pastoral Care*, 444
Gregory of Tours, 489
Gros, François, 385n8
Guha, Ranajit, 521, 521n42
Guha, Sumit, 511n21
Gujarat, 29, 228, 253, 484; Caulukyas of, 144–46, 174, 180–81, 416–17
Gujarati language: literization of, 391; Old Gujarati, 99, 326; standardization of, 552; vernacularization and, 292–93, 301, 400; vernacular polities and, 417
Gujarati literary culture: beginnings of, 285–86, 296; genre innovations in, 297; Islam and, 494; literary genres and, 285–86; literization in, 391; popular intelligibility and, 426; regional vernacularization in, 434–35; religion and, 428–29; vernacularization of, 326–27, 443
Gujarat-Rajasthan, 326–27
Gumbrecht, Hans-Ulrich, 24n25

guṇa (expression-form), 90, 188; Daṇḍin on, 211n41; *Kavirājamārgam* and, 344; *mārga* and, 207n32, 210; Rājaśekhara on origins of, 202–3; *rīti* and, 209n36
Guṇāḍhya, 93n45, 97
Guṇavarman, 124n21, 342, 361n67, 368n82; *Harivaṃśapurāṇam,* 426n96; *Śudrakam,* 426n96
Gupta dynasty: empire form in, 250–51, 252, 279, 280; power of, spatialized, 239, 243; *praśasti* poets in, 135; Śakas defeated by, 150–51; Sanskrit commercialized in, 74n70; Sanskrit cosmopolitan style and, 139; Sanskrit inscriptions in, 68; scholarship lacking on, 411
Gurjara Pratīhāra dynasty, 140–41, 150n66, 244–45
Gwalior, 393–94, 394n29
Gwaliyari language, 394, 394n28, 474
Gwaliyari literary culture: beginnings of, 394–95, 448; cosmopolitan verse experiments in, 396; *praśasti* in, 135–36; public inscriptions lacking in, 292; vernacular textualization in, 304, 394–95

Habermas, Jürgen, 8
Habinek, Thomas, 264n8
Hadrian's Wall (Great Britain), 275, 280, 556
Hāla, *Sattasaī,* 102–3n64
Halāyudha, 370n87; *Kavirahasya,* 173–74, 370; *Piṅgalasūtra,* 164
Halmiḍi inscriptions, 331–32, 332n2, 428
Halotti Beszéd, 451
Hangchow (China), 484
Hariṣeṇa (Gupta *praśasti* poet), 135
Harivaṃśa, 231
Harivara Vipra, *Jaiminibhārata,* 396
Harivṛddha, 102n61
Harṣavardhana (Kānyakubja king), 139
Harvey, David, 527
Hathigumpha cave inscription, 238
Hayagarva (Brahman poet), *Gadyarāja,* 382, 382n3, 396
Heersterman, Jan, 431n105
Hegel, G. W. F.: epic as national story in, 540–41, 544–47, 545n33; epicization and, 555; global reach of cultural analysis of, 548; novel as bourgeois epic in, 561–62; work: *Lectures on Aesthetics,* 544–45, 546;
Heidegger, Martin, 3, 57, 209, 545–46, 576; "Building Dwelling Thinking," 526–27; "Memorial Address," 527–28
Heine, Heinrich, 11n18
Heliand, 451, 477
Hellenization, 10
Hemacandra (Jain scholar): on Ardhamagadhi as original language, 44n15; on *deśī,* 401–5; grammar of, 181–82, 181n31, 189, 588–90; poetic self-explanations of, 87n33; vernacular *mahākāvya* recognized by, 99–100; works: *Deśīnāmamālā,* 402–5; *Dvyāśrayakāvya,* 174–75; *Kāvyānuśāsana,* 44n15, 181n31; *Siddhahemacandraśabdānuśāsana,* 181, 182, 189, 199, 401–2, 558
Hemādri, *Caturvargacintāmaṇi,* 190–91n3
Henry I (French king), 298, 448
Herder, Johann Gottfried von, 476, 505, 526
Hindavi, 304, 392–93, 429, 493
Hindi, 400n42, 500, 507
"Hindu," first use of, 492
Hinduism, 393, 393n27, 423, 488, 536, 575. *See also specific sect*
Hindutva (Hindu radicalism), 575
Hinüber, Oskar von, 93n45
Hitopadeśa, 293n19
Hock, Hans, 501–2
Holy Roman Empire, 261–62, 342, 464, 480
Homer, 297, 328; *Iliad,* 225; *Odyssey,* 225, 263
Horace, 268, 277, 456
Howlett, David, 447
Hoysaḷa dynasty: inscriptional discourse and lineage narrative of, 159n90, 523; Kannada grammaticization in, 27, 377–78; length of rule, 411; political/cultural domain of, 417–19; religion and politics in, 431; Sanskrit displaced in, 288–89, 336
Hoysaḷanāḍu, 419
Hundred Years' War, 465
Hungarian literary culture, 450, 451, 461, 491
Huntington, Samuel, 533, 534
hyperglossia, 50, 118, 127, 262, 432–33

Iberia, 271, 451
Iceland, 440, 471
ideology, 9, 33–34, 512, 514–16, 518–22
Ikṣvāku dynasty, 102, 116–17, 155n80

ilakkaṇam/ilakkiyam binary, 385, 385n8
Iḷampūraṇar, 386n10
Île-de-France, 465, 552
illiteratus, 82
imagination, political, 6–7, 18
immigration, 67, 79, 264–65, 277
imperialism. *See* empire/empire form
imperium romanum, 267, 274–80, 571–72
imperium sine fine, 31
India: anomalies of, 579–80; as civilizational nation, 562–63; communicative media in, 558; cosmopolitan vs. regional vernacularization in, 432–36; current cosmopolitanism/vernacularism dichotomy in, 575; "imaginary institution" of, 359; imperial model of, 482; Indianization of, 236, 512, 536; "linguistic provinces" reorganization of, 506–7, 507n13; names of, 192–93; nationalism in, 540, 562–63, 575; Persian linguistic influence in, 512n23; polities in, 523–24; "prepolitical," 6, 411; vernacularization in, northern vs. southern, 390–96, 471; Westernization and, 538
Indianization, 528–32, 535–38
Indian National Congress, 506–7
indigenism: civilizationalism and, 525–26, 532–33; cosmopolitan order and, 113; definition of, 525; discourse of, 533n17; nationalism and, 525–26, 539–40; theoretical problems of, 75; vernacular literary beginnings and, 75. *See also* civilizationalism; nationalism
indigenization, 435, 486
Indo-Aryan languages, 443, 472
Indo-Greeks. *See* Yavanas
Indonesia, 123
Indo-Scythians. *See* Śaka dynasty
Indrarāja III (Rāṣṭrakūṭa king), 134
industrialization, 543, 552, 562
inscriptional discourse, Sanskrit: features of, 130, 142; historical self-understanding in, 160–61; *kāvya* vs. *praśasti*, 134–37; in Khmer country, 125–30; legitimation theory and, 523; political goals of, 143–46; pragmatics of, 144, 148–61; *praśasti* genre and, 137–41; rhetoric of power in, 141–43; semantics of, 134–48; significance of, 147–48; workly vs. documentary aspects of, 146–47. See also *praśasti*
inscriptions: Khmer, 127n27; language choice for, 66–67, 98n56; origins of, 89; Prakrit, 101, 102, 116–20, 116n3, 238; Romanization and, 262; Sanskrit/regional division of labor in, 117–22, 117n7, 126–27; vernacular, 291n12. *See also* copperplate inscriptions
inscriptions, Sanskrit: criticism of, 147; as cultural-political decision, 500; early lack of, 59–62, 73, 79–80, 79n11; expressive/performative functions of, 147; Greek translations of, 265; immigrant influence on, 67–73, 72n66, 277; in Java, 130–32, 132n43, 294; in Khmer country, 125–30, 127n27, 531; political-cultural significance of, 147–48; political goals of, 148–49; public display of, 537; in Southeast Asia, 123–32, 148–49; trans-regional power projected in, 238–41
intellectual imperialism, 6
internationality, 577–78
Ireland, 392, 468
Iṟivabeḍaṅga Satyāśraya, 154, 155, 160, 357, 555
Islam: as agro-literate sphere, 553; European vernacularization and, 30, 440, 488–91; South Asian vernacularization and, 30, 392–93, 393n27, 429, 429n102, 488–89, 491–94
Islamic literary culture, 449n19
Islamization, 10, 514
Italian language, 392, 392n24, 471, 500
Italian literary culture: beginnings of, 451, 454, 471–72; language/power linkage in, 481, 481n22; Latin popularity in, 461; script vernaculars in, 469; vernacular anxiety in, 454–56; vernacular polities in, 464
Italy: Latin and language loss in, 271–72; Latin communicative competence in, 443, 478; nationalism and literary culture in, 541
itihāsa, 76, 224
Iṭṭage inscription, 432–33

Jaffrelot, Christophe, 514n25
Jagannātha (literary scholar), 175
Jahāngīr (Mughal emperor), 239
Jaimini, *Mīmāṃsāsūtra*, 40–41, 51
Jainism: Apabhramsha and, 103, 113, 338; Ardhamagadhi as sacred language in, 44n15; Bhoja and, 108n74; Brahman

Jainism *(continued)*
converts in, 58, 426, 426n95; Kannada literary culture and, 424–28, 426n96; language choices of, 65, 108n74, 424, 502, 513; literary language in, 98; *Nītivākyāmṛta* and, 422; philology and, 171; political impact of, 430–31; Prakrit defined in, 91n38; Rāṣṭrakūṭa court and, 338; Sanskrit rejected by, 55–56, 58–59; Sanskrit translations in, 105n69; *tadbhava* as viewed in, 108n73; vernacularization and, 289, 383, 424–25
Jai Singh II (Jaipur king), 233n16
Janabāī (Maharashtri poet), 307, 309
janapada (people-place), 352–54
Janna (Hoysaḷa court poet), 341, 368n82, 372n91; *Anantanāthapurāṇam*, 340
Jaṭācoḷa Bhīma, 160
jāti, 110, 111, 130, 211n40
Jasvant Siṃh, *Bhāṣābhūṣaṇ*, 471
Java: civilizationalism and Indianization of, 530, 532; educated king topos in, 166; epicizing of space in, 234–35; historical geography in, 235n18; *kāvya* status in, 135n47; *Mahābhārata* manuscripts in, 229; Sanskrit inscriptions in, 123, 124n22, 125, 130–32, 132n43, 294; Sanskrit linguistic influence in, 14; Sanskrit literary influence in, 127, 127–28n30, 162–64; trade and vernacularization in, 486n34; vernacularization in, 163, 294, 294n21, 325–26, 387–90
Javanese language, 387–88, 388–89n18, 512, 512n23
Javanese literary culture: beginnings of, 294, 294n21, 388; *bhakti* and, 429; literary territorialization in, 389–90; *Mahābhārata*'s influence on, 234; regional vernacularization in, 435; Sanskrit superposed on, 325–26, 326n76, 388–90; vernacularization of, 396, 426
Jayabandhu (Kannada prose writer), 339
Jayadeva, *Candrāloka*, 471
Jayadeva, *Gītagovinda*, 472
Jaya Indravarman I (Champa king), 166
Jayakīrti, *Chandonuśāsana*, 370
Jayānta Bhaṭṭa, 285, 285n3
jayapatra (edicts), 130
Jayāpīḍa (Kashmiri king), 171, 172, 173, 175, 183
Jayapratāpamalla, 293, 327–28
Jāyasenāpati, *Nṛttaratnāvali*, 407
Jayasiṃha Siddharāja (Caulukya king), 87n33; grammar envy of, 180–81; grammatical/political correctness and, 15, 174; literary textualization at court of, 134; political practices of, 252, 253; *praśasti* of, 144, 145, 174, 584–88; Sanskrit cosmopolis and, 182; script-mercantilism and, 558; spatialization of power and, 189
Jāyasī, *Padmāvat*, 493
Jayavarman charter (Tamilnadu), 64n49
Jayavarman VII (Khmer king), 127, 252n48
Jinasena II (Jain writer), 84; *Ādipurāṇa*, 207, 338, 338n13
Jinavallabha (Kannada poet), 356n57
Jīva Gosvāmin, 313
Jñāndev. See Jñāneśvar.
Jñāneśvar, 297, 311; *Jñāneśvarī*, 382
Joyce, James, *Ulysses*, 554
Junāgaṛh (Gujarat), Ashokan edicts at, 101
Junāgaṛh inscription, 67–70; as first *praśasti*, 68, 220; influence of, 120; *mārga* and, 220; power spatialized in, 239
jyotirliṅga, 192, 192n7

Kabīr, 393, 435, 435n111, 470
Kadamba dynasty: Bādāmi Cāḷukya lineage narrative and, 150–51; Kannada literized in, 288, 331–32, 332n2; Prakrit inscriptions in, 102, 116; *praśasti* as *kāvya* in, 135
Kaḍiri, 164
kāḍu, 478–79n16
kakasatriya, 390
kakawin: *bhakti* and, 429; definition of, 389; displacement of, 435; Javanese vernacularization and, 163; literary territorialization in, 389–90; *Mahābhārata* as model for, 162–63, 234; as political allegory, 390; Sanskrit and, 388–89, 396, 532, 536; Viṣṇudās *Mahābhārata* and, 394–95
kāku (intonation), 85
Kālacūris, 151n68
Kalhaṇa, *Rājataraṅgiṇī*, 171–73, 172n16, 225n3, 241–42, 511
Kali Age, 71, 145, 227
Kālidāsa: ancestry of, 194n11; Apabhramsha songs in, 92; as embodiment of *vaidarbha* literature, 220; influence of, 162, 163n1;

influences on, 240–41; *Kavirājamārgam* and, 339; *kāvya* textuality in, 86; as rootless, 576; works: *Raghuvaṃśa*, 240–42, 255, 266, 274, 279–80, 389, 536n22; *Śākuntala*, 213
Kalila wa Dimna, 469
Kaliyuga dating system, 225n3
Kalyāṇa Cāḷukya dynasty: Bādāmi Cāḷukya lineage narrative and, 145, 150, 154, 156–59, 411; inscriptional discourse and lineage narrative of, 14–15, 144–45, 154–61, 159n90, 523; inscriptions of, 153; Kannada inscriptions in, 332, 337n10; Kannada use of, 109, 332n3; length of rule, 411; *Mānasollāsa* composed during, 184–85; political/cultural domain of, 416–17; Sanskrit displaced in, 288, 332, 332n3; Sanskrit lineage narratives and, 337; vernacularization and, 155–56; war with Paramāras, 178
Kāmasūtra, 197–98, 197n17, 201, 221
kamma, 52
Kampaṉ, 85n28, 384, 536; *Rāmāyaṇa* adaptation of, 559
Kāñcīpuram, 153, 279, 290
kanda meter, 333n5
Kaniṣka (Kuṣāṇa king), 70, 169
Kannaḍabhāṣābhuṣaṇam, 26n26
Kannada language, 160; Cāḷukya records in, 149, 154, 156; cosmopolitanization of, 187; court patronage and, 523; Daṇḍin readapted in, 163; dictionaries, 368–69; inscriptions in, 330, 330n1, 421n86, 428; literary restrictions and, 301, 345–46; localization of, 99, 354, 432–33; and *Mānasollāsa*, 187; Medieval Kannada, 432–33; naturalistic view of development of, 500, 501; Old Kannada, 20, 348n36, 426, 432–33; "old Kannada," 339–40; as Prakrit, 374, 374n94; pure (*accagannaḍa*), 374–75, 405–6; Sanskrit vs., 375–76; standardization of, 342, 376–78, 471, 552; *tadbhava/ apabhraṃśa* words in, 374–75, 375n97; Telugu and, 415–16; textuality of, 331; transregionality of, 20–21; vernacularization and, 288–89; vernacular polities and, 415–17
Kannada literary culture: *ādikavi* in, 341–42; Apabhramsha as *kāvya* language in, 109; beginnings of, 286, 296, 338–42, 355–56; *campū*, 124n20, 361n67; ethnic fictions absent in, 475; Jainism and, 424–28, 426n96; Kannada political project lacking in, 421; *kāvya*, 289, 337; localization of, 352–56; *mārga* and, 347–48, 350–51; origins of, 424–25, 471–72; *praśasti*, 156, 334–35, 337; register synthesis in, 303; Sanskrit models for, 343–51, 396; *vacana*s, 433–34, 479; Virashaivism and, 436
Kannaḍanāḍu, 27, 560
Kannada philology: cultural/political goals of, 368; grammar in, 364, 371–77; *Kavirājamārgam* and, 363–66, 363–67, 371–72; lexicon in, 364, 368–69; literarization and, 378–79; prosody in, 364, 369–71; Sanskrit philological influence on, 367–68, 370–76, 449; standardization and, 377–78; vocabulary in, 374–75
Kannada-Telugu script, 159n89
Kannada, vernacularization of: beginnings of, 331; cosmopolitan, 368, 434; as defiance, 470; emulation in, 494; epic, 396, 559; European vernacularization compared with, 443, 469, 471; features of, 336–38; inscriptional discourse and, 176n22; Islam and, 491, 493; literacy and, 307–9; literarization, 26–27, 332–36, 355–56, 378–79; literization, 23, 331–32, 332n2; literization/literarization asynchrony, 331, 336, 378; pace of, 443; regional, 432–34, 436, 478–79; Sanskrit displacement and, 288–89
kaṇṭhastha, 82
Kānyakubja, 104, 141, 492
kāppiyam, 385
Karashima, Noboru, 411n68, 412n70
kārika, 215
Karimnagar Inscription, 356n57
karma, Buddhist redefinition of, 52
Karṇadeva (king), 145
Karnataka, premodern: Bādāmi Cāḷukya records in, 123–24, 145; *campū* in, 124, 124n20; cosmopolitan vernacularization in, 348; epigraphical history in, 330–31, 337; grammatical/political correctness in, 176; Hoysaḷas in, 417–18; Jain Brahmans in, 58, 426; Kadambas in, 116, 135; Kalyāṇa Cāḷukyas in, 144–45; Kannada use in, 109, 288–89, 523; kingliness in, 15; *laukika* genre in, 357; map,

Karnataka, premodern (*continued*) xix; metrics in, 370; multilingualism in, 509; Old Kannada as prestige dialect in, 20; Prakrit use in, 116; *praśasti* in, 135; Rāṣṭrakūṭas in, 176; regional vernacularization in, 328, 432–34, 475, 486; religious movements in, 430–32, 436; royal lineage narratives in, 144–45, 149–53; Sanskrit epic space localized in, 363; Sanskrit transregional power in, 238, 241–42, 243, 253; trade and vernacularization in, 485, 486; Tulu language in, 290; *vaidarbha* in, 209–10; vernacularization in, 29, 185, 445, 513; vernacular *kāvya* in, 109; vernacular polities in, 417–18, 421–22, 421n86; Vijayanagara empire in, 337. *See also* Kannada *entries*

Karṇāṭakapañcatantram, 426

Kashmir, 81; influence on Sanskrit literary theory, 105–6; literary science in, 201n14; *Mahābhārata* manuscripts in, 228, 559; Sanskrit cosmopolis and, 115, 133n44; Sanskrit translations in, 105n69; vernacularization in, 216–17, 492

Kāśikā, 169

Kātantra (Śarvavarman), 62n48; dating of, 170, 171n14; as divine inspiration, 97; educated king topos and study of, 166; grammatical/political relationship and, 169–70, 182; name variants of, 97, 97n54; significance of, 62; South Indian study of, 171, 171n13; structure of, Kēśirāja and, 373; as vernacular model, 471

kathāvinoda (entertainment of storytelling), 185, 187, 188

Kathmandu Valley, 115

Katti-Arasa, 150

Kātyāyana (grammarian), 47, 385, 385n8

Kauṇḍa Bhaṭṭa, 175, 400

Kauṇḍinya, 124n22

Kauthem plates, 156–57n83, 156–59, 159n90

Kauṭilya, 274

kavi (Vedic seer), 75

Kavibhūṣan, 175

Kavikarṇapūra, 102–3

kavipraśaṃsā (eulogy of past poets), 340–41

Kavirājamārgam (attr. Śrīvijaya), 330; authorship of, 343; cosmopolitan vernacular ideal of, 26–27, 357, 471; Daṇḍin readapted in, 163; Dante compared to, 342, 455; geography of styles in, 350; grammar in, 364, 365–66, 371–72; Kannada literary beginnings in, 339–42; Kannada literary culture localized in, 352–56; Kannada vernacularization and, 378–79; lexicon in, 364; literary models cited in, 338–39; *mārga* in, 346–51, 408; Pampa's reworking of, 357–58, 362, 367; past poets listed in, 340–41, 341nn19–n20, 366; philologization in, 363–67; prosody in, 364; purpose of, 338, 342; religion and, 426–27; Sanskrit models for, 343–51, 344n27; sociopolitical location of, 342–43, 371

Kaviraj, Sudipta, 423

Kavīśvara (Kannada poet), 339

kāvya: Bhoja's correctness in, 179; Bhoja's taxonomy of, 106–7, 582; binary theory of, 84; critical lexicon of, 205; definition of, 3–5, 90, 365; diffusion of, 16; empire form and, 256; example of, 582; first, 45; first vernacular, 292; grammatical/political correctness and, 162–64; immigrant influence on, 69, 69n58; intention in, 106; invention of, and Sanksrit cosmopolis, 13–14; invention of, Latin literary beginnings vs., 264–65; lack of, in Sanskrit, 62; lateness of, 89; *latinitas* and, 572; literacy and, 81–82, 83–84, 86–88, 86n30; literarization and, 25; literary beginnings and, 286; literary theory and, 89–90; localization of, 222; *Mahābhārata* as, 224; *Mānasollāsa* on, 185–88; manuscript culture and, 498; memorization of, 87–88; metrical structures in, 69n58; oral performance of, 84–86, 87–88, 87n33; origins of, 75–81, 88–89, 94, 202–4, 591–96; power-culture relationship and, 31, 39, 185–88; *praśasti* and, 114, 134–37, 148; professional reciters of, 85n28; qualifications for, 92; *rājya* and, 6, 18; Sanskrit cosmopolis and, 162–63, 257; *śāstra* vs., 3, 76; Veda and, 75–77; vernacular, 99–100, 109, 289, 292–93, 337, 389; vernacularization and, 27, 298–304, 385. See also *kāvya* language

Kāvyādarśa (Daṇḍin): commentaries on, 214, 344, 422; dissemination/influence of, 163, 343–44, 449; literary language

restrictions in, 90–91; on Sanskrit as sacred language, 44; Vedic background of, 171; vernacular adaptations of, 398–99, 399n40
kāvyadeva (deity of literature), 185
kāvya language: Bhoja's taxonomy of, 107–14; choice of, 111–12, 476, 504–5; cosmopolitanism and, 101, 103–4; definitions of, 90–93; *deśabhāṣā* and, 99–100; language-genre rules, 98–99, 99n58; ordering of, 104–5, 112–13; qualifications for, 100–105; religious affiliation and, 98–99, 424; restrictions on, 93–94n47, 94–98, 98n56, 108–9, 110–14, 112n81, 129, 269, 287–88, 298–304, 345–46; uniformity of, 220–22
Kāvyamīmāṃsā (Rājaśekhara): on literature, origins of, 201–4, 591–96; on oral performance, 85; Sanskrit geocultural matrix in, 193–94; spatialization of power in, 247
Kāvyapuruṣa (Poetry Man), 202–4, 210, 221
kāvyaśakti (literary talent), 320
kawi (Javanese genre), 388
Kedāra Bhaṭṭa, *Vṛttaratnākara*, 164
Kenney, E. J., 263n7
Kerala, 228, 232, 414, 469, 484, 559
Kern, H., 123–24
Keśavdās (poet), 314n56, 396n34, 409, 409n64
Kēśirāja (grammarian), 341, 375n97. See also *Śabdamaṇidarpaṇam*
Kētana, *Āndhrabhāṣābhūṣaṇamu*, 398
Khaljīs, 411, 487, 488
Khāravela (king), 79n11, 238, 417
Khmer country: civilizationalism and Indianization of, 530–32; epicizing of space in, 234–35; inscriptional discourse in, 125–30, 141–42; prevernacular universalist polity in, 420; Sanskrit cosmopolis and, 270, 515; Sanskrit inscriptions in, 147; Sanskrit linguistic influence in, 273; Sanskrit literature studied in, 162; vernacularization in, 294, 294n20
Khmer language: inscriptions in, 126–27, 127n27, 129; Sanskrit interaction with, 126–27, 127n27, 128, 142–43, 531
Khmer literary culture: beginnings of, 296–97; late development of, 129; literarization in, 25, 294n20; *Mahābhārata*'s influence on, 234; Sanskrit *praśasti* in, 132, 135, 138; vernacularization of, 502
Khotanese language, 100
Ḳhusrau, Amīr, 493
kidung (Javanese indigenous genre), 435
Kielhorn, Franz, 163n1, 169n9
kings/kingliness: divine status of, Roman vs. Sanskrit, 278–79, 278–79n41; educated king topos and, 166, 255–56, 267; grammar patronage and, 171–76; grammatical expertise as sign of, 173; legitimation theory and, 522–23; literature and, 15, 184–88, 232–33; royal biography and, 152; Sanskrit superposition in vernacular literature and, 322–23; in Southeast Asia, 531; uprooting/restoration of, 253; vernacularization and, 380, 384. *See also* courtly culture; court patronage; *specific dynasty*; *king*
Kirātas, 194
Kīrtivarman I (Cāḷukya king), 158
Kīrtivarman II (Cāḷukya king), 153, 155n79
Kloss, Heinz, 24n24
Kodagu language, 476
Konkani language, 20–21, 290, 446, 476
Korea, 487, 551
Koūhala, *Līlāvaī*, 402–3
Kroeber, Alfred, 529, 533n18
Kṛṣṇadāsa, 313, 314
Kṛṣṇadēvarāya (Vijayanagara king), 502; *Āmuktamālyadā*, 314–15, 422
Kṛṣṇa III (Rāṣṭrakūṭa king): death of, 370n87; Halāyudha on, 173–74; Kannada literary-cultural region and, 355; *praśasti* of, 333–35; religious affiliation of, 431; Sanskrit displaced during reign of, 332, 335; scholars/poets at court of, 214, 344, 422
Kṣemendra, 105n69; *Bṛhatkathāmañjarī*, 97
Kshatriya (caste), 41, 194, 202, 390
Kṣīrasvāmin (grammarian), 172
Kulacandra (king), 180n29
Kulaśekhara, *Mukundamālā*, 424
Kulke, Hermann, 420nn84–85, 484n29
Kulottuṅga Rājendra, 160
Kulottuṅga III (Cōḻa king), 176
Kumāradāsa, *Jānakīharaṇa*, 386n13
Kumāralāta (grammarian), 169, 170–71, 171n14
Kumārapāla (Gujarati king), 134, 174, 431
Kumārasambhava, 211n40
Kumāravyāsa, 363–64n72, 408n63; *Bhārata*, 306; *Karṇāṭabhāratakathāmañjarī*, 363, 559

Kumārī, 194
Kumārila Bhaṭṭa: Buddhist scriptural languages criticized by, 55–56, 92, 183; on learning the Veda, 500; Veda as transcendant in, 55–56, 56n36, 183; vernacular as corrupt in, 308–9
Kuntaka, 207n32, 218; *Vakroktijīvita*, 215–17, 350n40
Kūntaḷadeśa, 355
Kurkyāl Inscription, 356n57
Kurukṣetra, Battle of, 225n3
Kuṣāṇa dynasty: breakup of, 94n47; Buddhist language choices and, 499, 513; grammar/power relationship in, 169; Guptas and, 252; influence on Sanskrit reinvention, 67, 89; Prakrit inscriptions in, 116; Sanskrit Buddhist culture patronized by, 72–73, 277; Sanskrit cosmopolis and, 122; Sanskrit inscriptions in, 70; Sanskrit language use of, 69–70, 101
Kymlicka, Will, 577, 578

Lakoff, George, 531
lakṣaṇa (norms), 376, 385
Lakṣmadeva (Mālava king), 242
Lakṣmīśa, *Jaiminibhāratam*, 363
Lalitāditya Muktāpīḍa, 241–42
Lamotte, Etienne, 57
language change: intentionality in, 503–5, 503n6; naturalistic view of, 500–503
language choice: Bhoja's taxonomy and, 111, 116; ethnicity and, 564; functionalist view of, 512–13; intentionality in, 504–5; religion and, 55, 116–17, 423–24; Sanskrit vs. Prakrit, 64–66, 73–74, 116, 119; vernacularization and, 302
language loss, 567–68. *See also* multilingualism
Laos: Pali cosmopolitan formation in, 386; Sanskrit epic space in, 234, 235; Sanskrit inscriptions in, 123, 130, 137–38
Lati (Prakrit dialect), 91, 101
Latin cosmopolitan order, 236–37
Latinisms, 459
latinitas (Latinness), Sanskrit vs., 1, 19; comparative analysis and, 259–60, 280; cosmopolitanism, 571–72; language ideologies, 260–62; literary culture, 262–69; political order, 274–80; religion and, 572; transculturation processes, 269–74; vernacularization, 328, 391–92, 392n24, 572–74
Latin language: Arab conquests and, 489–90; Catholic monopolization of, 28–29, 477–78; as conquest language, 571; as cosmopolitan language, 254, 260–62, 267–68; as diglossic, 262; as first standardized language, 65n51; French and, 21; grammatical correctness in, 267, 268n16; Greek as challenge to, 21, 260–61, 263–64, 270n22; Greek influence on, 268n16, 458; historicism/localization of, 266–67; influence on literature, 262–63; interaction with local languages, 19, 261–62, 270, 271–72, 271n24, 472; linguistic cleansing of, 432n106; literacy in, 439, 442–43; multilingualism and, 272, 508; popularity of, 460–61, 478n14; pronunciation of, 392; Roman script, 273; spatial lexicon of, 479n17; spoken vs. written, 261; as superposed model, 328; vernacular anxiety and, 453; vernacularization and, 391–92, 392n24, 438, 444–45, 451–52; vernacular literization and, 440; as vernacular model, 448, 471; vernacular origins of, 20
Latin literary culture: beginnings of, 260, 262–64, 263n7, 264n8, 286, 297, 298, 447–48; decline of, 489, 492; emulation in, 449n19; epic vernacularization in, 396; influence of, 472; influence of non-Romans on, 537–38; *kāvya* origins vs., 264–65; literacy and, 263n7; manuscript culture and, 498; northward shift of, 492; political goals of, 266, 279–80; vernacularization and, 462, 508–9, 573
lāṭīya (southern Gujarat style), 210–11, 218
laukika (this-worldly): Bhoja on, 581; cosmopolitan vernacular and, 407, 479; *deśī* vs., 407; in Kannada literature, 357; *kāvya* as, 13; Prakrit used for, 72; precosmopolitan Sanskrit and, 46–49, 49n24; religion and, 407, 479; *saeculare* and, 571; Sanskrit used for, 74
laukika kāvya (this-worldly poetry), 425–28
Leach, Edmund, 515
Lefort, Claude, 520
legitimation/legitimacy, 9; Bourdieu on, 522n45; inapplicability of, to premodern South Asia, 516–24; Sanskrit cosmopolis and, 18; Western power-culture ideology and, 31–32, 512

Leon, 462, 491
Lévi, Sylvain, 69n58, 79n11, 80, 89
Levtzion, Nehemia, 429n102
Lewontin, R. C., 503n6
lexicons. *See* dictionaries
Leys d'amors, 465
Licchavi dynasty, 294
Lieberman, Victor, 486n34
Liebich, Bruno, 169n9
Līlātilaka, 409n66
lineage areas, 417, 417n79
linguism, 34, 506–9
linguistic diversity. *See* multilingualism
literacy, 267; Buddhism and, 82n19; European vernacularization and, 439–48; European vs. Sanskrit vernacularization and, 29, 469; first South Asian writing system, 59; *kāvya* and, 4–5, 81–82, 83–84, 86n30; Latin literature and, 263n7; Latin vs. Sanskrit literatures, 262; literary beginnings and, 287; orality vs., 4, 304–7; popular, 190; in Roman Empire, 262, 267; in South Asian local languages, 272; vernacular, 307
literae, 31
literarization: definition of, 5; Latin and, 261; literary beginnings and, 298; naturalistic view of, 499; Sanskrit literary-language exclusions and, 288; vernacularization process and, 23, 25–26, 283–84, 287, 295; vernacular polities and, 469–70
literary culture: definition of, 2; industrialization and, 552; nationalism and, 541–44, 543n32; vernacularization and, 23–25, 329
literary language. See *kāvya* language
literature, 31
Literaturfähigkeit, 439, 440n4
literization: definition of, 4; literarization vs., 5; literary beginnings and, 298, 305; naturalistic view of, 499; Sanskrit literary-language exclusions and, 288; of vernacular epics, 315–16; vernacularization process and, 23–25, 132, 283–84, 287, 295
litterae, 439
litteratus, 82, 83
Livius Andronicus, Lucius, 263, 264, 297, 298, 328, 537
local languages: Latin interaction with, 261–62, 270, 271–72, 271n24; Sanskrit interaction with, 115, 117–19, 126–27, 128–30, 142–43, 262, 272–74. *See also specific language*
Lōkapāla (Kannada poet), 339
Lokaprakāśa, 133n44
Lombard, Denys, 530, 532, 536–37
Louis XII (French king), 272
Ludden, David, 488n38
Lüders, Heinrich, 169, 170, 171
Luhmann, Niklas, 8, 498–501
Lukács, Georg, 544, 547, 549–50, 554
Lusignan, Serge, 480–81n21
Luther, Martin, 477; *Theses*, 450

Macaulay, Thomas Babington, 579
Madanapāla (Bengali king), 232
Mādhava Kandalī, 304, 424, 435; *Mahābhārata* adaptation of, 396, 428
Mādhva, 431, 436
Madhva, 430, 436
Madhyadeshiya, 327n77, 400, 443
māgadha (Maghada style), 218
Magadhi language: Ashokan edicts in, 101; in Bhoja's literary language taxonomy, 108; as Buddhist scriptural language, 55–56; grammaticization of, 56n36; literary restrictions and, 94, 95, 101, 112–13; Sanskrit geocultural matrix and, 221
Māgha, 339
Magyars, 489–90
Mahābhārata (attr. Vyāsa): commentaries on, 230n12, 231; conceptual space of, 237; dissemination of, 162, 232, 233–36, 233n16, 242, 558–60; editions of, 229–33; emulation of, 252; epic geosphere in, 226–37, 359–63, 394–95, 396n35; epic reiteration in, 554–55; epic vs. novel and, 554–55; Gwaliyari version of, 306; historicity of, 335; *kāvya* derived from, 80n14; literary genre of, 224–25; manuscript culture and, 316–17; manuscripts of, 228–30; as national story, 546; oral performance of, 86, 232–33; origins of, 224; patronage and, 231–33, 231n14; political narrative of, 225–28; power-culture relationship in, 17–18, 27; professional reciters of, 85, 85n28; Pune critical-edition project, 230, 558–59; puranic texts in, 193; purpose of, 554;

Mahābhārata (attr. Vyāsa) *(continued)*
regional scripts used for, 229–30; South Asian geography according to, 195; Southeast Asian space epicized by, 234–36; spatiality in, 223–24, 226–28; vernacularization and, 229
Mahābhārata, vernacular adaptations of: allegory in, 360–61; *bhakti* and, 429; cultural homogeneity in, 405; epic reiteration of, 554–55; Gwaliyari, 394–95, 394n28; Javanese, 388; Kannada, 358–62, 363, 381; literary-cultural emulation and, 469; Sanskrit epic world regionalized in, 396–97; Tamil, 384; Telugu, 398, 429. See also *Vikramārjunavijayam*
Mahābhārata war, 71
Mahābhāṣya (Patañjali): on corrupt language, 183; dating of, 168–69; educated king topos and study of, 166; grammar in, 47n20; grammatical/political relationship and, 168–69; literary works rarely cited in, 365n74; orality in, 83, 172; on regional Ways, 208n35; on Sanskrit as sacred language, 46–48; Sanskrit *kāvya* cited in, 80, 80–81n15; self-identification in, 169, 169n9; *vārttika* in, 385n8
Mahākāla temple (Ujjayinī), 177
mahākāvya (courtly epic), 70, 86, 98, 99–100, 302–3
Mahākūṭa Pillar Inscription, 158n86
Mahalingam, T. V., 119n10
Mahānubhāvas (religious community), 382–83, 429
Maharashtra: cosmopolitan miniaturization in, 236n20; Islam and vernacularization in, 493; *Mahābhārata* manuscripts in, 228; Marathi ungrammaticized in, 400; pilgrimage circuits and, 382–83; vernacular anxiety in, 453; vernacularization in, 289–90
Maharashtri Prakrit: Bhoja's taxonomy and, 108; grammaticization of, 101–2; Jain language choices and, 108n74; as *kāvya* language, 91, 95, 96, 113, 287–88; literary genre rules for, 302; Sanskrit geocultural matrix and, 221
Mahārthamañjarī, 108n74
Mahāvaṃsa, 387
Mahāvīra (Jain founder), 55, 59, 424
Mahāyāna Buddhism, 82n19, 431
Mahendrapāla of Kānyakubja (Pratīhāra emperor), 201
Mahīpati (Marathi biographer), 310–12
Mahīśāsaka Vinaya, 54n33
Mahmud of Ghazni, 493
Mahmūd Shāh II (Malwa king), 327n77
Maithili language, 294, 297n26
Maithili literature, 286, 391
Majapahit court (Java), 127, 127–28n30, 130
Majumdar, R. C., 529
Mālava, 178
Malayalam: civilizationalism and origins of, 500; *Līlātilaka* and, 409n66; *Mahābhārata* adaptations in, 229, 405; religion and vernacularization of, 429; script, 290n10
Malay language, 512n24
Malaysia, 123
Malla dynasty, 232, 293
Mallarmé, Stéphane, 508
Mallikārjuna, Cidānanda, 372n92, 418
Mallison, Françoise, 435n111
Mammaṭa, *Kāvyaprakāśa*, 365
Mānasāraśilpaśāstra, 265, 537
Mānasollāsa (Someśvara III): *deśabhāṣā* usage in, 25–26, 427–28n98; on kingliness and literature, 15, 184–88; religion and vernacularization in, 427; vernacularization and, 187–88, 300–304, 315, 391
Manchu dynasty, 535
Mandasor Inscription, 144nn58–59
Mandelstam, Osip, 442
Maṅgaleśa (Cāḷukya king), 155, 158, 158nn86–87, 232–33, 332, 332n2
Maṅgarāja, *Abhinavābhidhānam*, 369
Maṅikkuṟavaṉ, 315n57
maṇipravāla, 323, 366, 398, 409
Maṅkha (Kashmiri poet/lexicographer), 87; *Śrīkaṇṭhacarita*, 84–85
Mannheim, Karl, 519
mantra, 106–7, 581
Manu, 191, 194n11, 207, 225; *Dharmaśāstra*, 521n42
manuscript culture: beginning of, 4; communicative diffusion and, 558; literary vernacularization and, 315–17, 315n57; *Mahābhārata* and, 229–30; textuality and, 558–59
Mānyakheṭa, 338, 412, 412n69
maps, 190, 192n7

Maratha, 382, 511n21
Marathi language: grammaticization of, 400; inscriptions in, 149, 289–90, 381; Kannada merged into, 23; literary genre rules for, 302; Sanskrit interaction with, 154, 289–90; vernacular polities and, 416–17
Marathi literary culture: beginnings of, 296, 297, 298, 325, 381–83; genre restrictions in, 302; literization/literarization asynchrony in, 25, 446; regional vernacularization in, 479; Sanskrit as model for, 396; vernacularization of, 311, 493n45, 502
mārga (dramaturgical narrative element), 209n38
mārga (Way): Bhoja on, 110, 210–11, 211n40; as cosmopolitan cultural form, 220–22; cultural-historical significance of, 199, 208; *deśī* vs., 12, 208, 221, 357–58, 359, 405–10, 407n62; fourfold categorization of, 248; functional levels of, 207; imperial polity expressed in, 248; Kannada and, 348n37; in *Kavirājamārgam*, 346–51; kingliness and expertise in, 188; method of, 207–8; mode in, 208; multiplication of, 218–19; regional use of, 207, 208–22, 212n43; *rīti* vs., 207, 207n32, 409, 409n64; Sanskrit geocultural matrix and, 204–22, 237; tradition of, 205–7; in vernacular philology, 405–10
Martel, Charles, 492
Martial, 268
Marxism, 521, 521n43
Marx, Karl, 8, 545–46; *Eighteenth Brumaire*, 501
Master, Alfred, 93n45
Masʿūd Saʿd Salmān, 393, 493
Mathurā, 58, 66, 72n66, 116, 436
Maturai, 291
Maurya dynasty, 74, 81–82, 238, 252. *See also* Aśoka
May Fourth Movement, 487
Mayūra, 162, 163n1
Mayūraśarman (Kadamba overlord), 116, 116n3
McEwan, Ian, 284n1
McGregor, Stuart, 312n52, 393n27
Mebon Inscription, 125, 126, 129, 147
Medhāvin (Pallava praise-poet), 120–21, 332
Medici, Lorenzo de', 481, 552, 573
Medieval Kannada, 432–33
Mehta, Nandaśaṅkar, 328; *Karaṇaghelo*, 297
memorization, 82, 87–88
Menander (Indo-Greek king), 169
merchant guilds, 485
Meru, Mount, 16, 234, 246, 257
Merutuṅga, *Prabandhacintāmaṇi*, 178n25
Mesopotamia, 265, 537
metrics: of *deśabhāṣā*, 370–71; European vs. Sanskrit vernacularization and, 472; of *kāvya*, 69n58, 78, 202; Sanskrit used for, 39, 136; Southeast Asian study of, 163; vernacularization and, 395–96
Mewar *praśasti*, 326–27
meykkīrtti (literary/political genre), 323, 323n70
Mhāibhaṭa, 297; *Līḷacarita*, 382
Middle Indic, 56, 56n38, 60–61, 70. *See also* Prakrit
Mihirakūla (Hūṇa king), 138–39
Milindapanha, 100
Mīmāṃsā: Buddhist conflict with, 52–53, 53n32; dialect and, 102; grammar in, 66n53; grammatical authority and, 47; language ideology of, 52–53, 503n7; non-Sanskrit words in Veda and, 43n8; Sanskrit sociality and, 40–43; Veda as unauthored in, 76; written Veda prohibited in, 83, 83n23
mimesis, literary: *deśabhāṣā* used for, 96; Latin indifference to, 266–67; literariness defined by, 113; *mārga* and, 206, 209n38, 217; noncosmopolitan languages restricted to, 91, 94, 96, 109, 111–12, 287, 299; in vernacular songs, 303
Ming Rebellion, 484
Minnesänger, 452, 470
Mirashi, V. V., 72n66, 79n11
Mithilā, 492
modernity: complex categories of, 64–65; definition of, 8–10; elements of, 8–9; European cultural history and, 285; legitimation theory and, 517–21; nationalism and, 17; nation-states and, 251; power-culture practices of, 33–36
Monaguṇa, *Sumanasāntaka*, 389
Mongols, 487, 488
Montaigne, Michel Eyquem de, 457, 459, 465–66
Montesquieu, Charles Louis de, 521n42

More, Thomas, *Utopia*, 459
Moretti, Franco, 498n2
Morrison, Kathleen, 251n46
"mother language" trope, 318–19, 319n66, 472–73, 508
Mozarabs, 489
Mughals, 127, 168, 239, 252, 303n38
muktaka texts, 316n59
Muktāpīḍa (Kashmiri king), 249
Mūlarāja (king), 145
Müller, F. Max, 74n69
multiethnicity, 252
multilingualism: civilizationalism and, 503–4; European vernacularization and, 437; European vs. Sanskrit vernacularization and, 476–77, 480–81, 508, 511; impact of globalization on, 567–68; kingliness and, 173; South Asian cosmopolitanism and, 113, 173; South Asian empire form and, 252
multiscriptism, 229, 274n29
Muñja (Paramāra king), 154, 178, 178n25
music, 26, 199–200, 299–302, 300n29, 406–7
Muyangi, 160
My-son Stele inscription (Champa), 123n19, 124n20
mythomoteurs, 474, 526

nāḍu (culture-land), 352–55, 353n47, 478–79, 478–79n16
Naevius, 264, 266, 271, 298, 537
Nāgabhaṭa (Gurjara Pratīhāra king), 140–41, 245
Nāgara Brahmans, 434
Nāgarāja (king), 145
Nagari, 154, 159n89, 230, 289
Nāgārjuna, 339
Nāgārjuna, *Suhṛllekha*, 62n48
Nāgavarma I (Kannada scholar), 99, 160; *Chandōmbudhi*, 369–71, 378; *Karṇāṭakādambarī*, 109n75, 426
Nāgavarma II (Kannada scholar): as Jain Brahman, 426n95; *Kavirājamārgam* and, 342, 378; *mārga* and, 207n32, 212n43; multilingualism and, 509; on Ranna, 354–55; sources named by, 344n27; works: *Abhidhānavastukōśa*, 369; *Karṇāṭabhāṣābhūṣaṇa*, 372–73, 378, 398; *Kāvyāvalōkanam*, 348n37, 350n41, 351n43, 371–72; *Vīravardhamānapurāṇam*, 340, 372n91
Nāgeśa Bhaṭṭa, 175
Nagpur *praśasti*, 178
Nairn, Tom, 552n47, 577–78
Naiṣadīyacarita (Śrīharṣa), 88
Nakkiraṉār, 385n9
Namisādhu, 135n47
Nanddās (Brajbhasha poet), 312, 312n52, 502
Nandivarman II (Pallava king), 122n15
Nandivarman III (Pallava king), 358n63
Nannaya (Telugu poet), 93n45, 166, 171, 396, 536; *Āndhraśabdacintāmaṇi*, 364n73, 381, 398; *Mahābhāratamu*, 381, 398, 429
Narasimhacharya, R., 347–48
Narasiṃha I (Hoysaḷa king), 418, 419
Narasiṃha II (Hoysaḷa king), 418
Narasiṃha III (Hoysaḷa king), 159n90
Narasiṃha Mahetā, 296, 434–35, 436
Naravarman (Paramāra king), 177, 178, 183
Nārāyaṇa Bhaṭṭa, 144n59, 339; *Prakriyāsarvasva*, 175
Nārāyaṇapāla, 139–40, 220, 244
Narayana Rao, V., 86n30, 315–16, 315n57
Narmad, *Kavicaritra*, 296
Nasik cave inscription, 238
nāṭaka (epic drama), 86
Nāthamuni, *Divyaprabandham*, 384
Nāth yogis, 393
nationalism: colonialism and, 551n46; cosmopolitanism/vernacularism dichotomy and, 575–76; epic and, 544–47, 545n33, 554–58; epic space and, 556–58; historical origins of, 540, 541; Indian, 540; indigenism and, 525–26, 539–40; literary culture and, 541–44, 543n32; modernity and, 17; novel and, 544, 548–50; origins of, 551n46; philology and, 230, 558–59; Romantic, 543n32; theoretical problems of, 540–42, 550–51, 560–65; vernacularization and, 539–40, 576–78; vernacular literature and, 75, 297n26; Western power-culture ideology and, 9–10, 34–36, 565
nation-states: cultural effects of, 251; genealogy of, 540–42; origins of, 543; premodern empire form compared to, 251–52; print-capitalism and, 558; South Asian equivalent of, 31; vernacularity and, 525; Western criteria for, 562–63, 562n68
naturalism. *See* cultural naturalism
nāṭya (drama), 95

Nāṭyaśāstra (Bharata): *alaṅkāraśāstra* and, 90; on *deśabhāṣā*, 93–94; geocultural matrix and, 206; influence of, 164, 206; linguistic tripartition in, 93–94, 108; *mārga/deśī* dichotomy in, 406–7
Nayacandrasūri, *Hammīramahākāvya*, 394n29
Nāyannārs, 415n74
Nayasēna, *Dharmāmṛta*, 432
Nebrija, Antonio de, 165, 182, 463, 481, 481n23; *Gramatica Castellana*, 471
Nehru, Jawaharlal, 507n13, 560
neocolonialism, 533–34n18
Nepal, 133n44, 228, 232, 293–94, 469, 486
Nepali language, 293–94
Nepos, Cornelius, *Life of Hannibal*, 276
Newari language, 293–94, 293n19
Newari literary culture, 296, 297, 327–28, 391, 502
New Persian, 254–55, 262, 286, 287n4
nhātaka, 52n31
nidarśana (exemplification), 110
Niebelungenlied, 545
Nietzsche, Friedrich, 4
Nīlakaṇṭha Caturdhara, 230, 230n12, 231, 231n14
nirguṇa devotionalism, 432
Nirukta, 46n18
Nithard, 445
nomadic empires, 487–88
normative inversion, 51, 52
North Africa, Romanization of, 271
novel, European: beginnings of, 286; epic vs., 544, 547–50, 561–62; moral indeterminacy and, 547, 548; nationalism and, 544, 548–50
novel, Gujarati, 297
novelization, 542, 549
Nyāya, 53n32

Oaths of Strasbourg, 445
Occitan language, 448, 465, 467
Occitan literary culture: beginnings of, 297, 448, 452; as cosmopolitan vernacular, 448; emulation in, 573; Islam and, 491, 494, 538; Latin literacy and, 452; orality in, 442; script vernaculars in, 469; vernacular polities and, 465. *See also* French literary culture
Old English, 391, 447
Old French, 446, 447
Old Gujarati, 99, 326
Old Javanese, 388–89n18
Old Kannada, 20, 339–40, 348n36, 426, 432–33
Old Persian, 287n4
Old Tamil, 500
orality: epic vernacularization and, 363, 559–60; European vernacularization and, 440–42; *kāvya* and, 3–5, 84–86, 87–88, 87n32; literary beginnings and, 287; literization and, 23, 25, 315–16, 316n59; *Mahābhārata* and, 86, 232–33; in *Mahābhāṣya*, 83, 172; in *Rāmāyaṇa*, 78; royal lineages and, 155; in Sanskrit literary culture, 82–86; textualization and, 304–7; vernacularization and, 299–302
Oresme, Nicole, 480–81
Orientalism, 278, 284, 507, 521, 529–30
Orissa, 252–53
Oriya language, 292, 302
Oriya literary culture, 297n26, 302, 304, 391, 417
Ottomans, 252, 450, 491
ovī (song genre), 302, 325
Ovid, 276, 280

Padmagupta (poet), 178
Padmanābha, *Kānhaḍadeprabandha*, 493
Pagan, 515, 532
Pahlavas (Parthians), 70, 277
Pahlavi, 287n4
Paishachi: Bhoja's taxonomy and, 108, 110; *Bṛhatkathā* and, 92–93, 97; cosmopolitanism assigned to, 103–4; legendary status of, 92–93; in literary histories, 93n45; literary restrictions and, 95, 96–98; Rājaśekhara on origins of, 203
Pāla dynasty, 139–40, 220, 244, 252, 431n105
paḷagannaḍa (old Kannada), 339–40
palambang, 390n22
paleography, 123–24, 124n21
Pali: Buddhist turn to Sanskrit and, 56, 57; as cosmopolitan language, 386–87; Daṇḍin readapted in, 163; *kāvya* in, 386; philological works, 386n14, 399; philology and, 171; as sacred language, 44n15, 55
Pallava dynasty: Bhāsa plays dated in, 81; confederacy of, 153n75; Khmer inscriptions and, 124, 124n21; political self-

Pallava dynasty *(continued)*
identification of, 151; Prakrit grammaticization and, 102; Prakrit inscriptions in, 63–64, 63–64n49; royal icons in, 279; Śaka era and, 151n67; Sanskrit/regional division of labor in, 119–22, 119n10, 122n15; vernacularization in, 290–91
Pallava-Grantha script, 123–24
Palnāṭikathā, 314, 316
Pampa (Kannada poet): allegory used by, 360–62; as aristocrat, 486; career of, 355; eulogies to, 368n82; Indianization and, 536; influence of, 357; as Jain Brahman, 426n95; as Kannada *ādikavi*, 296, 341–42, 479; on Kannada as heartland, 354; *Kavirājamārgam* and, 357–58, 362, 367; learned audience of, 426; *mārga/deśī* dichotomy mediated by, 357–58, 359, 408, 408n63; as rooted, 576; Veṅgi Cāḷukya polities and, 160; vernacular epics of, 396; vernacular literarization and, 306, 308, 309; works: *Ādipurāṇa*, 340n18, 426n96. See also *Vikramārjunavijayam*
Pāñcāla, 154
pāñcāla (western style), 210, 212–13, 217–18, 221
Pañcanada, 191
Pañcatantra, 124n22
Paṇḍitacandra (Kannada poet), 339
paṇḍita lineages, 492
Pāṇḍuräṅga (Champa), 14
Pāṇini: *chandaḥ/bhāṣa* distinction and, 54n33, 66; educated king topos and study of, 166; grammatical/political relationship and, 168; influence of, 399; *Kātantra* and, 62; language studies of, 164; literacy and, 82; Ratneśvara on, 111n79. See also *Aṣṭādhyāyī*
Panjab, 228
Pannonius, Janus, 450
Pāṇṭiya dynasty, 291–92, 322–23, 335, 383–84, 384n6
paper revolution, 440
Parākramabāhu I (king), 387
Parākramabāhu II (king), 387; *Kavsiḷumiṇa*, 429
Paramāras, 177–78, 182, 219
pāramārthika sat, 2–3, 22, 65, 320–21
Pārasikas (Persians), 195
Parimala (court pandit), 180n29
Paris, University of, 470
Parthians, 277
parwa literature, 234, 388
Pāṭaṇ, 297
Patañjali: dating of, 70n60, 80, 80–81n15; on instantiations, 365; *Kātantra* and, 62; on quality of grammatical learning, 173; regional variation as prescriptive option in, 268; Śakas/Yavanas and, 70n60; South Asian geography according to, 191. See also *Mahābhāṣya*
patronage. *See* court patronage
Pavaṇanti, *Naṉṉūl*, 399
Peire d'Alvernha, 451
Peiteus, Guillem de, 448
Persia, 236; Achaemenid, 59, 482, 537
Persian language, 127, 318, 432n106, 512n23; New Persian, 254–55, 262, 286, 287n4; Old Persian, 287n4
Persian literary culture, 26, 254–55, 286, 287n4
Peruntēvaṉār (Tamil poet): *Pārataveṇpā*, 358n63, 384
Petrarch, 451
philology, 93, 101–2, 558–59. *See also* Kannada philology; Sanskrit philology; vernacular philology
phonetics, 39
Phukan, Shantanu, 393n27
pilgrimage circuits, 382–83
Piṅgala, *Chandaḥsūtra*, 171, 370, 370n87
Pirenne, Henri, 489
Plautus, 271, 537
Pléiade, 182, 467, 573
Pliny the Elder, 271–72
Poema de mio Cid. See *Cid, Poema de mio*
poesis, 31
Poetics Woman. *See* Sāhityavidyā
Poetry Man. *See* Kāvyapuruṣa
Poitiers, Arab defeat at (732), 492
polis, 12
politicization, 31–32
Ponna, 160, 341, 357, 368n82; *Bhuvanaikarāmābhyudayam*, 426n96; *Śāntipurāṇam*, 426n96
populus romanus, 276
Portuguese language, 500
postcolonialism, 577
Potana (Telugu poet), *Bhāgavatamu*, 351n44
power: aestheticization of, 133–34, 241, 258; definition of, 5–8; spatialization of, 189

Prabhācandra: *Prabhāvakacarita,* 87n32, 180n29, 181–82, 588–90
Prabhākara, 201n14
prabhātiyuṃ (lyrical morning prayer), 435
prācya, 66
Prakrit: Bhoja's taxonomy of, 107–8, 109, 110–11, 582; Buddhism and, 117, 118; "choice of," 64–67, 108n73; as cosmopolitan language, 104; definition of, 91; dialects of, 91; disappearance of, 116–20, 289, 338n13; grammar and ritual in, 46n17; grammatical/prosodical texts in, 108n74, 401n45; grammaticization of, 56n36, 101–3, 102n61, 102–3n64, 220–21, 401; inscriptions in, 60–64, 64n49, 101, 102, 116–20, 116n3, 238; intermediate stage theory, 66; Jainism and, 423–24; Kannada as, 374, 374n94; as *kāvya* language, 13, 26, 90, 91, 93–98, 98n56, 101, 113, 287–88, 299, 424; language-naming and, 474; literary genre rules for, 98–100, 302; as multiform, 66, 269; naturalistic view of development of, 500, 502; as political language, 499; political prose-poetry in, 79; power-culture practices and, 74; qualifications for *kāvya,* 100–104; Rājaśekhara on origins of, 203; regional dimension of, 91, 101; *saṃkīrṇakathā* genre in, 361n67; Sanskrit interaction with, 117–20, 117n7; Sanskrit vs., 13–14, 66, 74; Sātavāhana use of, 71–72; as second-order code, 104–5, 105n69; use of, on coins, 74n70; vernacularization and, 289–90, 395–96
Prākṛtaprakāśa, 56n36
prakṛti, 35, 91, 108
Prambanan (Java), 14, 115, 162, 163n1, 388n17
prāsa, 86n30
praśasti: aesthetic purpose of, 136, 137, 148; Cāḷukya, 151n68; diffusion of, 16; empire form and, 256; expressive resources of, 137–41; factual vs. mythical in, 141n55; first Kannada, 334–35; first Sanskrit, 220; genealogical succession in, 119, 157–58; grammaticality and, 167, 173–74; Javanese, 127–28n30, 130, 131–32; Junāgaṛh rock inscriptions as, 68; *kāvya* and, 114, 134–37, 148; Khmer Sanskrit, 125, 127; kingliness expressed in, 166; language restrictions on, 269; literary writers of, 134, 134–35n45; Mewar, 326–27; Nagpur, 178; Pallava inscriptions as, 119–20; political goals of, 143–46, 144n58, 148, 149, 182; power-culture relationship and, 39; power spatialized in, 243–45; Sanskrit cosmopolis and, 13, 14, 18, 257; Sanskrit/regional division of labor in, 120–22; Sanskrit theoretical neglect of, 135, 135n47; *śleṣa* and, 136, 139–41; as superposed model, 322–27; vernacular, 290, 292–93, 297, 337
Pratāparudrayaśobhūṣaṇa, 175
prātiśākhya literature, 170
Pravarasena, 117n6; *Setubandha,* 91n39, 333n5
pravṛtti (literary/dramatic costumes), 204, 205
premodernity: complex categories of, 64–65; legitimation theory and, 517–21; periodization of, 8–10
Pre Rup Inscription, 125, 129, 147, 163n1
primordialism, 505–8
Prinsep, James: *Corpus Inscriptionum Indicarum,* 69; *Epigraphia Indica,* 68–69
print-capitalism, 548, 552, 558, 562
print culture, 24n25, 552, 552n48
Pṛthivīcandracarita, 434
Pṛthvīdhāra (poet), 144n59
Pūjāvaliya, 387
Pulakeśin I (Cāḷukya king), 150n66, 155, 157, 252
Pulakeśin II (Cāḷukya king), 143, 151, 154, 156, 158, 243, 276
Pūlāṅkuṟicci, 291n12
Puligeṟe region, 354–56
Pune, 558–59
Punic Wars, 266
Pupphayanta, *Mahāpurāṇa,* 103, 425
purāṇa ("ancient lore"): Bhoja on, 107, 581–82; example of, 582; *mārga* and, 207; prediction as convention of, 70–71, 71n63; professional reciters of, 85n28; Sanskrit geography in, 193–96, 352
Purātanaprabandhasaṃgraha, 180n29
puruṣa (thought/spirit), 35
Puruṣa (Primal Being), 278
Puruṣapura (Peshawar), 14, 115
pūrvamīmāṃsā, 40, 41–42n4, 201n14
Pūrvottaramīmāṃsāvādanakṣatramālā, 51n30

Puṣpadanta, 338
Puṣṭimārga, 436
Puttamittiraṉ, *Vīracōḻiyakārikai*, 398
Pye, Lucian, 562n68

Rabelais, 459
Raghavan, 93n45, 110n77
Rahīm (Mughal court poet), 303n38
Raïdhū (Apabramsha poet), 394n29
Rājādhirāja (Cōḻa king), 291
Rājamalla (court poet), 292–93
Rājarāja I (Cōḻa king), 160, 291, 323, 383, 384
Rājarājanarenda (Telugu king), 166, 171
Rājaśekhara: ambivalence of, toward low-caste Sanskrit poets, 43n11; cosmopolitan literary system and, 105; on deity of literature, 185; geography of, 191, 194, 203; on Ghronṇa, 312; on grammatical/political correctness, 183; on *guṇas*, 210; influence of, 201; influences on, 206; *Kavirājamārgam* and, 341; on literary language choice, 111–12; on literature, origins of, 78, 94, 200–204, 221; regionalization in, 205–6, 219, 351; spatialization of power in, 247–49; on translocal codes, 103–4; Vālmīki *Rāmāyaṇa* and, 78; works: *Bālarāmāyaṇa*, 203. See also *Kāvyamīmāṃsā*
Rājendra Cōḻa (king), 246, 291
rājya: Bhoja's correctness in, 179; cultural elements of, 253; difficulty defining, 250; *imperium romanum* vs., 274–80, 572; *kāvya* and, 6, 18; vernacularization and, 27
Rakai Pikatan (Javanese king), 387–88, 390
Rāmacandra (Yādava king), 325
Rāmacandra Dīkṣita, 400
Ramanujan, A. K., 559–60
Rāmāyaṇa (Vālmīki), 44–45; dissemination of, 162–63, 163n1; as first Sanskrit *kāvya*, 13, 77–79, 202, 297; as Greek adaptation, 265; influence of, 174, 175; *kāvya* origins in, 77, 83, 286; as national story, 546; nonsacral Sanskrit use in, 48; orality and, 83, 88, 305, 441; professional reciters of, 85. See also *Rāmāyaṇa*, vernacular adaptations of
Rāmāyaṇa kakawin, 390
Rāmāyaṇa, vernacular adaptations of: Assamese, 396, 428, 449; Bangla, 449, 493n45; *bhakti* and, 428; emulation in, 449; epicization and, 396, 396n35; Islam and, 493, 493n45; Javanese, 388, 389, 396; Oriya, 449; professional reciters of, 85n28, 559; Tamil, 85n28, 384, 559
Ranna: as emperor-poet, 357; Kannada as heartland and, 354–55; *mārga/deśī* dichotomy and, 408; past poet eulogies and, 340n18, 341; vernacular epics of, 396, 555; works: *Ajitajinēśvaracaritam*, 354–55, 426n96; *Rannanighaṇṭu*, 364, 368–69. See also *Sāhasabhīmavijayam*
rasa (aestheticized emotion): components of, 217–18; *kāvya* and, 76, 95; kingliness and expertise in, 188; *mārga/deśī* dichotomy and, 408; regional use of, 348n37, 351n43; *rīti* and, 207n32; in Sanskrit literary theory, 84, 90, 198
rāsaka ("pastoral" genre), 98
rasokti ("affective" expression), 106, 106n71, 349, 350n40
Rāṣṭrakūṭa dynasty: Apabhramsha use of, 103; decline of, 370n87; destruction of, 154; emigration of, 356n56; grammar/power relationship in, 173–74, 176; Guptas and, 252; Kannada literarized in, 288–89, 332, 333–35, 355–56; Kannada/Sanskrit ratios in, 332n3; Kannada virtuosity and, 523; *Kavirājamārgam* and, 371; *praśasti* in, 125, 134; religion and politics in, 430–31; scholarship lacking on, 412; scholars/poets at court of, 207, 214; trade and vernacularization in, 485; transregional power of, 246, 246n38; vernacular polities and, 421–22
Ratnaprabhasūri, *Kuvalayamālākathā*, 105n69
Ratnaśrījñāna (commentator): Bhāmaha and, 212n43; on Daṇḍin, 214–15, 344; literary language restrictions in, 93n45; naturalizing interpretation of, 217, 320; on Prakrit as *kāvya* language, 91; regionalizing influences on, 216; Ruvan-mī and, 399n40; on Sanskrit uniformity, 269
Ratneśvara, 111n79, 209n36
Rāulavela, 304
Ravikīrti, 125
Raviṣena, *Padmapurāṇa*, 59
Rāyalasīma inscriptions, 289n6

Rēcarla dynasty, 219
Recent Style poetry, 163, 205, 535
Reconquista, 490–91
Redfield, Robert, 533–34n18
Reformation, 28, 450
regionalization: of *mārga*, 207, 208–22, 212n43; self-identification in, 219
Reid, Anthony, 486n34
religion: *kāvya* language and, 98–99, 424; language choice and, 113, 116–17, 423–24; Latin vs. Sanskrit cosmopolitanism and, 572; patronage of, 431, 431n105; regional vernacularization and, 433–36; royal authority and, 278–80; spatialization in, 190–91, 192; vernacularization and, 393, 393n27, 423–36, 429n102, 553n50, 564n71. See also *bhakti*; Buddhism; Hinduism; Islam; Jainism; Shaivism; *specific religion*
Renaissance, 272
Renou, Louis, 60, 62n48, 64
representation, historicity of, 7–8
Revatī island, 158
rex doctus topos, 267
Ṛgveda, 164, 202
Ṛgvedasaṃhitā, 75–76
Ricoeur, Paul, 518–19
Rīsthal Inscription, 144n59
rīti (Paths of literature), 110, 188; as *buddhyārambhānubhāva*, 217n50; *mārga* vs., 207, 207n32, 409, 409n64; mixed (*āndhra*), 218–19; Rājaśekhara on origins of, 204; regional use of, 207, 348n37; semantic range narrowed in, 208–9n36; tradition of, 207
rītikal, 409
ritualization, 12
Romance Europe, 440–41
Romance vernaculars: differentiation of, 485; Germanic vernacularization vs., 443–44; industrialization and, 552; Latin and, 261, 391–92, 471; metrics in, 472; vernacular polities and, 462–63; written forms/conventions in, 446n12
Roman de la Rose, 458
Roman des rois, 465
Roman Empire: center-periphery world system of, 270–71, 274–75, 276; ethnic fictions in, 474; foundational fiction of, 279–80; Greek influence on, 266; imperial model of, 482; Latin and, 19, 20; literacy in, 262, 267; literary beginnings in, 260, 262–64, 263n7, 264n8, 297; regional languages of, 271, 439; Sanskrit and, 1; Sanskrit cosmopolis and, 19; Sanskrit cosmopolis vs., 274–80; South Asia as categorized by, 192; South Asian empires incomparable to, 250; South Asian trade with, 122; spatialization in, 556
Romanization, 260; cosmopolitanism and, 10; of Germanic tribes, 489; influence of non-Romans on, 537–38; language loss caused by, 271–72, 271n24; literacy and, 442; military support for, 133; Sanskrit cosmopolitanism contrasted with, 133, 269–72
Roman script, 273
Romanticism, 319, 543n32
roma renovata, 275
Ronsard, Pierre, 458–59n31, 466–67
Rosenzweig, Franz, 505
royal court. *See* courtly culture
Ṛsabha, 194n11
Rudradāman (Śaka prince): empire form and, 253; grammatical/political correctness of, 255–56; influence of, 120, 151–52; literary beginnings and, 73, 297; public political inscription of, 500; as transcultured poet, 264. *See also* Junāgaṛh inscription
Rudraṭa: literary language restrictions in, 93n45, 94; *mārga* and *rasa* in, 217, 218, 220; past poet eulogies and, 344n27; work: *Kāvyālaṅkāra*, 135n47, 351n43
Rudravarman (Khmer king), 138
rūpaka (metaphor), 142
Russian language/literary culture, 512n23, 529n8, 547n40
Ruvan-mī, 399n40

Śabara, 42n5, 43, 83n22
Śabdamaṇidarpaṇam (Kēśirāja): *deśī* in, 405; Kannada grammaticization and, 372, 373–77, 378; Kannada literary culture and, 340; vernacularization and, 27, 372
"Śabdasmṛti," 376
sabhā (king's cultural assembly), 185–86
Sabhāpati II of Vijayanagara, 144n59
Ṣaḍbhāṣācandrikā, 103
Saddanīti (Pali grammar), 53, 53n32, 171, 386n14

sādhutva (correctness), 165
Safavids, 252
Śāhajī (Tancāvūr king), 233, 233n16
Sāhasabhīmavijayam (*Gadāyuddham*; Ranna): emendations of, 306n43; epic spatialization in, 363, 395; Kalyāṇa Cāḷukya lineage narrative in, 155–56, 155n79; literary norms and, 378; vernacular polities in, 425, 426n96
sāhitya, 31, 187
Sāhityamīmāṃsā, 198–99, 203
sāhityaśāstra (literary science), 89–90, 321–22
Sāhityavidyā (Poetics Woman), 204, 221
Sahṛdaya, Mutali, 128n30
Śaka dynasty: cosmopolitan culture crystallized in, 12–13, 67–73, 493; dating system of, 123–24n19, 150–51, 150n66, 151n67, 156; as foreigners, 70n60, 72n66; Guptas and, 252; *kāvya* origins and, 80, 89; political self-identification and, 151; power of, spatialized, 239; Sanskrit inscriptions in, 123, 277; Sanskrit language use of, 74n70, 101, 499
Śākambharī Chauhans, 303
Śākaṭāyana (grammarian), *Śabdānuśāsana*, 173, 338
sakāya niruttiyā, 54–55
Sa-skya Paṇḍita, 163
Saljuk Turks, 487
samasaṃskṛta (words equal with Sanskrit), 374
samāsokti (trope of abbreviation), 361
samavṛtta meter, 130
samaya, 53n32
Sāṃkhya (Indian philosophy), 284
saṃkīrṇakathā (Prakrit literary genre), 361n67
saṃpradāya (recension), 231
saṃskāra (ritual purification), 42, 45–46n17, 53
saṃskṛti, 12, 42, 44–46, 53
Samudragupta (Gupta overlord): empire form and, 252; as god-man, 278; influence of, 152; inscriptions of, 278; as learned king, 166; Sanskrit geocultural matrix and, 191, 239–40. *See also* Allahabad Pillar Inscription
saṃvṛti sat, 2–3
Sanctis, Francesco de, 543n32
sāndhivigrahika ("peace and war official"), 135, 135n46
Sangharakṣita, 163
saṅgīta (song/music/dance), 199–200, 406
Saṅgītadarpaṇa, 406
Sañjaya (Javanese king), 166, 242
Śaṅkara (philosopher), 36, 43n9, 430, 570
Śaṅkaradeva, 435
saṅketa, 52–53, 53n32
Sanskrit cosmopolis: analytical matrices in, 16–18; circulatory space of, 234–37; as colonization, 529–30; comparative analysis and, 18–19; cosmopolitanism/vernacularism dichotomy resolved in, 579–80; culture-power relationship in, 14–19, 30–31, 74, 256–58; Devanagari and, 229; development of, 12–13, 70, 74, 502; *digvijaya* and, 115; domination discourses in, 35–36; early manifestations of, 237–38; empire form in, 251–58; epic space in, 234–37, 557; foundational fiction of, 279–80; historical explanations for, 410; ideological view of, 515–16; *imperium romanum* vs., 274–80; *kāvya* and, 13–14, 18, 89, 162–63; Latin cosmopolitanism vs., 267–69; literary language in, 98–99; *mārga* and, 220–22; naturalistic view of, 499–501; political/grammatical correctness in, 165, 176, 182, 184; political inscription in, 115–16, 122, 146; Prakrit disappearance and, 116–20; *praśasti* and, 13, 14, 18; regional language practices in, 216–17, 510; regional self-understanding and, 219; role of literature/philology in, 184; Romanization vs., 269–72; in Southeast Asia, 123–32, 270, 512; spread of, 122–23, 132–33; use of term, 11–12, 21–22; vernacularization and, 21–22, 25–30, 317–18, 469
Sanskrit geocultural matrix: Bhāratavarṣa in, 191, 192–96, 199–200; *deśabhāṣā* in, 199–200, 299, 299n27; empire form in, 237–59; epic and, 226–37, 556; *kāvya* origins in, 200–204; localization of, 324; *mārga* and literary regionalization in, 204–22, 237; of Sanskrit knowledge systems, 189–200
Sanskritization, 126, 513–14, 514n25
Sanskrit language, 95; autochthony in, 527–28; *bhakti* and, 424; Bhoja's taxonomy and, 107, 110–11, 581–82; Brahmanism and, 28–29, 118; Buddhist resistance to, 51–56, 54n33, 61, 423–24; Buddhist

turn to, 56–59, 72, 100, 101; commercialization of, 74n70; communicative competence in, 478; as correct/true, 308–9; as cosmopolitan language, 104, 254–56, 262, 268–69, 571–72; court patronage and, 523; desacralization of, 62, 73–74, 74n70, 101, 170; discourse in, 15; displacement of, 288, 332, 336–37; eternal fame expressed in, 142–43, 146; excellence in, as sign of kingliness, 166–67, 255–56; first *kāvya* in, 77–79; first use of, 44–46; functionalist view of role of, 512–13; as hyperglossic, 50, 118, 127, 262, 432–33; interaction with local languages, 115, 117–22, 117n7, 122n15, 126–27, 128–30, 133n44, 142–43, 262, 272–74; intermediate stage theory, 66; Kannada vs., 375–76; as *kāvya* language, 13–14, 90, 93–98, 98n56, 110–14, 129, 287–88, 299; language-naming and, 474; Latin vs., 260–62; linguistic cleansing of, 432, 432n106; literarization and, 25; literary genre rules for, 98–100; "mother"/"father" language dichotomy and, 318; multilingualism and, 508–9; naturalistic view of development of, 499–500, 502; philology in, 15; political will expressed in, 133–34, 165–66; Prakrit grammatical/prosodical texts written in, 108n74; as *praśasti* language, 136–37; prestige economy of, 59, 72–74, 265; "proper," Prakrit vs., 64–67; public inscriptions absent in, 59–62, 79–80, 79n11; qualifications for *kāvya*, 100–104; Rājaśekhara on origins of, 203; regionalization of, 16; reinvention of, as literary/political code, 1, 11, 39, 67, 75; "revival" of, 74, 74n69; as sacred language, 28–29, 108n73, 502, 551; Śaka appropriation of, 70–73, 72n66; scripts of, 273–74, 274n29; *śleṣa* and, 139–40; spatial lexicon of, 479n17; spread of, 11, 14–15, 115–16, 189, 262; as standardized language, 552n48; as superposed model, 320; syllabary of, 176n22; translations into, 104–5, 105n69; transregionality of, 220–22; uniformity of, 107, 269; variations in, 64–66, 65n52, 66n54, 269; vernacular as challenge to, 1, 288–89

Sanskrit language, precosmopolitan: ambivalence about status of, 43–44; discursive ritualization of, 39–40, 44–50; grammar and, 44–49, 45–46n17; nonsacral use of, 48–50; social monopolization of, 39–44; speech community of, 40

Sanskrit literary culture: Chinese response to, 535; cosmopolitanism and, 19, 266; current relevance of, 568–70; definition of, 2–5; elite patronage of, 175–76; first systematized conceptualization of, 201; Greek influence on, 265; immigrant influence on, 69–70, 264–65, 277, 537; influence of, 162–63; Kashmiri role in, 105–6; language variety and, 95; *latinitas* vs., 262–69; literary theory and, 89–90; orality vs. literacy in, 3–4, 82–88, 304–7; origins of, 16; quasi-global context of, 143; reinvention of, 67, 89; in royal court, 184–88; Śaka appropriation of, 70; Sanskrit cosmopolis and, 89; Sanskrit/regional division of labor in, 117–19; southward shift of, 492; spatialization in, 16, 198–200, 223–24; spread of, 1, 16–17, 21, 89, 101; vernacularization and, 129, 130, 322–29, 478; vernacularization as rebellion against, 21, 470. See also *latinitas* (Latinness), Sanskrit vs.

Sanskrit literary theory. See *alaṅkāraśāstra*

Sanskrit literature: beginnings of, 75–79; Bhoja and, 178–79; deity of, 185; inscriptional aesthetics and, 134–37; kingliness and, 184–88, 232–33; *mārga* contradictions in, 219–20; oldest manuscripts of, 236; political goals of, 182–83, 279–80; regionality in, 214–15; in Sanskrit cosmopolis, 184, 220–22; social sites of, 184. See also *kāvya*; *specific genre*

Sanskrit philology: *alaṅkāraśāstra* and, 175; grammatical/political correctness and, 180; influence on Kannada, 367–68, 370–71, 370–76, 449; kingliness and, 166; *Mahābhārata* editions and, 231–32; nationalism and, 230; origins of, 171, 171n14; patronage and, 167–68, 175–76; and polity, historical relationship of, 171–76, 205; in Sanskrit cosmopolis, 184

Sanskrit political culture: early transregional power projections, 237–49; empire form in, 251–58; epic space in, 242, 249–50; imperial armies and, 246; inscriptional discourse and, 238–42; quasiuniversalism of, 242–46

Sanskrit studies, 11
Śāntivarman, 116–20
Śāradātanaya: on language-naming, 510; literary language restrictions in, 96, 99, 109; on *mārga*, 218; multilingualism and, 509; and *rīti*, 217n50; work: *Bhāvaprakāśana*, 95, 199–200, 299–300, 299n27, 315
Śaraḷadās, 396
sarpabandha (serpentine graph), 177
Sarvasena, *Harivijaya*, 117n6
Sarvāstivāda school, 56
Śarvavarman (grammarian), 62, 97, 169–70, 173. See also *Kātantra*
Sa-skya Paṇḍita, *The Scholar's Gate*, 399
śāstra: Bhoja on, 107, 582; example of, 582; *kāvya* vs., 3, 76, 107; literacy and, 83; literature as, 188; non-Sanskrit scriptural languages and, 55–56; universal reach of, 198; Vedic purpose, 42, 42n6, 46–47
śāstrakāvya, 162–63, 174–75, 389
śāstravinoda (entertainment of learned discourse), 15, 185–86, 188
Sātavāhana dynasty: grammar/power relationship in, 169–70; political prose-poetry of, 62n48, 79; political self-identification and, 61, 151; Prakrit use of, 61–62, 64, 66, 72, 79, 79n11, 97, 103n64, 502; Sanskrit language use of, 71–72; *Yugapurāṇa* and, 70–72
satkāryavāda (doctrine of preexistent effects), 284
Satya Khāna (Bengali lord), 231
Saurāṣṭra, 218
Saussure, Ferdinand de, 164
Scharfe, Hartmut, 167
Schieffer, Rudolf, 440n4
Scott, Walter, 328
script culture, 24n25
script-mercantilism, 558
script vernaculars, 469
secularization, 89
Sejong (Korean king), 487
senāpati ("master of the army"), 135
Senas, 134, 220, 411
Sequence of St. Eulalie, 451, 477
Servius, 266, 267
Setubandha (Pravarasena), 91
sexuality, Sanskrit taxonomy of, 197–98
Shackle, Christopher, 393n27
Shāh Jahān (Mughal emperor), 175
Shāh Nāmeh, 254, 432n106
Shaivism, 415n74; patronage of, 431n105; political impact of, 431; spatialization in, 192; vernacularization and, 289, 383–84, 425, 479–80
Sharada, 229
Shauraseni (Prakrit dialect), 91, 94, 95, 102, 108, 221
Shils, Edward, 506
Shrivaishnavism, 430, 431, 436
Shudras (caste): origins of, 202; precosmopolitan Sanskrit and, 40–41, 43–44; spatialization of, 194; Vedic ritual and, 41–42n4, 42n5, 43n9, 44n13; vernacularization and, 310–12
Siam, 555–56
Sicily, 494, 538
Sidatsaṅgarāva, 399
Siddhasena (monk), 58
Sidney, Philip, 457; *Apology for Poesie*, 459–60
Siete partidas, 463
Silk Road, 484, 486
Siṃhavarman III (Pallava king), 120–21
Siṃhaviṣṇu (king), 121
Sindh, Arab conquest of, 485, 489, 491
Sindhi language, 474
Śiṅgabhūpāla (king), 175, 218–19; *Rasārṇavasudhākara*, 218
Sinhala language, 163, 386, 399
Sinhala literary culture, 386–87, 429, 449, 471
Sinicization, 259–60
Sircar, D. C., 80, 89
Siri Saṅgbo (king), 387
Śivājī (Maratha king), 175
Śivaskandavarman (Pallava king), 63, 63–64n49, 119, 175
Sivathamby, Karthigesu, 384n6
Siyabaslakara, 26n26, 163, 399, 399n40, 471
Skandagupta (Gupta king), 68
Skandavarman IV (Pallava king), 120n13
skandhaka (courtly epic genre), 98, 333n5
Slavs, 489–90
śleṣa (pun): Bhoja on, 107, 110; cultural significance of, 147; factual vs. mythical in, 141n55; *praśasti* style and, 136, 139–41; regional use of, 208; Sanskrit/regional division of labor and, 121; vernacular uses of, 361
smārta, 190–91

Smith, Colin, 449–50
smṛti ("remembered" Vedic text), 107, 207, 225, 581
Smṛtisthala, 493n45
snātaka, 52n31
social theory, 32–33
societal culture, 577
sociolinguistics, 24
Śoḍāsa (Śaka lord), 69n58
Sogdian language, 55
Somadeva, *Kathāsaritsāgara*, 97n55
Somadevasūri, 431; *Nītivākyāmṛta*, 278–79n41, 421–22, 422n87; *Yaśastilakacampū*, 246, 421, 425
Somanātha, *Basavapurāṇa*, 382n4
Someśvara I (Cāḷukya king), 246
Someśvara III (Cāḷukya king), 160, 184–85, 477; *Vikramāṅkābhyudaya*, 302–3. See also *Mānasollāsa*
Song of St. Alexis, 452
songs, 26, 199–200, 299–302, 300n29
South Asia, premodern: cosmopolitanism in, 90; cosmopolitan vs. vernacular in, 6–7; current relevance of, 35–36, 568–70; documentary vs. workly language use in, 3, 25, 77, 146–47, 283; dynasties of, 597; empire form in, 251–54; European modernity vs., 9–10; geocultural matrix of, 189–200; glossary of peoples/places in, 597–600; historical representations of, 7–8; ideology and, 33–34; influence of orality on written literature in, 4; inscriptions in, 59–60; language-naming in, 473–74; language study in, 164–65; literacy in, 88, 190; the literary in, 2–5; maps, xvii-xviii; periodization of, 8–10; political self-identification in, 151; power in, 5–8; quasi-global formations in, 11; religion and language choice in, 423–24; Sanskrit as unity in, 65–66; Sanskrit cosmopolis and, 16, 122–23; Southeast Asian cultural-political order compared with, 132–34; the state in, 410–11; trade expanded in, 122; vernacularization in, 26–30, 250, 380–87, 390–96, 475–76. *See also* vernacularization, European vs. South Asian; *specific dynasty*; *person*; *place*
South Asia, premodern, Western theories of, 34–36; cultural naturalism, 497–505; ethnicity, 509–11; functionalism, 511–16, 522; ideology, 512, 514–16, 518–22; legitimation, 512, 516–24; linguism, 506–9; primordialism, 505–8; problems of, 550–51, 560–65; Sanskritization, 513–14, 514n25. *See also* civilizationalism; indigenism; nationalism
Southeast Asia, premodern: civilizationalism and Indianization of, 528–32, 535–38; educated king topos in, 166; empire form recreated in, 251–52; historical geography in, 235n19; legitimation theory and, 516–17; map, xx; Pali cosmopolitan formation in, 386; role of women in, 126, 126n25; Sanskrit cosmopolis and, 16, 123–32, 270; Sanskrit epic space in, 242; Sanskrit geocultural matrix and, 222, 234–36; Sanskrit linguistic influence on, 273, 478, 512; South Asian cultural-political order compared with, 132–34; South Asian trade with, 122; vernacularization in, 294, 387–90, 488. *See also* Angkor dynasty; Cambodia; Java; Khmer *entries*; Laos; Vietnam
Soviet Union, 529n8, 577
Spain: Arab invasion of, 440, 489; Reconquista, 490–91
Spanish language, 392, 489, 500
Spanish literary culture, 297; ethnic fictions in, 474; French influence on, 538; Islam and, 489–91, 493; vernacular emulation in, 449–50, 449n19; vernacular polities in, 462–64
Spartoi of Thebes, 567
Spengler, Oswald, 533
Spenser, Edmund, *The Faerie Queen*, 459
śrāddha (ancestor ceremony), 119
śrauta, 61–62, 581
Śravaṇabeḷgoḷa epigraphs, 367
śravya (recitative), 84
Śrīdharavarman, 69
Śrīharṣa (poet/philosopher), 88
Śrikaṇṭhapaṇḍita, 303–4
Sri Lanka: cosmopolitan vernacularization in, 399; Pali cosmopolitan formation in, 386–87; Sanskrit cosmopolis and, 115; Sanskrit literary influence in, 163, 228–29, 386, 386n13; vernacular polities in, 390
Śrīnāthuḍu (Andhra poet), 408–9, 442, 502; *Bhīmakhaṇḍamu*, 381; *Bhīmeśvaravilāsamu*, 313; *Palnāṭivīrabhāgavatamu*, 313–14, 316, 317; *Śṛṅgāranaiṣadhamu*, 313

Śrīpāla (*praśasti* poet), 134, 136, 144–46, 584–88
Śrīvijaya (Kannada poet): *Kavirājamārgam* and, 339, 341, 342; literary restrictions and, 99; Rāṣṭrakūṭa patronage and, 343; Sanskrit cosmopolis and, 16. See also *Kavirājamārgam*
Śṛṅgāraprakāśa (Bhoja): grammatical/political correctness in, 179; influences on, 201; Jayasiṃha's theft of, 181n31; *Kavirājamārgam* and, 349–50; on *kāvya* language, 581–82; literary analysis in, 105, 201; literary taxonomy in, 106–9; on *mārga*, 210–11, 349–50; on *rasa*, 84; southern orientation of, 350n40
Śṛṅgaverapura, 175
śruti ("heard" Vedic text), 76
state, definition of, 8
Stein, Burton, 411, 413–16, 414–15n74
stele, 149
Stephen I (Hungarian king), 450
Strasbourg, Oaths of, 445
Subodhālaṅkāra, 171
Sudarśana reservoir, 68
Sufism, 393, 429, 493–94, 553
sugṛhītanāmadheya, 150n66
Sukhotai, 532
Śukla, Rāmcandra, 409
Śukranītisāra, 422, 422n87
sūkta (Vedic hymn), 52, 75, 398
Śuṅga dynasty, 60, 252
Sūryakumāra (Khmer prince), 127, 135
sūryavaṃśa (solar dynasty), 280
Sūryavarman II, 235, 255–56
sūta, 48n24
sutta, 52
Suvarṇabhūmi (Malaysia), 16
Suvarṇanābha, 198
Suviśākha, 70
svabhāvokti ("natural"/direct expression): in Bhoja's literary language taxonomy, 106, 106n71, 110, 350n40; Daṇḍin on, 349n39; in *Kavirājamārgam*, 349, 350n41; *mārga* and, 212, 213, 214, 351n42; Pampa on, 358
systems-theory sociology, 498–501

tadbhava (Sanskrit derivatives): *deśabhāṣā* and, 404–5; European vs. Sanskrit vernacularization and, 472; Jain view of, 108n73; in Kannada philology, 368–69, 374–75, 375n97; Prakrit as, 108, 401
Tailapa II (king), 154, 155, 178, 178n25
Taittirīya Brāhmaṇa, 41n4
Tāḷagunda Pillar Inscription, 116, 116n3, 135
Tamilakam, 414, 414–15n74
Tamil language: court patronage and, 523; Daṇḍin readapted in, 163, 449; grammar in, 364n73, 366, 384–85, 401; grammaticization of, 398–99; *kāvya* in, 109; literary-cultural terminology in, 385, 385n8; literization of, 290–91; *Mahābhārata* adaptations in, 358–59, 358n63; Old Tamil, 500; philologization in, 384–85; political inscriptions in, 413–14, 421n86; *praśasti* in, 120–21; Sanskrit interaction with, 120–22, 122n15; as Southeast Asian koiné, 512, 512n24; superposition of, 26; vernacularization and, 289, 290–92
Tamil literary culture: *bhakti* and, 429; complex history of, 100; Daṇḍin readapted in, 163; emulation in, 449; intertextuality and, 351n44; Islam and, 491, 493; legitimation theory and, 516; *mārga/deśī* dichotomy and, 409; political space in, 553; prehistory of, 292; Shaivism and, 479–80; territorialization in, 385–86; textualization and, 314n55; vernacularization of, 322–23, 383–85, 396, 443
Tamilnadu: Cōḻa grammar halls in, 176, 176n22; Jayavarman charter of, 64n49; *Mahābhārata* manuscripts in, 228; Pallava rule of, 63; political regionality in, 413–15, 414–15n74; temples in, 252–53
Tamil philology, 398–99
tāmrapraśasti (copperplate grants), 130
Tanakung, *Wṛttasañcaya*, 164, 388
T'ang dynasty, 163, 205, 535
Taṇṭiyalaṅkāra, 399
tantra, 83n22
Tantu Panngelaran, 234
Tārikh-i Sistān, 286
Taruṇavācaspati, 344
Tasso, Torquato, *Gerusalemme liberata*, 469, 554
tatsama (Sanskrit loanwords): *deśī* words and, 401, 405; European vs. Sanskrit vernacularization and, 472; Prakrit as, 108, 401; in vernacular literary cultures, 374–75, 387, 388

Taylor, Charles, 506
technology, cultural change and, 498–501
Telugu language: grammar in, 364n73, 366, 381; grammaticization of, 398; inscriptions in, 149, 421n86; Kannada and, 23, 289, 415–16; naturalistic view of development of, 500; standardization of, 552
Telugu literary culture: beginnings of, 289, 297, 298, 380–81, 398; *bhakti* and, 429; cosmopolitan vernacularization of, 323–24, 435; emulation in, 448–49; epic vernacularization in, 396, 398; *mārga/deśī* dichotomy and, 408–9; popular intelligibility and, 426; *prāsa* in, 86n30; textualization in, 313–16
Telugu philology, 398
temples, 252–53
Temür, 394
Terence, 271, 537
Tertullian, 42n6
Tēvāram, 383
textualization, 283–84, 304–18
Thailand: Ayutthaya literary culture in, 132, 164, 205; Pali cosmopolitan formation in, 386; Sanskrit culture localized in, 270; Sanskrit inscriptions in, 123; Sanskrit literary influence in, 163–64, 205
Thai language, 396n34
thammasat, 270
Thoreau, Henry David, 319, 460
Tibet, 16, 98n56, 163, 205, 236, 399
Tikkana (Telugu poet), 396
Tilly, Charles, 2
Tinódi (Hungarian poet), 450
Tiṟukkuraḷ, 384–85, 385n8
Tocharian language, 55, 86
Tocqueville, Alexis de, 480n18
Tolkāppiyam, 338n12, 386n10, 398, 399n39
Tomars, 393–94, 412, 448
Tønnesson, Stein, 553n50, 564n71
Tours: Arab defeat at (732), 488–91; Council of (813), 261
Toynbee, Arnold, 533
trade, 30, 122, 484–87, 494
Trairājyapallava, 153n75
translatio studii et imperii, 480
Trivikramabhaṭṭa (*praśasti* poet), 134; *Nalacampū*, 361n67
troubadour poetry, 442, 442n6, 448n16, 465, 486. *See also* Occitan literary culture
Tukarām (Marathi poet), 310–12, 314, 502
Tulsīdās, 536; *Rāmcaritmānas*, 317
Tulu language, 20–21, 290, 446, 476
Tulu-Malayalam, 290n10
Turki, 429n102
Turkic tribes, 487–88
Turold (poet), 448, 490
Turuṣkas, 194, 194n11
Tuscany, 461, 481

Udayāditya (king), 183
Udbhaṭa (literary scholar), 175
Uddyotanasūri, 99, 299, 509; *Kuvalayamālā*, 96, 105n69, 289, 361n67
udīcya, 66
Ujjayinī, 70, 73, 151, 177, 220
ukti (modes of expressivity), 106, 106n71
Umāpatidhara (*praśasti* poet), 134
Umāsvāti, 58
Umayyad dynasty (Baghdad), 489
United States, neocolonial objectives of, 533–34n18, 575, 576
upamā (simile), 137–39
Utkalamāhātyma, 417n78
utprekṣā (imaginative conceits), 208
utraque lingua, 445n11
Uttaramīmāṃsā, 41–42n4

vacanas, 433–34, 479
vācya, 111
Vādijaṅghāla, 344, 422
Vaḍnagar, 144, 145
Vāgbhaṭa, 92, 112, 112n81
vāgmin, 83
vaidarbha (southern style): Ānandavardhana on, 217–18; Bhāmaha on, 211–12; Bhoja on, 210–11; definition of, 209–10; Kannada and, 348n37; in *Kavirājamārgam*, 346–51; Kuntaka on, 215–16; Maharashtri mapped against, 221; Ratnaśrījñāna on, 214; in Sanskrit literature, 220; Tamil and, 398; Vāmana on, 213. See also *mārga*
vaidika (Brahmanical) culture: Buddhist scriptural languages criticized in, 55–56; Buddhist transvaluation of, 51–56, 53n32; grammatical tradition in, 46–47; liturgy, preservation of, 71; naturalism of, 52; philology as originating in, 171, 171n14; prerequisites for participation in, 41, 44n13; Śakas and, 69–70; Sanskrit expansion and, 101, 254; Sanskrit inscrip-

vaidika (Brahmanical) culture *(continued)* tions and, 60–63, 63–64n49, 67, 72n66; sectarianism in, 170; spatialization of ritual in, 190–91
vaidika dharma, 405
Vaishnavism: *bhakti* and, 435; vernacularization and, 383–84, 427, 436, 479
Vaishya (caste), 41, 194, 202
Vaiśikatantram, 429
Vajrayāna Buddhism, 431
Vākāṭaka dynasty: dating system of, 151n67; end of Prakrit period during, 289–90; influence of, 150; Kālidāsa and, 220; poets of, 117n6; Prakrit inscriptions in, 117–19, 121; Sanskrit/regional division of labor in, 121
Vākpatirāja, 102, 104, 105n69
vakrokti ("indirect"/troped expression): in Bhoja's literary language taxonomy, 106, 106n71, 350n40; in *Kavirājamārgam*, 349, 350n41; *mārga* and, 213; Pampa on, 357–58
Vallabha, 312; Puṣṭimārga, 436
Vallabharāja (king), 145
Vālmīki, 77, 202, 314n56, 341. See also *Rāmāyaṇa* (Vālmīki)
Vāmana (literary scholar): grammatical/political relationship and, 175; on *mārga*, 212–13, 218, 220; *mārga/rīti* dichotomy in, 409; past poet eulogies and, 344n27; on *svabhāvokti*, 349n39; work: *Kāvyālaṅkārasūtra*, 209n36
vaṃśāvalī (line of succession), 155
vāṅmārga (ways of verbal mimesis), 209n38
vaṅmaya, 52–53
Varāhamihira, *Bṛhatsaṃhitā*, 196, 225
Varanasi, 559
Vararuci, 111n79; *Prākṛtasūtra*, 101–2
Vārkarīs (religious community), 382, 429
vārttika, 385n8
Vasantavilāsa, 293, 428
Vātsyāyana, 198
Vattelutu script, 289
Veda: Buddhist transvaluation of, 51–54; grammar in, 46–48; *Kātantra* and, 170; *kāvya* and, 5, 75–77; language of, 54n33; learning of, 500; lexical/semantic uniqueness of, 56n36; *Mahābhārata* believed derived from, 224–25; non-Sanskrit words in, 43, 43n8; precosmopolitan access to, 39, 41–44; purpose of, 42, 42n6, 46–47; register distinctions and, 107; ritual action in, 41–42, 41–42n4; Sanskrit used for, 108n73; written form prohibited, 83, 83n23
Vedānta, 41–42n4
Vēmaluvāḍa Cāḷukyas, 361
Veṅgi, 159–60, 356
Veṅgi Cāḷukya dynasty, 156–57, 166, 289, 297, 380–81
Veṅkāṭāppa Nāyaka, 168
Verdery, Katherine, 511n21
Vergil, *Aeneid*, 225, 266, 273, 279–80
vernacular: as *apabhraṣṭa*, 308–9; definition of, 19–20, 24; expansion of, 20–21; genre restrictions on, 299–302, 300n29; grammars in, 364n73; grammaticization of, 397–400, 471–73; *kāvya* in, 99–100, 109, 292–93, 304; literacy in, 307, 494; literarization of, 288; literary exclusion of, 298–304; literization of, 132, 288; *Mahābhārata* editions in, 229; as mimetic code, 304; novel and, 549; *praśasti* in, 290, 292–93, 297; Sanskrit cosmopolis and, 21–22; Sanskrit interaction with, 126–27; use of, as defiance, 310–12, 470. *See also* cosmopolitan vernacular; *deśabhāṣā*
vernacular anxiety, 451, 452–60, 470–71
vernacular epics, 559
vernacularization, 425; beginnings in, 22–23, 24–25, 283–88, 295–98; Bhoja and, 106; as courtly project, 430; as cultural-political decision, 499; of cultural/political spheres, 9; definition of, 20, 23, 283; divine authority for, 453; ethnicity and, 475–76, 511, 511n21; features of, 336–38, 380; gender and, 461n35; global trade/commerce and, 484–86, 494; grammatical norms and, 366–67, 471–73; Gujarati, 292–93; historical conditions and, 379; historical origins of, 30; inscriptional discourse and, 146–47; Islam and, 488–89, 488n38, 491–94; Javanese, 163; Kalyāṇa Cāḷukyas and, 155–56; in Karnataka, 185; in Kashmir, 216–17; *kāvya* and, 27, 298–304, 385; language/power linkage in, 481; literacy as part of, 307–9; literary territorialization in, 380, 385–86, 389–90; literization/literarization asynchrony in, 23, 25–26, 283–84, 287, 295, 502,

572; localization and, 283–84, 478–79; *Mānasollāsa* composed before, 187–88; manuscript culture and, 315–17; Marathi, 289–90; *mārga/deśī* dichotomy and, 208; mistaken accounts of, 423–26; multilingualism and, 477, 508–9; nationalism and, 539–40, 576–78; naturalistic view of, 498–99, 502–3; in Nepal, 293–94; nomadic empires and, 487–88; normativity and, 167; political place in, 553; political significance of, 295, 309–15; popular intelligibility and, 425–26; regional, 432–36, 432n106, 479–80, 573; religion and, 393, 393n27, 423–36, 429n102, 553n50; resistance to, 56; role of royal court in, 410; Sanskrit challenged by, 1; Sanskrit cosmopolis and, 25–30, 317–18; Sanskrit literary culture and, 129, 130; Sanskrit regionality and, 214–15; spread of, 469; superposition in, 320–29, 380; Tamil, 290–92; Telugu, 289; textualization and, 283–84, 304–18, 383–84. *See also* cosmopolitanism/vernacularism dichotomy; Europe, vernacularization of; Kannada, vernacularization of; literarization; literization; *specific vernacular*

vernacularization, European vs. South Asian: as connected Eurasian historical phenomenon, 482–92; cosmopolitan order and, 468–71, 481–82; differences in, 473–82, 572–74; ethnicity, 474–76, 480–81, 510–11; global trade/commerce and, 484–87, 494; grammar, 471–73; Islam and, 488–94; language choice, 476; language-naming, 473–74; language/power linkage, 480–82; linguistic distance, 443; literary-cultural emulation, 448–49, 469; multilingualism, 448n16, 476–77; nomadic empires and, 487–88; parallels in, 468–73; political space, 478–79, 479n17; religious influence, 477–80, 480n18, 564n71; theoretical problems of, 28–30, 438–39, 563–65; vernacular self-assertion, 456, 470–71

vernacular literary culture: beginnings of, 75, 95, 286–87, 297–98, 297n26, 314, 543; epic reiteration in, 554–55; industrialization and, 562; Jain, 425; literization in, 315–16; naturalness and, 318–20, 319n66; as political defiance, 309–16; political order and, 6–7, 396–97; Sanskrit as model for, 395–96; social dimension of writing and, 305–6; societal cultures and, 577

vernacular philology: *deśī* and, 397, 401–5; grammaticization, 397–400; Sanskrit conceptual framework for, 400–405

vernacular polities: European, 412–13, 460–67; features of, 418; historical trends toward, 420–21; regional orders of, 413–20, 420n84; role of royal court in, 421–23; scholarship lacking on, 410–12; vernacular literary production vs., 422–23

Verpoorten, Jean-Marie, 40n2

Vetruvius, 537

Vico, Giambattista, 2–3, 503, 503n7

Vidal, Peire, 470

Vidal, Raimon, *Razos de trobar*, 465

Vidyāpati, 286

Vidyāsāgara (editor), 230–31, 231n14

vidyātraya, 52

Vietnam: Chinese influence in, 21, 128, 128n33, 259–60; Sanskrit inscriptions in, 123; Sanskrit literary influence in, 21; standardized educational system in, 551; vernacularization in, 259–60, 486–87. *See also* Champa

Vijayāditya (Cāḷukya king), 153, 157, 332n2

Vijayanagara empire: cosmopolitan vernacularization in, 434; empire form and, 250–51, 251n46; grammatical/political linkage in, 232; Kannada use of, 337, 337n10; length of rule, 411; multiple vernacular character of, 420–21; religion and politics in, 431, 480; royal authority in, 279, 314

Vijayapura, 509

Vijayaskandavarman, 119–20

vijjā, 52

Vikings, 489–90

Vikramāditya I (Cāḷukya king), 151, 153, 156

Vikramāditya II (Cāḷukya king), 151n68, 152, 153

Vikramāditya V (Cāḷukya king), 156, 158–59, 161

Vikramāditya VI, 141n55, 150n66, 160, 220, 337

Vikramārjunavijayam (*Bhāratam*; Pampa), 316, 356–63, 555; epic spatialization in, 362–63, 378, 557; epic theme of,

Vikramārjunavijayam (continued)
358–62; influence of, 364; as *laukika* text, 426n96; linguistic register in, 357–58; surviving manuscripts of, 363n72; vernacularization process in, 357
Villers-Cotterêts, Ordinance of, 467, 481
Vimalōdaya (Kannada prose writer), 339
Vinayāditya I (Cāḷukya king), 153, 417
Vindhyaśakti II (Vākāṭaka king), 117
Vīracōḻiyam, 323, 364n73, 429
Vīrakumāra (Khmer prince), 127, 135
Virashaivism, 432, 433–34, 436, 476, 519
Vīrasōmēśvara (Hoysaḷa king), 418
Virāṭaparvan, 86
virodhābhāsa (apparent contradiction), 142
viṣama (inverted causality), 130, 142
viṣaya (political realm), 111, 352–53
Vishwa Hindu Parishad (World Hindu Council), 575
Viṣṇudās (vernacular poet): *bhakti* and, 429; *Mahābhārata* adaptation of, 306, 316, 394–95, 394n28; patron of, 292n17; vernacularization and, 292, 304, 309, 424
Viṣṇupurāṇa, 155n80
Viṣṇuvardhana (Hoysaḷa king), 157, 160, 167, 377, 417–19
Viṣṇuvarman (king), 130–31
Viśvāmitra (sage), 194n11
Viśvanātha, 135n47, 175
Viśveśvara (literary scholar), 175
Vitruvius, 265
Vivekasindhu, 382n3
Vo-cahn inscription, 124n21
Voltaire, 521n42
vṛtti (dance/musical modes), 204, 205, 215–16
Vuttodaya, 171, 386n14
vyākaraṇa (grammar), 46, 164
Vyāsa, 63, 224–25, 341, 554. See also *Mahābhārata*
vyatirekālaṅkāra (inverted simile), 143–44
vyāvahārika sat, 2–3, 5, 22, 65, 77, 321, 524

Walpole, Horace, *Castle of Otranto*, 297
Walther von der Vogelweide, 470
Warren, Austin, 543n32
wawachan (Javanese genre), 388
Weber, Max, 511; on culture/power, 8, 14; on ethnic fictions, 474; on India as "pre-political," 6, 411; on legitimation, 32–33, 517–19; on primordialism and linguism, 507–8
Wellek, René, 543n32
Wenceslas II (Polish king), 480, 573
Westernization, 538
Western Kṣtrapas, 67, 69–70, 69n58, 72n66, 150, 265n10
Wheatley, Paul, 235n19
Whitney, William Dwight, 164
Wolff, Philippe, 448n16
Wolters, O. W., 530–32, 536, 536n22
women: in Southeast Asian society, 126, 126n25; taxonomies of, 197–99
word species, threefold division of, 93
Wordsworth, William, "Preface to Lyrical Ballads," 319
Wright, Roger, 449n19
writing: Buddhism and, 82n19; invention of, *kāvya* and, 81–82, 305; vernacular textualization and, 304–7. *See also* literacy; literization

Xuangzang (Chinese pilgrim), 168–68, 170, 176n22, 192–93, 192n8, 234

Yādava dynasty: length of rule, 411; Marathi vernacularization in, 290, 297, 325, 381–83; political/cultural domain of, 416–17
Yaśodharapura (Khmer capital), 141–42
Yaśodharman (Mālava king), 138–39, 144nn58–59, 243
Yaśovarman (Khmer king), 127, 129n37, 141–43
Yavadvīpa (Java), 16
Yavanas (Indo-Greeks), 70n60, 71, 194, 194n11, 265n10
Yavaneśvara, 265, 265n10
Yching (Chinese pilgrim), 235n19
Yogeśvara (Pāla poet), 208
yogis, 393
Yuddhamalla (Cāḷukya prince), 323–24, 380–81
Yugapurāṇa, 62, 70–72, 71n63, 247
yuga theory, 70

Zoetmulder, P. J., 135n47, 163n1, 296
Zumthor, Paul, 24n25
Zvelebil, Kamil, 385n8

Compositor:	Integrated Composition Systems
Indexer:	Kevin Millham
Cartographer:	Bill Nelson
Text:	10/12 Baskerville
Display:	Baskerville
Printer and binder:	IBT Global